D0138200

AUDITING:
A RISK ANALYSIS APPROACH

5th Edition

LARRY F. KONRATH

University of Toledo

SOUTH-WESTERN

THOMSON LEARNING

Australia · Canada · Mexico · Singapore · Spain · United Kingdom · United States

Auditing: A Risk Analysis Approach, by Larry F. Konrath
Vice President/Publisher: Dave Shaut
Acquisitions Editor: Scott Person
Developmental Editor: Carol Bennett
Marketing Manager: Jennifer Codner
Production Editor: Margaret M. Bril
Manufacturing Coordinator: Doug Wilke
Media Technology Editor: Diane van Bakel
Media Development Editor: Sally Nieman
Media Production Editor: Lora Craver
Internal Design: Michael H. Stratton
Cover Design: Tin Box Studio/Cincinnati, Ohio
Cover Photographer: ©Gary Brettnacher/Adventure Photo & Film
Production House: Cover to Cover Publishing, Inc.
Compositor: Sandy Thomson, Cover to Cover Publishing, Inc.
Printer: Transcontinental

COPYRIGHT ©2002 by South-Western, a division of Thomson Learning. The Thomson Learning logo is a registered trademark used herein under license.

All Rights Reserved. No part of this work covered by the copyright hereon may be reproduced or used in any form or by any means—graphic, electronic, or mechanical, including photocopying, recording, taping, or information storage and retrieval systems—without the written permission of the publisher.

Material in the text is included from Certified Internal Auditor Examinations by The Institute of Internal Auditors, Inc. 249 Maitland Avenue, Altamonte Springs, Florida 32701 U.S.A. Reprinted with permission.

Material from the Uniform CPA Examination, Questions and Unofficial Answers, by the American Institute of Certified Public Accountants, Inc., is reprinted (or adapted) with permission.

Printed in Canada
1 2 3 4 5 04 03 02 01

For more information contact South-Western, 5101 Madison Road, Cincinnati, Ohio, 45227 or find us on the Internet at http://www.swcollege.com

For permission to use material from this text or product, contact us by
• **telephone: 1-800-730-2214**
• **fax: 1-800-730-2215**
• **web: http://www.thomsonrights.com**

Library of Congress Cataloging-in-Publication Data

Konrath, Larry F.
    Auditing : a risk analysis approach / Larry F. Konrath.–5th ed.
        p. cm.
    Rev. ed. of: Auditing concepts and applications : a risk analysis approach.
    Includes biblographical references and index.
    ISBN 0-324-05789-X
    1. Auditing. I. Konrath, Larry F. Auditing concepts and applications. II. Title.

HF5667 .K62 2001
657'.45–dc21   00-066184

brief contents

contents

Contents

Part 4
Reporting the Results of the Audit   581

p r e f a c e

OBJECTIVES AND APPROACH

Like its earlier editions, the fifth edition of *Auditing: A Risk Analysis Approach* stresses the important elements of risk-based auditing. In meeting this goal, the text offers an in-depth framework that addresses the concepts of audit evidence and materiality. Emphasis is given to the meeting of user expectations through audit risk analysis, application of audit judgment, and ethical considerations in auditing.

The fifth edition also addresses the broader aspects of assurance services that have gained increasing emphasis in contemporary auditing. Today's CPA applies a concept of assurance that is much broader than traditional financial statement auditing, performing such attest services as evaluating performance measurement systems, assessing the reliability of information systems, appraising an entity's business risk assessment function, and rating the integrity of electronic commerce.

The text strikes a balance between conceptual and applied aspects of auditing. In this regard, *Auditing: A Risk Analysis Approach* provides students with an effective preparation source for the auditing part of the Certified Public Accountants examination and is well documented with materials from pronouncements by the American Institute of Certified Public Accountants (AICPA).

To stress the importance of risk-based auditing, audit risk is introduced in Chapter 1, after which two entire chapters are devoted to audit risk (Chapters 5 and 7). After the topic is developed in Chapters 5 and 7, the concept of risk analysis and its relationship to the audit program is explored quantitatively in two chapters on statistical sampling (Chapters 9 and 10). The coverage of statistical sampling in auditing is extensive and affords the student the opportunity to visualize clearly the relationship between various levels of audit risk and their impact on the nature, timing, and extent of audit procedures.

To offer full coverage of audit risk, the text assigns much of the accounting systems details to useful chapter appendices. Since many senior-level accounting students have had a course in accounting information systems (AIS), assignment of systems details to appendices reduces unnecessary topic redundancy in the systems and the auditing courses. For those who have not had a prior systems course, the appendix following Chapter 7 should provide sufficient background information.

Changes in Fifth Edition

The fifth edition of *Auditing: A Risk Analysis Approach* retains and builds upon the framework developed in earlier editions. Major changes from the fourth edition include the following:

- The text is now divided into five distinct parts to promote continuity and structure:
    1. The Auditing Profession—Chapters 1-3
    2. Planning the Audit—Chapters 4-8
    3. Conducting the Audit—Chapters 9-13
    4. Reporting the Results of the Audit—Chapter 14
    5. Other Attestation and Assurance Services—Chapters 15-16
- Chapter 15 devotes greater attention to other assurance services, such as WebTrust, SysTrust, and ElderCare.

- The fifth edition offers several Internet assignments directing students to web sites such as the AICPA, the Independence Standards Board, the Public Register's Annual Report Service, the Australian Education Research Pty. Ltd., and 10K Wizard (an EDGAR database search engine).
- The fifth edition also provides numerous references to web sites as added sources of information.
- The *Biltrite Computer Audit Practice Case* has been revised to enable students to begin the case earlier in the course. This has been achieved by dividing the former Module I into two parts:

  Module I: Inherent Risk Analysis—to be completed following Chapter 5; and
  Module II: Control Risk Analysis—to be completed following Chapter 8.

  In addition, as part of analytical procedures, students are directed to the web site of Cannondale, an actual bicycle manufacturer, and are asked to compare key percentages and ratios with Biltrite.
- New essay questions and discussion cases involving actual companies are presented. Examples are Waste Management, Rite Aid, IBM, W.R. Grace, Bankers Trust, Sunbeam Corp., California Micro Devices, McKesson HBOC Inc., and Cendant Corp.
- The text has expanded coverage related to auditor independence, including greater attention to the work of the Independence Standards Board and the Panel on Audit Effectiveness. The SEC's concern about independence and management consulting is also discussed at some length.
- Increased attention is given to the topic of ethics and the concept of ethical behavior is discussed generally, followed by a more CPA-specific discussion of the Code of Professional Conduct
- Chapter 8, Internal Control and Computer-Based Information Systems, has been updated to reflect new audit approaches and techniques given changes in technology and the computer environment.
- The web site for *Auditing: A Risk Analysis Approach* (http://konrath. swcollege.com) has been upgraded and expanded. Online tutorials, PowerPoint presentation slides, links to web sites referred to in the text, and auditing terminology crossword puzzles are new, additional learning reinforcements.

.com
http://konrath.
swcollege.com

Learning Aids and Pedagogical Tools
Computer Audit Practice Case

The appendix following Chapter 16 contains a computer audit practice case, Biltrite Bicycles, Inc. The practice case is divided into fifteen modules that parallel related chapter topics. A CD containing partially completed audit workpapers in Excel is included with the textbook. The modules, which may be assigned individually or severally at the instructor's option, begin following Chapter 5. They continue at the end of succeeding chapters, ending with Chapter 14.

The practice case permits the student to discover how much of the typical financial audit can be automated with the computer. In addition, the student obtains hands-on exposure to computer auditing. The modules are sufficiently condensed that excessive amounts of computer time are not consumed. However, at the same time, the student must assess audit risk, analyze data, apply auditing procedures, and evaluate the results—all with the aid of the computer. These materials make *Auditing: A Risk Analysis Approach* unique in the auditing textbook market and add an exciting dimension to the study of auditing.

Audit Workpaper Templates

Excel templates contained on the Biltrite CD included with this textbook accompany six author-prepared essay/discussion case questions. The templates consist of partially completed audit workpapers. Students are asked to complete the workpapers by analyzing data, performing calculations, stating conclusions, and using audit legends to describe procedures applied. These mini cases give students the opportunity to simulate the audit field work experience and to learn how the computer assists in performing and documenting audits.

The cases, identified in the end-of-chapter materials by the Biltrite CD icon, are as follows:

Chapter 4: Discussion Case—Hanlon, Inc.
Chapter 5: Discussion Case IV—Marcus Publishing, Inc.
Chapter 11: Problem 11.10—Colorado Processing, Inc.
Chapter 12: Problem 12.12—Selfers Service Center
Chapter 13: Problem 13.15—Marvel Muffler Shops, Inc.
Chapter 13: Problem 13.16—Branson Manufacturing Company

Audit Objectives and Procedures Matrices

Matrices providing an integrated framework for analysis are included in appendices following Chapters 11 through 13.

The matrix approach helps to reinforce students' understanding of substantive audit testing by providing a framework for developing audit programs. This approach also enables students to build their own audit programs around careful risk analysis and formulation of specific objectives.

Use of Cases

To bring the material alive and to emphasize the importance of risk analysis in auditing, *Auditing: A Risk Analysis Approach* makes liberal use of case examples. Extensive references to cases involving auditors serves to reinforce students' mastery of concepts by relating a given concept to an actual company. Some of the cases are incorporated into the chapters, while others are included as end-of-chapter materials. All of the cases are based on actual events and are structured to contrast what should have been done with what actually was done.

Illustrations

Extensive use is made of diagrams, tables, and listings to ease the learning process. Internal control flowcharts and listings of necessary documents, records, and functions appended to the control chapters provide an easy review of control techniques without unnecessarily cluttering the chapter on internal control concepts.

Coverage of AICPA Professional Standards

The standards issued by the American Institute of Certified Public Accountants, referred to as AICPA Professional Standards, are given comprehensive coverage throughout the text as they impact given subject areas.

Chapter Organization

Careful attention has been given in the fifth edition to chapter organization in order to maintain maximum clarity and completeness. The study of auditing is organized into five major categories. Chapters 1 through 3 describe the auditing profession; Chapters 4 through 8 present a conceptual approach to planning the audit; Chapters 9 through 13 discuss the process of conducting the audit; Chapter 14 describes audit reports; and Chapters 15 and 16 consider other attestation and assurance services.

Chapter Overview and Learning Objectives

At the beginning of each chapter, an overview and a list of learning objectives are presented to introduce the reader to the major topics to be covered and to identify the major concepts to be learned from studying the chapter.

Key Terms and Glossary

A list of key terms is provided at the end of each chapter and serves as additional reinforcement of the learning process. Although auditing is related to accounting, it is not the same. The auditing student encounters many new terms, as well as familiar terms with a different connotation.

A glossary at the end of the textbook supplements the list of key terms and helps the student learn the language of auditing.

End-of-Chapter Materials

Essay questions, problems, and discussion cases, along with multiple choice questions from past CPA and CIA exams, are supplied at the end of each chapter. End-of-chapter review questions and applicable parts of the Biltrite computer audit practice case also are included. Flowcharting problems following Chapters 7 and 8 afford an opportunity to study an internal control narrative and graphically present it in the form of a flowchart. The template problems, together with the Biltrite practice case, offer a "hands-on" audit field work experience.

When considered collectively, these materials serve the dual purpose of solidifying the learning process and providing the student with questions important to CPA exam preparation. The multiple choice questions are especially effective in reviewing the contents of the Statements on Auditing Standards (SASs), a major component of the auditing part of the CPA exam. Answers to the multiple choice questions, along with the reasons for correct and incorrect choices, are given at the end of the textbook.

Supplements

Materials available to supplement this textbook include an *Instructor's Manual/ Solutions Manual, Examview Testing Software* (a computerized Test Bank), and an *Instructor's Resource CD* (IRCD). The Test Bank is also available in printed form and, in addition to multiple choice questions from past CPA and CIA examinations, contains author-prepared multiple choice, completion, matching, and essay questions.

The *Instructor's Manual* includes the following:

1. Answers to end-of-chapter materials: review questions, multiple choice questions, essay questions, problems (including the six template problems referred to earlier),

discussion cases, and Internet assignments. For CPA exam and CIA exam questions, the official answers are supplied. For multiple choice questions, narratives supporting correct choices and reasons other choices are incorrect accompany the answers.
2. Useful outlines for preparing lectures on the topics presented in each chapter.
3. Printout of solutions to the Biltrite Bicycles audit practice case modules.
4. Transparency masters highlighting important chapter topics.
5. Teaching suggestions at the beginning of each chapter, as appropriate, and for the Biltrite Bicycles audit practice case.

The *Instructor's Resource CD* contains:

1. The Instructor's Manual
2. The Solutions Manual
3. The Test Bank—Examview Testing Software
4. Completed workpapers for the Biltrite Bicycles audit practice case
5. Completed templates for the six case/problem assignments for which partial templates are provided on the student diskette.
6. PowerPoint presentation slides
7. Transparency Masters

.com

http://konrath.
swcollege.com

Web site Resources include: http://konrath.swcollege.com

Instructor Resources:
• Lecture outlines from the *Instructor's Manual*
• Solutions to essay questions, problems, and discussion cases
• Solutions to the Biltrite Bicycle case modules
• Internet activities solutions
• Teaching suggestions
• PowerPoint presentation slides
• PowerPoint transparency masters

Student Resources:
• Online tutorials
• PowerPoint slides
• Case spreadsheets in Excel
• Internet activities
• Links to web sites referenced in the text
• Auditing terminology crossword puzzles and solutions by chapter

In addition, the web site contains a link to the current Cannondale Corporation Annual Report and Form 10-K. Cannondale is introduced in an early Biltrite Case module for comparison purposes.

Acknowledgments

The author would like to thank the American Institute of Certified Public Accountants and the Institute of Internal Auditors for their generosity in granting permission to quote extensively from the professional literature, as well as for their permission to use past professional examination questions as a major part of the end-of-chapter materials.

The author gratefully acknowledges the valuable advice of the following persons who reviewed the textbook drafts: Charles Stanley, *Baylor University—Waco, Texas*; Anwer S. Ahmed, *Syracuse University*; Alex B. Ampadu, *State University of New York*; and Gail Wright, *Bryant College*. A special thanks goes to Harold O. Wilson, *Middle Tennessee State University*, who served as PowerPoint author.

The author also appreciates the assistance furnished by Scott Person, acquisitions editor, and Carol Bennett, developmental editor. Their helpful advice and diligent attention to detail have greatly enhanced the value of this textbook. I would also like to acknowledge Marge Bril, production editor, and Jennifer Codner, marketing manager, at South-Western for the fine job of producing and promoting the book.

Finally, I would like to thank my daughter, Jennifer, for her technical assistance in developing the PowerPoint transparency masters and my wife, Charn, for her constant encouragement and support in what has become a most enriching project over the years.

part 1

The Auditing Profession

biltrite

c h a p t e r 1

biltrite

l e a r n i n g   o b j e c t i v e s

After reading this chapter, you should be able to

1 Differentiate between attestation and assurance.
2 Identify the various kinds of assurance services performed by independent CPAs.
3 Define auditing as it relates to financial statements and identify the assertions contained in the financial statements.
4 Identify the attributes of a successful auditor and explain why these skills are necessary.
5 Differentiate between internal and independent auditing and between accounting and auditing.
6 Provide a broad overview of how audit evidence is collected and evaluated.
7 Describe the standard audit report, the types of departures from the standard report, and the reasons for the departures.
8 Enumerate and explain the steps in the audit process.

OVERVIEW

Auditing adds value to published financial statements by providing an independent expert opinion as to the fairness with which the statements present financial position, results of operations, and cash flows. For this reason, the securities laws require that public companies have their annual financial statements audited by an independent certified public accountant (CPA).

By studying auditing, you will learn how to gather and evaluate evidence supporting an entity's financial statements. Additionally, in assessing the fairness of financial presentation, you will have the opportunity to apply the myriad of accounting principles and concepts that you learned in previous accounting courses. Finally, by studying the materials presented in this textbook, you will have made substantial progress in your preparation for the auditing section of the Uniform CPA Examination.

Chapter 1 provides a broad audit perspective using a basic audit model or framework that is expanded on in subsequent chapters. The chapter begins with a general description of attestation and assurance services, and emphasizes financial statement auditing. Auditing is defined, followed by a discussion of the components contained within that definition. The requirements for an effective audit are then addressed in terms of necessary auditor training and proficiency.

The need for independent auditing is considered, and internal auditing is contrasted with independent auditing. Auditing is then differentiated from accounting, and generally accepted accounting principles (GAAP) are identified as the connecting link between the two disciplines.

The ensuing sections of the chapter deal with the collection and evaluation of audit evidence and the communication of the auditor's findings within the context of the standard audit report.

The next section of the chapter provides an overview of the audit process, with particular emphasis on audit risk analysis. This overview should be studied carefully—it provides the focal point for much of the discussion in the remaining chapters of the text.

The chapter's final section lists the nonaudit services that are increasingly important sources of revenue for accounting firms.

AUDITING, ATTESTATION, AND ASSURANCE

Auditing is a form of attestation. **Attestation**, in a general sense, refers to an "expert's" communication of a conclusion about the reliability of someone else's assertion. For example, an antiques expert might attest to the genuineness of a Duncan Phyfe table, an art expert might attest to the authenticity of a Matisse painting, and a food expert might attest to the ingredients in a newly introduced health food product. In a narrower sense, the American Institute of Certified Public Accountants (AICPA) has defined attestation as a "written communication that expresses a conclusion about the reliability of a written assertion that is the responsibility of another party."[1] As stated above, auditing is a form of attestation. Specifically, the CPA, in the role of auditor, attests to the fairness of an entity's financial statements. CPAs also perform other attestation services, such as reporting on internal control and reporting on prospective financial statements.

More recently, CPAs have begun to perform other types of assurance services. **Assurance services**, as defined by the AICPA Committee on Assurance Services, are "in-

---

1 *AICPA Professional Standards*, New York: AICPA, section AT 100.01.

dependent professional services that improve the quality of information, or its context, for decision makers."[2] Assurance services are broader in scope than either auditing or attestation. For example, a client may ask its independent CPA to evaluate the reliability of its information system, or to assess the adequacy of its system for managing business risk, or to appraise the effectiveness of its performance measurement system. With advances in computer technology, companies are transacting business electronically to an ever-increasing extent. Given the need for data security, the CPA may be asked to attest to the adequacy of controls over possible data manipulation or loss. Although this textbook concentrates primarily on independent financial audits, these other services are discussed in Chapter 15. If you wish to learn more about these newer types of assurance services now, you can visit the AICPA web site at http://www.aicpa.org/assurance/scas/newsvs/index.htm.

.com

http://www.
aicpa.org/assurance/
scas/newsvs/index.htm

Figure 1.1 provides a diagrammatic description of the relationship among assurance services, attestation services, and auditing. Note that auditing is a form of attestation which is a form of assurance.

FIGURE 1.1

Relationship Among Assurance, Attestation, and Auditing

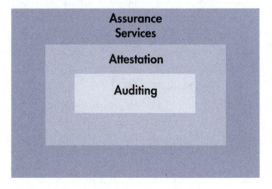

Assurance Services: Improve the quality of information or its context for decision makers

    Reliability of information systems

    Adequacy of risk management systems

    Effectiveness of performance measurement systems

    Adequacy of security over electronic commerce transactions

Attestation Services: Render an opinion as to the reliability of someone else's assertions

    Assertions regarding internal control

    Assertions regarding compliance with contract provisions

    Assertions regarding compliance with laws and regulations

    Auditing: Assertions regarding fairness of financial presentation

---

2   See *The Journal of Accountancy*, September 1996, p. 16.

Auditing, as used within the context of this textbook, may be defined as a systematic process of objectively obtaining and evaluating evidence regarding assertions about economic actions and events to ascertain the degree of correspondence between those assertions and established criteria and communicating the results to interested users.[3]

AUDITING AND MANAGEMENT ASSERTIONS

Assertions, as used in this context, are the *representations of management* as to the fairness of the financial statements. The Auditing Standards Board (ASB), a body established by the AICPA to formulate auditing standards and interpretations, has classified financial statement assertions as follows:

1. **Existence or occurrence:** Do all of the assets and equities on the balance sheet exist, and/or did all of the transactions represented on the income statement occur?
2. **Completeness:** Have any assets, equities, or transactions been omitted from the financial statements?
3. **Rights and obligations:** Are assets appearing on the balance sheet owned by the entity, and are reported liabilities obligations of the entity as of the balance sheet date?
4. **Valuation or allocation:** Are assets and equities properly valued in accordance with generally accepted accounting principles, and have amounts been fairly allocated between the balance sheet and the income statement (asset cost vs. depreciation expense, for example)?
5. **Presentation and disclosure:** Are classifications, such as current versus noncurrent assets and liabilities, and operating versus nonoperating revenues and expenses, properly reflected in the financial statements, and is footnote disclosure adequate for the financial statements not to be misleading?

The job of the auditor is to determine whether these representations (assertions) are indeed fair; that is, to "*ascertain the degree of correspondence between the assertions and established criteria.*" For financial reporting purposes, the *established criteria* are the body of generally accepted accounting principles (GAAP), as contained in the Statements of Financial Accounting Standards (SFASs), Accounting Principles Board Opinions (APBOs), Accounting Research Bulletins (ARBs), and other sources.

To evaluate fairness, the auditor must gather evidence either supporting or refuting the assertions. In gathering and evaluating audit evidence, the auditor adheres to a set of standards established by the Auditing Standards Board of the AICPA. These standards, referred to as *generally accepted auditing standards (GAAS)*, are addressed in Chapter 2. For auditing purposes, **evidence** consists of "the underlying accounting data and all corroborating information available to the auditor."[4]

The evidence must be gathered *objectively*. Most audits are performed on a test basis; that is, the auditor examines only a sample of the transactions and events that occurred during the period covered by the audit. In order for the samples to be representative of the respective populations tested, the auditor must be careful not to introduce bias into the selection process. For example, assume the auditor wishes to gain satisfaction concerning the existence of a client's surplus parts inventory by selecting a sample of the inventory and physically inspecting it. Assume further that both the

3   Committee on Basic Auditing Concepts, *A Statement of Basic Auditing Concepts*, Sarasota, FL: American Accounting Association, 1973, p. 2.
4   *AICPA Professional Standards*, op. cit., section AU 326.14.

auditor's office and the client's main warehouse are located in Phoenix, and that the client has a smaller warehouse, also containing surplus parts, in Houston. The auditor, given the distance involved, may find it inconvenient to include the Houston warehouse in the total population of surplus parts to be sampled. However, if the test count of surplus parts is limited to the main Phoenix warehouse, the sample will not have been objectively obtained and the results cannot be rationally extended to the population.

Auditing is a systematic process, consisting of a series of sequential steps that include (1) evaluating internal accounting control and (2) testing the substance of transactions and balances. The accounting system, including the necessary internal controls, produces the data appearing in the financial statements. A reliable system produces reliable financial statements. The auditor, therefore, studies and tests internal controls before testing the substance of transactions and balances (substantive testing). Strong internal control increases the level of auditor confidence and decreases the extent of transaction and balances testing (see Figure 1.2).

The auditor must evaluate the evidence gathered. To satisfy the definition, the evidence must be sufficient and competent. *Sufficient* means that "enough" evidence was examined. This determination is a function of the auditor's professional judgment and does not guarantee the accuracy of the financial statements; it simply expresses the auditor's opinion as to their fairness. The answer to the question, "How much evidence is adequate to support this opinion?", is not easily obtained and often requires significant training and experience as an auditor.

To be *competent*, evidence must be both valid and relevant. *Valid* evidence is reliable and convincing; validity is enhanced by an effective information system. *Relevance* means that the evidence relates to the audit objectives. Examining the surplus parts inventory, for example, helps establish the existence of inventory, but it does not provide a great deal of evidence concerning proper valuation of that inventory. Similarly, inspecting documents in support of recorded transactions is relevant for the purpose of locating errors in recorded transactions, but this procedure is not relevant in identifying transactions that have been omitted from the accounts. Rather, the tracing of documents forward to the accounts is a more effective procedure for detecting omissions.

FIGURE 1.2

Major Steps in the Systematic Process of Auditing

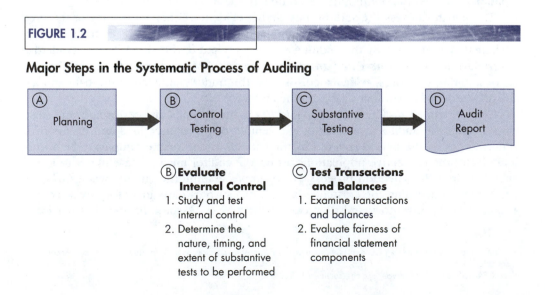

The auditor communicates the results of his or her audit work to interested users. Communication is the culmination of the attestation process, and its mechanism is the audit report. The **audit report** is included with the financial statements in the annual report to stockholders and describes the scope of the audit and the findings of the auditor. The findings are expressed in the form of an opinion concerning the fairness with which the financial statements present the firm's financial position, results of operations, and cash flows. Interested users are typically the stockholders and creditors of the client company, but may also include labor unions, regulatory agencies, and members of the general public.

EMPHASIS ON RISK-BASED AUDITS

In developing the financial auditing model in the ensuing chapters, emphasis will be placed on risk-based auditing. A **risk-based audit** is one in which the auditor carefully analyzes the entity and its existing internal control, identifies areas that pose the highest risk of financial statement errors, and allocates a greater proportion of audit resources to those areas. For example, discovery that a manufacturing client lacks perpetual inventory records should cause the auditor to place greater emphasis on the audit of materials, in process inventories, and finished goods inventories. Such factors as weak internal control, a declining industry, and client fixation on earnings growth contribute to the risk of financial misstatement, and should be areas of auditor concern translated into increased audit attention.

Recent cases involving financial reporting frauds not detected by the auditors have led the Securities and Exchange Commission to question the quality of independent auditing as currently practiced. These cases demonstrate the importance of risk-based auditing. Some of the cases and the related risk areas are presented in Exhibit 1.1. In virtually all of the cases one of two factors motivated the frauds:

- Management inflated earnings to meet the expectations of the financial community; or
- Management inflated earnings to boost the company's stock price in anticipation of a stock-for-stock acquisition of another entity.

Also, in most of the cases the auditors were either unaware of the fraud or agreed with the questionable accounting practices.

In the ensuing chapters we will explore many of these cases in greater depth and attempt to identify warning signs that should have alerted the auditors to the frauds. We will also examine the SEC's ongoing probe of auditor responsibility in these and other similar cases.

WHY INDEPENDENT AUDITING IS NECESSARY

Professions cannot exist without wide public acceptance, and independent auditing is no exception. Over the years, society has recognized the value added by audits of publicly held companies. With wide separation between ownership and management, a potential conflict of interest may be assumed to exist between management and stockholders regarding the financial statements. Management, knowing that it is being evaluated by the stockholders on the basis of the financial statements, desires to present the results of its stewardship in the most favorable light. Stockholders, on the other hand, are interested in financial statements that portray as closely as possible the true

EXHIBIT 1.1

Financial Reporting Fraud Cases and Related Risk Areas

Case	Type of Fraud
Cendant Corp.	Fictitious Revenues
Golden Bear Golf Company	Inflated percentage of completion for construction of golf courses
W. R. Grace & Co.	Used reserves to smooth earnings
Waste Management	Overestimated capacity of garbage dumps, thereby understating amortization charges
Telxon Corp.	Shipments to distributors booked as revenue
IBM Corp.	Reported nonoperating gain as reduction of selling, general, and administrative expenses
Premier Laser Systems, Inc.	Booked fictitious sales
Candie's, Inc.	Questionable barter transactions
Sunbeam Corp.	Recorded fictitious revenues, booked revenues early, and capitalized operating expenses
Rite Aid Corp.	Charged operating expenses to reserves established for acquisitions
	Related-party transactions treated as arm's-length
Bankers Trust Corp.	Diverted unclaimed customer funds to bolster earnings
Tyco International, Ltd.	Established reserves to be used later to increase earnings
Spectrum Information Technologies, Inc.	Booked licensing fees early as revenue, while deferring related advertising costs
Livent, Inc.	Shifted expenses of ongoing shows to preproduction costs of other shows
McKesson HBOC	Early recognition of revenue from sales of medical software
California Micro Devices Corp.	Recorded fictitious revenues
North Face Inc.	Understated accrued expenses and capitalized operating expenses
KnowledgeWare Inc.	Recorded fictitious software sales

financial position, results of operations, and cash flows of the company. Given these divergent attitudes toward financial reporting, the role of the independent auditor as impartial and competent attestor evolved.

As an expert in the application of generally accepted accounting principles, the independent auditor further enhances the quality of financial reporting. Figure 1.3 illus-

FIGURE 1.3

Role of the Independent Auditor

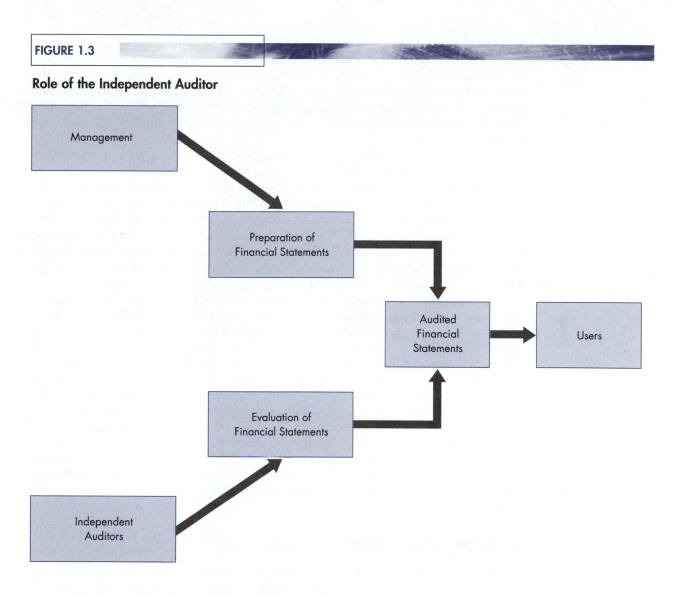

trates the independent auditor's role in adding quality to financial statements prepared by management.

The proper selection and application of GAAP have become increasingly complex over the years, given new types of transactions and new rules of accounting and disclosure pertaining to them. For this reason, the need for the professional auditor, knowledgeable in GAAP, has become more and more apparent to investors and creditors.

INDEPENDENT AUDITING VERSUS INTERNAL AUDITING

Up to this point, auditing has been considered only in the form of external, or independent, auditing. The main features of **independent audits** are that they are conducted by auditors who are independent of management and serve third-party users (e.g., stockholders and creditors). Also, they are limited to the auditee's financial statements and, therefore, are often referred to as *financial audits*. Although the national accounting firms perform most independent audits of large companies,[5] regional and local CPA firms also conduct audits. **Internal auditing** (discussed more fully in Chapter 16) is different from independent auditing in many significant respects. The major difference between internal auditing and independent auditing is that internal auditing serves management, while independent auditing serves third-party financial statement users. They are similar in that both involve collecting and evaluating evidence relating to assertions.

The Institute of Internal Auditors defines internal auditing as "an independent appraisal function established within an organization to examine and evaluate its activities as a service to the organization."[6] As the definition implies, internal auditing is broader in scope than independent auditing. Independent auditing is concerned exclusively with the financial statements prepared principally for external users. The internal auditor, by contrast, is concerned with all types of financial and other data generated for both internal and external users. The internal auditor also performs **operational audits**, which result in evaluating the efficiency of resource utilization and the effectiveness with which entity objectives are attained.

Although internal auditors participate in financial audits, one should note that their role is primarily that of assisting the external auditors by performing selected functions.

Another feature differentiating independent and internal auditing is reporting responsibility. The internal auditor is an employee of the entity being audited and does not possess the same degree of independence as the external auditor; the external auditor reports to the stockholders. A degree of internal independence must be present to compensate for lack of external independence. An important measure of the quality of internal auditing is the level within the organization to which the internal auditor reports (internal independence). A rule of thumb is that the internal auditor must report to a level sufficiently high that the audit findings will be implemented. Today, more and more companies are having their internal auditors report directly to the audit committee of the board of directors, thus providing maximum internal independence. Ordinarily, the **audit committee** consists mainly of outside directors having no management ties to the organization.

AUDITS BY GOVERNMENT ORGANIZATIONS

Several federal agencies perform a significant number of audits. These include the General Accounting Office (GAO), the Defense Contract Audit Agency (DCAA), and the Internal Revenue Service (IRS).

General Accounting Office

.com
http://www.gao.gov/

The **General Accounting Office (GAO)** is a federal agency that reports directly to Congress on the efficiency, effectiveness, and compliance of other government agencies, projects, and functions. GAO auditors frequently evaluate the effectiveness of management and will on occasion recommend in their reports substantial decreases in the level of funding or even discontinuance of various agencies and programs. The GAO has a set of

---

5 The national accounting firms at the time of this writing are as follows: Arthur Andersen, Deloitte & Touche, Ernst & Young, KPMG International, and PricewaterhouseCoopers.
6 Institute of Internal Auditors, Codification of Standards for the Professional Practice of Internal Auditing, Altamonte Springs, FL, 1993.

standards governing the conduct of its examinations, but these standards are considered to be beyond the scope of this book.

Defense Contract Audit Agency

The **Defense Contract Audit Agency (DCAA)** examines the records of entities fulfilling defense contracts for the federal government. The major goals of these examinations are to determine that only those costs pertaining to contract fulfillment have been charged to the government and that the entities have conformed to the contract terms. This type of auditing is referred to as compliance auditing. **Compliance auditing** may be defined as testing and reporting on conformity with laws and regulations relating to a specific entity or activity. As is more fully discussed in Chapter 16, independent auditors also engage in compliance auditing when examining the financial records of state and local governmental units and other nonprofit entities receiving federal financial assistance.

Internal Revenue Service

IRS audits affect businesses as well as individuals. A form of compliance auditing, IRS audits are designed to measure compliance with the federal tax laws.

The matrix in Figure 1.4 depicts the relationships of the types of auditing to classes of auditors. Note that financial audits remain the primary focus of independent auditing. The number of compliance audits, however, has increased rapidly in recent years. This may be attributed to an increased number of public-sector clients receiving federal

FIGURE 1.4

Auditors and Types of Auditing—Areas of Audit Emphasis

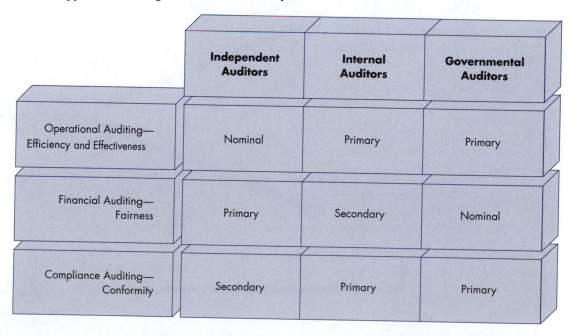

	Independent Auditors	Internal Auditors	Governmental Auditors
Operational Auditing— Efficiency and Effectiveness	Nominal	Primary	Primary
Financial Auditing— Fairness	Primary	Secondary	Nominal
Compliance Auditing— Conformity	Secondary	Primary	Primary

financial assistance. Compliance auditing is addressed more completely in Chapters 15 and 16.

HOW AUDITING DIFFERS FROM ACCOUNTING

Accounting students, who have not yet studied the subject, frequently think of auditing as another accounting course. Although auditing and accounting are related, they are distinct from each other. Accounting involves collecting, summarizing, reporting, and interpreting financial data. Auditing, by contrast, utilizes the theory of evidence—in much the same way as does the legal profession—to verify the overall reasonableness (fairness) of the financial statements presented. As shown in Figure 1.5, generally accepted accounting principles are the link between accounting and auditing. In assembling financial statements, accountants determine the best means for measuring, classifying, disclosing, and reporting financial information by referring to appropriate GAAP. In evaluating fairness of financial presentation, auditors use GAAP as the standard. Auditors, therefore, must be experts in accounting matters. The central thrust of auditing, however, is the collection and evaluation of evidence.

FIGURE 1.5

Accounting and Auditing Contrast

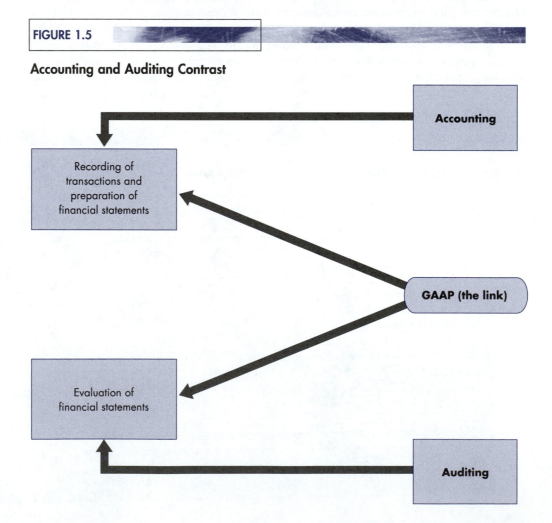

REQUIREMENTS FOR AN EFFECTIVE AUDIT

In order for an audit to be completed within the framework just discussed, certain attributes are required of the auditor. First, the auditor must have a *thorough understanding of the entity being audited and the industry* of which it is a part. As auditors have painfully learned from numerous legal actions filed against them by stockholders and creditors, complex transactions must be thoroughly understood if the auditor is to detect material errors and ensure adequate disclosure in the financial statements. In a case involving Golden Bear Golf, Inc., a company controlled by Jack Nicklaus, the auditors failed to detect the deliberate overstatement of profits relating to several construction projects undertaken by the company. As a result, the originally reported loss of $2.9 million for 1997 was later restated to $24.7 million. Under percentage of completion accounting, complex issues involving expenses incurred and stage of completion must be confronted and dealt with by the auditor. Apparently in this case not enough attention and audit resources were allocated to this high-risk audit area.[7]

The auditor must also have a *comprehensive knowledge of GAAP* in order to audit effectively. The body of GAAP is the standard by which fairness of financial presentation is judged by the auditor. Therefore, the auditor who is to formulate a rational opinion on the financial statements must be able to recognize material departures from GAAP, including errors in recording transactions and events, as well as inadequate disclosure. In satisfying this need, most auditing firms have extensive libraries containing SFASs, APBOs, ARBs, SEC pronouncements, and other sources of GAAP, as well as staff training programs to keep personnel informed of current developments in GAAP.

A solid *grasp of concepts of internal control* and a careful review and evaluation of internal accounting controls are also necessary ingredients to an effective audit. As will be discussed more fully in Chapter 6, **internal control** is the set of policies and procedures designed by an entity's management and board of directors to provide reasonable assurance regarding the achievement of entity objectives. The more effective the control system is in achieving its goals, the more confidence the auditor can place in it to prevent and detect material errors, both intentional and unintentional. One category of controls relates to the preparation of published financial statements. Therefore, in designing audit programs for testing transactions and balances, the auditor assesses the quality of internal controls within this category. The more effective the controls are, the lower the probability of material errors and fraud affecting the financial statements. This, in turn, leads to reduced need for examination of transactions and balances.

In addition to understanding the company, GAAP, and internal control, the auditor must also be *knowledgeable in the area of evidence gathering and evaluation*. The definition states that auditing is a "systematic process of . . . obtaining and evaluating evidence." In conducting the examination, the auditor has the opportunity of choosing among alternative forms of evidence and alternative means for gathering evidence: Some auditing procedures may be more costly to apply than others, some auditing procedures may be more effective in meeting specific objectives, and certain forms of evidence are more reliable under conditions of effective internal control. In choosing a particular way to satisfy audit objectives, therefore, the auditor must be able to exercise sound judgment based on an understanding of the characteristics of audit evidence. These characteristics will be addressed more fully in Chapter 4.

---

7 *The Wall Street Journal*, July 28, 1998, p. A9.

EVALUATION OF EVIDENCE

Generally accepted auditing standards require that the auditor gather sufficient competent evidential matter as a basis for the audit opinion.[8] Sufficiency of evidence is a matter of audit judgment, which requires the auditor to provide reasonable, rather than absolute, assurance that the financial statements are free from material misstatement, and the most effective means for assuring sound audit judgment are the training and experience of the auditor.

Although some guidelines are provided in the professional standards, a decision on whether the **audit evidence** is competent under the circumstances is subject to the seasoned judgment of the auditor. Competence of evidence pertains to the reliability of the evidence, or the degree to which the evidence is convincing. Some forms of evidence are, by their very nature, more competent than others. For example, examination of inventory for the existence of items produces more reliable evidence than a client's response to a question regarding its existence. Internal accounting control also has an impact on competence. The more reliable the controls are, the more valid the transaction evidence produced by them.

Evaluating audit evidence is a topic for further discussion throughout the text, since audit testing is related to transaction cycles. These guidelines are introduced here simply to provide an overview as part of the more exhaustive examination of audit evidence, audit procedures, and audit programs.

COMMUNICATION OF THE AUDITOR'S FINDINGS

The auditor's findings are communicated through the audit report. Exhibit 1.2 illustrates the standard audit report form recommended by the AICPA.[9] This report contains three main components: an introductory paragraph, a scope paragraph, and an opinion paragraph.

The introductory paragraph states that management is responsible for preparing the financial statements and the auditors are responsible for expressing an opinion as to the fairness of that presentation. The scope paragraph tells what the auditor did, that is, whether the audit was conducted in accordance with generally accepted auditing standards. The opinion paragraph contains the auditor's findings, that is, whether the financial statements are presented fairly, in accordance with generally accepted accounting principles.

The standard audit report, containing no exceptions, is rendered only under circumstances involving no material restrictions on the scope of the audit and no material departures from generally accepted accounting principles. Material scope restrictions and departures from GAAP necessitate qualifying the audit opinion.

Any material restrictions on the scope of the examination, for which the auditor is not able to obtain satisfaction by alternate means, would ordinarily cause the auditor to take exception in the audit report. These exceptions, or *qualifications*, are usually explained in a separate paragraph of the audit report. Depending on the severity of the restriction, the auditor may have to *disclaim* an opinion (i.e., render no opinion), on the grounds that insufficient evidence was obtained to render an opinion.

A material departure from GAAP may result in either a *qualified* or an *adverse* audit opinion, depending on how significantly the financial statements are affected by the de-

8 *AICPA Professional Standards*, op. cit., section AU 326.01.
9 Ibid, section AU 508.08.

EXHIBIT 1.2

Standard Audit Report

Report of Independent Auditors

To: Board of Directors and Stockholders
ABC Corporation

Introductory Paragraph

We have audited the accompanying balance sheet of ABC Corporation as of December 31, 2003, and the related statements of income, retained earnings, and cash flows for the year then ended. These financial statements are the responsibility of the Company's management. Our responsibility is to express an opinion on these financial statements based on our audit.

Scope Paragraph

We conducted our audit in accordance with generally accepted auditing standards. These standards require that we plan and perform the audit to obtain reasonable assurance about whether the financial statements are free of material misstatement. An audit includes examining, on a test basis, evidence supporting the amounts and disclosures in the financial statements. An audit also includes assessing the accounting principles used and significant estimates made by management, as well as evaluating the overall financial statement presentation. We believe that our audit provides a reasonable basis for our opinion.

Opinion Paragraph

In our opinion, the financial statements referred to above present fairly, in all material respects, the financial position of ABC Corporation as of December 31, 2003, and the results of its operations and its cash flows for the year then ended in conformity with generally accepted accounting principles.

Gibson and Keller, CPAs
March 2, 2004

parture. For example, failure to account properly for costs under a pension plan may result in a qualified opinion, whereas failure to capitalize financing leases, when virtually all plant assets are leased, may lead to an adverse opinion. The adverse opinion states that in the opinion of the auditor the financial statements do not fairly present the financial position, results of operations, and cash flows.

An explanatory paragraph must be added to the audit report when an inconsistency in the application of GAAP has occurred during the period under audit. A change in an accounting principle represents an **inconsistency**, and an explanatory paragraph must be added whenever there is a material change in an accounting principle. The purpose of the consistency paragraph is to alert the reader to the change, because it may materially affect the comparability of financial data among the periods presented in the annual report.

To summarize the discussion, the following conditions are necessary to warrant an unqualified audit opinion:

1. No material scope restrictions occurred for which the auditor was not able to obtain satisfaction by alternate means (other forms of evidence); and
2. The financial statements contain no material departures from GAAP (including adequacy of disclosure).

More extensive coverage of the audit report is provided in Chapter 14.

THE AUDIT PROCESS: AN OVERVIEW

Figure 1.6 summarizes the audit process in chronological fashion. The following paragraphs discuss the various steps shown in the diagram. The model will be refined in subsequent chapters as audit planning, control testing, substantive testing, and audit reporting are explored in depth.

Audit Planning

Preliminaries   After accepting an entity as an audit client, the independent CPA begins the audit process by gathering information concerning the operations of the entity,

---

FIGURE 1.6

The Audit Process

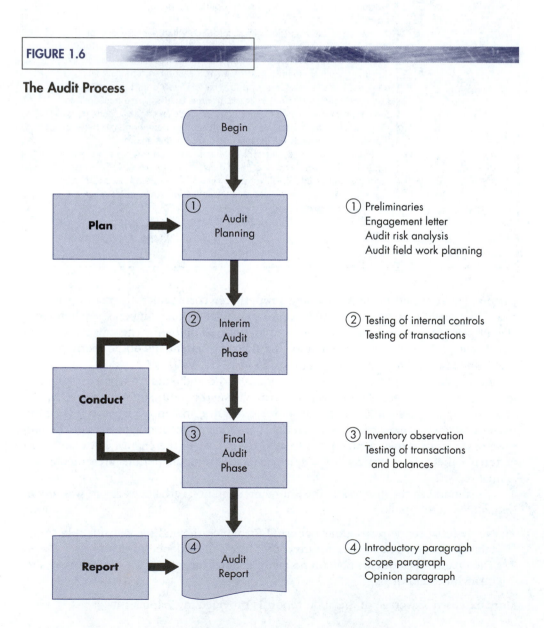

its organizational structure, its internal control system as related to the published financial statements, and the characteristics of its data processing applications. Referred to as **preliminaries**, this process enables the auditor to gain a working knowledge of the entity. It also assists audit planning by identifying those high-risk areas requiring special attention.

At the beginning of this section, **client acceptance** was assumed. During preliminary discussions with the client, however, the auditor may discover that she or he does not possess the technical expertise to conduct the audit, that management integrity is sufficiently lacking to preclude acceptance, or that certain mutual relationships rule out the necessary independence between the auditor and the client. If for any reason the auditor concludes that an audit is not feasible, the client should be so informed and the engagement declined.

Engagement Letter   Whether it concerns an initial or a recurring audit, both the client and the auditor should sign an engagement letter. Exhibit 1.3 illustrates a common form of engagement letter. The **engagement letter** summarizes the agreement of the parties formulated during the preliminaries, and states clearly the mutual understanding of the nature of the engagement. Its main function is to provide written evidence of agreement concerning the audit. Misunderstandings between auditor and client regarding the nature of the engagement may be more easily resolved given the engagement letter. Engagement letters are recommended regardless of the nature of the appointment and should be used for all types of assurance services performed by CPAs.

Audit Risk Analysis   Before performing tests of transactions and balances, the auditor should gain a thorough understanding of the client's business and the industry of which it is a part, and the existing internal accounting controls as they affect the assertions contained in the financial statements. A major trend in auditing, created by the rising incidence of cases alleging auditor negligence, has been the increased attention given by auditors to audit risk analysis. **Audit risk** may be defined as the probability of rendering an unqualified opinion on financial statements that are materially misstated. In order to adequately assess risk exposure, the auditor needs to understand the entity, the industry, and the economic substance of all significant transactions. The auditor also needs to obtain a sufficient understanding of the client's internal accounting control policies and procedures to permit planning of the audit.

Auditors must be alert to attempts by management to deliberately misstate the entity's financial position and results of operations, termed **fraudulent financial reporting**. These attempts have been prompted by such diverse factors as increased competition and the need to maintain earnings growth, liquidity problems and the attempt to conceal violations of restrictive covenants in loan agreements, a declining industry (defense contracting, for example) and resulting efforts to mask uncertainty about continued existence, and dishonesty in management (fabrication of earnings and assets through fraudulent transactions). The possibility of fraudulent financial reporting is a principal factor in audit risk. Analysis of the business and the industry, along with study and evaluation of the internal control, collectively represent the most significant part of audit risk analysis and assessment. These topics are addressed more fully in Chapters 5 and 6, respectively.

Audit Field Work Planning   Before the audit team can actually begin the field work (that part of the audit performed mainly on the client's premises), some preliminary **audit**

EXHIBIT 1.3

Engagement Letter

Mr. Howard Hill   September 6, 2003
ABC Corporation
2000 Expressway Drive North
Toledo, Ohio 43617

Dear Mr. Hill:

In accordance with the agreement reached in our conference on September 4, 2003, we are to perform an audit of the balance sheet of the ABC Corporation as of December 31, 2003, and of the related statements of income, retained earnings, and cash flows for the fiscal year then ended. The audit report will be mailed to you and the Board of Directors. We are also to prepare the federal and state income tax returns for the fiscal year ending December 31, 2003.

Our audit will be made in accordance with generally accepted auditing standards and, accordingly, will include such tests of the accounting records and such other auditing procedures as we consider necessary to enable us to express an opinion regarding your financial statements. It should be noted that such an examination is not primarily designed, and cannot be relied on, to disclose all errors, defalcations, and other similar irregularities, although they may be discovered as a result of the examination.

Our examination will include a study and review of your company's internal accounting control system. The purpose of the study and review of the internal accounting control system is to determine the scope of our audit engagement and is not to detect all errors in the processing of information. On the basis of our study and review of the internal accounting control system, we will make suggestions, where appropriate, for improving the system. If we should discover material weaknesses in the design or the execution of the system, we will disclose these weaknesses to you in writing before the conclusion of the audit.

Based on our discussion with your personnel and the predecessor auditor and a preliminary review of your accounting records, we estimate the cost of the audit engagement, including the preparation of the related tax returns, will be approximately $75,000. It should be recognized that the estimated fee could be affected by unusual circumstances we cannot foresee at this particular time. However, if we should encounter such problems, we will immediately contact you to discuss the implications of the new developments.

We appreciate the opportunity to serve your company. Do not hesitate to contact us if you have any questions about the engagement or desire other professional services.

If the terms designated in this letter are satisfactory, please sign in the space provided below and return the duplicate copy of the letter to us.

Sincerely,
James Gibson
James Gibson, CPA

Accepted by: *H. Hill*
Title: *Treasurer*
Date: *9/8/03*

planning of the field work needs to be done. First, preliminary audit programs need to be formulated. **Audit programs** are collections of audit procedures to be applied to meet specified audit objectives. At this stage in the audit, the programs will be based on the preliminaries, the analysis of the business and industry, and the auditor's understanding of internal accounting control, as discussed earlier. Further testing of the internal control procedures, which will be discussed later, may lead to subsequent modification of the audit programs.

Once the preliminary programs have been formulated, the *in-charge* (senior) auditor is in a position to determine the number of people needed to conduct the various phases of the audit. A **time budget**, which contains extensive detail concerning each phase of the audit and the number of hours of assistant, senior, manager, and partner time required, is prepared at this point.

After the time budget has been prepared and people have been selected for the audit, a **preaudit conference** with the audit team members may be convened by the audit partner to discuss significant aspects of the audit. Such matters as assignment of audit tasks, high-risk areas, information regarding the nature of the entity to be audited, and a general description of the internal accounting controls should be covered during the preaudit conference. Computer-based accounting applications and the possible need for computer audit specialists should also be considered at this time.

Interim Audit Work

Traditionally, **audit field work** (the actual application of auditing procedures) has been conducted in two major phases:

1. The **interim audit** phase, which consists of testing the client's internal accounting controls and performing substantive tests of transactions; and
2. The **final audit** phase, during which more substantive testing of transactions and substantive tests of balances are performed.

The nature, timing, and extent of transaction and balance testing depend primarily on the nature of the business and the industry and on the quality of the existing internal controls, as determined in the audit planning and control testing phases.

In recent years, certain changes in the information-processing environment have begun to alter the traditional approach to the interim audit phase. Instead of testing the internal control procedures during a single interim time period, auditors are applying these tests, along with tests of selected transactions, at frequent intervals throughout the year. This is sometimes referred to as **continuous auditing**. Continuous auditing is especially applicable to those clients with sophisticated computer-based accounting applications. Many of these systems do not retain permanent records of the *audit trail* (the means by which the auditor is able to follow a transaction from its source to the general ledger accounts). By frequently testing both control procedures and transactions during the year, the auditor is able to locate and substantiate controls and transactions before the audit trail is lost.

Final Audit Work

Inventory Observation   If the client has significant amounts of inventory and takes a physical inventory at or near year end, the independent auditor will plan to be present to observe the physical inventory. The main purpose for **inventory observation** and conducting test counts is to gain satisfaction concerning the inventory's existence.

Tests of Transactions and Balances   Many of the tests of transactions and most of the tests of balances are performed during the final audit phase, preferably at or close to year end. These procedures are referred to as **substantive tests** because the auditor examines evidence representing the *substance* underlying the transactions and balances. The tests include, but are not limited to, confirming accounts receivable with customers, determining the overall fairness of the inventory values assigned by the client, determining that amounts recorded as accrued and deferred are correct, and searching for unrecorded liabilities. Added control testing also may be necessary at this time if significant changes in the manner in which transactions are processed have occurred since the interim audit phase.

During both the interim and the final audit phases, the in-charge auditor should supervise all audit work of assistants. Upon completion of the final audit phase, the audit manager is usually called in to perform an overall review of the audit.

Audit Report

The audit report is the final step in the audit process. It summarizes the scope of the audit and presents the auditor's findings in the form of an audit opinion. The audit report has been discussed briefly in this chapter and will be covered more extensively in Chapter 14.

OTHER SERVICES PERFORMED BY CPA FIRMS

In addition to independent audits, CPA firms derive significant amounts of revenue from the following sources:

1. Tax services, including tax advising and tax return preparation
2. Other assurance services (discussed in Chapter 15)
3. Management consulting (discussed in Chapter 2)
4. Accounting and data processing

Although assurance services (including auditing) remain a major source of revenue for the national accounting firms (see Table 1.1), their share has declined in recent years

TABLE 1.1

Comparative Sources of Accounting Firm Revenue

| | | | | KPMG International Revenues (millions) | | | | |
	1996	% of Total	1997	% of Total	1998	% of Total	1999	% of Total
Assurance	$1,196	47%	$1,315	44%	$1,482	39%	$1,646	35%
Consulting	703	28%	926	31%	1,393	37%	1,963	42%
Tax	581	23%	688	23%	834	22%	1,028	22%
Other	45	2%	55	2%	92	2%	19	0%
Total	$2,525	100%	$2,984	100%	$3,801	100%	$4,656	100%

Source: KPMG International a Annual Report—1999.

in proportion to the total business of these firms. This may be attributed to the increasing incidence of client mergers, as well as pressure placed on firms by their clients to reduce audit fees. In contrast, management consulting services have increased both absolutely and in proportion to total firm revenues. Recognizing the changing nature of public accounting services, the AICPA established a Special Committee on Assurance Services, charging it with "analyzing and reporting on the current state and future of the audit/assurance function."[10] To date, the committee has identified types of assurance services with potential for CPAs. In addition to those addressed at the beginning of this chapter, others include evaluating the delivery of health care services, assessing elder care services, and providing assurance regarding policy compliance.

Smaller CPA firms realize an even lower percentage of their revenues from audits because their clients are nonpublic companies and, therefore, do not require independent audits. Instead, these firms derive most of their revenues from tax, accounting, and other assurance services.

KEY TERMS

Assertions, 5
Assurance services, 3
Attestation, 3
Audit committee, 10
Audit evidence, 14
Audit field work, 19
Audit planning, 18
Audit programs, 18
Audit report, 7
Audit risk, 17
Auditing, 5
Client acceptance, 17
Completeness assertion, 5
Compliance auditing, 11
Continuous auditing, 19
Defense Contract Audit Agency (DCAA), 11
Engagement letter, 17
Evidence, 5
Existence or occurrence assertion, 5

Final audit, 19
Fraudulent financial reporting, 17
General Accounting Office (GAO), 10
Inconsistency, 15
Independent audits, 9
Interim audit, 19
Internal auditing, 10
Internal control, 13
Inventory observation, 19
Operational audits, 10
Preaudit conference, 19
Preliminaries, 17
Presentation and disclosure assertion, 5
Rights and obligations assertion, 5
Risk-based audit, 7
Substantive tests, 20
Time budget, 19
Valuation or allocation assertion, 5

REVIEW QUESTIONS

1. Differentiate among the following terms:
    Auditing
    Attestation
    Assurance

2. Define *management's assertions*, as used in the definition of auditing cited in this chapter. List the assertions and give an example of each.

10 AICPA Special Committee on Assurance Services, New York: AICPA, 1996.

3. How does the auditor ascertain the degree of correspondence between management's assertions and established criteria?

4. What is meant by "systematically and objectively" obtaining evidence?

5. How does the auditor decide when evidence is sufficient and competent?

6. What is the communication mechanism used by the auditor?

7. How does internal auditing differ from independent auditing?

8. Name the governmental agencies involved in audits and briefly describe their respective audit activities.

9. How does auditing differ from accounting?

10. How is auditing related to accounting?

11. How does an audit enhance the quality of the financial statements?

12. Why is an understanding of the business and industry of the client necessary for an effective audit?

13. In addition to an understanding of the business and industry, what are the other requirements for an effective audit?

14. Differentiate between the scope and opinion paragraphs of the standard audit report.

15. What conditions are necessary for an unqualified opinion?

16. What is an engagement letter and why is it recommended prior to a CPA rendering professional services?

17. What function is served by the audit program?

18. Who participates in the preaudit conference and what topics should be discussed?

19. What distinguishes the interim audit phase from the final audit phase?

20. Why must the auditor test the internal controls prior to testing transactions and balances?

MULTIPLE CHOICE QUESTIONS FROM PAST CPA EXAMS

1. Which of the following statements relating to the competence of evidential matter is always true?
   a. Evidential matter gathered by an auditor from outside an enterprise is reliable.
   b. Accounting data developed under satisfactory conditions of internal control are more relevant than data developed under unsatisfactory internal control conditions.
   c. Oral representations made by management are not valid evidence.
   d. Evidence gathered by auditors must be both valid and relevant to be considered competent.

2. With respect to the auditor's planning of a year-end examination, which of the following statements is always true?
   a. An engagement should not be accepted after the fiscal year end.
   b. An inventory count must be observed at the balance sheet date.

    c. The client's audit committee should not be told of the specific audit procedures that will be performed.

    d. It is an acceptable practice to carry out substantial parts of the examination at interim dates.

3. Those procedures specifically outlined in an audit program are primarily designed to
    a. Gather evidence.
    b. Detect errors or fraud.
    c. Test internal systems.
    d. Protect the auditor in the event of litigation.

4. A typical objective of an operational audit is for the auditor to
    a. Determine whether the financial statements fairly present the entity's operations.
    b. Evaluate the feasibility of attaining the entity's operational objectives.
    c. Make recommendations for improving performance.
    d. Report on the entity's relative success in maximizing profits.

5. When, in the auditor's judgment, the financial statements are not presented fairly in conformity with generally accepted accounting principles, the auditor will issue a(n)
    a. Qualified opinion.
    b. Special report.
    c. Disclaimer of opinion.
    d. Adverse opinion.

6. In which of the following circumstances would an adverse opinion be appropriate?
    a. The auditor is not independent with respect to the enterprise being audited.
    b. A material uncertainty regarding litigation exists.
    c. The statements are not in conformity with APB Opinion No. 8 regarding pension plans.
    d. A client-imposed scope limitation prevents the auditor from complying with generally accepted auditing standards.

7. The primary purpose of the auditor's study and evaluation of internal control is to provide a basis for
    a. Determining whether procedures and records that are concerned with the safeguarding of assets are reliable.
    b. Constructive suggestions to clients concerning improvements in internal control.
    c. Determining the nature, extent, and timing of audit tests to be applied.
    d. The expression of an opinion.

8. The scope and nature of an auditor's contractual obligation to a client ordinarily is set forth in the
    a. Management letter.
    b. Scope paragraph of the auditor's report.
    c. Engagement letter.
    d. Introductory paragraph of the auditor's report.

ESSAY QUESTIONS AND PROBLEMS

1.1   Susan Hammer & Co., CPAs, has just accepted an engagement to audit Virtual, Inc., a small manufacturer of specialty computer games. Kurt Daglon has been selected as the in-charge auditor for the engagement, and Hanna Beach will be his assistant. In planning the audit field work, Daglon makes the following assignments of audit tasks:

	Kurt Daglon	*Hanna Beach*
Interim audit	Perform tests of sales transactions and accounts receivable balances	Perform tests of internal control over cash receipts
Final audit	Perform tests of cash receipts transactions and cash balances	Perform tests of internal control over sales and accounts receivable

Required:
a. Identify the steps to be followed in completing an audit.
b. What is meant by the term *systematic process* as contained in the definition of auditing?
c. Explain the strengths and weaknesses in Daglon's audit planning.

1.2   A student, newly enrolled in an auditing course, asks her instructor why auditing is a required course in the curriculum. She has already taken the income tax course, along with intermediate and advanced accounting, as well as cost and managerial accounting. "Don't I already have the knowledge and tools to examine the financial statements? Won't the auditing course be redundant?" she asks.

Required:
Assume the role of professor and respond to the student's questions.

1.3   During a staff training session, the participants were asked to identify characteristics of audit evidence and to explain how each characteristic assists the auditor in conducting the examination.

Required:
a. Identify the necessary characteristics of audit evidence.
b. Give an example of a type of audit evidence.
c. Discuss how that particular piece of evidence might help the auditor formulate an opinion on the financial statements.
d. How would you evaluate your evidence in terms of the characteristics just identified in (a)?

1.4   At the annual stockholders' meeting, the following question was raised by one of the minority shareholders and directed to the independent auditors: "Inasmuch as our company already has an internal audit staff, why is it necessary to be audited by outside CPAs? After all, the internal auditors know much more about the company's operations and are much more familiar with the personnel and the accounting system. It would appear that the internal auditors could do the job more effectively and at considerably less cost than the outside CPAs."

Required:
a. Respond to the shareholder's question.
b. How does the independent auditor fulfill a public need?

1.5   The auditor should obtain a level of knowledge of the entity's business, including events, transactions, and practices, that will enable the planning and performance of an examination in accordance with generally accepted auditing standards. Adhering to these standards enables the auditor's report to lend credibility to financial statements by providing the public with certain assurances.

Required:
a. How does knowledge of the entity's business help the auditor in the planning and performance of an examination in accordance with generally accepted auditing standards?
b. What assurances are provided to the public when the auditor states that the financial statements "present fairly . . . in conformity with generally accepted accounting principles"?

(AICPA adapted)

1.6   Feiler, the sole owner of a small hardware business, has been told that the business should have financial statements reported on by an independent CPA. Feiler, having some bookkeeping experience, has personally prepared the company's financial statements and does not understand why such statements should be examined by a CPA. Feiler discussed the matter with Farber, a CPA, and asked Farber to explain why an audit is considered important.

Required:
a. Describe the objectives of an independent audit.
b. Identify five ways in which an independent audit may be beneficial to Feiler.

(AICPA adapted)

1.7   An important measure of the quality of the internal auditing function concerns the level within the organization to which the internal auditor reports. A rule of thumb is that the internal auditor must report to a sufficiently high level so that his or her findings will be implemented.

Required:
a. How does reporting to a higher level within the organization improve the chances for the internal auditor's findings to be implemented?
b. Today, many companies have their internal auditors report directly to the audit committee of the board of directors. How does this practice enhance the effectiveness of internal auditing?

1.8   Following $3.54 billion in special charges and restatement of earnings over the previous seven years, Waste Management Inc. announced in March 1998 that the SEC had launched a formal investigation into the company's accounting practices. An area of particular interest in the SEC investigation concerned the company's estimate of garbage dump capacities. The value of a dump equals the number of tons of garbage the dump can accommodate over its estimated lifetime times the price per ton minus the cost of acquiring, improving, and developing the dump. Acquisition, improvement, and development costs are, of course, objectively determined, as is the price per ton of garbage. The capacity and life of the dump, in contrast, are based on engineering estimates and management's best guess as to whether a municipality will grant a permit to expand the dump at the end of its initial life. In the case of Waste Management, capacities and lives were greatly overstated, thereby inflating earnings by understating periodic amortization costs. Arthur Andersen, Waste Management's independent auditors, agreed with the estimates.

Following the SEC probe, shareholders initiated lawsuits against the company and its auditors. The cases were settled for $220 million to be paid jointly by the company and Arthur Andersen.

Required:

a. How does this case demonstrate the adversarial relationship between corporate management and its stockholders?

b. Do you think Arthur Andersen should have detected the overstatements of lives and dump capacities?

1.9   On June 1, 2001, Dibble & Beaudry, CPAs, was approached by Seeman Enterprises, Inc., to perform an audit of Seeman's financial statements for the fiscal year ending September 30, 2001. Donald Bear, an audit manager for Dibble & Beaudry, has completed a preliminary study of the company. The information documented in the preliminary study was gathered during discussions with client personnel, including the corporate controller, observation of company personnel, and study of company policy manuals and accounting manuals, as well as industry trade data. Some of Bear's findings follow.

Seeman Enterprises, incorporated in 1965, manufacturers and sells lawn furniture and garden equipment, such as lawn mowers, snow blowers, and leaf blowers. In addition, the company recently acquired a restaurant chain selling and servicing franchises on a nationwide scale. The company was previously audited by Franz & Johnson, CPAs. Although Bear hasn't yet contacted the previous auditors, Dennis Gaffney, Seeman's controller, cited the reason for the change in auditors as the failure of Franz & Johnson to provide needed management services, such as help with the new online computer system that Seeman hopes to install in the next year. In questioning Gaffney about Seeman's internal control, Bear couldn't seem to elicit specific information—only a general assurance by the controller that the system is "sound." The accounting system appears somewhat dated and transactions are entered in batches rather than online. Also, the company does not maintain perpetual inventory records. Bear finds this somewhat surprising in view of Seeman's size (2000 sales of $2.5 million and net assets of $12.6 million). Seeman does not have an internal audit staff and the accounting department seems small relative to the volume of transactions processed.

Required:

a. What is the significance of obtaining preliminary information prior to accepting an audit engagement?

b. Identify any concerns you have, based on Bear's preliminary study of Seeman. Discuss how your concerns might affect your acceptance decision and how it will impact the conduct of the Seeman's 2001 audit, assuming acceptance of the engagement. [Use the following format in answering (b).]

Concern	Affect Acceptance?	Audit Impact

1.10   In addition to financial auditing, the internal auditor is also engaged in evaluating the efficiency of operations (operational auditing) and the effectiveness of management (management, or performance, auditing).

Required:

a. Distinguish among the terms *financial auditing*, *operational auditing*, and *management auditing*.

b. Briefly describe the role of the General Accounting Office (GAO) in the performance of management audits.

c. The Internal Revenue Service and the Defense Contract Audit Agency perform compliance audits. Explain how this type of auditing differs from financial and operational auditing.

1.11   As used in the definition of auditing, assertions are representations of management as to the fairness of the financial statements. Each line item on the financial statements, therefore, represents management's assertions concerning such matters as existence and proper valuation of recorded assets, liabilities, revenues, and expenses.

Required:
a. Identify management's assertions related to fairness of financial presentation.
b. For each of the following balance sheet components, state how you would satisfy yourself as to existence and valuation (i.e., what evidence you might gather to gain reasonable assurance regarding those assertions).
   1. Inventories of finished goods
   2. Marketable equity securities
   3. Accounts receivable

1.12   Peter Martyn, CPA, has two audit clients, both of whom close their books on September 30. Both are recurring engagements (i.e., Martyn audited both clients for the year immediately preceding the current year). In developing preliminary audit plans, Martyn notes the following characteristics about each client.

Client A, a small computer manufacturer, conducts its operations at a single location. The company produces motherboards, keyboards, and cabinets, and buys such components as disk drives, monitors, and communication software from various manufacturers. The company sells direct to customers via catalog and other forms of advertising. Although the average investment in inventories is significant, internal control has been strong in the past and Martyn has recommended only a few audit adjustments in prior years. Increased competition, however, has caused some decline in profits, and cash flows have diminished to the point where the company is experiencing some difficulty in meeting its current obligations. Martyn has noted that while competitors have sustained losses through the third quarter of 1999, Client A has reported a small profit.

Client B, a film producer, creates syndicated programs and films for the television and movie industries. The company defers all direct production costs (those costs that can be identified with specific programs and films). When a program or film is sold to a television network or studio, revenue is recognized and previously deferred costs are expensed as part of the matching process. Films and programs are frequently rerun subsequent to the initial showing from which Client B earns additional revenue. If the company considers a rerun highly probable, a portion of the direct costs is deferred until a rerun contract is negotiated. If a pilot program or film cannot be sold, the direct costs are treated as a loss in the current accounting period. Client B's internal control procedures have been strong in the past.

Required:
Discuss how the given information might affect the audits of the two clients. Specifically, to minimize audit risk, what audit areas would you stress in each case? Where might you reduce audit emphasis?

Defining Professional Responsibility: Quality Standards and Ethics

c h a p t e r 2

biltrite

After reading this chapter, you should be able to

Understand how the following sources determine the quality of accounting services and impact the performance of CPAs:

- Generally accepted auditing standards (GAAS)
- Statements on Auditing Standards (SASs)
- Attestation Standards
- Statements on Standards for Accounting and Review Services (SSARSs)
- Statements on Standards for Consulting Services (CSs)
- Statements on Responsibilities in Tax Practice (TXs)
- Ethics and the Code of Professional Conduct

OVERVIEW

The means for achieving quality in the rendering of auditing and other professional services by CPAs are explored in this chapter. Maintaining the quality of performance is addressed in Chapter 3. Providing services at a level of competence expected by the recipients of those services is necessary if CPAs are to make a significant economic contribution. Appropriate levels of quality in auditing are defined by the ten generally accepted auditing standards (GAAS) and the Statements on Auditing Standards (SASs) promulgated by the AICPA. The Attestation Standards, Statements on Consulting Services, Statements on Responsibilities in Tax Practice, and Statements on Standards for Accounting and Review Services set quality guidelines for other professional services. Like the auditing standards, these statements and standards are also issued by the AICPA, and establish acceptable levels of quality for the conduct of these engagements.

Ethics define our attitudes and encourage us to observe the highest standards of moral conduct. The Code of Professional Conduct addresses ethics in terms of the necessary characteristics of the CPA practitioner and the proper conduct of a public accounting practice. The Code also makes the AICPA statements and standards binding on the CPA performing public accounting services.

STANDARDS GOVERNING THE QUALITY OF PROFESSIONAL ACCOUNTING SERVICES

How does auditing achieve the level of quality needed to preserve its professional status? Figure 2.1 summarizes the existing quality definition structure covering auditing and other accounting services rendered by CPAs and forms a basis for the discussion that follows. The various types of accounting services are listed on the left and the standards governing quality appear on the right. The Code of Conduct appears on the far right of the exhibit and extends to all public accounting services performed by CPA members of the AICPA. Although the remainder of this chapter may seem highly structured and somewhat formal, a careful scrutiny of the material is vital to an understanding of the accounting profession's quality control framework.

Auditing Standards

The ten **generally accepted auditing standards (GAAS)**, promulgated by the Auditing Standards Board (ASB) of the AICPA, establish a required level of quality for performing financial statement audits. These standards (see Figure 2.2) must be followed by the CPA in conducting audits. **Statements on Auditing Standards (SASs)** are interpretations of the ten standards. They are issued as necessary by the ASB and, like the standards, must be adhered to by CPAs performing independent audits. Auditing procedures are the means used by the CPA in attaining the quality required of the standards.

General Standards   The three **general standards** relate to the *character* and *competence* of the auditor. Adequate technical **training and proficiency as an auditor** assures clients that CPAs are able to adequately perform the services for which they represent themselves. If a client's accounting system contains complex computer-based applications, for example, the auditor must have an adequate understanding of computers and computer processing to permit examination of the system and the related financial data

FIGURE 2.1

Range of CPA's Services and Definition of Quality

Service	Quality Defined (Source)	
Auditing	Statement on Auditing Standards (SASs)	**C O D E O F C O N D U C T**
	Independence Standards Board (ISB)	
Other attest services: 　Financial projections 　Financial forecasts 　Pro forma statements 　Reports on internal control	Attestation Standards 　Statements on Standards for 　Attestation Engagements (SSAEs)	
Compilations and reviews	Statements on Standards for 　Accounting and Review Services 　(SSARs)	
Consulting engagements	Statements on Standards for 　Consulting Services (CSs)	
Tax services	Statements on Responsibilities in 　Tax Practice (TXs)	

flowing through the system. An auditor who undertakes to examine the financial statements of a client in a previously unfamiliar industry must attain a level of understanding of the transactions and accounting practices unique to that industry to afford a basis for successful completion of the audit.

Auditor independence means that auditors must be independent of management if they are to adequately serve the interests of financial statement users. For example, auditors cannot own stock in a public company they audit. Auditor independence has two aspects: **independence in fact** and **independence in appearance**. Auditor independence is discussed more fully in the *Rules of Conduct* section of this chapter.

Due professional care refers to the auditor's exercise of professional judgment during the conduct of an examination. Determining when evidence is sufficient or competent, categorizing an internal control weakness or a financial statement misstatement as material, and deciding on the form of audit report to render in the circumstances represent decisions that require the exercise of audit judgment. The standard of due care requires that the "prudent auditor" apply judgment in a conscientious manner, carefully weighing the relevant factors before reaching a decision.

Due care also suggests that the auditor make a reasonable effort to ensure that the financial statements are free from material misstatement. This aspect of due care is the concept most frequently cited by the courts in cases alleging auditor negligence. In these cases, the courts tend to address the questions of whether the auditor performed the examination with a reasonable degree of diligence and whether the auditor possessed the level of skill required by the profession in order to carry out the engagement.

FIGURE 2.2

Generally Accepted Auditing Standards

General Standards

1. The examination is to be performed by a person or persons having adequate technical training and proficiency as an auditor.
2. In all matters relating to the assignment, an independence in mental attitude is to be maintained by the auditor or auditors.
3. Due professional care is to be exercised in the performance of the examination and the preparation of the report.

Standards of Field Work

1. The work is to be adequately planned, and assistants, if any, are to be properly supervised.
2. A sufficient understanding of the internal control structure is to be obtained to plan the audit and to determine the nature, timing, and extent of tests to be performed.
3. Sufficient competent evidential matter is to be obtained through inspection, observation, inquiries, and confirmations to afford a reasonable basis for an opinion regarding the financial statements under examination.

Standards of Reporting

1. The report shall state whether the financial statements are presented in accordance with generally accepted accounting principles.
2. The report shall identify those circumstances in which such principles have not been consistently observed in the current period in relation to the preceding period.
3. Informative disclosures in the financial statements are to be regarded as reasonably adequate unless otherwise stated in the report.
4. The report shall either contain an opinion regarding the financial statements, taken as a whole, or an assertion to the effect that an opinion cannot be expressed. When an overall opinion cannot be expressed, the reasons therefore should be stated. In all cases where an auditor's name is associated with financial statements, the report should contain a clear-cut indication of the character of the auditor's examination, if any, and the degree of responsibility taken.

Source: *AICPA Professional Standards*, New York: American Institute of Certified Public Accountants, 1997, section AU 150.02.

In the case of *Escott vs. Bar Chris Construction Corporation* (see Chapter 3), the court held that the auditors had not exercised due care in the conduct of the examination. In this case, the auditors failed to gain an adequate understanding of certain complex sale and leaseback transactions entered into by Bar Chris. These transactions related to the construction, sale, leasing, and operation of bowling centers, the main activities of Bar Chris. Failure to comprehend the nature of these rather complex transactions, together with failure to identify certain related-party transactions, resulted in undetected material errors in the financial statements. As a result, assets and income were overstated, and related-party transactions were improperly classified on the balance sheet. The court, in finding the auditors guilty of negligence, stated that the in-charge senior auditor had not followed some of the steps set forth in the written audit programs and, more important, had been "too easily satisfied with glib answers to the auditor's questions."[1]

Due audit care does not require the auditor to make perfect judgment decisions in all cases, but it does require that the examination be completed with a reasonable degree of diligence by persons possessing the average skills required by the profession.

Given the increased incidence of cases similar to *Bar Chris* involving undetected management fraud, the ASB issued SAS 82, which requires the CPA to assess the probability of fraud when conducting a financial statement audit and consider that assessment in designing the audit procedures to be performed.[2] The SAS also provides guidance to the auditor in the form of identifying factors that are indicative of possible fraud and in modifying audit procedures in response to those factors.[3]

Field Work Standards   Whereas the general standards deal with the character and competence of the auditor, the **field work standards** are concerned with the *audit process*. As with the general standards, there are three standards of field work (see Figure 2.2).

Adequate **planning and supervision** are required if the audit is to proceed in a systematic fashion. Audit planning involves obtaining an understanding of the entity, assessing audit risk, and developing audit programs. Audit planning also encompasses such tasks as making arrangements with the client concerning the timing of the audit field work, use of the client's staff in completing certain phases of the audit, and coordinating the audit work with the internal auditors.

Preparation of a time budget estimating the hours required to complete the various parts of the audit provides the auditor with an effective structure for audit planning purposes. The preaudit conference, as described in Chapter 1, is also part of audit planning.

To ensure an adequate quality of auditing, assistants must be properly supervised. The in-charge senior auditor is the direct-line supervisor on the engagement. To ensure adequate supervision, the senior must assign to assistants only those audit tasks that the assistants are capable of performing. Also, the senior must be prepared to answer questions raised by the assistants in the performance of their assigned tasks. Finally, and perhaps most important, the senior must carefully review the workpapers prepared by the assistants, making certain that they are complete and conclusive in all material respects. The *Bar Chris* case, described previously, clearly illustrates the importance of proper training and adequate supervision of assistants.

Proper **study and evaluation of internal control** is needed because virtually all independent financial audits are **test-based audits**. This means that the auditor examines only a sample of transactions completed by the client during the period under audit. In determining the extent, as well as the nature and timing, of tests required, the auditor must determine the effectiveness of existing internal control policies and procedures as they affect the reliability of the assertions contained in the financial statements. Effective internal accounting control permits less substantive testing of transactions and balances than weak controls. Internal control concepts, as well as the auditor's ap-

---

1   Escott et al v. Bar Chris Construction Corp. et al, 283 F. Supp. 643 (S.D.N.Y. 1968).
2. Auditing Standards Board, *Consideration of Fraud in a Financial Statement Audit*, op. cit., para. 12.
3   Ibid, para. 16–32.

proach to study and evaluation of internal control, are more fully addressed in Chapters 6 through 8.

Sufficient competent evidential matter is the standard that comes closest to addressing the application of auditing procedures, but it does *not* constrain the auditor in the selection of which procedures to apply in particular circumstances. Instead, the standard, along with Statement on Auditing Standards (SAS) No. 31, identifies the various types of evidence available to the auditor, and offers guidelines for the auditor to follow in judging *sufficiency* and *competence* of evidential matter, as was described in Chapter 1.

Reporting Standards   The four **reporting standards** (see Figure 2.2) relate to the *attest function*—the end result of the audit. Specifically, these standards require the auditor to determine whether the financial statements are essentially in accordance with generally accepted accounting principles (GAAP), and whether informative disclosures are adequate. Additionally, the standards require that the auditor either formulate an opinion regarding the financial statements taken as a whole, or disclaim an opinion and give a reason for the disclaimer. These four standards are addressed at length in Chapter 14.

As stated previously, the ten auditing standards, along with the related statements on auditing standards (SASs), must be adhered to in the conduct of all audits. The SASs are authoritative pronouncements that are issued by the Auditing Standards Board (ASB) of the AICPA and represent interpretations of the standards; therefore, auditors must justify any material departures from them. SASs are covered throughout the text within the specific topics to which they relate.

Attestation Standards

Like audits, many nonaudit services (e.g., an engagement to determine an entity's compliance with laws, regulations, or contractual provisions; or an engagement to evaluate the adequacy of an entity's internal accounting control) also require some form of attestation (opinion) by the CPA. To define a proper level of quality in the performance of these services, the AICPA has established eleven **attestation standards**. Interpretations of these standards, referred to as Statements on Standards for Attestation Engagements, are also issued periodically by the AICPA, as they are considered necessary. These standards and interpretations, which are discussed in Chapter 15, do not supersede the ten generally accepted auditing standards. Rather, they complement them, and make explicit certain preconditions for the performance of nonaudit attest services.

Statements on Standards for Accounting and Review Services

In lieu of an audit, nonpublic clients, who are not responsible for filing reports with the SEC, may request the CPA to compile or perform a review of the financial statements. These engagements are significantly less in scope than audits, and consist mainly of reading the financial statements, making inquiries of management, and applying analytical procedures (discussed in Chapter 5). They do *not* entail study and evaluation of internal control or the application of auditing procedures that gather evidence supporting the financial statement assertions.

In order to achieve consistency in the rendering of these services, the AICPA, in 1977, established the Accounting and Review Services Committee. Equivalent to the Auditing Standards Board, the Accounting and Review Services Committee issues

Statements on Standards for Accounting and Review Services (SSARSs), which establish the framework and define acceptable quality for performing compilations and reviews. Like the SASs, the SSARSs are binding upon the profession, and the CPA must be prepared to justify departures from them. Compilations and reviews, along with the related SSARSs, are discussed more fully in Chapter 15.

Statements on Standards for Consulting Services

A CPA frequently may be asked by clients to render consulting services. These services have become quite diverse and may assume such forms as analyzing an accounting system, reviewing a profit plan, installing a computer system, analyzing a merger proposal, providing staff for computer programming services, selling packaged training programs, and various other functions for which the CPA possesses expertise. These services are collectively referred to as CPA **consulting services** and are governed by the **Statements on Standards for Consulting Services (CSs)** issued by the AICPA Management Advisory Services Executive Committee.

In performing consulting services for audit clients, the CPA must make sure that independence is not compromised. This is best achieved by avoiding situations in which the CPA is required to make management decisions that might impair objectivity. CS No. 1, issued by the committee in 1991, defines CPA consulting and provides guidelines for effectively performing consulting services without compromising independence. Six areas of consulting services are identified and defined in the statement (see Exhibit 2.1).

CSs, like the SASs, apply to CPAs who are members of the AICPA. Departures from the provisions of the CSs must be justified in the same manner as departures from GAAS and related SASs.[4]

EXHIBIT 2.1

Classification of CPA Consulting Services

1. *Consultations*—The practitioner's function is to provide counsel in a short time frame.

2. *Advisory services*—The practitioner's function is to develop findings, conclusions, and recommendations for client consideration and decision making.

3. *Implementation services*—The practitioner's function is to put an action plan into effect.

4. *Transaction services*—The practitioner's function is to provide services related to a specific client transaction.

5. *Staff and other support services*—The practitioner's function is to provide appropriate staff to perform tasks specified by the client.

6. *Product services*—The practitioner's function is to provide the client with a product and associated professional services in support of the installation, use, or maintenance of the product.

Source: *AICPA Professional Standards*, section CS 100.05.

---

4 *AICPA Professional Standards*, section CS 100.01–08.

Statements on Responsibilities in Tax Practice

The **Statements on Responsibilities in Tax Practice (TXs)**, issued by the Committee on Federal Taxation of the AICPA, provide guidance for CPAs in performing tax services and representing clients in tax matters before the Internal Revenue Service. Since its inception in 1964, the committee has issued several TXs, covering such topics as the circumstances under which the CPA may sign a return as preparer, appropriate actions when a client refuses to answer questions on a return, knowledge of errors in returns, and the CPA's approach when representing the client in administrative proceedings before the Internal Revenue Service.[5]

ETHICS AND THE CODE OF PROFESSIONAL CONDUCT

Ethics

Ethical behavior is a state of mind—not a collection of rules. **Ethics** may be defined as moral principles and concern such characteristics as honesty and integrity, reliability and accountability, as well as all other aspects of right versus wrong behavior. Although the Code of Professional Conduct (discussed in the next section) identifies what the CPA can and cannot do, only a person of character can decide what is right to do.

Notwithstanding the efforts of the AICPA and other bodies, quality of service will be achieved and maintained only to the extent that CPAs, individually and collectively, assume a positive approach to ethical behavior and strive to abide by the spirit, as well as the letter, of the professional standards.

The accounting profession, like any other profession, exists only through wide public acceptance. Public acceptance of a profession means that society perceives a need that can best be met by highly trained professionals who have met some minimally acceptable standard.

In the case of public financial reporting, the perceived need is for the independent audit function. Third-party users need to have the financial statements audited by accounting experts who are highly trained in evidence gathering and evaluation methods, and who are also independent of the statement preparers (management). The audit function, as performed by the independent CPA, adds this needed dimension to the financial statements in the form of enhanced reliability.

Independent auditing maintains its professional stature by striving for consistency of quality and by maintaining independence from management. If the quality of the audit function were to significantly deteriorate, or if the auditors were perceived as not being independent, users would no longer consider the independent audit as a factor adding economic value to the financial statements of publicly held companies.

Several bank failures, occurring in the 1980s, called into question the quality of audits. These cases caused the AICPA, the American Accounting Association (AAA), the Financial Executives Institute (FEI), the Institute of Internal Auditors (IIA), and Institute of Management Accountants (IMA) to jointly sponsor the National Commission on Fraudulent Financial Reporting. The Commission's purpose was to study the financial reporting system as it existed in the United States, identify causal factors that can lead to fraudulent reporting, and recommend steps to reduce its incidence. The results of this study were published in a report of the commission released in 1987. Referred to as the **Treadway Report**, after James Treadway, chairman of the Commission, the study

5   Ibid, sections TX 102.01–182.10.

contains recommendations aimed at improving the performance of CPAs, particularly in the area of fraud detection.[6] The earliest impact of the study was the 1988 and 1990 revisions to the Code of Professional Conduct and the bylaws of the AICPA, and the release of nine new Statements on Auditing Standards (SASs) by the Auditing Standards Board. These significant revisions are described briefly in the following paragraphs, and incorporated as appropriate throughout the text.

The revised Code of Conduct provided for a more positive approach to accountants' ethical behavior. The new set of principles and rules replaced the rules and interpretations contained in earlier codes, and were broadened to encompass all services rendered by CPAs. Prior to 1988, the code covered mainly audit services; however, as CPAs expanded the breadth of assurance services, the profession recognized the need to define and regulate the quality of these services.

The nine SASs, among other matters, produced significant changes in the auditor's study and evaluation of internal control, and in the form of the standard audit report. Despite these efforts, alleged "audit failures" continued during the 1990s. Some of the more notable ones involved Cendant Corp., Sunbeam Corp., Bankers' Trust Corp., W.R. Grace, Waste Management, Inc., Rite Aid Corp., Livent, Inc., and McKesson HBOC Inc. These cases, like those that occurred in the 1980s, caused the public to ask, "Where were the auditors?" In response, the Securities and Exchange Commission stepped up its scrutiny of the accounting profession. This, in turn, led the Auditing Standards Board to release an SAS in 1997 that further defined the auditor's responsibility for fraud detection and provided guidance for implementing it.[7] This SAS is given further consideration later in this chapter and is considered at length in Chapter 4.

As part of its probe of the accounting profession, the SEC has been highly concerned with whether auditor independence is being compromised as a result of auditors being compensated by the managements of auditees, increased competition for fewer audit clients, and by the accounting firms' increased emphasis on management consulting. To maintain public confidence, the auditing profession must demonstrate that it is independent of the management of audited companies. Some of the cases cited above, however, involved obvious and blatant financial statement distortions, begging the question of auditor complicity. More specifically, instances of premature revenue recognition, fictitious receivables, failure to disclose the existence of related parties and related-party transactions, and loans not secured by adequate collateral have surfaced in these cases.[8]

Because of these concerns over the possible compromise of auditor independence, and at the urging of the Securities and Exchange Commission, the AICPA, in 1997, established the **Independence Standards Board (ISB)**. The Board's purpose is to set independence standards for auditors of public companies. The functioning of the Board is discussed in the next chapter.

A CPA striving for proper ethical behavior in the practice of public accounting should make every attempt to serve the client for whom his or her services are being rendered. For financial statement audits of publicly held companies, the client is the financial statement user. The ethical CPA, therefore, must maintain an attitude of independence and professional skepticism and not subordinate his or her judgment to the

.com
http://www.
cpaindependence.org/

6   National Commission on Fraudulent Financial Reporting, *Report of the National Commission on Fraudulent Financial Reporting*, New York, October 1987.
7   Auditing Standards Board, Statement on Auditing Standards No. 82, *Consideration of Fraud in a Financial Statement Audit*, New York: AICPA, 1997.
8   These cases are covered in Chapter 3, which describes and discusses the auditor's legal liability.

wishes of management—particularly if the result of such subordination is a loss of fairness of financial presentation.

For other assurance services, CPAs should assess their ability to perform the services and decline engagements that they are unable to competently perform. An audit client, for example, may ask its independent CPA to evaluate several different health care delivery systems under consideration for its employees. If the CPA has no expertise in the field of health care, the proper ethical approach is to either attain the required expertise before performing the engagement, or to decline the engagement and recommend another practitioner specializing in health care assurance services.

The Code of Professional Conduct

The official and formal part of the framework defining the quality of auditing and other accounting services is the AICPA **Code of Professional Conduct**. Although the Code of Conduct permits CPAs to obtain clients presently being serviced by other CPAs, proper ethical behavior suggests that the CPA consider the impact of the change on the other CPA, as well as on the prospective client. Such questions as "Will the client be better served by the change in CPAs?" and "Will the change have a significant negative impact on the practice of the other CPA?" should be addressed by the new CPA before accepting the client.

The Code is divided between principles and rules of conduct, and governs the CPA's performance of all professional services rendered. The principles of conduct provide a framework for the rules. The rules are *binding upon the CPA, whether engaged in auditing or other professional accounting services*, such as tax practice or management consulting services. Departures from the rules of conduct must be justified by the member committing a violation. Material departures are subject to deliberations by the Professional Ethics Division and the Trial Board of the AICPA, and may lead to suspension or revocation of membership in the AICPA, and also to the suspension or revocation of the CPA's license.

In addition to principles and rules, the Executive Committee of the Professional Ethics Division issues "interpretations" and "ethics rulings" from time to time. The interpretations and rulings represent further clarification of the principles and rules of conduct. As with the SASs, departures from the interpretations and rulings must be justified by the CPA.

The following paragraphs address the principles and rules of conduct as contained in the code. Although interpretations and ethics rulings are not covered extensively in this chapter, the student may wish to visit the AICPA web site at http://www.aicpa.org/. At the "Site Directory for Information Solutions," choose "Ethics;" then scroll to the bottom of the page and click on "AICPA Code of Professional Conduct." At this site, click on "ET Topical Index" and you can study the various rules, interpretations, and examples that shed further light on the meaning of the rules of conduct. Some of the cases presented at the end of this chapter require further research into the interpretations and rulings to enhance this understanding. We might note that as one moves down the hierarchy of the code from principles to rules to interpretations to ethics rulings, the general concepts are transformed into specific guidelines (rules); then into further explanation of the rules (interpretations); and finally into examples of proper and improper conduct (ethics rulings). For example, Article III of the Principles addresses the question of integrity and states that "members should perform all professional responsibilities with the highest sense of integrity." Rule 102 goes a step further, defining

.com
http://www.aicpa.org/

objectivity and integrity as requiring freedom from "conflicts of interest, misrepresentation of facts, and/or subordination of judgment to others." Interpretation 102.03 clarifies what is meant by "conflicts of interest" as it pertains to public accounting services, and Ethics Ruling 191.001–002 states that if a member accepts "more than a token gift from a client, the appearance of independence may be lacking."[9] The relationship among the principles, rules, interpretations, and ethics rulings is portrayed in Figure 2.3.

Principles of Conduct   As discussed earlier, CPAs, in rendering professional services, must always promote the public interest that they are to serve. Public trust should never be subordinated to personal gain. The **principles of conduct** (see Exhibit 2.2) provide a framework for ensuring an appropriate level of services rendered by CPAs. The principles of objectivity, independence, integrity, and due care strongly suggest that the CPA perform competently and diligently. As stated previously, CPAs must strive continuously to conform to the *spirit* of these principles if public confidence in the profession is to be maintained.

Rules of Conduct   The **rules of conduct** presented in the following paragraphs flow from the principles. The bylaws of the AICPA require adherence to the rules. Where appropriate, interpretations of the rules are also included.

Section 100 Rules   This set of rules, set forth in Exhibit 2.3, relate to the *character* of the CPA. The first rule, dealing with independence, applies not only to audits, but also to other attest services, such as reviews of financial statements and reports on internal control.

   To fairly represent the users of his or her services, the CPA must be independent of the client's management. Independence has two facets: independence in fact and inde-

---

FIGURE 2.3

Relationship Among Principle, Rules, Interpretations, and Ethics Rulings

Principle—General concept

I.   Integrity and objectivity

Rule of Conduct—Specific guideline

Rule 102: Integrity and objectivity and freedom from conflicts of interest

Interpretation—Further explanation of the rule

102.03: Meaning of conflict of interest

Ethics Ruling—Example of proper or improper conduct

191.001–002: Accepting gifts from client creates conflict of interest and impairment of independence

---

9   Ibid, section ET 191.001–002.

EXHIBIT 2.2

Principles of Conduct

Principles

Article I: Responsibilities   In carrying out their responsibilities as professionals, members should exercise sensitive professional and moral judgments in all their activities.

Article II: The Public Interest   Members should accept the obligation to act in a way that will serve the public interest, honor the public trust, and demonstrate commitment to professionalism.

Article III: Integrity   To maintain and broaden public confidence, members should perform all professional responsibilities with the highest sense of integrity.

Article IV: Objectivity and Independence   A member should maintain objectivity and be free of conflicts of interest in discharging professional responsibilities. A member in public practice should be independent in fact and appearance when providing auditing and other attestation services.

Article V: Due Care   A member should observe the profession's technical and ethical standards, strive continually to improve competence and the quality of services, and discharge professional responsibility to the best of the member's ability.

Article VI: Scope and Nature of Services   A member in public practice should observe the Principles of the Code of Professional Conduct in determining the scope and nature of services to be provided.

Source: *AICPA Professional Standards*, section ET 52.01–57.03.

---

pendence in appearance. *Independence in fact* involves a state of mind. The CPA must be independent in mental attitude in all matters relating to the engagement. *Independence in appearance* relates to how financial statement users perceive independence. To illustrate, companies such as Enron Corp., Inland Steel Industries, Inc., and Unicom Corp. have "outsourced" their internal audit departments to national accounting firms.[10] If these firms also audit the companies, financial statement users may perceive a conflict of interest and a compromising of independence. To avoid the appearance of conflict, firms providing internal audit services should advisedly not perform independent audits for the same clients.[11]

Virtually all accounting firms perform consulting services. If these services are performed for audit clients, the question of independence surfaces. Specifically, can the firm objectively audit financial statements prepared by management while being compensated by the same management for consulting services? In a case illustrating this possible conflict, Ernst & Young had audited CUC International during the three years preceding CUC's merger with HFS, Inc., to form Cendant Corp. Ernst & Young had also performed consulting services for CUC. After the merger, Cendant's board of directors discovered that CUC had fraudulently recorded $511 million in revenues over a three-year period covered by Ernst & Young's audits. Although Ernst claimed that it had been a victim of a massive management fraud, the consulting arrangement led the public to

---

10 *The Wall Street Journal*, March 4, 1996.
11 This was a major factor considered by the SEC when deciding on the formation of the Independence Standards Board.

EXHIBIT 2.3

Independence, Integrity, and Objectivity Rules

RULE 101
Independence

A member in public practice shall be independent in the performance of professional services as required by standards promulgated by bodies designated by Council.

Interpretation 101-1. Independence shall be considered to be impaired if, for example, a member had any of the following transactions, interests, or relationships:

A. During the period of a professional engagement or at the time of expressing an opinion, a member or a member's firm
   1. Had or was committed to acquire any direct or material indirect financial interest in the enterprise.
   2. Was a trustee of any trust or executor or administrator of any estate if such trust or estate had or was committed to acquire any direct or material indirect financial interest in the enterprise.
   3. Had any joint, closely held business investment with the enterprise or with any officer, director, or principal stockholders thereof that was material in relation to the member's net worth or to the net worth of the member's firm.
   4. Had any loan to or from the enterprise or any officer, director, or principal stockholder of the enterprise.

B. During the period covered by the financial statements, during the period of the professional engagement, or at the time of expressing an opinion, a member or a member's firm
   1. Was connected with the enterprise as a promoter, underwriter or voting trustee, as a director or officer, or in any capacity equivalent to that of a member of management or of an employee.
   2. Was a trustee for any pension or profit-sharing trust of the enterprise.

The above examples are not intended to be all-inclusive.

RULE 102
Integrity and Objectivity

In the performance of any professional service, a member shall maintain objectivity and integrity, and shall be free of conflicts of interest, and shall not knowingly misrepresent facts or subordinate his or her judgment to others.

Source: *AICPA Professional Standards*, section ET 101.02–102.01.

accuse the firm of complicity in perpetrating the fraud. The appearance of independence, therefore, had been compromised.[12]

Officials of the Securities and Exchange Commission have warned the accounting profession to be careful in accepting those kinds of engagements that have the potential for creating a conflict of interest. SEC enforcement director, William McLucas, addressing a conference of the AICPA, asserted that "the complex entanglement of services with clients poses . . . A subtle but very real threat to independence."[13] During these

12 *The Wall Street Journal*, January 8, 1999.
13 Ibid, December 11, 1996.

same proceedings, SEC Chairman Arthur Levitt suggested that "auditors can't sell services that leave them auditing their own work."[14] As a result of these concerns, the AICPA has issued an ethics interpretation and rulings 103, 104, and 105 under Rule 101 of the Code of Conduct dealing with questions about client advocacy.[15]

While Rule 101 relates independence to auditing and other attest services, Rule 102 is broader, requiring integrity and objectivity in all services rendered by CPAs, such as management consulting and tax services. Independence is not so critical in the rendering of these other services. Indeed, in performing tax services and when dealing with the taxing authorities, the auditor is allowed to be an advocate of the client, representing the client's interests. The CPA, however, must not knowingly agree to false representations of the client, nor should the CPA simply carry out the wishes of management. Instead, an attitude of striving to provide honest and professional service to the client must be maintained.

In a case illustrating a possible conflict of interest, Ernst & Young, in 1993, entered into a consulting engagement with Merry-Go-Round Enterprises (MGR), a chain of retail clothing outlets catering to young buyers. MGR was having financial problems due to poor buying and marketing decisions. Creditors feared the only remedy was to close hundreds of money-losing stores. Ernst & Young, however, recommended adding different styles to the stores' inventories and keeping all of the stores open. This only worsened the company's cash flow problems and forced it to go out of business, causing thousands of employees to lose their jobs and leaving creditors with more than $200 million in uncollectible debts. The company sued Ernst & Young, alleging fraud and incompetence. Ernst & Young later settled for $185 million, but during the legal hearings two significant facts emerged. First, Ernst & Young had assigned an inexperienced partner to oversee the engagement—hence, the charge of incompetence; second, Ernst & Young provided tax services to Rouse Co., one of MGR's main landlords—the charge of conflict of interest. Had Ernst & Young recommended closing stores (as suggested by creditors), Rouse stood to lose rental income. Thus, although the firm's faulty advice probably resulted from inexperienced personnel assigned to the engagement, the *appearance* of conflict of interest was caused by the relationship with Rouse, and the public was led to believe that advising MGR to keep the money-losing stores open was done to protect Rouse.[16]

The Statements on Standards for Consulting Services (CSs) and the Statements on Responsibilities in Tax Practice (TXs), discussed earlier, provide further clarification of these issues.

Section 200 Rules   These rules, listed in Exhibit 2.4, apply to all public accounting services rendered by CPAs. Their collective effect is to *make the pronouncements of the AICPA binding* on the practitioner. Rule 201, entitled "general standards," is similar to, but should not be confused with, the general and field work auditing standards. Competence includes technical qualifications, the ability to supervise and evaluate work performed, and the ability to exercise sound judgment. The CPA does *not*, however, assume responsibility for infallibility of knowledge or judgment.

Rule 202 makes it mandatory for CPAs who are members of the Institute to abide by all of the standards issued by the various bodies so designated by the Institute that govern the practice of public accounting.

14 Ibid.
15 *The Journal of Accountancy*, August 1996, p. 62.
16 See *The Wall Street Journal*, August 10, 1999.

EXHIBIT 2.4

Standards and Principles Rules

RULE 201
General Standards

A member shall comply with the following standards and with any interpretations thereof by bodies designated by Council:

A. *Professional competence.* Undertake only those professional services that the member or the member's firm can reasonably expect to be completed with professional competence.

B. *Due professional care.* Exercise due professional care in the performance of professional services.

C. *Planning and supervision.* Adequately plan and supervise the performance of professional services.

D. *Sufficient relevant data.* Obtain sufficient relevant data to afford a reasonable basis for conclusions or recommendations in relation to any professional services performed.

RULE 202
Compliance with Standards

A member who performs auditing, review, compilation, management consulting, tax, or other professional services shall comply with standards promulgated by bodies designated by Council.

RULE 203
Accounting Principles

A member shall not (1) express an opinion or state affirmatively that the financial statements or other financial data of any entity are presented in conformity with generally accepted accounting principles or (2) state that he or she is not aware of any material modifications that should be made to such statements or data in order for them to be in conformity with generally accepted accounting principles, if such statements or data contain any departure from an accounting principle promulgated by bodies designated by Council to establish such principles that has a material effect on the statements or data taken as a whole. If, however, the statements or data contain such a departure and the member can demonstrate that due to unusual circumstances the financial statements or data would otherwise have been misleading, the member can comply with the rule by describing the departure, its approximate effects, if practicable, and the reasons why compliance with the principle would result in a misleading statement.

Source: *AICPA Professional Standards*, section 201.01–203.01.

Rule 203 makes the accounting principles binding upon the CPA in the same manner in which Rule 202 requires adherence to the professional standards. Since 1973, the "body designated by Council" has been the Financial Accounting Standards Board (FASB). Prior to that date, the Accounting Principles Board (1959–1973) and the Committee on Accounting Procedure (before 1959) had principle-setting authority. Thus, both FASB Statements of Financial Accounting Standards, as well as interpretations, and those Accounting Principles Board Opinions and Accounting Research Bulletins that have not been superseded by action of the FASB, constitute the first hierarchy of GAAP that are covered by Rule 203.

Except for unusual circumstances causing the financial statements to be otherwise misleading, the CPA may not agree with material departures from designated principles. "Unusual circumstances" are a matter of professional judgment. Circumstances that may justify a departure include new legislation or the evolution of a new form of business transaction. The existence of conflicting industry practices would not ordinarily justify a departure.

When, in an audit, the CPA agrees that application of the principle would cause the financial statements to be materially misleading, the departure must be disclosed in the auditor's report on the financial statements with specific information.

More recently, a Governmental Accounting Standards Board (GASB) has been established by the Financial Accounting Foundation and is responsible for issuing pronouncements on government accounting standards. In evaluating fairness of financial presentation for state and local government units, therefore, the auditor must consider the pronouncements of the GASB as being at the top in the hierarchy of generally accepted accounting principles.[17]

Section 300 Rules   These rules, listed in Exhibit 2.5, address *CPAs' relations with their clients*. The purpose of Rule 301 on **confidential client information** is to encourage clients to provide the CPA access to all information that is necessary to the successful completion of an engagement. The rule achieves this end by requiring the CPA to respect the confidentiality of this information. The information obtained during an engagement must not be disclosed to third parties unless it is necessary to the fairness of financial presentation or unless it is requested by the courts in cases involving clients. An exception to the confidentiality requirement is also included in order to provide for access to information by other CPAs during quality reviews of engagement workpapers.[18]

An interesting contrast to the U.S. Code of Conduct is the British practice of providing for confidential contacts between independent auditors and certain regulatory bodies. In the audit of the Bank of Credit & Commerce International (BCCI), for example, PricewaterhouseCoopers (then Price Waterhouse) was able to establish contact with the Bank of England as the auditors were uncovering evidence of fraud. Britain's 1987 Banking Act provides that "if a bank's management doesn't act to remedy a problem after being alerted by its auditors, then the auditors must go directly to the Bank of England."[19] In the United States this practice would generally be considered a breach of confidentiality. However, the Private Securities Litigation Reform Act of 1995 does require auditors to notify the SEC of any discovered illegal acts that are not properly addressed by managements of publicly held companies.[20]

Rule 302 generally prohibits CPAs from accepting fees contingent on the outcomes of assurance engagements. Such practices tend to undermine independence and objectivity. A fee, for example, based on a multiple of final audited net income or earnings per share figures would bias the auditor to favor those audit adjustments affecting income in the direction of increasing the audit fee. For this reason, arrangements involving **contingent fees** constitute violations of Rule 302 when related to audit and other attest engagements.

17 *AICPA Professional Standards*, section AU 411.12.
18 Quality reviews will be considered in Chapter 3 as a means for maintaining the quality of professional practice.
19 *The Wall Street Journal*, July 12, 1991.
20 See Chapter 3 for a more complete discussion of the Act.

EXHIBIT 2.5

Client Relations Rules

RULE 301
Confidential Client Information

A member in public practice shall not disclose any confidential information without the specific consent of the client.

This rule shall not be construed (1) to relieve a member of his or her professional obligations under rules 202 and 203, (2) to affect in any way the member's obligation to comply with a validly issued and enforceable subpoena or summons, or to prohibit a member's compliance with applicable laws and government regulations, (3) to prohibit review of a member's professional practice under AICPA or state CPA society or Board of Accountancy authorization, or (4) to preclude a member from initiating a complaint with, or responding to any inquiry made by, the professional ethics division or trial board of the Institute or a duly constituted investigative or disciplinary body of a state CPA society or Board of Accountancy.

Members of any of the bodies identified in (4) above and members involved with professional practice reviews identified in (3) above shall not use to their own advantage or disclose any member's confidential client information that comes to their attention in carrying out these activities. This prohibition shall not restrict members' exchange of information in connection with the investigative or disciplinary proceedings described in (4) above or the professional practice reviews described in (3) above.

RULE 302
Contingent Fees

A member in public practice shall not

A. Perform for a contingent fee any professional services for, or receive such a fee from, a client for whom the member or the member's firm performs
  1. an audit or review of a financial statement; or
  2. a compilation of a financial statement when the member expects, or reasonably might expect, that a third party will use the financial statement and the member's compilation report does not disclose a lack of independence; or
  3. an examination of prospective financial information.

B. Prepare an original or amended tax return or claim for a tax refund for a contingent fee for any client.

Source: *AICPA Professional Standards*, section ET 301.01–302.01.

The rule is not meant, however, to prevent the setting of fees according to the complexity of the engagement. Often, especially in initial audits, the fee quoted by the CPA is adjusted as the result of discovered weaknesses in internal accounting control that were not contemplated in the initial setting of the fee. These adjustments should be provided for in the engagement letter. Also, under a "consent agreement" between the AICPA and the Federal Trade Commission (FTC) completed in 1990, CPAs are permitted to accept contingent fees and referral commissions relating to nonattest engagements.[21]

Section 500 Rules   This set of rules (see Exhibit 2.6) *governs the conduct of the CPA's professional practice.* Rule 501 makes a general statement that prohibits members from

---

21 See *The Journal of Accountancy*, October 1990, p. 35.

EXHIBIT 2.6

CPA Practice Rules

RULE 501
Acts Discreditable

A member shall not commit an act discreditable to the profession.

RULE 502
Advertising and Other Forms of Solicitation

A member in public practice shall not seek to obtain clients by advertising or other forms of solicitation in a manner that is false, misleading, or deceptive. Solicitation by the use of coercion, over-reaching, or harassing conduct is prohibited.

RULE 503
Commissions and Referral Fees

A. Prohibited Commissions

   A member in public practice shall not for a commission recommend or refer to a client any product or service, or for a commission recommend or refer any product or service to be supplied by a client, or receive a commission, when the member or the member's firm also performs for that client
   1. an audit or review of a financial statement; or
   2. a compilation of a financial statement when the member expects, or reasonably might expect, that a third party will use the financial statement and the member's compilation report does not disclose a lack of independence; or
   3. an examination of prospective financial information.

This prohibition applies during the period in which the member is engaged to perform any of the services listed above and the period covered by any historical financial statements involved in such listed services.

B. Disclosure of Permitted Commissions

   A member in public practice who is not prohibited by this rule from performing services for or receiving a commission and who is paid or expects to be paid a commission shall disclose that fact to any person or entity to whom the member recommends or refers a product or service to which the commission relates.

C. Referral Fees

   Any member who accepts a referral fee for recommending or referring any service of a CPA to any person or entity or who pays a referral fee to obtain a client shall disclose such acceptance or payment to the client.

RULE 505
Form of Practice and Name

A member may practice public accounting only in a form of organization permitted by state law or regulation whose characteristics conform to resolutions of Council.

A member shall not practice under a firm name that is misleading. Names of one or more past owners may be included in the firm name of a successor organization. Also, an owner surviving the death or withdrawal of all other owners may continue to practice under a name which includes the name of past owners for up to two years after becoming a sole practitioner.

A firm may not designate itself as "Members of the American Institute of Certified Public Accountants" unless at least two-thirds of its owners are members of the Institute.

Source: *AICPA Professional Standards*, section ET 501.01–505.01.

committing discreditable acts. Professional stature can be achieved and maintained only through public acceptance and requires a level of conduct commensurate with this status. Although the rule itself is silent as to what specifically constitutes a **discreditable act**, Ethics Rulings ET 501.1.1 to ET 501.6 identify situations leading to membership suspension or termination. These include unauthorized retention of clients' records, discrimination in employment practices, failure to follow required standards in conducting government compliance audits, and unauthorized disclosure of CPA exam questions and answers.[22]

Rule 502, relating to CPA advertising, is much less restrictive than earlier codes. Prior to 1978, advertising was prohibited by the Code of Conduct. In 1977, the U.S. Supreme Court ruled that the American Bar Association could *not* prohibit advertising by lawyers. The AICPA then amended Rule 502 to permit advertising by accountants as well. Although most of the early advertising was quite subdued, in 1981, the AICPA Board of Directors saw fit to adopt a policy statement reading in part as follows:

> *The Board believes that members should exercise appropriate restraint if they elect to engage in the commercial practices of advertising and solicitation. Such self-restraint can be exercised through the application of common sense, good taste, moderation and individual responsibility. This exercise of self-restraint contributes to adherence to technical and ethical standards and, as a result, serves the public interest.*

The board's concern in this regard was that excesses in advertising and solicitation might jeopardize adherence to technical and ethical standards.

Advertising that is informative and objective is encouraged under Rule 502. Under the AICPA/FTC consent agreement referred to previously, however, the AICPA cannot prohibit members from engaging in "self-laudatory advertising, comparative advertising, testimonial advertising," or advertising that some members may believe is "undignified" or "lacking in good taste." In summary, Rule 502 encourages advertising that is informational, but given the consent agreement it cannot prohibit other forms of advertising that might be considered misleading.

Regarding Rule 503, members of a profession represent themselves as capable of providing services at a level of quality commensurate with that typified by the profession. Accordingly, CPAs have traditionally obtained new clients through the recommendations of other clients and associates. Recommendations have generally been based on the quality of service rendered by the CPA. Obtaining clients through referral commissions removes some of the incentive for increasing the quality of services provided to clients and, instead, permits growth through such devices as referral commissions and fee splitting. For this reason, the AICPA has seen fit to discourage the charging of **commissions and referral fees** relating to audits and other attest engagements, as well as to tax services and compilations where third-party use of the financial statements is expected. Here again, however, the AICPA/FTC consent agreement permits CPAs to accept contingent fees in performing nonattest engagements and permits the acceptance of referral fees and product recommendation commissions generally.[23]

Rule 505 defines the proper form of organization for public accounting firms. Prior to 1969, CPAs were not permitted to incorporate. Corporations provide for limited liability to their stockholders, while unlimited liability was traditionally considered a con-

---

22 *AICPA Professional Standards*, section ET 501.1–1.6.
23 *The Journal of Accountancy*, October 1990, p. 35.

dition of public sanction in the professions. In 1992, however, the AICPA membership voted to amend Rule 505 to permit CPA firms to organize themselves in any manner permitted by the state(s) in which they practice, provided the organizational form is not in conflict with Council resolutions.

Under Rule 505, as amended, if state law permits, a firm can organize itself as a *general corporation*, a *limited liability company (LLC)*, or a *limited liability partnership (LLP)*. When a firm is a general corporation or limited liability company or partnership, the individual partners' liability in firm negligence actions will be limited rather than unlimited (as before). In an LLP for example, the personal assets of partners *not* involved in alleged fraud or negligence are protected. Virtually all states now permit the formation of LLCs and LLPs. All of the national accounting firms are now organized as LLPs.

The major impetus behind the amendment and enabling legislation was the devastating effects of the "litigation explosion" on the personal assets of partners whose firms were being sued for negligence allegedly committed by other partners in their firms.[24]

With regard to firm name, the AICPA/FTC consent agreement now permits CPAs to practice under names that might otherwise be considered "misleading" under Rule 505. Such designations as "Quality CPA Services" or "Suburban Tax Services" are now permissible under the agreement, as long as there are no falsehoods.[25]

CODIFICATION OF PROFESSIONAL STANDARDS

The AICPA has codified all of its professional standards into sections containing abbreviations and section numbers according to the various types of public accounting service rendered by CPAs. The Code of Conduct principles, rules, interpretations, and ethics rulings are also included in the codification. The numbering system is such that changes in standards and interpretations can be inserted easily in the appropriate locations in the codification. The section abbreviations used in the **Codification of Professional Standards** are as follows:

AU—Auditing standards and interpretations
AT—Attestation standards and interpretations
AR—Statements on standards for accounting and review services
CS—Statements on standards for consulting services
ET—Code of professional conduct
QC—Quality control
TX—Tax practice

All footnotes in this textbook referencing the professional standards will contain the appropriate abbreviations followed by the section and paragraph number.

KEY TERMS

Attestation standards, 33	Confidential client information, 43
Auditor independence, 30	Consulting services, 34
Code of Professional Conduct, 37	Contingent fees, 43
Codification of Professional Standards, 47	Discreditable act, 46
Commissions and referral fees, 46	Due professional care, 30

---

24 See *The Journal of Accountancy*, October 1991, p. 45.
25 *The Journal of Accountancy*, October 1990, p. 35.

REVIEW QUESTIONS

1. How does the audit function enhance the quality of the financial statements?

2. Describe the framework that defines the quality of independent auditing.

3. Differentiate between auditing standards and auditing procedures.

4. Briefly describe each of the ten generally accepted auditing standards.

5. What is meant by "due professional care"?

6. The ten generally accepted auditing standards, along with the related Statements on Auditing Standards, must be adhered to in the conduct of an audit. The Code of Professional Conduct, however, is applicable to all services rendered by CPAs. Explain why.

7. Distinguish between independence in fact and independence in appearance.

8. Why is independence less critical in rendering tax and management consulting services than in performing an audit?

9. The attestation standards serve a different purpose than the auditing standards. Explain this difference.

10. Explain the significance of Rule 202 of the Code of Conduct—Compliance with Standards.

11. Rule 203 makes the accounting principles binding upon the auditor in the same manner as Rule 202 requires adherence to the professional practice standards. Explain how.

12. How do Rules 202 and 203 impact Rule 301—Confidential Client Information?

13. What purpose is served by the Statements on Standards for Accounting and Review Services?

14. In what way do the Statements on Responsibilities in Tax Practice differ from the SASs and SSARSs?

MULTIPLE CHOICE QUESTIONS FROM PAST CPA EXAMS

1. An auditor who accepts an audit engagement and does not possess the industry expertise of the business entity, should
   a. Engage financial experts familiar with the nature of the business entity.
   b. Obtain a knowledge of matters that relate to the nature of the entity's business.

    c. Refer a substantial portion of the audit to another CPA who will act as the principal auditor.

    d. First inform management that an unqualified opinion cannot be issued.

2. The authoritative body designated to promulgate standards concerning an accountant's association with unaudited financial statements of an entity that is *not* required to file financial statements with an agency regulating the issuance of the entity's securities is the

    a. Financial Accounting Standards Board.

    b. General Accounting Office.

    c. Accounting and Review Services Committee.

    d. Auditing Standards Board.

3. A CPA owes a duty to

    a. Provide for a successor CPA in the event death or disability prevents completion of an audit.

    b. Advise a client of errors contained in a previously filed tax return.

    c. Disclose client fraud to third parties.

    d. Perform an audit according to GAAP so that fraud will be uncovered.

4. Which of the following statements best describes the primary purpose of Statements on Auditing Standards?

    a. They are guides intended to set forth auditing procedures that are applicable to a variety of situations.

    b. They are procedural outlines that are intended to narrow the areas of inconsistency and divergence of auditor opinion.

    c. They are authoritative statements, enforced through the code of professional ethics, and are intended to limit the degree of auditor judgment.

    d. They are interpretations that are intended to clarify the meaning of "generally accepted auditing standards."

5. Which of the following general standards apply to consulting services engagements?

	Due professional care	Independence in mental attitude	Planning and supervision
a.	No	Yes	No
b.	No	Yes	Yes
c.	Yes	No	Yes
d.	Yes	No	No

6. Which of the following is the authoritative body designated to promulgate attestation standards?

    a. Auditing Standards Board

    b. Governmental Accounting Standards Board

    c. Financial Accounting Standards Board

    d. General Accounting Office

7. To exercise due professional care an auditor should

    a. Attain the proper balance of professional experience and formal education.

    b. Design the audit to detect all instances of illegal acts.

    c. Critically review the judgment exercised by those assisting in the audit.

    d. Examine all available corroborating evidence supporting management's assertions.

8. May a CPA hire for the CPA's public accounting firm a non-CPA systems analyst who specializes in developing computer systems?
   a. Yes, provided the CPA is qualified to perform each of the specialist's tasks.
   b. Yes, provided the CPA is able to supervise the specialist and evaluate the specialist's end product.
   c. No, because non-CPA professionals are not permitted to be associated with CPA firms in public practice.
   d. No, because developing computer systems is not recognized as a service performed by public accountants.

9. On completing an audit, Larkin, CPA, was asked by the client to provide technical assistance in the implementation of a new EDP system. The set of pronouncements designed to guide Larkin in this engagement is the Statements on
   a. Auditing Standards.
   b. Standards for Consulting Services.
   c. Quality Control Standards.
   d. Standards for Accountants' EDP Services.

INTERNET ACTIVITIES

Rule 101 of the Code of Professional Conduct requires the CPA to be independent in the performance of audit and other attest services for clients. The CPA may perform other nonattest services for audit clients provided these services do not impair independence in fact or appearance.

Required:

http://www.aicpa.org/

Go to the AICPA web site at http://www.aicpa.org/, click on "pubs" and determine which of the following activities would serve to impair auditor independence:

a. Using client time records, generate unsigned payroll checks and process client's payroll.

b. Sign client disbursement checks in emergency situations.

c. Approve vendor invoices for payment.

d. Perform record keeping of the client's investment portfolio.

e. Execute a transaction to buy or sell a client's investment.

f. Maintain custody of a client's securities.

g. Participate in employee hiring or compensation discussions in an advisory capacity.

h. Supervise client personnel in the daily operation of the client's information system.

ESSAY QUESTIONS AND PROBLEMS

2.1 Three weeks after the audit report has been released to the stockholders, Scott Skiver, CPA and auditor of Into Computers, learns that the client engaged in certain related-party transactions that may be in violation of the law. These transactions are not clearly disclosed in the recently released financial statements. Moreover, based on the newly discovered information, Skiver concludes that the reported profits of Into Computers are materially overstated by the inclusion of these transactions.

Skiver decides to approach the client and request that the stockholders be notified that the financial statements and an audit report are no longer to be relied upon, and that revised financial statements and an audit report will be forthcoming. The client refuses to comply on the grounds that the financial statements are fairly presented in all material respects. The president of Into Computers tells Skiver that the transactions are not illegal and that the parties are not directly related. Moreover, he informs Skiver that any information concerning the transactions conveyed by Skiver to the stockholders will be considered a violation of auditor–client confidentiality.

Required:
a. Discuss the requirements of Rule 301 dealing with confidential client information.
b. If you were Skiver what would you do in this case? Explain why you would assume the position that you have elected.

2.2   Eugene Franks, CPA, has several small clients for whom he provides bookkeeping services. The clients submit source documents to Franks for processing on Franks' computer. The source documents consist of sales invoices, vendors' invoices, payroll time cards, check stubs, and remittance advices. Franks' staff enter the documents into the computer where they are recorded and the results are stored for monthly printout of journals, ledgers, payroll summaries, earnings records, and financial statements. Franks also prepares various federal, state, and local tax returns for the clients, such as sales tax returns, payroll tax returns, and federal, state, and local income tax returns.

Mary's Boutique, one of the clients, has applied to the bank for a long-term loan and the bank has requested audited financial statements. Mary's requests Franks to perform the audit.

Required:
May Franks perform the audit, given that he renders bookkeeping services to Mary's? Support your answer by reference to appropriate rules, interpretations, and/or ethics rulings pertaining to the Code of Professional Conduct.

2.3   Vic Kapoor, CPA, is a partner in the firm of Kapoor, Moon, and Block, CPAs. Although most of the firm's clients are nonaudit, involving compilation and review services, management consulting, and tax advice and return preparation, a few audits are performed. During an annual fund-raising event drawing the participation of business and professional persons from various sectors, the president of the local cable provider asked Kapoor if his firm would be interested in conducting the annual audit of the company. None of the firm's present audit clients are cable companies or other kinds of communications providers. Kapoor does recall, however, participating as a senior auditor on a cable company audit when he was working for a "Big Five" accounting firm several years ago (before striking out on his own). Moreover, his firm has an extensive library of research materials that Kapoor might consult in preparing for the engagement. If the firm accepts the engagement, the interim work will need to begin within the next month or two.

Required:
Will Kapoor violate the Code of Professional Conduct or the auditing standards by accepting the engagement? Be specific in referring to parts of the Code and to auditing standards to support your position.

2.4   For each of the following independent situations, indicate the rule of professional conduct involved and the appropriate response to the question.
a. Manuel Hernandez, CPA, withdrew from an engagement on discovering irregularities in his client's tax return. May he reveal to the successor accountant why the relationship was terminated?

    b. Lanny Solomon, CPA, is requested by one of his audit clients, Sports Productions, Inc., to perform certain services in addition to the annual audit. Although internal auditors normally carry out these functions, the company's size does not permit maintaining a separate internal audit function. The specific services requested of Solomon are as follows:

        1. Perform a special engagement to detect a suspected defalcation of major proportions.

        2. Review production contracts with football and baseball teams and recommend approval or denial of contracts submitted to Sports Productions.

2.5   You are a newly hired assistant auditor in the firm of Autry & Rogers, CPAs. On your first audit you have been assigned to the sales and accounts receivable transaction cycle. Two matters trouble you about your assignment:

    a. The audit program calls for examining accounts receivable at an interim date instead of at year end. Based on what you learned in your auditing course, you think this is improper and you inform the in-charge senior auditor. She tells you to follow the audit program as written.

    b. The engagement time budget allows six hours for examining the documentation for 200 sales transactions. Despite working as fast as you can, you have completed only 45 in five hours. Given your previous encounter with the in-charge auditor, you do not want to bother her again. You are considering the following alternative courses of action:

        1. Complete the remaining transactions as called for in the audit program, regardless of the time involved.

        2. Complete as many sales transactions as you can in the six hours allowed.

        3. Examine all 200 sales transactions but in much less detail than followed to date.

        4. Come in on Saturday (without pay) to complete the assigned work.

You know that audit efficiency is valued highly in your firm and you don't want to look bad in comparison to the assistant who did the work last year.

Required:

Discuss the proper course of action to take in the present situation. Refer to the Code of Conduct as appropriate.

2.6   Kramer & Reuben, CPAs, assigned Julia Brinks, a newly promoted senior staff person, as auditor in charge of the initial examination of Forrester, Inc., a small construction firm. Brinks had participated in prior audits of Forrester as an assistant. As the audit progressed, Brinks discovered some rather complex contracts accounted for on a percentage of completion basis. Although she wasn't sure whether the profits should have been recognized in this manner, the controller of Forrester assured her that these contracts did indeed constitute sales and that the profits had been properly booked in accordance with GAAP. Brinks accepted the controller's assurances, having been satisfied during past audits with his integrity. Following the audit, an unqualified opinion accompanied the financial statements of Forrester, Inc. Shortly thereafter, Forrester filed for bankruptcy and Kramer & Reuben were sued for negligence by the minority stockholders. The contracts that had concerned Brinks were, in reality, sale and leaseback transactions, followed by subleasing and extensive discounting of notes with banks and factors. Title to most of the properties resulting from the projects had remained with Forrester, therefore the profits should not have been recognized. When asked by Reuben, one of the senior partners, why she had not detected the fictitious nature of the profits, Brinks replied that, given the audit team's past experience with the corporate controller, she assumed he was being truthful and she therefore relied on his assurances.

Required:

a. Identify any auditing standards and professional conduct rules that, in your opinion, have been violated in this case. Explain why you feel the standard or rule in question was not observed.

b. What should Brinks have done after examining the contracts?

c. What should the audit manager (Brinks' supervisor) have done upon examining Brinks' workpaper supporting the contracts?

2.7   Li, CPA, has been requested by an audit client to perform a nonrecurring engagement involving the implementation of an EDP information and control system. The client requests that in setting up the new system and during the period prior to conversion to the new system, Li:

• Counsel on potential expansion of business activity plans.
• Search for and interview new personnel.
• Hire new personnel.
• Train personnel.

In addition, the client requests that during the three months subsequent to the conversion, Li:

• Supervise the operation of the new system.
• Monitor client-prepared source documents and make changes in basic EDP-generated data as Li may deem necessary without concurrence of the client.

Li responds that she may perform some of the services requested, but not all of them.

Required:

Which of these services may Li perform and which of these services may Li not perform? Explain.

(AICPA adapted)

2.8   You have two clients, Hickory and Maple. Hickory is considering a monetary advance to Maple as part of a long-term contractual arrangement. It is not public knowledge, but you know that Maple is in very "shaky" financial condition. While the advance and long-term contract would be very good for Maple and might save that company, you think that this undertaking would be a big mistake for Hickory, given the risks involved. You wonder whether you should inform Hickory of the potential danger.

Required:

Should you inform Hickory? Justify your answer by referring to the appropriate section(s) of the Code of Conduct.

2.9   For each of the following independent situations, indicate the auditing standard(s) violated.

a. In auditing Dayton Contractors, Inc., Gloria James, CPA, failed to detect a major inventory shortage. The shortage was made possible because Dayton did not maintain perpetual inventory records and did not restrict access to materials inventories. In performing the audit, James limited her inventory auditing procedures to test counting Dayton's physical inventory.

b. Although Lake Manufacturing maintained significant inventories of finished goods in remote locations, approximately two-thirds of its inventory was stored in Birmingham, the company's manufacturing base. James Jackson, a CPA and Lake's independent auditor, examined only the Birmingham inventory, given that it represented the majority of Lake's finished goods. He rendered an unqualified opinion on the company's financial statements. Shortly thereafter, Lake filed for bankruptcy. The trustee in bankruptcy, appointed by the court, discovered that the inventory purported to be located outside Birmingham did not exist, and the 2002 reported profit of $3.6 million was in fact a loss of $960,000.

c. Although he discovered several significant errors and frauds while auditing the records of Brendon, Inc., Jarrod Mohler, CPA, did not include them in his audit workpapers, nor did he bring them to the attention of senior management, because, in the aggregate, the errors and frauds did not materially affect Brendon's financial statements. Also, his brother was controller for Brendon and Mohler did not wish to be the cause of his brother's termination or possible arrest for fraud. Subsequently, the assistant controller discovered the misstatements and reported them to the chief executive officer. Jarrod Mohler's brother was prosecuted for fraud and Mohler's accounting firm was also named in the charge.

d. Marilyn Kane, CPA, rendered an unqualified opinion on the financial statements of Tycor International, Inc. Tycor's financial statements were essentially correct, but contained no footnote disclosing that the company's working capital had fallen below the amount specified in a major loan agreement. Shortly after release of the financial statements, First National Bank foreclosed on the Tycor loan and forced the company into bankruptcy. Kane's firm was sued by the stockholders for negligence.

e. Chandler Art Museum, an audit client of Triplett & Wilson, CPAs, maintained its portfolio of investment securities with three local brokerage firms. Reginald Dawson, a newly hired assistant auditor for Triplett & Wilson, was assigned to audit Chandler's investment portfolio. Although he was able to obtain confirmation of securities from two of the brokerage firms, Dawson failed to obtain a response to his confirmation request from the third firm. He noted this in his audit workpaper, but failed to follow up. Juanita Lopez, the in-charge senior auditor, did not review that particular workpaper. After release of the audit report (unqualified opinion), the museum discovered that a significant number of securities was missing. Michael Hennings, the museum controller, had misappropriated the securities and misrepresented them as being held by a nonexistent brokerage firm—the firm that had not responded to Reginald Dawson's request for confirmation. The museum sued Triplett & Wilson for negligence in not detecting the fraud.

2.10   For each of the following situations, indicate whether or not auditor independence has been impaired. Explain your reasoning in each case.

a. While examining the financial statements of a major retail clothing chain, the auditor discovers major weaknesses in the client's system of internal control. Correcting the weaknesses results in significant cost savings. As a reward, the client extends to the auditor the same store discount privileges enjoyed by the company's employees.

b. At age 55, Hugh Carlson, senior partner, departs under the CPA firm's mandatory retirement policy. He then accepts an appointment to the board of directors of Lake Park, Inc., the largest of his former firm's audit clients. In addition, Carlson, as recognition for his years of service, is granted an office in the Lake Park suite and a computer connected to the company's local area network, along with email privileges. The CPA firm also retains him as a paid consultant.

c. Reginald Green, CPA, audits the financial statements of Jackson Corp., a local automobile dealer. Green's sister-in-law (his wife's sister) is the vice president and sales manager of Jackson. Green's sister-in-law also owns stock in the company.

      d. Franz and Schroeder, CPAs, have financed the purchase of the building housing their firm's offices by issuing a first mortgage to Bank Six, an audit client.

2.11   As an independent auditor, one often becomes aware of matters not known by the general public. For example, the following two situations have recently arisen:

    a. Janice George, the assistant controller of Murphy, an audit client, has told you that she would like to change jobs. You know that Janson, another audit client, wishes to replace its controller and has asked your firm to make recommendations. This would be a good promotion for George and you think she would be capable. However, you are concerned about fairness to Murphy if you inform George of the Janson position opening, particularly since the position is *not* known to the general public.

    b. The controller of Hoag, Inc., thinks he is underpaid. Based on what you know from similar clients, he is. He has asked you, as a friend, to tell him what you think a fair salary would be.

Required:

For each of the above situations, identify the course of action that you believe is appropriate relative to the Code of Conduct. Cite appropriate principles, rules, and interpretations to support your position.

2.12   In examining the financial statements of Tamminy Valley, Inc., a major leasing company, the auditor discovers that gross profits, recognized from certain sales-type leases, include contingent rentals yet to be realized. The rentals are based on a percentage of the lessee's monthly sales above a minimum dollar level. The controller, upon inquiry, explains that the lessees in question have consistently earned adequate revenues to more than cover the contingent rentals included in the "gross lease payments receivable" account. Further, he asserts that not to include the contingent rentals in the sales price would make the financial statements materially misleading.

Required:

    a. Under what circumstances may an auditor agree to a departure from a principle "promulgated by the body designated by Council"?

    b. Assuming that you were the auditor in this case, how would you respond to the controller's assertion?

    c. If you agree to the company's accounting treatment, what effect would this have on your audit report? What effect would it have if you do *not* agree?

2.13   BP Amoco recently announced that it was transferring much of its U.S. Accounting operations to PricewaterhouseCoopers LLP. Such outsourcing is becoming more popular, given enhanced computer and communications technology permitting such practices. As part of the arrangement, approximately 1,200 BP Amoco employees were transferred to the offices of PricewaterhouseCoopers.

    PricewaterhouseCoopers has assumed the financial reporting, accounts payable, and accounting responsibilities for BP Amoco's U.S. chemical and oil exploration activities. PwC also took over the information systems maintenance and upgrading functions.

Required:

    a. What determines which functions, in addition to examining the financial statements, a CPA may perform for an audit client? Cite specific rules and interpretations of the Code of Conduct in your answer.

    b. May PwC also perform the audit for BP Amoco? Explain.

DISCUSSION CASES

CASE I

IBM

IBM, long regarded as "leader of the blue chips," was experiencing the effects of a "profit squeeze" in the mid-1980s. This was caused by increased competition in the personal computer industry and by an erosion of the role played by IBM's big mainframe computers in the business sector. In 1984, anticipating possible losses, IBM management began changing to less conservative accounting policies.

Thornton O'Glove, a San Francisco accounting expert, stated in 1993 that "since the mid-1980s, IBM has been borrowing from the future to bolster today's profits."[26] According to O'Glove, the company was predicting a return to mainframes in the future and a resumption of high profits—a prediction that never materialized. O'Glove further estimated that the accounting changes made to liberalize accounting policies were responsible for 26 percent of IBM's 1984 profits.[27]

Financial experts alleged that the switch to less conservative accounting caused financial analysts to miss the beginning of IBM's "profit slide" because they believed that the company was still following conservative accounting policies. This allegation may well be true: the company's common stock price didn't peak until 1987, three years after the profit slide had begun. From a high of $175 in 1987, the stock began to fall and reached a low of $43 by August 1993.

Two of the accounting changes involved the timing of revenue recognition and the treatment of computer leases. With regard to revenue recognition, IBM began in 1984 to recognize revenue upon shipment of products to dealers, even though a right of return existed. In some instances, the company recognized shipments to its own warehouses as sales. The company was also booking revenue at full price while promising customers that if price cuts occurred, customers need pay only the reduced prices.

In a strongly worded memo to management, Donald Chandler, the Price Waterhouse partner in charge of the IBM audit at the time, stated that the revenue recognition changes seemed "clearly inappropriate."[28] IBM countered by saying that it made allowances for returns and that the "earning process [was] substantially complete upon shipment." For shipments to warehouses, the company said it recognized revenue only when "installation at the customer" was "expected within 30 days."[29]

Concerning lease accounting, IBM treated the leases of its mainframe computers as sales-type leases, recognizing gross profit upon signing of the leases. To apply this method of accounting, the company needed to meet the 90 percent test; that is, the net present value of minimum lease payments had to equal at least 90 percent of the computer's fair value at the date of the lease. To help IBM meet the 90 percent test, Merrill Lynch sold the company "7D insurance" (named after paragraph 7D of Statement of Financial Accounting Standards No. 52). The insurance guaranteed a value at the end of the lease term that was at least enough to push IBM over the 90 percent mark. An accounting professor reflected that "structuring a lease to violate the spirit of the accounting rule . . . is weaseling, hokey, and totally inappropriate for a company of IBM's stature."[30] Price Waterhouse, IBM's auditors, responded by saying that 7D insurance is "acceptable accounting, and it was thoroughly reviewed before it was implemented." Chandler, the former audit partner, however, noted in his memo (referred to above) that these transactions "rarely qualify" as sales-type leases without the help of a third party such as Merrill Lynch.

Daniel Gough, a former IBM accounting manager, left the company presumably because he didn't approve of its accounting policies. Moreover, in the late

26 *The Wall Street Journal*, April 3, 1993.
27 Ibid.
28 Ibid.
29 Ibid.
30 Ibid.

1980s, IBM's executives received big raises and bonuses, partly pegged to reported earnings. By 1989, IBM's return on equity had declined from a high of 26.5 percent in 1984 to 9.6 percent. This was followed by losses in 1991 and 1992.

Required:
Although Chandler, the Price Waterhouse partner in charge of the IBM audit, expressed his reservations concerning the company's liberalization of its ac-

counting policies, the firm nevertheless rendered an unqualified opinion on IBM's 1984 financial statements.

a. Explain the apparent inconsistency between the partner's strongly worded memo and the unqualified audit opinion.

b. Do you feel the auditors in this case fairly represented the interests of third-party users by agreeing with management's changes?

CASE II

Tambrands, Inc.

Several years ago, the accounting profession and the financial community introduced the concept of the "audit committee" as a means for strengthening internal control, promoting auditor independence, and better representing the interests of third-party shareholders and creditors. Ideally, the audit committee, a committee of the board of directors consisting mainly of outside directors, has oversight responsibility for the entity's internal control system and is responsible for arbitrating disputes between management and the independent auditors—particularly disputes involving disagreements regarding financial statement presentation. Often these disputes are sufficiently serious as to produce a qualified audit opinion or a change in auditors if not resolved.

Although the concept appears sound, its implementation in practice has had mixed results. A question might be raised, for example, as to how effectively audit committee members can maintain independence from management when they are compensated by the same managers for whom they have oversight responsibility. Two sides of this issue were presented in an article appearing in *The Wall Street Journal*, entitled "While Outside Directors' Pay Increases, Independence from Managers May Fade." Donald P. Jacobs, dean of Northwestern University's Kellogg School of Management, and an outside director for several companies, offered the following argument supporting the independence concept:

There are enough potential plaintiffs out there that would attack a director for failing to act independently, that the risk is too great for compromise.

Robert Monks, a shareholder-rights activist, in contrast, asserted:

A chief executive officer runs a board by overpaying them. The phenomenon of the independent director is being diluted to the point of illusoriness.

The Tambrands, Inc., case lends support to Monks' assertion that boards of directors may *not* be sufficiently independent. In this case, Martin Emmett, during his four-year term as president and chief executive officer of Tambrands, had channeled millions of dollars of consulting business annually to Personnel Corp. of America (PCA), a human resources consulting firm managed by two of Emmett's long-time friends, David Meredith and Jack Lederer. Moreover, former PCA executives said that Meredith and Lederer were placed on the Tambrands' board of directors and received annual retainers that exceeded the salaries of most Tambrands officers. By the end of Emmett's term as CEO, Tambrands business accounted for 30 percent of PCA's annual revenue. During this same period, Tambrands' market share in Tampax tampons had decreased by 8 percent and the market value of its shares had declined drastically. Much of this was due to a decision by Emmett to capitalize on consumer brand loyalty by raising retail prices of Tampax and reducing the number of tampons in a box.

In response to the loss of market share, Tambrands reduced its workforce by one-third. At the same time, however, in response to recommendations contained in studies completed by the PCA consultants, the Tambrand board of directors voted itself a pay raise and awarded Emmett a package of unusually attractive stock options and other benefits.

By June 1993, Tambrands' shares had lost nearly one-third of their market value and Emmett was forced to resign. Immediately following the resignation, Tambrands severed its contracts with PCA.

Required:

a. In your opinion, do the means by which directors are appointed and compensated contribute to a loss of independence from management? Explain.
b. How might selection and compensation be improved to make the board of directors more responsive to third-party needs?
c. What is the independent auditors' responsibility in cases like this?

c h a p t e r 3

biltrite

l e a r n i n g   o b j e c t i v e s

After reading this chapter, you should be able to

1 Recognize the means by which the profession regulates itself and maintains the necessary level of quality in rendering auditing and accounting services.

2 Define the expectations gap and recognize the importance of self-regulation in any attempt to narrow the gap.

3 Understand the impact on quality maintenance flowing from external regulation.

4 Identify and define the sources and types of auditor legal liability and relate them to one another.

5 Describe the key cases illustrating specific sources and types of auditor liability.

6 Develop a plan for preventing legal actions and dealing with liability that does arise.

OVERVIEW

Maintaining the quality of service requires a mechanism for monitoring the activities of CPAs in rendering professional services, and for invoking disciplinary action in those situations involving substandard performance. One component of quality maintenance is regulation. Regulation is considered in this chapter in terms of self-regulation and external regulation. The self-regulation mechanism is housed within the AICPA and the various state boards of accountancy. External regulation emanates primarily from the Securities and Exchange Commission (SEC). Both sectors are instrumental in monitoring performance by CPAs and in imposing discipline where appropriate.

A second component of quality maintenance is legal liability. The courts have been instrumental in defining auditor responsibility in terms of ordinary negligence, gross negligence, and fraud. This chapter discusses maintenance of quality in terms of both regulation and legal liability.

INTRODUCTION

Although the standards and ethics define the quality of services rendered by CPAs, some mechanism is needed for monitoring professional practice. Monitoring is necessary to ensure that the defined level of quality is maintained. If CPAs are to be held accountable for departures from the standards and ethics, a means must exist for identifying those departures. The AICPA and the various state boards of accountancy, along with the Securities and Exchange Commission and the courts, have all played significant roles in maintaining quality control (see Figure 3.1).

Traditionally, the monitoring mechanism has been housed mainly within the AICPA, with the SEC and the courts intervening where internal efforts are perceived to have failed. Internal enforcement of the standards and ethics by the AICPA is referred to as **self-regulation**. Oversight and corrective action by the SEC and the courts is known as **external regulation**.

The AICPA monitoring mechanism consists of the bylaws and Trial Board of the Institute, along with the Quality Control Standards Committee, the Division for CPA Firms, and the Independence Standards Board. The state boards of accountancy regulate public accounting practice by administering the CPA examination, issuing and revoking licenses to practice, and enforcing continuing education requirements.

The SEC monitors the accounting profession primarily through the Office of the Chief Accountant. Although absolute regulatory power is granted the Commission through the Securities Acts, this body has generally opted for self-regulation by the profession.

The first half of this chapter describes the monitoring functions of the AICPA, the state boards of accountancy, and the SEC. The last half of the chapter discusses the CPA's legal liability and the role played by the courts in monitoring performance.

The courts represent the ultimate determinant of CPA liability. The legal liability section of the chapter defines and illustrates various aspects of liability confronting auditors. The section begins by identifying and discussing types of liability. This is followed by a similar consideration of sources of liability. The relationship between types and sources of liability is then addressed, and finally summarized in the form of a relational exhibit. Key cases are used to clarify the nature of auditor liability.

Following the consideration of auditor liability, the CPA's liability for unaudited statements is described and illustrated. The *1136 Tenants* case is used as a focal point for the discussion.

FIGURE 3.1

Regulation Structure

I. Self-Regulation

American Institute of Certified Public Accountants
  Bylaws
    Continuing professional education requirement
    Quality Review Division
  AICPA Trial Board
    Admonish members who have violated standards or rules
    Suspend or expel from membership
  Quality Control Standards Committee
    Statements on Quality Control Standards
  Division for CPA Firms
    Quality maintenance
    Peer review
    Public Oversight Board (POB)
      Monitors SEC Practice Section of Division for CPA Firms
  Independence Standards Board
    Statements on Independence Standards

State Boards of Accountancy
  Issue and revoke CPA certificate
  Issue and revoke license to practice
  Impose continuing professional education requirements

II. External Regulation

Securities and Exchange Commission
  Office of the Chief Accountant
    Monitors the Auditing Standards Board
    Monitors the Independence Standards Board
    Oversees the SEC Practice Section of the Division for CPA Firms
    Investigates alleged audit failures
  Change in auditors must be reported to the SEC (Form 8-K)

The courts
  Liability for negligence
  Criminal liability

The section concludes by enumerating means for preventing legal actions and for dealing with liability as it confronts the CPA. Risk analysis and the exercise of due audit care are the most effective preventives. Adequate audit documentation, on the other hand, is the best defense in the event of legal action against the CPA.

SELF-REGULATION AND QUALITY MAINTENANCE

The AICPA, the State Boards of Accountancy, and Quality Maintenance

Provision is made in the bylaws of the AICPA for disciplining members who are found by the Trial Board to be in violation of the rules of conduct of the Code of Professional Conduct. Disciplinary action may take the form of admonishment, suspension, or expulsion from membership within the Institute. Given the broad coverage of Rule 202 of the Code, virtually all forms of auditing, accounting, and consulting services rendered by CPAs fall within this regulatory mechanism. Departures from any of the respective standards expose the CPA to the threat of a hearing before the Trial Board and the possibility of disciplinary action. Membership in the Institute is voluntary and its authority extends only to its members.

The CPA is also subject to the requirements of the board of accountancy of the state in which she or he is licensed to practice. Regulatory powers are most critical to the CPA. The legal right to practice as a CPA is obtained through a license granted by the state board. In order to retain and periodically renew this license, the CPA must abide by the state laws that govern the practice of accountancy.

In addition to the AICPA continuing education requirements, many of the states have also prescribed continuing professional education requirements to encourage CPAs to keep abreast of changes occurring within the profession, and to provide the best possible service to their clients.

Violations of the state licensing statutes are subject to varying degrees of disciplinary action, including suspension or revocation of the CPA certificate and/or suspension or revocation of the CPA's license to practice.

The AICPA Quality Control Standards Committee

AICPA Professional Standards require firms to design and implement quality control systems. Failure to do so constitutes a violation of GAAS.[1] A system of quality control is defined as "the firm's organizational structure and the policies adopted and procedures established to provide the firm with reasonable assurance of conforming with professional standards."[2] Moreover, as described earlier, the bylaws of the institute require members to be enrolled in practice-monitoring programs. Firms, therefore, need to establish quality control policies and procedures that will provide reasonable assurance of conformance with generally accepted auditing standards (GAAS). These policies and procedures should apply also to attestation engagements, accounting and review services, and other engagements for which professional standards have been established.

In 1979, Statement on Quality Control Standard No. 1 (SQCS-1) was issued by the **AICPA Quality Control Standards Committee**, the body responsible for issuing **Statements on Quality Control Standards**. SQCS-2, issued in 1997, amended the first statement and consists of five broad elements defining appropriate standards of quality control for member firms. These elements relate to maintaining independence, integrity, and objectivity; managing personnel; establishing guidelines for accepting and continuing clients; performing engagements; and monitoring the existing quality control policies and procedures.[3]

Accounting firms use various means in conforming to these guidelines. In helping to ensure independence, for example, the firm might elect to distribute a list of clients and have staff members sign a statement of independence. Advance planning can help in assigning qualified personnel to engagements. Most firms designate specific persons as experts in areas such as auditing, taxation, and management consulting services. This provides a mechanism for obtaining answers to technical questions that arise during engagements. Requiring all workpapers to be reviewed by supervisory or technical per-

---

1   *AICPA Professional Standards*, New York: AICPA, section QC 10.
2   Ibid, section QC 10.03.
3   Ibid, section QC 10.07.

sonnel supports the supervision guideline. Providing minimum qualifications for hiring of personnel, establishing continuing education requirements, and evaluating the performance of staff members help to ensure quality maintenance in hiring, development, and promotion of personnel within the firm.

To ensure that the firm does not associate with clients whose managements lack integrity, present clients should be reviewed for continuance, and prospective clients should be reviewed for acceptance. In reviewing prospective clients for acceptance, the auditor may make inquiries of predecessor auditors, bankers, attorneys, and other business associates.[4]

The Division for CPA Firms

In 1977, the AICPA created the **Division for CPA Firms** for the purpose of promoting quality and consistency in the rendering of professional services. The Division comprises two sections: the SEC Practice Section and the Private Companies Practice Section. Firms with clients who are subject to SEC filing requirements (publicly held companies) enroll in the **SEC Practice Section**, while those with only non-SEC clients seek membership in the **Private Companies Practice Section**. Although membership in the Private Practice Section is voluntary, CPA firms with public clients must enroll in the SEC Practice Section. The conditions for membership in both sections include agreement to participate in peer (or quality) review, to conform to specified continuing professional education requirements, and to maintain adequate levels of liability insurance.

Peer (quality) reviews are to be performed every three years. Other CPAs who are members of the Division conduct reviews. The review consists mainly of examination of the documentation supporting audits and other accounting services rendered by the firm being reviewed. Whether a CPA is performing an audit or rendering other professional services, all work must be fully documented. Documentation in the form of appropriately indexed workpapers is the only evidence of the CPA's adherence to professional standards. In cases involving alleged negligence, these workpapers may be the CPA's principal defense.[5]

The continuing professional education requirement consists of 120 hours of credit every three years. Division members practicing in states lacking mandatory continuing professional education for licensing purposes are still required to undertake formal professional development to maintain membership in the Division.

The **Public Oversight Board (POB)** of the AICPA supervises the SEC Practice Section. The majority of POB members are not accountants. The Board may recommend that the executive committee of the Section impose sanctions for failure to maintain compliance with membership requirements. Sanctions assume the form of corrective measures to be implemented by the firm in violation, required continuing professional education, special peer review, and suspension and/or expulsion from membership in the Section. The POB must report annually to the Chief Accountant of the SEC.

Independence Standards Board

In 1997, the AICPA, in conjunction with the Securities and Exchange Commission, formed the **Independence Standards Board (ISB)** for the purpose of establishing

.com
http://www.
cpaindependence.org/

4   The client acceptance decision is addressed more fully in Chapter 5.
5   Audit workpapers are discussed and illustrated in Chapter 4.

independence standards for auditors of public companies. The SEC's concern that the profession's broadening of assurance services to encompass a wide range of nonaudit engagements might compromise independence led to the formation of the ISB.

The ISB, an eight-member private-sector body, is composed of four certified public accountants and four public members from which the chairman is elected. The Board is responsible for three tasks:

1. Developing a conceptual framework for evaluating CPA independence;
2. Identifying independence issues through the **Independent Issues Committee (IIC)**, a support group for the ISB consisting of eight members, all of whom are practicing accountants; and
3. Issuing standards and rules that prevent public accounting firms from accepting engagements that could affect the quality and independence of their audits of public companies' financial statements.[6]

The SEC has oversight responsibility over the ISB's operations (in a manner similar to the SEC's oversight of the ASB and the FASB).

In 1999, the ISB issued ISB Standard No. 1 requiring the CPA to disclose to the audit committee of the client, in writing, all relationships between the auditor and its related entities and the company and its related entities that in the auditor's judgment might bear on independence. Additionally, the standard requires that the auditor meet annually with the audit committee of the client to discuss issues bearing on auditor independence.[7] The combination of a written communication and the annual meeting is meant to provide the audit committee input for assessing auditor independence.

SELF-REGULATION AND THE EXPECTATIONS GAP

For self-regulation to prevail, users must perceive a level of quality of services rendered by CPAs equal to their expectations. A disparity between users' and CPAs' perceptions of the quality of CPA services, especially regarding the attest function, is referred to as an **expectations gap** (see Figure 3.2).

The independent auditor's responsibility for detecting fraud in auditing is one of the major areas contributing to the expectations gap. Many financial statement users believe that an unqualified audit opinion means that the auditor has detected all material errors and/or fraud that may have occurred during the period under audit. Statements on Auditing Standards, however, are at variance with this view, and hold the auditor responsible only for exercising due care in the conduct of the examination.[8] Management override of internal accounting controls and other forms of management misrepresentation fraud may occur and be so cleverly concealed that the exercise of due audit care fails to detect the financial statement misstatements produced by these means.

Phar-Mor, Comptronix, JWP, Lincoln Savings and Loan, Crazy Eddie, and MiniScribe are cases involving significant financial statement misrepresentations that were not detected by the independent auditors, cases that have tended to widen the expectations gap. Although management override of internal control was involved in all of these cases, the significance of the resulting losses caused investors to raise the question, "Where were the auditors?"

---

6 *Journal of Accountancy*, May 1999, p. 32.
7 Ibid, April 1999, p. 102.
8 *AICPA Professional Standards*, op. cit., section AU 316.01–08.

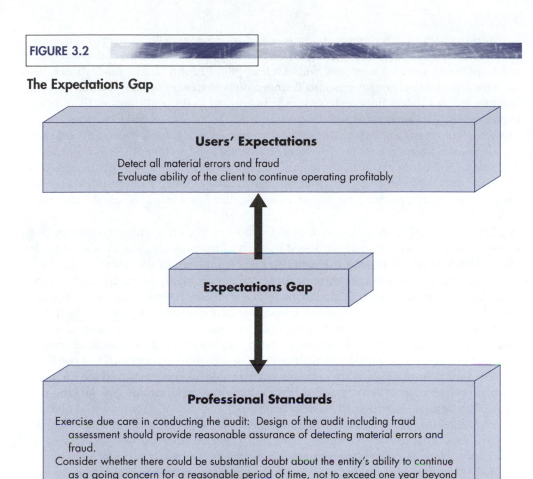

FIGURE 3.2

The Expectations Gap

Users' Expectations

Detect all material errors and fraud
Evaluate ability of the client to continue operating profitably

Expectations Gap

Professional Standards

Exercise due care in conducting the audit: Design of the audit including fraud
    assessment should provide reasonable assurance of detecting material errors and
    fraud.
Consider whether there could be substantial doubt about the entity's ability to continue
    as a going concern for a reasonable period of time, not to exceed one year beyond
    the date of the audited financial statements.

In a 1994 address to the AICPA's Annual National Conference on Current SEC
Developments, Walter Schuetze, SEC Chief Accountant, described these and other situations as cases in which auditors appear to have "subordinated their judgment on accounting and reporting issues to their clients." He raised the question, "How can
registrants (companies) and their auditors ignore the literature and then expect investors, regulators, Congress, and the public generally to put credence in what they
say?" Schuetze concluded his address by imploring the profession to "let nothing stand
in the auditor's way of telling the truth as he or she sees it."[9]

In response to these concerns the Auditing Standards Board issued a new Statement
on Auditing Standards that provides more explicit guidance for detecting fraud and communicating the findings to management and the board of directors.[10] This SAS, as well
as fraud detection and audit risk analysis in general, will be discussed in Chapter 5.
These concerns, as well as the broadening of assurance services, also led to formation
of the Independence Standards Board discussed earlier.

---

9   Schuetze, Walter P., "Commentary—A Mountain or a Molehill?" *Accounting Horizons*, Vol. 8, No. 1, March 1994,
pp. 69–75.
10   *AICPA Professional Standards*, op. cit., section AU 316.

Another area of differing perceptions of auditor responsibility concerns the ability of a company to continue as a going concern. Most users believe that an unqualified audit opinion provides a company with a "clean bill of health." If a company later files for bankruptcy or otherwise gets into financial difficulty, users often question why the auditors did not detect the conditions and cover them in the audit report. In an effort to narrow the expectations gap in this area, in 1989 the Auditing Standards Board issued SAS 59 relating to the ability of the client to continue as a going concern. Specifically, the standard requires the auditor to consider whether the results of the audit indicate that substantial doubt exists as to the entity's ability to continue as a going concern for a period not to exceed one year from the balance sheet date. If doubt does exist, an explanatory paragraph must be added following the opinion paragraph of the audit report.[11]

The appointment of audit committees by most public companies has also helped to narrow the expectations gap by providing the auditor with a means for resolving disputes with management. An **audit committee** is a committee of the board of directors consisting mainly of outside directors—those not having management positions in the company. This external perspective helps to ensure their independence from management.[12] Among other duties, the audit committee is responsible for overseeing the internal control system and arbitrating disagreements between the auditors and management. Disagreements usually concern accounting measurement or disclosure issues that could result in a qualified audit opinion or a change in auditors if not resolved.

Changes in the AICPA's bylaws also have been made in an effort to reduce the number of so-called audit failures, and to further narrow the expectations gap. Members of the AICPA must enroll in an institute-approved practice-monitoring program. A division has been established to conduct the quality review program for the AICPA, and to conduct reviews of firms enrolled in the program.[13] Another AICPA bylaw requires members to complete **continuing professional education** requirements as established by the Council.[14] The requirement that persons applying for AICPA membership after the year 2000 must have completed 150 semester hours of undergraduate study is also the result of an AICPA bylaw.[15] For most students, this translates into a five-year accountancy program.

These efforts taken by the AICPA recognize the risk of increased external regulation of the profession if the expectations gap is permitted to widen further. Increased external regulation means a decline in the governing power of the AICPA and could lead to assumption of absolute regulatory authority by the SEC or some other agency established by Congress. The next section discusses the present and potential impact on quality maintenance of the SEC and the courts.

EXTERNAL REGULATION

The Securities and Exchange Commission (SEC)

The SEC possesses broad authority over the accounting profession. It has the power to set accounting and auditing standards and the authority to take disciplinary action

---

11 Ibid, section AU 341.12.
12 Some concern has been expressed over the granting of such benefits as pension plans and high retainer fees to outside directors; these benefits, it is alleged, may compromise independence.
13 *AICPA Professional Standards*, op. cit., section PR 100.01–06.
14 Ibid, section CPE 100.
15 Ibid, section BL 220.01.2.2.4.

when requirements are violated. The SEC derives its authority from the Securities Act of 1933 and the Securities Exchange Act of 1934. These acts require that the securities of most publicly held companies be registered with the Commission and that independent CPAs audit the financial statements accompanying the registration statements.

The **Chief Accountant of the SEC** conducts investigations of alleged audit failures and is empowered to impose sanctions as considered necessary. In 1998, SEC Chairman Arthur Levitt voiced concern over possible earnings management by public companies and announced a program of increased investigation of suspected instances.[16]

Although the SEC may fine or censure accounting firms for violations of standards, or prohibit them from conducting audits, sanctions typically take the form of temporarily prohibiting the CPA from accepting new SEC clients (usually for a period of from six months to one year). Required special peer review or continuing professional education or both also may be invoked as disciplinary measures by the Chief Accountant.

In addition to the investigative and disciplinary powers just described, the Chief Accountant has the authority to monitor the activities of the Financial Accounting Standards Board, Auditing Standards Board, and the Independence Standards Board, as well as the peer review program of the SEC Practice Section of the Division for CPA Firms. FASB monitoring by the SEC is accomplished through SEC representation on the **Emerging Issues Task Force (EITF)** of the FASB. The EITF is composed of 17 members; its purpose is to reach consensus on how to account for new and unusual financial transactions. The SEC views consensus solutions as the preferred accounting treatment; material departures must be justified. Auditing Standards Board monitoring is done through the POB (as described previously). As discussed above, monitoring of the Independence Standards Board is achieved through the Independence Issues Committee (IIC). Figure 3.3 summarizes the SEC's role in setting accounting, auditing, and independence standards.

The SEC must be notified when a company changes auditors. Form 8-K is the required format for notification. In 1998, for example, Ernst & Young announced its resignation as independent auditor for Premier Laser Systems Inc. because of "serious disagreements" with the company's accounting practices.[17] The 8-K filing must include the reason for the change and any disagreements with the former auditors over the previous two years. In addition, the former auditors must submit a response letter, either agreeing or disagreeing with the company's version of why the change has occurred, and of past disagreements.

In addition, AICPA Professional Standards require that the new auditor attempt to communicate with the former auditor. **Communication with predecessor auditor** may be instituted only with the prospective client's permission. Discussions with the predecessor auditor should include, among other matters, the reason for the change in auditors, any major disagreements between the former auditors and the management of the client firm, the integrity of management, and any other factors having a significant impact on audit risk.[18]

Although the SEC is given broad regulatory authority under the securities laws, the Commission has opted to permit the profession to regulate itself through the various means described earlier. Self-regulation efforts of the profession, however, are under

16 *The Wall Street Journal*, December 9, 1998.
17 *The Wall Street Journal*, May 27, 1998.
18 *AICPA Professional Standards*, op. cit., section AU 315.03–09.

FIGURE 3.3

The Role of the SEC in Setting Accounting and Auditing Standards

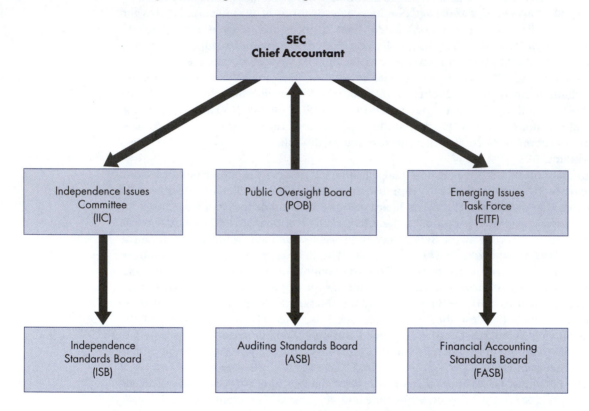

continuous review by the SEC. For example, earnings restatements of such companies as Cendant Corp., Sunbeam Corp., and Livent Inc., believed to have been caused by fraudulent financial reporting, have prompted the SEC to question auditor independence.[19] More recently, the Commission notified 150 public companies that it would review their latest financial statements for possible accounting irregularities.[20] The threat of public regulation, therefore, exists and will continue to exist as long as questions arise concerning the ability of the accounting profession to regulate itself.

.com
http://www.sec.gov/

The SEC maintains a web site at http://www.sec.gov/. This site provides updates on current SEC rulings and deliberations, as well as filings by registrants including quarterly and annual financial reports required of publicly held companies.

AUDITOR LIABILITY: THE COURTS

In addition to the AICPA, the various state boards of accountancy, and the SEC, the courts have also played a role in maintaining the quality of auditing. To cite some ex-

19 *The Wall Street Journal*, Sept. 23, 1998.
20 Ibid, Jan. 22, 1999.

amples, in December 1998, Arthur Andersen agreed to share in a $220 million settlement of a series of lawsuits brought by the shareholders of Waste Management. The lawsuits alleged that the company defrauded investors by overstating its profits over several years.[21] In April 1999, BDO Seidman lost a $44 million jury verdict in a trial alleging negligence for failing to detect a $70 million overstatement of a scrap metal inventory. The overvalued inventory caused Mindis Acquisition Corp. To pay an inflated price to acquire the metals company.[22] In March 1999, Jackson National Life Insurance Co. sued Ernst & Young for negligence in the audit of Kent International Associates, a company to whom Jackson had extended a substantial loan in 1997. The suit alleged that Kent inflated sales in order to obtain the loan amounts and the auditors failed to detect the overstatements. Specifically, the complaint stated that a large number of Kent's customers had addresses corresponding to the company's Brooklyn location, and that Kent was making substantial sales to its vendors.[23]

In 1998 alone 235 companies were named as defendants in federal class action securities fraud lawsuits.[24] This statistic along with the cases cited in this chapter reveal the litigious environment faced by today's independent auditor. In many of the cases, the company has been "fleeced" by its management and the auditors are the only source of relief for hungry lawyers and angry investors. Moreover, unlike the BDO Seidman case described above, CPA firms generally prefer to settle the claims without going to trial because most juries extend little sympathy to the accountants and do not understand some of the complex accounting and auditing issues involved in the cases.

The litigation process begins when clients or third parties sue auditors for negligence or fraud. During the proceedings, lawyers and judges often consider the meaning of such auditing and accounting concepts as "due care," "present fairly," "related parties," "GAAP," "independence," "internal control," and "sufficiency and competence of evidence." These deliberations result in conclusions that are either in agreement or at variance with existing standards (GAAS and GAAP). If the court's findings do *not* agree, the Auditing Standards Board (ASB) or the Financial Accounting Standards Board (FASB) may wish to reconsider the matters dealt with by the court. The result may be a new Statement on Auditing Standards (SAS), a new Statement of Financial Accounting Standards (SFAS), or a reaffirmation of existing pronouncements. In the *Continental Vending Machine Corporation* case, for example (see the appendix following this chapter), the judge instructed the jury to look beyond GAAP, if necessary, in determining whether the financial statements were fairly presented.[25] Auditors had previously been accustomed to using GAAP as the framework within which to evaluate fairness. SAS 5, The Meaning of Present Fairly in Conformity with Generally Accepted Accounting Principles in the Independent Auditor's Report, which resulted from this case, reaffirmed GAAP as the appropriate framework for judging fairness. SAS 69, although superseding SAS 5, retains the reaffirmation of GAAP.[26]

Clients may sue their auditors for failing to detect employee fraud; stockholders and creditors may sue because they relied on audited financial statements that were materially misstated, and were injured by the reliance. This section of the chapter defines

21 *The Wall Street Journal*, December 10, 1998, p. B15.
22 Ibid, April 26, 1999, p. B4.
23 Ibid, March 30, 1999, p. B5.
24 Based on statistics produced by the *Stanford Securities Class Action Clearinghouse*.
25 U.S. vs. Simon et al., 425 F. 2d 796 (2d Cir. 1969).
26 *AICPA Professional Standards*, op. cit., section AU 411.03.

the sources and types of auditor liability and concludes by suggesting ways of preventing and dealing with legal actions. An appendix identifying and discussing the more significant auditor liability cases follows.

Types of Liability

Auditors may be found guilty of ordinary negligence, gross negligence, or fraud in actions relating to the audit of financial statements and other assurance services. In negligence actions, plaintiffs must prove the following:

- The financial statements contain one or more material misstatements;
- The plaintiff relied on the financial statements;
- The plaintiff was injured by such reliance; and
- The application of generally accepted auditing standards should have detected the misstatement(s).

Ordinary negligence actions allege that the auditor failed to exercise **reasonable care** that would be expected to be exercised by a reasonable auditor in the same or a similar situation. **Gross negligence** means that the auditor failed to exercise **minimum care** that would be expected to be exercised by a reasonable auditor in the same or a similar situation. **Fraud** actions allege **intent to deceive**, and accuse the auditor of complicity in misrepresenting financial position and/or results of operations. Figure 3.4 is a diagrammatic representation of auditor liability.

Ordinary Negligence versus Gross Negligence   *Ordinary negligence*, or failure to exercise reasonable care, occurs when an auditor fails to detect an error or fraud that application of generally accepted auditing standards *may or may not* have uncovered. *Gross negligence*, or failure to exercise minimum care, occurs when material errors or fraud that *should have* been detected by the application of GAAS go undetected. Distinguishing between these two types of negligence is important because auditors are always liable for gross negligence, but are *not* always liable for ordinary negligence.

Two concepts are helpful in differentiating between auditor liability for ordinary negligence and liability for gross negligence: *materiality* and *internal control*. The more material a misstatement, the greater the likelihood of detection by the auditor. The application of standard auditing procedures (as described in subsequent chapters), for example, should alert the auditor to material amounts of fictitious sales recorded by the client at year end to inflate earnings. Failure to detect this type of intentional misstatement, referred to as *management misrepresentation fraud*, might be interpreted as gross negligence in a legal action brought against the auditor.

Understating several expense accounts, each by a small amount, might effect a similar misstatement of earnings. Assume that none of the misstatements is material by itself, but the aggregate effect on income is material. The application of standard audit procedures in this instance is not likely to disclose unusual abnormalities. The probability of detection by the auditor, therefore, is much smaller. Under these circumstances, failure to detect may be construed by the courts as ordinary negligence, given the material aggregate effect on income, but *not* as gross negligence.

Internal accounting control, as it relates to auditing, is also helpful in distinguishing between ordinary and gross negligence. As defined in Chapter 1, internal accounting control is that part of internal control designed to enhance the reliability of financial records and safeguard assets. Errors or fraud may occur within the system due to con-

FIGURE 3.4

Types of Auditor Liability

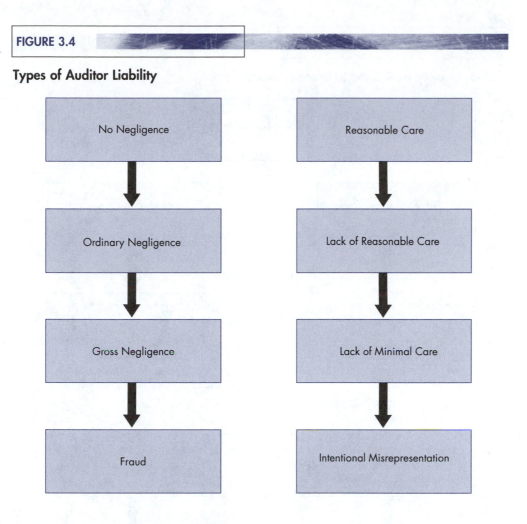

trol weaknesses. Under generally accepted auditing standards, material accounting control weaknesses should be identified by the auditor and tests of transactions and balances should be extended in those areas. Thus, one might expect the auditor to detect significant financial statement misstatements that occur because of major control weaknesses.

Misstatements resulting from fraud may also result from conditions existing outside the internal controls, through collusion (employees working together to circumvent the system) and management override of internal control (see Figure 3.5). These conditions are much more difficult for auditors to detect, given enhanced concealment means. For this reason, plaintiffs' allegations of negligence are more difficult to sustain under these circumstances.

To summarize, material errors and fraud occurring within the control system due to significant weaknesses are more likely to be detected in the course of the audit than those occurring outside the system. This likelihood results from auditors expanding their tests of transactions and balances under conditions of weak internal accounting control. Therefore, as a generality, one might postulate that failure to detect inside control misstatements is more indicative of gross negligence than failure to detect outside control misstatements.

FIGURE 3.5

Auditor Liability as Related to Internal Control

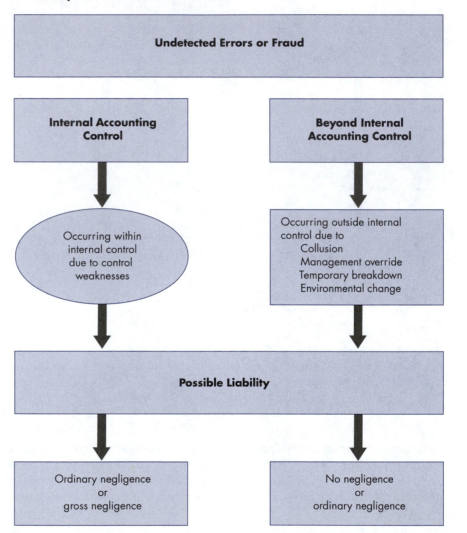

In the case of *Cenco vs. Seidman & Seidman*, the auditors did not detect a $25 million inventory fraud that had been well concealed by management. Clearly, this is an example of management override, with the fraud occurring outside the internal control system. In this case, the court found the auditors not guilty. In his decision, the judge stated that auditors cannot be expected to detect misrepresentation fraud when management turns the company "into an engine of theft against outsiders."[27]

Gross Negligence versus Fraud   Fraud is intentional deceit. A charge of fraud, therefore, accuses the auditor of complicity in the deception. In the *Continental Vending*

27 Cenco, Incorporated vs. Seidman & Seidman, 686 F.2d 449 (CA 7 1982).

Machine Corporation case, the auditors were charged and convicted of knowingly drawing up and rendering an unqualified opinion on a false and misleading financial statement of Continental Vending for the year ending September 30, 1962.[28] In the *National Student Marketing Corporation* and *ESM Government Securities* cases, the auditors were also found guilty of fraud (see the appendix following this chapter).

Negligence does not involve deceit. The auditor may have failed to do what a reasonable auditor would have done to detect the error or fraud, but he or she did not intentionally contrive with the client to deceive third-party financial statement users.

The courts have defined different levels of negligence. The distinction between ordinary and gross negligence was described earlier. Negligence may be so flagrant, however, as to border on deceit. The courts have termed this level of negligence **constructive fraud**. If the auditor ignores that which is obvious, or if the auditor has no reason to believe that the financial statements are fairly presented, yet renders an unqualified audit opinion, the court likely will find the auditor guilty of reckless misconduct and interpret the negligence as constructive fraud. In *Ultramares vs. Touche* (see the appendix), for example, the auditors were found not guilty of intentional deceit. In finding them guilty of negligence, however, the court held that negligence might be so gross as to be construed as fraud.

Table 3.1 summarizes the various types of auditor liability by relating each level of liability to the characteristics associated with it. Figure 3.6 presents a flowchart identifying the types and levels of auditor liability.

Sources of Auditor Liability

The two sources of auditor liability are *common law* and *statutory law*. Under common law, auditors are liable to their clients for breach of contract. They are also subject to civil liability to third parties. Under statutory law, auditors may be held liable for violating the provisions of the Securities Act of 1933 and the Securities Exchange Act of 1934. These four subsets of sources are discussed in the following paragraphs.

Common Law

Contractual Liability to Client The CPA has an agreement with the client to perform, for consideration, whatever services are described in the engagement letter. This agreement (contract) is breached whenever one or both parties violate the provisions. Under contract law, auditors have **contractual liability** to their clients for ordinary negligence, gross negligence, and fraud. Failure to detect employee fraud is the most common cause for actions brought by clients against their auditors. Liability does *not* generally extend to third parties. This limitation of liability under contract law is known as **privity of contract**.

An exception to the rule of privity is made when a third party is a primary beneficiary and is specifically known to the auditor to be relying on the financial statements. Two cases illustrating the extension of privity are the *Rusch Factors* and *Rhode Island Hospital Trust* cases (see the appendix). Three later cases further strengthened and upheld the doctrine of privity. Two of these cases, *Credit Alliance Corporation vs. Arthur Andersen & Co.* (1985), and *Bily vs. Arthur Young & Co.* (1992), are included in the appendix following this chapter. The third case, decided in 1994, involved the firm of Seidman & Seidman. In this case a Florida court of appeals also upheld the doctrine of

28 U.S. vs. Simon et. Al., op. cit.

TABLE 3.1	

Summary of Types of Auditor Liability

No Negligence

Audit conducted in accordance with generally accepted auditing standards

Management override of internal control

Fraud well concealed

Collusive fraud

Ordinary Negligence

Undetected errors or fraud occurring outside internal control

Material management fraud that is concealed by spreading of the misstatements over several financial statement components

Gross Negligence (Constructive Fraud)

Material management fraud not well concealed

Material errors and/or fraud occurring within internal control

Reckless misconduct

Application of generally accepted auditing standards should have disclosed the errors or fraud

Fraud

Intentional deceit

Auditor complicity

privity. The plaintiffs, three individuals, had invested in First American Bank and Trust, which had been audited by Seidman & Seidman. The plaintiffs' investments were subsequently lost when the bank failed. The court held that the law "extends liability to an accountant only when the accountant knows at the time the work is done that a limited group of third parties intends to rely on the work for a specific transaction."[29]

In contrast, a 1998 case decided by the North Carolina Court of Appeals ruled that in certain instances, a CPA may be expected to *infer* that one or a limited number of creditors are relying on the client's financial statements. In this case, one of the client's major suppliers had extended credit to the client based on materially misstated financial statements audited by Price Waterhouse. PW had issued an unqualified audit opinion on the statements. Although PW did not have direct knowledge that the creditor was relying on the statements, they knew, according to the court, that the client intended to supply financial information to a limited group of creditors.[30]

Privity is important in these cases because if privity is extended to the known third party, the auditor can be held liable for ordinary negligence. Under common law, as discussed below, third parties may hold auditors liable for fraud and gross negligence, but *not* for ordinary negligence.

29 Machata vs. Seidman & Seidman, 644 So. 2d 114 (Fla. App. 4 Dist. 1994).
30 Marcus Brothers Textiles, Inc. v. Price Waterhouse, LLP, 498 S.E. 2d 196, 1998 N.C. App. LEXIS 428.

FIGURE 3.6

Legal Liability Flowchart

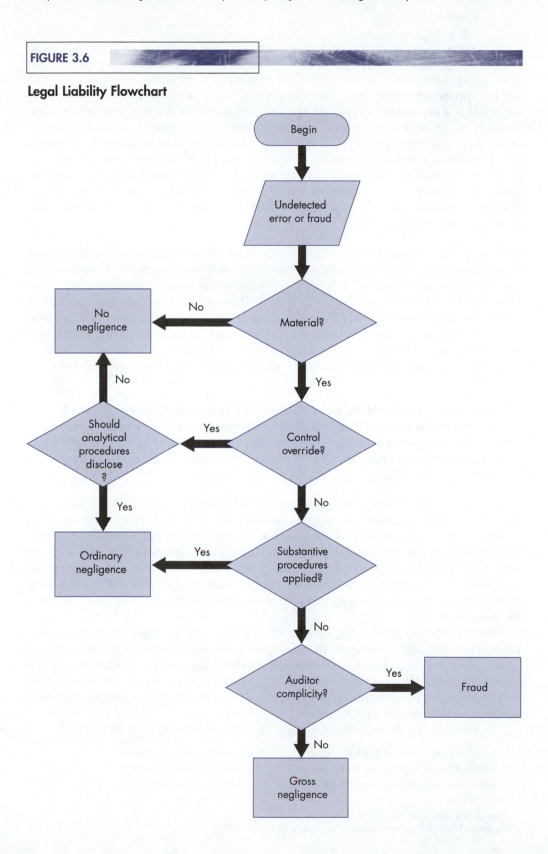

If a client sues the auditor for failure to detect fraud, the burden of proof is on the plaintiff (the client) to demonstrate that failure to detect resulted from auditor negligence. The auditor, in turn, may plead the defense of contributory negligence by the client. **Contributory negligence**, an assertion that the client's own negligence gave rise to the fraud, is a particularly strong defense if the fraud occurs at a high level in the organization or involves management override of the control system. In the *Cenco vs. Seidman & Seidman* case, cited earlier, the auditors were found not guilty for failure to detect inventory fraud perpetrated by management.[31] In a similar case, *Cedars of Lebanon Hospital vs. Touche*, the auditors were sued by the new management for failure to detect massive embezzlements committed by their predecessors. The court ruled in this case that management cannot sue an auditor for failing to detect a fraud that management itself perpetrated.[32]

Civil Liability to Third Parties   Under common law, no contractual relationship exists between the auditors and third parties. Therefore, with the exceptions to privity noted above, auditors generally are *not* liable to third parties for ordinary negligence. They are liable, however, for gross negligence and fraud. These distinctions between contractual liability to clients and **civil liability** to third parties are most clearly described in *Ultramares vs. Touche* (see the appendix). As in contract law, in civil liability actions the burden of proof is placed upon the third party to demonstrate that reliance was placed on financial statements that were materially misstated and that injury resulted from the reliance.

Statutory Law   The **Securities Act of 1933** and the **Securities Exchange Act of 1934** are the two primary sources of auditor liability under **statutory law**, referred to as statutory liability. The 1933 act covers new securities offerings, while the 1934 act establishes recurring reporting requirements for public companies once their securities have been registered with the SEC.

The Securities Act of 1933   In registering a new securities offering, a company must file a registration statement and prospectus with the SEC. The prospectus, which includes much of the information contained in the registration statement, must be furnished to purchasers of the securities. Materials accompanying the statement are to include audited balance sheets, income statements, and statements of cash flows for the last three years. In addition, an unaudited balance sheet and income statement within 90 days of the filing date must be included if "90 days prior to the filing date" falls after the latest audit.

   The registration process begins with the company's filing of the registration statement. The statement is reviewed by the Division of Corporate Finance and a *letter of comments* is issued, setting forth deficiencies in the statement. Upon receiving the letter of comments, the company makes the necessary corrections and additions and resubmits the statement. Upon final review, the SEC declares the registration *effective*, whereupon the underwriters may issue the securities.

   To illustrate the above process, assume the following dates:

Most recent audited balance sheet	December 31, 2001
Filing date of registration statement	September 30, 2002
Effective date of registration statement	November 30, 2002

31 Cenco, Incorporated vs. Seidman & Seidman, op. cit.
32 Cedars of Lebanon Hospital Corporation vs. Touche Ross & Co. (1981).

Given these assumptions, the registrant must include the December 31 audited balance sheets for 2000 and 2001, and audited statements of income and cash flows for the years ending on December 31, 1999, 2000, and 2001. In addition, an unaudited balance sheet as of a date no earlier than June 30, 2002, and an unaudited income statement and statement of cash flows for the partial year must be included.

The 1933 act is the most stringent in terms of potential auditor liability. Under this act, liability is increased in the following ways:

1. The burden of proof shifts from the third party to the auditor to demonstrate due care; that is, the auditor had reasonable grounds for believing the statements were presented fairly;
2. The auditor is liable to injured third parties for ordinary as well as gross negligence; and
3. Auditor liability extends to the effective date of the registration statement.

In view of item 3, the auditor should extend the subsequent events review to the effective date of the registration statement. As defined and discussed in Chapter 13, the subsequent events review requires that the auditor search for events occurring after the balance sheet date that may require adjustment or disclosure in the financial statements being audited. In the present case, the review should extend through November 30, 2002.

Because underwriters usually request a **comfort letter**, the auditor will likely apply certain limited procedures to the unaudited data, in addition to searching for subsequent events up to the effective date of the registration statement. As described and illustrated in Chapter 15, the comfort letter is usually addressed to the underwriters. It is dated as of the effective date of the registration statement and provides limited assurance with respect to

1. Adequacy of disclosure concerning events occurring subsequent to the date of the most recent audited balance sheet; and
2. Unaudited data included in the interim financial statements.

Escott vs. Bar Chris Construction Corporation is an example of a case brought under Section 11 of the Securities Act of 1933 (see the appendix). The auditors were found guilty of negligence in this case.[33] In finding for the plaintiffs, the court held that the auditors had *not* exercised due care in the conduct of their audit. Moreover, the opinion of the court found the auditors lacking due diligence in conducting the "S-1 review" (**subsequent events review**) covering the period extending to the effective date of the registration statement.[34]

The Securities Exchange Act of 1934   The Securities Exchange Act of 1934 requires companies whose securities are registered with the SEC to file quarterly and annual reports with the commission. The quarterly reports (Form 10-Q) include unaudited financial statements, and the annual report (Form 10-K) includes audited financial statements. In addition, special events, such as changes in principal stockholders and changes in auditors, must be promptly reported (Form 8-K).

Much of the financial statement information in form 10-K is identical to the information contained in the annual report to shareholders. Given the concept of **integrated**

---

33 Escott et al. vs. Bar Chris Construction Corp. et al., 283 F. Supp. 643 (S.D.N.Y. 1968).
34 Ibid.

disclosure, as defined by the SEC, this information may be incorporated by reference in Form 10-K.[35] This has greatly simplified SEC reporting requirements.

Prior to the 1976 U.S. Supreme Court decision in *Ernst & Ernst vs. Hochfelder* (see the appendix), the auditor's liability under Rule 10B-5 of the 1934 act was thought to be generally the same as that under common law. Given this interpretation, the auditor was considered liable for gross negligence and fraud, but *not* for ordinary negligence. *Ernst & Ernst vs. Hochfelder* changed this interpretation significantly. The decision in this case set a precedent requiring the plaintiff to prove **scienter**—intent to deceive—in order for the auditors to be held liable under 10B-5.[36] This decision has been interpreted to mean that auditors are liable only for fraud (intentional deceit) under 10B-5. The Supreme Court, however, did not address the question of whether reckless conduct produces negligence so gross as to constitute fraud. Cases brought subsequent to Hochfelder have generally supported the doctrine of scienter as defined in the Hochfelder case.[37]

Recall that under common law actions, the plaintiff must show that he or she relied on financial statements that were materially misstated, and that the reliance caused damage to the plaintiff. With regard to *reliance*, under the 1934 act, the **fraud on the market theory** may impute fraud to management and the auditors even if the plaintiff did not rely *directly* on fraudulent financial statements. This theory stems from the "efficient market" theory, which states that the market price of a publicly traded security reflects all public information impacting that security. Under the fraud on the market theory, if a fraudulent statement or act causes the market to price a security improperly, the parties responsible for the fraud can be liable to investors relying on the efficient market. For example, if an investor buys securities on the advice of a broker, never having examined the financial reports of the company, and it is later discovered that the company had intentionally overstated its reported earnings, the investor may find relief under 10B-5, given the impact of the fraud on the efficient market. In other words, reliance can be imputed, given acceptance of the efficient market theory.[38]

Another important difference between the Securities Act of 1933 and the Securities Exchange Act of 1934 relates to burden of proof. Under the Securities Act of 1933, the burden of proof rests upon the auditor to demonstrate due care in performing the audit. Under the Securities Exchange Act of 1934, however, the burden shifts back to the plaintiff to prove negligence by the auditor. For current information about SEC civil suits in Federal Court and descriptions of selected criminal proceedings, visit the SEC Enforcement Division web site at www.sec.gov/enforce.htm.

The **Private Securities Litigation Reform Act of 1995** has reduced the extent of auditor liability under Section 10B of the 1934 act. Prior to this legislation, auditors were held jointly and severally liable to injured shareholders for auditor negligence. *Joint and several liability* means that one of several defendants found guilty of negligence may be held liable for damages sustained by the plaintiff even if these damages exceed that portion caused by that one defendant's negligence.

.com

http://www.
sec.gov/enforce.htm

---

35 Incorporation by reference directs the reader's attention to information included in the annual report to shareholders, rather than reporting such information in Form 10-K.

36 Ernst & Ernst vs. Hochfelder, 425 U.S. 185, 96 S Ct. 1375, 47 L Ed 2d 668 (1976).

37 See, for example, SEC v. Price Waterhouse (797 F. Supp. 1217 [S.D.N.Y. 1992]) , Shields v. Citytrust Bankeom, Inc. (25 F3d 1124 [2d Cir. 1994]), and Zucker v. Sasaki, CCH Securities Law Reporter, para 99,493, U.S. District Court S.D.N.Y., no. 95 Clv. 10517 [SWK]).

38 For an excellent discussion of the fraud on the market theory, see "Measuring Damages on Securities Actions: Understanding the Fraud on Market Theory," "Supplement: Banking & Financial Mangement," *Massachusetts Lawyer Weekly*, April 5, 1993, p. 51.

Often the companies whose financial statements were misstated were insolvent and the auditors provided the only relief for recovering damages. Joint and several liability thus resulted in damages that far exceeded substantive auditor responsibility. The 1995 act changes auditor liability from joint and several to proportionate. Under *proportionate liability*, responsibility is allocated among the defendants found to be responsible for the loss suffered by the plaintiffs. Given that many of these cases involve management misrepresentation fraud and auditor negligence, auditors will be found less culpable than management and, under these conditions, the bulk of the damage award will be assigned to management.

The 1995 act does *not* cover fraud. Therefore, auditors found guilty of knowing misrepresentation remain jointly and severally liable.[39] Moreover, the act requires an auditor to report an illegal act to the client "as soon as practicable." In 1997, the SEC adopted rules to assist in implementing this rule. Under these rules, an auditor must report directly to the board of directors if

1. The illegal act has a material effect on the financial statements;
2. Appropriate remedial action has not been taken by senior management; and
3. This failure is expected to result in the auditor's resignation or a departure from their standard audit report.[40]

Summary of Sources and Types of Auditor Liability

Auditors are liable to their clients, under contract law, for ordinary negligence, gross negligence, and fraud. Under common law, auditors are liable to third parties for gross negligence and fraud. Additionally, they are liable for ordinary negligence to specifically identified third parties known to be relying on the financial statements. Under the Securities Act of 1933, auditors are liable to third-party purchasers of securities for ordinary negligence, gross negligence, and fraud. Moreover, the 1933 act requires the auditor to prove due care and extends liability to the effective date of the registration statement. Under the Securities Exchange Act of 1934, auditors are liable to third parties for fraud, but *not* for negligence. Moreover, the 1934 act shifts the burden of proof back to the plaintiff for proving either fraud or constructive fraud on the part of the auditor (see Table 3.2).

Liability for Unaudited Statements

The CPA must exercise due care, regardless of the type of service performed. For unaudited financial statements, due care is exercised by adhering to those standards designed to maintain the quality of unaudited statements. These standards are addressed in Chapter 15. Further, a CPA who is aware of material errors or fraud in unaudited financial statements has a duty to inform the owners.

In addition to defining the accountant's liability for unaudited financial statements, the 1971 case of *1136 Tenants Corporation vs. Max Rothenberg & Co.* (see the appendix) demonstrates the need for reaching a clear understanding with the client regarding the type of service to be performed. SAS No. 26, Association with Financial Statements, was issued as the direct result of *1136 Tenants*. The Accounting and Review

---

39 For a more complete discussion of the act, see Pincus, Andrew J., "The Reform Act: What CPAs Should Know," *The Journal of Accountancy*, September 1996, pp. 55–58.
40 *Deloitte & Touche Review*, March 31, 1997.

TABLE 3.2

Sources and Types of Auditor Liability

Sources	Ordinary Negligence	Gross Negligence	Fraud
Common Law			
Contractual Liability	X	X	X
Civil Liability (to third parties)		X	X
Statutory Law			
1933 Act	X	X	X
1934 Act		X ?	X

Services Committee was also formed, and Statements on Standards for Accounting and Review Services No. 1, Compilation and Review of Financial Statements, was issued following this case.[41]

Prevention of Legal Action

Concerned over the increasing number of alleged audit failures, SEC Chairman Arthur Levitt in 1999 urged the formation of the **Panel on Audit Effectiveness**, under the Public Oversight Board, to determine whether the audit practices of CPA firms adequately support the interests of investors and creditors. Specifically, the SEC asked the panel to "focus on the problem of managed earnings, cookie-jar reserves, purchased R&D write-offs and abuse of the materiality concept."[42] After conducting its research and holding public hearings, the panel will issue recommendations directed toward improving the quality of independent audits, thereby reducing the number of undetected frauds. Undetected frauds, of course, lead to lawsuits against CPAs. Until the panel reports its findings and recommendations, the question of liability prevention remains.

The best approach to preventing lawsuits is to remove the basis for legal actions. Allocating resources to areas of high audit risk helps to ensure that the auditor detects material errors and fraud.

Detection by itself, however, is not enough. Auditors must also follow through to determine that the client has corrected material errors detected by the auditors. Otherwise, injury to third parties relying on materially misstated financial statements will result. Auditor insistence on proper treatment in financial statements of discovered errors and fraud, including footnote disclosure of related-party transactions, is significant in preventing third-party injury.

Chapter 5 presents an approach to risk analysis that supports these efforts. The approach evaluates audit risk by analyzing the business and industry to gain a better understanding of transactions and events completed by the client, noting unusual

---

41 The attestation standards and the statements on standards for accounting and review services collectively define the quality of attest services, other than audited financial statements, as well as unaudited financial statements. These standards, along with the various forms of professional services performed by CPAs, are addressed fully in Chapter 15.
42 *Journal of Accountancy*, op. cit., p. 12.

relationships among accounting data that may be indicative of financial statement mis-statements, and studying and evaluating internal accounting control to determine its effectiveness. These audit risk elements are then considered collectively in planning the audit and designing procedures for testing transactions and balances (substantive audit testing). This approach provides a systematic means for detecting errors and fraud and reduces the overall audit risk of expressing an unqualified opinion on financial statements that are materially misstated. Other measures that can help in preventing legal actions include the following:

1. Utilize the audit committee of the board of directors wherever possible. The audit committee, composed of nonmanagement board members, typically has responsibility for monitoring the internal control system and arbitrating disputes arising between the independent auditors and management.
2. Carefully supervise assistants and thoroughly review their work. Audit personnel who are new to the engagement do not possess extensive knowledge of the business and may not readily recognize questionable transactions and other unusual circumstances.
3. Don't submit to time pressure during the audit. Clients sometimes press the auditors to finish the engagement earlier than is warranted by existing conditions. Although early completion reduces the cost to the client and minimizes disruption of the client's staff, it may also prevent the auditor from detecting significant financial statement errors because of failure to apply necessary auditing procedures.
4. For initial audits, communicate with predecessor auditors (in accordance with section AU 315 of the AICPA Professional Standards) and carefully consider whether to accept the engagement. Auditors should not be associated with the financial statements of entities whose managements lack integrity. Such association is in violation of the Code of Professional Conduct and also increases the risk of undetected errors or fraud in the financial statements.
5. Review clients annually for continuance, for the same reasons just cited.
6. Always observe the spirit of ethical behavior and make a positive effort to serve the interests of third-party users of audited financial statements. Be particularly conscious of Rule 102, which requires the CPA to "*maintain objectivity and integrity, be free of conflicts of interest, and not knowingly misrepresent facts or subordinate his or her judgment to others.*"[43]

Dealing with Liability

Regardless of the extent of due care, the auditor can never be absolutely assured that all material errors and fraud have been detected and properly reflected in the financial statements. The audit is, after all, test-based and therefore includes some risk that material errors and fraud will occur and go undetected. For this reason, even the most diligent auditor may be sued by third parties that have been injured by relying on materially misstated financial statements. Auditors need to be prepared to defend themselves in the event of legal actions brought by clients or third parties.

The best defense is demonstration of due care in the conduct of the audit, which is best evidenced by thorough documentation of the audit. Workpapers that are particularly helpful in establishing due care include the following:

---

43 *AICPA Professional Standards*, op. cit., section ET 102.01.

1. Documentation of discovered control weaknesses and the thought processes leading to modification of substantive audit programs in light of the weaknesses;
2. Documentation of the auditor's specific fraud assessment and actions taken in light of such assessment;[44]
3. An engagement letter clearly setting forth the nature of the services to be performed by the CPA;[45]
4. Evidence that the work of assistants was properly reviewed, and that all unanswered questions were cleared prior to issuing the audit report.

Audit workpapers are addressed more fully in Chapter 4.

In addition to the due care defense, auditors should also plan for adequate liability insurance as protection in the event of lawsuits. As noted in Chapter 2, CPA firms can also protect themselves by forming limited liability companies or limited liability partnerships. Although this form of organization does *not* protect the CPA from third-party negligence and fraud actions, it does shield the personal assets of CPA partners or shareholders that were not involved in the alleged wrongdoing. Most state laws governing these forms of organization, however, do require the firm to carry adequate liability insurance to cover potential losses.

APPENDIX

LEGAL CASES INVOLVING AUDITORS

Preface to Cases

Most of the cases cited in this appendix were adjudicated prior to 1980. Virtually all cases involving auditors and occurring subsequent to 1980 have been settled out of court. The reason for the out-of-court settlements has been ostensibly to avoid the exorbitant cost of prolonged litigation, combined with the high risk of an unfavorable outcome. Some of the more significant recent settlements involving national firms are the following:

Year of Settlement	Firm	Amount of Settlement	Nature of Client
1999	Ernst & Young	$185 million	Merry-Go-Round
1994	Deloitte & Touche	$312 million	Failed S&Ls
1992	Ernst & Young	$400 million	Failed S&Ls
1992	Coopers & Lybrand	$95 million	MiniScribe Corp.

In addition to the monetary settlements, the firms must often agree to certain restrictions on future practice. The 1992 Ernst & Young settlement, for example, required the firm to increase training for auditors of depository institutions, submit certain work of

---

44 Chapter 5 defines and discusses the concept of fraud assessment.

45 Although *1136 Tenants* demonstrated the importance of engagement letters, the 1994 case of Congregation of the Passion, Holy Cross Province vs. Touche Ross & Co., 159 Ill. 2d 137, 636 N.E. 2d 503 (1994) expanded the CPA's liability to include extra contractual responsibilities in addition to those specified in the engagement letter. See *The Journal of Accountancy*, December 1995, pp. 89–90 for the details surrounding this case.

audit partners to external third-party review, and more closely "scrutinize accounting decisions in sensitive, high-risk areas."[46]

Notwithstanding the supposedly lower cost of out-of-court settlements, the national firms estimate that litigation settlements in 1992 alone reduced total audit revenue by 9 percent.

Cases Under Common Law

ULTRAMARES VS. TOUCHE (1931)[47]

The *Ultramares* case established that auditors are *not* liable to unknown third-party users for ordinary negligence. The court did hold, however, that auditors might be held liable for gross negligence, which the judge equated with "constructive fraud."

In this case, the firm of Touche, Niven & Co. (now Deloitte & Touche) had been retained by Fred Stern & Co. To prepare and certify the company's December 31, 1923, balance sheet. The balance sheet reflected assets and liabilities approximating $2.5 million and $1.5 million, respectively. In fact, the company was insolvent, and its liabilities exceeded assets by $200,000.

The auditors were held negligent in not examining documentation supporting penciled debit postings to accounts receivable in the general ledger. These unsupported entries, posted after the regular month-end postings had been completed, represented fictitious sales. Other factors, according to the court decision, also should have alerted the auditors to material errors and fraud by Stern & Co.

The plaintiff, Ultramares, had made numerous loans to the company on the basis of the certified balance sheet. Fred Stern & Co. subsequently collapsed and declared bankruptcy on January 2, 1925.

Although deciding in favor of the plaintiffs (Ultramares), the court did uphold the doctrine of privity. In the words of Justice Cardozo, who wrote the court's opinion: "If liability for negligence exists, a thoughtless slip or blunder, the failure to detect a theft or forgery beneath the cover of deceptive entries, may expose accountants to a liability in an indeterminate amount for an indeterminate time to an indeterminate class."[48] The court then declared that *constructive fraud* exists if the plaintiffs can prove gross negligence. The court found the defendants guilty of gross negligence in this case. The auditors, according to the decision, should have further investigated the added postings to accounts receivable. Instead, they accepted the numbers without any form of verification.

RUSCH FACTORS VS. LEVIN (1968)[49]

This case further clarified the *Ultramares* decision by extending privity to specifically identified third parties known by the auditor to be relying on the audited financial statements. In 1963, the plaintiff, a New York banker and factor, had made substantial loans to a Rhode Island corporation. Leonard Levin, a CPA, had issued an unqualified opinion on the financial statements that were, in fact, materially misstated. Rusch Factors lent more than $300,000 to the corporation on the basis of those statements. The company subsequently went into receivership, and Rusch recovered only a portion of the loans.

---

46 *The Wall Street Journal*, November 24, 1992.
47 Ultramares vs. Touche, 255 N.Y. 170, 174 N.E. 441 (N.Y. Ct. App. 1931).
48 Ibid.
49 Rusch Factors, Inc. vs. Levin, 248 F. Supp. 85 (D.R.H. 1968).

The court held that "an accountant should be liable in negligence for careless financial misrepresentation relied upon by actually foreseen and limited classes of persons."[50] Because the plaintiffs proved negligence, the court found for the plaintiffs.

RHODE ISLAND HOSPITAL TRUST NATIONAL BANK VS. SWARTZ (1972)[51]

This case is similar to *Rusch Factors* in holding auditors liable to known third parties in negligence actions. Rhode Island Hospital Trust National Bank had extended and enlarged a line of credit to a company on the basis of reported increases in earnings per share. The increases, as later established, were gained by debiting operating expenses to leasehold improvements accounts. The leasehold improvements were ostensibly related to port facilities used by the company in grain-handling operations. The improvements, in fact, did not exist, and documentation supporting the debits was lacking.

Although the auditors disclaimed an opinion on the financial statements, the court found them negligent in not clearly explaining the reasons for the disclaimer. The reasons given by the auditors were as follows: "Additions to fixed assets in 1963 were found to include principally warehouse improvements and installation of machinery and equipment....Practically all of this work had been done by employees....Complete detailed cost records were not kept of these improvements and no exact determination could be made as to the actual cost of said improvements."[52] The court held that the auditors should have addressed the question of existence, as well as valuation, in citing reasons for the disclaimer. The auditors, therefore, were found guilty of ordinary negligence, and privity was extended to Rhode Island Trust as a specifically identified third party.

CREDIT ALLIANCE CORPORATION VS. ARTHUR ANDERSEN & CO. (1985)[53]

In this case, the New York Court of Appeals defined what is perhaps the most stringent test for determining when privity is to be extended to third parties. Credit Alliance provided substantial financing to L. B. Smith, a Virginia company and audit client of Arthur Andersen. Shortly after the transaction was completed, Smith declared bankruptcy and Credit Alliance sued Arthur Andersen for negligence, alleging that the financial statements "materially overstated Smith's assets, net worth, and general financial health, and that Andersen, by failing to comply with generally accepted auditing standards, failed to discover Smith's precarious financial condition and the possibility that it might not survive as a going concern."[54] Credit Alliance also alleged that Andersen knew or should have known that Smith was using the audited financial statements to induce Credit Alliance and other companies to make credit available to Smith. In finding for Andersen, the court stated that three prerequisites must be satisfied before accountants may be held liable to noncontractual parties relying on inaccurate financial reports:

1. The accountants must have been aware that the financial reports were to be used for a particular purpose or purposes;
2. In the furtherance of which a known party or parties was intended to rely; and
3. Some conduct on the part of the accountants linking them to that party or parties, which evinces the accountants' understanding of that party or parties' reliance.[55]

50 Ibid.
51 Rhode Island Hospital Trust National Bank vs. Swartz, 455 F. 2d. 847 (4th Cir. 1972).
52 Ibid.
53 Credit Alliance Corp. vs. Arthur Andersen & Co., No. 218 (N.Y. Ct. App. July 2, 1985).
54 Ibid.
55 Ibid.

The court then held that, in the present case, there was "no allegation that Andersen had any direct dealings with the plaintiffs, had specifically agreed with Smith to prepare the report for the plaintiffs' use, or had specifically agreed with Smith to provide the plaintiffs with a copy or actually did so." In other words, there was no conduct evidencing Andersen's knowledge of Credit Alliance's reliance on the financial statements.[56]

BILY VS. ARTHUR YOUNG & CO. (1992)[57]

In this case, decided by the California Supreme Court, the plaintiffs were individuals and pension and venture capital funds that had provided "bridge financing" to Osborne Computer Corporation. Osborne was founded in 1980. The investments were in anticipation of an initial public offering planned by Osborne for 1983 to raise capital for the manufacture and distribution of the first portable personal computer. The investments, consisting of warrants issued in exchange for direct loans or letters of credit, allegedly were made on the basis of the 1981 and 1982 audited financial statements, regarding which the defendants, Arthur Young (now Ernst & Young), had rendered unqualified audit opinions.

At trial, the plaintiffs' expert witness identified more than forty instances of negligence in AY's 1982 audit, resulting, in his opinion, in a $3 million understatement of Osborne's liabilities, turning its reported modest profit into a loss of more than $3 million. Although the jury returned a verdict for the plaintiffs, based on a doctrine of "reasonable foreseeability," the California Supreme Court reversed the verdict, rejecting the broad foreseeable plaintiff rule. In a footnote, however, the court did allow "in theory" for the possibility that a third party who is expressly identified in the "audit engagement contract" might sue "under appropriate circumstances" as a third-party beneficiary of that contract.[58]

Cases Under Statutory Law

ESCOTT VS. BAR CHRIS CONSTRUCTION CORPORATION (1968)[59]

This case involved a civil action brought under the Securities Act of 1933. The securities being registered consisted of 15-year convertible subordinated debenture bonds. The case is meaningful in that it emphasizes the significance of gaining a thorough understanding of the business and industry in which the client operates. It also demonstrates the importance of exercising due diligence in conducting the S-1 (subsequent events) review.[60]

Bar Chris was in the business of constructing, selling, leasing, and occasionally operating bowling establishments. The company financed some of the sales, but often sold the notes to a factor in order to satisfy immediate cash needs. Given the overbuilding of bowling establishments in the 1960s, Bar Chris began to encounter difficulties in collecting from its customers, and ultimately filed under the Bankruptcy Act.

The court action brought against the auditors by third-party purchasers of the debentures alleged lack of due care in performing the audit, and lack of due diligence in performing the S-1 review. Assets and income were found to be overstated because

---

56 Ibid.
57 Bily vs. Arthur Young & Co., No. SO17199 (Cal. Aug. 27, 1992).
58 Ibid.
59 Escott et al vs. Bar Chris Construction Corp. et al, 283 F. Supp. 643 (S.D.N.Y. 1968).
60 Remember that under the 1933 act, auditors are liable for both ordinary and gross negligence and liability extends to the effective date of the registration statement.

of incorrect application of the percentage of completion method, and recording transfers to related parties as sales. Other transactions with related parties were found to be improperly classified on the December 31, 1960, balance sheet. The unaudited financial statements, covering the 1961 period prior to the filing date, were also deemed misstated.

The court found the auditors guilty of negligence, both in the performance of the audit and in the conduct of the S-1 review. With respect to the audit, the court held that the auditors depended too heavily on oral responses to their questions and did not further corroborate the answers. Concerning the S-1 review, the auditor's review program was considered adequate, but the court held that it was not properly carried out. In ruling on the due diligence question, the judge stated:

> There had been a material change for the worse in Bar Chris's financial position. That change was sufficiently serious so that the failure to disclose it made the 1960 figures misleading. Beradi (the senior auditor on the engagement) did not discover it. As far as results were concerned, his S-1 review was useless.
>
> Accountants should not be held to a standard higher than that recognized in their profession. I do not do so here. Beradi's review did not come up to that standard. He did not take some of the steps, which the written (audit) program prescribed. He did not spend an adequate amount of time on a task of this magnitude. Most important of all, he was too easily satisfied with glib answers to his inquiries.
>
> This is not to say that he should have made a complete audit. But there were enough danger signals in the materials, which he did examine, to require some further investigation on his part. Generally accepted accounting (auditing) standards required such further investigation under these circumstances. It is not always sufficient merely to ask questions.[61]

FISCHER VS. KLETZ (THE YALE EXPRESS CASE) (1967)[62]

Yale Express demonstrates the importance of auditor follow-up when facts are later discovered that, if known at the time the audit report was released, might have affected the auditor's opinion. The subsequently discovered facts, in this case, related to accounts receivable reported on the year-end audited balance sheet. A substantial portion of the receivables was determined to be fictitious. The accounting firm's management advisory personnel who were engaged to perform systems work following the audit engagement made this discovery. The management advisory services people promptly reported their findings to the audit partner. The auditors notified Yale Express management, but neither management nor the auditors took further action.

Yale Express was engaged in trucking and freight forwarding services. Its 1963 financial statements showed a profit of $1.14 million. Had the statements been adjusted for the fictitious receivables, a loss of $1.2 million would have been reflected. In conjunction with their 1964 audit report, the auditors mentioned the 1963 loss. Yale Express filed for bankruptcy in May 1965. Upon discovering the 1963 loss, purchasers of Yale's securities sued the auditors for deceit under Rule 10B-5 of the Securities Exchange Act of 1934.

Although settled out of court, this case demonstrates the importance of the auditor's responsibility to third parties. At that time, there had been no auditing pro-

61 Escott et al vs. Bar Chris Construction Corp. et al, op. cit.
62 Fischer vs. Kletz, 266 F. Supp. 180 (S.D.N.Y. 1967).

nouncements dealing with information discovered subsequent to the audit report date. As a result of Yale Express, Statement on Auditing Procedure No. 41, Subsequent Discovery of Facts Existing at the Date of the Auditor's Report was released by the AICPA. This SAP was later incorporated into Statement on Auditing Standards No. 1.

UNITED STATES VS. SIMON (THE CONTINENTAL VENDING MACHINE CORPORATION CASE) (1969)[63]

The stockholders of Continental Vending, like those of Yale Express, alleged that the auditors engaged in willful deceit by expressing an unqualified opinion on financial statements that were materially misleading. In contrast to *Yale*, however, this case involved disclosure standards rather than measurement standards.

Harold Roth was president and chief executive officer of Continental Vending. He was also president of Valley Commercial Corporation, a wholly owned subsidiary of Continental. He was the controlling stockholder in both companies, and used them to channel funds to his own personal use. Extensive movements ("laundering") of the funds concealed the diversions. Continental issued notes to Valley, and Valley discounted the notes at various banks. The proceeds were then transferred by Valley to Continental, whereupon Continental made advances to Valley. Finally, Valley made loans to Harold Roth from the advances received from Continental (see Figure 3.7).

At the fiscal year end, September 30, 1962, the amount payable to Valley was $1.03 million, and the amount receivable from Valley was $3.5 million. By the date of the audit report, the auditors had learned that Valley was unable to meet its obligation to Continental. Shortly after release of the 1962 financial statements and audit report, Continental collapsed and the SEC halted trading in the company's securities.

The defendants in this case, two audit partners and a manager, were prosecuted for allegedly participating in a conspiracy to defraud Continental's stockholders. The action was brought under Section 32 of the Securities Exchange Act of 1934. They were convicted in 1968 and the judge imposed prison terms. They received a presidential pardon in 1973.

A central question surrounding the *Continental Vending* case is that of "legal form versus economic substance" of transactions. Although technically a loan to an affiliate, secured by collateral, the receivable was, in fact, an advance to an officer. Moreover, the loan was uncollectible, because it was secured by Continental's own stock and Roth was unable to pay. A sort of "catch-22" existed with regard to the collectibility of the receivable. Since Roth was unable to pay, collectibility became dependent on the collateral. However, given the magnitude of the receivable relative to total assets, the value of the collateral (Continental stock) was dependent on the collectibility of the receivable.

Note 2 to the consolidated financial statements described the receivable as follows:

> *The amount receivable from Valley Commercial Corp. (an affiliated company of which Mr. Harold Roth is an officer, director, and stockholder) bears interest at 12% a year. Such amount, less the balance of the notes payable to that company, is secured by the assignment to the company of Valley's equity in certain marketable securities. As of February 15, 1963, the amount of such equity at current market quotations exceeded the net amount receivable.*

Although expert witnesses from other national accounting firms testified that the note constituted adequate disclosure, the government argued that the note did not clearly

---

63 U.S. vs. Simon et al, op. cit.

FIGURE 3.7

Continental Vending Scheme

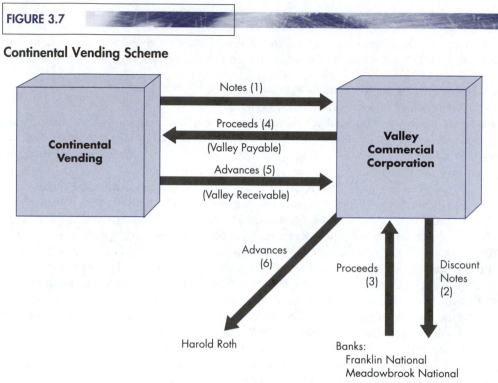

9/30/62:

Valley payable: $1.03 million (50% of current liabilities)

Valley receivable: $3.5 million
(secured mainly by Continental stock pledged as collateral by Harold Roth)

(1) – (6) = The chronology of transactions.

reflect the *substance* of the transactions. Instead, they presented the following as pre-ferred wording of the footnote:

> *The amount receivable from Valley Commercial Corp. (an affiliated company of which Mr. Harold Roth is an officer, director, and stockholder), which bears in-terest at 12% a year, was uncollectible at September 30, 1962, since Valley had loaned approximately the same amount to Mr. Roth who was unable to pay. Since that date, Mr. Roth and others have pledged as security for the repayment of his obligation to Valley and its obligation to Continental (now $3,900,000 against which Continental's liability to Valley cannot be offset) securities which, as of February 14, 1963, had a market value of $2,978,000. Approximately 80% of such securities are stock and convertible debentures of the Company.*

Continental's board of directors had not been informed of the loans, and when they did learn of them, they disapproved.

A significant result of the *Continental Vending* case was the issuance by the Auditing Standards Board of Statement on Auditing Standards No. 6, Related Party Transactions. This statement (later superseded by SAS 45) defines the auditor's responsibility for identifying and auditing transactions similar to the Continental-Valley-Roth transactions. Moreover, it requires the auditor to insist upon adequate disclosure of the substance of the transactions.

UNITED STATES VS. NATELLI (THE NATIONAL STUDENT MARKETING CASE) (1975)[64]

This is another case in which the auditors were charged with intentional deceit under Section 32 of the Securities Exchange Act of 1934. National Student Marketing Corporation (NSM) was engaged in developing advertising for clients wishing to market their products on college campuses. Based on increased earnings, the price of the company's stock had increased dramatically within a six-month period. NSM was taking advantage of the favorable market performance by using its stock to acquire other companies in "pooling of interests" transactions.

Demonstrating to the auditors that most of the revenue-producing effort was expended "up front" in identifying media, developing layout, and producing the ads, NSM recognized revenue upon completion of these activities. Given the time lag between completion of production and appearance of the ads in the media, revenue was frequently recognized in one year, while the ads actually appeared in a subsequent year. This method of revenue recognition is acceptable, provided firm contracts with clients exist and the revenue has been substantially earned. In the absence of written contracts, however, 1968 commitments totaling $1.7 million were reflected as revenue. The auditors agreed with this, only to discover that approximately $1 million of these revenues were written off in 1969. In fact, the amounts written off represented nonexistent 1968 contracts.

In adjusting for the "error" the auditors allegedly agreed to the following plan:

Charged to 1969 earnings	$350,000
Subtracted from 1968 sales of pooled companies	$678,000

In addition, the auditing firm's tax department recommended a reversal of a tax deferral in the amount of $189,000, thus changing the income effect from $(210,000) to $(21,000). The apparent reason for "spreading" the adjustments was to avoid any breakdown in merger negotiations taking place in 1969 between NSM and prospective pooling candidates. A significant downward adjustment of previously reported 1968 earnings would have materially increased the number of NSM shares to be given up in exchange.

In light of these circumstances, the court found the auditors guilty of conspiring with NSM management in misrepresenting the 1968 financial statements and intentionally concealing the errors.

ERNST & ERNST VS. HOCHFELDER (1976)[65]

More than any other case to date, the *Hochfelder* case clearly defines the auditor's liability under Section 10B-5 of the 1934 act. The Supreme Court decided in this case that under the act, auditors are not liable for negligence, but only for fraud. Although

---

64 U.S. vs. Natelli, F. 2d.f (2d Cir. 1975).
65 Ernst & Ernst vs. Hochfelder, op. cit.

auditors had never been held liable for ordinary negligence under 10B-5, the courts had begun to lean towards a broad definition of gross negligence. The Supreme Court decision in *Hochfelder* served to halt this trend.

Investors in nonexistent escrow accounts sued Ernst & Ernst, the auditors of First Securities Corporation of Chicago, a small brokerage firm. The plaintiffs charged that the auditors should have notified the Midwest Stock Exchange of a weakness in internal accounting control. The weakness allegedly permitted the chief executive officer of First Securities to misappropriate escrow funds during the period 1942–1966.

In addition to being CEO of First Securities, Leston Nay also owned 92 percent of the stock in the corporation. Nay had induced friends and associates to invest in certain "escrow accounts" that promised to pay higher-than-normal rates of return. He requested that the investors make the checks payable to him in order to promote flexibility in investing in those accounts promising the highest rates of return. The moneys were never invested. Instead, Nay misappropriated the funds.

Nay concealed the fraud by insisting that all of his mail be placed on his desk unopened, even if he happened to be absent at the time. In this way, no one but Nay and the investors knew that the checks were payable to Nay. The fraud was never discovered, and came to light only as a result of a letter written by Nay shortly before his suicide.

The plaintiffs asserted that Ernst & Ernst (now Ernst & Young) was negligent in not detecting and reporting the "mail rule" to the SEC as a material weakness in internal control. Ernst & Ernst responded by stating that the mail rule was *not* relevant to internal control and that, in fact, First Securities had an adequate system of internal control. The fraud perpetrated by Nay was actually made possible through management override— not by any weakness in internal control.

The trial court decided for Ernst & Ernst and dismissed the case. Upon appeal, the trial court's decision was reversed. This prompted Ernst & Ernst to appeal to the U.S. Supreme Court, which found for the auditors on the basis of "no scienter (i.e., no intent), no liability."

Cases subsequent to *Ernst & Ernst vs. Hochfelder* have generally upheld the doctrine of scienter. (See, for example, SEC v. Price Waterhouse [797 F. Supp. 1217 (S.D.N.Y. 1992)], Shields v. Citytrust Bankeom, Inc. [25 F3d 1124 (2d Cir. 1994)], and Zucker v. Sasaki, [U.S. District Court S.D.N.Y., no. 95 Clv. 10517].)

ESM GOVERNMENT SECURITIES VS. ALEXANDER GRANT & CO. (1986)[66]

Alexander Grant & Co. (now Grant Thornton), a CPA firm and auditor of ESM, was charged with complicity in a scheme to defraud savings and loan institutions and municipalities out of millions of dollars of their temporary investments in ESM. Among the municipalities so affected was the city of Toledo, Ohio, and among the thrift institutions was Home State Savings Bank of Cincinnati, which advanced an estimated $150 million in unsecured loans to ESM.

ESM Government Securities and ESM Securities, Inc., formed in 1975, were related brokerage firms licensed by the Securities and Exchange Commission and the National Association of Securities Dealers. They purportedly invested funds for thrifts and municipalities in various types of government and other securities offering relatively high rates of return. In 1976, ESM Financial Group was formed, and in 1977, ESM Group was formed, both to be holding companies for the other two firms. By the recording of fic-

66 Tew vs. Gomez, No. 85-6219—Civ-Jay (S.D. Fla. 1986).

titious transactions between the brokerage firms and the holding companies, losses incurred by ESM Government Securities were transferred to ESM Financial. The transactions were supported by false documentation purporting loans by Government to Financial. Not only were the losses thus concealed, but ESM Government was also able to accrue interest on the fictitious loans. Moreover, the partner in charge of the ESM audit, a young and ambitious CPA, allegedly accepted bribes from ESM management in return for aiding in concealing the fraud.

In 1984, ESM collapsed and charges were filed against several of the parties involved, including Alexander Grant & Co. Although the case was never tried in court, the out-of-court settlement with Alexander Grant was reportedly in excess of $50 million. The CPA firm partner involved in the fraud was ultimately terminated and subsequently prosecuted by the state of Florida.

Association with Unaudited Financial Statements

1136 TENANTS CORPORATION VS. MAX ROTHENBERG & CO.[67]

In this case, 1136 Tenants Corporation owned a cooperative apartment complex and retained Max Rothenberg & Co., a CPA firm, to prepare financial statements. While preparing the statements, the accountants noted that documentation supporting certain disbursements was missing. They did not try to locate the missing documents. Moreover, they did not notify the client of the "missing invoices." The invoices, in fact, had never existed. Indeed, Riker, the managing agent for the apartment complex, had embezzled over $1 million and concealed the embezzlement with fraudulent journal entries debiting operating expenses and crediting cash. In deciding for the plaintiffs, the Appellate Division of the Supreme Court of New York stated: "Even if a firm of certified public accountants was hired only to perform 'write-up' services for owners of (an) apartment building, when accountants became aware that material invoices purportedly paid by the manager of the building were missing, the accountants were negligent in failing to inform owners of the building of that fact." Given the lack of a formal engagement letter and the fact that the accountants had performed some limited auditing procedures, the court was also unclear as to whether the defendants had been retained to prepare audited or unaudited statements. This further weakened the accountants' due care defense.

KEY TERMS

AICPA Quality Control Standards Committee, 62

Audit committee, 66

Chief Accountant of the SEC, 67

Civil liability, 76

Comfort letter, 77

Communication with predecessor auditor, 67

Constructive fraud, 73

Continuing professional education, 66

Contractual liability, 73

Contributory negligence, 76

Division for CPA Firms, 63

Emerging Issues Task Force (EITF), 67

Expectations gap, 64

External regulation, 60

Fraud: Intent to deceive, 70

Fraud on the market theory, 78

Gross negligence, 70

Independence Issues Committee (IIC), 64

Independence Standards Board (ISB), 63

Integrated disclosure, 77

Minimum care, 70

---

67 1136 Tenants Corporation vs. Max Rothenberg & Co., 36 App. Div. 2d, 30 N.Y. 2d 804, 319 N.Y.S. 2d 1007.

Ordinary negligence, 70
Panel on Audit Effectiveness, 80
Peer (quality) review, 63
Private Companies Practice Section, 63
Private Securities Litigation Reform Act of
    1995, 78
Privity of contract, 73
Public Oversight Board (POB), 63
Reasonable care, 70

Scienter, 78
SEC Practice Section, 63
Securities Act of 1933, 76
Securities Exchange Act of 1934, 76
Self-regulation, 60
Statements on Quality Control Standards, 62
Statutory law, 76
Subsequent events review, 77

REVIEW QUESTIONS

1. Differentiate between self-regulation and external regulation. What are the major vehicles for self-regulation? For external regulation?

2. The AICPA has contributed to the maintenance of audit quality through the various bodies housed within the Institute. The courts have similarly furthered the quality of auditing. Discuss how the courts have enhanced audit quality, citing specific cases in support of your answers.

3. How does the expectations gap relate to quality control?

4. How does the Division for CPA Firms promote quality control?

5. Describe the function of the Public Oversight Board.

6. What role does the SEC play in the maintenance of quality in auditing?

7. What are the duties of the Chief Accountant of the SEC that relate to independent audits?

8. Describe the role of the AICPA Quality Control Standards Committee. What authority do its pronouncements have?

9. Describe the function of the Independence Standards Board.

10. Differentiate between ordinary negligence and gross negligence in terms of the following:
    a. due care
    b. materiality
    c. internal control

11. Give two examples of errors or fraud occurring outside internal control.

12. How did the *Cenco vs. Seidman & Seidman* case further clarify the auditor's liability for negligence?

13. Differentiate between gross negligence and fraud.

14. What is the principal difference, in terms of auditor liability, between the court's findings in the *Bar Chris* case and the *Continental Vending Machine Corporation* case? (See the appendix.)

15. Identify the sources of auditor liability and the subsets within each source.

16. Define *privity of contract*. Under what conditions does privity extend to injured third parties?

17. How does the *Rhode Island Trust* case further define the concept of privity? (See the appendix.)

18. What is the major difference, in terms of auditor liability, between contract law and common law?

19. How do the reporting requirements of the Securities Act of 1933 and the Securities Exchange Act of 1934 differ?

20. How is the auditor's liability more extensive under the 1933 act?

21. Define the following terms:
    a. 10-K
    b. Integrated disclosure
    c. Incorporation by reference
    d. 10-Q

22. What major point of law, in terms of auditor liability, emerged from the *Ernst & Ernst vs. Hochfelder* case?

23. Describe the fraud on the market theory. How does this impact auditor liability?

24. Briefly describe the impact of the Private Securities Litigation Reform Act of 1995 on auditor liability.

25. Successful defenses to legal actions that do arise require that the auditor demonstrate due care in the conduct of the examination. How can auditors, during the conduct of their examinations, ensure an adequate due care defense?

MULTIPLE CHOICE QUESTIONS FROM PAST CPA EXAMS

1. King Enterprises, Inc., engaged the accounting firm of Jackson, Jackson, and Green to perform its annual audit. The firm performed the audit in a competent, nonnegligent manner and billed DMO for $16,000, the agreed fee. Shortly after delivery of the audited financial statements, Beaudry, the assistant controller, disappeared, taking with him $28,000 of DMO's funds. It was then discovered that Beaudry had been engaged in a highly sophisticated, novel defalcation scheme during the past year. He had previously embezzled $35,000 of King's funds. King has refused to pay the accounting firm's fee and is seeking to recover the $63,000 that was stolen by Beaudry. Which of the following is correct?
   a. The accountants cannot recover their fee and are liable for $63,000.
   b. The accountants are entitled to collect their fee and are not liable for $63,000.
   c. King is entitled to rescind the audit contract and thus is not liable for the $16,000 fee, but it cannot recover damages.
   d. King is entitled to recover the $28,000 defalcation, and is not liable for the $16,000 fee.

2. If a stockholder sues a CPA for common law fraud based upon false statements contained in the financial statements audited by the CPA, which of the following is the CPA's best defense?
   a. The stockholder lacks privity to sue.
   b. The CPA disclaimed liability to all third parties in the engagement letter.
   c. The contributory negligence of the client.
   d. The false statements were immaterial.

3. Draheim and Co., CPAs, issued an unqualified opinion on the 2002 financial statements of Karl Corp. These financial statements were included in Karl's annual report and Form 10-K filed with the SEC. Draheim did not detect material misstatements in the financial statements as a result of negligence in the performance of the audit. Based upon the financial statements,

Ponds purchased stock in Karl. Shortly thereafter, Karl became insolvent, causing the price of the stock to decline drastically. Ponds has commenced legal action against Draheim for damages based upon Section 10B and Rule 10B-5 of the Securities Exchange Act of 1934. Draheim's best defense to such an action would be that

a. Ponds lacks privity to sue.

b. The engagement letter specifically disclaimed all liability to third parties.

c. There is no proof of scienter.

d. There has been no subsequent sale for which a loss can be computed.

4. A CPA firm would be reasonably assured of meeting its responsibility to provide services that conform with professional standards by

a. Adhering to generally accepted auditing standards.

b. Having an appropriate system of quality control.

c. Joining professional societies that enforce ethical conduct.

d. Maintaining an attitude of independence in its engagements.

5. Which one of the following, if present, would support a finding of constructive fraud on the part of a CPA?

a. Privity of contract

b. Intent to deceive

c. Reckless disregard

d. Ordinary negligence

6. Rodriguez Corp. desired to acquire the common stock of Marrin Corp. And engaged Latez & Co., CPAs, to audit the financial statements of Marrin Corp. Latez failed to discover a significant liability in performing the audit. In a common law action against Latez, Rodriguez at a minimum must prove

a. Gross negligence on the part of Latez.

b. Negligence on the part of Latez.

c. Fraud on the part of Latez.

d. Latez knew that the liability existed.

7. To recover in a common law action based upon fraud against a CPA with regard to an audit of financial statements, the plaintiff must prove among other things

a. Privity of contract.

b. Unavailability of any other cause of action.

c. That there was a sale or purchase of securities within a six-month period that resulted in a loss.

d. Reliance on the financial statements.

8. Before accepting an engagement to audit a new client, an auditor is required to

a. Make inquiries of the predecessor auditor after obtaining the consent of the prospective client.

b. Obtain the prospective client's signature to the engagement letter.

c. Prepare a memorandum setting forth the staffing requirements and documenting the preliminary audit plan.

d. Discuss the management representation letter with the prospective client's audit committee.

9. In which of the following statements concerning a CPA firm's action is scienter or its equivalent absent?

a. Reckless disregard for the truth

b. Actual knowledge of fraud

    c. Intent to gain monetarily by concealing fraud

    d. Performance of substandard auditing procedures

10. An auditor who discovers that client employees have committed an illegal act that has a material effect on the client's financial statements most likely would withdraw from the engagement if

    a. The illegal act is a violation of generally accepted accounting principles.

    b. The client does not take the remedial action that the auditor considers necessary.

    c. The illegal act was committed during a prior year that was not audited.

    d. The auditor has already assessed control risk at the maximum level.

11. Rosen and Co., CPAs, issued an unqualified opinion on the 2001 financial statements of Hartman Corp. Late in 2002, Hartman determined that its treasurer had embezzled over $1 million. Rosen was unaware of the embezzlement. Hartman has decided to sue Rosen to recover the $1 million. Hartman's suit is based upon Rosen's failure to discover the missing money while performing the audit. Which of the following is Rosen's best defense?

    a. That the audit was performed in accordance with GAAS.

    b. Rosen had no knowledge of the embezzlement.

    c. The financial statements were presented in conformity with GAAP.

    d. The treasurer was Hartman's agent and as such had designed the internal controls that facilitated the embezzlement.

12. A CPA firm evaluates its personnel advancement experience to ascertain whether individuals meeting stated criteria are assigned increased degrees of responsibility. This is evidence of the firm's adherence to which of the following prescribed standards?

    a. Professional ethics

    b. Supervision and review

    c. Accounting and review services

    d. Quality control

13. Conrad purchased Alpha Corp. bonds in a public offering subject to the Securities Act of 1933. Kramer and Co., CPAs, rendered an unqualified opinion on Alpha's financial statements, which were included in Alpha's registration statement. Kramer is being sued by Conrad based upon misstatements contained in the financial statements. In order to be successful, Conrad must prove

	Damages	Materiality of the misstatement	Kosson's scienter
a.	Yes	Yes	Yes
b.	Yes	Yes	No
c.	Yes	No	No
d.	No	Yes	Yes

14. Champion, Inc. engaged Spillman, CPA, to audit Wyandott Company. Champion purchased Wyandott after receiving Wyandott's audited financial statements, which included Spillman's unqualified auditor's opinion. Spillman was negligent in the performance of the Wyandott audit engagement. As a result of Spillman's negligence, Champion suffered damages of $75,000. Champion appears to have grounds to sue Spillman for

	Breach of contract	Negligence
a.	Yes	Yes
b.	Yes	No
c.	No	Yes
d.	No	No

INTERNET ACTIVITIES

The Independence Standard Board is a private body established jointly by the AICPA and the SEC to address issues of auditor independence. The board is charged with issuing standards and interpretations relating to situations and conditions that may impair auditor independence. One of these issues concerns CPA firm professionals who leave the firm for employment with clients.

Required:

Go to the Independence Standards Board web site at http://www.cpaindependence.org/ and summarize the issues to be considered both before and after a CPA firm professional obtains employment with a client. (Hint: The Board has issued a standard that deals specifically with these issues.)

.com

http://www.
cpaindependence.org/

ESSAY QUESTIONS AND PROBLEMS

3.1   AICPA Professional Standards require accounting firms to establish quality control policies and procedures. To assist the firms in this endeavor, the AICPA Quality Control Standards Committee was established.

Required:
a. What authority do the pronouncements of the Quality Control Standards Committee have with respect to the CPA?
b. Briefly describe the five elements of quality control as set forth in Statements on Quality Control Standards No. 2.
c. What are the implications to an accounting firm for failure to establish quality control policies?

3.2   Dibble & Dabble, CPAs, were the accountants for China Corporation, a closely held corporation. Dibble & Dabble had been previously engaged by China to perform certain compilation and tax return work. Kray, China's president, indicated he needed something more than the previous type of services rendered. He advised Dibble, the partner in charge, that the financial statements would be used internally, primarily for management purposes, and also to obtain short-term loans from financial institutions. Dibble recommended that a review of the financial statements be performed. Dibble did not prepare an engagement letter.

In the course of the review, Dibble indicated some reservations about the financial statements. Dibble indicated at various stages that "he was uneasy about certain figures and conclusions" but that "he would take the client's word about the validity of certain entries since the review was primarily for internal use in any event and was not an audit."

Dibble & Dabble did not discover a material act of fraud committed by management. The fraud would have been detected had Dibble not relied wholly on the representations of management concerning the validity of certain entries about which he had felt uneasy.

Required:
a. What is the role of the engagement letter when a CPA has agreed to perform a review of a closely held company? What points should be covered in a typical engagement letter that would be relevant to the parties under the facts set forth above?
b. What is the duty of the CPA in the event suspicious circumstances are revealed as a result of the review?
c. What potential liability does Dibble & Dabble face and who may assert claims against the firm?
(AICPA adapted)

3.3   Match the following terms with their definitions:

a. Chief Accountant of the SEC
b. Division for CPA Firms
c. Due audit care
d. Expectations gap
e. Field work standards
f. Peer review
g. Reporting standards
h. SEC Practice Section
i. General standards
j. Rules of conduct
k. ISB

1. Monitors the activities of accounting profession
2. Relate to the attest function
3. The process whereby one accountant or firm reviews the work of another accountant or firm
4. The major parts of the Code of Professional Conduct
5. The auditor must perform the examination at a reasonable level of skill and with a reasonable degree of care
6. That part of the Division of CPA Firms consisting of firms with SEC clients
7. The disparity between auditor and user perceptions of the role of the independent audit
8. A body, consisting of two sections, established by the AICPA for the purpose of promoting self-regulation
9. Relate to the character and competence of the auditor
10. Relate to the audit process
11. A board established by the AICPA for the purpose of setting independence standards for auditors of public companies

3.4   Weinraub & Kim, CPAs, had been auditing Haughton Pharmaceuticals for many years. They rendered an unqualified opinion on Haughton's financial statements for the current year ended December 31, 2002. The audited financial statements reflected a net income of $4.6 million and earnings per share of $6.23.

Ken Kim, the partner in charge of the audit, was aware that Haughton had applied to Lazy Days Bank in January 2002 to expand the company's line of credit from $7 million to $12 million, and to extend the current due date from 1/15/2003 to 1/15/2005. Lazy Days agreed on the condition that Haughton's 2002 earnings performance improve substantially relative to 2001. Kim had so informed the in-charge senior, Cheryl Bane, and instructed her to be alert to any attempt to fabricate reported earnings. Bane, in turn, had relayed this information to the audit team during the preaudit conference that precedes each Weinraub & Kim audit.

At the beginning of 2002, Haughton had purportedly decided to expand the capacity of its Albany warehouse by constructing a major addition. In the process of verifying debits to "Construction in Progress," relating to the addition, Steve Klein, one of the staff auditors assigned by Bane, was unable to locate invoices supporting many of the charges appearing on "Construction Work Order A1016," the work order pertaining to the Albany warehouse addition. Upon inquiry, Jack Hammer, the corporate controller, told Klein that the invoices had been sent to Albany for verification purposes and would be returned to headquarters by March 15 (well after the completion of audit field work). Bane said not to worry inasmuch as the addition had not been completed by the 2002 year end. The team would examine the invoices during the 2003 interim audit.

Because the 2002 audited financial statements showed a major increase in earnings over 2001, Lazy Days Bank expanded and extended the line of credit as agreed. Shortly thereafter, Haughton became insolvent and filed for bankruptcy under Chapter 11. The line-of-credit expansion had been used to fight a hostile takeover. Moreover, the trustee in bankruptcy learned that the Albany warehouse addition did not exist. Instead, the debits to "Construction in Progress" were really operating expenses that had been fraudulently capitalized in order to achieve the earnings increase necessary to effect the line-of-credit adjustments. Lazy Days Bank sued Haughton Pharmaceuticals and also brought action against Weinraub & Kim for negligence in not detecting the fraud.

Required:
a. What sources and types of liability confront the auditors in the present case?
b. Do you think the auditors were negligent? Support your answer.
c. Does privity extend to Lazy Days Bank? Explain why.

3.5   Shirley Brown is the chief executive officer of Brown Cosmetics, a small but rapidly growing manufacturer of lotions and cosmetics. For the past several years, Gingrich & Starr, CPAs, had been engaged to do compilation work, to provide a systems improvement study, and to prepare the company's federal and state income tax returns. In 2001, Brown decided that due to the growth of the company and requests from bankers, it would be desirable to have an audit. Moreover, Brown had recently received a disturbing anonymous letter that stated: "Beware, you have a viper in your nest. The money is literally disappearing before your very eyes! Signed: A friend."

Brown believed that the audit was entirely necessary and easily justifiable on the basis of the growth and credit factors mentioned above. She decided she would keep the anonymous letter to herself.

Therefore, Brown on behalf of Brown Cosmetics engaged Gingrich & Starr, CPAs, to render an opinion on the financial statements for the year ended June 30, 2002. She told Gingrich she wanted to verify that the financial statements were "accurate and proper." She did not mention the anonymous letter. The usual engagement letter providing for an audit in accordance with generally accepted auditing standards was drafted by Gingrich & Starr and signed by both parties.

The audit was performed in accordance with GAAS. The audit did not reveal a clever defalcation plan by which Biden, the assistant treasurer, was siphoning off substantial amounts of Brown Cosmetics' money. The defalcations occurred both before and after the audit. Biden's embezzlement was discovered in October 2002. Although the scheme was fairly sophisticated, it could have been detected had Gingrich & Starr performed additional checks and procedures. Brown Cosmetics demands reimbursement from Gingrich for the entire amount of the embezzlement, some $150,000 of which occurred before the audit and $275,000 after. Gingrich has denied any liability and refuses to pay.

Required:
a. In the event Brown Cosmetics sues Gingrich & Starr, will it prevail in whole or in part?
b. Might there be any liability to Brown Cosmetics on Brown's part and, if so, under what theory?
(AICPA adapted)

3.6   The Securities and Exchange Commission possesses broad authority over the accounting profession, in terms of the power to set accounting and auditing standards, and the authority to take disciplinary action where requirements are violated.

Required:
a. From where does the SEC derive this authority?
b. To what extent has the SEC exercised its authority?
c. Through what means does the SEC monitor the accounting profession's efforts at self-regulation?
d. Discuss the role of the Chief Accountant of the SEC as it affects the accounting profession.

3.7   Abel Corporation decided to make a public offering of bonds to raise needed capital. On June 30, 2002, it publicly sold $63 million of 7 percent debentures in accordance with the registration requirements of the Securities Act of 1933.

The financial statements filed with the registration statement contained the unqualified opinion of Chavez & Co., CPAs. The statements overstated Abel's net income and net worth. Through negligence Chavez did not detect the overstatements. As a result the bonds, which originally sold for $1,000 per bond, have dropped in value to $700.

Brown is an investor who purchased $10,000 of the bonds. He promptly brought an action against Chavez under the Securities Act of 1933.

Required:
Will Brown prevail on his claim under the Securities Act of 1933? Give the reasons for your conclusions. (AICPA adapted)

3.8   Drewcarey Place is a large condominium complex located in Shaker Heights, Ohio. Residential units have been sold primarily to retired individuals and those contemplating retirement. Lander Lee was hired by the Drewcarey Owners' Association to manage the complex, comply with the various employment and tax laws, and issue annual financial statements to the homeowners. Matthews & Donaldson, CPAs, were engaged by the association to review (not audit) the financial statements prepared by Lee's accountant. The CPAs did not draft an engagement letter.

While reviewing the accounts, Burt Matthews, Stanley Matthews' son and newly hired staff auditor, was unable to locate invoices supporting disbursements to several vendors for condominium repairs. Not knowing whether to pursue the matter further, he prepared a workpaper entitled "Missing Invoices" and placed it in the current workpaper file. He later asked his father what to do about the missing invoices. The elder Matthews replied that nothing need be done inasmuch as the firm was engaged to review the financial statements, and *not* to conduct an audit. A review, he reminded his son, consists primarily of analyzing relationships among financial statement components and inquiring of management, and does *not* involve the application of procedures normally associated with an audit. "Furthermore," he said, "we're going to disclaim an opinion, anyway, on the basis that the numbers are strictly management's representations."

Shortly after releasing the financial statements, Lee informed the Drewcarey Owners' Association that he had found another position and would be resigning as manager effective immediately. The following week (Lee had already left the country), creditors began to request payment of allegedly significant balances owing them, and the bank notified the association of a $30,000 overdraft that needed to be settled immediately. Lee had told the association prior to his departure that the complex was in sound financial condition and that the owners should be contemplating temporary investment sources for excess funds and possibly rebating maintenance fees to the condominium owners. Alarmed at this sudden liquidity crisis, the association requested that Matthews & Donaldson conduct an investigation of whatever events had contributed to the current problems. The CPAs discovered that Lee had been embezzling funds and concealing the thefts by recording fraudulent disbursements. The fraud had been perpetrated over a number of years, and had become so significant that Lee felt he couldn't "cover it" any longer. This threat of exposure had led to his resignation and self-imposed exile.

The association subsequently filed an action against Matthews & Donaldson for recovery of $1.8 million, the best estimate of loss from Lee's embezzlement. The action alleged that Matthews & Donaldson was negligent in failing to discover the fraud. Matthews & Donaldson responded that it was not engaged to conduct an audit, notwithstanding the absence of an engagement letter supporting its position. Upon subpoena of Matthews' workpapers, lawyers for the plaintiffs discovered the workpaper entitled "Missing Invoices."

Required:
a. Who should prevail in this case? Give reasons for your answer.
b. What does this case demonstrate as to the importance of an engagement letter?
c. What is the responsibility of a CPA when his or her suspicions are aroused during an engagement? How does this responsibility differ as to type of engagement?

3.9   Webledger Inc. Applied for a substantial bank loan from Charter Two Bank. In connection with its application, Webledger engaged Justison & Co., CPAs, to audit its financial statements. Justison completed the audit and rendered an unqualified opinion. On the basis of the financial statements and Justison's opinion, Charter Two granted Webledger a loan of $2,500,000.

Within three months after the loan was granted, Webledger filed for bankruptcy. Charter Two promptly brought suit against Justison for damages, claiming that it had relied to its detriment on misleading financial statements and the unqualified opinion of Justison.

Justison's audit workpapers reveal negligence and possible other misconduct in the performance of the audit. Nevertheless, Justison believes it can defend itself against liability to Charter Two based on the privity defense.

Required:
a. Explain the privity defense and evaluate its application to Justison.
b. What exceptions to the privity defense might Charter Two argue?
(AICPA adapted)

DISCUSSION CASE

PHAR-MOR, INC.

Michael (Mickey) Monus, president and chief executive officer of Phar-Mor, once the nation's largest discount drug chain, was regarded as somewhat of a folk hero in his hometown of Youngstown, Ohio. After all, he had created thousands of jobs in a city that had lost 50,000 jobs to the dying steel industry. In addition, he had endowed a chair in the business school at Youngstown State University, served on the board of trustees, and founded the World Basketball League

(WBL), bringing one of the teams to Youngstown. Suddenly, in July 1992, Monus' world came tumbling down. The first "domino" fell when WBL team owners rebelled because players and referees had not been paid for nearly two months. Monus then issued two checks, both of which bounced. Shortly thereafter, Phar-Mor officials received a tip that money had been channeled from the company to the WBL. An in-house investigation uncovered some questionable transactions; this prompted Phar-Mor to call in federal authorities to conduct a more intensive investigation. This investigation uncovered one of the largest fraud and embezzlement schemes in the history of U.S. business, totaling nearly $1 billion.

Phar-Mor was founded in 1982 by Michael Monus and David Shapira. Shapira's family owned Giant Eagle, a supermarket chain headquartered in Pittsburgh. Giant Eagle was also the largest Phar-Mor stockholder. Phar-Mor had grown, within a decade, from a single store in Niles, Ohio (a Youngstown suburb), to 300 stores employing 23,000 employees and achieving sales of $3 billion. The stores were warehouse size and sold everything from prescription drugs to office furniture, electronics, sportswear, and videotapes. The fraud allegedly was perpetrated by Monus, who enlisted the services of Patrick Finn, chief financial officer, as well as two former staff members of Coopers & Lybrand, the Phar-Mor auditors. The former Coopers staff members, Jeff Walley and Stan Cherelstein, had been hired by Phar-Mor as vice president for finance and comptroller, respectively. Of the missing $1 billion, $15 million supposedly consisted of embezzled funds channeled to the failing WBL and to Monus' personal use. Blain Howe, a CPA who headed Phar-Mor's small business division, stated that the division had a check-writing machine with Monus' signature that was routinely used to move Phar-Mor funds to the WBL and elsewhere.

The remaining $985 million consisted of misrepresentation fraud in the form of earnings overstatement. According to investigators, the purpose of the overstatement was to maximize executive bonuses based on reported profits, and generally to make Phar-Mor look good to investors and potential investors. The fraud initially took the form of improper accounting for large initial payments, totaling approximately $140 million, from such vendors as The Coca-Cola Company and Fuji Film Company, in exchange for limited-term exclusive supply arrangements. Phar-Mor reported the payments as revenue upon receipt, rather than as purchases discounts amortized over the life of the arrangements. By 1990 this scheme did not adequately increase underbudget earnings, whereupon the fraud assumed the form of inventory inflation.

Phar-Mor hired an outside company to take inventory. Upon completion, the company turned its figures over to Monus and his assistants, who allegedly increased the quantities. Two sets of books were maintained. One contained the correct inventory figures. The other set, for the auditors' use, included unexplained inventory increase adjustments. The adjustments were spread over hundreds of stores. In addition to the inventory overstatement, a smaller amount of earnings overstatement was said to have been concealed through uncollectible accounts receivable not written off, underestimates of liabilities, and improperly claimed assets.

Patrick Finn, Phar-Mor's chief financial officer, allegedly prepared two versions of the monthly financial report. The first version was the true report and showed staggering losses. According to investigators, this report was known only to Monus, Finn, Walley, and Cherelstein and was kept hidden. The second version, referred to as "David's Report" (because it was prepared for David Shapira), showed ever-increasing profits.

The impact of the fraud was to overstate 1989, 1990, and 1991 figures to show profits when, in fact, large losses were sustained in each of the three years. In 1991, for example, the company reported a $50 million profit rather than the $150 million loss that had actually been incurred.

Upon discovery of the fraud, Phar-Mor fired Monus, as well as Coopers & Lybrand, its auditors since 1984. Additionally, the company took a $350 million charge in the second quarter of 1992. The fraud investigation was conducted jointly by the Federal Bureau of Investigation and the Internal Revenue Service. David Shapira, who apparently had no knowledge of the fraud perpetrated by his longtime friend, replaced Monus as chief executive officer, and Deloitte & Touche were engaged to replace Coopers & Lybrand as independent auditors. In June 1993 Monus was indicted on 129 counts of fraud, filing false income tax returns, and money laundering.

A subsequent legal action was filed by Phar-Mor against Coopers & Lybrand. This suit accused the auditors of looking no further than the inventory summary sheets, thereby missing the unexplained adjustments. The suit also alleged that Coopers observed physical inventory-taking at only five to ten stores and informed Phar-Mor management in advance as to which stores it was going to test (Coopers responded by stating that Monus had informed it that the company had to know in advance in order to close the stores during inventory observation). The perpetrators, of course, were careful not to adjust inventory in any of the stores tested by the auditors.

Phar-Mor filed for bankruptcy protection under Chapter 11 of the U.S. Bankruptcy Code in August 1992. The company was forced to close 132 of its 300 stores and terminated nearly 13,000 employees. In addition, the office furniture and equipment, sportswear, and consumer electronics lines were dropped from the remaining stores. In February 1993 the company hired "turnaround specialist" Antonio Alvarez as president and chief operating officer. By April, Phar-Mor appeared to be making a comeback, having amassed $200 million cash from operations and having negotiated a $150 million debtor financing agreement. Its accounting and reporting system had been greatly improved, and the company was planning for chainwide installation of point-of-sale (POS) scanners for better inventory control.

Required:

a. What must Phar-Mor prove in order to prevail in this case? What must Coopers & Lybrand demonstrate in order to successfully defend itself?

b. The following statements have been extracted from various articles and reports covering the Phar-Mor saga. The statements have been recast in the form of charges by Phar-Mor representatives and responses by Coopers & Lybrand representatives. Comment on the validity and strength of each of the charges and responses.

Charges:

1. "The auditors should have detected the inventory fraud. This is basic accounting. This is Auditing 101." (Paul A. Manion, Phar-Mor's lawyer)

2. "The auditors looked no farther than the cover sheets on detailed inventory records. Had they investigated a little more, they would have found adjustments to inventory made without explanation. They (Coopers) virtually missed the entire company. Some of the things that they failed to do are of the most fundamental nature." (Paul Manion)

3. Phar-Mor accused Coopers of malpractice and negligence by failing to uncover massive fraud and for misrepresenting Phar-Mor's finances in audit opinions and reports. Phar-Mor said it based major decisions on Coopers' reports, such as expanding the size and number of its stores from 81 to 300 and obtaining a $600 million line of credit and $155 million in long-term financing. *(Pittsburgh Post-Gazette, 2 February 1993)*

4. "(David) Shapira trusted Monus more than he should have—but he had no reason not to trust him. David's not a flamboyant type of guy, but I think Shapira tolerated him (Monus) over the years because of what Mickey had seemingly accomplished." (Attorney for Shapira)

Responses:

1. "The company hired an auditor. If it wanted a private investigator, it should have hired one of those instead." (Coopers & Lybrand)

2. "The fraud was not simply a matter of overlooking a few hundred million dollars worth of soap and toothpaste. Rather, Phar-Mor's finance department tinkered with complex accounting formulas, adjusting carrying values and gross margins— schemes that aren't easily detected. Also, the fraud was collusive. Coopers was hoodwinked by not one or two low-level employees, but by the company's president and its top finance executives. Had we any inkling that senior management was doing something fraudulent, we would have immediately expanded our audit procedures and dug deeper." (David McLean, Coopers' associate general counsel)

3. Coopers called the lawsuit a "shameless attempt to shift the burden of its own corporate wrongdoing from itself and its management to an accounting firm which was a victim of corporate

fraud. . . . Phar-Mor has functioned as an engine of fraud for the benefit of its senior management." (*Pittsburgh Post-Gazette*, 2 February 1993)

4. "(David) Shapira should have known there was something amiss. He was a very sophisticated retailer. He was the famous hands-on executive. . . . How can he accuse (the auditors) of being negligent when he was CEO (of Giant Eagle)? He's the guy on whose desk the buck stops." (David McLean)

p a r t 2

Planning the Audit

biltrite

c h a p t e r 4

biltrite

l e a r n i n g o b j e c t i v e s

After reading this chapter, you should be able to

1 Develop a framework, in terms of objectives, evidence, and procedures, for conducting an independent financial audit.

2 Identify and describe the various forms of audit evidence, the procedures for gathering evidence, and how to relate the evidence and procedures to audit objectives.

3 Define audit programs and understand the need for them, how they are prepared, and how they are classified.

4 Understand the nature and purpose of audit workpapers and know the difference between the current file and permanent file workpapers.

5 Recognize the attributes of the complete audit workpaper, and know why each is important to adequate documentation of the audit.

6 Differentiate, in terms of the nature, timing, and extent of audit procedures, between an initial audit and a recurring audit.

OVERVIEW

Chapter 4 begins by identifying the objectives relating to an independent financial statement audit. The chapter then describes audit evidence in terms of its characteristics and how these characteristics relate to the audit objectives. The third section of the chapter focuses on the procedures auditors use to gather audit evidence, and audit programs are defined and related to the audit planning standard.

Chapter 4 concludes by introducing the student to audit workpapers and the need for complete documentation of the audit. Workpapers are classified as "permanent" file workpapers and "current" file workpapers.

INTRODUCTION

The third standard of audit field work requires that "sufficient competent evidential matter is to be obtained through inspection, observation, inquiries, and confirmations to afford a reasonable basis for an opinion regarding the financial statements under examination."[1] To satisfy this standard, the auditor must first identify audit objectives for the engagement and then select the kinds of audit evidence and procedures necessary to meet those objectives. The audit plan containing the specified objectives and procedures is referred to as an "audit program." Audit workpapers are the documentary evidence that the auditor has satisfied the objectives set forth in the audit program.

AUDIT OBJECTIVES

Before determining the kinds of audit evidence to gather and the procedures to be applied in a particular engagement, the auditor must clearly identify the appropriate **audit objectives**. Audit objectives may be classified into two categories: understanding the client's environment—audit planning objectives, and audit of transactions and balances—and substantive audit objectives.

Understanding the Client's Environment

Understanding the client's environment consists of two parts:

1. Understanding the client's business and the industry of which it is a part; and
2. Understanding the existing internal control system.

Understanding the Business and the Industry   Effective allocation of audit resources requires that the auditor have a clear understanding of the client's business and the industry of which it is a part. Understanding the business and industry enables the auditor to concentrate audit resources in those areas of high audit risk.

Audit risk is defined as "the risk that the auditor may unknowingly fail to appropriately modify his/her opinion on financial statements that are materially misstated."[2] The misstatements may be the result of errors (unintentional) or fraud (intentional).

Analysis of the client's business and the industry assists in audit risk assessment in three ways. First, it directs the auditor's attention toward areas suggesting intentional misstatements by management. The analysis is also helpful in identifying factors that

---

1   *AICPA Professional Standards*, New York: AICPA, section AU 150.02.
2   Ibid, section AU 312.02.

may lead the auditor to question the ability of the entity to continue as a going concern.[3] Finally, study of the client's business and industry can help to identify complex transaction areas contributing to higher probabilities of recording errors.

Some of the specific risk areas that may be identified by analyzing the nature of the client's business are the following:

1. *Competition within the industry.* Today's so-called high-tech industries are very competitive. Within this environment, companies may be "pressured" by the financial community to maintain earnings growth. The auditor must be alert, under these conditions, to the possibility of premature recognition of revenue or unjustified deferral of costs as a means for misrepresenting earnings growth.

2. *Declining industry.* The airline industry suffered during the 1990s following deregulation and declining demand. Competition increased due to deregulation, and at the same time, given downsizing and cost-cutting efforts by businesses, the demand for air travel slackened markedly. The problem was so severe that companies such as Pan Am and Eastern Airlines were forced out of business. Circumstances like these raise the question of whether other companies in the industry can survive in the face of increasing competition and declining demand. When auditing companies in declining industries, the auditor needs to ascertain specifically how the client is dealing with the situation and assess the ability of the client to continue as a going concern. Another basis of accounting may be suggested if the "going concern" assumption is not appropriate in the circumstances.

3. *Idle capacity.* Frequently, companies or entire industries (steel, for example, in the 1980s) experience idle capacity due to declining demand, increased competition from imports, or some combination of factors. Within this environment, the auditor must determine that inventories are not excessive (suggesting possible obsolescence). Even where the inventories are not deemed excessive, the auditor must determine that they do not contain excessive amounts of fixed overhead more appropriately charged to current operations as a capacity loss.

4. *Related parties. A **related party**,* within the context of auditing, is a person or entity having the potential to influence the auditee and to prevent the auditee from fully pursuing its own interests. In 1998, for example, a company controlled by Rite Aid CEO Martin Grass and his brother-in-law purchased a parcel of land that they allegedly intended to sell or lease to the company as the new Rite Aid headquarters site. The Grass family also had ownership interests in other land parcels leased to Rite Aid stores, as well as partial ownership of some Rite Aid suppliers.[4]

    Shell companies, subsidiaries, executives, and their families are all related parties. The economic substance of transactions with related parties is sometimes at variance with legal form. The auditor, under these circumstances, must ensure that economic substance takes precedence.[5] In the Rite Aid example, the auditor must be alert to all significant transactions between the company and the enterprises controlled by the Grass family. The auditor's principal objective here is to determine

---

3   SAS 59 requires the auditor to consider whether the aggregate results of all audit procedures performed during planning, performance, and evaluation indicate that there could be substantial doubt about the entity's ability to continue as a going concern for a reasonable period of time, not to exceed one year beyond the date of the audited financial statements. If such doubt exists, the auditor is required to add an explanatory paragraph following the opinion paragraph in the audit report (see Chapter 14).

4   *The Wall Street Journal,* February 19, 1999.

5   *AICPA Professional Standards,* op. cit., section AU 334.02.

that disbursements to these enterprises represent arm's-length transactions for which the company receives due consideration in exchange for the consideration given up. Do the leased properties exist? Are the rentals reasonable in amount? Do the suppliers exist? Are the disbursements for goods actually received and are the amounts reasonable compared with prices paid to other suppliers?

Given the magnitude of related-party transactions, the professional standards require that audit procedures be applied for the purpose of identifying related parties and related-party transactions and ensuring proper disclosure of the economic substance of these transactions.

Understanding the Existing Internal Control System   In addition to performing business and industry analysis, the auditor also assesses the probability of material financial statement errors or fraud by studying and evaluating the internal accounting control system. This study and evaluation, referred to as *assessment of control risk*, is described below and discussed at length in Chapters 7 and 8.

The second standard of field work states that a sufficient understanding of the internal control system should be obtained by the auditor in order to determine the nature, timing, and extent of the audit tests to be performed. Specifically, the auditor studies the internal control system in order to identify types of potential financial statement misstatements and assess control risk. A strong system reduces the probability of material misstatements. This, in turn, leads to a reduction in the quantity of audit evidence necessary to satisfy the audit objectives.

In studying internal controls, the auditor must obtain an understanding of each element of the system. The Treadway Commission (see Chapter 2) identified three categories and five components of internal control.[6] The auditor's understanding of the internal control system is then used to

1. Identify the types of potential misstatements;
2. Consider the factors that may affect the risk of material misstatement; and
3. Design substantive tests (of transactions and balances).[7]

Significant weaknesses in internal control systems may be likened to those areas of high audit risk discussed in the preceding section. Each type of environment (the business and industry environment and the internal control environment) poses a threat in terms of potential misstatement in the financial statements. Both, therefore, suggest the need for additional audit resources to adequately manage the associated audit risk.

Audit of Transactions and Balances

With an understanding of the business and industry and of the internal control system, the auditor can proceed with the **audit of transactions and balances**. Figure 4.1 summarizes the following discussion and provides a framework for relating auditing procedures to various forms of audit evidence and audit objectives. Note that audit evidence is a function of audit objectives, and that auditing procedures are dependent on the nature and amount of evidence needed to satisfy the specific audit objectives. The procedures, therefore, should flow logically from the objectives.

---

6 Committee of Sponsoring Organizations of the Treadway Commission, *Internal Control–Integrated Framework*, New York: COSO, 1994.
7 *AICPA Professional Standards*, op. cit., section AU 319.

FIGURE 4.1

Audit Objectives, Evidence, and Procedures

Audit Objectives
Understanding the Client's Environment—Audit Planning Objectives
    Understand the client's business and industry
    Understand the client's internal accounting control
        Identify types of potential misstatements
        Consider factors that may affect the risk of material misstatement
        Design substantive tests
Audit of Transactions and Balances—Substantive Audit Objectives
    Existence or occurrence (misstatements due to commission)
    Completeness (misstatements due to omission)
    Rights and obligations
    Valuation or allocation
    Presentation and disclosure

Audit Evidence
Physical	Sufficient
Confirmation	Competent
Documentary	Valid and
Mathematical	Relevant
Analytical	
Hearsay	

Auditing Procedures (Examples)
Observe inventory taking
Confirm accounts receivable
Vouch plant asset additions
Calculate accrued interest
Compare gross profit with that of prior year
Inquire as to contingent liabilities

Auditing objectives and procedures are not necessarily related on a one-to-one basis. Some audit procedures satisfy many objectives, while in other audit applications, a combination of procedures may be required to satisfy a single objective.[8]

Substantive audit testing consists of examining evidence that substantiates the items appearing on the financial statements. Because the nature, timing, and extent of substantive audit tests are dependent on the nature of the business and the quality of existing internal control, the *client understanding objectives necessarily precede the substantive audit objectives.*

In the third paragraph of the standard audit report, the auditor expresses an opinion as to the fairness with which the financial statements present the financial position, results of operations, and cash flows. As described in Chapter 1, five specific manage-

8   Ibid, section AU 326.10.

ment assertions have been identified by the auditing profession as necessary in order to support fairness of financial presentation:

1. Existence or occurrence;
2. Completeness;
3. Rights and obligations;
4. Valuation or allocation; and
5. Presentation and disclosure.[9]

Given that the auditor's task is to assess the fairness with which these assertions are represented in the financial statements, *the assertions become the objectives* for the audit of transactions and balances. These objectives (assertions) are now considered in terms of how they support financial statement fairness.

Existence or Occurrence The financial statements contain management's representations concerning assets, equities (used hereafter to mean liabilities and ownership equity), revenues, expenses, gains, and losses. The auditor must, through substantive audit testing, determine **existence or occurrence**. He or she must establish that all of the asset and equity balances represented on the balance sheet existed at the balance sheet date, and that all of the revenues, expenses, gains, and losses reflected in the income statement occurred during the period being audited. Inclusion of nonexistent items results in overstatements of these components; such overstatements may be referred to as **misstatements due to commission**.

Auditors ordinarily consider audit risk involving misstatements due to commission to be most critical in the areas of assets and revenues, given the past tendencies of some companies to inflate income by overstating these financial statement components.

Completeness Just as assets and revenues are more often overstated than understated, liabilities and expenses are more frequently understated than overstated. It is therefore imperative that the auditor ascertains **completeness**. Misstatements that understate financial statement components may be referred to as **misstatements due to omission**. In both cases, the result is overstatement of net assets and net income. To this end, most audit programs contain procedures for identifying unrecorded liabilities, as well as procedures dealing with possible asset overstatements.

The completeness objective is more difficult to satisfy than the existence objective. In determining existence, the auditor has a starting point: the representations contained in the financial statements. In ascertaining completeness (omissions), on the other hand, the auditor must begin the search from outside the statements. The auditor, in other words, must determine whether any material transactions or events have occurred during the period under audit that are *not* reflected in the financial statements.

Rights and Obligations In addition to existence and completeness, the auditor must establish the client's **rights and obligations**. The auditor must ascertain that the assets are owned by the client (rights) and that the liabilities are those of the client (obligations). In examining recorded assets, for example, the auditor should be aware that although the inventories held by the client under consignment arrangements exist, they are *not* owned by the client. The auditor must determine, therefore, that "inventories"

9 Ibid, section AU 326.03.

as represented on the balance sheet do *not* contain significant amounts of consigned goods. In examining recorded liabilities, the auditor may discover that the client has recorded operating leases as capital leases, resulting in a liability on the balance sheet that is not yet an obligation of the client.

Valuation or Allocation   In assessing fairness of financial statement presentation, the auditor must determine proper **valuation**. Acceptable valuation requires that assets and equities are properly valued in accordance with GAAP. Reporting inventories or plant assets at current or constant dollar cost, for example, represents a departure from GAAP and would ordinarily lead to an adverse audit opinion.

The auditor must also be satisfied that **allocations** are within GAAP. Prime costing, for example, under which only materials and direct labor are included in manufacturing inventories as product costs, whereas overhead is charged to expense, is also a violation of GAAP. Other examples involving allocation of costs include interest during construction, ordinary as opposed to extraordinary repairs, depreciation and amortization policies, and treatment of past service cost under pension plans.

Presentation and Disclosure   The auditor must be satisfied that *presentation and disclosure* are adequate. **Presentation** of components within the financial statements relates mainly to proper classification. **Disclosure** is ordinarily associated with the footnotes to the financial statements.

With regard to classification, the auditor must determine that the distinctions between "current" and "noncurrent" and between "operating" and "nonoperating" have been properly observed in the balance sheet and income statement, respectively. Significant classification errors can materially distort liquidity and profitability ratios.

Concerning footnotes, the auditor must be satisfied that disclosure is adequate in order not to make the financial statements misleading. In the *Continental Vending Machine Corporation* case, for example (see Chapter 3), the court held that the footnote describing the Valley Commercial Corporation receivable was deficient—it did not adequately describe either the nature of the transactions involved or the collateral securing the loans.[10]

The main theme associated with the five objectives discussed previously is that the financial statements are the representations of management;[11] the job of the auditor is to gather evidence that will be useful in testing the five hypotheses (assertions) for acceptance or rejection.

Another way of viewing the relationship between management's assertions and audit objectives is in terms of **account versus substance**. The financial statements (accounts) might be viewed as being symbolic of the actual substance underlying them. The line item labeled "inventories," for example, represents the investment in the substance called inventories; the "accounts receivable" component of the balance sheet likewise symbolizes the amounts owed to the client by trade customers of the company. Referring to the financial statement components as accounts, one might describe the job of the auditor as determining that the accounts are, in all material respects, representative of the underlying substance to which they relate. Table 4.1 supports this framework by including some examples of "accounts" and related "substance."

---

10 U.S. vs. Simon et al, 425 F. 2d, 796 (2d Cir. 1969).
11 *AICPA Professional Standards*, op. cit., section AU 326.03.

TABLE 4.1

Account versus Substance (Examples)

Account	Substance (as Evidenced by)
Cash in bank	Bank statement, canceled checks, deposit tickets
Marketable securities	Securities in vault or in safekeeping, brokers' advices
Inventories	Goods in warehouses, goods out on consignment
Accounts receivable	Customers' confirmation of amounts owed
Notes receivable	Makers' notes payable
Property, plant, and equipment	Plant assets at various locations, vendors' invoices
Accounts payable	Vendors' records of accounts receivable, vendors' invoices, vendors' statements
Notes payable	Payees' confirmation of amounts owed to them
Capital stock	Records maintained by registrar and transfer agent
Sales revenue	Sales invoices, shipping documents, cash register tapes
Operating expenses	Vendors' invoices, canceled checks
Wages and salaries expense	Payroll summaries, time cards, clock cards, canceled checks, personnel records

CHARACTERISTICS OF AUDIT EVIDENCE

Factual versus Inferential Evidence

Audit evidence consists of those facts and inferences that influence the auditor's mind with respect to financial presentation. **Factual evidence** is direct and generally considered to be stronger than inferential evidence. Observation of inventory to ascertain its existence is an example of factual evidence. By examining the inventory, the auditor may conclude directly that it exists. **Inferential evidence**, by contrast, does *not* lend itself to direct conclusions. Noting what appear to be excessive quantities of particular stock items, for example, may lead the auditor to suspect that the inventory is obsolete. This is inferential evidence. It is *not* conclusive or direct evidence. The auditor only infers obsolescence. Additional evidence, either supporting or refuting the initial inference of obsolescence, may be obtained through inquiry of client personnel and tests of inventory turnover.

Underlying Accounting Data and Corroborating Information

Section 326 of the AICPA Professional Standards describes evidential matter supporting the financial statements as consisting of "the underlying accounting data and all corroborating information available to the auditor."[12] **Underlying accounting data** include

---

12 Ibid, section AU 326.15.

the books of original entry, ledgers, and supporting worksheets. **Corroborating information** includes such documentation as canceled checks, bank statements, sales invoices, vendors' invoices, vouchers, time cards, requisitions, purchase orders, bills of lading, and shipping orders. It also includes evidence developed by the auditor, such as confirmations, calculations, observation, and reconciliations.

Sufficiency and Competence of Evidence

Evidence must be both sufficient and competent. **Sufficient evidence** is evidence that is adequate to support the auditor's opinion on the financial statements. Sufficiency is a matter of audit judgment, and is usually based on materiality and the adequacy of the existing internal control system. The auditor will generally require greater amounts of evidence for major account balances and transaction classes. Plant asset additions for a manufacturing entity, for example, will be audited more intensely than miscellaneous expenses.

The stronger the internal control system policies and procedures are, the more reliable the accounting data produced by that system. Under these conditions, the auditor may examine a smaller number of transactions or test count a smaller proportion of inventory than under conditions of weak internal control.

Competent evidence is evidence that is both valid and relevant.[13] **Validity** is a function of three qualities:

1. *The independence and competence of the source from whom the evidence was obtained.* Evidence obtained from external sources (e.g., confirmation of customer account balances) possesses greater validity than that obtained from internal sources (e.g., client-prepared documents).
2. *The conditions under which the evidence was obtained.* A sales invoice produced under conditions of satisfactory internal control possesses greater validity than one produced under conditions of weak internal control.
3. *The manner in which the evidence was obtained.* Evidence obtained directly by the auditor (e.g., observation of inventory for existence) is more reliable than that obtained indirectly (e.g., questioning of client personnel).

Relevance means that the evidence must pertain to specific audit objectives. Observing the taking of the physical inventory, for example, provides evidence concerning existence of the inventory, but it is *not* relevant to determining ownership.

Figure 4.2 summarizes the qualities of audit evidence just described. Note the importance of internal control in determining both sufficiency and competence of evidential matter.

AUDIT EVIDENCE AND RELATED AUDITING PROCEDURES

Figure 4.1 classified audit evidence into six types:

1. Physical evidence;
2. Evidence obtained through confirmation;
3. Documentary evidence;
4. Mathematical evidence;

---

13 Ibid, section AU 326.21.

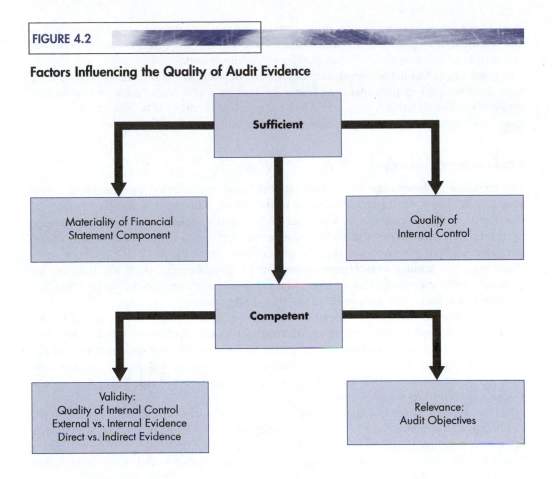

FIGURE 4.2

Factors Influencing the Quality of Audit Evidence

5. Analytical evidence; and
6. Hearsay evidence.

Each of these forms of evidence, together with related auditing procedures, is considered in the following paragraphs.

Physical Evidence

Physical evidence consists of everything that can be counted, examined, observed, or inspected; it provides, through **direct** (or factual) **evidence**, primary support for the existence objective. The auditor counts cash on hand at year end and traces it to the cash receipts record and bank statement in order to determine that cash receipts transactions have been recorded in the proper accounting period. The auditor examines securities held by the client for the purpose of determining that the balance sheet listing of "marketable securities" fairly represents the underlying substance.

The auditor observes the taking of the physical inventory by the client. The auditor tests the client's physical counts and compares these with the recorded amounts in order to gain satisfaction concerning the existence and condition of recorded inventories.

Observing the functioning of the internal control system is a further example of obtaining physical evidence. Observation of internal control is applied prior to substantive testing as a basis for determining the nature, timing, and extent of tests to be applied in the circumstances. The extent of inventory test counting, for example, is a function of the quality of internal control over purchases and inventories.

If the client has made significant acquisitions of plant assets during the year, the auditor may wish to inspect major additions, at least on a test basis. As with inventories and marketable securities, the purpose of this set of procedures is to determine that the assets, as represented in the accounts, actually exist.

Confirmation Evidence

Confirmation evidence consists of obtaining evidence of existence, ownership, or valuation directly from third parties *external* to the client. The most common example of this form of evidence relates to trade accounts receivable. In confirming accounts receivable, the client, under the auditor's direction, typically sends a copy of the client-prepared customer statement to the customer and requests that the customer reply directly to the auditor concerning agreement or disagreement with the balance appearing on the statement. The strength of this form of evidence lies in the fact that it is obtained directly by the auditor from the third-party source.

In addition to the confirming of accounts receivable, many other forms of confirmation are utilized in the normal audit. Notes receivable and notes payable are confirmed with the makers and payees, respectively; inventories out on consignment are confirmed with the consignee; goods in public warehouses, as well as securities in safe-keeping, are confirmed with the respective agents; accounts payable balances are confirmed with vendors on a test basis.

The *lawyer's letter* obtained by the auditor directly from the client's outside legal counsel is also a form of confirmation. The purpose of this letter is to provide evidence regarding pending litigation and the possible need for journal entries or footnotes relating to asserted and unasserted claims. The lawyer's letter is described more completely in Chapter 12.

Documentary Evidence

Documentary evidence consists of the accounting records and all of the underlying documentation supporting the transactions and events recorded in these records. Vendors' invoices, customer sales invoice copies, and journal entries are examples of documentary evidence. Exhibit 4.1 contains a more complete listing.

Documentary evidence is *internal*, as contrasted with evidence obtained through confirmation. Moreover, unlike physical evidence, much of it is *inferential* rather than factual; that is, conclusions often cannot be drawn directly from the evidence. Notwithstanding these weaker qualities, documentary evidence plays a significant role in the conduct of most audits. Documentation constitutes an integral element of the so-called audit trail. The **audit trail** consists of that stream of evidence that enables the auditor to trace and vouch transactions and events from source to ledger and vice versa. **Tracing** supports the completeness objective and consists of following a transaction or event forward from its inception (documentation) to the appropriate ledger account(s). **Vouching** supports the existence objective and involves pursuing a posting backward from the ledger account to the inception of the transaction or event. The process of vouching and tracing transactions and events represents a very important phase of any audit program (see Figure 4.3, p. 118). Because the document provides evidence of

---

EXHIBIT 4.1

Examples of Documentary Evidence

Ledgers and journals

Supporting workpapers

Purchase orders, requisitions, receiving reports, vendors' invoices, and vouchers

Sales orders, sales invoices, shipping orders, bills of lading, and freight bills

Time cards, clock cards, employee earnings records, and payroll summaries

Inventory tags and listings

Cash receipts listings, remittance advices, cash register tapes, and deposit tickets

Canceled checks and bank statements

Correspondence

Contracts

Monthly financial statements

---

transaction inception, adequate documentation is imperative to effective tracing and vouching.

The auditor's study and evaluation of internal control is closely related to the importance of documentary evidence. The degree of confidence that the auditor places in the internal documentation of transactions and events is a function of the quality of the related controls over the documentation. For example, if internal control over sales and cash receipts is strong, the auditor can rely more heavily on sales invoices, bills of lading, cash receipts listings, and the accounts receivable subsidiary ledger (i.e., the internal documentation), and will need to confirm a smaller proportion of customers' accounts than would be necessary if internal control were weak.

Some parts of the audit would not be feasible in the absence of adequate documentation. Transactions such as plant asset additions, payroll, cash receipts, and cash disbursements require documentation if they are to be examined and evaluated by the auditor.

Mathematical Evidence

Mathematical evidence consists of calculations, recalculations, and reconciliations performed by the auditor. In auditing the client's final inventory amounts, for example, extensions (price × quantity) and footings of inventory listings must be tested. These tests produce mathematical evidence. Mathematical evidence is a *direct* form of audit evidence, because the auditor performs the computations on the data. Computers are used to a large extent by auditors in performing mathematical computations on large quantities of data.

An important category of mathematical evidence relates to allocations and accruals. Examples of allocations and accruals tested through calculation or recalculation are interest, depreciation, taxes, payroll accruals, and gains and/or losses on asset disposals.

GAAS requires that the auditor carefully evaluate the reasonableness of accounting estimates developed by management and suggests utilizing one or more of the following approaches:

FIGURE 4.3

Vouching and Tracing: A Two-Way Process

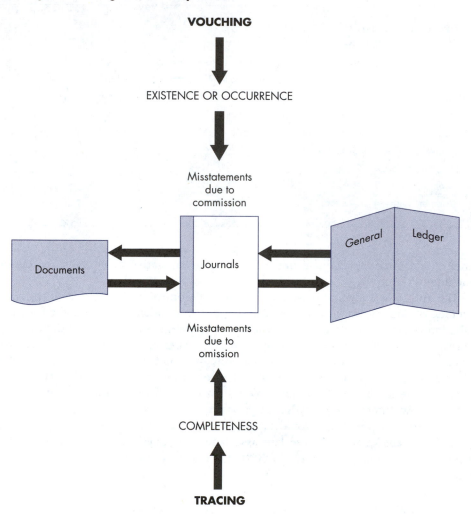

1. Review and test the process used by management to develop the estimate; and/or
2. Develop an independent expectation of the estimate to corroborate the reasonableness of management's estimate; and/or
3. Review subsequent events or transactions occurring prior to the completion of field work.[14]

The second choice results in a form of mathematical evidence. The auditor, for example, may recalculate warranty expense, net realizable value of inventories, the allowance for loan losses, or potential losses on purchase commitments.

14 Ibid, section AU 342.

Reconciliations, given that they involve numerous computations, may also be categorized as mathematical evidence. Examples include bank reconciliations, ensuring agreement of subsidiary ledgers with control accounts, and reconciling inter- and intra-company accounts of those clients with subsidiaries and/or divisions. Establishing agreement between subsidiary ledgers and control accounts, like testing inventory extensions and footings, involves numerous calculations, and the auditor may use computer software to automate the process.

Analytical Evidence

Purpose for Applying   **Analytical evidence** procedures are substantive tests of financial information performed by studying and comparing relationships among data.[15] They must be applied during the planning stages of the audit, prior to applying the main body of substantive testing procedures.[16] They also must be applied at the end of audit field work, as part of the overall audit review.[17] During the *planning phase*, the objective is to identify areas of high audit risk. High-risk areas are suggested by unusual relationships within or between periods being audited, and by unaudited amounts that differ significantly from predetermined auditor expectations. Having identified significant unexplained abnormalities, the auditor plans to apply substantive procedures more intensively to these areas. The abnormalities may have been caused by a change in the environment, or errors may have been made or fraud committed in recording or classifying data. In either case, the auditor must determine the cause and suggest corrections for any material misstatements discovered in the process.

As part of the *overall review phase*, the auditor evaluates the reasonableness of audited transactions and balances. Having audited the finished goods inventory, for example, the auditor may elect to apply the gross profit method in arriving at an estimate of the ending inventory using historic gross profit rates. Proximity of the audited and estimated inventories will lend added assurance to the auditor concerning the final audited inventory figures. A wide disparity, on the other hand, will form a basis for further examination.

The following paragraphs describe typical applications of analytical procedures and state whether the procedures are applied in the planning or review stages of the audit.

Trend (Horizontal) Analysis   **Trend analysis** requires examining changes in data over time. The underlying premise is that past trends may be expected to continue into the future unless conditions change materially. The auditor may, for example, observe absolute changes in revenues and expenses over time, or may observe changes in relationships. Another trend analysis technique involves regression analysis to predict revenue and expense components based on observed relationships.

An application involving trend analysis might be to *compare major components of the current financial statements with those of prior years and investigate significant variations*. Although this procedure can be applied to all the financial statements, it is most useful when related to comparative income statements. To maximize usefulness of the approach, the statement components should be expressed in both dollars and percentages. If the gross profit rate, for example, has increased significantly during

15 Ibid, section AU 329.02.
16 Ibid, section AU 329.04.
17 Ibid.

the current year, this could be the result of a change in product mix or a cost reduction program—or it could reflect inflated inventories caused by the failure to relieve the inventory accounts for goods sold at year end. This analytical procedure is ordinarily applied as part of the audit planning stage.

As a further example of horizontal analysis, the auditor might *compare sources of revenue and expense and investigate new sources and elimination of prior sources.* Sources of miscellaneous revenue and expense may vary from year to year. Investigation of these changes, together with comparison of amounts, may be the only procedure applied to these accounts. If the amounts have *not* changed materially in relation to the other income statement components, and if the sources are the same as those of the prior year, the auditor may conclude properly that miscellaneous revenues and expenses are fairly stated.

Common Size (Vertical) Analysis   **Common size financial statements** express all components as percentages of a common base. On the balance sheet, for example, an asset amount may be expressed as a percentage of total assets. Income statement components are usually expressed as percentages of sales.

As an example of vertical analysis, the auditor, having prepared a set of common size financial statements, might decide to *develop auditor expectations by analyzing relationships among data within the period being audited.* Some financial statement balances are dependent on other transactions or balances. These relationships are said to be "plausible," or expected to exist. For example, if the sales commission rate is 5 percent and sales for the year is $6 million, the auditor reasonably may expect sales commissions to approximate $300,000. A significantly lower amount may be indicative of either a failure to record accrued sales commissions at year end, or inflated sales. Other revenues and expenses, known to have a plausible relationship to sales or cost of sales, can be similarly analyzed. Certain classes of payroll expense, for example, as well as repairs and maintenance expenses and revenue from scrap sales, may bear a fixed relationship to cost of goods manufactured. This set of procedures may be applied during the overall review stages of the audit, as well as during the planning phase.

As another example of vertical analysis, the auditor may *examine performance reports and investigate significant variations from the budget.* Most companies have budgetary control systems whereby budgets are formulated *ex ante*, and performance reports comparing budgeted and actual amounts are prepared *ex post.* In analyzing the reports, the entity is interested in controlling costs and improving profitability. The auditor, in contrast, is interested in abnormal variations as possible indicators of errors or fraud. If sales have fallen materially short of budget expectations, for example, two concerns face the auditor. First, if production was *not* curtailed in the face of declining sales, there may be a problem of inventory overstock and possible obsolescence. Second, if production was cut back, an abnormal volume or capacity variance is probable, and the auditor must determine that the variance has been accounted for as a charge to the current period's operations, and *not* treated either as a deferred charge or as a part of inventory cost on the balance sheet. Applying these analytical procedures should lead the auditor to discover the cause and effect of all significant budget variations. This is another example of a set of analytical procedures applied during the planning stages of an audit.

Ratio Analysis   **Ratio analysis** compares relationships among account balances. Although this is most useful when comparing the entity with other companies or with industry averages, the auditor should also observe changes in the ratios over time. Ratios may be classified as:

1. **Liquidity ratios**, which are indicators of the firm's short-term debt-paying ability. Examples of liquidity ratios are the current ratio and the quick ratio.
2. **Profitability ratios**, which are used for gauging operating efficiency. Examples of profitability ratios are operating margin and return on assets.
3. **Leverage ratios**, which portray the firm's financial flexibility. Percentage of long-term liabilities to total capital structure (long-term liabilities plus stockholders' equity) and times interest earned are examples of leverage ratios.
4. **Asset management ratios**, which show how effectively management has controlled operating assets. Examples of asset management ratios are inventory turnover, accounts receivable turnover, and number of days' sales in accounts receivable.

Like trend analysis, these ratios are of interest to the auditor in highlighting abnormalities suggesting possible errors or fraud. For example, negative cash flows accompanied by positive earnings may be the result of an expanding business with heavy investments in inventories and accounts receivable; or it may be due to overstated revenues or understated expenses in an effort to mask an operating loss. In either case, the auditor must determine the reason for the abnormal relationship.

In addition, weaknesses in the liquidity and/or leverage ratios could indicate a possible financial crisis. As is discussed more fully in Chapter 14, the auditor must evaluate each client for its ability to continue as a going concern (i.e., its ability to meet its obligations as they mature over the next year); when substantial doubt exists, the auditor must add an explanatory paragraph to the audit report.[18]

The ratios described above are useful only when compared with appropriate standards, such as prior periods, other companies, and/or industry averages. Such sources as Dunn & Bradstreet and Robert Morris Associates contain key ratios and percentages that can be used for comparison purposes. Significant differences between the client and industry averages may be due to the unique nature of the client's operations. Alternatively, the variations could be the result of errors or fraud committed in recording or classifying data.

Exhibits 4.2 through 4.4 (pp. 122–124) illustrate the application of vertical, horizontal, and ratio analysis to a hypothetical set of financial statements. Note that the comparative financial statements are presented in both dollars and percentages. Exhibit 4.2 contains comparative income statements over a five-year period; Exhibit 4.3 presents comparative balance sheets as of the end of the current and preceding years. In Exhibit 4.4, the ratios described earlier are shown for Jones Manufacturing, as well as for a competitor and for the industry. Based on an analysis of this data, one might observe the following "auditor alerts":

1. Inventories and profit margins have increased significantly in 1999 and are well above those of prior years and the industry averages. This condition may be indicative of overstated inventories and understated cost of goods sold, and suggests that the auditor should devote extra time to the inventory audit.
2. As indicated by the quick ratio, cash and accounts receivable are significantly less than total current liabilities. This condition may cause the auditor to have doubts concerning the ability of the entity to continue as a going concern.

18 See for example, Mills, John R. and Jeanne H. Yamamura, "The Power of Cash Flow Ratios," *The Journal of Accountancy*, October 1998, pp. 53–61.

EXHIBIT 4.2

Jones Manufacturing Corporation: Comparative Income Statements

Years ending December 31, 2001–2005 (in thousands of dollars)

| | Unaudited | | | | Audited | | | | | |
	2005		2004		2003		2002		2001	
Sales	$222,344	100.00%	$206,000	100.00%	$245,000	100.00%	$288,900	100.00%	$312,400	100.00%
Cost of Goods Sold	132,680	59.67	145,606	70.68	171,500	70.00	196,452	68.00	203,060	65.00
Gross Profit	89,664	40.33	60,394	29.32	73,500	30.00	92,448	32.00	109,340	35.00
Operating Expenses	26,170	11.77	25,035	12.15	24,556	10.02	23,890	8.27	23,200	7.43
Operating Income	63,494	28.56	35,359	17.16	48,944	19.98	68,558	23.73	86,140	27.57
Interest Expense	4,426	1.99	3,720	1.81	3,600	1.47	3,450	1.19	3,890	1.25
Net Income before Taxes and Extraordinary Items	59,068	26.57	31,639	15.36	45,344	18.51	65,108	22.54	82,250	26.33
Income Taxes	5,092	2.29	9,492	4.61	13,603	5.55	19,532	6.76	24,675	7.90
New Income before Extraordinary Items	53,976	24.28	22,147	10.75	31,741	12.96	45,576	15.78	57,575	18.43
Extraordinary Gain (Loss)—Net of Tax	0	0.00	(1,540)	-0.75	0	0.00	3,400	1.18	0	0.00
Net Income	$ 53,976	24.28%	$ 20,607	10.00%	$ 31,741	12.96%	$ 48,976	16.96%	$ 57,575	18.43%

EXHIBIT 4.3

Jones Manufacturing Corporation: Comparative Percentage Balance Sheets

As of December 31, 2004 and 2005 (in thousands of dollars)

	(Unaudited) 12/31/05	Percentage	(Audited) 12/31/04	Percentage
ASSETS				
Current Assets:				
Cash on hand and in banks	$ 5,321	1.69%	$ 12,400	4.56%
Accounts and notes receivable—trade	19,600	6.21	16,700	6.15
Inventories	44,200	14.00	22,180	8.16
Total current assets	69,121	21.90	51,280	18.88
Property, Plant, and Equipment:				
Land	2,000	0.63	2,000	0.74
Buildings and equipment (net)	215,800	68.37	209,000	76.93
Autos and trucks (net)	380	0.12	500	0.18
Total property, plant, and equipment	218,180	69.13	211,500	77.85
Investments and other assets	28,327	8.97	8,900	3.28
TOTAL ASSETS	315,628	100.00	271,680	100.00
LIABILITIES				
Current Liabilities:				
Accounts payable	13,350	4.23	21,540	7.93
Income taxes payable	7,900	2.50	1,800	0.66
Other	6,995	2.22	3,962	1.46
Total current liabilities	28,245	8.95	27,302	10.05
Mortgage Note Payable	70,600	22.37	74,000	27.24
TOTAL LIABILITIES	98,845	31.32	101,302	37.29
STOCKHOLDERS' EQUITY				
Common stock:				
13,000 shares @ $10 par	130,000	41.19	130,000	47.85
Additional paid-in capital	20,000	6.34	20,000	7.36
Retained earnings	66,783	21.16	20,378	7.50
TOTAL STOCKHOLDERS' EQUITY	216,783	68.68	170,378	62.71
TOTAL LIABILITIES AND STOCKHOLDERS' EQUITY	$ 315,628	100.00%	$ 271,680	100.00%

Analytical Procedures and the Completeness Assertion A final comment concerning analytical procedures relates to the completeness assertion. Application of analytical procedures is perhaps the most effective means for the auditor to become initially aware of material omissions from the accounting records. As noted earlier, one of the objectives of substantive audit testing is to detect material misstatements of omission as well as misstatements due to commission. Omissions are generally more difficult to

EXHIBIT 4.4

Jones Manufacturing Corporation: Ratio Analysis

	Jones Manufacturing 2005 (unaudited)	2004 (audited)	Company B 2005	Industry Avg. 2005
LIQUIDITY RATIOS:				
Current Ratio				
(current assets/current liabilities)	2.45	1.88	2.25	2.36
Quick Ratio				
(cash and receivables/current liabilities)	0.88	1.07	1.15	1.12
LEVERAGE RATIOS:				
Percentage of debt in capital structure				
(long-term liabilities/total LTL+SE)	0.25	0.30	0.35	0.25
Times Interest Earned				
(net income before interest and				
taxes/interest)	14.35	9.51	6.33	7.72
PROFITABILITY RATIOS:				
Operating Margin				
(net income before extraordinary				
items/sales)	0.24	0.11	0.09	0.10
Return on Assets				
(net income before extraordinary				
items/total assets)	0.17	0.08	0.07	0.09
ASSET MANAGEMENT RATIOS:				
Inventory Turnover				
(cost of goods sold/average inventory)	4.00	6.56	9.00	11.00
Accounts Receivable Turnover				
(credit sales/average				
accounts receivable)	12.25	12.34	14.00	12.00
Days' Sales in Accounts Receivable				
(360/accounts receivable turnover)	29.39	29.18	25.71	30.00

detect because, in contrast to commissions, there is no convenient starting point for testing a hypothesis. If the auditor suspects that accounts receivable are inflated (misstatement due to commission), confirmation of accounts selected from the subsidiary ledger should reveal any significant misstatements. If, on the other hand, significant amounts of sales revenue have gone unrecorded, analytical procedures, by disclosing the decrease, will direct the auditor's attention to the possibility of omitted revenues. In the absence of analytical procedures, the chances for detecting this type of misstatement are substantially lessened.

To summarize, analytical procedures serve two functions for the auditor. First, they assist in detecting unusual relationships that suggest possible errors or fraud in recording or classifying data. These areas are labeled *high-audit-risk areas*. Audit resources may then be allocated accordingly. Second, they enable the auditor to evaluate the reasonableness of final audited transactions and balances during the overall review stages of the audit.

Hearsay Evidence

Hearsay (oral) **evidence** consists of answers to questions posed by the auditor to client personnel. Hearsay is the weakest form of audit evidence and must be further corroborated. It is, however, applied extensively by the auditor throughout the examination. During the study and evaluation of internal control, for example, the auditor questions client personnel concerning duties and responsibilities, as well as the specific workings of internal control procedures.

In addition to questions regarding internal control, the auditor also inquires about contingent liabilities, inventory obsolescence, consignments, contracts, commitments, guarantees of indebtedness, related parties, illegal acts, and subsequent events. Like analytical procedures, hearsay evidence often leads the auditor toward areas requiring further investigation.

Sometimes the questions are suggested as a result of applying analytical procedures. For example, a significant decrease in inventory turnover should lead to the questioning of inventory and production personnel concerning inventory obsolescence. Similarly, a decrease in accounts receivable turnover suggests that the auditor question the credit manager as to changes in credit terms or the existence of doubtful accounts.

Some Concluding Observations

Some observations can be made at this point concerning the various forms of audit evidence just discussed. First, some forms of evidence are more reliable than others (see Figure 4.4). Physical, mathematical, and confirmation evidence, for example, are direct forms of audit evidence, in that the auditor obtains the evidence directly through observation, calculation, or formal inquiry of third parties. Documentary and hearsay evidence, on the other hand, are forms of **indirect evidence** and are *not* as conclusive as the former types. One should note that documentary evidence gathered under strong internal control is more reliable than that obtained under weak internal control.

Although certain forms of evidence are more reliable than others, other forms of evidence may be more relevant in terms of specific audit objectives. Documentary evidence, for example, is frequently the only means available to the auditor for the purpose of determining proper valuation or allocation. For these reasons, all of the audit evidence forms considered are significant, and all of the forms are used to greater or lesser degrees in most financial audits.

A second observation concerns how the auditor gathers evidence, and the form the evidence assumes. Much of the evidence discussed in this chapter may be gathered by computer-assisted means. Testing of inventory footings and extensions, reconciling of subsidiary ledger and control accounts, and application of analytical procedures all can be automated and extended with the aid of computers.

Evidence may be either in written or in electronic form. In the absence of hard copy, the auditor may be able to examine and analyze electronic evidence only with the aid of a computer. Also, many forms of electronic evidence exist for only a short time. Under these conditions, the auditor may need to gather and analyze evidence at frequent intervals.[19]

---

19 For a further discussion of the implications of electronic audit evidence, see *The Journal of Accountancy*, February 1997, pp. 69–71.

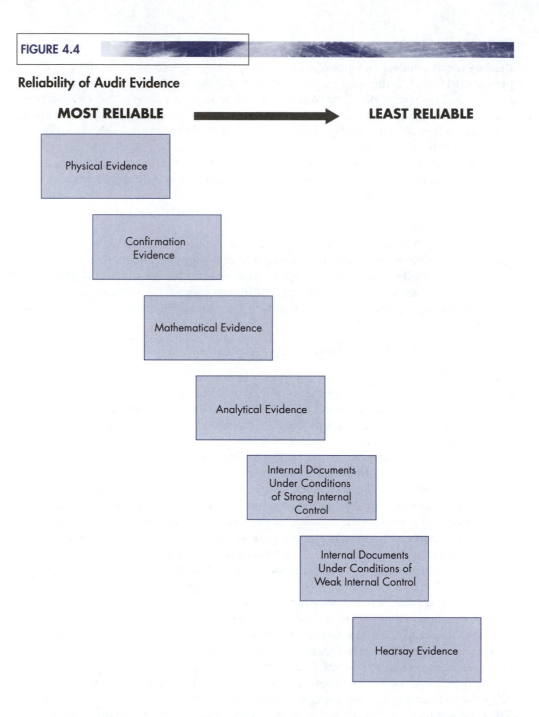

FIGURE 4.4

Reliability of Audit Evidence

MOST RELIABLE ➡ LEAST RELIABLE

Physical Evidence

Confirmation Evidence

Mathematical Evidence

Analytical Evidence

Internal Documents Under Conditions of Strong Internal Control

Internal Documents Under Conditions of Weak Internal Control

Hearsay Evidence

AUDIT PLANNING AND AUDIT PROGRAMS

The first standard of audit field work states that "the work is to be properly planned and assistants, if any, are to be properly supervised."[20] **Audit planning** begins prior to the

20 *AICPA Professional Standards*, op. cit., section AU 150.02.

client acceptance decision as the CPA gathers information concerning the client's business, industry, and management personnel. Planning continues as the CPA assesses inherent risk (Chapter 5) and control risk (Chapter 7). At the conclusion of the planning process, the auditor develops programs for the conduct of the audit. An **audit program** is an outline of procedures to be followed in performing an audit and is usually classified according to transaction cycles. A **transaction cycle** consists of a group of related transactions affecting essentially the same set of general ledger accounts. By focusing on transaction cycles rather than just account balances in assessing risk and applying substantive procedures, the auditor obtains greater assurance of testing all of management's assertions contained in a given set of financial statements. The following transaction cycles are used throughout this textbook as a framework for audit testing:

1. **Revenue cycle**
   a.   Sales revenue and accounts receivable balances
   b.   Cash receipts from customers and cash balances
2. **Expenditure cycle**
   a.   Purchases, operating expenses, depreciation expense, and plant asset balances
   b.   Payments to vendors and accounts payable balances
   c.   Payroll
   d.   Capital stock and dividend transactions
3. **Financing and investing cycle**
   a.   Borrowing from others, interest expense, and liability balances
   b.   Lending to others, interest revenue, and notes receivable balances
   c.   Acquisitions and disposals of financial assets
   d.   Capital stock and dividend transactions

In the appendix following Chapter 7, this format will be used to categorize tests of internal control systems policies and procedures affecting transactions and balances. Similarly, in the appendices following Chapters 11, 12, and 13, the format will be used to illustrate substantive tests of transactions and balances.

Exhibit 4.5 contains a partial program for the audit of cash receipts. It is important that the auditor tailor audit programs to reflect each client's unique business, industry, and internal control characteristics. The AICPA offers a computerized audit program generator for creating tailored audit programs and for guiding auditors through various kinds of engagements.[21]

Developing Audit Programs

The nature, timing, and extent of auditing procedures to be applied (i.e., the content of the audit programs) depends on the following:

1. Study and evaluation of existing internal controls;
2. Materiality of transactions and balances;
3. Nature of client's activities; and
4. Cost–benefit.

Study and Evaluation of Internal Controls   Audit programs should be reflective of the quality of the client's internal controls. Therefore, the study and evaluation of internal

21 AICPA, *Audit Program Generator.*

EXHIBIT 4.5

Partial Audit Program

A.B. Smith, Inc.
Partial Audit Program
Cash Receipts

Audit Workpaper Reference	Procedure	Auditor	Date
A	Evaluate internal controls relating to the processing and recording of cash receipts and modify audit program accordingly	LK	11/5/01
1.1	Count and list cash on hand at year end	MR	12/31/01
1.3	Trace year-end cash count to cutoff bank statement	SJ	1/20/02
WTB 1	Identify sources of miscellaneous cash receipts and investigate any changes for proper approval and authenticity	LK	1/15/02
12.3	Vouch nonrecurring cash receipts transactions in excess of $1,000 by examining remittance advice and receipted deposit ticket	RN	1/26/02
1.2	Reconcile bank accounts	SJ	1/20/02
1.3	Obtain cutoff bank statement and trace reconciling items to cutoff statement	SJ	1/20/02
1.2	Confirm bank balances	SJ	12/31/01

accounting control must precede substantive testing of transactions and balances if the collection and evaluation of audit evidence is to proceed in a systematic manner.

The stronger the internal control system is, the lower the probability of errors in processing transactions and events. Under these circumstances, the auditor may justifiably reduce the extent of substantive testing that otherwise would be necessary. For example, if purchases of goods are fully documented and properly approved, if the perpetual inventory records are reliable, and if the physical inventory is carefully planned and taken by the client, the auditor may limit test counts and comparisons of inventory to a few major items plus a small sample of the remainder.

Materiality of Transactions and Balances   Heavier concentrations of audit resources are needed for the more significant categories of transactions and balances. **Materiality** may be defined as the amount of misstatement that would affect the decisions of a reasonably informed financial statement user, and should be related to the various measures used by financial analysts and others in gauging an entity's liquidity and profitability. Preliminary audit programs for each transaction cycle subset should reflect the auditor's judgment regarding materiality. Materiality is considered in greater detail in the next chapter.

Nature of Client's Activities   Audit programs must be tailored to fit the unique characteristics of the entity being examined. An audit program for a commercial bank, for example, differs significantly from one developed for a manufacturing client. For the bank, extensive audit resources are concentrated in the areas of loans receivable, loan loss reserves, and tests for solvency and liquidity. These are the areas of highest audit risk. In auditing the manufacturer, more attention is devoted to inventories, purchases, manufacturing operations, and the cost accounting system.

Overall audit objectives relating to the assertions of existence, completeness, rights and obligations, valuation, and disclosure are the same regardless of the nature of the auditee. The more specific subsets of objectives, however, must relate more closely to the unique operations of the entity. In examining the financial statements of the commercial bank, for example, the auditor will view the valuation assertion as most critical to loans receivable. In auditing a manufacturing client, the auditor relates the valuation assertion mainly to inventories and plant assets.

Cost–Benefit   Some auditing procedures are more costly to apply than others. To illustrate, in auditing inventories for existence, the cost involved in visiting the locations of inventories stored off the premises exceeds the cost of confirming the existence of those inventories by corresponding directly with the custodian. Although cost should never be an overriding factor limiting the collection of sufficient, competent evidential matter, neither should it be ignored. A recommended guideline regarding the **cost–benefit** rule is the following: Given two or more sets of audit procedures, each of which is satisfactory in attaining the specified audit objectives, the auditor should select the least costly from among the sets.

To summarize the preceding discussion, audit programs need to be developed in light of existing internal control, materiality of balances and transactions, and the nature of the entity's activities; and cost should be a determining factor when audit objectives can be attained by alternate means.

Documentation of Audit Programs

A final observation with respect to audit programs concerns documentation. The audit workpapers should fully document the thought processes leading to the procedures contained in the final audit programs. Of particular significance is the impact of audit risk analysis, including fraud assessment, on the content of audit programs. If the nature of the entity's activities or the auditor's suspicions regarding fraud produce conditions of high audit risk leading to the modification of audit programs, it is not enough to simply modify the programs. Rather, a description of the conditions, together with the underlying rationale for modifying the programs, should be clearly set forth in the workpapers. This type of documentation provides effective evidence that the auditors have exercised due care in the conduct of the examination.

AUDIT WORKPAPERS

The collection and evaluation of audit evidence are documented in the form of **audit workpapers**. Audit workpapers constitute the principal record of the evidence that the auditor has gathered and evaluated in support of the audit opinion.[22]

Audit workpapers consist of two types—*permanent file* workpapers and *current file* workpapers. They are covered in the following sections.

---

22 *AICPA Professional Standards*, op. cit., section AU 339.01.

Audit Workpaper Files

Permanent File   Figure 4.5 lists the contents of the audit workpaper files. Audit workpapers that have ongoing significance are placed in the **permanent file**. A copy of a long-term capital lease agreement containing a contingent rental clause, for example, is relevant to future audits as well as to the current year's audit, and would be contained in the permanent file. Copies of contracts, articles of incorporation, and narrative descriptions of the client's principal activities are examples of other workpapers contained in the permanent file. The contents of the permanent file are reviewed and updated during the conduct of each annual audit.

Current File   Those audit workpapers that support only the period being examined are classified as **current file** workpapers. The working trial balance and the results of audit tests comprise the major part of the current file. These workpapers are considered in the ensuing paragraphs.

FIGURE 4.5

Audit Workpaper Files

Current File (Workpapers applicable exclusively to current period under audit):

Working trial balance
Lead schedules
Supporting schedules
Audit adjustments
Reclassification entries
Audit report
Financial statements and footnotes
Internal accounting control questionnaires, flowcharts, and conclusions resulting from study and
    evaluation of control structure
Audit programs (substantive testing procedures)
Audit risk analysis workpapers

Permanent File (Workpapers of ongoing significance):

Analysis of business and industry
Organization charts
Charts of accounts
Copies of contracts (that affect future periods)
Corporate charter and bylaws
Excerpts from minutes of meetings
Labor-management agreement
Information concerning related parties
Accounting systems information (including flowcharts)
Duties and composition of internal audit staff
Descriptions of complex business transactions and/or unique accounting treatments
Copies of pension plans, stock option plans, and employee bonus and profit-sharing plans
Analyses of capital and retained earnings
Descriptions of tax temporary differences and method of calculating change in deferred taxes

Working Trial Balance   The focal point of the current file is the **working trial balance**. Exhibit 4.6 illustrates a balance sheet working trial balance. A similar workpaper is prepared for the income statement accounts. The working trial balance might be likened to a table of contents found at the beginning of a book. Each line corresponds to a "line item" on the financial statements (in this instance, the balance sheet of Bold, Inc.). The letters or numbers in the far right column indicate the location of the items.

Lead Schedules   Exhibit 4.7 presents a **lead schedule** for cash. A lead schedule lists all of the general ledger accounts comprising a single "line item" on the financial statements. A lead schedule, of course, is not necessary where the financial statement line item consists of only one account. In this case, three accounts make up the line item "cash" on the 12/31/02 Bold, Inc., balance sheet. In addition to listing the accounts, the lead schedule also summarizes the audit adjustments affecting the accounts. Note the index numbers in the second column of Exhibit 4.7. These numbers—subsets of the lead schedule index—are the workpaper references of the supporting workpapers. To complete the link to the current file workpapers, the page number of the working trial balance on which the lead schedule total appears is listed below that figure.

Supporting Schedule   The **supporting schedule** workpapers are perhaps the most important component of the current file. Exhibit 4.8 (p. 134) illustrates a supporting workpaper; in the present case, this is the workpaper containing the reconciliation of the City Bank account of Bold, Inc. The substantive tests performed by the auditor, together with the results of those tests and the auditor's conclusions, are contained in the supporting schedule workpapers. The tests, the results, and the conclusions constitute the body of "sufficient, competent evidential matter" supporting the auditor's opinion on the financial statements. If, at a future point in time, the auditor needs to demonstrate that due care was exercised in the conduct of the audit, the supporting audit workpapers are the single most important source of that evidence.

How Audit Workpapers Are Interconnected

The workpaper reference column in the working trial balance (see Exhibit 4.6) tells the reader where in the current workpaper file to find the related lead schedule that describes the contents of the line item. The lead schedule for "cash," for example, is to be found at Workpaper A in the current file (see Exhibit 4.7). The lead schedule, in turn, is linked to the supporting schedules, and is also cross-referenced to the working trial balance. This rather extensive referencing and cross-referencing found in most audit workpapers (see Figure 4.6, p. 135) is for the purpose of facilitating effective review by those in charge of the audit field work. Lead schedule numbers appear in the working trial balance; supporting schedule numbers, as well as working trial balance page numbers, appear in the lead schedule; and lead schedule numbers appear in the supporting schedules. This system of **indexing** permits the reviewer to proceed from working trial balance to lead schedule to supporting schedule and vice versa.

Within the working trial balance itself, the first column of numbers represents the previous year's audited financial statement balances, as taken from the last year's working trial balance. The auditor compares these balances with the general ledger balances at the previous year end in order to determine that the client posted all of last year's agreed-upon audit adjustments. The second column of numbers in Exhibit 4.6, headed 12/31/02, contains the company's current year-end unaudited general ledger balances.

EXHIBIT 4.6

Working Trial Balance

Bold, Inc.—Balance Sheet
Working Trial Balance
12/31/02

Workpaper	General Ledger 12/31/01 (Audited)	12/31/02 (Unaudited)	Adjustments	Reclassifications	Audited Financial Statements 12/31/02	Reference
ASSETS						
Cash	$ 75,000	$ 86,268	$ 421		$ 86,689	A
Trade Receivables	240,000	280,000	(515)		279,485	B
Inventories	300,000	400,000			400,000	C
Total Current Assets	615,000	766,268			766,174	
Property, Plant, and Equipment (Net)	1,200,000	1,300,000			1,300,000	D
Other Assets	20,000	20,000			20,000	E
Total Assets	1,835,000	2,086,268	(94)		2,086,174	
LIABILITIES AND STOCKHOLDERS' EQUITY						
Notes Payable—Short-term	50,000	60,000		50,000	110,000	F
Accounts Payable	150,000	230,000	(90)		229,910	G
Accrued Expenses	70,000	80,000			80,000	H
Total Current Liabilities	270,000	370,000			419,910	
Notes Payable—Long-term	150,000	150,000		(50,000)	100,000	I
Total Liabilities	420,000	520,000			519,910	
Common Stock	600,000	600,000			600,000	J
Retained Earnings	815,000	966,268	(4)		966,264	K
	$1,835,000	$2,086,268	$ (94)		$2,086,174	

EXHIBIT 4.7

Lead Schedule

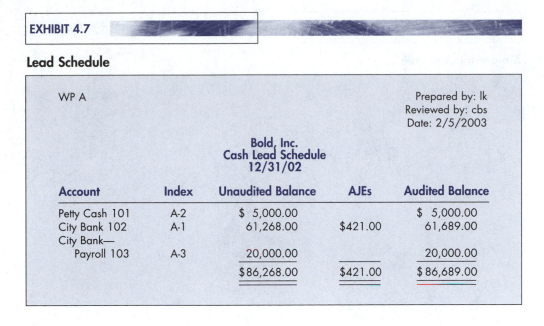

WP A

Prepared by: lk
Reviewed by: cbs
Date: 2/5/2003

Bold, Inc.
Cash Lead Schedule
12/31/02

Account	Index	Unaudited Balance	AJEs	Audited Balance
Petty Cash 101	A-2	$ 5,000.00		$ 5,000.00
City Bank 102	A-1	61,268.00	$421.00	61,689.00
City Bank—				
Payroll 103	A-3	20,000.00		20,000.00
		$86,268.00	$421.00	$ 86,689.00

These numbers, of course, are the numbers that are the subject matter for the current year's audit.

The *adjustments* column contains the effects of **audit adjustments** on the financial statement line items. The underlying details supporting these adjustments may be found in the supporting schedule workpapers (see Exhibit 4.8, for example) and also in the audit adjustments workpaper (see Exhibit 4.9, p. 135). The audit adjustments are journal entries proposed by the auditor to the client. The purpose of the entries is to correct the general ledger accounts and the financial statements for material misstatements discovered during the examination. Because the financial statements are the representations of management, the client must agree to the adjustments before they are actually posted to the general ledger accounts and incorporated into the financial statements.

The *reclassifications* column contains **audit reclassifications**—additional entries necessary to assure proper presentation of items in the financial statements. Significant credit balances in trade accounts receivable, for example, should be reclassified as current liabilities. Similarly, current installments of long-term liabilities, as well as bank overdrafts, should be reclassified as current liabilities if material in amount. Because the general ledger accounts are *not* in error, the client does not post the reclassifications to the accounts. Therefore, they are displayed in a column separate from the audit adjustments in the working trial balance.

The final column of numbers represents the audited figures that are to appear on the financial statements. These figures are the algebraic sum of the unaudited numbers plus or minus audit adjustments and reclassifications. The analyses supporting the fairness of these numbers may be found in the workpapers indicated in the *workpaper reference* column.

Guidelines for Preparing Adequate Audit Workpapers

Some guidelines for the preparation of audit workpapers, particularly directed at supporting schedules, are noted at this point. Using Exhibit 4.8 as a reference, note the

EXHIBIT 4.8

Supporting Schedule

WP A-1   Prepared by: lfk Date: 1/20/03
                                                             Reviewed by: cbs Date: 2/5/03

Bold, Inc.
Bank Reconciliation City Bank—A/C 102
12/31/02

Balance per bank		$62,765.18 *
Add deposit in transit		1,452.20 &
		64,217.38
Deduct outstanding checks:		
2345	$ 87.10 &	
2853	232.90 &	
2857	17.20 &	
2866	619.75 &	
2867	1,100.00 &	
2868	472.19 &	
Adjusted balance		2,529.14
		61,688.24
Balance per ledger		61,267.69 !
AJE 12: Bank collection		515.00 ×
		61,782.69
AJE 13: December bank charges		(4.45)#
AJE 14: To correct error on check #2802		(90.00)~
Adjusted balance		$61,688.24

To WP A

EXPLANATION OF AUDIT LEGENDS:
* Agreed to bank confirmation
& Traced to January bank statement
! Compared with ledger balance
Examined debit memo
~ Examined cash disbursements entry
× Examined bank credit memo

workpaper number, the preparer's initials, the reviewer's initials, and the dates of preparation and review in the upper section. The workpaper number facilitates location of the workpaper by those wishing to review it. The preparer's initials fix responsibility for the preparation of the workpaper, and the reviewer's initials indicate that the workpaper has been reviewed and by whom and when the review was made.

The workpaper heading identifies the client, the account being examined (name and number), and the balance sheet date. Although each supporting workpaper corresponds to an account in the general ledger, it is not necessary for each account or financial statement line item to be supported by a workpaper. Materiality of the balance,

FIGURE 4.6

Linking of Audit Workpapers through Cross-referencing

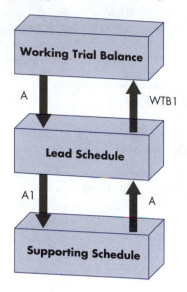

EXHIBIT 4.9

Audit Adjustments

Bold, Inc.
Audit Adjustments
12/31/02

AJE 12

City Bank 102	$515.00	
Notes Receivable		$515.00

To record collection of non-interest
note by the bank.

AJE 13

Miscellaneous Expenses	4.45	
City Bank 102		4.45

To record December bank charge
not recorded by client.

AJE 14

Accounts Payable	90.00	
City Bank 102		90.00

To correct error in recording
Check No. 2802:
Recorded as $890
Should be $980

the volume of transactions processed through the account, and associated audit risk determine whether the amounts involved warrant a supporting workpaper. Those procedures performed, however, do need to be documented. In the absence of a supporting workpaper, this documentation may appear on the lead schedule, or even on the appropriate line of the working trial balance.

The analysis contained in the body of the supporting schedule workpaper must be complete and self-contained in order to provide adequate evidence of due audit care. To be self-contained, the workpaper should clearly display the following:

1. The composition of the balance or transactions;
2. The auditing procedures performed;
3. The findings of the auditor;
4. The auditor's evaluation, conclusions, and recommended adjustments, if any; and
5. An explanation of all audit legends.

Adherence to these guidelines for workpaper preparation provides assurance that anyone reviewing the workpaper will be able to clearly identify the procedures performed by the auditor and the rationale supporting the auditor's conclusions and recommendations. As stated earlier, the audit workpapers provide the only source for determining whether the auditor gathered "sufficient, competent evidence supporting the audit opinion." Faced with the prospect of possible litigation involving auditor negligence, auditing firms and practitioners consider adequate workpaper documentation to be imperative.

In addition to affording effective review and possible legal protection, complete and properly indexed audit workpapers also facilitate future audits of the same client. The previous year's audit workpaper files provide an effective starting point for new staff members assigned to the audit. In order to familiarize themselves with the client, the staff members may review last year's current file workpapers together with the permanent file. In addition, many firms hold a **preaudit conference** following this review. The purpose of the preaudit conference is to gather together all those assigned to the audit to discuss the essential characteristics of the client, including areas of high audit risk. The major components of the audit and tentative staff assignments also are covered during the preaudit conference.

INITIAL VERSUS RECURRING AUDITS

A final word with regard to audit evidence and audit workpapers concerns initial versus recurring audits. An **initial audit** is a first-time examination; a **recurring audit** is a repeat examination of the same client in the following year. Generally, the nature, timing, and extent of audit evidence for an initial audit are not the same as those for a recurring audit. In an initial audit, the *study and evaluation of internal control and the study of the business and industry* require more time, because the auditor is not familiar with the client's environment. In a recurring audit, the auditor is looking for *significant changes in the control system and operations*, but is familiar with the essential characteristics.

In order to determine the fairness of *real* (balance sheet) account balances, the auditor in an initial audit must begin at the origin of the respective balances. For such assets as machinery and equipment, buildings, autos and trucks, and other plant assets, this usually involves examining several years' transactions. In a recurring audit, the auditor must obtain evidence regarding the ending inventory; in an initial audit, the beginning inventory, as well as the ending inventory, must be audited if the auditor is to express an opinion on the income statement. If the auditor cannot obtain satisfaction regarding the beginning inventory, a disclaimer of opinion is in order.

In conforming to GAAS relating to audit reports, the auditor must determine that accounting principles have been *applied consistently* in the current year relative to the preceding year. If material changes in principle application have occurred in the year under examination, the auditor must add an explanatory paragraph following the opinion paragraph of the audit report. In an initial audit, as contrasted with a recurring audit, this involves examining the previous year as well as the current year, at least to the extent of identifying the accounting principles applied in both years.

In the event that a new client previously was audited by another CPA, communication with the predecessor auditor, as discussed in Chapter 2, greatly facilitates the evidence-gathering problems for an initial audit. If the client has never been audited, however, the task is much more extensive.

KEY TERMS

Account versus substance, 112
Allocation, 112
Analytical evidence, 119
Asset management ratios, 121
Audit adjustments, 133
Audit evidence, 113
Audit objectives, 107
Audit planning, 126
Audit program, 127
Audit reclassifications, 133
Audit risk, 107
Audit trail, 116
Audit of transactions and balances, 109
Audit workpapers, 129
Common size financial statements, 120
Competent evidence, 114
Completeness, 111
Confirmation evidence, 116
Corroborating information, 114
Cost–benefit, 129
Current file, 130
Direct evidence, 115
Disclosure, 112
Documentary evidence, 116
Existence or occurrence, 111
Expenditure cycle, 127
Factual evidence, 113
Financing and investing cycle, 127
Hearsay evidence, 125
Indexing, 131
Indirect evidence, 125
Inferential evidence, 113

Initial audit, 136
Lead schedule, 131
Leverage ratios, 121
Liquidity ratios, 121
Materiality, 128
Mathematical evidence, 117
Misstatements due to commission, 111
Misstatements due to omission, 111
Permanent file, 130
Physical evidence, 115
Preaudit conference, 136
Presentation, 112
Profitability ratios, 121
Ratio analysis, 120
Reconciliations, 119
Recurring audit, 136
Related party, 108
Relevance, 114
Revenue cycle, 127
Rights and obligations, 111
Substantive audit testing, 110
Sufficient evidence, 114
Supporting schedule, 131
Tracing, 116
Transaction cycle, 127
Trend analysis, 119
Underlying accounting data, 113
Understanding the client's environment, 107
Validity, 114
Valuation, 112
Vouching, 116
Working trial balance, 131

REVIEW QUESTIONS

1. Differentiate between factual evidence and inferential evidence, giving an example of each.

2. Describe the two aspects of competence as related to audit evidence.

3. How does the auditor determine when sufficient evidence has been obtained?

4. How does an understanding of the client's business promote effective auditing?

5. Why must the client's environment be considered prior to substantive testing?

6. Identify the specific objectives related to the audit of transactions and balances.

7. Differentiate between the audit objectives of existence and completeness.

8. Why is the completeness objective generally more difficult to satisfy than the existence objective?

9. How does the valuation objective relate to GAAP?

10. What is meant by *correspondence between accounts and related substance*?

11. Name the primary objective served by the gathering of physical evidence. Give three examples of physical evidence.

12. What is the major form of confirmation evidence obtained by the auditor?

13. What is the principal factor determining the strength of documentary evidence?

14. Define *audit trail*.

15. How are the audit procedures referred to as *vouching* and *tracing* related to the audit trail?

16. Mathematical evidence consists of calculations, recalculations, and reconciliations. Give an example of each.

17. How does the application of analytical procedures assist the auditor in becoming aware of major omissions from the financial statements?

18. Define the term *transaction cycle* as it is used in auditing.

19. What factors should the auditor consider when developing audit programs?

20. Differentiate between current and permanent audit workpaper files.

21. In what way is the working trial balance like a table of contents found at the beginning of a book?

22. What is a lead schedule? What is a supporting schedule? How are they linked together? Give an example of each.

23. What are the components of a complete workpaper?

24. What is the major function of audit workpapers?

MULTIPLE CHOICE QUESTIONS FROM PAST CPA EXAMS

1. The audit workpaper that reflects the major components of an amount reported in the financial statements is the

a. Interbank transfer schedule.
b. Carryforward schedule.
c. Supporting schedule.
d. Lead schedule.

2. Which of the following elements ultimately determines the specific auditing procedures necessary under the circumstances to afford a reasonable basis for an opinion?
a. Auditor judgment
b. Materiality
c. Relative risk
d. Reasonable assurance

3. A basic premise underlying the application of analytical procedures is that
a. The study of financial ratios is an acceptable alternative to the investigation of unusual fluctuations.
b. Statistical tests of financial information may lead to the discovery of material errors in the financial statements.
c. Plausible relationships among data may reasonably be expected to exist and continue in the absence of known conditions to the contrary.
d. These procedures *cannot* replace tests of balances and transactions.

4. In testing the existence assertion for an asset, an auditor ordinarily works from the
a. Financial statements to the potentially unrecorded items.
b. Potentially unrecorded items to the financial statements.
c. Accounting records to the supporting evidence.
d. Supporting evidence to the accounting records.

5. An auditor ordinarily uses a working trial balance resembling the financial statements without footnotes, but containing columns for
a. Reclassifications and adjustments.
b. Reconciliations and tickmarks.
c. Accruals and deferrals.
d. Expense and revenue summaries.

6. The auditor will most likely perform extensive tests for possible understatement of
a. Revenues.
b. Assets.
c. Liabilities.
d. Capital.

7. The current file of an auditor's workpapers most likely would include a copy of the
a. Bank reconciliation.
b. Pension plan contract.
c. Articles of incorporation.
d. Flowchart of the internal control procedures.

8. As a result of analytical procedures, the independent auditor determines that the gross profit percentage has declined from 30 percent in the preceding year to 20 percent in the current year. The auditor should
a. Document management's intentions with respect to plans for reversing this trend.
b. Evaluate management's performance in causing this decline.
c. Require footnote disclosure.
d. Consider the possibility of an error in the financial statements.

9. An auditor's analytical procedures most likely would be facilitated if the entity
   a. Corrects material weaknesses in internal control before the beginning of the audit.
   b. Develops its data from sources solely within the entity.
   c. Segregates obsolete inventory before the physical inventory count.
   d. Uses a standard cost system that produces variance reports.

10. Which of the following statements is generally correct about the competence of evidential matter?
    a. The more effective the internal control system, the more assurance it provides about the reliability of the accounting data and financial statements.
    b. Competence of evidential matter refers to the amount of corroborative evidence obtained.
    c. Information obtained indirectly from independent outside sources is more persuasive than the auditor's direct personal knowledge obtained through observation and inspection.
    d. Competence of evidential matter refers to the audit evidence obtained from outside the entity.

11. Which of the following statements concerning evidential matter is correct?
    a. Competent evidence supporting management's assertions should be convincing rather than merely persuasive.
    b. An effective internal control system contributes little to the reliability of the evidence created within the entity.
    c. The cost of obtaining evidence is *not* an important consideration to an auditor in deciding what evidence should be obtained.
    d. A client's accounting data *cannot* be considered sufficient audit evidence to support the financial statements.

12. Which of the following statements relating to the competence of evidential matter is *always* true?
    a. Evidential matter gathered by an auditor from outside an enterprise is reliable.
    b. Accounting data developed under satisfactory conditions of internal control are more relevant than data developed under unsatisfactory internal control conditions.
    c. Oral representations made by management are *not* valid evidence.
    d. Evidence gathered by auditors must be both valid and relevant to be considered competent.

13. Which of the following best describes the primary purpose of audit procedures?
    a. To detect errors or fraud
    b. To comply with generally accepted accounting principles
    c. To gather corroborative evidence
    d. To verify the accuracy of account balances

14. Which of the following circumstances is most likely to cause an auditor to consider whether a material misstatement exists?
    a. Transactions selected for testing are not supported by proper documentation.
    b. The turnover of senior accounting personnel is exceptionally low.
    c. Management places little emphasis on meeting earnings projections.
    d. Operating and financing decisions are dominated by several persons.

INTERNET ACTIVITIES

The Public Register's *Annual Report Service* is a web site containing annual reports for over 2,000 companies. These reports may be viewed online or a free copy of the report may be requested.

Required:
Go to http://annualreportservice.com, select two companies of your choice, and calculate the following ratios for each:

http://
annualreportservice.
com

1. Two liquidity ratios

2. Two profitability ratios

3. One leverage ratio

4. Two asset management ratios

ESSAY QUESTIONS AND PROBLEMS

4.1   IBM, in reporting its first nine months' operating results for 1999, showed a of 12 percent increase in revenue and a 53 percent increase in operating income. These results, along with an announcement by IBM CEO Louis Gerstner citing "strong expense management," caused the company's stock price to advance markedly.

The footnotes to the quarterly financial statements stated that the company included in its operating results $4 billion in gains from the sale of its Global Network business to AT&T during the second and third quarters. These gains were reflected in "selling, general and administrative expenses." Had the gains not been included, the after-tax operating income for the nine-month period would have been $6.5 billion rather than the reported $8.9 billion.

Required:
a. Is IBM's financial statement presentation of the gains in accordance with GAAP? Discuss.
b. How would the independent CPA auditing IBM's annual financial statements for the year ended December 31, 1999, initially become aware of the company's treatment of the gains?

4.2   In analyzing the business activities of Rubiatt Inc., a small computer manufacturer, Jameel Brown, CPA and auditor of Rubiatt, discovered that due to declining sales volume in the face of increased competition, Rubiatt has been unable to maintain minimum cash balances as required by a major loan agreement. Moreover, a significant fourth-quarter loss appeared imminent. Due to the probable magnitude of the loss, Rubiatt will probably sustain a loss for the year. This will be the first time in its five-year history that Rubiatt has suffered a loss and the effect on its stock price is expected to be material. This prospect is especially bleak in that Rubiatt was planning an initial public offering of its stock as a means for dealing with its severe liquidity problems.

In generally analyzing the computer industry, Brown has discovered that many small computer manufacturers have failed during the past five years. At the present time, Rubiatt is one of the few remaining members of an increasingly competitive industry. Rubiatt's management, however, assures Brown that it is prepared to compete actively and anticipates no problems in marketing its stock issue.

Required:
a. Based on this information, what specific audit risk factors present themselves?
b. Discuss the effects the analysis may have on Jameel Brown's audit programs.

4.3   For each of the following specific audit objectives, identify the related financial statement assertion, the type of evidence required, and the audit procedure to be applied. Your answers should assume the following format:

ASSERTION:

FORM OF EVIDENCE:

AUDIT PROCEDURE(S):

a. To determine that year-end recorded inventories are on hand.

b. To obtain satisfaction regarding proper accrual of officers' year-end bonuses.

c. To assess adequacy of disclosure related to employee stock options.

d. To determine that all cash receipts were deposited in the bank.

e. To verify proper classification of property and repairs expenditures as to asset versus expense.

f. To establish validity of year-end accounts receivable balances.

4.4   Exhibit 4.10 is an audit workpaper prepared by Sarah Hughes, a member of the audit team examining the records of Harkness, Inc. Hughes prepared the workpaper to document her analysis of additions, disposals, and depreciation related to "Office Furniture and Equipment."

Required:

a. Referring to the *Guidelines for Preparing Adequate Audit Workpapers* section in the chapter, identify the weaknesses in the workpaper.

b. Name the audit procedures associated with each of the audit legends.

4.5   Application of analytical procedures is an effective means for the auditor to become initially aware of material omissions from the accounting records.

Required:

Explain how each of the following applications of analytical procedures assists in identifying material omissions.

a. Comparison of the current year's sales, cost of sales, and gross profit by months with those of the preceding year.

b. Comparison of amounts and sources of miscellaneous revenue with those of the prior year.

EXHIBIT 4.10

Problem 4.4 Workpaper

Banner, Inc.
Office Furniture and Equipment

	Asset	Accumulated Depreciation	Depreciation Expense	Gain or (Loss)
Beginning ledger balances	$130,000^	75,000^		
Purchases	65,000*			
Disposals	(42,000)*&	(37,000)*&		6,000%
Depreciation		17,000%	17,000%	
Ending ledger balances	$153,000	$ 55,000	$17,000	6,000
	F	F	F	F

   c. Calculation of accounts payable turnover and comparison with that of the prior year.

   d. Calculation of accounts receivable turnover and comparison with that of the prior year.

   e. Comparison of return on operating assets with the industry average.

4.6   Explain why each of the following situations is or is not a proper application of the concept of cost–benefit in auditing.

   a. For clients with material amounts of inventory, the auditor generally is required to observe the client's taking of the physical inventory, if feasible. Assume that P. Skiver, CPA, has a client with inventory located at two branch locations in addition to its headquarters location. Given the distances involved, the lack of audit personnel, and the fact that the branch inventories collectively represent only 15 percent of the total, Skiver decides to restrict inventory observation to the headquarters location only.

   b. In auditing marketable securities, the objectives of existence and ownership are of major importance. Conway, Inc., an audit client, has significant holdings of securities, both in a vault on the premises and in safekeeping with the trust department of a distant bank. The auditor decides to examine the securities on the premises, but due to the cost of traveling to the distant location and the lack of correspondent auditors in that area, the existence and ownership of the securities in safekeeping will be determined by confirmation rather than by physical examination.

4.7   The audit trail is defined as "the stream of evidence that enables the auditor to follow a transaction or event forward from its inception to the appropriate ledger account(s) (tracing)—or, conversely, backward from the ledger account to the inception of the transaction or event (vouching)."

Required:

For each of the following specific audit objectives, indicate whether the recommended procedure should assume the form of vouching or tracing.

   a. To obtain satisfaction that all shipments of merchandise have been billed to the respective customers of the client.

   b. To determine that all billings to customers are supported by shipments of merchandise.

   c. To verify additions to plant and equipment by examining underlying documentation.

   d. To gain assurance that credits to vendors' accounts in the accounts payable subsidiary ledger are supported by documentation evidencing receipt of goods or services.

   e. To determine that vendors' invoices have been posted to the proper account.

4.8   Auditing procedures are the means used by the auditor in gathering audit evidence.

Required:

   a. Using the classification of audit evidence presented in the chapter, identify the type of evidence produced by each of the following procedures.

     1. Examined vendor's invoice supporting debit to "machinery and equipment."

     2. Reconciled payroll bank account.

     3. Recalculated accrued interest on short-term notes receivable.

     4. Observed the taking of the client's physical inventory.

     5. Mailed confirmations to a sampling of the client's customers.

     6. Compared "sales," "cost of goods sold," and "gross profit" with prior year and investigated material changes for cause.

     7. Inquired of credit manager as to collectibility of certain customers' accounts receivable.

     8. Examined and listed marketable securities held for the client by a local bank.

     9. Mailed letters to consignees requesting verification of goods held by them.

10. Obtained response to letter of audit inquiry from the client's outside legal counsel.

11. Vouched a sampling of postings from customers' accounts in the subsidiary ledger to sales invoices and credit memos. Also traced a sample of invoices and credit memos to the subsidiary ledger.

b. For each of the 11 procedures, identify the financial statement assertion(s) tested by the resulting evidence.

4.9   *Part a.* The first generally accepted auditing standard of field work requires, in part, that "the work is to be adequately planned." An effective tool for the auditor in adequately planning the work is an audit program.

Required:

What is an audit program, and what purposes does it serve?

Part b. Auditors frequently refer to the terms *standards* and *procedures*. Standards deal with measures of the quality of the auditor's performance and specifically refer to the ten generally accepted auditing standards. Procedures relate to those acts that are performed by the auditor while trying to gather evidence and specifically refer to the methods or techniques used by the auditor in the conduct of the examination.

Required:

List at least two types of procedures that an auditor would use during an examination of financial statements. For example, a type of procedure that an auditor would frequently use is the observation of activities and conditions. Do *not* discuss specific accounts. (AICPA adapted)

4.10   Identify all of the deficiencies in the Exhibit 4.11 audit workpaper analyzing additions to Machinery and Equipment.

EXHIBIT 4.11

Problem 4.10 Workpaper

W. P. Index_____
Prepared by _____
Date_____
Reviewed by_____
Date_____

Kalbo, Inc.
Machinery and Equipment
December 31, 2002

Date	Description	Amount
12/31/01	Balance per General Ledger	$134,985
2002	Additions	57,630
2002	Disposals	(42,650)
12/31/02	Balance per General Ledger	$149,965
12/31/02	Balance per General Ledger (as above)	$149,965
	Audit adjustment to correct disposal	(12,350)
12/31/02	Adjusted Balance	$137,615

DISCUSSION CASE

biltrite

HANLON, INC.

Hanlon, Inc., manufactures and sells personal computers. Manufacturing operations are conducted at the company's sole plant in Hoopshire, New Hampshire, where general offices are also located. Products are distributed nationally through such retail outlets as Abcess III and Computer Country. Many large discount chains also handle Hanlon computers. The company has just completed its seventh year of operations. Your firm has audited Hanlon since its inception. Financial statements for the past three years, along with certain industry data, are presented in Exhibits 4.12 and 4.13.

EXHIBIT 4.12

Hanlon, Inc., Balance Sheets

	Hanlon, Inc.		
	Unaudited 12/31/X7	Audited 12/31/X6	Audited 12/31/X5
Cash in bank—general	$ 4,000	$ 12,000	$ 53,000
Cash in bank—payroll	4,000	4,000	8,000
Petty cash	500	500	500
Notes receivable—current	8,000	6,000	10,000
Accounts receivable—trade	300,000	150,000	220,000
Allowance for doubtful accounts	(12,000)	(12,000)	(15,000)
Interest receivable	600	400	500
Investments—current	7,000	2,000	6,000
Raw materials and purchased parts inventories	270,000	80,000	100,000
Goods in process	4,500	12,000	30,000
Finished goods inventory	300,000	180,000	266,000
Prepaid expenses—current	8,000	5,900	7,800
Plant assets—net	1,620,000	1,210,000	1,200,000
Intangible assets—net	350,000	115,000	120,000
Other assets	7,000	4,000	6,000
Total assets	$2,871,600	$1,769,800	$2,012,800
Notes payable—trade	$ 2,000	$ 7,000	$ 3,000
Accounts payable—trade	199,086	113,586	120,000
Taxes payable	8,000	6,000	20,000
Accrued liabilities	5,800	6,500	7,800
Mortgage note payable—current	200,000	200,000	147,000
Note payable—10%—current	100,000		
Note payable—10%—due 19X9	900,000		
Mortgage note payable—8%	400,000	520,000	720,000
Common stock—no par	300,000	300,000	300,000
Additional paid-in capital	120,000	120,000	120,000
Retained earnings	636,714	496,714	575,000
Total liabilities and stockholders' equity	$2,871,600	$1,769,800	$2,012,800

EXHIBIT 4.13

Hanlon, Inc., Income Statements

	Hanlon, Inc. For the Years Ending		
	Unaudited 12/31/X7	Audited 12/31/X6	Audited 12/31/X5
Sales	$1,800,000	$1,300,000	$2,860,000
Cost of goods sold	800,000	620,000	1,700,000
Gross profit	1,000,000	680,000	1,160,000
Operating expenses	600,000	488,954	520,000
Income before income taxes	400,000	191,046	640,000
Income taxes	180,000	154,332	250,000
Net income	220,000	36,714	390,000
Retained earnings—BOY	496,714	575,000	300,000
Total	716,714	611,714	690,000
Dividends	80,000	115,000	115,000
Retained earnings—EOY	$ 636,714	$ 496,714	$ 575,000
Selected Industry Averages:			
Inventory turnover	3.00		
Accounts receivable turnover	10.00		
Profit margin	5.00%		
Debt: equity ratio	50.00%		
Current ratio	2:1		

Hanlon, one of the first companies to manufacture personal computers, experienced substantial growth during the first five years of its existence. As more companies entered the field, however, Hanlon's earnings began to decline. By its sixth year, Hanlon was struggling with severe cash flow problems and the threat of a net loss. Negotiating a $1 million term loan with the Hoopshire National Bank and Trust Company temporarily averted the liquidity problems. The loan bears interest at 10 percent, and is payable in $100,000 annual installments, beginning in X8.

Required:

a. Copy the comparative financial statements and add columns for expressing balance sheet amounts as a percent of total assets, and income statement amounts as a percent of sales.

b. Compute the following ratios for each of the three years:

1. Inventory turnover
2. Accounts receivable turnover
3. Operating margin
4. Percentage of long-term debt to total capital structure (long-term debt plus stockholders' equity)
5. Current ratio
6. Quick ratio

c. Enter the given industry averages for these ratios and

1. Compare company and industry.
2. Compare current and prior years.
3. Identify areas requiring further investigation.
4. Identify possible causes of disparities cited in 3.

NOTE: The solution to this case can be greatly expedited by retrieving and completing the spreadsheet template entitled "Hanlon." This file is included on the student CD.

Audit Planning: Assessment of Inherent Risk and Materiality

c h a p t e r 5

biltrite

l e a r n i n g   o b j e c t i v e s

After reading this chapter, you should be able to

1 Define audit risk.
2 Identify and describe the three components of audit risk.
3 Quantify audit risk as a joint probability of the components.
4 Discuss the quantitative and qualitative aspects of materiality as they affect financial statement audits.
5 Describe inherent risk assessment in terms of audit planning, study of the business and industry, analytical procedures, and fraud assessment.
6 Describe the thought processes leading to the client acceptance decision.
7 Identify the sources of information available to the auditor in analyzing inherent risk.
8 Identify the warning signs providing evidence of inherent risk.
9 Understand the relationships among risk, materiality, and evidence and how these relationships are reflected in the development of audit programs.
10 Understand how audit risk analysis affects the development of audit programs.
11 Develop an approach to identifying and responding to the risk of fraud in a financial statement audit.

OVERVIEW

Chapter 4 defined the basic characteristics of audit evidence, audit programs, and audit work-papers. This chapter examines the concepts of materiality and audit risk as they relate to developing audit programs and gathering and evaluating audit evidence.

The chapter begins by defining audit risk and subdividing it into its three components: inherent risk, control risk, and detection risk. A means for quantifying audit risk is presented to promote consistency in analyzing risk. The chapter then considers materiality in terms of its individual item and aggregate impact on the financial statements. A model for dealing with materiality is presented and examples are used to illustrate the model. The relationships among audit risk, audit evidence, and materiality are also explored.

The remaining sections of the chapter develop an approach to analyzing and assessing inherent risk. Guidance provided by SAS 82, *The Auditor's Consideration of Fraud in a Financial Statement Audit*, is highlighted in the discussion. The audit planning function, including a study of the business and industry, and the application of analytical procedures provide the structure for inherent risk assessment.[1] The client acceptance decision is also an integral part of audit planning.

Cases are presented to emphasize the importance of heeding the warning signs revealed by risk analysis. In addition to demonstrating the significance of risk analysis, the cases also permit the student to assume the role of senior auditor and experience typical audit judgment situations. Suggested solutions to the first two cases are presented at the conclusion of each case. Solutions for the last two cases are contained in the *Instructor's Manual* and at the Instructor Resource Center on the web site *http://konrath.swcollege.com*. In addition, several discussion cases are presented as end-of-chapter materials.

A risk analysis matrix, matching warning signs with sources of information, is provided following this discussion. The purpose of the matrix is to ensure that all major risk areas are taken into account during the audit planning phase.

.com

http://
konrath.swcollege.com

INTRODUCTION

Audit risk was addressed briefly in Chapter 1 as part of the overall audit process. Figure 1.6 portrayed the process diagrammatically. This figure is now reproduced as Figure 5.1 with emphasis on that part of the process—inherent risk assessment—addressed in this chapter. To provide perspective regarding the placement of the subject matter of specific chapters in the overall audit process, the figure is also presented at the beginning of subsequent chapters as appropriate. Each reproduction is color-coded to highlight that part of the audit process to be covered in the respective chapters.

AUDIT RISK DEFINED

Audit risk has been defined as "the risk that auditors may unknowingly fail to appropriately modify their opinion on financial statements that are materially misstated."[2] Material misstatements may be the result of errors or fraud. **Errors** are *unintentional* mistakes; these were classified in Chapter 4 as omissions (transactions and/or balances

---

1   Control risk, the other component of audit risk, is covered in Chapters 6 through 8.
2   *AICPA Professional Standards*, New York: AICPA, section AU 312.02.

FIGURE 5.1

The Audit Process

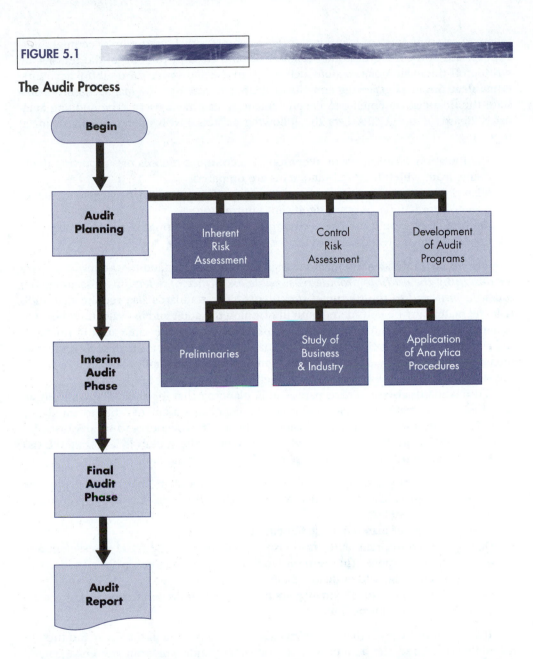

excluded from the financial statements) and commissions (erroneous transactions and/or balances included in the financial statements). In testing for omissions the auditor is concerned with management's assertion of completeness. Errors of commission relate to the existence or occurrence assertion. Errors may result from failing to record a transaction, recording a transaction in the wrong accounting period, recording a transaction at the wrong amount, or debiting or crediting the wrong account. Errors can be minimized through effective internal control, a topic addressed in Chapter 6.

Misstatements due to **fraud** are *intentional* and may involve misappropriation or fraudulent financial reporting. **Misappropriation** is the fraudulent transfer of assets from the firm to one or more dishonest employees. The transfer is either preceded or followed by some form of concealment. For example, a dishonest employee might misappropriate unrecorded customer remittances and attempt to conceal the transfer by writing off the customer's account, debiting it to the allowance for doubtful accounts. **Fraudulent financial reporting** consists of deliberate attempts by management to misstate the financial statements to deceive financial statement users. The Auditing Standards Board of the AICPA lists the following as acts involving fraudulent financial reporting:

- Manipulation, falsification, or alteration of accounting records or supporting documents from which financial statements are prepared.
- Misrepresentation in, or intentional omission from, the financial statements of events, transactions, or other significant information.
- Intentional misapplication of accounting principles relating to amounts, classification, manner of presentation, or disclosure.[3]

The AICPA Professional Standards assign the independent auditor the *responsibility for designing the audit to provide reasonable assurance of detecting* (misstatements) *that are material to the financial statements*.[4] The standards also require that audit risk and materiality be considered both in planning the audit and in evaluating the audit results.[5] As discussed later, the levels of materiality may be the same at both points in the audit. If, however, in the process of evaluating audit evidence, the materiality thresholds are lowered below those set at the planning stage, the auditor should "reevaluate the sufficiency of auditing procedures, which have been applied."[6]

The standards also require, as part of audit planning, that the auditor "specifically assess the risk of material misstatement of the financial statements due to fraud and should consider the assessment in designing the audit procedures to be performed."[7] SAS 82, issued by the ASB in 1997, provides guidance to the auditor in assessing the risk of fraud and responding to the assessment. Specifically, the auditor must:

1. Consider the presence of risk factors relating to fraudulent financial reporting and misappropriation of assets (labeled "warning signs," these risk factors are considered later in the chapter).
2. Assess the risk of material misstatement due to fraud.
3. Develop an appropriate audit response as indicated by the fraud assessment and document the response (in the audit workpapers).
4. Perform audit tests and evaluate results.
5. Communicate the results to management (or to the audit committee if senior management is a party to the fraud).[8]

If the auditor believes that senior management is involved in the fraud and there is no audit committee, the auditor should consider withdrawal from the engagement. As related in an earlier chapter, KPMG resigned from the audit of Rite Aid for this very reason.[9]

---

3   Ibid, section AU 316.
4   Ibid.
5   Ibid.
6   Ibid, section AU 312.22.
7   Ibid, section AU 316.
8   Barnett, Andrew, James Brown, Robert Fleming, and William Read, "The CPA as Fraud-Buster," *The Journal of Accountancy*, May 1998, pp. 69–73.
9   *The Wall Street Journal*, November 19, 1999.

The following paragraphs expand on the definitions of audit risk and audit risk analysis and explain how risk analysis can reduce the probability of material undetected errors and fraud in the financial statements and satisfy the requirements of SAS 82.

COMPONENTS OF AUDIT RISK

Inherent Risk

Inherent risk relates to the "susceptibility of an assertion to a material misstatement assuming that there are no related controls."[10] Inherent risk is a function of management integrity, management's attitude toward reliable financial reporting, and the complexity of the client's business. If the auditor perceives the managers to be persons of high integrity with genuine concern for proper financial reporting, the probability of fraudulent financial reporting is greatly reduced.

Inherent risk is often increased by unique characteristics of the business or industry that can contribute to audit complexity and uncertainty, thereby increasing the likelihood of undetected misstatements in the financial statements. Clients operating in the oil and gas exploration and the casualty insurance industries, for example, given specialized accounting treatment relating to income determination, present greater audit complexity than the more typical manufacturing, merchandising, or service clients. The existence of related parties, leases, financial derivatives, and other complicated contracts and agreements also contribute to audit complexity.

Clients in declining industries present a higher inherent risk than clients in stable or thriving industries. Audits of these clients may raise questions of uncertainty regarding the ability to continue as a going concern. Depending on the degree of uncertainty, the audit report may need to be modified. Clients in industries experiencing business declines also present a higher risk of fraudulent financial reporting. Pressures to maintain stable earnings in the face of a business downturn may lead management to begin using accounting principles that maximize earnings per share, or to classify ordinary losses as extraordinary. Violations of restrictive covenants in loan agreements (e.g., minimum cash balance and/or working capital requirements) are also more likely if diminishing revenues have given rise to liquidity problems.

Control Risk

Control risk is the risk that "a material misstatement that could occur in an assertion will not be prevented or detected on a timely basis by the entity's internal control."[11] Failure to adequately review transactions; inadequate documentation; unlimited access to negotiable securities, cash, and inventories; and lack of perpetual inventory records are examples of control weaknesses that contribute to financial statement errors or fraud. Auditing standards require the auditor to assess control risk.[12]

Together, inherent risk and control risk determine the probability that the financial statements will be materially misstated.[13] As discussed in Chapter 4, these risk elements also affect the validity of internal audit evidence. Before determining the nature, timing,

---

10 *AICPA Professional Standards*, op. cit., section AU 312.27.
11 Ibid.
12 Ibid, section AU 319.
13 Ibid, section AU 312.27.

and extent of substantive audit testing to be performed, the auditor must carefully analyze these two risk factors, as well as assess the probability of fraud.

Detection Risk

Detection risk is the risk that "the auditor will not detect a material misstatement that exists in an assertion."[14] Detection risk can be reduced through the application of substantive audit procedures. The auditor manages detection risk by first assessing inherent risk and control risk. If either or both of these risk levels is high, the auditor increases the extent of substantive testing to minimize overall audit risk.

QUANTIFYING AUDIT RISK

Audit risk analysis directly confronts inherent risk, control risk, and detection risk. It is an audit approach that attempts to identify those areas presenting the highest probability of material errors or fraud, and those areas of greatest audit complexity. Once identified, audit risk, including the risk of fraud, must be evaluated, and audit resources must be allocated more liberally to those areas presenting the highest risk. A means for quantifying audit risk is presented in this section. Although auditors do not necessarily quantify audit risk for each engagement, the concept of quantification enhances one's understanding of the risk components and provides a consistent approach to risk analysis.

Audit risk can be viewed as a joint probability of inherent risk, control risk, and detection risk. The following equation expresses this interpretation of audit risk.

$$AR = IR \times CR \times DR$$

where

AR = overall audit risk
IR = inherent risk
CR = control risk
DR = detection risk

Overall audit risk is that level of risk the auditor considers acceptable. It should be set low because the complement of this risk factor forms the basis for the audit opinion. If, for example, audit risk is set at 5 percent, the auditor's opinion will be expressed with 95 percent confidence that the financial statements are not materially misstated. A good rule of thumb is to set the overall audit risk $\leq$ 10 percent.[15]

Conservatism would suggest that inherent risk be set initially at 100 percent. One reasonably may assume, in other words, that in the absence of internal control, the probability of occurrence of material misstatements is 100 percent. This is *not* an unreasonable assumption when one considers what might happen when transactions are not properly approved, bank accounts are not reconciled, assets are not adequately safeguarded, and transactions lack documentation.

Control risk is assessed on the basis of the auditor's study and evaluation of internal control. Detection risk is the controllable variable in the equation, and it is a func-

---

14 Ibid.
15 AU section 312 of the *AICPA Professional Standards* requires the auditor to limit audit risk to a low level "that is, in the auditor's professional judgment, appropriate for expressing an opinion on the financial statements."

tion of the auditor's evaluation of inherent risk and control risk. More specifically, detection risk is determined by the assessed levels of control risk and inherent risk, in conjunction with the auditor's acceptable level of overall audit risk, such that the joint probability of the three risk elements produces the desired overall audit risk. The level of detection risk is inversely related to the extent of substantive audit testing to be performed under the circumstances.

Given the equation expressing audit risk as a joint probability, and given that detection risk is controllable through increasing or decreasing substantive audit testing, the equation may be rearranged so that the controllable (dependent) variable (detection risk) is on the left side of the equation, and the uncontrollable (independent) variables are on the right side. This may be accomplished by dividing both sides of the equation by $IR \times CR$. The equation may now be expressed as

$$DR = \frac{AR}{IR \times CR}$$

If IR is assumed to be 100 percent, then the equation may be shortened to

$$DR = \frac{AR}{CR}$$

Assume that the auditor has determined the following percentages:

$AR = 10\%$ (set low because it forms the basis for the audit opinion)
$CR = 30\%$ (based on study and testing of internal control)

Therefore,

$$DR = 0.10/0.30 = 33\%$$

If study and testing of internal controls revealed weaker controls than those indicated above, CR might be assessed at, say, 60 percent rather than 30 percent. Detection risk would then decrease to $16\frac{2}{3}$ percent, requiring a substantial increase in the amount of substantive testing (confirmation of accounts receivable, vouching and tracing, observation and test counting of inventories, inspection of securities, etc.) in order to compensate for weaker controls and yet maintain the overall audit risk at the specified 10 percent.

The analysis of inherent risk, as will be discussed, enables the auditor to *reduce inherent risk below 100 percent.* By concentrating audit resources in the high-risk areas, the probability of undetected misstatements decreases. Both inherent risk assessment and control risk assessment, therefore, affect the nature, timing, and extent of substantive audit testing. As stated in the AICPA Professional Standards, "The less the inherent and control risk the auditor believes exists, the greater the detection risk that can be accepted. Conversely, the greater the inherent and control risk the auditor believes exists, the less the detection risk that can be accepted."[16]

Figure 5.2 summarizes this discussion of errors, fraud, and audit risk analysis, and sets the course for the discussion that follows. As indicated in the figure, inherent risk is covered in this chapter. The audit planning phases involving inherent risk assessment are

---

16 *AICPA Professional Standards*, op. cit., section AU 312.28.

FIGURE 5.2

Audit Planning and Risk Analysis

I. Factors Contributing to Audit Risk

A. *Errors*
   1. Commission
   2. Omission

B. *Fraud*
   1. Misappropriation
   2. Misrepresentation

II. Components of Audit Risk

A. Inherent Risk:
   A function of management integrity and the unique characteristics of the business or industry that contribute to audit complexity and uncertainty

B. Control Risk:
   Risk that a material misstatement will not be prevented or detected by internal control

C. Detection Risk:
   Risk that the auditor will not detect a material misstatement that exists in an assertion

---

III. Audit Risk Analysis

Risk Component	Audit Phase	Chapter
Inherent Risk	Audit planning	5
	Study of the business and industry	
	Analytical procedures	
Control Risk	Further testing of selected controls	6–8
Detection Risk	Substantive audit testing (as modified based on analysis of inherent risk and control risk)	10–13

- Preliminary phase of audit planning;
- Study of the business and industry; and
- Analytical procedures.

MATERIALITY AND ITS IMPACT ON AUDIT EVIDENCE

In deciding whether to recommend an audit adjustment or reclassification, the auditor must consider materiality in terms of both the income statement and the balance sheet. Qualitative factors relating to misstatement (e.g., related parties and management override of internal control) may also need to be considered when absolute amounts are not material. The following paragraphs explore materiality issues.

The Meaning of Materiality as Applied to Auditing

In management's opinion, the Medical Care Inc. unit of W.R. Grace was experiencing a too-rapid earnings growth, so they transferred part of the profit to a "reserve" for use in later years when profits were not so robust. Clearly a violation of GAAP, the company's auditors PricewaterhouseCoopers so informed management. Despite management's refusal to correct the accounts, the auditors rendered an unqualified opinion on the basis that the amounts involved *were not material*. As a result, the SEC brought action against Grace and also considered action against PwC as part of the agency's ongoing efforts to thwart the "games companies play to tweak results to avoid missing Wall Street's quarterly earnings estimates."[17] In addition, the SEC issued a Staff Accounting Bulletin stating that "managers should not direct or acquiesce in immaterial misstatements in the financial statements for the purpose of managing earnings."[18] **Materiality** has been defined as that amount of misstatement that would affect the decisions of a reasonably informed user of the financial statements.[19] The auditor considers materiality while planning the audit, conducting the audit, and evaluating the results of the audit.

In the planning phase, the auditor considers materiality in developing audit programs. Materiality of particular classes of transactions and account balances helps to determine the extent and type of audit evidence to gather. In conducting the audit, the auditor considers whether or not discovered misstatements are sufficiently material to warrant proposing them to the client as audit adjustments or reclassifications. In evaluating audit results, the auditor must decide whether in light of discovered misstatements preliminary material levels need to be revised, and whether sufficient audit evidence has been obtained.

In deciding materiality, the auditor should consider the impact of possible misstatements on those profitability and liquidity measures typically applied by financial statement users in making investing and lending decisions. Net operating income as a percentage of net sales, gross profit margin, net income as a percentage of operating assets, net income as a percentage of stockholders' equity, inventory turnover, accounts receivable turnover, earnings per share, times interest earned, current ratio, quick ratio, and net working capital are examples of ratios and percentages that the auditor should consider when establishing materiality levels. Because these ratios and percentages are based on both balance sheet and income statement components, materiality considerations should give equal weight to both statements. Materiality and its influence on the audit process are considered in the following paragraphs.

For *audit planning purposes*, appropriate materiality levels and areas of audit emphasis vary with different engagements and are a matter of audit judgment. To illustrate, assume two separate audit clients: one is a wholesale distributor and the other is a service organization. One would expect a greater proportion of audit resources to be dedicated to the audit of inventory balances for the wholesale distributor, given the relative materiality of the investment in inventories. In contrast, primary emphasis might be given to testing the appropriateness of revenue recognition for the service client. Proper timing of revenue recording relative to earning and realization is of utmost importance to the fair statement of assets and income for service organizations.

For *proposed audit adjustment and reclassification purposes*, the auditor should consider materiality in both the planning and evaluation phases of the audit. In the planning stage, preliminary judgments about materiality levels are made. These judgments

17 See *The Wall Street Journal*, April 7, 1999.
18 *Securities and Exchange Commission*, Staff Accounting Bulletin (SAB) No. 99.
19 *AICPA Professional Standards*, op. cit., section AU 312.10.

typically are based on the smallest aggregate level of misstatement that could be considered material to any one of the financial statements. These levels are hereafter referred to as **materiality thresholds**. For example, if a $100,000 misstatement is considered material to net income, while a $200,000 misstatement is material to financial position, the auditor should select the $200,000 threshold for misstatements affecting the balance sheet only (e.g., audit reclassifications), and $100,000 as the appropriate threshold for all other misstatements.

Consideration of materiality in the evaluation phase of the audit differs from its consideration in the planning stage in two respects. First, materiality thresholds may change between the planning and the evaluation stages. Using the above example, assume that proposed audit adjustments developed during the course of the field work have lowered net income by $300,000. If the original $100,000 materiality threshold was derived by applying a percentage to unaudited net income, that threshold has now decreased and the auditor must question the sufficiency of audit evidence in light of the revised materiality level. This would suggest that if during the audit planning phase the auditor suspects earnings overstatement, lower materiality thresholds should be set to prevent underauditing.

Materiality judgments during the evaluation phase also differ from those made during audit planning due to qualitative factors arising during the implementation of audit programs. Examples of qualitative factors that impact materiality judgments are illegal payments, fraud detected during the audit, and contingencies. To illustrate, a small illegal payment discovered during the audit of transactions and balances may be insignificant by itself, but it could result in fines, lawsuits, or court injunctions, producing subsequent expenditures or loss of revenues in substantial amounts. Likewise, fraud may be immaterial in quantitative terms, but may raise major questions regarding management integrity. In the W.R. Grace case cited above, the amounts involved may indeed have been immaterial, but the fact that management intentionally created the reserve for the purpose of "smoothing" earnings should cause the auditor to question the reliability of management's representations.

The auditor cannot anticipate all of the qualitative materiality factors during the audit planning phase and build them into the audit programs. Rather, she or he must also consider them as they arise during substantive audit testing and evaluate their overall financial statement implications during audit evaluation.

To summarize, the auditor should consider both quantitative and qualitative factors in establishing materiality thresholds for financial statement auditing purposes. To emphasize this point, the SEC stated in SAB No. 99 that "the use of a percentage ceiling (quantitative) test alone to make materiality determinations is not acceptable."[20]

Individual Item versus Aggregate Materiality

Materiality thresholds may be further classified as to individual item and aggregate. **Individual item materiality** concerns the impact of a single misstatement on the financial statements. Along with individual item materiality, the auditor also must consider **aggregate materiality**: the total effect of two or more misstatements, each of which is not material by itself. Assume that the magnitude of classification errors between the repairs and maintenance accounts and the plant asset accounts is immaterial in the judgment of the auditor. Assume further, however, that the auditor discovers classifica-

20 SAB No. 99, op. cit.

tion errors between other asset and expense accounts. If each account is misstated to some degree, the aggregate effect on total operating expenses and net income could well be significant. To ensure proper consideration of aggregate materiality, the auditor should set a second materiality threshold measure. This level is then used for selecting misstatements to be included as *potential* audit adjustments or reclassifications.

A special audit workpaper may be prepared for accumulating these adjustments. The auditor will refer to this workpaper in the evaluation phase to gauge the aggregate impact of the individual misstatements. If the individual item materiality threshold for net income, for example, is $100,000, the auditor may decide on a lower aggregate materiality threshold—say $10,000—and accumulate, in a separate audit workpaper, net income misstatements less than $100,000 and more than $10,000 for later aggregate evaluation. If the combined effect of the potential adjustments equals or exceeds the individual item materiality threshold ($100,000), the auditor should present these adjustments, as well as the individual item adjustments, to the client for posting and inclusion in the audited financial statements. Figure 5.3 and Exhibits 5.1 and 5.2 illustrate some of the considerations involved in aggregate materiality determinations. Figure 5.3 uses four thresholds—two for the income statement and two for the balance sheet. For misstatements affecting the income statement, the individual item and aggregate thresholds are $100,000 and $10,000, respectively; for balance sheet only adjustment and reclassification purposes, the amounts are $300,000 and $30,000, respectively. Income misstatements that are less than $10,000 will be ignored as immaterial, and balance sheet only misstatements under $30,000 will likewise be ignored.

Income statement materiality thresholds are generally based on the auditor's judgment as to what constitutes a material misstatement of net income. Balance sheet materiality, on the other hand, relates to errors within the balance sheet that have no impact on net income. As an example, the auditor may need to decide whether to reclassify credit balances in trade accounts receivable as current liabilities. Because net income and net assets are not affected, balance sheet thresholds are usually set at *higher* levels than income statement thresholds.

Note that Exhibit 5.2 analyzes audit adjustments affecting the income statement. A similar workpaper may also be developed to accumulate possible audit adjustments and reclassifications affecting the balance sheet only.

FIGURE 5.3

Materiality Thresholds

	Affects Net Income and Net Assets	Affects Balance Sheet Only	Audit Adjustment?
Individual Item Materiality	≥$100,000	≥$300,000	Yes
Aggregate Materiality	≥$10,000 <$100,000	≥$30,000 <$300,000	Maybe
Less than Aggregate Materiality	<$10,000	<$30,000	No

EXHIBIT 5.1

Aggregate Materiality Workpaper

WP Z
Prepared by:
Reviewed by:

Brandt Manufacturing
Aggregate Materiality
12/31/XX

Individual item materiality threshold (firm policy):
   2% of net income
   1% of net assets
   Qualitative considerations:
      Intent
      Volume of transactions
Brandt Manufacturing—Unaudited:
   Net income . . . . $5 million
   Net assets . . . . $30 million

Materiality thresholds as related to Brandt:
   As related to net income $100,000
   As related to net assets $300,000

Individual item materiality for Brandt Manufacturing audit:
   For audit adjustment purposes $100,000
   For balance sheet reclassification purposes $300,000

Aggregate materiality as based on audit risk assessment:
   For high control risk and/or inherent risk environments, firm policy is to set aggregate
      materiality threshold at 1% of individual item materiality
   For low-risk environments, firm policy is to set the level at 15% of individual item
      materiality
   Risk assessment for Brandt (see control and inherent risk assessment workpapers at
      Index 1-A):
   Control risk . . . . Medium
   Inherent risk . . . . Low

Based on firm policy and the Brandt assessment, aggregate materiality is set at $10,000
for the income statement and $30,000 for balance sheet reclassification purposes (10% of
individual item materiality, given the approximation to the low-risk environment). Therefore,
any income statement error greater than $10,000 and lower than $100,000, and/or any
balance sheet error greater than $30,000 and lower than $300,000 will be documented
on this workpaper as a proposed audit adjustment. If the proposed adjustments and/or reclassifications aggregate more than $100,000 or $300,000, respectively, they will be presented to Brandt management along with the other audit adjustments and reclassifications.

(See workpaper Z-1 for list of adjustments and conclusions.)

The establishment of the aggregate materiality threshold at $10,000 or at some other amount higher or lower than $10,000 is a function of the auditor's preliminary judgments concerning audit risk. As a general rule, the *more misstatements the auditor expects, the lower should be the aggregate materiality threshold*. For example, if the auditor perceives during the audit planning phase that transactions are processed accurately and in accordance with GAAP, the aggregate materiality threshold will be set

EXHIBIT 5.2

Possible Audit Adjustments

WP Z-1
Prepared by:
Reviewed by:

Brandt Manufacturing
Aggregate Materiality
Possible Audit Adjustments
12/31/XX

WP Ref.	Description	Income Effect
D-1	Product development costs incorrectly capitalized as intangible assets	$ 23,500
L-3	Understatement of estimated product warranty liability	44,600
E-1	Added depreciation on disposals of machinery and equipment	63,200
	Total	$131,300

Inasmuch as these possible adjustments, each greater than $10,000 and less than $100,000, sum to an amount exceeding the individual item materiality threshold, they should be presented to the client as audit adjustments. They have therefore been transcribed to the "Audit Adjustments" workpaper (see WP X).

higher than if he or she suspects numerous processing errors. If expectations subsequently change as the audit progresses, the threshold should be raised or lowered as appropriate. A preliminary expectation of few errors, for example, followed by the subsequent discovery of numerous errors, should lead to a decrease in the aggregate materiality threshold.

For auditing purposes, *materiality must be applied to transactions as well as to balances.* A bank account, for example, may have become inactive during the period under audit, with only a nominal balance remaining at year end. Suppose, however, that prior to the account becoming inactive and during the year under audit, a large volume of cash receipts and disbursements transactions were processed through this account. Were the auditor to consider materiality in light of balances only, this account would receive inadequate audit attention. When the concept of materiality is extended to transactions as well as balances, a more rational allocation of audit resources results.

A final point regarding materiality considerations in auditing relates to *discovered* versus *projected* misstatements. If the auditor examines only a portion of the transactions relating to a given balance sheet or income statement class, detected misstatements must be extended to the population represented by the evidence examined. An audit of a sampling of debits to repairs and maintenance expense, for example, may detect $20,000 of capital expenditures erroneously debited to expense. When projected to the population of debits to the account, however, the auditor may project a $150,000 overstatement of repairs expense for the period under audit. Although the detected misstatements aggregating $20,000 are not significant when compared with a $100,000 materiality threshold, the projected error becomes substantial ($150,000) when extended to the population. Statistical sampling procedures, discussed in Chapters 9 and 10, provide a means for systematically projecting to the related populations errors discovered in audited samples.

Having considered the characteristics of materiality as related to financial statement auditing, attention will now be focused on audit risk and the relationship between risk and materiality.

RELATIONSHIP AMONG AUDIT RISK, AUDIT EVIDENCE, AND MATERIALITY

Chapter 4, along with the preceding paragraphs, discussed the concepts of audit evidence, materiality, and audit risk. In addition to gaining a thorough understanding of these three concepts, the auditor must also recognize the direct relationships that exist among them.

In developing a rational audit approach that conforms to the "due care" concept as stated in Rule 201 of the Code of Professional Conduct, the auditor must exercise **professional skepticism**—"an attitude that includes a questioning mind and critical assessment of audit evidence."[21] In exercising skepticism, the auditor first must evaluate audit risk, after which materiality thresholds can be set and the nature, timing, and extent of audit evidence can be determined. To evaluate risk, the auditor studies the business and industry, applies analytical procedures, and studies and evaluates internal control. Audit risk related to the various aspects of the business and industry is referred to as *inherent risk*, and is defined and explained more fully below. Audit risk related to weaknesses in the internal control system is referred to as *control risk*, and is the subject of Chapters 6 through 8.

Given the concepts of audit evidence, risk, and materiality, the auditor should combine these three components in developing substantive audit programs. Figure 5.4 presents these relationships and considerations diagramatically. If, for example, inherent risk is high because of auditor suspicion of intentional management misrepresentation of financial position and/or results of operations, aggregate materiality levels must be reduced and the auditor *cannot* rely so heavily on internal evidence. The reason for reducing aggregate materiality levels under these conditions is the increased probability that several accounts or transaction classes will be misrepresented in order to effect concealment of the initial misrepresentation. The reason for obtaining greater amounts of external evidence is because internal documentation may have been intentionally altered or fabricated.

If control risk is high, the probability of numerous unintentional errors is increased and aggregate materiality levels must be decreased accordingly. Weak internal control also lowers the validity (reliability) of internal documentation and suggests that the auditor rely more heavily on external evidence, such as confirmations, physical inspection, calculations, and reconciliations.

Understanding the above relationships is critical to the exercise of due care and to the maintenance of an attitude of professional skepticism in planning and conducting the audit. This understanding is also a basic premise of risk-driven audits.[22]

21 *AICPA Professional Standards*, op. cit., section AU 316.27.
22 The concept of the risk-driven audit is defined and described in a later section of this chapter.

FIGURE 5.4

Relationships Among Audit Evidence, Audit Risk, and Materiality

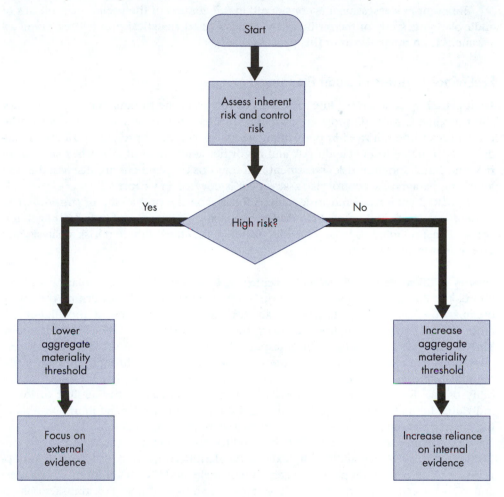

ANALYSIS OF INHERENT RISK

Inherent risk, as defined earlier, is the susceptibility of a financial statement assertion to a material misstatement, assuming that there are no related controls. Inherent risk may be compounded or mitigated by the auditor's specific fraud assessment as well as by the unique characteristics of the business and industry. The fraud assessment addresses the risk of misstatement from two types of fraud:

- Misstatements arising from *fraudulent financial reporting*; and
- Misstatements arising from *misappropriation of assets*.

The inherent risk discussion contained in this chapter will be confined to that part of the fraud assessment directed at fraudulent financial reporting. Asset misappropriation relates more to control weaknesses and will be covered in the next chapter.

Business and industry characteristics contribute to audit complexity and uncertainty and influence the incidence of material errors and fraud in the financial statements. The following paragraphs demonstrate how the auditor can manage inherent risk through analysis of these factors.

Inherent risk assessment is considered in the context of the preliminary phases of audit planning, study of the business and industry, and analytical procedures. Fraud assessment is an integral part of this process.

Preliminary Phases of Audit Planning

Audit planning, as described in Chapter 1, culminates in the formulation of preliminary audit programs. An audit program, as defined in Chapter 4, represents an outline of the procedures to be followed in performing an audit. The audit program reflects the auditor's acceptable level of audit risk and his or her assessment of inherent risk, control risk, and fraud. Inherent risk assessment and fraud risk assessment are discussed in the following paragraphs; control risk assessment is covered in Chapter 7.

As stated earlier, inherent risk analysis focuses on the probability of *fraudulent financial reporting* and on *audit complexity* posed by business and industry characteristics. The preliminary phase of audit planning facilitates inherent risk analysis and assessment in the following ways.

Inquiry of Client Personnel Assists in Identifying Risk Areas   The audit planning phase affords the auditor the opportunity to question client personnel concerning the entity organization. Questioning directs the auditor's attention to some of the higher-risk areas. For example, the auditor may learn that the existence of excess capacity, combined with strong competition from imports, has placed a "squeeze" on profits. These conditions make the auditor alert to possible earnings inflation through premature revenue recognition, expense deferral, or a combination of the two. The increased probability of this form of fraudulent financial reporting also causes the auditor to lower individual item and aggregate materiality thresholds and consider the merits of obtaining greater amounts of external evidence relative to internal evidence.

The preliminary discussions between auditor and client also facilitate early identification of areas of high audit complexity. Early identification affords the auditor an opportunity to modify audit programs accordingly, make audit team additions or changes, and plan for effective coverage of these areas. Examples of complex transactions requiring special attention are a lease containing contingent rental clauses, modification of an existing pension plan, a corporate restructuring, and inventory requiring special expertise for counting or valuation.

Use of Client Personnel Enables the Auditor to Concentrate on High-Risk Areas   Part of audit planning involves arrangements between the auditor and client concerning use of client personnel on the engagement. By using client personnel in a judicious manner, the auditor is able to devote more time to areas of high audit risk. Virtually any audit task, short of audit judgment decision making, may be assigned to client personnel, provided the auditor reviews and verifies their work on at least a test basis. The auditor must, of course, use employees capable of performing the assigned tasks.

The Client Acceptance Decision Serves as Part of Risk Analysis   The auditor's consideration of the risk of material misstatement due to fraud may "indicate such a significant risk of fraud that the auditor should consider withdrawing from the engagement."[23] In November 1999, KPMG announced that the firm would no longer audit the financial statements of Rite Aid Corp. because the firm decided it could no longer rely on management's representations.[24] In May 1998, Ernst & Young resigned as independent auditor for Premier Laser Systems Inc. because of disagreements with management over accounting practices.[25] In June 1998, Deloitte & Touche resigned as auditors for YBM Magnex International Inc. because of concern over illegal acts that might have materially affected the 1997 financial statements.[26] During 1996, Coopers & Lybrand discontinued twenty-eight public clients; Arthur Andersen & Co. dropped forty-seven between 1994 and 1996; and Price Waterhouse terminated forty-six during the same period.[27]

The exercise of due audit care, as required by the Code of Professional Conduct, may not be possible in an environment of management dishonesty and widespread fraud. The quality control guidelines issued by the AICPA Quality Control Standards Committee (see Chapter 2) include a provision for **client acceptance** that requires the auditor not only to evaluate new clients for acceptance, but also to review existing clients periodically for continuance. The policies and procedures adopted for this purpose should provide reasonable assurance that the firm will not be associated with clients whose managements lack integrity.[28] In the event that new clients previously have been audited by other CPAs, the new auditors, in accordance with the AICPA Professional Standards, should obtain permission from the prospective client to contact the predecessor auditors. The primary purpose of the communication is to obtain further information concerning the accounting system and management integrity that may impact the acceptance decision.[29]

The AICPA recommends that the auditor complete a "Client Acceptance Checklist" prior to submitting the engagement letter and use this completed form to determine whether a prospective client should be accepted. Some of the items included in the form are presented in Exhibit 5.3.

PricewaterhouseCoopers, one of the Big 5 national accounting firms, uses a two-tier client screening program to reduce the firm's overall liability exposure. At the first level, the local engagement partner goes over an extensive checklist to verify the prospect's business history, current operations, internal controls, and top management. The decision of the partner is then reviewed at a second level for final approval. In addition to looking at the prospective client's reputation in the marketplace, its financial condition, and the state of the industry, the reviewer focuses on the integrity of the principal owners, top management's expertise, the legality of business activities, and the financial viability of the entity.[30]

Study of the Business and Industry

Careful analysis of the client's business and the industry of which it is a part provides an effective means for the auditor to gain a better understanding of the client's organi-

23 *AICPA Professional Standards*, op. cit., section AU 316.36.
24 *The Wall Street Journal*, November 19, 1999.
25 Ibid, May 27, 1998.
26 Ibid, June 29, 1998.
27 Ibid, April 25, 1997.
28 A news article appearing in the *Los Angeles Times* reported that the auditor for Home Theater Products resigned citing "significant weaknesses in internal controls and concerns about management integrity." October 10, 1995, p. D-6.
29 *AICPA Professional Standards*, op. cit., section AU 315.
30 *International Bank Accountant 92*, No. 37, October 5, 1992, p. 3.

EXHIBIT 5.3

Client Acceptance Checklist

- What additional staff or expertise will be required?

- Might any possible related-party transactions affect the engagement?

- Does it appear that the accounting system provides records sufficient to permit application of cost-effective audit procedures? If not, are there possible scope limitations?

- What are the potential effects on the auditor's report and likely management reaction?

- Who is the current (or former) independent CPA over the previous five years? (Obtain the company's permission to contact them.) Were there any disputes over accounting matters?

- Has the company sued prior auditors or other professionals?

- If we have no prior knowledge of the company, its management, or its officers, were references checked? What were their comments? Contacts include the company's principal lawyer, its banker, the Chamber of Commerce, and the Better Business Bureau. Was a Dun & Bradstreet report obtained? What experiences have firm members had with the company's lawyers?

- Would service to this company cause independence problems or conflicts of interest?

- Have any of the following circumstances raised any concerns about management's integrity?
  (a) Difficulty in obtaining information from management or evasive, guarded, or glib responses to inquires
  (b) Apparent difficulty in meeting financial operations or a deteriorating financial position that might predispose management to undertake fraudulent financial reporting
  (c) Disputes about accounting principles, engagement procedures, or similarly significant matters with an existing or former auditor, or doubts of the predecessor auditor about management integrity
  (d) Comments by bankers, attorneys, creditors, or others in a business relationship with the potential client

- Is the company operating in an industry that might put the firm at a high-level risk of litigation or unfavorable publicity?

- Why is management changing auditors?

- Is there any reason to suspect that management would be uncooperative, unreasonable, or otherwise unpleasant to work with?

Source: *AICPA Audit and Accounting Manual*, New York: AICPA.

zation and operations. This, in turn, assists the auditor in identifying those transaction areas posing the greatest threat of material misstatement. In the process of studying the organizational structure and conducting preliminary discussions with the client's management personnel, the auditor already gained some grasp of the client's organization and the nature of its operations. A more penetrating study is needed, however, now that the client has been accepted.

Study of the business and industry also enables the auditor to identify complex transaction areas and more clearly differentiates between the form and the substance of transactions. The *Bar Chris* case (cited in Chapter 3) involved highly complex sale and leaseback transactions that the company had treated as sales in the ordinary course of business. Accordingly, revenue was recognized upon signing of the leases. Although legally (i.e., in form) these were sales, in substance the criteria for revenue recognition were not met and, therefore, the revenue was recognized prematurely. The court determined in this case that the in-charge auditor did not have a thorough understanding of the substantive nature of these transactions and found the auditors negligent for (among other things) not recommending deferral of the revenue.

Classifying Business and Industry Information   Sources of information that should be consulted by the auditor in studying the client's business and industry are listed in Figure 5.5.

The information to be gathered from these sources may be classified as follows:

1. Information concerning the economy;
2. Information concerning the industry; and
3. Information concerning the business.

The procedures to be applied in obtaining the necessary information are discussed in the following paragraphs.

Information Concerning the Economy   Familiarity with current economic conditions promotes risk analysis in several ways. A downturn in the economy, for example, may

---

FIGURE 5.5

Sources of Business and Industry Information

1. The permanent file (if a recurring audit) and last year's current file

2. Correspondence files and minutes of directors' meetings

3. Prior year's financial statements and related footnotes

4. AICPA industry audit and accounting guides

5. Industry publications describing the nature of the industry and economic, political, and other events affecting the industry at the time of the audit

6. Government publications relating to the industry, including those containing industry statistics and economic factors affecting the industry (many such publications are available through the Government Printing Office)

7. Tax laws unique to the industry

8. Annual reports of other companies in the industry

9. Discussions with predecessor auditor (if a new client was previously audited by another CPA firm)

10. Credit reports from such sources as Dun & Bradstreet and commercial banks

11. Corporate manuals, such as accounting manuals, chart of accounts and policy, and procedures manuals

12. Computer databases containing industry information (e.g., NEXIS, COMPACT DISCLOSURE, etc.)

13. Business periodicals

create problems in collecting customer accounts receivable and may suggest that increased audit time be devoted to the allowance for uncollectible accounts.

Many of the savings and loan failures occurring in the 1980s were the result of accepting risky loans during the more prosperous times immediately following government deregulation of the industry and preceding the recession years that followed. Faced with these portfolios, auditors began to concentrate their resources on evaluating portfolio quality, and devoted particular attention to the adequacy of loan loss reserves. Case 5.1, involving United Bank of Seattle, emphasizes the auditor's need for understanding the impact of economic conditions on the client's business.[31] In this case, the abnormal increase in the loan portfolio and the heavy concentration in a single area should have raised a red flag for the auditors. Specifically, it should have alerted them to high inherent risk relative to the loans receivable and the loan loss reserve subset of the revenue cycle.

CASE 5.1

UNITED BANK OF SEATTLE
Case Description

George Brenner, CPA and senior auditor for Jackson, Brewster, and Hampton, CPAs, was the in-charge auditor for the 1986 financial statement audit of United Bank of Seattle. His audit team consisted of a semi-senior auditor and three assistants. Brenner and his team began the final audit work on January 4, 1987, and completed the examination on January 26.

United Bank had experienced rapid growth in its loan portfolio from 1983 to 1985. Most of these loans were related to the Seattle Sesquicentennial, held at that time. Moreover, nearly half of the loans were to friends and relatives of Lauren Knox, chief executive of United Bank and chairman of the Sesquicentennial. By 1986, most of these loans were found to be uncollectible, given the heavy losses suffered by the Sesquicentennial sponsors. As a result, the bank was insolvent.

Knox and his brother operated several banks besides United Bank. To conceal the gravity of the situation from the auditors and bank examiners, Knox attempted to transfer problem loans to some of these other banks before the auditors arrived.

What Would You Do?

Industry analysis should have alerted the auditors to the abnormal portfolio growth of United Bank and the heavy concentration of Sesquicentennial loans. Together with the existence of significant related-party transactions, these findings should have raised red flags for the auditors and examiners. Specifically, they should have caused the auditors to be concerned about the assertions of valuation and presentation. Related parties in this case included not only friends and relatives to whom loans had been made, but also the other banks operated by the Knox brothers, as well as the Sesquicentennial Committee, inasmuch as Lauren Knox was chairman.

31 This is the first of four cases presented in Chapter 5 to illustrate the importance of audit risk analysis. Suggested solutions are presented for the first two cases. To provide an opportunity for class discussion, the suggested solutions to Cases 5.3 and 5.4 are provided in the *Instructor's Manual*. Although the proper course of action for the auditor to have taken might seem obvious, one needs to recognize that only the pertinent factors in the cases have been isolated for illustrative purposes. In the actual situations, the auditors may have been faced with several issues requiring the exercise of audit judgment as to the adequacy of audit evidence supporting existence or occurrence, completeness, rights and obligations, valuation or allocation, and presentation and disclosure. One must also recognize that most facts seem more obvious when viewed *ex post facto*—that is, hindsight is 20/20. The auditor, however, is in an *ex ante facto* position and must evaluate the adequacy of audit evidence and the cost–benefit tradeoff of gathering additional evidence.

Such warning signs as those mentioned should have caused the auditors to concentrate heavily on analysis of the loan portfolio for quality and collectibility. Critical attention should also have been given to the loan loss reserves, which, in this instance, proved quite inadequate.

Federal bank examiners were on the premises during much of the audit investigating the loan portfolio and applying selected solvency measures. These means enabled the examiners to detect many of the more significant problem loans and determine the inadequacy of the loan loss reserves. Given the circumstances of this case, the auditors should have questioned the examiners as to any findings concerning loan quality.

What Was Done?

Brenner and his team applied standard audit procedures without concentrating audit resources on loan quality. Judgment regarding the adequacy of the loan loss reserve was applied essentially in terms of a percentage of outstanding loans. As a result, the problem loans were not identified, and the auditors issued a "clean" opinion. Moreover, the federal examiners reported that, notwithstanding their common presence on the premises for two weeks in January 1987, neither Brenner nor any member of the audit team questioned them concerning their investigation and findings.

Consequences

On February 14, 1987, shortly after the auditors had issued their opinion on United Bank's financial statements, the bank was found to be insolvent and was closed by the state banking commissioner. The auditors later were sued for negligence for not disclosing the problem loans.

Another sector affected by economic conditions in the 1990s was the farm equipment manufacturing industry. Deere & Co., Case Corp., Cummins Engine Co., and others dependent on the agricultural sector experienced financial hardship as a result of changing economic conditions in the farming industry. During this period the prices of most crops and livestock fell to their lowest levels in decades.[32] Declining export markets due to the Asian financial crisis, combined with declining crop and livestock revenues, forced farmers to retain old equipment rather than replace it with new equipment. As a result, new equipment sales declined drastically. Faced with a serious decline in revenue and experiencing large inventories of farm equipment and heavy debt service on outstanding loans, farm equipment manufacturers were forced to drastically curtail production and lay off thousands of employees. Auditors, under similar circumstances, should consider such information as a further sign of inherent risk and be particularly alert as to the proper valuation of inventories and accounts receivable. Economic slumps of this nature increase the probability of inventory overstocking and uncollectible receivables.

National Harvester Company, a farm equipment manufacturer, is used in Case 5.2 to illustrate the added inherent risk posed by this type of economic environment and the kind of audit approach needed to cope with it.

Information Concerning the Industry   Certain characteristics of the client's industry can also assist in inherent risk assessment. For example, in today's high-tech industries, large amounts of money are expended for research and development costs. CPAs performing audits of clients in these industries must therefore be alert to improper

32 *The Wall Street Journal,* August 18, 1999.

CASE 5.2

NATIONAL HARVESTER COMPANY
Case Description

National Harvester Company, for years a leader in the manufacture of farm equipment, had seen its revenues and profits grow steadily during the mid 1980s and early 1990s. Favorable commodity prices combined with booming export markets produced healthy cash flows for farmers. Given increased demand relative to supply, farmland prices began to regain some of the declines experienced during the farm recession of the late 1970s and early 1980s. As a result, farmers began to cultivate more acres and acquire more and bigger farm equipment. Tractors, combines, corn pickers, and "six-bottom" plows were in heavy demand. National Harvester, as was typical in the industry, financed many, if not most, of such purchases by farmers.

As long as interest rates were low and commodity prices stable, the farmers were able to meet the debt service payments on commodity and equipment loans. When commodity prices began to decline in the 1990s, however, farmers faced a liquidity crisis. The result was an inability to pay their loans and foreclosures by banks.

National Harvester, along with other farm equipment manufacturers, also experienced mounting liquidity problems as equipment sales declined and farmers defaulted on their equipment loans. As a result, the company filed under Chapter 11 shortly after the 1998 financial statements were released.

Compounding the liquidity problems, National Harvester had not adjusted production quickly enough in light of decreased demand. As a result, the 1998 financial statements reported inventories containing significant amounts of obsolete equipment. Had this equipment been adjusted to net realizable value, the reported profit of $1.2 million would have been transformed into a loss of $2.3 million.

What Would You Do?

The "economic gloom" surrounding this industry should have raised significant uncertainty questions in the minds of the auditors. Moreover, the steadily mounting inventories and declining quality of notes receivable should have caused them to question the valuation assertion. Specific concerns should have centered on collectibility of the notes and the increased risk of inventory obsolescence. This, in turn, should have led to increased audit concentration in the areas of inventories, notes receivable, and long-term liabilities.

What Was Done?

Susan Trimline, a four-year senior auditor for DeNutt & Stevens, CPAs, had been in charge of the 1998 audit of National. Harry Mack was the manager, and William DeNutt was the partner in charge. Five weeks of audit field work culminated in an unqualified opinion issued on February 16, 1999.

Instead of utilizing a risk-based approach, Trimline and her audit team conducted the standard examination. They did not examine loan collateral, and did not evaluate collectibility beyond applying standard percentages to outstanding receivables. These were the same percentages, incidentally, used during the years when farmers were prosperous and National's loan losses were insignificant. Moreover, the auditors applied standard procedures to test the costing of the inventories and did not test extensively for obsolescence. As a result, they took no exception to management's reporting of the inventories at full cost.

Consequences

Shortly after the company declared bankruptcy, the stockholders and creditors of National Harvester sued the auditors for negligence. In finding for the plaintiffs, the court held that study of the business and industry should have prompted the auditors to concentrate audit resources on examining inventories for obsolescence and loan collateral for adequacy.

capitalization of internally generated R&D costs as a means to inflate profits. Conversely, mergers of technology-based companies have given rise to questionable write-offs of purchased R&D as a means for avoiding goodwill amortization and also for the purpose of lowering the asset base of the combined companies. In 1995, for example, when IBM purchased Lotus Development Corporation, it charged nearly 60 percent of the purchase price to "purchased research and development" and included this in operating expenses in its 1995 income statement.[33] This treatment served to lower IBM's total asset base and thereby enabled the company to increase its percentage return on operating assets in subsequent years.

Auditors must also be alert to cyclical or seasonal factors unique to the industry. A textbook publisher, for example, ordinarily should not experience high revenues in June; ice cream sales should not peak in February; revenues from the sale of bicycles are usually low in January; and tax service revenues are not expected to be high in September. High reported revenues during traditionally low-revenue months should alert the auditor to possible revenue inflation.

Case 5.3, involving a major toy manufacturer, illustrates the importance of seasonal analysis and the need to allocate audit resources to areas of high audit risk, as revealed by the analysis. In this case, the company reported the heaviest sales of the year in December, which is traditionally the slowest month for this industry.

CASE 5.3

HIGHBELL TOY COMPANY
Case Description

Highbell Toy Company was one of the largest toy manufacturers in the United States. Over the years the company had experienced considerable success and steadily increasing profits. Expanded product lines, however, coupled with increasing severity of competition within the industry, had begun to put a squeeze on Highbell's profitability and liquidity.

In 1996, while the toy industry was suffering substantial losses in sales, Highbell found itself especially threatened. Unless additional financing could be obtained, the company faced the prospect of a cash flow crisis and possible loan defaults.

In the opinion of Highbell's management, however, additional financing could not be obtained unless the 1996 income statement showed an increase in profit over that of the preceding year. To effect the increase, Highbell's controller, in collusion with the

marketing vice president, fabricated a substantial number of fictitious December sales. Sales orders, shipping orders, bills of lading, and invoices were prepared for nonexistent sales. The customers were real, but the sales and shipments were not.

As an illustration of management's desperate attempts at profitability, the company purported to have shipped over $2 million of toys during the last Saturday in December. This would have been virtually impossible, given Highbell's shipping facilities at that time!

What Would You Do?

1. What warning signs should the auditors have identified, and what procedures would have enabled them to do so?
2. What assertions should the auditors have questioned relative to their findings in (1) above?
3. What procedures should the auditors have applied to satisfy themselves?

33 See *The Wall Street Journal*, December 2, 1996 and *1995 IBM Annual Report*.

The auditor should ascertain whether the client's industry is labor or capital intensive. Increasing labor costs, along with burgeoning technology, have prompted U.S. manufacturers to become increasingly automated. A capital-intensive, or highly automated, industry enjoys greater operating leverage due to high fixed costs relative to variable costs. This causes earnings to increase rapidly once the break-even point has been reached, but companies in these industries also face higher risk during periods of declining revenues because certain fixed costs remain stable regardless of the level of activity achieved. Under conditions of excess capacity, therefore, auditors must be alert to the increased probability of excessive amounts of fixed costs in ending inventories. In the presence of underutilization, the auditor needs to devote greater attention to analysis of overhead rates and the extent of capacity loss for the year.

The auditor also should be alert to the degree of competition within an industry, and how successfully the client is meeting the challenge posed by competitors' actions. An intensely competitive industry may suggest questions concerning inventory valuation. Large amounts of inventory carried at full cost, for example, may pose a valuation problem at a time when competition is forcing the industry to lower prices.

Companies in the computer, clothing, and toy industries face a greater risk of product obsolescence than companies in other industries. Auditors examining the financial statements of such companies, therefore, should be aware of the increased probability of inventory overstatement resulting from obsolescence.

Auditors frequently encounter accounting practices that are unique to the client's industry (e.g., banks, brokerage firms, film producers, and cable broadcasters). Under these circumstances, the auditor needs to determine whether the practice is in accordance with GAAP. The fact that other companies in the industry are applying the same accounting treatment to a particular class of transactions, or to a particular category of assets or equities, does *not* necessarily qualify the application as being in accordance with GAAP. Material departures from SFASs, APBs, ARBs, and other official pronouncement are assumed to be violations of GAAP, unless the client can demonstrate that application of GAAP would make the financial statements materially misleading.

A company engaged in manufacturing custom-made refrigeration equipment for ships and hospitals, decorating hotels and casinos, and building food service systems used a method referred to as "cost-to-cost percentage of completion" accounting. Under this method profits were recognized in proportion to the amount of money spent on materials, regardless of whether the materials had been used in existing projects. This practice was clearly at variance with GAAP, since revenues were recognized prior to having been either earned or realized. In one instance, the company borrowed $4 million to finance deck planking, most of which was still in the form of trees growing in forests at the time revenue was recognized.

Information Concerning the Business   In addition to gaining familiarity with the client's industry and economic conditions as they affect the industry, the auditor must gain a thorough understanding of the client's business operations, the kinds of transactions that occur, how the transactions are processed and recorded, and any other characteristics of the business that affect inherent risk. Inquiry of client personnel and discussions with predecessor auditors are means commonly utilized for obtaining business information.

If the client is new and was previously audited by other CPAs, an attempt should be made by the new auditor to communicate with the predecessor auditor. The purpose of the communication is to learn more about the nature of the client's business, and to elicit information from the predecessor auditor concerning management integrity and possible disagreements between the predecessor auditor and management. This information, in turn, provides further input into the client acceptance decision described earlier.

Communication usually assumes the form of discussions and examination of audit reports and the audit workpapers of the predecessor. AICPA Professional Standards require that the successor auditor attempt to communicate with the predecessor, but only with the client's permission.[34] If the client will not grant permission, the auditor generally should decline the engagement.

As an example of failure to communicate, a brokerage firm had overstated its assets by $45 million, when in reality the firm was insolvent and soon thereafter declared bankruptcy. Because the former auditors would not agree to the questionable asset valuation, the brokerage firm switched auditors. The rendering of an unqualified opinion by the successor auditors shortly before bankruptcy proceedings began raises a question as to whether or not the communication process, as required by GAAS, was even attempted by the successor auditors.

In addition to the preliminary discussions with the client and consultation with predecessor auditors, other means of gaining familiarity with the client's business include visiting major locations and talking with personnel; reviewing the prior year's financial statements and audit report (noting particularly any scope limitations or uncertainties); and obtaining and reviewing tax returns, policy and procedures manuals, and company forms and documents.

Analytical Procedures

Analytical procedures are used to highlight abnormalities, and hence provide another important mechanism for identifying high inherent risk areas. As discussed in Chapter 4, the most frequently applied analytical procedures include horizontal (trend) analysis, vertical (common size) analysis, and ratio analysis.

Although analytical procedures do *not* provide conclusive evidence, they do comprise a powerful means for identifying abnormalities caused by material errors or fraud. As applied in the audit planning stage, they also provide a basis for lowering materiality thresholds where significant earnings inflation is indicated. Computer software has enabled auditors to apply analytical procedures to a much greater extent than they could before. A recent application of the use of analytical procedures to assist in risk assessment involves the use of regression analysis to predict account balances and to evaluate differences between predicted and reported balances. If, for example, the auditor wishes to predict cost of sales by month in the period under audit, she or he might use regression analysis to determine the historical rate of change in cost of sales that is dependent on changes in sales. If reported and predicted sales differ markedly, the regression model can be utilized further to evaluate quantitatively the significance of the difference.[35]

In the Highbell Toy Company case involving the recording of fictitious December sales, application of analytical procedures would have revealed a material change relative to the prior year, as well as a monthly sales pattern significantly at variance with the

---

34 *AICPA Professional Standards*, op. cit., section AU 315.07-08.
35 For an excellent discussion of the use of regression analysis in audit risk assessment, see Robert J. Campbell and Larry J. Rankin, *The Ohio CPA Journal*, 49, No. 3, Autumn 1990, pp. 7–12.

industry norm. This, in turn, should have alerted the auditors to the increased probability of fraudulent financial reporting and caused them to place less reliance on internal evidence (sales orders, sales invoices, and bills of lading).

In another case, Bankers Trust Corp., a large investment and commercial bank (now a unit of Deutsche Bank AG), diverted $15.5 million of unclaimed customer funds to reserves that were used to bolster sagging earnings of future periods. The unclaimed funds arose as a result of client dividend and benefit checks not cashed by the payees. Rather than sending these unclaimed monies to the state after a specified period, as required by law, the company transferred them to the reserve accounts. The auditors, in applying analytical procedures to 1994 unaudited data, noticed that the unclaimed funds accounts had dropped from $10.2 million in 1993 to $3.9 million in 1994. Although they asked for records explaining the decline, these records were not forthcoming and the auditors ultimately detected the fraud by other means.[36] Case 5.4 presented below illustrates the pitfalls for the auditor who does not utilize analytical procedures as an integral part of the engagement.

Figure 5.6 summarizes the three phases of inherent risk assessment, as described in the preceding paragraphs. A means for classifying the risk factors identified previously is presented in the following section.

CASE 5.4

JOHNSON GRAIN HANDLERS
Case Description

Johnson Grain Handlers, a midwestern company, was a principal exporter of corn, wheat, and soybeans. Dock space was leased at Duluth and Chicago. Grain-handling facilities had been constructed by the company and were carried in the accounts as leasehold improvements. In 2000, Johnson expanded its operations to include Toledo and Cleveland. At the same time, the company decided to construct improved handling facilities at all locations to provide for more efficient loading of bulk grain.

In January 2000, Johnson's management requested National Illinois Bank of Chicago to increase an existing line of credit to help finance the expansion. The bank initially turned down the application, but later reversed its decision on the basis of Johnson's assurance that increased profitability would result from the improved handling facilities.

During 2000, as predicted, the company's reported income and earnings per share increased by 25 percent. The increase was effected primarily through significant decreases in operating expenses relative to gross revenues. Shortly after the financial statements were released, however, the company defaulted on its line of credit and was unable to meet further interest and principal payments. An investigation later determined that the reported increase in profits was fictitious and had resulted from capitalizing operating expenses as leasehold improvements. The purported improvements did *not* exist.

What Would You Do?

1. What warning signs should the auditors have identified, and what procedures would have enabled them to do so?
2. What assertions should the auditors have questioned relative to their findings in (1) above?
3. What procedures should the auditors have applied to satisfy themselves?

36 *New York Times*, May 30, 1999.

FIGURE 5.6

Inherent Risk Analysis

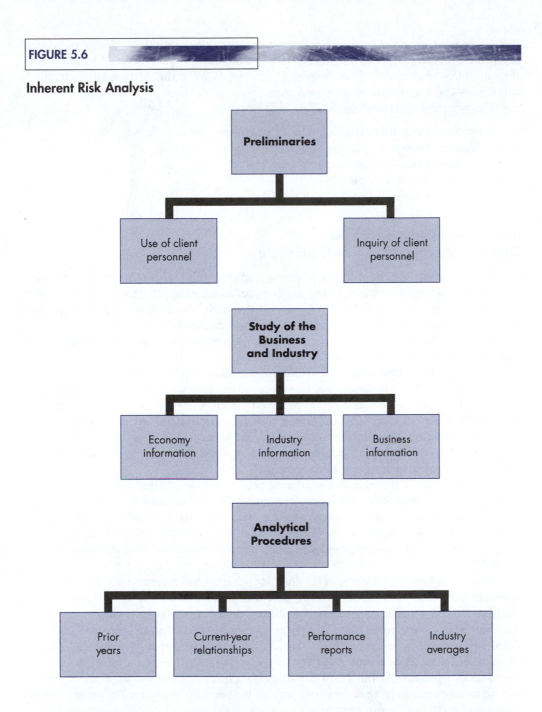

CLASSIFYING THE WARNING SIGNS

During the preliminary audit planning phase, the study of the business and industry, and the application of analytical procedures, the auditor documents all factors, referred to hereafter as **warning signs**, that are indicative of significant audit risk. AICPA Professional Standards specifically require the auditor to document "evidence of the performance of the assessment of the risk of material misstatement due to fraud."[37] Moreover, where high risk is present, the documentation "should include the risk factors identified and the auditor's response."[38] The "response" should address the setting of materiality thresholds and the design of audit programs.

The warning signs can be classified as follows:

1. Indicators of possible material financial statement errors or fraud;
2. Indicators of forces impacting earnings or liquidity;
3. Indicators of possible disclosure requirements;
4. Indicators of audit complexity; and
5. Indicators of possible fraudulent financial reporting.

Indicators of Possible Material Financial Statement Errors or Fraud

Perhaps the most important of the warning signs are the indicators that raise serious questions regarding errors or fraud in the financial statements. Such factors as abnormal ratios or trends and related-party transactions generally should lead to further investigation, given the high probability of errors or fraud caused by the occurrences.

Of somewhat lesser importance, but useful nevertheless as possible indicators of material misstatement, are IRS audits in progress and compensation or stock options tied to reported performance over which management has control. Significant adjustments presented by an IRS audit may be indicative of financial statement misstatements. Compensation or stock options tied to reported earnings always carry the risk that managers having control over the accounting process may be inclined to maximize their own compensation by selecting accounting principles that maximize reported earnings. Therefore, auditors must be particularly alert to the increased probability of earnings overstatement under these circumstances.

AOL (America Online) announced a "special one-time charge" to earnings in the amount of $385 million representing previously capitalized and deferred marketing costs. While these costs were being deferred, stock options that had been awarded to AOL executives as compensation continued to increase in value. By treating the write-off as a special one-time charge, management was able to avoid future earnings impairment.[39]

Other companies taking special one-time charges in recent years include Tyco International Ltd., Kerr-McGee Corp., SPX Corp., Halliburton Co., Citigroup Inc., Seagram Co., J.P. Morgan & Co., Amerada Hess Corp., Lear Corp., and Quaker Oats Co. Although special one-time charges due to corporate restructuring are permissible under GAAP, auditors must be alert to the inclusion of recurring operating expenses in these charges and also to write-downs of legitimate assets still possessing future economic benefit. SEC Chairman Arthur Levitt has labeled such restructuring charges as "big bath" hits to current earnings that pave the way to higher future profits. By writing assets down and including future operating expenses in the current one-time charge, future periods are relieved of expenses otherwise chargeable to them.[40] The thinking is that if

---

37 *AICPA Professional Standards*, op. cit., section AU 316.37.
38 Ibid.
39 See *The Wall Street Journal*, October 30, 1996 and November 7, 1996.
40 Levitt, Arthur, *The Numbers Game*, remarks delivered at the NYU Center for Law and Business, New York, NY, September 28, 1998.

a loss in the current year is imminent, take the "big bath" now and pave the way for an illusory earnings rebound in future periods.

Indicators of Forces Affecting Earnings or Liquidity

Certain factors over which management has little or no control can often produce a severe squeeze on earnings or liquidity. Intense competition from imports, a sluggish economy along with excess capacity, government regulations, highly inflexible debt agreements, high technology causing a threat of product obsolescence, and dependence on a single product or a small number of products or customers are all representative of this class of warning signs. Auditors need to consider these factors in audit planning for two reasons. First, asset valuation questions and possible violations of debt agreements may require audit adjustments or special footnote disclosures. Second, the present and projected impact on working capital may be so significant as to produce doubt about whether the entity can continue as a going concern. Under these circumstances, the auditor must consider whether to add an explanatory paragraph to the audit report expressing such doubt to financial statement users.

Indicators of Possible Disclosure Requirements

During discussions with the client and study of the business and industry, the auditor may discover circumstances requiring disclosure in the form of footnotes to the financial statements. An IRS audit or litigation in progress represents possible loss contingencies, and—depending on materiality, measurability, and degree of uncertainty—may require footnote disclosure or even accrual of the loss.

The existence of related parties and related-party transactions also might be discovered during this phase of the audit. If the transactions are material, footnote disclosure is required. The disclosures must identify the related party and the nature of the relationship, as well as the type, amounts, and volume of transactions involved. Rite Aid Corp. was questioned recently about certain real estate transactions between the company and its then CEO, Martin Grass, as well as Mr. Grass's financial interests in certain of the company's suppliers. These relationships had not been disclosed in the financial statements and were revealed in a lawsuit filed by a former executive who had been fired by the company.[41]

Indicators of Audit Complexity

Study of the client's business and industry may reveal conditions creating higher-than-normal audit complexity. Certain types of inventory, for example, may require special expertise for valuation; or the auditor may discover that a major part of the client's accounting system is online, posing complex computer audit questions. Early identification of the conditions permits the auditor to retain specialists well in advance and otherwise modify audit programs in consideration of the complexities involved. In these cases, an appraiser may be needed for inventory valuation and a computer audit specialist may be required for assistance in evaluating computer controls and in performing substantive audit tests.

41 *The Wall Street Journal*, February 19, 1999 and March 2, 1999.

Discovery of unique accounting practices utilized by the client in recording and re-porting significant classes of transactions also may produce conditions of high audit complexity—especially if other companies in the industry also use the unique practices and appear to be at variance with GAAP. Under these circumstances, the auditor must determine whether the "departure from a principle promulgated by the body desig-nated by Council" can be justified on the basis that conformity to the principle desig-nated by Council would make the financial statements materially misleading, or whether the principle is being inappropriately applied. The complexities presented by the application of unique practices usually require that extended audit procedures be applied to the transaction cycles affected. In this regard, early identification permits more effective audit planning, both in terms of the nature and extent of the procedures to be applied.

Indicators of Possible Management Dishonesty

Warning signs that cause the auditor to question management integrity must be taken seriously and pursued vigorously. The auditor must determine whether the suspicions aroused by the warning signs have validity and, if so, whether under the circumstances the auditor can continue to be associated with the financial statements.[42] AICPA Professional Standards suggest that the auditor "may conclude that it is not practicable to modify the (audit) procedures . . . sufficiently to address the risk. In that case with-drawal from the engagement with communication to the appropriate parties may be an appropriate course of action."[43] KPMG's withdrawal from the Rite Aid audit, as dis-cussed earlier, and notification of the SEC is an example of inability to rely on manage-ment's representations. Additionally, the auditor has a responsibility to communicate illegal acts, as well as other findings of this nature, to the audit committee of the client's board of directors.[44]

Examples of warning signs raising questions concerning management integrity in-clude the following:

1. Increasing interest by management in earnings-per-share effects of accounting al-ternatives;
2. Changes in accounting principles that favorably impact reported earnings;
3. Indications of personal financial difficulty on the part of senior management;
4. A complex corporate structure not warranted by corporate size;
5. Sale of real estate with complex or unusual terms;
6. High turnover rate in key management positions;
7. Material transactions with related parties;
8. Large or unusual transactions at year end;
9. Judgmental allowances (e.g., bad debts, inventory obsolescence, and product war-ranty) consistently estimated at or near the low end of reasonableness;
10. Recent significant sales of stock by insiders; and
11. Progressive deterioration in the quality of earnings.[45]

42 As an example, the independent auditor for Home Theater Products resigned in 1995 citing "significant weaknesses in internal control and *concerns about management integrity* [italics added]." *Los Angeles Times*, October 10, 1995.
43 *AICPA Professional Standards*, op. cit., section AU 316.26.
44 Ibid, section AU 317.
45 With respect to the last warning sign (no. 11), "quality of earnings" relates to the accounting principles applied by the entity. Principles that produce early revenue recognition or excessive deferral of costs are viewed by the financial statement users as reducing the quality of reported earnings through possible overstatement, as contrasted with reported earnings re-sulting from the application of more conservative accounting practices.

With regard to No. 9, judgmental allowances, SEC Chairman Levitt suggested that some companies create "cookie jar reserves" by overestimating the allowances in profitable periods to provide a buffer against possible earnings declines in future periods.[46] The result is *income smoothing*, which enables the companies to report constant earnings growth over several accounting periods.

RISK ANALYSIS MATRIX

Table 5.1 incorporates the discussion contained in the preceding pages into a risk analysis matrix, matching warning signs with sources of information available to the auditor for identifying the warning signs. The matrix is organized as follows:

Warning Signs
- Indicators of possible material financial statement errors or fraud
- Indicators of external or internal forces affecting earnings or liquidity
- Indicators of possible disclosure requirements
- Indicators of audit complexity
- Indicators of possible management dishonesty

Sources of Information
- Management inquiry
- Auditor's workpapers
- Internal documents
- External documents
- Predecessor auditor
- Analytical procedures

TABLE 5.1

Risk Analysis Matrix

	Source of Information					
Warning Sign	**Mgmt. Inquiry 1**	**Auditor's Workpapers 2**	**Internal Documents 3**	**External Documents 4**	**Predecessor Auditor**	**Analytical Procedures**
I. INDICATORS OF POSSIBLE MATERIAL FINANCIAL STATEMENT ERRORS OR FRAUD						
a. IRS audit	x		x		x	
b. Related-party transactions	x	x	x		x	
c. Abnormal ratios or trends						x
d. Compensation or stock options tied to reported performance over which management has control	x	x	x		x	
e. Inventory increase without comparable sales increase						x
II. INDICATORS OF EXTERNAL OR INTERNAL FORCES AFFECTING EARNINGS OR LIQUIDITY						
a. Import competition	x	x	x	x	x	
b. Sluggish economy or excess capacity	x		x	x	x	x

(continued)

46 Remarks of Arthur Levitt, op. cit., September 28, 1998.

TABLE 5.1

(continued)

Warning Sign	Mgmt. Inquiry 1	Auditor's Workpapers 2	Internal Documents 3	External Documents 4	Predecessor Auditor	Analytical Procedures
c. Government regulations affecting the company or industry	x	x	x	x	x	
d. Highly inflexible debt agreements	x	x	x		x	
e. Narrowing profit margins due to declining sales volume, cost increases, etc.			x		x	x
f. Decreasing working capital causing liquidity squeeze			x			x
g. High-technology industry causing threat of product obsolescence	x	x		x	x	
h. Reduction in sales order backlog					x	x
i. Slowdown in customer collections					x	x
j. Difficulty in obtaining credit			x	x	x	
k. Dependence on a single product or small number of products or customers	x	x		x	x	
l. Rapidly growing or declining industry		x		x	x	
III. INDICATORS OF POSSIBLE DISCLOSURE REQUIREMENTS						
a. IRS audit	x		x			
b. Pending litigation	x		x		x	
c. Existence of related parties and related-party transactions	x	x	x		x	
IV. INDICATORS OF AUDIT COMPLEXITY						
a. Inventories requiring special expertise for valuation	x	x	x	x	x	
b. Complex EDP applications	x	x	x		x	
c. Unique industry accounting practices	x	x	x	x	x	
d. Prior year's audit report qualified because of scope limitation		x	x			
e. Ineffective board of directors or audit committee	x	x	x			
V. INDICATORS OF POSSIBLE MANAGEMENT DISHONESTY						
a. Indications of control override		x			x	x

TABLE 5.1

(continued)

Warning Sign	Source of Information					
	Mgmt. Inquiry 1	Auditor's Workpapers 2	Internal Documents 3	External Documents 4	Predecessor Auditor	Analytical Procedures
b. Increasing interest by management in EPS effects of accounting alternatives	x	x	x		x	
c. Indications of personal financial difficulty of senior management	x		x		x	
d. Proxy contests	x		x		x	
e. Complex corporate structure not warranted by corporation's size		x	x		x	
f. High turnover rate in key positions	x	x	x		x	
g. Frequent change of auditors or legal counsel	x	x	x		x	
h. Material transactions with related parties	x	x	x		x	
i. Large or unusual transactions at year end			x			x
j. Client pressure to complete audit in unusually short time		x			x	
k. Management reluctance to provide auditors with clear explanations	x	x			x	
l. Progressive deterioration in the "quality" of earnings		x			x	x
m. Existence of significant litigation, especially between shareholders and management	x		x		x	
n. Significant tax adjustments by IRS, especially if a regular occurrence	x	x	x		x	
o. Unmarketable collateral	x	x	x		x	

Key to Sources:

1. Management inquiry:
   a. Preliminary discussions with management
   b. Discussion during tour of major locations

2. Auditor's workpapers:
   a. Permanent file
   b. Current file (last year)

3. Internal documents:
   a. Correspondence files and minutes of meetings
   b. Prior financial statements and audit report
   c. Accounting manuals

   d. Policy and procedures manuals
   e. Company forms and documents
   f. List of stockholders (if small or closely held company)

4. External documents:
   a. AICPA audit and accounting guides
   b. Industry trade publications
   c. Government publications
   d. Moody's, Standard & Poor's, Robert Morris Associates
   e. Credit reports (Dun & Bradstreet, banks, etc.)

The permanent audit workpaper file contains much of the information referenced in the matrix; for this reason, it can be very helpful to the auditor in analyzing inherent risk. The existence of related parties and types of related-party transactions, compensation or stock option plans tied to reported earnings, debt agreements, nature of operations and competition, computer-based information systems applications, unique inventories requiring special expertise for valuation, the corporate structure, and unique industry accounting practices are all contained in the permanent file. New staff members assigned to the audit for the first time should be asked to review the permanent file along with the prior year's current file in order to gain some familiarity with the client's operations prior to engaging in the audit field work.

Both internal and external documents also contain information essential to effective inherent risk assessment. Correspondence files and minutes of directors' meetings may reveal related parties and related-party transactions. These sources may also disclose possible loan defaults, as well as authorization of new loan agreements. Minutes of the board of directors' meetings frequently discuss earnings performance and liquidity problems, both of which are of interest to the auditor in analyzing risk.

AICPA audit and accounting guides, along with industry publications, shed light on unique accounting practices and particular audit complexities that might be encountered due to the unique characteristics of the client's industry. To the extent that the client has experienced difficulties in obtaining credit or in meeting the terms of existing debt agreements, the reports of such credit agencies as Dun & Bradstreet will reflect the relevant conditions and circumstances.

In summary, the matrix, although not meant to be exhaustive, contains the major warning signs and sources of information that are significant in assessing inherent risk. Use of this type of matrix, therefore, ensures that all aspects of inherent risk are taken into account during the audit planning phase.[47]

INCORPORATING INHERENT RISK ASSESSMENT INTO THE AUDIT

Risk-Driven versus Procedures-Driven Audits

In 1988, the General Accounting Office (GAO) completed a review of the quality of audits of savings and loan associations in the Dallas Federal Home Loan Bank District. The GAO study focused on eleven audits of savings and loans (S&Ls) that failed during the 1985–1987 period. The GAO concluded that six of the eleven audits were substandard in *not* adequately assessing and dealing with audit risk.[48] The lesson to be learned from this study is that if auditors are to narrow the expectations gap and fulfill their responsibility for detecting material errors and fraud, audits must be "risk driven." A **risk-driven audit** is one that carefully analyzes audit risk, sets materiality thresholds based on audit risk analysis, and develops audit programs that allocate a larger proportion of audit resources to high-risk areas. A **procedures-driven audit**, on the other hand, utilizes standard audit programs regardless of varying levels of audit risk. This approach has two

---

47 For further discussion and listing of warning signs, see Vicky B. Heiman-Hoffman, Kimberly P. Morgan, and James M. Patton, "The Warning Signs of Fraudulent Financial Reporting," *The Journal of Accountancy*, October 1996, pp. 75–77; see also Howard Groveman, "How Auditors Can Detect Financial Statement Misstatement," *The Journal of Accountancy*, October 1995, pp. 83–86.

48 United States General Accounting Office, *CPA Audit Quality*, Report to the Chairman, Committee on Banking, Finance, and Urban Affairs, House of Representatives, Washington, D.C., February 1989.

major weaknesses. First, it results in over-auditing in low-risk areas and underauditing in high-risk areas. Second, procedures-driven audits, by not concentrating resources in high-risk areas, greatly increase the probability of undetected errors and fraud. The findings in the GAO report referred to earlier suggest that some, if not most, of the S&L audits covered in the report were procedures driven.

Generally accepted auditing standards currently require CPAs to conduct risk-driven audits. Section AU 316 of the AICPA Professional Standards, as amended in 1997, states that the auditor should "specifically assess the risk of material misstatement of the financial statements due to fraud and should consider that assessment in designing the audit procedures to be performed." Given this requirement, the thrust of this and the ensuing chapters will be in the direction of careful analysis of audit risk and the development of audit programs that fully account for assessed risk.

Preliminary Audit Programs

Based on the discussions with the client, the auditor's study of the client's business and industry, application of analytical procedures, and study of internal control, **preliminary audit programs** may be designed. These programs should reflect the auditor's acceptable level of audit risk, his or her assessment of inherent risk and control risk, and the resulting impact on detection risk.

Figure 5.7 is an expansion of the audit risk equation presented previously, and provides guidance for relating the auditor's assessment of inherent risk and control risk to varying levels of detection risk, given a constant level of overall audit risk. In this model, inherent risk is a function of the results of analytical procedures, the auditor's assessment of fraud, and the auditor's assessment of audit complexity.

As discussed earlier, low detection risk requires expanded substantive procedures, while high detection risk permits minimal substantive testing. Note that under conditions of both high inherent and high control risk, the auditor performs a **primarily substantive audit**. Conversely, the combination of low inherent and low control risk may limit substantive testing to little more than analytical procedures. The latter situation is rare in practice, and the auditor should exercise caution in pursuing such a program.

As an example of high inherent risk, a sharp decline in accounts receivable turnover, as revealed by the application of analytical procedures during the audit planning stage, may be the result of a weakness in the credit and collection function, or it may be indicative of inflated accounts receivable. Detection risk, therefore, should be set at a relatively low level, and the audit program for sales and accounts receivable, under these circumstances, should be extended—particularly in the areas of evaluating the adequacy of the allowance for doubtful accounts and determining the validity of accounts receivable. If accounts receivable are materially inflated, extending the confirmation process (using external evidence) should detect the overstatements. Increased attention to sales transactions recorded at or near year end may likewise detect the recording of next year's sales during the current year. The auditor may elect to confirm the more significant of these recorded transactions. The importance of this form of confirmation reflects the need to rely more heavily on external (confirmation) evidence relative to internal (documentary) evidence when fraudulent financial reporting is suspected.

If the declining receivables turnover is the result of a weakening of the credit and collection function, the probability of uncollectible accounts increases, and the analysis of the allowance for doubtful accounts should be expanded accordingly. Expansion

FIGURE 5.7

Determining the Required Level of Detection Risk for Planning and Substantive Audit Tests

(1) Results of Analytical Procedures	(2) Auditor's Assessment of Fraud	(3) Auditor's Assessment of Audit Complexity (based on study of the business)	(4) Auditor's Assessment of Inherent Risk (1), (2), and (3)	(5) Auditor's Assessment of Control Risk	(6) Required Level of Detection Risk (4) and (5)
Significant Abnormalities	High	High	High	High	Very low [a]
No Significant Abnormalities	Low	Moderate	Low	High	Low
Significant Abnormalities	High	Moderate	High	Low	Low
No Significant Abnormalities	High	High	High	Low	Moderate to low
Significant Abnormalities	Low	Low	Moderate	Low	Moderate to high
No Significant Abnormalities	Low	Low	Low	Low	_ _ _ _ _ [b]

[a]A primarily substantive audit is indicated.

[b]Substantive tests may be limited essentially to analytical procedures.

might assume the form of extended analysis of subsequent collections of year-end accounts receivable.

The procedures cited in the illustration are not unique. They are, however, selected and applied by the auditor based on the unique characteristics of the client being audited. The problem areas, revealed by inherent risk analysis, prompt an expansion of the procedures beyond the degree normally applied, and also impact the form of audit evidence. The auditor, in other words must vary the nature or timing, as well as the extent, of audit procedures in order to deal adequately with identified audit risk. As another example, a material decline in "revenue from scrap sales" might prompt the auditor to confirm the nonexistence of transactions with the client's scrap dealers (testing for omissions), a procedure that would *not* be applied under ordinary circumstances.

A final point needs to be considered relative to preliminary audit programs. As discussed in Chapter 4, a major factor considered by the auditor in the design of audit programs is the potential for misstatement, as revealed by the study and testing of the client's system of internal control. At this stage in the audit process, however, testing of internal control has not yet been completed. During the audit planning phase, the auditor will have obtained a basic understanding of the client's internal control and will have made a preliminary assessment of control risk. This assessment is subject to further modification, however, if the auditor decides to test the controls (this process is covered at length in Chapter 7). For this reason, the programs developed upon completion of audit planning are referred to as *preliminary audit programs*. The programs as modified after testing of selected internal controls are referred to as *final audit programs*. Recall the sequence of audit steps leading to the rendering of the audit report:

1. Audit *planning* and risk assessment;
2. Modification of assessed control risk through testing;
3. *Conducting* the audit through substantive audit testing; and
4. Preparation of the audit *report*.[49]

In simplified terms, the auditing model may now be expressed thus:

> PLAN
> CONDUCT
> REPORT

The current file of audit workpapers, as described in Chapter 4, should provide ample evidence of completing these three phases of the audit.

Time Budgets and Staff Scheduling

Having reached a preliminary assessment of inherent risk and control risk (Chapter 7) and having designed preliminary audit programs in light of this assessment, the auditor now may prepare a **time budget** and determine audit staff needs for the engagement. Exhibit 5.4 illustrates an audit time budget. The time budget estimates the hours required to complete each phase of the audit. It is broken down as to audit area and level of staff person (e.g., assistant, senior auditor, manager, partner). The timing of specific needs (i.e., interim audit work, inventory observation and other year-end procedures, final audit work) should also be included in the time budget in order to facilitate staff scheduling.

The time budget is usually prepared by the in-charge auditor, subject to review by the manager or audit partner. Factors to be considered in its preparation are as follows:

1. Nature of the audit client;
2. Assessment of inherent risk (including fraud assessment);

---

49 This sequence is not rigid. Analytical procedures, for example, are substantive audit procedures, notwithstanding their application during both the audit planning and the review phases. Moreover, control weaknesses overlooked during the internal control study and evaluation phase may come to light during substantive testing and require further audit program modification at that point.

EXHIBIT 5.4

Time Budget

Jones and Journey, Inc.
Time Accounting and Budget
December 31, 2001

Audit Area	Staff Assistant 1	Staff Assistant 2	In-Charge Senior	Manager	Partner	Support Staff	Budgeted Hours	Actual Hours	Explanation of Variance
Cash	30		2				32	28	
Accounts receivable		60	5				65	110	See WP 20: Many exceptions to confirmation requests
Inventory	30	30	5				65	96	
Plant assets	20		10				30	33	
Investments			5				5	7	
Other assets			5				5	3	
Accounts payable	10	10	3				23	22	See WP 30: Failure to achieve proper cutoff
Long-term debt and equity			10				10	20	Debt restructuring required more audit hours
Revenue and expense accounts			5				5	7	
Payroll	10		5				15	12	
Pension, profit sharing, etc.			20				20	23	
Planning, review and supervise			25	10	5		40	38	
Reports				10	5		15	15	
Taxes	20		5		3		28	26	
Typing and proofreading						8	8	7	
	120	100	105	20	13	8	366	447	

3. Preliminary assessment of control risk (subject to modification resulting from testing of controls);
4. Prior year's time budget and its relationship to actual time (if a recurring audit);
5. Whether staff members have previous audit experience with the client; and
6. Required expertise.

Once the time budget has been prepared, personnel may be assigned to the audit. In scheduling people, the firm should take into account the degree of participation by the client's employees.

As various parts of the audit are completed, the actual times should be posted to the time budget and compared with the projected times. Comparison assists in two ways. First, it serves as input into the preparation of next year's time budget. Second, to the extent that overruns result from weaknesses in the client's accounting system, the added hours may be considered chargeable and included in the client billing. However, additional hours that are the result of using inexperienced audit staff personnel should *not* be billed to the client.

In recurring engagements, the prior year's budget may be used as a starting point for preparing the current budget. Times then can be modified for changed conditions (e.g., changes in inherent risk, changes in internal accounting control, changes in client personnel, or changes in audit personnel).

The Preaudit Conference

Given its significance and complexity, much of the inherent risk assessment, including the preliminary discussions with the client, will be performed by the in-charge senior auditor, with the possible participation of the audit manager. Once this phase of the audit has been completed, and the client has been accepted, a **preaudit conference** should be convened by the in-charge auditor. All persons involved in the audit field work should be included in the conference. The purpose of the preaudit conference is to increase the effectiveness of the audit by discussing the results of risk analysis with the staff members comprising the "audit team." The nature of the client's business, the organizational structure, major locations of operations, and key features of the accounting system and control procedures should also be covered during the preaudit conference.

Of major importance during the conference is the identification of warning signs detected during audit planning and risk analysis, making certain that the persons assigned to the audit are fully aware of the high-risk areas associated with their respective assignments.

KEY TERMS

COMPUTER AUDIT PRACTICE CASE

Biltrite Bicycles, Inc.

As part of the end-of-chapter materials for Chapters 5 through 14, optional assignments will be made from the Biltrite Bicycles audit practice case presented in the appendix following Chapter 16. This case consists of fifteen modules. Each module relates to one or more audit phases and can be completed with the aid of a computer. The assignments at the end of each chapter parallel the chapter discussion and require the student to analyze files, make changes where appropriate, and draft audit adjustments and reclassifications. Several questions concerning specific audit issues also must be answered in completing the modules included in each assignment.

Completing the assignments requires the use of a data CD containing partially completed audit workpapers. This CD is provided free of charge by South-Western College Publishing. The workpapers on the CD may be accessed and completed by using Excel or Excel-compatible spreadsheet software. Instructions for completing the workpapers as well as meeting other requirements are contained in the Biltrite appendix.

For Chapter 5 purposes, complete Module I: Assessment of inherent risk.

REVIEW QUESTIONS

1. The auditor considers materiality while planning the audit, conducting the audit, and evaluating audit results. Explain.

2. Differentiate between individual item materiality and aggregate materiality.

3. How does the expected number of errors affect aggregate materiality?

4. In Staff Accounting Bulletin (SAB) 99, the SEC stated that the use of a quantitative method alone to assess materiality is not acceptable. Explain.

5. Why are the relationships among materiality, risk, and audit evidence important considerations in the development of audit programs?

6. Differentiate between errors and fraud. Identify and define the types of errors and fraud.

7. AICPA standards require that the auditor design the audit to provide reasonable assurance of detecting material misstatements. In assessing the risk of misstatement due to fraud, how does the auditor meet the above requirement?

8. Define the terms *audit risk*, *inherent risk*, *control risk*, and *detection risk*.

9. In what way is materiality related to audit risk?

10. State audit risk in equation form.

11. Which of the audit risk components is controllable by the auditor?

12. Why is overall audit risk set low?

13. Restate the audit risk equation in a form more useful to the auditor. Why is this form of the equation more useful?

14. Assuming that overall audit risk is set at 5 percent, and control risk is estimated at 30 percent, calculate the detection risk percentage (assume inherent risk = 100 percent).

15. At what point in the audit process does the auditor deal with inherent risk? Control risk?

16. How does audit planning assist in assessing inherent risk?

17. What are the three phases of inherent risk assessment? How does each phase assist in inherent risk assessment?

18. Name three sources of business and industry information.

19. SAS No. 84 requires the successor auditor to request permission from the client to communicate with the predecessor auditor. How does this form of communication assist in audit risk assessment?

20 Discuss analytical procedures in terms of their audit risk assessment features.

21. What are warning signs and how are they useful to the auditor?

22. Name the five classes of warning signs of importance to the auditor, giving two examples of each class.

23. Warning signs that cause the auditor to question management integrity must be taken seriously and pursued vigorously. Explain.

24. Differentiate between preliminary and final audit programs.

25. What is the purpose of the audit time budget?

26. How does the preaudit conference increase the effectiveness of the audit?

27. Differentiate between risk-driven audits and procedures-driven audits. How does SAS No. 82 support the concept of risk-driven audits?

28. Name and briefly define the three steps in the audit process model.

MULTIPLE CHOICE QUESTIONS FROM PAST CPA EXAMS

1. For which of the following judgments may an independent auditor share responsibility with an entity's internal auditor who is assessed to be both competent and objective?

	Materiality of misstatements	*Evaluation of accounting estimates*
a.	Yes	No
b.	No	Yes
c.	No	No
d.	Yes	Yes

2. An auditor assesses control risk because it
    a. Indicates where inherent risk may be the greatest.
    b. Affects the level of detection risk the auditor may accept.
    c. Determines whether sampling risk is sufficiently low.
    d. Includes the aspects of nonsampling risk that are controllable.

3. The acceptable level of detection risk is inversely related to the
   a. Assurance provided by substantive tests.
   b. Risk of misapplying auditing procedures.
   c. Preliminary judgment about materiality levels.
   d. Risk of failing to discover material misstatements.

4. Inherent risk and control risk differ from detection risk in that inherent risk and control risk are
   a. Elements of audit risk while detection risk is not.
   b. Changed at the auditor's discretion while detection risk is not.
   c. Considered at the individual account balance level while detection risk is not.
   d. Functions of the client and its environment while detection risk is not.

5. Analytical procedures used in planning an audit should focus on identifying
   a. Material weaknesses in the internal control system.
   b. The predictability of financial data from individual transactions.
   c. The various assertions that are embodied in the financial statements.
   d. Areas that may represent specific risks relevant to the audit.

6. Before accepting an audit engagement, a successor auditor should make specific inquiries of the predecessor auditor regarding
   a. Disagreements the predecessor had with the client concerning auditing procedures and accounting principles.
   b. The predecessor's evaluation of matters of continuing accounting significance.
   c. The degree of cooperation the predecessor received concerning the inquiry of the client's lawyer.
   d. The predecessor's assessments of inherent risk and judgments about materiality.

7. As the acceptable level of detection risk decreases, an auditor may change the
   a. Timing of substantive tests by performing them at an interim date rather than at year-end.
   b. Nature of substantive tests from a less effective to a more effective procedure.
   c. Timing of tests of controls by performing them at several dates rather than at one time.
   d. Assessed level of inherent risk to a higher amount.

8. The audit work performed by each assistant should be reviewed to determine whether it was adequately performed and to evaluate whether the
   a. Audit has been performed by persons having adequate technical training and proficiency as auditors.
   b. Auditor's system of quality control has been maintained at a high level.
   c. Results are consistent with the conclusions to be presented in the auditor's report.
   d. Audit procedures performed are approved in the Professional Standards.

9. The element of the audit planning process most likely to be agreed upon with the client before implementation of the audit strategy is the determination of the
   a. Timing of inventory observation procedures to be performed.
   b. Evidence to be gathered to provide a sufficient basis for the auditor's opinion.
   c. Procedures to be undertaken to discover litigation, claims, and assessments.
   d. Pending legal matters to be included in the inquiry of the client's attorney.

10. On the basis of audit evidence gathered and evaluated, an auditor decides to increase the assessed level of control risk from that originally planned. To achieve an overall audit risk level that is substantially the same as the planned audit risk level, the auditor would

    a. Increase inherent risk.

    b. Increase materiality levels.

    c. Decrease substantive testing.

    d. Decrease detection risk.

11. As the acceptable level of detection risk decreases, the assurance directly provided from

    a. Substantive tests should increase.

    b. Substantive tests should decrease.

    c. Tests of controls should increase.

    d. Tests of controls should decrease.

12. Which of the following audit risk components may be assessed in nonquantitative terms?

	Control risk	Detection risk	Inherent risk
a.	Yes	Yes	Yes
b.	No	Yes	Yes
c.	Yes	Yes	No
d.	Yes	No	Yes

13. Which of the following is ordinarily designed to detect possible material dollar errors on the financial statements?

    a. Control testing

    b. Analytical procedures

    c. Computer controls

    d. Postaudit workpaper review

14. In considering materiality for planning purposes, an auditor believes that misstatements aggregating $10,000 would have a material effect on an entity's income statement, but that misstatements would have to aggregate $20,000 to materially affect the balance sheet. Ordinarily, it would be appropriate to design auditing procedures that would be expected to detect misstatements that aggregate

    a. $10,000.

    b. $15,000.

    c. $20,000.

    d. $30,000.

15. Which of the following procedures would an auditor least likely perform in planning a financial statement audit?

    a. Coordinating the assistance of entity personnel in data preparation

    b. Discussing matters that may affect the audit with firm personnel responsible for nonaudit services to the entity

    c. Selecting a sample of vendors' invoices for comparison to receiving reports

    d. Reading the current year's interim financial statements

16. Which of the following statements best describes an auditor's responsibility to detect errors and fraud?

    a. The auditor should study and evaluate the client's internal control system, and design the audit to provide reasonable assurance of detecting all errors and fraud.

    b. The auditor should assess the risk that errors and fraud may cause the financial statements to contain material misstatements, and determine whether the necessary internal control procedures are prescribed and are being followed satisfactorily.

    c. The auditor should consider the types of errors and fraud that could occur, and determine whether the necessary internal control procedures are prescribed and are being followed.

    d. The auditor should assess the risk that errors and fraud may cause the financial statements to contain material misstatements, and design the audit to provide reasonable assurance of detecting material errors and fraud.

17. Which of the following comparisons would be most useful to an auditor in evaluating the results of an entity's operations?

    a. Prior year accounts payable to current year accounts payable

    b. Prior year payroll expense to budgeted current year payroll expense

    c. Current year revenue to budgeted current year revenue

    d. Current year warranty expense to current year contingent liabilities

INTERNET ACTIVITIES

.com

http://
annualreportservice.com

Using the same companies that you selected in the Chapter 4 Internet assignment, return to the Public Register's *Annual Report Service* at http://annualreportservice.com and calculate the following materiality thresholds:

1. Individual item for audit adjustment purposes;
2. Individual item for audit reclassification purposes;
3. Aggregate for audit adjustment purposes; and
4. Aggregate for audit reclassification purposes.

For purposes of this assignment, assume the thresholds are:

Individual item:
    4% of net income
    1% of net assets

Aggregate:
    High risk environment: 5% of individual item threshold
    Low-risk environment: 15% of individual item threshold

The percentages you select should be based in your findings in the Chapter 4 Internet assignment (i.e., evaluate inherent risk based on the ratios you calculated in that assignment.)

ESSAY QUESTIONS AND PROBLEMS

5.1   For each of the following situations explain how audit risk has been increased, and how risk can be reduced through the modification of audit programs (i.e., what kinds of auditing procedures should be applied in each case in order to keep audit risk within acceptable bounds).

    a. While conducting a study of the business, Kenneth Hammer, the in-charge auditor on the newly acquired Colony audit, discovers that Colony owns 60 percent of the stock of Yonkers, Inc., and that Yonkers has never been audited.

    b. Jamison International Products Company, an audit client of Pharmley & Associates, CPAs, completed construction of three highly automated plants during the current year. Funding of the construction required some rather unique financing arrangements, including sale and leaseback of two of the plants. Much of Jamison's present production is being transferred to the new, more efficient plants.

    c. Agrimachines, Inc., a farm equipment manufacturer, follows a policy of guaranteeing the indebtedness of farm operators purchasing Agrimachines' farm equipment. Given the significance of some of the loans, Agrimachines has seen fit to require collateral in the form of second mortgages on some of the farms owned by the purchasers. Because of depressed land and commodity prices, combined with increased liquidity problems faced by the operators, a significant portion of the loans are in danger of default.

    d. In applying analytical procedures to the financial data of Sonic Software, Jared Mohler, a newly assigned assistant auditor, discovers that Sonic's net profit margin has remained at approximately 12 percent, while, for the most part, the industry has been suffering losses.

5.2   The board of directors of Danson Corp. asked Jameel & Solen, CPAs, to audit Danson's financial statements for the year ended December 31, 1999. Jameel & Solen explained the need to make an inquiry of the predecessor auditor and requested permission to do so. Danson's board refused to honor the request on the grounds that relations with the predecessor had deteriorated so significantly that Jameel & Solen would receive biased and defamatory information from the predecessor.

Required:

a. What is the purpose of the communication between the successor and predecessor auditors?

b. How does communication aid in assessing audit risk?

c. What position should Jameel & Solen assume in the present situation? How should they respond to Danson's refusal to permit communication with the predecessor?

5.3   Sarah Slagle is the in-charge auditor with administrative responsibilities for the upcoming annual audit of RS Company, a continuing audit client. Slagle will supervise two assistants on the engagement and will visit the client before the field work begins.

    Slagle has started the planning process by preparing a list of procedures to be performed prior to the beginning of field work. The list includes the following:

1. Review correspondence and permanent files.
2. Review prior years' audit workpapers, financial statements, and auditor's reports.
3. Discuss with CPA firm personnel responsible for audit and nonaudit services to the client matters that may affect the examination.
4. Discuss with management current business developments affecting the client.

Required:

Complete Slagle's list of procedures to be performed prior to the beginning of field work. (AICPA adapted)

5.4   Schafer, CPA, audited Sloan Company's financial statements for the year ended December 31, 2001. On November 1, 2002, Sloan notified Schafer that it was changing auditors and that Schafer's services were being terminated. On November 5, 2002, Sloan invited Anderson, CPA, to make a proposal for an engagement to audit its financial statements for the year ended December 31, 2002.

Required:

a. What procedures concerning Schafer should Anderson perform before accepting the engagement?

b. What additional procedures should Anderson consider performing during the planning phase of this audit (after acceptance of the engagement) that would *not* be performed during the audit of a continuing client?

(AICPA adapted)

5.5   Olson & Treuhaft, CPAs, presented the following audit risk analysis exercise during a staff training seminar:

	AR	CR	IR
Client A:	5%	70%	80%
Client B:	5%	55%	50%
Client C:	10%	30%	40%

Required:

a. Calculate detection risk for each client.

b. Explain how audit emphasis might be different for each of the three clients.

5.6   Assume that during the audit planning phase for a client that manufactures audio components, the auditor sets materiality thresholds based on the following unaudited balances:

Total assets	$25.0 million
Net income	$4.0 million
Liabilities	$7.0 million
Current assets	$9.0 million
Current liabilities	$3.5 million
Net working capital	$5.5 million

Required:

a. Assuming the auditor considers misstatements of net assets of 3 percent or more and misstatements of net income of 7 percent or more to be material, determine the individual item materiality threshold to be used for audit planning purposes. How would this threshold change if, based on past experience with this client, the auditor suspects significant amounts of earnings inflation?

b. During the implementation of audit programs developed on the basis of (a), the auditor discovered the following errors.

1. The allowance for doubtful accounts is understated by approximately $200,000.

2. Nonreimbursable research and development expenditures totaling $420,000 were debited to a noncurrent asset account titled "deferred development costs."

3. The liability for product warranty is understated by approximately $755,000.

Draft the audit adjustments suggested by the above errors. What impact do the adjustments have on the materiality threshold set in part (a)? What are the auditing implications, if any, of the possible change in materiality threshold?

5.7   Although analytical procedures do *not* provide conclusive evidence, they do constitute a powerful means for identifying abnormalities caused by material errors or fraud.

Required:

For each of the following "abnormalities," indicate the type of error or fraud that might have occurred and how you would resolve your doubts. Organize your answers as to the type of error or fraud and the audit procedure(s) to be applied.

a. December 2002 sales are 12 percent higher than December 2001 sales.

b. Revenue from scrap sales has declined by 45 percent this year.

c. Inventory turnover has declined from 5.0 times to 2.5 times during the current year, while sales have increased by 25 percent.

d. Although production has declined by 60 percent in the current year, an insignificant volume (capacity) variance appears in the general ledger.

e. Accounts receivable turnover decreased from 12 times to 7 times during the current year, while sales increased by 40 percent.

f. In past years, the company has had substantial amounts of inventory out on consignment. Although management has stated that the consignment arrangements have been discontinued, inventory turnover has declined significantly during the current year.

g. Repairs and maintenance expense, as a percentage of sales, has increased from 6 percent to 12 percent during the current year.

5.8   Jackson Hall & Associates, CPAs, has established the following materiality parameters as firm policy.

Individual item materiality:

Income statement—6 percent of net income from continuing operations

Balance sheet—3 percent of net assets

Aggregate materiality floor:

Income statement—5 to 25 percent of individual item materiality

Balance sheet—30 percent of individual item materiality

These percentages are modified as conditions warrant.

Required:

For each of the following independent scenarios relating to Jackson Hall clients:

a. Indicate the appropriate materiality percentages to be used for determining audit adjustments and reclassifications, and justify the percentages selected.

b. Decide whether you would increase or decrease the net income and/or net asset base and justify your recommendation.

c. Decide whether you would place more emphasis on external evidence or internal evidence in carrying out your audit objectives.

Scenarios

1. Client A, a large midwest clothing chain, has strong internal control, but Darlene King, the in-charge senior auditor, suspects management misrepresentation fraud in the form of earnings inflation. King's suspicions are based on a pending merger between Client A and an eastern clothing chain. Client A will complete the merger early next year by exchanging its stock for that of the other company. King has noted that Client A's unaudited income for the current year has increased by 12 percent, while industry earnings have declined. The earnings increase has caused the company's stock price to rise, thereby requiring fewer shares to accomplish the merger.

2. Client B, a small airplane manufacturer and a recurring audit client, has been known in the past for its weak internal control. The control weaknesses have caused perpetual inventory records to be unreliable, and revenue and expense accounts to be generally misstated. Year-end accruals of revenues and expenses, as well as allocation adjustments, have been incorrect and/or omitted altogether. Although John Harley, the in-charge senior auditor for the past several years, has recommended specific improvements, the company has *not* made any serious effort to correct the control weaknesses.

5.9   Risk and materiality should be considered when planning and performing an audit of financial statements in accordance with generally accepted auditing standards. Audit risk and materiality also should be considered in determining the nature, timing, and extent of auditing procedures and in evaluating the results of those procedures.

Required:
a. 1. Define *audit risk*.
   2. Describe its components of inherent risk, control risk, and detection risk.
   3. Explain how these components are interrelated.
b. 1. Define *materiality*.
   2. Discuss the factors affecting its determination.
   3. Describe the relationship between materiality for planning purposes and materiality for evaluation purposes.

(AICPA adapted)

5.10   Your firm has recently accepted Domitec, Inc., as an audit client. You have been assigned as the in-charge auditor and are in the process of conducting a preliminary review. During inquiry and the application of analytical procedures, you discover several aspects of the company, some of which may affect the audit programs to be developed for the Domitec audit. The company is a large, diversified manufacturer of pet supplies, hardware, and building materials. Moreover, it has recently acquired a company that manufactures toys and computer games, having accounted for the acquisition as a pooling of interests. Most of the manufactured building materials are sold to home builders, and Domitec has been guaranteeing loans by local banks to the home builders to finance purchases from Domitec. Domitec was previously audited by Johnson and Associates, a local CPA firm. The company has decided to retain your firm because it is anticipating a public offering of securities within the next couple of years, and your firm is more widely known and already has several public clients.

In applying analytical procedures, you note that the firm's profit margin appears to be significantly higher than the industry average in the building materials segment, while inventory turnover is substantially lower.

Required:
a. What questions are raised by the narrative that, in your opinion, might have an impact on the audit programs to be developed for the Domitec audit?
b. What kinds of audit procedures would you apply in addressing the questions just identified?

5.11   Analytical procedures consist of evaluations of financial information made by a study of plausible relationships between both financial and nonfinancial data. They range from simple comparisons to the use of complex models involving many relationships and elements of data. They involve comparisons of recorded amounts, or ratios developed from recorded amounts, to expectations developed by the auditors.

Required:
a. Describe the broad purposes of analytical procedures.
b. Identify the sources of information from which an auditor develops expectations.
c. Describe the factors that influence an auditor's consideration of the reliability of data for purposes of achieving audit objectives.

(AICPA adapted)

5.12   a. In applying analytical procedures, a common practice is to compare monthly income statement components with the preceding year. What is the purpose for the comparisons?

b. Joan Koley, staff auditor for Bohn and Associates, CPAs, discovers during the application of analytical procedures that Samson's Hardware Store, an audit client, experienced a significant decline in inventory turnover during the current year. What might have caused the decrease? What steps might Koley take to pursue the matter further? How might this discovery affect the audit program? Be specific in terms of audit area affected and possible added procedures.

5.13   Powermate, Inc., manufactures and sells a complete line of power tools and small hand tools to wholesale distributors and retail hardware stores throughout the United States. The company has five plants serving the Northeast, the Southeast, the Midwest, the Southwest, and the West Coast. In planning the 2002 audit, Jolly & Weaver, Powermate's auditors, used the following unaudited amounts in setting materiality thresholds:

Sales revenue	$75 million
Cost of goods sold	$50 million
Operating expenses	$15 million
Net financing expense	$4 million
Current assets	$70 million
Noncurrent assets	$150 million
Current liabilities	$30 million
Noncurrent liabilities	$50 million

Misstatements equal to or exceeding 2 percent of net assets and 5 percent of net income, either individually or in the aggregate, are considered by the auditors to be material. Any misstatement equal to or exceeding 1/2 percent of net assets and net income will be subject to aggregate materiality consideration during the audit evaluation and review phase occurring at the end of audit field work.

Required:
a. What factors might the auditors have considered in setting the materiality percentages? Using the selected percentages, determine the dollar amounts of materiality thresholds for balance sheet and income statement purposes.
b. The audit team discovers the following errors during the audit.
   1. An invoice for $150,000 from Powermate's legal counsel for 2002 legal services was *not* recorded until 2003.
   2. 2003 sales in the amount of $1,300,000 were recorded in 2002. The goods were properly included in the ending inventory.
   3. A portion of Powermate's mortgage note ($16 million), payable in 2003, was included in long-term liabilities.
   4. Powermate did *not* record any adjustment for product warranty for 2002. Based on past experience, the auditors have decided that 3/4 percent of net sales is an appropriate percentage for determining the provision.
   5. Powermate incorrectly capitalized the roof replacement for two of its plants during 2002. The combined amount of the expenditures was $220,000.
   Record the necessary audit adjustment and reclassification journal entries (include only those that meet the individual or aggregate materiality thresholds set by the auditors).
c. As the audit progresses, the auditors will have identified audit adjustments and reclassifications that will be proposed to the client for reflection in the financial statements. What effect, if any, will these adjustments and reclassifications have on the materiality thresholds set in the planning stages of the audit?
d. What are your recommendations regarding aggregate materiality adjustments; that is, will you include them in your proposed audit adjustments, or ignore them?

DISCUSSION CASES

CASE I

Coppers & Reams

Your firm, M.E. Rhone, CPAs, has accepted a new audit client, Coppers & Reams (hereafter referred to as C&R). You will be in charge of the audit field work for this engagement. The company's fiscal year ends August 31, 2001. C&R previously has been audited by the firm of Dodd & Smith, CPAs. Prior to acceptance of the engagement, Roger Short, the M.E. Rhone partner responsible for the audit, obtained permission from the management of C&R and communicated with Dodd & Smith concerning its experience with the client. Short provided you with the following information, obtained from his conference with Jennifer Louden, the Dodd & Smith partner previously in charge of the C&R audit.

1. C&R develops, produces, and sells proprietary and ethical drugs in the United States, Canada, Mexico, and portions of Europe.
2. Increasing competition and continued regulation by the Food and Drug Administration have placed a severe strain on the company's liquidity and profitability.
3. Management has been quite aggressive in maximizing reported income and earnings per share in light of the "profit squeeze." Louden indicated that the 2000 audit resulted in downward adjustments of income in the amount of $1.2 million, or 30 percent.
4. Louden also indicated an unwillingness on the part of C&R management to accept audit adjustments readily; lack of an audit committee of the board of directors made the auditors' task all the more difficult.
5. Internal control policies and procedures in most transaction cycle subsets are adequate, but inventory control is weak; perpetual inventory records, recently computerized, are not very accurate. Moreover, the company does *not* have an internal audit staff and bank accounts are *not* reconciled on a regular basis.

In examining the company's annual reports for the past three years, you note a pattern of declining earnings. You also note that the auditors added an explanatory paragraph to the 2000 audit report expressing doubt as to the ability of C&R to continue as a going concern. Also, a footnote to the 2000 financial statements described a lawsuit by users of a subsequently banned C&R drug used by arthritis sufferers, which was found by the FDA to be a possible cause of cancer. C&R's audited 2000 net income was $2.7 million, down from $3.6 million in 1999. The 2001 unaudited net income is $4.1 million. Audited net assets at August 31, 2000 totaled $110 million and unaudited net assets at August 31, 2001 were $114 million.

Required:

a. Using Figure 5.4 and the related chapter discussion as a focal point, discuss inherent and control risk levels, the types of audit evidence you might emphasize in the C&R audit, and the types of audit evidence you might de-emphasize.
b. Using the same framework as that in (a), give your thoughts about the appropriate levels of materiality.
c. Assume the following M.E. Rhone policy regarding materiality thresholds:

Individual item materiality:

3 percent of net income
2 percent of net assets

Aggregate materiality:

- For high control risk and/or inherent risk environments—5 percent of individual item materiality
- For low-risk environments—25 percent of individual item materiality
- For environments falling between these extremes, the auditor should select an appropriate level between the above levels.

Referring to Exhibit 5.1 (the aggregate materiality workpaper) and the related chapter discussion, set what you consider to be reasonable dollar thresholds for the following:

1. Individual item for income statement purposes;
2. Individual item for balance sheet reclassification purposes; and

3. Aggregate materiality.

Justify the levels you consider appropriate.

CASE II

Sunbeam Corp.

Sunbeam Corp. a Boca Raton, Florida, manufacturer of camping goods and consumer products, prospered quickly under its new CEO, Albert Dunlap. After assuming the top role in 1996, Dunlap ("Chainsaw Al" as he came to be called) proceeded to downsize the company by laying off 12,000 workers and closing 80 of Sunbeam's 114 plants, offices, and warehouses. Although the downsizing produced a special one-time restructuring charge of $337 million, the subsequent earnings boost caused the company's stock price to advance rapidly from $12.50 a share on the date Dunlap took over in July 1996 to a high of $53.00 by March 1998. In 1997, Sunbeam reported earnings of $109.4 million, or $1.41 per share, on sales of $1.2 billion. Given this stellar performance, the company began shopping for a buyer. With the stock selling in the 50s, however, the price seemed too high and no takers appeared.

Then, just as rapidly as the star rose, it suddenly fell to earth when the company announced a loss of $44.6 million for the first quarter of 1998 on a sales decline of 3.6 percent, and its stock price fell to $22.00. Moreover, the reported earnings from Sunbeam's 1997 record year, according to an article appearing in the June 8, 1998, issue of *Barron's*, may have been overstated. Indicators of possible earnings inflation are the following:

1. The company's 1996 restructuring charge of $337 million before taxes included $90 million of inventories of discontinued products written down to zero. Even if these products were sold in 1997 at a 50 percent markdown, the proceeds would account for about a third of Sunbeam's 1997 earnings.

2. On the 1997 year-end balance sheet, prepaid expenses and other current assets declined to $17.2 million from $40.4 million in 1996. Again, as part of the 1996 restructuring charge, Sunbeam wrote off some costs having future economic benefit extending well into 1997. These write-downs produced an additional $15 million in income for 1997.

3. Amounts provided for in product warranty allowances and other "reserves" as part of the 1996 restructuring were reversed in 1997, adding approximately $25 million to the company's earnings.

4. As part of the 1996 restructuring charge, Sunbeam wrote down its property, plant, and equipment accounts by $92 million. Some of this write-down applied to assets the company was selling, but much of it applied to assets used in its ongoing operations. This allowed Sunbeam to reduce its depreciation charges and added approximately $9 million to its earnings.

5. Sunbeam's advertising and promotion expense dropped from $71.5 million in 1996 to $56.4 million in 1997 as the result of increased capitalization of advertising and product promotion charges.

6. The allowance for doubtful accounts dropped from $23.4 million in 1996 to $8.4 million in 1997, suggesting a less than conservative approach to accounts receivable valuation.

7. Sunbeam's inventories increased by 40 percent during 1997—an increase not justified by order backlogs. The increased production, however, permitted the company to capitalize manufacturing overhead in inventories that would otherwise have been charged to 1997 earnings as a capacity loss.

8. The company delayed recording 1996 sales (a loss year anyway) and recognized the revenue in 1997. Then, at the end of 1997, $35 million of sales were booked that were in fact "bill and hold" sales that hadn't left the warehouses by year end.

The items described above added approximately $120 million to Sunbeam's income. The statement of cash flows, however, reflected negative operating cash flows of $8.2 million.

The company fired Dunlap in June 1998 and the SEC launched an investigation into the company's accounting practices. In the meantime, Arthur Andersen, Sunbeam's independent auditors, advised the company that it remained comfortable with its unqualified opinion on Sunbeam's 1997 financial statements. Although the board of directors was satisfied that the company's accounting confirmed to GAAP, the audit committee expressed concern about the quality of the numbers.

Required:
a. For each of the items listed, identify accounting standards that may have been violated.
b. How might the auditors have become aware of each of the items?
c. Do you think the auditors were justified in rendering an unqualified opinion on Sunbeam's 1997 financial statements? Explain.

CASE III

Hughes Aircraft Company

The following quote is from an article appearing in the October 29, 1990, issue of *The Wall Street Journal*:

> *Hughes Aircraft Co., faced with cost overruns on a fixed-price contract to develop a radar system for the F-15 jet fighter, improperly charged expenses to other government contracts, a government audit alleged.*

The Air Force audit team had discovered that Hughes had charged $21.4 million of development costs of the radar system to a contract with Grumman Corp. for an advanced F-14 radar and to a contract with Northrop Corp. for the B-2 bomber's radar. These costs should have been charged to the F-15 project under the control of prime contractor McDonnell Douglas Corp. Hughes' motive, as alleged by the auditors, was to reduce losses on the F-15 contract, a fixed-price contract that was already in a cost overrun condition, by charging the costs to other projects that would permit reimbursement.

Hughes had created a system whereby all development costs, regardless of whether they were directly related to a specific contract, were charged to a "common pool" and subsequently charged out to contracts. Hughes rebutted that the auditors were incorrect in their allegations of wrongdoing in that many, if not most, of the development costs were general in nature and therefore applicable to all of the contracts jointly, and should *not* have been charged to single contracts as maintained by the Air Force auditors. The government report stated, however, that while Grumman and Northrop had agreed that certain components in their radar systems would be identical to those used in others, the decision to distribute these costs and the ratio for the distribution were made internally by Hughes, with no input from the contractors or the appropriate government offices.

Required:
a. One of the factors increasing inherent risk is audit complexity. How does audit complexity relate to the Hughes Aircraft Co. case?
b. How might auditors be alerted to a situation such as that described in this case? In other words, what sounds the "warning whistle"?
c. Having been alerted to a possible error or fraud in a case like this, how should the auditors proceed in gathering evidence to resolve their suspicions? To answer this question, recall the various forms of audit evidence and types of procedures described in Chapter 4.

CASE IV

Marcus Publishing, Inc.

You are currently planning the audit for Marcus Publishing, Inc., a closely held company that prints and publishes a diverse line of college textbooks. Given increased competition from multimedia publishers and a continued decline in college enrollments, the college textbook industry has experienced a drop in revenue and profits for 2001. Exhibits 5.5 through 5.8 (pp. 200–202) contain financial data for Marcus and the industry in general. The increase in "long-term notes payable" occurred in August 2000 when Marcus' management, faced with inadequate liquid resources to finance 2000–2001 textbook production, obtained a long-term credit line increase of $1,000,000 from its primary bank.

The balance sheet account "deferred publishing costs" represents unamortized printing and promotional costs associated with textbooks still in their current editions. These costs are amortized over three or four years, depending on whether the related textbook is revised every three years or every four years. Costs pertaining to unsuccessful books are expensed in the year in which the loss occurs.

The company's sales representatives are compensated on a commission basis. Editors receive a salary plus a share of gross profit on titles that have surpassed their break-even volume. Production employees are paid on an hourly basis. Marcus' top management staff receive a salary plus a bonus of 30 percent of any increase in net income over the preceding fiscal year.

Required:

a. Prepare comparative percentage income statements for the years 1997 through 2001.

b. Calculate the following ratios for 2001:
   1. Current ratio
   2. Accounts receivable turnover
   3. Inventory turnover
   4. Ratio of deferred publishing costs to cost of sales
   5. Gross profit margin
   6. Net income margin

c. Using the data contained in Exhibits 5.5 through 5.8, along with the data developed in parts (a) and (b), identify any warning signs that warrant further investigation. What might have caused the abnormality in each instance?

d. How might your findings influence the audit plan?

Note: The solution to this case can be greatly expedited by retrieving and completing the spreadsheet template entitled "Marcus." This file is included on the same Student CD that contains the Biltrite Bicycle templates.

CASE V

JWP, Inc.

In January 1993, shareholders filed a class action suit against JWP, Inc., and Ernst & Young, its auditors, charging that management had intentionally inflated earnings and assets, and that the auditors were negligent in *not* detecting the fraud. The suit alleged that the financial statements were overstated because executive bonuses were tied to reported earnings.

JWP, a diversified technical services company, was begun by Martin Dwyer as Jamaica Water Properties, a small water utility. Dwyer died in 1987 and was succeeded by his son, Andrew T. Dwyer, who transformed the company, through dozens of acquisitions, into one of the fastest-growing technical services contractors in the country. JWP's main business involved mechanical and electrical services related to large commercial construction projects. The company wired buildings, installed surveillance systems and escalators, and maintained the systems. In addition, JWP bought Businessland, Inc., a computer retailer, in 1991.

After a period of rapidly increasing sales and profits, revenues began to plummet as a result of computer price wars and the construction downturn of the early 1990s. According to the lawsuit, the company failed to write off a significant amount of

---

EXHIBIT 5.5

Case IV—Revenue and Expense Data

Marcus Publishing, Inc.
Comparative Income Statement Data
(1997–2001)
(in thousands of dollars)

	(unaudited)	(audited)			
	2001 Dollars	2000 Dollars	1999 Dollars	1998 Dollars	1997 Dollars
Sales	$5,500	$4,800	$5,000	$4,800	$4,500
Cost of sales	2,300	2,400	2,700	2,500	2,300
Gross profit	$3,200	$2,400	$2,300	$2,300	$2,200
Operating expenses	1,500	1,400	1,400	1,300	1,200
Net income before taxes	$1,700	$1,000	$900	$1,000	$1,000
Income taxes	600	350	320	350	350
Net income	$1,100	$650	$580	$650	$650

---

uncollectible accounts receivable and obsolete inventories. The receivables were related to construction projects and had been uncollectible for several years due to customer bankruptcies. In addition, the suit revealed that the internal auditors had raised questions about the value of spare parts and raw materials inventories acquired from Businessland in the 1991 acquisition. The inventories were significantly overvalued because of obsolescence and the computer price wars.

The impact of the alleged management fraud, according to the lawsuit, was to create an illusion of profitability for 1991 and 1992. In October 1992, JWP's president and chief operating officer, David L. Sokol, resigned because of the "magnitude and pervasiveness of accounting irregularities." He had uncovered the irregularities with the aid of Deloitte & Touche, CPAs. The writedown of the receivables and inventories produced a $500 million loss for 1992 and a net worth of zero as of year end. In addition, the company was carrying $484 million in debt, on which interest payments were suspended in March

1993. The market price of JWP stock dropped 90 percent in the 18 months ending July 1993. The auditors, Ernst & Young, were named in the suit on the grounds that they should have detected the overvalued inventories and the uncollectible accounts receivable.

In early 1993, Andrew Dwyer resigned as chief executive officer and was replaced by Edward Kosnik. The company then divested itself of its information services unit, including Businessland, Inc., as well as 12 other previous acquisitions, and returned to concentrating on the technical services area, where its primary expertise lay. As of July 1993, JWP had a customer order backlog of $1.2 billion and was on the verge of a restructuring agreement.

Required:
a. Were the auditors negligent in this case? Support your answer.
b. Discuss the ethical questions raised when an accounting firm, such as Deloitte & Touche, joins in the investigation of another accounting firm.

EXHIBIT 5.6

Case IV—Balance Sheet Data

Marcus Publishing, Inc.
Comparative Balance Sheets
June 30, 2001 and 2000
(in thousands of dollars)

	2001 (unaudited)	2000 (audited)
ASSETS		
Cash on hand and in banks	$ 200	$ 1,000
Accounts receivable (net)	2,400	1,400
Textbook inventory	1,400	500
Total current assets	$ 4,000	$ 2,900
Deferred publishing costs	2,500	1,600
Property, plant, and equipment (net)	5,200	4,600
Total assets	$11,700	$ 9,100
LIABILITIES AND STOCKHOLDERS' EQUITY		
Accounts payable	$ 223	$ 100
Interest payable	460	208
Accrued liabilities	200	575
Total current liabilities	$ 883	$ 883
Long-term notes payable (8%)	3,600	2,600
Total liabilities	$ 4,483	$ 3,483
Common stock	3,000	2,000
Retained earnings	4,217	3,617
Total liabilities and stockholders' equity	$11,700	$ 9,100

CASE VI

Brooke Group, Ltd.

Bennett S. LeBow, chairman and 60 percent stockholder of Brooke Group, Ltd., was allegedly "milking" the company of its resources in order to fund his own personal and business ventures. Brooke Group is a Miami, Florida, corporation listed on the New York Stock Exchange. At the time of this writing, the company manufactured Ligett cigarettes and computer software. Brooke was also engaged in helicopter maintenance and was a major seller of sports trading cards.

Although the entity reported losses of $149.6 million in 1991 and $75.8 million in 1992, finally halting dividends in late 1992, LeBow was alleged to have continued channeling corporate monies, especially from the cash-rich Ligett Group, into his personal accounts. He borrowed $5 million in February 1991 and $6.5 million during 1992. He owed the company nearly $18 million by July 1993. Between 1989 and 1993 Brooke's cash position dwindled from a high of $228 million to about $14 million.

In addition to using direct loans, Bennett LeBow was accused of devising other means for siphoning funds from Brooke. In 1990, for example, Brooke

EXHIBIT 5.7

Case IV—Cash Flow Data

Marcus Publishing, Inc.
Statement of Cash Flows
For the Year Ended June 30, 2001
(unaudited)

Cash Flows from Operating Activities:		
Net Income		$ 1,100
Add:		
Depreciation		100
Increase in accounts payable		123
Increase in interest payable		252
Total		$ 1,575
Deduct:		
Increase in accounts receivable	$ 1,000	
Increase in textbook inventory	900	
Increase in deferred publishing costs	900	
Decrease in accrued liabilities	375	
		$(3,175)
Net cash flow from operating activities		$(1,600)
Cash Flows from Investing Activities:		
Acquisition of equipment		$ (700)
Cash Flows from Financing Activities:		
Proceeds from issuance of long-term note payable	$ 1,000	
Proceeds from issuance of common stock	1,000	
Dividends paid	(500)	
Net cash flows from financing activities		$ 1,500
Increase (decrease) in cash		$ (800)
Cash—July 1, 2000		1,000
Cash—June 30, 2001		$ 200

EXHIBIT 5.8

Case IV—Industry Data

Industry Data for Textbook Publishers	
Current ratio	2.1
Accounts receivable turnover	10
Inventory turnover	8
Ratio of deferred publishing costs to cost of sales	50%
Gross profit margin	45%
Net income margin	5%

bought LeBow's airplane, appraised at $8 million. The purchase was financed by assuming $5.9 million of LeBow's debt and paying him $1.4 million in cash. The plane was maintained by L Aviation, Inc., a private company controlled by LeBow. Even though Brooke now owned the airplane, the company continued paying rent on it to two LeBow-controlled private companies, L Aviation and Brooke Aviation ($441,000 was paid in 1991 and $594,000 in 1992).

In March 1991, Brooke bought back some of LeBow's convertible preferred stock that the company had issued to him as part of a merger, paying him $1.4 million. Also in 1991, LeBow sold the company a $2.6 million option to buy his last airplane. Although LeBow found another buyer, he supposedly did not repay the option money to Brooke. At the end of 1992, one of LeBow's private companies owed a Brooke Group subsidiary $300,000 for 1992 medical plan payments.

In 1988, the company that was building LeBow a $25 million yacht was collapsing. To avoid failure of the company prior to completing his boat, LeBow bought the company and then sold it to Brooke after the yacht was finished.

Although LeBow received no salary or bonuses from Brooke Group, he and four other associates received salaries from one of his private companies, Brooke Management, Inc., which presented itself as a consulting firm and charged Brooke Group, their sole client, over $10 million in 1990 and over $10 million in 1991 for "services" and "expenses." In mid-1991, Brooke Group paid LeBow $2.5 million for an option to buy 80 percent of Brooke Management (Brooke Management assets consisted of LeBow and his associates). The company exercised the option in 1992 by paying $9.6 million for the 80 percent and $2.4 million for the remaining 20 percent. After Brooke Management was sold, LeBow began receiving salary and bonus from Brooke Group.

Filings with the Securities and Exchange Commission showed many transfers involving millions of dollars from the company to LeBow. The transfers may have been facilitated by the fact that LeBow, in addition to being chief executive officer and controlling stockholder, was also president and treasurer of the Group. Moreover, in 1990 and 1991 Brooke had only two outside directors on the board. One held a consulting contract with a Brooke subsidiary and the other was LeBow's neighbor. At July 30, 1993, the company had only three directors—LeBow and two other Brooke officers.

After dividends were halted in late 1992, minority shareholders brought a lawsuit against Brooke alleging that the company "(had) been denuded of tens of millions of dollars of corporate assets in transactions that personally benefited and enriched" management. By July 1993, the company was "sinking" under $400 million of debt and reported a $490 million deficit. Its stock price had declined from a high of $10 in 1990 to $2 by May 1993. For the latest year-end audit, Coopers & Lybrand expressed substantial doubt about Brooke Group's ability to continue as a going concern.

Required:

a. Discuss the auditor's responsibility in cases of this nature. Must the auditor be a "whistle blower," informing stockholders that management is *not* exercising proper stewardship over their resources?

b. What are the "warning signs" in the present case that might arouse the auditor's suspicions concerning the existence of the transactions described in this case?

c. Do you feel that the auditor's responsibility, as set forth in the AICPA Professional Standards, is adequate in this regard?

c h a p t e r 6

biltrite

l e a r n i n g   o b j e c t i v e s

After reading this chapter, you should be able to

1 Define internal control and describe its five components.
2 Relate the components to management's assertions regarding financial statement presentation.
3 Understand the need for a minimum audit, given the limitations inherent in any control system.
4 Identify the ingredients comprising effective internal control for a small business, and understand how they differ from the control systems found in larger entities.

OVERVIEW

Chapter 5 described an approach to evaluating inherent risk by incorporating audit risk analysis into the planning phase. Chapter 6 discusses internal control system components, and Chapter 7 shows how the auditor can assess control risk through studying and evaluating the firm's internal control system.

Chapter 6 begins by defining internal control and describing its five components: control environment, risk assessment, information and communication, control activities, and monitoring. The chapter emphasizes those aspects of internal control that are relevant to a financial statement audit. Because the auditor's direct concern is with management's assertions contained in the financial statements, the discussion emphasizes control elements relating to those assertions: existence or occurrence, completeness, rights and obligations, valuation or allocation, and presentation and disclosure.

Inherent limitations give rise to opportunities for errors and fraud, even in situations for which the auditor assesses control risk at a relatively low level. These limitations require the auditor to perform minimum substantive tests, regardless of internal control effectiveness. Given the impact of limitations inherent in all control systems on the independent audit, the topic is covered in a separate section of the chapter.

The chapter concludes with a discussion of internal control as modified to meet the needs of small businesses where the owner/manager must assume a more active role in defining and achieving control objectives.

INTERNAL CONTROL SYSTEM DEFINED

AICPA Professional Standards define **internal control** as the process effected by an entity's board of directors, management, and other personnel designed to provide reasonable assurance regarding the *achievement of objectives* in the following categories:

- **Operations controls**—relating to the effective and efficient use of the entity's resources;
- **Financial reporting controls**—relating to the preparation of reliable published financial statements; and
- **Compliance controls**—relating to the entity's compliance with applicable laws and regulations.[1]

This is a broad definition and pervades all of an organization's activities. Inasmuch as the auditor's primary concern is with those controls impacting the reliability of the published financial statements, this chapter emphasizes financial reporting controls.[2]

Because people affect internal control, all systems contain certain inherent limitations. As a result, internal control provides **reasonable assurance** (not absolute assurance) as to the achievement of control objectives.

COMPONENTS OF INTERNAL CONTROL

AICPA Professional Standards identifies five internal control components:

- Control environment;
- Risk assessment;

---

1   *AICPA Professional Standards*, New York: AICPA, section AU 319.06.
2   As will be discussed in Chapter 16, the independent auditor is also concerned with compliance controls when auditing governmental and other not-for-profit entities receiving federal financial assistance.

- Information and communication;
- Control activities; and
- Monitoring.[3]

These components are defined and discussed in the following paragraphs.

Controls that enhance the reliability of the financial statements may be *prevention controls* or *detection controls*. **Prevention controls** (e.g., input editing of data introduced into the system) avoid errors and fraud; **detection controls** (e.g., monthly bank reconciliations), while recognizing that errors and fraud will occur even under ideal conditions, provide for a "double-check" to locate significant occurrences after the fact.

In evaluating financial reporting controls, the auditor's primary consideration is whether a specific control affects the **financial statement assertions**.[4] Those assertions were identified in Chapter 1 as the following:

- Existence or occurrence;
- Completeness;
- Rights and obligations;
- Valuation or allocation; and
- Presentation and disclosure.

The following paragraphs discuss the five components of internal control in terms of their impact on the above assertions.

Control Environment

The first component, the **control environment**, forms the foundation for the others (see Figure 6.1). The absence of one or more significant elements of the control environment will cause the system to be ineffective, notwithstanding the strength of the remaining four components.

The control environment is determined by the attitudes of the persons in charge of the internal control system. Management's attitude toward control has a significant impact on control effectiveness; thus, management must be *strongly supportive* of internal control and must *communicate that support* throughout the organization. Management that does not possess a control-conscious attitude will serve to undermine the system. One of the reasons cited by KPMG for resigning from the Rite Aid audit was the multitude of weaknesses in the company's financial reporting controls, caused by management's indifference regarding sound control.[5]

The reliability of management's assertions regarding the fairness of financial presentation depends strongly on a continuous pattern of management support of internal control and concern for proper financial reporting. When combined with management integrity and sound ethical values, the result is the selection of accounting principles that fairly portray financial position, results of operations, cash flows, and accounting estimates that are reasonable and complete. Lack of concern for accurate accounting can negate other controls and cause the entire system to be ineffective.

Internal control is only as strong as the *ethics* and *competence* of the persons who are responsible for it. Achievement of sound internal control, therefore, requires a commitment to high integrity and strong ethical values. If internal controls are to be prop-

3   *AICPA Professional Standards*, op. cit., section AU 319.07.
4   Ibid, section AU 319.14.
5   See *The Wall Street Journal*, November 19, 1999.

FIGURE 6.1

Components of Internal Control

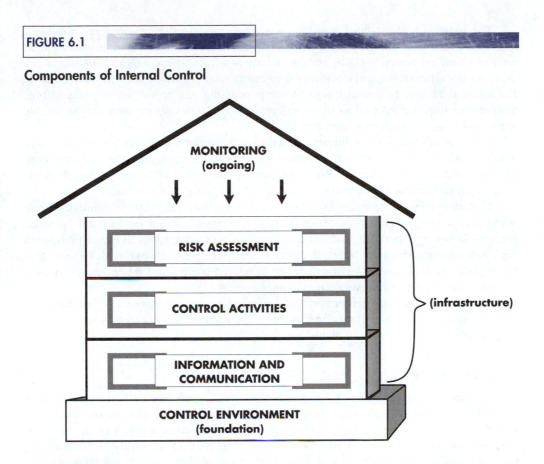

erly designed and implemented, that commitment must start at the top with the chief executive officer and permeate the entire organization. In the Rite Aid case cited above, numerous related-party transactions between the company and its CEO, along with questionable accounting practices, resulted in a virtual breakdown in control.

Many companies have established written **codes of corporate conduct** as a means of communicating to their employees the entities' ethical values. A written code of conduct typically defines conflicts of interest, illegal acts, improper payments, and other behavior considered unacceptable to the entity. Penalties for violations of code provisions also may be specified in the written document.

Competence is achieved by *effective personnel policies*. Failure to maintain a sound human resources function that emphasizes effective employee hiring and training policies leads to the assignment of control duties to persons not capable of performing them properly. This, in turn, often leads to material misstatements due to commission (existence or occurrence), omission (completeness), valuation or allocation, and/or presentation in the financial statements.

Included in the control environment is management's *attitude toward risk taking*. Assets (real estate, for example) obtained in high-risk ventures may be overvalued in terms of cost versus current market value, or sales to customers who are high credit risks may result in receivables that are improperly classified as current, given their questionable collectibility. An attitude that encourages the assumption of unwarranted risk may adversely affect the presentation and/or valuation assertions.

The existence of *internal auditing*, a positive aspect of the control environment, assists in preventing and detecting misstatements due to omission and commission, as well as valuation errors. Periodic review of transactions and events, examination of underlying documentation, and comparison of assets with recorded accountability enable the internal auditor to detect errors in the processing and recording of transactions. Knowledge that the internal auditors will review transactions increases employee diligence and discourages errors and fraud.

To be most effective, the internal auditing department should report to persons at a sufficiently high level within the organization to ensure implementation of their conclusions and recommendations. Preferably, the auditors should report to the chief executive officer and/or to the audit committee of the board of directors.

Certain *external factors* also may affect the firm's internal financial controls. While some may strengthen controls, other factors may place a strain on internal controls. Internal Revenue Service regulations and the Foreign Corrupt Practices Act provisions for maintaining adequate internal control are examples of external factors that strengthen internal control.[6] The existence of related parties and related-party transactions are factors that could weaken existing controls.

To summarize, a management philosophy emphasizing the importance of sound internal control creates a control consciousness throughout the organization that serves to strengthen the system at all levels.

Risk Assessment[7]

Just as auditors assess audit risk—the risk of expressing an unqualified opinion on financial statements that are materially misstated—managers assess **business risk**—"the risk that an entity's business objectives will not be attained as a result of the external and internal factors, pressures, and forces brought to bear on the entity and, ultimately, the risk associated with the entity's survival and profitability."[8] Entity objectives cannot be achieved without some risk. Effective internal control should help managers in assessing and managing business risk.

For risk management controls to be operable, control objectives must be specific and clearly defined. *Operating objectives* relate to the entity's effective and efficient use of resources. These objectives need to be entity-wide, be reasonably attainable, and contain implementation strategies. Examples of risks threatening the achievement of operating objectives include new technology, changing customer needs or expectations, competition, new legislation, natural catastrophes, and economic changes.[9] *Financial reporting objectives* address the preparation of reliable published financial statements. These goals are defined by generally accepted accounting principles and by the assertions underlying an entity's financial statements. Changes in the information processing system, accounting personnel changes, and downsizing of the internal audit staff are examples of factors impacting the risk associated with reliably prepared financial state-

6   See Chapter 16 for added discussion of the Foreign Corrupt Practices Act of 1977.
7   Students need to be careful not to confuse risk assessment as a component of internal control with the auditor's assessment of audit risk in connection with planning and conducting the audit.
8   Bell, Timothy, Frank Marrs, Ira Solomon, and Howard Thomas, *Auditing Organizations Through a Strategic-Systems Lens,* New York: KPMG Peat Marwick LLP, 1997, p. 15.
9   Committee of Sponsoring Organizations of the Treadway Commission, *Internal Control—Integrated Framework,* New York: COSO, 1992, p. 40.

ments. *Compliance objectives* depend on external factors such as tax laws and the requirements of regulatory agencies. Changes in the applicable laws and regulations create compliance risk.

Risk assessment for financial reporting purposes should identify, analyze, and manage risks relevant to the preparation of financial statements.[10] Risks relevant to financial reporting include "external and internal events and circumstances that may occur and adversely affect an entity's ability to record, process, summarize, and report financial data consistent with the [financial statement] assertions."[11]

Financial controls are strongest when conditions giving rise to errors and fraud are minimized. An effective control system, therefore, should provide for timely identification and correction of these conditions. The following paragraphs discuss this aspect of risk assessment.

To reduce the risk of unrecorded transactions, the internal control system should provide for an adequate audit trail that provides reasonable assurance that all completed transactions have been identified and recorded. To minimize the risk of fraudulent transactions, the system should provide for proper approval and review of transactions. To avoid overlooking necessary accounting adjustments and the risk of making unrealistic accounting estimates, the controls should include a systematic set of end-of-period closing procedures.

Another factor impacting financial reporting risk relates to budgetary goals and the risk of intentional misstatement. If operating objectives regarding costs, revenues, and profitability are not reasonably attainable, persons with budgetary responsibility may be inclined to misrepresent actual results to achieve favorable budget comparisons. The risk of misstatement increases when wage and salary incentives are tied to favorable budget variances. The existence or occurrence, completeness, and valuation assertions can be seriously compromised under these conditions.

To reduce misrepresentation risk, entities should institute planning and budgetary systems that encourage the setting of attainable objectives with clearly defined implementation strategies. These objectives and strategies are then communicated clearly to those persons with specific budgetary responsibility. Moreover, significant risks affecting the achievement of profitability objectives are assessed carefully and incorporated into the budgets.

Financial reporting risk also involves the ability to manage change. As the entity's environment changes, new risks and opportunities are presented. New accounting personnel and/or new or revamped accounting information systems increase the short-term risk of misstated financial reports. For this reason, effective internal control should provide for new personnel to be adequately trained and carefully supervised until they are proficient in the accounting and/or financial control aspects of their employment.

Proposed changes in the accounting information system should be carefully analyzed and properly implemented; during the design and installation of the new system, attention should be directed toward installing all of the controls necessary to achieve the control objectives. Once the changes have been installed, the former system should continue to operate in parallel fashion until the new system functions as designed.

10 *AICPA Professional Standards*, op. cit., section AU 319.28.
11 Ibid, section AU 319.29.

Information and Communication

To be effective, an internal control system must provide relevant and timely **information and communication**. The system should identify the information requirements and create an information system that provides the needed data and reports. In evaluating the appropriateness of an information system, an entity should consider the following issues:

- Obtaining external and internal information and providing management with necessary reports on the entity's performance relative to established objectives;
- Providing information to the right people in sufficient detail and on time to enable them to carry out their responsibilities efficiently and effectively;
- Development or revision of information systems (as needed); and
- Management's support for the development of necessary information systems, demonstrated by the commitment of appropriate resources.[12]

Note that these components encompass both internal and external information requirements.

Information System Elements   Because the financial statements are produced by the information system, **information system elements** directly affect the financial reporting set of control objectives.

The essential elements of a sound information system are as follows:

- Identification of information;
- Capture of information;
- Processing of information; and
- Reporting of information.[13]

The following paragraphs discuss these elements in relation to accounting data, stipulating how each element supports management's financial statement assertions.

Identification of Information   Proper identification of all economic transactions and events supports the completeness assertion by preventing omissions. Input editing, transaction documentation, prenumbered documents, analysis of relationships, and reconciliations strengthen this element of the accounting information system.

Capture of Information   Once identified, accounting data must be accessed and captured by whatever device is used to store and assemble it while awaiting classification and recording by the storage device. The "capture" device may be a computer terminal, a document, or a set of manual accounting records. Preventing and detecting access and/or capture errors supports the completeness assertion by ensuring that all transactions and events are secured and moved intact to the point of recording.

Processing of Information   Accounting information is processed by the recording of transactions in journals and their posting to ledger accounts. From the external auditor's perspective, transactions and events need to be properly classified as to type and ownership, and recorded according to generally accepted accounting principles. Adequate

12 COSO, *Internal Control—Integrated Framework*, op. cit., p. 67.
13 Ibid, p. 60.

internal controls over recording of transactions support the valuation assertion. Proper control over classification supports the presentation and disclosure assertion and the rights and obligations (ownership) assertion. Computerized recording and posting, given adequate attention to programmed controls, greatly enhances reliability, thereby strengthening internal control over transaction processing.

A set of **standard journal entries** for recurring month-end transactions and events also improves internal control by providing reasonable assurance that material adjustments are *not* overlooked in the preparation of monthly, quarterly, or annual financial statements. The standard entries may be numbered (for example, Standard Entry No. 1 may be for monthly depreciation of plant assets; No. 2 may be for bad debts) and prewritten, except for amounts. Month-end accruals of taxes, product warranty, and interest, as well as entries to cost production and sales, might be recorded monthly through standard journal entries.

Reporting of Information   The external auditor is concerned that the internal control system accurately converts accounting data from ledger format to financial statements (reports) prepared in accordance with generally accepted accounting principles, including necessary end-of-period adjustments and adequate footnote disclosure. Most computer software programs used for capturing and processing accounting data are also designed to produce periodic financial statements from the ledger balances.

In addition to preparing financial statements and schedules, the internal control system must provide for retaining the accounting data, together with underlying documents, for later examination by the internal and external auditors.

Communication   Financial reporting controls require that specific duties be communicated clearly to employees responsible for implementing the control procedures. Every affected employee needs to know how the controls work, their role and responsibility in the system, and the importance of performing their tasks in a consistent and efficient manner. Clear job descriptions, accounting manuals, policy and procedures manuals, and employee training programs are means for effecting **communication**.

Control Activities

Control activities are the policies and procedures that help ensure that management directives are carried out. They also help ensure that necessary actions are taken to address risks to the achievement of entity objectives.[14]

Control activities designed to prevent and detect errors in accounting data strengthen the accounting information system, contributing to reliable financial statements. These control activities and their ability to enhance proper identification, capture, processing, and reporting of accounting information are discussed in the following paragraphs.

Documentation, Approval, Verification, and Reconciliations   This set of control activities is designed to prevent and detect both completeness and existence errors, and to ensure that transactions are properly recorded in accordance with GAAP. Table 6.1 lists the essential control activities that support financial statement assertions.

14 *AICPA Professional Standards,* op. cit., section AU 319.32.

TABLE 6.1

Control Activities Supporting the Financial Statement Assertions

1. Documentation of transactions;

2. Creating a chart of accounts (listing of accounts and account numbers) and accounting manuals (that define accounts and transactions) to facilitate proper recording of unusual transactions;

3. Proper approval and review of transactions prior to recording;

4. Input editing for transactions and events processed by computer;

5. Employee verifications, reconciliations, and reviews;

6. Developing a system of budgeting, standard costs, and variance analysis;

7. Using prenumbered documents and periodic numerical sequence checks;

8. Maintaining transaction logs for data entered via terminal;

9. Implementing a system of standard journal entries or checklists for ensuring that all necessary monthly, quarterly, and year-end adjustments are recorded;

10. Careful review of the general ledger trial balance by responsible accounting personnel for needed monthly and year-end adjustments;

11. Proper control over data center operations, including separation of systems analysis and programming from data operations;

12. Careful attention to systems and program development, including documentation, review, and approval of changes;

13. Careful follow-up and controlled reprocessing of errors that occur in the initial recording of data; and

14. Provision for identifying consigned-in inventory and/or assets held as collateral, such that these are not misrepresented as assets.

Certain of these controls—input editing, data center control, systems and program controls, and controlled reprocessing—are directly related to computer-based information systems. These controls are described and discussed in Chapter 8.

Reporting   Internal control activities supporting the reporting elements of an adequate accounting information system include the following:

- **Chart of accounts** listing all accounts and account numbers;
- **Accounting manuals** defining accounts and transactions and describing proper valuation and classification within the financial statements, as well as addressing the need for footnote disclosure;
- A system of standard journal entries for recurring adjustments, and provision for analysis of the end-of-period unadjusted trial balance and supporting files for additional adjustments and/or reclassifications;
- Policies providing for a reasonable approach to the development of management's estimates contained in the financial statements; and
- Documentation and record retention policies that provide for storage until records are released by the external auditors.

Security of Assets (Safeguard Controls)   **Safeguard controls**, designed to protect the firm's assets, support the existence assertion by helping to ensure that recorded assets have not been misappropriated. Examples of safeguard controls include policies limiting access to valuable and portable assets, background investigation and bonding of employees in positions of trust, adequate insurance coverage, and environmental management. In addition to limiting access to valuable and portable assets, the controls should limit access to documents authorizing the use or disposition of assets and fix responsibility over custody of assets and documents.

Safeguard controls may be classified further into *access* and *accountability controls*. **Access controls** limit admission to areas containing portable and valuable assets such as inventory, small tools, negotiable securities, and cash receipts. **Accountability controls** assign responsibility over the custody of each class of these assets to specified individuals.

Limiting access to assets without limiting access to documents authorizing the use or disposition of assets does *not* constitute adequate physical control. Assume, for example, that a company has installed limited-access controls over merchandise in the warehouse, has fixed responsibility over merchandise, and prohibits shipments without a properly approved shipping order. These controls will be effective only if unused shipping order forms are also under physical control. If access to shipping orders is unlimited, goods may be removed from the warehouse through fabricated shipping orders. For this reason, all documents authorizing the use or disposition of assets (e.g., shipping orders, sales invoices, vouchers, disbursement checks, and receiving reports) should be placed under the same physical control as the assets to which they relate. Table 6.2 lists some of the specific control techniques classified as safeguard controls.

Segregation of Duties   Proper separation of duties supports financial control by helping to prevent and detect errors and fraud. First, segregation of the accounting and treasury functions prevents a single person from accessing and misappropriating assets and concealing the misappropriation by making false entries in the accounting records. Such separation means that accounting personnel do *not* have access to financial assets, and treasury personnel do *not* have access to accounting records.

Separation of computer programmers from computer operators serves the same purpose. In addition to the prevention aspect, proper separation also serves as a double check in manual systems, enabling one person to verify the work of another. For example, in accounting for vouchers processed in a manual accounting system, one employee may determine the account(s) to be debited for a given transaction, after which a second employee verifies the correctness of the debit(s). Other examples of appropriate separation of duties include reconciliation of bank accounts by an employee who does not have access to cash receipts and who does not record cash receipts, and distribution of computer output by persons not responsible for input or processing of data.

Monitoring Financial Reporting Controls

To be certain that internal controls are effective over time, they must be monitored on a recurring basis. For some controls, **monitoring** can be performed on a "real-time" basis; that is, the monitoring is ongoing and virtually automatic. Examining operating data, comparing budget with actual performance, and then taking corrective action is an example of **ongoing monitoring**. Other examples include mailing statements to customers

TABLE 6.2

Examples of Asset Safeguard Controls

Access Controls

1. Creating secure areas for merchandise, small tools, supplies, securities, and so on;

2. Requiring use of cash registers with locked-in tapes;

3. Limiting access to unused documents and proper cancellation of used documents;

4. Daily intact deposits of cash receipts;

5. Limiting access to computers, access codes to terminals, disk files, and elements of data-bases (as discussed in Chapter 8); and

6. Requiring dual access to negotiable securities and other valuable portable assets (unauthorized removal could occur only through collusion, under these circumstances).

Accountability Controls

1. Prelisting incoming cash receipts for later comparison with the daily cash receipts journal entry and bank deposit ticket;

2. Fixing responsibility for custody over prenumbered documents;

3. Periodic accounting for the numeric sequence of used documents;

4. Establishing imprest funds for petty cash and payroll accounts and fixed responsibility for custodianship;

5. Recording serial numbers, and affixing tags with recorded numbers to assets not having serial numbers, to prevent removal and temporary substitution of similar assets; and

6. Bonding employees in positions of trust.*

*Bonding serves a dual purpose. First, it compensates the entity in the event of loss. Second, some companies consider bonding to be a psychological deterrent against theft, in that the bonded employee would have to contend with the bonding company should misappropriation be suspected.

and responding to exceptions, clearing exceptions to vendors' statements, responding to questions posed by regulators, a system of double-checking whereby one employee reviews the work of another in order to minimize errors, and periodic inventories and comparison with recorded accountability.

Other controls are not conducive to ongoing monitoring and require **separate evaluations**. Integrity, ethical values, competence, and the control environment cannot be monitored on a real-time basis, but require recurring review for effectiveness.

Provision for periodic evaluation of these controls by various levels of management, as well as by the internal auditors, is recommended if the system is to remain strong. Responding to input from external auditors and regulators also serves as a positive influence in maintaining effective control over factors not amenable to ongoing monitoring.

Because control activities vary according to the transaction cycles to which they relate, ongoing monitoring of these activities should maintain a transaction cycle focus. For example, controls over cash receipts and cash balances may be adequate, while payroll controls are weak. To be effective, therefore, the monitoring mechanism should recognize these variations in control activities and provide immediate feedback for correction purposes. Specifically, monitoring should focus on transaction cycle subsets (e.g., cash receipts and cash balances, sales and accounts receivable, purchases and accounts payable, production, payroll, financing and investing transactions, etc.).

Table 6.3 lists some of the more common monitoring controls that may be applied to specific transaction cycle subsets. Item 4 in Table 6.3, **periodic counts and comparisons**, strengthens the completeness and existence assertions and also helps to establish ownership of assets (rights and obligations assertion).

Failure to institute these or similar monitoring controls can result in the misappropriation of assets and concealment of the transfer. Concealment might assume the form of **alteration of accounts** (e.g., customer remittances may be misappropriated and concealment effected through overstatement of discounts or charging the account against the allowance for doubtful accounts). Alternately, concealment might be achieved through **alteration of substance** (e.g., negotiable securities or inventories may be misappropriated and concealment effected through substitution of similar assets for the missing assets during physical counts and inspections). Case 6.1 illustrates a situation in which a dishonest treasurer was able to misappropriate large amounts of cash from the sale of securities and conceal the misappropriation through substitution.

ANOTHER LOOK AT FINANCIAL CONTROLS

Another approach to viewing financial reporting controls relates to their accuracy, safeguarding, prevention, and detection characteristics. Table 6.4 presents this view in the form of an internal control matrix that relates accuracy and safeguard controls to their

---

TABLE 6.3

Monitoring Controls for Financial Reporting Purposes

1. Investigation of budget variances as to cause;

2. Follow-up of customer exceptions to statements;

3. Determining reasons for differences between creditor statements and subsidiary ledger balances;

4. Periodic counts of inventories, securities, plant assets, and other valuable portable assets and comparisons with recorded accountability. The following are typical of the counts and comparisons to be found in an effective set of control monitoring procedures:
   a. Perpetual inventory records and periodic counts and comparisons;
   b. Subsidiary ledgers for such general ledger accounts as accounts receivable, accounts payable, investments, and plant assets, and periodic comparisons of subsidiary ledgers with the control accounts in the general ledger and the underlying substance (customer exceptions to monthly statements, monthly creditors' statements, examination of securities, and periodic inspection of plant assets);
   c. Monthly bank reconciliations;
   d. Daily cash register audit (counting cash in registers and comparing it with cash register tapes, then forwarding cash register tapes to the person responsible for comparing cash receipts with entry and deposit); and
   e. Comparison of deposit slip with cash receipts entry and prelisting

5. Implementation of financial control recommendations submitted by internal and external auditors.

LARSON HOSPITAL SUPPLY
Case Description

Larson Hospital Supply, located in Yuma, Arizona, was the principal distributor of surgical equipment and hospital supplies for the hospitals located in Yuma and the surrounding area. Annual sales were approximately $10 million; net income for the latest fiscal year was $2.3 million. Chalmers and Pierson, CPAs, had been auditing the financial statements of Larson for the past several years. Judy Riemsnyder, a newly appointed senior auditor, was placed in charge of the 2001 audit for the first time.

Lars Nielson, the corporate treasurer, was responsible for managing Larson's rather sizable investment portfolio. In order to provide maximum flexibility, Larson placed its accounts at the various brokerage houses in Nielson's name. Nielson authorized all purchases and sales; checks for sales proceeds were written to the order of Lars Nielson and mailed to him c/o Larson Hospital Supply. Brokers' advices and other items of correspondence from brokers similarly were mailed directly to Nielson. Nielson maintained the investment ledger supporting the portfolio. Hubert Pompano, Larson's controller, maintained the general ledger.

Given the weaknesses in control over purchases and sales of securities, Lars Nielson misappropriated $350,000 of proceeds from the sale of securities over a two-year period ending with the close of the 2001 fiscal year. Nielson effected the defalcations by depositing checks from brokerage firms into his own bank accounts and destroying the brokers' advices. In the absence of brokers' advices, Pompano had not recorded the sales. To maintain correspondence between the investment ledger and the general ledger control account, Nielson did not credit the investment ledger for the fraudulent sales. Prior to the annual audits, Nielson would transfer cash and securities from his personal accounts with brokers to the company accounts to cover the year-end discrepancies between the accounts with brokers and the investment ledger.

Neither Riemsnyder nor her predecessor on the Larson audit extended their substantive audit procedures. They did confirm the balances with brokers but, as long as the totals agreed with those in the investment ledger, no further procedures were applied and the shortages were not detected.

Discussion Questions

1. What control weaknesses were present in this case that permitted misappropriation and concealment of such a large sum?
2. What course of action should the auditors have taken upon discovering the weaknesses? How might they have modified their substantive testing procedures, given the discovered weaknesses?

prevention and detection characteristics. **Accuracy controls** are designed to prevent and detect errors in recording and presenting financial statement data. They are most supportive of the valuation and presentation assertions. *Safeguard controls* prevent and detect misappropriation of assets and emphasize the existence, completeness, and ownership assertions. Note that many of the controls have both accuracy and safeguard characteristics, as well as both prevention and detection characteristics.

INHERENT LIMITATIONS OF INTERNAL CONTROL SYSTEMS

An internal control system, regardless of how carefully designed and implemented it is, contains certain **inherent limitations**. This is the reason the system is said to provide "reasonable" rather than "absolute" assurance of preventing and detecting errors and fraud. This is also the reason the independent auditor must perform a **minimum audit**

TABLE 6.4

Financial Reporting Control Characteristics

	Prevention Controls	Detection Controls
ACCURACY CONTROLS	Management support of internal control Input editing Electronic data interchange Accounting manuals Chart of accounts Hiring and training policies Proper documentation of transactions Proper documentation of computer programs and systems Proper authorization and documentation of program and system changes Standard journal entries	System of budgeting and variance analysis Analysis of relationships Reconciliations Document review prior to payment Audit trail review Internal audit staff

SAFEGUARD CONTROLS	Management support
	Restrictive endorsements on incoming checks
	Cash prelistings
	Intact daily deposits
	Prenumbered documents
	Recorded serial numbers
	Limited access to assets and documents
	Limited access to computer databases
	Fixing of responsibility:
	    Assets
	    Documents
	    Database elements
	Computer backup files
	Separation of duties:
	    Accounting/Treasury
	    Programmers/Operators
	Voucher system
	Cancellation of used documents
		Employee rotation
		Inventories and comparisons
		System of budgeting and variance analysis
		Analysis of relationships
		Internal audit staff
		Monthly bank reconciliations
		Comparison of bank deposit ticket with prelisting
		Controlled reprocessing of errors

(i.e., perform some substantive testing), no matter how effective the control system is. The inherent limitations are classified and discussed in the following paragraphs.

Collusion to Circumvent Control

Adequate separation of functional responsibilities provides reasonable assurance against a single individual's perpetration and concealment of a misappropriation fraud, but this class of controls can be circumvented by **collusion**, involving two or more individuals working together to effect the misappropriation and concealment. A person having custody over incoming cash receipts, for example, might conspire with a person responsible for processing and recording those receipts. Together, these individuals could effect a fraudulent diversion of cash receipts, accompanied by its concealment. Concealment might assume the form of failure to record the cash receipts, overstatement of discounts, recording of fictitious returns, writing off of accounts receivable, or some combination of these or other possible means.

Management Override

The accounting information system and related internal control activities may be referred to collectively as an *arm of management*. As such, the controls are as effective or as ineffective as management wishes them to be. They cannot be expected, therefore, to prevent or detect frauds perpetrated by those members of management responsible for monitoring the internal control system.

Management override may assume the form of either fraudulent financial reporting or misappropriation. Misappropriation, the fraudulent transfer of assets accompanied by concealment, was discussed earlier. **Fraudulent financial reporting** (discussed in Chapter 5) occurs when management intentionally attempts to misstate financial position or results of operations. In a case that surfaced in 1998, executives of Bankers Trust Corp. unlawfully diverted millions of dollars in unclaimed client funds to bolster the company's earnings. Officers and employees in the company's client processing services unit, responding to earnings pressure from top management, asked employees to transfer unclaimed client monies to reserve accounts. Employees then falsified the records to conceal the diversions from bank regulators.

The client processing services unit functioned as a disbursing agent for the bank's clients by writing and mailing dividend and pension checks to investors and retirees. The diverted funds represented checks that had been returned because the payees had either moved or were deceased. By law, the bank should have remitted these unclaimed monies to the state after a reasonable waiting period. Instead, the bank transferred the unclaimed funds to reserve accounts. The reserve accounts were then used to increase the company's earnings.

During their investigation, federal prosecutors found evidence suggesting that the managing director, the financial controller, and several other executives had known about the transfers since 1994. The evidence consisted of emails from the financial controller to the managing director and the other executives.[15] Whatever controls may have been in place to secure the unclaimed funds, they were ineffective given the override by the top management of Bankers Trust.

Although misappropriation of assets by lower-level employees can be prevented effectively through documentation, limited access, and separation of duties, misappropriation by members of top management cannot be prevented, given the opportunity for override.

Case 6.2 illustrates how an effective control system breaks down under conditions of management override.

Temporary Breakdown of the System

The functioning of the internal control system and related internal control activities is only as effective as the performance of the people administering the controls. People

15 See *The Wall Street Journal*, March 15, 1999.

CASE 6.2

MAPLES OF SINGAPORE HOSPITAL

Case Description

Maples of Singapore Hospital, with 1,200 beds, was one of the largest hospitals in the Atlanta metropolitan area. It was considered by other hospitals in the region to be one of the best-managed and most competitive health care institutions. The management team consisted of Wade Holloway, chief executive officer; Nolan Tuckerman, vice president and chief operating officer; Jack Hanlan, controller; and Georgiann Bartells, treasurer. Gerald Smile & Associates, CPAs, had been performing the annual audit of Maples for several years, the latest having been the fiscal year ending June 30, 1999.

For as long as Smile & Associates had been auditing Maples, the management team had conspired to perpetrate material defalcations of monies received from insurers and patients. The frauds primarily involved inflating insurance claims. Claims for actual patients were padded, and claims for nonexistent patients were filed. The frauds involved millions of dollars annually, and had been cleverly concealed through false documentation—all properly approved by the management team.

The frauds were discovered after Hanlan became ill and was replaced temporarily by Jason Drew, assistant controller. Not having been included in the conspiracy, Drew became suspicious upon reviewing insurance claims for patients alleged to be in rooms known by Drew to be vacant on the dates referenced in the claims. Drew had visited Hanlan in the hospital on the dates in question and had noted specifically the unusual vacancy rate on Hanlan's floor. Upon questioning Tuckerman, Drew was told that he must be mistaken and not to pursue the matter further. Being confident of his facts, Drew took the matter to Wade Holloway, who also tried to convince him that he was wrong.

Finding no other avenue open to him, Drew contacted one of the outside members of the board of directors. An emergency board meeting was called, and Holloway admitted the fraud when confronted by the board. An investigation was conducted by Smile & Associates, who later estimated the defalcation at $35 million over a five-year period.

Holloway, Tuckerman, Hanlan, and Bartells were all terminated, prosecuted by the state of Georgia, and sentenced to terms in prison. Smile & Associates were sued by the new hospital administrators for negligence in not detecting the defalcations.

What Do You Think?

Should management be prevented from recovering damages for the negligence of auditors in not detecting frauds committed by a different management? Will your answer be influenced by the type of fraud committed?

---

cannot be expected to perform the control functions in a consistent manner at all times. Misunderstandings, mistaken judgment, carelessness, distraction, and fatigue are some factors causing **temporary breakdowns** of the system. A significant extension (price × quantity) error on the face of a vendor's invoice may go undetected, a shipment of merchandise may fail to be billed to a customer, or an unauthorized disbursement may be made because the check signer did not adequately review the accompanying documentation. These "control failures" are certain to happen occasionally, whenever people are charged with administering control functions.

Chapter 8 offers a means for minimizing the incidence of temporary breakdowns through effective computer controls. Computers, unlike people, perform programmed functions in a consistent manner. Therefore, if they are properly programmed to perform comparisons, recalculations, and reconciliations, the magnitude of temporary control breakdowns can be dramatically reduced.

Temporary breakdowns also occur as a result of changing environments not accompanied by immediate control adaptation. Examples of environmental changes affecting internal control include acquiring other companies; opening branches in other locations; and adding or dropping divisions, departments, or product lines. When these changes occur, the accounting system and other control procedures frequently do not adapt immediately to the new environment. Until they do, errors or fraud may occur. A company, for example, may require that all incoming cash receipts be prelisted, and that the prelisting be compared to the daily deposit ticket received from the bank. A newly opened branch may have overlooked this requirement and failed to prelist cash receipts or otherwise maintain proper accountability over cash. The situation may go undetected until the internal auditors arrive from the home office and inform the branch manager of the "gap" in control.

A related type of change occurs when the environment remains stable while the accounting system changes. Computerizing a portion of the accounting system, for example, may result in a temporary loss of control—or it may result in temporary control redundancy. Assume that a manual payroll system provides for double-checking pay rates, hours, and withholdings. Assume further that the company replaces the manual system with a computerized payroll system. The new system may include programmed routines for verifying rates, hours, and withholdings, in which case the manual checking becomes unnecessary. Retention of the manual controls beyond the normal "debugging" stage would result in control redundancy.

A more serious matter would present itself, however, if the manual checking were eliminated and the new system did not contain the verification routines. For this reason, most companies require that computer-based information (CBI) systems be operated alongside manual systems until the CBI systems are functioning adequately, and all controls are in place and working.

INTERNAL CONTROL FOR A SMALL BUSINESS

Small firms, given personnel constraints, cannot justify on the basis of cost–benefit analysis many of the accounting system features and control activities found in larger entities. Separation of functional responsibilities, for example, which is present in large entities, is not found in smaller businesses due to the added employee cost of effecting separation. In addition, smaller companies cannot afford to maintain the internal audit personnel found in larger businesses. Given these constraints, **compensating controls** are needed to achieve adequate internal control in a cost-effective manner. Active participation by the owner or manager is usually the best form of compensating control. Active involvement should include at least the following functions:

1. *Examine all documentation before signing checks and mail checks directly upon signing.* The owner/manager's knowledge of the business should enable him or her to recognize documents that are fabricated, altered, or otherwise not representative of transactions completed by the entity. Also, by mailing signed checks directly, the owner/manager is preventing accounting personnel from having access to financial assets (signed disbursement checks) for possible misappropriation and concealment.

2. *Mail customer statements directly after careful review.* The purpose of reviewing customer statements is to identify significant past-due balances for follow-up with

customers. Whether the past-due balances are the result of lapping[16] or actually are delinquent accounts, the owner/manager's review and follow-up should reveal the cause. Moreover, knowledge of the owner/manager's review and follow-up policy should discourage accounting personnel from fraudulently lapping customer's remittances and should encourage vigorous collection policies.

3. *Examine purchase orders before their submission to vendors.* By examining purchase orders before they are forwarded to vendors, the owner/manager can prevent or detect purchasing abuses such as buying goods and services of inferior quality, buying at excessive prices (whether or not kickbacks are involved), or failing to buy in quantities that satisfactorily balance order cost and carrying cost.

4. *Apply analytical procedures and investigate unusual relationships.* By requiring budgets along with monthly financial statements and performance reports, the owner/manager can apply analytical procedures similar to those discussed in Chapter 4. This, in turn, should enable him or her to identify significant abnormalities and investigate them for cause. Ratios and percentages of particular interest include gross profit rates, budget variances, current and quick ratios, accounts receivable turnover, inventory turnover, and times interest earned. Whether significant declines are the result of deteriorating economic conditions, increased competition, errors, or fraud, by investigating for cause and following up for correction, the owner/manager is able to achieve effective control.

5. *Control cash receipts and compare them with daily deposit tickets obtained from the bank.* To ensure that all incoming cash receipts are deposited intact, the owner/manager should require the following:
   a. Incoming checks should be restrictively endorsed by someone *not* having access to accounting records (e.g., the owner/manager's secretary or a receptionist) and listed for later comparison with the deposit ticket;
   b. The owner/manager or the person responsible for incoming checks should audit cash registers;
   c. Cash register tapes and sales slips should be forwarded to the accountant;
   d. Checks and cash register receipts should be deposited by the person endorsing checks and auditing the cash registers, and receipted deposit tickets should be forwarded to the owner/manager; and
   e. The owner/manager should compare each deposit ticket total for agreement with the cash receipts entry, the sum from the cash register tapes, and the listing of checks received by mail.

6. *Reconcile bank accounts or have accounts reconciled by someone other than the cashier or bookkeeper.* As a further control to detect errors or irregularities relating to cash, the owner/manager should reconcile the bank accounts monthly or assign this task to someone not having access to either cash receipts or accounting records.

7. *Approve all write-offs of customer accounts.* To guard against premature write-offs of otherwise collectible accounts, and to prevent dishonest employees from writing off accounts to conceal misappropriated remittances, the owner/manager should contact customers and/or collection agencies prior to approving write-offs of presumably uncollectible accounts.

---

16 Lapping is a form of concealment whereby current customer remittances are credited to customers whose previous remittances have been misappropriated. Lapping is discussed in Chapter 11.

8. *Test-count inventory periodically and compare results with perpetual records.* Significant disparities between physical inventories and perpetual inventory records may result from either inventory shortages or inadequate perpetual records. If the result of a shortage, the cause may be due to fraud or waste. Whatever the cause, the result is loss of inventory control. By performing recurring test counts and comparisons, the owner/manager can quickly detect shortages and investigate for cause. This practice should also strengthen inventory accounting by encouraging the person(s) maintaining the perpetual records to exercise care in minimizing errors.

9. *Review payroll checks prior to signing them and perform an occasional surprise distribution of payroll checks.* In a small business, the owner/manager should be familiar with his or her labor force, as well as with normal working hours and rates of pay. By reviewing payroll checks before signing them, he or she should be able to identify errors and fraud relating to hours, rates of pay, fictitious employees, and/or terminated employees who remain on the payroll. If the number of employees is too great for ready recognition, the owner/manager can compensate for lack of familiarity by distributing checks occasionally and retaining unclaimed checks for follow-up.

10. *Retain an independent CPA for recurring review of the accounting system and related financial statements.* Although small businesses are not typically audited by independent CPAs, reviews are quite common. Further defined in Chapter 15, a review, although more limited in scope than an audit, does provide a degree of assurance regarding the financial statements. Moreover, although the CPA is not required to study and evaluate internal control as part of a review, significant control weaknesses should be sufficiently obvious to the trained professional, enabling him or her to so inform the owner/manager.

In essence, the owner/manager, in performing the above activities, is acting in the capacity of internal auditor, thus strengthening the control environment and providing compensating controls in the absence of separation. Systematic application of these procedures requires little of the owner/manager's time, while providing much-needed control of the firm's assets and accounting system.

KEY TERMS

Access controls, 213

Accountability controls, 213

Accounting manuals, 212

Accuracy controls, 216

Alteration of accounts, 215

Alteration of substance, 215

Business risk, 208

Chart of accounts, 212

Codes of corporate conduct, 207

Collusion, 217

Communication, 211

Compensating controls, 220

Compliance controls, 205

Control activities, 211

Control environment, 206

Detection controls, 206

Financial reporting controls, 205

Financial statement assertions, 206

Fraudulent financial reporting, 218

Information and communication, 210

Information system elements, 210

Inherent limitations, 216

Internal control, 205

Management override, 218

Minimum audit, 216

Monitoring, 213

REVIEW QUESTIONS

1. Define *internal control systems*.

2. Identify the five components of internal control.

3. Name and briefly describe the three categories of internal control.

4. Of the three categories of controls, which is/are of interest to the external auditor?

5. Why is internal control said to provide only "reasonable assurance" as to the attainment of the entity's objectives?

6. Discuss the importance of management's support of internal control.

7. How does the human resources function impact internal control?

8. An effective control system is said to have both prevention and detection aspects. Explain.

9. What factors impact financial reporting risk and how can effective internal control minimize the impact of financial reporting risk?

10. Identify the essential components of an information system.

11. How does communication affect financial reporting risk?

12. How does monitoring differ from other aspects of internal control? Differentiate between on-going monitoring and separate evaluations.

13. Differentiate between access controls and accountability controls.

14. Why must access to documents, as well as assets, be limited?

15. How does fixing responsibility enhance control?

16. Why is a minimum audit necessary, notwithstanding an effective control system?

17. How does the internal control system in a small entity differ from that in a large entity?

MULTIPLE CHOICE QUESTIONS FROM PAST CPA AND CIA EXAMS

1. Mailing disbursement checks and remittance advices should be controlled by the employee who
   a. Approves the vouchers for payment.
   b. Matches the receiving reports, purchase orders, and vendors' invoices.
   c. Maintains possession of the mechanical check-signing device.
   d. Signs the checks last.

2. Which of the following controls would an entity most likely use in safeguarding against the loss of marketable securities?

a. An independent trust company that has no direct contact with the employees who have record-keeping responsibilities has possession of the securities.

b. The internal auditor verifies the marketable securities in the entity's safe each year on the balance sheet date.

c. The independent auditor traces all purchases and sales of marketable securities through the subsidiary ledgers to the general ledger.

d. A designated member of the board of directors controls the securities in a bank safe-deposit box.

3. An entity with a large volume of customer remittances by mail could most likely reduce the risk of employee misappropriation of cash by using
   a. Employee fidelity bonds.
   b. Independently prepared mailroom prelists.
   c. Daily check summaries.
   d. A bank lockbox system.

4. When the shipping department returns nonconforming goods to a vendor, the purchasing department should send to the accounting department the
   a. Unpaid voucher.
   b. Debit memo.
   c. Vendor invoice.
   d. Credit memo.

5. Which of the following departments most likely would approve changes in pay rates and deductions from employee salaries?
   a. Personnel
   b. Treasurer
   c. Controller
   d. Payroll

6. The authority to accept incoming goods in receiving should be based on a(n)
   a. Vendor's invoice.
   b. Materials requisition.
   c. Bill of lading.
   d. Approved purchase order.

7. Which of the following factors are included in an entity's control environment?

	Audit committee	Internal audit function	Organizational structure
a.	Yes	Yes	No
b.	Yes	No	Yes
c.	No	Yes	Yes
d.	Yes	Yes	Yes

8. Immediately upon receipt of cash, a responsible employee should
   a. Record the amount in the cash receipts journal.
   b. Prepare a remittance listing.
   c. Update the subsidiary accounts receivable records.
   d. Prepare a deposit slip in triplicate.

9. Which of the following internal control activities is *not* usually performed in the treasurer's department?

a. Verifying the accuracy of checks and vouchers
b. Controlling the mailing of checks to vendors
c. Approving vendors' invoices for payment
d. Canceling payment vouchers when paid

10. For effective internal control, the accounts payable department generally should
    a. Obliterate the quantity ordered on the receiving department copy of the purchase order.
    b. Establish the agreement of the vendor's invoice with the receiving report and purchase order.
    c. Stamp, perforate, or otherwise cancel supporting documentation after payment is mailed.
    d. Ascertain that an authorized employee approves each requisition as to price, quantity, and quality.

ESSAY QUESTIONS AND PROBLEMS

6.1   Juanita Alvarez joined Grimley Metals as assistant controller in March 1995 after having been with Giese and Zurk, CPAs, for six years. At the end of her employment with the accounting firm, Alvarez was the in-charge auditor on several engagements, including the Grimley Metals audit. She progressed in the company even faster than anticipated by Grimley management and assumed the title of controller in 1999 following the former controller's retirement. As corporate controller, Alvarez was in charge of the accounting system, encompassing the internal as well as the external reporting functions. She was considered by Homer Otto, Grimley's chief executive officer, as a "very loyal, devoted employee, who earned a lot of trust from us." She also had earned the highest respect from the firm of Giese and Zurk, her former employer and continuing independent auditors of Grimley.

Acting on an anonymous tip, however, Grimley Metals officials became suspicious about their controller's lifestyle, being concerned that she was living well beyond her $85,000-a-year salary. Of particular interest was the $350,000 houseboat recently purchased by Alvarez and moored at the private lake that was part of the subdivision where she lived, and the expensive sports car that she had recently acquired. The anonymous tipster informed Otto that Alvarez had paid cash for both the boat and the automobile.

Otto, after discussing the matter with his executive staff, decided to engage Giese and Zurk to conduct a special audit of the books to determine if the company's financial assets were secure. Cheryl Bench, the in-charge auditor for the Grimley Metals engagement (Alvarez's replacement), was placed in charge of the special investigation. She and her audit team quickly discovered that at least $900,000 was missing. Upon being informed of the finding, Otto asked for and received a court freeze on Alvarez's assets.

The amount had been misappropriated over a period of eleven months, from mid-2000 to mid-2001, and equaled the company's first-half profits for 2001. The fraud had been perpetrated through overbuying from Grimley's suppliers and subsequently returning the excess and requesting a refund. Alvarez had opened an account with a local bank in the name of the company and for which she was the sole signatory—only she could withdraw funds from the account. She then deposited the unrecorded refund checks in this account and drew checks on the account to fund her personal purchases. To conceal the overstatement in the "receivable from vendors" account, set up as excess inventory that was returned to the suppliers, Alvarez debited various operating expense accounts. In this manner, none of the expenses appeared to be "out of line" and the auditors would have a difficult time detecting the fraud.

Required:

a. What kinds of controls are needed to prevent and/or detect this type of misappropriation?

b. What responsibility do you think the independent auditors have for detecting misappropriation of this nature?

6.2   The management of Swan, Ltd., has engaged you to review internal control over the purchase, receipt, storage, and issue of raw materials. You have prepared the following comments that describe Swan's procedures.

Raw materials, which consist mainly of high-cost electronic components, are kept in a locked storeroom. Storeroom personnel include a supervisor and four clerks. All are well trained, competent, and adequately bonded. Raw materials are removed from the storeroom only upon written or oral authorization of one of the production supervisors.

There are no perpetual inventory records; hence, the storeroom clerks do not keep records of goods received or issued. To compensate for the lack of perpetual records, a physical inventory count is taken monthly by the storeroom clerks, who are well supervised. Appropriate procedures are followed in making the inventory count.

After the physical count, the storeroom supervisor matches quantities counted against predetermined reorder levels. If the count for a given part is below the reorder level, the supervisor enters the part number on a materials requisition list and sends this list to the accounts payable clerk. The accounts payable clerk prepares a purchase order for a predetermined reorder quantity for each part and mails the purchase order to the vendor from whom the part was last purchased.

When ordered materials arrive at Swan, they are received by the storeroom clerks. The clerks count the merchandise and agree the counts to the shipper's bill of lading. All vendors' bills of lading are initialed, dated, and filed in the storeroom to serve as receiving reports.

Required:

Describe the weaknesses in internal control and recommend improvements in Swan's procedures for the purchase, receipt, storage, and issue of raw materials. Organize your answer sheet into two columns: *Weakness* and *Recommended Improvements*. (AICPA adapted)

6.3   The Dollyfield Zoological Society operates a zoo for the benefit and enjoyment of the community. During hours when the zoo is open to the public, two clerks, who are positioned at the entrance, collect a $5 admission fee from each nonmember patron. Members of the Dollyfield Zoological Society are permitted to enter free of charge upon presentation of their membership cards.

At the end of each day, one of the clerks delivers the proceeds to the treasurer. The treasurer counts the cash in the presence of the clerk and places it in a safe. Each Friday afternoon the treasurer and one of the clerks deliver all cash held in the safe to the bank and receive an authenticated deposit slip, which provides the basis for the weekly entry in the cash receipts journal.

The board of directors of the Dollyfield Zoological Society has identified a need to improve the internal control over cash admission fees. The board has determined that the cost of installing turnstiles or sales booths, or otherwise altering the physical layout of the zoo entrance, will greatly exceed any benefits that may be derived. However, the board has agreed that the sale of admission tickets must be an integral part of its improvement efforts. Wright has been asked by the board of directors of the Dollyfield Zoological Society to review the internal controls over cash admission fees and provide suggestions for improvement.

Required:

Indicate the weaknesses in existing internal control over cash admission fees that Wright should identify, and recommend one improvement for each of the weaknesses identified. Organize your answer into two columns: *Weakness* and *Recommendation*. (AICPA adapted)

6.4   Laser Beams, Inc., produces high-priced precision equipment used in laser eye surgery. The specifications of component parts are vital to the manufacturing process. Laser Beams buys valuable electronic subcomponents and large quantities of plastic and screws. Screws and subcomponents are ordered by Laser Beams and billed by the vendors on a unit basis. Plastic is ordered by Laser Beams and is billed by the vendors on the basis of weight. The receiving clerk is responsible for documenting the quality and quantity of inventory received. A preliminary review of the internal control system indicates that the procedures used are as follows:

Receiving Report: Properly approved purchase orders, which are prenumbered, are filed numerically. The copy sent to the receiving clerk is an exact duplicate of the copy sent to the vendor. The receiving clerk records receipts of inventory on the duplicate copy.

Plastic: The company receives plastic by railroad. The railroad independently weighs the plastic and reports the weight and date of receipt on a bill of lading (waybill) that accompanies each delivery. The receiving clerk checks only the weight on the waybill against that on the purchase order.

Screws: The receiving clerk opens cartons containing screws, then inspects and weighs the contents. The weight is converted to number of units by means of conversion charts. The receiving clerk then checks the computed quantity against the purchase order.

Electronic subcomponents: Each subcomponent is delivered in a separate corrugated carton. Cartons are counted as they are received by the receiving clerk and the number of cartons is checked against each purchase order.

Required:
a. Explain why the internal control activities, as they apply individually to receiving reports and the receipt of plastic, screws, and electronic subcomponents, are adequate or inadequate. Do not discuss recommendations for improvements.
b. What financial statement distortions may arise because of the inadequacies in Laser Beams' internal controls and how may they occur?
(AICPA adapted)

6.5   Each of the following cases relate to internal control for a small business.

Required:
Identify the internal control(s) that should have prevented or detected the error or fraud for each case.
a. The bookkeeper for Harley Clothing misappropriated customer checks in payment of outstanding accounts receivable. The checks were endorsed by the bookkeeper and deposited in her personal checking account. To conceal the fraud, the bookkeeper charged the accounts to bad debts expense.
b. Jason James, controller of Burlington Housewares, established a fictitious vendor and fabricated purchase orders, receiving reports, and vendor's invoices for goods purportedly purchased from the vendor. After Abe Burlington, owner of the business, signed the disbursement checks payable to the vendor, James restrictively endorsed the checks

and deposited them in a bank account that he had opened in the name of the vendor. The debit to inventory was later written off to the inventory shrinkage account.

c. Lara Finnegan, the cashier/bookkeeper for Carl's Pharmacy, systematically withheld recorded cash receipts. To cover the disparity between the general ledger cash balance and the bank account balance, Finnegan, in reconciling the bank account, added a nonexistent deposit-in-transit equal to the shortage.

d. Funways Amusement Park employs several seasonal employees, and employee turnover is high. Recognizing this, Lowel Schroeder, the company controller, retained employees on the payroll who no longer worked for the company. After reviewing the payroll and signing the checks, the owner, Potter, forwarded the signed payroll checks to Schroeder, who withheld the fraudulent checks, endorsed them, and deposited them in his personal checking account. Over a ten-year period, Schroeder was able to misappropriate $220,000 in this manner. The fraud was finally detected when a terminated employee complained that he had received a Form W-2 withholding statement reporting more wages than he had earned that year.

6.6   The Franz Company produces a variety of chemical products for use by cleaning supply manufacturers. The plant operates on two shifts, five days per week, with maintenance work performed on the third shift and on Saturdays, as required.

An audit conducted by the staff of the new corporate internal audit department was recently completed; comments on inventory control were not favorable. Audit comments were directed particularly to the control of raw material ingredients and maintenance materials.

Raw material ingredients are received at the back of the plant, signed for by one of the employees of the batching department, and stored near the location of the initial batching process. Receiving tallies are given during the day to the supervisor, who then forwards them to the inventory control department at the end of the day. The inventory control department calculates ingredient usage using weekly reports of actual production and standard formulas. Physical inventories are taken quarterly. The inventory control department prepares purchase requisitions and rush orders are frequent. In spite of the need for rush orders, the production superintendent regularly gets memos from the controller stating that there must be excess inventory because the ingredient inventory dollar value is too high.

Maintenance parts and supplies are received and stored in a storeroom. There is a storeroom clerk on each operating shift. Storeroom requisitions are to be filled out for everything taken from the storeroom; however, this practice is not always followed. The storeroom is not locked when the clerk is out because of the need to get parts quickly. The storeroom also is open during the third shift for the maintenance crews to get parts as needed. The storeroom clerk prepares purchase requisitions and physical inventory is taken on a cycle count basis. Rush orders are frequent.

Required:

a. Identify the weaknesses in Franz Company's internal control procedures for ingredients inventory and maintenance material and supplies inventory. Then, recommend improvements to be instituted for each of these areas.

b. What procedures would the internal auditors use to identify the weaknesses in Franz Company's inventory control?

(AICPA adapted)

6.7   Each of the following independent narratives describes one or more misstatements that occurred in the financial statements of Sanford Manufacturing.

Required:

For each narrative, determine whether the misstatement(s) resulted from an internal control weakness or from an inherent weakness in internal control. Remember the inherent weaknesses described in this chapter: collusion, management override, and temporary breakdown.

If the misstatement was caused by an internal control weakness, recommend an appropriate remedy. If the misstatement was due to an inherent limitation, identify the limitation. Use the following format in addressing each narrative:

Inherent Weakness or Control Weakness	Type of Control Remedy

a. The company recently installed a new CBI payroll system. Although some errors in payroll classification appeared in the 2001 financial statements, the errors were not material and the system is currently performing without error.

b. Because of numerous classification errors in recording plant and equipment acquisitions and repair expenditures, the property accounts, along with depreciation expenses, are significantly understated, while repairs and maintenance expenses are materially overstated.

c. Although the control system provided for detailed cutoff procedures to ensure proper recording of year-end sales, Sean O'Brian, Sanford's chief executive officer, together with his three vice presidents, arranged for 2002 sales to be recorded in 2001, prior to shipment. The goods were included in the 12/31/01 inventory. The early recording inflated reported net income by the selling price times the quantity of goods. This, in turn, increased the amount of profit-based bonuses awarded the four executives. As a result, sales revenue and bonus expense were overstated in the 2001 income statement, and accounts receivable was overstated on the balance sheet.

d. Unbilled shipments were made to customers during the year. Inasmuch as the shipments were not invoiced, the sales were not recorded. As a result, accounts receivable, sales, and cost of goods sold were understated, while inventory was overstated.

e. A significant amount of cash receipts from customers was misappropriated by billing clerks. To avoid detection, the clerks charged the related customer accounts to allowance for uncollectible accounts. As a result, bad debts expense was overstated on the income statement and cash was understated on the balance sheet.

f. A computer programmer and a computer operator were able to program the computer to print checks payable to each of them. The debits were to such accounts as inventory, repairs, and miscellaneous expense. Although the amounts involved were not material to overall financial presentation, the dishonest employees were able to misappropriate more than $50,000 during 2001.

6.8 A company uses expensive metals in manufacturing its products. Production is highly efficient, but large amounts of scrap metal are generated. The company sells the scrap to a large scrap metal dealer who counts it, picks it up, and sends the company a check. The storage facility is physically secure and personnel record on blank forms what and how much is sold, based on the purchaser's record. The total quantity of scrap sales for each quarter is reviewed for reasonableness and compared to that for prior periods.

Required:

Identify three strengths and six weaknesses in the internal control over scrap metal.
(IIA adapted)

6.9   The following short cases describe some specific internal control weaknesses.

Required:

For each case, determine whether the weakness is relevant to an independent financial audit. If a weakness is relevant to an audit, identify the financial statement assertion(s) affected by the weakness and how they are affected. Use the following format in addressing each weakness:

Relevant to Audit?   Assertion Affected   How Affected?

a. In choosing among alternative long-term investment opportunities, Dowley, Ltd., selects those projects that promise the highest accounting rate of return. Discounted cash flow and payback methods are ignored.

b. Jackson, Inc., does not utilize a set of standard journal entries or journal vouchers for recording monthly allocations and accruals.

c. All Hardware Corp. sells hardware and small appliances to selected retailers throughout the United States and Canada. Terms are 2/10; n/30. In addition to customer accounts, All Hardware's accounts receivable includes employee receivables, customer credit balances, and other nontrade receivables, such as returnable container deposits, utility deposits, and amounts receivable from sale of assets other than inventory. These other amounts are considered material, but no effort is made to identify them separately for either monthly or annual financial statement purposes.

d. Although Jupiter Warehouses, Ltd., maintains perpetual inventory records, monthly counts and comparisons are not made. To satisfy the independent auditors, a thorough physical inventory is taken annually and the perpetual records are adjusted to agree with the physical inventory.

e. Ovally, Inc., makes and sells unassembled silos to farm supply distributors in the midwest. Upon credit approval and determination of available inventory, Ovally bills the distributor. The sales invoice, together with customer order and evidence of credit approval, are filed in an open invoice file awaiting payment by the customer.

f. Barnes, Inc., a small manufacturer of water pumps, does not formally train its accounting personnel. Moreover, although the company has a chart of accounts, accounting manuals describing appropriate debits and credits to the various accounts have not been developed.

g. Although Discovery, Inc., has embarked on several new ventures in recent years, the company does not have a formal strategic planning function in place. As a result, some of the endeavors have resulted in significant losses.

h. Litehouse Pools, Inc., manufactures and sells in-ground pools, pumps, filters, and supplies to retailers east of the Mississippi River. All sales are on open account, and customer checks are received through the mail on a daily basis. The checks are forwarded to data processing where they are posted to the general ledger and to individual customer accounts by computer. The checks then are transferred to the corporate treasurer where the daily deposits are prepared and sent to the bank.

i. All payments to vendors for purchases of goods and services by Grambling, Inc., require a properly approved voucher. Although the vouchers are prenumbered, the numeric sequence of used vouchers is not monitored and neither used vouchers nor paid invoices are canceled.

6.10   The following functions are enhanced by the presence of certain internal control procedures:

1. Error prevention
2. Error detection
3. Fraud prevention
4. Fraud detection

Required:

For each of the following specific controls, indicate by appropriate number or numbers the function(s) served by the control.

a.   Prelisting incoming cash receipts

b.   Monthly bank reconciliations

c.   Cash disbursements made only with properly approved voucher supported by necessary documentation

d.   Time cards approved by supervisor at the end of each day

e.   Account distributions (debits and credits) appearing on the face of vouchers that are double-checked by a second person

f.   Review of pay rates, hours, extensions, and withholdings prior to distribution of payroll checks

g.   Written job descriptions for all clerical positions

h.   Custody of accounting records separate from custody of cash and negotiable securities

i.   Receiving reports required for all incoming goods, including sales returns

j.   Chart of accounts and accounting manuals

k.   Prenumbering of all documents

l.   All inventories in physically secured areas

m.   Responsibility for physical control over inventories assigned to the store's manager

n.   Daily intact deposits of cash receipts

o.   Inventories periodically "spot-checked" and compared with perpetual records

c h a p t e r 7

biltrite

l e a r n i n g   o b j e c t i v e s

After reading this chapter, you should be able to

1 Explain the reason for the auditor's assessment of control risk.
2 Describe an approach to assessing control risk.
3 Differentiate between an initial understanding of the design and implementation of internal control and tests of controls for operating effectiveness.
4 Determine the need for testing internal controls.
5 Develop the methodology for testing internal controls.
6 Develop the necessary documentation of the auditor's understanding of a client's internal control.
7 Develop the necessary documentation supporting an assessed level of control risk below the maximum level.
8 Describe both a quantitative and a qualitative approach to the design of substantive audit procedures, after having assessed inherent risk and control risk.
9 Understand the meaning of "reportable conditions" and how and to whom to report them.

OVERVIEW

Chapter 7 presents the auditor's approach to assessing control risk through the study and evaluation of internal control policies and procedures relevant to an audit. To assess control risk, the auditor must obtain a sufficient understanding of the client's internal control system to be able to evaluate the probability that material misstatements exist. This understanding of the client's internal control is gained through inquiry, observation, and by studying its organizational structure. Documentation of this understanding is generally in the form of narrative memoranda, internal control flowcharts, internal control checklists or questionnaires, or a combination of these.

Based on the initial understanding, the auditor may decide to assess control risk as being at the maximum level or below the maximum level. In addition, the auditor may elect to test certain controls as a means of further reducing the assessed level of control risk. Tests of controls may be in the form of transaction reprocessing, added observation, document examination and testing, or a combination of these. Whenever control risk is assessed below the maximum level, the auditor must document the basis for the assessment.

The assessment of control risk combined with the assessment of inherent risk (Chapter 5) forms the basis for setting detection risk and designing substantive audit programs. The level of risk assessment affects the nature, timing, and extent of the procedures incorporated into the programs. Significant internal control weaknesses identified by the auditor during the assessment of control risk must be communicated—orally or in writing—to the client's audit committee.

AUDITOR'S ASSESSMENT OF CONTROL RISK

The second standard of audit field work requires the auditor to obtain a sufficient understanding of a client's internal control system to plan the audit and to determine the nature, timing, and extent of tests to be performed. Chapter 5 defined the three components of audit risk and presented a model for assessing inherent risk (the susceptibility of an assertion to a material misstatement, assuming that there are no related controls)[1] as part of the overall audit process. The essence of this part of the audit model involves a thorough study of the company and the industry and application of analytical procedures. In order to complete the planning phase of the audit, the auditor must also assess control risk (the probability that a material misstatement that could occur in a financial statement assertion will not be prevented or detected on a timely basis by the entity's internal control).[2] Together, the assessment of inherent risk and control risk enables the auditor to set detection risk and develop substantive audit programs based on such risk assessment.

The ensuing paragraphs address the auditor's assessment of control risk through study and evaluation of internal control policies and procedures relevant to an audit (hereafter the term *internal control* is considered the same as *financial reporting controls*).

Figure 7.1 shows where control risk assessment fits into the overall audit process. Control risk assessment, like inherent risk assessment, is initially conducted in the planning stages of the audit.[3] Once inherent risk and control risk have been assessed, the auditor can determine the level of detection risk (the risk that an auditor will not

1   *AICPA Professional Standards*, New York: AICPA, section 312.27.a.
2   Ibid, section AU 312.27.b.
3   Ibid, section AU 319.02–03.

FIGURE 7.1

The Audit Process

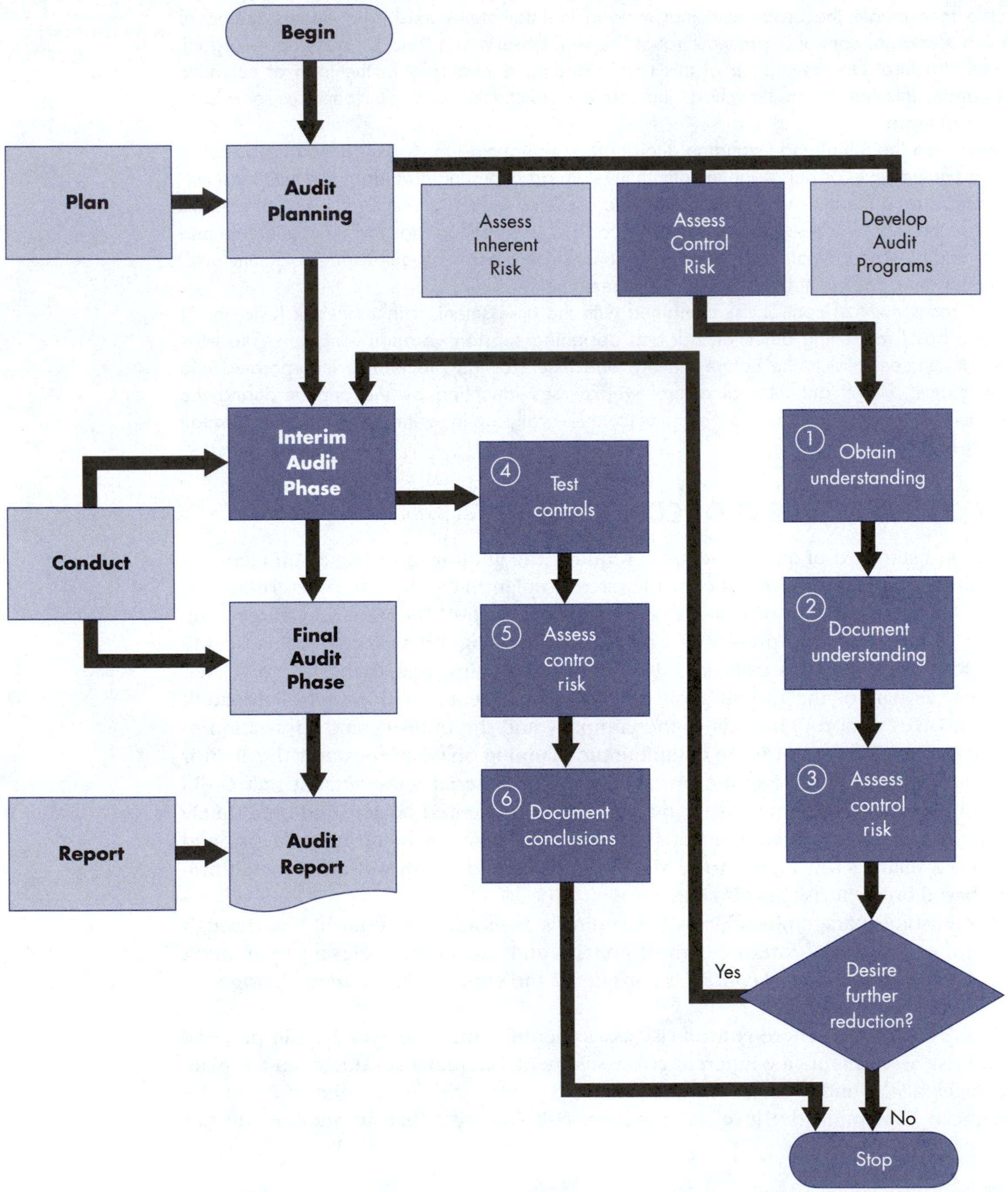

detect a material misstatement that exists in an assertion)[4] needed to maintain overall audit risk within acceptable bounds.[5] Note that if the auditor decides to perform tests of controls, control risk assessment extends from audit planning into the interim audit phase.

In addition to providing a basis for developing substantive audit programs, study of the financial reporting controls serves as a basis for offering constructive suggestions to the client concerning control weaknesses. Referred to as "reportable conditions," these weaknesses are considered in the concluding section of this chapter.

AUDITOR'S APPROACH TO ASSESSING CONTROL RISK

Figure 7.2 presents a flowchart that summarizes the auditor's approach to assessing control risk and defines the assessed level of control risk. The flowchart serves as a focal point for the ensuing discussion.

Obtain an Understanding of the Control System

In order to plan the audit, the auditor obtains an understanding of the design and implementation of the financial reporting controls of the client. Financial reporting controls, as described in Chapter 6, consist of those internal control policies and procedures having an impact on the assertions contained in the financial statements.

The auditor's objective in studying the client's financial reporting controls is to obtain sufficient evidence to identify the types of potential material misstatements of financial statement components, and the risks associated with each. Accordingly, for each of the transaction cycles identified in Chapter 4 (revenue cycle, expenditure cycle, financing and investing cycle) the auditor should

- Consider the types of errors or fraud that could occur in the absence of necessary controls;
- Determine the financial reporting controls necessary to prevent or detect those errors or fraud;
- Determine whether the necessary controls have been designed and whether they have been placed in operation;
- Identify weaknesses (potential errors and fraud not covered by financial reporting controls);
- Design substantive audit programs to reflect the weaknesses identified; and
- Communicate weaknesses identified as reportable conditions to the audit committee.

Much of the auditor's understanding of the client's financial reporting controls is gained during the initial planning phases of the audit. The auditor may at this point evaluate certain aspects of the system, such as the following:

- Communication of management support of internal control;
- Competence and objectivity of the internal audit staff;
- Separation of functional responsibilities;

---

4   Ibid, section AU 312.27.c.
5   Chapter 5 presented a way of quantifying audit risk in equation form. After the auditor has established inherent risk and control risk, detection risk is set such that the overall audit risk objective can be achieved.

FIGURE 7.2

Control Risk Assessment Flowchart

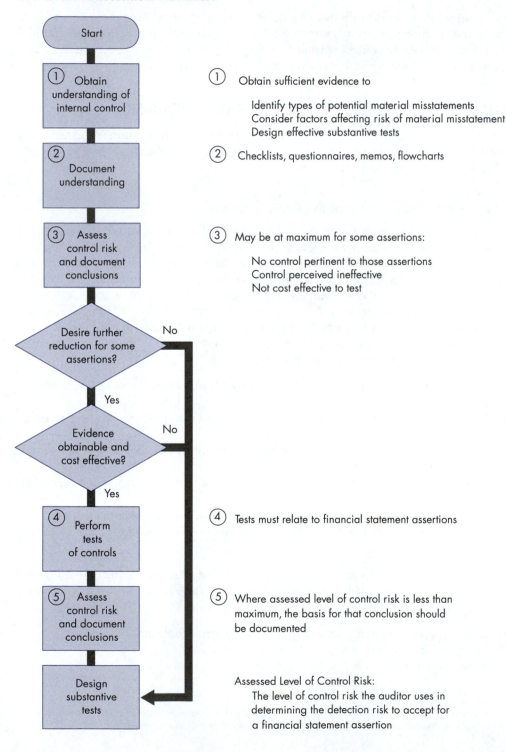

- Competence of persons performing accounting functions and control procedures; and
- Existence of safeguard controls that provide limited access to assets and accountability through fixing of responsibility.

Evidence concerning these aspects may have been obtained by either or both of the following means during the initial planning phases of the audit.

1. *Study of the organizational structure as a basis for rational inquiry.* The auditor identifies the persons involved in the performance of various accounting and control procedures. For a recurring audit, much of the information will be available in prior workpapers and in the permanent file, but it should be verified as up to date and accurate. For an initial audit, study of the business and industry, as described in Chapter 5, should provide the answer.
2. *Inquiry of management about necessary controls and whether those controls exist.* The focal point of the questioning should be the various classes of transactions and the methods by which the transactions are authorized, executed, and recorded. The means of data processing should also be determined, along with management's methods for supervising the system.

Identify Control Points

In determining the design and implementation of a client's internal control policies and procedures, the auditor needs to identify the necessary control points. A **control point** exists wherever an error or fraud could occur in the capturing and processing of data and wherever assets need to be safeguarded against loss through theft or other causes. Prenumbered documents, for example, together with required approvals and reviews and evidence of the same, provide reasonable assurance that only properly approved transactions will occur and that the transactions will be documented at the point of occurrence (indicating control over the capturing of data).

For control point identification purposes, the auditor should classify controls as either accuracy controls or safeguard controls (see Chapter 6). Accuracy controls support the valuation, ownership, and classification assertions. Assigning competent persons to tasks involving cost allocation and account distributions (debits and credits) provides greater assurance concerning the correct processing of data. Installing a system of double-checking, whereby a second person reviews transactions for proper assignment of debit and credit, also supports processing accuracy. Safeguard controls relate to the completeness and existence assertions. Restricted access, point-of-sale (POS) terminals, and separation of duties provide asset protection and are examples of safeguard controls. Because accuracy and safeguard controls directly support the financial statement assertions, auditor concentration on these controls is a cost-effective approach to studying financial reporting controls.

The auditor, who identifies a control point for which the suggested accuracy or safeguard control is lacking, should determine whether or not a **compensating control** exists. For example, monthly statements to customers and follow-up of resulting exceptions help to ensure the accuracy of accounts receivable balances. Although failure to mail monthly statements suggests a control weakness, the following actions (compensating controls) serve to mitigate the weakness:

1. Past-due invoices are carefully reviewed and all customer exceptions are promptly followed up; and

2. Adequate computer editing controls during input of customer orders greatly reduce the probability of errors in processing sales.

Document Understanding

The auditor must fully document his or her understanding of the financial reporting controls.[6] The purpose of documentation is to provide evidence of compliance with the second field work standard. As stated earlier, this standard requires the auditor to obtain an understanding of the internal control policies and procedures sufficient to plan the audit and to afford a basis for designing substantive audit procedures.

Documentation may assume various forms. The most common are internal control checklists, internal control questionnaires, internal control flowcharts, and internal control memoranda. These are briefly described in the following paragraphs.

The **internal control memorandum** (see Exhibit 7.1) consists of a narrative description of a transaction cycle. The processing of cash receipts, sales transactions, payroll, purchases and vouchering, and cash disbursements might each be the subject of an internal control memorandum. Together, the various memoranda constitute the documentation of the auditor's understanding of the financial reporting controls.

The advantage of the memorandum approach lies in its rigor of analysis, and the financial control understanding this rigor promotes. This means of financial control analysis, however, does not lend itself readily to quick review and ready comprehension

EXHIBIT 7.1

Internal Control Memorandum: Sales Processing

Prenumbered sales orders, including evidence of proper credit approval, are based on customer orders, approved by the regional sales manager, received from the regional sales offices via remote terminals, and reviewed by one of the three product managers. These orders are sent to accounting for a completeness review, including evidence of credit approval. After reviewing the orders, accounting prepares an input recording form. The recording form contains customer number, sales representative number, stock number, and quantity of each stock item ordered by the customer. The recording forms are then forwarded daily to EDP, where they form the basis for entry into the system. A copy of the sales order is forwarded by EDP to shipping to trigger processing of the shipment to the customer. The computer prepares the sales invoice set after editing the order for the customer number, existence of customer credit approval, customer credit limit vs. existing customer balance, stock number, and availability of products. As part of the sales processing, the computer inserts the customer's name and address, product descriptions and prices, and extensions and footings. Terms of payment and discount availability are also determined by the computer and included on the invoice. For each order processed, the computer records the transaction, including costing the sale, and updates the accounts receivable and inventory modules. EDP then forwards the invoice sets to accounting, where they are filed awaiting notification from shipping that the goods were shipped to the customer. Upon receipt of the shipping order and signed bill of lading from shipping, accounting reviews all documents (sales invoice, sales order, shipping order, and bill of lading) for completeness and agreement, and mails the invoice to the customer.

6   *AICPA Professional Standards*, op. cit., section 319.44.

by someone other than the author of the memorandum. The narrative form of documentation, if not presented in combination with internal control flowcharts, as described later and in the appendix to this chapter, does not quickly convey a clear image of the system. This is especially critical when new people are assigned to the audit and wish to review the financial reporting controls. The memorandum, by itself, also presents a problem for the audit manager in reviewing the audit field work.

The **internal control questionnaire** and the **internal control checklist** supplement the memorandum as part of the documentation of the auditor's understanding of financial reporting controls. A partial internal control questionnaire is presented as Exhibit 7.2. As used in an actual audit, the questionnaire is quite extensive and detailed, often consisting of several pages for each transaction cycle. Checklists, as an alternative to the questionnaire, consist of lists of controls rather than questions and answers. Checklists are illustrated in the appendix to this chapter. (See, for example, Table 7.2, p. 255.) Questionnaires and checklists attempt to cover all pertinent control points in a given transaction cycle and are designed to identify weaknesses in financial reporting controls. In the questionnaire, questions usually are worded so that "yes" answers denote strengths and "no" answers identify weaknesses. The advantage of the questionnaire or checklist approach lies in its thoroughness of coverage. Virtually every aspect of the transaction cycle being analyzed is covered. Moreover, these devices are easy to apply and portray control weaknesses clearly to whoever is reviewing the documentation. A possible disadvantage is the tendency toward cursory review, given the ease of completing the questionnaire or checklist. New or inexperienced auditors who may not comprehend the reasons for including certain questions or points are often assigned the task of administering parts of the questionnaire or verifying the existence of points contained in checklists. If they are not carefully instructed and supervised, lack of full

EXHIBIT 7.2

A Partial Internal Control Questionnaire for Processing Sales Orders and Shipping Goods

Question	Yes	No	Remarks
Processing Sales Orders:			
Are prenumbered sales order forms used in preparing sales orders?	✓		
Is proper credit approval noted on sales order forms?	✓		
Are prices on customer order compared with authorized price list?	✓		
Are customer orders properly approved for quantities, shipping, and discount terms?	✓		
Shipping Goods:			
Are properly approved and prenumbered sales orders required in order for goods to leave the warehouse?	✓		
Are prenumbered bills of lading used?	✓		
Are bills of lading signed by the carrier evidencing shipment?	✓		
Invoicing Customers:			
Do copies of the sales order and bill of lading go to accounting?		✓	BOL only
Are sales invoices prepared only on the basis of properly approved sales orders and bills of lading?	✓		

understanding may result in failure to detect inconsistencies in responses to questions and result in serious control weaknesses that are not revealed in the process.

The **internal control flowchart** is another means for documenting the auditor's understanding of financial reporting controls. The internal control flowchart lends itself to easy review of the accounting information system and the control procedures applied during the processing and review of transactions and events. By presenting the processing steps pictorially in terms of actions, documents, and people performing the control procedures, it provides a quick and easy method for grasping the essential features of how transactions and events are processed and for identifying the major control strengths and weaknesses associated with each transaction cycle subset. Internal control strengths and weaknesses are shown in Figure 7.3 by the symbols S-n and W-n, respectively. Exhibit 7.3 describes each of the strengths and weaknesses.

The flowchart approach by itself, however, does not provide the level of detail necessary for the auditor to fully assess control risk; nor does it provide adequate documentation of the auditor's understanding of internal control. For this reason, most auditors combine the internal control flowcharts with memoranda, questionnaires, or checklists.

The use of flowcharting in the design of CBI systems may be cited as a reason for the widespread use of internal control flowcharts by auditors. The flowchart has enhanced the understanding of accounting information systems and transaction processing in the same fashion in which it has facilitated development and comprehension of complex CBI systems. Many of the CBI system flowcharts, with slight modification, can be converted to internal control flowcharts, thereby reducing the auditor's time invested in internal control description and documentation. Automated flowcharting techniques contained in computer software packages reduce the time required in preparing flowcharts, while expanding the depth of analysis.

EXHIBIT 7.3

Explanation of Internal Control Strengths and Weaknesses as Identified in Figure 7.3

Strengths	Explanation
S-1	Credit approval required on face of sales order before goods are released by the warehouse.
S-2	Sales invoice not prepared and mailed to customer until bill of lading evidencing shipment has been received by billing.
S-3	Several numeric files indicate prenumbering of documents, such as sales orders, sales invoices, and bills of lading.
Weaknesses	
W-1	No indication of procedure for review and approval of customer order.
W-2	No formal procedure for handling out-of-stock conditions; that is, whether goods are back-ordered, whether customers are notified, and whether partial shipments are made.
W-3	Sales invoices are not reviewed for proper pricing, quantities, and extensions before being mailed to customers.

FIGURE 7.3

Internal Control Flowchart for Sales Orders and Inventory

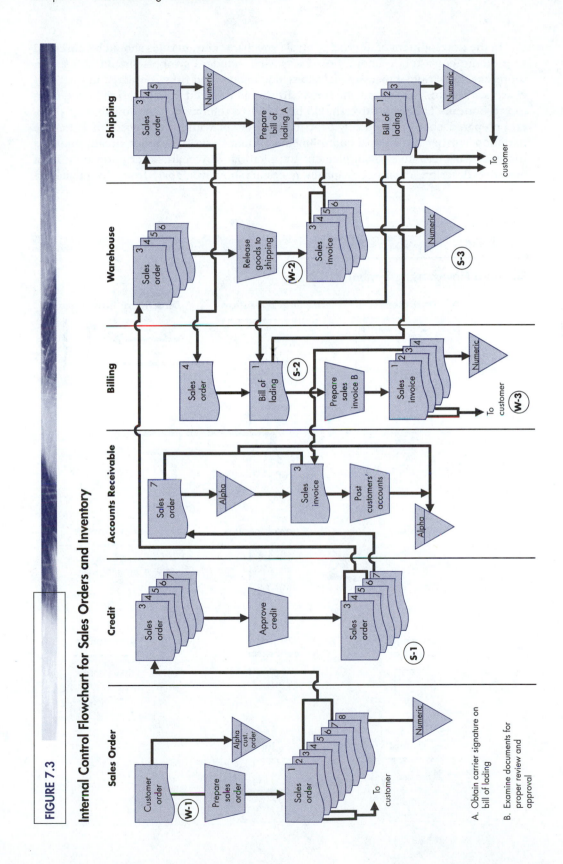

A. Obtain carrier signature on bill of lading

B. Examine documents for proper review and approval

In the development of internal control flowcharts, certain rules should be observed to promote consistency among flowcharts. First, standard symbols should be used to represent the various processes, decisions, documents, and flows depicted in the flowchart (see Figure 7.4). Second, the flowchart should proceed from left to right and from top to bottom. Third, narrative should be kept to a minimum. The flowchart, if properly prepared, should adequately describe the system without the need for extensive narration. Further, the internal control memorandum, described earlier, already contains the necessary narrative to supplement the pictorial flowchart description fully. Brief narrative descriptions are occasionally necessary, however, apart from the memoran-

FIGURE 7.4

Standard Flowcharting Symbols

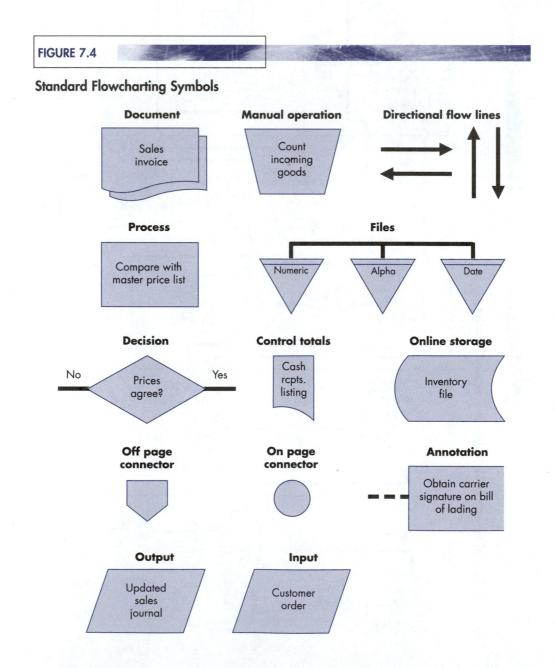

dum. The narrative is identified by annotation within the flowchart and presented outside the main body.

Internal control memoranda, internal control questionnaires and checklists, and internal control flowcharts all have unique merits and shortcomings. For this reason, auditors generally prefer to use a combination of approaches. The flowchart approach, with its ease of review, combines effectively with a questionnaire or checklist for thoroughness of coverage. The memorandum approach can provide an in-depth analysis and documentation of a modified transaction cycle in which significant changes have been made by the client. Some CPAs follow the practice of performing an in-depth analysis of a financial control segment (e.g., financial reporting controls for a given transaction cycle) each year. The analysis, in the form of flowcharts and detailed narrative memoranda, is then placed in the permanent file and updated in subsequent years as the internal control system changes. The appendix to this chapter presents examples of checklists and flowcharts categorized by transaction cycle.

Assess Control Risk and Document Conclusions

The auditor's **assessed level of control risk** is defined as "that level of control risk used by the auditor in determining the detection risk to accept for a financial statement assertion and, accordingly, in determining the nature, timing, and extent of substantive tests."[7] This level may vary along a range from maximum to minimum as long as the auditor has obtained evidential matter to support that assessed level. **Maximum control risk** is defined as "the greatest probability that a material misstatement that could occur in an assertion will not be prevented or detected on a timely basis by the entity's internal control structure."[8] The assessed level of control risk also may vary by transaction cycles.

For those assertions assessed at the maximum level, a **primarily substantive audit** approach is suggested. Emphasis on substantive testing requires the auditor to examine a larger proportion of transactions and balances than he or she would under conditions of lower-than-maximum control risk assessment. If, for example, controls over cash receipts and cash balances are weak, the auditor may elect to assess control risk at maximum and perform extended tests of cash receipts transactions.

The auditor's assessment of control risk may be based on the initial understanding of internal control, or the auditor may wish to lower the assessed level of control risk further by testing controls. This, in turn, will enable the auditor to further reduce the amount of substantive testing related to the affected transaction cycles and assertions. If, for example, payroll controls appear strong, the auditor may decide to test the controls further as a means for limiting the extent of substantive testing.

As indicated in Figure 7.2, if the auditor assesses control risk at maximum for a given set of assertions, only his or her understanding of the financial reporting controls need be documented. If control risk is assessed below maximum, however, the auditor must also document the basis for the reduction. Moreover, the auditor may not assess control risk below maximum without obtaining an understanding of the operating effectiveness of the internal financial control policies and procedures related to that set of assertions. Because operating effectiveness is best defined by performing tests of con-

---

7   Ibid, section 319.55. As defined in Chapter 4, substantive testing consists of obtaining evidence in support of transactions and balances. Observing the client's physical inventory, reconciling bank accounts, and vouching plant asset additions are examples of substantive audit testing.
8   Ibid, section AU 319.47.

trols, most auditors hesitate to assess control risk below maximum without having performed tests.

Reduce the Assessed Level of Control Risk through Control Testing

Tests of controls require the auditor to identify the pertinent financial reporting controls in a given transaction cycle subset and examine them on a test basis for the period covered by the audit. The purpose of the tests is to determine whether the controls functioned effectively during the period.

While the initial understanding of internal control provides evidence concerning design effectiveness, tests of controls enable the auditor to evaluate the **operating effectiveness of financial reporting controls**. Operating effectiveness provides increased evidence as to the proper functioning of controls during the period under audit.

Whether or not tests of controls will be performed depends on the auditor's perception of control effectiveness and the cost effectiveness of the tests. The auditor may decide *not* to perform tests because the overall internal financial control system design is perceived to be inadequate (i.e., the controls have already been perceived as ineffective). Discovery during the initial planning phase, for example, that bank accounts have not been reconciled properly during the year is convincing evidence as to the weakness of this control, and the auditor would ordinarily elect not to test the control for operating effectiveness. The auditor may decide *not* to test a control after concluding that testing is not cost effective (i.e., the cost of testing the control exceeds the cost savings associated with reduced substantive testing). A few major plant asset additions occurring during the year, for example, might be audited more effectively through examination of the assets and underlying purchase documentation (a primarily substantive audit approach) than by testing control policies and procedures covering plant asset additions.

In audits of small businesses, given the combining of functional responsibilities and the lack of an internal audit staff, auditors frequently follow a primarily substantive audit approach; that is, the auditor obtains an understanding of those financial reporting controls that do exist, and then assesses control risk at maximum and applies substantive audit procedures extensively. Even in the presence of controls, substantive testing may be more cost effective, given the relatively small volume of transactions completed by a small business. In other words, examining virtually 100 percent of the entity's transactions may be less costly than testing controls for the purpose of reducing substantive testing.

If the auditor decides that the assessed level of control risk can be reduced through cost-effective means, tests of controls are designed and performed for this purpose. For example, based on the initial understanding, the auditor may believe that internal controls over sales transactions and accounts receivable balances are designed to be effective. By testing the controls for operating effectiveness, the auditor may be able to greatly reduce the extent of substantive testing in the form of accounts receivable confirmation.

Tests of controls may assume the forms of reprocessing, further observation, and document examination and testing. These approaches are described below.

Reprocessing   The auditor may determine whether transactions are being properly executed and recorded by introducing hypothetical transactions into the system. In a set of procedures referred to as **reprocessing**, the transactions are designed by the auditor to test the system's ability to identify and correct errors in the capturing and processing of data. Hypothetical sales transactions, for example, may contain incorrect selling prices, new customers without credit approval, customers exceeding credit limits, sales invoices without attached shipping orders, and extension or footing errors. Similar transaction sets can be designed for expenditure, production, payroll, and financing and investing transactions.

Having designed hypothetical transactions that violate all significant controls within a given transaction cycle, the auditor next introduces the transactions into the client's system and observes the results of processing. Based on testing, the auditor may conclude that certain controls, indicated in the questionnaire or flowcharts as existing, are either missing or ineffective. Compensating controls, as described earlier, may also be discovered.

Reprocessing as a means of tests of controls is particularly useful in a computer based information systems environment. For this reason, this approach is considered again in Chapter 8, "Internal Control and Computer-Based Information Systems."

Observation   In addition to, or in place of, reprocessing, the auditor may test financial reporting controls by **observation** of the control activities. Observation is particularly appropriate for clients with complex CBI systems. Transaction documentation is often less extensive in these systems, requiring the auditor to apply alternate means for testing the design and operating effectiveness of certain controls, often in the form of observing transaction processing at the input stage. The auditor may elect to perform these observations at numerous points throughout the year under audit.

Document Examination and Testing   Where extensive documentation exists, the auditor may elect to test controls by examining documents supporting selected transactions that occurred during the period under audit. The objective of **document examination and testing** is to determine that the documents contain evidence of proper approvals, reviews, and account distribution, and are without material errors. Documents supporting disbursements, for example, might be examined for the following control features:

- Proper review and approval of prices, quantities, and vendors;
- All necessary documentation (requisition, purchase order, receiving report, vendor's invoice) attached to voucher;
- Agreement of types of goods and quantities appearing on the receiving report with quantities on vendor's invoice;
- Agreement of prices on vendor's invoice with prices appearing on the purchase order;
- Correctness of account distributions (debits and credits); and
- Correctness of extensions (quantity × price) and footings (total of extended amounts).

Documents supporting sales, cash receipts, payroll, and production transactions and events are similarly examined for proper execution and recording. A listing of all necessary control points and careful definition of what constitutes an error are important prerequisites to selecting and examining documents for purposes of testing controls. The details concerning selection and examination of documents for testing financial reporting controls are covered in Chapter 9.

As stated earlier, auditors must document their understanding of internal control. Similarly, the results of the auditor's tests of controls—whether obtained through re-processing of transactions, observation, or document examination and testing—must also be fully documented. Documentation is critical and should include the thought processes leading to any reduction in the assessed level of control risk below maximum and the resultant effect on the design of substantive audit procedures.

DESIGN OF SUBSTANTIVE AUDIT PROGRAMS

Adjusting Materiality Thresholds Based on Risk Analysis

As discussed in Chapter 5, the nature, timing, and extent of substantive audit testing is a function of auditor judgment based on materiality and risk. Having set materiality thresholds and having assessed inherent risk and control risk, the auditor has the infor-mation necessary to design substantive audit programs. In approaching program design, the auditor should observe the following guidelines:

1. Proportionately more audit resources should be allocated to areas of high audit risk, as evidenced by the auditor's study of the business and industry, application of ana-lytical procedures, and fraud assessment (inherent risk assessment), and her or his study and evaluation of the internal control system (control risk assessment).
2. Material account balances and transactions generally should receive more substan-tive audit attention than less material areas.
3. If, based on the study of the business, application of analytical procedures, and fraud assessment, the auditor suspects earnings inflation, *individual item materiality* thresholds should be *decreased* and the auditor should place less emphasis on in-ternal evidence and more on external evidence (see Chapter 5 and Figure 5.4).
4. For transaction cycle subsets where internal control is weak and numerous errors are expected, *aggregate materiality* thresholds—materiality levels for including smaller errors in the audit workpaper for later audit adjustment consideration—should be *set low*, relative to those applicable to strong internal control subsets. The purpose is to lower the probability of overlooking numerous small errors that, in the aggregate, could exceed the individual item threshold. Also, as in (3) above, the au-ditor should obtain greater amounts of external evidence relative to internal evi-dence in satisfying specific audit objectives.

Assume that an auditor initially assesses internal control as satisfactory and sets ag-gregate and individual item materiality thresholds for income reporting purposes at $20,000 and $200,000, respectively. Errors of $200,000 or greater will be considered material and incorporated into proposed audit adjustments, errors ranging between $20,000 and $200,000 will be accumulated in an audit workpaper for later evaluation as to aggregate materiality, and errors of less than $20,000 generally will be ignored. Assume further that, after obtaining an understanding and performing tests of financial reporting controls for a given internal control subset, the auditor lowers the assessment of control from satisfactory to weak. The resulting increase in the assessed level of con-trol risk suggests a need to decrease the aggregate materiality threshold level. The un-derlying rationale is as follows. Under weak internal control, errors are more likely to have occurred and, given more numerous errors, the probability increases that errors less than $20,000 will aggregate to $200,000 or more (the individual item threshold). The auditor, therefore, should consider lowering the aggregate level in proportion to the number of errors anticipated. Given an assumption of satisfactory internal control, an aggregate threshold of $20,000, and an individual item level of $200,000, the auditor expects ten or fewer errors aggregating $200,000 or less. Discovering internal control to be weak, the auditor may elect to lower the threshold to $10,000 (assuming that the error incidence expectation has increased from ten or fewer to twenty or fewer). This will result in documenting a greater number of smaller errors and, in turn, lowers the probability of ignoring small errors that, in the aggregate, would exceed the $200,000 individual item threshold.

In designing substantive audit programs based on risk assessment and materiality considerations, the auditor generally needs to modify the nature, timing, and/or extent of audit procedures contained in the preliminary audit programs. In determining the necessary modifications, the auditor may adopt a qualitative or a quantitative approach.

Qualitative Approach to Designing Substantive Tests

The second standard of audit field work requires the auditor to gather sufficient, competent, evidential matter to afford a basis for the audit opinion.[9] For substantive testing purposes, audit procedures applied to gather evidence may vary as to nature, timing, and extent, according to the auditor's judgment.[10] The auditor typically utilizes a **qualitative approach** in modifying the nature and timing of audit procedures (i.e., in determining the types of procedures to apply and when to apply them). A **quantitative approach** is used in altering the extent of audit procedures (e.g., how many customer accounts to confirm or how many machinery and equipment additions to vouch).

As discussed in Chapter 5 and illustrated in the Highbell Toy Company case (Case 5.3), if internal control is weak, suggesting numerous errors, or if the auditor suspects fraudulent financial reporting, less emphasis should be placed on internal evidence relative to external evidence. Thus, the nature of audit evidence is altered on the basis of inherent and control risk assessment. In the Highbell case, the auditors should have pursued confirmation evidence (external) instead of relying on sales and shipping documents (internal). As another example, if the auditor suspects that unrecorded revenues from scrap sales have been misappropriated, internal documents in the form of sales invoices and remittance advices possess limited validity. For this reason, the auditor may decide to mail confirmations to the client's scrap buyers, requesting verification of scrap purchases by the buyers. This is not a standard procedure in the ordinary financial audit; however, circumstances such as those cited here and in the Highbell case frequently suggest altering the *nature* of auditing procedures.

Ordinarily, trade accounts receivable are confirmed by the auditor as of the client's balance sheet date, due to materiality and the difficulty of "working forward" to year end. Under conditions of excellent internal control over sales and cash receipts, however, the auditor may consider confirming the accounts receivable at an interim date (change in *timing* of audit procedures). Interim application of substantive audit procedures is cost effective in that it reduces the time required, following year end (the auditor's "busy season"), to complete the final audit phase.

The application of principal substantive procedures (e.g., accounts receivable confirmation and inventory observation) at an interim date does increase audit risk. The degree of incremental risk is a function of the time interval beginning with the interim

9   Ibid, section AU 326.01.
10 Ibid, section AU 326.13.

date and ending with the balance sheet date (i.e., the longer the interval, the greater the increase in audit risk).[11] For this reason, these procedures should not be applied at interim dates, except under the following conditions:

1. Internal control is excellent;
2. The auditor can identify substantive tests to cover the remaining period; and
3. The cost savings resulting from interim application are not exceeded by the cost of substantive tests to cover the remaining period.[12]

Quantitative Approach to Designing Substantive Tests

Inherent and control risk assessment also may suggest modifying the *extent* of substantive auditing procedures to be applied. Chapter 5 presented the audit risk equation:

$$AR = IR \times CR \times DR$$

Chapter 5 then presented a means for assessing inherent risk (*IR*) based on a study of the business and industry, the application of analytical procedures, and assessing the risk of fraud. Overall audit risk (*AR*) is set low because it is the basis for the auditor's opinion. An approach to assessing control risk (*CR*) by evaluating those elements of the internal control system relating to the financial statement assertions has been presented in this chapter. Having set three of the four equation components, the auditor can determine detection risk by solving for *DR*. For example, assume the following values for the equation components:

$$IR = 70\%$$
$$CR = 50\%$$
$$AR = 10\%$$

DR can be solved as follows:

$$DR = \frac{AR}{IR \times CR}$$
$$= 0.10/(0.70 \times 0.50) = 0.2857 = 29\%$$

The detection risk of 29 percent may be used as input for determining the number of items to be included in a sample drawn for the purpose of evaluating the reasonableness of a specific financial statement component. To expand upon this example, assume that during document examination (a form of testing controls) the auditor discovered that repairs and maintenance expenses were charged to various plant asset accounts, or vice versa. In addition, the client did not calculate and account for gains and losses on disposals correctly. Under these circumstances, control risk for the plant assets subset of the expenditure cycle might be assessed at 100 percent rather than 50 percent as initially set. The resulting detection risk would then be calculated as 14 percent [0.10/(0.70 × 1.00)], rather than 29 percent. A lower detection risk percentage, as input into the sample size equation for substantive audit testing purposes, will produce a larger sample size. Stated differently, the weaker the financial reporting controls, the more extensive the substantive testing must be to maintain overall audit risk at a pre-

11 Ibid, section AU 313.03
12 Ibid, section AU 313.05–07.

determined level. This approach to calculating sample size is explored in greater depth in Chapter 10.

SUMMARY OF AUDIT RISK ASSESSMENT

Figure 7.5 summarizes the auditor's approach to risk assessment as presented in Chapters 5 through 7. The combination of inherent risk and control risk determines the probability of material misstatements in the financial statements, enabling the auditor to set detection risk and design substantive audit programs as appropriate.

FIGURE 7.5

Audit Risk Assessment Summary

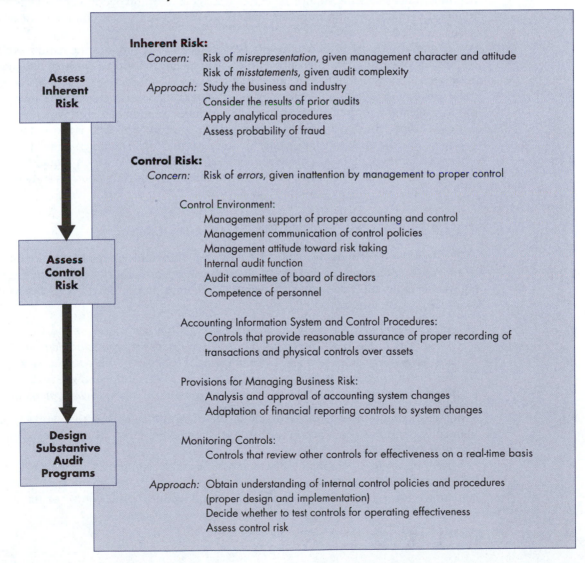

Assess Inherent Risk

Inherent Risk:

Concern: Risk of *misrepresentation*, given management character and attitude
Risk of *misstatements*, given audit complexity

Approach: Study the business and industry
Consider the results of prior audits
Apply analytical procedures
Assess probability of fraud

Assess Control Risk

Control Risk:

Concern: Risk of *errors*, given inattention by management to proper control

Control Environment:
Management support of proper accounting and control
Management communication of control policies
Management attitude toward risk taking
Internal audit function
Audit committee of board of directors
Competence of personnel

Accounting Information System and Control Procedures:
Controls that provide reasonable assurance of proper recording of transactions and physical controls over assets

Provisions for Managing Business Risk:
Analysis and approval of accounting system changes
Adaptation of financial reporting controls to system changes

Design Substantive Audit Programs

Monitoring Controls:
Controls that review other controls for effectiveness on a real-time basis

Approach: Obtain understanding of internal control policies and procedures (proper design and implementation)
Decide whether to test controls for operating effectiveness
Assess control risk

A point to be noted in the risk assessment summary presented in Figure 7.5 is the degree to which management attitude and character affect both inherent and control risk. In assessing inherent risk, for example, the auditor's assessment of management integrity (character) is important for assessing the probability of fraud. If management is perceived to be "earnings aggressive," the chances for intentional misstatement of financial position and/or results of operations (fraudulent financial reporting) are increased significantly. In evaluating control risk, the auditor is concerned with both management integrity and management support of internal control. The auditor must ascertain management support of internal control (attitude) as a major input in assessing the probability of material financial statement errors. If the auditor concludes that management is strongly committed to sound internal control, the probability of material financial statement errors is greatly reduced. Stated differently, if the auditor concludes that management is honest and committed to sound internal control, the chances for both fraudulent financial reporting and material errors are greatly reduced. If, on the other hand, the auditor perceives management to be overly aggressive toward reported earnings, significant misstatements are likely, even under conditions of otherwise sound internal control.

To summarize the preceding discussion, the auditor determines the nature, timing, and extent of substantive audit procedures after having set individual item and aggregate materiality thresholds, and after having assessed inherent risk and control risk. Clear and complete documentation of these determinations, including the judgment processes leading to the decisions, should be included in the audit workpapers. An important component of that documentation, as discussed in Chapter 5, is the auditor's assessment of the risk of fraudulent financial reporting. Documentation provides evidence of compliance with the second standard of field work, which requires the auditor to obtain an understanding of the client's financial reporting controls sufficient to plan the audit and design substantive audit programs.

COMMUNICATION OF REPORTABLE CONDITIONS

AICPA Professional Standards require the auditor to communicate reportable conditions to the audit committee or to individuals with a level of authority and responsibility equivalent to an audit committee in organizations that do not have one.[13] **Reportable conditions** are defined as

> *matters coming to the auditor's attention that, in his/her judgment, should be communicated to the audit committee because they represent significant deficiencies in the design or operation of the internal control (system), which could adversely affect the organization's ability to record, process, summarize, and report financial data consistent with the assertions of management in the financial statements.*[14]

Reportable conditions may relate to any of the control elements as they impact management's assertions contained in the financial statements. Table 7.1 contains examples of reportable conditions.

It is important to emphasize that auditors are not required to search for and/or identify reportable conditions. The auditor must, however, communicate reportable conditions when they come to her or his attention during the course of the audit.

---

13 Ibid, section AU 325.01.
14 Ibid, section AU 325.02.

TABLE 7.1

Examples of Reportable Conditions

1. Inadequate overall internal control system design;

2. Absence of appropriate segregation of duties consistent with appropriate control objectives;

3. Absence of appropriate reviews and approvals of transactions, accounting entries, or systems output;

4. Inadequate procedures for appropriately assessing and applying accounting principles;

5. Absence of other control techniques considered appropriate for the type and level of transaction activity;

6. Evidence that a system fails to provide complete and accurate output consistent with objectives and current needs because of design flaws;

7. Evidence of failure of identified controls to prevent or detect misstatements of accounting information;

8. Evidence that a system fails to provide complete and accurate output consistent with the entity's control objectives because of the misapplication of control procedures;

9. Evidence of failure to safeguard assets from loss, damage, or misappropriation;

10. Evidence of intentional override of the internal control system by those in authority, to the detriment of the overall objectives of the system;

11. Evidence of failure to perform tasks that are part of the internal control system, such as reconciliations not prepared or not prepared in a timely manner;

12. Evidence of willful wrongdoing by employees or management;

13. Evidence of manipulation, falsification, or alteration of accounting records or supporting documents;

14. Evidence of intentional misapplication of accounting principles;

15. Evidence of misrepresentation by client personnel to the auditor;

16. Evidence that employees or management lack the qualifications and training to fulfill their assigned functions;

17. Absence of a sufficient level of control consciousness within the organization;

18. Failure to follow up and correct previously identified internal control deficiencies;

19. Evidence of significant or extensive undisclosed related-party transactions; and

20. Evidence of undue bias or lack of objectivity by those responsible for accounting decisions.

Source: *AICPA Professional Standards*, New York: AICPA, section AU 325.21.

Although the communication may be written or oral, written communication of reportable conditions is preferred. Moreover, whether it is written or oral, the auditor must document the reportable conditions in the audit workpapers. The distribution of any written communication must be limited to the audit committee of the board of directors, management, and others within the organization.[15] An illustration of the

15 Ibid, section AU 325.10.

recommended wording of a written communication of reportable conditions is contained in Exhibit 7.4. The Auditing Standards Board requires that in the report, the auditor do the following things:

- Indicate that the purpose of the audit was to report on the financial statements and not to provide assurance on the internal control system;
- Include the definition of reportable conditions;

EXHIBIT 7.4

Reportable Conditions Communication

To: Mr. James Brosley
        Chair, Audit Committee
        ABC Corporation

Subject: Reportable conditions resulting from the 2002 audit

In planning and performing our audit of the financial statements of the ABC Corporation for the year ended December 31, 2002, we considered its internal control system in order to determine our auditing procedures for the purpose of expressing our opinion on the financial statements, and not to provide assurance on the internal control system. However, we noted certain matters involving the internal control system and its operation that we consider to be reportable conditions under standards established by the American Institute of Certified Public Accountants. Reportable conditions involve matters coming to our attention relating to significant deficiencies in the design or operation of the internal control system that, in our judgment, could adversely affect the organization's ability to record, process, summarize, and report financial data consistent with the assertions of management in the financial statements.

The conditions that we consider to be material weaknesses in ABC Corporation's internal control system are as follows:

1. Sales invoices and bills of lading forms are not prenumbered, a condition that precludes verifying that all shipments have been billed or that all billed orders have been shipped. We recommend that these forms be prenumbered, that security be maintained over unused forms, and that used documents be canceled effectively and that numeric sequence be accounted for periodically.
2. Statements are not mailed to customers on a monthly basis. As a result, analysis of unpaid balances in terms of specific invoices is difficult. Moreover, the company does not perform a monthly aging analysis of customer balances and, as a result, follow-up and collection of past-due accounts is somewhat lax. We recommend a policy of monthly statements and monthly accounts receivable aging analysis to enhance the reliability of recorded balances, to facilitate evaluation of uncollectibility, and to improve the follow-up and collection of past-due accounts.

This report is intended solely for the information and use of the audit committee (board of directors, board of trustees, or owners in owner-managed enterprises), management, and others within the organization (or specified regulatory agency or other specified third party).

Samuel Chase
Dual & Chase
February 18, 2003

- Describe the internal financial control weaknesses comprising the reportable conditions; and
- Include the restriction on distribution of the report.[16]

If the auditor discovers no reportable conditions during the course of the audit, no written representation should be made.[17]

APPENDIX

TRANSACTION CYCLES AND RELATED TESTS OF CONTROLS

Internal control concepts were discussed in Chapter 6. Chapter 7 addressed the auditor's approach to obtaining an understanding of internal control policies and procedures relevant to an audit (financial reporting controls). Under certain conditions, the auditor may elect to test controls to obtain knowledge about the entity's operating effectiveness and possibly reduce the assessed level of control risk to a point below the maximum level. This appendix presents an in-depth analysis of the main control features that should be present and that the auditor should be looking for, and the related tests associated with further exploration of financial reporting controls. The following transaction cycles, as described in Chapter 4, provide the framework for discussion:

1. *Revenue cycle*
   a.   Sales revenue and accounts receivable balances
   b.   Cash receipts from customers and cash balances
2. *Expenditure cycle*
   a.   Purchases, operating expenses, depreciation expense, and plant asset balances
   b.   Payments to vendors and accounts payable balances
   c.   Payroll
   d.   Production and inventory balances
3. *Financing and investing cycle*
   a.   Borrowing from others, interest expense, and liability balances
   b.   Lending to others, interest revenue, and notes receivable balances
   c.   Acquisitions and disposals of financial assets
   d.   Capital stock and dividend transactions

The format used in discussing control features and control testing is as follows:

1. The transactions within each cycle subset are described;
2. Documents associated with the transactions are identified;
3. A model flowchart is presented that depicts the appropriate documents, people, and actions that should be associated with the transactions;
4. The major control features that should be present are considered within the framework of the control concepts discussed in Chapter 6;
5. Procedures are recommended for testing those controls the auditor wishes to study for operating effectiveness; and
6. Design of substantive audit procedures is considered in light of the understanding obtained.

---

16 Ibid, section AU 325.11
17 Ibid, section AU 325.17.

REVENUE CYCLE

Sales

Transactions   Sales transactions, as considered here, are limited to sales to customers on account. Cash sales are considered in the next section, along with collections from customers on account.

Documents   Documents commonly associated with account sales to customers are as follows:

1. *Customer order:* The customer order is transmitted by the customer to the salesperson, indicating the type and quantity of product(s); prices, payment terms, shipping date, and means of transport may also appear on the customer order.
2. *Sales order:* A formalization of the customer order, the sales order, in addition to the information appearing on the customer order, contains evidence of credit check and approval.
3. *Bill of lading:* Evidence of shipment of goods, the bill of lading identifies the carrier, the customer, the type of goods, and the shipping date.
4. *Sales invoice:* The sales invoice is the billing rendered to the customer. The information in the preceding documents is presented, together with extended amounts (price × quantity) of the charges.

Control Features and Internal Control Flowchart   Table 7.2 lists the main control features applicable to the processing of sales transactions. Figure 7.6 incorporates the control features into a flowchart portraying a suitable set of control procedures covering sales processing. The purpose of the flowchart is to assist in identifying control points and the necessary control features related to each point.

Both documentation of each step in the processing cycle and evidence of proper reviews and credit approval have been provided for in the model system. These control features help to ensure that sales transactions are authentic and have been accurately recorded.

The bill of lading, signed by the carrier, provides evidence of shipment. Forwarding copies of this document to billing ensures that all shipments of goods are billed to customers. Requiring all sales invoices to be accompanied by a copy of the signed bill of lading ensures that customers will be invoiced only for goods actually shipped.

Functional responsibilities have been separated such that persons performing the order, billing, credit, and accounting functions do not have access to the goods being shipped to customers. Similarly, persons handling goods do not have access to the accounting records.

A complete audit trail has been provided, in the form of file copies, together with evidence of review and approval of transactions. The audit trail permits one to trace the processing from point of origin to recording of the transaction and vice versa.

Perpetual inventory records, in combination with periodic inventory test counts and comparisons, facilitate early detection of errors or fraud relating to inventories. In the same manner, the accounts receivable subsidiary ledger, together with monthly statements to customers, and careful investigation of customer exceptions facilitate error detection in processing sales and cash receipts.

Limited access to inventories and related documents helps to prevent unauthorized use or disposition of inventories, either through direct removal or by fabricating docu-

TABLE 7.2

Control Principles and Techniques: Revenue Cycle for Sales Transactions

Control Principle	Control Feature	Control Principle	Control Feature
(1) Competence of personnel	Approving credit Approving write-offs of customer accounts Preparing sales invoices Recording sales and accounts receivable Approving returns and allowances	(4) Recording in accordance with GAAP	Chart of accounts and accounting manual Account distribution on face of document Review of account distributions
(2) Separation of duties	Processing sales orders Approving credit Shipping Billing Issuing credit memos Accounting	(5) Safeguard controls	Limited access to finished goods Limited access to documents Fixed responsibility for custody over goods and documents

(3) Execution in accordance with authorization	Adequate documentation for:
	    Customer order
	    Sales order
	    Sales invoice
	    Shipping order
	    Bill of lading signed by carrier
	    Credit memo
	Documents prenumbered
	System of reviews and approvals and evidence of same on face
		(6) Periodic inventories and comparisons	Subsidiary accounts receivable ledger agreed to control account on a monthly basis
			Monthly statements to customers
			Clear exceptions to customer statements
			Perpetual inventory records
			Periodic test counts and comparisons with perpetual records
			Annual physical inventory and adjustment of perpetual records (after investigating significant shrinkages)

mentation permitting removal. Limiting access to customer records prevents employees from concealing misappropriation through alteration of customer accounts.

Tests of Controls   As described earlier in this chapter, control testing may assume one or more of the following forms: additional observation and inquiry, reprocessing, or document examination and testing. The third form, document examination and testing, involves examining documentation underlying transactions and events and identifying errors committed during processing. This form of testing is discussed here as it relates to the processing of account sales transactions.

By identifying errors in a sample of transactions, the auditor is able to project the errors to the population. The projection permits the auditor to better assess the operating effectiveness of financial reporting controls and thereby modify the assessed level of control risk. This, in turn, provides a basis for designing substantive audit procedures. An approach to determining proper sample size, selecting items for inclusion in the

FIGURE 7.6

Sales Flowchart

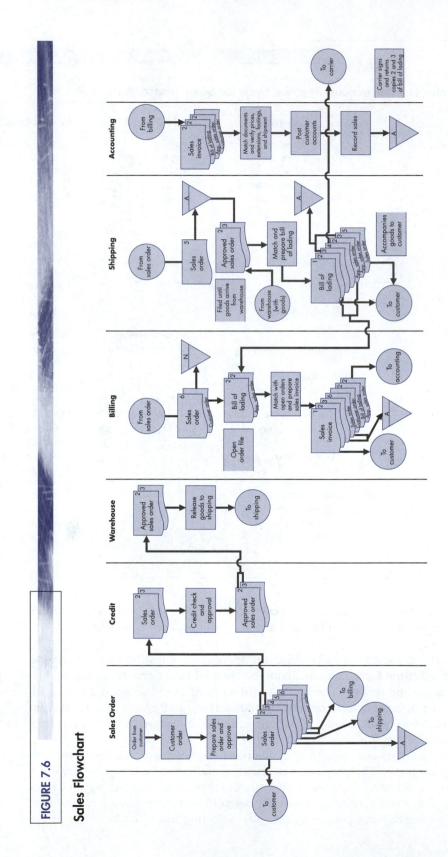

sample, examining sample items, and evaluating results of the sampling is presented in Chapter 9, as part of sampling for attributes. The present discussion is limited to describing those control testing procedures that will assist the auditor in identifying control weaknesses.

The rate of error in executing and recording transactions increases under the following conditions, all of which constitute control weaknesses.

1. Transactions are not adequately documented;
2. Documents are not prenumbered or the numeric sequence of used documents is not accounted for periodically;
3. Transactions are not reviewed for adequacy of documentation, proper approvals, and correctness of debits and credits;
4. Persons reviewing documents and determining account distributions are not competent or adequately trained;
5. Accounting manuals either do not exist, or are not used in determining correctness of debits and credits; and
6. Write-offs of customers' accounts or returns and allowances are not properly approved.

Table 7.3 identifies the types of errors and fraud associated with these weaknesses and describes possible tests of controls. The first set of tests requires examining the documents underlying completed sales transactions for the presence of necessary controls. The second set of tests is directed toward identifying misstatements due to *omission*—tracing from shipping documentation to related journal entries—and misstatements due to *commission*—vouching recorded sales to underlying documentation. The purpose of these tests is to determine that all shipments of goods have been billed and recorded and that recorded sales are authentic.

Design of Substantive Audit Procedures   Discovery of weaknesses in processing sales transactions should prompt the auditor to consider the following substantive audit tests.

1. Expand confirmation of customer balances as of year end;
2. Consider confirming sales transactions, as well as receivable balances;
3. Confirm all accounts receivable write-offs with customers; and
4. Expand year-end cutoff tests to obtain assurance that sales were recorded in the proper accounting period.

In addition to designing substantive audit procedures, the auditor should update the reportable conditions audit workpapers to include major weaknesses discovered during control testing.

Substantive audit testing is covered in depth in Chapters 11 through 13. They are introduced in this appendix in order to illustrate the impact of control testing on the design of substantive audit procedures.

Cash Receipts

Transactions   Cash receipts transactions included in this section are of three types:

1. Cash received from customers on account;
2. Cash sales; and
3. Miscellaneous cash receipts, such as cash from disposals of plant assets or investments; dividends or interest constituting investment revenue; financing receipts

TABLE 7.3

Control Weaknesses and Related Tests: Revenue Cycle for Sales Transactions

Control Weakness	Possible Errors	Tests of Controls
Inadequate documentation of sales transactions	Customer billed for goods not shipped Goods shipped and not billed	Select a sample of documented sales transactions and examine for prenumbering of documents
Lack of numeric control over the following forms: Sales orders Sales invoices Shipping orders Credit memos Bills of lading	Fictitious transactions recorded Failure to record completed sales transactions Unauthorized use of shipping orders or bills of lading to remove goods from premises	Evidence of proper reviews and approvals: Customer credit Selling prices Account distribution Inclusion of all necessary documentation:
Customer credit approval not indicated on sales order	Goods shipped to customers whose credit has not been approved	Customer order Sales order Sales invoice
Selling prices not compared with master price list	Goods billed to customers at incorrect prices	Shipping order Bill of lading
Accounting manuals not used or account distribution (debit and credit effects of transactions and events) not double-checked	Transactions and events incorrectly recorded	Correctness of account distributions Agreement of selling prices with master price lists Trace the selected transactions to journal entries and customer account postings to determine proper recording To ascertain validity of recorded sales, select a sample of recorded sales and trace to documentation, including sales invoice and bill of lading To determine that all shipments are billed and recorded, select a sample of bills of lading and trace to invoice and books of original entry
Write-off of customer accounts receivable not properly approved	Collectible accounts written off as uncollectible Customer account intentionally written off to conceal misappropriation of customer remittances	Examine all documentation underlying accounts receivable write-offs for the year Determine that the write-offs were properly recorded Determine that the write-offs were properly approved
Returns and allowances lacking proper approval	Credit memos issued for unauthorized returns Credit memos issued for goods not returned Credit memos written and recorded to conceal misappropriation of customer remittances	Select a sample of credit memos processed during the year, and examine for the following characteristics: Proper approval and review Receiving report attached if credit memo involves returned goods Prenumbered credit memos Ensure proper recording

(borrowing, collections on loans made to others); cash from disposals of scrap, waste, and returnable containers; and other miscellaneous cash receipts.

Documents   Documents commonly associated with cash receipts transactions are as follows:

1. *Remittance advice:* The lower part of a check, usually separated from the check by a perforation; the remittance advice contains details of charges covered by the check.
2. *Prelisting of incoming checks:* The prelisting is prepared daily by someone independent of the cash receipts recording function and includes the checks received by mail for the day.
3. *Cash receipts summary:* The summary lists cash receipts contained in the daily bank deposit and is the basis for recording daily cash receipts.
4. *Receipted deposit ticket:* This provides evidence of the daily deposit of cash.
5. *Cash register tapes:* These provide evidence of cash sales for the day.

Control Features and Internal Control Flowchart   Table 7.4 lists the main control features applicable to the processing of cash receipts. Figure 7.7 is a flowchart describing a model set of procedures for processing and recording mail cash receipts. Although the flowchart includes only cash from customers, *all* incoming cash receipts should be controlled similarly.

Maintaining proper security and accountability during processing is the principal concern in providing effective control over cash receipts. Accountability is provided by the prelisting for mail receipts and by locked-in cash register tapes for cash sales. As indicated in the flowchart, the controller's office compares daily the receipted deposit ticket with the prelisting and register tapes to determine that all incoming cash receipts are deposited in the bank. The monthly bank reconciliation, prepared by someone having neither custodial nor cash-recording responsibility, provides further accountability control over cash.

Requiring that all incoming checks be restrictively endorsed immediately upon receipt provides security over mail cash receipts. Requiring the use of cash registers with locked-in tapes strengthens security over cash sales receipts. Fixing custodial responsibility over cash and requiring that cash receipts be deposited intact on a daily basis offers added security in addition to accountability.

The procedures described in Figure 7.7 provide for separating the cash custodial function from the cash recording function. The cashier, in this model, does *not* have access to accounting records and the accounting personnel have no access to cash receipts. Postings are made from remittance advices and cash register tapes rather than from checks and currency. This form of separation is critical in preventing misappropriation accompanied by concealment through account alteration.

The flowchart in Figure 7.7 also separates the function of posting customer accounts from the recording of cash receipts and the posting of the general ledger. Separation, accompanied by reconciling of the accounts receivable subsidiary ledger with the controlling account on a monthly basis, provides a double-check of the recording and posting functions.

As indicated in Table 7.4, a chart of accounts, accounting manuals, and use of competent persons to record cash receipts are necessary controls for ensuring proper recording. Cash receipts from sources other than collections from customers are especially susceptible to recording errors. File copies of prelistings, cash receipts summaries,

TABLE 7.4

Control Principles and Techniques: Revenue Cycle for Cash Receipts Transactions

Control Principle	Control Feature
Competence of personnel	Reconciling bank accounts Recording cash receipts Preparing deposits Opening mail and prelisting cash receipts Auditing cash registers Comparing deposit ticket with cash entries
Separation of duties	Receiving and prelisting cash Recording cash Depositing cash Reconciling bank accounts
Execution in accordance with authorization	Documentation of cash receipts Prelistings Cash register tapes Remittance advices Deposit tickets
Recording in accordance with GAAP	Chart of accounts and accounting manual Double-checking of credits relating to miscellaneous cash receipts Sales coding on cash register tapes
Safeguard controls	Daily intact deposits Cash registers for cash sales Restrictive endorsements on incoming checks Prelisting of incoming checks
Periodic inventories and comparisons	Comparison of prelisting and cash register tapes with deposit ticket from bank and entry to record cash receipts Monthly bank reconciliations

remittance advices, and deposit tickets provide the audit trail necessary for reconstructing transactions and tracing the processing flows.

Tests of Controls   In designing tests of cash receipts controls, the auditor is interested mainly in the adequacy of security over cash receipts and proper recording. Table 7.5 describes several tests aimed at identifying errors in processing cash receipts. Note that the control tests are directed at detecting undeposited cash receipts, as well as recording errors.

Undeposited receipts may or may not have been recorded. If they were recorded, the cash receipts record will not agree with the deposit ticket. If they were unrecorded, the prelisting will not agree with the deposit ticket or the cash receipts record. Unrecorded cash receipts are especially difficult to detect if cash is not prelisted. Under these circumstances, auditors may elect to prepare their own prelisting on a surprise basis and compare details with the cash receipts entries and the deposit ticket. If

FIGURE 7.7

Cash Receipts from Customers Flowchart

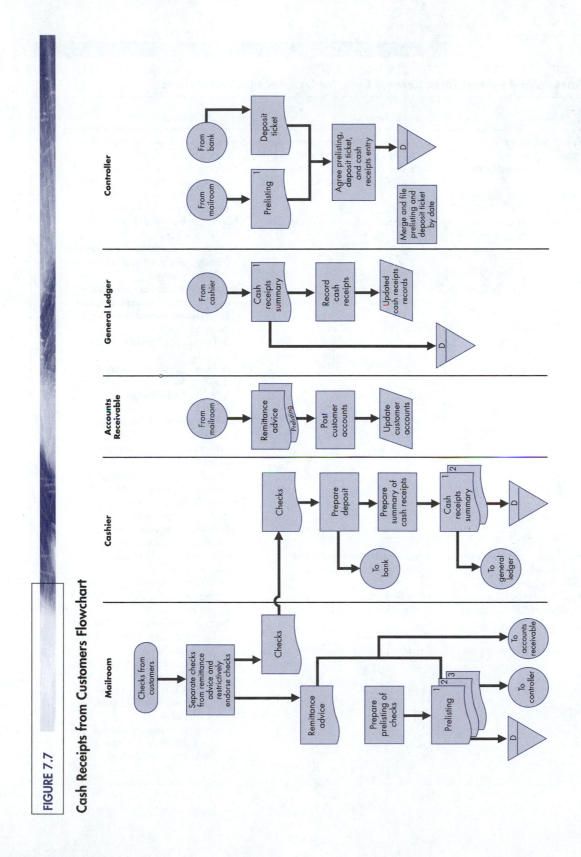

TABLE 7.5

Control Weaknesses and Related Tests: Revenue Cycle for Cash Receipts Transactions

Control Weakness	Possible Errors	Tests of Controls
Bank accounts not properly reconciled	Cash receipts processing errors not located on a timely basis	Examine several months' reconciliations for possible errors
Incoming cash receipts not prelisted	Recorded cash receipts are not deposited in the bank	If mail cash receipts are prelisted, select a sample of prelisting and cash register tapes representing several days' cash receipts
Cash registers and tapes not properly controlled		
Bank deposit ticket not compared with prelisting and cash register tapes	Unrecorded cash receipts are not deposited in the bank	Trace to bank statement and cash receipts record
		Test postings to customers' accounts by tracing from remittance advice to subsidiary ledger
		If mail cash receipts are not prelisted, select a sample of deposit tickets representing several days' cash receipts
		Trace from deposit ticket to cash receipts record
		Trace from cash receipts record to underlying documentation (cash register tapes and remittance advice)
		Trace from remittance advice to subsidiary ledger
		To test for unrecorded cash receipts, given the absence of prelistings, consider intercepting and prelisting cash receipts on a surprise basis
		Trace prelisting to cash receipts record and bank statement
		Trace prelisting to customers' accounts in subsidiary ledger
Accounting manuals not used to assist in properly recording miscellaneous cash receipts	Miscellaneous cash receipts credited to incorrect amounts	Use the same sample of cash receipts prelistings to
		Identify all cash receipts, other than customer payments on account
Credits arising from miscellaneous cash receipts not double-checked	Miscellaneous cash receipts credited to incorrect accounts	
		Trace to cash receipts record and determine that proper accounts were credited
Sales not coded on cash register tapes	Credits to wrong sales accounts	Select a sample of cash register tapes representing several days' sales
		Determine proper sales categories represented by each day's sales
		Trace to cash receipts record and determine that proper accounts were credited

the auditor does suspect employee misappropriation of cash receipts, management is so informed.

Material errors in recording cash receipts from sources other than collections from customers on account are generally of two types: errors in recording miscellaneous cash receipts transactions and errors involving credits to the wrong revenue accounts. First, because of the nonrecurring nature of miscellaneous receipts, recording errors are more likely to occur. A system of review and approval, as well as use of accounting manuals, is needed to minimize the incidence of this form of error. Second, if several categories of sales revenue are present, controls are needed to ensure credits to the proper sales accounts. Cash registers programmed to record product codes and summarize sales by category assist in minimizing these errors.

If material errors of the above types have occurred, analytical procedures should have raised the auditor's suspicions prior to performance of the control tests noted in Table 7.5. As a result, a larger sample of prelistings and cash register tapes will be selected for testing, given the higher expected error rate.

Design of Substantive Audit Procedures   Control weaknesses relating to cash receipts should lead to one or more of the following audit program approaches.

1. Expand the review of bank reconciliations to cover several months;
2. Extend accounts receivable confirmation; and
3. Increase testing of cash receipts from miscellaneous revenues, as well as disposals of noninventory assets (e.g., plant assets and marketable securities).

EXPENDITURE CYCLE

Purchases

Transactions   Purchases transactions, as defined here, include purchases of materials, merchandise for resale, supplies, services (other than payroll), and plant assets. Given their materiality, payroll transactions are addressed as a separate section within the expenditure cycle.

Documents   Documents associated with purchases transactions are as follows:

1. *Purchase requisition:* This form is prepared and signed by the person requesting goods or services and approved by someone authorized to do so.
2. *Purchase order:* This is a formal order, based on the approved requisition, and sent to the appropriate vendor.
3. *Receiving report:* Prepared by receiving department employees, this form is evidence of the receipt of purchased goods, as well as sales returns.
4. *Vendor's invoice:* This is the billing document received from the vendor.
5. *Voucher:* This form contains evidence of approval of vendors' invoices for payment.
6. *Daily voucher summary:* A compilation of vouchers approved for payment on a given day, the voucher summary serves as the basis for recording the daily vouchers.

Control Procedures and Internal Control Flowchart   Table 7.6 identifies the features necessary to achieve satisfactory control over purchase transactions. Figure 7.8 configures the model into a flowchart depicting the purchasing and vouchering functions.

The use of prenumbered documents, including requisitions, purchase orders, receiving reports, and vouchers, enhances accountability for purchases. It also provides

TABLE 7.6

Control Principles and Techniques: Expenditure Cycle for Purchase Transactions

Control Principle	Control Feature
Competence of personnel	Purchasing Receiving Managing stores Preparing vouchers (including account distribution) Approving vouchers Recording vouchers Maintaining accounts payable ledger
Separation of duties	Requisitioning goods and services Purchasing Receiving Custody over inventory Recording purchases

Execution in accordance with authorization	Voucher system
	Documentation of purchases
	    Requisition
	    Purchase order
	    Receiving report
	    Voucher
	Prenumbered documents
	Evidence of proper review and approval appearing on document
	Purchase order prepared only on basis of properly approved requisition
	Voucher prepared only after:
	    Determining presence of all necessary documents
	    Agreeing prices, quantities, footings, and extensions on documents

Recording in accordance with GAAP	Chart of accounts and accounting manuals Account distribution on face of voucher Double-checking account distributions (and evidence of same on face of voucher)
Safeguard controls	Limited access to inventories, negotiable securities, small tools and other valuable and portable assets Limited access to documents authorizing acquisitions of assets or services Fixed responsibility over assets and documents Documentation of asset movements for proper accountability Prenumbered documents

Periodic inventories and comparisons	Periodic count and comparison of the following on a test basis:
	    Inventories of materials, goods, tools, etc.
	    Negotiable securities
	    Plant assets
	    Supplies
	Numeric sequence of used documents accounted for on a regular basis
	Comparison of creditors' statements with subsidiary ledger to clear exceptions

FIGURE 7.8

Purchases Flowchart

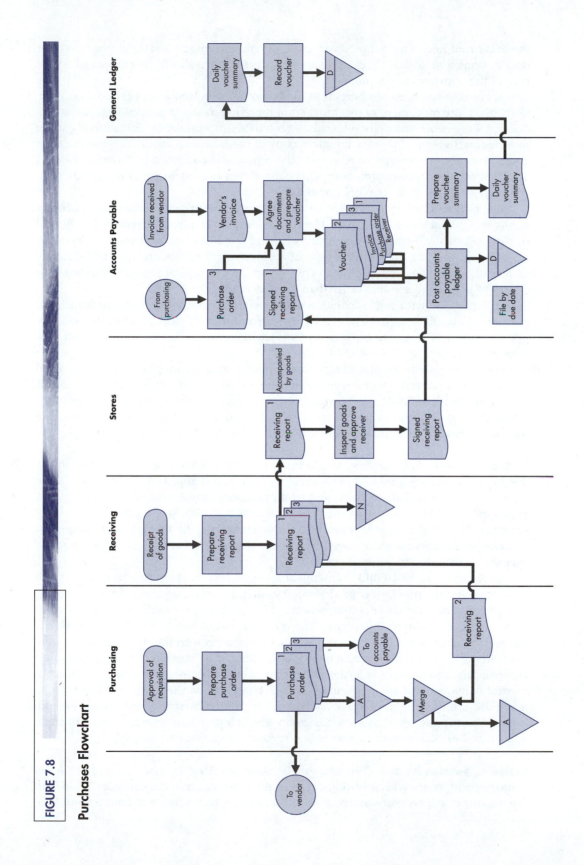

the audit trail necessary for reconstructing purchase transactions. Approvals, account distributions, and double-checking of account distributions should be evidenced on the face of the appropriate documents.

Accountability is also important in the inventory purchasing and production functions, given the movement of inventory from receiving to stores and from stores to production. Proper documentation increases accountability control by documenting these movements. In Figure 7.8, for example, a copy of the receiving report accompanies the goods from the receiving area to stores. The report is then signed by stores personnel and forwarded to accounts payable. This copy serves as evidence that the goods were received by stores in satisfactory condition.

Use of a voucher system helps to ensure that only properly authorized disbursements will be made. As depicted in Figure 7.8, vendors' invoices are paid only when all of the documents, including a voucher evidencing review and approval, are present. Accounting manuals, along with review of account distributions, enhance the accuracy of recording purchase transactions. This is particularly critical for nonrecurring purchases of goods and services other than stock in trade.

As is the case with cash, separation of custodial and record-keeping functions is important to maintaining proper security over inventories of materials, goods, and supplies. If the assets are portable, limited access and fixed responsibility for inventories are even more critical to effective control.

Periodic test counts and comparisons, perpetual inventory records, and annual physical inventories also support inventory security and accountability. These controls permit timely identification and investigation of abnormal losses from shrinkage. In addition, the use of perpetual inventory records leads to more effective cost control, and thereby enhances the accuracy of inventory and cost of sales amounts.

Tests of Controls   For purchase transactions, internal control tests are focused on the documents evidencing receipt of goods and services and approval for payment. Table 7.7 identifies errors that are associated with purchase control weaknesses and suggests appropriate tests for evaluating the controls. Control weaknesses leading to recording errors are the most critical in terms of possible impact on the financial statements. For this reason, auditors consider tests for completeness of documentation and accuracy of account distribution to be most critical.

In obtaining an initial understanding of financial reporting controls, the auditor will have observed the purchasing procedures for adequacy of separation, physical controls, and periodic inventories and comparisons. The auditor also evaluates competence of personnel during the review phase. The effectiveness of this last control, however, is further tested during the document examination phase, given the decision to test controls. Frequent errors in recording or lack of agreement between receiving reports, purchase orders, and invoices is further indication of lack of competence. Because internal control consists of people performing various functions, weaknesses involving competence are critical. Auditors, therefore, should expand substantive procedures accordingly when the client's organization is composed of individuals who are *not* adequately trained and *not* competent to review and record transactions accurately.

Design of Substantive Audit Procedures   Because purchase transactions affect the inventory, plant assets, and operating expense accounts, control weaknesses should lead the auditor to expand substantive tests in these areas. Extending test counts during in-

TABLE 7.7

Control Weaknesses and Related Tests: Expenditure Cycle for Purchase Transactions

Control Weakness	Possible Errors	Tests of Controls
Inadequate documentation of purchases	Vendors paid for goods and services not received by the client	Select a sample of documented purchase transactions and examine for the following characteristics:
Documents not properly approved or reviewed	Unauthorized purchases	Prenumbering of documents
Documents not prenumbered	Goods received and paid for that were not ordered	Evidence of proper reviews and approvals:
	Invoicing errors undetected	Approval of requisition
Accounting manuals not used	Errors in recording purchase transactions	Approval of purchase order
		Signatures on receiving report evidencing inspection by receiving and receipt by stores
Account distribution not appearing on face of voucher or not subject to review	Errors in recording purchase transactions	Review of account distribution on face of voucher
Creditors' statements not examined for possible errors	Undetected errors in recording purchase transactions	Inclusion of all necessary documentation:
Lack of perpetual inventory records	Undetected errors in recording inventory transactions	Purchase requisition
		Purchase order
		Receiving report
		Voucher
		Vendor's invoice
		Agreement of type of goods or services and prices appearing on purchase order with those items on vendor's invoice
		Agreement of quantities and types appearing on receiving report with those items on vendor's invoice
		Correctness of account distribution

ventory observation, increasing inventory pricing and extension tests, and devoting greater attention to possible inventory obsolescence are possible extensions of procedures relating to inventories. Reviewing documentation for a larger proportion of plant asset additions and of repairs and maintenance, as well as recalculating depreciation expense, may be adequate for extending substantive procedures relating to plant assets, repairs, and depreciation. If prior application of analytical procedures indicates major changes in operating expenses, control weaknesses in the purchases subset of the expenditure cycle become even more critical. Under these conditions, the auditor should intensify substantive tests of the major components of operating expenses.

In addition to affecting inventories, plant assets, depreciation, and operating expenses, the control weaknesses also affect accounts payable. For this reason, the auditor may consider extending auditing procedures relating to accounts payable. Possibilities include reconciling vendors' accounts with year-end vendors' statements and increased confirmation of creditors' accounts.

Payments to Vendors

Transactions   Payments to vendors for purchases of materials, supplies, merchandise, services, and other nonrecurring expenditures are considered in this section. The discussion assumes that the control procedures require a properly approved voucher for every disbursement, and that all disbursements are made by check. Given this assumption, all of the transactions involving payments to vendors will result in debits to accounts payable and credits to cash in bank.

Documents   Documents associated with disbursement transactions are as follows:

1. *Voucher:* This is an authorization to pay one or more vendors' invoices. The approved voucher should be accompanied by the invoice, purchase order, requisition, and receiving report relating to the expenditure.
2. *Disbursement check:* This is the payment of the approved voucher.

Control Features and Internal Control Flowchart   Table 7.8 lists the features necessary for effective control over cash disbursements transactions. Figure 7.9 portrays the flow

TABLE 7.8

Control Principles and Techniques: Expenditure Cycle for Payments to Vendors

Control Principle	Control Feature
Competence of personnel	Reviewing documents and signing checks Recording disbursements
Separation of duties	Recording disbursements Signing and mailing checks Posting creditors' accounts Reconciling bank accounts
Execution in accordance with authorization	No checks signed without adequate documentation (including approved voucher) Review of all documentation prior to signing checks All payments (except petty cash) by check
Recording in accordance with GAAP	Chart of accounts and accounting manuals Voucher system such that all debits for cash disbursements are to accounts payable
Safeguard controls	Limited access to disbursement checks Mailing of disbursements checks immediately upon signing No checks signed in advance Limited access to check-signing devices Fixed responsibility for custody of checks and check-signing devices Cancellation of paid invoices and vouchers
Periodic inventories and comparisons	Monthly bank reconciliations Agreement of currency, checks, and vouchers in petty cash box to authorized fund amount before reimbursing

FIGURE 7.9

Payments to Vendors Flowchart

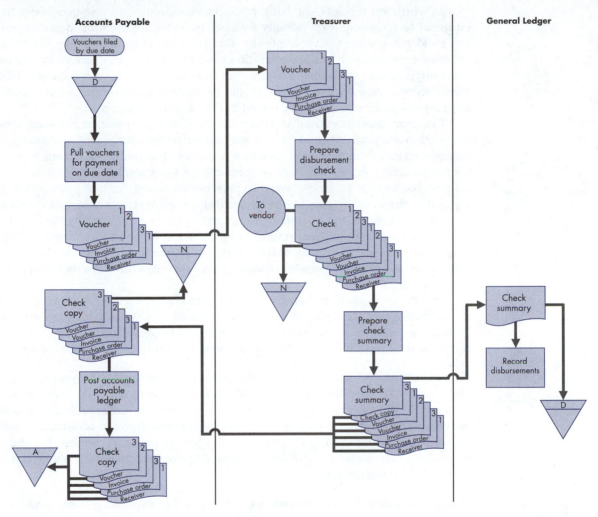

of documents, the functions performed, and the separation of these functions needed to achieve proper control.

The foremost concern in designing control procedures for payments to vendors is preventing unauthorized disbursements. Requiring that all cash disbursements be made by check and that a properly approved and documented voucher be submitted as a prerequisite for check signing are the controls most critical in meeting this concern. The documents to be submitted along with the approved voucher include the vendor's invoice, the purchase order, and the receiving report (if purchases of goods are involved). Review of the documentation for completeness and evidence of review and approval further strengthens control over disbursements.

Limited access to vouchers and disbursement checks and effective cancellation of paid invoices are also necessary to adequately control disbursements (prevention controls). Unlimited access to these documents can lead to the submission of fraudulent disbursement checks, supported by previously paid invoices and fabricated vouchers. In the absence of effective document cancellation, previously paid invoices might be paid a second time, intentionally or unintentionally.

As with cash receipts, the bank reconciliation, prepared by someone not having custodial or recording responsibility for cash, provides a means for identifying errors and fraud in recording cash receipts and disbursements (a detection control). To attain maximum effectiveness, the reconciliation procedures should require careful examination of paid checks for agreement of payees and endorsements with the cash disbursements record. Also, voided checks should be examined for proper cancellation, and bank statement credits should be traced to the cash receipts record.

The procedures portrayed in Figure 7.9 provide for separation between voucher preparation and payment. In addition to preparation of the voucher, the accounts payable function includes the posting of creditors' accounts. The treasury function is responsible for preparing and signing disbursement checks. Once signed, a disbursement check assumes the form of a financial asset. To preserve accountability and maintain adequate separation, the treasurer should mail signed disbursement checks directly to vendors.

Dual signing of checks by the treasurer and a person authorized by the board of directors is advisable to further prevent errors and fraud. Moreover, to preserve adequacy of document review, checks should not be signed in advance. Designating three or more individuals as check signers, while requiring only two signatures, is a means of avoiding advance signing.

As with previous flowcharts, the model portrayed in Figure 7.9 provides an audit trail in the form of file copies of disbursement documents. When combined with Figure 7.8, the model permits expenditure transactions to be reconstructed and traced from the point of requisition to vouchering, payment, and posting of the creditor's account.

Tests of Controls   Table 7.9 extends the control tests described for purchasing to include cash disbursements. Attributes of interest in examining paid invoices include adequacy of documentation, proper reviews and approvals, cancellation of used documents, and correctness in recording disbursement transactions. In addition, the auditor, through observation during the initial understanding phase, ascertains that disbursement checks are mailed immediately upon signing and that checks are not signed in advance of the payment date.

Design of Substantive Audit Procedures   In addition to expanding bank reconciliation procedures, as described earlier in the section discussing substantive procedures related to cash receipts, the auditor also needs to be alert to recording errors. This is especially critical in the absence of a formal voucher system. Under these circumstances, the auditor should consider extending the analysis of nontrade cash disbursements.

Payroll

Transactions   Payroll transactions include recording the payroll, vouchering net pay and the various withholdings as they become due, writing disbursement checks to transfer net pay to the payroll bank account, and issuing individual payroll checks to employees.

Documents   Documents necessary for achieving proper control over payroll and for complying with the various laws requiring the maintenance of adequate payroll records are as follows:

TABLE 7.9

Control Weaknesses and Related Tests: Expenditure Cycle for Payments to Vendors

Control Weakness	Possible Errors	Tests of Controls
Inadequate documentation of cash disbursements	Unauthorized disbursements	Select a sample of paid invoices and examine for the following characteristics:
Disbursements not always based on approved vouchers (debits not always to accounts payable)	Errors in recording cash disbursements	Adequacy of documentation: Voucher
Access to disbursement checks not limited and responsibility not fixed	Unauthorized disbursements	Purchase order Requisition Receiving report Vendor's invoice
Disbursement checks returned to accounts payable for mailing to vendors	Unauthorized disbursements	Proper review and approval of documents
Checks sometimes signed in advance	Unauthorized disbursements	Correctness of account distribution
Documents not effectively canceled upon payment of vendors' invoices	Unauthorized disbursements	Effective cancellation of documents

1. *Time cards:* The time card is a record of the time worked by an employee. The card may be prepared manually or it may be automated by use of computers or time clocks.
2. *Employee earnings record:* The employee earnings record is a document maintained for each employee, showing hours worked, gross pay, deductions, and net pay for each pay period.
3. *Payroll summary:* The payroll summary is a listing, by employee, of gross pay, deductions, net pay, and check number. A payroll summary is prepared for each pay period. Exhibits 7.5 and 7.6 illustrate the employee earnings record and payroll summary.
4. *Payroll voucher:* The payroll voucher is a voucher authorizing a check to be drawn on the general account for deposit in the payroll bank account. The check will equal the net pay for the payroll period.
5. *Payroll checks:* After the net pay has been transferred to the payroll bank account, individual payroll checks are written for each employee.

Control Features and Internal Control Flowchart   Table 7.10 on page 274 lists the features that are most important in effecting proper control over payroll transactions. Figure 7.10 on page 275 incorporates the features into a payroll processing model flowchart.

Because of the extent of calculations involved in payroll processing, error prevention becomes increasingly difficult for entities with large numbers of employees. For this reason, computer processing of payroll frequently offers the most effective control. When properly programmed to verify input data, a CBI payroll system provides consistency, accuracy, and speed in calculating and processing payroll transactions. Chapter 8 explores the general impact of CBI processing on internal control systems.

EXHIBIT 7.5

Employee Earnings Record

						Withholding Class:	Single			
Name:	Lance Bannister					Exemptions:	1			
Employee Number:	272 45 6809					Department:	Maintenance			
Address:	3020 Harvest Road					Wage Rate:	$8.00 per hour			
	Alandale, Ohio 44568									

Hours	Date	Employee Name	Gross	FICA	FIT	Health Ins.	Union Dues	Other	Net Pay	Check Number
40	1/6/02	Lance Bannister	$ 320.00	$ 22.88	$39.00	$ 5.00	$ 3.00	$0.00	$ 250.12	37089
42	1/13/02	Lance Bannister	336.00	24.02	41.00	5.00	3.00	0.00	262.98	38121
38	1/20/02	Lance Bannister	304.00	21.74	39.00	5.00	3.00	0.00	235.26	40664
			*	*	*	*	*	*	*	
			*	*	*	*	*	*	*	
			*	*	*	*	*	*	*	
Quarter Total			$4,300.00	$307.45	$460.00	$60.00	$36.00	$0.00	$3,436.55	

EXHIBIT 7.6

Payroll Summary

Period Ended 1/6/02

Employee Number	Employee Name	Gross	FICA	FIT	Health Ins.	Union Dues	Other	Net Pay	Check Number
348 90 8765	Sarah Allen	$ 344.00	$ 24.60	$ 42.00	$ 5.00	$ 3.00	$0.00	$ 269.40	37087
197 88 0956	Joshua Anderson	356.00	25.45	44.00	8.00	3.00	0.00	275.55	37088
272 45 6809	Lance Bannister	320.00	22.88	39.00	5.00	3.00	0.00	250.12	37089
234 98 7689	Carlos Alivita	383.00	27.38	48.00	8.00	3.00	0.00	296.62	37090
321 67 8854	James Jackson	266.00	19.02	25.00	8.00	3.00	0.00	210.98	37091
		*	*	*	*	*	*	*	
		*	*	*	*	*	*	*	
		*	*	*	*	*	*	*	
Totals		$10,500.00	$750.75	$1,350.00	$210.00	$90.00	$0.00	$8,099.25	

TABLE 7.10

Control Principles and Techniques: Expenditure Cycle for Payroll Transactions

Control Principle	Control Feature

Competence of personnel	Timekeeping and approving time cards
	    Calculating gross pay, deductions, and net pay
	    Preparing payroll tax returns
	    Reconciling payroll bank accounts
	    Maintaining employee personnel records

Separation of duties	Authorizing hiring, termination, and pay rates
	    Maintaining employee personnel records
	    Reconciling bank accounts
	    Timekeeping
	    Preparing payroll checks
	    Signing checks and distributing payroll

Execution in accordance with authorization	Time cards or clock cards required
	    Time cards approved and signed by supervisor
	    Payroll prepared on basis of current list of employees
	      received from personnel

Recording in accordance with GAAP	Review of payroll calculations, including gross pay,
	      deductions, and net pay
	    Review of payroll entries for correctness of account
	      distributions
	    Standard journal entries for monthly payroll accruals

Safeguard controls	Payrolls paid by check
	    Distribution of payroll checks immediately upon signing
	    Use of imprest payroll bank accounts
	    Control over unclaimed checks
	    Limited access to time cards, clock cards, and unused
	      payroll checks

Periodic inventories and comparisons	Payroll bank reconciliations on a monthly basis
	    Periodic comparison of entries in payroll summary with
	      authorized list of employees maintained in personnel

Error prevention in payroll systems is enhanced through a system of double-checks attained through separation of functional responsibilities. As described in Table 7.10 and illustrated in Figure 7.10, the following duties should be assigned to the functions indicated:

Function	Duties
Timekeeping	Reviewing time cards for proper hours and approvals, and comparing control totals of time cards with a copy of the payroll summary received from payroll.
Payroll	Preparing payroll on the basis of time cards received from timekeeping and the current list of employees and pay rates received from human resources, and double-checking calculations of gross pay, withholdings, and net pay.

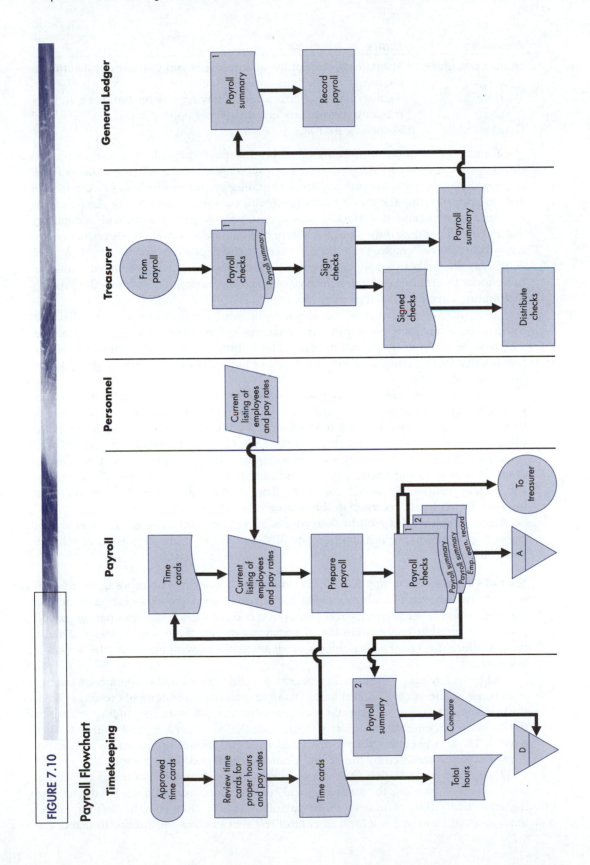

FIGURE 7.10

Payroll Flowchart

Function	Duties
Human resources	Maintaining current list of employees and pay rates, and authorizing hires, terminations, and pay rates.
Treasurer	Signing payroll checks after reviewing payroll summary, and distributing payroll checks immediately upon signing.
General ledger	Recording payroll.

Separation of duties also helps in preventing payroll fraud. The various means through which most payroll frauds have been accomplished are referred to collectively as *payroll padding*. Payroll padding involves adding employees or hours to the payroll and misappropriating the monies associated with padding. Separation of the functions of check signing and distribution, production, payroll preparation, and accounting makes payroll padding difficult in the absence of collusion. Automatic direct deposit of payroll checks (i.e., employees authorize checks to be deposited directly into their bank accounts) also makes payroll padding more difficult by eliminating the need to distribute checks to employees. Under this system, payroll distribution assumes the form of distributing check stubs rather than checks.

Requiring the human resources department, which maintains no custodial access to financial assets, to approve hires, terminations, and pay rates is another control device designed to prevent payroll padding. This control ensures a current listing of employees that can be compared with the listing of payroll checks actually written for any given payroll period.

A set of standard journal entries such as those illustrated in Exhibit 7.7 helps to ensure accuracy in recording the payroll and the employer's payroll taxes. The entries can be drafted one set for each month, in advance for the year, and only the amounts for each debit and credit need be entered at the end of the month when they are known.

Paying the payroll by check and depositing net pay in an imprest payroll bank account also assist in preventing payroll errors and fraud. Under this type of system, payroll checks cannot be issued for more than a maximum specified amount, and unclaimed checks are returned to the treasurer for safekeeping.

Reconciliation of payroll bank accounts by persons not having responsibility for preparing, recording, or distributing payroll assists in detecting payroll processing errors and fraud.

Tests of Controls   In testing payroll controls for risk assessment purposes, the auditor is concerned primarily with evaluating the accuracy of payroll processing, including calculation and recording of payroll. Discovered control weaknesses that permit payroll padding is brought to the attention of management, but these weaknesses ordinarily do not affect the financial statements as significantly as weaknesses in the accuracy controls.

Table 7.11 relates control weaknesses to possible errors, and recommends control tests to assist the auditor in evaluating possible material misstatements resulting from the weaknesses. In performing the recommended control tests, the auditor examines the primary documentation underlying the calculation, recording, and distribution of payroll. These procedures, therefore, should assist the auditor in evaluating the materiality of errors committed by the client in calculating or recording payroll.

If inadequate separation of duties or lack of physical controls increases the probability of payroll padding, the auditor should consider accompanying the paymaster during the distribution of one or more payrolls. This is done by the auditor on an unannounced basis and is a form of control test that enables the auditor to detect the

EXHIBIT 7.7

Standard Journal Entries for Payroll

Journal Voucher Number 21 Payroll Distribution	Month/Year 3/02	
Account Title	Debit	Credit
Direct labor	X	
Manufacturing overhead	X	
General and administrative	X	
Accrued payroll		X

Journal Voucher Number 22 Monthly Payroll Taxes	Month/Year 3/02	
Account Title	Debit	Credit
FICA tax expense	X	
Workers' compensation expense	X	
State unemployment tax expense	X	
Federal unemployment tax expense	X	
Payroll taxes payable		X

TABLE 7.11

Control Weaknesses and Related Tests: Expenditure Cycle for Payroll

Control Weakness	Possible Errors	Tests of Controls
Lack of care in calculating payroll, and failure to review and double-check calculations	Errors in calculating gross pay, deductions, net pay, and payroll taxes	Select a sample of payroll summaries from the period under audit and perform the following procedures: Examine time cards for proper approval
Lack of competent personnel in areas of payroll calculation, payroll tax return preparation, or reconciliation of payroll bank accounts	Errors in calculating gross pay, deductions, net pay, and payroll taxes	Compare time cards with payroll summary for agreement of hours, employee name, and employee number
Standard journal entries not drafted for monthly payroll entries	Errors in recording payroll and payroll taxes	Compare pay rate with authorized list of rates maintained by personnel department
Journal entries to record payroll and payroll taxes not reviewed for correctness	Errors in recording payroll and payroll taxes	Recalculate gross pay, deductions, and net pay
Inadequate separation of duties among timekeeping, personnel, production, payroll accounting, and check distribution	Payroll padding	Trace from payroll summary to standard journal entry for correctness of payroll recording Review payroll tax returns for correctness Review payroll bank reconciliations for correctness

presence of improper payroll checks. Checks that are unclaimed at the completion of payroll distribution are compared with current human resources records to determine whether the employees are still on the payroll, and the ultimate disposition of unclaimed checks is ascertained. Comparison of hours and rates, as recommended in Table 7.11, also assists in detecting payroll padding.

Design of Substantive Audit Procedures   Weaknesses in payroll control lead the auditor to extend testing of the year-end accruals of payroll, payroll withholdings, and employer payroll tax expense. If the client is a manufacturer, goods in process and finished goods inventories also may be affected by payroll recording errors. In this case the auditor should determine, on the basis of the audited payroll balances, whether standard labor and overhead rates are reasonable.

Production

Transactions   The transactions that make up the production cycle are internal in nature. They are as follows (the journal entries associated with the respective transactions assume that perpetual inventory records are used to maintain accountability over the production flows):

1. Movement of materials from stores to production
   Debit: Goods in Process
   Credit: Raw Materials Inventory
2. Conversion of materials into finished goods
   Debit: Goods in Process
   Credit: Direct Labor Applied
                Manufacturing Overhead Applied
3. Transfer of finished goods to inventory
   Debit: Finished Goods Inventory
   Credit: Goods in Process

Documents   Documents normally associated with these transactions are as follows:

1. *Materials requisition:* This is a formal written materials request from production to stores.
2. *Production order:* This document authorizes and initiates the production of goods to fill a customer's order or for stock.
3. *Production report:* This is a summary of materials, labor, and overhead inputs and finished goods output for a given time period.
4. *Monthly cost summary:* This is a journal entry summarizing material, labor, and overhead inputs and finished goods output for the month.

Control Features and Internal Control Flowchart   Table 7.12 and Figure 7.11 identify and describe the principal components of internal control over production. Maintaining accountability as materials proceed through the production process is critical to effective control. This is accomplished through perpetual inventory records for materials, goods in process, and finished goods. Documentation of the flows, including evidence of proper authorizations at each stage of the process, helps promote accountability.

TABLE 7.12

Control Principles and Techniques: Expenditure Cycle for Production

Control Principle	Control Feature
Competence of personnel	Setting standard costs Recording inventory cost flows Maintaining inventory records Determining overhead application rates Costing physical inventory
Separation of duties	Maintaining inventory records Custody over inventories Taking of physical inventories Production Accounting for inventory cost flows
Execution in accordance with authorization	Production initiated only on the basis of properly approved production order accompanied by signed requisitions Documentation of all inventory movements
Recording in accordance with GAAP	Job order or process cost system for recording cost flows Incorporation of standard costs and variances into the accounting system Maintenance of detailed manufacturing overhead ledger Standard journal entries for costing monthly production
Safeguard controls	Daily production and scrap reports Orderly arrangement of goods in warehouses Limited access to inventories and fixed responsibility Limited access to inventories of repair parts, small tools, and supplies, and fixed responsibility
Periodic inventories and comparisons	Periodic test counts of inventories and comparison with perpetual records Monthly agreement of subsidiary ledgers (materials, goods in process, finished goods, and manufacturing overhead) with control accounts

Perpetual inventory records, along with standard costs and variance analysis, are also helpful in identifying major errors and fraud involving inventory.

Limiting access to inventories, fixing custodial responsibility over inventories, and conducting periodic test counts and comparisons all enable prompt identification and follow-up in the event of major inventory shortages.

Proper recording of inventory cost flows is enhanced through assignment of competent personnel to inventory accounting, the use of standard journal entries for monthly cost summaries, and monthly comparisons of perpetual inventory records with the related controlling accounts.

Tests of Controls The auditor's major concern in testing the production cycle for risk assessment purposes is the adequacy of the system in accurately recording inventory

FIGURE 7.11

Production Flowchart

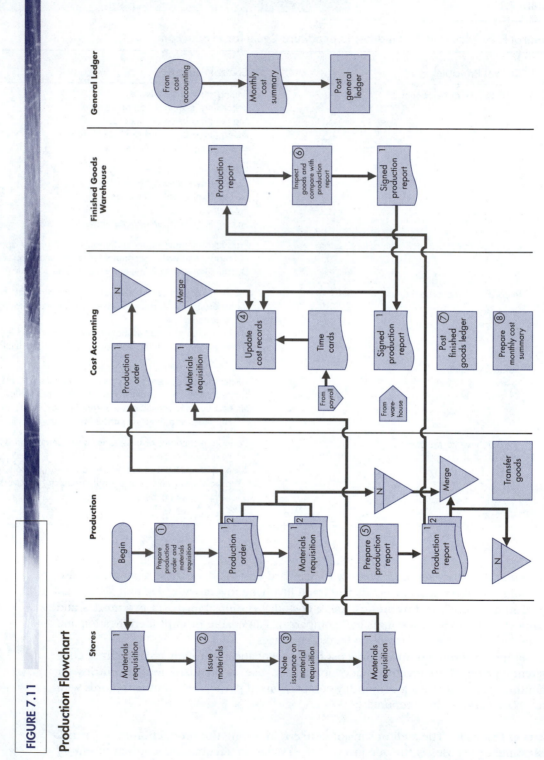

Note: Circled numbers denote sequence in which functions are performed.

cost flows. Testing the inventory costing model by recalculating standard cost for a sample of finished products and tracing a sample of production orders through the system are effective means for obtaining the necessary evidence.

Table 7.13 suggests control tests that the auditor can use to evaluate the production control procedures. The recommended tests assume that the client has developed standard costs for finished products and uses perpetual inventory records in accounting for inventory flows.

The first set of procedures is designed to test the standard cost system for reasonableness. In applying these procedures, the auditor might proceed as follows:

TABLE 7.13

Control Weaknesses and Related Tests: Expenditure Cycle for Production

Control Weakness	Possible Errors	Tests of Controls
Persons recording inventory cost flows, maintaining inventory records, determining overhead application rates, setting standard costs, or costing physical inventory not competent to do so	Errors in recording inventory cost flows	Select a sample of finished products and test for the following attributes:
	Errors in costing inventory and cost of sales	Proper determination of material types and quantities needed to produce finished product
	Errors in perpetual inventory records	Proper determination of labor operations and times required to produce finished product
Inadequate documentation of inventory movements	Unauthorized issuance of materials	Current materials prices and labor rates used to cost products
Lack of rigorous cost accounting system, as evidenced by:	Inaccurate inventory records	Reasonableness of rates used in applying overhead to finished products
Absence of journal entries recording cost flows	Inventory recording errors	Select a sample of completed production orders and test for the following attributes:
Failure to incorporate standard costs and variance analysis into the accounting system	Errors in calculating and recording cost of sales	Adequacy of documentation of production flows, as evidenced by
Failure to maintain detailed manufacturing overhead ledger	Failure to promptly locate and correct unfavorable variances	Materials requisition
		Production order
Failure to use standard journal entries in costing monthly production		Job order cost sheet or departmental production reports
		Time cards
Lack of periodic test counts and comparison of physical inventory with perpetual records	Undetected inventory shrinkage or recording errors	Recording and posting accuracy (trace from requisition to materials ledger, from materials ledger to cost sheets, and from production reports to finished goods ledger)
Failure to agree subsidiary inventory and overhead ledgers to controlling accounts on a regular basis	Undetected errors in recording or posting overhead accounts	Evidence of proper authorization of production orders and approval of requisitions
		Accuracy in posting production reports to monthly cost summary

Objective	Procedure
1. Determine reasonableness of types and quantities of materials used in finished product	Examine bill of materials describing the type and amount of each material used in finished product.
2. Determine reasonableness of direct labor operations and time required to produce a unit of finished product	Examine routing sheets describing each step in the manufacture of a given product, expressed in terms of: Labor operation / Labor time and rate / Material input and cost at each step in the process
3. Determine reasonableness of materials prices used to cost finished products	Trace from bill of materials to current vendors' invoices.
4. Determine that proper labor rates are used to cost finished products	Trace from routing sheets to listing of labor rates provided by human resources department.
5. Determine reasonableness of overhead rates applied to finished products	Recalculate overhead rates on a test basis by relating actual overhead to base (labor hours, labor dollars, machine hours, etc.). Compare calculated rates with standard rates. Consider capacity utilization.

The second set of tests described in Table 7.13 is concerned with the adequacy of documentation supporting inventory cost flows and the accuracy of recording the flows. These tests require the auditor to select a sample of completed production orders, examine for proper documentation, and trace the cost flows through the recording and posting process. Assuming that standard costs are incorporated into the general ledger, the auditor must determine that inventories are recorded at standard cost. Tracing the inventory debits to the audited standard cost records can do this. The auditor also should recalculate variances on a test basis and obtain explanations for significant variances occurring in the sample of production orders.

Design of Substantive Audit Procedures   Material weaknesses in inventory and production controls should lead to extended testing of the year-end physical inventories. This is particularly important if the perpetual inventory records are unreliable because of the weaknesses. Extended testing should consist mainly of expanding inventory test counts during the observation of physical inventory taking. In addition, depending on the nature of the weaknesses, the auditor may elect to recalculate direct labor and overhead included in ending goods in process and finished goods inventories.

FINANCING AND INVESTING CYCLE

Financial control policies and procedures and the auditor's tests of controls, as related to the financing and investing cycle, are discussed in this section according to the following categories of transactions:

1. *Borrowing from others*, excluding open trade accounts with creditors. The transactions may involve long-term or short-term notes, bonds payable, mortgages payable, or long-term financing leases.

2. *Lending to others*, excluding open trade accounts with customers.
3. *Acquisitions and disposals of financial assets.* Purchases of marketable securities, such as common stocks, preferred stocks, corporate bonds, and government securities fall into this category of transactions.
4. *Capital stock and dividend transactions.* Stock issuance and reacquisition, stock retirement, and dividend declarations are the principal transactions involving stockholders' equity.

Borrowing from Others

Transactions   Issuance of debt instruments, accrual of interest, and repayment of debt are the transaction classes comprising borrowing activities.

Documents   Documents associated with borrowing transactions are as follows:

1. *Remittance advice or bank credit memo:* This evidences receipt of loan proceeds.
2. *Copy of the debt instrument (note payable, bond indenture, lease agreement):* This specifies the terms under which the debt is to be repaid.
3. *Voucher authorizing payment of interest, principal, or both:* This authorizes payment by the entity.
4. *Standard journal entry or journal voucher for monthly interest accrual:* This ensures that all interest charges will be reflected in the monthly financial statements.

Control Features   The major features in effective internal control over borrowing activities are the proper authorization of borrowing and the control of cash receipts and disbursements resulting from borrowing and repayment. Borrowing authority should be clearly defined in policy and procedures manuals in terms of the person and the maximum amount of borrowing authority delegated to that person. The control procedures should provide that amounts in excess of the specified maximum be authorized by the board of directors and recorded in the directors' minutes.

Cash receipts from borrowing should be subject to the same control procedures as those described previously for the revenue cycle (see Figure 7.7). They should be included in the prelisting of cash receipts and compared with the deposit ticket and cash receipts entry related to that day's receipts.

Disbursements for interest and principal repayments should be supported by properly approved vouchers. Documentation in the form of copies of the debt instruments or calculations of interest should accompany the vouchers. Evidence of review and approval should appear on the face of the vouchers (see Figure 7.9).

Tests of Controls   The control tests related to borrowing and repayment already have been described in the section dealing with the revenue cycle (cash receipts) and the expenditure cycle (cash payments). In addition, as part of the initial internal control understanding phase, the auditor should review policy and procedures manuals for proper definition of borrowing authority. The auditor also should question management concerning control procedures related to miscellaneous cash receipts and disbursements.

Borrowing transactions are fewer in number than purchases and sales, and they are more likely to be individually significant. For this reason, the auditor examines the majority of these transactions during the substantive testing phase of the audit, regardless of the effectiveness of internal control. The amount of attention devoted to control testing of the borrowing cycle, therefore, is usually less than that accorded the revenue and expenditure cycle.

Design of Substantive Audit Procedures   If the control procedures do not provide for adequate authorization and approval of borrowing transactions, the auditor should consider the following substantive procedures.

1. Examine loan agreements for authenticity of nontrade liabilities;
2. Examine board of directors' minutes for recorded authorization of debt issuance;
3. Inquire of management as to proper authorization of liabilities not authorized in the board of directors' minutes; and
4. Consider confirming all material transactions and balances in nontrade liability accounts.

Lending to Others

Transactions   Lending transactions consist of the following:

1. Transfers of cash or other assets to others in exchange for some form of debt instrument—usually a note receivable;
2. Accrual of interest on notes receivable; and
3. Collection of notes receivable or interest.

Documents   Documents relating to lending transactions are as follows:

1. *Notes receivable:* These are the debt instruments.
2. *Canceled checks:* These are evidence of the lending transactions.
3. *Supporting calculations of interest accruals.*
4. *Cash receipts listings, remittance advices, and deposit tickets:* These are evidence of receipt and deposit of interest, principal, or both.

Control Features   Financial reporting controls over lending transactions should contain the following features:

1. Lending transactions should be subject to proper authorization and approval. The policies and procedures manuals should clearly define authority, and the system should provide for board approval and the recording of loan authorizations in the minutes of the directors' meetings.
2. A properly approved voucher and a copy of the note receivable authorizing the payment (see Figure 7.9) should accompany disbursement of loan proceeds.
3. Cash receipts resulting from interest and principal remittances should be controlled in the same manner as cash receipts from customers. To this end, they should be included in the daily cash receipts listings and compared with deposit tickets and cash receipts entries (see Figure 7.7).
4. Monthly interest accruals should be provided for by means of a standard journal entry or journal voucher. This control prevents inadvertent omission of necessary adjustments.

Tests of Controls   As with borrowing transactions, the auditor evaluates the effectiveness of internal control over the receipt and disbursement of loan proceeds during the control testing of the revenue and expenditure cycles. Reviewing the policies and procedures manuals and questioning management during the initial understanding phase complete the control testing of lending activities.

Design of Substantive Audit Procedures   As with borrowing transactions, failure to provide for proper loan authorization is the control weakness of greatest concern. Under these circumstances, the auditor should consider extending the following substantive audit procedures.

1. Examine loan agreements for all material year-end balances in nontrade receivables;
2. Examine board of directors' minutes for recorded authorization of all material year-end balances in nontrade receivables;
3. Inquire of management as to authorization of those loans not recorded in the board of directors' minutes; and
4. Consider confirming year-end balances in nontrade receivables.

Acquisitions and Disposals of Financial Assets

Transactions   The principal transactions in this category are the following:

1. Purchases of marketable securities and long-term investments; and
2. Sales of securities and investments.

Documents   Documents associated with asset acquisition and disposals are as follows:

1. *Brokers' advices and canceled checks:* These documents are evidence of the purchase of assets.
2. *Brokers' advices, receipted deposit tickets, cash receipts listings, and remittance advices:* These documents evidence the sale of financial assets.

Control Features   The following control features should be included in an effective system of internal control over the acquisition and disposal of financial assets.

1. Proper authorization of purchases and sales;
2. Review and approval of vouchers and documentation supporting purchases of financial assets;
3. Effective control over cash receipts from disposals; and
4. Provision for reviewing calculations in support of gains and losses on disposals and interest accruals.

The policies and procedures manuals should identify responsibility for the purchase and sale of investment securities. Moreover, provision should be made for board of director approval of transactions exceeding predetermined levels.

Cash receipts and disbursements associated with disposals and acquisitions should be subject to the same controls as receipts and disbursements relating to normal operating activities (see Figure 7.7). Standard journal entries or journal vouchers should be drafted for monthly interest accruals. Accounting manuals should provide guidance in calculating gain or loss from disposals.

Tests of Controls   Control over the purchase and sale of financial assets is evaluated as part of the auditor's control tests of cash receipts transactions and payments to vendors. During the initial understanding phase of financial reporting controls, the auditor should review the policies and procedures manuals for provisions relating to authorizations for acquisition or disposal. Accounting manuals should be examined for adequacy of instructions for calculating gains and losses on disposals. In reviewing standard journal entries, the auditor should determine that provision has been made for proper interest accrual.

Design of Substantive Audit Procedures   As with borrowing and lending transactions, failure of the client to provide for proper authorization of acquisitions and disposals prompts the auditor to inquire of management as to the propriety of the transactions. The auditor even may consider confirming the more significant transactions with brokers or with buyers and sellers for transactions not processed through securities dealers.

Control weaknesses that suggest material errors in calculating gains and losses and accrued interest should lead to extended tests in computing year-end balances. The accounts affected include gain or loss on the disposal of securities, interest receivable, and interest revenue. By applying analytical procedures, the auditor is able to evaluate the extent of possible misstatement.

Capital Stock and Dividend Transactions

Transactions   The principal transactions relating to capital stock and dividends are the following:

1. Issuance, reacquisition, and retirement of capital stock;
2. Declaration and payment of cash dividends; and
3. Stock dividends and stock splits.

Documents   Documents associated with stock transactions are as follows:

1. *Board of directors' minutes:* The minutes provide evidence that stock issuance and reacquisitions have been properly authorized.
2. *Remittance advices, cash receipts listings, and deposit tickets:* Cash receipts from stock issuance are evidenced by remittance advices attached to checks received from brokers or investment bankers, cash receipts listings, and bank deposit tickets.
3. *Disbursement vouchers and canceled checks:* The disbursement vouchers and canceled checks support reacquisitions of stock and dividend payments.

Control Features   The main control features related to capital stock transactions are the following:

1. All stock issuances and reacquisitions, as well as dividend declarations, should require board approval;
2. Cash receipts from stock issuance should be subject to the same control as other cash receipts (see Figure 7.7);
3. Disbursements for reacquisition of stock should be controlled in the same manner as other cash disbursements (see Figure 7.9); and
4. Imprest accounts should be used for paying dividends, and a single voucher and check should be written to transfer the total amount of a dividend declaration from the general to the imprest account.

Tests of Controls   Control tests of capital stock and dividend transactions should consist of evaluating the effectiveness of receipts and disbursements controls, as well as the adequacy of authorizations and approvals of stock issuance, reacquisitions, and dividends. Control testing of the revenue and expenditure cycles, as described earlier, provides the information necessary for evaluating the effectiveness of controls over receipts and disbursements related to capital stock transactions. Examining policy and procedures manuals and examining board of directors' minutes for approvals enables the auditor to determine the adequacy of authorizations and approvals.

Design of Substantive Audit Procedures   Failure to provide for proper authorization of capital stock issuance, reacquisition, and/or dividend declarations suggests that the auditor proceed as follows (this is covered more fully in Chapter 13):

1. Examine minutes for board of director approval of capital stock and dividend transactions;
2. Confirm with the board those transactions not recorded in the minutes; and
3. Examine stock certificates supporting treasury stock balances.

Control weaknesses affecting cash receipts and disbursements related to capital stock and dividend transactions suggest the following substantive audit procedures:

1. Examine remittance advices, brokers' advices, cash receipts listings, deposit tickets, and bank statement credits for all cash receipts arising from stock issuance;
2. Examine brokers' advices, vouchers, and canceled checks supporting stock reacquisitions; and
3. Reconcile dividend bank accounts for one or more months of the year under audit.

KEY TERMS

Assessed level of control risk, 243	Observation, 245
Compensating control, 237	Operating effectiveness of financial reporting
Control point, 237	controls, 244
Document examination and testing, 245	Primarily substantive audit, 243
Internal control checklist, 239	Qualitative approach, 247
Internal control flowchart, 240	Quantitative approach, 247
Internal control memorandum, 238	Reportable conditions, 250
Internal control questionnaire, 239	Reprocessing, 245
Maximum control risk, 243	Tests of controls, 244

REVIEW QUESTIONS

1. Define and give an example of a control point.

2. Define *reprocessing*. What is the purpose for this procedure?

3. What is meant by *the auditor's understanding of a client's internal control*?

4. How does the auditor obtain an initial understanding of a client's financial control policies and procedures?

5. What kind of documentation is required relative to the auditor's understanding of a client's financial reporting controls?

6. How does testing of financial reporting controls help in the design of substantive audit procedures?

7. Under what circumstances might an auditor decide *not* to test internal controls beyond obtaining an initial understanding?

8. Identify alternative means for testing of financial reporting controls.

9. Differentiate between fraudulent financial reporting and misappropriation.

10. Give an example of how a control weakness may lead to an expansion of substantive audit procedures.

11. What is meant by *reportable conditions*? What purpose is served by the letter to the audit committee communicating internal control related matters?

12. What is meant by *assessed level of control risk*?

13. Summarize the steps involved in the auditor's approach to obtaining an understanding of financial reporting controls and assessing control risk.

14. How does an internal control flowchart assist in evaluating the controls within a given transaction cycle?

15. Describe how the memorandum, questionnaire or checklist, and flowchart approaches might be used in combination to provide an effective means for studying and evaluating a client's financial reporting controls.

16. Explain how management characteristics affect both inherent risk and control risk.

17. Define the term *primarily substantive audit* and describe the conditions suggesting a primarily substantive audit.

MULTIPLE CHOICE QUESTIONS FROM PAST CPA AND CIA EXAMS

1. Reportable conditions are matters that come to an auditor's attention, which should be communicated to an entity's audit committee because they represent
   a. Material frauds or illegal acts perpetrated by high-level management.
   b. Significant deficiencies in the design or operation of the internal control system.
   c. Flagrant violations of the entity's documented conflict-of-interest policies.
   d. Intentional attempts by client personnel to limit the scope of the auditor's field work.

2. The objective of tests of details of transactions performed as tests of controls is to
   a. Detect material misstatements in the account balances of the financial statements.
   b. Evaluate whether financial reporting controls operated effectively.
   c. Determine the nature, timing, and extent of substantive tests for financial statement assertions.
   d. Reduce control risk, inherent risk, and detection risk to an acceptably low level.

3. When an auditor increases the planned assessed level of control risk because certain control procedures were determined to be ineffective, the auditor would most likely increase the
   a. Extent of substantive testing.
   b. Level of inherent risk.
   c. Extent of tests of controls.
   d. Level of detection risk.

4. When an auditor assesses control risk below the maximum level, the auditor is required to document the auditor's

	Basis for concluding that control risk is below the maximum level	*Understanding of the entity's internal control system elements*
a.	No	No
b.	Yes	Yes
c.	Yes	No
d.	No	Yes

5. Which of the following is *not* a reason an auditor should obtain an understanding of the elements of an entity's financial reporting controls in planning an audit?

  a. Identify types of potential misstatements that can occur
  b. Design substantive tests
  c. Consider the operating effectiveness of the controls
  d. Consider factors that affect the risk of material misstatements

6. An auditor's primary consideration regarding an entity's internal control system policies and procedures is whether the policies and procedures
  a. Affect the financial statement assertions.
  b. Prevent management override.
  c. Relate to the control environment.
  d. Reflect management's philosophy and operating style.

7. In a study and evaluation of financial reporting controls, the completion of a questionnaire is most closely associated with which of the following?
  a. Tests of control
  b. Substantive tests
  c. Obtaining an initial understanding of the system
  d. Review of the system design

8. During consideration of the internal control system in a financial statement audit, an auditor is *not* obligated to
  a. Search for significant deficiencies in the operation of the internal control system.
  b. Understand the internal control environment and the accounting system.
  c. Determine whether the control procedures relevant to audit planning have been placed in operation.
  d. Perform procedures to understand the design of the internal control policies.

9. An advantage of using internal control flowcharts to document information about financial reporting controls instead of using internal control questionnaires is that flowcharts
  a. Identify internal control weaknesses more prominently.
  b. Provide a visual depiction of clients' activities.
  c. Indicate whether control procedures are operating effectively.
  d. Reduce the need to observe clients' employees performing routine tasks.

10. When control risk is assessed at the maximum level for all financial statement assertions, an auditor should document the auditor's

	Understanding of the entity's internal con- trol elements	*Conclusion that control risk is at the maximum level*	*Basis for concluding that control risk is at the maximum level*
a.	Yes	No	No
b.	Yes	Yes	No
c.	No	Yes	Yes
d.	Yes	Yes	Yes

11. When there are numerous property and equipment transactions during the year, an auditor who plans to assess control risk at a low level usually performs
  a. Analytical procedures for property and equipment balances at the end of the year.
  b. Tests of controls and extensive tests of property and equipment balances at the end of the year.
  c. Analytical procedures for the current year property and equipment transactions.
  d. Tests of controls and limited tests of current year property and equipment transactions.

12. The primary objective of procedures performed to obtain an understanding of the internal control system is to provide an auditor with
   a. Evidential matter to use in reducing detection risk.
   b. Knowledge necessary to plan the audit.
   c. A basis from which to modify tests of controls.
   d. Information necessary to prepare flowcharts.

13. After obtaining an understanding of an entity's financial reporting controls, an auditor may assess control risk at the maximum level for some assertions because the auditor
   a. Believes the internal control policies and procedures are unlikely to be effective.
   b. Determines that the pertinent financial reporting control elements are *not* well documented.
   c. Performs tests of controls to restrict detection risk to an acceptable level.
   d. Identifies internal control policies and procedures that are likely to prevent material misstatements.

14. Which of the following audit techniques most likely would provide an auditor with the most assurance about the effectiveness of the operation of an internal control procedure?
   a. Confirmation with outside parties
   b. Inquiry of client personnel
   c. Recomputation of account balance amounts
   d. Observation of client personnel

15. An auditor uses the knowledge provided by the understanding of the financial reporting controls and the assessed level of control risk primarily to
   a. Determine whether procedures and records concerning the safeguarding of assets are reliable.
   b. Ascertain whether the opportunities to allow any person to both perpetrate and conceal frauds are minimized.
   c. Modify the initial assessments of inherent risk and preliminary judgments about materiality levels.
   d. Determine the nature, timing, and extent of substantive tests for financial statement assertions.

16. Which of the following statements describes why a properly designed and executed audit may *not* detect a material fraud?
   a. Audit procedures that are effective for detecting an unintentional misstatement may be ineffective for an intentional misstatement that is concealed through collusion.
   b. An audit is designed to provide reasonable assurance of detecting material errors, but there is *no* similar responsibility concerning material fraud.
   c. The factors considered in assessing control risk indicated an increased risk of intentional misstatements, but only a low risk of unintentional errors in the financial statements.
   d. The auditor did *not* consider factors influencing audit risk for account balances that have effects pervasive to the financial statements taken as a whole.

17. After obtaining an understanding of an entity's financial reporting controls and assessing control risk, an auditor may next
   a. Perform tests of controls to verify management's assertions that are embodied in the financial statements.
   b. Consider whether evidential matter is available to support a further reduction in the assessed level of control risk.

c. Apply analytical procedures as substantive tests to validate the assessed level of control risk.

d. Evaluate whether the internal control system policies and procedures detected material misstatements in the financial statements.

18. In developing a preliminary audit strategy, an auditor should consider

a. Whether the allowance for sampling risk exceeds the achieved upper precision limit.

b. Findings from substantive tests performed at interim dates.

c. Whether the inquiry of the client's attorney identifies any litigation, claims, or assessments *not* disclosed in the financial statements.

d. The planned assessed level of control risk.

19. The ultimate purpose of assessing control risk is to contribute to the auditor's evaluation of the risk that

a. Specified controls requiring segregation of duties may be circumvented by collusion.

b. Senior management may override entity policies.

c. Tests of controls may fail to identify procedures relevant to assertions.

d. Material misstatements may exist in the financial statements.

INTERNET ACTIVITIES

ABREMA, an acronym meaning Activity Based Risk Evaluation Model of Auditing, was developed by the Australian Educational Research Pty Ltd. The web site at http://www.abrema.net/abrema/index.html is meant to assist auditors in cognitive decision making, particularly in the area of risk analysis. The model is divided into four steps:

Planning
Evidence gathering
Evidence evaluation
Decision making (audit report decision)

Required:

Go to the ABREMA web site and, after reading the Executive Summary, answer the following questions:

1. Define AR1* and AR1.
2. Differentiate between AR1 and AR2.
3. How do the above concepts assist the auditor in reaching a decision regarding client acceptance?
4. Define CR2 and CR3.
5. How does one get from CR2 to CR3?

ESSAY QUESTIONS AND PROBLEMS

7.1   A partially completed charge sales systems flowchart appears in Figure 7.12. The flowchart depicts the charge sales activities of Ferdo Distributors, Inc.

A customer's purchase order is received and a six-part sales order is prepared from it. The six copies are initially distributed as follows:

Copy No. 1—Billing copy to billing department.
Copy No. 2—Shipping copy to shipping department.
Copy No. 3—Credit copy to credit department.

.com

http://www.
abrema.net/abrema/
index.html

FIGURE 7.12

Flowchart of Credit Sales for Problem 7.1

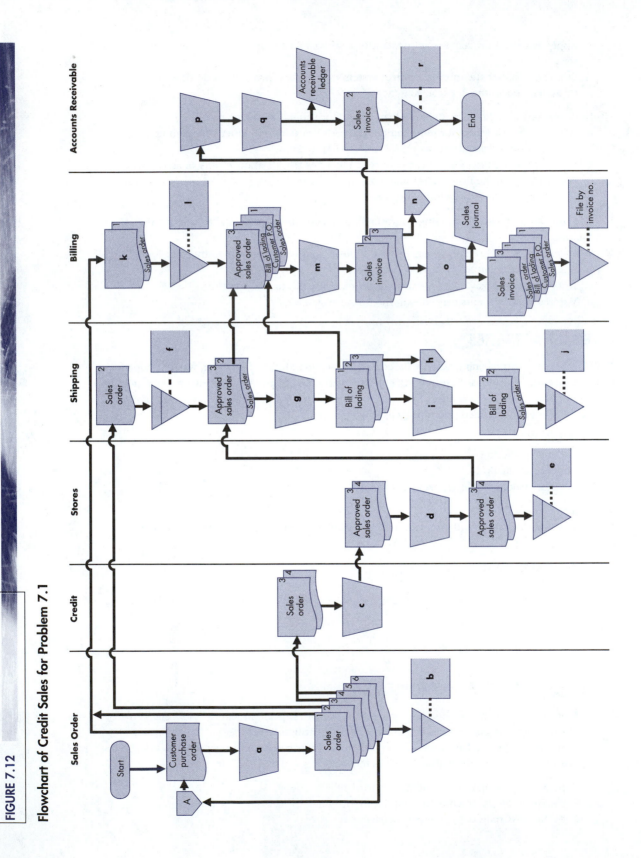

Copy No. 4—Stock request copy to credit department.

Copy No. 5—Customer copy to customer.

Copy No. 6—Sales order copy filed in sales order department.

When each copy of the sales order reaches the applicable department or destination, it calls for specific internal control procedures and related documents. Some of the procedures and related documents are indicated on the flowchart. Other procedures and documents are labeled **a** to **r**.

Required:

a. List the procedures or the internal documents that are labeled **c** to **r** in the flowchart of Ferdo Distributors' charge sales system.

   Organize your answer as follows (note that an explanation of the **a** and **b** that appear in the flowchart are entered as examples):

Flowchart Symbol Letter	Procedures or Internal Document
a	Prepare six-part sales order.
b	File by order number.

b. Describe the procedures the auditor might use to test the internal controls over charge sales processing. What financial statement assertions are supported by each of the controls tested?

(AICPA adapted)

7.2   Sportsman, Ltd., a recurring audit client of Kamp & Hike, CPAs, is a large manufacturer of hunting and fishing equipment and camping supplies. Based on past audits, Joel Banks, the senior auditor in charge of audit field work for this engagement, believes internal control to be strong in all areas. He also hopes to reduce inherent risk below 100 percent, based on past experience with Sportsman's management team.

   Sportsman's unaudited net income for 2002 is $150 million and its unaudited assets equal $3.5 billion. Kamper & Hike's firm policy regarding materiality thresholds is as follows:

Individual item materiality—5%–7% of net income for audit adjustment purposes
                             2%–4% of total assets for audit reclassification purposes

Aggregate materiality—8%–22% of individual item materiality (depending on the levels of assessed inherent and control risk)

Based on this policy, Banks has set the following preaudit planning thresholds:

Individual item materiality—6% and 3%, respectively, for adjustment and reclassification purposes

Aggregate—20% of individual item, given low inherent risk and control risk

Study of the business and industry and application of analytical procedures produces no unusual complexities or abnormalities and thus supports Banks' plan to reduce inherent risk below 100 percent. In studying internal control and performing control tests, however, Banks and his audit team found that financial reporting controls have deteriorated significantly in most transaction cycle subsets. The company's controller resigned in January 2002 and has not yet been replaced. Also, as part of a downsizing effort, the internal audit staff was reduced from 32 to 4 members.

Required:

a. Calculate the dollar amount of individual item and aggregate materiality thresholds for the Sportsman audit.

b. Given the audit team's assessment of inherent risk and its findings regarding internal control, what do you suggest regarding:
   1. Changes in materiality thresholds
   2. Types of audit evidence

7.3   An auditor is required to obtain a sufficient understanding of each of the elements of an entity's internal control system to plan the audit of the entity's financial statements and to assess control risk for the assertions embodied in the account balance, transaction class, and disclosure components of the financial statements.

Required:
a. Identify the elements of an entity's financial reporting controls.
b. For what purposes should an auditor's understanding of the internal control elements be used in planning an audit?
c. Explain the reasons an auditor may assess control risk at the maximum level for one or more assertions embodied in an account balance.
d. What must an auditor do to support assessing control risk at less than the maximum level when the auditor has determined that controls have been placed in operation?
(AICPA adapted)

7.4   During the preaudit conference for Kleene, Inc., the senior auditor described for the new staff persons assigned to this year's audit the essential characteristics of Kleene's financial reporting control system. In the payroll cycle, controls have been found severely lacking; however, the auditors have been reasonably satisfied with the controls within the other cycles. In the past, the controls over cash receipts have been evaluated as excellent.

Within the payroll area, material errors and fraud can occur readily. Supervisors do *not* review time cards prepared by employees; pay rates, hours, extensions, and withholdings are *not* reviewed independently. Paychecks, after being signed, are returned to department supervisors for distribution.

Required:
a. What alternatives are available to auditors for dealing with weak financial control subsets? What possible effects might the absence of payroll controls have on the financial statements in this case?
b. What steps should the auditor take if, based on the initial review, controls are thought to be adequate?
c. Describe procedures the auditor might apply in testing the payroll controls.
d. Although the control procedures relating to cash receipts have been excellent in the past, they should be reevaluated again this year.
   1. Why is it necessary for the auditors to study and evaluate internal control each year?
   2. Why is a minimum audit necessary notwithstanding excellent controls?

7.5   A CPA's audit workpapers contain a narrative description (below) of a segment of the Bergdon Chemicals, Inc., payroll system and an accompanying flowchart.

NARRATIVE

The internal control system with respect to the department of human resources is functioning well and is not included in the accompanying flowchart (Figure 7.13).

At the beginning of each work week, payroll clerk no. 1 reviews the payroll department files to determine the employment status of production employees, then prepares time cards and distributes them as each individual arrives at work. This payroll clerk,

FIGURE 7.13

Factory Payroll System for Problem 7.5

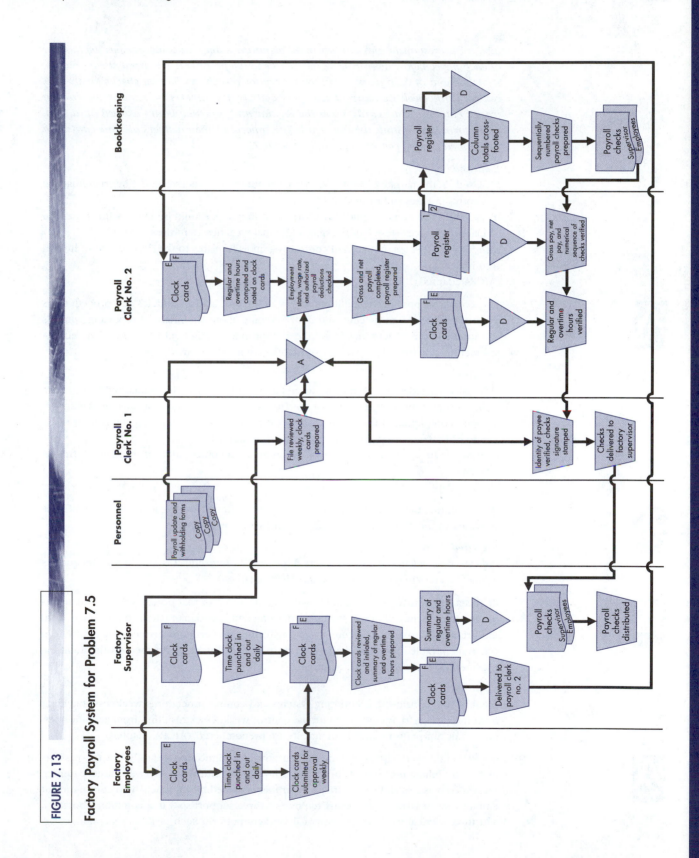

who is also responsible for custody of the signature stamp machine, verifies the identity of each payee before delivering signed checks to the processing department supervisor.

At the end of each work week, the supervisor distributes payroll checks for the preceding work week. Concurrent with this activity, the supervisor reviews the current week's employee time cards, notes the regular and overtime hours worked on a summary form, and initials the time cards. The supervisor then delivers all time cards and unclaimed payroll checks to payroll clerk no. 2.

Required:
a. Based on the narrative and flowchart, what are the weaknesses in the internal financial control policies and procedures?
b. Based on the narrative and flowchart, what inquiries should be made with respect to clarifying the existence of possible additional weaknesses in the controls?

Note: Do *not* discuss the internal control system as it relates to the department of human resources.

(AICPA adapted)

7.6 The overall purpose of the auditor's review of internal control policies and procedures is to obtain sufficient knowledge and understanding about the financial reporting controls and internal control activities to aid the auditor in assessing control risk, so that such assessment can be used in designing substantive audit procedures.

Required:
a. What knowledge should the auditor obtain from the initial understanding phase of the internal control study and evaluation? How does the auditor obtain this knowledge?
b. Upon completion of the initial phase, what possible conclusions may the auditor reach and how would each affect the auditor's substantive tests?
c. What is the appropriate extent of the auditor's documentation of internal control review?

(AICPA adapted)

7.7 While auditing Big Lots, Inc., the auditor prepared a flowchart (Figure 7.14) of credit sales activities. In this flowchart code letter **A** represents the customer.

Required:
Indicate what each of the code letters **B** through **P** represents. Do *not* discuss adequacies or inadequacies in the control system. (AICPA adapted)

7.8 Rebecca James, CPA, prepared the flowchart in Figure 7.15 that portrays the raw materials purchasing function of one of James' clients, a medium-sized manufacturing company, from the preparation of initial documents through the vouchering of invoices for payment in accounts payable. The flowchart was a portion of the work performed on the audit engagement to evaluate internal control.

Required:
Identify and explain the accounting systems and control procedures weaknesses evident from the flowchart. Include the internal control weaknesses resulting from activities performed or not performed. All documents are prenumbered. (AICPA adapted)

7.9 A CPA's audit workpapers include the narrative description on page 299 of the cash receipts and billing portions of the financial reporting controls of Parkway Surgery Center, Inc. Parkway is a small health care provider that is owned by a publicly held corporation. It employs seven salaried physicians, ten nurses, three support staff in a common laboratory, and three clerical workers. The clerical workers perform such tasks as reception, corre-

FIGURE 7.14

Flowchart of Credit Sales Activities for Problem 7.7

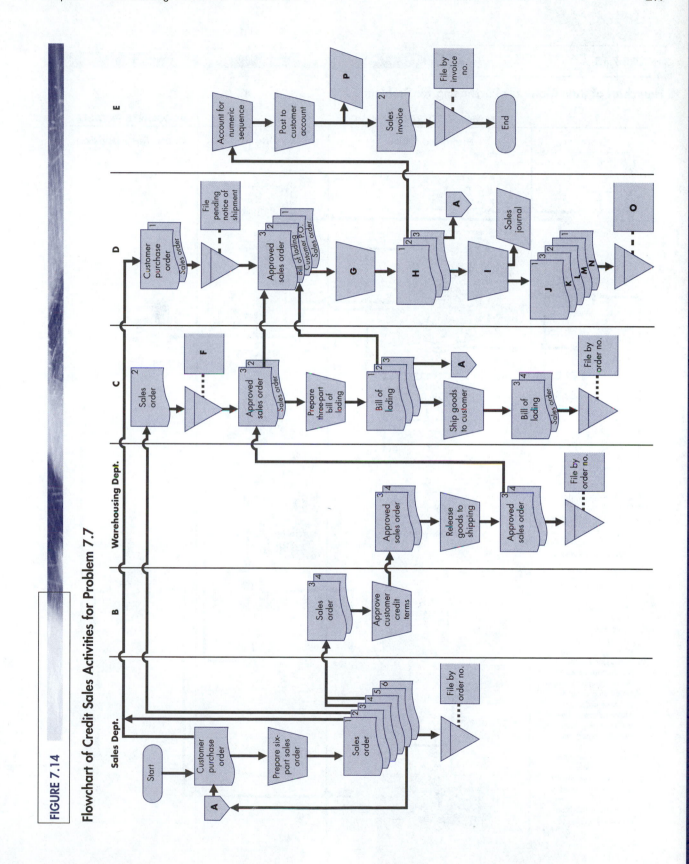

FIGURE 7.15

Flowchart of Raw Materials Purchasing for Problem 7.8

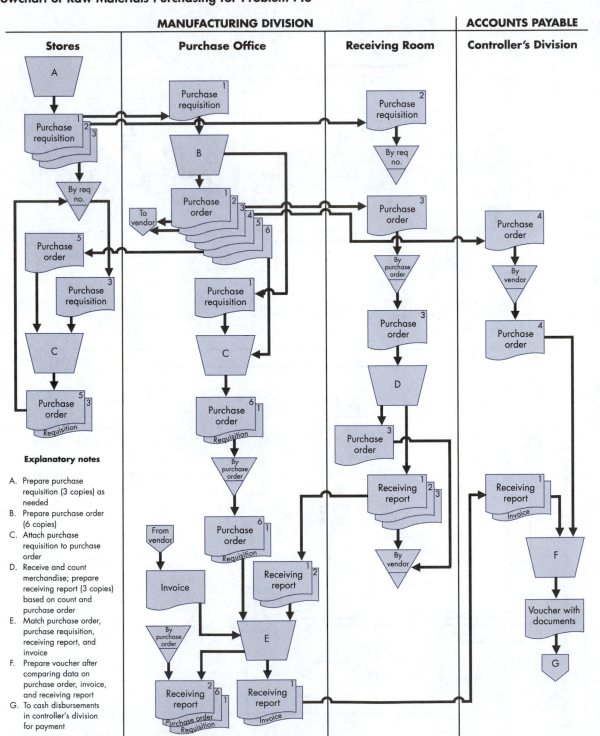

Explanatory notes

A. Prepare purchase requisition (3 copies) as needed
B. Prepare purchase order (6 copies)
C. Attach purchase requisition to purchase order
D. Receive and count merchandise; prepare receiving report (3 copies) based on count and purchase order
E. Match purchase order, purchase requisition, receiving report, and invoice
F. Prepare voucher after comparing data on purchase order, invoice, and receiving report
G. To cash disbursements in controller's division for payment

spondence, cash receipts, billing, and appointment scheduling and are adequately bonded. They are referred to in the narrative as "office manager," "clerk no. 1," and "clerk no. 2."

NARRATIVE

Most patients pay for services by cash or check at the time services are rendered. Credit is not approved by the clerical staff. The physician who is to perform the respective services approves credit based on an interview. When credit is approved, the physician files a memo with the billing clerk (clerk no. 2) to set up the receivable from data generated by the physician.

The servicing physician prepares a charge slip that is given to clerk no. 1 for pricing and preparation of the patient's bill. Clerk no. 1 transmits a copy of the bill to clerk no. 2 for preparation of the revenue summary and for posting in the accounts receivable subsidiary ledger.

The cash receipts functions are performed by clerk no. 1, who receives cash and checks directly from patients and gives each patient a prenumbered cash receipt. Clerk no. 1 opens the mail, immediately stamps all checks "for deposit only," and lists cash and checks for deposit. The cash and checks are deposited daily by the office manager. The list of cash and checks, together with the related remittance advices, is forwarded by clerk no. 1 to clerk no. 2. Clerk no. 1 also serves as receptionist and performs general correspondence duties.

Clerk no. 2 prepares and sends monthly statements to patients with unpaid balances. Clerk no. 2 also prepares the cash receipts journal and is responsible for the accounts receivable subsidiary ledger. No other clerical employee is permitted access to the accounts receivable subsidiary ledger. Uncollectible accounts are written off by clerk no. 2 only after the physician who performed the respective services believes the account to be uncollectible and communicates the write-off approval to the office manager. The office manager then issues a write-off memo which clerk no. 2 processes.

The office manager supervises the clerks, issues write-off memos, schedules appointments for the doctors, makes bank deposits, reconciles bank statements, and performs general correspondence duties.

Additional services are performed monthly by a local accountant, who posts summaries prepared by the clerks to the general ledger, prepares income statements, and files the appropriate payroll forms and tax returns. The accountant reports directly to the parent corporation.

Required:
Based on the information in the narrative:
a. Prepare an internal control flowchart that portrays the revenue cycle (billing and cash receipts) for Parkway Surgery Center.
b. Based on the narrative and your completed flowchart, describe the reportable conditions and one resulting misstatement that could occur and *not* be prevented or detected by Parkway's financial reporting controls over the cash receipts and billing function. Do *not* describe how to correct the reportable conditions and potential misstatements. Use the format illustrated below.

Reportable condition	Potential misstatement
There is no control to verify that fees are recorded and billed at authorized rates and terms.	Accounts receivable could be overstated and uncollectible accounts understated because of the lack of controls.

(AICPA adapted)

CASE I

California Steakhouse

Your company, a national CPA firm, has been retained to audit California Steakhouse, a large restaurant franchiser with 300 outlets located throughout the United States. You have been assigned as the in-charge senior auditor responsible for the audit field work. California Steakhouse was previously audited by a smaller firm of CPAs, but because the company desires to go public in a couple of years, its management decided to hire a national CPA firm to assist in the registration of securities. You obtained management's permission to communicate with the predecessor CPAs and learned that the predecessors had a disagreement with the company's management concerning the timing of revenue recognition.

Your analytical procedures indicate that California's profits have been increasing steadily over the past several years, but that growth has slowed in the past two years. Unaudited net income for this year, however, has rebounded and the percentage increase significantly exceeds that of the preceding year.

You also have studied the company's organizational structure, talked with various members of management concerning the nature of the company's business and its internal control system, and obtained an initial understanding of those control policies and procedures relevant to an audit. The contents of that study are contained in the following paragraphs.

Upon signing a franchising agreement, the franchisee must pay California Steakhouse $50,000 cash and sign a five-year variable rate note (prime rate plus 1%) payable for $200,000. In exchange for this fee, the company provides marketing research and site location, arranges for construction of the restaurant, provides fixtures and equipment, helps train new employees, and arranges for initial promotion of the new facility.

Franchisees must buy all ingredients from California Steakhouse and must also pay royalties on revenue in excess of a stated minimum. California Steakhouse personnel periodically visit the sites to inspect for cleanliness and integrity of food products. The company's internal auditors also periodically visit franchisees to examine the records and verify the accuracy of royalties.

Although California Steakhouse appears to have good internal control over cash receipts, policies appear rather "loose" with regard to revenue recognition. Moreover, the deferred franchise costs (construction costs, initial promotion, site location, etc.) as a percent of total assets appear high relative to other similar restaurant franchisers.

Required:

a. In what areas would you be willing to reduce inherent risk below 100 percent? Why?

b. Based on your evaluation of inherent risk and control risk, where would you concentrate audit resources? Why?

c. Given your evaluation of internal control, can you identify any transaction cycle subsets warranting a minimum audit? What should you do before proceeding with the minimum audit in the selected area(s)?

d. Should you test revenue recognition controls for operating effectiveness? If so, why? If not, why not?

CASE II

Jack's Appliances

Jack's Appliances is a large appliance store located in a small midwestern city. The company is owned and managed by its founder, Jack Morrison. The store sells a complete line of kitchen appliances, as well as audio and video equipment. Employees consist of twelve salespersons, six appliance repair employees, an office/store manager, and a bookkeeper. As part of a recently completed loan agreement with one of the local banks, Jack's is required to have an annual audit.

Jack Morrison has arranged with you, a local CPA, to conduct the audit. As part of your audit planning, you wish to obtain an understanding of Jack's internal control system. This case concentrates on the purchases and payment subset of the expenditure cycle, which is described in the following paragraphs.

Appliances and repair parts are purchased from several wholesale warehouses located within a radius of 150 miles from Jack's. Perpetual inventory records are maintained in quantities and dollars by the bookkeeper. The "first-in first-out" method is used in costing credits to the inventories. Debits are entered on the basis of matched bills of lading and vendors' invoices. Copies of sales invoices form the basis for credits to the perpetual records.

Jack Morrison orders goods after his weekly inspection of the storage area, located to the rear of the building behind the sales floor. Based on his inspection, he prepares a list of goods and repair parts to be purchased. This list is forwarded to the bookkeeper, who prepares purchase orders for Morrison's signature. Vendors are selected by the bookkeeper on the basis of product availability and vendor proximity. After examining the purchase orders, Morrison signs them and returns them to the bookkeeper for mailing. The bookkeeper files copies of all purchase orders alphabetically by vendor.

All appliances are delivered to Jack's by truck. The truck drivers unload the products with the assistance of one or more repair employees or salespersons, depending on who is available. The employee(s) assisting in unloading sign the bill of lading after the unloading is complete. The signed bill of lading serves as a receiving report and is forwarded to the bookkeeper. The bookkeeper files the bill of lading alphabetically awaiting receipt of the vendor's in-voice. Upon receipt of the vendor's invoice, the bill of lading is removed and compared with the invoice as to type and quantity of goods. Perpetual inventory records are updated at this time and matched invoices and bills of lading are filed chronologically by due date.

On the date an invoice is due to be paid, the bookkeeper removes the documents from the chronological file and prepares a disbursement check for the invoice price less the discount. The documents, along with the checks, are then forwarded to Jack Morrison for his signature. Morrison signs the checks manually after examining the documents and comparing the check amount. The checks, along with the documents, are returned to the bookkeeper, who mails the checks to the vendors, marks the invoices "paid," and files the paid invoices, bills of lading, and check copies alphabetically in a "paid invoice" file.

Required:

a. Prepare a flowchart of Jack's purchasing, receiving, and payment subset of the expenditure cycle. Identify internal control strengths and weaknesses on your flowchart. Remember, you are concerned only with strengths and weaknesses having a material impact on Jack's financial statements.

b. For each internal control strength, indicate the financial statement assertion(s) affected and how the strength promotes financial statement reliability.

c. For each internal control weakness, indicate the financial statement assertion(s) affected, recommend improvements, and discuss the possible impact of the weakness on substantive audit testing.

Internal Control and Computer-Based Information Systems (CBIS)

c h a p t e r 8

biltrite

After reading this chapter, you should be able to

1 Differentiate between auditing around and auditing through the computer.
2 Classify and describe the different types of CBIS.
3 Classify and define the major CBIS accounting controls.
4 Develop an approach to assessing control risk through review of internal control policies and procedures, given significant CBIS accounting applications.
5 Evaluate and manage audit risk factors uniquely associated with CBIS accounting applications.

OVERVIEW

Computer-based information systems (CBIS) accounting applications have an impact on the auditor in two ways. First, they affect the auditor's review of internal control policies and procedures; this topic is covered in this chapter. Second, they influence the nature of substantive audit testing; this aspect is addressed in Chapters 11 through 13. As shown in Figure 8.1, this chapter is concerned with the same segment of the audit process as Chapter 7. While Chapter 7 emphasized controls associated with accounting information systems generally, Chapter 8 considers CBIS environments exclusively.

CBIS are diverse in practice, and for this reason, have different control features. The systems vary as to method of processing, file integration, and hardware configuration. Whatever the nature of the system, the auditor must determine that the necessary controls are properly designed and implemented.

CBIS controls may be classified according to three types:

1. General controls;
2. Application controls; and
3. User controls.

General controls cover all computer-processing tasks and are more pervasive than application controls that relate to specific tasks performed by the computer. User controls consist of manual controls (e.g., control totals) applied by departments whose transactions are processed by the computer. The purpose of user controls is to verify the completeness and accuracy of computer output.

Although many techniques exist for testing CBIS controls, they may be classified broadly as either auditing around the computer or auditing through the computer. Auditing *around* the computer compares input with output and treats the computer as a "black box," ignoring the means by which transactions are processed. Auditing *through* the computer (the "white box" approach) directly tests the CBIS controls. Most auditors use a combination of methods in testing CBIS controls.

Auditors should consider the unique ways by which CBIS impact audit risk. Centralized systems, distributed systems, and electronic commerce systems affect audit risk in two ways. First, direct input of transactions, internal storage of files and data, and lack of hard-copy transaction documentation pose increased risk to the auditor. Second, the existence of adequate controls in the supervisory programs of these systems mitigates risk by assuring consistent and correct processing of transactions. These issues, together with the methods for dealing with increased risk, are covered in the final section of the chapter.

AUDIT APPROACHES

CBIS and Audit Risk

Computers are being used to an ever-increasing extent to process transactions and to store accounting data. Systems range from simple personal computer (PC) systems to complex electronic commerce systems. The trend in computer use affects two aspects of audit risk:

1. Assessing control risk, given the need for CBIS controls; and
2. Managing detection risk, by substantiating transactions processed by the computer and balances stored in computer files.

The first area concerns the **phases of processing** and is the subject matter of the current chapter. The second area deals with the **results of processing** and is covered in Chapters 11 through 13.

FIGURE 8.1

The Audit Process

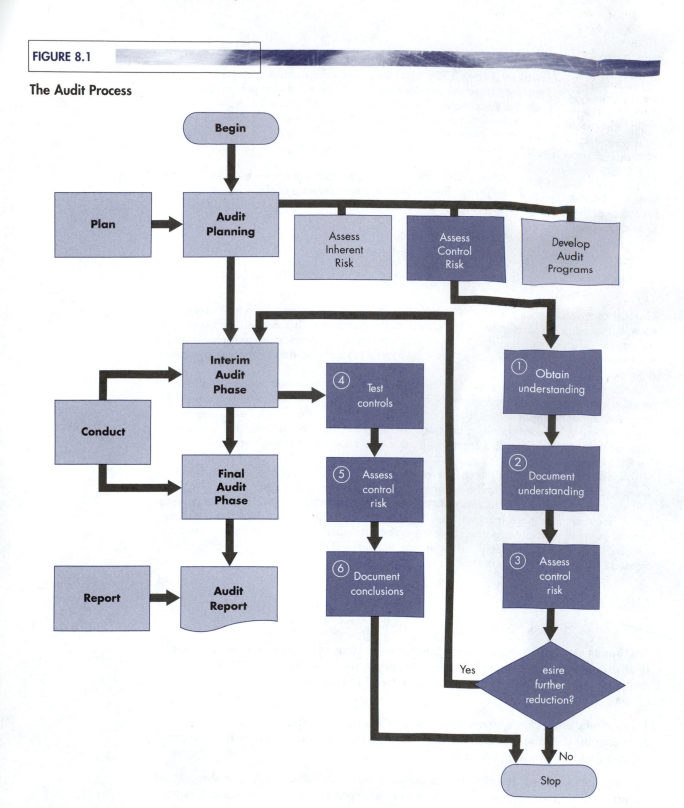

Impact of CBIS on the Audit Approach

The type of accounting system used by the client, as addressed in Chapter 4, does not affect auditing objectives. The audit approach, however, may need to be modified to accommodate CBIS accounting applications. The reasons for modification are discussed in the following paragraphs.

Change in the Audit Trail   The audit trail frequently assumes a different form when transactions are processed by the computer. The more advanced computer systems produce less documentation than manual systems, but the decrease in documentation is offset by programmed controls to ensure consistent and accurate processing of transactions. Moreover, internal storage of transactions and files reduces the need for permanent retention of hard copy.

Remote sales order processing is a common example of programmed controls replacing manual controls. In this environment, sales orders are inputted at terminal locations, with the computer performing most of the verification procedures involving customer number, credit limit, price, terms, and so on. Computer verification, as contrasted with manual checking, reduces the need for extensive documentation, and also makes permanent retention of the hard copy unnecessary once all verification procedures have been performed and documented internally. The visible audit trail, under these conditions, has been transformed into a computer audit trail. Performing tests of controls, therefore, may shift from examination of documents to inspection of transaction logs and observation of control activity performed during input, because the internal processing by computers is not visible to the human eye.

Referred to as **paperless offices**, some companies are using optical scanners to transfer transaction documents to "computer file cabinets." Software programs called **document management systems** then are used for scanning, retrieving, and managing the documents stored in the file cabinets.[1] Under these circumstances, the auditor needs to test computer controls more extensively, and perform substantive audit procedures by retrieving internally stored documents.

Combining of Functions   In addition to audit trail modification, computer processing of transactions permits the combining of functions that ordinarily are separated in manual systems. Using the sales order example, CBIS processing enables the computer to validate the customer number, credit limit, price, stock number, credit terms, and so on through input editing. A manual system, on the other hand, validates through visual checking followed by second-party review. In a computerized payroll system, the computer internally checks the employee number to determine whether the person is a valid employee, and also tests the correctness of labor rates and the reasonableness of hours worked; hence, it replaces the more traditional manual performance of these control procedures.

Combining of functions that are normally separated in manual systems, like the audit trail modifications, requires a somewhat different approach to performing tests of controls by the auditor. Testing the validation controls through observation, tracing

---

1   For an excellent description of paperless offices, see Weiss, Mitchell Jay, "The Paperless Office," and Hunton, James E., "Setting Up a Paperless Office," both articles appearing in *The Journal of Accountancy*, November 1994. For an audit approach, given the paperless office environment, see Pearson, Michael A., "Auditing in a Paperless Environment," *The Ohio CPA Journal*, June 1996.

transactions through the system, or auditing around the computer is necessary, given the absence of separation under these circumstances.

Alternative Approaches

In testing the phases of processing (assessing control risk, given CBIS accounting controls), the auditor has a choice of auditing around the computer or auditing through the computer. In **auditing around the computer**, the auditor concentrates on input and output, and ignores the specifics of how the computer processes data. Here the auditor does not test the CBIS controls, arguing that if inputs and outputs are correct, then the processing must have been accurate. In testing payroll applications, for example, the auditor first might examine selected time cards for hours and employee earnings records for rates, and then trace these to the payroll summary output to compare hours, rates, and extensions. The comparison of inputs and outputs may be done manually or with the assistance of the computer. The computer-assisted approach has the advantage of permitting the auditor to make more comparisons than would be possible manually.

Auditing through the computer involves direct testing of the programmed controls used in processing specific applications. In the above payroll example, the auditor would identify the controls included in the payroll application program (e.g., limit tests, validity tests, and check digits) and test them by directly observing the control functions during data processing.

Auditing around the computer has the advantage of ease of comprehension, in that the tracing of source documents to output does not require any in-depth study of application programs. A major disadvantage, however, is that the auditor, not having directly tested the controls, cannot make assertions about the underlying process. Moreover, in some of the more complex CBIS, intermediate printouts may not be available for making the needed comparisons.

Auditing through the computer has the advantage of enabling the auditor to test CBIS controls in both simple and complex systems. This approach also enables the auditor to make direct assertions about the processing of transactions. If the controls over transaction processing are determined to be reliable through direct testing of the relevant controls, the auditor may conclude that the records have an increased probability of being accurate. In practice, auditors usually use a combination of auditing around and through the computer.

These audit approaches are applied later in this chapter as part of the control testing discussion. First, however, we will examine the various types of CBIS and the kinds of controls to be found in them.

TYPES OF CBIS

Many types of computer systems are currently in use. These systems may be centralized or distributed systems; they may be real-time or batch processing systems; they may be multi-user or flat file systems; and they may interact with vendors and customers as electronic commerce systems.

Centralized versus Distributed Systems

Centralized Data Processing Systems   In a **centralized data processing system**, the data processing group controls the recording of transactions at a central location utilizing one or more large computers. Data is transmitted by functional or geographical areas to data processing either in the form of paper documents or electronic transmittals using terminals connected to the central computing center. (See Figure 8.2) If in the form of paper documents, the data must be converted to a form suitable for computer processing. In a centralized system, systems analysis and development, programming, and data control are all housed in the central location. End users may receive information from computer services in the form of hard copy or by utilizing terminals with read only access to centralized databases.

Most entities with centralized systems place the computer services function under the control of an officer with a title such as "vice president of computer services." The significant financial reporting controls over the processing of data are designed and implemented at the central location. The advantages of a centralized system lie in its cost savings through consolidation; the consistent processing of data; and the heightened internal control provided by concentrating systems development, programming, and data

FIGURE 8.2

Centralized Data Processing System

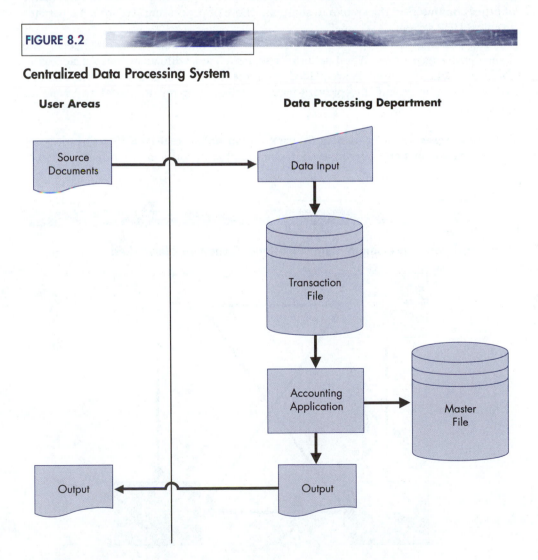

processing in one central location. Removing information design and data processing from end users can result in failure to meet unique user information needs and is therefore the main disadvantage of such systems.

Distributed Data Processing Systems   **Distributed data processing (DDP) systems** consist of several data processing units within the entity, each under the control of end users. The units may be based on function, such as marketing, finance, production, and human resources; or they may be geographically based. For better internal control, some entities centralize systems development, programming, and database administration while maintaining computers and databases at the user locations. Other entities distribute all computer functions to end users.

Distributed data processing systems may be linked to one another through a system of **networking** utilizing telephone lines. Networks enable the computers to communicate with one another and share workloads. A division faced with an unusually large number of transactions to be processed, for example, may decide to enlist the assistance of other computers in the system to share the chore of processing. Figure 8.3 illustrates a typical DDP system.

The principal advantage of DDP systems is their focus on end users' needs. The main disadvantage is increased security risk associated with unauthorized access to databases. Where computers are placed at remote locations and linked to one another, controls must be designed to prevent users from initiating unauthorized or erroneous file changes.

Real-Time versus Batch Processing Systems   In an **online real-time (OLRT) processing system**, transactions are entered as they occur, and are processed as they are entered.

FIGURE 8.3

Distributed Data Processing System—Divisional Computers Networked

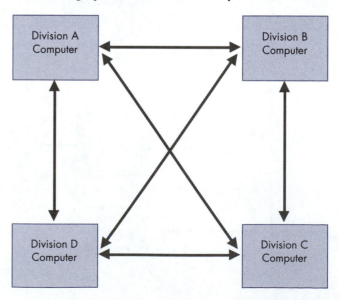

Transactions are typically entered through terminals and processed electronically. In a **batch processing system**, transactions are accumulated and processed in groups. Companies that rely on paper documents to evidence transactions are more likely to utilize batch processing systems for recording purposes. Given the use of PCs and point-of-sale terminals, batch systems are rarely found in today's systems environment.

Real-time processing forms the heart of management information systems. Given the continuous updating of the database as transactions are entered, the status of such files as accounts receivable, accounts payable, and inventory may be determined at any time. Although powerful in terms of information capability, OLRT systems are more complex than batch processing systems. Moreover, they do not provide the extent of audit trail documentation produced by batch systems. For this reason, they are more difficult to audit in terms of obtaining satisfaction concerning the existence of necessary controls, and of designing substantive testing procedures. Notwithstanding complexity, present-generation computer systems are characterized more and more by their real-time processing capabilities. Figure 8.4 illustrates a real-time processing system.

Multi-User versus Flat File Systems

Flat File Systems   In a **flat file system**, users own their own data; that is, the user has exclusive access to and use of his or her set of data. Typically associated with distributed

---

FIGURE 8.4

Online Real-Time System

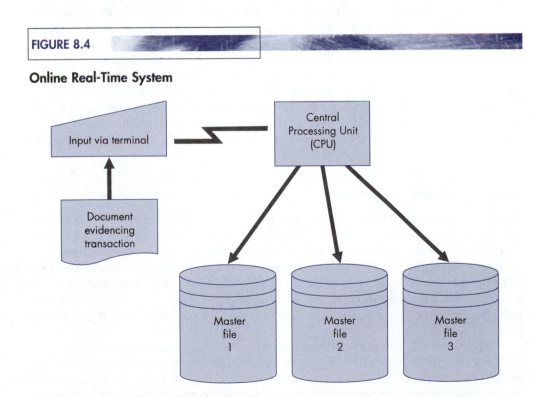

Transactions are entered as they occur, usually at a location remote from the CPU. Hard copy (the document) is retained at the location of transaction origin. Several files (e.g., sales, accounts receivable, inventory) are updated simultaneously as transactions are processed.

data processing, flat file systems produce redundancy in that several users may require the same set of data. Many data sets may need to be updated for a single transaction or group of transactions. The data processing and storage cost associated with flat file systems can be quite expensive, given heavy data volume.

Multi-User Systems   In a **multi-user system**, functional and geographical units share a single operating system housed in a central location. Such systems are characterized by real-time processing and a database approach whereby data is entered only once and shared by a multitude of users. An **integrated database system** contains a set of interrelated master files that are integrated in order to reduce data redundancy. The software used to control input, processing, and output, referred to as the *database management system* (DBMS), handles the storage, retrieval, updating, and maintenance of data in the database. These systems update many files simultaneously as transactions are processed. Processing of a sales order, for example, updates the accounts receivable control account as well as the subsidiary ledger; inventory control and the related subsidiary ledger also are updated, and the sales control and sales detail are posted as the sales order is processed.

Integrated files are associated most often with real-time systems and pose the greatest challenge for auditors. Controls within these systems are harder to test and assess due to the danger of file destruction. The internal storage of data in random, rather than sequential, order increases the difficulty involved in performing substantive tests.

Data warehousing, a form of integrated system, collects in one database immense volumes of data detailing every aspect of a company's operations and cross-indexes it. The system then uses clusters of parallel computers together with warehousing software that extracts data from mainframes, cross-indexes it for rapid searching, and analyzes and presents the results. The system can also search masses of data to locate unanticipated patterns and relationships. Although data warehousing greatly enhances the ability of managers to access data and information for decision-making purposes, the inclusion of large amounts of nonfinancial data along with transactions data poses additional challenges to the auditor in testing CBIS controls and in performing substantive tests.

Electronic Commerce Systems

Electronic commerce involves the trading of goods and services through the use of computers. Much electronic commerce is transacted on the Internet. Books, videos, general merchandise, and clothing are marketed electronically by such companies as Amazon.com, Wal-Mart, and L.L. Bean; securities are bought and sold on the Internet; CPAs provide bookkeeping services for their clients via the Internet; tax returns are filed electronically; banking is done on the Internet; and the list goes on. The growth of this industry fueled the dramatic rise in stock prices of the so-called "high-tech" companies in the 1990s.

Control risk is increased in companies engaged in electronic commerce due to access by customers as well as by employees. Data security therefore becomes paramount in such environments. As will be discussed in Chapter 15, CPAs have become involved in providing assurance services to clients engaged in electronic commerce. These services focus on systems and data security given widespread access.

Electronic data interchange (EDI), one of the earliest forms of electronic commerce, is the computer-to-computer exchange of intercompany business documents in a "public standard format." More specifically, it is a technique by which a company's computer system is linked to those of its suppliers and customers, and transactions—such as purchases, sales, and cash receipts and payments—may be initiated automatically by the system. Companies such as Chevron, DuPont, and Mobil have begun programs to do away with checks entirely, and companies such as General Electric and Burlington Northern Railroad have urged customers to send payments electronically.[2]

In an EDI system, documents such as purchase orders, invoices, receiving acknowledgments, and checks are converted into public standard format, permitting the other company's computer to read and accept them. Public standard format, facilitated in development by the Accredited Standards Committee of the American National Standards Institute, is a set of uniform standards for electronic communications. Called ANSI X12, the standards establish rules for data transmission that specify which documents and information can be transmitted and in which formats. EDI eliminates the need to reenter data into the accounting system. This results in fewer errors and more timely information. These systems, however, also require greater attention to proper controls over input of transactions.

.com
http://www.
ansi.org/

Two methods are available for implementing EDI. The first, referred to as the "direct" method, directly links the computers of Company A and Company B—a manufacturer and one of its parts suppliers, for example (see Figure 8.5). The second, called the "indirect" method (see Figure 8.6), utilizes a network for linking several companies' computers by providing a "mailbox" for each participant. The network, through what is called *protocol conversion*, transforms the senders' messages into the format preferred by the receivers. The advantage of the indirect method is that the sender company can transmit documents to several receiver companies without having to change its document form each time a message is sent to a different receiving company. Instead, the network protocol conversion will make sure the document is received in the proper form.

KINDS OF CBIS CONTROLS

CBIS controls can be classified into three major categories: general controls, application controls, and user controls. Control procedures that are interactive with two or more control objectives are classified as **general controls**; those designed to achieve specific control objectives are classified as **application controls**. General controls are broader in scope than application controls and relate to all or many computerized

FIGURE 8.5

Electronic Data Interchange System: Direct Approach

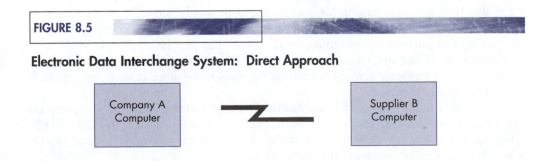

FIGURE 8.6

Electronic Data Interchange System: Indirect Approach

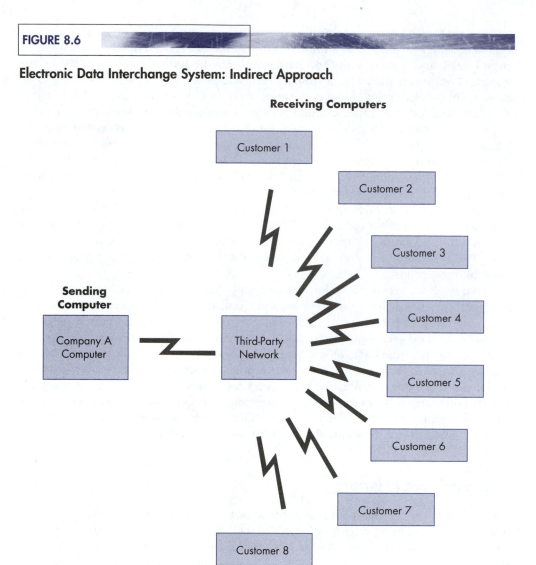

accounting activities. They are concerned with the organizational structure of the CBIS function, the safeguarding of data files and programs, and the adequate documentation of systems, programs, and program changes. Application controls relate to individual computerized accounting applications and are generally classified into input, processing, and output controls. Because general controls affect all applications, auditors usually consider general control weaknesses to be more critical than application control weaknesses.

The third category of controls, **user controls**, includes those controls established by departments outside data processing whose transactions are processed by a computer. They consist of control totals to check the accuracy of data processing, as well as provision for approval of input and review of output.

Each of these types of controls is discussed in the following paragraphs, after which the auditor's approach to control risk assessment is examined.

General Controls

Organization and Operation Controls   Because such tasks as editing, comparing, and reviewing are combined within CBIS, care must be taken to ensure adequate separation of duties within the CBIS function. Moreover, CBIS should be separate from user departments, and CBIS personnel should *not* initiate transactions. Separation within the CBIS function should include at least the following employees:

1. **CBIS Manager:** Has overall charge of the data processing activity.
2. **Systems Analysts:** Design new systems and modify existing systems in accordance with the information needs of the users.
3. **Programmers:** Write and test programs based on the system design and/or modification.
4. **Computer Operators:** Process transactions through the system in accordance with the operator instructions for the application being updated.
5. **Input Preparation Group:** Converts input data to a machine-readable form.
6. **Librarian:** Maintains custody over master files and programs. Permits access only on the basis of proper authority.
7. **Data Control Group:** Distributes output, monitors reprocessing of errors, and compares input with output on a test basis.

Figure 8.7 is a partial organization chart showing a recommended structure for the CBIS function. Note that the CBIS manager reports to a sufficiently high level to ensure the necessary breadth of computer applications within the entity. Reporting to only the chief accountant or the sales manager, for example, might restrict computing goals and prevent maximum usage of CBIS capabilities.

Systems Development and Documentation Controls   The processing of transactions by computer requires increased dependence on the computer systems and software for accuracy and completeness of processing. This reliance creates a need for effective control over the definition, design, development, testing, and documentation of the systems and programs constituting each application.

In order to ensure the reliability of financial data, user groups, as well as the accounting and internal auditing staffs, should participate in the system design. To an increasing extent, especially in the design of the more complex online real-time systems, independent auditors also are becoming involved in system design. The nature of independent auditor involvement is advisory—it focuses on ensuring that necessary controls are incorporated into the system.

Once a system has been designed and developed, it must be thoroughly tested before being used to process transactions on a routine basis. Testing usually is performed by the programmers who wrote the software to be used in the application.

Systems and programs, as well as modifications, must be adequately documented and properly approved before being used. Documentation ordinarily assumes the following forms:

1. System flowcharts;
2. Program flowcharts;
3. Data flow diagrams;
4. Decision tables;
5. Program changes (including evidence of proper approval);

FIGURE 8.7

Organization Chart for CBIS Function

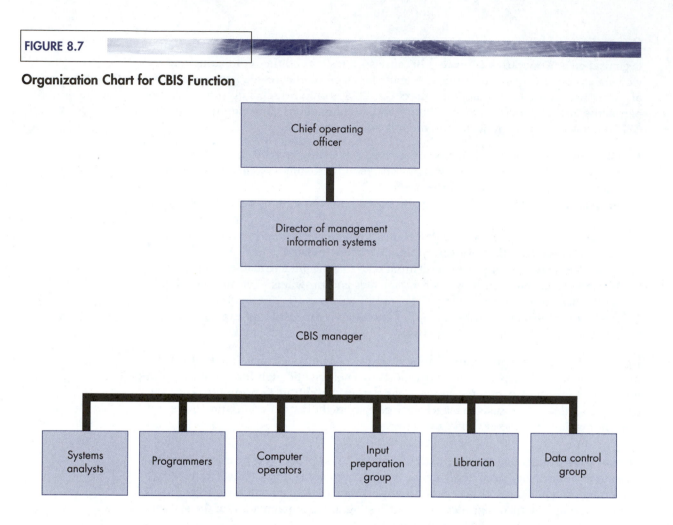

6. Operator instructions; and
7. Program descriptions explaining the purpose for each part of a program.

Appropriate documentation and its approval facilitate reviewing and updating systems and programs as the environment changes. Also, good documentation makes it easier for new CBIS personnel to familiarize themselves with the systems and programs in place. Finally, adequate documentation evidencing approval of changes minimizes the probability of unauthorized system and program changes that could result in loss of control and decreased reliability of financial data.

Access Controls   In order to prevent unauthorized use of files and programs, access must be limited to authorized individuals. Access controls encompass files, programs, documentation, and hardware. In an online, integrated file system and/or EDI, access limitation is achieved through control over **passwords**, which are codes used for accessing various parts of the database. Some of the passwords permit examining the database (read only), whereas other codes permit updating of files (read and write capabilities). Database control includes voiding the passwords of individuals leaving the employ of the company, and periodic changing of passwords to ensure that only current employees with properly approved passwords may access databases. Database control also provides for fixing responsibility over the various elements of the database to facilitate identifying the source of any problems regarding access to and changes in database files.

In a batch processing system, control may be achieved by assigning responsibility to the librarian. The librarian then institutes a formal "checkout" system, whereby only authorized persons may remove files and programs.

Data and Procedural Controls   This set of controls is for the purpose of controlling daily computer operations. A system of backup files stored both on and off the premises, to guard against loss of valuable files and data due to casualty or other factors, is an example of data control. Environmental controls, including temperature, humidity, and dust control, are other examples of data and procedural controls.

Given the increased use of networking and EDI, added controls are needed to prevent loss of data during transmission. Events such as power outages, computer viruses, transmission errors, and sabotage can cause data to be altered or lost between origin and destination. **Network monitoring software**, such as Lantern by Novell, Inc., and Net by Xtree Co., is designed to monitor data flow and detect weak points in hardware and software configurations that are likely to cause transmission errors. **Protocol controls**, which direct the receiving and sending computers to acknowledge the transmission link and verify the accuracy of the data transmitted, are another means for controlling data transmission. **Data encryption**, a control that breaks messages into fragments, requires special hardware at both ends of the transmission line to encode the outbound data and then decode it once it has been delivered. Although rather expensive, this type of control prevents loss of data through sabotage. To prevent loss of data caused by weak communication links, many companies have upgraded to **conditioned telecommunication lines**, which are clearer and less likely to produce loss through partial outages. **Fiber optic cable**, whereby data is transmitted in the form of high-speed pulses of light, produces the optimum transmission capability.[3]

Application Controls

A separate set of application controls is required for each computer application (e.g., sales order processing, cash receipts, vouchers, cash disbursements, and payroll). Application controls are classified into input controls, processing controls, and output controls.

Input Controls   **Input controls** are concerned with the accuracy and completeness of data entered into the data processing system. Examples of input controls are computer editing and audit trails provided by transaction logs.

Computer editing is the process of including programmed routines for computer checking of the validity and accuracy of input. Examples of computer editing include the following:

1. **Numeric field tests:** These determine that only numeric data were entered in numeric fields, and that only alphabetic data were entered in alphabetic fields.

---

3   For a more comprehensive discussion of data transmission security, see Ewer, Wills, and Nichols, "How Safe Are Your Data Transmissions?" *The Journal of Accountancy*, September 1993, pp. 66–70.

2. **Tests for valid codes:** These are routines that test the accuracy of code numbers entered as input into the system (e.g., customer number, product code, and employee number).
3. **Tests for reasonableness:** These are routines that cause the computer to reject input that is abnormal in amount ("employee hours in excess of 60 per week" is an example of a reasonableness test).
4. **Completeness tests:** These are routines that determine that all necessary fields contain data (e.g., name, address, and social security number for employees on the active payroll).
5. **Check digit:** This is a digit added to a number, the value of which is computed by a formula when data are entered, then recalculated and compared to the original value whenever the field is used. The purpose is to verify the correctness of input or output. Account numbers, customer numbers, employee numbers, and vendor numbers are examples of check digit applications. The check digit is based on the values of the other digits in the field; when the digit produced by the routine differs from the check digit in computer memory, an apparent input or output error has occurred.

Computer editing is a vital ingredient of the supervisory program controls in online real-time and EDI systems. Given the combining of functions within the supervisory programs, computer editing compensates for the lack of control totals that are present in batch systems and manual checking that is performed in noncomputerized systems.

Transaction logs that record transaction input and other forms of database access are vital to providing an audit trail of significant computer activity. Transaction logs are of critical importance to the auditor in reconstructing transactions and events as part of control testing and substantive auditing. The logs should record the IDs of users accessing the system, the time and duration of access, the files and programs used during the activity, and any modifications of files or databases.

Processing Controls   **Processing controls** are those controls concerned with the proper processing of the data once they are entered into the computer. An example of a processing control is the inclusion of header and trailer label information, consisting of file name, record counts, and other data for comparison purposes. Another example of a processing control is an echo check. An **echo check** occurs when the receiving computer sends the message back to the sender for verification. This control is particularly useful in distributed processing systems.

Output Controls   **Output controls** are concerned with the verification and proper distribution of the computer output. Examples of output controls include having the control group distribute printed output only to authorized recipients, adding batch totals to beginning balances and comparing the results with the ending balances, and maintaining an error log accessible only to the control group for the purpose of monitoring the reprocessing of errors.

Because application controls are often dependent on general controls, the auditor may find it more efficient to review general controls before reviewing application controls. Figure 8.8 illustrates the interdependence of general and application controls and highlights the pervasive nature of general controls. Unlimited access to data files (a general control weakness), for example, affects all applications, whereas failure to compare sales prices appearing on sales orders with master price lists affects only the sales processing application program.

FIGURE 8.8

General Controls versus Application Controls

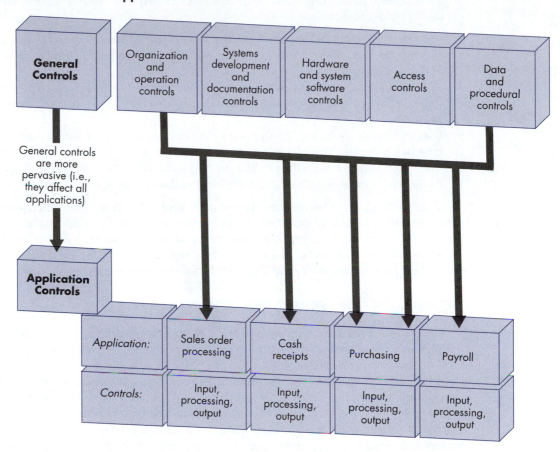

User Controls

User controls are manual control procedures applied by organizational units (user groups) whose data are processed by CBIS. These controls consist mainly of control totals. **Control totals** are calculated totals developed prior to submission of data for processing and later compared with the computer output. The payroll department, for example, may develop control totals for gross pay, number of checks to be processed, or total hours worked in the pay period. These totals then are compared with the payroll summary output received from CBIS. Sales departments may calculate totals relating to sales orders entered into the system and compare them with sales reports received from data processing.[4]

Control totals may consist of dollar totals (e.g., cash receipts listings), record counts (e.g., number of time cards to be processed), or hash totals. Hash totals have no significance other than as control totals. The sum of account numbers for those accounts to

---

4   These calculations may be automated as part of computer editing during input.

be updated, for example, may be compared with a computer-generated total of account numbers updated in a processing run. Because control totals and hash totals are compared with computer output, they are also considered input controls.

In designing substantive audit programs, auditors may elect to rely on user controls for the following reasons:

1. As part of the overall decision regarding evaluation of internal control policies and procedures, the auditor gains maximum efficiency by evaluating a mixture of CBIS and user controls.
2. The CBIS controls may be weak, thereby giving the auditor no alternative but to evaluate user controls as possible compensating controls for control risk assessment purposes.
3. User controls may be less costly than CBIS controls for the auditor to test in more complex systems. This election may be justified only if the necessary audit objectives are attainable, notwithstanding the bypassing of CBIS controls. It is *not* justifiable on the basis of lack of auditor understanding of the CBIS.

In evaluating user controls and assessing control risk, the auditor determines that separation of functional responsibilities within user departments is adequate, identifies the controls that reconcile input with output, and obtains satisfaction that the necessary reconciliations are being made. Ordinarily, this is accomplished through observation, inquiry, and testing of a sample of the documented reconciliations.

TECHNIQUES FOR TESTING CBIS CONTROLS

To assess control risk for clients with CBIS accounting applications, auditors first obtain a sufficient understanding of the CBIS controls to enable them to determine the significant accounting applications and to identify the essential financial reporting control features.[5] After obtaining an understanding of the system, the auditor identifies those general and application controls for which tests of controls are to be performed. The next step is to test the controls as necessary. A final assessment is made of control risk, together with documentation of the auditors' understanding of the system and the basis for any reduction in the assessed level of control risk below the maximum level, after which substantive audit programs may be developed. Figure 8.9 is a flowchart of the steps involved.

Understanding the System

The auditor can best gain an understanding of the essential accounting and control features by observing the system, asking questions of client personnel, and studying the system and program documentation.

Observation and Inquiry   Observation of the system and inquiry of client personnel helps the auditor to identify and evaluate the general controls. The following specific features of the system should be covered during this phase of the review:

• The organization and operation of the CBIS function;
• The extent to which access to data files, programs, and computer hardware is limited;

---

5   GAAS requires that some consideration be given to a computer system when it processes significant accounting applications.

FIGURE 8.9

Evaluating CBIS Controls for Control Risk Assessment Purposes

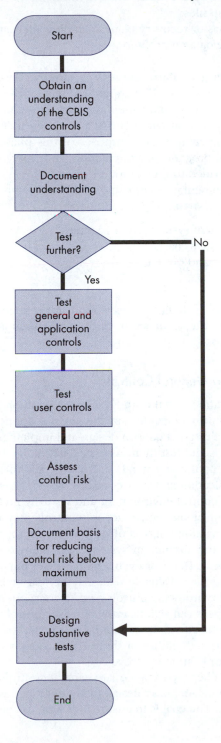

- The process by which new programs and program modifications are authorized, documented, and tested;
- The process by which systems are designed, documented, and tested;
- The existence of hardware controls and environmental controls;
- The extent of backup files;
- The existence of disaster recovery plans, including alternate processing sites; and
- The functions of the data control group.

Study of Systems and Program Documentation   Narrative descriptions and flowcharts of all systems and programs should be an integral part of the documentation for each CBIS application. Study of the documentation enables the auditor to identify and initially evaluate the application controls that have been included in the systems and program designs. Documentation, for purposes of this phase of the review, includes systems documentation, program documentation, and operations documentation (involving information provided to the computer operator).

In studying the documentation for each significant accounting application, the auditor might include the following specifications:

- Narrative descriptions of systems and programs;
- System and program flowcharts;
- Descriptions of input and output;
- File descriptions;
- Control features; and
- Operator instructions, including a description of programs to be used, inputs and outputs required, and the sequence of cards, tapes, disks, and other files applicable to the processing run.

Evaluating and Testing General Controls

Through inquiry, observation, and the study of documentation, as just described, the auditor is able to obtain an understanding of the general, application, and user controls that are vital to adequate internal control design and implementation. The next step is to evaluate these controls and test them, as necessary.

Given the pervasive nature of general controls, the auditor evaluates and tests these before focusing on application and user controls. Weaknesses in general controls can significantly impact the control environment and virtually nullify application controls. For example, nonexistent or ineffective access controls may result in intentional manipulation of data files, resulting in loss of data or misappropriation of assets through fraudulent transfers. In the absence of systems documentation and/or backup files, a catastrophe such as a fire or flood, or even a mere power outage, can cause permanent loss of data, systems, and files. Valuable data may be lost or intercepted during transmission without adequate protocol controls or data encryption. The presence of these kinds of control weaknesses can significantly increase control risk and may lead the auditor to conclude either that an audit cannot be conducted or that a primarily substantive audit must be performed. Either of these conclusions would, of course, preempt evaluating and testing application controls.

To help ensure that clients have adequate general controls, many accounting firms offer design phase auditing services. **Design phase auditing** involves the auditor in the auditee's systems design. The goal is to ensure inclusion of controls that will detect exceptional or unusual conditions and record and log information about the initiating transactions. The special controls are intended to compensate for the loss of documentary evidence (hard copy audit trail), given online real-time systems and distributed processing systems. Because the systems associated with design phase auditing are usually complex, computer audit specialists may be needed to assist in designing the necessary controls, as well as monitoring and reviewing the control functions. A **computer audit specialist** is an employee of the CPA firm who, typically, will have served on the audit staff for a period of time, then have received specialized training in computer system design and control and CBIS auditing. Virtually all public accounting firms that perform financial statement audits employ one or more computer audit specialists for this purpose.[6]

Once the necessary controls have been designed and incorporated into the system, frequent visits by the auditor to the client's premises are necessary. The purpose of the visits is to determine, through observation of the data processing activity, that the controls are functioning properly.

A major advantage of design phase auditing is that it addresses the audit trail problems associated with the more complex online real-time systems. The importance of transaction logs as replacement for hard-copy documents and substitution of computer checking for manual checking necessitates increased attention by the auditor to CBIS accounting controls for assurance as to reliability of accounting data. This need is met by auditor participation in system design and frequent auditor monitoring of control activity.

A possible disadvantage of design phase auditing relates to the independence issue, given auditor monitoring and review of a system that she or he helped to design. One might observe, however, that making control recommendations during the system design phase is really no different from making auditor recommendations for control improvements after the fact, when documented in the reportable conditions letter.

The following paragraphs suggest possible auditor approaches to evaluating and testing general controls. In some instances, depending on the complexity of the accounting information system, the auditor may elect to utilize one or more computer audit specialists to assist in the evaluation and testing process.

Organizational Controls   The main concern with regard to organizational controls is the degree to which duties have been adequately segregated. To obtain satisfaction as to proper segregation, the auditor relies primarily on inquiry, observation, and study of the organizational structure.

The auditor must be particularly alert to the separation between systems analysis, design, and programming on the one hand, and data processing on the other. Combining these functions greatly increases the entity's exposure to misappropriation fraud. In reviewing job descriptions, the auditor should be alert for possible incompatible functions. The auditor should also examine and test programmer access codes to determine that functions are restricted to testing and debugging programs. By interviewing the CBIS manager, the auditor may obtain clarification of exceptions detected by the above testing means.

---

6   Computer audit specialists can also assist in providing assurance services to clients regarding the adequacy of existing management information systems. Most of the national accounting firms have created Computer Assurance Services sections within their firms for this purpose.

Access Controls   The auditor tests access controls by comparing passwords with documented password descriptions and with job descriptions. In performing this test, the auditor focuses on whether authorized access is consistent with the person's need to know, and that only appropriate persons are authorized to alter databases. Branch managers, for example, should not have passwords permitting them to alter account balances. As a further test of access controls, auditors may attempt to gain entry to computer databases and alter them using existing passwords, voided passwords, or improper passwords.

Systems Development and Documentation Controls   In studying policies and procedures covering systems development and documentation, the auditor should be particularly alert to the client's authorization policy and policies describing the required documentation of systems and systems modifications. In testing the controls, the auditor studies the documentation for existing systems and modifications, being especially alert to adequacy of documentation and evidence of proper authorization. The auditor also considers the extent of internal auditor involvement in monitoring the systems development function. An effective internal audit function provides added assurance for the independent auditor regarding proper authorization and documentation of systems design and modification.

Data and Procedural Controls   In evaluating the data and procedural controls, the auditor inquires as to policies and procedures for backing up files and controlling the physical computer environment. The auditor also determines that current versions of antivirus software are available and used on a regular basis. Inspecting backup files and observing environmental conditions provides added assurance as to data restoration and file protection. Selecting a sample of microcomputers and testing for the existence of current antivirus software serves to verify the presence of this form of program and file protection.

To the extent the client engages in EDI or other forms of electronic commerce, the auditor needs to gain satisfaction regarding data and file protection during the processing of transactions. Inquiry and examination of systems documentation is a starting point for evaluating this set of controls. Examining printouts from the application of any network monitoring software in use and observing data input for the proper functioning of protocol controls and data encryption provides assurance regarding the protection of data during transmission and processing.

Evaluating and Testing Application Controls

The auditor can test application controls by auditing either around the computer or through the computer. These two approaches were defined earlier. Figure 8.10 summarizes and compares the two methods of further control testing.

Gaining adequate assurance that the client programs tested by the auditor are, in fact, the programs used to process client data presents a major problem in auditing through the computer. This problem is addressed in the ensuing discussion of techniques for auditing through the computer. Each of the approaches has advantages and disadvantages. For this reason, auditors have discovered that some combination of two or more of the techniques best serves the control-testing objectives.

Test Data Approach   The **test data approach** requires the preparation of simulated input data (transactions) that are processed, under the auditor's control, by the client's pro-

FIGURE 8.10

Auditing Around the Computer versus Auditing Through the Computer

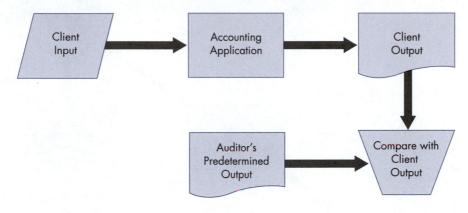

Auditing Around the Computer

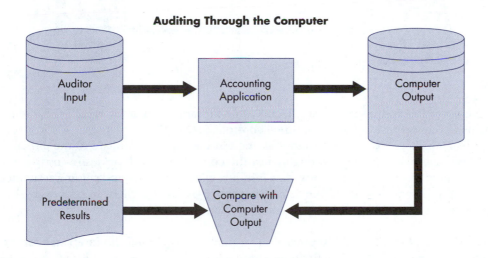

Auditing Through the Computer

cessing system. The hypothetical transactions contain errors that should be detected by the controls the auditor wishes to test. The test data ideally should contain a combination of all inputs required to execute all of the logic contained in the process. Examples of errors that might be included in testing a payroll application are an employee credited with working 98 hours in a single week, an incorrect social security number, or a recently terminated employee included in the current payroll. The results of the processing are then compared with the auditor's predetermined output to verify that the errors have been logged by the computer for follow-up and correction. Figure 8.11 diagrams the test data approach.

Base case system evaluation (BCSE) is a special application of the test data approach whereby a comprehensive set of test data is developed to test all possible data processing conditions within a given application. Because it is time-consuming and

FIGURE 8.11

Test Data Approach

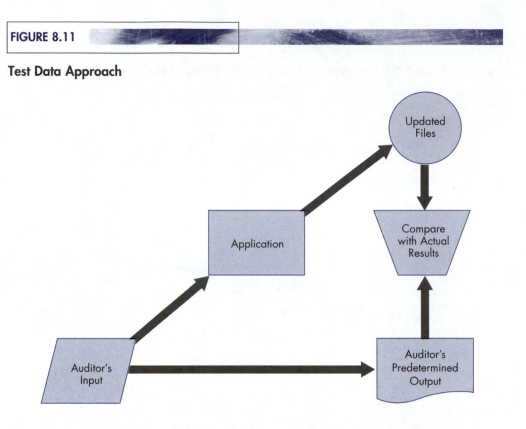

expensive, this approach is cost effective only for large clients for whom the auditor plans to rely extensively on the internal control system.

The major problems associated with the test data approach relate to the difficulty in designing test data that thoroughly test the controls the auditor desires further understanding of, eliminating the test data from the client's records, and gaining assurance that the programs tested are the same programs used by the client in processing live transactions. The ITF approach overcomes the latter problem.

Integrated Test Facility (ITF) Approach   The auditor, in applying the **integrated test facility (ITF) approach**, creates a fictitious entity within the client's actual data files during the systems design phase. Hypothetical data for the fictitious entity are then processed as part of the client's ongoing data processing activity. A fictitious customer account, for example, is created and integrated into the accounts receivable ledger. The auditor introduces artificial (unusual or abnormal) transactions into the data processing system while live data are being processed. The company is instructed to handle routinely the business involved, without actually shipping goods or mailing customer invoices to the fictitious entity.

The auditor compares the results of processing with the anticipated results as a basis for evaluating the effectiveness of accounting control over customer billings, shipment, and remittances. The ITF approach, particularly useful for testing EDI systems, is portrayed in Figure 8.12.

The principal advantage of the ITF approach is the assurance gained by the auditor that the programs tested are the same programs used by the client to process live data.

FIGURE 8.12

ITF Approach

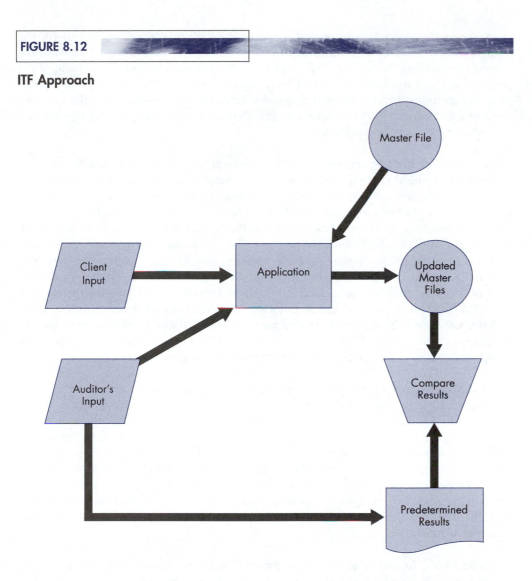

The more frequently the auditor applies the test procedures during the period under audit, the stronger the assurance. A major disadvantage, however, is the risk of damaging the client's files by failing to purge them completely of the hypothetical transactions. Two alternative approaches are available for assuring that ITF transactions are removed promptly from the files. First, a filtering system can be used to mark the transactions; these transactions can be automatically removed from the processing stream before culmination of a hypothetical transaction. A disadvantage of the filtering approach, when people are inputting transactions, is that it reveals the test transactions to the data processing employees. An alternative approach that retains the anonymity of test transactions is for the auditor to prepare a set of reversing journal entries for manually removing the test data at the culmination of the processing runs.

Tagging and Tracing   Tagging and tracing is a technique whereby an identifier or "tag" is affixed to a transaction record. This tag triggers "snapshots" during the processing of transactions. The snapshots are stored, are accessible only by the auditor, and enable the auditor to examine transactions at the intermediate steps in processing. Following the tagged transactions through the system permits the auditor to evaluate the logic of the processing steps and the adequacy of programmed controls. The advantage of the tagging and tracing approach lies in the use of actual data and elimination of the need for reversing journal entries. The disadvantage is that the auditor analyzes the transactions only after processing is completed.

Systems Control Audit Review File (SCARF)   A **systems control audit review file (SCARF)** is an audit log used to "collect information for subsequent analysis and review."[7] An imbedded audit module monitors selected transactions as they pass by specific processing points. Client programs need to be modified in order to identify the criteria (e.g., a particular type of transaction or a specified dollar amount) for inclusion in the SCARF. The module then captures the input data so that relevant information (hard copy) is displayed at key points in the processing system. The hard copy is available only to the auditor and may describe such inputs as hours worked in a pay period in excess of 60, or sales orders processed in excess of $100,000. Like tagging and tracing, the SCARF approach uses real transaction data. The disadvantage is that erroneous data will not necessarily be captured. An effective combination approach may be to use the ITF approach for a few hypothetical transactions, and the tagging and tracing approach along with SCARF files to follow live data through a complex system.

Parallel Simulation   **Parallel simulation** requires the auditor to create a set of application programs that simulates the processing system and compares the output from the real and the simulated systems. Figure 8.13 illustrates parallel simulation.

Although a control testing technique, parallel simulation is, in fact, an automated version of auditing around the computer. The comparison of input with output ignores the essential characteristics of the processing system and assumes that if the outputs are identical the system is processing transactions accurately. Using the computer to make the comparisons, however, significantly increases the number of data records that can be simulated. For this reason, the approach may be useful in combination with design phase auditing.

Surprise Audit   In using this technique, the auditor, on an unannounced basis—during neither the scheduled interim nor the final audit phases—requests duplicate copies of client programs at the conclusion of specific processing runs. The programs are copied onto spare disks or magnetic tape reels that the auditor brings for this purpose. The "in-use" programs are then compared with the "authorized" versions that have been acquired previously by the auditor for checking purposes. Special computerized programs are available for making the comparisons.

Surprise auditing assists the auditor in determining whether client personnel are using authorized versions of programs in processing data. This approach also provides a means for assessing whether program modifications have been properly authorized and documented.

For surprise auditing to be effective, the client must notify the auditor whenever program changes are made. Otherwise, the auditor's copy of the client's programs will not be current, and the comparison will not be relevant.

---

7 AICPA, *Auditing With Computers*, New York: AICPA, 1994, p. 84.

FIGURE 8.13

Parallel Simulation

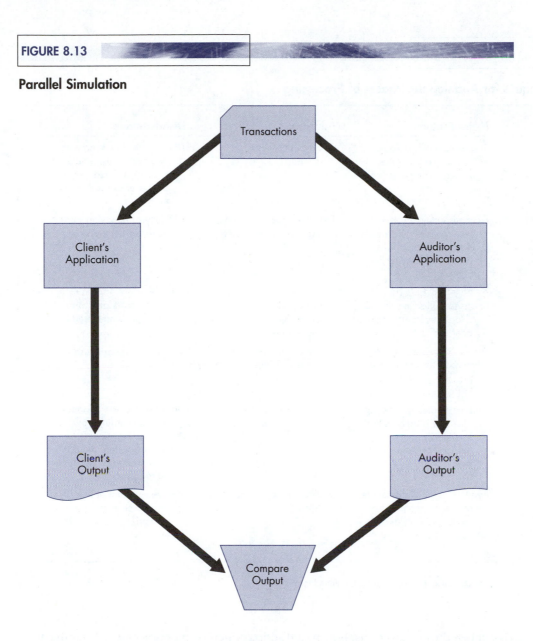

Table 8.1 summarizes techniques for testing CBIS controls. Although all of the approaches have strong points, they also all have weak points, and the best course for the auditor is to utilize a combination of the methods in order to gain satisfactory assurance as to the proper functioning of the controls.

CBIS AND AUDIT RISK IMPLICATIONS

Audit Trail Modification

Online real-time systems, network systems, and electronic commerce, as described earlier, pose increased risk to the auditor, due mainly to lack of hard-copy documentation,

TABLE 8.1

Summary of Techniques for Auditing the Phases of Processing

Technique*	Major Feature	Advantage	Disadvantage
Test Data Approach (T)	Preparation of simulated input data processed under auditor's control	Good test of existing controls	Difficulty in designing comprehensive test data; programs tested may not be the ones used during the year
ITF Approach (T)	Fictitious entity created within client's data files; fictitious transactions processed against the entity during live processing	Tests the actual system during operation	Difficulty in removing transactions from the system
Tagging and Tracing (T)	Snapshots enabling the auditor to evaluate controls after the fact	Use of actual data eliminates the need for reversing entries	Analysis occurs after processing is completed
SCARF (T)	Process of monitoring selected transactions that pass by specific processing points	Use of actual data eliminates need for reversing entries	Will not necessarily tag erroneous data
Parallel Simulation (A)	Auditor creates a set of application programs that simulates processing system and compares output	Increases the number of data records that can be compared	Does not provide information concerning how transactions are processed and the controls housed in the application programs
Surprise Audit (T)	Request for duplicate copies of client's programs and compares with authorized version	Discloses program modifications	Auditor may not always have a current copy of authorized version of program

*T indicates auditing through the computer; A indicates auditing around the computer.

risk of loss during data transmission, and added difficulty in performing substantive tests of transactions and balances.

OLRT systems process transactions as they occur (some automatically), and several files (e.g., sales, accounts receivable, inventory) are updated simultaneously by a single transaction input. Electronic commerce and distributed data processing systems transmit data from multiple locations and result in less hard-copy documentation of transactions.[8]

---

8 Although paperless offices, discussed earlier, also result in less hard-copy documentation, the documents still exist, but in computerized form. For this reason, audit risk is *not* increased by internal storage of documents representing completed transactions. In fact, well-designed computerized document management systems, by increasing document security, actually may lower audit risk and facilitate substantive testing.

To review, some of the more common characteristics of advanced CBIS are the following:

- The use of online terminals for entering transactions from remote locations;
- Integrated databases maintained in the form of disk files;
- Supervisory programs (e.g., DBMS) for storing programs and managing the system; and
- Absence of hard-copy documentation (e.g., when EDI processes transactions directly from sending computer to receiving computer).

Figure 8.14 illustrates an advanced electronic data processing system.

FIGURE 8.14

Online Real-Time System

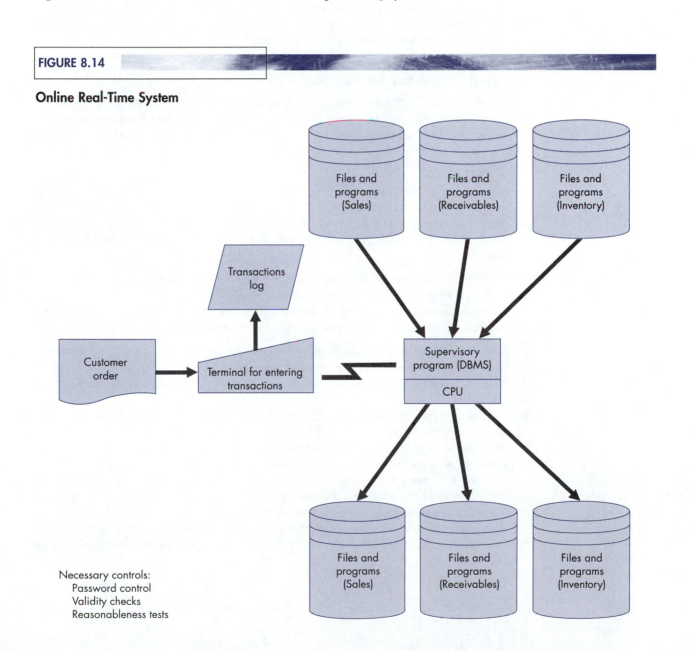

With DDP and EDI, transactions are entered at remote locations and transactions and balances are stored internally. Therefore, the need for the more traditional documentation is reduced. Moreover, documents used to enter information into the computer for processing may, for the reasons cited earlier, exist for only a short period. In some computer systems, input documents may not exist at all, because information is entered directly into the system.[9]

Temporary, rather than long-term, retention of documents may require that the auditor visit the client's premises frequently during the year and audit transactions while the hard copy still exists. Situations in which no documentation exists require increased attention to transaction logs and to the controls housed in the supervisory programs. To justify assessing risk below maximum, more testing needs to be performed by the auditor. Testing is more difficult, however, given the increased vulnerability of the client's files to destruction during the testing process.

Reducing Control Risk for Advanced CBIS

The section of the AICPA Professional Standards concerning evidential matter suggests that certain electronic systems may prohibit the auditor from reducing detection risk by performing only substantive tests for a given financial statement assertion. Such systems leave no alternative but to reduce the assessed level of control risk through control testing. An excerpt from that modification reads as follows:

> *The potential for improper initiation or alteration of information to occur and not be detected may be greater if information is produced, maintained, or accessed only in electronic form. In such circumstances, the auditor* should perform tests of controls *to gather evidential matter to use in assessing control risk.*[10]

Given this modification of the standards, the various control testing techniques described earlier have assumed increased importance.

In addition to auditor testing of client controls, the following means are suggested for strengthening financial reporting controls associated with OLRT and DDP systems:

1. Systems, programs, and modifications should be well-documented, and modifications should be properly approved and reviewed.
2. Transaction logs should contain adequate detail and be readily accessible for audit purposes.
3. Access to input terminals should be restricted by effective control over passwords and by assigning responsibility for elements of the database. In distributed systems utilizing networking, specially designed software is available to strengthen input controls. Referred to generally as the *PC-mainframe link*, the software controls the flow of data between a mainframe and a PC. This is achieved by "change controllers" within the programs that limit access to either all or specified files through a system of passwords as well as user identification codes.
4. Passwords should be changed frequently and former passwords voided.
5. Passwords assigned to employees should be voided upon termination of their employment.

---

9 *AICPA Professional Standards*, New York: AICPA, section AU 326.18.
10 Ibid, section AU 326.14.

6. In designing advanced systems, careful attention should be given to input editing. Examples of input editing controls are validity tests for checking customer or employee numbers, stock numbers, prices or pay rates, vendor numbers, and so on; limit or reasonableness tests; echo checks; and balance checks (e.g., debits should equal credits for each transaction entered).
7. All computer activities should be logged into a history file with user identification, terminal identification, time, and date.
8. Journal files should be maintained for backup (the files may be kept on tape or on disk).

Like OLRT and DDP, electronic commerce generally and EDI systems in particular increase audit risk. Although EDI should increase processing accuracy, lower inventory investment through reduced lead times, and provide for more timely information, this means of processing transactions poses serious control and audit challenges. First, as with other OLRT systems, the need for hard-copy documentation is diminished. Moreover, given automatic initiation of certain transactions (e.g., inventory reorder when minimum levels are reached), authorizations may be difficult to verify and the risk of unauthorized persons transmitting messages increases. To compensate for these challenges, compensating controls should be in place, and the auditor needs to obtain an understanding of these controls and test them as appropriate. The following are examples of possible controls:

• Strict identification and password controls housed in the software can permit only specified individuals to perform given types of transactions.
• Terminals can be limited to perform only certain tasks.
• Software can be programmed to produce a log of transactions showing date, time, type of transaction, and operator.
• Data encryption, as described earlier, can be used whereby an encoding key is used by the sender to scramble the message. The receiver must have the corresponding key to unscramble and read the message. With data encryption, strict security must be maintained over the encoding keys.
• The EDI software should contain input and receiving edit controls (protocol controls) that detect errors and print them in the form of an error log. The CBIS control group should handle the reprocessing of the errors.
• An echo check also may be programmed into the software, whereby the receiving computer returns the message to the sending computer for confirmation that information received is the same as information sent.

Case 8.1, involving computer fraud, illustrates the importance of unique controls for OLRT, DDP, and EDI systems, and the need for auditor evaluation of these controls in CBIS.

Although the characteristics of systems described in this section pose risk problems for the auditor, other aspects of these systems serve to strengthen internal control. Input editing features that test transaction input for validity, reasonableness, and proper account distribution ensure that all transactions will be processed uniformly. Processing consistency virtually eliminates the occurrence of clerical errors normally associated with manual systems.[11]

---

11 Such assurance, one might note, is not limited to OLRT systems, but is present whenever transactions are processed by CBI systems containing the necessary programmed control features.

CASE 8.1

SHENANDOAH VALLEY WHOLESALERS
Case Description

Shenandoah Valley Wholesalers sold furniture and appliances to retailers located in the southeastern United States, primarily Virginia. The company's two hundred salespersons were all paid on a commission basis. Sales commissions were paid biweekly on the basis of a computer printout of commission checks. The computer also printed out a commission listing register.

Shenandoah used an online system for processing sales orders and calculating commissions. Sales orders were entered into terminals located at the company's twenty regional sales offices. The computer was programmed to check for proper salesperson number, customer number, product code, price, and customer credit limit. In addition, commission rates for each product code were stored in the computer, thereby permitting automatic calculation and storage of commissions for each sales order. In printing the biweekly commission checks and listing, the computer also was programmed to print checks only for sales orders that had been shipped and billed.

Kerry Gold, the Richmond regional sales manager, was a trained accountant and computer programmer, and before joining Shenandoah's marketing group she had been a computer audit specialist for a large regional CPA firm. Her CPA certificate and license to practice was revoked in 1984 upon her conviction for accepting bribes from a client. After joining Shenandoah, she had made it a point to become familiar with the company's sales processing system. As such, she thoroughly understood the programmed controls and knew that a sales invoice number and shipping order number were needed in order to complete a sales commission transaction. Although the regional sales managers were not entitled to earn commissions, Gold devised a scheme for paying herself fraudulent commissions. Using the employee number of one of her recently terminated sales representatives, she entered fictitious sales orders, ship-

ping orders, and sales invoice numbers. To conceal the overstatement of sales, she reversed the entries prior to the monthly sales printouts.

Martha Hennings & Associates, CPAs, had been auditing Shenandoah for several years. They were not aware of Gold's thefts, which had been occurring since 1995. Gary Harvey, a recently promoted senior auditor for Martha Hennings, was designated the in-charge auditor for the 2001 Shenandoah audit. Harvey decided, as part of his analytical procedures, to apply commission rates to sales by each regional sales office, and compare these with commissions paid. This had not been done previously, and Harvey wished to perform the test, given the significance of "commissions expense" in the 2001 income statement. He also was concerned with the apparent lack of control over passwords permitting access to the home-office computer database, and the failure to log and periodically account for sales order and shipping order numbers. Failure to perform a record count and comparison with currently active employees at the conclusion of the commission-processing computer run also troubled Harvey.

Harvey's test revealed that commissions paid materially exceeded the calculated commissions for the Richmond office. Suspecting possible fraud, Harvey arranged a conference with Herbert Mills, the audit manager for the Shenandoah audit. They agreed that the amounts involved did not materially impact the 2001 financial statements, but that they should notify Charles Gibbons, Shenandoah's corporate controller, of the control weaknesses and possible fraud. Upon learning of the situation, Gibbons directed the internal audit staff to conduct an investigation. After a lengthy investigation, the internal audit manager, accompanied by Gibbons, confronted Gold, who admitted to stealing approximately $500,000 in fraudulent commissions since 1995. Shenandoah's management and board of directors decided to sue Martha Hennings & Associates for not having detected the fraud during its audits from 1995 to 2001.

What Would You Have Done?

1. What control weaknesses made this fraud possible?

2. Evaluate Gary Harvey's approach in this case.

3. Do you think the auditors were negligent in prior years?[12]

Managing Detection Risk

To maintain detection risk within reasonable bounds when auditing clients with complex information processing systems, the auditor should give careful consideration to the following system characteristics and internal control testing alternatives:

1. Auditors need to become more involved in system design, given the lack of hard-copy documentation associated with OLRT and EDI systems. This participation is necessary in order to ensure adequate transaction logs and to determine that supervisory programs contain the necessary controls for proper input editing. Auditor participation also may provide for tagging certain types of transaction conditions for later follow-up by the audit team and for supplying the auditor with copies of all programs and program modifications relating to significant accounting applications.

2. Greater use by the audit team of computer audit specialists may be necessary in light of the complexities associated with advanced electronic systems and the related danger of file destruction during testing. The primary role of the specialist is to assist in the design phase; however, assistance during testing of internal controls is also common in practice.

3. Performing tests of controls and substantive tests of transactions by means of more frequent (quarterly or monthly) visits to the client's premises may become necessary as systems become more advanced. Termed **continuous auditing**, this transition in form of testing is necessitated by both the lack of documentation and the more temporary nature of document retention associated with advanced systems.

4. Auditors must be alert to the increased potential for management fraud, given computer capability for altering databases and fabricating documentation for nonexistent transactions.

Focusing on the above factors also supports the auditing standards modification cited earlier requiring that auditors test controls rather than rely on substantive testing when auditing clients with complex systems and those engaged in electronic commerce.

Case 8.2 illustrates how a client enlisted the aid of the computer in facilitating the manufacture of fraudulent insurance policies.

EXPERT SYSTEMS AS A MEANS OF MANAGING AUDIT RISK

In addition to automating routine tasks and permitting fuller analysis of client data, computers are also being used to an increasing degree to assist the auditor in making various kinds of judgment decisions. For example, one large accounting firm uses Notes, an

---

12 The solution to this case is in the *Instructor's Manual*.

VENTURE INSURANCE COMPANY
Case Description

Jonathon Crane, the partner in charge of the Venture Insurance Company audit, could not understand how his audit team could have overlooked $255 million of fictitious insurance policies during the 2001 audit. Gardiner Mill & Associates, CPAs, had been conducting the Venture audit for five years, and this was the first knowledge they had of the fraud.

A business practice called *reinsurance* is common in the life insurance industry. Under reinsurance, one company sells its policies to another insurance company, receiving the discounted value of future premiums less a service charge. The buying company then collects the premiums and pays any claims resulting from death or other causes. Since 1997, Venture, with the support and guidance of its CEO, Gerald Kidd, and with the aid of its latest-generation computer, had been "manufacturing" fictitious insurance policies and selling them to other insurance companies under the guise of reinsurance. Venture, of course, would have to remit the premiums from its own assets, because the purported policyholders did not exist. The company also filed occasional claims based on the death of fictitious policyholders. Actuarial tables, stored in the computer, provided the information necessary to determine an appropriate number of, as well as the timing of, claims for, death benefits.

Venture began the fraudulent reinsurance practice in 1997 as a means for solving a short-term liquidity problem. Gerald Kidd later decided to use the practice to achieve growth and leadership status in the insurance industry. By 2001, the portfolio of fic-

titious policies had grown to $255 million, nearly 40 percent of Venture's outstanding policies.

Inasmuch as the buying companies did not follow the practice of confirming the policies with individual holders, the probability of detection from that source was remote. The independent auditors, on the other hand, presented a threat of detection. They followed the practice of selecting a sample of policies and examining them in detail, including their underlying documentation. They also confirmed the selected policies with the policyholders. Inclusion of one or more of the fictitious policies in the sample could lead to detection. To overcome this threat, Kidd and his management team looked through the auditors' workpapers during lunch breaks until they discovered the auditors' sampling plan, including policy numbers for which documentation was to be requested. Then, Venture employees, with the aid of the computer, manufactured all the necessary supporting documentation for all bogus policies included in the plan. Addresses of employees who were part of the fraud were used as policyholders' addresses, thus ensuring return of auditor confirmation requests. The files were then held ready until requested by the auditors.

The fraud continued for four years, and only came to light when a disgruntled ex-employee granted an interview to a leading financial periodical. During the interview, the employee described the fraud and admitted his own role in Gerald Kidd's plan for growth.

What Would You Do?

Discuss the auditors' responsibility to third-party financial statement users in this case.[13]

IBM software package that runs on networks of IBM-compatible PCs. Used by upwards of two thousand of the firm's auditors, Notes permits staff auditors to analyze complex accounting and tax issues by utilizing the stored knowledge of the firm's auditing and tax experts.[14]

13 The solution to this case is in the *Instructor's Manual.*
14 *Business Week*, March 29, 1993, p. 84.

Termed **expert systems**, these software packages have the ability to make expert quality decisions within specialized domains. Their advantages in facilitating financial audits are twofold. First, they allow increased accessibility to expert knowledge. Second, they assist in achieving consistency in task performance and increase the efficiency in training new decision makers.

Expert systems consist of a body of expert knowledge and a set of decision parameters for solving problems. Experts in the specialized domain (tax experts, pension accounting specialists, bank audit specialists) develop the **knowledge base** portion of the software package. Formulation of the base may be completed by such techniques as verbal protocol analysis or gaming and simulation techniques. The decision parameters, known as the knowledge representation framework, can be purchased as an expert systems shell package. Based on rules, frames, or logic, the **expert systems shell** is basically an expert system awaiting a knowledge base. Once the software has been developed, it is tested through system validation, which compares the system's performance to that of other experts. This can be a lengthy process. In adopting Notes, for example, the accounting firm mentioned above required nearly two years to install and customize the software, and train staff persons to use it properly.[15]

Some of the ways in which CPAs currently are making use of expert systems are in predicting the likelihood of bankruptcy, developing audit strategies and generating audit programs, determining the likelihood of fraud, evaluating internal control policies and procedures and assessing control risk, and doing tax planning and developing tax strategies.

A variant of expert systems, neural networks, are more advanced in that they require no knowledge base programming. A **neural network** is a computer system designed to replicate the functioning of the human brain.[16] Unlike expert systems, neural networks do not require the formulation of a knowledge base programming rule. Instead, they learn by example. Large numbers of examples, consisting of pairs of alternatives, together with historical outcomes are housed in the system. The network then uses the examples in combination with the outcomes to make decisions, given real input examples.[17] Auditing firms are just beginning to use neural networks to evaluate clients' internal control systems and to detect various types of fraud.

Although they constitute a relatively new form of computer application in auditing, expert systems and neural networks hold out promise for revolutionizing auditing in years to come. The list of possible system applications in auditing is limited only by the imagination of the CPA.

KEY TERMS

Application controls, 311

Auditing around the computer, 306

Auditing through the computer, 306

Base case system evaluation (BCSE), 323

Batch processing system, 309

CBIS manager, 313

Centralized data processing system, 306

Check digit, 316

Completeness tests, 316

Computer audit specialist, 321

---

15 Ibid.

16 Hall, James A., *Accounting Information Systems*, 2nd ed., Cincinnati, OH: South-Western College Publishing, 1998, p. 528.

17 For an excellent description of neural networks, see Hall, *Accounting Information Systems*, op. cit., pp. 528–532.

COMPUTER AUDIT PRACTICE CASE

Biltrite Bicycles, Inc.

Module II requires the student to assess control risk after studying Biltrite's accounting information system and financial controls. You may complete the module at this time.

REVIEW QUESTIONS

1. Define and give an example of each of the following: general controls, application controls, and user controls.

2. Differentiate between auditing around and auditing through the computer.

3. Explain why the audit approach may need to be modified, given the existence of significant CBIS accounting applications.

4. In what respects does the audit trail assume a different form when transactions are processed by computer?

5. Differentiate between batch processing systems and real-time processing systems.

6. What is an EDI system and what are its advantages and disadvantages?

7. What constitutes adequate separation of functional responsibilities within the CBIS function?

8. Why are systems and program documentation important to effective internal control?

9. How does electronic commerce affect the CPA?

10. What function does a transaction log serve? What information should be included?

11. Why might the auditor prefer to review general controls before reviewing application controls?

12. List three possible reasons for auditor testing of user controls.

13. Describe the sequence of steps to be followed by the auditor in studying internal financial control policies and procedures for clients with CBIS accounting applications.

14. How does the auditor gain an understanding of the essential accounting and control features of a CBIS?

15. How does the auditor review and test user controls?

16. Why do auditors prefer to apply a combination of techniques in testing application controls?

17. Identify the advantages and disadvantages of each of the following techniques for testing computer controls:
    a. Test data approach
    b. ITF approach
    c. Tagging and tracing
    d. SCARF

18. Parallel simulation is thought to be an automated version of auditing around the computer. Explain why.

19. OLRT, DDP, and EDI systems affect audit risk in two offsetting ways. Explain how.

20. Why should auditors become more involved in OLRT systems design?

21. What are expert systems?

22. What are the components of expert systems? How are these components developed?

23. Identify two possible audit applications for expert systems.

MULTIPLE CHOICE QUESTIONS FROM PAST CPA AND CIA EXAMS

1. When an auditor tests a computerized accounting system, which of the following is true of the test data approach?
   a. Test data must consist of all possible valid and invalid conditions.
   b. The program tested is different from the program used throughout the year by the client.
   c. Several transactions of each type must be tested.
   d. Test data are processed by the client's computer programs under the auditor's control.

2. When CBIS programs or files can be accessed from terminals, users should be required to enter a(n)
   a. Parity check.
   b. Personal identification code.
   c. Self-diagnosis test.
   d. Echo check.

3. Which of the following computer-assisted auditing techniques allows fictitious and real transactions to be processed together without client operating personnel being aware of the testing process?
   a. Parallel simulation
   b. Integrated test facility approach

    c. Test data approach

    d. Exception report tests

4. Which of the following most likely represents a significant deficiency in the internal control system?

    a. The systems analyst reviews applications of data processing and maintains systems documentation.

    b. The systems programmer designs systems for computerized applications and maintains output controls.

    c. The control clerk establishes control over data received by the CBIS department and reconciles control totals after processing.

    d. The accounts payable clerk prepares data for computer processing and enters the data into the computer.

5. To obtain evidence that online access controls are properly functioning, an auditor most likely would

    a. Create checkpoints at periodic intervals after live data processing to test for unauthorized use of the system.

    b. Examine the transaction log to discover whether any transactions were lost or entered twice due to a system malfunction.

    c. Enter invalid identification numbers or passwords to ascertain whether the system rejects them.

    d. Vouch a random sample of processed transactions to assure proper authorization.

6. Which of the following types of computer documentation would an auditor most likely utilize in obtaining an understanding of the internal control system?

    a. Systems flowcharts

    b. Record counts

    c. Program listings

    d. Record layouts

7. To obtain evidence that user identification and password controls are functioning as designed, an auditor would most likely

    a. Attempt to sign on to the system using invalid user identifications and passwords.

    b. Write a computer program that simulates the logic of the client's access control software.

    c. Extract a random sample of processed transactions and ensure that the transactions were appropriately authorized.

    d. Examine statements signed by employees stating that they have not divulged their user identifications and passwords to any other person.

8. Which of the following types of evidence would an auditor most likely examine to determine whether internal control policies and procedures are operating as designed?

    a. Confirmations of receivables verifying account balances

    b. Letters of representations corroborating inventory pricing

    c. Attorneys' responses to the auditor's inquiries

    d. Client records documenting the use of CBIS programs

9. In auditing an online perpetual inventory system, an auditor selected certain file updating transactions for detailed testing. The audit technique that will provide a computer trail of all relevant processing steps applied to a specific transaction is described as

    a. Simulation.

    b. Snapshot.

    c. Code comparison.

    d. Tagging and tracing.

10. Which of the following statements most likely represents a disadvantage for an entity that keeps computer-prepared data files rather than manually prepared files?

    a. Random error associated with processing similar transactions in different ways is usually greater.

    b. It is usually more difficult to compare recorded accountability with a physical count of assets.

    c. Attention is focused on the accuracy of the programming process rather than errors in individual transactions.

    d. It is usually easier for unauthorized persons to access and alter files.

11. To obtain evidential matter about control risk, an auditor ordinarily selects tests from a variety of techniques, including

    a. Analysis.

    b. Confirmations.

    c. Reprocessing.

    d. Comparison.

12. Processing data through the use of simulated files provides an auditor with information about the operating effectiveness of control policies and procedures. One of the techniques involved in this approach makes use of

    a. Controlled reprocessing.

    b. An integrated test facility.

    c. Input validation.

    d. Program code checking.

13. An auditor who is testing CBIS controls in a payroll system would most likely use test data that contain conditions such as

    a. Deductions *not* authorized by employees.

    b. Overtime *not* approved by supervisors.

    c. Time tickets with invalid job numbers.

    d. Payroll checks with unauthorized signatures.

14. To gain access to a bank's online customer systems, users must validate themselves with a user identification code and password. The purpose of this procedure is to provide

    a. Data security.

    b. Physical security.

    c. Context-dependent security.

    d. Write-protection security.

15. An auditor wishes to perform tests of controls on a client's cash disbursements procedures. If the control procedures leave *no* audit trail of documentary evidence, the auditor most likely will test the procedures by

    a. Inquiry and analytical procedures.

    b. Confirmation and observation.

    c. Observation and inquiry.

    d. Analytical procedures and confirmation.

16. Which of the following controls most likely would assure that an entity can reconstruct its financial records?

    a. Hardware controls are built into the computer by the computer manufacturer.

    b. Backup diskettes or tapes of files are stored away from originals.

c. Personnel who are independent of data input perform parallel simulations.

d. System flowcharts provide accurate descriptions of input and output operations.

17. A CBIS input control is designed to ensure that
    a. Machine processing is accurate.
    b. Only authorized personnel have access to the computer area.
    c. Data received for processing are properly authorized and converted to machine-readable form.
    d. CBI processing has been performed as intended for the particular application.

18. When erroneous data are detected by computer program controls, the data may be excluded from processing and printed on an error report. This error report should be reviewed and followed up by the
    a. Computer operator.
    b. Systems analyst.
    c. CBIS control group.
    d. Computer programmer.

19. An auditor would most likely be concerned with which of the following controls in a distributed data processing system?
    a. Hardware controls
    b. Systems documentation controls
    c. Access controls
    d. Disaster recovery controls

20. Which of the following is a general control that would most likely assist an entity whose systems analyst left the entity in the middle of a major project?
    a. Grandfather–father–son record retention
    b. Input and output validation routines
    c. Systems documentation
    d. Check digit verification

21. Internal control is ineffective when computer department personnel
    a. Participate in computer software acquisition decisions.
    b. Design documentation for computerized systems.
    c. Originate changes in master files.
    d. Provide physical security for program files.

22. In a computerized payroll system environment, an auditor would be *least* likely to use test data to test controls related to
    a. Missing employee numbers.
    b. Proper approval of overtime by supervisors.
    c. Time tickets with invalid job numbers.
    d. Agreement of hours per clock cards with hours on time tickets.

23. Which of the following most likely represents a weakness in the financial controls of a CBIS?
    a. The systems analyst reviews output and controls the distribution of output from the CBIS department.
    b. The accounts payable clerk prepares data for computer processing and enters the data into the computer.
    c. The systems programmer designs the operating and control functions of programs and participates in testing operating systems.
    d. The control clerk establishes control over data received by the CBIS department and reconciles control totals after processing.

24. Which of the following is *not* a major reason for maintaining an audit trail for a computer system?
    a. Deterrent to fraud
    b. Monitoring purposes
    c. Analytical procedures
    d. Query answering

25. An auditor anticipates assessing control risk at a low level in a computerized environment. Under these circumstances, on which of the following procedures would the auditor initially focus?
    a. Programmed control procedures
    b. Application control procedures
    c. Output control procedures
    d. General control procedures

ESSAY QUESTIONS AND PROBLEMS

8.1   Bernath, Inc., an audit client, recently installed a new CBIS to process more efficiently the shipping, billing, and accounts receivable records. During interim work, an assistant completed the review of the accounting system and the internal controls. The assistant determined the following information concerning the new CBIS and the processing and control of shipping notices and customer invoices.

Each major computerized function, that is, shipping, billing, accounts receivable, and so on, is permanently assigned to a specific computer operator who is responsible for making program changes, running the program, and reconciling the computer log. Responsibility for the custody of and control over the magnetic tapes and system documentation is rotated randomly among the computer operators on a monthly basis, to prevent any one person from having access to the tapes and documentation at all times. Each computer programmer and computer operator has access to the computer room via a magnetic card and a digital code that is different for each card. The systems analyst and the supervisor of the computer operators do *not* have access to the computer room.

The CBIS documentation consists of the following items: program listing, error listing, logs, and record layout. To increase efficiency, batch totals and processing controls are omitted from the system.

Bernath ships its products directly from two warehouses, which forward shipping notices to general accounting. There, the billing clerk enters the price of the item and accounts for the numerical sequence of the shipping notices. The billing clerk also prepares daily adding machine tapes of the units shipped and the sales amount. Shipping notices and adding machine tapes are forwarded to the computer department for processing. The computer output consists of a three-copy invoice that is forwarded to the billing clerk, and a daily sales register showing the aggregate totals of units shipped and sales amounts that the computer operator compares to the adding machine tapes.

The billing clerk mails two copies of each invoice to the customer and retains the third copy in an open invoice file that serves as a detailed accounts receivable record.

Required:
    a. Prepare an internal control flowchart for Bernath's shipping and billing subset of the revenue cycle.
    b. Based on the narrative and your flowchart, identify the control weaknesses.

c. Describe one specific recommendation for correcting each condition in internal controls in the new CBIS and for correcting each condition or inefficiency in the procedures for processing and controlling shipping notices and customer invoices.
(AICPA adapted)

8.2   The flowchart presented in Figure 8.15 depicts part of a client's revenue cycle. Some of the flowchart symbols are labeled to indicate control procedures and records.

Required:

For each symbol numbered 61 through 73, select one response from the answer lists below. Each response in the lists may be selected only once; not every response may be selected.

ANSWER LISTS

Operations and Control Procedures

A. Enter shipping data
B. Verify agreement of sales order and shipping document
C. Write off accounts receivable
D. To warehouse and shipping department
E. Authorize accounts receivable write-off
F. Prepare aged trial balance
G. To sales department
H. Release goods for shipment
I. To accounts receivable department
J. Enter price data
K. Determine that customer exists
L. Match customer purchase order with sales
M. Perform customer credit check
N. Prepare sales journal
O. Prepare sales invoice

Documents, Journals, Ledgers, and Files

P. Shipping document
Q. General ledger master file
R. General journal
S. Master price file
T. Sales journal
U. Sales invoice
V. Cash receipts journal
W. Uncollectible accounts file
X. Shipping file
Y. Aged trial balance
Z. Open order file

(AICPA adapted)

8.3   Programmed control procedures may be tested by using one or more of the following means: test data approach, ITF approach, tagging and tracing, SCARF, and surprise audit.

Required:

a. Briefly define each of the above testing alternatives and identify the primary advantage and disadvantage of each.

FIGURE 8.15

Flowchart for Problem 8.2

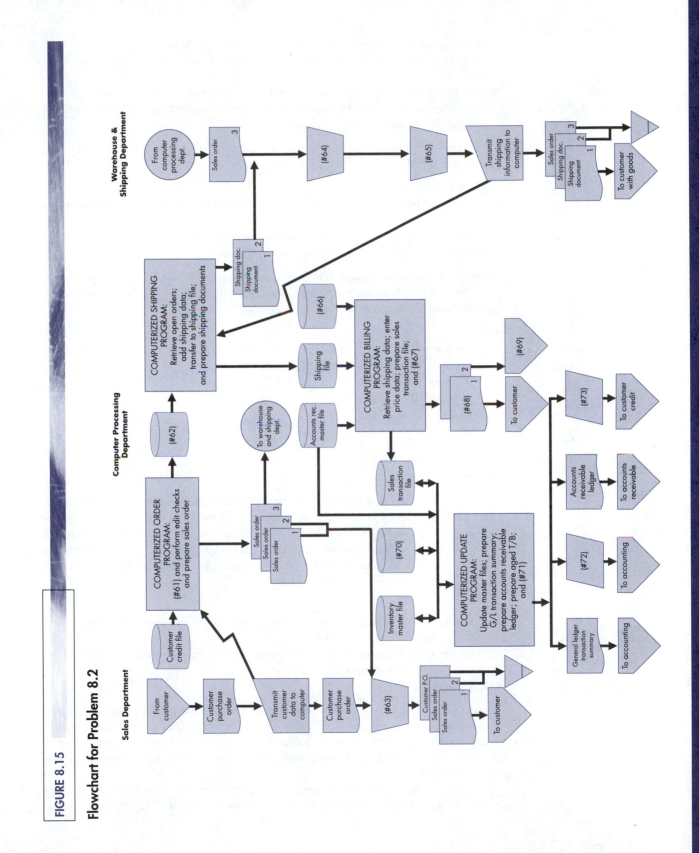

    b. Why is some combination of the above approaches usually advisable?

    c. Differentiate between auditing around the computer and auditing through the computer.

    d. Parallel simulation has been characterized as an "automated version of auditing around the computer." Explain why. Under what circumstances might the auditor elect to use parallel simulation?

8.4   User controls are manual control procedures applied by organizational units (user groups) whose data is processed by CBIS applications.

Required:

    a. Give two examples each of user controls for a payroll application and a sales order processing application.

    b. Under what circumstances might an auditor elect to test user controls?

    c. Discuss the auditor's approach to testing user controls.

8.5   Auditors have various CBIS audit techniques available to aid in testing computer-based systems. Included in these audit techniques are (a) test decks (data), (b) parallel simulation, (c) integrated test facility (ITF), and (d) tagging and tracing and SCARF.

Required:

Describe each of the four identified audit techniques and list two situations where they are most appropriately used. Use the following format:

    a. Test Decks:

        1. Description

        2. Uses

          A.

          B.

    b., c., d.: same format as (a).

    (IIA adapted)

8.6   Whipple, a CPA, was engaged to examine the financial statements of Meister, Incorporated. During the preliminary review, Whipple found that Meister lacked proper segregation of the programming and operating functions. As a result, Whipple intensified the study and evaluation of the internal control procedures surrounding the computer and concluded that the compensating general controls provided reasonable assurance that the objectives of the internal control system were being met.

Required:

    a. In a properly functioning CBIS environment, how is the separation of the programming and operating functions achieved?

    b. What are the compensating general controls that Whipple most likely found? Do not discuss hardware and application controls.

    (AICPA adapted)

8.7   Conan Products manufactures a line of men's and women's shaving products, including razors, shaving creams and gels, deodorants, after-shave lotions and creams, and colognes. These products are shipped to wholesalers and to retail chain warehouses throughout North America. The sales processing subset of the revenue cycle is described in the following narrative.

    All sales are made on open account and payment terms are 2/10; n/30, unless other arrangements have been negotiated with credit manager approval. Conan maintains accounts receivable and inventory as part of an online real-time computer database. Official selling prices are housed in computer memory, and are updated as changes are made by the respective product managers and approved by the sales vice president. Customer orders are received by regional sales managers and entered into the system from remote terminals. The regional managers can override official prices after the computer questions deviations. New customers require official credit approval by both the regional sales manager and the home office credit manager before an order can be processed. Although each customer has an established line of credit, the computer does *not* have a routine for checking whether a sales transaction exceeds the line. Instead, a monthly report compares customer balances with existing credit lines and a halt is placed on further sales if the line has been exceeded.

Upon entering a customer order and checking for credit approval, the computer program determines inventory availability. If the inventory is available, shipping is notified immediately to reserve that quantity of inventory and hold it for a shipping order. If the customer order reduces the inventory below the reorder point, the computer automatically generates a purchase order. If the goods are not in stock, they are back-ordered and the customer is notified immediately as to the back-order.

If the goods are in stock and reserved for shipment, a prenumbered combination sales invoice/shipping order set is printed. At the same time, the computer records the sale, costs the sale, and relieves the inventory for the goods to be shipped. The invoice/order set consists of four copies:

- Original mailed to customer;
- Copy to accounting;
- Copy to shipping; and
- Copy to accounts receivable.

The copy to accounting is filed in an open invoice file awaiting receipt of the bill of lading evidencing shipment. Upon receipt of a bill of lading, the invoice copy and bill of lading are matched and filed alphabetically. The accounts receivable copy is filed alphabetically.

Upon receipt of the invoice copy, shipping prepares the order and completes a prenumbered three-part bill of lading set. The bill of lading is signed by the carrier as evidence of acceptance and the copies are distributed as follows:

- Original accompanying goods to customer;
- Copy to accounting (for matching with invoice copy); and
- Copy filed numerically in shipping.

Required:
a. Prepare a flowchart of the sales order, shipping, and invoicing process. Identify internal control strengths and weaknesses on your flowchart.
b. For internal control strengths, identify the financial statement assertions to which they relate and state how you would proceed to test them for operating effectiveness.
c. For internal control weaknesses, identify the assertion affected, state how you would correct the weakness, and give the impact of the weakness on substantive audit testing.

8.8 A nationwide sportswear retailer is preparing to implement electronic data interchange (EDI) of invoices, purchase orders, and delivery schedules with its suppliers. The retailer has a single distribution center for all the stores. The stores transmit sales and inventory positions daily to the distribution center. When conversion is complete, EDI will be used to transfer all business documents between the retailer and its suppliers. If EDI is really successful, management will implement EDI in its other lines of business.

Management has asked the director of internal auditing to plan for auditing the sportswear division to (1) compare its performance with and without EDI and (2) audit the new system on a continuing basis after its installation. The director consulted the audit staff, who suggested considering the following techniques for the continuing audit:

1. Test data method;
2. Integrated test facility; and
3. Parallel simulation.

Before responding to management, the director wants the audit staff to agree on the best approach and has decided to prepare a memorandum to the audit staff as a basis for further discussion.

Required:
a. Assume the role of the director of internal audit in consulting with the internal audit staff. Specifically, you are to write a memorandum to your staff that proposes:
  1. Data that internal auditors could use to compare performance with and without EDI;
  2. The best of the suggested computer audit techniques for the continuous audit, and justification for the choice; and
  3. An explanation of why the other techniques are inadequate.
b. Assume the role of independent auditor. In reviewing the work of the internal auditing staff, as part of acquiring an understanding of the client's internal control, would you be more interested in the role of the internal auditors in comparing performance with and without EDI, or in their continuous auditing efforts? Explain.
(IIA adapted)

8.9   As more and more clients install complex CBIS, independent auditors are participating to an increasing extent in systems design. At the same time, the independent auditor's use of computer audit specialists is growing.

Required:
a. What is design phase auditing and why is it important?
b. In what way does design phase auditing affect auditor independence?
c. What function does the computer audit specialist serve?
d. To what extent may the independent auditor rely on the computer audit specialist?

8.10   The importance of input editing increases with the complexity of CBIS.

Required:
a. What is meant by input editing?
b. Give two examples each of input editing routines for payroll processing and for sales order processing.
c. Why does input editing become increasingly significant as the complexity of CBIS increases?

8.11   You are reviewing the audit workpapers containing a narrative description of Overland Inc.'s factory payroll system. A portion of that narrative is as follows:

Factory employees punch time clock cards each day when entering or leaving the shop. At the end of each week, the timekeeping department collects the time cards and prepares duplicate batch-control slips by department, showing total hours and number of employees. The time cards and original batch-control slips are sent to the payroll accounting section. The second copies of the batch-control slips are filed by date.

In the payroll accounting section, payroll transaction cards are keypunched from the information on the time cards, and a batch total card for each batch is keypunched from the batch-control slip. The time cards and batch-control slips then are filed by batch for possible reference. The payroll transaction cards and batch total card are sent to data processing where they are sorted by employee number within each batch. Each batch is edited by a computer program that checks the validity of employee number against a master employee tape file, and the total hours and number of employees against the batch total card. A detail printout by batch and employee number is produced that indicates batches that do not balance and invalid employee numbers. This printout is returned to payroll accounting for resolution of all differences.

In searching for documentation you have found a flowchart of the payroll system that included all appropriate symbols, but was only partially labeled. The portion of this flowchart described by the above narrative appears as Figure 8.16.

Required:
a. Number your answer 1 through 17. Next to the corresponding number of your answer, supply the appropriate labeling (document name, process description, file order) for each numbered symbol on the flowchart.
b. A flowchart is one of the aids an auditor may use to determine and evaluate a client's internal control system. List the advantages of using flowcharts in this context.
(AICPA adapted)

8.12 The following independent narratives describe controls the auditor wishes to test for operating effectiveness.

1. Mary Todd, CPA, wishes to test her client's cash receipts for completeness, that is, whether all cash receipts are deposited in the bank.
2. McKee, Inc., has a computerized payroll system. The auditor wishes to test the controls for integrity and accuracy of processing.
3. Denatric, Ltd., has installed an integrated database and distributed processing for capturing and recording division and branch transactions. Robert Murray, CPA and independent auditor, wishes to test database security.
4. To support its just-in-time inventory control system, Merriweather Corporation uses an electronic data interchange system (EDI) with protocol conversion and data encryption to purchase most of the raw materials used in its manufacturing process. Juanita Gomez, Merriweather's independent auditor, wishes to test the effectiveness of the data encryption portion of the system.
5. Jack's Wholesale Distributors has a batch processing system for sales and accounts receivable. Sales and cash receipts for a given day are processed the next working day. Maggie Clover, the independent auditor, wishes to test the accuracy of debits to sales discounts and credits to accounts receivable for customer remittances.
6. Amanda Krantz, CPA, is concerned about documentation and approval of systems, programs, and program changes, given her client's newly installed computerized accounting and management information system.
7. Marple Hardware Supply has a computerized vouchering system as a component of its integrated database system. As part of control risk assessment, Raymont Brown, Marple's auditor, wishes to test repairs and maintenance expense accounts for

348 Part 2 Planning the Audit

FIGURE 8.16

Flowchart for Problem 8.11

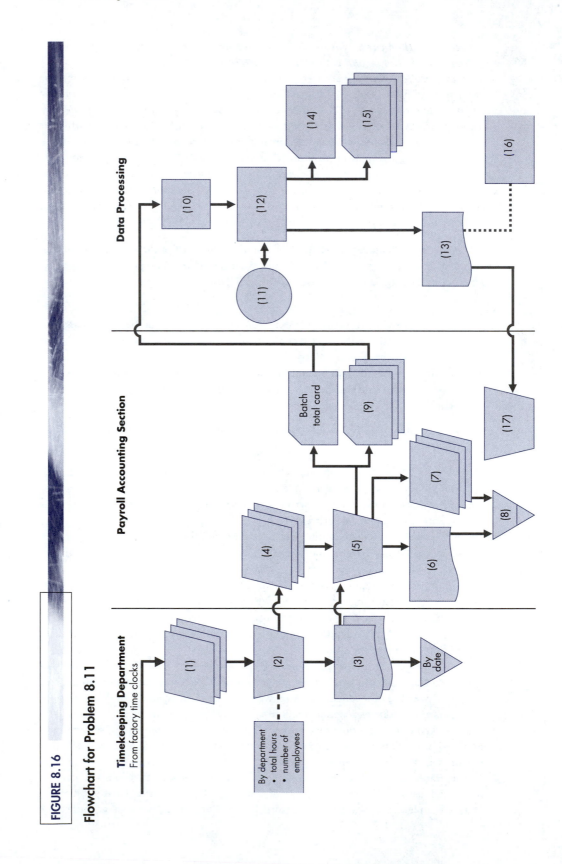

possible debits that should have been made to property accounts. Company policy states that all expenditures below $10,000 are to be expensed, and Brown has agreed to this policy.

8. Although Ron Lozer believes that his client's computer operators who process purchases transactions are competent, he wishes to apply control tests to support a reduction in the assessed level of control risk within the purchasing subset of the expenditure cycle.

Required:

For each narrative:

a. Choose, from the following alternatives, the most efficient means for testing the controls:
   1. Observation
   2. Document examination and testing
   3. Reprocessing
b. Describe more precisely how you would test the controls. In each case, the auditor believes the controls to be reliable, but needs to test them for operating effectiveness before reducing the assessed level of control risk.

8.13   Increasing use of sophisticated CBIS has produced significant changes in the accounting environment. Some of these changes are the following:

1. Documents that are used to enter information into the computer may exist for only a short time or only in computer-readable form. In some computer systems, input documents may not exist at all, because information is entered directly into the system.
2. Computer processing uniformly subjects like transactions to the same processing instructions.
3. Many internal control procedures, once performed by separate individuals in manual systems, may be concentrated in systems that use computer processing.
4. The potential for individuals to gain unauthorized access to data or assets may be greater in computerized accounting systems than in manual systems.

Required:

For each of the changes, discuss the impact on the internal control system and the independent audit.

Conducting the Audit

part3

biltrite

chapter 9

biltrite

learning objectives

After reading this chapter, you should be able to

1 Identify the audit areas in which sampling is appropriate.
2 Differentiate between statistical and nonstatistical sampling.
3 Define expected occurrence rate, tolerable occurrence rate, risk of underassessment, and upper occurrence limit.
4 Apply attribute sampling to a control testing example.
5 Relate attribute sampling to audit risk.
6 Quantify audit risk as an input to variables sampling for substantive testing purposes.

OVERVIEW

Chapter 9 is the first of two chapters devoted to statistical sampling in auditing. The discussion in Chapter 9 is restricted to sampling as it is applied to the auditor's assessment of control risk. Figure 9.1 identifies that part of the audit process occupied by this discussion. Chapter 10 considers sampling applications for substantive testing purposes.

Chapter 9 begins by comparing statistical with nonstatistical sampling, noting that although both approaches are permitted by GAAS, the coverage in Chapters 9 and 10 is restricted to statistical sampling. The ability of statistical sampling to assist the auditor in evaluating audit risk, by providing a means for partially quantifying it, is the reason for limiting the discussion to this means of audit sampling.

After identifying attribute sampling as the appropriate method for performing tests of controls and for control risk assessment purposes, the chapter proceeds to define sampling terms and outline the steps involved in the sampling process.

The means by which statistical sampling assists in audit risk quantification are described at length, and an extended example is presented at the end of the chapter to clarify the concepts further.

SAMPLING APPLICATIONS IN AUDITING

Virtually all independent audits are test based. A test-based audit permits the auditor to draw conclusions by examining only a portion of an organization's transactions and events. Detailed audits requiring the examination of all transactions were common in the early stages of auditing. However, as entities grew in size, the volume of transactions became too great for a detailed audit to be cost effective. For this reason, auditors began to recognize the importance of internal control policies and procedures for preventing and detecting material errors and fraud, and auditing gradually evolved from detailed to test based in nature. At the same time, audit reports shifted from guaranteeing the accuracy of the accounts to providing reasonable assurance as to the overall fairness of the financial statements.

In test-based auditing, the selection of those transactions to be examined requires some sampling methodology. Currently, generally accepted auditing standards permit either statistical or nonstatistical sampling.[1]

Sampling methods are used by auditors in performing both tests of controls and substantive testing. For tests of controls, sampling is used to estimate error rates and thereby assist in evaluating the effectiveness of internal control procedures. In substantive testing, sampling is used to estimate the dollar amount of account balances and transactions. Sampling for tests of controls is covered in this chapter. Sampling for substantive testing is examined in Chapter 10.

HOW SAMPLING CAN ASSIST IN TESTING OF CONTROLS

Sampling provides a systematic approach to estimating error rates in certain kinds of populations. The error rates provide evidence of control weaknesses and assist the auditor in assessing control risk within each of the transaction cycle subsets.

Forms of Control Testing

As presented in Chapter 7, internal control testing assumes three forms in the typical independent financial statement audit. Where there is a visible audit trail, the auditor

---

1 *AICPA Professional Standards*, New York: AICPA, section AU 350.03.

FIGURE 9.1

The Audit Process

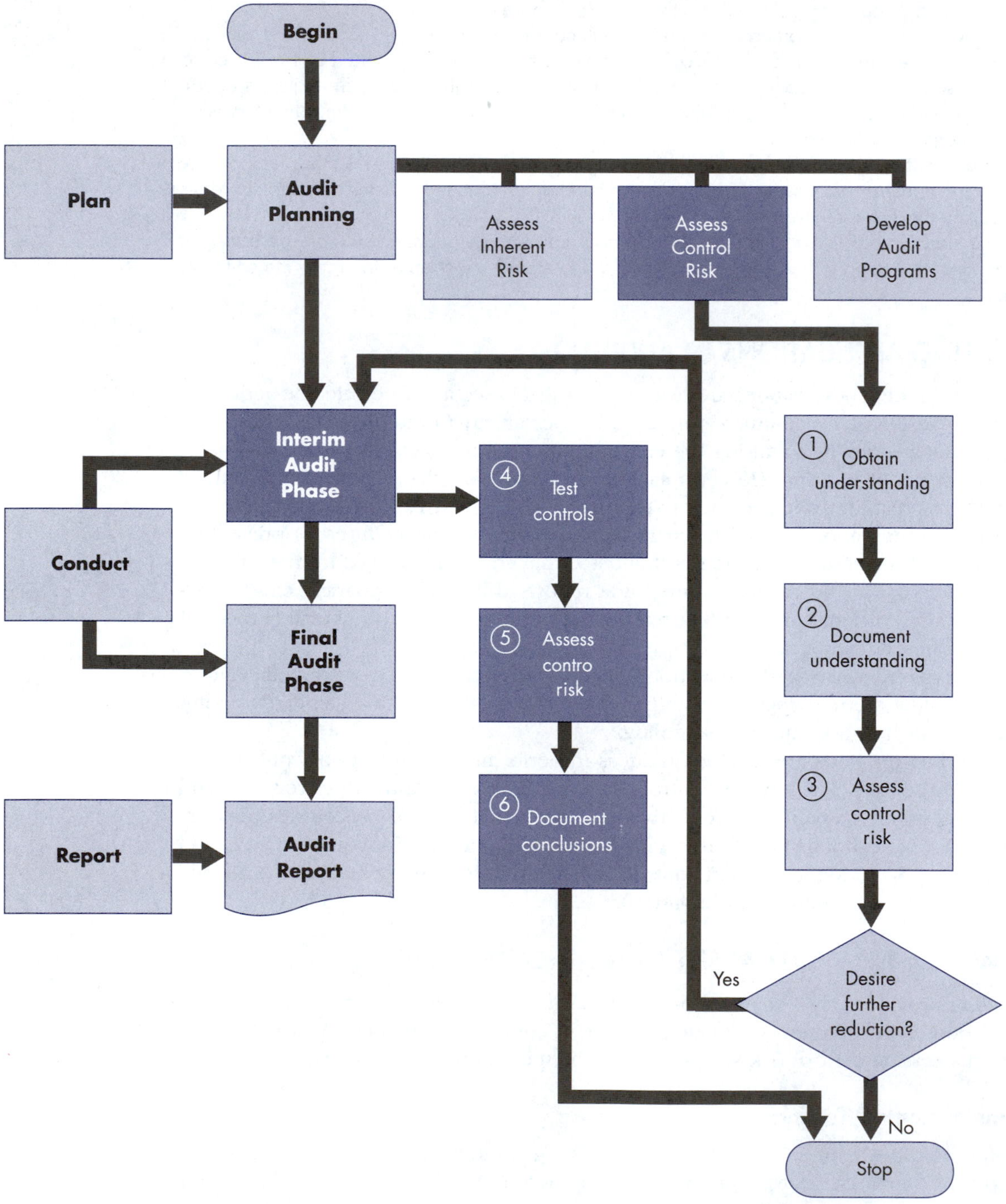

examines documents, as appropriate, to verify the effectiveness of internal control procedures. Evidence as to whether transactions have been executed in accordance with management's authorization and recorded in accordance with GAAP is gathered through this examination. In the absence of an audit trail, the auditor *observes* the control environment and control activities, and possibly *reprocesses* selected transactions. Management support of internal control, adequacy of separation of duties, competence and integrity of personnel, and existence of periodic inventories and comparisons are verified by the auditor through observation. Password security, user identification codes, and input editing controls are tested through reprocessing.

Sampling to Test Controls with Documentation

Sampling methods commonly are applied to the first form of control tests, that is, in verifying the existence of proper reviews, approvals, and recording where there is an audit trail in the form of documentation.[2] Observation for control effectiveness ordinarily does not require the use of audit sampling. Although transaction reprocessing may involve a form of sampling, the auditor utilizes judgment sampling rather than probability sampling in testing a few selected transactions designed to violate controls.

Sampling can assist the auditor during the examination of documentary evidence for the purpose of testing controls in the following ways:

• Determining the number of documents to examine in testing for a specific attribute;
• Selecting the documents to be tested;
• Evaluating the sample results; and
• Further assessing control risk.

STATISTICAL VERSUS NONSTATISTICAL SAMPLING

When confronted with a task requiring the application of sampling methods, the auditor must elect to apply either statistical or nonstatistical sampling. As stated earlier, auditing standards permit either approach. In order to make a rational selection, the auditor must recognize the distinction between the two methods.

Statistical sampling is a mathematical approach to inference involving the calculation of sample sizes, population values, and precision ranges, given set parameters relating to required reliability and precision. In determining sample size, in selecting the sample, and in evaluating the sample results, a consistent and orderly approach is followed. The setting of precision ranges and reliability levels, as defined and discussed in Chapter 10, is important in applying this approach.

Large populations providing ready access to each item are more conducive to statistical sampling methods than smaller populations or populations containing items not readily accessible by the auditor. A large population of prenumbered vouchers, for example, all of which are filed sequentially, may be tested for control effectiveness through the use of statistical sampling.

For auditing applications, the statistical sampling methods commonly used are as follows:

• **Attribute sampling:** An estimate of *frequency* of events (errors or fraud). This method is covered in the current chapter as it is used for performing tests of controls.

---

2   Ibid, section AU 350.32.

- **Variables sampling:** An estimate of *amount* (account balance or dollar amount of errors). Variables sampling is used for substantive testing purposes and is covered in Chapter 10.
- **Discovery sampling:** An orderly approach to locating a *particular event*. In auditing applications, this method is used to find an example of an error or fraud when the auditor's suspicions are aroused. Related more to detection of employee fraud, discovery sampling is beyond the scope of this textbook.

Nonstatistical sampling is a more subjective approach to inference, in that mathematical techniques are not used consistently in determining sample size, selecting the sample, or evaluating sample results. Instead, the auditor exercises professional judgment in making these determinations. Smaller populations, or populations containing items not readily accessible by the auditor, are often more conducive to the application of nonstatistical sampling techniques. Given a relatively small number of customer accounts, for example, the auditor may find it cost effective to examine a larger percentage of the accounts than would be required by the application of statistical sampling methods. Similarly, a large population of vouchers processed by an online real-time system may not be filed in a manner that lends itself to random selection. Under these conditions, nonstatistical sampling methods may be more appropriate.

Although both methods are permitted under GAAS, the discussion in this chapter and the next is restricted to statistical sampling. In addition to being a more consistent approach to audit sampling, statistical sampling provides the most effective means for quantifying audit risk. Therefore, it fits more neatly into the risk analysis framework of this textbook.

STATISTICAL SAMPLING AND AUDIT JUDGMENT

Although statistical sampling involves the application of mathematical techniques in determining sample size and in evaluating sample results, it does *not* replace audit judgment. In determining sample size, for example, the auditor must exercise judgment in selecting a tolerable rate of error beyond which the assessed level of control risk would not be reduced. Audit judgment also is required in determining an acceptable risk of incorrectly assessing control risk below the maximum level. In evaluating sample results, the auditor must exercise judgment in assessing the materiality of control weaknesses. Statistical sampling does provide for greater consistency in the application of audit judgment. By providing a uniform framework for determining sample size, selecting the sample, and evaluating results, statistical sampling permits the auditor to make audit judgments within the bounds of consistent parameters.

STATISTICAL SAMPLING FOR TESTING OF CONTROLS

The goal of control testing is to determine whether the controls the auditor wishes to test were functioning effectively during the period under audit. Some controls are tested through observation, some are tested by transaction reprocessing, and some are tested by examining documents. Statistical sampling techniques, as discussed in the following paragraphs, are applicable to the latter method.

Some **attributes** (control features) of interest to the auditor in testing controls by examining documents are as follows:

- Are purchase invoices properly approved for payment?

- Are account distributions (debit/credit) correct?
- Do vouchers contain the necessary documentation?
- Are proper labor rates being used to compute payroll?
- Do time cards agree with the payroll summary regarding hours?
- Are all sales invoices properly approved and accompanied by shipping orders and bills of lading?
- Do selling prices agree with published price lists?

Statistical sampling techniques will assist in determining the number of documents to be examined for each attribute of interest, in selecting the documents, and in evaluating the results of the sampling.

Calculating the Sample Size

In applying statistical sampling techniques, the auditor is trying to draw conclusions about a population by looking at only part of it. The question is, how much does the auditor need to examine? In applying attribute sampling to tests of controls, sample size is a function of the following factors.

Population Size   For attribute sampling purposes, **population size** (e.g., the number of vouchers processed during the period, the number of employee time cards submitted, or the number of sales invoices written) has a material influence on sample size *only* if the population contains fewer than one thousand items (see Table 9.1). However, because virtually all attribute sampling applications in auditing involve population sizes in excess of one thousand, tables for determining sample size ignore population size.

Expected Occurrence Rate   The **expected occurrence rate** is the anticipated error rate. For example, an attribute of interest, for control testing purposes, is whether the proper accounts were debited for vouchers processed, that is, testing for proper account distribution. The expected occurrence rate, for purposes of this test, is the estimated per-

TABLE 9.1

Effects of Population Size on Sample Size

Population Size	Sample Size
50	45
100	64
500	87
1,000	90
2,000	92
5,000	93
100,000	93

Source: AICPA, *Audit Sampling Guide*, New York: AICPA, 1983, p. 35.

centage of vouchers containing account distribution errors. The estimate may be based on the initial understanding phase of the internal control review and evaluation, on the prior year's audit if this is a recurring audit, or on a pilot sample selected for the purpose of estimating the population occurrence rate. The expected occurrence rate positively affects sample size in that a high expected rate requires a larger sample than would be appropriate were a low rate of error expected.

Tolerable Occurrence Rate   The **tolerable occurrence rate** is the maximum rate of error acceptable to the auditor, while still warranting a lowering of assessed control risk below the maximum level. It is inversely related to sample size; that is, the lower the tolerable rate of error, the larger the sample size. The decision about whether the rate is to be set high or low depends on audit judgment.

In setting the tolerable occurrence rate, the auditor considers the importance of the attribute being tested: The more critical an attribute is to those control policies and procedures relevant to an audit, the lower the tolerable occurrence rate. Account distribution errors, for example, may be considered more critical to accurate financial statements than lack of initials evidencing approval of purchase requisitions. The setting of a lower tolerable occurrence rate when examining vouchers for erroneous debits increases the sample size and thereby recognizes the materiality of control weaknesses involving account distribution errors.

The expected occurrence rate and the tolerable occurrence rate together define **precision**, which is the range within which the true answer most likely falls. The narrower the precision range (i.e., the closer the two rates are), the larger the sample size (see Table 9.2). Given a specified expected occurrence rate, the lower the tolerable occurrence rate, the larger the sample size. Likewise, given a specified tolerable occurrence rate, the higher the expected occurrence rate, the larger the sample size.

Acceptable Level of Risk of Underassessing Control Risk   As discussed in Chapter 5, audit risk may be classified as the risk that material errors or fraud exist (inherent risk and

TABLE 9.2

Precision and Sample Size

Expected Occurrence Rate (%)	Tolerable Occurrence Rate (%)	Precision (%)	Sample Size
1	4	3	156
1	5	4	93
1	6	5	78
1	7	6	66
1	8	7	58
2	8	6	77
3	8	5	95
4	8	4	146

control risk), and the risk that material errors or fraud will go undetected and the audit opinion will not be appropriately modified (detection risk). The auditor studies the business and industry and applies analytical procedures (as discussed in Chapter 5) as a basis for assessing inherent risk, studies and evaluates internal control policies and procedures relevant to an audit for assessing control risk, and designs substantive audit procedures to reduce detection risk to an acceptable level. In this context, detection risk represents the amount of risk the auditor is willing to accept that his or her procedures will fail to detect errors beyond the internal control system.

A weak set of internal financial controls (maximum level of control risk) increases overall audit risk. A high level of audit risk, however, needs to be reduced to a reasonably acceptable level; thus, more substantive testing is required (lower detection risk) than if the internal financial controls are satisfactory.[3] In a test-based audit, the auditor must assess control risk by examining a sample and extending the results to the population (Chapter 9). The assessment, when combined with the auditor's evaluation of inherent risk, then will serve as an input into calculating sample sizes for substantive testing purposes (Chapter 10).

The **risk of underassessment** is the risk of incorrectly assessing control risk below the maximum level and is also a function of audit judgment. Stated differently, the risk of underassessment is the risk that the sample supports the auditor's lowering of assessed control risk when the true error rate in the population does not justify a reduction. In nonstatistical terms, it is the probability that the auditor will assess control risk at a lower level than is justified for a subset of the client's internal financial controls. Risk of underassessment (assessing control risk too low) relates to *reliability*, or the confidence level, defined as the likelihood that the true answer falls within the range (precision) established through sampling. It is inversely related to sample size; that is, the lower the acceptable risk of underassessment, the larger the required sample size. Stated differently, the greater the confidence the auditor wishes to place in the results of sampling, the larger the number of items to be included in the sample.

Risk of underassessment is similar to **beta risk**, defined in statistics as the risk of incorrect acceptance. Given that it represents a primary basis for the audit opinion, the risk of underassessment should be set at a low level. Most auditors, as a rule of thumb, accept a risk of underassessment of less than or equal to 10 percent ($\leq$ 10%). The risk of overassessment is termed **alpha risk**. Together, alpha risk and beta risk comprise **sampling risk**, defined as the risk that the auditor's conclusions about a population will be incorrect. The auditor controls sampling risk by specifying a low overall audit risk and by increasing or decreasing detection risk on the basis of control risk and inherent risk evaluation. Alpha risk and beta risk are discussed at greater length in Chapter 10.

The expected occurrence rate, the tolerable occurrence rate, and the acceptable risk of underassessment as just defined are the inputs contained in the sample size tables (Tables 9.3 and 9.4) presented in this chapter. The effects on sample size as these parameters increase are as follows:

Parameter	*Effect on Sample Size*
Population size	Positive
Expected occurrence rate	Positive
Tolerable occurrence rate	Inverse
Acceptable risk of underassessment	Inverse

3   Overall audit risk is the joint probability of inherent risk, control risk, and detection risk. It was represented in Chapter 5 by the notation $IR \times CR \times DR$.

TABLE 9.3

Statistical Sample Sizes for Control Testing at 5 Percent Risk of Underassessment (with Number of Expected Errors in Parentheses)

Expected Population Deviation Rate#	Tolerable Rate											
	2%	3%	4%	5%	6%	7%	8%	9%	10%	15%	20%	
0.00%	149(0)	99(0)	74(0)	59(0)	49(0)	42(0)	36(0)	32(0)	29(0)	19(0)	14(0)	
.25	236(1)	157(1)	117(1)	93(1)	78(1)	66(1)	58(1)	51(1)	46(1)	30(1)	22(1)	
.50	*	157(1)	117(1)	93(1)	78(1)	66(1)	58(1)	51(1)	46(1)	30(1)	22(1)	
.75	*	208(2)	117(1)	93(1)	78(1)	66(1)	58(1)	51(1)	46(1)	30(1)	22(1)	
1.00	*	*	156(2)	93(1)	78(1)	66(1)	58(1)	51(1)	46(1)	30(1)	22(1)	
1.25	*	*	156(2)	124(2)	78(1)	66(1)	58(1)	51(1)	46(1)	30(1)	22(1)	
1.50	*	*	192(3)	124(2)	103(2)	66(1)	58(1)	51(1)	46(1)	30(1)	22(1)	
1.75	*	*	227(4)	153(3)	103(2)	88(2)	77(2)	51(1)	46(1)	30(1)	22(1)	
2.00	*	*	*	181(4)	127(3)	88(2)	77(2)	68(2)	46(1)	30(1)	22(1)	
2.25	*	*	*	208(5)	127(3)	88(2)	77(2)	68(2)	61(2)	30(1)	22(1)	
2.50	*	*	*	*	150(4)	109(3)	77(2)	68(2)	61(2)	30(1)	22(1)	
2.75	*	*	*	*	173(5)	109(3)	95(3)	68(2)	61(2)	30(1)	22(1)	
3.00	*	*	*	*	195(6)	129(4)	95(3)	84(3)	61(2)	30(1)	22(1)	
3.25	*	*	*	*	*	148(5)	112(4)	84(3)	61(2)	30(1)	22(1)	
3.50	*	*	*	*	*	167(6)	112(4)	84(3)	76(3)	40(2)	22(1)	
3.75	*	*	*	*	*	185(7)	129(5)	100(4)	76(3)	40(2)	22(1)	
4.00	*	*	*	*	*	*	146(6)	100(4)	89(4)	40(2)	22(1)	
5.00	*	*	*	*	*	*	*	158(8)	116(6)	40(2)	30(2)	
6.00	*	*	*	*	*	*	*	*	170(11)	50(3)	30(2)	
7.00	*	*	*	*	*	*	*	*	*	68(5)	37(3)	

#Same as "expected occurrence rate."
*Sample size is too large to be cost effective for most audit applications.
Note: This table assumes a large population.
Source: AICPA, *Audit Sampling Guide,* New York: AICPA, 1983, p. 106.

TABLE 9.4

Statistical Sample Sizes for Control Testing at 10 Percent Risk of Underassessment (with Number of Expected Errors in Parentheses)

Expected Population Deviation Rate#	Tolerable Rate										
	2%	3%	4%	5%	6%	7%	8%	9%	10%	15%	20%
0.00%	114(0)	76(0)	57(0)	45(0)	38(0)	32(0)	28(0)	25(0)	22(0)	15(0)	11(0)
.25	194(1)	129(1)	96(1)	77(1)	64(1)	55(1)	48(1)	42(1)	38(1)	25(1)	18(1)
.50	194(1)	129(1)	96(1)	77(1)	64(1)	55(1)	48(1)	42(1)	38(1)	25(1)	18(1)
.75	265(2)	129(1)	96(1)	77(1)	64(1)	55(1)	48(1)	42(1)	38(1)	25(1)	18(1)
1.00	*	176(2)	96(1)	77(1)	64(1)	55(1)	48(1)	42(1)	38(1)	25(1)	18(1)
1.25	*	221(3)	132(2)	77(1)	64(1)	55(1)	48(1)	42(1)	38(1)	25(1)	18(1)
1.50	*	*	132(2)	105(2)	64(1)	55(1)	48(1)	42(1)	38(1)	25(1)	18(1)
1.75	*	*	166(3)	105(2)	88(2)	55(1)	48(1)	42(1)	38(1)	25(1)	18(1)
2.00	*	*	198(4)	132(3)	88(2)	75(2)	48(1)	42(1)	38(1)	25(1)	18(1)
2.25	*	*	*	132(3)	88(2)	75(2)	65(2)	42(1)	38(1)	25(1)	18(1)
2.50	*	*	*	158(4)	110(3)	75(2)	65(2)	58(2)	38(1)	25(1)	18(1)
2.75	*	*	*	209(6)	132(4)	94(3)	65(2)	58(2)	52(2)	25(1)	18(1)
3.00	*	*	*	*	132(4)	94(3)	65(2)	58(2)	52(2)	25(1)	18(1)
3.25	*	*	*	*	153(5)	113(4)	82(3)	58(2)	52(2)	25(1)	18(1)
3.50	*	*	*	*	194(7)	113(4)	82(3)	73(3)	52(2)	25(1)	18(1)
3.75	*	*	*	*	*	131(5)	98(4)	73(3)	52(2)	25(1)	18(1)
4.00	*	*	*	*	*	149(6)	98(4)	73(3)	65(3)	25(1)	18(1)
5.00	*	*	*	*	*	*	160(8)	115(6)	78(4)	34(2)	18(1)
6.00	*	*	*	*	*	*	*	182(11)	116(7)	43(3)	25(2)
7.00	*	*	*	*	*	*	*	*	199(14)	52(4)	25(2)

#Same as "expected occurrence rate."
*Sample size is too large to be cost effective for most audit applications.
Note: This table assumes a large population.
Source: AICPA, *Audit Sampling Guide*, New York: AICPA, 1983, p. 107.

The tables provide for two possible levels of risk of underassessment of control risk: 5 percent and 10 percent.

Case Study

As a means for applying the concepts just discussed, consider the following example. In testing internal control policies and procedures relevant to the purchases subset of the expenditure cycle, the auditor wishes to examine the client's vouchers to determine whether the necessary controls are present and functioning effectively. One of the attributes to be tested is proper documentation of transactions. With respect to a specific voucher, the absence of any one of the following documents is considered an error:

* Purchase requisition;
* Purchase order;
* Receiving report; and
* Vendor's invoice.

Based on last year's audit and this year's preliminary internal control study and evaluation, the CPA believes that the client's vouchers contain a 3 percent error rate with respect to inadequate documentation (expected occurrence rate). The CPA wishes to gain assurance, with 95 percent confidence (risk of underassessment = 5%), that the population error rate is ≤ 6 percent (tolerable occurrence rate). An upper error limit greater than 6 percent, in other words, will preclude the lowering of the assessed control risk below the maximum level. Tables 9.3 and 9.4 list sample sizes based on risk of underassessment, expected occurrence rate, and tolerable occurrence rate. In Table 9.3, the sample size corresponding to the intersection of a 3 percent expected occurrence rate and a 6 percent tolerable occurrence rate is 195. This means that the auditor must select 195 vouchers, and examine each one for completeness of documentation.

Drawing the Sample

In the application of statistical sampling methods, the items to be included in the sample must be drawn on a probability basis; that is, every item in the population must have a known or equal chance of being included in the sample. This is referred to as **random selection**. Techniques available to the auditor for this purpose are random number tables and systematic sampling.

Random number tables (see Table 9.5) or computer-generated random numbers are most appropriate when documents are prenumbered and filed in numerical sequence for ready access. Before random number tables are used, two determinations are necessary. First, some form of correspondence between the document numbers and the random number tables must be established. If the documents contain four digits, for example, and the random numbers are five-digit numbers, the auditor must determine which four digits of the random numbers to use, and apply the method consistently in drawing the sample. If a chosen number in the table did not conform to a document number used during the period, the auditor would discard that number and proceed sequentially to the next usable number in the table.

In addition to establishing correspondence between the random number tables and the document numbers, the auditor must determine a consistent route through the tables in order to ensure systematic movement. The route may be vertical, horizontal, or

TABLE 9.5								

Illustration of Table of Random Numbers

	(01)	(02)	(03)	(04)	(05)	(06)	(07)	(08)
(0001)	9492	4562	4180	5525	7255	1297	9296	1283
(0002)	1557	0392	8989	6898	1072	6013	0020	8582
(0003)	0714	5947	2420	6210	3824	2743	4217	3707
(0004)	0558	8266	4990	8954	7455	6309	9543	1148
(0005)	1458	8725	3750	3138	2499	6017	7744	1485
(0006)	5169	6981	4319	3369	9424	4117	7632	5457
(0007)	0328	5213	1017	5248	8622	6454	8120	4585
(0008)	2462	2055	9782	4213	3452	9940	8859	1000
(0009)	8408	8697	3982	8228	7668	8139	3736	4889
(0010)	1818	5041	9706	4646	3992	4110	4091	7619
(0011)	1771	8614	8593	0930	2095	5005	6387	4002
(0012)	7050	1437	6847	4679	9059	4139	6602	6817
(0013)	5875	2094	0495	3213	5694	5513	3547	9035
(0014)	2473	2087	4618	1507	4471	9542	7565	2371
(0015)	1976	1639	4956	9011	8221	4840	4513	5263
(0016)	4006	4029	7270	8027	7476	7690	6362	1251
(0017)	2149	8162	0667	0825	7353	4645	3273	1181
(0018)	1669	7011	6548	5851	8278	9006	8176	1268
(0019)	7436	5041	4087	1647	7205	3977	4257	9008
(0020)	2178	3632	5745	2228	1780	6043	9296	4469

Source: Dan M. Guy, *Statistical Sampling in Auditing*, New York: John Wiley & Sons, 1982, p. 24.

diagonal, but once it is determined, the route must be followed consistently for a particular sample.

After the auditor has determined numeric correspondence and route, she or he may select the first number from the table. This selection must be made at random. Thereafter, each succeeding item in the table (using the predetermined route) is drawn, until the number of documents selected is equal to the sample size.

The auditor must determine whether a particular number (document) may be selected more than once (sampling with replacement), or whether a document may be drawn only once for inclusion in the sample (sampling without replacement). Although both methods are statistically acceptable, most auditors prefer to sample without replacement.

When documents are not prenumbered, an acceptable alternative to the use of random number tables or computer-generated numbers is systematic sampling with a random start. **Systematic sampling** involves choosing every *n*th item in the population until the requisite sample size has been reached. Two requirements in applying this method are that the starting point be random and that the entire field be covered. If, for example, the population of vouchers is 19,500 and the sample size is 195, the auditor will select the first voucher at random and every 100th voucher thereafter (19,500/195).

Examining the Sample Items

Having drawn the sample on a probability basis, the auditor must examine each item in the sample for the chosen attribute. A prerequisite to effectively performing this step in the sampling process is a clear definition by the auditor of deviations from the attribute being tested. The absence of a receiving report, for example, may be defined as a deviation (error) if the related voucher is for goods purchased, but does *not* constitute an error if purchased services are the subject matter of the voucher. Similarly, lack of an approved requisition is *not* an error if certain inventory items are automatically reordered when the minimum stock level has been reached.

The preceding discussion has been based on a single attribute: proper documentation. In examining a particular type of document, however, the auditor is usually interested in more than a single attribute. In the testing of vouchers, for example, the following attributes may be relevant:

- Proper documentation;
- Evidence of proper authorizations, approvals, and reviews;
- Proper account distribution (correctness of debits and credits);
- Agreement of receiver and vendor's invoice as to type and quantity of goods received and billed;
- Agreement between the purchase order and vendor's invoice as to price; and
- Correctness of extensions and footings on vendor's invoice.

Rather than drawing six different samples for testing these attributes, the auditor need draw only a single sample equal to the maximum sample size. Exhibit 9.1 presents a sampling plan worksheet for the purpose of testing vouchers for the six attributes just listed. Note that the sample sizes are not the same for all attributes because expected occurrence rate, tolerable occurrence rate, and precision are not the same for all attributes. These parameters are a function of the preliminary evaluation of internal financial controls and the auditor's judgment concerning materiality, which may vary for different attributes.

In following the sampling plan outlined in Exhibit 9.1, the auditor randomly draws a sample equal to the maximum sample size presented in the worksheet (195). In examining the vouchers for errors, the auditor proceeds as follows, examining the documents in the order drawn:

1. Vouchers 1–95 are examined for all attributes;
2. Vouchers 96–129 are examined for attributes 1, 2, 3, 4, and 6;
3. Vouchers 130–156 are examined for attributes 1, 2, 3, and 6;
4. Vouchers 157–181 are examined for attributes 1 and 2; and
5. Vouchers 182–195 are examined for attribute 1.

This plan satisfies each of the sample size requirements and is cost effective.

Evaluating Sample Results

Having examined each item in the sample for the attributes being tested, the auditor next must evaluate the sample results. Three steps are involved in this process:

1. The auditor calculates the upper occurrence limit (Exhibit 9.2);
2. The upper occurrence limit is compared with the tolerable occurrence limit; and
3. The impact on substantive audit programs is considered.

EXHIBIT 9.1

Attribute Sampling Plan Worksheet 1

XYZ Company
Voucher Testing for Control Effectiveness
12/31/01

Index: S.1
Prepared by: LFK
Date: 9/3/01
Reviewed by: SEL
Date: 9/15/01

Attribute Tested	Risk of Under-assessment (%)	Expected Occurrence Rate (%)	Tolerable Occurrence Rate (%)	Precision (%)	Sample Size	Number of Detected Errors	Upper Occurrence Limit (%)
1. Proper documentation	5	3	6	3	195		
2. Proper reviews and approvals	5	2	5	3	181		
3. Proper account distribution	5	1	4	3	156		
4. Agreement of receiver and vendor's invoice as to type and quantity of goods received and billed	5	3	7	4	129		
5. Agreement between purchase order and vendor's invoice as to price	5	3	8	5	95		
6. Correctness of extensions and footings on vendor's invoice	5	1	4	3	156		

EXHIBIT 9.2

Attribute Sampling Plan Worksheet 2

XYZ Company
Voucher Testing for Control Effectiveness
12/31/01

Index: S.1
Prepared by: LFK
Date: 9/3/01
Reviewed by: SEL
Date: 9/15/01

Attribute Tested	Risk of Under-assessment (%)	Expected Occurrence Rate (%)	Tolerable Occurrence Rate (%)	Precision (%)	Sample Size	Number of Detected Errors	Upper Occurrence Limit (%)
1. Proper documentation	5	3	6	3	195	3	4
2. Proper reviews and approvals	5	2	5	3	181	3	5
3. Proper account distribution	5	1	4	3	156	5	7
4. Agreement of receiver and vendor's invoice as to type and quantity of goods received and billed	5	3	7	4	129	2	5
5. Agreement between purchase order and vendor's invoice as to price	5	3	8	5	95	2	7
6. Correctness of extensions and footings on vendor's invoice	5	1	4	3	156	1	3

The **upper occurrence limit** is the calculated maximum error rate based on the results of sampling. It is a function of the number of errors detected in the sample relative to the sample size and the designated risk of underassessment. Tables 9.6 and 9.7 are provided for calculating the upper occurrence limit.

The point at which sample size and number of deviations intersect determines the upper occurrence limit.[4] If the upper occurrence limit exceeds the tolerable occurrence rate, the auditor should consider maintaining assessed control risk at the maximum level for that set of attributes. For all attributes except (3), the upper occurrence limit, as determined by sampling, is equal to or less than the tolerable occurrence rate, thus indicating an apparent justification for lowering assessed risk. Attribute (3), however, is indicative of a control weakness that may, in turn, require modification of substantive audit programs. Under these conditions, the auditor must address the following questions:

- How might the weakness affect the financial statements?
- Is the probability of material impact on the financial statements high?

TABLE 9.6

Statistical Sample Results Evaluation Table for Control Tests

(Upper Limits at 5 Percent Risk of Underassessment)

Sample Size	Actual Number of Deviations Found										
	0	1	2	3	4	5	6	7	8	9	10
25	11.3	17.6	*	*	*	*	*	*	*	*	*
30	9.5	14.9	19.6	*	*	*	*	*	*	*	*
35	8.3	12.9	17.0	*	*	*	*	*	*	*	*
40	7.3	11.4	15.0	18.3	*	*	*	*	*	*	*
45	6.5	10.2	13.4	16.4	19.2	*	*	*	*	*	*
50	5.9	9.2	12.1	14.8	17.4	19.9	*	*	*	*	*
55	5.4	8.4	11.1	13.5	15.9	18.2	*	*	*	*	*
60	4.9	7.7	10.2	12.5	14.7	16.8	18.8	*	*	*	*
65	4.6	7.1	9.4	11.5	13.6	15.5	17.4	19.3	*	*	*
70	4.2	6.6	8.8	10.8	12.6	14.5	16.3	18.0	19.7	*	*
75	4.0	6.2	8.2	10.1	11.8	13.6	15.2	16.9	18.5	20.0	*
80	3.7	5.8	7.7	9.5	11.1	12.7	14.3	15.9	17.4	18.9	*
90	3.3	5.2	6.9	8.4	9.9	11.4	12.8	14.2	15.5	16.8	18.2
100	3.0	4.7	6.2	7.6	9.0	10.3	11.5	12.8	14.0	15.2	16.4
125	2.4	3.8	5.0	6.1	7.2	8.3	9.3	10.3	11.3	12.3	13.2
150	2.0	3.2	4.2	5.1	6.0	6.9	7.8	8.6	9.5	10.3	11.1
200	1.5	2.4	3.2	3.9	4.6	5.2	5.9	6.5	7.2	7.8	8.4

*Over 20%.
Note: This table presents upper limits as percentages. This table assumes a large population.
Source: AICPA, *Audit Sampling Guide*, New York: AICPA, 1983, p. 108.

4   For those sample sizes in Exhibit 9.2 not contained in the evaluation tables, the number in the table most nearly corresponding to actual sample size was selected.

TABLE 9.7

Statistical Sample Results Evaluation Table for Control Tests

(Upper Limits at 10 Percent Risk of Underassessment)

Sample Size	Actual Number of Deviations Found										
	0	1	2	3	4	5	6	7	8	9	10
20	10.9	18.1	*	*	*	*	*	*	*	*	*
25	8.8	14.7	19.9	*	*	*	*	*	*	*	*
30	7.4	12.4	16.8	*	*	*	*	*	*	*	*
35	6.4	10.7	14.5	18.1	*	*	*	*	*	*	*
40	5.6	9.4	12.8	16.0	19.0	*	*	*	*	*	*
45	5.0	8.4	11.4	14.3	17.0	19.7	*	*	*	*	*
50	4.6	7.6	10.3	12.9	15.4	17.8	*	*	*	*	*
55	4.1	6.9	9.4	11.8	14.1	16.3	18.4	*	*	*	*
60	3.8	6.4	8.7	10.8	12.9	15.0	16.9	18.9	*	*	*
70	3.3	5.5	7.5	9.3	11.1	12.9	14.6	16.3	17.9	19.6	*
80	2.9	4.8	6.6	8.2	9.8	11.3	12.8	14.3	15.8	17.2	18.6
90	2.6	4.3	5.9	7.3	8.7	10.1	11.5	12.8	14.1	15.4	16.6
100	2.3	3.9	5.3	6.6	7.9	9.1	10.3	11.5	12.7	13.9	15.0
120	2.0	3.3	4.4	5.5	6.6	7.6	8.7	9.7	10.7	11.6	12.6
160	1.5	2.5	3.3	4.2	5.0	5.8	6.5	7.3	8.0	8.8	9.5
200	1.2	2.0	2.7	3.4	4.0	4.6	5.3	5.9	6.5	7.1	7.6

*Over 20%.
Note: This table presents upper limits as percentages. This table assumes a large population.
Source: AICPA, *Audit Sampling Guide*, New York: AICPA, 1983, p. 109.

- Do compensating controls exist?
- If the auditor believes that the weakness is material, and compensating controls do not exist, what substantive audit procedures are necessary in order to determine whether, in fact, the weaknesses have affected one or more financial statement assertions, and to what extent?[5]

Applying this approach to attribute (3), assume that the auditor decides to extend substantive audit testing, given the significance of account distribution errors relating to vouchers. The form of this extension may vary. For example, the auditor may elect to extend the examination of vouchers for proper account distribution by selecting all credits to accounts payable in excess of a specified dollar amount. Alternatively (or in addition), the auditor may increase the extent of analytical procedures applied to certain expense and asset accounts, comparing the balances in selected accounts with the prior year. This comparison will highlight significant changes, which may have resulted from account distribution errors.

---

5   As discussed in Chapter 7, the auditor who plans to consider compensating controls must also examine those controls for effectiveness.

Sometimes, when auditors are evaluating sample results as presented, they elect to use a "shortcut" that enables them to avoid using the evaluation tables and determining the upper occurrence limit. This procedure involves comparing the number of expected deviations with the actual deviations. The expected number of deviations may be calculated by multiplying the expected occurrence rate by the sample size. If the number of expected deviations is greater than the number of detected errors, the auditor may conclude that the upper occurrence limit does *not* exceed the tolerable occurrence rate, and need *not* proceed to the tables. For example, for attribute (1), the expected number of deviations is 6 (195 × .03), while the number of detected errors is 3. Based on this comparison, the auditor may conclude that the upper occurrence limit does not exceed the tolerable rate of 6 percent and, therefore, the assessed level of control risk may be lowered.

Summary of Steps in Applying Attribute Sampling

Figure 9.2 summarizes the sampling process described in the preceding paragraphs and highlights the link between performing tests of controls and substantive testing. Defining sampling objectives, attributes, the sampling unit, the population, and what constitutes errors is critical to a successful attribute sampling plan. The **sampling unit** defines the nature of the population items making up the sample. For example, given a choice in sampling units of either shipping orders or sales invoices, if the auditor wishes to test for unbilled shipments, he or she would choose shipping orders as the sampling unit and trace the sample to sales invoices to determine that the shipment has been properly billed to the customer. If the sampling objective is to determine that all invoices are accompanied by shipments to customers, the sampling unit would be the sales invoice. In applying the sampling plan in this case, the auditor traces sales invoices to shipping orders to confirm shipments to customers.

Comparison of the upper occurrence limit with the tolerable occurrence rate is vital to the development of sampling plans for substantive testing purposes that reflect the auditor's control risk assessment. If the upper limit is below the tolerable rate, the auditor may elect to reduce the assessed level of control risk further. If the upper occurrence limit exceeds the tolerable rate, however, the assessed level of control risk should not be reduced, and may even be increased beyond the level based on the auditor's initial understanding. This final link between performing tests of controls and substantive testing will be described in Chapter 10.

STATISTICAL SAMPLING AND AUDIT RISK IMPLICATIONS

Statistical sampling, by offering a means for partially quantifying audit risk, provides a useful framework for risk analysis. The following paragraphs explain the approach and procedures to be applied to quantification and analysis.

Review of Audit Risk and Reason for Quantifying

As presented in Chapter 5, audit risk consists of the following three components, all of which must be dealt with by the CPA in conducting a financial audit:

1. Inherent risk;
2. Control risk; and
3. Detection risk.

FIGURE 9.2

Summary of Steps in Applying Attribute Sampling

1. Define:
   a. Sampling objectives
   b. Sampling unit
   c. Population
   d. Errors (attributes)

2. Set Parameters:
   a. Expected occurrence rate
   b. Tolerable occurrence rate (TOR)
   c. Risk of underassessment

3. Calculate sample size

4. Draw the sample on a probability basis

5. Examine the sample and list errors

6. Evaluate the sample results:
   a. Determine the observed error rate and the upper occurrence limit (UOL)
   b. Compare UOL and TOR. Is UOL ≤ TOR?
      1. If yes, lower assessed level of control risk
      2. If no, maintain or increase assessed level of control risk

7. Design substantive audit programs

8. Develop sampling plans for substantive testing (Chapter 10)

Both inherent risk and control risk are considered and evaluated during the audit planning phase. The auditor's study of the business and industry and the application of analytical procedures provide an effective basis for assessing inherent risk and for budgeting added audit resources to those areas posing higher-than-average risk. Control risk is assessed by the auditor as a result of studying and evaluating the client's internal financial controls and, if it is deemed appropriate, performing of tests of controls during the interim audit work.

Given the equation $DR = AR/(IR \times CR)$, detection risk (DR) is the dependent variable and is determined by the assessed levels of inherent risk (IR) and control risk (CR). Its resulting magnitude will affect the nature, timing, and extent of substantive audit testing.

Although GAAS do not require the quantification of audit risk, quantification of the risk components is necessary if the auditor wishes to design and implement statistical sampling plans for substantive audit testing purposes. The following paragraphs demonstrate how attribute sampling aids in quantifying these types of audit risk, thereby providing the inputs needed in designing variables sampling plans, as discussed in Chapter 10.

How to Quantify Control Risk

Relate Upper Occurrence Limit to Qualitative Evaluation   The first step in quantifying control risk is to relate possible upper occurrence limits to a qualitative assessment of the client's internal financial controls. The assessment should be made for each transaction cycle segment. For example, assume that the following limits and qualitative assessments have been assigned by the auditor preparatory to testing the sales order processing phase of the revenue cycle for effectiveness:

Upper Occurrence Limit	Internal Control Evaluation
≤1%	Excellent
>1% to ≤3%	Good
>3% to ≤5%	Fair
>5% to ≤7%	Poor
>7%	Unreliable

Determination of the maximum upper occurrence limit beyond which the auditor will elect *not* to reduce control risk assessment below the maximum level is a function of audit judgment. The significance of given attributes relative to the financial statement assertions serves as an input into the decision. Significance relates to the auditor's assessment of the importance of error types. The auditor, for example, might consider errors in processing sales orders to have little impact on the financial statements. Sales pricing errors, conversely, might be judged to be more critical in terms of financial statement impact. For the more critical variables, the auditor relates acceptable internal control to an upper occurrence limit that is lower than what he or she assigns to the less critical variables. In the above example, a computed upper occurrence limit of 3 percent may be necessary for internal control over sales pricing to be rated as "good," while a 5 percent limit may suffice for other aspects of sales processing.

Relate Qualitative Evaluation to Quantitative Assessment of Control Risk   The qualitative evaluation of internal control can now be translated into a quantitative assessment of control risk. Continuing the above illustration, the analysis may be expanded as follows:

Upper Occurrence Limit (%)	Internal Control Evaluation	Control Risk (%)
≤1	Excellent	10
>1 to ≤3	Good	30
>3 to ≤5	Fair	50
>5 to ≤7	Poor	70
>7	Unreliable	100

The more effective the internal control policies and procedures are relative to a given subset of a transaction cycle, as evidenced by the auditor's tests of controls, the lower the auditor may justifiably set the assessed level of control risk. Excellent internal control warrants substantial reduction below the maximum level and produces minimal control risk. Unreliable internal control, conversely, warrants no reduction, and the auditor may assume a 100 percent probability that material errors will occur under such conditions.

How to Quantify Inherent Risk

Inherent risk is the risk that, internal financial controls absent, material errors and/or fraud will occur. Most auditors begin with a conservative estimate of inherent risk equal to 100 percent and subsequently modify the estimate, based on analytical procedures and the auditor's study of the business and industry.

As an example, assume that the auditor in performing control tests of sales orders and invoices discovers numerous errors of a material nature, and decides to set control risk at a relatively high level (70%).[6] Assume further, however, that analytical procedures indicate no material changes in relationships or proportions. Sales volume, both in total and by months, was essentially the same as that in the prior year, and appears to be justified by existing economic conditions. Moreover, no changes in the client's operations occurred in the current year that would warrant material changes in volume. These findings give the auditor added assurance as to the absence of material errors and justify a reduction in inherent risk assessment below the initial 100 percent.

Assume that in the present case the auditor reduces the inherent risk estimate to 70 percent. The reduction reduces the extent of substantive testing that the auditor otherwise would have to perform under conditions of weak or unreliable internal financial controls.

How to Quantify Detection Risk

Detection risk was defined in Chapter 5 as the probability that the auditor will not detect material errors that occur and are not detected by internal control procedures. It is a function of the risk the auditor is willing to accept for expressing an unqualified opinion on financial statements that are materially misstated (overall audit risk), as well as of the assessed levels of inherent risk and control risk. The following equation for determining detection risk was presented in Chapter 5:

$$DR = \frac{AR}{CR \times IR}$$

where
AR = overall audit risk
DR = detection risk
CR = control risk
IR = inherent risk

The weaker the internal control policies and procedures are (the higher the control risk is) and the more closely inherent risk approaches 100 percent, as modified by analytical procedures and study of the business and industry, the lower will be the detection risk facing the auditor.

---

6   Under conditions of unreliable internal control, control risk is set equal to 100 percent.

Given the quantification of inherent risk and control risk, as explained in the preceding paragraphs, the above equation expresses detection risk as a percentage. For example, if control risk, inherent risk, and audit risk are set at 50, 70, and 5 percent, respectively, detection risk equals 14 percent. Table 9.8 displays detection risk percentages given various combinations of control risk and inherent risk, and assumes an overall audit risk of 5 percent.[7]

Detection risk is inversely related to the extent of substantive audit procedures to be applied to a given transaction cycle subset. A low detection risk, based on weak internal control policies and procedures and high inherent risk, requires extended substantive testing in order to minimize the risk of accepting a book value that is materially misstated. The following relationships exist between the level of detection risk and the quantity of evidence to be gathered and examined by the auditor in evaluating management's assertions:

Detection Risk	*Quantity of Evidence*
High	Minimal
Moderate	Moderate
Low	Substantial

Detection risk, as just quantified, is used in Chapter 10 as input in calculating the sample size for substantive testing. A significant advantage of quantifying inherent risk, control risk, and detection risk is that quantification provides a concrete link between audit planning and the design of substantive audit programs. Risk quantification does *not* replace audit judgment, but it promotes greater consistency in the application of professional judgment.

TABLE 9.8

Table for Determining Detection Risk (5 Percent Audit Risk Assumed)

Upper Occurrence Limit	Internal Control Evaluation	Control Risk (%)	Inherent Risk (%)				
			10%	30%	50%	70%	100%
≤ 1	Excellent	10	*	*	*	71	50
> 1 to ≤ 3%	Good	30	*	55	33	24	16
> 3 to ≤ 5%	Fair	50	*	33	20	14	10
> 5 to ≤ 7%	Poor	70	71	24	14	10	7
> 7%	Unreliable	100	50	16	10	7	5

*The allowable level of audit risk of 5 percent exceeds the product of *CR* and *IR*; thus, the planned substantive test of details may not be necessary.
Source: Adapted from SAS No. 39.

7   Recall from Chapter 5 that overall audit risk should generally be set ≤10 percent, inasmuch as it forms the basis for the audit opinion.

EXTENDED EXAMPLE

An example is presented here in order to further illustrate the concepts just discussed and to determine how the assessment of both inherent risk and control risk serves as input to the design of substantive audit procedures. Performance of tests of controls within the sales order and invoicing segment of the revenue cycle is used as a basis for the illustration.

Hotsaws, Inc., manufactures chain saws and space heaters. The products are sold directly to large retailers and wholesale hardware distributors. A staff of 40 sales representatives markets the units and submits orders to the home office. A prenumbered sales invoice is prepared after each order has been examined for correctness of prices, approval of customer credit, and availability of stock. One of the staff auditors for Hawkins, CPAs, Hotsaws' independent auditors, prepared the flowchart depicted in Exhibit 9.3. Based on the flowchart and discussions with the personnel involved in the sales order, shipping, and billing process, Gerald Kolb, the in-charge senior auditor for the Hotsaws' engagement, arrived at the following conclusions regarding financial control weaknesses and possible errors resulting from the weaknesses:

1. Customers are invoiced before billing is notified of shipment. This control weakness could result in customers being billed for goods not received. Moreover, fictitious sales may be recorded, given that evidence of shipment is not required for recording purposes.
2. Shipping does not compare the sales invoice and customer order with the goods received from stores. Customers could be shipped goods not ordered.
3. Accounts receivable does not review and compare documents before posting customers' accounts. Therefore, the following errors might occur that otherwise would have been detected by review and comparison:
   a. Quantities and/or types of goods appearing on the customer order may not agree with the sales invoice or bill of lading;
   b. Extensions and/or footings on the sales invoice may be in error;
   c. Shipping mode or terms may not agree with customer specifications; and
   d. Credit and discount terms may be in violation of company policy.

Given these weaknesses and the high probability of resulting errors, Kolb tentatively plans to reduce his assessment of control risk relative to billing and shipping only slightly below the maximum level. He also decides to apply attribute sampling methods for the purpose of testing the controls for effectiveness. The tests of controls should either add further support to the preliminary assessment or provide a basis for further modification of assessed control risk.

Kolb identifies the sampling unit for control testing purposes as the population of 10,000 prenumbered sales invoices processed during the fiscal year and decides to sample the invoices for the following attributes:

1. Sales invoice is accompanied by a bill of lading evidencing shipment;
2. Goods per invoice agree with bill of lading as to type and quantity;
3. Prices appearing on sales invoice agree with master price list;
4. Evidence of credit approval appears on face of invoice;
5. Proper sales accounts have been credited;
6. Extensions and footings on face of invoice are correct;
7. Credit and discount terms are in accordance with company policy; and
8. Goods per invoice agree with customer order as to type and quantity.

EXHIBIT 9.3

Hotsaws, Inc., Customer Order, Shipping, and Billing Flowchart

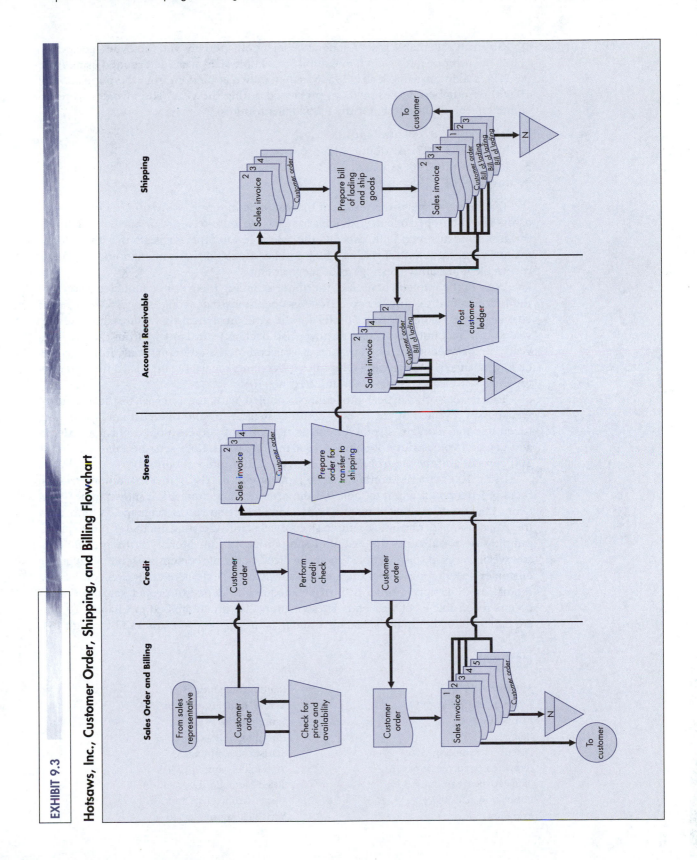

Given an acceptable risk of underassessment of 5 percent and the expected and tolerable occurrence rates shown in Exhibit 9.4, sample sizes were determined using Table 9.3. The maximum sample size, 195, was then drawn at random from the population of 10,000 prenumbered sales invoices processed during the year. The invoices were examined in the order drawn for the following attributes:

1. Invoices 1–78: All attributes;
2. Invoices 79–127: Attributes 1, 2, 3, 6, 7, and 8;
3. Invoices 128–146: Attributes 1, 2, 6, and 8; and
4. Invoices 147–195: Attribute 1.

Exhibit 9.5 displays the results of the sampling in terms of the number of detected errors and the upper occurrence limit for each attribute tested. For attributes 2 and 8, the upper occurrence limit exceeds the tolerable rate; this suggests that the auditor maintain assessed control risk at a high level and extend the examination of accounts receivable (substantive testing) as of the year end.

Prior to the implementation of the above sampling plan, Kolb conducted a study of the business and discovered no change in operations that would suggest a significant change in the volume or mix of sales for the year. Analytical procedures, however, revealed that accounts receivable turnover had declined substantially from the previous year. The balance in trade receivables at year end increased dramatically from the preceding balance sheet date, and days' sales in accounts receivable increased from 30 days to 60 days (Hotsaws' credit terms are 2/10; net 30).

The results of analytical procedures, coupled with the internal financial control weaknesses revealed by the tests of controls, suggest to Kolb that customers' accounts receivable may contain disputed items in the form of goods shipped but not ordered and goods invoiced but not shipped. For these reasons, Kolb sets the inherent risk at 100 percent and the control risk at 70 percent (poor internal control).

Using 100 percent inherent risk, 70 percent control risk, and a risk of underassessment of 5 percent as input to Table 9.8, the resulting detection risk is shown to be 7 percent. Chapter 10 will demonstrate how a low detection risk percentage, as input into the equation for determining sample size for substantive testing, increases the required sample size, and thereby the extent of substantive testing. Moreover, the specific control weaknesses in this example (goods invoiced not in agreement with bill of lading or customer order) suggest that the nature, as well as the extent, of audit procedures may require modification in order to provide adequate evidence of proper valuation of accounts receivable as of year end. These matters also are addressed in Chapter 10, and are explored further in the substantive audit testing chapters (Chapters 11 through 13).

KEY TERMS

EXHIBIT 9.4

Attribute Sampling Plan Worksheet 1

Hotsaws, Inc.
Sales Orders and Invoicing
12/31/01

Index: S.1
Prepared by: LFK
Date: 9/3/01
Reviewed by: SEL
Date: 9/15/01

Attribute Tested	Risk of Under-assessment (%)	Expected Occurrence Rate (%)	Tolerable Occurrence Rate (%)	Precision (%)	Sample Size	Number of Detected Errors	Upper Occurrence Limit (%)
1. Goods were shipped	5	3	6	3	195		
2. Goods agree with bill of lading as to type and quantity	5	4	8	4	146		
3. Invoice price agrees with master price list	5	2	6	4	127		
4. Credit approval noted on face of invoice	5	1	6	5	78		
5. Proper sales account(s) credited	5	1	6	5	78		
6. Correctness of extensions and footings on face of invoice	5	4	8	4	146		
7. Credit and discount terms agree with company policy	5	2	6	4	127		
8. Goods agree with customer order as to type and quantity	5	4	8	4	146		

EXHIBIT 9.5

Attribute Sampling Plan Worksheet 2

Hotsaws, Inc.
Sales Orders and Invoicing
12/31/01

Index: S.1
Prepared by: LFK
Date: 9/3/01
Reviewed by: SEL
Date: 9/15/01

Attribute Tested	Risk of Under-assessment (%)	Expected Occurrence Rate (%)	Tolerable Occurrence Rate (%)	Precision (%)	Sample Size	Number of Detected Errors	Upper Occurrence Limit (%)
1. Goods were shipped	5	3	6	3	195	5	5
2. Goods agree with bill of lading as to type and quantity	5	4	8	4	146	9	10
3. Invoice price agrees with master price list	5	2	6	4	127	3	6
4. Credit approval noted on face of invoice	5	1	6	5	78	1	6
5. Proper sales account(s) credited	5	1	6	5	78	0	4
6. Correctness of extensions and footings on face of invoice	5	4	8	4	146	1	3
7. Credit and discount terms agree with company policy	5	2	6	4	127	2	5
8. Goods agree with customer order as to type and quantity	5	4	8	4	146	10	11

COMPUTER AUDIT PRACTICE CASE

Biltrite Bicycles, Inc.

Module III of the Biltrite audit practice case (in the appendix following Chapter 16) contains an exercise requiring the application of attribute sampling to the sales processing system. This exercise may be completed at this time.

REVIEW QUESTIONS

1. In what ways can sampling assist the auditor in performing tests of a client's internal control policies and procedures?

2. Differentiate between statistical sampling and nonstatistical sampling.

3. Differentiate between attribute sampling and variables sampling.

4. Define *expected occurrence rate* and *tolerable occurrence rate*, explaining how they are set and how they affect sample size.

5. Why is the risk of underassessment usually set at ≤ 10 percent?

6. What is meant by random selection of samples?

7. How does systematic sampling result in random selection?

8. Why are sample sizes not necessarily the same for all attributes tested in a sampling plan?

9. Define *upper occurrence limit*.

10. How does the relationship between the tolerable occurrence rate and the upper occurrence limit affect the auditor's decision concerning control risk assessment?

11. Name and define the three factors comprising overall audit risk.

12. Which of the three risk factors is usually set at 100 percent, and how might it be reduced below 100 percent?

13. How does risk quantification serve as a link between audit planning and the design of substantive audit procedures?

14. Define *sampling risk*. How can the auditor control sampling risk?

MULTIPLE CHOICE QUESTIONS FROM PAST CPA AND CIA EXAMS

1. To determine the sample size for a test of controls, an auditor should consider the tolerable occurrence rate, the allowable risk of assessing control risk too low, and the
   a. Expected occurrence rate.
   b. Upper precision limit.
   c. Risk of incorrect acceptance.
   d. Risk of incorrect rejection.

2. Which of the following combinations results in a decrease in sample size in a sample for attributes?

	Risk of assessing control risk too low	Tolerable rate	Expected population error rate
a.	Increase	Decrease	Increase
b.	Decrease	Increase	Decrease
c.	Increase	Increase	Decrease
d.	Increase	Increase	Increase

3. Which of the following models expresses the general relationship of risks associated with the auditor's assessment of control risk (*CR*), the application of analytical procedures and other relevant substantive tests (*IR*), and overall audit risk (*AR*), that would lead the auditor to conclude that additional substantive tests of details of an account balance are not necessary?

	IR	CR	AR
a.	20%	40%	10%
b.	20%	60%	5%
c.	10%	70%	4.5%
d.	30%	40%	5.5%

Questions 4 and 5 are based on the following:

An auditor desired to test credit approval on 10,000 sales invoices processed during the year. The auditor designed a statistical sample that would provide a 1 percent risk of assessing control risk too low (99 percent confidence) that not more than 7 percent of the sales invoices lacked approval. The auditor estimated from previous experience that about $2\frac{1}{2}$ percent of the sales invoices lacked approval. A sample of 200 invoices was examined and 7 of them were lacking approval. The auditor then determined the upper occurrence limit to be 8 percent.

4. In the evaluation of this sample, the auditor decided to increase the level of the preliminary assessment of control risk because the
   a. Tolerable rate (7%) was less than the achieved upper occurrence limit (8%).
   b. Expected occurrence rate (7%) was more than the percentage of errors in the sample ($3\frac{1}{2}$%).
   c. Achieved upper occurrence limit (8%) was more than the percentage of errors in the sample ($3\frac{1}{2}$%).
   d. Expected occurrence rate ($2\frac{1}{2}$%) was less than the tolerable rate (7%).

5. The allowance for sampling risk (precision) was
   a. $5\frac{1}{2}$ percent.
   b. $4\frac{1}{2}$ percent.
   c. $3\frac{1}{2}$ percent
   d. 1 percent.

6. An auditor who uses statistical sampling for attributes in testing internal controls should increase the assessed level of control risk when the
   a. Sample occurrence rate is less than the expected occurrence rate used in planning the sample.
   b. Tolerable rate less the allowance for sampling risk exceeds the sample occurrence rate.
   c. Sample occurrence rate plus the allowance for sampling risk exceeds the tolerable rate.
   d. Sample occurrence rate plus the allowance for sampling risk equals the tolerable rate.

7. What is an auditor's evaluation of a statistical sample for attributes when a test of 100 documents results in 4 errors if the tolerable rate is 5 percent, the expected occurrence rate is 3 percent, and the allowance for sampling risk is 2 percent?
   a. Accept the sample results as support for lowering the assessed level of control risk because the tolerable rate less the allowance for sampling risk equals the expected occurrence rate.
   b. Do not decrease the assessed level of control risk because the sample occurrence rate plus the allowance for sampling risk exceeds the tolerable rate.
   c. Do not decrease the assessed level of control risk because the tolerable rate plus the allowance for sampling risk exceeds the expected occurrence rate.
   d. Accept the sample results as support for lowering the assessed level of control risk because the sample occurrence rate plus the allowance for sampling risk exceeds the tolerable rate.

8. An auditor plans to examine a sample of 20 checks for countersignatures as prescribed by the client's internal control procedures. One of the checks in the chosen sample of 20 cannot be found. The auditor should consider the reasons for this limitation and
   a. Evaluate the results as if the sample size had been 19.
   b. Treat the missing check as an error for the purpose of evaluating the sample.
   c. Treat the missing check in the same manner as the majority of the other 19 checks, that is, countersigned or not.
   d. Choose another check to replace the missing check in the sample.

9. Which of the following controls would be most effective in assuring that recorded purchases are free of material errors?
   a. The receiving department compares the quantity ordered on purchase orders with the quantity received on receiving reports.
   b. An employee who is independent of the receiving department compares vendors' invoices with purchase orders.
   c. Receiving reports require the signature of the individual who authorized the purchase.
   d. Purchase orders, receiving reports, and vendors' invoices are independently matched in preparing vouchers.

10. To determine whether accounts payable are complete, an auditor performs a test to verify that all merchandise received is recorded. The population of documents for this test consists of all
   a. Vendors' invoices.
   b. Purchase orders.
   c. Receiving reports.
   d. Canceled checks.

11. The sampling unit in a test of controls pertaining to the existence of payroll transactions ordinarily is a(n)
   a. Clock card or time ticket.
   b. Employee Form W-2.
   c. Employee personnel record.
   d. Payroll register entry.

12. Samples to test internal control procedures are intended to provide a basis for an auditor to conclude whether
   a. The control procedures are operating effectively.
   b. The financial statements are materially misstated.

c. The risk of incorrect acceptance is too high.

d. Materiality for planning purposes is at a sufficiently low level.

13. The following table depicts the auditor's estimated upper occurrence limit compared with the tolerable rate, and also depicts the true population occurrence rate compared with the tolerable rate.

	True state of population	
Auditor's estimate based on sample results	Upper occurrence limit is less than tolerable rate	Upper occurrence limit exceeds tolerable rate
Upper occurrence limit is less than tolerable rate	I.	III.
Upper occurrence limit exceeds tolerable rate	II.	IV.

As a result of tests of controls, the auditor assesses control risk higher than necessary and thereby increases substantive testing. This is illustrated by situation

a. I.

b. II.

c. III.

d. IV.

14. Which of the following statements is correct concerning statistical sampling in tests of controls?

a. Deviations from control procedures at a given rate usually result in misstatements at a higher rate.

b. As the population size doubles, the sample size should also double.

c. The auditor does not consider the qualitative aspects of deviations.

d. There is an inverse relationship between the sample size and the tolerable occurrence rate.

15. What is an auditor's evaluation of a statistical sample for attributes when a test of 50 documents results in 3 deviations if the tolerable occurrence rate is 7 percent, the expected occurrence rate is 5 percent, and the allowance for sampling risk is 2 percent?

a. Modify the planned assessed level of control risk because the tolerable rate plus the allowance for sampling risk exceeds the expected occurrence rate.

b. Accept the sample results as support for the planned assessed level of control risk because the sample occurrence rate plus the allowance for sampling risk exceeds the tolerable rate.

c. Accept the sample results as support for the planned assessed level of control risk because the tolerable rate less the allowance for sampling risk equals the expected occurrence rate.

d. Modify the planned assessed level of control risk because the sample occurrence rate plus the allowance for sampling risk exceeds the tolerable rate.

16. An entity's internal control system requires for every check request that there be an approved voucher, supported by a prenumbered purchase order and a prenumbered receiving report. To determine whether checks are being issued for unauthorized expenditures, an auditor most likely would select items for testing from the population of all

a. Purchase orders.

b. Canceled checks.

c. Receiving reports.

d. Approved vouchers.

17. In planning a statistical sample for a test of controls, an auditor increased the expected occurrence rate from the prior year's rate because of the results of the prior year's tests of controls and the overall control environment. The auditor most likely would then increase the planned
    a. Tolerable rate.
    b. Allowance for sampling risk.
    c. Risk of assessing control risk too low.
    d. Sample size.

18. As a result of tests of controls, an auditor assessed control risk too low and decreased substantive testing. This assessment occurred because the true occurrence rate in the population was
    a. More than the risk of assessing control risk too low based on the auditor's sample.
    b. More than the occurrence rate in the auditor's sample.
    c. Less than the risk of assessing control risk too low based on the auditor's sample.
    d. Less than the occurrence rate in the auditor's sample.

19. In performing tests of controls over authorization of cash disbursements, which of the following statistical sampling methods would be most appropriate?
    a. Variables
    b. Stratified
    c. Ratio
    d. Attributes

20. As a result of sampling procedures applied as tests of controls, an auditor incorrectly assesses control risk lower than appropriate. The most likely explanation for this situation is that
    a. The occurrence rates of both the auditor's sample and the population exceed the tolerable rate.
    b. The occurrence rates of both the auditor's sample and the population is less than the tolerable rate.
    c. The occurrence rate in the auditor's sample is less than the tolerable rate, but the occurrence rate in the population exceeds the tolerable rate.
    d. The occurrence rate in the auditor's sample exceeds the tolerable rate, but the occurrence rate in the population is less than the tolerable rate.

ESSAY QUESTIONS AND PROBLEMS

9.1   a. Explain how each of the following factors affects sample size for attribute sampling purposes.
        1. Population size
        2. Expected occurrence rate
        3. Tolerable occurrence rate
        4. Acceptable level of risk of underassessment
    b. Explain how the auditor determines factors (2), (3), and (4).

9.2   Although statistical sampling involves the application of mathematical techniques in determining sample size and evaluating sample results, it does not replace audit judgment.

   Required:
   Assuming that you are examining the revenue cycle for control risk assessment purposes and that your client is a wholesale distributor of lumber products, discuss how audit judgment enters into each of the following determinations.

a. Allowable selling price deviations from master price lists
b. Acceptable risk of underassessment of control risk relative to the processing of sales transactions
c. Determining the materiality of identified control weaknesses

9.3   For each of the following attributes, identify the sampling unit and carefully define what constitutes an error.

a. Approval of purchase invoices for payment
b. Correctness of account distributions (debits and credits)
c. Receiving report attached to paid vouchers
d. Correctness of labor rates used in computing payroll
e. Agreement of hours on time cards with payroll summary
f. Approval of customer credit
g. Agreement of sales prices with master price list
h. Shipping order attached to sales invoice

9.4   a. Attribute sampling is appropriate for testing certain types of controls to assess control risk, but is not appropriate for testing others. Explain why.
b. Of the following controls, indicate those that might be tested by the application of attribute sampling methods. For those controls *not* amenable to attribute sampling, state the control objective for each and identify alternative means of testing for effectiveness.
   1. Correctness of pay rates and hours used in preparing the payroll summary
   2. Competence of the EDP manager
   3. Preventing the systems analyst from accessing programs and updating transaction files
   4. Correctness of debits resulting from the processing of vendors' invoices
   5. Monthly reconciliation of all bank accounts
   6. Completeness of receiving reports for incoming goods
   7. Prenumbering of sales invoices and periodic checks as to numeric sequence
   8. Retention of voided documents
   9. Agreement of selling prices appearing on customer invoices with company price lists
   10. Ability of the cashier to access cash receipts records and customer accounts

9.5   Sampling can assist the auditor in various ways during the examination of documentary evidence for tests of internal controls. Using a payroll application as an example, assume that you are interested in evaluating internal control policies and procedures relative to the processing of a client's hourly payroll. Specifically, you wish to determine the correctness of rates and hours and the genuineness of listed employees. Discuss how attribute sampling might assist you in the following phases of your tests of payroll controls.

a. Determining the number of payroll transactions to test
b. Selecting the transactions for testing
c. Evaluating the results of the payroll test
d. Assessing audit risk associated with the payroll cycle

9.6   Prior to performing substantive tests for Dura, Inc., a mid-size manufacturer of specialty steel, Marilyn Glass and her audit team conducted a study of the business and industry, applied analytical procedures, and obtained an initial understanding of Dura's internal control policies and procedures. Profits in the industry had declined during 2002. Countering the pattern, Dura reported a net profit (unaudited) for 2002. The remaining companies in the industry reported losses ranging from minimal to substantial. One of the companies, Gemsteel, Inc., was in receivership by year end. Analytical procedures revealed higher-than-normal sales in August, the last month of Dura's fiscal year. In addition, the gross profit rate increased from 27 percent in 2001 to 38 percent in 2002. The preliminary study of internal control in the area of sales and shipments led the auditors to conclude that the controls were generally adequate to prevent unauthorized shipments or billings and, therefore, should be tested further for possible lowering of the assessed control risk.

Required:
a. Discuss the audit risk implications of the Dura engagement.
b. How does the possibility of management override affect the auditor's determination of acceptable detection risk?
c. How would you deal with inherent risk in the present circumstances?
d. In what way(s) might statistical sampling assist Glass and her audit team in quantifying the various audit risk factors confronting them in the Dura engagement?

9.7   Brown, a CPA, is planning to use attribute sampling in order to determine whether the assessed level of control risk can be lowered relative to sales processing. Brown has begun to develop an outline of the main steps in the sampling plan as follows:

1. State the objective(s) of the audit test (e.g., to test the effectiveness of internal control policies and procedures relative to sales processing).
2. Define the population.
3. Define the sampling unit (e.g., client copies of sales invoices).

Required:
a. What are the remaining steps in the above outline that Brown should include in the statistical test of sales invoices? Do not present a detailed analysis of tasks that must be performed to carry out the objectives of each step. Parenthetical examples need not be provided.
b. How does statistical methodology help the auditor to develop a satisfactory sampling plan?
(AICPA adapted)

9.8   The use of statistical sampling techniques in an examination of financial statements does *not* eliminate judgmental decisions.

Required:
a. Identify and explain four areas where a CPA may exercise judgment in planning a statistical sampling test.
b. Assume that a CPA's sample shows an unacceptable error rate. Describe the various actions that she or he may take based on this finding.
c. A sample of 160 accounts payable vouchers is to be selected from a population of 9,000. The vouchers are numbered consecutively from 31211 to 40210 and are listed, 30 to a page, in the voucher register. Describe two different techniques for selecting a random sample of vouchers for review.
(AICPA adapted)

9.9   The following factors are often identified in comparing statistical and nonstatistical sampling:

1. Statistical sampling is a mathematical approach to inference, whereas nonstatistical sampling is a more subjective approach to inference.

2. Statistical sampling is a more consistent approach to sampling.
3. Statistical sampling is a more effective means than nonstatistical sampling for quantifying audit risk.

Required:
a. Explain each of the above statements, using examples as appropriate.
b. Notwithstanding the advantages of statistical sampling, under what circumstances might nonstatistical sampling be appropriate?

9.10   Craburn, Inc., an audit client of Randy Shay, CPA, manufactures and sells window coverings, carpeting, and floor tile. Products are sold directly to retailers, including some rather large chain outlets. All sales are on account and invoices are payable by the 10th of the month following the sale. A 2 percent cash discount is available for invoices paid within 15 days of the invoice date.

Shay wishes to test the sales order, invoice, and shipping procedures for control effectiveness as part of his assessment of control risk within the revenue cycle. To this end, he elects to apply attribute sampling to the population of 70,000 prenumbered sales invoices processed during 2002. Having decided on an acceptable risk of underassessment of 5 percent, Shay plans to test for the following attributes:

1. Proper documentation of sales, as evidenced by existence of prenumbered and approved sales order, sales invoice, and shipping order;
2. Agreement of quantity and type of goods shipped on sales invoice and shipping order;
3. Agreement of price on sales invoice with company price lists;
4. Evidence of proper credit approval;
5. Correctness of credits to the various revenue accounts; and
6. Correctness of extensions and footings on face of invoice.

Based on last year's audit and this year's initial understanding of Craburn's internal control, Shay believes the sales invoices to contain a 2 percent error rate with respect to attributes 1, 3, 5, and 6; and a 1 percent error rate as to attributes 2 and 4. He is willing to accept a tolerable occurrence rate of 5 percent as a condition for lowering his assessment of control risk relative to the sales processing system.

Required:
a. Determine the sample size.
b. Discuss the audit risk factors and the audit judgment process leading to the determination of sample size in the present case. In other words, what prompted Shay to decide on the values chosen as determinants of sample size?
c. Develop a sampling plan worksheet similar to Exhibit 9.5.
d. Assume that the following errors were discovered in examining the sample:

Attribute	Errors
1	6
2	3
3	2
4	1
5	4
6	1

Calculate the upper occurrence limit and evaluate the sample results.
e. What impact might the evaluation have on substantive audit testing?

9.11   Hanks, a CPA, was engaged to audit Deel Company's financial statements for the year ended September 30, 2002. After obtaining an understanding of Deel's internal control, Hanks decided to obtain evidential matter about the effectiveness of both the design and operation of the policies and procedures that might support a low assessed level of control risk concerning Deel's shipping and billing functions. During prior years' audits Hanks had used nonstatistical sampling, but for the current year he used a statistical sample in the tests of controls, to eliminate the need for judgment.

Hanks wanted to assess control risk at a low level, so a tolerable occurrence rate of 15 percent was established. To estimate the population occurrence rate and the achieved upper occurrence limit, Hanks decided to apply a discovery sampling technique of attribute sampling that would use a population expected occurrence rate of 6 percent for the 18,000 shipping documents, and decided to defer consideration of risk of underassessment of control risk until evaluating the sample results. Hanks used the tolerable rate, the population size, and the expected population occurrence rate to determine that a sample size of 140 would be sufficient. When it was subsequently determined that the actual population was about 21,000 shipping documents, Hanks increased the sample size to 160.

Hanks' objective was to ascertain whether Deel's shipments had been properly billed. He took a sample of 160 invoices by selecting the first 40 invoices from the first month of each quarter. Hanks then compared the invoices to the corresponding prenumbered shipping documents.

When he tested the sample, 12 errors were discovered. Additionally, one shipment that should have been billed at $10,443 was actually billed at $10,434. Hanks considered this $9 to be immaterial and did not count it as an error.

In evaluating the sample results, Hanks made the initial determination that a 5 percent risk of underassessment was desired and, using the appropriate statistical sampling table, determined that for 12 observed errors from a sample size of 160, the achieved upper occurrence limit was 10 percent. Hanks then calculated the allowance for sampling risk to be 1.5 percent, the difference between the actual sample occurrence rate (7.5%) and the expected occurrence rate (6%). Hanks reasoned that the actual sample occurrence rate (7.5%) plus the allowance for sampling risk (1.5%) was less than the achieved upper occurrence limit (10%); therefore, the sample supported a low level of control risk.

Required:
Describe each incorrect assumption, inaccurate statement, and inappropriate application of attribute sampling in Hanks' procedures. (AICPA adapted)

9.12   Justgross, Inc., is a tax preparation service with offices in 20 cities. The company's staff consists of 80 full-time salaried employees and approximately 700 part-time hourly employees. The hourly employees are hired for the period from January through April. Rates for these employees vary by level and experience and range from $6.75 to $10.75 per hour. Justgross pays overtime for hours worked in excess of 40 in a single week. The overtime rate is $1^1/_2$ times the regular rate. Time cards are completed manually and approved by the office manager at the end of each working day. The time cards are forwarded to corporate headquarters each week, where the payroll is processed by computer.

Data entry operators, also part-time employees, enter employee numbers and hours into the computer. Pay rate and withholding data are entered once for each new employee on the basis of withholding certificates (W-4s). Changes in hourly rates are submitted by the local office manager and approved by the corporate controller. Upon entry of employee number and hours, the computer calculates regular pay, overtime pay, gross pay, withholdings, and net pay. Computer output consists of payroll checks and a printed payroll summary.

Lee Merriweather, Justgross's independent auditor for the past two years, believes that internal controls over payroll accuracy are reliable, and he wishes to test them for operating effectiveness as a basis for reducing the assessed level of control risk below maximum. He decides to use attribute sampling in conducting this set of tests, and wishes to concentrate on the part-time payroll. For the fiscal year ended May 31, 2002, the year under audit, Merriweather will test the payroll controls for the period January through April. This period contains sixteen payrolls with a total of 13,000 entries on the sixteen payroll summary printouts (one printout for each weekly pay period).

Required:

a. What are the sampling objectives for purposes of this exercise? Given your stated objectives, what is the most logical sampling unit? What is the population?
b. Assume that Merriweather identifies the following attributes to be tested:

1. Proper employee number
2. Approval of hours by office manager
3. Hours per time card in agreement with payroll summary
4. Proper pay rates
5. Hours times pay rate, including overtime, correctly calculated
6. Correctness of withholding calculations
7. Gross pay minus withholdings equal to net pay

The expected occurrence rate is 1 percent for each of the attributes. The tolerable occurrence rate for attributes (3), (4), and (5) is 4 percent; for attributes (6) and (7) the tolerable rate is 5 percent; and for attributes (1) and (2) the tolerable rate is 6 percent. If Merriweather specifies a 10 percent risk of underassessment of control risk, what is the appropriate sample size for each attribute?

c. What method should Merriweather use to draw the samples? How should he proceed through the samples?
d. Assume that Merriweather discovered the following errors in examining the sample items.

Error	Number of incidents
1. Office manager approval lacking	2
2. Withholdings understated	1
3. Pay rate too high	5

Evaluate the sample results. Assume that no other errors were discovered. (In using the sampling results evaluation tables, select the sample size in the table that most nearly approximates your sample size.)

9.13   German and French, the independent auditors for Clapons Plumbing Supply, are conducting a test of control procedures over sales processing. During the year to date (1/1/02 to 6/30/02), Clapons issued 22,600 prenumbered sales invoices ranging in number from 12664 to 35263. Each sales invoice is accompanied by a combination shipping order/bill of lading form signed by the carrier. These forms are also prenumbered and range from 13662 to 36678. The warehouse manager has informed Megan Will, the in-charge auditor assigned to the Clapons' audit, that shipping orders are frequently voided, and this explains the overusage of these forms relative to sales invoice forms.

Based on her initial understanding of Clapons' internal control, Will believes that controls over sales processing, billing, and collection are adequate to permit reducing the assessed level of control risk below the maximum level, but she is not willing to reduce her assessment without testing the controls for operating effectiveness. Specifically, she is concerned with the following attributes related to sales to customers:

1. Proper approval of customer credit prior to shipment
2. A sales invoice exists for every shipment
3. The bill of lading was signed by the carrier
4. Prices on the invoice are in accordance with official price lists
5. The sale was properly recorded and posted to the customer's account

Will asks you to develop and implement a sampling plan for determining whether the assessed level of control risk relating to sales can be reduced below maximum. Given an acceptable risk of underassessment of 5 percent, you have set the following percentages for expected occurrence rate and tolerable occurrence rate:

Attribute Number	Expected Occurrence Rate (%)	Tolerable Rate (%)
1	0.75	3.00
2	0.50	3.00
3	0.75	3.00
4	0.75	3.00
5	0.50	3.00

Required:
a. What is the population and sampling unit for purposes of your sampling plan? (*Hint:* It is either the sales invoice or the shipping order/bill of lading.) Justify your answer.
b. Calculate the sample size for each of the attributes.
c. How would you draw the sample to conform to random sampling rules?
d. Assuming the following discovered errors, calculate the upper occurrence limit. (In using the sample results evaluation tables, select the sample size that most nearly approximates your sample size.)

Attribute Number	Errors
1	0
2	8
3	0
4	2
5	0

e. To what extent, if any, can you advise Will relative to reducing the assessed level of control risk in the area of sales processing?

9.14   Sampling for attributes is often used to allow an auditor to reach a conclusion concerning a rate of occurrence in a population. A common use in auditing is to test the rate of deviation from a prescribed internal control procedure to determine whether the planned assessed level of control risk is appropriate.

Required:
a. When an auditor samples for attributes, identify the factors that should influence the auditor's judgment concerning the determination of:
   1. Acceptable level of risk of assessing control risk too low;
   2. Tolerable occurrence rate; and
   3. Expected occurrence rate.

b. State the effect on sample size of an increase in each of the following factors, assuming all other factors are held constant:
1. Acceptable level of the risk of assessing control risk too low;
2. Tolerable occurrence rate; and
3. Expected occurrence rate.
c. Evaluate the sample results of a test for attributes if authorizations are found to be missing on 10 check requests out of a sample of 120 tested. The population consists of 5,000 check requests, the tolerable occurrence rate is 8 percent, and the acceptable level of risk of assessing control risk too low is considered to be 5 percent.
d. How may the use of statistical sampling assist the auditor in evaluating the sample results described in (c) above?

(AICPA adapted)

chapter 10

biltrite

l e a r n i n g   o b j e c t i v e s

After reading this chapter, you should be able to

1 Determine the appropriate sampling method to apply under varying circumstances.

2 Apply any of the three sampling methods—mean per unit, difference estimation, and probability-proportional-to-size—discussed in the chapter.

3 Evaluate sample results and draw conclusions:

a Accept the book value as fairly representative of the true population value, given a tolerable level of risk of incorrect acceptance (beta risk); or

b Reject the book value as being materially misstated, given a tolerable level of risk of incorrect rejection (alpha risk).

OVERVIEW

Chapter 10 discusses the auditor's use of statistical sampling for substantive testing purposes. Figure 10.1 identifies the chapter subject matter within the framework of the overall audit process.

Three variations of statistical sampling are commonly used by auditors for substantive audit testing. Two of these, mean per unit and difference estimation sampling, are discussed in the

FIGURE 10.1

The Audit Process

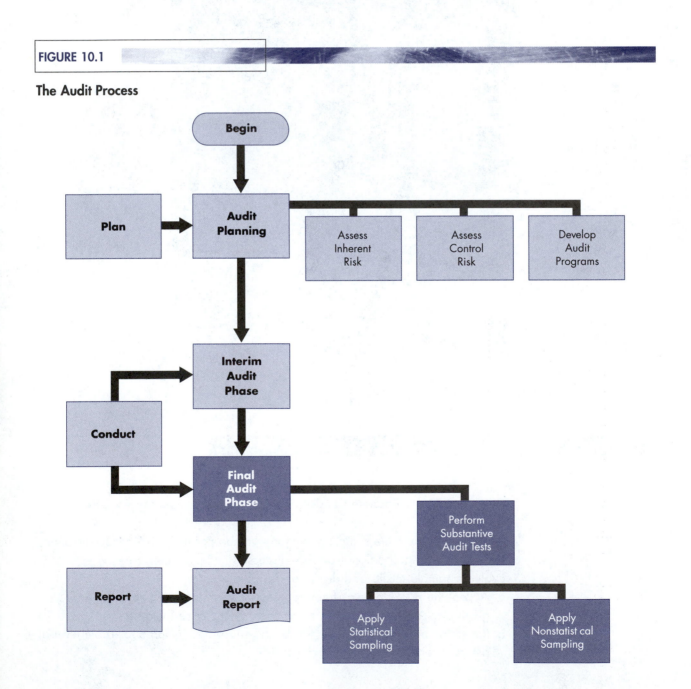

first part of this chapter; the third, probability-proportional-to-size sampling, is covered in the last part.

Mean per unit, often referred to as classical variables sampling, calculates a mean value for a sample and extends this value to the population. The population, for substantive testing purposes, might consist of inventories, accounts receivable, plant asset additions, or some other dollar amount for transactions or balances. Difference estimation, a variation of mean per unit, compares audited value and book value for a sample and imputes the dollar difference to the population. It is usually more cost effective than mean per unit, since the sample sizes are smaller.

Probability-proportional-to-size (PPS) sampling, a variation of attribute sampling, calculates an upper error limit (expressed in dollars rather than as a percentage) and compares it with the tolerable error as set by the auditor. PPS sampling is more cost effective than either mean per unit or difference estimation sampling, and therefore should be used where conditions warrant.

INTRODUCTION

Attribute sampling for performing tests of controls was examined in Chapter 9 as a means of assisting the auditor in estimating error *percentages* and assessing control risk. Chapter 10 explores the application of statistical sampling for substantive testing purposes, and concentrates on *dollar* estimates rather than percentages.

In performing substantive tests, the auditor's goal is to determine whether the financial data appearing in the client's general ledger are presented fairly in accordance with GAAP. To this end, the auditor examines, confirms, calculates, and inquires. Statistical sampling techniques assist the auditor by providing a consistent approach to judging the fairness of the dollar representations.

The two methods most commonly used by auditors in applying sampling for substantive testing purposes are *variables sampling* and *probability-proportional-to-size sampling*. Classical **variables sampling** is used to estimate the dollar amount of transactions or account balances through examination of a sample and extending the results to the population. It is commonly applied to such balance sheet components as trade accounts receivable and inventories, given the large number of postings to these accounts. Variables sampling approaches are covered in the first part of this chapter. **Probability-proportional-to-size sampling (PPS)**, a variation of attribute sampling, is used to estimate the dollar amount of overstatement errors; it is discussed in the second part of the chapter.

APPROACHES TO VARIABLES SAMPLING

Two alternative approaches are available to the auditor in applying variables sampling—mean per unit and difference estimation. **Mean per unit (MPU)** consists of calculating the sample mean and multiplying by the number of items in the population in order to arrive at the audited value of the population. **Difference estimation** involves calculating the average difference between the audited value and the client's book value and multiplying by the number of items in the population. The result is the estimated total difference between the audited and book values. A positive value (AV > BV) represents an understated book value, while a negative value (AV < BV) is indicative of an overstated book value.

Difference estimation often results in smaller sample sizes than MPU and is more cost effective under those circumstances. These two variations of classical variables sampling are discussed in the following paragraphs.

MEAN PER UNIT (MPU)

In applying mean per unit sampling, the auditor must calculate sample size after giving due consideration to risk and materiality. Detection risk, an important ingredient in determining sample size for mean per unit sampling purposes, has been defined as the risk that material errors or fraud that are not prevented or detected by the client's internal control system will not be discovered by the auditor. It is a function of control risk, inherent risk, and overall audit risk; it was expressed in Chapter 9 by the following equation:

$$DR = \frac{AR}{CR \times IR}$$

where

AR = Audit risk
CR = Control risk
IR = Inherent risk

Detection risk is referred to as **beta risk** by statisticians. This is defined as the risk of incorrect acceptance. For auditing applications, this means incorrectly accepting a book value that is materially misstated. The opposite of beta risk is **alpha risk**, the risk of incorrect rejection (i.e., incorrectly rejecting a book value that is fairly stated). As described in Chapter 9, these two risks may be referred to collectively as **sampling risk**: the risk that the auditor's conclusions regarding a population are incorrect.

Beta and alpha risks, as related to substantive audit testing, may be represented in terms of classical hypothesis testing as follows:

	S_0	S_1
	B.V. Correct	*B.V. Materially Misstated*
H_0 Accept book value	X	beta risk
H_1 Reject book value	alpha risk	X

The null hypothesis (H_0) accepts the book value as being fairly stated, whereas the alternate hypothesis (H_1) rejects the book value as being materially misstated. If the null hypothesis is chosen and the book value is fairly stated (true state = S_0), a correct judgment has been made. If, on the other hand, the book value is materially misstated (S_1), an incorrect decision has been made. The risk of accepting the null hypothesis when the alternate state exists is the beta risk. The risk of accepting the alternate hypothesis (H_1) when the true state (S_0) exists is the alpha risk.

Recall from Chapter 9 that beta risk is equated with the risk of underassessing control risk and alpha risk is synonymous with overassessing control risk. In terms of audit effectiveness and audit efficiency, assessing control risk too low and/or assessing detection risk too high may affect **audit effectiveness** adversely by causing the auditor to gather insufficient evidence to support an audit opinion. The worst possible result occurs if the auditor renders an unqualified audit opinion on financial statements that are materially misstated. Conversely, assessing control risk too high and/or detection risk too low impacts **audit efficiency** if, as a result, the auditor gathers more evidence than is needed under the true circumstances. This adds unnecessary cost to the audit in terms of the time and effort expended in gathering and evaluating excessive amounts of evidence. These risk combinations can be summarized as follows:

	Lowers Audit Effectiveness	Lowers Audit Efficiency
Beta Risk:		
Assessing control risk too low	X	
Accepting a population that is materially in error	X	
Alpha Risk:		
Assessing control risk too high		X
Rejecting a population that is reasonably stated		X

This analysis demonstrates once again the importance of exercising care in assessing risk. One might note at this point that if the auditor is to err, a sacrifice of efficiency is less harmful than a sacrifice of effectiveness. In other words, too much evidence is preferable to insufficient evidence.

Calculating Sample Size

Both beta and alpha risks must be set by the auditor as a condition for determining sample size. As discussed in Chapter 9, beta risk (referred to as *detection risk* in that chapter) is a function of the auditor's study of the business, application of analytical procedures, and study and evaluation of internal control policies and procedures. It serves as the link between audit planning and substantive audit testing. Table 10.1 is a reproduction of Table 9.8, except for the substitution of the term *beta risk* for *detection risk*.

Alpha risk, the risk that the sample results will lead the auditor to conclude improperly that a materially correct book value is significantly in error, is a function of overall audit risk. Most auditors simply equate alpha risk with overall audit risk, setting it at ≤ 10 percent.

In addition to beta and alpha risks, the other factors influencing sample size for mean per unit variables sampling are as follows.

TABLE 10.1

Table for Determining Beta Risk (5 Percent Audit Risk Assumed)

Upper Occurrence Limit	Internal Control Evaluation	Control Risk (%)	Inherent Risk (%)				
			10%	30%	50%	70%	100%
$\leq 1\%$	Excellent	10	*	*	*	71	50
> 1 to $\leq 3\%$	Good	30	*	55	33	24	16
> 3 to $\leq 5\%$	Fair	50	*	33	20	14	10
> 5 to $\leq 7\%$	Poor	70	71	24	14	10	7
> 7%	Unreliable	100	50	16	10	7	5

*The allowable level of audit risk of 5 percent exceeds the product of *CR* and *IR*; thus, the planned substantive test of details may not be necessary.
Source: Adapted from SAS No. 39.

Population Size   Population size (e.g., the number of customer accounts in the accounts receivable subsidiary ledger, or the number of line items on inventory listings) has a positive influence on sample size; that is, the larger the population, the larger the sample size.

Standard Deviation   The **standard deviation** is a measure of population variability. More specifically, it is defined as the degree of variation of individual values about the population mean. As can be seen in Figure 10.2, the more narrowly dispersed the values in the population are, the smaller the standard deviation.

Like population size, the standard deviation positively influences sample size; that is, the greater the variation, the larger the sample size. The standard deviation of the sample may be expressed by the following equation:

$$ SD = \sqrt{\frac{\Sigma(\bar{x} - x_i)^2}{n-1}} $$

where

$\bar{x}$ = Mean value
x_i = Individual values
n = Sample size

FIGURE 10.2

Normal Probability Distribution with Varying Degrees of Standard Deviation

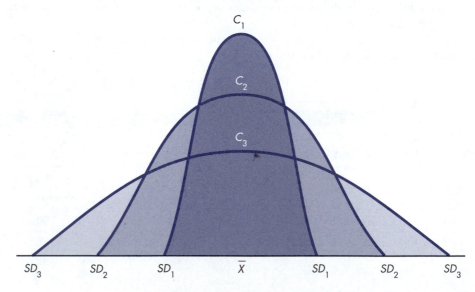

SD_1: Standard deviation for population represented by C_1 (curve 1).
SD_2: Standard deviation for population represented by C_2.
SD_3: Standard deviation for population represented by C_3.
$\bar{X}$: Population mean.

In Figure 10.2, C_3 (curve 3), which is flat and wide, denotes a large standard deviation, whereas C_1 (curve 1), which is high and narrow, indicates little variation about the mean. Variables sampling attempts to describe the population in terms of its mean and standard deviation.

Precision   **Precision** is defined as the range (plus or minus) within which the true answer most likely falls. It is set by the auditor as a function of materiality and those levels of beta and alpha risks deemed acceptable. Precision has a negative influence on sample size. The narrower the range of precision, the larger the sample size. A narrow precision range is associated with risk aversion and a conservative concept of materiality.

Reliability   Also referred to as *confidence level*, **reliability** is the likelihood that the sample range contains the true value. It is based on overall audit risk—that is, the degree of confidence the auditor wishes to place in the sampling results. As stated earlier, the overall audit risk and alpha risk are usually maintained at ≤ 10 percent. The **confidence level** is the complement of audit or alpha risk. An alpha risk of 5 percent, for example, is associated with a 95 percent confidence level. Like the population size and standard deviation, the confidence level has a positive influence on sample size; that is, the greater the degree of confidence set by the auditor, the larger the sample size.

To summarize, the parameters described above affect sample size as follows:

As these factors INCREASE	Sample Size INCREASES	Sample Size DECREASES
Population size	X	
Standard deviation	X	
Precision (narrowing)	X	
Reliability	X	
Materiality		X
Beta risk		X
Alpha risk		X

Equation for MPU Sample Size

Given the above sample size determinants, the following equation may be used to express sample size for MPU:

$$n = \left(\frac{N \times SD \times U_r}{A} \right)^2$$

where

N = Population size (number of customer accounts, number of inventory line items, etc.)

SD = Standard deviation (can be estimated by examining a **pilot sample** of 30 to 40 items at random or by using the book value and a computer program for calculating SD)

U_r = Reliability factor related to the confidence level selected. Referred to as coefficients of reliability, the factors most commonly used in auditing applications are as follows:

Reliability	Audit (Alpha) Risk	U_r Coefficient
.99	.01	2.58
.95	.05	1.96
.90	.10	1.65

The U_r factor may be understood most clearly as the number of standard deviations from the mean for a given confidence level (see Figure 10.3).

A = **Desired precision**, a function of audit judgment, based on materiality and acceptable risk levels. It may be expressed by the following equation:

$$A = M \left(\frac{1}{1 + \frac{Z_b}{Z_a/2}} \right)$$

where

M = Materiality expressed in dollars

Z_b = Z value corresponding to acceptable level of beta risk (see Table 10.2).

Z_a = Z value corresponding to acceptable level of alpha risk divided by 2 (see Table 10.2).

Example Illustrating Mean per Unit Sampling

The following example is used to illustrate the application of mean per unit sampling and to clarify further the equations just presented. In auditing the inventories of Xano, Inc., a toy manufacturer, John Halter, the in-charge senior auditor for Alright, CPAs, decides to apply MPU sampling in estimating the value of Xano's raw materials inventory. The physical inventory is taken by Xano and observed by Halter and his team of staff auditors. Several test counts are made, and Halter is satisfied with the physical inventory quantities appearing on the inventory tags.

FIGURE 10.3

Probability Distribution Showing the Relationship between Confidence Levels and U_r Factors

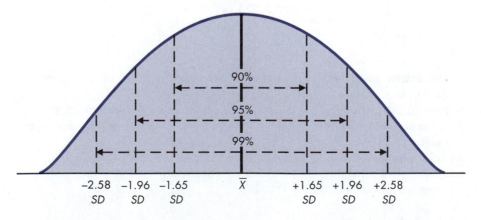

TABLE 10.2

Z Values Related to Alpha and Beta Risk

Alpha/2 or Beta (%)	Z Value	Alpha/2 or Beta (%)	Z Value	Alpha/2 or Beta (%)	Z Value
1.00	2.33	17.00	.96	34.00	.42
2.00	2.06	18.00	.92	35.00	.39
2.50	1.96	19.00	.88	36.00	.36
3.00	1.89	20.00	.85	37.00	.34
4.00	1.76	21.00	.81	38.00	.31
5.00	1.65	22.00	.78	39.00	.28
6.00	1.56	23.00	.74	40.00	.26
7.00	1.48	24.00	.71	41.00	.23
8.00	1.41	25.00	.68	42.00	.21
9.00	1.35	26.00	.65	43.00	.18
10.00	1.29	27.00	.62	44.00	.16
11.00	1.23	28.00	.59	45.00	.13
12.00	1.18	29.00	.56	46.00	.11
13.00	1.13	30.00	.53	47.00	.08
14.00	1.09	31.00	.50	48.00	.06
15.00	1.04	32.00	.47	49.00	.03
16.00	1.00	33.00	.44	50.00	.00

The quantities as evidenced by the tags are translated into a computer printout of the raw materials inventory. In addition to the quantities, the printout includes prices and extended (price × quantity) inventory costs. The costed inventory has been recorded by Xano's controller, Lonnie Mack, and posted to the general ledger. Perpetual records are not maintained for raw materials or finished goods.

In sampling terms, Halter wishes to estimate the value of the raw materials inventory by computing an average value for a sample and imputing this value to the population. The following values have been identified or set by Halter:

- *Population Size:* 20,000 line items on the computer printouts.
- *Book Value:* $20 million, as taken from the general ledger and also appearing as the total on the computer printout.
- *Materiality:* $1 million.
- *Alpha Risk and Audit Risk:* 5 percent (confidence level and the U_r factor are therefore 95 percent and 1.96, respectively).
- *Beta Risk:* 7 percent. Halter found internal control over the processing of raw materials purchases to be poor and, therefore, assesses control risk at 70 percent (see Table 10.1). Inherent risk = 100 percent.
- *Standard Deviation:* $370. This preliminary estimate of standard deviation was determined by examining a pilot sample of 40 line items, selected at random from the computer printout, and calculating the standard deviation.

Given these values, the sample size equation is as follows:

$$n = \left(\frac{20{,}000 \times \$370 \times 1.96}{\$569{,}768} \right)^2 = 648$$

The denominator, \$569,768, is calculated by using the following equation for precision:

$$A = \$1{,}000{,}000 \left(\frac{1}{1 + 1.48/1.96} \right) = \$569{,}768$$

The Z values were taken from Table 10.2.

Whenever the sample size equation produces a sample size ≥ 5 percent of the population size (N), the following **finite correction factor** should be applied:

$$n' = \frac{n}{1 + n/N}$$

where

n' = sample size adjusted for the finite correction factor.

The finite correction factor is necessary because the sample size equation, for purposes of simplicity, assumes sampling with replacement, and this produces larger sample sizes than more complex equations based on sampling without replacement. Because auditors do not replace an item in the population to avoid possible repeat selection after selecting it once, the finite adjustment is made to larger sample sizes to reduce them to acceptable amounts.

In the present example, 648 is less than 5 percent of 20,000, and the correction factor is not needed.

Drawing the Sample and Evaluating the Sample Results

Continuing with the example, 608 additional items need to be selected at random from the computer listings. The pilot sample, drawn for the purpose of estimating the standard deviation, may be considered part of the final sample. Assuming that Halter used a set of random number tables in drawing the pilot sample of 40, he will draw the remaining items by beginning in the random number table at the stopping point for the 40 and proceeding until 608 additional line items have been selected.

In practice, auditors often stratify populations for MPU sampling purposes, by examining 100 percent of the larger dollar value items and sampling the remainder. The purpose of **stratified sampling** is to permit the auditor to vary the intensity of examination for certain subsets of the population. In these cases the subsets are considered as two populations rather than one and are evaluated separately. For example, in the present case, assume that the book value of the total raw materials inventory was \$30 million and consisted of the following two subsets:

- 100 line items with a total book value of \$10 million; and
- 20,000 line items with a total book value of \$20 million.

Under these circumstances, the audit team may elect to audit all 100 items comprising the \$10 million of book value, and randomly sample the second subset, because the average value of the first subset is much higher (\$100,000) than that of the second subset (\$1,000).

Once the sample is drawn, the next step is to calculate its audited value and impute this value to the population. This entails examining each item carefully for the audit objectives (e.g., existence, ownership, and valuation) being tested. In the present example, Halter is interested in the following aspects of Xano's raw materials inventory:

1. The items appearing on the inventory listings were transcribed correctly as to type and quantity from the inventory tags;
2. The inventory items were costed in accordance with GAAP and on a basis consistent with the preceding year; and
3. Unit costs were multiplied correctly by quantities and extended amounts were footed correctly.

Once each item in the sample has been audited for these characteristics, the sample mean, $(\bar{y})$ may be calculated by the following equation:

$$\bar{y} = \frac{\Sigma\, y_i}{n}$$

Assuming the mean audited value of the sample is $990, the estimated population value is determined as follows:

$$Y = \bar{y} \times N = \$990 \times 20{,}000 = \$19{,}800{,}000$$

The final step in evaluating the sample results is to compute achieved precision and draw conclusions. **Achieved precision** is the calculated range within which the true value of the population most likely falls. The equation for computing achieved precision (A') is as follows:[1]

$$A' = N \times U_r \left(\frac{SD}{\sqrt{n}}\right)$$

Assuming the standard deviation of the sample is $360, the equation assumes the following form:

$$A' = 20{,}000 \times 1.96 \times \frac{360}{\sqrt{648}} = \$554{,}368$$

Achieved precision (A') must be $\leq$ desired precision (A). Otherwise, the actual beta risk will be higher than that specified in the sampling plan, and further sampling will be necessary in order to reduce the risk to an acceptable level. In this case, $554,368 < $569,768. Therefore, the beta risk is within acceptable bounds.

Having imputed the sample results to the population and having computed precision, Halter now may express the following conclusion: "I am 95 percent confident that the true value of Xano's raw materials inventory is $19,800,000 plus or minus $554,368." This conclusion also may be expressed in terms of a range, as follows:

$Y - A'$	Y	$Y + A'$
$19,245,632	$19,800,000	$20,354,368

[1] If the finite correction factor is needed in adjusting the initial sample size, this equation must be modified and becomes

$$A = N \times U_r\left(\frac{SD}{\sqrt{n'}}\right)\left(\sqrt{\frac{N-n'}{N-1}}\right)$$

Having calculated the precision range, Halter next should determine the **range of acceptability**, defined as the range of possible book values considered acceptable to the auditor. The lower end of the range (i.e., the lowest acceptable book value) equals the upper level of the precision range reduced by materiality (*M*). The upper end of the range (i.e., the highest acceptable book value) equals the lower level of the precision range increased by *M*. In this example, the range may be represented by the following continuum:

$Y + A' - M$		$Y - A' + M$
\$19,354,368	\$20,000,000	\$20,245,632
(\$20,354,368 – \$1,000,000)	Book Value	(\$19,245,632 + \$1,000,000)

Because the book value falls within the range of acceptability, Halter may accept Xano's inventory value as being fairly stated. Had the book value of the inventory fallen outside this range, an audit adjustment would be necessary in order to bring the book value to an amount no greater than the upper level of acceptability and no smaller than the lower level. For example, a book value of \$20,500,000 would require a downward adjustment of \$254,368 (\$20,500,000 – \$20,245,632). Conversely, a book value of \$19,000,000 would necessitate an upward adjustment of \$354,368 (\$19,354,368 – \$19,000,000).

DIFFERENCE ESTIMATION

Difference estimation, a variation of MPU, is used to project the total dollar error in a population. This is done by comparing audited value (*AV*) and book value (*BV*) for a sample, and imputing the difference to the population. If *AV – BV* is positive, book value is understated; if negative, book value is overstated.

Where usable, difference estimation is more cost effective than MPU, because sample sizes are smaller. The reason for smaller sample sizes is that the standard deviation of differences is less than the standard deviation of individual item values about the mean.

The following conditions must exist in order for difference estimation sampling to be appropriate:

1. A book value must be available for each population item (e.g., customer account balances in the accounts receivable subsidiary ledger);
2. The total book value must be the sum of the individual book values (i.e., the sum of the subsidiary ledger accounts must be equal to the control account in the general ledger);
3. The sample must be large enough to produce a normal distribution; and
4. There must be a large population of non-zero differences divided approximately equally between overstatement and understatement.

Steps in Applying Difference Estimation

In applying the difference estimation sampling approach, the following steps are necessary:

1. Sum the individual book values and compare the result with total book value.
2. Draw a pilot sample containing at least 30 differences and estimate the standard deviation as follows:

$$SD_d = \sqrt{\frac{\Sigma(\bar{d} - d_i)^2}{n - 1}}$$

where

SD_d = Standard deviation of the differences
d_i = Individual differences
$\bar{d}$ = Mean of the differences
n = Number of items in the pilot sample

Differences, for difference estimation purposes, are calculated by this equation:

$$d_i = AV - BV$$

where

AV = Audited value
BV = Book value

As stated above, a positive value points to understatement, and a negative value to overstatement.

3. Having estimated the standard deviation of the differences between audited value and book value, calculate the sample size as follows:

$$n = \left(\frac{N \times U_r \times SD_d}{A}\right)^2$$

Note that the sample size equation for difference estimation is identical to the MPU equation, except that SD_d, a lower number, is substituted for SD. As in the MPU equation, the finite correction factor

$$n' = \frac{n}{1 + n/N}$$

is required if $n \geq 5$ percent of N.

4. Randomly select the additional sample items.
5. Audit the sample, listing all differences, and calculate the mean of the differences ($\bar{d}$):

$$\bar{d} = \frac{\Sigma d_i}{n}$$

where

$\bar{d}$ = Mean of the differences
d_i = Individual differences, as represented by $AV_i - BV_i$

6. Calculate the standard deviation of the differences (SD_d):

$$SD_d = \sqrt{\frac{\Sigma(\bar{d} - d_i)^2}{n - 1}}$$

7. Calculate achieved precision (A'):

$$A' = N \times U_r\left(\frac{SD_d}{\sqrt{n}}\right)$$

8. Calculate the estimated population difference (D):

$$D = N \times \bar{d}$$

9. Calculate the estimated audited value (*EAV*):

$$EAV = BV \pm D$$

10. State your conclusions. This is done in the same manner as for MPU, but with a smaller sample size.

Example Illustrating Difference Estimation

White Wash, Inc., a large wholesale distributor of appliances and bathroom fixtures, distributes its products to retail outlets on a nationwide basis. Helen Kane, a CPA and senior auditor with Proud, Tall, and Straight, CPAs, has been assigned to the White Wash account as the in-charge auditor.

White Wash has 14,000 customer accounts with a total book value of $22.4 million. Jerry Crash, one of Kane's assistants on the audit, has determined that the sum of the book values agrees with the accounts receivable control account in the general ledger.

A study of internal control policies and procedures relative to the revenue cycle has led Kane to conclude that internal control over sales and accounts receivable is fair, and she has assessed control risk at 50 percent. Because the application of analytical procedures produced no unusual numbers, Kane decides on an inherent risk of 50 percent. Assuming the alpha risk is set at 5 percent, beta risk becomes 20 percent (see Table 10.1).

Kane wishes to confirm a sample of customer accounts and apply difference estimation sampling for the purpose of evaluating the fairness of White Wash's accounts receivable book value. As stated in Chapter 4, confirmation consists of a written communication from the client to the customer, requesting that the customer notify the auditor directly concerning the correctness or incorrectness of the balances as represented by the client.

Before calculating sample size, Kane must estimate the standard deviation of the differences between audited and book value. To this end, she confirms a sample of 75 customer accounts drawn at random. A careful audit of the replies produces a standard deviation of $464. Sample size now may be calculated as follows:

$$n = \left(\frac{14,000 \times 1.96 \times \$464}{A}\right)^2$$

Assuming that Kane considers $800,000 to be a material misstatement of accounts receivable, precision (*A*) may be calculated as follows:

$$A = M \left(\frac{1}{1 + \dfrac{Z_b}{Z_a/2}}\right)$$

$$= \$800,000 \times .7$$
$$= \$560,000 \text{ (See Table 10.2 for Z values.)}$$

Substituting for *A*, the sample size becomes

$$n = \left(\frac{14,000 \times 1.96 \times \$464}{\$560,000}\right)^2 = 517$$

To complete the sample, Kane selects 442 additional customer accounts at random for confirmation and carefully audits the replies. For customers not responding to second and third requests for confirmation, alternate procedures (e.g., examining shipping orders, bills of lading, and remittance advice) are applied in order to obtain satisfaction concerning valuation, existence, and classification.[2]

Assume that Kane applies the following equation to the sample results, which produces a negative mean of the differences in the amount of $61.34:

$$\bar{d} = \frac{\Sigma d_i}{n}$$

Imputing of the mean to the population by the equation

$$D = \bar{d} \times N$$

produces an estimated overstatement of accounts receivable in the amount of $858,760 ($61.34 × 14,000).

The estimated audited value (*EAV*) now may be computed as follows:

$$EAV = BV \pm D = \$22,400,000 - \$858,760 = \$21,541,240$$

Assuming that the standard deviation of the differences (SD_d) for the completed sample of 517 equals $410, achieved precision is determined as follows:

$$A' = 14,000 \times 1.96 \left(\frac{\$410}{\sqrt{517}}\right) = \$494,620$$

Inasmuch as $A' < A$, further sampling is not necessary.

Kane may now state, with 95 percent confidence, that the true value of the accounts receivable of White Wash, Inc., at year end is $21,541,240 ± $494,620. This conclusion may be expressed diagrammatically as follows:

EAV – A'	EAV	EAV + A'
$21,046,620	$21,541,240	$22,035,860

The range of acceptability may be represented as follows:

EAV + A' – M	EAV – A' + M	
$21,235,860	$21,846,620	$22,400,000
($22,035,860 – $800,000)	($21,046,620 + $800,000)	Book Value

A minimum audit adjustment of $553,380 is therefore necessary in order to reduce the book value to an amount equal to the upper level of acceptability ($22,400,000 – $21,846,620). This adjustment may be made directly to individual customer accounts to the extent of actual errors discovered in the sample. Any remaining adjustment, in order for the total to equal $553,380, may be credited to Allowance for Doubtful Accounts.

PROBABILITY-PROPORTIONAL-TO-SIZE SAMPLING (PPS)

Probability-proportional-to-size (PPS) sampling (also known as dollar unit sampling) is a variation of attribute sampling. In applying PPS, the auditor estimates the dollar amount

---

2   See Chapter 11 for a more detailed discussion of substantive audit procedures applied to trade accounts receivable.

of error (rather than error percent) by examining a sample and calculating an upper error limit for the population, based on the sample results.

Advantages of PPS

PPS is easier to use than classical variables sampling, and therefore more cost effective. Some of the advantages of PPS over classical variables sampling are the following:

1. The standard deviation calculation is not required, thereby eliminating the need for pilot samples;
2. Because the population is automatically stratified, large dollar errors have a higher probability of being detected; and
3. Sample size is usually smaller than either MPU or difference estimation.

A significant limitation of PPS sampling is that it is most applicable to populations for which the auditor suspects few errors, and those of *overstatement* only. Given automatic stratification of the population, units that are understated (i.e., low book values) have a much lower probability of being included in a sample than units that are overstated.

The following situations are candidates for PPS sampling:

1. The auditor expects the inventory to contain few but significant overpricing errors;
2. Analytical procedures and study of the business lead the auditor to suspect that accounts receivable are materially inflated; or
3. Based on past experience with the client, the auditor believes that a substantial amount of repairs and maintenance expense has been capitalized.

Although PPS sampling also can be used when both overstatement and understatement errors exist, it is more difficult to apply; thus, it is therefore considered beyond the scope of this textbook.[3]

Given its cost effectiveness in testing for overstatement errors, however, PPS sampling should be used whenever conditions warrant its use.

Steps in Applying PPS

For PPS purposes, the sampling unit is the individual dollar. The sum of the dollars constitutes the account balance (e.g., accounts receivable) or the total of transactions processed during the period under audit (e.g., debit postings to machinery and equipment). Given random selection, each dollar in the population has an equal chance of being included in the sample.

The **logical sampling unit** is the item to which the randomly selected dollar attaches. Referred to as a *hook*, the "snagged" item might assume the form of a customer account, a line item on an inventory listing, or a posting to a plant asset account.

The sequence of steps required in applying PPS sampling is presented next, followed by a case illustrating the application.

Calculate the Sample Size   Sample size is determined by the following equation:

$$n = \frac{BV \times RF}{TE - (AE \times EF)}$$

where

BV = Book value of the population

RF = **Reliability factor** corresponding to the level of incorrect acceptance (beta risk) as set by the auditor, and assuming zero errors

TE = **Tolerable error** acceptable to the auditor (expressed in dollars)

AE = **Anticipated error**, the amount of error expected by the auditor. Also expressed in dollars, anticipated error is a function of the auditor's judgment concerning inherent risk and control risk.

EF = **Expansion factor**, related to the reliability factor, assumes a positive value only when errors are expected. The expansion factor provides for additional sampling error where some errors are expected.

The denominator of the sample size equation determines desired precision and is a function of audit judgment.

Draw the Sample   The first step in drawing the sample is to calculate the **sampling interval**. The sampling interval, the distance between two consecutive sample items, is expressed by the following equation:

$$SI = \frac{BV}{n}$$

Once the sampling interval has been determined, systematic sampling is applied in drawing the sample. A number between 1 and SI is chosen at random and is the first item selected for the sample. Logical units containing every SIth dollar thereafter are then drawn to complete the sample selection process. This results in stratified sampling—logical units that are greater than the sampling interval have a 100 percent chance of being selected, and other logical units have a chance dependent on size.[4]

Evaluate the Sample Results   The auditor evaluates sample results in three steps:

1. Calculate the projected error;
2. Compute precision; and
3. Determine the upper error limit.

The **projected error** relates to the errors discovered in the logical units included in the sample. A logical unit containing one or more errors is said to be "tainted." Moreover, if the book value of the logical unit is less than the sampling interval, a "tainting" percentage must be applied in order to project the error to the entire sampling interval containing the logical unit.

Computed precision consists of the following components:

1. **Basic precision** (BP), expressed by the equation

$$BP = RF \times SI$$

4   This explains the term "probability-proportional-to-size" as applied to this form of sampling.

where

RF = Reliability factor corresponding to the risk of incorrect acceptance

SI = Sampling interval

2. **Incremental precision allowance** (*IA*), where errors are found in logical units that are smaller than the sampling interval.

The sum of $BP + IA$ = **Allowance for sampling risk**.

The auditor now can determine the **upper error limit** (UEL), which is the sum of the projected error and the allowance for sampling risk. The upper error limit should be less than the tolerable error in order for the book value to be acceptable to the auditor.

These PPS concepts are applied in the following case study.

Example Illustrating the Application of PPS Sampling

Alice Holden, the in-charge auditor for Jole, Inc., a manufacturer of original and replacement mufflers, suspects that material amounts of repairs and maintenance charges have been capitalized in the Machinery & Equipment account. Her suspicions are founded on the results of analytical procedures showing a significant decrease in Repairs & Maintenance. This expense, as a percentage of sales, fell from 8 percent in 1999 to 4 percent in 2000. Moreover, her study of the business and industry has revealed a severe "profit squeeze" during the current year, which may have prompted the company to capitalize repairs intentionally in the plant asset accounts. Jole always has followed a policy of debiting repair and maintenance parts and supplies to expense at the point of purchase.

Internal control procedures relative to the processing of vendors' invoices have been found to be strong, and this leads Holden to believe that the problem may be one of management override rather than unintentional errors.

Holden decides to use PPS sampling in determining the extent to which expenses have been capitalized improperly in 2000. The sampling unit for this application is each individual dollar debited to Machinery & Equipment during the year. (The Machinery & Equipment account is selected because the auditor suspects an overstatement resulting from debits of ordinary repairs to this account.) The logical sampling unit is each debit posting to the account. Because many of the invoices from vendors contain both repair items and capital items, postings often are made to both Repairs & Maintenance and Machinery & Equipment from a single invoice.

The total of the debit postings to Machinery & Equipment for 2000 equals $3.5 million and consists of 3,980 individual postings made to the account during the year. The dollar postings total ($3.5 million) represents the book value (*BV*) for PPS sampling purposes. Based on her evaluation of internal control procedures relative to the processing of invoices, the results of analytical procedures, and the problem of deteriorating profits, Holden decides on a 5 percent risk of incorrect acceptance, and an anticipated error of $60,000. The tolerable error, given her best judgment as to materiality, is set at $111,000. A calculated upper error limit exceeding $111,000, in other words, will be construed as a material overstatement of the Machinery & Equipment account and will require a downward adjustment.

The sample size now may be calculated as follows:

$$n = \frac{BV \times RF}{TE - (AE \times EF)} = \frac{\$3,500,000 \times 3.00}{\$111,000 - (\$60,000 \times 1.6)} = 700$$

(See Table 10.3 for the reliability and expansion factors relating to a 5 percent risk of incorrect acceptance.)

The sampling interval becomes

$$SI = \frac{BV}{n} = \frac{\$3,500,000}{700} = \$5,000$$

Given the sample size of 700 and the sampling interval of $5,000, Holden now picks a number at random between 1 and 5000 (assume 2124), and proceeds to select that logical unit and every 5,000th dollar thereafter. Exhibit 10.1 displays the results of the first five invoices selected. Note that one of the invoices contained billings for repairs as well as equipment, and another invoice was for repair parts only.

Exhibit 10.2 summarizes all invoices containing posting errors. The next step is to calculate the projected error. For each logical unit containing an error and having a book value of less than the sampling interval ($5,000), Holden must apply a *tainting percentage* to the sampling interval (see Exhibit 10.3), thereby extending the error projection to the entire interval.[5]

Having calculated the projected error, the final step is to calculate the allowance for sampling risk and the upper error limit. This is done as follows.

TABLE 10.3

**Reliability Factors and Expansion Factors for PPS Sampling
(By Risk of Incorrect Acceptance)**

Over-Statement Errors	Risk of Incorrect Acceptance								
	1%	5%	10%	15%	20%	25%	30%	37%	50%
Reliability Factors									
0	4.61	3.00	2.31	1.90	1.61	1.39	1.21	1.00	0.70
1	6.64	4.75	3.89	3.38	3.00	2.70	2.44	2.14	1.68
2	8.41	6.30	5.33	4.72	4.28	3.93	3.62	3.25	2.68
3	10.05	7.76	6.69	6.02	5.52	5.11	4.77	4.34	3.68
4	11.61	9.16	8.00	7.27	6.73	6.28	5.90	5.43	4.68
5	13.11	10.52	9.28	8.50	7.91	7.43	7.01	6.49	5.58
6	14.57	11.85	10.54	9.71	9.08	8.56	8.12	7.56	6.67
7	16.00	13.15	11.78	10.90	10.24	9.69	9.21	8.63	7.67
8	17.41	14.44	13.00	12.08	11.38	10.81	10.31	9.68	8.67
9	18.79	15.71	14.21	13.25	12.52	11.92	11.39	10.74	9.67
10	20.15	16.97	15.41	14.42	13.66	13.02	12.47	11.79	10.67
Expansion Factors									
	1.90	1.60	1.50	1.40	1.30	1.25	1.20	1.15	1.00

Source: *AICPA Audit Sampling Guide*, New York, AICPA, 1983, p. 117.

5   If no errors are found in the sample, the projected error is zero, and the auditor may conclude that the population is not overstated by more than the tolerable error at the specified risk of incorrect acceptance.

EXHIBIT 10.1

Sample Selection: First Five Selections

$ Number	Vendor	Invoice Amount	Company Posting M&E	Company Posting Repairs	Correct Posting M&E	Correct Posting Repairs
2124	Jermain, Inc.	$6,382	$6,382	$0	$6,382	$ 0
7124	Martin Equipment	4,247	4,257	0	4,257	0
12124	Holert, Inc.	3,112	3,112	0	3,112	0
17124	Ubba Tools	1,217	1,217	0	800	417
22124	Herol Industrial Supplies	4,985	4,985	0	0	4,985
27124	Knock Motors	2,786	2,786	0	2,786	0

EXHIBIT 10.2

Summary of Errors

$ Number AV	Vendor	Machinery & Equipment Posting Company Posting (BV)	Correct Posting (AV)	BV −
17124	Ubba Tools	$ 1,217	$ 800	$ 417
22124	Herol Industrial Supplies	4,985	0	4,985
52124	Lott Industries	12,863	3,456	9,407
962124	Jerrod Enterprises	72,350	0	72,350
2102124	Terry Trees	2,134	1,100	1,034
3222124	International Hoes	3,260	900	2,360

1. Calculate *basic precision* (*BP*):

$$BP = RF \times SI$$

   where
   - RF = Reliability factor corresponding to the risk of incorrect acceptance
   - SI = Sampling interval
   - BP = 3.00 × $5,000 = $15,000

2. Calculate the *incremental allowance for precision*. This calculation need be made only where errors are found in logical units that are smaller than the sampling interval. Exhibit 10.4 calculates the incremental allowance for the Jole sample. Note the ranking of projected errors from high to low. This is so because PPS sampling produces the *maximum* rate of error at the specified confidence level. The incre-

EXHIBIT 10.3

Projected Error

		(1)	(2)	(3)	(4) Tainting %	(5)	(6) Projected
		Book	Audited	Error	(BV – AV)/	Sampling	Error
$ Number	Vendor	Value	Value	(BV – AV)	BV	Interval	(4) × (5)
17124	Ubba Tools	$ 1,217	$ 800	$ 417	34.26	$5,000	$ 1,713
22124	Herol Industrial Supplies	4,985	0	4,985	100.00	5,000	5,000
52124	Lott Industries	12,863	3,456	9,407	N/A*	N/A*	9,407
962124	Jerrod Enterprises	72,350	0	72,350	N/A*	N/A*	72,350
2102124	Terry Trees	2,134	1,100	1,034	48.45	5,000	2,423
3222124	International Hoes	3,260	900	2,360	72.39	5,000	3,620
				$90,553			$94,513

EXHIBIT 10.4

Incremental Allowance for Precision

		(1) Ranked Projected	(2) Incremental Reliability	(3) Incremental Allowance
$ Number	Vendor	Errors	Factor – 1	(1) × (2)
22124	Herol Industrial Supplies	$5,000	0.75	$3,750
3222124	International Hoes	3,620	0.55	1,991
2102124	Terry Trees	2,423	0.46	1,115
17124	Ubba Tools	1,713	0.40	685
				$7,541

mental reliability factors are found in Table 10.3, beginning with an assumption of one overstatement error. The reliability factor given one overstatement error and a 5 percent risk of incorrect acceptance (4.75) minus the reliability factor associated with zero errors (3.00) equals 1.75. The incremental factor is then reduced by 1.00 to arrive at the first number in column 2 of Exhibit 10.4.

3. Calculate the *allowance for sampling risk*. Basic precision plus the incremental allowance equals the allowance for sampling risk. For the Jole Machinery & Equipment account, the allowance for sampling risk is calculated as follows:

$$ASR = BP + IA$$

where
    ASR = Allowance for sampling risk
    BP = Basic precision
    IA = Incremental allowance

$$ASR = \$15,000 + \$7,541 = \$22,541$$

4. Compute the *upper error limit* and compare it with the tolerable error:

$$UEL = PE + ASR$$

where
    UEL = Upper error limit
    PE = Projected error
    ASR = Allowance for sampling risk

In this example, the calculation is as follows:

$$UEL = \$94,513 + \$22,541 = \$117,054$$

Because the upper error limit ($117,054) exceeds the tolerable error ($111,000), Holden concludes that the Machinery & Equipment account is materially overstated and, conversely, that the Repairs & Maintenance Expense account is materially understated. In statistical terms, Holden may conclude, with 95 percent confidence, that the book value is not overstated by more than $117,054.

By drafting an audit adjustment in the amount of $90,553 (the total amount of the overstatement errors contained in the sample), she will have reduced the audited value of the Machinery & Equipment account to an amount that is within the bounds of acceptance.

COMPUTER-ASSISTED SAMPLING

Many of the statistical sampling procedures described in this chapter can be performed more efficiently with the use of computers and statistical software. Moreover, most of the software is currently available for use with PCs, thus significantly broadening its audit applicability. The software can be used to:

1. Calculate sample sizes;
2. Select items to be included in samples; and
3. Evaluate sampling results.

For determining sample size, most of the programs require only that the auditor specify the confidence level and precision required. For attribute sampling, precision will be expressed as a percentage; for variables sampling and PPS sampling, precision will be stated in dollars.

The computer also can be used to assist in selecting the items to be included in the sample. The auditor enters the highest and lowest numbers, for example, in a group of prenumbered documents representing a given population, and also enters the sample size from the sample size calculation procedure. The computer then will produce a worksheet that lists the items to be selected for examination.

After the sample items have been examined and audited, the statistical software can calculate such measures as the best estimate of population value, precision range, range of acceptability, and upper error limit.

In addition to broadening and expediting sampling applications in auditing, statistical software offers the advantage of enabling auditors with little or no training in statistical sampling to utilize the procedures, inasmuch as the calculations are performed by the computer with limited input by the auditor. The auditor must, of course, be able to interpret the results and exercise judgment in determining the need for modifying the assessed level of control risk and/or the need for audit adjustments based on the sampling results.[6]

KEY TERMS

Achieved precision, 401	Mean per unit (MPU), 393
Allowance for sampling risk, 408	Pilot sample, 397
Alpha risk, 394	Precision, 397
Anticipated error, 407	Probability-proportional-to-size sampling (PPS), 393
Audit effectiveness, 394	
Audit efficiency, 394	Projected error, 407
Basic precision, 407	Range of acceptability, 402
Beta risk, 394	Reliability, 397
Computed precision, 407	Reliability factor, 407
Confidence level, 397	Sampling interval, 407
Desired precision, 398	Sampling risk, 394
Difference estimation, 393	Standard deviation, 396
Expansion factor, 407	Stratified sampling, 400
Finite correction factor, 400	Tolerable error, 407
Incremental precision allowance, 408	Upper error limit, 408
Logical sampling unit, 406	Variables sampling, 393

COMPUTER AUDIT PRACTICE CASE

Biltrite Bicycles, Inc.

Module IV of the Biltrite audit practice case contains an exercise requiring the application of probability-proportional-to-size sampling to factory equipment additions. This exercise may be completed at this time.

REVIEW QUESTIONS

1. Differentiate between classical variables sampling and probability-proportional-to-size sampling.

2. Identify and distinguish between the two approaches to variables sampling used by auditors.

3. What is another term for *detection risk*?

4. How does detection risk affect sample size in substantive testing?

5. What is the standard deviation and how does it affect the sample size?

6   Sampling software available to auditors includes *Idea: Interactive Data Extraction and Analysis*, available from the AICPA. This program performs MPU and PPS sampling, as well as difference estimation. Other packages are available from several of the accounting firms.

6. How does the auditor estimate the standard deviation for calculating the sample size?

7. Differentiate between alpha risk and beta risk.

8. How are alpha and beta risks set by the auditor, and how do they influence the sample size?

9. Define *precision* and *reliability* for variables sampling.

10. Why is stratification of populations often useful for substantive testing purposes?

11. Differentiate between achieved precision and desired precision.

12. Why must achieved precision be $\leq$ desired precision?

13. Why are sample sizes usually smaller for difference estimation purposes than for MPU?

14. What conditions must be met for difference estimation sampling to be appropriate?

15. How does PPS sampling differ from attribute sampling?

16. Under what conditions may PPS sampling be used?

17. Define the following terms as used in PPS sampling:
    a. Logical sampling unit
    b. Sampling interval
    c. Projected error
    d. Basic precision
    e. Incremental precision allowance
    f. Allowance for sampling risk
    g. Upper error limit

18. Name three areas of computer application in sampling. How does the computer facilitate sampling in each of the areas?

MULTIPLE CHOICE QUESTIONS FROM PAST CPA EXAMS

1. While performing a substantive test of details during an audit, the auditor determined that the sample results supported the conclusion that the recorded account balance was materially misstated. It was, in fact, not materially misstated. This situation illustrates the risk of
   a. Alpha risk.
   b. Beta risk.
   c. Assessing control risk too low.
   d. Assessing control risk too high.

2. In a probability-proportional-to-size sample with a sampling interval of $5,000, an auditor discovered that a selected account receivable with a recorded amount of $10,000 had an audit amount of $8,000. If this were the only error discovered by the auditor, the projected error of this sample would be
   a. $1,000.
   b. $2,000.
   c. $4,000.
   d. $5,000.

3. What is the primary objective of using stratification as a sampling method in auditing?
   a. To increase the confidence level at which a decision will be reached from the results of the sample selected

    b. To determine the occurrence rate for a given characteristic in the population being studied

    c. To decrease the effect of variance in the total population

    d. To determine the precision range of the sample selected

4. Which of the following courses of action would an auditor most likely follow in planning a sample of cash disbursements if the auditor is aware of several unusually large cash disbursements?

    a. Increase the sample size to reduce the effect of the unusually large disbursements.

    b. Continue to draw new samples until all the unusually large disbursements appear in the sample.

    c. Set the tolerable rate of deviation at a lower level than originally planned.

    d. Stratify the cash disbursements population so that the unusually large disbursements are selected.

5. When using classical variables sampling for estimation, an auditor normally evaluates the sampling results by calculating the possible error in either direction. This statistical concept is known as

    a. Precision.

    b. Reliability.

    c. Projected error.

    d. Standard deviation.

6. Which of the following most likely would be an advantage in using classical variables sampling rather than probability-proportional-to-size (PPS) sampling?

    a. An estimate of the standard deviation of the population's recorded amounts is not required.

    b. The auditor rarely needs the assistance of a computer program to design an efficient sample.

    c. Inclusion of zero and negative balances generally does not require special design considerations.

    d. Any amount that is individually significant is automatically identified and selected.

7. Statistical sampling provides a technique for

    a. Exactly defining materiality.

    b. Greatly reducing the amount of substantive testing.

    c. Eliminating judgment in testing.

    d. Measuring the sufficiency of evidential matter.

8. If the achieved precision range of a statistical sample at a given reliability level is greater than the desired range this is an indication that the

    a. Standard deviation was larger than expected.

    b. Standard deviation was less than expected.

    c. Population was larger than expected.

    d. Population was smaller than expected.

9. Which of the following sampling methods would be used to estimate a numerical value measurement of a population, such as a dollar value?

    a. Discovery sampling

    b. Numerical sampling

    c. Sampling for attributes

    d. Sampling for variables

10. In the application of statistical techniques to the estimation of dollar amounts, a preliminary sample is usually taken primarily for the purpose of estimating the population
    a. Variability.
    b. Mode.
    c. Range.
    d. Median.

11. The theoretical distribution of means from all possible samples of a given size is a normal distribution, and this distribution is the basis for statistical sampling. Which of the following statements is *not* true with respect to the sampling distribution of sample means?
    a. Approximately 68 percent of the sample means will be within 1 standard deviation of the mean for the normal distribution.
    b. The distribution is defined in terms of its mean and its standard error of the mean.
    c. An auditor can be approximately 95 percent confident that the mean for a sample is within 2 standard deviations of the population mean.
    d. The items drawn in an auditor's sample will have a normal distribution.

12. If the auditor is concerned that a population may contain exceptions, the determination of a sample size sufficient to include at least one such exception is a characteristic of
    a. Discovery sampling.
    b. Variables sampling.
    c. Random sampling.
    d. Dollar-unit sampling.

13. When planning a sample for a substantive test of details, an auditor should consider tolerable misstatement for the sample. This consideration should
    a. Be related to the auditor's assessment of inherent risk.
    b. Not be adjusted for qualitative factors.
    c. Be related to preliminary judgments about materiality levels.
    d. Not be changed during the audit process.

14. In a probability-proportional-to-size sample with a sampling interval of $10,000, an auditor discovered that a selected account receivable with a recorded amount of $5,000 had an audit amount of $2,000. The projected error of this sample was
    a. $3,000.
    b. $4,000.
    c. $6,000.
    d. $8,000.

15. A sampling method that can be used to estimate overstatement error of an account balance but which is not based on normal-curve mathematics is
    a. Discovery sampling.
    b. Mean per unit sampling.
    c. Attributes sampling.
    d. Probability-proportional-to-size sampling.

16. Which of the following is designed to estimate a numerical measurement of a population, such as a dollar value?
    a. Sampling for variables
    b. Sampling for attributes
    c. Discovery sampling
    d. Numerical sampling

17. PPS sampling is less efficient if
    a. Computerized account balances are being audited.
    b. Statistical inferences are to be made.
    c. The audit objective is oriented to understatements.
    d. The account contains a large number of transactions.

INTERNET ACTIVITIES

Required:

Go to the ABREMA web site at http://www.abrema.net/abrema/index.html. Click on the "Tabular Representation of the ABREMA Framework."

An equation appears at the intersection of "audit planning" and "evidence evaluation."

1. Compare this equation with a similar one appearing in Chapter 10. How does ABREMA define the equation?
2. How do the values of the components of the equation impact the statistical model?

.com
http://www.abrema.
net/abrema/index.html

ESSAY QUESTIONS AND PROBLEMS

10.1   Gloria Robinson, the in-charge senior auditor for the Dew Chemicals audit, has developed the following statistical sampling plan for the finished goods inventory audit. Finished goods consists of 25 categories of chemicals, all of approximately equal value. There are several grades within each category. The final unaudited inventory value, as determined by Dew employees, is $47,500,000. The audit team observed the physical inventory taking and is satisfied as to physical quantities. The inventory was "tagged" and the auditors have retained their copies of the inventory tags. The final inventory is in the form of a computer printout consisting of the following headings:

Stock number
Description
Location
Quantity
Unit cost
Extended cost

To facilitate random selection, Robinson requested and obtained from Dew a copy of the printout with the stock numbers in sequential order. A total of 2,100 stock numbers comprised the final printout. Given good internal control within the purchasing and production subsets of the expenditure cycle, an effective physical inventory by Dew, and the absence of abnormalities from the application of analytical procedures, Robinson set the following parameters for statistical sampling of the finished goods inventory:

Alpha risk and audit risk		10%
Beta risk		40%
Materiality	$2,000,000	

A preliminary standard deviation, based on Dew Chemicals' final inventory, was calculated by the computer at $4,800.

Required:
a. Calculate the sample size.
b. How would you draw the sample? Be as specific as you can.

    c. What audit procedures would you apply to the sample items?

    d. Assume the following sample results:

Mean value	$6,200
Standard deviation	$4,200

      Calculate the

      1. Best estimate of population value; and

      2. Achieved precision.

    e. What conclusions can Robinson draw with regard to Dew's finished goods inventory? In answering this question, calculate the

      1. Precision range; and

      2. Range of acceptability.

    f. What course should Robinson pursue as a next step?

10.2   Mohler, CPA, was engaged to audit Delta Co.'s financial statements for the year ended August 31, 2002. Mohler is applying sampling procedures.

NARRATIVE

During the prior years' audits, Mohler used classical variables sampling in performing tests of controls on Delta's accounts receivable. For the current year she decided to use probability-proportional-to-size (PPS) sampling in confirming accounts receivable because PPS sampling uses each account in the population as a separate sampling unit. Mohler expected to discover many overstatements, but presumed that the PPS sample still would be smaller than the corresponding size for classical variables sampling.

Mohler reasoned that the PPS sample should result automatically in a stratified sample because each account would have an equal chance of being selected for confirmation. Additionally, the selection of negative (credit) balances would be facilitated without special consideration.

Mohler computed the sample size using the risk of incorrect acceptance, the total recorded book amount of the receivables, and the number of misstated accounts allowed. She divided the total recorded book value of the receivables by the sample size to determine the sampling interval. Mohler then calculated the standard deviation of the dollar amounts of the accounts selected for evaluation of the receivables.

Mohler's calculated sample size was 60 and the sampling interval was determined to be $9,600. However, only 55 different accounts were selected because five accounts were so large that the sampling interval caused each of them to be selected twice. Mohler proceeded to send confirmation requests to 53 of the 55 customers. Each of two selected accounts had insignificant recorded balances of under $30. Mohler ignored these two small accounts and substituted the two largest accounts that had not been selected in the sample. Each of these accounts had balances in excess of $6,000, so Mohler sent confirmation requests to those customers.

The confirmation process revealed two differences. One account with an audited amount of $6,000 had been recorded at $8,000. Mohler projected this to be a $2,000 error. Another account with an audited amount of $1,000 had been recorded at $3,000. Mohler therefore added $2,000 to the projected error.

In evaluating the sample results, Mohler determined that the accounts receivable balance was not overstated, because the projected misstatement was less than the allowance for sampling risk.

Required:

Describe each incorrect assumption, statement, and inappropriate application of sampling in Mohler's procedures. (AICPA adapted)

10.3   In order to minimize its tax liability, Wauseon Manufacturing Company, a publicly held manufacturer of chain saws and leaf blowers, has been rather liberal in treating maintenance and repairs expenditures as ordinary expense items. Shannon Gergen, of Sam Samson & Co., CPAs, the in-charge auditor for the Wauseon engagement, decides to apply probability-proportional-to-size (PPS) sampling to test the Repairs and Maintenance account for possible overstatement. Given higher-than-normal profits arising from heavy sales of chain saws during the severe storm season just ended, Gergen suspects that material amounts of capital expenditures once again have been charged to the Repairs and Maintenance account. Her suspicions are further supported by the application of analytical procedures. In past years preaudited repairs and maintenance expenditures have ranged from 8 to 10 percent of net sales. The audited values have been considerably lower, ranging from 4 to 5 percent of net sales. For the current year, the unaudited amount, $2,566,000, equals 12 percent of net sales. A total of 1,385 postings to the Repairs and Maintenance account make up the balance in the account. No credits were posted to repairs during the year. In the past, vendors' invoices have frequently included both capital and repair expenditure charges.

Given effective internal control over the processing of vendors' invoices, Gergen believes the problem to be one of possible management override rather than weak control. She decides on a risk of incorrect acceptance of 10 percent and an anticipated error of $60,000.

Required:

a. Assuming that Gergen is willing to accept a tolerable error of $110,000, calculate the sample size and the sampling interval.
b. What is the sampling unit in the present case? What is the logical unit? Using the sample size and sampling interval determined in (a), discuss the steps required in drawing and evaluating the sample.
c. Assuming the following errors are discovered in the sample, calculate the projected error, basic precision, the incremental allowance for sampling risk, and the upper error limit. What conclusions can be drawn from the sampling results?

$ Number	Vendor	Book Value ($)	Audited Value ($)
4,531	Challenge, Inc.	2,622	1,875
71,181	Tools Unlimited	17,344	3,160
157,826	Triple Tier Enterprises	1,360	0
297,791	Buntworth Brown, Inc.	20,231	0
586,452	Johnsons Wholesalers	14,761	2,356
996,785	Truncated Tools, Inc.	5,389	890
1,363,790	Chalmers Repair Parts	16,122	1,088
1,793,456	Kaiser Suppliers	7,988	1,867
2,122,988	Hapworth, Ltd.	43,668	0

10.4   For each of the following situations, identify the most appropriate sampling method and the reason for selecting that method.

a. The auditor believes that the client has intentionally inflated inventory dollar amounts. She suspects that the overstated amounts involve just a few line items on the final inventory printouts.

b. The auditor wishes to estimate the balance in the account Trade Accounts Receivable. He has assessed control risk at maximum and believes that an equal probability exists for overstated and understated account balances.

c. Same as (b) except the auditor believes that the client has intentionally overstated several customer accounts and intentionally understated a few others in order to mislead the auditors. The auditor believes the net effect is a significant inflation of accounts receivable.

10.5   Dogmatics, Inc., manufactures earth movers and other construction equipment. Tires and engines comprise the bulk of Dogmatic's materials and components inventory. Two general ledger accounts, Tires and Engines, are used for these components. These accounts are supported by detailed perpetual inventory records.

Kenneth Gramling of Harrison & Associates, CPAs, is a member of the audit team performing the Dogmatic audit for the fiscal year ended October 31, 2002. The auditors observed the physical inventory taken by Dogmatic employees on October 30 and 31 and were satisfied with the inventory counts. Gramling has been assigned the task of auditing the final tires and engines inventories as costed by Dogmatic. Dogmatic's perpetual inventory records have been adjusted to agree with the costed physical inventories.

Gennifer Mauk, the in-charge auditor for the engagement, is concerned about the smallness of the inventory adjustments for the tires and engines inventories. Based on the results of her analytical procedures, the unaudited inventories before adjusting to physical inventories were abnormally high relative to the preceding years' audited figures. To Mauk, this suggested inventory overstatement; she therefore expected much higher downward adjustments of perpetual to physical inventories. Inventory turnover statistics for the current and preceding years, for example, were as follows:

	Unaudited *2002*	*Audited* *2001*
Tires	8	14
Engines	8	13

The significant decline in turnover for 2002, suggesting inventory overstatement, led Mauk to suggest that Gramling apply probability-proportional-to-size sampling in estimating the amount, if any, by which Dogmatic's final tires and engines inventories are overstated.

The unaudited inventory amounts at October 31, 2002, after adjustment to physical counts, were as follows:

Tires	$3,460,000
Engines	8,300,000

The final inventories are documented in computer printouts and classified as either "tires" or "engines." Within each broad category, the inventories are further categorized as to type of tire and type of engine. Gramling, with Mauk's approval, decides on 5 percent as the risk of incorrect acceptance. The anticipated and tolerable errors for each component are as follows:

	Anticipated *error*	*Tolerable* *error*
Tires	$15,000	$ 80,000
Engines	30,000	120,000

Required:

a. What is the sampling unit for purposes of this exercise? What is the logical unit?

b. Calculate the sample size and sampling interval for each inventory class.

c. Assume that Gramling finds the following errors in auditing the randomly drawn samples:

TIRES

$ Number	Book Value ($)	Audited Value ($)	Error ($)
356,663	500,000	120,000	380,000
628,259	12,400	1,000	11,400
967,754	550,000	210,000	340,000
1,533,579	14,000	6,500	7,500
2,393,633	20,000	8,000	12,000
3,298,953	1,300,000	300,000	1,000,000
4,792,731	11,000	2,000	9,000
6,784,435	170,000	30,000	140,000

ENGINES

$ Number	Book Value ($)	Audited Value ($)	Error ($)
667,300	245,000	30,000	215,000
1,006,770	14,700	-0-	14,700
3,247,272	1,780,000	480,000	1,300,000
5,114,357	9,500	0	9,500
7,253,018	1,860,000	940,000	920,000
10,308,248	4,600	2,400	2,200

Calculate the

1. Projected error;

2. Basic precision;

3. Incremental allowance for precision; and

4. Estimated upper error limit.

d. What conclusions can you draw with respect to each of the two inventory components? What do you recommend as the next step for the audit team?

10.6 During the course of an audit engagement, a CPA attempts to ascertain that there are no material misstatements in the accounts receivable of a client. Statistical sampling is a tool that the auditor often uses to obtain representative evidence to verify accounts. On a particular engagement an auditor determined that a material misstatement in a population of accounts would be $35,000. To obtain satisfaction the auditor had to be 95 percent confident that the population of accounts was *not* in error by more than $35,000. The auditor decided to use MPU sampling and took a preliminary random sample of 100 items (n) from a population of 1,000 items (N). The sample produced the following data:

Arithmetic mean of sample items, $\bar{y}$	$4,000
Standard deviation of sample items, SD	$200

Required:

a. Define the statistical terms *reliability* and *precision* as applied to auditing.

b. If all necessary audit work is performed on the preliminary sample items and no errors are detected, what can the auditor say about the total amount of accounts receivable at the 95 percent confidence level, and at what confidence level can the auditor say that the population is *not* in error by $35,000?

c. Assuming that the preliminary sample was sufficient, compute the auditor's estimate of the population total, and indicate how the auditor should relate this estimate to the client's recorded amount.

The following list of U_r and reliability factors may be used as needed in completing the above requirements.

Confidence Level (%)	U_r Factor
91.086	1.70
91.988	1.75
92.814	1.80
93.568	1.85
94.256	1.90
94.882	1.95
95.000	1.96
95.450	2.00
95.964	2.05
96.428	2.10
96.844	2.15

(AICPA adapted)

10.7 Standard deviation is defined as the degree of variation of individual item values from the population mean; precision is defined as the range within which the true answer most likely falls.

Required:
a. How are standard deviation and precision related?
b. What factors would you consider in specifying precision?
c. How do standard deviation and precision affect sample size?

10.8 John Daniels, of Bowers and Hahn, CPAs, is the in-charge auditor for the Breckenridge Furniture Company audit. In planning for the finished goods inventory audit, Daniels decides to use mean per unit sampling in evaluating the quantities, prices, and extended amounts on the inventory listings. The inventory listings consist of 12,000 line items on computer printouts. Each line item is identified by stock number and includes quantity, price, and extended amount of that specific furniture item. Daniels and his audit team observed the year-end physical inventory and were concerned about the lack of control during inventory taking. Operations continued during the physical counting, goods were moved from storeroom to production area and from production to finished goods, obvious overstocking conditions were observed by the "team," and inventory tags were *not* prenumbered. With considerable effort, however, Daniels and his staff assistants were able to satisfy themselves as to physical quantities. This required counting approximately 60 percent of the estimated dollar value of finished goods. In addition to the identified control weaknesses during inventory, Daniels had observed other weaknesses in maintaining perpetual inventory records (the inventory adjustment reflected a 10 percent shrinkage factor) and in processing sales orders.

Diana Drew, one of Daniels' assistants, traced the total appearing on the printouts, $2,632,400, to the general ledger.

Required:

a. How might the apparent lack of control over finished goods inventory affect the sampling plan in the present situation?

b. Assuming the audit team decides to assess both inherent risk and control risk at 100 percent, and chooses a 10 percent risk of incorrect rejection, what is the beta risk?

c. If a pilot sample of 40 line items from the inventory listings produces a preliminary estimate of standard deviation in the amount of $90, and $110,000 is considered to be the minimum acceptable misstatement of finished goods inventory, what is the sample size?

d. What audit procedures should the team apply to the sample items?

e. Assuming a sample mean of $160 and a standard deviation of $85, what is the achieved precision and the estimated audited value of the population? State the conclusions to be drawn based on the audit sampling.

10.9   Ken McMurray of McMurray and McMurray, CPAs, is planning the merchandise inventory audit of Smithers, a large retail chain. Computer printouts of priced inventory, categorized by line of merchandise, have been provided to McMurray for audit purposes. Based on past audits and also because profit declines have been an ongoing problem for Smithers during the last quarter, McMurray anticipates some significant inventory overpricing errors. His suspicions are aroused further through the application of analytical procedures. Historical gross profit rates, as applied to different lines of Smithers' merchandise, produced estimated inventory figures significantly below the values booked by Smithers' controller, Homer Scanlon. Results of the test are as follows:

	Ending Inventory Based on	
Merchandise Line	*Gross Profit Test*	*Smithers Book Value*
Appliances and Furniture	$23,456,000	$27,478,933
Housewares	$12,600,000	$14,575,456
Sporting Goods	$16,750,000	$22,489,345
Audio-Video	$34,400,000	$41,348,990
Clothing	$56,788,000	$62,788,800

McMurray decides to apply probability-proportional-to-size sampling (PPS) to each merchandise line in order to estimate the extent of overstatement error (if any) attributable to each. Satisfaction regarding inventory quantities already has been obtained by observing the ending inventory counts at several locations.

Both internal control over the processing of inventory purchases and store security measures instituted over the years have led McMurray to evaluate overall control within the purchasing and inventory cycle as good. The major concern, therefore, is one of possible management override in the form of intentional inventory overpricing.

The following sampling plan has been developed for each line of merchandise:

Merchandise Line	*Risk of Incorrect Acceptance (%)*	*Anticipated Error*	*Tolerable Error*
Appliance and Furniture	20	$500,000	$1,300,000
Housewares	20	$180,000	$1,000,000
Sporting Goods	20	$230,000	$1,000,000
Audio-Video	15	$900,000	$2,200,000
Clothing	15	$2,200,000	$4,100,000

Required:

a. What is the sampling unit for purposes of the test? What is the logical sampling unit? What is the sample size for each line?

b. Calculate the sampling interval for each of the sample sizes determined in (a).

c. Assuming the following sample results for the clothing line, calculate projected error, basic precision, and incremental precision allowance.

$ Number	Line	Book Value ($)	Audited Value ($)
590,603	Suzzanna Jackets	435,980	363,200
8,169,587	Glenn Browning Sport Coats	3,476,962	1,450,480
16,380,153	Floorshine Shoes	1,529,800	987,954
21,432,809	Fruit of the Limb Underwear	211,000	56,765
28,380,211	London Rain Top Coats	1,580,327	1,076,400
36,590,777	Roy Rogers Wallets	847,000	56,842
44,801,343	Bigtex Romper Suits	631,000	102,877
47,327,671	Pierre Cardex Suits	5,160,000	2,620,900
54,906,655	Spear Dress Shirts	1,223,545	478,954
61,854,057	Lee High Jeans	4,876,544	1,897,665

d. What conclusions can be drawn based on the sample results? Are any further procedures indicated? Explain.

10.10 As a staff training exercise, Heather Lohman wishes to demonstrate the cost effectiveness of difference estimation sampling by calculating and contrasting sample size for mean per unit and difference estimations. She has developed the following data and assumptions as inputs for the exercise.

Application: Trade accounts receivable
Number of customer accounts: 3,500
Total book value: $7,200,000
Control risk: 60%
Inherent risk: 50%
Alpha risk: 5%
Preliminary estimate of standard deviation (based on pilot sample): Standard deviation is $750; standard deviation of differences is $380
Individual item materiality: $320,000

Required:

a. Calculate sample size for both MPU and difference estimation purposes.

b. Why do the sample sizes differ?

c. If difference estimation is more cost effective than MPU, why would MPU ever be used in auditing applications?

10.11 Alpha and beta risks are important ingredients in determining sample size for variables sampling.

Required:

a. Differentiate between alpha risk and beta risk.

b. Discuss the relevance of alpha and beta risks for audit hypothesis testing purposes.

c. Identify and discuss the factors considered by the auditor in quantifying alpha and beta risks in variables sampling applications.

10.12 The Hillsdale College of Hillsdale, Oklahoma, has a common endowment fund in the amount of $52 million. This fund consists of the common stocks of 1,350 publicly held companies. James Todd, the in-charge senior auditor for the Hillsdale College audit, wishes to apply difference estimation sampling in evaluating the fairness of the fund's book value. The approach will be to select a sample from the 1,350 accounts in the investment ledger, audit them carefully as to type, quantity, ownership, cost, and market value, and extend the results to the population.

One of Todd's assistants has obtained a computer printout of the investment ledger and determined that the sum of the accounts equals $52 million, the control account balance in the general ledger. Thomas Walters, the college controller, has assured Todd that the securities have been adjusted to market value as of the balance sheet date in accordance with generally accepted accounting principles.

Prior audits and the current year's testing of control procedures relative to the processing of securities transactions have led Todd to believe that the population contains numerous differences divided equally between overstatement and understatement. As a result, he concludes that internal control is poor, and assesses control risk at 70 percent for substantive testing purposes. Inherent risk and alpha risks are set at 90 percent and 5 percent, respectively. A pilot sample of 40 securities drawn at random from the computer printout produces a standard deviation of the differences between audited and book values in the amount of $3,200.

Required:
  a. Assuming Todd and the audit team have established $800,000 as individual item materiality, calculate the sample size.
  b. State the conclusions given the following sampling results: Mean of the differences is ($4,600) (negative); standard deviation of the differences is $2,800.
  c. What alternatives are available to the audit team as indicated by the sample results?

10.13 You are auditing a company offering both department store and catalog sales. You are designing a variables sampling plan to estimate the amount of revenue resulting from catalog sales. Company records indicate that 85,000 catalog sales were completed during the year ending December 31, 2002. The total sales recorded for the same period were equal to $15,682,000. *Catalog sales are not separately recorded.* A pilot sample of 30 catalog sales resulted in the following:

Estimated population standard deviation	$9.00
Average billing amount	$27.50

The appropriate statistical sampling table indicates that a desired precision of $1.38 (5 percent of average billed amount) and the pilot sample standard deviation of $9.00 will require testing a sample of 121 transactions. It is the policy of your firm to conduct such tests at the 90 percent confidence level ($Z = 1.65$).

Required:
  a. Can the 30 items used as a pilot sample also be used as part of the sample of 121? Explain.
  b. What are the factors that impact the precision of the estimate of a population value?
  c. Given the pilot sample results, what can the auditor do to decrease the size of the sample standard deviation?
  d. The standard error of the mean can be computed by dividing the population standard deviation by the square root of the sample size (ignoring the finite population

correction factor). Assuming no change in the estimated population standard deviation after considering all 121 items, what is the value of:

- The standard error of the mean?
- The achieved precision?

e. Assuming no change in the estimated average billing amount after considering all 121 items, compute the estimated total catalog sales.

f. Compute the 90 percent confidence interval for estimated total catalog sales.

(IIA adapted)

10.14 In conjunction with the potential acquisition of a manufacturing firm, the auditor has been asked to verify the book value of equipment of the company to be acquired. The auditor has decided to use a mean per unit variables sampling technique to estimate the book value.

The reported book value of the equipment is $5,550,000. An error of more than $200,000 will be considered material. The auditor has chosen to use a confidence level of 95 percent (1.96 Z factor) for the sample.

A pilot sample of equipment records yields a preliminary estimated standard deviation of $300. Based on the above parameters, the auditor computes a required sample size of 160 from the 3,400 items listed in the company's equipment inventory. The results of the sample are:

Sample standard deviation $280
Total audit value of sampled items $262,400

Required:

a. Identify the factors impacting sample size. Briefly explain each.

b. Using the sample data, compute the value of the equipment account. Include a measure of reliability (confidence interval) achieved.

c. Briefly state whether the sample results support the reported book value.

d. Identify the two types of sampling risk that the auditor might have considered in formulating the statistical sample and briefly state how to control each.

(IIA adapted)

c h a p t e r 1 1

biltrite

After reading this chapter, you should be able to

1 Define substantive testing.
2 Identify specific audit objectives related to the revenue cycle.
3 Develop for the revenue cycle audit programs that relate audit procedures to audit objectives for each component of the cycle.
4 Modify audit programs, as necessary, in light of warning signs that surface during a study of the business and industry, the application of analytical procedures, or a study of internal control policies and procedures.

OVERVIEW

Substantive testing is the process of obtaining evidence in support of transactions and balances. Chapters 11, 12, and 13 discuss substantive testing according to transaction cycles.

In determining the nature, timing, and extent of substantive testing procedures to be applied in the circumstances, the auditor must consider audit risk, materiality, and cost effectiveness. Although most substantive testing is done after the balance sheet date, a certain amount may be completed during the interim audit phase.

This chapter covers substantive testing of the revenue cycle in two parts:

1.   Sales transactions and accounts receivable balances; and
2.   Cash receipts transactions and cash balances.

For each part, specific audit objectives are identified. This is followed by a discussion of audit evidence and procedures necessary to meet the specified objectives.

SUBSTANTIVE TESTING VERSUS TESTS OF CONTROLS

Substantive audit testing is the process of obtaining evidence in support of transactions and balances. The nature, timing, and extent of substantive testing is a function of the auditor's judgment concerning audit risk and materiality. The substantive procedures selected by the auditor are incorporated into audit programs, which are designed at the conclusion of the audit planning phase based on the auditor's assessment of inherent risk and control risk. They may be modified further as conditions warrant.

As described in Chapter 7, tests of controls precede substantive testing and constitute the process whereby the auditor tests transactions, observes task performance, and inquires of client personnel. The auditor performs tests of controls to reduce the assessed level of control risk below the maximum level. Where tests of controls are *not* applied, control risk is assessed at maximum and a primarily substantive audit is performed.

Note that both substantive tests and tests of controls incorporate observation and inquiry, as well as transaction testing. Tests of controls, however, do *not* include analytical procedures or balance testing. In summary, these two forms of testing may be compared as follows:

	Substantive Testing	*Control Testing*
Transaction testing	Yes	Yes
Balance testing	Yes	No
Analytical procedures	Yes	No
Observation and inquiry	Yes	Yes

This chapter and the two that follow are concerned with substantive testing as it applies to the following transaction cycles:

Chapter 11—Revenue Cycle: includes sales transactions, accounts receivable balances, cash receipts transactions, and cash balances.

Chapter 12—Expenditure Cycle: includes purchases, cash payments, operating expenses, inventories, plant assets, intangible assets, and accounts payable.

Chapter 13—Financing and Investing Cycle: includes borrowing and investing transactions, interest revenue and expense, dividends, notes receivable, notes payable, bonds payable, capital stock, and retained earnings.

These are the same transaction cycles that were introduced in Chapter 4 and used in Chapter 7 for discussing tests of controls. The appendices that follow these chapters consist of a matrix relating auditing objectives to audit evidence and procedures within the appropriate transaction cycle. Each appendix thereby provides a framework for applying substantive testing within the given cycle. Although not intended to be all-inclusive, the appendices may serve as models for developing comprehensive programs for substantive audit testing.

REVIEW OF THE AUDIT PROCESS

Figure 11.1, like its counterparts in previous chapters, shows where the chapter material fits into the overall audit process. As illustrated, the current chapter discusses substantive testing relative to the revenue cycle. Those steps in the audit process preceding substantive testing were covered in Chapters 5 through 10. They are as follows:

1. Inherent risk was assessed by means of discussions with management, a study of the business and industry, and the application of analytical procedures.
2. Internal control policies and procedures were studied and evaluated by observation of the control environment; inquiry of management and employees; completion of questionnaires, checklists, memoranda, and flowcharts; examination of documents for errors; and reprocessing of transactions through the accounting system. The auditor's understanding of internal control was documented, control risk was assessed, and the auditor documented the basis for reducing assessed control risk below the maximum level (the results of the auditor's tests of controls).
3. Detection risk was set based on the auditor's acceptable level of audit risk and his or her assessment of inherent risk and control risk.

Next, the auditor develops substantive audit programs, based on the results of the preceding steps. These programs were introduced in Chapter 4 and will be elaborated on in this and the two ensuing chapters. While Chapters 5 through 7 considered various levels of inherent risk and control risk, Chapters 11 through 13 discuss substantive testing under the assumptions that inherent risk is less than 100 percent and that internal control is adequate to permit the auditor to reduce control risk below maximum. These assumptions are given in the concluding section of each chapter, where audit risk associated with each of the transaction cycles is considered. Warning signs are identified that should arouse the auditor's suspicions concerning possible misstatements of financial statement components; cases that illustrate the warning signs are cited and discussed.

OVERVIEW OF SUBSTANTIVE TESTING

Timing of Substantive Testing

In collecting evidence in support of transactions and account balances (substantive testing), the auditor must determine the nature, timing, and extent of procedures to be applied under the circumstances. These determinations are based on audit judgment, and influenced by audit risk, materiality, and cost effectiveness.

Although most substantive audit tests are applied as of the balance sheet date, a limited amount of substantive testing may be performed during the interim audit phase to conserve time on the final audit phase. A rule of thumb is that the auditor performs tests of balances (e.g., confirming accounts receivable, observing inventory taking, and

FIGURE 11.1

The Audit Process

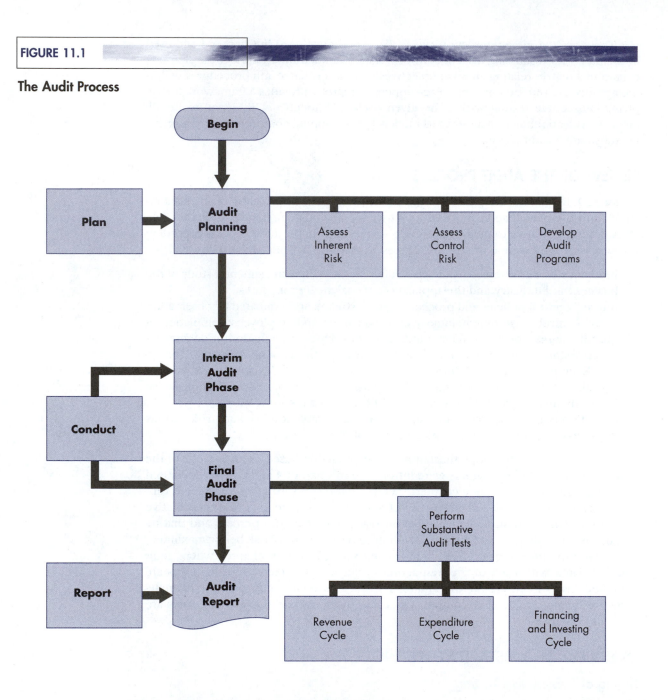

reconciling bank balances) as of the balance sheet date, and tests transactions (e.g., plant asset additions and disposals, research and development expenditures, operating revenues and expenses, purchases and sales of marketable securities) during both the interim and the final audit phases. An exception to this general rule may be made under conditions of excellent internal control within given transaction cycle subsets. Under these conditions, the auditor may decide to test certain balances at interim points prior to the balance sheet date. If internal control over sales processing, billing, and collection, for example, has been evaluated as excellent, the auditor may elect to confirm customers' accounts receivable at an interim date. AICPA Professional Standards, however, caution against performing excessive amounts of substantive testing during interim periods. Too much substantive testing during the interim audit phase may increase detection risk to an unacceptable level as of the balance sheet date.[1] A good rule, therefore, is to increase interim balance testing under conditions of excellent internal control, and to perform minimal balance testing during the interim audit phase under conditions of fair to weak internal control.

Cost–Benefit and Substantive Testing

In considering cost effectiveness, the auditor recognizes that if an opinion is to be expressed, sufficient, competent evidence must be obtained, regardless of the cost involved. Given alternate means for achieving a specific audit objective, however, the auditor should choose the less costly procedures. For example, assume that the auditor wishes to ascertain the existence and ownership of securities purportedly owned by the client. Assume further that these securities are in safekeeping at a distant location. Obviously, the objective can be satisfied by the auditor's visiting the location and physically examining the securities. However, the auditor could meet the objective more economically and just as effectively by confirming the securities' existence and ownership with the custodian. If two or more alternate methods for obtaining evidence are equally effective in meeting the stated audit objective, the auditor should choose the least costly from among the alternatives.

Analytical Procedures and Substantive Testing

Chapter 5 discussed the application of analytical procedures as part of the auditor's analysis of inherent risk. Analytical procedures help to identify unusual relationships that may be investigated further with substantive audit programs. A material decline in accounts receivable turnover, for example, may be indicative of collection problems. This, in turn, affects net realizable value and may warrant extending the confirmation of customers' accounts, expanding the analysis of customer remittances subsequent to the balance sheet date, and/or increasing attention to the adequacy of the allowance for uncollectible accounts.

   In addition to requiring the application of analytical procedures during the planning phase of the audit, AICPA Professional Standards also require that analytical procedures be applied as part of the overall audit review.[2] This assists the auditor in assessing conclusions and in determining the sufficiency of audit evidence.[3] Upon conclusion of the audit of inventories, for example, the auditor may estimate the ending inventory using historical gross profit rates. If the estimated inventory is materially at variance with the audited inventory, the auditor may have to audit the inventories further to resolve the disparity.

Audit Objectives, Evidence, and Procedures

Figure 11.2 summarizes the audit objectives evidence and procedures model as presented in Chapter 4. Note that audit objectives relate to management's assertions as to

1   *AICPA Professional Standards*, New York: AICPA, section AU 313.03.
2   Ibid, section AU 329.
3   Ibid.

FIGURE 11.2

Substantive Audit Testing Model for Designing Audit Programs

1. Audit Objectives
Specify Audit Objectives—related to management's financial statement assertions

Existence or Occurrence   Valuation or Allocation
Completeness   Presentation and Disclosure
Rights and Obligations

2. Audit Evidence
Identify Relevant Types of Evidence for Each Objective

Physical   Mathematical
Confirmation   Analytical
Documentary   Hearsay

3. Audit Procedures
Develop Audit Programs

Observe   Vouch   Recalculate
Examine   Inspect   Trace
Count   Inquire   Compare
Confirm   Calculate Reconcile
Analyze

the reasonableness of the financial statements. The auditor's objective is to verify each of the assertions. Audit evidence is the corroborative matter needed to meet the audit objectives, and audit procedures are the detailed steps necessary for gathering and evaluating the evidence. In the chapters to follow, each transaction cycle is addressed within this framework. Accordingly, each subset of the transaction cycle is considered in the following order:

1. The specific *audit objectives* relevant to that part of the cycle;
2. The types of *audit evidence* needed to satisfy the objectives; and
3. The *audit procedures* that can be used to collect the necessary evidence.

Emphasis and Direction of Substantive Testing

Before considering the transaction cycles in depth, a word of caution regarding the emphasis and direction of substantive testing is in order. In analyzing audit risk, auditors frequently discover conditions that lead them to suspect that assets and revenues may be intentionally overstated or that liabilities and expenses may be understated. Under these conditions, attention is directed to developing programs that will aid in detecting various types of fraudulent financial reporting. Over the past several years, a significant number of frauds of asset/earnings inflation have surfaced in the courts. Accordingly, considerable attention is devoted in this text to audit procedures designed to detect asset overstatements and liability understatements.

At the same time, however, the emphasis needs to be properly balanced. Companies that are successful in terms of profits and cash flows, for example, may seek to understate revenues or overstate expenses. The goal may be to avoid a major spurt in the current year's earnings and, instead, maintain a more gradual and continued growth in profits; or, as in the case of IBM's write-off of costs related to the acquisition of Lotus Development Corporation, an entity may elect to take a major nonrecurring charge to earnings in a given year in order to "pave the way" to increased future earnings.[4] Moreover, unintentional errors, resulting from internal control weaknesses, may materially misstate financial statements in either direction. If, therefore, the auditor suspects material understatement, audit programs should be modified accordingly.

Table 11.1 presents a **balanced audit approach**, designed to avoid overemphasizing either extreme in audit direction. By testing assets and expenses for overstatement and liabilities and revenues for understatement, the auditor is considering both directions of possible misstatement. The model presented in Table 11.1 represents a neutral position regarding emphasis of direction, which should be modified when specific risk analysis factors lead the auditor to strongly suspect misstatement in one specific direction.

USE OF COMPUTERS IN PERFORMING SUBSTANTIVE AUDIT TESTS

As defined in Chapter 4, substantive audit testing consists of examining evidence in support of the assertions contained in the financial statements. Use of the computer to assist in gathering and evaluating audit evidence enhances the effectiveness of substantive testing by permitting the auditor to examine increased quantities of evidence in support of management's financial statement assertions. By examining larger quantities of evidence and by enlisting the aid of the computer in analyzing and evaluating evidence, the auditor is able to manage detection risk more effectively.

TABLE 11.1

Audit Balance Matrix

Account	Audit Emphasis	
	Test for Overstatement	Test for Understatement
Assets	X	
Liabilities		X
Revenues		X
Expenses	X	

4   See *The Wall Street Journal*, December 6, 1996. In this instance, IBM acquired Lotus Development Corporation for $3.2 billion and immediately wrote off $1.8 billion as "purchased R&D." Although a major "hit" to the 1995 earnings of the consolidated entity, this write-off significantly reduced the entity's asset base, thereby providing for decreased amortization charges in future years and a lower asset base against which to compare earnings for ROI purposes.

Computer Advantage: Speed and Clerical Accuracy

Speed and clerical accuracy are features that make the computer especially advantageous in performing substantive audit tests. In examining inventories, for example, the auditor must gather evidence in support of the client's calculations of final inventory costs. This process includes determining that the proper prices were applied to the various categories of inventory and recalculating the product of price per unit times quantity of units for a sample of inventory line items. The extended amounts also must be added on a test basis and compared with the client's totals. In applying these procedures, the auditor can harness the ability of the computer to manipulate large amounts of data quickly and in an error-free manner, permitting a larger number of inventory prices, extensions, and footings to be tested.

The capacity of the computer to store large amounts of data for multiple purposes permits the auditor to expand the breadth and depth of analytical procedures. Trend and proportional analysis, as well as comparison with industry averages, can be performed quickly and accurately with computer programs designed for that purpose.

The computer can also increase the cost effectiveness of auditing. Determining sample sizes, as well as drawing samples and evaluating sample results (described in Chapters 9 and 10), can be accomplished more efficiently and accounts and transactions may be audited more quickly with the aid of a computer. Moreover, given computerized data files and the necessary programs, the cost of using the computer in completing these audit tasks is much lower than performing them manually, using expensive audit staff hours.

Several software programs designed specifically for auditing with the computer are currently available. The programs require minimal staff training and are relatively inexpensive considering the enhanced audit effectiveness they provide.[5]

Personal Computers and Auditing

A significant development in auditing during recent years has been the increasing use of the personal computer (PC), which has become smaller and more portable, as well as faster and more powerful. In using PC software packages to analyze the client's data, the auditor first must transfer accounting data from the client's files to the computer. Although this may be done by entering the data manually into the computer, a more efficient approach, if feasible, is to download the data directly from the client's files to the auditor's computer. However the transfer is effected, the auditor utilizes the power of the PC to perform substantive tests on the data.

The PC may be used whether or not the client's system is computerized. The tests are performed more efficiently, however, on computerized client files, as downloading becomes relatively automated. If the client's system is manual, the auditor must arrange for the manual entering of client data into the computer prior to performing substantive testing. This task has been facilitated, however, by the increasing availability of **optical scanning devices** that read data and enter it into the computer without the need for keyboarding.

As discussed and illustrated in Chapter 4, the PC also offers the ability to automate the audit workpapers. With an electronic spreadsheet or database package, the working trial balance, lead schedules, supporting schedules, and working copies of financial

5   For examples of audit software see Lanxa, Richard B., *Journal of Accountancy*, New York: AICPA, June 1998, p. 33.

statements can be linked. With linkage, changes in supporting schedules and audit adjustments are automatically reflected in the related lead schedules and the working trial balance. Within the revenue cycle, for example, an increase in the allowance for bad debts can be entered in the supporting schedule analyzing this account, and the change will be replicated in the accounts receivable lead schedule and the balance sheet as well as the income statement components of the working trial balance. In Chapters 11 through 13, the illustrative workpapers are based on spreadsheet templates.

AUDITING THE REVENUE CYCLE

Substantive testing of the **revenue cycle** (sales revenue, cash receipts, cash balances, and accounts receivable) is discussed in the following two sections. The steps involved in processing revenue cycle transactions are diagrammed in Figure 11.3. At this time, you may wish to review that portion of the appendix following Chapter 7 that identifies control points and tests of controls related to the revenue cycle. The significant control policies and procedures are summarized as follows:

1. All incoming customer orders should be properly approved for credit;
2. Sales order/sales invoice sets should be generated only on the basis of properly approved customer orders;
3. Shipments to customers should be made only on the basis of properly approved sales order/invoice sets accompanied by credit approval;
4. All shipments should be evidenced by bills of lading signed by the carrier;
5. Invoices should be mailed to customers only on the basis of signed bills of lading;
6. Sales should be recorded only after receipt of bills of lading evidencing shipment and sales invoices with customer orders attached, evidencing order approval, credit approval, and billing;
7. Customer remittances should be endorsed restrictively and prelisted upon receipt;
8. Customer remittances, along with other cash receipts, should be deposited intact daily;
9. Cash receipts should be recorded daily by persons who are competent and who do *not* have access to cash or checks;
10. Receipted bank deposit tickets should be compared with prelistings and cash receipts journal entries daily;
11. All bank accounts should be reconciled monthly by persons *not* having access to cash or accounting records;
12. Internal documents such as customer order forms, sales order/sales invoice sets, shipping orders, and bills of lading should be prenumbered and the numeric sequence of used documents should be periodically accounted for; and
13. To the extent to which the revenue cycle is computerized, adequate input editing, processing, and output controls should be designed and implemented to provide reasonable assurance as to proper recording of transactions and security over the resulting databases.

In designing risk-based audit programs for the revenue cycle, the auditor must keep these controls in mind, along with specifically identified risk factors associated with each.

The first of the two sections that follow deals with sales transactions and accounts receivable balances. The second section covers cash receipts transactions and cash balances. Each section is divided further into two parts: audit objectives and audit evidence/procedures.

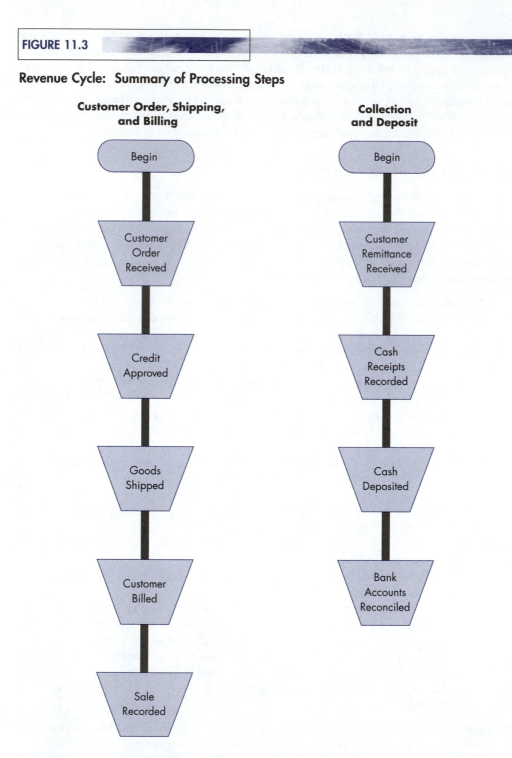

FIGURE 11.3

Revenue Cycle: Summary of Processing Steps

Sales Transactions and Accounts Receivable Balances

Audit Objectives   The audit objectives relating to sales transactions and accounts receivable balances may be classified as follows:

1. *Existence and completeness assertions.* The auditor needs to determine that all sales are recorded in the proper accounting period, and that all debits to accounts receivable represent actual sales transactions.

2. *Valuation or allocation assertion.* The auditor must ascertain that sales are recorded at proper amounts in accordance with GAAP. These require that only completed sales are recorded and that consignments be excluded from sales, that sales be recognized only on the basis of revenues having been substantially earned, and that sales revenue *not* be recognized before realization is complete or reasonably predictable. The auditor also must determine, by evaluating the allowance for doubtful accounts, that accounts receivable balances are stated at amounts *not* exceeding estimated net realizable value.

3. *Presentation and disclosure assertions.* Credit balances in accounts receivable should be reclassified as current liabilities, if material. Similarly, significant amounts of nontrade receivables and receivables from related parties should be reported separately. Related-party transactions, moreover, need to be disclosed fully in footnotes to the financial statements. Pledging or assignment of accounts receivable as loan collateral also must be disclosed in the body of the financial statements or in footnotes.

Audit Evidence and Procedures   Analytical procedures, applied earlier in the audit process, will have revealed any significant changes in patterns of sales, cost of sales, or gross profit. This, along with a study of industry sales patterns and tests of controls within the revenue cycle, will influence the extent of application of the procedures addressed in the following paragraphs.

Sales Cutoff Tests   To obtain satisfaction that sales are recorded in the proper accounting period, the auditor should apply **sales cutoff** procedures. Cutoff tests require examination of documentary evidence supporting sales transactions for a few days before and after year end. Sales orders, sales invoices, shipping orders, and bills of lading form the necessary documentary evidence. In examining the evidence, the auditor should note shipping dates and freight terms, making certain that sales reflected in the year under audit were shipped before year end, and that sales in transit at year end and recorded as revenue were shipped F.O.B. shipping point. The auditor also must determine consistency of the current year-end sales cutoff with that of the preceding year. If the cutoff is *not* consistent, the current year may contain a greater or smaller number of days' sales than the number of working days in the year. Cutoff is addressed more extensively in Chapter 12 as part of the inventory audit discussion.

Confirmation of Accounts Receivable   **Confirmation of accounts receivable** on a test basis helps the auditor to substantiate the genuineness of receivables and to evaluate correctness of valuation of the year-end balances. Confirmation is defined in the AICPA Professional Standards as "the process of obtaining and evaluating a direct communication from a third party in response to a request for information about a particular item affecting financial statement assertions."[6] As applied to trade accounts receivable, confirmation consists of customers' direct replies to auditors concerning the accuracy of the receivable balances, as reflected by the clients. Two types of confirmation are utilized in practice. **Positive confirmation** requests the customer to respond as to

6 *AICPA Professional Standards*, op. cit., section AU 330.04.

agreement or disagreement with the reported balance (see Exhibit 11.1). **Negative confirmation** requests the customer to reply only in the event of disagreement (see Exhibit 11.2). A disadvantage of the negative confirmation is that nonreplies may signify either agreement or simply failure to respond. For this reason, GAAS permits the negative form of confirmation only where the auditor has assessed the level of inherent risk and control risk as low, the auditor has no reason to believe that the recipient will not review the confirmation request, and a large number of small balances are involved.[7] If the first two conditions are met and customers' accounts include both large and small balances, auditors frequently stratify the population of customer accounts as to size, requesting positive confirmation for most of the large balances, and relying on negative confirmation for a sample of the smaller accounts.

After the subsidiary accounts receivable ledger has been compared with the general ledger control account, and customer statements that accompany the confirmation form have been prepared, the auditor must control the mailing of the confirmation requests. To maintain control, the auditor either mails the forms directly or carefully supervises the client's mailing of the confirmations. For both positive and negative confirmation requests, an envelope addressed to the CPA firm is included with the customer statement and confirmation request to ensure that customer replies are received directly by the auditor (a form of external evidence).

EXHIBIT 11.1

Positive Accounts Receivable Confirmation Request

(control number) 108

Jarol, Inc.
2334 Oak Street
Phoenix, Arizona

January 12, 2003

Roberts Discount Stores
835 Mound Street
Los Angeles, California

Gentlemen:

Our auditors, Arfol & Tick, CPAs, are making an examination of our financial statements. Please examine the accompanying statement and either confirm its correctness or report any differences to our auditors.

Your prompt attention to this request will be appreciated. An envelope is enclosed for your reply.

Very truly yours,

John Saling

John Saling
Credit Manager

7   Ibid, section AU 330.20.

EXHIBIT 11.2	

Negative Accounts Receivable Confirmation Request

> **Trane, Inc.**
> **4555 Pheasant Point**
> **Julio, Texas**
>
> January 12, 2003
>
> Links Bakeries
> 434 Tenth Street
> Libo, Louisiana
>
> Gentlemen:
>
> Please examine the accompanying statement. If it does not agree with your records, please report any exceptions directly to our auditors, Rightly & Wrongly, CPAs, who are making an examination of our financial statements.
>
> Very truly yours,
>
> *Stephen Jurs*
>
> Stephen Jurs
> Credit Manager

As the replies are received, they are logged into a control worksheet (see Exhibit 11.3), and all exceptions are cleared. Many exceptions consist of goods or remittances in transit and, assuming proper cutoff, do *not* require audit adjustment. Exceptions that are indicative of genuine disputes concerning prices, discounts, allowances, or returns should be explored in depth and may require audit adjustment, if material.

For customers *not* responding to the initial requests for positive confirmation, the auditor should mail second and possibly third requests. In the absence of replies to second and third requests, the auditor should apply alternate procedures. The procedures may be in the form of examining billing and shipping documents or remittance advices (the lower part attached to the customer's check and detailing the invoices paid by the remittance) in support of subsequent collections. If customers cannot confirm balances because the sales and accounts receivable systems restrict information to transactions, the auditor should consider confirming selected transactions with these customers.

Auditors must be careful not to rely too heavily on client documentation of sales where numerous nonreplies to confirmation requests are experienced. Confirmations are a form of external evidence and, therefore, provide greater assurance as to existence and valuation than internal evidence in the form of client documentation. Under conditions of significant nonreplies, the concept of due audit care should lead the auditor to consider whether an unqualified audit opinion can be rendered. The case presented later in this chapter illustrates how overreliance on internal evidence can lead to significant audit risk.

Lapping of Customers' Accounts Receivable   If one or more employees have misappropriated customer remittances with access to customer accounts, a form of conceal-

EXHIBIT 11.3

Confirmation Control Worksheet

W.P. No.	C.3
Prepared by:	lfk 1/15/03
Reviewed by:	gfg 1/22/03

Jarol, Inc.
Accounts Receivable—Trade
Confirmation Control Worksheet
12/31/02

Confirmation Number	Customer	Balance	Date Returned	Comments
100	Congre Wholesalers	$ 2,688	2/6	No exceptions
101	Trac Two	12,357	2/3	No exceptions
102	House of Glass	6,654		(1)
103	General Arts	34,890	2/8	(2)
104	Uler Office Supply	4,532	3/1	No exceptions
105	Jolly News	1,388	2/20	No exceptions
106	Riker Gifts	7,760		(3)
107	Lila's Pharmacy	5,235	2/13	No exceptions
108	Roberts Discount Stores	66,890	2/2	(4)
109	Usher, Inc.	54,378	3/2	No exceptions
110	Save More	8,697	2/5	No exceptions

(1) No response to second and third requests.
   Examined shipping documents and subsequent collections—No exceptions.
(2) Credit not given for returned merchandise.
   Customer has issued debit memo for $1,870.
   Credit manager indicates that CM is forthcoming.
(3) No response to second and third requests.
   Examined shipping documents and subsequent collections—No exceptions.
(4) Remittance of $12,346 in transit at year end.
   Traced to January cash receipts (see WP B.2).

ment known as *lapping* may have been applied. **Lapping** involves crediting current remittances to the accounts of customers who have remitted previously. The purpose is to keep all accounts current in order to avoid auditor suspicion and unusual customer exceptions to confirmation requests. For example, assume that Customer A remitted $2,000 on November 1, and the remittance was misappropriated by an accounts receivable clerk prior to recording. Assume further that Customer B remitted $5,000 on December 30 and that the company closes its books on December 31. The dishonest clerk may elect to credit $2,000 of B's remittance to Customer A, and only $3,000 to Customer B's account in the subsidiary ledger. The effect is to lessen the probability of detection by transferring the fraudulent debit from a past due to a current customer account. The auditor is less likely to be suspicious of the Customer B confirmation exception, given the current status of the account. He or she might assume the difference represents a remittance in transit.

In addition to confirming customer accounts and clearing all exceptions, an auditor who suspects lapping because of control weaknesses should consider tracing the details of year-end cash receipts to remittance advices and the accounts receivable subsidiary ledger. Any credit to an account other than that of the customer remitting will thereby be detected. This procedure also may be applied to cash receipts for the first couple of days following year end. This set of procedures is another example of modifying the nature of substantive audit procedures under conditions of weak internal control.

Use of the Computer to Assist in Accounts Receivable Confirmation and Analysis
Auditors frequently utilize computer capability to assist in determining sample size for confirmation purposes and in selecting customers' accounts to be confirmed. The computer can print confirmation requests for selected accounts, and final results can be evaluated. The auditor usually relies on statistical sampling software packages, spreadsheet templates, or database systems in applying these procedures. A **relational database software package**, for example, may be used to assist in performing the following tasks relative to the audit of accounts receivable:

1. Select and list customer balances above a certain balance for purposes of stratifying the population of customer accounts;
2. List all accounts with credit balances for further follow-up;
3. Select balances for confirmation and print confirmation requests;
4. Sort accounts by account number, dollar balance, customer class, or location;
5. Check for valid account number;
6. Compare credit limit to the current balance for each account and list exceptions;
7. Compare cash receipts after year end to invoices at the balance sheet date; and
8. Calculate ratios as part of the application of analytical procedures (e.g., turnover, returns and allowances to sales, bad debts expense to accounts receivable, and average balance per customer).

Accounts Receivable Aging Analysis   An **accounts receivable aging analysis** is useful in evaluating the adequacy of the allowance for doubtful accounts (see Exhibits 11.4 and 11.5). Note that Exhibit 11.4 includes post-balance sheet collections of customers' year-end balances. Subsequent remittance by the customer is the best evidence of collectibility at the balance sheet date.

The aging analysis can be automated in the form of an electronic spreadsheet template. Cell equations may be inserted for performing the following calculations:

1. Footing and crossfooting of the columns;
2. Calculating outstanding balances after application of subsequent collections; and
3. Applying expected loss percentages to the various categories of receivables, to assist the auditor in evaluating collectibility.

Tests for Proper Presentation and Disclosure   In addition to ensuring completeness, existence, and valuation, the auditor must gather evidence in support of proper presentation and adequacy of disclosure relative to sales revenue and trade accounts receivable. Credit balances in customers' accounts, nontrade receivables, and related-party receivables must be classified separately, if material, and are detected best through inquiry of management. Inquiry is further corroborated by analysis of the accounts receivable subsidiary ledger as part of the confirmation process. The standard bank

EXHIBIT 11.4

Accounts Receivable Aging Analysis

WPC

Auditee, Inc.
Accounts Receivable Aging Analysis
12/31/02

Prepared by: LFK Date: 2/5/03
Reviewed by: CCK Date: 2/15/03

Customer	Total	Current	Past Due: 1–60 days	Past Due: 61–90 days	Past Due: 91–120 days	Past Due: 121 + days	Subsequent Collections (through 1/31/03)
Audobon, Inc.	$100,000	$ 0	$ 30,000	$ 70,000			$ 40,000&
Bando	0	0					0&
Crail, Ltd.	260,000	60,000	200,000				60,000&
Dorodiak, Inc.	210,000	0	100,000	30,000		$80,000	100,000&
Klarion Chief	40,000	20,000	20,000				20,000&
Laubers	80,000	80,000					80,000&
Mastalon, Inc.	30,000	0	30,000		—		0&
12/31/02							
Total Accounts Receivable	$720,000	$160,000*	$380,000*	$100,000*	$0*	$80,000*	$300,000
Subsequent collections	300,000	160,000	130,000	10,000	0	0	
Uncollected at 1/31/03	$420,000	$ 0	$250,000	$ 90,000	$0	$80,000	
Estimated uncollectible (%)			10%	20%		100%	
Estimated uncollectible ($)	$123,000		$ 25,000	$ 18,000	$0	$80,000	

& Traced to remittance advice
* Obtained from subsidiary ledger

EXHIBIT 11.5

Allowance for Doubtful Accounts

		WP C.1
	Prepared by:	LFK
	Date:	2/3/03
	Reviewed by:	CG
	Date:	2/15/03

Auditee, Inc.
Accounts Receivable—Trade
Allowance for Doubtful Accounts
12/31/02

1/1/02	Balance per ledger	$ 97,000&	
1/1–12/31/02	Write-offs	(76,000)*	
12/31/02	Balance per ledger	$ 21,000	
	AJE 6	102,000	See WP C
12/31/02	Final balance	$123,000	To WP C
	AJE 6		

Bad debts expense	$102,000	
Allowance for doubtful accounts		$102,000

To adjust allowance for doubtful accounts to amount
  considered reasonable in the circumstances.

Discussed adequacy of allowance for doubtful accounts with credit manager, in light of aging
analysis (see WP C). The above balance, as adjusted, appears to be adequate.

& Traced to WTB
* Examined documentation, and discussed with credit manager and legal counsel.

---

confirmation, described later in the chapter, may disclose pledging or assignment of accounts receivable as collateral in securing loans.

Miscellaneous Revenue Tests   Substantive testing of trade accounts receivable provides evidence in support of operating revenue transactions. The auditor also should apply substantive procedures to miscellaneous revenues. The first step in auditing miscellaneous revenues is to apply analytical procedures that compare balances in the accounts with those of the prior year, for both amount and source of revenue. Assuming no major abnormalities, substantive procedures may be limited to vouching credits on a test basis by examining underlying documentation.

If analytical procedures reveal major changes in amount or source, the auditor should consider confirming transactions. If revenues have declined significantly, transactions should be confirmed for nonexistence as well as for existence. Confirming for nonexistence requires identifying the historic sources of miscellaneous revenues (e.g., scrap dealers) and requesting the companies so identified to provide the auditors with the dollar volume of transactions with the client during the year.

Figure 11.4 summarizes the preceding discussion by presenting a model audit program for performing substantive tests of the sales and accounts receivable portion of

FIGURE 11.4

Model Audit Program for Sales Transactions in Revenue Cycle

Analytical Procedures
1. Compare sales, cost of sales, and gross profit with those in the prior year, on a month-by-month basis, and account for major changes.
2. Compare sales patterns and gross profit rates with industry averages.
3. Calculate turnover of accounts receivable, and compare with prior-year turnover and industry average.
4. Compare sales returns and allowances and miscellaneous revenues with those of prior year and account for significant changes.
5. Compare sales, cost of sales, and gross profit with budgeted amounts and account for significant variances.

Other Substantive Audit Procedures
1. Perform sales cutoff procedures by examining documentary evidence for a few days before and after year end.
2. Vouch credits to miscellaneous revenue accounts on a test basis by examining underlying documentation.
3. Confirm accounts receivable balances on a test basis:
   • Agree subsidiary ledger to control account in general ledger.
   • Consider stratifying population and confirming larger accounts and credit balances on a positive basis.
   • Examine evidence of shipment and remittance advice for those customers not responding to second and third requests for positive confirmation.
4. Prepare an aging analysis of accounts receivable, and evaluate the adequacy of the allowance for doubtful accounts.
5. Inquire of management, and examine directors' minutes, correspondence, contracts, and bank confirmation for evidence of:
   • Pledging or assigning accounts receivable as collateral for loans.
   • Existence of related parties and related-party transactions.

the revenue cycle. If the auditor discovers increased or decreased audit risk as a result of analytical procedures, study of the business and industry, or the internal control study and evaluation, the program would need to be modified.

Cash Receipts Transactions and Cash Balances

Audit Objectives   The audit objectives related to cash receipts transactions and cash balances may be classified as follows:

1. *Existence and completeness assertions.* The auditor must be reasonably assured that all cash receipts and only cash receipts of the period under audit have been recorded and deposited prior to year end. The auditor must also be satisfied that all cash balances and only cash balances of the client are reflected on the ending balance sheet.

2. *Presentation and disclosure assertions.* The auditor should be alert to the possibility of bank overdrafts and recommend reclassification as current liabilities, if material in amount.

Restricted funds, such as sinking funds, should be classified as noncurrent assets because they are unavailable for payment of current obligations. When the obligation becomes current, the balances should be classified as current assets.

Loan agreements frequently require the borrower to maintain minimum levels in demand deposit accounts. Referred to as *compensating balance requirements*, these restrictions, along with other restrictive covenants contained in the agreements, should be disclosed in footnotes to the financial statements.

Audit Evidence and Procedures

Bank Confirmation   The **standard bank confirmation** form (see Exhibit 11.6) should be used for all bank accounts, both active and inactive.[8] The form is signed by the client, completed by the bank, and returned directly to the auditor. The bank confirmation provides evidence of the existence and valuation of the accounts. It also requests the bank to confirm outstanding loans to the company, as well as collateral used for securing the loans. Note that the standard bank confirmation form does not cover contingent items such as client guarantees of loans to related parties. Auditors frequently request banks to confirm the existence or nonexistence of these contingencies and draft separate confirmation letters for this purpose.

Bank Reconciliation and the Cutoff Bank Statement   If the client has reconciled bank accounts as of year end, the auditor should examine the reconciliations for evidence of proper valuation and cutoff. If the client has *not* reconciled the accounts, the auditor should consider this a control weakness and complete the reconciliations as an extended audit procedure (see Exhibit 11.7).

The auditor also should obtain a **cutoff bank statement** directly from the bank. The client requests the bank to forward the statement directly to the auditor. A cutoff bank statement is identical to the normal monthly bank statement, but covers a two- or three-week period immediately following year end. Obtaining the statement permits the auditor to examine evidence in support of the reconciling items appearing on the year-end bank reconciliation. Deposits in transit, outstanding checks, and other reconciling items are traced to the cutoff bank statement and to the canceled checks returned with the statement. All canceled checks dated prior to year end are traced to the list of outstanding checks appearing on the year-end bank reconciliation to determine if they were recorded in the proper accounting period. Payees, endorsements, and clearing dates appearing on canceled checks should all be noted carefully during examination of the cutoff bank statement. Payees are compared with the cash disbursements record for agreement and endorsements are compared with payees appearing on the face of the check. Lack of agreement may be indicative of efforts to conceal defalcations or other forms of fraud. Late clearing dates, appearing on canceled checks dated before year end, may result from holding the cash disbursements record open after year end.

8   Although inactive accounts may contain zero or nominal balances, the volume of transactions flowing through the accounts during the year may have been substantial. For this reason, auditors should guard against underauditing inactive bank accounts.

EXHIBIT 11.6

Standard Form to Confirm Account Balance Information with Financial Institutions

Financial Institution's Name and Address

First National Bank
201 Marchal Street
Meridian, MS

Auditee, Inc.
_____
Customer Name

We have provided to our accountants the following information as of the close of business on ___December 31, 2002___ , regarding our deposit and loan balances. Please confirm the accuracy of the information, noting any exceptions to the information provided. If the balances have been left blank, please complete this form by furnishing the balance in the appropriate space below.* Although we do not request nor expect you to conduct a comprehensive, detailed search of your records, if during the process of completing this confirmation additional information about other deposit and loan accounts we may have with you comes to your attention, please include such information below. Please use the enclosed envelope to return the form directly to our accountants.

1. At the close of business on the date listed above, our records indicated the following deposit balance(s):

Account Name	Account No.	Interest Rate	Balance*
Auditee, Inc.—General	65-2318-431	—	$450,000.00
Auditee, Inc.—Payroll	81-6713-562	—	10,000.00

2. We were directly liable to the financial institution for loans at the close of business on the date listed above as follows:

Account No./ Description	Balance*	Date Due	Interest Rate	Date Through Which Interest Is Paid	Description of Collateral
1013864	$850,000	12/31/03	9 1/2%	12/31/02	None

_____John Helmoil—Controller_____   _____1/8/03_____
(Customer's Authorized Signature)   (Date)

The information presented above by the customer is in agreement with our records. Although we have not conducted a comprehensive, detailed search of our records, no other deposit or loan accounts have come to our attention except as noted below.

_____George Kennedy_____   _____1/12/03_____
(Financial Institution Authorized Signature)   (Date)

_____Commercial Account Officer_____
(Title)

Exceptions and/or Comments

Please return this form directly to our accountants:

Double of Toil, CPAs
1023 Mercury Rd
Meridian, MS

*Ordinarily, balances are intentionally left blank if they are not available at the time the form is prepared. Approved 1990 by American Bankers Association, American Institute of Certified Public Accountants, and Bank Administration Institute. Additional forms available from: AICPA— Order Department, P.O. Box 1003, NY, NY 10108-1003

EXHIBIT 11.7

Bank Reconciliation

			WP A.1
		Prepared by:	LFK
		Date:	1/23/03
		Reviewed by:	JRG
		Date:	2/5/03

Auditee, Inc.
Bank Reconciliation
Cash in Bank—General
12/31/02

12/31/02	Balance per bank		$450,000*
	Add deposits in transit		50,000&
	Total		500,000
	Deduct:		
	Outstanding checks	30,000&	
	Restricted balance	10,000!	
			40,000
12/31/02	Balance per reconciliation		$460,000
12/31/02	Balance per general ledger		$420,000
	AJE No. 1—bank collection of customer note		50,000+
	RJE No. A—restricted balance		(10,000)
12/31/02	Balance per reconciliation		$460,000 to WPA

		AJE 1	
Cash in bank—general		50,000	
Notes receivable			50,000
To record bank collection of customer note.			

		RJE A	
Cash in bank—restricted		10,000	
Cash in bank—general			10,000
To reclassify restricted cash as a noncurrent asset.			

* Traced to bank confirmation attached
& Traced to cutoff bank statement obtained directly from bank
! Examined loan agreement (see permanent file)
+ Examined bank credit memo included with bank statement

Cash Receipts Cutoff   The auditor also should apply **cash receipts cutoff** tests to year-end cash transactions. Cash receipts on the last business day of the year should be examined by reference to cash receipts listings, remittance advices, and deposit tickets. The cash should also be traced to the bank statement, if deposited before year end. If the cash receipts were not deposited by year end, they should be traced to the bank reconciliation and to the cutoff bank statement. For deposits in transit, the auditor should determine that the bank credited the deposit within one or two working days after year end. Credits dated later than this may be indicative of faulty cutoff procedures and, possibly, inflated year-end cash balances.

Proof of Cash   Auditors who determine that internal control over cash transactions is weak may elect to prepare a **proof of cash** for one or more months of the year under audit. This is a time-consuming and costly audit procedure and for this reason should be completed only under conditions of weak internal control over cash. The proof of cash (see Exhibit 11.8) performs the same function as the bank reconciliation and in addition reconciles the client's recorded receipts and disbursements with bank statement credits and debits. If cash receipts have been misappropriated or erroneously recorded,

---

EXHIBIT 11.8

Proof of Cash

		WP A.3
Prepared by:		LFK
Date:		2/17/03
Reviewed by:		CCK
Date:		2/22/03

Biochem, Inc.
Proof of Cash
12/31/02

	6/30/02 Bank Reconciliation	Receipts	Disbursements	12/31/02 Bank Reconciliation
Balance per bank statement	$ 167,183.23	$1,234,652.16	$1,312,589.80	$ 89,245.59C
Deposits in transit				
Beginning	66,839.60	(66,839.60)		
Ending		123,678.90		123,678.90
Outstanding checks				
Beginning	(125,456.98)		(125,456.98)⊕	
Ending			77,982.12⊕	(77,982.12)
Bank collection of note receivable plus interest		(22,314.50)E		(22,314.50)
Balance per books	$ 108,565.85	$1,269,176.96	$1,265,114.94	$112,627.87
	GL	✓	~	GL
	F	F	F	F
				CF

C Traced to bank confirmation
✓ Traced to cash receipts record
~ Traced to cash disbursement record
E Examined bank credit memo
F Footed
CF Crossfooted
⊕ See lists of outstanding checks attached
GL Traced to general ledger

therefore, the receipts per books will *not* reconcile with the receipts per the bank statement. Similarly, if cash disbursements have been misrecorded, the disbursements per books will *not* reconcile with bank statement debits. In summary, this extended audit procedure should help in the detection of errors or fraud involving cash receipts or disbursements under conditions of weak internal control. It will also aid in the detection of omitted entries.

Analysis of Interbank Transfers   If the client has more than one bank account, the auditor should complete an **analysis of interbank transfers** for one or two weeks before and after year end (see Exhibit 11.9). The purpose of this test is to detect errors or fraud involving year-end checks in transit between banks.

Kiting, a type of fraud used to conceal bank overdrafts or cash misappropriations, as well as to obtain interest-free loans, may be detected by analyzing interbank transfers. **Kiting** occurs when a company draws a check on one bank for deposit in another bank, but does not record the transaction, or records only a part of the transaction before year end. In the case of overdrafts, the following scenario may occur: A journal entry is made to record the receipt, and the check is listed as a deposit in transit to conceal the overdraft. The disbursement side of the transaction is not recorded until after year end, and the check is not listed as outstanding in the reconciliation of the disbursing bank account. In Exhibit 11.9, Check #1668, drawn on Huron Bank—Duluth for deposit in First Bank—Chicago, is apparently a form of kiting because the cash receipt was recorded in 2002.

A highly publicized check kiting case occurring in the mid-1980s involved the president and chief executive officers of Transit Mix Concrete Corporation and two large banks, Marine Midland and Citibank. The officers drew checks on the Transit Mix Concrete account at Citibank and deposited those checks in an account at Marine Midland for Water Tunnel Associates, a "dummy" company also operated by Halloran and Madden, the officers of Transit Mix Concrete. Of the $9.2 billion transferred between the two banks, the two officers were charged with stealing $23 million.[9]

In another case, the use of **float**, defined as the time lag for cash transfers to clear between the disbursing bank and the payee bank, permitted the brokerage firm of E.F. Hutton to fraudulently obtain interest-free loans exceeding $8 million between 1980 and 1982 from some 400 banks.[10]

In addition to analyzing interbank transfers, the auditor should also examine cash receipts and disbursements for a few days before and after the balance sheet date. This procedure assists in the detection of other errors or fraud. Repayment of officers' loans prior to year end, for example, followed by relending after year end, will surface during the analysis. Checks in transit between divisions, with the disbursement but not the receipt having been recorded, will also be detected.

Other Tests   By examining loan agreements and the bank confirmation, and through inquiry of client personnel, the auditor should be able to identify compensating balance requirements and other cash restrictions. These restrictions require disclosure in footnotes to the financial statements.

Audit attention also should be directed toward cash receipts derived from sources other than from customers. These include sales of plant assets, sales of securities or other investments, sales of scrap materials, proceeds from stock issuance, and so on.

9   Chambers, Marcia, "Two Face Charges in a Bank Theft of $23 Million," *The New York Times*, June 28, 1985, p. B3.
10 Alexander, Charles P., "Crime in the Suites," *Time*, June 10, 1985, p. 56.

EXHIBIT 11.9

Analysis of Interbank Transfers

Prepared by: lfk
Date: 2/3/03
Reviewed by: jrg
Date: 2/10/03

WP A.3

Hublee Motors
Analysis of Interbank Transfers
12/31/02

Check Number	Drawn on	Deposited in	Check Amount	Date of Check (1)	Date of Receipt (1)	Date Credited by Depository Bank	Date Debited by Payor Bank
1067	First Bank—Chicago	City Bank—Cleveland	$10,000	12/30/02	12/31/02	1/2/03*	1/5/03 *
2079	1st Bank—Knoxville	Huron Bank—Duluth	22,354	12/31/02	1/3/03	1/4/03*	1/9/03
3063	City Bank—Cleveland	1st Bank—Knoxville	30,000	12/30/02	1/2/03	1/3/03*	1/5/03
1668	Huron Bank—Duluth	First Bank—Chicago	44,000	1/2/03	12/31/02	1/2/03*	1/4/03

AJE 3
Cash in Bank—Duluth $22,354
    Receivable from Knoxville Branch $22,354

AJE 4
Cash in Bank—Knoxville $30,000
    Receivable from Cleveland Branch $30,000

AJE 5
Receivable from Duluth $44,000
    Cash in Bank—Chicago $44,000

Examined check registers and cash receipts records for the period December 15, 2002, to January 15, 2003. All interbank transfers, detected by the above examination, are listed above.

(1) Same as date recorded.
* Traced to cutoff bank statement. Compared payees and endorsements with check register.

Cash receipts of this nature are identified in analyzing the related accounts and noting credit postings to plant assets, investment accounts, notes payable, capital stock, and notes receivable. Once identified, the cash receipts should be vouched on a test basis by reference to the underlying documentation and traced to the cash receipts record and to the bank statement.

In addition to cash in bank accounts, other forms of cash, such as petty cash funds, change funds, and various forms of undeposited cash on hand, are included in "Cash" on the balance sheet. Although audit procedures may be applied to these items, they usually are limited, given the concepts of relative risk and materiality. Counting of the funds on a test basis and comparison of balances with those of prior years may be the extent of procedures applied.

Figure 11.5 contains a model audit program for substantive testing of cash receipts transactions and cash balances. The analytical procedures serve as input to further modification of the nature, timing, and extent of the other substantive procedures.

AUDIT RISK ANALYSIS AND THE REVENUE CYCLE: SOME WARNING SIGNS

In the preceding discussion of audit procedures, unless otherwise noted, it was assumed that the auditor did *not* discover any unusual conditions that would indicate a higher-

---

FIGURE 11.5

Model Audit Program for Cash Receipts Transactions and Cash Balances in the Revenue Cycle

Analytical Procedures
1. Compare cash accounts with those of prior year and investigate additions or deletions of accounts.
2. Compare cash receipts from miscellaneous sources with those of prior year and account for major changes.

Other Substantive Procedures
1. Count and list cash on hand at year end and trace to cash receipts record and bank statement.
2. Vouch significant cash receipts from sources other than customers and trace to deposit tickets and bank statements on a test basis.
3. Confirm bank balances directly with bank.
4. Compare balance on confirmation with year-end bank statement.
5. Reconcile bank accounts as of year end.
6. Obtain cutoff bank statement(s) directly from banks and trace reconciling items from bank reconciliation to cutoff statement.
7. Prepare analysis of interbank transfers for a few days before and after year end.
8. Examine loan agreements and directors' minutes for compensating balance requirements and consider reclassifying as noncurrent if significant.
9. Inquire as to status of inactive bank accounts.

than-normal audit risk situation. The following paragraphs consider some warning signs that might cause the auditor to suspect that certain components of the revenue cycle have been intentionally misstated. Auditing procedures that the auditors might apply, given the warning signs, are also identified.

Bartered Web-Site Advertising

A practice prevalent among dot-com companies advertising on the Internet is to trade advertising with other companies. The sold advertising is then treated as revenue while the purchased advertising appears as expense. The popularity of these noncash barter transactions stems from the financial community's focus on revenues of Internet startup companies that are still incurring losses. Financial analysts often calculate a stock price to revenue ratio for these companies in lieu of a price/earnings ratio. Although the Financial Accounting Standards Board permits revenue recognition in barter transactions, a significant caveat prohibits revenue recognition if the company hasn't sold similar advertising for cash within the previous six months. The CPA, therefore, must be alert to bartered advertising transactions when auditing Internet companies with recurring losses.

Inflated Sales or Fictitious Accounts Receivable

If sales or accounts receivable were materially inflated, the application of analytical procedures should reveal abnormal sales patterns, reduced accounts receivable turnover, or both. Moreover, if sales were inflated by holding the sales record open after year end, sales cutoff procedures should assist the auditor in detecting the misrepresentation.

In a case brought to light several years ago, a major toy manufacturer fabricated several invoices at year end in order to inflate sales and accounts receivable and thereby avoid reporting losses for the year.[11] Although other toy companies were reporting declining sales for the year, Company X enjoyed a sizable increase. January sales (the last month of the fiscal year, normally the lowest month for sales volume) reflected an especially heavy volume. The company reported $2.9 million (1.3 million pounds) of toys shipped on the last day of the fiscal year, Saturday, January 31! In this case, the auditors apparently did not pursue abnormalities that should have been brought to their attention by the application of analytical procedures. Moreover, the auditors did not adequately clear exceptions to confirmation requests returned by customers. Instead of investigating allegations of nonshipment, as evidenced by the returned confirmations, the auditors relied on management's assertions. Indeed, they accepted the fabricated sales orders, sales invoices, and bills of lading at face value, and ignored the confirmations. In essence, the auditors "went through the motions" but did not really confirm accounts receivable.

The lesson in this case for auditors is that warning signs should be heeded, and audit resources allocated accordingly. The auditors should have performed a more thorough sales cutoff test. Also, given the presence of both external and internal evidence, accompanied by control weaknesses and/or abnormalities revealed by analytical procedures, auditors should formulate their audit conclusions on the basis of the stronger external evidence (recall Chapter 5, Figure 5.4). In the toy company case, the auditors

---

11 Johnson, Alan P., *Auditing Judgment—A Book of Cases*, Homewood, IL: Richard D. Irwin, 1980, pp. 112–24.

elected to accept management's assertions (internal evidence) and to ignore the confirmation exceptions (external evidence).

In a case that surfaced in the 1990s, California Micro Devices Corp., a manufacturer of computer chips, also inflated income by recording fictitious sales to nonexistent customers, resulting in a significant overstatement of earnings. Nevertheless, the auditors, Coopers Lybrand, rendered an unqualified opinion on the company's financial statements for the fiscal year ended September 30, 1994. In addition to the fictitious sales, Cal Micro was recognizing revenue from products shipped before customers wanted them. Moreover, the company didn't reverse the sales when the customers returned the products. The company later attributed massive write-offs of the inflated receivables to uncollectible accounts.[12]

As in the toy company case cited above, the auditors, according to SEC investigators, ignored the multitude of exceptions taken by customers to accounts receivable confirmation requests. Some of the replies stated that the customers hadn't received the products until well after year end; others indicated disputes over credits for returned merchandise; and one stated that Cal Micro had shipped the products to them on consignment and the goods had yet to be sold. A further warning sign apparently ignored or overlooked by the auditors was the fact that Cal Micro's reported operating earnings far exceeded its operating cash flow for the fiscal year.[13]

A New York money manager questioned the earnings projections of Boston Chicken, the fast-food rotisserie chicken franchiser. He alleged that the company had inflated its earnings by including royalties and fees from franchisees who were "essentially subsidiaries." The franchise agreements permitted franchisees to convert their loans to equity after two years and become 66 percent-owned subsidiaries of Boston Chicken. The royalties and fees, given the loan/equity conversion provisions, were, in substance, cash transfers rather than revenues, as reported by the company.[14] This is but another example of the auditor's need to be continuously alert to possible conflicts between legal form and economic substance when auditing revenue transactions. The lesson in this case, for auditors with franchising clients, is that the agreements should be examined carefully in determining proper timing and valuation of revenues.

Inadequate Loan Loss Reserves

Commercial banks and savings and loan associations derive most of their revenue from interest on loans made to their customers. For many years relatively modest "loan loss reserves," established through debits to bad debts expense, proved adequate to absorb losses from uncollectible loans. As certain industries (agriculture and energy, for example) began to decline, however, and as the loan portfolios included increasing numbers of real estate loans and foreign loans, loan loss reserves as they had been maintained traditionally were insufficient at many institutions. In several cases, the losses were so great that they threatened the solvency of the banks. In some instances (the cases involving Lincoln Savings, United American Bank of Knoxville, First Oklahoma Bancorp, and Penn Square Bank of Oklahoma City, for example), the auditors were sued for failing to detect the problem loans.

---

12 MacDonald, Elizabeth, "What's Revenue?" *The Wall Street Journal*, January 6, 2000, p. A1.
13 Ibid.
14 *Business Week*, July 18, 1994, p. 70.

454

In one of the cases, a land developer purchased a bank and completed several real estate sales and financing transactions with related parties. The real estate was mostly desert land but, given the existence of related parties, the inflated prices enabled the bank to record large "paper" gains on the sales. Moreover, the loans to finance the sales were significantly in excess of the appraised values of the properties. These transactions allowed the bank to record large profits, and the bank-backed loans provided a conduit for channeling funds from the bank to a parent company also controlled by the land developer and controlling stockholder of the bank. This in turn allegedly allowed cash flow to the developer's family.

Auditors in this case were accused of actually approving the related-party transactions.[15] At the very least, they did not devote adequate audit resources to examining the related-party transactions. The rapid increase in the investment portfolio, the rising proportion of real estate transactions accompanied by loan guarantees by the bank, and the high incidence of and amounts in cash transfers from the bank to the parent company should have alerted the auditors to the heightened risk of fraud.

As a result of these and similar cases, auditors who examine the financial statements of commercial banks and savings and loan associations devote increased attention to loan portfolios and to evaluating the adequacy of loan loss reserves.

Unclaimed customer funds is another area of critical importance in bank audits. In a case that came to light in the 1990s, Bankers Trust, an investment and commercial bank, was charged with illegally diverting over $19 million in cash and other assets to a "slush" fund for the purpose of bolstering the bank's sagging earnings. The funds represented uncashed dividend and benefit checks that had been issued by the bank to stockholders and employees of clients serviced by the bank's processing services division. Most state laws require that such funds be transferred to the state after a reasonable time period. The auditors became suspicious when the unclaimed funds accounts had decreased dramatically from $10 million to $4 million in 1994. Although the auditors requested documents explaining the decrease, management did not immediately provide the documents. Using alternate means such as inquiring of employees and subpoenaing documents, the auditors finally developed enough evidence of fraud to spawn a Federal investigation.

Early Revenue Recognition

Auditors should be alert to the possibility of **early revenue recognition**, which occurs when clients recognize revenue before the point of sale. The percentage of completion method of accounting for construction contracts and the proportional method for recognizing revenue from service contracts are acceptable alternatives to recognizing revenue at the point of sale. Certain conditions must be met, however, in order for these methods to be appropriate under the circumstances. First, the earning process must be substantially complete; second, realization must be reasonably assured; and third, the revenue and related costs must be capable of reasonable measurement. Several cases have surfaced over the years in which companies, recognizing revenue without having met all of these conditions, have received unqualified audit opinions.

In the case of Frigitemp Corporation, a company engaged in manufacturing custom-made refrigeration equipment for ships and hospitals, decorating hotels and casinos, and

---

15 Thomas, Paulette, "Auditors Say Lincoln S&L 'Sham' Deals Were Approved by Arthur Young & Co.," *The Wall Street Journal*, November 15, 1989, p. A2.

building food service systems, a method for revenue recognition referred to as "cost-to-cost percentage of completion" was used. Under this method, revenue was recognized in proportion to the amount of money spent on raw materials. As a result, the company purchased excessive amounts of materials in order to maximize reported profits. In one instance, a supplier gave Frigitemp an invoice for $4.2 million in deck planking, most of which was still growing in forests on the West Coast.[16]

Another case of premature revenue recognition involved the HBO division of McKesson HBOC Inc. McKesson had recently acquired the division, formerly HBO & Co., a developer of medical software. HBO had been a fast-growing company selling hospitals and doctors software to handle financial and clinical data. Completing the acquisition before an in-depth audit of HBO, McKesson failed to detect substantial earnings inflation caused by early revenue recognition. In most of the cases, the software sales included side contracts covering contingencies that were not met by HBO. After adjusting for the overstatement of revenue, fiscal 1999 earnings for the combined companies was reduced from $237 million to $85 million.

Careful examination of the contracts and confirmation requests returned by customers alerted the auditors to the overstatements. These procedures prompted the auditors to further investigation and subsequent detection.[17]

Another case of early revenue recognition involved Orion Pictures Corp., producer of *Dances with Wolves* and *Silence of the Lambs*. Between 1983 and 1990, Orion reported profits every year. During the same period, however, the balance in its "deferred television and movie costs," an asset, was also increasing. The rate of increase was so significant that by 1990 the balance in the account, $766 million, exceeded its 1990 revenues of $584 million. For other filmmakers, reported revenues significantly exceeded the balance in deferred assets. Paramount Pictures and Disney, for example, reported revenues during the same period that were approximately four times the balances in their respective deferred asset accounts.

Further analysis determined that Orion was not writing off failed films, thus accounting for the continued increase in the asset carrying value. Perhaps the most flagrant abuse of revenue accounting occurred in 1990 when Orion received $175 million from Columbia Pictures as an advance against future international distribution of Orion films, most of which had *not* yet been made. Although it was clearly unearned, Orion recorded $50 million of the advance as revenue. This allowed the company to report a $20 million pretax profit for 1990, rather than a $30 million loss.

Although accounting for revenue from the sale of television shows and movies is complex and not structured like other types of revenue, this was clearly a case that should have alerted the auditors to possible earnings inflation. Moreover, the auditors' suspicions should have been aroused by the application of analytical procedures. The steady increase in the deferred asset balance, the excess of the balance over 1990 revenue, and the opposite pattern from those of other filmmakers in the industry should have led the auditors to devote increased attention to Orion's revenue recognition policies and to carefully analyze the deferred asset account.[18]

16 Fialka, John J., "Why Arthur Andersen Failed to Detect Accounting Fraud at Frigitemp," *The Wall Street Journal*, September 21, 1984, p. A1.
17 King, Ralph T., "Soft Numbers," *The Wall Street Journal*, July 15, 1999, p. A1.
18 As a result of this and similar instances of revenue recognition abuse in the film industry, the Financial Accounting Standards Board has tightened the rules for recognizing revenue and deferring costs related to films produced by film and television companies.

The warning signs just cited are examples of conditions that auditors are most likely to identify while studying the business and industry and applying analytical procedures. The audit implications of the above findings make it imperative that all members of the audit team be made aware of identified high-risk situations and that audit programs be modified accordingly. This is the essence of audit risk analysis and audit program modification, as presented in Chapter 5.

APPENDIX

AUDITING OBJECTIVES AND PROCEDURES: REVENUE CYCLE

This appendix consists of a matrix that relates audit objectives to audit evidence and procedures within the revenue cycle. Specific audit objectives are listed below the related management assertions, and the audit procedures are listed next to the set of objectives to which they relate. Although not intended to be all-inclusive, the matrix may serve as a model for developing comprehensive programs for substantive audit testing.

Sales Transactions and Accounts Receivable Balances

Assertions and Audit Objectives	Audit Evidence and Procedures
Existence, Completeness, and Valuation	***Analytical Evidence***
Are customers valid?	• Compare sales, cost of sales, and gross profit with those of prior year, on a month-by-month basis, and account for major changes.
Are accounts receivable reported at net realizable value?	• Compare sales, cost of sales, and gross profit with budgeted amounts and investigate significant variances.
Are sales reported in the proper accounting period?	• Compare sales patterns and gross profit rates with industry averages.
Have sales been omitted?	• Calculate turnover of accounts receivable and compare with that of prior year and industry average.
	• Compare sales returns and allowances as a percentage of sales with prior year and account for material changes.
	• Compare miscellaneous and other nonoperating revenue accounts with those of prior year for both source and amount and investigate significant changes.
	Documentary Evidence
	• Review accounts receivable subsidiary ledger for large balances, unusual balances, credit balances, and related-party balances.
	• Perform sales cutoff procedures by examining documentary evidence (e.g., shipping orders, in-

voices, and bills of lading) for a few days before and after year end.

- Vouch credits to miscellaneous revenue accounts on a test basis by examining underlying documentation.

Confirmation Evidence

- Confirm accounts receivable on a test basis. Use positive confirmation requests, except for smaller balances where inherent risk and control risk are assessed at low levels.
- Consider stratifying population and confirming a higher percentage of larger accounts.
- Examine evidence of shipment and remittance advice for those customers *not* responding to second and third requests for positive confirmation.
- Confirm year-end credit balances and accounts written off during the year.
- Consider confirming miscellaneous revenue transactions, if material, or if analytical procedures indicate major changes.

Mathematical Evidence

- Agree accounts receivable subsidiary ledger to controlling account.
- Prepare an aging analysis of accounts receivable and evaluate the adequacy of the allowance for doubtful accounts.

Presentation and Disclosure

Any credit balances?

Any receivables from related parties?

Any pledging of receivables as collateral?

Any significant noncurrent or nontrade receivables?

Documentary Evidence

- Examine directors' minutes, correspondence, and contracts for evidence regarding pledging or assignment of accounts receivable.
- Scan subsidiary ledger for credit balances.
- Examine SEC "conflict of interest statements" for possible existence of related-party receivables.

Confirmation Evidence

- Examine bank confirmation for evidence of pledging or assigning receivables as collateral for loans.

Hearsay Evidence

- Inquire of management as to related-party transactions and nontrade receivables included in accounts receivable.
- Inquire of credit manager as to extended credit terms that may require noncurrent classification of certain receivables.

Cash Receipts Transactions and Cash Balances

Assertions and Audit Objectives	Audit Evidence and Procedures

Existence, Completeness, and Valuation

Do all cash accounts exist?
Have all cash transactions been properly recorded?
Have all cash receipts been deposited?

Analytical Evidence

- Compare cash receipts from miscellaneous sources with prior year and account for major changes.

Physical Evidence

- If present for inventory observation at year end, count and list cash on hand.

Documentary Evidence

- Trace count of year-end cash on hand to cash receipts record and to bank statement.
- Determine that above cash count agrees with final entry in cash receipts record for the year.
- Vouch significant cash receipts from sources other than customers, such as sales of plant assets or investments, and loan proceeds. Trace to remittance advices, deposit tickets, and bank statements on a test basis.

Mathematical Evidence

- Reconcile bank accounts as of year end.
- Prepare proof of cash if internal control over cash is weak.
- Prepare analysis of interbank transfers to detect kiting and errors resulting in unrecorded cash.

Confirmation Evidence

- Confirm bank balances directly with banks.
- Compare balance on confirmation with year-end bank statement.
- Obtain cutoff bank statements directly from banks.
- Trace reconciling items on year-end reconciliations to cutoff bank statements, noting especially
  1. Agreement of payees appearing on returned checks with cash disbursements record.
  2. Agreement of payees on face of returned checks with endorsements on back of checks.
  3. Outstanding checks at year end cleared bank within reasonable period.
  4. Deposits in transit at year end were credited by bank within reasonable period.

Presentation and Disclosure

Any bank overdrafts?
Any restricted cash balances?

Documentary Evidence

- Examine loan agreements and directors' minutes for compensating balance requirements, and consider reclassifying as noncurrent if significant.

Confirmation Evidence

- Examine bank confirmation for other information provided by bank, such as outstanding indebtedness.
- Consider mailing confirmation requests to banks for guarantees of indebtedness, pledging, and/or loan commitments.

Hearsay Evidence

- Inquire as to status of inactive bank accounts.

KEY TERMS

COMPUTER AUDIT PRACTICE CASE

Biltrite Bicycles, Inc.

The Biltrite audit practice case contains several exercises pertaining to the revenue cycle. They may be completed at this time and are as follows:

> *Module V:* Dallas Dollar Bank—bank reconciliation
> *Module VI:* Analysis of interbank transfers
> *Module VII:* Accounts receivable aging analysis and evaluation of allowance for doubtful accounts

REVIEW QUESTIONS

1. Define *substantive testing*.

2. What factors influence the amount of substantive testing to be applied during the interim audit phase?

3. Define *balanced auditing* and discuss its importance.

4. How do analytical procedures assist in the evaluation and review stages of the audit?

5. How does the auditor gain assurance as to proper sales cutoff?

6. Why is consistency of cutoff important?

7. Differentiate between positive and negative forms of confirmation.

8. Distinguish between confirmation replies requiring audit adjustment and those *not* requiring audit adjustment.

9. What alternate procedures might the auditor apply if replies to confirmation requests were not received?

10. Of what significance to the auditor is the accounts receivable aging analysis?

11. How are miscellaneous revenues audited?

12. What is the purpose of requesting a bank confirmation?

13. Why does the auditor request a cutoff bank statement in addition to reconciling the bank account?

14. Discuss the purpose for auditing interbank transfers.

15. What kinds of documentary evidence are examined in auditing sales transactions?

16. What kinds of mathematical evidence are obtained in auditing cash receipts transactions?

17. Auditors usually analyze subsequent collections from customers as part of the audit program for accounts receivable. What audit objective(s) is (are) served by this procedure?

18. What determines the number of positive or negative confirmation requests to be mailed to customers in a particular engagement?

19. Define *early revenue recognition*. Why is the risk of early revenue recognition greater in some industries than in others?

20. Identify the principal classification and disclosure issues pertaining to the revenue cycle.

MULTIPLE CHOICE QUESTIONS FROM PAST CPA EXAMS

1. Cutoff tests designed to detect credit sales made before the end of the year that have been recorded in the subsequent year provide assurance about management's assertion of
   a. Presentation.
   b. Completeness.
   c. Rights.
   d. Existence.

2. Which of the following most likely would be detected by an auditor's review of a client's sales cutoff?
   a. Shipments lacking sales invoices and shipping documents
   b. Excessive write-offs of accounts receivable
   c. Unrecorded sales at year end
   d. Lapping of year-end accounts receivable

3. An unrecorded check issued during the last week of the year would most likely be discovered by the auditor when the

    a. Check register for the last month is reviewed.

    b. Cutoff bank statement is reconciled.

    c. Bank confirmation is reviewed.

    d. Search for unrecorded liabilities is performed.

4. Which of the following procedures would an auditor most likely perform for year-end accounts receivable confirmations when replies to second requests are not received?

    a. Review the cash receipts journal for the month prior to year end

    b. Intensify the study of internal financial controls concerning the revenue cycle

    c. Increase the assessed level of detection risk for the existence assertion

    d. Inspect the shipping records documenting the merchandise sold to the debtors

5. An auditor should trace bank transfers for the last part of the audit period and first part of the subsequent period to detect whether

    a. The cash receipts journal was held open for a few days after year end.

    b. The last checks recorded before year end were actually mailed by year end.

    c. Cash balances were overstated because of kiting.

    d. Any unusual payments to or receipts from related parties occurred.

6. The primary purpose of sending a standard confirmation request to financial institutions with which the client has done business during the year is to

    a. Detect kiting activities that may otherwise not be discovered.

    b. Corroborate information regarding deposit and loan balances.

    c. Provide the data necessary to prepare a proof of cash.

    d. Request information about contingent liabilities and secured transactions.

7. The auditor will most likely perform extensive tests for possible understatement of

    a. Revenues.

    b. Assets.

    c. Liabilities.

    d. Capital.

8. Which of the following procedures would an auditor most likely perform to verify management's assertion of completeness?

    a. Compare a sample of shipping documents to related sales invoices

    b. Observe the client's distribution of payroll checks

    c. Confirm a sample of recorded receivables by direct communication with the debtors

    d. Review standard bank confirmations for indications of kiting

9. In the context of an audit of financial statements, substantive tests are audit procedures that

    a. May be eliminated under certain conditions.

    b. Are designed to discover significant subsequent events.

    c. May be either tests of transactions, direct tests of financial balances, or analytical tests.

    d. Will increase proportionately with increases in assessed control risk.

10. Which of the following procedures is least likely to be performed before the balance sheet date?

    a. Observation of inventory

    b. Review of internal control over cash disbursements

    c. Search for unrecorded liabilities

    d. Confirmation of receivables

11. Cooper, CPA, is auditing the financial statements of a small rural municipality. The receivable balances represent residents' delinquent real estate taxes. The internal control system at the municipality is weak. To determine the existence of the accounts receivable balances at the balance sheet date, Cooper would most likely
   a. Send positive confirmation requests.
   b. Send negative confirmation requests.
   c. Examine evidence of subsequent cash receipts.
   d. Inspect the internal records such as copies of the tax invoices that were mailed to the residents.

12. If the objective of a test of details is to detect overstatements of sales, the auditor should trace transactions from the
   a. Cash receipts journal to the sales journal.
   b. Sales journal to the cash receipts journal.
   c. Source documents to the accounting records.
   d. Accounting records to the source documents.

13. Which of the following most likely would give the most assurance concerning the valuation assertion of accounts receivable?
   a. Tracing amounts in the subsidiary ledger to details on shipping documents
   b. Comparing receivable turnover ratios to industry statistics
   c. Inquiring about receivables pledged under loan agreements
   d. Assessing the allowance for uncollectible accounts for reasonableness

Questions 14 and 15 are based on the following:

Miles Company
Bank Transfer Schedule
December 31, 2002

Check Number	Bank Accounts From	To	Amount	Date Disbursed per Books	Date Disbursed per Bank	Date Deposited per Books	Date Deposited per Bank
2020	1st National	Suburban	$32,000	12/31	1/5 *	12/31	1/3&
2021	1st National	Capital	21,000	12/31	1/4 *	12/31	1/3&
3217	2nd State	Suburban	6,700	1/3	1/5	1/3	1/6
0659	Midtown	Suburban	5,500	12/30	1/5 *	12/30	1/3&

14. The audit legend "*" most likely indicates that the amount was traced to the
   a. December cash disbursements journal.
   b. Outstanding check list of the applicable bank reconciliation.
   c. January cash disbursements journal.
   d. Year-end bank confirmations.

15. The audit legend "&" most likely indicates that the amount was traced to the
   a. Deposits in transit of the applicable bank reconciliation.
   b. December cash receipts journal.
   c. January cash receipts journal.
   d. Year-end bank confirmations.

ESSAY QUESTIONS AND PROBLEMS

11.1   A customary procedure in examining cash balances is to request the client's bank(s) to send a cutoff statement directly to the auditor. The cutoff bank statement generally covers a portion of the month following the balance sheet date.

Required:
a. What is the purpose of obtaining a cutoff bank statement?
b. In tracing reconciling items to the cutoff bank statement, the auditor notes payees, endorsements, and clearing dates for checks and notes date of credit for deposits. What, specifically, is the auditor looking for in applying these procedures?
c. In tracing reconciling items to the cutoff statement, the auditor lists the following exceptions:
1. 12/31/02 deposit in transit cleared bank on 1/9/03.
2. Outstanding $10,000 check payable to K. Burkee, Inc., was endorsed by Jules Lavern, client controller.
3. Checks 1099, 1100, 1101, and 1102, recorded as of 12/31/02, did not clear the bank until 1/22/03, 1/23/03, 1/24/03, and 1/25/03, respectively.
Discuss the possible errors or fraud associated with each of the above items. Are any audit adjustments necessary? Explain why or why not.

11.2   Exhibit 11.10 (p. 464), a client-prepared bank reconciliation, is being examined by MacKenzie Dean, a CPA, during an examination of the financial statements of Healthtex Company.

Required:
Indicate one or more audit procedures that should be performed by Dean in gathering evidence in support of each of the items (a) through (f) as identified in the reconciliation. (AICPA adapted)

11.3   The CPA firm of Buffington and Bean is in the process of examining Jackson Corporation's 2002 financial statements. The following matter must be resolved before the audit can be completed.

No audit work has been performed on nonresponses to customer accounts receivable confirmation requests. Both positive and negative confirmations were used. A second request was sent to debtors who did not respond to the initial positive request.

Required:
What alternative audit procedures should Buffington and Bean consider performing on the nonresponses to customer accounts receivable confirmation requests? (AICPA adapted)

11.4   You have been engaged to audit the books of Earthnet, Inc., a manufacturer of computer software and computer disk drives. Although the industry has been suffering losses during the past few years, Earthnet shows unaudited net income of $1.87 million for the current year. In applying analytical procedures, you discover that Earthnet's sales have increased by 20 percent over the preceding year, and the gross profit margin has risen from 18 to 25 percent.

In confirming accounts receivable, you have encountered difficulty in obtaining replies to positive requests and the replies you have received are similar to the following response:

EXHIBIT 11.10

Problem 11.2 Client-Prepared Bank Reconciliation

Healthtex Company
Bank Reconciliation—Village Bank Account 2
December 31, 2002

Balance per bank (a)		$ 18,375.91
Deposits in transit (b)		
12/30	1,471.10	
12/31	2,840.69	4,311.79
Subtotal		22,687.70
Outstanding checks (c)		
837	6,000.00	
1941	671.80	
1966	320.00	
1984	1,855.42	
1985	3,621.22	
1987	2,576.89	
1991	4,420.88	(19,466.21)
Subtotal		3,221.49
NSF check returned 12/29 (d)		200.00
Error Check No. 1932		5.50
Customer note collected by the bank		
($2,750 plus $275 interest) (e)		(3,025.00)
Balance per books (f)		$ 401.99

According to our records, we owed Earthnet $22,100 as of 12/31/02. We cannot seem to account for the following invoices, and request copies be sent to us for comparison with our documentation:

Invoice No.	Date	Amount
4566	12/30/02	$12,000
4567	12/31/02	14,500
4568	12/31/02	52,800

The receivable from the customer, according to Earthnet's records, was $106,000. Of 112 positive confirmations mailed, the following results were obtained:

Type of Response	Number	Amount
No exception	3	$ 96,000
Exception indicated	12	420,000
No reply	97	3,678,000

The 112 accounts selected for confirmation constituted 75 percent of the dollar amount of accounts receivable as of 12/31/02.

While performing sales cutoff tests, you noted that $1 million of disk drives and software were shipped on 12/31/02, a Saturday. Much of the supporting documentation for these shipments lacks the required initials of the shipper.

Required:

a. As an auditor exercising professional skepticism, what do you think may have accounted for Earthnet's robust earnings for 2002?

b. What additional evidence is needed with regard to sales and accounts receivable?

c. Identify the substantive audit procedures you would apply in completing the examination of sales and receivables.

11.5   As part of the audit of accounts receivable, Raymond George, a CPA and in-charge auditor for the Baumann, Inc., engagement, requested the client to prepare an aging analysis of the receivables as of 12/31/02, Baumann's year end. The following data are taken from that analysis:

Status	Amount	Estimated Uncollectible
Current	$3,200,000	1%
1–30 days past due	1,600,000	3
31–60 days past due	925,000	5
61–90 days past due	670,000	12
Over 90 days past due	1,700,000	20

The percentages appearing in the last column have been used in the past in estimating uncollectibility of customers' accounts. The current balance in the allowance for uncollectible accounts is $72,000. The credit manager informs you that this amount is adequate in light of successful collection efforts relating to the 61–90 and the over 90-days past-due accounts.

Required:

a. Why is it necessary for the auditor to address the question of adequacy of the allowance for uncollectible accounts?

b. Discuss the procedures you would apply to ascertain the adequacy of the allowance in the present instance.

c. If you discover that the allowance is inadequate, how would you convince the Baumann controller and credit manager of the need for adjustment?

11.6   After determining that computer controls are valid, Jennings is reviewing the sales system of Norland Corporation in order to determine how a computerized audit program may be used to assist in performing tests of Norland's sales records.

Norland sells crude oil from one central location. All orders are received by mail and indicate the preassigned customer identification number, desired quantity, proposed delivery date, method of payment, and shipping terms. Since price fluctuates daily, orders do *not* indicate a price. Price sheets are printed daily and details are stored in a permanent disk file. The details of orders are also maintained in a permanent disk file.

Each morning the shipping clerk receives a computer printout that indicates details of customers' orders to be shipped that day. After the orders have been shipped, the shipping details are entered in the computer, which simultaneously updates the sales journal, perpetual inventory records, accounts receivable, and sales accounts.

The details of all transactions, as well as daily updates, are maintained on disks that are available for use by Jennings during the audit.

Required:

a. How may a computerized audit program be used by Jennings to perform substantive tests of Norland's sales records in their machine-readable form? Do *not* discuss accounts receivable and inventory.

b. After performing these tests with the assistance of the computer, what other auditing procedures should Jennings perform in order to complete the examination of Norland's sales records?

(AICPA adapted)

11.7   In applying substantive tests to transaction cycles, auditors emphasize the importance of determining proper cutoff. Sales cutoff, purchases cutoff, cash receipts cutoff, and cash disbursements cutoff all must be tested by the auditor.

Required:

a. What is the significance of proper cutoff?
b. Design an audit program for determining the reasonableness of sales cutoff for a bookstore.
c. Under what circumstances would you extend sales cutoff procedures? Under what conditions would you restrict them?
d. Why is consistency of cutoff important?

11.8   A company owns several shopping centers. The standard lease with all tenants requires that they pay a fixed rent plus a percentage of net sales. It also provides that the tenant get an audit opinion on the tenant's reported sales figure or allow the lessor company's internal auditor to audit the sales figure and charge the tenant for the audit.

A tenant restaurant owner decided to have the lessor company's internal auditor perform this service. You, as the internal auditor, have been asked by the head of the internal auditing department to verify the sales figures presented by the restaurant.

You have determined that there are ten waiters or waitresses employed. Only food and soft drinks are served to patrons. No carry-out orders are filled. All orders are filled by the use of handwritten, prenumbered restaurant checks. All restaurant checks and cash register tapes are retained. A record of daily sales and the general ledger are maintained by the owner.

Required:

Develop four specific objectives for the audit of the tenant restaurant and at least two audit program steps for each objective. (IIA adapted)

11.9   Carijay, Inc., maintains bank accounts at the following branch locations: Minneapolis—First Minnesota Bank & Trust, Milwaukee—Second Milwaukee Bank, Chicago—Intercontinental Bank, and Detroit—Motor City Bank & Trust. Interbank transfers occur among the banks in settlement of interbranch transactions. For example, goods might be shipped from Minneapolis to Detroit. Detroit pays for the goods by drawing a check on the Motor City account and the Minneapolis branch deposits the check in the First Minnesota account. These and similar transactions occur among the branches during the year. In analyzing interbank transfers at the end of 2002 and the beginning of 2003, Nancy Lau, CPA, identified the following checks:

Ck. No.	Date of Check	Drawn On	Deposited In	Amount
1066	12/30/02	First Minnesota	Second Milwaukee	$10,000
2033	12/31/02	Intercontinental	Motor City Bank	$35,466
3099	1/2/03	Motor City Bank	Second Milwaukee	$55,000
1067	1/3/03	First Minnesota	Intercontinental	$12,000

Checks generally require two days before being received by the payee. All checks are deposited on the date received. In examining cash receipts records, Lau learned that check

1066 was recorded and deposited in the payee account on 1/2/03; check 2033 also was recorded and deposited on 1/2/03; check 3099 was recorded by the payee (the Milwaukee branch) and deposited on 12/31/02, but not credited by the bank until 1/2/03; and check 1067 was recorded by the recipient on 1/4/03, but was credited on the bank statement as of 12/31/02.

Required:
a. Which of the checks are indicative of kiting?
b. What is the probable reason for the kiting in each instance?
c. Draft any audit adjustments necessitated by this analysis.

11.10 Stephen Trinity, of Spillman & Splash, CPAs, has been assigned to the Colorado Processing, Inc., audit for the fiscal year ended October 31, 2002. He currently is completing the audit of accounts receivable by reviewing returned accounts receivable confirmations and evaluating the adequacy of the allowance for doubtful accounts. Colorado Processing buys beef, pork, and poultry from local slaughterhouses, processes it, and sells it to area grocery retailers and restaurants. As of October 31, the company had 450 customer accounts with a combined balance of $365,000. Trinity stratified the population of accounts so that all balances equal to or greater than $2,000 were selected for confirmation. From the remaining 420 accounts, he drew a random sample of 50 accounts. Trinity then mailed positive confirmation requests to the 80 customers. Exhibit 11.11 summarizes the confirmation replies.

Required:
a. Comment on the adequacy of Trinity's workpaper as presented in Exhibit 11.11.
b. Assuming all amounts are considered material, draft any audit adjustments that you consider necessary. Include journal explanations. (Assume that Colorado Processing maintains perpetual inventory records.)
c. Exhibits 11.12 and 11.13 reproduce the audit workpapers for the Accounts Receivable Aging Analysis and Allowance for Uncollectible Accounts, respectively.
  1. Using two sheets of paper, reproduce, on the first workpaper, the last line of Exhibit 11.12, which represents the aged totals of Colorado Processing's accounts receivable. Add an audit legend describing how Trinity obtained the $365,000 balance in accounts receivable. On the second workpaper, reproduce the last line of Exhibit 11.13, the October 31 general ledger balance in allowance for doubtful accounts.
  2. Post your adjustments from part (b) to the two workpapers.
  3. Record subsequent collections on the aging analysis, assuming the following cash receipts for the period 11/1/02 through 11/27/02:

Current	$210,113
1–30 days past due	13,353
Total	$223,466

  4. Add an audit legend describing the procedures you would apply to the subsequent collections.
  5. Calculate estimated uncollectible accounts receivable on the aging analysis, assuming that the following percentages are used by Colorado Processing and have been agreed to by the auditors:

Current	10%
Past due:	
1–30 days	25%
31–60 days	70%
Over 60 days	100%

EXHIBIT 11.11

Problem 11.10

W.P. No.   C.3
Prepared by: J.K. 12/6/02
Reviewed by: L.W. 12/8/02

Colorado Processing, Inc.
Accounts Receivable—Trade
Confirmation Control Worksheet
October 31, 2002

Conf. No.	Customer	Balance	Date Returned	Comments
106	Crulls Grocery	$ 4,256	11/6	Balance per customer, $1,256. Oct. 28 remittance of $3,000 not received until Nov. 2.
112	Consolidated Foods	12,380	11/8	Balance per customer, $1,280. Month-end meat order, shipped 10/31 F.O.B. destination, not received until 11/2. Invoice amount, $11,100. Cost, $8,600.
117	Jilley's Steak House	1,277	11/10	Balance per customer, $0. Jilley has filed for Chapter 11 bankruptcy and, according to Colorado's legal counsel, this account will not be collected.
125	Amalgamated Stores, Inc.	22,234	11/14	Balance per customer, $18,600. Customer submitted debit memo in early October for $3,634 representing meats that spoiled in transit. Although Colorado acknowledges the spoilage, the company did not issue a credit memo until 11/2. Cost of the spoiled meat, $2,400.
138	Smitty's Meat Market	1,056	11/17	Balance per customer, $0. $1,000 remitted 10/30; not received by Colorado until 11/1. Remainder represents discount taken by Smitty in error.
151	Appolo Restaurants	8,600	11/20	No response to second and third requests.
155	General Foods Discount Grocers	13,468	11/22	Balance per customer, $468. Remittance of $13,000 sent 10/24. Traced to 10/26 cash receipts. Credited to Sales Revenue in error.
162	Beaver Hills Market	1,123	11/23	No response to second and third requests.
171	Kim's Fresh Meats	2,334	11/23	Balance per customer, $1,260. Invoice for $1,074 shipped 10/31 F.O.B. shipping point.
177	Joey's Supper Club	866	11/26	Balance per customer, $532. 10/30 shipment, $334, rejected by customer because order was incorrect. Meat was returned to Colorado and received 10/31 in good condition. Return not recorded until 11/1. Cost of returned meat, $250.
	Confirmations returned without exception	184,300		
	Total confirmation requests	$252,894		

EXHIBIT 11.12

Problem 11.10

WP No.   C.2
Prepared by: J.K. 11/30/02
Reviewed by: L.W. 12/2/02

Colorado Processing, Inc.
Accounts Receivable—Trade
Aging Analysis
October 31, 2002

Cust. No.	Customer Name	Balance	Current	Past Due (Days) 1–30	31–60	Over 60
1060	Culley's Meats	$ 1,330	$ 1,330			
1061	Jolly Roger Restaurant	466		$ 466		
1064	Crulls Grocery	4,256	3,000	1,256		
	(Other)	329,433	280,763	33,467	$12,324	$2,879
1602	Rudy's Deli	378			378	
1603	General Foods Discount Grocers	13,468	13,000			468
1607	Kim's Fresh Meats	2,334	1,074	1,260		
1608	Dills Discount Grocery	12,469	12,469			
1612	Joey's Supper Club	866	334		532	
10/31	Balance per ledger	$365,000	$311,970	$36,449	$13,234	$3,347

EXHIBIT 11.13

Problem 11.10

WP No.   C.4
Prepared by: J.K. 12/8/02
Reviewed by: L.W. 12/10/02

Colorado Processing, Inc.
Accounts Receivable—Trade
Allowance for Doubtful Accounts
October 31, 2002

11/1/01	Balance per general ledger	$ 28,000#
11/1–10/31	Monthly provision	24,000&
11/1–10/31	Write-offs	(37,000)@
10/31/02	Balance per general ledger	$ 15,000

Traced to last year's WTB-audited balance
& Traced to standard journal entries
@ Examined documentation and discussed with credit manager and legal counsel

6. Evaluate the adequacy of the allowance for doubtful accounts and record any necessary audit adjustment on the allowance for doubtful accounts workpaper.

7. Add an audit legend presenting your conclusion regarding the adequacy of the allowance for doubtful accounts.

Note: The solution to this case can be expedited greatly by retrieving and completing the spreadsheet template entitled "Colorado." This file is included on the same Student CD that contains the Biltrite Bicycle templates.

11.11 Skiver & Robinson, CPAs, has reviewed the financial statements of Delta Internet Access, Inc., for the past several years. This year, the company has requested an audit to meet the requirements of a pending loan from Hofer Venture Capital. The loan, if granted, will be used to replace equipment and install new fiber optic lines to expand the company's subscriber base.

Delta Internet Access is a local Internet provider with approximately 30,000 subscribers. The company maintains demand deposit accounts with two local banks. The accounts and their year-end (December 31, 2002) general ledger balances are as follows:

Fifth/Fourth Bank	$23,440
Farmington Trust	$42,000

The balances according to the 12/31/02 bank statements were as follows:

Fifth/Fourth Bank	$4,800
Farmington Trust	$17,300

The company's internal financial controls require that all cash receipts be deposited intact daily. Cash receipts consist of remittances from subscribers who are billed on a cycle basis according to the first letter of the subscribers' last names. Revenue is recorded on the billing date and remittances are credited to Accounts Receivable. Monthly cash receipts approximate $600,000, averaging around $20,000 per day. All of the cash is deposited in Fifth/Fourth Bank, the account from which Delta Internet Access pays its creditors. The company is required, however, to maintain a balance of $10,000 in Farmington Trust in order to comply with a loan agreement previously negotiated with the bank. For this reason, Delta Internet Access uses the Farmington Trust account to meet its monthly payroll, transferring monies from Fifth/Fourth Bank, as necessary.

Marlene Parker, CPA, the in-charge auditor for the Delta Internet Access engagement, has obtained the company's year-end bank reconciliations. She also has obtained cutoff bank statements directly from the banks as of January 20, 2003. The reconciliations and cutoff statements are reproduced in Exhibits 11.14 through 11.17. Upon further inquiry, Parker learned that check no. 1734, drawn on Fifth/Fourth Bank, dated 12/28/02 and recorded on the same date, was not deposited in Farmington Trust until 1/6/03 and was credited by the bank on the same date. The Delta Internet Access entry to record this check was:

12/28/02	Cash in bank—Farmington Trust	$66,000	
	Cash in bank—Fifth/Fourth Bank		$66,000
	To record payroll transfer.		

Required:

a. Based on the above narrative and your analysis of Exhibits 11.14 through 11.17, draft any audit adjustments that you consider necessary. Explain the reason for your proposed adjustments.

b. Identify possible disclosure requirements resulting from your analysis.

EXHIBIT 11.14

Problem 11.11 Fifth/Fourth Bank Reconciliation

Delta Internet Access, Inc.
Bank Reconciliation
Fifth/Fourth Bank
December 31, 2002

12/31/02	Balance per bank		$ 4,800
	Add deposits in transit		112,000
			116,800
	Deduct outstanding checks:		
	1731 Bundy Theaters	1,560	
	1733 Columbus Publishing	4,200	
	1734 Farmington Trust (payroll)	66,000	
	1737 Edison Electric	6,300	
	1738 Covington Treasurer (property taxes)	9,600	
	1739 United Health Care	5,700	
			93,360
12/31/02	Balance per general ledger		$ 23,440

EXHIBIT 11.15

Problem 11.11 Farmington Trust Bank Reconciliation

Delta Internet Access, Inc.
Bank Reconciliation
Farmington Trust
December 31, 2002

12/31/02	Balance per bank		$17,300
	Add deposits in transit		66,000
			83,300
	Deduct outstanding checks (all payroll):		
	2152	2,200	
	2155	2,200	
	2156	3,000	
	2162	2,400	
	2163	3,100	
	2167	2,700	
	2168	2,300	
	2171	4,400	
	2172	2,200	
	2173	3,200	
	2176	2,600	
	2177	3,000	
	2178	2,200	
	2179	2,700	
	2180	3,100	
			41,300
12/31/02	Balance per general ledger		$42,000

EXHIBIT 11.16

Problem 11.11 Cutoff Bank Statement

Fifth/Fourth Bank
Delta Internet Access, Inc. Bank Statement
Account # 1005688
January 20, 2003

	Debits	Credits	
Balance 12/31/02			$ 4,800
1/2/01	1,560	17,000	
1/5/01		18,000	
1/6/01	4,200	22,000	
1/7/01	9,600	26,000	
1/8/01	6,300	29,000	
1/9/01	66,000	32,000	
1/12/01	12,300	22,000	
1/13/01	7,800	16,000	
1/14/01	23,500	15,000	
1/15/01	33,400	12,000	
1/16/01	41,700	10,000	
	206,360	219,000	
Balance 1/20/03			$17,440

EXHIBIT 11.17

Problem 11.11 Cutoff Bank Statement

Farmington Trust
Delta Internet Access, Inc. Bank Statement
Account # 2377210
January 20, 2003

	Debits	Credits	
Balance 12/31/02			$17,300
1/2/03	2,400		
	2,200		
	3,000		
	2,200		
	3,100		
	2,700		
1/5/03	2,600		
	2,200		
	4,400		
	2,700		
	3,100		
1/6/03	3,000	66,000	
	3,200		
	36,800	66,000	
Balance 1/20/03			$46,500

11.12 Shannon Moore, CPA, is engaged to audit the financial statements of Cridon Wholesalers for the year ended December 31, 2002. Moore obtained and documented an understanding of internal control relating to accounts receivable and has assessed control risk at the maximum level. She requested and obtained from Cridon an aged accounts receivable schedule listing the total amount owed by each customer as of December 31, 2002, and sent positive confirmation requests to a sample of the customers.

Required:

What additional substantive audit procedures should Moore consider applying in auditing the accounts receivable? (AICPA adapted)

DISCUSSION CASES

CASE I

Cendant Corp.

Facilitated by the bull market of the 1990s, HFS, Inc. had experienced annual revenue growth of 25 percent through stock-for-stock acquisitions of companies such as Avis, Travelodge, Days Inn, Ramada, Century 21, and Coldwell Banker. With Henry Silverman at the helm, the stock price of HFS, Inc., had risen from $4.75 in 1992 to $77 in December 1997. In January 1998 the company merged with CUC International to form Cendant Corp. CUC was in the business of selling travel, shopping, and dining discount memberships. Walter Forbes, formerly CEO of CUC, became CEO of the combined companies.

Not long after the merger, two former managers of CUC who had stayed on after the merger approached Michael Monaco, CFO of Cendant, and informed him that CUC management, including the former CFO, had been manufacturing earnings in order to bolster the company's stock price. Specifically the company, for quarterly reporting purposes, had been setting up fictitious accounts receivable and crediting revenue accounts for nonexistent membership sales. Prior to the end of the fourth quarter, the fictitious revenue entries were reversed. To compensate for the revenue reversals and thereby inflate earnings for the fiscal year, management ordered the accounting staff to recognize all new membership sales as revenue for the current year while deferring the related expenses over one to three years. The company also reduced the allowance for future membership cancellations. Finally, substantial portions of reserves created to cover charges related to acquisitions (e.g., costs of dismissing employees, closing of facilities, and executive travel) were used to further fabricate earnings.

As news of the fraud penetrated the financial community, Cendant's stock price decreased from $41 in April 1998 to $13 by August of that year. Cendant's audit committee engaged Arthur Andersen to conduct a special fraud audit, which determined that 61 percent of CUC's reported 1997 earnings were fabricated. Walter Forbes resigned as Cendant's CEO and stockholders proceeded to sue the company.

Ernst & Young, CUC's auditors, had rendered an unqualified opinion on the 1997 financial statements. Cendant, therefore, sued the auditors for negligence because they had relied on the firm's audit when they were denied access to CUC's books prior to the merger. In addition, Ernst & Young was named in two separate class action suits by the stockholders of Cendant. The firm denied liability on the basis that management had engaged in collusive fraud, that documents had been fabricated, and that access to documentation substantiating fictitious journal entries had been denied them.

Required:

a. Discuss the auditor's responsibility for detecting this type of fraudulent financial reporting.

b. Do you think the auditors should be held liable to Cendant? To the stockholders? Explain.

c. What procedures, if any, should have alerted the auditors to possible fraud?

CASE II

College Bound

College Bound, a Florida corporation, operated a chain of test centers to help prepare high school students to take college entrance exams. The firm was begun in 1980 by George and Janet Ronkin as a neighborhood enterprise; news of the Ronkin's effectiveness spread and the business grew quickly. In 1988 the company went public and raised approximately $30 million from European investors in the form of convertible notes. To avoid the rigors of an initial public offering and the stringent regulatory review by the Securities and Exchange Commission, College Bound merged into an existing shell company. This practice also avoided the scrutiny of underwriters who can be held liable for misstatements in a registration statement. Beginning as a "penny" stock, the share price rose rapidly to $4.75 in December 1990 and peaked at $24 by August 1991. The high share price enabled the company to acquire other companies more cheaply in stock-for-stock exchanges. One of the acquired companies, ACSI, provided professional testing services, such as preparing candidates for the bar examination, and accounted for 38 percent of the combined entity's 1991 revenue.

By August 1991, the company claimed to be operating more than 150 test centers throughout the United States. For the fiscal year ended August 31, 1991, College Bound reported a net income of $5.5 million on revenues of $22.5 million. For the quarter ended November 30, 1991, reported net income was $2.3 million on revenues of $9.6 million. However, in a lawsuit filed April 24, 1992, the SEC charged that $5 of every $6 of revenue was "bogus," and that the corporate bank accounts had only a quarter of the cash purported in April 1992. The Commission even questioned whether College Bound really operated 150 test centers, suggesting that some were fabricated by the Ronkins. One analyst called nineteen College Bound Centers to confirm their existence. Eight of the responses were recorded messages—four by the same person in different locations. At two locations the phone was answered by an operator saying the number was being checked for trouble. Other ana-

lysts visited locations and found only one or two employees.

As a result of the SEC lawsuit, which also included allegations that the Ronkins had deposited $500,000 of College Bound funds into their personal bank accounts and transferred $625,000 more of College Bound money into Swiss bank accounts in December 1992, a Federal judge froze the Ronkin's assets. In April 1992, the Ronkins resigned from the company, College Bound filed for bankruptcy protection, and a receiver was appointed to run the company. On May 3, 1992, the firm was delisted by NASDAQ, the company's only avenue for public trading.

The fraud allegedly consisted of recording interbank transfers as revenue. As proceeds were received from the European convertible note issues, College Bound properly recorded the debit to Cash and the credit to Notes Payable. The company would then transfer funds from the corporate bank accounts to the various test centers without recording the transfers. The test centers, however, recorded the receipts as revenue. The result was inflated revenues by the test centers and cash shortages in the corporate bank accounts. According to the SEC suit, Janet Ronkin made the transfers herself, with the knowledge of her husband.

College Bound's independent auditor, a close friend of Mrs. Ronkin's twin brother, rendered an unqualified opinion on the company's 1991 net income of $5.5 million. In reality, the company had suffered a loss. In January 1993 the Securities and Exchange Commission filed a complaint against the auditor, charging that he did not follow generally accepted auditing standards when he examined the company's 1991 financial statements. The complaint also sought permanent injunction and civil monetary penalties against the auditor.

Required:

a. Assuming the outside auditor was part of a scheme to intentionally deceive investors, fraud concealment was *not* a problem for College Bound management. Had the auditor been truly independent, however, College Bound management would have been compelled to develop more effective concealment means. How might company management have concealed the fraud effectively?

b. Given your answer to part (a), how might an astute auditor nevertheless become suspicious and ultimately detect the concealment? At what point does concealment become so effective as to relieve the auditor of detection responsibility?

Substantive Audit Testing: Expenditure Cycle

c h a p t e r 1 2

biltrite

l e a r n i n g   o b j e c t i v e s

After reading this chapter, you should be able to

1 Identify specific audit objectives related to the expenditure cycle.
2 Develop for the expenditure cycle audit programs that relate audit procedures to audit objectives for each component of the cycle.
3 Modify audit programs as necessary, in light of warning signs that surface during the study of the business and industry, analytical procedures, or the study and evaluation of internal control policies and procedures.

OVERVIEW

This chapter discusses substantive testing of the expenditure cycle. Figure 12.1 displays this part of the audit within the overall audit process. The expenditure cycle substantive audit is addressed in four parts:

1. Purchases, production, and inventories;
2. Plant assets;
3. Intangible assets; and
4. Current liabilities and operating expenses.

FIGURE 12.1

The Audit Process

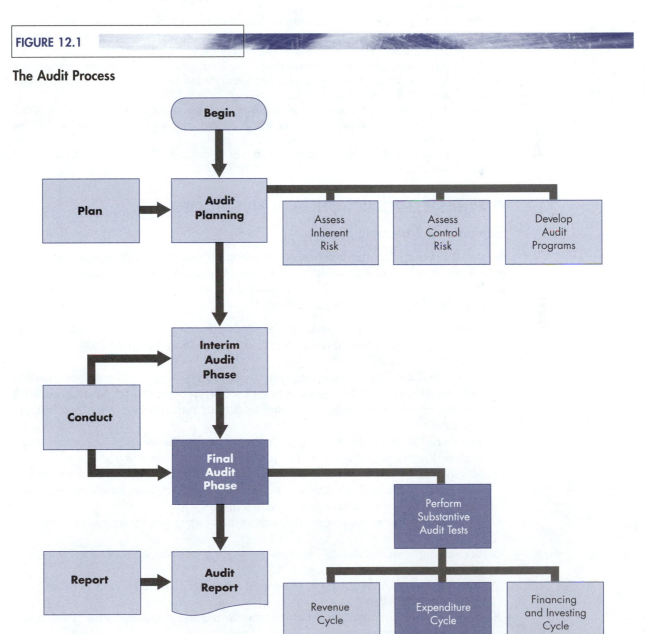

As in Chapter 11, the processing steps in the expenditure cycle are enumerated and a summary flowchart is presented. Audit objectives then are identified for each part of the transaction cycle. This discussion is followed by a consideration of audit evidence and procedures available for meeting the objectives.

To achieve consistency with the balanced audit approach described in Chapter 11 and portrayed graphically in Table 11.1, in testing inventories, plant assets, and intangible assets auditors should emphasize testing for overstatement unless they have cause to suspect understatement. In testing liabilities auditors should emphasize testing for understatement unless they have cause to suspect overstatement. Accordingly, auditors test inventories extensively for existence and valuation.

Plant assets and intangible assets are audited in conjunction with the repairs expense accounts and research and development expense. Simultaneous examination helps to identify errors in classifying expenditures as to asset additions or expenses.

In testing current liabilities for understatement, auditors should concentrate on completeness (i.e., locating errors of omission). A set of procedures referred to as the "search for unrecorded liabilities" is applied to meet this objective.

The chapter concludes with a consideration of audit risk associated with the expenditure cycle. As in Chapter 11, warning signs are identified and their impact on various parts of the cycle is discussed.

An appendix relating audit objectives to types of evidence and procedures is presented at the end of the chapter.

PURCHASES, PRODUCTION, AND INVENTORIES

Summary of Processing Steps

Figure 12.2 summarizes the significant processing steps included in purchases, payment of vendors' invoices, and production. The more important control policies and procedures related to this part of the expenditure cycle, as more fully described in the appendix following Chapter 7, are as follows:

1. Documents, such as purchase orders, vouchers, receiving reports, disbursement checks, production orders, and production reports, should be prenumbered and periodically accounted for;
2. For manual and batch processing systems, approvals, account distributions (debits and credits), and double checks of account distributions should be evidenced on the face of the documents to provide for proper authorization, recording, and accountability;
3. For online EDP systems, proper input editing controls should provide reasonable assurance that transactions are authorized and properly recorded;
4. All movements of inventory (e.g., from receiving to stores, from stores to production, from production to finished goods, and from finished goods to shipping) should be documented to provide accountability;
5. A voucher system should be used to ensure that only properly authorized disbursements will be made;
6. Accounting manuals should be available to facilitate proper recording of unique and/or nonrecurring purchases;
7. Inventories should be physically secured, with access limited and responsibility fixed to ensure safety;
8. Perpetual inventory records should be maintained and compared with physical test counts on a recurring basis;

FIGURE 12.2

Expenditure Cycle—Summary of Processing Steps

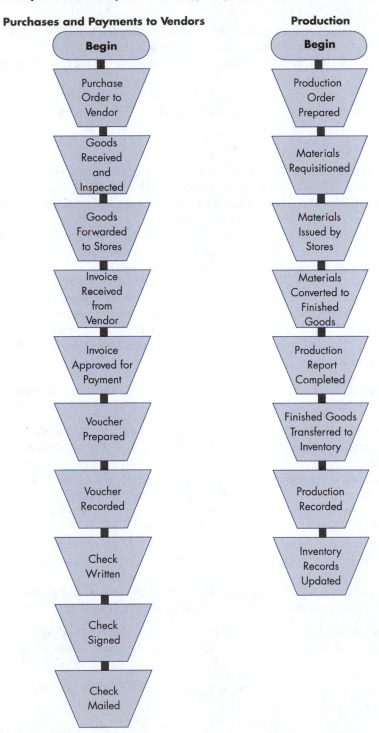

Purchases and Payments to Vendors

- Begin
- Purchase Order to Vendor
- Goods Received and Inspected
- Goods Forwarded to Stores
- Invoice Received from Vendor
- Invoice Approved for Payment
- Voucher Prepared
- Voucher Recorded
- Check Written
- Check Signed
- Check Mailed

Production

- Begin
- Production Order Prepared
- Materials Requisitioned
- Materials Issued by Stores
- Materials Converted to Finished Goods
- Production Report Completed
- Finished Goods Transferred to Inventory
- Production Recorded
- Inventory Records Updated

9. An annual physical inventory should be conducted with the independent auditors present to observe;

10. All cash disbursements should be made by check, and checks should be signed only upon submission of properly documented and approved vouchers authorizing the disbursements;

11. Access to unused vouchers and disbursement checks should be limited and responsibility for custody of these documents should be fixed;

12. Upon payment, vouchers, purchase orders, vendors' invoices, and receiving reports should be effectively canceled; and

13. If check-signing machines are used, they should be secured and responsibility should be fixed to prevent unauthorized access.

Audit Objectives

Existence and Completeness Assertions   In applying the balanced approach described in Chapter 11, the auditor tests assets for possible overstatement. Reporting nonexistent inventories on the balance sheet is one way of overstating assets; therefore, a major part of the audit program for inventories should concentrate on determining that the inventories exist. Factors such as inventories at numerous locations, manufacturing inventories, inventories in public warehouses, and inventories out on consignment further complicate the auditor's task in verifying existence.

Rights and Obligations Assertions   The auditor also must determine that the client owns the inventories, as represented on the balance sheet. Inventories in transit, consigned goods, and special orders require particular attention in the determination of ownership. Reporting consignments-in as part of the ending inventory is another possible means for inflating assets.

Valuation Assertions   In auditing inventories for proper valuation, the auditor must determine the following:

1. That raw materials are valued at the lower of cost or market. Typically, this will equal current vendor's price, less applicable cash discount, plus an allowance for transportation;

2. That the cost accounting system is adequate in terms of assigning the proper amount for materials, labor, and overhead to finished products;

3. That the cost accounting system permits ready identification of cost at various stages of completion, to allow work-in-process valuation;

4. That the client uses an acceptable method for assigning costs to products during the acquisition, production, and disposal stages. First-in, first-out; average cost; and last-in, first-out are all acceptable valuation methods;[1] and

5. That slow-moving and obsolete goods, as well as other inventories, are reported on the balance sheet at amounts not to exceed net realizable value.[2]

A cost accounting system that assigns too much overhead to ending inventories and too little to cost of goods sold, and that reflects obsolete and slow-moving inventories

---

1   Financial Accounting Standards Board, *Accounting Standards: Current Text*, 1996/97 ed., New York: John Wiley & Sons, Inc., 1996, section I 78.107.
2   Ibid, section I 78.109.

at full cost, are further means of inflating reported assets and net income. Given a balanced audit approach, the auditor needs to test carefully for these eventualities.

Presentation and Disclosure Assertions   The balance sheet should disclose inventories by major classes (e.g., raw materials, work in process, and finished goods) and the costing method used for valuing the inventories. If inventories are pledged as collateral for outstanding loans, this fact also must be disclosed. Significant amounts of inventory held for purposes other than manufacture or resale should be classified separately on the balance sheet.[3]

Audit Evidence and Procedures

Inventory Observation   Observing the annual taking of the physical inventory is the most effective way for the auditor to obtain satisfaction regarding existence. For this reason, inventory observation is required by generally accepted auditing standards.[4] **Inventory observation** requires that the auditor be present during the inventory taking and that she or he perform test counts and evaluate the overall control exercised by the client in performing the physical inventory task.

If goods are contained in sealed boxes, the auditor should open some of the boxes to ascertain that they contain the proper inventory items. Moreover, if the boxes are stacked, the auditor should examine the stacks to ascertain that hollow areas do not exist within the stacks. For inventories that cannot be counted, such as chemicals stored in tanks, the auditor should estimate inventory quantities using alternative measures. For example, chemical container volume might be estimated on the basis of container dimensions, weight, and/or the fullness of the container.

In selecting items for counting, auditors should stratify the population, test-counting most of the expensive inventory items and sampling the remainder. If inventory is unique (e.g., precious metals), the auditor may want to consult with a specialist concerning the quality and value of the inventory.

Before the actual physical count of goods on hand, the auditor should review the inventory instructions prepared by the client (see Exhibit 12.1). The **inventory instructions** are directed to the client's personnel who will be involved in the inventory-taking procedures. The instructions should cover the date and location of counts; counting procedures, including how counts will be documented and provision for double-checking of counts; arrangement of goods, including physical separation of consigned and obsolete goods; and production during inventory taking. Clear and complete inventory instructions provide the auditor added assurance concerning accuracy of counts, exclusion of consignments-in, and proper identification of obsolete and slow-moving goods.

Prenumbered **inventory tags or sheets** are used by the client for documenting the counts. If a tagging system is used, the tags (Exhibit 12.2) are physically attached to the merchandise, and are removed at the instruction of the auditor after all test counting has been completed. Regardless of whether tags or sheets are used, duplicates should be provided to the auditor. To exercise proper control, the auditor should account for all tag numbers, both used and unused, and retain the auditor copies for later comparison with the client's final inventory listings (discussed as follows).

3   Ibid, section I 78.102-3.
4   *AICPA Professional Standards*, New York: AICPA, section AU 331.01.

EXHIBIT 12.1

Inventory Instructions

Jallo, Inc.
Instructions for Physical Inventory Taking
Fiscal Year Ended 6/30/02

Our physical inventory will be taken in its entirety on June 29 and 30, 2002. Manufacturing operations will be halted during the inventory taking.

Raw materials and finished goods inventories are located in the warehouse at 12131 Messenger Road. A minimal amount of partially completed goods will be at various locations on the factory floor. In addition, some materials may be in the receiving area and/or in railroad cars on the company siding. Similarly, a limited amount of finished goods may be on the shipping dock, either in the shipping bays or loaded on company trucks.

The inventory will be counted by two-person count teams and double-checked by a third person. Prenumbered tags will be used for recording the counts. The tags will be issued to the count teams in packets of 100. Issued numbers will be recorded by the stores manager on a control sheet. Tags not used should be returned for proper notation on the control sheet. The teams and checkers should exercise utmost care to ensure accuracy of the counts. Obsolete materials and finished goods should be so indicated on the tags to facilitate proper pricing. The count team, as well as the checker, will initial the tags. The tags will remain on the goods until the independent auditors have completed their testing, pulled their copies of tags, and cleared the areas for resumption of operations.

Vendors have been instructed not to ship materials after June 28, and the company will not ship goods to customers after June 28. Goods will not otherwise be shipped or received during the physical inventory taking.

Similar goods should be *located together* to maximize efficiency in counting. They should also be physically arranged in a manner that facilitates ease of counting.

Consignments-in and other goods not owned by Jallo should not be tagged or otherwise included in the physical inventory.

At the conclusion of the inventory, the independent auditors, along with the internal auditors, will account for all tag numbers, used and unused, and will tour the warehouse and factory to ensure that all inventory has been counted and tagged. They will then clear the area for removal of tags and authorize return to normal operations.

Joel Keller
Corporate Controller

The auditor should document the **inventory test counts** on a worksheet for later comparison with the client's final inventory listings. Exhibit 12.3 (p. 484) illustrates an inventory count worksheet.

While observing the physical inventory, the auditor must exercise control over movements within the areas to be tested to prevent possible double counting. The auditor also should be alert to possible obsolescence or overstocking. Signs of physical deterioration or what may appear to be excessive quantities of goods may evidence these conditions. The related tags or sheets should be marked for later follow-up as to final costing.

The auditor also should inquire about obsolescence, as well as consigned-in goods, and ascertain that consignments-in are *not* included in the inventory. Environmental

EXHIBIT 12.2

Inventory Tag

Tag No. 21306

Inventory Class: *Finished Goods*

Location: *Warehouse #1*

Counted by: *OJ*

Checked by: *RM*

Description: *Model 56A Toaster Ovens*

Quantity: *612*   Unit of Measure: *Units*

Comments: *Outdated model—write down to net realizable value*

conditions, such as physical arrangement of goods and security within inventory areas, should be noted for possible inclusion in the reportable conditions letter.

Before concluding the inventory observation, the auditor should account for all used inventory tags (including voided tags) and sheets, according to numeric sequence, and list all unused tag or sheet numbers. This procedure provides for prevention or detection of the adding of nonexistent goods to tags or sheets after the counting is completed.

Inventory Confirmation   The auditor may elect to confirm goods held in public warehouses or goods out on consignment. If the amounts involved are significant, however, the auditor should arrange for physical inspection of the inventories.

Inventory Cutoff Tests   As described in Chapter 11, the purpose of **cutoff tests** is to ascertain that transactions are recorded in the proper accounting period. The auditor applies the tests to purchases, sales, cash receipts, and cash disbursements transactions. The discussion in the following paragraphs is limited to **inventory cutoff**, **purchases cutoff**, and **sales cutoff**. Cash receipts and disbursements cutoff were addressed in Chapter 11.

In testing purchases and sales for proper cutoff, the auditor must be satisfied that

1. Goods purchased before year end have been recorded as purchases and included in the ending inventory; and
2. Goods sold by year end have been recorded as sales and excluded from the ending inventory.

EXHIBIT 12.3	

Auditor Documentation of Inventory Counts

WP D.1
Prepared by: MRB
Date: 12/31/02
Reviewed by: SLM
Date: 1/12/03

Hodek Manufacturing, Inc.
Inventory Observation
Test Counts
12/31/02

Tag Number	Location	Inventory Type	Description	Client Count*	Auditor Count*	Comments
21306	Whse #1	FG	Mod. 56A Toaster Ovens	612	612	Appears overstocked. To be priced at net realizable value.
23487	Whse #1	FG	Mod. 431 Blenders	124	86	Count corrected by client.
25679	Whse #1	FG	Mod. 886 Microwave Ovens	1,277	1,277	
26669	Whse #2	RM	Part 345 Hinges	2,344	2,344	Weigh counted. Count appears reasonable.
26701	Whse #2	RM	Part 873 Oven Glass	134	123	Sheets 8 × 12 ft. Client corrected count on tag.
27333	Factory	WIP	Mod. 890 Microwave Ovens	76	76	Stamped and formed. Not assembled.

* All counts represent units.

The significance of errors involving inconsistencies in purchases, sales, and inventory cutoff is illustrated in Exhibit 12.4.

In determining whether a purchase or sale has occurred prior to year end, the auditor must examine documentation for evidence of passage of title. The date of receipt or shipment of goods and the freight terms are the principal factors determining transfer of ownership. If the freight terms are *F.O.B. shipping point*, title passes to the buyer upon acceptance by the shipper. If the terms are *F.O.B. destination*, title passes to the buyer upon receipt of goods. Receiving reports, vendors' invoices, bills of lading, freight bills, and sales invoices provide needed evidence.

As part of the test for purchases and sales cutoff, the auditor's attention should be directed to the shipping and receiving areas during inventory observation. The auditor should record the last document numbers (shipping order, sales invoice, receiving report, voucher) and relate them to the goods shipped or received. Later, during the final audit phase, these numbers should be traced to the sales and purchases records to verify their inclusion as the last sales and purchase entries of the year.

In addition to matching goods with documents as of year end, the auditor should also test purchases and sales transactions for a few days before and after year end. The documents to be examined for this purpose include sales invoices, shipping orders, bills of lading, receiving reports, vendors' invoices, and freight bills covering the period

EXHIBIT 12.4

Effects of Cutoff Errors

	Significance of Cutoff Errors Year Ended 12/31/02			
Description of Error	Ending Inventory	Purchases	Sales	2002 Income Effect*
I. A 2002 purchase in the amount of $30,000 was not recorded				
A. Included in ending inventory	No Effect	Understated	No Effect	Overstated by $30,000
B. Excluded from ending inventory	Understated	Understated	No Effect	No Effect
II. A 2003 purchase in the amount of $30,000 was recorded in 2002				
A. Included in ending inventory	Overstated	Overstated	No Effect	No Effect
B. Excluded from ending inventory	No Effect	Overstated	No Effect	Understated by $30,000
III. A 2003 sale in the amount of $66,000 was recorded in 2002. Cost = $40,000				
A. Included in ending inventory	No Effect	No Effect	Overstated	Overstated by $66,000
B. Excluded from ending inventory	Understated	No Effect	Overstated	Overstated by $26,000
IV. A 2002 sale in the amount of $66,000 was recorded in 2003. Cost = $40,000				
A. Included in ending inventory	Overstated	No Effect	Understated	Understated by $26,000
B. Excluded from ending inventory	No Effect	No Effect	Understated	Understated by $66,000

Note: Consistent errors (IB, IIA, IIIB, and IVA) have less effect on income than inconsistent errors.
Rules: Recorded purchases must be included in inventory. Recorded sales must be excluded from inventory.
* Before taxes.

shortly before and after the balance sheet date. The reason for examining the documents is to determine the point at which title passed. This, in turn, identifies the period in which the transaction should be recorded. Shipping dates, receiving dates, and freight terms will assist the auditor in determining passage of title. Regarding, for example, **inventory in transit** from client to customer at year end, if the freight terms are F.O.B. destination, the goods should be included in the client's ending inventory and the sales transaction should be reversed. Similarly, if incoming materials or goods are in transit at year end and have been shipped by the vendor F.O.B. shipping point, title has passed to the client; the goods should be included in the ending inventory, and the purchase should be recorded.

In selecting the transactions to be tested, the auditor should proceed both from documents to accounting records and from accounting records to documents. This provides greater assurance of detecting errors of commission as well as errors of omission. Table 12.1 summarizes the records, documents, and substance to be examined in the test for proper sales and purchases cutoff.[5]

---

5   Chapter 4 defined substance as "that which is represented by an account." The substance supporting a sales transaction, for example, is the customer's record of the purchase, as evidenced by a returned confirmation request. The substance underlying a purchase is the inventory resulting from the transaction.

TABLE 12.1

Records, Documents, and Substance for Cutoff Tests

Transaction	Records	Documents	Substance
Purchases	Voucher Register	Vouchers Vendors' Invoices Receiving Reports Bills of Lading Freight Bills	Inventories
Sales	Sales Register Customers' Ledger	Sales Invoices Shipping Orders Bills of Lading	Inventories Confirmations
Cash Receipts	Cash Receipts Record	Remittance Advice Cash Receipts Prelisting Cash Register Tapes (year end)	Cash Count Bank Statement Cutoff Bank Statement
Cash Disbursements	Check Register	Bank Reconciliation Paid Vouchers	Canceled Checks Cutoff Bank Statement

Procedures:

1. *Trace* from documents to records and *vouch* from records to documents, to detect errors of omission and errors of commission.
2. *Examine substance* at year end, record last document numbers (sales invoice, voucher, receiving report, shipping order, disbursement check, etc.), and determine consistency with recording of transactions.
   a. Include in inventory any inventory in receiving area at year end, listed on last receiver number for the year, and recorded as last purchase in voucher register.
   b. Exclude from inventory any inventory shipped out on date of inventory, billed on last sales invoice number for the year, and recorded as last sale in sales register.
   c. Trace last document numbers recorded at year end to accounting records: sales invoice to sales record, voucher and receiving report to voucher register, and check to check register.

Test Pricing of Ending Inventory The auditor verifies existence by observing the taking of the physical inventory. Ownership is determined by the performance of cutoff tests. The auditor also must determine that the ending inventories have been properly valued in accordance with GAAP. Two inputs govern valuation: price and quantity. Tests of quantities have already been discussed as part of verifying existence. Satisfied as to the physical inventory, however, the auditor next must trace the quantities to the final inventory listings, to ensure that the client has not committed errors or fraud in transferring the counts to the listings. In performing this procedure the auditor should trace both quantities counted and quantities not counted. The direction of testing should proceed from the auditor's copies of tags or sheets to the final listings. As a further quantity test, the auditor should scan the client's inventory listings for large dollar amounts and trace the related quantities to the auditor's copies of tags or sheets. The purpose of this procedure is to detect material overstatements by the client, intentional or unintentional, in transferring quantities to the final inventory listings.

Before testing the prices appearing on the final inventory listings (the second input to valuation, referred to as **inventory pricing tests**), the auditor must be satisfied that the cost accounting system produces reliable inventory cost data. The auditor ordinarily tests the cost accounting system during the interim audit phase as part of the tests of controls. Raw materials and purchased parts price lists, bills of material and routing sheets for manufactured goods, and perpetual inventory records all should be examined and tested for reliability. Satisfied as to prices and costing methods, the auditor can rely on the cost records as to unit prices used in valuing the final inventory.

Next the auditor should, on a test basis, trace the prices on the final inventory listings to the audited price lists, and test extensions and footings appearing on the listings. If the inventories are computerized, the auditor may elect to use the computer to assist in these tests.

In determining whether inventories are properly valued at lower of cost or market, the auditor should test for possible obsolete or slow-moving inventory. **Tests for inventory obsolescence** may begin with analytical procedures directed at inventory turnover for various classes of goods. A significant decline in turnover relative to prior years or relative to other similar inventory items is further evidence of obsolescence. The auditor should inquire of stores personnel as to cause where turnover rates are unusually low. Turnover calculations and inquiry also should be applied to apparent overstocking noted by the auditor during inventory observation.

Summary Audit Program

Figure 12.3 presents a summary audit program for the examination of inventories. The program is not intended to be exhaustive, but rather incorporates the more significant procedures applied to the audit of inventories. Those procedures related to inventory observation (existence) and inventory pricing (valuation and ownership) are most critical to the auditor's opinion concerning inventories.

PLANT ASSETS

Audit Objectives

Existence and Completeness Assertions   In testing for misstated or omitted plant assets, the auditor must concentrate on such factors as whether new assets have been placed in service as of year end, whether all disposals have been recorded, and whether financing leases have been properly included among plant assets. The possibility of off-balance sheet financing (failure to record financing leases) poses a significant threat to fairness of financial presentation, given material amounts of leased assets in today's business world.

Rights and Obligations Assertions   The auditor must ascertain that the client owns the existing plant assets as of the balance sheet date. In addition, the auditor must determine that all mortgages and other forms of outstanding indebtedness relating to the assets are included on the balance sheet. Financing leases with contingent rental clauses must be examined carefully for year-end accruals. If, for example, a lease contract specifies, in addition to minimum lease payments, an additional amount calculated as a percentage of net sales in excess of a specified monthly amount (contingent rentals), the auditor should recalculate the added amounts on a test basis, and determine that they

FIGURE 12.3

Model Audit Program for Expenditure Cycle: Inventory, Purchases, and Production

Analytical Procedures
1. Compare purchases, inventories, and gross profit percentages with prior year and industry averages, and account for significant fluctuations.
2. Calculate inventory turnover by major classes, compare with prior year and industry averages, and account for major fluctuations.

Other Substantive Audit Procedures
1. Review client's inventory-taking instructions for completeness and adequacy.
2. Observe the taking of the client's physical inventory, and observe or confirm goods not on premises, as necessary.
3. Test for purchases and sales cutoff.
4. Determine that client has properly adjusted general ledger inventory amounts to agree with physical inventory.
5. Test the costing of the physical inventory by tracing to audited price lists and cost records.
6. Trace quantities from tags or count sheets to final inventory listings.
7. Scan inventory listings for extended amounts in excess of $10,000. Trace related quantities to auditor's copy of inventory tag.
8. Test final inventory extensions and footings.
9. Inquire as to inventory obsolescence and pledging of inventories as collateral for outstanding loans.

have been properly recorded as expenses, and that unpaid amounts have been reflected as current liabilities at year end.

Valuation or Allocation Assertion   For valuation purposes, the auditor must determine that plant assets are properly reflected on the balance sheet at cost less accumulated depreciation. Although more applicable to intangible assets (see next section), the auditor must also determine client compliance with provisions of SFAS No. 121 relating to impairment of assets held for sale or used in operations.[6] SFAS 121 requires a "test for impairment if events or circumstances indicate the carrying amount of an asset to be held or used may not be recoverable."[7] With respect to leased assets, the valuation objective requires attention to the calculation of minimum lease payments and the discount rate used in determining present value.

A balanced audit approach that focuses on overstatement of assets requires that the auditor be alert to methods used to inflate plant assets and understate depreciation. Proper classification of capital and revenue expenditures for costs incurred subsequent to the acquisition of plant assets addresses plant asset inflation, while the evaluation of

6 FASB, *Accounting Standards: Current Text,* op. cit., section 108.
7 Ibid.

the appropriateness of depreciation methods as well as the consistency of application focuses on depreciation understatement. A further valuation objective is establishing the correctness of computed gains or losses on disposals.

Presentation and Disclosure Assertions   Major classes of plant assets, the accumulated depreciation related to each, and depreciation methods used must be disclosed clearly, either in the body of the balance sheet or in footnotes thereto. Leased assets involve added disclosure as to future cash flows required under the lease agreements. Pledging of assets as security for outstanding loans also must be disclosed clearly in the body of the balance sheet or in its footnotes.

Assets removed from production for other than standby purposes, as well as assets purchased for investment purposes, must be classified separately on the balance sheet. These are nonoperating assets and should *not* be included in plant assets.

Changes in depreciation methods for existing classes of plant assets also must be disclosed. The cumulative effect change, net of tax, is shown separately, after extraordinary items on the income statement; the nature of the change and its justification must be incorporated in a footnote.[8]

Audit Evidence and Procedures

Plant Assets Lead Schedule   To provide a focal point for applying substantive tests, the auditor should prepare or obtain a schedule of plant assets and accumulated depreciation. Exhibit 12.5 illustrates a **plant assets lead schedule**. Exhibit 12.6, "Autos and Trucks," is one of the six supporting schedules accompanying the "Plant Assets" lead schedule. The supporting schedule contains a record of the audit procedures applied and the evidence gathered. Note that depreciation expense and gain or loss on disposals are analyzed, along with the related plant asset accounts. This supports the transaction cycle approach to substantive audit testing. By auditing income statement accounts in conjunction with the related balance sheet accounts, the auditor gains greater assurance as to proper matching and cutoff. The approach also enhances audit efficiency by permitting the auditor to examine simultaneously both the balance sheet and the income statement effects of transactions.

After the beginning balances have been entered in the plant assets lead schedule, the auditor should reconcile the plant assets subsidiary ledger with the controlling accounts in the general ledger. Although the audit testing will be performed on the subsidiary ledger, any audit adjustments will be posted by the client to the controlling accounts. It is imperative, therefore, that agreement be established at the outset. This procedure is applicable, incidentally, whenever subsidiary ledgers support controlling accounts in the general ledger, and often can be automated with computer assistance.

Analytical Procedures   Before vouching and recalculating, the auditor should compare depreciation and repairs and maintenance charges with those of the prior year and with budgeted amounts, and investigate major changes. A significant decrease in repairs, for example, could indicate errors in classifying repairs as capital expenditures and should prompt the auditor to direct more attention toward the vouching of plant asset additions. A material increase in repairs expense, alternately, suggests possible expense

8   Ibid, section A106.116.

EXHIBIT 12.5

Plant Assets Lead Schedule

		WP G
	Prepared by:	LK
	Date:	1/11/03
	Reviewed by:	JR
	Date:	1/15/03

Jallo, Inc.
Plant Assets
Lead Schedule
12/31/02

Description	Final Balances 12/31/01	Additions	Disposals	Final Balances 12/31/02	WP #
Assets					
Land	$ 130,000	60,000	30,000	160,000	G.1
Land improvements	50,000			50,000	G.2
Buildings	786,000	160,000	86,000	860,000	G.3
Machinery and equipment	345,000	85,000	45,000	385,000	G.4
Autos and trucks	120,000	30,000	28,000	122,000	G.5
Office furniture and equipment	86,000	12,000	6,000	92,000	G.6
	$1,517,000	347,000	195,000	1,669,000	
			WTB 1		
Accumulated Depreciation and Amortization					
Land improvements	$ 20,000	5,000		25,000	G.2
Buildings	453,000	40,000	72,000	421,000	G.3
Machinery and equipment	126,000	35,000	42,000	119,000	G.4
Autos and trucks	65,000	24,000	25,000	64,000	G.5
Office furniture and equipment	43,000	17,000	3,000	57,000	G.6
	$ 707,000	121,000	142,000	686,000	
			WTB 1		

overstatement, and should result in the direction of added audit resources towards the vouching of debits to the repair accounts.

Recurring operating losses and decreasing cash flows suggest auditor attention to possible asset impairment. Under these conditions, the auditor must determine that the client has completed the necessary tests for asset impairment, and has reduced carrying values of impaired assets to amounts not exceeding recoverability.[9]

Vouching of Additions and Disposals   On a test basis, the auditor should examine documentation supporting plant asset additions and disposals. Vendors' invoices and freight

9 Ibid, section 108.

EXHIBIT 12.6

Plant Assets Supporting Schedule

			WP G.5
		Prepared by:	LK
		Date:	1/10/03
		Reviewed by:	JR
		Date:	1/15/03

Jallo, Inc.
Autos and Trucks
12/31/02

	Final Balances 12/31/01	Additions	Disposals	Final Balances 12/31/02
Assets				
Salespersons' autos	$130,000⊕			30,000
Delivery trucks	50,000⊕	30,000~	28,000	52,000
Service trucks	40,000⊕			40,000
	$120,000	30,000	28,000	122,000
	F	F	F	To WP G F
Accumulated Depreciation				
Salespersons' autos	$ 10,000⊕	7,000C		17,000
Delivery trucks	35,000⊕	9,000C	25,000C	19,000
Service trucks	20,000⊕	8,000C		28,000
	$ 65,000	24,000	25,000	64,000
	F	F	F	To WP G F

Gain or Loss on Disposals

Selling Price	Book Value	Gain (Loss)
$6,700	$3,000	$3,700
√		
		To WP S

⊕ Tracked to 12/31/01 working trial balance
F Footed and crossfooted
~ Examined title and canceled check
C Recomputed
√ Traced to deposit ticket and bank statement

bills provide evidence supporting proper valuation and ownership of purchased assets. Work orders provide the detail covering materials, labor, and overhead applied to constructed plant assets. Materials, labor, and direct overhead charges should be traced to requisitions and time tickets on a test basis. Fixed overhead should be recalculated to support the reasonableness of the application rates. Generally accepted accounting principles require that a proportionate share of fixed overhead be applied to constructed plant assets. The auditor also should determine whether interest should be capitalized as part of the projects.

Remittance advices, deposit tickets, and bank statements should be examined in support of plant asset disposals. Control over miscellaneous cash receipts is evaluated during the control risk assessment phase of the audit. The goal of applying substantive tests is to verify that material amounts of miscellaneous receipts were properly recorded and deposited intact.

As part of the vouching process, the auditor should also examine the minutes of directors' meetings for proper authorization of major acquisitions and disposals. Purchase and sale agreements should be examined for proper recording and for the existence of indebtedness, contingent liabilities, or other restrictions arising from the transactions.

Recalculation of Depreciation   After evaluating the appropriateness of depreciation methods used by the client, the auditor should recalculate the depreciation charges on a test basis. Depreciation recorded on additions and disposals should be examined for consistency with company policy and the prior year.

Accelerated Cost Recovery System (ACRS) charges and Modified Accelerated Cost Recovery System (MACRS) charges for tax purposes should be recalculated on a test basis and the temporary differences traced to the deferred tax account. In addition to depreciation charges, ACRS charges, and MACRS charges, the auditor should recalculate gains or losses on disposals of plant assets. Gains and losses for accounting and tax purposes then should be reconciled.

Vouching of Repairs and Maintenance Charges   Repairs and maintenance accounts should be analyzed along with plant asset accounts. Major expenditures should be vouched to vendors' invoices and work orders. The performance of this procedure in conjunction with vouching additions and disposals of plant assets increases the probability of locating material classification errors (i.e., ordinary repairs capitalized or extraordinary repairs expensed). The auditor should examine and evaluate company policy regarding capitalization of extraordinary repairs and should apply analytical procedures, as described above, before beginning the vouching process.

Examination of Leases and Loan Agreements   The auditor must determine, by examining the contracts, whether leases have been properly classified as financing versus operating leases. For financing leases, the auditor should recalculate minimum lease payments and evaluate the appropriateness of the discount rates used in capitalizing the leases.

Loan agreements should be examined for possible pledging of plant assets as collateral. The auditor also should inquire of legal counsel and examine bank confirmations for evidence of pledging. To the extent to which plant assets have been pledged as security, balance sheet disclosure is required.

Summary Audit Program

Figure 12.4 summarizes the principal audit procedures applicable to plant asset additions, disposals, and balances. Note that the program also covers such related income statement accounts as depreciation, gain or loss on disposals, and repairs and maintenance.

FIGURE 12.4

Model Audit Program for Expenditure Cycle: Plant Assets

> **Analytical Procedures**
> 1. Compare depreciation expense with that of prior year and account for major changes.
> 2. Compare maintenance and repair expense with that of prior year, both in total and as a percentage of sales, and account for major changes.
> 3. Compare maintenance and repair expense with budgeted amounts and investigate significant variances as to cause.

> **Other Substantive Audit Procedures**
> 1. Consider inspecting major additions to verify existence.
> 2. Prepare a lead schedule of plant assets and accumulated depreciation by major classes of assets.
> 3. Reconcile subsidiary plant ledger with controlling accounts and agree to ending balances appearing on plant assets lead schedule.
> 4. Examine directors' minutes and purchase and sale agreements for proper authorization and accounting for major acquisitions and disposals.
> 5. Vouch plant asset additions and disposals on a test basis. Be particularly alert to possible capitalization of ordinary repairs.
> 6. Vouch repair and maintenance expenditures on a test basis. Be particularly alert to possible expensing of plant asset additions.
> 7. Evaluate appropriateness and consistency of depreciation method(s).
> 8. Recalculate depreciation and gain or loss on disposals on a test basis.
> 9. For self-constructed assets, recalculate overhead allocation and interest during construction, if applicable.
> 10. Examine plant ledger for fully depreciated assets, and inquire as to status. Remove from accounts if disposed of or otherwise no longer in use.
> 11. Examine all lease agreements and determine proper classification as to financing versus operating.
> 12. For financing leases:
>   a. Evaluate appropriateness of discount rate used in calculating net present value of minimum lease payments;
>   b. Recalculate minimum lease payments; and
>   c. Recalculate contingent rentals, as necessary, on a test basis.
> 13. Examine loan agreements for possible pledges of plant assets as collateral.

INTANGIBLE ASSETS

Audit Objectives

Existence and Completeness Assertions   Intangible assets do *not* possess physical substance, as do inventories and plant assets. Examples of intangible assets include patents, copyrights, trademarks, goodwill, and franchises. Despite their lack of physical substance, the auditor must verify the existence of the recorded intangibles. As to completeness, the auditor must be satisfied that no significant amounts of purchased intangibles, possessing future economic benefit, have been expensed.

Rights and Obligations Assertions   The auditor must ascertain ownership of purchased intangibles. Real and contingent liabilities arising from the intangible assets also need to be identified.

Valuation or Allocation Assertion   Purchased intangible assets should be valued at acquisition cost less accumulated amortization. Costs of developed intangibles generally should be expensed. In accordance with the balanced audit approach of testing assets for overstatement, the auditor should determine that no research and development costs have been improperly capitalized as intangible assets.

Determining proper valuation also requires an assessment of future economic benefit to be derived from the assets. In this respect, the auditor must evaluate the reasonableness of the amortization periods selected for given classes of intangible assets.

The auditor also should determine, by reference to historical data and budgeted cash flows, whether the client is in conformity with the requirements of SFAS 121 relating to asset impairment. Intangibles, under conditions of recurring operating losses and declining cash flows, are usually the first assets to materially decline in value.

Presentation and Disclosure Assertions   The nature of intangible assets and valuation and amortization methods all need to be disclosed in the financial statements. Contingent liabilities related to the intangibles also need to be disclosed.

Audit Evidence and Procedures

Analytical Procedures   In auditing intangible assets, the auditor should begin by applying analytical procedures to the current year's amortization expense and to research and development (R&D) expense. Significant abnormalities should be pursued to ascertain cause. Abnormal decreases in amortization may be indicative of disposals or write-offs of intangibles. Unusual decreases in R&D expense may have been caused by improper capitalization of expenditures.

Inquiry and Examination of Underlying Documentation   The existence objective may be satisfied through the examination of the underlying documentation in support of intangibles. Patents, copyrights, trademarks, franchise agreements, and merger agreements constitute necessary documentation. The auditor also should examine directors' minutes for authorization of material purchases of intangible assets.

Inquiry of management and legal counsel may assist the auditor in identifying possible contingencies relating to intangible assets. Contingencies frequently assume the form of lawsuits alleging infringement of patents, copyrights, trademarks, or franchises.

In determining client compliance with the provisions of SFAS 121, relative to impairment testing, the auditor should determine that the carrying amounts of affected intangible assets have been appropriately reduced.[10]

10 Auditor requirements under SFAS No. 121 are explored more fully in the "Audit Risk Analysis and the Expenditure Cycle" section presented at the end of this chapter.

The auditor also may inquire of management generally as to future economic benefit accruing from recorded intangibles. The relating of copyrights, franchises, patents, trademarks, and goodwill to the revenues produced by these assets may corroborate answers to auditor inquiry. Continued revenue-producing trends are good evidence of future benefit.

Vouching of Additions and Disposals   The auditor should examine correspondence, contracts and agreements, legal documents, and canceled checks related to acquisitions of intangible assets. Errors in valuing intangibles are likely to be detected by these procedures. For example, in examining merger agreements, the auditor should evaluate the reasonableness of valuations placed on intangible assets. To the extent that any excess of cost over book value has been improperly charged to goodwill, it should be reclassified to the appropriate tangible assets.

Research and development costs also should be vouched, along with additions to intangible assets. Improperly capitalized R&D costs should be reclassified as expenses. Likewise, material amounts of purchased intangibles that have been expensed as part of R&D costs should be capitalized.[11]

Credits to intangible asset accounts may represent amortization, write-offs, or disposals. In vouching disposals, the auditor should trace recorded cash receipts, arising from sales of intangibles, to the bank statement.

Recalculation of Gains, Losses, and Amortization   Gains or losses on disposals, as well as amortization expense, should be recalculated on a test basis. If analytical procedures indicate abnormal changes in these accounts, the degree of testing may be intensified.

Summary Audit Program

Figure 12.5 summarizes these procedures in the form of a summary audit program for intangibles. Note that research and development expenditures are audited in conjunction with intangible assets as a means of detecting material classification errors.

CURRENT LIABILITIES

Audit Objectives

Existence and Completeness Assertions   A balanced audit approach requires testing liabilities for possible understatement. A common form of management misrepresentation fraud involves omitting liabilities from the balance sheet and the related expenses from the income statement. Moreover, given the large number of accruals arising at year end, together with difficulties in achieving a proper cutoff, liabilities may be omitted unintentionally from the balance sheet. For these reasons, auditing for completeness (i.e., determining that no significant amounts of liabilities have been omitted from the balance sheet) is a major goal in the audit of current liabilities. The auditor must also determine that contingent liabilities are properly disclosed in footnotes to the financial statements.

---

11 As part of its acquisition of Lotus Development Corp. in 1995, IBM wrote off more than half the cost ($1.8 billion) to expense, including it in operating expenses as part of "research, development and engineering." Although technically in accordance with GAAP, one might question the fairness of this practice, given the probable future economic benefit associated with these costs.

FIGURE 12.5

Model Audit Program for Expenditure Cycle: Intangible Assets and Research and Development Expenditures

Analytical Procedures

1. Compare amortization expense with that of prior year and investigate material changes.
2. Compare research and development expense with that of prior year, both in absolute terms and as a percentage of sales, and account for material changes.
3. Compare research and development expense with budgeted amounts and investigate significant variances as to cause.
4. Evaluate future economic benefit of recorded intangibles by relating assets to revenue produced by them.

Other Substantive Audit Procedures

1. Determine existence of recorded intangibles by examining underlying documentation (patents, copyrights, trademarks, franchise agreements, merger agreements, etc.).
2. Vouch additions to and disposals of intangible assets on a test basis.
3. Examine legal documents, canceled checks, etc.
4. Recalculate gain or loss on disposals.
5. Evaluate appropriateness of amortization period for recorded intangibles, and recalculate amortization on a test basis.
6. Examine minutes of directors' meetings for proper authorization of acquisitions and disposals of intangible assets.
7. Vouch research and development expenditures on a test basis and determine appropriateness of classification.
8. Inquire of management and legal counsel as to possible contingencies relating to intangible assets.

Valuation or Allocation Assertion   Accruals and loss contingencies pose the greatest challenge to the auditor in verifying valuation. Examples of accruals requiring audit attention are taxes, pension liability, profit sharing and bonus accruals, and vacation pay. Another common loss contingency, requiring accrual at year end, is the estimated allowance for doubtful accounts (previously covered in Chapter 11). Other loss contingencies, such as product warranty provision and pending litigation, may or may not be pertinent to a given engagement.

Many of the accruals and loss contingencies (e.g., pension liability, warranty provision, and allowance for loan losses) are based on management estimates. The auditor is responsible for evaluating the reasonableness of these estimates.[12] If the internal control system supports the reliability of management's estimates, the auditor may elect to simply review and test the process used by management. Under conditions of weak control, however, the auditor may wish to develop independent estimates.[13]

Presentation and Disclosure Assertions   The major presentation objective in the audit of current liabilities is determining that no significant classification errors confusing

---

12 *AICPA Professional Standards*, op. cit., section AU 342.
13 Ibid.

current and noncurrent liabilities have occurred. Current installments of long-term debt, for example, should be reflected in the current liability section of the balance sheet. Conversely, short-term obligations expected to be refinanced should be reclassified as long-term liabilities, provided the conditions set forth by FASB in SFAS 6 have been met.[14]

Proper adherence to footnote disclosure requirements relating to leases, pensions, and contingencies also must be tested.

Audit Evidence and Procedures

Search for Unrecorded Liabilities   In testing for completeness, the auditor should conduct a **search for unrecorded liabilities**. The auditor does this by examining invoices and the voucher register for a short period after the balance sheet date. The purpose of this procedure is to determine, by reference to vouchers, invoices, and receiving reports, that recording took place in the proper accounting period. If the client has prepared year-end adjustments for accruals and other previously unrecorded liabilities, the auditor should trace invoices and vouchers processed shortly after year end to the adjusting entries.

If purchases cutoff is found to be inadequate, the auditor should consider examining vendors' invoices, on a test basis, to the date of audit field work completion. This extended procedure should further assist the auditor in locating material amounts of unrecorded liabilities.

Analytical procedures applied to operating expenses such as interest, payroll taxes, product warranty expense, pensions, vacation pay, legal and accounting fees, rent, and so on also will assist in the location of possible omissions. In a recurring audit, examination of the prior year's audit adjustments for unrecorded liabilities likewise may reveal obligations that otherwise would be overlooked.

Confirmation   As part of the accounts payable audit, auditors typically request **accounts payable confirmation** statements from the client's vendors. Similar to a positive accounts receivable confirmation, the statement provides detail that the auditor can use to determine completeness of recorded accounts payable. Like the accounts receivable confirmation, the **request for vendor's statement** is drafted by the client and mailed to the vendor with a request that the statement be returned directly to the auditor.

In selecting vendors for statement requests, the auditor should include those customary and frequent vendors with zero balances. Inclusion of these vendors prevents the overlooking of omitted liabilities.

Contingent liabilities also should be confirmed with the client's legal counsel. SFAS No. 5 sets forth the conditions under which contingent liabilities should be recorded in the accounts, disclosed in a footnote, or neither recorded nor disclosed. The criteria for making the determination are measurability of possible loss and probability of unfavorable outcome.

A type of loss contingency frequently encountered by auditors is threatened or pending litigation. Because auditors are not legal experts, they rely on the client's legal counsel for evaluating the possible outcome of litigation. Termed a **letter of audit**

14 To qualify for reclassifying the liability as long term, management must intend to refinance and demonstrate an ability to refinance. Ability may be evidenced by either actual refinancing or completing an agreement to refinance prior to issuing the financial statements.

inquiry to the client's legal counsel,[15] the auditor begins by requesting management to draft a letter to legal counsel. The letter contains a listing of pending or threatened litigation and unasserted claims, together with management's evaluation of possible outcomes. Management may request legal counsel to provide the listing. Exhibit 12.7 illustrates the letter of audit inquiry. The lawyers are requested to examine the listing and respond directly to the auditor regarding agreement or disagreement with management's listing and views. Having examined management's letter of inquiry and the lawyer's response, the auditor may better evaluate whether the contingencies deserve recognition in the financial statements.

The auditor also should examine the bank confirmation(s) for the existence of outstanding loans that may require interest accrual and possibly disclosure of collateral securing the loans. If guarantees of related-party indebtedness are indicated, the auditor also should consider drafting separate confirmation request letters to the lending banks.

Mathematical Evidence   To gain assurance as to proper valuation of current liabilities, the auditor should recalculate accruals on a test basis. Examples of the more common accruals for which recalculation is applied are interest on notes, accrued payroll taxes and withholdings, income and property tax accruals, product warranty accruals, pension and profit-sharing accruals, and vacation pay.

Summary Audit Program

Figure 12.6 summarizes, in the form of a model audit program for current liabilities and operating expenses, the audit procedures just described.

AUDIT RISK ANALYSIS AND THE EXPENDITURE CYCLE

The auditing procedures discussed in the preceding section assume no significant modifications of the initial audit programs. The implication is that neither the application of analytical procedures and study of the business and industry nor internal control study and evaluation aroused the auditor's suspicions. This section addresses some risk factors that may be suggestive of material errors or fraud relating to the expenditure cycle. These factors, along with extended audit procedures that might be applied in the circumstances, are discussed in the following paragraphs.

Some warning signs that should prompt further investigation and possible program modification are as follows:

1. Significant amounts of idle capacity;
2. Inventory increases without comparable sales increases;
3. Significant increase in plant asset additions;
4. Possible asset impairment;
5. Nonrecurring special charges (used for possible "smoothing" purposes); and
6. Existence of related parties.

Idle Capacity

Under conditions of idle capacity, the auditor must be particularly alert to the reasonableness of fixed overhead included in the ending inventories. If overhead is applied

---

15 *AICPA Professional Standards*, op. cit., section AU 337.

EXHIBIT 12.7

Letter of Audit Inquiry to the Client's Legal Counsel

Jallo, Inc.
34 Spring Street
Omaha, Nebraska 66567

January 22, 2003

Wrepre and Zent, Attorneys
8756 Whiteway Blvd.
Omaha, Nebraska 66545

Gentlemen:

In connection with an examination of our financial statements at December 31, 2002, and for the year then ended, the management of Jallo has furnished to our auditors, Went and Saw, CPAs, a description and evaluation of certain contingencies, including those set forth below involving matters with respect to which you have devoted substantial attention on behalf of Jallo in the form of legal consultation or representation. For the purpose of your response to this letter, we believe that, as to each contingency, an amount in excess of $5,000 would be material, and in total, $25,000. Your response should include matters that existed at December 31, 2002, and during the period from that date to the date of completion of their examination, which is anticipated to be on or about February 15, 2003.

PENDING OR THREATENED LITIGATION, CLAIMS AND ASSESSMENTS (EXCLUDING UNASSERTED CLAIMS AND ASSESSMENTS):

Product Liability Claim. The Company is a defendant in a suit brought by Piney Woods Amusement Park resulting from injuries sustained by patrons during a ride on equipment installed by Jallo. The plaintiffs are seeking $3,000,000 in damages. Management is of the opinion that Jallo can find relief in the manufacturer of the equipment for any damages awarded by the court.

Nebraska Tax Assessment. An additional assessment for Nebraska income taxes has been levied as a result of a recently completed audit by the Nebraska tax division. The amount of the added assessment, applicable to 1998–2000, is $1,300,000 plus interest and penalties. The Company is appealing the finding and expects to prevail.

UNASSERTED CLAIMS AND ASSESSMENTS CONSIDERED BY MANAGEMENT TO BE PROBABLE OF ASSERTION AND THAT, IF ASSERTED, WOULD HAVE AT LEAST A REASONABLE POSSIBILITY OF AN UNFAVORABLE OUTCOME:

Threatened Expropriation of Chilean Subsidiary. Due to a change in the ruling government of Chile, Jallo faces loss of its manufacturing holdings in that country. The carrying value of the properties, including inventories and equipment, is $4,600,000 at December 31, 2002. Although some recovery from the new government is expected in the event of nationalization of the facility, it is impossible to estimate the amount of recovery at this time.

Please furnish our auditors such explanation, if any, that you consider necessary to supplement the foregoing information, including an explanation of those matters on which your views may differ from those stated.

We understand that when in the course of performing legal service for us with respect to a matter recognized to involve an unasserted possible claim or assessment that may call for financial statement disclosure, if you have formed a professional conclusion that we should disclose or consider disclosure concerning such possible claim or assessment, as a matter of professional responsibility to us, you will so advise us and will consult with us concerning the question of such disclosure and the applicable requirements of Statement of Financial Accounting Standards No. 5. Please specifically confirm to our auditors that our understanding is correct.

OTHER MATTERS:

Please specifically identify the nature of and reasons for any limitations on your response.

Please indicate the amount owed to you for services and expenses, billed and unbilled, at December 31, 2002.

Very truly yours,

Harold McMillan
President

FIGURE 12.6

**Model Audit Program for Expenditure Cycle:
Current Liabilities and Operating Expenses**

Analytical Review
1. Compare year-end accruals with those of prior year, and account for significant changes or omissions.
2. Compare operating expenses with those of prior year, in terms of both absolute amount and percentage of sales, and account for major changes.

Other Substantive Audit Procedures
1. Inquire as to contingent liabilities.
2. Obtain lawyer's letter to identify contingencies requiring adjustment or footnote disclosure.
3. Conduct a search for unrecorded liabilities.
4. Confirm accounts payable on a test basis by requesting that vendor statements be mailed directly to the auditor.
5. Recompute loss contingencies and accruals on a test basis.
6. Obtain client representation letter (defined and illustrated in Chapter 13).

on the basis of normal volume over a multiyear operating cycle, a portion of the volume variance may be reported as a deferred charge. If the idle capacity is abnormal, however, a loss should be recognized in the current period. The auditor, therefore, should carefully evaluate the client's policy for applying overhead to inventory and ascertain that the policy is in accordance with GAAP and has been followed consistently during the current period. As part of the examination of inventories, the auditor should compare overhead as a percentage of inventory cost with that of the preceding year. A higher-than-normal percentage suggests that a capacity loss may have been capitalized.

Abnormal Inventory Increase

An unusual increase in inventory may be detected when the auditor is applying analytical procedures related to comparing inventory turnover with that of preceding years and with industry averages. The increase may be due to expected sales increases for the upcoming year, accompanied by projected inventory supplier shortages. Overstocking in anticipation of current sales that never materialized also may be a cause. Finally, the increase may be the result of management's deliberate attempt to overstate earnings by inflating inventories.

Given an abnormal inventory increase, the auditor should inquire of management as to the cause. If management's response is satisfactory, the auditor should further corroborate it. On the other hand, if management's response does *not* provide a reasonable explanation of the increase, the auditor should expand the substantive testing of inventories. Extended testing in the following areas will assist in identifying the cause:

1. Search for evidence of overstocking, obsolescence, or quantity inflation during inventory observation;

2. Increase the proportion of test counts during inventory observation;
3. Expand purchases and inventory cutoff procedures;
4. Extend the tests of inventory prices and quantities appearing on the final inventory listings (prices may be inflated or quantities may be increased in the transfer from inventory tags or sheets to the final listings); and
5. Arrange for observation, rather than confirmation, of significant amounts of inventory on consignment or in public warehouses.

Significant Increase in Plant Assets

Companies in the rebuilding process, or new and rapidly growing companies, may expend large sums on capital assets. Companies in mature or declining industries, on the other hand, usually replace worn-out assets, but are not expected to add heavily to the plant asset base.

Given a client in the former category, the auditor should plan to examine the underlying documentation supporting debits to plant asset accounts, evaluate the accounting for and valuation of the additions, and perhaps inspect some of the assets on a test basis. Suspicions ordinarily should not be aroused concerning asset inflation.

In the latter category, however, the auditor, upon discovering significant plant asset additions, should consider the possibility that ordinary repairs have been capitalized rather than expensed. Expanding the tests of smaller debits to the plant asset accounts, in conjunction with analyzing the repairs and maintenance accounts, should assist in determining whether the expenditures have been classified properly.

Asset Impairment

SFAS No. 121, "Accounting for the Impairment of Long-Lived Assets and for Long-Lived Assets to Be Disposed Of," applies to both plant assets and intangible assets, and requires impairment testing of these assets when circumstances indicate carrying amounts may not be recoverable. The auditor, therefore, must be aware of impairment indicators, examine management's test for impairment, and verify that an impairment loss equal to the difference between the assets' carrying value and estimated fair value has been recognized.

Impairment indicators include:

1. A significant decrease in an asset's market value;
2. A significant change in the manner in which an asset is being used; and
3. A current period operating or cash flow loss combined with either past losses or projected future losses.

In examining management's test for impairment, the auditor should review appraisal reports and management's projections of future income and cash flows. Additionally, the auditor should review subsequent events prior to the date of the audit report.[16]

Special Charges

A process known as **smoothing** occurs in accounting when an entity attempts to minimize peaks and valleys in earnings over time. The goal typically is to reflect a steady in-

16 FASB, *Accounting Standards: Current Text,* op. cit., section 108.

crease in income and earnings per share, thereby satisfying lenders and stockholders. One form of smoothing consists of establishing reserves during times of prosperity to be used to enhance profits during a downturn. The SEC recently warned banks about padding loan loss reserves in a healthy economy to be used to smooth earnings during an economic downturn.[17] Other smoothing devices assume the guise of deferring expenses such as research and development, advertising, employee training, and other intangible costs and amortizing them over future periods. Because this practice is considered a violation of GAAP, the auditor must be alert to conditions suggesting smoothing and recommend expensing any material charges inappropriately deferred.

The common practice, in today's environment of acquisitions and downsizing, of "taking special charges," although technically in accordance with GAAP, is alleged by some to be a form of smoothing. IBM, for example, charged $1.8 billion of the cost of acquiring Lotus Development Corporation (over half the purchase price) to expense in 1995, the year of acquisition. At the prodding of the SEC, FASB considered repealing standards permitting companies to expense such acquisition costs (classified as "purchased in-process research and development"). Upon further consideration, however, the rule was permitted to stand on the basis that the change would produce an inconsistency in the treatment of R&D costs.

Companies such as Haliburton, CitiGroup, Seagram, J.P. Morgan, Amerada Hess, and Lear took special charges in the late 1990s related to "restructuring and downsizing." Kerr-McGee Corp. took a $250 million charge in 1999 for previously capitalized oil and gas acquisition and development costs.[18] In all of these instances, the special charges affect only the year in which they are taken and relieve future periods of any impact related to the event. Although GAAP condones these practices on the precept that losses be recognized in the periods in which they are sustained, the auditor must be alert to the inappropriate inclusion of current and future operating expenses in the special charges. Such improper inclusion may be considered a form of smoothing because it relieves current and future accounting periods of operating expense charges applicable to those periods. Also, by overstating the special charge, management creates a "reserve" that may be partially reversed to mitigate the impact of lackluster earnings occurring in future periods.[19]

Existence of Related Parties

The existence of related parties may serve as a conduit for transferring expenses from one company to another. Research and development costs, for example, may be transferred improperly by the sale of the results of completed projects to related parties. In one case, a company reported a substantial increase in earnings per share by selling an allegedly valuable patent that had been obtained by developing a new product internally to a "shell" company. The sale was completed on the basis of the parent company's guarantee of loans to the related party and the loan proceeds then were used to buy the patent from the parent.

Related-party transactions, as in this case, often produce variances between legal form and economic substance, and when these variances occur, economic substance must take precedence. In this case, the legal form of the transaction was a sale at a

17 *Journal of Accountancy*, September 1999, p. 17.
18 *The Wall Street Journal*, January 15, 1999.
19 See, for example, "Write-Offs May Become 'Write-Ons,'" *The Wall Street Journal*, December 30, 1996, p. C2.

profit; the economic substance of the transaction, however, was a loan from the bank to the parent company, given that the shell company had no resources to repay the loan. Because of these possible occurrences, auditors must examine related-party transactions carefully, especially if analytical procedures disclose significant improvements in profitability.[20]

APPENDIX

AUDITING OBJECTIVES AND PROCEDURES: EXPENDITURE CYCLE

This audit objectives-evidence-procedures matrix, like the one in the appendix to Chapter 11, lists management assertions and specific audit objectives in the left column. Forms of audit evidence and selected audit procedures relating to the assertions and objectives are then listed in the right column of the matrix.

Purchases, Production, and Inventories

Assertions and Audit Objectives   **Audit Evidence and Procedures**

Existence and Completeness

Do inventories exist?

Documentary Evidence

- Review inventory-taking instructions for such matters as:
  1. Timing and location of inventory taking;
  2. Counting procedures;
  3. How counts are documented (tags, sheets, cards, etc.);
  4. Arrangement of obsolete inventory and consignments-in; and
  5. Control over production during inventory.

Physical Evidence

- Observe physical inventory taking:
  1. Test count and compare with sheets or tags;
  2. Keep record of test counts for later comparison with final inventory listings;
  3. Control movements within areas to be tested;
  4. Account for numeric sequence of tags or sheets, and control auditor's copies;
  5. Note possible obsolescence or overstocking (mark tags or listings for later follow up on final audit);
  6. Note environmental conditions as to arrangement and security over areas;

20 See Chapter 13 for a description of the auditor's approach to examining related-party transactions.

7. Note stage of completion for work in process;
8. Verify that consigned-in goods are not inventoried; and
9. Include loading docks and receiving areas in inventory observation.

Confirmation Evidence

- Confirm goods in public warehouses and goods out on consignment.

Rights, Obligations, and Valuation

Are inventories owned by the client?

Are inventories properly valued at lower of cost or market?

Are inventory transactions recorded in the proper accounting period?

Documentary Evidence

- Test for proper cutoff:
  1. During inventory observation, record document numbers of last receiving report, sales invoice, shipping order, and bill of lading;
  2. During inventory observation, trace substance (goods) to receiving area or shipping area;
  3. On final audit, trace to purchase and sales records (should be last entry of the year);
  4. Examine documents for a few days before and after the balance sheet date (especially sales invoices, sales orders, shipping orders, and bills of lading; receiving reports, vouchers, and freight bills) and determine when title passed; and
  5. Trace and vouch from documents to accounting records for errors of omission, and from accounting records to documents for errors of commission.
- Examine inventory adjustment to determine that book inventory has been properly adjusted to physical inventory.
- Test pricing of final inventory:
  1. Cost accounting system will have been examined as part of control testing during interim audit;
  2. Trace final inventory prices to audited price lists. Audited materials price lists should include a charge for freight and be exclusive of discount; finished goods price lists ordinarily assume the form of audited standard cost records; and work in process, given stage of completion, should be traced to audited routing sheets that accumulate costs by stage of production;
  3. Perform "lower of cost or market value" test; and

4. Determine proper valuation of goods appearing on tags or sheets marked "obsolete" or "slow-moving."
- Trace auditor's copies of tags or sheets to final inventory listings:
  1. Perform this test for tags representing both inventory counted and inventory not counted; and
  2. Determine that client has not added digits, tags, or sheets.
- Scan final inventory listings for large dollar amounts and trace related quantities to auditor's copies of tags or count sheets to detect significant inventory inflation errors.

Mathematical Evidence

- Test extensions and footings:
  1. Include most large-value items and sample remainder; and
  2. Use computer to assist in this procedure.

Analytical Evidence

- Use the "gross profit" method to estimate ending inventory:
  1. Compare with audited inventory; and
  2. Investigate further if this procedure produces wide variance.

Presentation and Disclosure

Hearsay Evidence

- Inquire about:
  1. Obsolescence;
  2. Pledging;
  3. Consigned goods;
  4. Cutoff; and
  5. Inventory held for use or consumption rather than for manufacture or resale.

Plant Assets

Assertions and Audit Objectives

Audit Evidence and Procedures

Existence and Completeness

Do recorded additions exist?
Have existing additions been recorded?
Have retirements been recorded?

Physical Evidence

- Inspect major additions—especially if internal control over plant assets is weak.

Analytical Evidence

- Compare depreciation expense and maintenance and repairs expense with those of prior year and with budgeted amounts and account for major changes:

1. Increase in depreciation may denote additions to plant assets (decrease may denote retirements);
2. Increase in maintenance and repairs expense may be the result of plant asset additions having been erroneously expensed (decrease may be indicative of ordinary repairs having been erroneously capitalized); and
3. A favorable maintenance and repair expense budget variance also suggests possible capitalization of ordinary repairs.

Hearsay Evidence

- Examine plant ledger for fully depreciated assets:
  1. Inquire as to status; and
  2. If no longer in use, or disposed of, an entry is needed to remove these.

Documentary Evidence

- Vouch repairs and maintenance accounts along with plant assets:
  1. The audit objective is to locate possible misclassifications (plant assets debited to repairs expense or ordinary repairs debited to plant assets); and
  2. Vouch major expenditures and test the remainder.

Valuation and Ownership

Are all assets valued at historical cost less accumulated depreciation?

Have impaired assets been properly reflected at fair value?

Have expenditures been properly classified as asset versus expense?

Mathematical Evidence

- Prepare a lead schedule of plant assets and accumulated depreciation by major classes:
  1. This should reflect beginning balances, additions, disposals, and ending balances; and
  2. It should be classified according to major categories of plant assets (e.g., land, buildings, equipment, autos and trucks, leasehold improvements, leased assets, and office equipment).
- Reconcile subsidiary ledger with controlling accounts and agree to ending balances appearing on plant assets lead schedule.
- Evaluate appropriateness and consistency of depreciation methods.
- Recalculate depreciation and gain or loss on disposals.

- Calculate change in deferred taxes related to temporary differences between book and tax depreciation.
- For self-constructed assets, recalculate:
  1. Overhead allocation; and
  2. Interest during construction, if applicable.
- Determine existence of impaired assets and determine that carrying amounts do *not* exceed fair value.

Documentary Evidence

- Vouch plant asset additions and disposals, along with repairs and maintenance accounts, on a test basis:
  1. Examine vendors' invoices and freight bills for purchased assets;
  2. Examine work orders for constructed assets;
  3. Trace receipts from disposals to bank statement; and
  4. Compare method of recording depreciation in year of acquisition and disposal with company policy for consistency.
- Examine directors' minutes and purchase and sale agreements for proper authorization and accounting for major acquisitions and disposals.

Presentation and Disclosure

Have financing leases been properly capitalized?

Hearsay Evidence

- Inquire as to assets not used in production:
  1. Assets on standby;
  2. Those awaiting disposal; and
  3. Those held for investment purposes.

Documentary Evidence

- Examine all lease agreements and determine proper classification as to financing versus operating.
- Examine loan agreements for possible pledging of plant assets as collateral.

Mathematical Evidence

- Evaluate appropriateness of discount rate used in calculating net present value of minimum lease payments.
- Recalculate minimum lease payments of financing leases.
- Recalculate contingent rentals on a test basis.

Intangible Assets (Patents, Copyrights, Trademarks, Franchises, Goodwill, etc.)

Assertions and Audit Objectives	Audit Evidence and Procedures

Existence and Completeness

Do recorded intangible assets exist?

Documentary Evidence

- Examine documentation supporting intangible assets:
  1. Patents, copyrights, and trademarks; and
  2. Franchise and merger agreements.
- Vouch additions and disposals:
  1. Include research and development expense; and
  2. Be alert to the possibility of purchased intangibles being debited to research and development expense and/or research and development expenses debited to intangible asset accounts.
- Examine minutes for proper authorization of acquisitions and disposals.

Analytical Evidence

- Apply analytical procedures to amortization and R&D expense by comparing with those of prior year and with budgeted amounts, and investigate material changes and/or variances.

Valuation and Ownership

Are purchased intangible assets properly recorded at acquisition cost less accumulated amortization?
Have research and development expenditures been charged to expense in accordance with GAAP?

Documentary Evidence

- Vouch additions and disposals on a test basis:
  1. Examine agreements;
  2. Examine canceled checks;
  3. Be particularly alert to the possibility of capitalized R&D or related-party transactions; and
  4. Trace receipts from disposals to bank statements.

Mathematical Evidence

- Recalculate gain or loss on disposal.
- Evaluate appropriateness of amortization period, and recalculate amortization on a test basis.

Presentation and Disclosure

Do reported intangibles possess future economic benefit?

Analytical Evidence

- Evaluate future economic benefit by relating assets to revenue produced by them.
- Determine need for asset impairment test in accordance with FASB 121:
  1. Examine management's documentation of test;
  2. Examine appraisal reports and cash flow forecasts; and

3. Determine that carrying amounts of impaired assets do not exceed fair values.
- Compare research and development expense with that of prior year and investigate major changes (may be the result of errors in classifying expenditures).

Hearsay Evidence

- Inquire of management and legal counsel as to possible contingencies relating to intangible assets (e.g., patent infringement suit).
- Inquire of management as to possible "asset impairment" if conditions so suggest.

Current Liabilities

Assertions and Audit Objectives	Audit Evidence and Procedures

Existence and Completeness

Are all significant liabilities reflected on the balance sheet?

Confirmation Evidence

- Obtain lawyer's letter to identify contingencies requiring adjustment or footnote disclosure.
- Examine bank confirmation for loans.

Documentary Evidence

- Search for unrecorded liabilities:
  1. Examine paid and unpaid invoices for a short period following the balance sheet date, and determine that recording took place in the proper period;
  2. Trace to client's year-end adjustment for unrecorded liabilities;
  3. Examine loan agreements for possible existence of imputed interest.

Analytical Evidence

- Compare year-end accruals with those of prior year and account for significant changes or omissions.

Hearsay Evidence

- Inquire as to contingencies.
- Obtain client representation letter.

Valuation

Are management's estimates reasonable?

Mathematical Evidence

- Recompute the following, as applicable, on a test basis:
  1. Interest accruals;
  2. Tax accruals;

3. Liability for product warranty;
4. Pension cost and liability;
5. Vacation pay; and
6. Profit sharing and bonuses.

Presentation and Disclosure	*Documentary Evidence*
Have significant contingencies been properly reflected?	• Determine that contingent liabilities are properly disclosed.

Analytical Evidence

• Examine prior year's financial statements for possible footnote disclosures required in the current year's statements.

KEY TERMS

Accounts payable confirmation, 497
Cutoff tests, 483
Inventory cutoff, 483
Inventory in transit, 485
Inventory instructions, 481
Inventory observation, 481
Inventory pricing tests, 487
Inventory tags or sheets, 481
Inventory test counts, 482

Letter of audit inquiry to the client's legal counsel, 497
Plant assets lead schedule, 489
Purchases cutoff, 483
Request for vendor's statement, 497
Sales cutoff, 483
Search for unrecorded liabilities, 497
Smoothing, 501
Tests for inventory obsolescence, 487

COMPUTER AUDIT PRACTICE CASE

Biltrite Bicycles, Inc.

The following expenditure cycle substantive testing assignments from the Biltrite audit practice case may be completed at this time:

Module VIII: Sales and purchases cutoff tests
Module IX: Search for unrecorded liabilities
Module X: Estimated liability for product warranty
Module XI: Plant asset additions and disposals

REVIEW QUESTIONS

1. How does the auditor verify the existence of inventories?

2. Why is it important for the auditor to review the client's inventory-taking instructions?

3. Why is it necessary for the auditor to control inventory tags and inventory movements during the physical inventory?

4. What purpose is served in auditing cutoff?

5. How does the auditor gain assurance that quantities appearing on the final inventory listings are correct?

6. How does the auditor test inventory for obsolescence?

7. How does the application of analytical procedures assist in the audit of plant assets?

8. Identify the audit objectives and procedures concerning plant asset disposals.

9. How does the auditor ascertain proper authorization of major additions and disposals?

10. Why should the repairs and maintenance accounts be audited simultaneously with the plant asset accounts?

11. Why are lease agreements examined along with plant assets?

12. Research and development expenditures should be examined as part of the audit of intangible assets. Explain why.

13. How does the auditor ascertain the future economic benefit of recorded intangibles?

14. Briefly describe the search for unrecorded liabilities.

15. What is the purpose of the letter of audit inquiry to the client's legal counsel?

16. How might a company manipulate overhead in order to understate losses during a period of abnormally low-volume operations? How should the auditor respond to such a situation?

17. How does the auditor determine whether an inventory increase is normal or abnormal?

MULTIPLE CHOICE QUESTIONS FROM PAST CPA EXAMS

1. An auditor most likely would analyze inventory turnover rates to obtain evidence concerning management's assertions about
   a. Existence or occurrence.
   b. Rights and obligations.
   c. Presentation and disclosure.
   d. Valuation or allocation.

2. An auditor most likely would perform substantive tests of details on payroll transactions and balances when
   a. Cutoff tests indicate a substantial amount of accrued payroll expense.
   b. The assessed level of control risk relative to payroll transactions is low.
   c. Analytical procedures indicate unusual fluctuations in recurring payroll entries.
   d. Accrued payroll expense consists primarily of unpaid commissions.

3. Which of the following questions would most likely be included in an internal control questionnaire concerning the completeness assertion for purchases?
   a. Is an authorized purchase order required before the receiving department can accept a shipment or the vouchers payable department can record a voucher?
   b. Are purchase requisitions prenumbered and independently matched with vendor invoices?
   c. Is the unpaid voucher file periodically reconciled with inventory records by an employee who does not have access to purchase requisitions?
   d. Are purchase orders, receiving reports, and vouchers prenumbered and periodically accounted for?

4. A client maintains perpetual inventory records in both quantities and dollars. If the assessed level of control risk is high, an auditor would probably
   a. Insist that the client perform physical counts of inventory items several times during the year.

    b. Apply gross profit tests to ascertain the reasonableness of the physical counts.

    c. Increase the extent of tests of controls of the inventory cycle.

    d. Request the client to schedule the physical inventory count at the end of the year.

5. Which of the following is a substantive test that an auditor most likely would perform to verify the existence and valuation of recorded accounts payable?

    a. Investigating the open purchase order file to ascertain that prenumbered purchase orders are used and accounted for

    b. Receiving the client's mail, unopened, for a reasonable period of time after year end to search for unrecorded vendors' invoices

    c. Vouching selected entries in the accounts payable subsidiary ledger to purchase orders and receiving reports

    d. Confirming accounts payable balances with known suppliers who have zero balances

6. To determine whether accounts payable are complete, an auditor performs a test to verify that all merchandise received is recorded. The population of documents for this test consists of all

    a. Payment vouchers.

    b. Receiving reports.

    c. Purchase requisitions.

    d. Vendors' invoices.

7. Which of the following procedures is *least* likely to be performed before the balance sheet date?

    a. Testing of internal control over cash

    b. Confirmation of receivables

    c. Search for unrecorded liabilities

    d. Observation of inventory

8. Which of the following is the best audit procedure for determining the existence of unrecorded liabilities?

    a. Examine confirmation requests returned by creditors whose accounts appear on a subsidiary trial balance of accounts payable

    b. Examine unusual relationships between monthly accounts payable balances and recorded purchases

    c. Examine a sample of invoices a few days prior to and subsequent to year end to ascertain whether they have been properly recorded

    d. Examine a sample of cash disbursements in the period subsequent to year end

9. Which of the following most likely would be detected by an auditor's review of a client's sales cutoff?

    a. Unrecorded sales for the year

    b. Lapping of year-end accounts receivable

    c. Excessive sales discounts

    d. Unauthorized goods returned for credit

10. Which of the following combinations of procedures would an auditor most likely perform to obtain evidence about fixed asset additions?

    a. Inspecting documents and physically examining assets

    b. Recomputing calculations and obtaining written management representations

    c. Observing operating activities and comparing balances to prior period balances

    d. Confirming ownership and corroborating transactions through inquiries of client personnel

11. An auditor who selects a sample of items from the vouchers payable register for the last month of the period under audit and traces these items to underlying documents is gathering evidence primarily in support of the assertion that
    a. Recorded obligations were paid.
    b. Incurred obligations were recorded in the correct period.
    c. Recorded obligations were valid.
    d. Cash disbursements were recorded as incurred obligations.

12. Which of the following control procedures most likely would assist in reducing control risk related to the existence or occurrence of manufacturing transactions?
    a. Perpetual inventory records are independently compared with goods on hand.
    b. Forms used for direct material requisitions are prenumbered and accounted for.
    c. Finished goods are stored in locked limited access warehouses.
    d. Subsidiary ledgers are periodically reconciled with inventory control accounts.

13. Inquiries of warehouse personnel concerning possible obsolete or slow-moving inventory items provide assurance about management's assertion of
    a. Completeness.
    b. Existence.
    c. Presentation.
    d. Valuation.

ESSAY QUESTIONS AND PROBLEMS

12.1   Robinson, CPA, is auditing Atlantic Contractors' financial statements and is about to perform substantive audit procedures on Atlantic's trade accounts payable balances. After obtaining an understanding of Atlantic's internal control system for accounts payable, Robinson assessed control risk at near the maximum. She requested and received from Atlantic a schedule of the trade accounts payable prepared using the trade accounts payable subsidiary ledger (voucher register).

Required:
Describe the substantive audit procedures Robinson should apply to Atlantic's trade accounts payable balances (AICPA adapted)

12.2   The purpose of all auditing procedures is to gather sufficient competent evidence for an auditor to form an opinion regarding the financial statements taken as a whole.

Required:
    a. In addition to the following example, identify and describe five means or techniques of gathering audit evidence used to evaluate a client's inventory balance.

Technique	*Description*
Observation	An auditor watches the performance of some functions, such as a client's annual inventory count.

    b. Identify the five general assertions regarding a client's inventory balance and describe one *different* substantive auditing procedure for each assertion. Use the format illustrated below.

Assertion	**Substantive Auditing Procedure**

(AICPA adapted)

12.3   In examining Exhibit 12.8, a worksheet for machinery and equipment, you note that the audit legends are *not* explained. List the legends and identify the audit procedures represented by each.

EXHIBIT 12.8

Problem 12.3 Worksheet

		WP C.2
Prepared by:	lfk	
Date:	1/23/03	
Reviewed by:	jcf	
Date:	1/29/03	

Laurlee, Inc.
Machinery & Equipment
12/31/02

	M&E	Accum. Dept.	Gain/(Loss)
12/31/01 Final Balances	$1,234,600*	$ 658,900*	
Additions:			
Stable Press	126,000@		
Computer-Controlled Welder	267,890@		
Disposals:			
Tracer Bed	(174,000)^	(152,000)^	8,000!
2002 Depreciation		226,500!	
12/31/02 Final Balances	$1,454,490&	$ 733,400&	$8,000&
	f	f	f
	To WP C	To WP C	To WP C

12.4   In conducting the search for unrecorded liabilities, Jason Lopez, senior auditor on the Charn Stitcheries audit, performed the following procedures. He obtained the client's year-end adjustment for unrecorded invoices vouchered in the following accounting period, vouched to underlying documentation, and traced to general ledger accounts. He also obtained a client representation letter.

Required:
a. Identify the audit objective(s) served by the search for unrecorded liabilities, and discuss its overall significance.
b. Assuming that the auditors judged Charn's internal control over purchases and accounts payable to be acceptable, what added procedures should Jason Lopez apply? Explain the reason(s) for each procedure recommended.

12.5   You are the in-charge auditor for the Channin, Inc., examination. Channin manufactures commercial pumps, primarily for industrial applications. In observing the taking of the year-end inventory by Channin personnel, you noted the following:

1. All inventories, except for work in process, which is minor, are housed in the central warehouse.

2. Inventory tags are prenumbered and show description and quantity of inventory. They were attached upon counting and removed only upon authorization by the independent auditors. The tags were issued to the two-person count teams and each number series issued was recorded by the plant superintendent on a control sheet.

3. Although the auditors did not test count one of the six finished goods bays, they walked through the area, accompanied by the plant superintendent, to ensure that all goods were tagged.

4. Inasmuch as no provision was made for auditors' copies of the inventory tags, the auditors recorded all of their test counts on inventory count sheets (part of the audit workpapers).

5. No provision was made by the client for double-checking the original inventory counts.

6. At the end of the inventory taking and observation, the auditors did not consider it feasible to account for all of the issued and unissued inventory tags. They did have the client furnish them with a copy of the control sheet maintained by the superintendent.

Required:

a. Comment on the effectiveness of the inventory taking by Channin and the inventory observation by the auditors. Can you identify specific warning signs in this case that might have alerted the auditors to possible inventory inflation?

b. Consistent with your answer to (a), list any added substantive audit procedures that you would recommend.

12.6   Jackson, CPA, was engaged to audit the financial statements of Natural Accents, Inc., a continuing audit client. Jackson is about to audit Natural Accents' payroll transactions. Natural Accents uses an in-house payroll department to compute payroll data and prepare and distribute payroll checks.

During the planning process, Jackson determined that the inherent risk of overstatement of payroll expense is high. In addition, he obtained an understanding of the internal control system and assessed control risk at the maximum level for payroll-related assertions.

Required:

Describe the audit procedures Jackson should consider performing in the audit of Natural Accents' payroll transactions to address the risk of overstatement. Do *not* discuss Natural Accents' internal control system. (AICPA adapted)

12.7   George Ruiz,, a recent addition to the staff of Gonzalez and Haft, CPAs, is a member of the audit team examining the accounts of Young Manufacturing for the year ended December 31, 2002. Gonzalez and Haft have audited Young for the past five years. Ruiz has just been assigned the task of searching for unrecorded liabilities. He has already determined that all payroll, payroll taxes, income and property taxes, sales taxes, and interest have been properly reflected by the company. In addition, he has obtained the following copy of Young's 12/31/02 adjusting journal entry to reflect other unrecorded liabilities at year end:

Raw materials inventory	$23,675	
Utilities expense	6,400	
Professional fees	33,690	
Manufacturing supplies	8,900	
Accounts payable		$72,665

To record the following invoices unpaid at 12/31/02:

Follet Manufacturing	$23,675
Consolidated Gas	2,760
Cay City Electric	3,640
Gonzalez and Haft (consulting)	33,690
Wemlo Suppliers	7,700
Hammer and Nail	1,200

Although the Wemlo Suppliers invoice was received in December, the supplies were shipped to Young on January 2 and received on January 4.

In addition to a copy of this journal entry and the supporting documentation, Ruiz requested all invoices vouchered during the period 1/2/03 to 1/21/03 and all unvouchered invoices as of 1/21/03. In examining these invoices and vouchers, Ruiz found the following:

Gemco Industries	$17,200	Raw materials shipped F.O.B. destination on 12/30/02 and received by Wooley on 1/2/03.
Rubicon & Sellers Advertising	$27,430	Production and layout for 2002 promotional campaign.
Fuller & Fuller	$64,000	2002 legal services.
Wemlo Suppliers	$2,355	Manufacturing supplies shipped F.O.B. shipping point on 12/30/02 and received by Wooley on 1/2/03.
Cay City Department of Public Utilities	$1,200	January water bill.
Hefty Manufacturers	$132,000	Five lift trucks received and placed in service December 12.
Second District Court	$27,500	Payment for judgment rendered 1/4/03, applicable to product liability lawsuit brought against Young in February 2002.
Computers, Limited	$13,800	Two computers received in January 2003.
American Office Warehouse	$3,900	Office supplies purchased in November.
Wichita Laboratories	$22,100	Manufacturing royalties for October through December, $15,100; and royalty advance on January through March royalties, $7,000.
Holea Equipment	$166,800	Robotic equipment invoiced by Holea in January 2003 but received and placed in service in December 2002.
Todco Custodial Services	$14,670	Contract services for November and December.
Diedrich Employment Agency	$6,770	Employment fee for marketing vice president hired in January.

Required:

a. Draft all necessary audit adjustments based on your analysis of the above data.

b. Can you identify any other procedures Ruiz should apply in completing the search for unrecorded liabilities?

12.8 Consider the auditing objectives related to the following management assertions:

1. Existence or occurrence
2. Completeness
3. Rights and obligations
4. Valuation or allocation
5. Presentation and disclosure

These objectives have varying degrees of importance when related to specific subsets of transaction cycles. Assuming that circumstances suggest a balanced audit approach, as described in Chapter 11, identify the most critical objective for each of the following subsets of the expenditure cycle:

a. Purchases, production, and inventories
b. Plant assets
c. Intangible assets
d. Current liabilities and operating expenses

Justify your choice in each instance.

12.9 Gretta Gaines, an independent auditor, was engaged to examine the financial statements of Lake Erie Construction, Inc., for the year ended December 31, 2002. Lake Erie's financial statements reflect a substantial amount of mobile construction equipment used in the firm's operations. The equipment is accounted for in a subsidiary ledger. Gaines performed a study and evaluation of Lake Erie's internal control policies and procedures and found them to be satisfactory.

Required:
Identify the substantive audit procedures that Gaines should utilize in examining mobile construction equipment and related depreciation in Lake Erie's financial statements. (AICPA adapted)

12.10 Martin Bailes, a CPA, is engaged in the audit of Iowa Wholesalers for the year ended December 31, 2002. Bailes performed a proper study of internal control policies and procedures relating to the purchasing, receiving, trade accounts payable, and cash disbursement cycles, and has decided *not* to test controls. Based on analytical procedures, Bailes believes that the trade accounts payable balance on the balance sheet as of December 31, 2002, may be understated.

He requested and obtained a client-prepared trade accounts payable schedule listing the total amount owed to each vendor.

Required:
What additional substantive audit procedures should Bailes apply in examining the trade accounts payable? (AICPA adapted)

12.11 You have been engaged for the audit of Granite Tire for the year ended December 31, 2002. Granite is engaged in the wholesale auto parts business. All sales are made at cost plus 30 percent of cost. Granite maintains perpetual inventory records and adjusts the records annually after taking a physical inventory.

Shown in Exhibit 12.9 are portions of Granite's sales and inventory accounts for tires, the single most important (40 percent of total sales) product handled by the firm.

EXHIBIT 12.9

Problem 12.11 Tire Sales and Inventory Accounts

Tire Sales

Date	Reference	Amount	Date	Reference	Amount
12/31	Closing entry	$11,460,200		Balance Forward	$11,250,000
			12/27	SO# 1278	16,400
			12/28	SO# 1279	48,600
			12/28	SO# 1280	20,100
			12/31	SO# 1281	56,800
			12/31	SO# 1282	17,600
			12/31	SO# 1283	42,700
			12/31	SO# 1284	8,000
		$11,460,200			$11,460,200

Tire Inventory

Date	Reference	Amount	Date	Reference	Amount
	Balance Forward	$780,680	12/31	Adjustment to physical	$120,480
12/28	RR# 2060	6,400			
12/30	RR# 2062	22,600			
12/31	RR# 2063	10,800			

You observed the physical inventory and are satisfied that it was taken properly. The tire inventory is located in two adjacent bays in the company's central warehouse.

When performing a sales and purchases cutoff test, you found that at December 31, 2002, the last receiving report used was #2063. Moreover, you determined that no shipments had been made on any shipping orders with numbers larger than 1281.

You also obtained the following information:

1. Included in the physical inventory at December 31, 2002, were tires that had been purchased and received on receiving report #2061 but for which an invoice was *not* received until 2003. The cost was $14,200.
2. In the warehouse at December 31, 2002, were tires that had been sold and paid for by the customer but that were *not* shipped until 2003. They were all sold on sales invoice/shipping order #1278. The tires were included in the physical inventory.
3. On the evening of December 31, 2002, two cars were on the Granite company railroad track. Both cars contained tires that were included in the 12/31/02 physical inventory: Car #SA877560 was unloaded on January 2, 2003, and received on receiving report #2064 (cost of tires, $16,800). The freight was paid by the vendor. Car #EE455621 was loaded and sealed on December 31, 2002, and because the freight was paid by the customer, title passed when the car was switched off the Hedley track on January 2, 2003. The sales price was $56,800. This order was sold on sales invoice/shipping order #1281.
4. Temporarily stranded on a railroad track at December 31, 2002, were two cars of tires in transit to Grambling Tires of St. Louis. They were sold on sales invoice/shipping order #1279 and the terms were F.O.B. shipping point.

5. En route to Granite Tire on December 31, 2002, was a truckload of tires that was received on receiving report #2065. The tires were shipped F.O.B. shipping point and freight of $1,600 was paid by Granite. However, the freight was deducted from the purchase price of $32,100.

6. Included in the physical inventory were tires damaged by excessive heat in transit and deemed unsalable. Their invoice cost was $16,300; freight charges of $960 had been paid on the tires. Granite filed a claim against the shipper in January 2003.

Required:

a. Draft the auditor's adjustments that are required as of 12/31/02.

b. Calculate the corrected physical inventory at 12/31/02.

c. Comment on any control weaknesses indicated by these procedures.

12.12 Selfers Service Center is a wholly owned subsidiary of Selfers Federated Stores. The company's function is to deliver furniture and appliances sold by the parent and to service electronics and appliances, also sold by the parent company. Selfers Federated Stores, the parent, operates twelve retail outlets in a large tri-county metropolitan area. The service center uses three delivery trucks and fifteen service vehicles for delivering goods and for making service calls related to large appliances and electronic equipment. Customers typically bring small appliances and electronics to the service center for repair.

At January 1, 2002, Selfers Service Center reported audited balances of $720,000 and $350,000 for "Trucks" and "Accumulated Depreciation—Trucks," respectively. The vehicles consisted of five delivery trucks costing $72,000 each and fifteen service trucks costing $24,000 each. Accumulated depreciation was $200,000 for delivery trucks and $150,000 for service trucks.

The company depreciates all trucks on a straight-line basis, using a six-year life and zero salvage value. One-half year's depreciation is taken in the year of acquisition and in the year of disposal.

During 2002, the following transactions and journal entries were completed by the company.

2/2/02:   Sold one delivery truck for $4,000. The truck was fully depreciated at 12/31/01.

Cash	$4,000	
Truck		$4,000

3/1/02:   Bought one delivery truck for $84,000.

Truck	$84,000	
Cash		$84,000

3/15/02:   Sold one service truck for $7,000. This truck was purchased 8/15/99 for $24,000 and the accumulated depreciation, according to Selfer's subsidiary ledger, at the date of sale was $10,000.

Cash	$7,000	
Truck		$7,000

7/25/02:   Bought one service truck for $26,000.

Truck	$26,000	
Cash		$26,000

12/31/02:   Recorded depreciation for 2000:

Four delivery trucks @ $12,000 each =	$ 48,000	
Fifteen service trucks @ $4,000 each =	60,000	
Total	$108,000	
Depreciation Expense—Trucks	$108,000	
Accumulated Depreciation—Trucks		$108,000

Required:

a. Prepare an audit workpaper analyzing the following accounts:
   - Trucks
   - Accumulated depreciation—trucks
   - Depreciation expense—trucks
   - Gain (loss) on disposal of trucks

   Start with the audited balances at the beginning of the year. Reflect the transactions as they should have been recorded during 2002 to arrive at audited balances at the end of the year. Then compare these with the December 31, 2002 client balances and record necessary audit adjustments.

b. What are the audit objectives for purposes of this exercise? What audit procedures should be applied in meeting these objectives?

c. Add audit legends. Explain them at the bottom of your workpaper, describing the procedures that you identified in (b) above.

Note: The solution to this problem can be greatly expedited by retrieving and completing the spreadsheet template entitled "Selfers." This file is included on the same Student CD that contains the Biltrite Bicycle templates.

DISCUSSION CASES

CASE 1
Crazy Eddie

Crazy Eddie, Inc., a company operating forty-two electronics stores in the eastern United States, had reported significant gains in sales and earnings since going public in 1984. At that time, the company raised $124 million by issuing subordinated debenture bonds and capital stock. Bear, Stearns & Co. and Salomon Brothers, Inc., were among the underwriters for these securities issues. According to Eddie Antar, the firm's founder, chief executive officer, and principal stockholder, Crazy Eddie's success resulted from rapid expansion of its electronics stores, skillful sales floor techniques, and lively commercials. An investigation by the Securities and Exchange Commission and third-party legal proceedings, how-

ever, revealed the sales and earnings growth, for the most part, to be fabricated. Reported profits of $33 million for the combined fiscal years ending February 28, 1984–87, were followed by a loss of $109 million in 1988. The 1988 loss included items that should have been charged to prior years, but neither the new management nor the auditors could reasonably determine the years to which specific charges applied.

The fraud was effected by inflating inventories by $65 million and understating accounts payable by approximately $10 million. The inventory overstatement was accomplished by fabricating count sheets for nonexistent inventory, by including in inventory goods that already had been recorded as purchases returns and were awaiting shipment back to vendors, and by including unrecorded inventories in stores prior to physical inventory counts and auditor observation of the counts. That is, the purchases had *not* been recorded, but the goods were included in the ending inventory.

Sales also were inflated by including in a given store's sales goods that were shipped to other stores. Sales growth at new stores was a key success indicator emphasized by financial analysts promoting Crazy Eddie stock and debentures.

CASE II

Comptronix Corporation

In August 1992, the three top officers of Comptronix Corporation—William Hebding, chief executive officer; Allen Shifflett, president and chief operating officer; and Paul Medlin, treasurer–controller— voluntarily disclosed to the board of directors that serious accounting irregularities had occurred over the past three years. An ongoing IRS audit may have prompted the disclosure.

Comptronix, based in Guntersville, Alabama, was founded in 1984 by William Hebding, who is also a certified public accountant, and by Allen Shifflett. The company was engaged in contract manufacturing. At the peak of its operations it employed 1,800 people at plants in San Jose, California, and Guntersville. Contract manufacturing in the U.S. electronics market is estimated at $4 billion annually; it is a rapidly growing industry, dominated by small companies. The rate of growth has been estimated most recently at 12 percent per year. Contract manufacturers build parts and components for large companies that once performed these operations themselves but, after downsizing, found it more cost effective to subcontract to the smaller component manufacturers. Comptronix manufactures components for computers, medical devices, and communications equipment. One of its main lines consists of circuit boards used in such products as medical CAT scan machines and personal computers.

Reported sales and earnings had been growing briskly. In 1991, for example, net income was reported at $5.1 million or $0.51 per share, a 67 percent increase over 1990 income. Sales were $102

Required:

a. What, in your opinion, should the auditors' responsibility have been for detecting the Crazy Eddie fraud?

b. What procedures might the auditors have applied that would have enabled them to detect the fraud?

million, a 45 percent increase over 1990. For the third quarter of 1992, reported sales were $40 million, a 43 percent increase over those of the same quarter in 1991. Earnings increased 48 percent to $2.2 million. The price per share of common stock increased from $3 per share at the end of 1990 to $22 per share by the end of 1992. Comptronix had been audited by the firm of KPMG Peat Marwick.

The accounting irregularities disclosed by the three officers resulted in grossly overstated profits for the years following 1989, when the company first went public. For 1992, the reported profit of $5.3 million should have been a loss of $1.5 million. For the preceding three years, profits were overstated by $10 million; by the end of 1992 shareholders' equity was overstated by 50 percent, or $45.6 million. The company had a good reputation among its competitors, who apparently never questioned the impressive earnings.

Based on an investigation conducted jointly by Arthur Andersen, CPAs, and the Securities and Exchange Commission, the fraud was perpetrated as follows:

1. At the end of each month the company inflated inventory by making the following entry:

   Debit: Inventory
     Credit: Cost of sales

   Presumably this entry was explained as an adjustment of book to physical inventory.

2. In addition, the company periodically made the following entry:

   Debit: Equipment
     Credit: Accounts payable

All documentation for fictitious purchases of equipment was fabricated. As will be seen below, this entry provided a vehicle for transferring the inventory overstatement to the equipment account where the probability of auditor detection was less likely.

3. To get rid of the inventory overstatement, the company recorded bogus sales with the following entries:

Debit: Accounts receivable
   Credit: Sales

Debit: Cost of sales
   Credit: Inventory

As with equipment purchases, all documentation supporting the fictitious sales transactions was fabricated.

4. To avoid auditor scrutiny regarding the fictitious accounts payable and accounts receivable, Comptronix wrote checks to the bogus vendors, deposited the checks in the bank, and credited the accounts of the bogus customers. The following set of entries achieved this goal:

Debit: Accounts payable
   Credit: Cash

Debit: Cash
   Credit: Accounts receivable

As to why the bank did not become suspicious about the deposit of vendor checks in the company's own account, a possible explanation lies in the fact that the president of the depository bank was a Comptronix director.

The end result of the above entries was a set of debits to Equipment and credits to Sales (the other debits and credits canceled one another). The financial statement effect was a revenue overstatement of $20 million and $20 million of nonexistent equipment in the accounts ($35 million of actual equipment cost compared with a total reported value of $55 million).

Following disclosure of the fraud, the price of Comptronix stock declined from $22 to $6 per share in a single day's trading. The three officers were suspended, and William Hebding was ultimately fired for refusing to cooperate in the investigation. The company was also in violation of certain loan agreements because of overstated shareholders' equity.

Required:

a. What might have prompted the fraud described in this case?

b. Why didn't the auditors find it? Were they negligent? Were obvious warning signs ignored?

CASE III

Laribee Wire

Laribee Wire was able to convert a $6.5 million loss into a $3 million profit by inflating inventories. The fraud was allegedly perpetrated by top management to assist LW Industries, Laribee's parent, in obtaining a $130 million loan from a group of six banks. Much of the collateral for this loan consisted of Laribee's copper rod inventory.

Laribee Wire manufactured copper rod and copper wire for use in the construction industry. LW Industries, in turn, was controlled by New York investor Martin Wright and his son Jordan Wright, who were also involved in real estate ventures. LW Industries had grown through several acquisitions, and the group bank loan was for the purpose of funding yet another. At this point in time (1989), sales to the construction companies were declining due to the recession in that industry. By inflating inventories, therefore, LW Industries was able to misrepresent to the banks both its profit and the value of the collateral securing the loans.

The loans were obtained in April 1990. By October of that year, LW Industries had defaulted on the loans, and in February 1991 the company and its five subsidiaries, including Laribee, filed for bankruptcy protection. LW Industries ceased operating on March 31, 1991; at that time, it owed $50 million to its copper suppliers alone. The Wrights resigned after the U.S. Bankruptcy Court in New York approved the turnover of management to Hampton Group, a firm that managed businesses in crisis. John Turbidy, a member of Hampton Group, was named new chief executive officer.

Stating that they had relied on the unqualified opinion rendered by Deloitte & Touche (LW Industries' auditors) on the 1989 financial statements, the banks sued Deloitte, charging the firm with gross negligence for failing to detect the inventory fraud. Among the banks bringing the lawsuit were First Union Commercial, a leasing and asset-based lending subsidiary of First Union Corp., and Bankers' Trust of New York.

An investigation into the fraud showed that much of the inventory didn't exist, and that some was carried at overstated values.   Certain wire-product stocks, carried on Laribee's books at $2.20 per pound, were selling at $1.70 per pound; shipments between plants were reported as stocks located at both plants; and 4.5 million pounds of copper rod, supposedly worth $5 million, was reported by Laribee in two warehouses in upstate New York. Further investigation showed that the space occupied by this inventory would have required three times the capacity of these buildings. In addition, the Wrights were alleged to have transferred much of the borrowed money from LW Industries to their troubled real estate operations.

John Turbidy, the court-appointed trustee and new chief executive officer, said that some of the auditors who showed up at Laribee's plants for inventory observation were "fresh out of college." The auditors checking the upstate New York inventory had three years' or less experience. "The faces kept changing and there was little continuity," said James Simmons, Laribee's former vice president for operations.[21] Mr. Dobrichovsky, the in-charge partner, never showed up at the plants during annual inventory counts. Sometimes the auditors permitted company officials to follow them and record the spots where they were making test counts.

Required:
a. Discuss whether or not, in your opinion, the following findings are evidence of negligence by the auditors:
    1. Some of the auditors were "fresh out of college."
    2. The upstate New York inventory observers had three years' or less experience.
    3. The faces kept changing and there was little continuity.
    4. The in-charge partner never showed up at the plants during inventory observation.
    5. The auditors permitted company officials to follow them and record where they were making test counts.
b. What warning signs, if any, should have aroused the auditors' suspicions?
c. What degree of negligence do the banks need to demonstrate in this case?

21 *The Wall Street Journal,* December 14, 1992.

Substantive Audit Testing: Financing and Investing Cycle
and Completing the Audit

c h a p t e r 1 3

biltrite

After reading this chapter, you should be able to

1 Identify specific audit objectives related to the financing and investing cycle.

2 Develop audit programs for the financing and investing cycle that relate audit procedures to audit objectives for each component of the cycle, and that include procedures for

    a identifying related parties and auditing related-party transactions; and

    b locating Type I and Type II subsequent events.

3 Modify audit programs, as necessary, in light of warning signs that surface during the study of the business and industry, application of analytical procedures, or the study and evaluation of internal control policies and procedures.

4 Complete audit field work by searching for subsequent events, performing analytical procedures as part of overall audit review, clearing open items, obtaining a client representation letter, drafting a reportable conditions letter outlining significant internal control weaknesses, and communicating with the client's audit committee.

OVERVIEW

This chapter discusses substantive testing of the financing and investing cycle. This part of the audit process, depicted in Figure 13.1, is presented in three parts:

1. Investing transactions;
2. Borrowing transactions; and
3. Stockholders' equity transactions.

FIGURE 13.1

The Audit Process

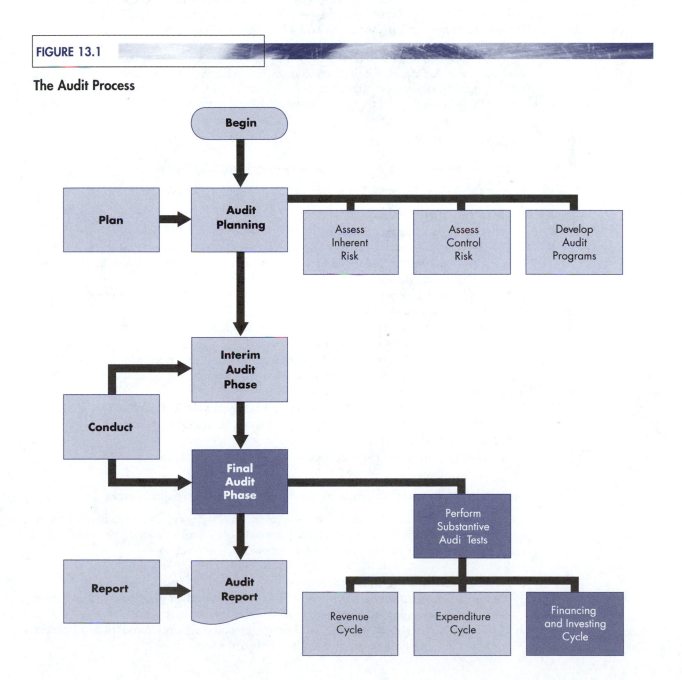

The format used is similar to that of Chapters 11 and 12, including the appendix at the end of each chapter.

This chapter emphasizes the testing of investments for overstatement and liabilities for understatement. Accordingly, attention is given to such procedures as examining or confirming securities, reading loan agreements and directors' minutes, and recalculating accruals. Disclosure of details surrounding debt agreements and stockholders' equity transactions also is stressed.

The audit risk analysis section of the chapter begins with the identification and examination of related-party transactions. Because related-party transactions occur more frequently within the financing and investing cycle, the chapter covers this topic in depth. The case of Rite Aid and its former CEO is used as an example of the significance of identifying and auditing related-party transactions.

The chapter concludes by addressing those steps necessary for completing the audit field work. Of particular importance, and therefore treated as the main topics in that section, are the need to apply analytical procedures as part of overall audit review, possible modification of materiality thresholds based on audited financial data, and the search for subsequent events.

INTRODUCTION

Types of Transactions in the Financing and Investing Cycle

The financing and investing cycle includes the following sets of transactions:

1. *Investing transactions*:
   a. Lending to others, interest revenue, and notes receivable balances;
   b. Acquisitions and disposals of financial assets, including marketable equity securities (long-term and short-term), investments in bonds, interest revenue, and gain/loss on disposals; and
   c. Investments in other assets (e.g., real estate) not held for operating purposes.
2. *Borrowing transactions*:
   a. Borrowing from others, including bonds and mortgages payable;
   b. Liabilities under capital leases;
   c. Deferred taxes arising from depreciation timing differences; and
   d. Interest expense and liability related to borrowing transactions.
3. *Stockholders' equity transactions*:
   a. Cash and stock dividends, and retained earnings balances;
   b. Stock issues, stock retirements, capital stock balances, and treasury stock transactions and balances; and
   c. Stock options and earnings per share.

Summary of Processing Steps in the Financing and Investing Cycle

Figure 13.2 is a flowchart summarizing the processing steps typically included in the financing and investing cycle. The essential control policies and procedures, which were more fully described in the appendix following Chapter 7, follow.

Borrowing and Investing Transactions

1. Borrowing and investing transactions should be properly authorized, and authority should be clearly defined in policy and procedures manuals;
2. Control policies should provide that borrowing and investing transactions in excess of specified amounts be authorized by the board of directors;

FIGURE 13.2

Financing and Investing Cycle: Summary of Processing Steps

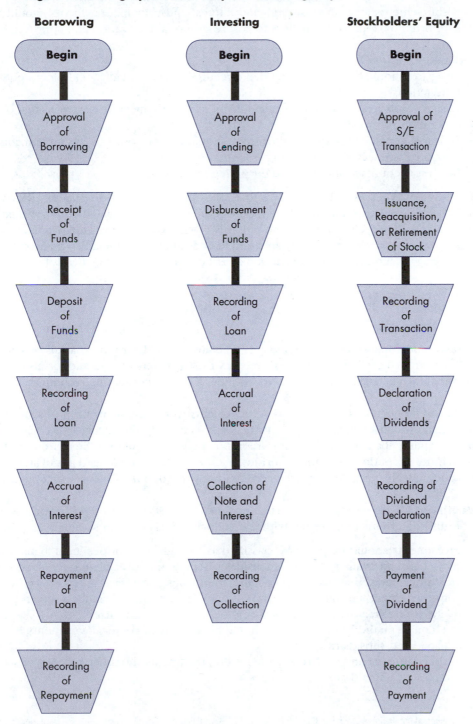

3. Cash receipts from borrowing and investing transactions should be subject to the same control procedures as those used in the revenue cycle;
4. Monthly interest accruals should be provided for by standard journal entries or journal vouchers to prevent inadvertent omission of necessary adjustments; and
5. Disbursements for loans to others and interest and principal payments should be supported by approved vouchers to ensure proper authorization and approval.

Stockholders' Equity Transactions
1. Provision should be made for board of directors' approval of all stockholders' equity transactions;
2. Cash receipts from stock issuance should be subject to the same control as that over other cash receipts;
3. Disbursements for reacquisition of stock should be controlled in the same manner as other cash disbursements; and
4. Imprest accounts should be used for paying dividends.

This chapter addresses audit objectives first, followed by a discussion of audit evidence and procedures. This is followed by an analysis of audit risk associated with the financing and investing cycle. Particular attention is given to locating related-party transactions, violations of restrictive covenants, and loan defaults. Attention also is directed to the increase in audit risk in the event of disposal of a segment of the client's business.

INVESTING TRANSACTIONS

Audit Objectives

Existence and Completeness Assertions   The auditor must determine that all securities represented in the client's investment records exist (existence). The auditor also must verify that the client's investment records include all securities examined (completeness).

Rights and Obligations Assertions   The auditor must verify the ownership of securities included in the investment records. If the client is holding the securities as **collateral** for outstanding loans receivable, they are *not* owned and should *not* be represented as such. If the client does own the securities, but they have been pledged as collateral on outstanding loans payable, this fact needs to be disclosed in the financial statements.

Valuation or Allocation Assertion   In testing financial assets for proper valuation, the auditor must determine compliance with the following measurement standards:

1. Investments should be properly classified as to trading securities, held-to-maturity securities, and available-for-sale securities. Trading and available-for-sale securities are to be reported at market, with unrealized gains and losses reflected in the income statement and the stockholders' equity section of the balance sheet, respectively. Held-to-maturity securities should be reported at amortized cost.[1]
2. The equity method of accounting should be applied to certain investments in unconsolidated subsidiaries.
3. Accrued interest and declared dividends on investments should be recognized as of the balance sheet date.

---

1   Statement of Financial Accounting Standards No. 115, Accounting for Certain Investments in Debt and Equity Securities.

4. Discounts or premiums on fixed-maturity investments classified as held to maturity should be amortized. The effective interest method should be used unless straight-line amortization produces an immaterial difference.
5. Realized gains or losses on disposals should be recognized in the income statement.
6. Notes receivable should be carried at net realizable value and estimated losses from uncollectible notes receivable should be reflected in the income statement.

Presentation and Disclosure Assertions   Of critical importance is how to classify securities investments in the balance sheet. In deciding whether securities are to be classified as current or noncurrent assets, the auditor should consider marketability and management intent. Both conditions must be satisfied in order for the securities to be classified as current assets; that is, they must be readily marketable, and management must intend to hold them for the short term only.

The income statement should report income from interest and dividends, except for dividends on stock accounted for under the equity method, as other income. Dividends on stock accounted for under the equity method should be reflected as an investment recovery.

In addition to the investment amount, the financial statements should present the following information clearly, either in the body of the statements or in footnotes:

1. Method of valuation;
2. Pledging, if any;
3. Realized and unrealized gains and losses;
4. The percentage of ownership of stock in affiliated companies; and
5. The market value of all financial instruments.

In addition, the footnotes should clearly disclose details surrounding transactions with related parties. Finally, the annual report should include the financial position and operations and cash flows of unconsolidated subsidiaries accounted for by the equity method.

The following paragraphs describe the means for acquiring evidence supporting these objectives.

Audit Evidence and Procedures

Physical Examination   The auditor usually examines securities in the client's possession to verify existence and ownership. As part of this procedure, the auditor should exercise control over all negotiable securities, cash on hand, and cash funds on the premises. Simultaneous control prevents client substitution of cash or securities to conceal shortages.

In the **examination of securities**, the auditor should record serial numbers for later comparison with the investment records. If securities have been misappropriated, the investment records will contain securities that are no longer in the client's portfolio. Temporary substitution of similar securities for the missing securities is one way of concealing the shortage. Comparison of serial numbers as recorded in the investment records with those appearing on the securities examined will reveal the substitution.

Determining that the securities are registered in the name of the client and noting evidence of pledging as loan collateral are also a necessary part of the physical examination of securities.

Confirmation   **Confirmation of securities** *not* on the premises (held in safekeeping or by a broker) is an acceptable alternative to physical examination in most instances. The auditor must request information as to name of issuer, number of shares (of stock) or par value (of bonds), registered name of owner, and serial numbers.

If the investment in securities not on the premises is substantial, the auditor may elect to examine rather than confirm them. In addition to confirming securities not on the premises, the auditor should confirm notes receivable with the makers of the notes. The confirmation request should cover the details of the notes as well as collateral requirements and defaults on interest or principal, if applicable in the circumstances.

Documentary Evidence   The auditor should trace from the count sheets, prepared as part of the physical examination of securities (or from returned confirmation forms, in the absence of physical inspection), to the investment records. Comparison of serial numbers, as just noted, will assist the auditor in detecting the substitution of similar securities for missing ones. Tracing in the opposite direction, from the investment records to the count sheets, reveals shortages not covered by substitution or other means.

On a test basis, the auditor should vouch additions and disposals of securities by reference to the underlying documentation. Brokers' advices, remittance advices, and canceled checks are representative of documentation.

The auditor should also examine documentation to corroborate management's statement of intent to hold securities for short-term purposes. Corroborating evidence might consist of written records of investment strategies, instructions to portfolio managers, and minutes of meetings of the board of directors. Similarly, the auditor must corroborate management's ability to exercise effective control over entities whose investments are being accounted for by the equity method. Minutes of management executive committee meetings and the board of directors' meetings constitute possible sources of corroborating evidence.

Correctness of recorded dividends may be ascertained by reference to one of the dividend reporters (e.g., *Standard & Poor's* or *Moody's*). Although the client may elect to accrue dividends that have been declared by the issuing corporation, the auditor must determine, by reference to the previous year's workpapers, that this practice has been applied consistently.

Transactions with affiliates should be audited carefully for two reasons:

1. They constitute **related-party transactions** and there may be disparities in **form versus substance**. An advance to a principal stockholder, for example, may be represented as a loan (legal form) when, in fact, it is a dividend (economic substance) because neither the corporation nor the stockholder expects the "advance" to be repaid. Where legal form and economic substance are different, audit adjustments or special disclosures may be necessary.
2. Intercompany and intracompany transactions occurring near year end must be examined carefully to ascertain that both sides of the transactions were recorded. Lack of **accounting symmetry** could distort assets, liabilities, or income.

For notes receivable transactions, the auditor should examine the notes for details relating to maturity date, principal amount, interest rate, and collateral. The auditor also should vouch lending transactions by reference to authorizations in the minutes, disbursement vouchers, and canceled checks. Note and interest collections should be vouched by reference to the cash receipts record, remittance advices, deposit tickets, and bank statement credits.

Mathematical Evidence   If the client maintains a subsidiary **investment ledger**, the auditor should reconcile it with the general ledger control account. As emphasized earlier, whenever the auditor plans to use a subsidiary ledger as an evidence-gathering base, agreement with the related control account must be determined. This form of mathematical evidence, therefore, is often obtained before other procedures are applied within a transaction cycle subset.

Other forms of mathematical evidence relating to investments and notes receivable include recomputation of gains and losses on disposals, interest accruals, and implicit interest, where applicable. Calculation of market value by reference to listed quotations as of the balance sheet date is another form of mathematical evidence supporting proper valuation of securities. If the client has already performed this procedure, the auditor should test the client's schedule.

Hearsay Evidence   Critical areas of auditor inquiry relate to the nature of investments and notes receivable and the length of time management intends to hold them. The auditor should determine that the securities are properly classified and accounted for, and also should determine whether any of the investments or notes involves related parties. Responses must be corroborated, but a logical starting point is to question management regarding these areas.

Analytical Evidence   Analytical procedures relating to investments and notes receivable involve comparing interest and dividends with the prior year. Differences not suggested by increases, decreases, or mix changes in the investment portfolio should be investigated for possible errors.

Exhibit 13.1 illustrates a lead schedule for investments, and Exhibit 13.2 is a supporting schedule for the audit of marketable securities. The supporting schedule contains the procedures discussed in the preceding paragraphs.

Summary Audit Program

Figure 13.3 (p. 534) summarizes the above procedures in a model audit program for investment transactions. The most critical procedures are examination of securities, determination of year-end market value, recalculation of income, and vouching of acquisitions and disposals.

BORROWING TRANSACTIONS

Audit Objectives

Existence and Completeness Assertions   As with current liabilities, the auditor must minimize the risk that the client has failed to record material amounts of long-term liabilities (errors of omission). Treating a capital lease as an operating lease, for example, can cause the debt-to-equity ratio to appear significantly lower than it is. Failure to make provision for the tax impact of differences in timing between book and tax depreciation similarly may understate long-term liabilities.

Valuation or Allocation Assertion   Long-term liabilities, as a general rule, should be reflected on the balance sheet at net present value. Accordingly, the auditor must determine that appropriate methods are being used to amortize premiums or discounts on long-term debt. Because the effective interest method more closely approximates net present value than does the straight-line amortization method, the effective interest method should be used, unless the difference between them is immaterial.

EXHIBIT 13.1

Lead Schedule—Investments

			WP H
		Prepared by:	LK
		Date:	1/8/2003
		Reviewed by:	CK
		Date:	1/20/2003

Jallo, Inc.
Investments—Long Term
12/31/02

Description	Audited Balances 12/31/01	Additions	Disposals	Audited Balances 12/31/02	WP #
Investment in Alley Oops common	$ 750,000	$150,000		$ 900,000	H.1
Investment in Bringhall common	160,000	40,000		200,000	H.2
Investment in Bringhall preferred	55,000			55,000	H.3
Investment in Morganthal 8% debenture bonds	225,000		$ 50,000	175,000	H.4
Investment in U.S. treasury notes	100,000	150,000	50,000	200,000	H.5
	$1,290,000	$340,000	$100,000	$1,530,000	
				WTB 1	

A **troubled debt restructuring** may cause valuation problems if it requires a new implicit interest rate or produces a gain on restructuring. The auditor must determine, under these circumstances, that the resulting liability is reported in accordance with SFAS No. 15.

Presentation and Disclosure Assertions   Correct classification of liabilities as current or noncurrent is an important objective in the audit of liabilities. Current installments of long-term debt should be reclassified as current. Conversely, short-term obligations expected to be refinanced should be reclassified as long-term, if they meet the provisions of SFAS No. 78.

Details surrounding various aspects of long-term liabilities must be disclosed, either in the body of the financial statements or in footnotes. Some of these are the following:

1. Defaults on bonds or violations of restrictive covenants in loan agreements;
2. Details of leases;
3. Pension disclosures;
4. Nature of tax and book temporary differences; and
5. Details regarding bonds and mortgages payable (e.g., term, interest rate, collateral).

Audit Evidence and Procedures

Documentary Evidence   Most long-term liabilities (bonds, notes, leases, and mortgages payable) are supported by contracts or agreements entered into by the client. Careful

EXHIBIT 13.2

Supporting Schedule—Investments

	WP H.1
Prepared by:	LK
Date:	2/2/2003
Reviewed by:	CK
Date:	2/10/2003

Jallo, Inc.
Investments
Alley Oops Common
12/31/02

			No. of Shares
12/31/01:	Audited balance	$750,000~	150,000
1/3/02:	Purchased additional shares	100,000*ⅹ̌	15,000
12/31/02:	Ledger balance	850,000	
	AJE #5	50,000	
12/31/02:	Audited balance	$900,000	165,000
		to WP H	√

AJE #5		
Investment in Alley Oops Common	$ 50,000	
Dividend Revenue	50,000	
Equity in income of unconsolidated		
subsidiary		$100,000
To adjust investment account for excess		
of Jallo's share of income over		
dividends received, as follows:		
Dividends:		
3/1/02	(10,000)o	
6/1/02	(10,000)o	
9/1/02	(10,000)o	
12/1/02	(20,000)o	
		(50,000)
Net income of subsidiary	303,000⊕	
Jallo's share (33%)	100,000	100,000
		$ 50,000

~ Compared with 12/31/01 workpapers
* Vouched to brokers' advice and canceled check
ⅹ̌ Examined minutes for directors' authorization
√ Examined stock certificates
o Traced to cash receipts record and bank statement
⊕ Examined audited income statement of Alley Oops

examination of debt agreements and comparison with accounting records assist the auditor in identifying necessary accruals and disclosures. Cash flow requirements under lease agreements, for example, must be disclosed in a footnote. The amount and timing

FIGURE 13.3

Model Audit Program for Investment Transactions

Analytical Procedures
Compare interest and dividends with those of prior year and investigate significant changes.

Other Substantive Audit Procedures
1. Agree subsidiary investment ledger with related general ledger control account(s).
2. Examine securities and record serial numbers for later comparison with recorded accountability (investment ledger).
3. Examine notes receivable on a test basis.
4. Confirm securities held in safekeeping.
5. Trace from count sheets or returned confirmations to investment ledger (note serial numbers to detect substitution).
6. Trace from investment ledger to count sheets or returned confirmations for evidence of missing securities.
7. Confirm notes receivable with makers on a test basis.
8. Vouch additions and disposals by reference to the following underlying documentation: broker's advice; remittance advice, cash receipts record, and bank statement; and canceled checks.
9. Vouch lending transactions by reference to vouchers, canceled checks, and bank statements.
10. Vouch collections of notes and interest by reference to the cash receipts record, remittance advices, deposit tickets, and bank statements.
11. Examine minutes for proper authorization of major lending transactions and purchases and sales of investments.
12. Examine income statements of unconsolidated subsidiaries accounted for on an equity basis.
13. Verify dividends by reference to *Standard & Poor's* or *Moody's* dividend reporter.
14. Recalculate interest received or accrued.
15. Recalculate premium or discount amortization on long-term investments in interest-bearing securities.
16. Recalculate gain or loss on disposal.
17. Calculate implicit interest where applicable.
18. Perform cost or market test for marketable securities.
19. Inquire of management as to nature of investments and notes receivable and reasons for holding.
20. Inquire as to related-party transactions.

of these flows can be determined by examination of the lease. Similarly, the lessor's interest rate (if stated in the lease), contingent rentals, purchase options, renewal options, and the lease term all can be identified by reading the lease.

By examining long-term debt agreements, the auditor can identify restrictive covenants (retained earnings restrictions, restrictions on the issuance of additional debt), compensating balance requirements, note collateral, note repayment terms, and interest rates. The auditor also should evaluate the reasonableness of interest rates and, given a low rate or no rate, consider the need for related-party disclosure, or imputed interest.

Exhibits 13.3 through 13.5 illustrate workpapers supporting the audit of leases and long-term debt. The significance of examining the lease and loan agreements is evident by the frequency of audit legends supported by that procedure.

Mathematical Evidence   Mathematical evidence is useful in evaluating accruals and apportionments commonly associated with long-term liabilities. For example, the auditor should recalculate the following, as necessary, on a test basis:

EXHIBIT 13.3

Capital Leases Audit Workpaper

	WP P.2
Prepared by:	LFK
Date:	1/13/2003
Reviewed by:	JER
Date:	1/26/2003

Jallo, Inc.
Capital Leases
12/31/02

Description	Date of Agreement	Termination Date	Implicit Interest Rate	Liability 1/1/02	2002 Payments
Phoenix warehouse&	1/1/00	12/31/2006	8.00√	$1,230,000*	$ 371,400^
Memphis warehouse#&	1/1/02	12/31/2007	10.00√&	2,800,000&	643,000^
Tractors and trailers&	1/1/01	12/31/2005	10.00√	870,000*	349,840^
				$4,900,000	$1,364,240

Interest	Principal	Liability 12/31/02	Current Portion	Noncurrent Portion	Contingent Rentals
$ 98,400√	$273,000	$ 957,000	$294,840√	$ 662,160	$ 0
280,000√	363,000	2,437,000	399,300√	2,037,700	0
87,000√	262,840	607,160	289,124√	318,036	80,000√
$465,400	$898,840	$ 4,001,160	$983,264	$3,017,896	$80,000
@			@	@	

*   Agreed to 12/31/01 workpapers and final balances.
& Examined lease agreement.
^   Examined canceled checks.
√   Recomputed.
@ Agreed to 12/31/02 general ledger balance.
# Examined minutes for directors' authorization.

Minimum rentals are paid at year end on all leases.

The lease agreement covering the tractors and trailers requires added rentals of $0.20/mile in excess of 40,000 miles annually for each truck.

EXHIBIT 13.4

Long-Term Debt Audit Workpaper

			WP P.1
		Prepared by:	LFK
		Date:	1/21/2003
		Reviewed by:	JER
		Date:	2/2/2003

Jallo, Inc.
12% Mortgage Bonds Payable
12/31/02

	Bonds Payable	Interest Payment	Interest Expense	Discount Amortization	Unamortized Discount	Issuance Price
12/31/01	-0-					
1/1/02	$2,000,000				$213,551	$1,786,449&
3/31/02		$60,000^	$ 62,526*	$2,526*	211,025	
6/30/02		60,000^	62,614*	2,614*	208,411	
9/30/02		60,000^	62,706*	2,706*	205,705	
12/31/02		60,000^	62,800*	2,800*	202,905√	
	$2,000,000√		$250,646√			

& Traced proceeds to cash receipts record and to bank statement.
* Per amortization schedule (see WP PF P.1 in permanent file).
√ Agreed to general ledger.
^ Examined canceled check payable to trustee.

---

1. Premium or discount amortization;
2. Lease amortization;
3. Contingent rentals;
4. Interest accruals;
5. Gain or loss on bond redemptions;
6. Change in deferred taxes;
7. Pension liability; and
8. Implicit interest.

Analytical Evidence   The auditor should compare lease amortization, interest expense, and pension liability with their counterparts in the prior year and investigate significant changes. These procedures assist in identification of unrecorded liabilities resulting from overlooking necessary accruals.

Summary Audit Program

Figure 13.4 (p. 539) illustrates a model audit program for borrowing transactions. Analytical procedures comparing the current and prior year's expenses relating to long-term liabilities are most important for locating significant errors of omission.

EXHIBIT 13.5	

Long-Term Debt, Permanent File Workpaper

	WP PF P.1
Prepared by:	LFK
Date:	1/21/2003
Reviewed by:	JER
Date:	2/2/2003

Jallo, Inc.
12% Mortgage Bonds Payable
Amortization Schedule

Period	Cash Credit	Interest Expense Debit	Unamortized Premium (debit) Discount (credit)	Carrying Value of Bonds
0				$1,786,449.28
1	$60,000.00	$62,525.72	$(2,525.72)	1,788,975.00
2	60,000.00	62,614.13	(2,614.13)	1,791,589.13
3	60,000.00	62,705.62	(2,705.62)	1,794,294.75
4	60,000.00	62,800.31	(2,800.31)	1,797,095.06
5	60,000.00	62,898.33	(2,898.33)	1,799,993.39
6	60,000.00	62,999.77	(2,999.77)	1,802,993.16
7	60,000.00	63,104.76	(3,104.76)	1,806,097.92
8	60,000.00	63,213.43	(3,213.43)	1,809,311.35
9	60,000.00	63,325.90	(3,325.90)	1,812,637.25
10	60,000.00	63,442.30	(3,442.30)	1,816,079.55
11	60,000.00	63,562.78	(3,562.78)	1,819,642.33
12	60,000.00	63,687.48	(3,687.48)	1,823,329.81
13	60,000.00	63,816.54	(3,816.54)	1,827,146.35
14	60,000.00	63,950.12	(3,950.12)	1,831,096.47
15	60,000.00	64,088.38	(4,088.38)	1,835,184.85
16	60,000.00	64,231.47	(4,231.47)	1,839,416.32
17	60,000.00	64,379.57	(4,379.57)	1,843,795.89
18	60,000.00	64,532.86	(4,532.86)	1,848,328.75
19	60,000.00	64,691.51	(4,691.51)	1,853,020.26
20	60,000.00	64,855.71	(4,855.71)	1,857,875.97
21	60,000.00	65,025.66	(5,025.66)	1,862,901.63
22	60,000.00	65,201.55	(5,201.55)	1,868,103.18
23	60,000.00	65,383.61	(5,383.61)	1,873,486.79
24	60,000.00	65,572.04	(5,572.04)	1,879,058.83
25	60,000.00	65,767.06	(5,767.06)	1,884,825.89
26	60,000.00	65,968.91	(5,968.91)	1,890,794.80
27	60,000.00	66,177.82	(6,177.82)	1,896,972.62
28	60,000.00	66,394.04	(6,394.04)	1,903,366.66
29	60,000.00	66,617.83	(6,617.83)	1,909,984.49
30	60,000.00	66,849.46	(6,849.46)	1,916,833.95
31	60,000.00	66,089.18	(7,089.18)	1,923,923.13
32	60,000.00	67,337.31	(7,337.31)	1,931,260.44
33	60,000.00	67,594.12	(7,594.12)	1,938,854.56
34	60,000.00	67,859.91	(7,859.91)	1,946,714.47
35	60,000.00	68,135.01	(8,135.01)	1,954,849.48
36	60,000.00	68,419.73	(8,419.73)	1,963,269.21

(continued)

EXHIBIT 13.5

(continued)

Period	Cash Credit	Interest Expense Debit	Unamortized Premium (debit) Discount (credit)	Carrying Value of Bonds
37	60,000.00	68,714.42	(8,714.42)	1,971,983.63
38	60,000.00	69,019.43	(9,019.43)	1,981,003.06
39	60,000.00	69,335.10	(9,335.10)	1,990,338.16
40	60,000.00	69,661.84	(9,661.84)	2,000,000.00

DEBT TERMS:

Principal	$2,000,000E
Term (years)	10E
Times interest paid/year	4E
Nominal interest rate	12.00%E
Per interest period	3.00%
Effective interest rate	14.00%C
Per interest period	3.50%C
Interest payment	$60,000C
Collateral	Land and buildingsE
Date of issuance	1-1-02
Due date	12/31/2011
Interest payment dates	3/31E
	6/30E
	9/30E
	12/31E
Dividend restrictions	None
NPV = Issuance Price	$1,786,449.28C

E = Examined bond indenture.
C = Computed.

STOCKHOLDERS' EQUITY TRANSACTIONS

Audit Objectives

Valuation Assertion   The valuation assertion is not generally as important as presentation and disclosure in the audit of stockholders' equity transactions. The occurrence of certain transactions, however, may require some audit attention to specific valuation aspects. If the client issues stock for noncash assets, for example, the auditor must be satisfied as to the values assigned to the assets. Treasury stock transactions and stock dividends also raise valuation issues. Regarding stock dividends, the auditor must verify the appropriateness of the amount transferred from retained earnings (market value for small stock dividends; par or stated value for large stock dividends).

Presentation and Disclosure Assertions   The major presentation issue regarding stockholders' equity involves separation between contributed capital and retained earnings. The most significant disclosure issue is how to calculate and present earnings per share. Although the earnings per share figures appear on the income statement, their deter-

FIGURE 13.4

Model Audit Program for Borrowing Transactions

Analytical Procedures
Compare liabilities and related expenses with those of prior year and investigate significant changes.

Other Substantive Audit Procedures
1. Confirm bonds payable and pension plan liability with respective trustees.
2. Examine bank confirmation for possible unrecorded liabilities or guarantees of indebtedness.
3. Examine lease agreements for contingent rentals.
4. Examine pension agreements for vesting provisions.
5. Examine loan agreements for possible need to impute interest.
6. Examine loan agreements, bond indentures, and pension agreements for the following: restrictive covenants, collateral requirements, or other disclosure requirements (future cash flows under lease agreements, details surrounding bond issues, pension provisions, etc.).
7. Vouch the following on a test basis: interest payments, lease payments, and pension plan contributions.
8. Recompute the following on a test basis: premium and discount amortization, lease amortization, contingent rentals, interest accruals, gain or loss on bond redemptions, change in deferred taxes, and pension liability.
9. Compute implicit interest, if applicable.

mination requires a careful analysis of all components of long-term debt and stockholders' equity. A complex capital structure requires a dual presentation that includes diluted earnings per share and basic earnings per share, as well as a reconciliation of the two figures.

Additional disclosure questions relate to such features as restrictions on dividend availability and dividends in arrears on cumulative preferred stock. Details regarding stock option plans, as well as the fair value of stock options at date of grant, also need to be disclosed.

Audit Evidence and Procedures

Documentary Evidence   Because most stockholders' equity transactions require director approval, the auditor should examine minutes of directors' meetings for authorization of such events as stock issuance, stock reacquisition or retirement, dividends, and stock options. Satisfied that the transactions were properly approved, the auditor should vouch them by examining the underlying documentation (cash receipts entries and deposit slips for stock issuance, exercise of stock options, or sale of treasury stock; cash disbursement records and canceled checks for reacquisitions and dividends).

Stock option agreements should be examined for disclosure requirements (employees eligible, number of shares involved, option prices, exercise dates, and fair value at date of grant). By examining the option agreement(s), the auditor also can identify the measurement date, and determine the amount of deferred compensation, if any.

Mathematical Evidence   The auditor should recompute the following, on a test basis, where applicable:

1. Dividend declarations—particularly those involving participating preferred stock;
2. Debits to retained earnings—cash dividends, as well as stock dividends;
3. Debits to deferred compensation for stock option credits;
4. Earnings-per-share computations; and
5. Computations pertaining to treasury stock transactions.

Summary Audit Program

Figure 13.5 presents a model audit program for stockholders' equity transactions.

FIGURE 13.5

Model Audit Program for Stockholders' Equity Transactions

Analytical Procedures
1. Compare dividends with those of prior year and investigate significant fluctuations.
2. Compare capital stock accounts with those of prior year and account for all changes.
3. Compare stock option credits with those of prior year and account for increases.

Other Substantive Procedures
1. Confirm stock issuance and dividends with registrar and transfer agent.
2. Examine minutes of directors' meetings for dividend declarations.
3. Examine minutes of directors' meetings for proper authorization of the following: stock issuance, stock reacquisition, stock retirements, stock options, and stock splits.
4. Vouch dividend declarations and payments.
5. Vouch treasury stock transactions.
6. Examine evidence of valuation where stock is issued for noncash assets.
7. Recalculate earnings per share, stock option credits and amortization, and stock dividends.
8. Examine loan agreements and directors' minutes for possible restrictions on retained earnings, and determine that appropriate disclosures have been made in the financial statements.
9. Examine stock option agreements and determine that proper disclosure has been made concerning employees participating, shares involved, option prices, and exercise dates.
10. Examine corporate charter for description of various classes of stock, and determine that proper financial statement disclosure has been made concerning participating or cumulative features of preferred stock and dividends in arrears on preferred stock.

AUDIT RISK ANALYSIS AND THE FINANCING AND INVESTING CYCLE

Search for Related-Party Transactions

Significant related-party transactions occur more frequently within the financing and investing cycle than within the other transaction cycles. Loans to and from related parties, repayments or refunding of these loans, stock issued for noncash assets, and stock reacquisitions are examples of transactions involved.

In accordance with the AICPA Professional Standards, the auditor must

1. Identify related parties;
2. Identify material transactions; and
3. Examine identified material related-party transactions.[2]

The major audit risk factor associated with related-party transactions is the potential disparity between legal form and economic substance. When the two are in conflict, GAAP requires that substance take precedence over form. The auditor must determine, therefore, that the financial statements clearly reflect the economic substance of material related-party transactions.[3]

In a recent case, former Rite Aid CEO Martin Grass and his brother-in-law were alleged to have purchased an 83-acre site with plans to sell the parcel to Rite Aid for construction of its new headquarters complex. In addition, the Grass family, founders of Rite Aid, owned other interests in real estate leased to Rite Aid stores as well as in vendors supplying Rite Aid.[4] Such conflicts of interest may significantly affect stockholder investments and pose questions regarding proper asset valuation. When these relationships are not openly disclosed by management to the auditor, they raise questions regarding management integrity and the degree to which the auditor can rely on management representations.

In another case, the chairman of Guarantee Security Life Insurance Co., a Florida company, was able to complete related-party transactions with Guarantee's principal securities broker, Merrill Lynch & Co. Beginning in 1984, upon its acquisition by Mark Sanford, who subsequently was appointed chairman, Guarantee offered abnormally high interest rates to purchasers of its annuities and also paid high commissions to independent agents marketing the annuities. To finance the high interest rates, the company bought high-yielding junk bond investments. To conceal the risky nature of its investment portfolio, Guarantee temporarily exchanged hundreds of millions of dollars of junk bonds for U.S. Treasury securities in year-end trades with Merrill Lynch. The trades then were reversed at the beginning of the following year. This practice was followed from 1984 through 1988. Florida insurance regulators alleged that the securities swaps weren't bona fide trades, but just paper transactions. Indeed, Coopers & Lybrand, the company's auditors, said in 1985 that the swaps couldn't be recognized under GAAP. But Coopers later relented and agreed to recognize the swaps for regulatory reporting purposes only. Accordingly, financial statements submitted to the Florida Insurance Commission reported primarily U.S. government securities rather than the junk bonds.

---

2   *AICPA Professional Standards*, New York: AICPA, section AU 334.07–10.
3   Ibid, section AU 334.02.
4   *The Wall Street Journal*, February 19, 1999, p. A4.

Given the problems encountered by the companies holding junk bonds in the 1980s, Guarantee, with its top-heavy portfolio of these securities, became insolvent in August 1991, and its 57,000 policyholders were temporarily prevented from collecting on their annuities. Subsequently, the company was seized by the State of Florida, and accused of fraud in attempting to conceal the true nature of its investment portfolio. At the same time, the SEC began investigating Guarantee, Merrill Lynch, and Coopers & Lybrand. The suit filed by the Florida Insurance Commission accused Merrill Lynch of fraud and also accused Coopers & Lybrand, Guarantee's auditors, of malpractice and breach of fiduciary duty.[5]

In a similar case, United American Bank of Knoxville used other banks, all controlled by the same family, as a means for transferring problem loans, thus keeping them from being detected by the auditors. In fact, FDIC examiners reported that the "bank had about $377 million, or nearly half its total assets, in loans the FDIC classed as partly or totally uncollectible. . . . Nearly half the problem loans were made to United American's former chairman, Jake F. Butcher, his family and associates and their interests."[6]

The lesson for auditors in these cases is that when legal form and economic substance of material transactions are at variance, the *auditors must be emphatic in their insistence on the precedence of substance over form.* To do otherwise places the auditor in violation of Rule 102 of the Code of Professional Conduct, which states that "the member shall maintain objectivity and integrity, shall be free of conflicts of interest, and *shall not knowingly misrepresent facts or subordinate his or her judgment to others*" [emphasis added].[7] If the year-end financial statements had reflected the true nature of the investment and loan portfolios of Guarantee and United Bank, respectively, the companies would have been required to increase their loss reserves substantially. Indeed, had Guarantee done this, according to the deputy receiver, the company would have been insolvent by 1985.[8]

In addition to misrepresentation fraud, companies have also used related-party transactions as conduits for transferring assets out of the entity. In the Continental Vending Machine Corporation case (see Chapter 3), the president of Continental used a wholly owned subsidiary to obtain bank loans. The loan proceeds were transferred back and forth between the companies to "muddy" the audit trail. Finally, they were loaned to the president, who used the money to finance his personal transactions, mainly in the stock markets. His inability to repay the loans, together with the insufficiency of collateral, forced the company into receivership.[9]

In view of the large number of significant cases involving related-party transactions, Section 334 provides extensive guidance in identifying related parties and related-party transactions, and examining the transactions for possible disparities between form and substance.[10]

An AICPA Practice Alert identified indicators pointing to the possible existence of related-party transactions:

1.   Complex corporate capital structure;

5   See "Castle in the Sand," *The Wall Street Journal*, December 23, 1991.
6   Colvin, Geoffrey, et. al., "Jake Butcher's Fall," *Fortune*, March 21, 1983, p. 7.
7   *AICPA Professional Standards*, op. cit., section ET 102.02.
8   "Castle in the Sand," op. cit.
9   *U.S. v. Simon et. al.*, 425 F.2d. 796 (2d Cir. 1969).
10 *AICPA Professional Standards*, op. cit., section AU 334.07–10.

2. Audit responsibilities for entities that have material intercompany transactions with one another divided among two or more auditing firms, or in which one of the entities is not audited;

3. Highly complex business practices that enhance the ability of management to mask their economic substance; and

4. The existence of unique, highly complex, and material transactions close to year end that pose difficult "substance over form" questions.[11]

As can be seen from the previous discussion, related-party transactions are often difficult to identify. For this reason, auditors need to stretch their analytical abilities to capacity in seeking them out and determining the substance of these potentially elusive transactions.

Loan Defaults

If clients have significant amounts of loans outstanding, the auditor must be particularly alert to violations of restrictive covenants or failure to meet required interest or principal payments. Failure to meet the terms of a loan agreement constitutes a **loan default** and often makes the entire amount of the loan, together with any accrued interest, immediately due. This, in turn, may cast doubt on the ability of the firm to continue as a going concern.

In a recent press release, Supercuts, Inc., a San Francisco-based hair-care chain, announced that significant declines in its earnings and cash flow may have placed the company in violation of a covenant between the company and a consortium of banks, and that this would constitute default on a $30 million credit line issued by the consortium, a group of three banks headed by Bank of America.[12]

Auditors should read carefully all loan agreements and extract portions covering working capital, cash flow, or retained earnings restrictions, maintenance of collateral, repayment schedules, and any other provisions relating to potential loan defaults.

If liquidity problems have prevented the client from meeting interest or principal repayment schedules, the auditor must inquire of management concerning steps taken toward restructuring the loan agreements. If loan restructuring has been completed before issuance of the audit report, the auditor should examine the agreements to determine whether any gain should be recognized, and whether the going concern issue has been satisfactorily resolved.

Derivatives

Derivatives are complex financial instruments whose values depend on the values of one or more underlying assets or financial indexes. Entities invest in derivatives, such as asset-backed securities, in order to enhance yield, liquidity, marketability, or some combination of these. Other derivatives, such as forward contracts and currency swaps, are used to hedge against financial risks associated with fluctuating interest rates, foreign exchange rates, and commodity prices.

The audit risk associated with derivatives arises when entities attempt to profit from buying and selling these instruments, rather than simply hedging against possible

---

11 *AICPA Practice Alert*, New York: AICPA, No. 95-3, November 1995.
12 *The San Francisco Chronicle*, January 9, 1996, p. C1.

future losses. In 1994, for example, Procter & Gamble recognized a one-time pretax charge of $157 million to close out two interest rate swap contracts it had made.[13] MG Corporation, a unit of Metallgesellschaft AG, a German company, sustained a 1994 loss of more than $1 billion in energy derivatives in an attempt to lower the risks of its oil distribution business.[14] Orange County, California, became insolvent after losing billions of dollars from speculation in derivatives.[15]

Given the increasing incidence of derivatives, auditors should inquire of clients as to the existence of these instruments and examine the contracts carefully for possible risk exposure and the need to recognize losses, and determine that all derivatives are reflected at market value as of the balance sheet date. The auditor also should ascertain adequacy of footnote disclosure regarding company policy relating to investments in derivatives.

Disposal of a Segment

If a client is reporting a segment disposal for the period under examination, the auditor first should determine whether the transaction meets the **disposal of a segment** requirements, as set forth in APBO No. 30.[16] If so, "gain (loss) from discontinued operations" and "gain (loss) from disposal" should be reflected *below the line* (i.e., after income from continuing operations).

In addition to determining proper classification, the auditor must verify that the amounts reported as discontinued operations do *not* include expenses relating to continuing operations. The application of analytical procedures by segment usually will disclose major classification errors of this type.

COMPLETING THE AUDIT

Having covered substantive audit testing in Chapters 11, 12, and this chapter, we now turn our attention to a few remaining, but significant, factors requiring the auditor's attention in completing the audit field work.

Analytical Procedures as Part of Audit Review

Generally accepted auditing standards require the auditor to apply analytical procedures in the final review stages of the audit.[17] The purpose of applying analytical procedures during audit review is to ascertain that the auditor has gathered adequate evidence to resolve suspicions arising during the planning stages of the audit. For example, assume that analytical procedures applied to unaudited data during the planning stages of the audit revealed a material decline in repairs and maintenance expense, relative to the preceding year. If audit adjustments for ordinary repairs improperly capitalized have reduced the decline to insignificant proportions, analytical procedures applied as part of overall audit review will provide the needed assurance to the auditor that prior suspicions have been resolved. If, however, analytical procedures applied dur-

13 *The Wall Street Journal*, April 14, 1994.
14 Ibid.
15 *The New York Times*, January 18, 1995.
16 Financial Accounting Standards Board, *Accounting Standards: Current Text, 1996/97*, New York: John Wiley & Sons, Inc., 1996, section 113.404.
17 *AICPA Professional Standards*, op. cit., section AU 329.04.

ing audit review continue to produce abnormalities, the auditor should pursue the disparities until his or her suspicions are resolved. The auditor, upon further investigation, may be able to obtain a satisfactory (and documented) explanation for the abnormality, or he or she may need to modify the audit programs and apply extended substantive procedures to determine the cause of the disparity.

Further Materiality Considerations

As discussed in Chapter 5, the auditor should set individual item and aggregate materiality thresholds as a part of the audit planning. The levels chosen are dependent on inherent risk, control risk (the quality of internal control), and the dollar amounts of unaudited financial statement components, such as net income, total assets, and net assets. Chapter 5 also suggested that the auditor may need to modify these levels subsequently, depending on the significance of proposed audit adjustments. One or more adjustments that materially reduce net income, for example, may require a decrease in the dollar amount of both individual item and aggregate materiality thresholds. Because of the possible need for modification, therefore, the auditor must reevaluate materiality levels as part of the audit review. If the review suggests lower thresholds, the auditor must reevaluate possible audit adjustments not meeting the initial thresholds based on unaudited data and determine if they fall within the bounds of the modified thresholds based on audited income and net assets. Assume, for example, that the auditor discovered $30,000 of nonrecurring fixed overhead capacity loss improperly included in the ending inventories of goods in process and finished goods. Assume further that based on unaudited net income of $2,000,000, the auditor established an individual item materiality threshold of 2 percent, or $40,000. Based on this criterion, the auditor would not likely propose an audit adjustment for the overhead capitalization error. If, however, other audit adjustments meeting the materiality threshold reduced net income from $2,000,000 to $1,000,000, the error would meet the modified individual item materiality threshold based on audited income (2 percent of $1,000,000 equals $20,000, versus the error of $30,000). The auditor, under these circumstances, might elect to include the error correction in the set of proposed audit adjustments.

Subsequent Events

Certain events or transactions that occur after the balance sheet date, but before the completion of audit field work, may have an impact on the audited financial statements. If the effects are material, adjustment of the statements or disclosure may be necessary.

AICPA Professional Standards classify subsequent events as follows:

1. **Type I subsequent events**: Those events that provide additional evidence with respect to conditions that existed at the date of the balance sheet and affect the estimates inherent in the process of preparing the financial statements.
2. **Type II subsequent events**: Those events that provide evidence with respect to conditions that *did not* exist at the date of the balance sheet being reported on, but arose subsequent to that date.[18]

Type I events, if material, require adjustment of the financial statements. For example, assume that certain inventories on hand at year end and reported at full cost are

18 Ibid, section AU 560.02–05.

believed by the auditor to be obsolete. Assume further that these inventories are sold at distress prices materially below cost, after the balance sheet date, but before the end of audit field work. The distress sale provides conclusive evidence supporting obsolescence, and the inventories, therefore, should be adjusted to reflect net realizable value as of the balance sheet date.

Type II subsequent events *do not* require adjustment. For example, assume that uninsured inventories were destroyed by fire during the subsequent period. In this case, the conditions giving rise to the loss occurred after the balance sheet date and before the end of audit field work. Although the financial statements do not require adjustment, footnote disclosure of events of this nature may be required, depending on materiality.

Given the adjustment and disclosure requirements associated with subsequent events, the auditor must seek to identify those of significance. Certain auditing procedures (e.g., cutoff tests and the search for unrecorded liabilities) assist in detecting subsequent events. In addition, the AICPA Professional Standards list the following procedures to be applied in the subsequent period:

1. Read the latest available interim financial statements.
2. Inquire of and discuss with officers and other executives having responsibility for financial and accounting matters as to
   a. Whether any substantial contingent liabilities or commitments existed at the date of the balance sheet being reported on or at the date of inquiry;
   b. Whether there was any significant change in the capital stock, long-term debt, or working capital to the date of inquiry;
   c. The current status of items in the financial statements being reported on that were accounted for on the basis of tentative, preliminary, or inconclusive data; and
   d. Whether any unusual adjustments were made during the period from the balance sheet date to the date of inquiry.
3. Read the available minutes of meetings of stockholders, directors, and appropriate committees issued subsequent to the balance sheet date.
4. Obtain from legal counsel a description and evaluation of any litigation, impending litigation, claims, and contingent liabilities that existed at the date of the balance sheet of which he or she has knowledge.
5. Obtain a letter of representations, dated as of the date of the auditor's report . . . as to whether any events occurred subsequent to the date of the financial statements being reported on . . . that in the officer's opinion would require adjustment or disclosure in these statements.
6. Make additional inquiries or perform procedures as he or she considers necessary and appropriate to dispose of questions that arise in carrying out the foregoing procedures, inquiries, and discussions.[19]

Statement of Cash Flows

As part of the audit completion process, the auditor should examine the statement of cash flows. The transactions reflected in the statement already have been subjected to audit as part of the examination of the transaction cycles covered in this and the two

19 Ibid, section AU 560.12.

preceding chapters. The auditor needs to determine, however, that the amounts and descriptions have been properly reflected in the statement.

Audit procedures applied specifically to the statement of cash flows should include the following:

1. Reviewing the comparative balance sheets and the current year's income statement to determine that all significant cash flows have been properly calculated and reflected in the statement;
2. Determining that a proper distinction has been made among cash flows from operations, cash flows from investing transactions, and cash flows from financing transactions;
3. Identifying significant noncash financing and investing transactions, and determining that they have been properly reflected in the statement; and
4. Determining that a statement of cash flows has been included for each year for which an income statement is included in the annual report.

Workpaper Review

The first standard of audit field work requires that the work be adequately planned and assistants, if any, be properly supervised. An important ingredient of supervision is the need for careful review of all audit workpapers. The in-charge senior auditor is responsible for reviewing workpapers prepared by assistants; the audit manager and the audit partner conduct an overall review of the audit workpapers.

As a first step, the reviewer should examine the workpapers for completeness of indexing. As described and illustrated in Chapter 4, supporting schedules, lead schedules, and the working trial balance must be cross-indexed so that the reviewer can proceed in either direction from supporting schedule to working trial balance, or vice versa.

Having determined accuracy and completeness of indexing, the reviewer should ascertain that the workpapers fully describe all procedures applied, and clearly display auditor conclusions and audit adjustments. The **workpaper review** also should determine that the audit procedures evidenced by the workpapers are consistent with the audit objectives specified in the audit programs for that part of the examination.

Open Items

As part of virtually every audit, certain questions arise during the examination that cannot be answered immediately. Information suggesting the existence of inventories out on consignment needs to be pursued further, certificates representing stock investments held in safekeeping off the premises need to be examined, certain documents cannot be located, or an intercompany account has not been reconciled because the workpapers have not been received from the divisional auditors. These types of questions should be listed on an **open items** workpaper and cleared as the information becomes available. Exhibit 13.6 illustrates an open items workpaper. Note the initials, date, and comment of the person clearing each question.

When all of the open items have been cleared, the workpaper may be included as part of the current file or may be discarded (the information having been incorporated into the respective supporting schedules). Retaining the workpaper has the advantage of encouraging the auditor to dispose fully of each open item documented during the course of the examination. It also gives the audit manager an opportunity during the

EXHIBIT 13.6

Open Items Workpaper

WP 1

Prepared by: LK   Date: 2/22/2003
Reviewed by: GF   Date: 3/2/2003

Jallo, Inc.
Open Items
12/31/02

Description of Item	Disposition of Item	Cleared
Shares represented by Treflen investment allegedly held by broker.	Examined 1/14/2003 See WP F.3	LFK
Conference with client's legal counsel needed in order to clarify product liability suit.	Held 1/22/2003 See WP P.6	JER
Examine debt restructuring agreement to be signed by client by 1/25/2003. Determine if short-term obligations may be reclassified as long-term.	Examined 1/30/2003 See WP P.4	JER
Ask credit manager to contact Seels, Inc., and request return of accounts receivable confirmation.	Received 1/31/2003 See WP C.2	MEL
Examine and evaluate collateral securing loan to Ralph Proudsell, president.	Examined 2/1/2003 See WP D.2	JER
Obtain minutes of November directors' meeting.	Legal counsel will forward	MEL
Have Detroit office visit location of Alma Motors and determine if Alma is an operating company or a "shell" company.		
Contact broker as to ask-and-bid price for Bool Mines stock.		

workpaper review to perform a separate evaluation of open items and their resolution by the audit team.

Auditor/Client Conference

Auditors ordinarily discuss proposed audit adjustments and internal control weaknesses with the client as these adjustments and weaknesses are discovered. At the close of audit field work, these discussions are summarized in a formal conference. Given the nature of the subject matter, the **auditor/client conference** is usually attended by the audit partner, the audit manager, the in-charge senior auditor, and one or more members of the client's top management.

In addition to providing a forum for presenting and discussing audit adjustments and internal control weaknesses, the conference also covers recommended footnote disclosures and the type of audit report to be rendered. The form of audit report, as described by the auditors, is conditional upon client acceptance of the audit adjustments and recommended footnote disclosures.

Clients may object to the income statement effects of certain proposed audit adjustments, or may deem certain footnote disclosures too "harsh." Nevertheless, proper ethical behavior requires the independent auditors to insist on fairness of financial presentation and disclosure—or take exception in their audit reports. Occasionally, compromise is possible, but compromise should not result in a sacrifice of fairness or integrity.

Communication with the Audit Committee

In addition to holding the auditor/client conference just referred to, the auditor is required to communicate certain matters discovered during the audit to the audit committee or similar body with designated financial statement oversight authority.[20] The following are among the more important matters to be covered in the **communication with the audit committee**:

1. The auditor's responsibility for internal control and for financial statements under GAAS. It is important for the audit committee to recognize that the auditor is providing *reasonable* rather than *absolute* assurance about the financial statements;
2. Selection of and changes in significant accounting policies;
3. Management's process in formulating estimates and the auditor's evaluation of the resulting estimates;
4. Significant audit adjustments;
5. Disagreements with management about matters that could be significant to the financial statements or the auditor's report; and
6. Difficulties encountered in performing the audit, such as delays in commencing the audit, withholding of information, undue time pressures imposed by management, unavailability of client personnel, and failure of client personnel to complete client-prepared schedules on a timely basis.[21]

Communicating these matters enables the audit committee to perform its oversight function more effectively. Communication also assists the auditor by providing a mechanism for resolving possible disputes with management.

The communication may be oral or written. If it is oral, the auditor should document the communication in the workpapers.

Client Representation Letter

GAAS requires that the auditor obtain a **client representation letter** from management. Failure to provide the letter is considered a scope limitation that would impact the audit report. The letter is dated as of the close of audit field work and should be signed by the chief executive officer and the chief financial officer of the client. Its stated purpose is to "confirm oral representations given to the auditor, indicate and document the continued appropriateness of such representations, and reduce the possibility of misunderstanding concerning the matters that are the subject of the representations."[22] Some companies choose to include the management representation letter in the annual report to stockholders.

---

20 Ibid, section AU 380.
21 Ibid.
22 Ibid, section AU 333.02.

The letter does not relieve the auditor from corroborating the written representations through the application of standard or extended auditing procedures. It does assist in making management more aware of its primary responsibility for fairness of financial presentation. AICPA standards require that the auditor carefully consider the reliability of a representation made by management if other audit evidence contradicts that representation.[23] Refusal by management to provide the auditor with a representation letter constitutes a scope limitation and should usually result in a disclaimer of opinion.[24]

Exhibit 13.7 illustrates the recommended form. Specific representations should relate to the following matters:

Financial Statements

1. Management's acknowledgment of its responsibility for the presentation in the financial statements of financial position, results of operations, and cash flows in conformity with generally accepted accounting principles; and
2. Management's belief that the financial statements are fairly presented in conformity with generally accepted accounting principles.

EXHIBIT 13.7

Client Representation Letter

February 26, 2003

Ricks and Hanley, CPAs
1213 South Bing
Houston, TX 73705

Attention: J. Rindley, Partner

Dear Mr. Rindley:

We are providing this letter in connection with your audit(s) of the financial statements of Jallo, Inc. for the years ended December 31, 2002 and 2001 for the purpose of expressing an opinion as to whether the financial statements present fairly, in all material respects, the financial position, results of operations, and cash flows of Jallo, Inc. in conformity with generally accepted accounting principles. We confirm that we are responsible for the fair presentation in the financial statements of financial position, results of operations, and cash flows in conformity with generally accepted accounting principles.

Certain representations in this letter are described as being limited to matters that are material. Items are considered material, regardless of size, if they involve an omission or misstatement of accounting information that, in the light of surrounding circumstances, makes it probable that the judgment of a reasonable person relying on the information would be changed or influenced by the omission or misstatement.

We confirm, to the best of our knowledge and belief, as of February 26, 2003, the following representations made to you during your audits.

---

23 Ibid, section AU 333.04.
24 Ibid, section AU 333.13.

EXHIBIT 13.7	

(continued)

1. The financial statements referred to above are fairly presented in conformity with generally accepted accounting principles.
2. We have made available to you all—
   a. Financial records and related data.
   b. Minutes of the meetings of stockholders, directors, and committees of directors, or summaries of actions of recent meetings for which minutes have not been prepared.
3. There have been no communications from regulatory agencies concerning noncompliance with or deficiencies in financial reporting practices.
4. There are no material transactions that have not been properly recorded in the accounting records underlying the financial statements.
5. There has been no—
   a. Fraud involving management or employees who have significant roles in internal control.
   b. Fraud involving others that could have a material effect on the financial statements.
6. The company has no plans or intentions that may materially affect the carrying value or classification of assets and liabilities.
7. The following have been properly recorded or disclosed in the financial statements:
   a. Related-party transactions, including sales, purchases, loans, transfers, leasing arrangements, and guarantees, and amounts receivable from or payable to related parties.
   b. Guarantees, whether written or oral, under which the company is contingently liable.
   c. Significant estimates and material concentrations known to management that are required to be disclosed.
8. There are no—
   a. Violations or possible violations of laws or regulations whose effects should be considered for disclosure in the financial statements or as a basis for recording a loss contingency.
   b. Unasserted claims or assessments that our lawyer has advised us are probable of assertion and must be disclosed in accordance with FASB Statement No. 5, Accounting for Contingencies.
   c. Other liabilities or gain or loss contingencies that are required to be accrued or disclosed by FASB No. 5.
9. The company has satisfactory title to all owned assets, and there are no liens or encumbrances on such assets nor has any asset been pledged as collateral.
10. The company has complied with all aspects of contractual agreements that would have a material effect on the financial statements in the event of noncompliance.

To the best of our knowledge and belief, no events have occurred subsequent to the balance sheet date and through the date of this letter that would require adjustment to or disclosure in the aforementioned financial statements.

Joel Adams
Joel Adams
President and Chief Executive Officer

Jeremy Slade
Jeremy Slade
Chief Financial Officer

Jallo, Inc.

Source: Adapted from *AICPA Professional Standards*, section AU 333.16.

Completeness of Information

3. Availability of all financial records and related data;
4. Completeness and availability of all minutes of meetings of stockholders, directors, and committees of directors;
5. Communications from regulatory agencies concerning noncompliance with or deficiencies in financial reporting practices; and
6. Absence of unrecorded transactions.

Recognition, Measurement, and Disclosure

7. Information concerning fraud involving (1) management, (2) employees who have significant roles in internal control, or (3) others where the fraud could have a material effect on the financial statements;
8. Plans or intentions that may affect the carrying value or classification of assets or liabilities;
9. Information concerning related-party transactions and amounts receivable from or payable to related parties;
10. Guarantees, whether written or oral, under which the entity is contingently liable;
11. Significant estimates and material concentrations known to management that are required to be disclosed;
12. Violations or possible violations of laws or regulations whose effects should be considered for disclosure in the financial statements or as a basis for recording a loss contingency;
13. Unasserted claims or assessments that the entity's lawyer has advised are probable of assertion and must be disclosed in accordance with FASB Statement No. 5, Accounting for Contingencies;
14. Other liabilities and gain or loss contingencies that are required to be accrued or disclosed by FASB Statement No. 5;
15. Satisfactory title to assets, liens or encumbrances on assets, and assets pledged as collateral; and
16. Compliance with aspects of contractual agreements that may affect the financial statements.

Subsequent Events

17. Information concerning subsequent events.[25]

Communication of Matters Related to Internal Control

Auditing standards require that the auditor communicate any material internal control matters discovered during the audit. The communication should be to the audit committee or to individuals with a level of authority and responsibility equivalent to that of an audit committee in organizations that do not have one, such as the board of directors, the board of trustees, an owner in an owner-managed enterprise, or others who may have engaged the auditor.[26]

The matters required to be reported to the audit committee are referred to as **reportable conditions**. Reportable conditions are matters coming to the auditor's attention

25 *AICPA Professional Standards,* op. cit., section AU 333.06.
26 Ibid, section AU 325.

that, in her or his judgment, represent significant deficiencies in internal financial controls that could adversely affect the entity's ability to record, process, summarize, and report financial data consistent with the assertions of management in the financial statements.[27] Deficiencies may relate to any one or a combination of the internal control components (e.g., integrity and ethical values, the control environment, the accounting information system, control procedures, adapting to change, or monitoring).

The report preferably should be in writing, and should state that the communication is intended solely for the information and the use of the audit committee, management, and others within the organization. The **reportable conditions letter** should

1. Indicate that the purpose of the audit was to report on the financial statements and not to provide assurance on the internal control system;
2. Include the definition of reportable conditions;
3. List the reportable conditions discovered; and
4. Include the restriction on distribution.[28]

If the auditor discovers no reportable conditions during the course of the audit, no written representation should be made.[29] Exhibit 13.8 illustrates a recommended form for the reportable conditions letter.

In addition to ensuring proper notification of the audit committee, the letter also provides protection to the auditor. Through its incorporation into the audit workpapers, the letter provides evidence that the auditor discovered internal control deficiencies and suggested ways for rectifying the conditions. This can serve as an effective defense in the event of future legal actions against the auditor involving undetected errors or fraud caused by uncorrected control weaknesses.

Another type of letter that the auditors may choose to issue to the client is a **management letter**. As contrasted with the reportable conditions communication, the management letter covers all auditor-discovered weaknesses, not just those materially affecting the financial statement assertions. The purpose of the letter is to provide constructive suggestions to management concerning improvements in the internal controls. Although it is not required by GAAS, most auditors and their clients find the letter to be useful in contributing to maximum control effectiveness. Exhibit 13.9 illustrates a typical management letter, addressed to the president of the company.

APPENDIX

AUDITING OBJECTIVES AND PROCEDURES: FINANCING AND INVESTING CYCLE

Investing Transactions

This audit objectives-evidence-procedures matrix, like the ones following Chapters 11 and 12, lists management assertions and specific audit objectives in the left column.

27 Ibid.
28 Ibid.
29 Ibid.

EXHIBIT 13.8

Communication of Reportable Conditions

February 26, 2003

To the Audit Committee of the Board of Directors of Jallo, Inc.

In planning and performing our audit of the financial statements of Jallo, Inc., for the year ended December 31, 2002, we considered its internal control structure in order to determine our auditing procedures for the purpose of expressing our opinion on the financial statements and not to provide assurance on the internal control structure. However, we noted certain matters involving the internal control structure and its operation that we consider to be reportable conditions under standards established by the American Institute of Certified Public Accountants. Reportable conditions involve matters coming to our attention relating to significant deficiencies in the design or operation of the internal control structure that, in our judgment, could adversely affect the organization's ability to record, process, summarize, and report financial data consistent with the assertions of management in the financial statements.

Our study and evaluation disclosed the following conditions that we believe result in more than a relatively low risk that errors or irregularities in amounts that would be material in relation to the financial statements of Jallo, Inc., may occur and not be detected within a timely period. Programmed controls have not been developed for editing computer input. As a result, we found numerous posting errors during our tests of customer accounts, creditor accounts, and inventory accounts. We also noted that the company does not require data entry forms for the input of transactions into the EDP system. This weakness is compounded by a general lack of security over access to computer terminals and leads us to conclude that significant errors or irregularities could occur and go undetected given the absence of an adequate audit trail. We discussed these conditions with Elizabeth Benton, corporate controller of Jallo. Ms. Benton assured us that steps were being taken to correct the situation.

This report is intended solely for the information and use of the audit committee (board of directors, board of trustees, or owners in owner-managed enterprises), management, and others within the organization (or specified regulatory agency or other specified third party).

Source: *AICPA Professional Standards*, section AU 325.12.

Forms of audit evidence and selected audit procedures relating to the assertions and objectives are then listed in the right column of the matrix.

Assertions and Audit Objectives	Audit Evidence and Procedures
Existence and Completeness	*Physical Evidence*
Do the securities exist?	• Assume control over all negotiable securities, cash on hand, and cash funds (to prevent substitution).
	• Examine securities and record serial numbers for later comparison with recorded accountability (investment ledger).
	• Examine notes receivable.
	• Obtain receipt upon return of cash and securities.

EXHIBIT 13.9

Management Letter

March 1, 2003

Mr. Joel Adams, President
Jallo, Inc.
1010 Plaza Tower
Houston, TX 73775

Dear Mr. Adams:

We have audited the financial statements of Jallo, Inc., for the year ended December 31, 2002, and have issued our report thereon dated February 26, 2003. As part of our audit, we made a study of control structure policies and procedures only to the extent we considered necessary to determine the nature, timing, and extent of our auditing procedures.

We have submitted to the chief financial officer a detailed report of our suggestions for improvements in control structure policies and procedures. Our recommendations were discussed with personnel responsible for the various areas and many of them currently are being implemented. Summarized below are our suggestions of importance which we believe warrant your attention.

COMPUTER CONTROLS

Adequate input controls over the processing of purchases and sales transactions do not exist. As a result, numerous errors are made in posting customer, creditor, and inventory accounts. We strongly urge installing such controls as validity tests, reasonableness tests, check digits, and control totals as part of the transaction editing procedures. In addition, access to computer terminals is generally unlimited and recording forms are not utilized in inputting transactions into the system. These weaknesses can result in erroneous or unauthorized transactions being processed by the system. We recommend a policy of establishing passwords and codes to ensure security over computer databases. We also suggest that the company design and require the use of recording forms for all transactions input directly into the EDP system.

INVENTORY CONTROL AT BRANCHES

Although branch managers are responsible for inventory control at their respective locations, we noted significant adjustments of the perpetual records, maintained at the home office, to the year-end physical inventories at several of the branches. We recommend that the internal audit staff be assigned the task of test counting inventories at branches during the year and comparing such counts with the perpetual records. Such periodic "spot-checking" on an unannounced basis should strengthen inventory control.

CREDIT APPROVAL

Inasmuch as Mr. Reece, credit manager, retired in January 2002, and has not yet been replaced, customer orders have been processed without credit approval. Our aging analysis of trade accounts receivable indicated a significant increase, over the previous year end, of past-due accounts. We recommend that either a new credit manager be hired or an existing staff person be assigned the responsibility for credit approval.

We appreciate the opportunity to present these comments for your consideration and we are prepared to discuss them at your convenience.

Sincerely,

J. Rindley

Ricks and Hanley, CPAs

Confirmation Evidence

- Confirm existence of securities not on premises.

Rights and Obligations

Are the securities owned by the client?

Physical Evidence

- Examine securities for evidence that client is the registered owner.
- Examine for evidence of pledging as collateral on loans.

Confirmation Evidence

- Confirm ownership with holders of securities not on premises.
- Confirm notes receivable with makers.

Valuation

Are securities properly valued?
- *Market for trading and available for sale*
- *Amortized cost for held to maturity*
- *Equity for significant interest*
- *Net realizable value for notes receivable*

Documentary Evidence

- Perform cutoff tests:
  1. Verify dividends by reference to *Standard & Poor's* or *Moody's*; and
  2. Analyze intercompany accounts, making certain both sides of intercompany transactions have been consistently recorded, and look for related-party transactions.
- Trace and vouch securities examined or confirmed:
  1. Trace from count sheets or returned confirmations to investment ledger (note serial numbers to detect substitution); and
  2. Vouch from investment ledger to count sheets or returned confirmations for evidence of missing securities.
- Vouch additions and disposals by reference to the following, as necessary:
  1. Broker's advice;
  2. Remittance advice, cash receipts record, and bank statement; and
  3. Canceled check.
- Examine minutes for proper authorization of major purchases and sales and to corroborate management's intent and ability as to holding period for securities.
- Examine income statements of unconsolidated subsidiaries accounted for on an equity basis.
- Determine market value as of the balance sheet date.

Mathematical Evidence

- Recompute premium or discount amortization on long-term bond investments.

- Recompute gain or loss on disposal.
- Recompute interest accrual.
- Calculate implicit interest, where applicable.
- Determine year-end market value for marketable securities:
    1. Do separate analysis for long-term and short-term portfolios; and
    2. Determine proper adjustment to market.

Analytical Evidence

- Compare interest and dividends with those of prior year and investigate significant changes.

Presentation and Disclosure

Are securities and notes receivable properly classified as to current or noncurrent?

Have necessary disclosures been made as to pledging, and gains and losses on transactions?

Hearsay Evidence

- Inquire of management as to nature of investments and reasons for holding them.
- Inquire as to pledging of securities as loan collateral.
- Inquire as to related-party transactions.

Documentary Evidence

- Examine minutes for evidence of pledging or related-party transactions.
- Determine, by vouching, that dividends on stock reported under the equity method have been reflected as reductions in the investment account.
- Examine minutes and other pertinent documentation to corroborate management's intent and ability relative to declared holding periods for short-term and long-term investments.

Borrowing Transactions

Assertions and Audit Objectives	Audit Evidence and Procedures

Existence and Completeness

Are there any unrecorded liabilities?

Are liabilities properly authorized?

Documentary Evidence

- Examine the following for possible failure to record long-term liabilities:
    1. Lease agreements;
    2. Pension and profit-sharing plans;
    3. Bank confirmations;
    4. Bond indentures and mortgage agreements; and
    5. Directors' minutes.
- Examine directors' minutes for evidence of loan authorizations.

Hearsay Evidence

- Obtain client representation letter.

Valuation

Are long-term liabilities reflected at net present value?

Confirmation Evidence

- Confirm liabilities, as appropriate.

Documentary Evidence

- Examine lease agreements for contingent rentals.
- Examine pension agreements for vesting provisions.
- Examine loan agreements for possible need to impute interest.
- Vouch the following on a test basis:
  1. Interest payments;
  2. Lease payments; and
  3. Pension plan contributions.

Mathematical Evidence

- Recompute the following on a test basis:
  1. Premium and discount amortization;
  2. Lease amortization;
  3. Contingent rentals;
  4. Interest accruals;
  5. Gain or loss on bond redemptions;
  6. Change in deferred taxes; and
  7. Pension liability.
- Compute implicit interest, if applicable.

Analytical Evidence

- Compare liabilities and related expenses with those of prior year and investigate significant changes.

Hearsay Evidence

- Obtain client representation letter.

Presentation and Disclosure

Have current portions of long-term debt been reclassified as current?

Documentary Evidence

- Examine liability agreements for the following:
  1. Restrictive covenants; consider adequacy of disclosure given violations of restrictive covenants;
  2. Collateral requirements; consider adequacy of disclosure given collateral requirements; and
  3. Other disclosure requirements (future cash flows under lease agreements, details surrounding bond issues, pension provisions, etc.).

Stockholders' Equity Transactions

Assertions and Audit Objectives	Audit Evidence and Procedures

Valuation

Physical Evidence

Have gains or losses on stock-holders' equity transactions been improperly recognized?

- Examine treasury stock certificates.

Confirmation Evidence

- Confirm stock issuance and dividends with registrar and transfer agent.

Are capital stock transactions properly authorized?

Documentary Evidence

- Examine minutes for dividend declarations and proper authorization of the following:
  1. Stock issuance;
  2. Stock reacquisition;
  3. Stock retirements; and
  4. Stock options.
- Vouch dividend declarations and payments.
- Vouch treasury stock transactions.
- Trace treasury stock issuance proceeds to bank statement.
- Examine evidence of valuation where stock is issued for noncash assets.

Mathematical Evidence

- Recompute earnings per share.
- Recompute stock option credit.
- Recalculate debit to retained earnings for stock dividends.

Presentation and Disclosure

Documentary Evidence

Proper distinction between invested capital and earned capital?

Have restrictions been adequately disclosed?

Have details relating to capital structure components been adequately disclosed?

- Examine loan agreements and directors' minutes for possible restrictions on retained earnings.
- Examine stock option agreements for details surrounding the options:
  1. Employees participating;
  2. Shares involved;
  3. Option prices; and
  4. Exercise dates.
- Examine corporate charter for description of various classes of stock:
  1. Whether preferred is participating or cumulative;
  2. Dividends in arrears on cumulative preferred; and
  3. Liquidation values of preferred, if different from par.

KEY TERMS

Accounting symmetry, 530
Auditor/client conference, 548
Client representation letter, 549
Collateral, 528
Communication with the audit committee, 549
Confirmation of securities, 529
Derivatives, 543
Disposal of a segment, 544
Examination of debt agreements, 533
Examination of securities, 529
Form versus substance, 530

Investment ledger, 530
Loan default, 543
Management letter, 553
Open items, 547
Related-party transactions, 530
Reportable conditions, 552
Reportable conditions letter, 553
Troubled debt restructuring, 532
Type I subsequent events, 545
Type II subsequent events, 545
Workpaper review, 547

COMPUTER AUDIT PRACTICE CASE

Biltrite Bicycles, Inc.

As part of the audit of the financing and investing cycle, you may now complete the following exercises contained in the Biltrite audit practice case:

Module XII: Analysis of marketable securities
Module XIII: Mortgage note payable and note payable to Bank Two
Module XIV: Working trial balance

REVIEW QUESTIONS

1. In examining investment securities, the auditor vouches from investment records to count sheets or returned confirmations, and traces from count sheets or returned confirmations to investment records. Why are both vouching and tracing necessary?

2. As part of the examination of investment securities, the auditor should record serial numbers in the workpapers on which the counts are recorded. Explain why this is necessary.

3. What specific audit objectives can be met by examining long-term debt agreements?

4. How does the reading of directors' minutes assist the auditor in satisfying the objectives related to the audit of stockholders' equity?

5. What is the auditor's responsibility relative to related-party transactions?

6. State two ways in which financial statements might be distorted by the existence of related-party transactions.

7. Why must the auditor be concerned about restrictive covenants contained in loan agreements?

8. If the client is reporting a "disposal of a segment," the auditor must obtain satisfaction concerning two aspects of classification. Explain which aspects and why.

9. Why is it necessary for the auditor to apply analytical procedures as part of overall audit review?

10. What impact might a modification of materiality thresholds have on the audit?

11. Differentiate between a Type I and Type II subsequent event.

12. What is the auditor's responsibility for locating subsequent events?

13. How does the auditor locate subsequent events?

14. Explain the importance of the workpaper review.

15. Define the *open items workpaper* and explain its significance.

16. What topics are commonly covered during the auditor/client conference held at the close of audit field work?

17. To what extent does the client representation letter relieve the auditor of responsibility?

18. Differentiate between the reportable conditions communication and the management letter.

MULTIPLE CHOICE QUESTIONS FROM PAST CPA EXAMS

1. To satisfy the valuation assertion when auditing an investment accounted for by the equity method, an auditor most likely would
   a. Inspect the stock certificates evidencing the investment.
   b. Examine the audited financial statements of the investee company.
   c. Review the broker's advice or canceled check for the investment's acquisition.
   d. Obtain market quotations from financial newspapers or periodicals.

2. An auditor's purpose in reviewing the renewal of a note payable shortly after the balance sheet date most likely is to obtain evidence concerning management's assertions about
   a. Existence or occurrence.
   b. Presentation and disclosure.
   c. Completeness.
   d. Valuation or allocation.

3. To which of the following matters would materiality limits *not* apply when obtaining written client representations?
   a. Losses from sales commitments
   b. Unasserted claims and assessments
   c. Fraud involving management
   d. Noncompliance with contractual agreements

4. In testing long-term investments, an auditor ordinarily would use analytical procedures to ascertain the reasonableness of the
   a. Completeness of recorded investment income.
   b. Classification between current and noncurrent portfolios.
   c. Valuation of marketable equity securities.
   d. Existence of unrealized gains or losses in the portfolio.

5. For all audits of financial statements made in accordance with generally accepted auditing standards, the use of analytical procedures is required to some extent

	In the planning stage	As a substantive test	In the review stage
a.	Yes	No	Yes
b.	No	Yes	No
c.	No	Yes	Yes
d.	Yes	No	No

6. Which of the following matters is an auditor required to communicate to an entity's audit committee?

	Significant audit adjustments	Changes in significant accounting policies
a.	Yes	Yes
b.	Yes	No
c.	No	Yes
d.	No	No

7. An auditor would most likely verify the interest earned on bond investments by
   a. Vouching the receipt and deposit of interest checks.
   b. Confirming the bond interest rate with the issuer of the bonds.
   c. Recomputing the interest earned on the basis of face amount, interest rate, and period held.
   d. Testing the internal controls over cash receipts.

8. Analytical procedures used in the overall review stage of an audit generally include
   a. Considering unusual or unexpected account balances that were *not* previously identified.
   b. Performing tests of transactions to corroborate management's financial statement assertions.
   c. Gathering evidence concerning account balances that have *not* changed from the prior year.
   d. Retesting control procedures that appeared to be ineffective during the assessment of control risk.

9. Which of the following procedures would an auditor most likely perform to obtain evidence about the occurrence of subsequent events?
   a. Recomputing a sample of large-dollar transactions occurring after year end for arithmetic accuracy.
   b. Investigating changes in stockholders' equity occurring after year end.
   c. Inquiring of the entity's legal counsel concerning litigation, claims, and assessments arising after year end.
   d. Confirming bank accounts established after year end.

10. The primary objective of analytical procedures used in the final review stage of an audit is to
    a. Obtain evidence from details tested to corroborate particular assertions.
    b. Identify areas that represent specific risks relevant to the audit.
    c. Assist the auditor in assessing the validity of the conclusions reached.
    d. Satisfy doubts when questions arise about a client's ability to continue in existence.

11. An auditor most likely would inspect loan agreements under which an entity's inventories are pledged to support management's financial statement assertion of
    a. Existence or occurrence.
    b. Completeness.
    c. Presentation and disclosure.
    d. Valuation or allocation.

12. Which of the following documentation is required for an audit in accordance with generally accepted auditing standards?
    a. An internal control questionnaire
    b. A client engagement letter

    c. A planning memorandum or checklist

    d. A client representation letter

13. A purpose of a management representation letter is to reduce

    a. Audit risk to an aggregate level of misstatement that could be considered material.

    b. An auditor's responsibility to detect material misstatements only to the extent that the letter is relied on.

    c. The possibility of a misunderstanding concerning management's responsibility for the financial statements.

    d. The scope of an auditor's procedures concerning related-party transactions and subsequent events.

14. An auditor's program to examine long-term debt most likely would include steps that require

    a. Comparing the carrying amount of the debt to its year-end market value.

    b. Correlating interest expense recorded for the period with outstanding debt.

    c. Verifying the existence of the holders of the debt by direct confirmation.

    d. Inspecting the accounts payable subsidiary ledger for unrecorded long-term debt.

15. Which of the following most likely would indicate the existence of related parties?

    a. Writing down obsolete inventory just before year end

    b. Failing to correct previously identified internal control deficiencies

    c. Depending on a single product for the success of the entity

    d. Borrowing money at an interest rate significantly below the market rate

16. An auditor should request that an audit client send a letter of inquiry to those attorneys who have been consulted concerning litigation, claims, or assessments. The primary reason for this request is to provide

    a. The opinion of a specialist as to whether loss contingencies are possible, probable, or remote.

    b. A description of litigation, claims, and assessments that have a reasonable possibility of unfavorable outcomes.

    c. An objective appraisal of management's policies and procedures adopted for identifying and evaluating legal matters.

    d. The corroboration of the information furnished by management concerning litigation, claims, and assessments.

17. Which of the following statements ordinarily is included among the written client representations obtained by the auditor?

    a. Management acknowledges that there are no material weaknesses in internal control.

    b. Sufficient evidential matter has been made available to permit the issuance of an unqualified opinion.

    c. Compensating balances and other arrangements involving restrictions on cash balances have been disclosed.

    d. Management acknowledges responsibility for illegal actions committed by employees.

18. During an audit of an entity's stockholders' equity accounts, the auditor determines whether there are restrictions on retained earnings resulting from loans, agreements, or state law. This audit procedure most likely is intended to verify management's assertion of

    a. Existence or occurrence.

    b. Completeness.

    c. Valuation or allocation.

    d. Presentation and disclosure.

19. An auditor searching for related-party transactions should obtain an understanding of each subsidiary's relationship to the total entity because
   a. This may permit the audit of intercompany balances to be performed as of concurrent dates.
   b. Intercompany transactions may have been consummated on terms equivalent to arm's-length transactions.
   c. This may reveal whether particular transactions would have taken place if the parties had *not* been related.
   d. The business structure may be deliberately designed to obscure related-party transactions.

ESSAY QUESTIONS AND PROBLEMS

13.1   During the examination of the annual financial statements of Jorgens.com, Beth Anderson, the company's president, and Marjory Rinck, the auditor, reviewed matters that were supposed to be included in a written representation letter. Upon receipt of the client representation letter in Exhibit 13.10, Rinck contacted Anderson to state that it was incomplete.

Required:
Identify the other matters that Anderson's representation letter should confirm specifically. (AICPA adapted)

EXHIBIT 13.10

Problem 13.1 Client Representation Letter

To M. Rinck, CPA

In connection with your audit of the balance sheet of Jorgens.com, as of December 31, 2002 and the related statements of income, retained earnings, and cash flows for the year then ended, for the purpose of expressing an opinion as to whether the financial statements present fairly the financial position, results of operations, and cash flows of Jorgens.com, in conformity with generally accepted accounting principles, we confirm, to the best of our knowledge and belief, the following representations made to you during your examination. There were no

1. Plans or intentions that may materially affect the carrying value or classification of assets and liabilities.
2. Communications from regulatory agencies concerning noncompliance with, or deficiencies in, financial reporting practices.
3. Agreements to repurchase assets previously sold.
4. Violations or possible violations of laws or regulations whose effects should be considered for disclosure in the financial statements or as a basis for recording a loss contingency.
5. Unasserted claims or assessments that our lawyer has advised are probable of assertion and must be disclosed in accordance with Statement of Financial Accounting Standards No. 5.
6. Capital stock repurchase options or agreements or capital stock reserved for options, warrants, conversions, or other requirements.
7. Compensating balance or other arrangements involving restrictions on cash balances.

B. Anderson
President
Jorgens.com
March 14, 2003

13.2   For each of the following situations, identify the auditing procedures that should have alerted the auditor to the risk associated with the examination, and those procedures that should have assisted the auditor in locating the fraud.

1. Kipling, Inc., a producer and distributor of auto replacement parts, has experienced difficulty in maintaining income levels due to competition from foreign producers. In a desperation move to ward off a possible proxy fight with dissident stockholders, Jacob Brady, Kipling's CEO, formed a shell company. Piko Auto Repair Centers, Inc., as the company was named, supposedly operated a regional chain of auto repair shops. Documents were fabricated in support of fictitious sales transactions with Piko, the new customer. As a result, Kipling's earnings increased significantly over the preceding year. Others in the industry were recording declines and even losses for the same period.

2. Lou Rolla, the president and chief executive officer of Feloney, Inc., had been living well beyond his means. As a result, he had several short positions to cover with his stockbrokers, and his creditors were becoming aggressive in their attempts to collect the amounts owed them. Although Rolla could have "weathered the storm" by cutting back on his lavish lifestyle, he had come to enjoy the "high living." Instead of reducing his spending, therefore, he borrowed the needed funds from the corporation. In order to confuse the auditors, he used a wholly owned subsidiary and several banks as conduits for moving the funds. The usual procedure was to have Feloney issue a note to Dorite Corp., the wholly owned subsidiary. Dorite discounted the note at one of the banks, and transferred the money to Feloney. Feloney then loaned the funds to Dorite, which loaned them in turn to Rolla. Although Rolla pledged his stock in Feloney as collateral, the stock's intrinsic value rested upon Rolla's ability to repay the loans (the loans receivable amounts represented 35 percent of Feloney's total assets), and Rolla was insolvent due to his continued run of bad luck in the stock market, as well as his trips to Europe.

13.3   Juarez, CPA, is auditing the financial statements of Hunters, Inc., a privately held corporation with 300 employees and 5 stockholders, three of whom are active in management. Hunters has been in business for many years, but has never had its financial statements audited. Juarez suspects that the substance of some of Hunters' business transactions differs from their form because of the pervasiveness of related-party relationships and transactions in the local building supplies industry.

Required:
Describe the audit procedures Juarez should apply to identify related-party relationships and transactions. (AICPA adapted)

13.4   The schedule in Exhibit 13.11 was prepared by the controller of World Wholesalers for use by the independent auditors during their examination of World's year-end financial statements. All procedures performed by the audit assistant were noted in the bottom "Legend" section, and it was properly initialed, dated, and indexed, and then submitted to a senior member of the audit staff for review. The client's internal control was reviewed and considered to be satisfactory.

Required:
a. What information that is essential to the audit of marketable securities is missing from this schedule?
b. What essential audit procedures were not noted as having been performed by the audit assistant?
   (AICPA adapted)

EXHIBIT 13.11

Problem 13.4 Securities Schedule

World Wholesalers
Marketable Securities
Year Ended December 31, 2002

Description of Security	%	Year Due	Serial No.	Face Value of Bonds	Gen. Ledger 1/1	Purch. in 2002	Sold in 2002	Cost	Gen. Ledger 12/31	12/31 Market	Dividend & Interest Pay Date(s)	Amount Received	Accruals 12/31
Corp. Bonds													
A	6	2012	21-7	$10,000	$ 9,400 a				$ 9,400	$ 9,100	7/15	$ 300 b,d	$ 275
D	4	2004	73-0	30,000	27,500 a				27,500	26,220	12/1	1,200 b,d	100
G	9	2019	16-4	5,000	4,000 a				4,000	5,080	8/1	450 b,d	188
Rc	5	2006	08-2	70,000	66,000 a		$57,000 b	$66,000					
Sc	10	2020	07-4	100,000		$100,000 e			100,000	101,250	7/1	5,000 b,d	5,000
					$106,900 a,f	$100,000 f	$57,000 f	$66,000 f	$140,900 f,g	$141,650 f		$6,950 f	$5,563 f
Stocks													
P common 1000 shares			1044		$ 7,500 a				$ 7,500	$ 7,600	3/1	$ 750 b,d	
											6/1	750 b,d	
											9/1	750 b,d	
											12/1	750 b,d	$ 250
U common 50 shares			8530		9,700 a				9,700	9,800	2/1	800 b,d	
											8/1	800 b,d	667
					$ 17,200 a,f				$ 17,200 f,g	$ 17,400 f		$4,600 f	$ 917 f

Legends and comments relative to above
a = Beginning balances agreed to 2001 working papers
b = Traced to cash receipts
c = Minutes examined (purchase and sales approved by the board of directors)
d = Agreed to 1099
e = Confirmed by tracing to broker's advice
f = Totals footed
g = Agreed to general ledger

13.5   Discuss the significance of the auditor's review of subsequent events, and differentiate between Type I and Type II subsequent events. Explain how each of the following procedures assists the auditor in locating subsequent events. Be specific in describing the kinds of events revealed by each set of procedures.

1. Obtaining a letter from the client's legal counsel.
2. Reading the minutes of the directors' meetings since year end.
3. Reading the latest interim financial statements since year end.

13.6   Jensing, Inc., a developer and producer of cooking and baking appliances, leases factory and office space at its only location in St. Paul, Minnesota. Quarterly lease payments of $100,000 are charged to rent expense as paid or accrued. The lease is noncancellable and was signed on January 1, 2002, with the first rent due and paid on April 1, 2002. The present value of the future lease payments at 1/1/02 was $2,346,833. This amount was based on the 8 percent interest rate stated in the lease agreement.

Required:

a. As the in-charge auditor examining the Jensing financial statements for the year ended 12/31/02, what additional information do you need in order to determine whether the lease is a capital or operating lease?
b. What audit procedures would you apply in gathering the information needed in (a)?
c. Assuming that the lease is considered a capital lease, and the estimated useful life and salvage value of the property are 8 years and $400,000, respectively, prepare an audit workpaper for the lease liability. Assume that the quarterly payments are due on April 1, July 1, October 1, and January 1. Include all necessary audit legends as evidence of procedures performed.
d. Draft any audit adjustments indicated by the workpaper prepared in (c).

13.7   Tania Jackson, a CPA and the continuing auditor of Barnes, Inc., is beginning the audit of the common stock and treasury stock accounts. Jackson has decided to design substantive tests without testing Barnes' internal control procedures.

Barnes has no par, no stated value common stock, and acts as its own registrar and transfer agent. During the past year Barnes both issued and reacquired shares of its own common stock, some of which the company still owned at year end. Additional common stock transactions occurred among the shareholders during the year.

Common stock transactions can be traced to individual shareholders' accounts in a subsidiary ledger and to a stock certificate book. The company has *not* paid any cash or stock dividends. There are no other classes of stock, stock rights, warrants, or option plans.

Required:
What substantive audit procedures should Jackson apply in examining the common stock and treasury stock accounts? (AICPA adapted)

13.8   Lemming, CPA, is auditing the financial statements of Zelon Corporation for the year ended December 31, 2002. Lemming plans to complete the field work and sign the auditor's report about May 10, 2003. Lemming is concerned about events and transactions occurring after December 31, 2002, that may affect the 2002 financial statements.

Required:

a. What are the general types of subsequent events that require Lemming's consideration and evaluation?
b. What are the auditing procedures Lemming should consider performing to gather evidence concerning subsequent events?

(AICPA adapted)

13.9   Exhibit 13.12 (pp. 570–571) contains a long-term liabilities workpaper (indexed K-1). The workpaper was prepared by client personnel and audited by AA, an audit assistant, during the calendar year 2002 audit of Indiana Corp., a continuing audit client. The engagement supervisor is reviewing the audit workpapers thoroughly.

Required:

Identify the deficiencies in the workpaper that the engagement supervisor should discover. (AICPA adapted)

13.10   Sean O'Reilly, a CPA, has been engaged to examine the financial statements of Journeys End, Inc., for the year ended December 31, 2002. During the year, Journeys End obtained a long-term loan from a local bank pursuant to a financing agreement that provided that the:

1. Loan was to be secured by the company's inventory and accounts receivable;
2. Company was to maintain a debt-to-equity ratio not to exceed 2 to 1;
3. Company was not to pay dividends without permission from the bank; and
4. Monthly installment payments were to commence July 1, 2003.

In addition, during the year the company also borrowed amounts, on a short-term basis, from the president of the company, including substantial amounts just prior to year end.

Required:

a. For the audit of the financial statements of Journeys End, Inc., what procedures should O'Reilly employ in examining the described loans? Identify the audit objective served by each of the procedures.
b. What financial statement disclosures should O'Reilly expect to find with respect to the loans from the president?
    (AICPA adapted)

13.11   To test financial statement assertions, an auditor develops specific audit objectives. The auditor then designs substantive tests to satisfy or accomplish each objective.

Required:

Items (1) through (10) represent audit objectives for the investments, accounts receivable, and property and equipment accounts. To the right of each set of audit objectives is a listing of possible audit procedures for that account. For each audit objective, select the audit procedure that would primarily respond to the objective. Select only one procedure for each audit objective. A procedure may be selected only once, or not at all.

Example:

The following is an example of the manner in which the answer sheet should be marked.

Audit Objectives for Cash	*Audit Procedures for Cash*
11. Recorded cash represents cash on balance sheet date.	C. Count cash on hand.

Items to be answered:

Audit Objectives for Investments	*Audit Procedures for Investments*
1. Investments are properly described and classified in the financial statements.	A. Trace opening balances in the subsidiary ledger to prior year's audit workpapers.

Audit Objectives for Investments	*Audit Procedures for Investments*
2. Recorded investments represent investments actually owned at the balance sheet date.	B. Determine that employees who are authorized to sell investments do not have access to cash.
3. Investments are properly valued at the balance sheet date.	C. Examine supporting documents for a sample of investment transactions to verify that prenumbered documents are used.
	D. Determine that changes in investment value have been properly recorded.
	E. Verify that transfers from one class to another in the investment portfolio have been properly recorded.
	F. Obtain positive confirmations as of the balance sheet date of investments held by independent custodians.
	G. Trace investment transactions to minutes of the board of directors' meetings to determine that transactions were properly authorized.

Audit Objectives for Accounts Receivable	*Audit Procedures for Accounts Receivable*
4. Accounts receivable represent all amounts owed to the entity at the balance sheet date.	H. Analyze the relationship of accounts receivable and sales and compare it with relationships for preceding periods.
5. The entity has legal right to all accounts receivable at the balance sheet date.	I. Perform sales cutoff tests to obtain assurance that sales transactions and corresponding entries for inventories and cost of goods sold are recorded in the same and proper period.
6. Accounts receivable are stated at net realizable value.	J. Review the aged trial balance for significant past due accounts.
7. Accounts receivable are properly described and presented in the financial statements.	K. Obtain an understanding of the business purpose of transactions that resulted in accounts receivable balances.
	L. Review loan agreements for indications of whether accounts receivable have been factored or pledged.
	M. Review the accounts receivable trial balance for amounts due from officers and employees.
	N. Analyze unusual relationships between monthly accounts receivable balances and monthly accounts payable balances.

Audit Objectives for Property and Equipment	*Audit Procedures for Property and Equipment*
8. The entity has legal right to property and equipment acquired during the year.	O. Trace opening balances in the summary schedules to the prior year's audit workpapers.

EXHIBIT 13.12

Problem 13.9 Schedule of Long-Term Liabilities

Indiana Corp.
WORKPAPERS
December 31, 2002

Index: K-1
Date: 3/22/2003
Prepared By:
Approved By: AA

Lender	Interest Rate	Payment Terms	Collateral	Balance 12/31/01	2002 Borrowings	2002 Reductions	Balance 12/31/02	Interest Paid To	Accrued Interest Payable 12/31/02	Comments
Ø First Commercial Bank	12%	Interest only on 25th of month, principal due in full 1/1/2006; no prepayment penalty	Inventories	$ 50,000√	$300,000 A 1/31/02	$100,000⊕ 6/30/02	$ 250,000 CX	12/25/02	$2,500 NR	Dividend of $80,000 paid 9/2/02 (W/P N-3) violated a provision of the debt agreement, which thereby permits lender to demand immediate payment; lender has refused to waive this violation
Ø Lender's Capital Corp.	Prime plus 1%	Interest only on last day of month, principal due in full 3/5/2004	2nd Mortgage on Park St. Building	100,000√	50,000 A 2/29/02		200,000 C	12/31/02	—	Prime rate was 8% to 9% during the year
Ø Gigantic Building & Loan Assoc.	12%	$5,000 principal plus interest due 5th of month, due in full 12/31/2013	1st Mortgage on Park St. Building	720,000√	—	60,000⊕	660,000 C	12/5/02	5,642 R	Reclassification entry for current portion proposed (See RJE-3)
Ø J. Lott, majority stockholder	0%	Due in full 12/31/2005	Unsecured	300,000√	—	100,000 N 12/31/02	200,000 C	—	—	Borrowed additional $100,000 from J. Lott on 1/7/2003
				$1,170,000√ F	$350,000 F	$260,000 F	$1,310,000 T/B F		$8,142 T/B F	

EXHIBIT 13.12

(continued)

Interest costs from long-term debt

Interest expense for year	$281,333T/B
Average loan balance outstanding	$1,406,667R

Five-year maturities (for disclosure purposes)

Year end	
12/31/2003	$ 60,000
12/31/2004	260,000
12/31/2005	260,000
12/31/2006	310,000
12/31/2007	60,000
Thereafter	360,000
	$1,310,000
	F

Overall conclusions

Long-term debt, accrued interest payable, and interest expense are correct and complete at 12/31/02.

Tickmark legend

F	Readded, foots correctly
C	Confirmed without exception, W/P K-2
CX	Confirmed with exception, W/P K-3
NR	Does not recompute correctly
A	Agreed to loan agreement, validated bank deposit ticket, and board of directors' authorization, W/P W-7
N	Agreed to cash disbursements journal and canceled check dated 12/31/02, clearing 1/8/2003
T/B	Traced to working trial balance
√	Agreed to 12/31/02 workpapers
∅	Agreed to interest rate, term, and collateral to copy of note and loan agreement
⊕	Agreed to canceled check and board of directors' authorization, W/P W-7

Audit Objectives for Property and Equipment	*Audit Procedures for Property and Equipment*
9. Recorded property and equipment represent assets that actually exist at the balance sheet date.	P. Review the provision for depreciation expense and determine that depreciable lives and methods used in the current year are consistent with those used in the prior year.
10. Net property and equipment are properly valued at the balance sheet date.	Q. Determine that the responsibility for maintaining the property and equipment records is segregated from the responsibility for custody of property and equipment.
	R. Examine deeds and title insurance certificates.
	S. Perform cutoff tests to verify that property and equipment additions are recorded in the proper period.
	T. Determine that property and equipment are adequately insured.
	U. Physically examine all major property and equipment additions.

(AICPA adapted)

13.12 Trimbley, CPA, has been engaged to audit the financial statements of Seaway Distributors, Inc., a continuing audit client, for the year ended September 30, 2002. After obtaining an understanding of Seaway's internal control system, Trimbley assessed control risk at the maximum level for all financial statement assertions concerning investments. Trimbley determined that Seaway is unable to exercise significant influence over any investee and none are related parties.

Trimbley obtained from Seaway detailed analyses of its investments in domestic securities showing:

- The classification between current and noncurrent portfolios;
- A description of each security, including the interest rate and maturity date of bonds and par value;
- A notation of the location of each security, either in the treasurer's safe or held by an independent custodian;
- The number of shares of stock or face amount of bonds held at the beginning and end of the year;
- The beginning and ending balances at cost and at market, and the unamortized premium or discount on bonds;
- Additions to and sales from the portfolios for the year, including date, number of shares, face amount of bonds, cost, proceeds, and realized gain or loss;
- Valuation allowances at the beginning and end of the year and changes therein; and
- Accrued investment income for each investment at the beginning and end of the year, and income earned and collected during the year.

Trimbley then prepared the following partial audit program of substantive auditing procedures:

1. Foot and crossfoot the analyses;

2. Trace the ending totals to the general ledger and financial statements;
3. Trace the beginning balances to the prior year's workpapers;
4. Obtain positive confirmation as of the balance sheet date of the investments held by any independent custodian;
5. Determine that income from investments had been properly recorded as accrued or collected by reference to published sources, by computation, and by tracing to recorded amounts;
6. For investments in nonpublic entities, compare carrying value to information in the most recently available audited financial statements;
7. Determine that all transfers between the current and noncurrent portfolios have been properly authorized and recorded; and
8. Determine that any changes in investment value have been properly accounted for.

Required:

a. Identify the primary financial statement assertion relative to investments that would be addressed by each of the procedures 4 through 8 and describe the primary audit objective of performing that procedure. Use the format illustrated below.

Primary Assertion   **Objective**

b. Describe three additional substantive auditing procedures Trimbley should consider in auditing Seaway's investments.
   (AICPA adapted)

13.13 Bennie & June, CPAs, have completed the field work for the PartyCrest Deli audit, and are considering the impact on PartyCrest's audited financial statements of certain events occurring between the balance sheet date, December 31, 2002, and the date of field work completion, February 12, 2003. PartyCrest's audited net income for 2002 was $15.6 million. The following occurrences are the subject of consideration.

1. On January 22, 2003, PartyCrest settled a lawsuit filed by a consumer who was made ill by a PartyCrest salami bar that somehow had been tainted. The customer consumed the salami in 2002 and brought legal action in June of that year. The original lawsuit asked for medical reimbursement and damages totaling $12 million. The January settlement was for $1.26 million.
2. On November 20, 2002, Carly's Party Stores, a PartyCrest competitor, sued PartyCrest for alleged patent infringement. The infringement relates to a meat storage process, patented by Carly's, for longer and safer storage of meats and other refrigerated products. PartyCrest's defense is that although their process also provides for longer storage it differs markedly from Carly's process. On January 22, 2003, a judge awarded the plaintiffs $5.5 million in damages. PartyCrest's outside legal counsel, in a letter to the auditors, stated their intent to appeal the decision and believe the defendant will ultimately prevail.
3. On January 30, 2003, PartyCrest was forced to recall assorted beefstick and cheese boxes produced by its Cleveland factory and sold in 2002 to wholesale distributors and retail outlets on the east coast. Although the products posed no health hazard, they had been inadvertently processed without salt. The products subject to recall had cost PartyCrest $3.7 million and sold for $5.5 million. The meats and cheeses had no residual value and were discarded upon return to Cleveland.
4. On February 5, 2003, PartyCrest acquired Hamels Meats, Limited, a Canadian meat processor. The transaction was completed by exchanging PartyCrest stock and cash for Hamels stock and was accounted for as a purchase.

5. Although in previous years the auditors had never considered the need for a year-end allowance adjustment for future sales returns and allowances, they are seriously considering one for 2002. Their concern arises from the abnormal incidence of price adjustments occurring in January 2003 and related to December 2002 sales. An examination of January credit memos issued to customers revealed total adjustments of $877,000 relating to December sales.

6. An examination of the January 2003 board of directors' meeting minutes disclosed approval of a bonus equal to 10 percent of audited net income before bonuses.

Required:

a. Assuming the auditors have set the individual item materiality threshold at 5 percent of audited net income, classify each of the mentioned subsequent events as Type I, Type II, or not material. Justify your choice in each instance. (You may ignore the effects of income taxes.)

b. For Type I events, draft the necessary audit adjustments.

c. For Type II events, draft any footnotes that you consider necessary to support adequacy of informative disclosure.

13.14 At the completion of audit field work, before departing the client's premises, the audit manager should conduct an overall review of the audit workpapers. The purpose of this review is to determine that all necessary evidence has been collected, evaluated, and documented, and that all necessary audit adjustments, reclassifications, and disclosures have been prepared. Assume that you are the audit manager in charge of the Perfect Kitchens audit, and that Megan Parlens, the in-charge senior auditor, has presented you with an open items audit workpaper describing the following unresolved issues:

1. We observed the physical inventory taken at the end of Perfect Kitchens' fiscal year, December 31, 2002. In addition, Perfect Kitchens had inventory stored in a public warehouse in Salem, Oregon, awaiting shipment to retailers during the spring buying season. We requested the warehouse to confirm the existence and ownership of the inventory, but a reply has not been received as of the close of audit field work, February 17, 2003. The goods represent 8 percent of the total finished goods inventory.

2. According to company representatives, Perfect Kitchens, in order to expedite shipments to its customers, has constructed upgraded conveyor systems at its five regional warehouses. Although the materials, labor, and overhead costs debited to machinery and equipment are considered significant, we have been unable to obtain the work orders documenting construction of the facilities. According to Kyle Wingate, corporate controller, the internal audit staff has been reviewing the charges and is in possession of the work orders.

3. The company is being sued by a competitor for manufacturing and selling a popular cupboard cabinet allegedly protected by a patent held by the competitor. The suit seeks to recover $3,000,000 in lost revenues and punitive damages. Although Perfect Kitchens management believes the plaintiff's case is weak, we have been unable to obtain a lawyer's letter from the company's outside legal counsel.

4. The company's accounts reflect a large portfolio of marketable securities as of December 31, 2002. These securities purportedly are held by a Portland, Oregon, brokerage firm. Because the company headquarters are located in Sacramento, we mailed a confirmation request to the brokerage firm. As of February 17 we have yet to receive a reply.

5. The account "Gain on Sale of Patent" had a balance of $7.3 million (23 percent of unaudited net income) at December 31, 2002. According to management, the gain resulted

from the sale of a recently acquired patent to King Cabinets, Inc. The patent covers a technically advanced flooring designed and produced by Perfect Kitchens. Given its current liquidity problems, however, the company decided to sell the patent rather than manufacture and market the flooring. Although we examined the bank deposit ticket and the $7.3 million bank statement credit, we have not been able to determine whether King Cabinets is an operating company.

Required:

a. For each of the open items described above, identify the primary audit risk if the issue is not satisfactorily resolved.

b. How would you resolve each item (i.e., what audit procedure(s) would you recommend)?

13.15 Marvel Muffler Shops, Inc., leases its single warehouse from State-Line Leasing Company. The terms of the lease provide for minimum lease payments of $350,000 every six months payable at the beginning of each six-month period. The initial lease term runs for fifteen years with no renewal or purchase options. Marvel is responsible for paying property taxes and also for any needed repairs to the warehouse. The cost of the warehouse to State-Line was $3,800,000 and the market value at date of completion was $5,649,374. The explicit interest rate stated in the lease agreement is 10 percent. The lease was signed and the warehouse occupied on January 2, 2002.

Geiger & Half, CPAs, have audited the accounts of Marvel since 1998. The company closes its books on December 31. Eric Johnson is in charge of the 2002 audit. He has asked you to audit the State-Line warehouse lease.

Required:

a. Assuming that this is a capital lease, prepare an amortization schedule for the period 1/2/02 through 12/31/04.

b. Based on your completed amortization schedule, is this a capital lease or an operating lease? Justify your response.

c. What are the objectives in the audit of the State-Line lease?

d. Draft an audit workpaper, in good form, analyzing the account Obligation Under Long-Term Lease. Incorporate all of the objectives that you identified in (c) above, and assume that Marvel has accounted for the obligation as follows:

1/2/02	Credit	$5,649,374
1/2/02	Debit	350,000
7/1/02	Debit	350,000
12/31/02	Balance	$4,949,374

Note: The solution to this case can be greatly expedited by retrieving and completing the spreadsheet template entitled "Marvel." This file is included on the same Student CD that contains the Biltrite Bicycle templates.

13.16 Amy Robinson, of Bancroft & Jury, CPAs, is in charge of the Branson Manufacturing Company audit for the year ended December 31, 2002. The firm also audited Branson last year. Branson manufactures airplane parts and owns 30 percent of the voting stock of Franklin Industries, a leasing company. At December 31, 2001, the end of the preceding year, Branson held 5 percent of the shares and reported the investment at cost, which equaled the market value of the shares at that date. During 2002, Branson acquired an additional 25 percent of the voting shares. December 31, 2001 balances and 2002 transactions related to this investment are as follows:

12/31/01:   Balance in Investment in Branson, 500 shares at a cost of $30 per share.

1/2/02:   Purchased 2,500 shares of Franklin at a cost of $450 per share.

4/1/02:   Franklin declared a first-quarter dividend of $30,000.

7/1/02:   Franklin declared a second-quarter dividend of $30,000.

10/1/02:   Franklin declared a third-quarter dividend of $40,000.

At December 31, the investment account appeared as follows in Branson's general ledger:

Investment in Franklin Common

| 12/31/01 | Balance | 15,000 |
| 1/2/02 | Purchase | 100,000 |

Branson recorded its share of Franklin dividends as Dividend Revenue.

Franklin's income statement for 2002 reflected the following revenue and expense components:

Leasing revenues	$15 million
Cost of equipment for sales-type leases	$9 million
Operating expenses	$3 million
Extraordinary loss from casualty (net of tax)	$1 million
Income taxes	$1 million

Required:

a. What specific audit objectives should Robinson identify in examining the Franklin account? What audit procedures should she apply?

b. What level of satisfaction does Robinson require with respect to Franklin's income statement components?

c. Prepare an audit workpaper, in good form, for the Franklin investment. Be sure to include any necessary audit adjustments.

d. Does the Franklin investment raise any "warning signs" that the auditors should pursue?

Note: The solution to this case can be greatly expedited by retrieving and completing the spreadsheet template entitled "Branson." This file is included on the same Student CD that contains the Biltrite Bicycle templates.

DISCUSSION CASES

CASE I

Chambers Development Company

Chambers Development Company saw its 1991 profits plummet to $1.5 million after taking a $27 million after-tax charge against earnings. Chambers is a waste management concern in the business of obtaining landfill permits, collecting waste for deposit in the landfills, and treating the landfills. Until the special charge, Chambers had followed the practice of deferring certain indirect costs related to new landfills. Unlike other companies in the industry (Browning-Ferris Industries, Inc., Waste Management, Inc., Sanifill, Inc., and Laidlaw, Inc.), Chambers considered itself a development stage company and thereby justified deferring such costs as executive salaries related to time spent on new landfills, public relations costs, legal fees, and executive travel. For 1991, however, Richard Knight, Chambers' chief financial officer and former partner with Grant Thornton, Chambers' independent accountants, determined that the company was now an operational, rather than a development-stage, enterprise. Therefore, the change in accounting principle from deferral to expensing of indirect costs was made. Charles Fallon, the Grant Thornton partner in charge of the Chambers audit, concurred with the change. Indeed, Grant Thornton refused to render an unqualified audit opinion unless Chambers made the change.

When the change was announced, Chambers' Class B stock fell 40 percent, from $19 to $11.50 per share. Following the drop in reported earnings, the board of directors decided in a special meeting to rescind all executive bonuses for 1991.

Required:

a. Comment on the appropriateness of Chambers' practice of cost deferral as a "development-stage enterprise." Cite appropriate authoritative pronouncements to support your position.

b. Why do you suppose the auditors agreed with the practice prior to 1991? Does this case raise any ethical issues? Explain.

CASE II

Leslie Fay

Don Kenia, Leslie Fay's corporate controller, admitted during the year-end audit that he and the fifteen divisional controllers had been making false entries in the company's books starting in the last quarter of 1991 and continuing throughout 1992. Correction of the fraud, relating to inventories and cost of goods sold, would eliminate 1992 net income and require a substantial downward restatement of 1991 net income.

At that time, Leslie Fay was the nation's second largest maker of women's apparel sold to department stores. The company was founded in 1944 by Fred Pomerantz, who had designed uniforms for the Women's Army Corps during World War II. Leslie Fay went public in 1952. John Pomerantz, current CEO and son of the founder, took Leslie Fay private in a 1982 leveraged buyout, but the company went public again in 1986.

Although corporate headquarters are in New York, the accounting records were maintained in Wilkes-Barre, Pennsylvania. According to some analysts, internal financial controls at the company were somewhat lax. The chief financial officer at the time was Paul Polishan and employees referred to Wilkes-Barre as "Poliworld." Immediately upon graduation from college, Polishan had been hired by Fred

Pomerantz, company founder. He was described by employees as autocratic and very demanding.

The specific nature of the fraud consisted of inflating inventory and decreasing cost of goods sold. This was accomplished by overstating the number of garments made while understating the manufacturing cost of each item. The company then flooded stores with the discounted dresses to further inflate profits. Retailers accepted the dresses after being granted substantial discounts by Pomerantz. In addition to the discounts, Pomerantz had been offering to pay "markdown money" to compensate for potential further price reductions by the retailers after dresses were on the racks for an extended time period.

Although Pomerantz and Polishan insisted that the fraud was perpetrated solely by Kenia and other mid-level employees, executive bonuses were a function of reported profits. Between 1986 and 1992, for example, Pomerantz received total compensation of $18.6 million, mainly in bonuses. He was said to have little financial acumen. Instead he enjoyed mingling in the fashion world, loved the good life, and was quite flamboyant in his life style. Alan Golub, chief operating officer, and Polishan also received profit-driven bonuses in 1991. Kenia received a bonus ($20,000) as well, but it was at the discretion of Polishan and was *not* related to reported profits. One analyst raised the question of top management involvement, inasmuch as the practice of shipping discounted dresses, given the understated unit costs, helped to inflate Leslie Fay's profits. Kenia's attorney suggested that others were also involved. "Kenia did not all by his lonesome conceive of this plan," he said. Other officials at Leslie Fay described Kenia as a "straight arrow," a "real decent guy" and suggested that "something doesn't add up" and that they were puzzled as to why Kenia and the divisional controllers would make false entries when they had nothing to gain from the fraud.[30] What is known is that Leslie Fay was experiencing severe competition from such companies as Liz Claiborne and Jones New York, that the company's orders were declining, and that retailers were being forced to mark down Leslie Fay apparel in order to move it.

Reported income for 1991, $29.3 million on sales of $836.6 million, was lowered to $17 million, but sales were correctly stated. The 1992 income, first estimated at $24 million by analysts, was adjusted to reflect a loss of $13.7 million. The price per common share of Leslie Fay common fell from $12 to $5.25 in March 1993, following announcement of the fraud. Leslie Fay's independent auditors were from the firm of BDO Seidman of New York. Arthur Andersen, CPAs, was assigned the task of investigating the fraud.

By April 1993, Polishan had been dismissed—with no reason given for the termination—and a former partner of Arthur Andersen was named to replace him. Although the company filed for bankruptcy protection in 1993, management and the board of directors had no plans to liquidate. In fact, at this time the company was solvent with reported assets of $390 million and liabilities of $280 million.

Required:

a. Can you identify any "warning signs" in this case that might have alerted the auditors to the existence of fraud?

b. In your opinion were the BDO Seidman auditors negligent in not detecting the fraud prior to the end of 1992?

CASE III

Dell Computer Corporation

According to David Korus, senior vice-president and technology analyst at Kidder, Peabody & Co., Dell Computer Corporation lost millions of dollars speculating in foreign currency options and may have attempted to hide the losses, thereby overstating profits.[31] Dell makes, sells, and services personal computers and had grown rapidly since its founding in 1984 by then 19-year-old Michael Dell.

The currency transactions in question occurred mainly during the summer of 1992. Trades allegedly involved hundreds of transactions per week, totaling as much as $1 billion. Dell's treasurer, convinced that the company could make money by trading currency options, incurred $38 million in realized and unrealized losses by July 31, the end of the second quarter. The losses were particularly painful inasmuch as they were sustained during an intense price-cutting war among computer manufacturers.

The board of directors ordered management to end currency trading. A month later, James R. Daniel, chief financial officer of Dell and a strong proponent of the heavy currency trading, resigned for "personal" reasons.

Although Dell maintained that the transactions were strictly "hedging," a report in *Derivatives Strategy & Tactics*, a New York newsletter devoted to hedging issues, stated that "Dell was crossing the border between hedging and speculation all along." Bobby Inman, a Dell board member and chairman of the audit committee, asked Price Waterhouse, the company's auditors, to investigate as to whether the company had adhered to generally accepted accounting principles in its treatment of the currency losses. Price Waterhouse determined that the treatment was proper.[32]

---

30 *Business Week*, March 15, 1993.
31 *Business Week*, March 22, 1993.
32 *The Wall Street Journal*, November 30, 1992.

Korus hired bankers, accountants, and foreign currency analysts to assist in his investigation of Dell's foreign currency activity. He learned that Dell had sold currency option contracts worth $435 million as of February 2, 1992, the end of the fiscal year. This total was more than twice the amount ($200 million) of Dell's international sales for that year. Korus shared his concerns in a conference call with 200 brokers and institutional investors on November 20, 1992.

Dell's stock fell 10 percent following the news. Because the company had just announced record profits and was preparing to raise $150 million by selling 4 million shares of its common stock, its reaction to Korus's allegations was an angry rebuttal and a threat to sue Kidder Peabody. Management asserted that the firm was growing rapidly and that its hedging practices were in line with Dell's expected exposure to foreign currency fluctuations. They also maintained that the $435 million worth of sold options was offset by an equal amount in purchased options, and that the $38 million loss cited by Korus had shrunk to $1 million by year end. As to the allegations of improper accounting, Dell claimed that this issue never could be resolved completely. Price Waterhouse, as indicated previously, apparently agreed.

Dell even attempted to discredit David Korus, suggesting that he routinely took extreme positions in the companies he covered for his clients. The public relations manager at Dell said that Korus's clients "include(d) a lot of hedge funds who might not be displeased to see the (Dell) stock go down." (Hedge funds often engage in selling stock short in the belief that prices will fall. Short sales involve selling borrowed shares and later replacing them with shares purchased at the lower price.) Dell management even hinted that Korus's personal relationship with a New York hedge fund analyst somehow might have influenced his Dell story.[33]

Dell's stock did quickly recover from the news and had achieved new highs for the year within a couple of weeks following the adverse news.

Required:

a. How does one differentiate between hedging and speculation? How does the accounting treatment differ
   1. For quarterly reporting purposes?
   2. For annual financial reporting purposes?
   Document your answer by reference to appropriate accounting pronouncements.

b. 1. Assuming that Dell did *not* report losses from foreign currency transactions in its quarterly reports covering the year ended January 31, 1993, but did report the net effect of the transactions in its annual report for that year, was it in compliance with GAAP?
   2. What responsibility do the auditors have for determining whether the accounting treatment was correct?

c. Apart from the technical differences in accounting treatment for quarterly reporting purposes, are Dell's stockholders properly served when management engages in foreign currency speculation? What responsibility does the auditor have to inform the stockholders, given that the annual financial statements give no indication as to whether foreign currency gains or losses are from hedging or speculation?

33 Ibid.

part 4

Reporting the Results of the Audit

biltrite

Chapter 14 Audit Reports

chapter 14

biltrite

learning objectives

After reading this chapter, you should be able to

1 Describe the standard audit report and the conditions under which it is issued.
2 Differentiate among unqualified opinions, qualified opinions, adverse opinions, and disclaimers of opinion.
3 Distinguish between an explanatory paragraph and a qualified opinion.
4 Describe situations in which an explanatory paragraph might be included in the audit report.
5 Define and give examples of material scope limitations.
6 Define and give examples of departures from GAAP.
7 Define continuing auditor and describe the updating of audit reports.

OVERVIEW

The audit report is the culminating step in the audit process and expressing an audit opinion is the auditor's overriding goal. Figure 14.1 emphasizes the placement of the audit report at the end of the audit process. The audit report concisely describes the auditor's responsibility, the nature of the examination, and the auditor's findings. Chapter 14 begins by presenting the

FIGURE 14.1

The Audit Process

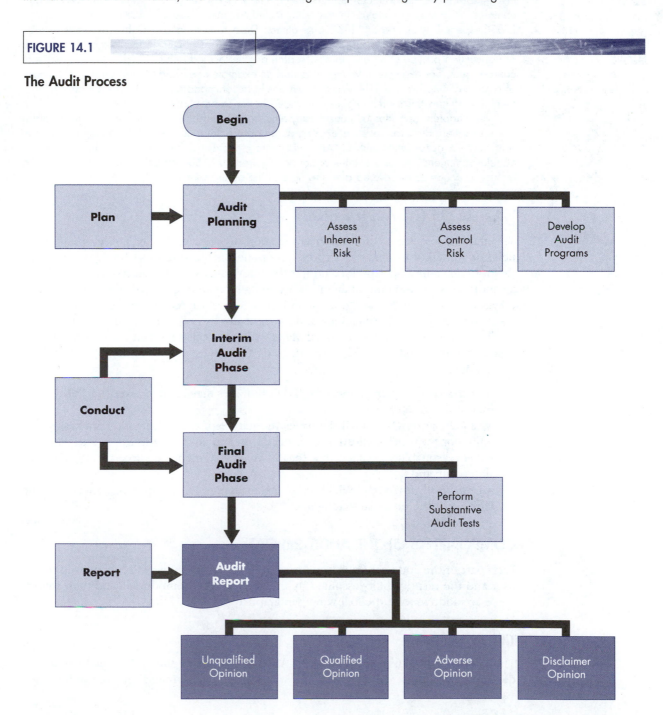

standard audit report and describing the conditions that justify its issuance. The discussion then turns to departures from the standard report in the form of qualified opinions, adverse opinions, and disclaimers of opinion. Explanatory paragraphs, as distinguished from qualified opinions, are also considered.

Many of the audit reports included as exhibits in this chapter were taken from the SEC EDGAR database. EDGAR can be accessed at http://www.sec.gov/edaux/searches.htm, and contains all company filings with the SEC, including annual reports (10K), quarterly reports (10Q), special events reports (8K), and others. Data regarding a specific company can be found by accessing this database and entering the company's name. To locate a particular type of transaction or type of report, an SEC search engine located at http://www.tenkwizard.com can be used. For example, if you want to find an example of an audit report qualified because of a scope limitation, the 10K Wizard can easily accommodate the task. An Internet assignment that utilizes this search engine is included in the end-of-chapter materials.

The chapter concludes by considering other topics that affect audit reports. These topics are subsequent discovery of facts existing at the date of the audit report, the meaning of "present fairly in accordance with GAAP," other information in documents containing audited financial statements, supplemental information required by FASB, related-party transactions, and omitted procedures discovered after the date of the audit report.

.com

http://www.sec.gov/
edaux/searches.htm

.com

http://
www.tenkwizard.com

NATURE OF THE AUDIT REPORT

The audit report is the culmination of the audit process. Gathering and evaluating sufficient competent evidence to express an opinion is the auditor's overriding goal, and the opinion cannot be expressed until the auditor has assessed audit risk and completed all audit tests. In addition, an audit report containing an unqualified opinion cannot be released to stockholders and others until the client has agreed to reflect the necessary audit adjustments, reclassifications, and footnote disclosures in the financial statements.

Exhibit 14.1 illustrates an actual **standard audit report** for Sun Microsystems, Inc. This is the standard form specified by the AICPA, and is composed of the following three paragraphs:

1. An *introductory paragraph*, which differentiates management's responsibility from that of the auditor;
2. A *scope paragraph*, which describes the nature of the examination, including any limitations on the application of procedures, and acknowledges that an audit provides reasonable assurance that the financial statements are free of material misstatement; and
3. An *opinion paragraph*, which contains an expression of opinion concerning the fairness of the financial statements.

COMPONENTS OF THE AUDIT REPORT

Each part of the audit report is significant in terms of the information conveyed to the user and the responsibility assumed by the auditor. The components and their importance are addressed in the following paragraphs.

Title

The audit report must contain a title. Also, except when the auditor lacks independence, the title must include the word *independent*, to distinguish it from other kinds

EXHIBIT 14.1

Standard Audit Report

INDEPENDENT AUDITORS' REPORT

To the Board of Directors and Stockholders
Sun Microsystems, Inc.

We have audited the accompanying consolidated balance sheet of Sun Microsystems, Inc., as of June 30, 1999 and 1998, and the related consolidated statements of income, stockholders' equity, and cash flows for each of the three years in the period ended June 30, 1999. These financial statements are the responsibility of the Company's management. Our responsibility is to express an opinion on these financial statements based on our audits.

We conducted our audits in accordance with generally accepted auditing standards. Those standards require that we plan and perform the audit to obtain reasonable assurance about whether the financial statements are free of material misstatement. An audit includes examining, on a test basis, evidence supporting the amounts and disclosures in the financial statements. An audit also includes assessing the accounting principles used and significant estimates made by management, as well as evaluating the overall financial statement presentation. We believe that our audits provide a reasonable basis for our opinion.

In our opinion, the financial statements referred to above present fairly, in all material respects, the consolidated financial position of Sun Microsystems, Inc., at June 30, 1999 and 1998, and the consolidated results of their operations and their cash flows for each of the three years in the period ended June 30, 1999, in conformity with generally accepted accounting principles.

ERNST & YOUNG LLP
Palo Alto, California

July 21, 1999

Source: SEC EDGAR database.

of reports rendered by CPAs.[1] Inclusion of the word *independent* also emphasizes the auditor's objectivity.

Addressee

The audit report may be addressed to the company, the stockholders, the board of directors, or some combination of these. If the auditor is appointed by the stockholders at the annual meeting, the report should be addressed to them.

Introductory Paragraph

The **introductory paragraph** identifies the financial statements covered by the audit report and clearly differentiates management's responsibility for preparing the financial statements from the auditor's responsibility for expressing an opinion on them. Management's responsibility is direct, whereas the auditor has an indirect responsibility for exercising due care in conducting the audit and expressing an opinion on the financial statements.

1   *AICPA Professional Standards*, New York: AICPA, section AU 508.

Scope Paragraph

The **scope paragraph** describes what the auditor did. Specifically, it states whether or not the audit was conducted in accordance with generally accepted auditing standards (GAAS). It also states the GAAS requirement that an audit be planned to provide reasonable assurance that the financial statements are free of material misstatement. Material scope restrictions should be identified in the scope paragraph and described further in a fourth paragraph, between the scope and opinion paragraphs, of the audit report. These matters are discussed more fully below.

Opinion Paragraph

The **opinion paragraph** conveys the auditor's findings. If, in the auditor's opinion, the financial statements are presented fairly in accordance with GAAP, the standard opinion paragraph (unqualified opinion) should be rendered. Material departures from GAAP, including inadequate footnote disclosure, should prompt the auditor to depart from the standard wording. The departures may require a qualified or adverse opinion.

Signature and Date

The report should be signed by the auditor and usually is dated as of the close of audit field work. The date is significant, because it represents the time limit on the auditor's responsibility for locating Type I and Type II subsequent events.[2] The auditor does not have responsibility to make any inquiries or to conduct any audit procedures after this date.

If a material event that occurred after this date, but prior to issuance of the audit report, comes to the auditor's attention *and* requires footnote disclosure, the auditor may elect to dual-date the audit report. The two relevant dates in a **dual-dated audit report** are the date of completion of audit field work and the date of the subsequent event.[3] Exhibit 14.2 illustrates a dual-dated audit report. The September 28 subsequent event referred to an investment in the company by General Electric Company that enabled Advanced Lighting Technology to liquidate certain short-term liabilities. In exchange GE received warrants to purchase Advanced Lighting Stock. The details of the acquisition were fully described in Note U, to which reference was made in the dual-dating line of the audit report. In the case of a dual-dated audit report, the auditor's liability for events subsequent to the close of audit field work is limited to the single event covered by the later date.

KINDS OF AUDIT OPINIONS

Upon completion of the audit field work, the auditor must decide whether an opinion can be rendered. If an opinion cannot be rendered, the auditor must clearly disclaim an opinion and give the reasons for the disclaimer. If an opinion can be rendered, the auditor must decide whether to issue an unqualified, qualified, or adverse opinion. These alternatives are discussed in the following paragraphs.

2   See Chapter 13 for a description of Type I and Type II subsequent events.
3   *AICPA Professional Standards,* op. cit., section AU 530.05.

EXHIBIT 14.2

Dual-Dated Report

INDEPENDENT AUDITORS' REPORT

To the Board of Directors and Shareholders
Advanced Lighting Technologies, Inc.

We have audited the accompanying consolidated balance sheet of Advanced Lighting Technologies, Inc., as of June 30, 1999, and the related consolidated statements of operations, shareholders' equity, and cash flows for the year then ended. These financial statements are the responsibility of the Company's management. Our responsibility is to express an opinion on these financial statements based on our audit.

We conducted our audits in accordance with generally accepted auditing standards. Those standards require that we plan and perform the audit to obtain reasonable assurance about whether the financial statements are free of material misstatement. An audit includes examining, on a test basis, evidence supporting the amounts and disclosures in the financial statements. An audit also includes assessing the accounting principles used and significant estimates made by management, as well as evaluating the overall financial statement presentation. We believe that our audit provides a reasonable basis for our opinion.

In our opinion, the financial statements referred to above present fairly, in all material respects, the consolidated financial position of Advanced Lighting Technologies, Inc., as of June 30, 1999, and the consolidated results of its operations and its cash flows for the year then ended, in conformity with generally accepted accounting principles.

GRANT THORNTON LLP
Cleveland, Ohio

September 24, 1999
(except for note U, as to which the date is September 28, 1999)

Source: SEC EDGAR database.

Unqualified Opinion

Exhibit 14.1 contains an **unqualified opinion**. For the auditor to issue an unqualified audit opinion, the following conditions must exist:

1. No material scope restrictions, client-imposed or otherwise, have prevented the auditor from collecting sufficient, competent evidence; and
2. The financial statements, including footnote disclosures, contain no material departures from GAAP.

An unqualified audit opinion expresses the auditor's belief that the financial statements are presented fairly in conformity with GAAP. The words *presented fairly* mean free from material misstatement. The phrase *in conformity with GAAP* means that fairness has been evaluated within the framework of generally accepted accounting principles.[4] Section AU 411 of the AICPA Professional Standards provides further guidance as to preferred sources of GAAP, by ranking them in the following order:

I. Established Accounting Principles:
    A. FASB Statements and Interpretations, APB Opinions, GASB (Governmental Accounting Standards Board) Statements and Interpretations, and AICPA Accounting Research Bulletins;

---

4 Ibid, section AU 411.03.

B. FASB and GASB Technical Bulletins, AICPA Industry Audit and Accounting Guides, and AICPA Statements of Position;

C. Consensus positions of FASB and GASB Emerging Issues Task Forces and AICPA Practice Bulletins; and

D. AICPA Accounting Interpretations, "Qs and As" published by FASB and GASB staffs, as well as industry practices widely recognized and prevalent.

II. Other Accounting Literature:

A. FASB and GASB Concepts Statements;

B. APB Statements;

C. AICPA Issues Papers;

D. International Accounting Standards Committee Statements;

E. Pronouncements of other professional associations or regulatory agencies;

F. AICPA Technical Practice Aids; and

G. Accounting textbooks, handbooks, and articles.[5]

Audit judgment determines which accounting principles should be used in any situation. In exercising judgment, the auditor must be satisfied that the principles selected have general acceptance, that they are appropriate in the circumstances, that the financial statement components are properly classified, that disclosure is adequate, and that the economic substance of all material transactions and events has been reflected in the statements.[6]

In terms of audit risk, an unqualified opinion means that the auditor was able to manage detection risk effectively, given the assessed levels of inherent risk and control risk. That is, the auditor gathered sufficient, competent evidence to express an unqualified opinion at that level of confidence complementing the overall audit risk level required by the auditor. In addition, the evidence supported management's assertions and, if applicable, management agreed to the auditor's recommended modifications in the form of audit adjustments, reclassifications, and/or footnote disclosures.

Qualified and Adverse Opinions

Whenever financial statements contain a material departure from GAAP or a material scope restriction, the auditor must, at the very least, render a **qualified audit opinion**. For a departure from GAAP, the auditor must decide whether to render an unqualified opinion, a qualified opinion, or an adverse opinion. Materiality is the criterion used in deciding among these alternatives. Materiality is judged according to whether the departure might significantly affect the business decisions of the various users of the financial statements. A departure that does *not* result in a material distortion of the financial statements does *not* warrant a qualification of the auditor's opinion.

Qualified and adverse opinions require a fourth paragraph more fully describing the reason for the opinion modification. The auditor places this **explanatory paragraph between the scope and opinion paragraphs** of the audit report (see Exhibit 14.3). Departures from GAAP may result from the application of an accounting principle that is at variance with the one prescribed by the body designated by the AICPA to formu-

---

5 Ibid, section AU 411.16.

6 Some auditors believe that technical compliance with GAAP falls short of "fairness" and would evaluate fairness beyond the framework outlined above. For an excellent discussion of this controversial topic, see Kirk, Donald and Arthur Siegel, "How Directors and Auditors Can Improve Corporate Governance," *The Journal of Accountancy*, January 1996, pp. 53–57.

EXHIBIT 14.3

Qualified Opinion: Departure from GAAP

INDEPENDENT AUDITORS' REPORT

To the Board of Directors
GulfWest Oil Company

We have audited the accompanying consolidated balance sheets of GulfWest Oil Company (a Texas Corporation) as of December 31, 1996 and 1995, and the related consolidated statements of operations, stockholders' equity, and cash flows for the years then ended. These consolidated financial statements are the responsibility of the Company's management. Our responsibility is to express an opinion on these financial statements based on our audits.

We conducted our audits in accordance with generally accepted auditing standards. Those standards require that we plan and perform the audit to obtain reasonable assurance about whether the financial statements are free of material misstatement. An audit includes examining, on a test basis, evidence supporting the amounts and disclosures in the financial statements. An audit also includes assessing the accounting principles used and significant estimates made by management, as well as evaluating the overall financial statement presentation. We believe that our audits provide a reasonable basis for our opinion.

The Company's financial statements do not disclose pro forma results of operations for the years ended December 31, 1996 and 1995, relating to certain significant business acquisitions in 1996, as further described in Note 3 to the consolidated financial statements. In our opinion, disclosure of this information is required to conform with generally accepted accounting principles.

In our opinion, except for the omission of the information discussed in the previous paragraph, the consolidated financial statements referred to above present fairly, in all material respects, the consolidated financial position of GulfWest Oil Company at December 31, 1996 and 1995, and the consolidated results of their operations and their cash flows for the years then ended in conformity with generally accepted accounting principles.

WEAVER & TIDWELL, LLP
Dallas, Texas

April 19, 1997

Source: SEC EDGAR database.

late accounting principles—for example, a departure from a statement issued by the Financial Accounting Standards Board—or from inadequate footnote disclosure. Exhibit 14.3 illustrates an opinion qualified because the client failed to include pro forma financial data relating to acquisitions of other companies.

Failure to disclose adequately the circumstances related to material uncertainties is another condition warranting qualification of the auditor's opinion. In some instances, management cannot reasonably estimate the outcome of future events that may affect the financial statements. These are termed **uncertainties**. They may or may not be considered material. Examples of uncertainties are pending lawsuits, for which legal counsel cannot predict the outcome; IRS audits in progress; and the violation of one or more restrictive covenants contained in loan agreements, which could result in a demand by the lender for immediate payment of principal and accrued interest. If the resulting losses from these contingencies could be material, they should be described in appropriate footnotes to the financial statements. The absence of such footnote disclosure constitutes a departure from GAAP, and the auditor must qualify the opinion accordingly.

An **adverse opinion** is issued whenever financial statements contain departures from GAAP that are too material to warrant only a qualification. Omission of all footnotes, for example, ordinarily require an adverse audit opinion. In rendering an adverse opinion, the auditor states that the financial statements *do not present fairly* financial position, results of operations, and cash flows in conformity with GAAP. An adverse opinion is the subject of much graver user concern than is a qualified opinion and, hence, is seldom issued in practice. Exhibit 14.4 illustrates an adverse opinion resulting from a material departure from GAAP.

EXHIBIT 14.4

Adverse Opinion

INDEPENDENT AUDITORS' REPORT

To the Stockholders and Directors
ABC Company

We have audited the accompanying balance sheet of ABC Company as of December 31, 20XX, and the related statements of income, retained earnings, and cash flows for the year then ended. These financial statements are the responsibility of the Company's management. Our responsibility is to express an opinion on these financial statements based on our audit.

We conducted our audit in accordance with generally accepted auditing standards. Those standards require that we plan and perform the audit to obtain reasonable assurance about whether the financial statements are free of material misstatement. An audit includes examining, on a test basis, evidence supporting the amounts and disclosures in the financial statements. An audit also includes assessing the accounting principles used and significant estimates made by management, as well as evaluating the overall financial statement presentation. We believe that our audit provides a reasonable basis for our opinion.

As discussed in Note X to the financial statements, the company carries its property, plant, and equipment accounts at appraisal values, and provides depreciation on the basis of such values. Further, the company does not provide for income taxes with respect to temporary differences between financial income and taxable income arising because of the use, for income tax purposes, of the installment method of reporting gross profit from certain types of sales. Generally accepted accounting principles require that property, plant, and equipment be stated at an amount not in excess of cost, reduced by depreciation based on such amount, and that deferred income taxes be provided. Because of the departures from generally accepted accounting principles identified above, as of December 31, 20XX, inventories have been increased $_____ by inclusion in manufacturing overhead of depreciation in excess of that based on cost; property, plant, and equipment, less accumulated depreciation, is carried at $_____ in excess of an amount based on the cost to the Company; and allocated income tax of $_____ has not been recorded, resulting in an increase of $_____ in retained earnings and in appraisal surplus of $_____. For the year ended December 31, 20XX, cost of goods sold has been increased $_____ because of the effects of the depreciation accounting referred to above and deferred income taxes of $_____ have not been provided, resulting in an increase in net income and earnings per share of $_____ and $_____, respectively.

In our opinion, because of the effects of the matters discussed in the preceding paragraph, the financial statements referred to above do not present fairly, in conformity with generally accepted accounting principles, the financial position of ABC Company as of December 31, 20XX, or the results of its operations and cash flows for the year then ended.

(Signature)

(Date)

Source: *AICPA Professional Standards*, section AU 508.60.

The third standard of reporting states that informative disclosures in the financial statements are to be regarded as adequate unless otherwise stated in the audit report. When disclosure is inadequate, the auditor should provide the needed information in the audit report, if practicable. The opinion still should be qualified or adverse, because the information is not disclosed in the financial statements or footnotes. In addition to omitted or misrepresented footnotes, inadequate disclosure also may assume the form of omitted financial statements. Failure to include the statement of cash flows, for example, results in inadequate disclosure, and should lead to a qualified audit opinion.

Qualified Opinions and Disclaimers of Opinion

Given material scope restrictions, the independent auditor should either qualify or disclaim an opinion. A **disclaimer of opinion** means that the auditor is unable to express an opinion on the financial statements. A **scope restriction** means that the auditor has not gathered sufficient competent evidential matter to support an audit opinion.

Client-imposed scope restrictions may exist. For example, management may not permit the auditors to examine securities purportedly held as investments, or management may prohibit the auditors from confirming accounts receivable. Other scope restrictions may be circumstantially imposed. For example, the auditors may be unable to observe the taking of the physical inventory because they were engaged by the client after year end, or the client's outside legal counsel may be unable or unwilling to respond to a letter of audit inquiry.

In the event of material client-imposed scope restrictions, the auditor ordinarily should disclaim an opinion on the financial statements.[7] Client-imposed restrictions, whether one or more, cast a negative reflection on the overall reliability of management's assertions contained in the financial statements. The resulting increase in inherent risk is usually sufficient to preclude the rendering of an audit opinion.

For nonclient-imposed scope limitations, the auditor may or may not be able to obtain the necessary evidence by means of alternate auditing procedures. In an audit of the Drug Enforcement Administration, for example, KPMG Peat Marwick stated that they were unable to satisfy themselves as to the fair presentation of (several) transactions and balances, and therefore could not form an opinion as to whether the agency's books were accurate.[8] If the auditor is able to obtain satisfaction by other means, the audit report should not be modified. If the auditor cannot obtain satisfaction by other means, either a qualified opinion or a disclaimer is in order, depending on the materiality of the limitations.

Exhibit 14.5 illustrates an actual qualification of opinion related to a material scope restriction that was *not* client imposed. In this instance, the auditors were unable to obtain information pertaining to future cash flows relating to oil and gas properties. Also, the auditors were unable to determine the client's share of revenues and expenses from a partnership investment.

Exhibit 14.6 illustrates the proper wording for a disclaimer of opinion resulting from a scope restriction, combined with uncertainty as to the ability of the client to continue as a going concern. The scope restriction occurred because the auditors could not obtain written representations from outside legal counsel regarding pending or

7   *AICPA Professional Standards*, op. cit., section AU 508.24.
8   "Audit rips anti-drug agency's accounting," *The Blade*, Toledo, Ohio, July 15, 1998.

EXHIBIT 14.5

Qualified Opinion: Scope Limitation

INDEPENDENT AUDITOR'S REPORT

To the Board of Directors and Stockholders
Mountains West Exploration, Inc.

We have audited the accompanying balance sheet of Mountains West Exploration, Inc., (a New Mexico corporation) (MWEX) as of December 31, 1996, and the related statements of operations, stockholders' equity, and cash flows for the years ended December 31, 1996 and 1995. These financial statements are the responsibility of MWEX's management. Our responsibility is to express an opinion on these financial statements based on our audits.

Except as discussed in the following paragraphs, we conducted our audits in accordance with generally accepted auditing standards. Those standards require that we plan and perform the audit to obtain reasonable assurance about whether the financial statements are free of material misstatement. An audit includes examining, on a test basis, evidence supporting the amounts and disclosures in the financial statements. An audit also includes assessing the accounting principles used and significant estimates made by management, as well as evaluating the overall financial statement presentation. We believe that our audits provide a reasonable basis for our opinion.

We were unable to obtain information pertaining to the discounted future net cash flows relating to MWEX's interest in an oil and gas property as described in Note 3 to the financial statements; nor were we able to satisfy ourselves as to the carrying value of the oil and gas property by other auditing procedures.

We were also unable to determine MWEX's portion of revenues and expenses of the partnership investment described in Note 10; therefore, no revenues and expenses are recorded in the statement of operations for this investment for the year ended December 31, 1996, and the investment recorded on the balance sheet as of December 31, 1996, has not been adjusted for MWEX's portion of the revenues and expenses of the partnership.

In our opinion, except for the effects of such adjustments, if any, as might have been determined to be necessary had we been able to examine the evidence regarding the discounted future net cash flows and carrying value of an oil and gas property and had the financial information necessary to determine MWEX's portion of the revenues and expenses of the partnership investment been available to properly record this investment, the financial statements referred to above present fairly, in all material respects, the financial position of Mountains West Exploration, Inc., as of December 31, 1996, and the results of its operations and its cash flows for the years ended December 31, 1996 and 1995, in conformity with generally accepted accounting principles.

ERICKSON ALLEN, P.C.
Albuquerque, New Mexico

March 4, 1997

Source: SEC EDGAR database.

threatened litigation; nor could the auditors obtain written confirmation of certain related-party transactions, notes receivable, and notes payable.[9]

In addition to scope restriction disclaimers, CPAs also issue disclaimers of opinion when associated with financial statements of clients for whom audits were not performed. As discussed more fully in Chapter 15, accounting services such as compilations and reviews result in unaudited financial statements. To clearly convey to users that the statements are unaudited, the CPA attaches a disclaimer of opinion.

9 This disclaimer also covers uncertainty regarding the ability of the entity to continue as a going concern. This type of uncertainty is discussed in a later section of the chapter.

EXHIBIT 14.6

Disclaimer of Opinion: Scope Restriction Combined with Uncertainty

INDEPENDENT AUDITORS' REPORT

To the Board of Directors and Stockholders
Lafayette Industries, Inc.
New York, New York

We were engaged to audit the accompanying consolidated balance sheet of Lafayette Industries, Inc., and its subsidiaries as of December 31, 1996, and the related consolidated statements of operations, shareholders' deficit, and cash flows for each of the two years in the period ended December 31, 1996. These consolidated financial statements are the responsibility of the Company's management.

We were unable to obtain written representations from certain of the Company's outside legal counsel regarding pending or threatened litigation, or obtain confirmation regarding certain related-party transactions. In addition, we were not able to confirm the existence of certain notes receivable and payable. The Company's records do not permit the application of other auditing procedures to determine the existence and/or completeness of the aforementioned assets and liabilities.

The accompanying consolidated financial statements have been prepared assuming that the Company will continue as a going concern. As discussed in Notes 3, 12, and 22 to the financial statements, the Company has suffered recurring losses since its inception, has an accumulated deficit of $6.5 million, has a total shareholders' deficit of $6.9 million, is in default on substantially all of its debt, and is party to various litigation, including but not limited to financial guarantees. These conditions raise substantial doubt about the Company's ability to continue as a going concern. Management's plans in regard to these matters are also described in Note 3. The outcome of these events and management's plans are subject to substantial uncertainty. The financial statements do not include any adjustment that might result from the outcome of these uncertainties.

Because of the significance of the matters described in the preceding paragraph, and the scope limitations described in the second paragraph, and our inability to apply other auditing procedures to satisfy ourselves regarding the fair presentation of the consolidated financial statements in conformity with generally accepted accounting principles, the scope of our work was not sufficient to enable us to express, and we do not express, an opinion on the consolidated financial statements referred to in the first paragraph.

MOORE STEPHENS, P.C.
Certified Public Accountants
Cranford, New Jersey

April 9, 1997

Source: SEC EDGAR database.

Table 14.1 and Figure 14.2 summarize this discussion in terms of the conditions under which each type of audit report is rendered. The nature of the condition (i.e., scope restriction versus departure from GAAP) and the auditor's judgment as to materiality of the condition's impact on lending and investment decisions are the key ingredients in deciding among the alternatives.

If an entity is required to file quarterly and annual reports with the SEC, financial statements on which the opinion is modified for either client-imposed scope restrictions or GAAP violations (including inadequate disclosure) are unacceptable. Under either of these conditions, the entity is in violation of the securities laws and subject to fines and penalties. Moreover, if its securities are traded publicly on one of the exchanges, trading is likely to be halted.

TABLE 14.1

Types of Audit Reports

	Type of Audit Report			
Conditions	Unqualified	Qualified	Adverse	Disclaimer
Scope limitation:				
Not material	X			
Material		X		
Very material				X
Departure from GAAP:				
Not material	X			
Material		X		
Very material			X	

DIVIDED RESPONSIBILITY

If a client has one or more subsidiaries that are included in the consolidated financial statements, other CPAs frequently are retained to audit the subsidiaries. Under these circumstances, the principal auditor must decide whether to accept full responsibility for the audit or to divide responsibility. A **principal auditor** is one who has examined the major portion of the combined entity. For example, assume Company A has a relatively small subsidiary, Company B. Assume also that Company A is audited by Auditor I and Company B is audited by Auditor II. Under these circumstances, Auditor I is the principal auditor. In some instances, identifying the principal auditor is not so easy, but consideration of more nebulous circumstances is outside the scope of this textbook. **Full responsibility** means that the principal auditor accepts responsibility for all work performed on the audit. Under **divided responsibility**, the principal auditors are responsible for the components of the group they themselves audit, and the other auditors are responsible for the subsidiaries that they audit.[10] If responsibility is divided, the audit report must identify the division clearly.

The principal auditor may decide to accept full responsibility if the other auditors are associated or correspondent firms or the portion examined by other auditors is not material to the overall financial statements. Regardless of whether the decision is to divide responsibility or to accept full responsibility, the principal auditor must obtain satisfaction concerning the other auditors' independence and professional reputation.[11] Additionally, if the decision is to accept full responsibility, the principal auditor should consider whether it will be necessary to visit the other auditors to discuss the audit and review the audit programs and workpapers of the other auditors.[12]

If the principal auditor decides to accept full responsibility, the wording of the audit report need not be modified. A decision to divide responsibility, on the other hand, requires that reference be made to the work of the other auditors in all three paragraphs of the audit report. Exhibit 14.7 represents an actual audit report that illustrates the

10 *AICPA Professional Standards*, op. cit., section AU 543.03.
11 Ibid, section AU 543.10.
12 Ibid, section AU 543.12.

FIGURE 14.2

Audit Reporting Decision Analysis

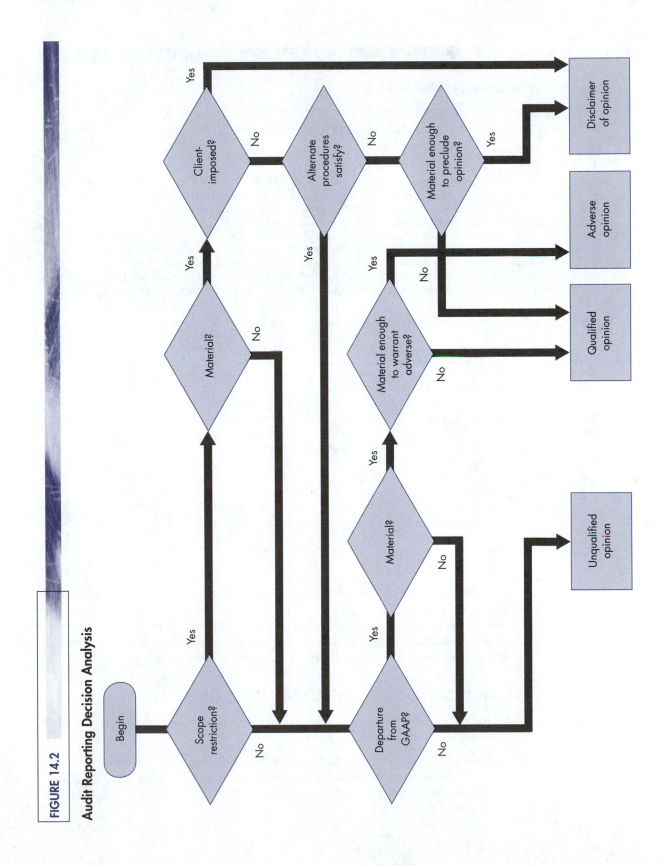

EXHIBIT 14.7

Opinion Based in Part on Report of Other Auditors

INDEPENDENT AUDITORS' REPORT

To the Board of Directors and Shareholders
ALPNET, Inc., and Subsidiaries

We have audited the accompanying consolidated balance sheets of ALPNET, Inc., and subsidiaries as of December 31, 1998 and 1997, and the related consolidated statements of operations, shareholders' equity, and cash flows for each of the three years in the period ended December 31, 1998. These financial statements are the responsibility of the Company's management. Our responsibility is to express an opinion on these financial statements based on our audits. We did not audit the financial statements of ALPNET Canada Inc., a subsidiary of ALPNET, Inc., which statements reflect total assets constituting 19 percent as of December 31, 1998, and 13 percent as of December 31, 1997, and total revenues constituting 18 percent in 1998, 15 percent in 1997, and 14 percent in 1996 of the related consolidated totals. Those statements were audited by other auditors whose report has been furnished to us, and our opinion, insofar as it relates to data included for ALPNET Canada Inc., is based solely on the report of the other auditors.

We conducted our audit in accordance with generally accepted auditing standards. Those standards require that we plan and perform the audit to obtain reasonable assurance about whether the financial statements are free of material misstatement. An audit includes examining, on a test basis, evidence supporting the amounts and disclosures in the financial statements. An audit also includes assessing the accounting principles used and significant estimates made by management, as well as evaluating the overall financial statement presentation. We believe that our audits and the report of other auditors provide a reasonable basis for our opinion.

In our opinion, based on our audits and the report of other auditors, the financial statements referred to above present fairly, in all material respects, the consolidated financial position of ALPNET, Inc., and subsidiaries at December 31, 1998 and 1997, and the consolidated results of their operations and their cash flows for each of the three years in the period ended December 31, 1998, in conformity with generally accepted accounting principles.

ERNST & YOUNG LLP
Salt Lake City, Utah

March 5, 1999

Source: SEC EDGAR database.

proper wording for divided responsibility. Note that the magnitude of the statements audited by the other auditors, expressed as a percentage of total assets and revenues, is set forth in the introductory paragraph, and that the division of responsibility does *not* constitute a qualification of the auditor's opinion. The report should not be viewed as inferior to a report that does not contain a reference to other auditors.

EXPLANATORY PARAGRAPH: UNQUALIFIED OPINION

Under the following conditions, an auditor may depart from the standard audit report wording without qualifying the opinion:

1. Departure from principle promulgated by body designated by Council;
2. Ability of entity to continue as a going concern;
3. Change in accounting principle; or
4. Emphasis of a matter.

Any of these departures normally assumes the form of an **explanatory paragraph following the opinion paragraph**. This is in contrast to the explanatory paragraph placed between the scope and opinion paragraphs and describing a qualified or adverse opinion. The conditions giving rise to an explanatory paragraph following the opinion paragraph are discussed in the following sections.

Departure from a Designated Principle

The first condition under which an audit report modification is accompanied by an unqualified opinion is an agreed-upon **departure from a designated principle**—that is, a principle promulgated by the body designated by Council of the AICPA. Although fairness of financial presentation is to be judged within the framework of GAAP,[13] the auditor occasionally may discover an appropriate departure from a prescribed Statement of Financial Accounting Standards, Accounting Principles Board Opinion, or Accounting Research Bulletin. The auditor may agree with the departure if it can be demonstrated that application of the prescribed standard would cause the financial statements to be materially misleading. Rule 203 of the Rules of Conduct states that

> *A member shall not (1) express an opinion or state affirmatively that the financial statements or other financial data of any entity are presented in conformity with generally accepted accounting principles or (2) state that he or she is not aware of any material modifications that should be made to such statements or data in order for them to be in conformity with generally accepted accounting principles, if such statements or data contain any departure from an accounting principle promulgated by bodies designated by Council to establish such principles that has a material effect on the statements or data taken as a whole. If, however, the statements or data contain such a departure and the member can demonstrate that due to unusual circumstances the financial statements or data would otherwise have been misleading, the member can comply with the rule by describing the departure, its approximate effects, if practicable, and the reasons why compliance with the principle would result in misleading statements.*[14]

If the auditor agrees with a material departure, the audit report must be modified accordingly. Exhibit 14.8 contains the proper report wording for an *auditor-agreed* departure from a designated principle. Note how the added paragraph both describes and justifies the departure. If the financial statement effects of the departure can be determined readily, they also should be disclosed in the explanatory paragraph. The resulting opinion, however, is unqualified.

Ability of Entity to Continue as a Going Concern

The following is an excerpt from an article appearing in a recent issue of *The Blade*, a Toledo, Ohio, newspaper:

> *Ohio Art Co.'s auditors have questioned the company's future in a new government-required financial report submitted by the firm. The report reveals that the*

13 Ibid, section AU 411.03.
14 Ibid, section ET 203.01.

EXHIBIT 14.8

Departure from a Designated Principle

INDEPENDENT AUDITORS' REPORT

To the Board of Directors and Stockholders
U.S. Healthmart, Inc.

We have audited the accompanying consolidated balance sheets of U.S. Healthmart, Inc., and consolidated subsidiaries as of December 31, 1997 and 1996, and the related consolidated statements of income, retained earnings, and cash flows for the years then ended. These financial statements are the responsibility of the Company's management. Our responsibility is to express an opinion on these financial statements based on our audits.

We conducted our audits in accordance with generally accepted auditing standards. Those standards require that we plan and perform the audit to obtain reasonable assurance about whether the financial statements are free of material misstatement. An audit includes examining, on a test basis, evidence supporting the amounts and disclosures in the financial statements. An audit also includes assessing the accounting principles used and significant estimates made by management, as well as evaluating the overall financial statement presentation. We believe that our audits provide a reasonable basis for our opinion.

In our opinion, the financial statements referred to above present fairly, in all material respects, the consolidated financial position of U.S. Healthmart, Inc., and consolidated subsidiaries as of December 31, 1997 and 1996, and the results of its operations and its cash flows for the years then ended in conformity with generally accepted accounting principles.

As explained in Note 9, the corporation's health spa subsidiaries have changed their method of recording revenues from the recognition of revenue at the time of sale to the recognition of revenue over the membership term and have applied this change retroactively in their financial statements. Accounting Principles Board (APB) Opinion Number 20, "Accounting Changes," provides that such a change be made by including, as an element of net earnings during the year of change, the cumulative effect of the change on prior years. Had APB Opinion Number 20 been followed literally, the cumulative effect of the accounting change would have been included as a charge in the 1997 statement of income. Because of the magnitude and pervasiveness of this change, we believe a literal application of APB Opinion Number 20 would result in a misleading presentation, and that this change should therefore be made on a retroactive basis. Accordingly, the accompanying consolidated financial statements for 1996 have been restated.

(Signature)

(Date)

maker of Etch A Sketch and other toys defaulted on a loan by a chief lender in the spring.

The company's recurring operating losses and limited working capital "raise substantial doubt about the company's ability to continue as a going concern," reads the statement by Ernst & Young accounting firm in the filing.[15]

Under GAAS, the auditor has a responsibility to evaluate whether there is substantial doubt about a client's **ability to continue as a going concern** for a reasonable period of time, not to exceed one year beyond the date of the financial statements being audited.[16] Section AU 341 also provides guidance concerning whether substantial doubt

15 "Ohio Art filing sheds light on firm's finances," *The Blade*, Toledo, Ohio, September 8, 1999.
16 *AICPA Professional Standards*, op. cit., section AU 341.

exists. The auditor's consideration of the client as a going concern ordinarily relates to the ability of the client to meet its continuing obligations as they come due. If the client can meet these obligations only by disposing of substantial portions of its assets or restructuring of its debt, going concern ability would appear to be seriously impaired. Examples of conditions and events raising doubt in the auditor's mind are the following:

1. Negative trends, such as recurring operating losses;
2. Defaults on loans or similar agreements;
3. Internal matters, such as work stoppages; and
4. External matters, such as legal proceedings, legislation, or similar matters that might impair the client's ability to operate.

Careful analysis of a client's cash flows can also provide useful information as to going concern ability.[17] Weakening ratios or negative cash flows, notwithstanding continuing earnings, should raise going concern doubts in the auditor's mind.

The auditor's evaluation is based on the aggregate results of all audit procedures performed during the planning and performance of the audit. In resolving doubt about these conditions, the auditor should obtain information concerning management's plans to deal with the conditions giving rise to uncertainty. These plans may include the following:

1. Plans to dispose of assets;
2. Plans to borrow money or restructure debt;
3. Plans to reduce or delay expenditures; or
4. Plans to increase ownership equity.

If doubt remains, an explanatory paragraph may have to be added, following the opinion paragraph in the audit report. The words *substantial doubt about the ability of the entity to continue as a going concern* must be used in the explanatory paragraph.[18] Exhibit 14.9 contains an actual audit report in which an explanatory paragraph is used to describe doubt as to going concern.

If doubt about the ability of an entity to continue as a going concern is so great as to call into question whether assets should be valued at going concern or liquidation values, the auditor may elect to disclaim an opinion due to uncertainty. During the 1980s, a number of savings and loan associations, faced with risky investments following deregulation, experienced capital declines below statutory minimums. Under these circumstances, auditors were compelled to disclaim opinions. Exhibit 14.10 contains an audit report that illustrates this type of disclaimer.

Change in Accounting Principle

The auditor's standard report implies that accounting principles have been applied consistently during or between periods. A material change in accounting principles or method of application between periods represents an **inconsistency** that the auditor must describe in an explanatory paragraph of the audit report. A change in accounting principle may assume any of the following forms:

1. Change in accounting principle;

17 For an excellent approach to cash flow analysis for going concern purposes, see Mills, John R. and Jeanne H. Yamamura, "The Power of Cash Flow Ratios," *The Journal of Accountancy*, October, 1998, pp. 53–61.
18 *AICPA Professional Standards*, op. cit., section AU 341.12.

EXHIBIT 14.9

Doubt as to Going Concern Ability Cited in Independent Auditors' Report

INDEPENDENT AUDITORS' REPORT

To the Board of Directors and Stockholders
The Maxim Group, Inc.

We have audited the accompanying consolidated balance sheets of The Maxim Group, Inc., (a Delaware corporation) and subsidiaries as of January 31, 1999 and 1998, and the related consolidated statements of operations, stockholders' equity, and cash flows for each of the three years in the period ended January 31, 1999. These financial statements are the responsibility of the Company's management. Our responsibility is to express an opinion on these financial statements based on our audits.

We conducted our audits in accordance with generally accepted auditing standards. Those standards require that we plan and perform the audit to obtain reasonable assurance about whether the financial statements are free of material misstatement. An audit includes examining, on a test basis, evidence supporting the amounts and disclosures in the financial statements. An audit also includes assessing the accounting principles used and significant estimates made by management, as well as evaluating the overall financial statement presentation. We believe that our audits provide a reasonable basis for our opinion.

In our opinion, the financial statements referred to above present fairly, in all material respects, the financial position of The Maxim Group, Inc., and subsidiaries as of January 31, 1999 and 1998, and the results of their operations and their cash flows for each of the three years in the period ended January 31, 1999, in conformity with generally accepted accounting principles.

The accompanying financial statements have been prepared assuming that the Company will continue as a going concern. As discussed in Note 1 to the financial statements, the Company is not in compliance with a certain restricted payment covenant contained in the indenture which references the Company's $100 million Senior Subordinated Notes due October 2007 (the "Senior Notes") and, as a result, the trustee or the holders of not less than 25 percent of the Senior Notes may declare all unpaid principal plus any accrued interest of all of the Senior Notes due and payable. The Company's available borrowings under its Senior Credit Facility plus cash on hand are not sufficient to repay the Senior Notes if declared due and payable. These matters raise substantial doubt about the Company's ability to continue as a going concern. Management's plans in regard to these matters are also described in Note 1. The financial statements do not include any adjustments relating to the recoverability and classification of asset carrying amounts or the amount and classification of liabilities that might result should the Company be unable to continue as a going concern.

ARTHUR ANDERSEN LLP
Atlanta, Georgia

October 11, 1999

Source: SEC EDGAR database.

2. Change in reporting entity;
3. Correction of an error in principle; or
4. Change in principle inseparable from change in estimate.[19]

A change in principle is material when the effect on comparability of the client's financial statements is significant.

The explanatory paragraph should identify the nature of the change and refer the reader to the footnote in the financial statements that discusses the change in detail.[20]

19 Ibid, section AU 420.06–12.
20 Ibid, section AU 508.16.

EXHIBIT 14.10

Disclaimer Due to Uncertainty Regarding Going Concern Ability

INDEPENDENT AUDITORS' REPORT

To the Board of Directors and Stockholders
National Micronetics, Inc.

We have audited the accompanying consolidated balance sheets of National Micronetics, Inc., and subsidiaries as of June 29, 1996, and June 24, 1995, and the related consolidated statements of operations, changes in stockholders' deficiency, and cash flows for each of the years in the three-year period ended June 29, 1996. These consolidated financial statements are the responsibility of the Company's management. Our responsibility is to express an opinion on these consolidated financial statements based on our audits.

We conducted our audits in accordance with generally accepted auditing standards. Those standards require that we plan and perform the audit to obtain reasonable assurance about whether the financial statements are free of material misstatement. An audit includes examining, on a test basis, evidence supporting the amounts and disclosures in the financial statements. An audit also includes assessing the accounting principles used and significant estimates made by management, as well as evaluating the overall financial statement presentation. We believe that our audits provide a reasonable basis for our opinion.

The accompanying consolidated financial statements have been prepared assuming that National Micronetics, Inc., and subsidiaries will continue as a going concern. The Company has suffered recurring losses from operations and has net capital deficiencies. As a result of these recurring losses, the Company has suffered a significant deterioration in liquidity. The Company has received funding for operations from its parent, Newmax Co., Ltd., and affiliated companies in the current and prior years; however, the Company has no guarantee that this funding will continue. These circumstances raise substantial doubt about the Company's ability to continue as a going concern. Management's plans in regard to these matters are described in Note 2. The consolidated financial statements do not include any adjustments that might result from the outcome of this uncertainty.

Because of the effects on the consolidated financial statements of such adjustments, if any, as might have been required had the outcome of the uncertainty discussed in the preceding paragraph been known, we are unable to, and do not, express an opinion on the accompanying consolidated financial statements as of June 29, 1996, and June 24, 1995, and for each of the years in the three-year period ended June 29, 1996.

KPMG PEAT MARWICK, LLP
Albany, New York

August 28, 1996

Source: SEC EDGAR database.

Exhibit 14.11 contains an audit report that illustrates the appropriate wording for a change in principle. If the change in principle is not properly accounted for or is inadequately disclosed, the auditor should consider issuing a qualified or adverse opinion.

Emphasis of a Matter

Although financial statements and the accompanying footnotes may be stated fairly, the auditor may still wish to bring a matter of importance to the reader's attention. Significant related-party transactions, or a subsequent event, for example, may be properly accounted for and adequately disclosed in a footnote to the financial statements. Yet, given the nature or magnitude of the transactions, the auditor may wish to direct the reader to the appropriate footnote to prevent possible oversight. **Emphasis of a matter**,

---

EXHIBIT 14.11

Change in Accounting Principle Cited in the Independent Auditors' Report

INDEPENDENT AUDITORS' REPORT

To the Board of Directors and Shareholders
Cendant Corporation

We have audited the accompanying consolidated balance sheets of Cendant Corporation and subsidiaries (the "Company") as of December 31, 1999 and 1998, and the related consolidated statements of operations, cash flows, and shareholders' equity for each of the three years in the period ended December 31, 1999. These consolidated financial statements are the responsibility of the Company's management. Our responsibility is to express an opinion on the consolidated financial statements based on our audits.

We conducted our audits in accordance with generally accepted auditing standards. Those standards require that we plan and perform the audit to obtain reasonable assurance about whether the financial statements are free of material misstatement. An audit includes examining, on a test basis, evidence supporting the amounts and disclosures in the financial statements. An audit also includes assessing the accounting principles used and significant estimates made by management, as well as evaluating the overall financial statement presentation. We believe that our audits provide a reasonable basis for our opinion.

In our opinion, the consolidated financial statements referred to above present fairly, in all material respects, the consolidated financial position of the Company at December 31, 1999 and 1998, and the consolidated results of its operations and its cash flows for each of the three years in the period ended December 31, 1999, in conformity with generally accepted accounting principles.

As discussed in Note 1 to the consolidated financial statements, effective January 1, 1997, the Company changed its method of recognizing revenue and membership solicitation costs for its individual membership business.

DELOITTE & TOUCHE LLP
New York, New York

February 28, 2000

Source: SEC EDGAR database.

as illustrated in the audit report in Exhibit 14.12, is achieved by adding an explanatory paragraph, following the opinion paragraph, to the audit report. Like the preceding examples, the report contains a departure from the standard wording, while the opinion remains unqualified.

The preceding paragraphs have addressed the most frequent causes for modifying the audit report or opinion. Table 14.2 summarizes the causes and the effects of each on the audit report. Figure 14.3 shows the proper placement of the explanatory paragraph. If the report contains a qualified or adverse opinion, or if the report disclaims an opinion, the explanatory paragraph follows the scope paragraph. If the paragraph is merely explanatory and the audit opinion is not qualified, the explanatory paragraph follows the opinion paragraph.

AUDITED STATEMENTS PREPARED ON A BASIS OTHER THAN GAAP

Some entities elect to prepare financial statements using an accounting basis not in conformity with generally accepted accounting principles. Regulatory bodies having jurisdiction over certain industries, for example, require that the financial statements be

---

EXHIBIT 14.12

Emphasis of a Matter in the Independent Auditors' Report

INDEPENDENT AUDITORS' REPORT

To the Board of Directors
Rite Aid Corporation

We have audited the accompanying consolidated balance sheets of Rite Aid Corporation and subsidiaries as of February 27, 1999, and February 28, 1998, and the related consolidated statements of income, stockholders' equity, and cash flows for each of the years in the three-year period ended February 27, 1999. These consolidated financial statements are the responsibility of the Company's management. Our responsibility is to express an opinion on these consolidated financial statements based on our audits.

We conducted our audits in accordance with generally accepted auditing standards. Those standards require that we plan and perform the audit to obtain reasonable assurance about whether the financial statements are free of material misstatement. An audit includes examining, on a test basis, evidence supporting the amounts and disclosures in the financial statements. An audit also includes assessing the accounting principles used and significant estimates made by management, as well as evaluating the overall financial statement presentation. We believe that our audits provide a reasonable basis for our opinion.

In our opinion, the consolidated financial statements referred to above present fairly, in all material respects, the financial position of Rite Aid Corporation and subsidiaries as of February 27, 1999, and February 28, 1998, and the results of operations and their cash flows for each of the years in the three-year period ended February 27, 1999, in conformity with generally accepted accounting principles.

As discussed in Note 2, the accompanying consolidated balance sheet as of February 28, 1998, and the consolidated statements of income, stockholders' equity, and cash flows for each of the years in the two-year period ended February 28, 1998, have been restated.

KPMG LLP
Harrisburg, Pennsylvania

May 28, 1999

Source: SEC EDGAR database.

---

prepared in accordance with rules they prescribe. Cable broadcasting companies regulated by the Federal Communications Commission and insurance companies regulated by state insurance commissions are two examples. Other examples, not involving specific industries, are financial statements prepared on a tax basis or on a cash basis.

This type of engagement is an audit in which fairness is evaluated within the framework of the "other basis," rather than GAAP. Tests of controls and substantive tests are performed as deemed necessary. Often referred to as a **special report**, an opinion is expressed as to whether the financial statements are fairly presented in accordance with the appropriate basis.

Exhibit 14.13 illustrates the recommended form of special report to be issued by the CPA for a client using a **comprehensive basis of accounting other than GAAP**. The following characteristics, which distinguish this report from the standard audit report, should be noted. First, in the introductory paragraph, the terms *balance sheet*, *income statement*, and *statement of retained earnings* are not used, inasmuch as these terms imply that the financial statements were prepared in accordance with GAAP. Instead, other titles that are more descriptive of the basis are used. Second, a

TABLE 14.2

Summary of Audit Report Modifications

	MODIFICATION					
Condition	Unqualified Opinion	Qualified Opinion	Adverse Opinion	Disclaimer of Opinion	Explanatory Paragraph Following Scope Paragraph	Explanatory Paragraph Following Opinion Paragraph
1. No material scope limitation	X					
2. No material departure from GAAP	X					
3. Material scope limitation		X		X	X	
4. Material departure from GAAP		X	X		X	
5. Divided responsibility	X					
6. Auditor agrees with departure from designated principle	X					X
7. Doubt as to going concern ability	X			X		X
8. Change in accounting principle	X					X
9. Emphasis of a matter	X					X

FIGURE 14.3

Placement of Fourth Paragraph of Audit Report

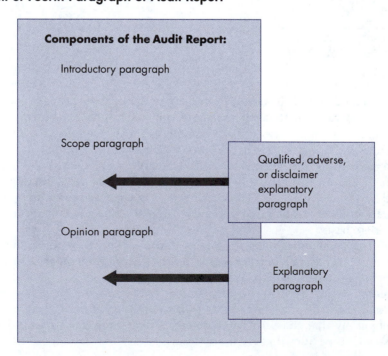

EXHIBIT 14.13

Report on a Comprehensive Basis of Accounting Other Than GAAP

INDEPENDENT AUDITORS' REPORT

The GMAC 1995—A Grantor Trust, its Certificate Holders, Capital Auto Receivables, Inc., and The First National Bank of Chicago, Trustee:

We have audited the accompanying Statement of Assets and Liabilities of the GMAC 1995—A Grantor Trust as of December 31, 1996 and 1995, and the related Statement of Distributable Income for the year ended December 31, 1996, and the period March 16, 1995, (inception) through December 31, 1995. These financial statements are the responsibility of the Trust's management. Our responsibility is to express an opinion on these financial statements based on our audit.

We conducted our audit in accordance with generally accepted auditing standards. Those standards require that we plan and perform the audit to obtain reasonable assurance about whether the financial statements are free of material misstatement. An audit includes examining, on a test basis, evidence supporting the amounts and disclosures in the financial statements. An audit also includes assessing the accounting principles used and significant estimates made by management, as well as evaluating the overall financial statement presentation. We believe that our audits provide a reasonable basis for our opinion.

As described in Note 1 to the financial statements, these financial statements are prepared on the basis of cash receipts and disbursements, which is a comprehensive basis of accounting other than generally accepted accounting principles.

In our opinion, such financial statements present fairly, in all material respects, the assets and liabilities of the GMAC 1995—A Grantor Trust at December 31, 1996 and 1995, and its distributable income and distributions for the year ended December 31, 1996, and the period March 16, 1995, (inception) through December 31, 1995, on the basis of accounting described in Note 1.

DELOITTE & TOUCHE, LLP
600 Renaissance Center
Detroit, Michigan 48243

March 3, 1997

Source: SEC EDGAR database.

paragraph referring the reader to the footnote that describes the basis other than GAAP is inserted between the scope and opinion paragraphs. Third, the opinion paragraph states whether the auditor believes the financial statements are fairly presented in accordance with the described basis. Finally, when the statements are prepared in accordance with the requirements of a regulatory body, a fifth paragraph that restricts the use of the financial statements to management, the board of directors, and the regulatory agency must be added.

OTHER TOPICS AFFECTING AUDIT REPORTS

Updating the Audit Report

When financial statements of the prior year are presented together with those of the current year, a continuing auditor should report on the statements of the prior year, as well as those of the current year. A **continuing auditor** is one who has audited the financial statements of the current period and one or more consecutive periods immediately prior to the current period.[21]

In this process, referred to as **updating the audit report**, the continuing auditor must decide whether to use the prior report in its same form or modify it. The most frequent reason for modification is the correction of a prior departure from GAAP. If a GAAP departure in previous financial statements has been corrected for inclusion in the current year's annual report, the auditor should change the qualified opinion of the prior year to an unqualified opinion when updating. Exhibit 14.14 illustrates an audit report that has been updated to reflect the resolution of a prior uncertainty regarding the ability of the client to continue as a going concern. The resolution enabled the auditors to issue an opinion to replace the prior disclaimer.

EXHIBIT 14.14

Updated Audit Report

INDEPENDENT AUDITORS' REPORT

To the Board of Directors and Stockholders
Marvel Enterprises, Inc.

We have audited the accompanying consolidated balance sheets of Marvel Enterprises, Inc., (formerly Toy Biz, Inc.) and subsidiaries (the "Company") as of December 31, 1997 and 1998, and the related consolidated statements of operations, stockholders' equity, and cash flows for each of the three years in the period ended December 31, 1998. These financial statements are the responsibility of the Company's management. Our responsibility is to express an opinion on these financial statements based on our audits.

We conducted our audits in accordance with generally accepted auditing standards. Those standards require that we plan and perform the audit to obtain reasonable assurance about whether the financial statements are free of material misstatement. An audit includes examining, on a test basis, evidence supporting the amounts and disclosures in the financial statements. An audit also includes assessing the accounting principles used and significant estimates made by management, as well as evaluating the overall financial statement presentation. We believe that our audits provide a reasonable basis for our opinion.

Since the date of completion of our audit of the accompanying financial statements and initial issuance of our report thereon dated February 5, 1999, which report contained an explanatory paragraph regarding the Company's ability to continue as a going concern, the Company, as discussed in Note 1, has completed the issuance of a $250 million notes offering and repaid all outstanding balances under its Bridge loan. Therefore, the conditions that raised substantial doubt about whether the Company will continue as a going concern no longer exist.

In our opinion, the financial statements referred to above present fairly, in all material respects, the consolidated financial position of Marvel Enterprises, Inc., and subsidiaries at December 31, 1997 and 1998, and the consolidated results of their operations and their cash flows for each of the three years in the period ended December 31, 1998, in conformity with generally accepted accounting principles.

ERNST & YOUNG LLP
New York, New York

February 5, 1999

Source: SEC EDGAR database.

21 Ibid, section AU 508.65.

In the event that a **predecessor auditor** examined the financial statements of the prior period, the predecessor auditor's report may or may not be included with the comparative statements. The predecessor auditor who agrees to the inclusion of the earlier report must consider whether the previously issued report is still appropriate. Reading the statements, comparing with the prior period, and obtaining a letter of representation from the successor auditor are means for determining the suitability of the prior report.

If the predecessor's report is *not* included, the successor auditor should include the following information in the introductory paragraph of the audit report:

1. That another auditor audited the prior-period financial statements;
2. The date of the predecessor's report;
3. The type of report issued by the predecessor auditor; and
4. If it was other than a standard report, the substantive reasons for this.[22]

Exhibit 14.15 contains an audit report that illustrates the proper wording when the predecessor auditor's report is not included.

Subsequent Discovery of Facts Existing at the Date of the Audit Report

After issuing the audit report, the auditors may become aware of information that might have affected the audit report had it been known at the time it was issued. This situation is called a **subsequent discovery of facts**. For example, assume that after the auditors have completed their field work and released the audit report, a team of management consulting services personnel from the same accounting firm is retained to develop a more effective system for processing customer billings and collections. While performing this engagement, the team discovers that a substantial portion of reported accounts receivable was fictitious. They immediately inform the audit team. The auditors determine that the impact of the fictitious receivables is to transform a reported income (audited) of $2 million into a loss of $1.6 million. The action that the firm should take, if any, and the responsibility to third parties are the subjects addressed in the following paragraphs.

The auditors first should ascertain whether the information is reliable and whether the facts existed at the date of the audit report. If reliability and existence are affirmed, the auditors, given the significance of financial statement impact, have a duty to inform third parties known to be relying on the audit report that such reliance is no longer appropriate. Requesting the client to disclose the newly discovered facts and their impact on the financial statements satisfies this duty.

If the client cooperates and the effects can be determined promptly, revised financial statements and a revised audit report should be issued. The reason for the revision should be described in a footnote to the financial statements and referred to in the auditor's report. If issuance of financial statements and the audit report for a subsequent period is imminent, revision can be made in such statements. If the effects cannot be determined promptly, the client should notify third persons known to be relying on the financial statements, instruct them not to so rely on them, and inform them that revised statements and an audit report are forthcoming.[23]

22 Ibid, section AU 508.74.
23 Ibid, section AU 561.01–06.

EXHIBIT 14.15

Predecessor Audit Report Not Included

INDEPENDENT AUDITORS' REPORT

To the Board of Directors
Texas Gas Transmission Corporation

We have audited the accompanying balance sheet of Texas Gas Transmission Corporation as of December 31, 1996 and 1995, and the related statements of income, retained earnings and paid-in capital, and cash flows for the year ended December 31, 1996, and the periods from January 1, 1995, to January 17, 1995, and from January 18, 1995, to December 31, 1995. These financial statements are the responsibility of the Company's management. Our responsibility is to express an opinion on these consolidated financial statements based on our audits. The statements of income, retained earnings and paid-in capital, and cash flows for the period ended December 31, 1994, were audited by other auditors whose report dated February 20, 1995, expressed an unqualified opinion on those statements.

We conducted our audits in accordance with generally accepted auditing standards. Those standards require that we plan and perform the audit to obtain reasonable assurance about whether the financial statements are free of material misstatement. An audit includes examining, on a test basis, evidence supporting the amounts and disclosures in the financial statements. An audit also includes assessing the accounting principles used and significant estimates made by management, as well as evaluating the overall financial statement presentation. We believe that our audits provide a reasonable basis for our opinion.

In our opinion, the financial statements referred to above present fairly, in all material respects, the consolidated financial position of Texas Gas Transmission Corporation at December 31, 1996 and 1995, and the results of its operations and its cash flows for the year ended December 31, 1996, and the periods from January 1, 1995, to January 17, 1995, and from January 18, 1995, to December 31, 1995, in conformity with generally accepted accounting principles.

ERNST & YOUNG, LLP
Tulsa, Oklahoma

February 7, 1997

Source: SEC EDGAR database.

If the client refuses to inform third parties, the auditor must notify each member of the board of directors and also perform the following steps:

1. Notify the client that the auditor's report no longer can be associated with the financial statements;
2. Notify regulatory agencies (e.g., the SEC and stock exchange) having jurisdiction over the client that the auditor's report no longer can be relied upon; and
3. Notify each person known by the auditor to be relying on the financial statements that the auditor's report no longer can be relied upon.[24]

If the client is publicly held, third-party notification by the auditor on an individual basis may not be possible. Under these circumstances, notifying the SEC and the appropriate stock exchange, and requesting that these agencies make appropriate third-party disclosure, usually satisfies the auditor's disclosure responsibility.

24 Ibid, section AU 561.08.

Other Information in Documents Containing Audited Financial Statements

In addition to the financial statements and footnotes, most annual reports contain other information of interest to the shareholders. The information may be contained in **management's discussion and analysis (MD&A)**, a supplemental letter from management in the annual report to shareholders. In the letter, management elaborates on the audited financial statements by explaining the more significant changes in financial statement components occurring during the year. Exhibit 14.16 illustrates a portion of Owens Corning's 1998 MD&A. The president's letter and the reports of divisional vice presidents are also sources of other information, some of which may consist of financial data (e.g., segment earnings, earnings per share, and long-term debt). In expressing an opinion on the financial statements, the auditor's responsibility does *not* extend beyond the financial information that he or she has identified in the audit report. The auditor, therefore, has no obligation to perform any procedures to corroborate the other information. The auditor should, however, read the information and consider whether material inconsistencies exist between the other data and the financial statements. When inconsistencies exist, the auditor must consider whether the financial statements, the audit report, or both require revision.[25]

Supplemental Information Required by FASB

In drafting financial accounting standards, the Financial Accounting Standards Board occasionally has included requirements calling for certain supplemental information to accompany the financial statements; for example, disclosures of mineral reserves and oil and gas reserves by companies in the extractive industries. Because FASB considers the information to be an essential part of the financial reporting of the entity, the auditor should apply certain limited procedures and should report deficiencies in or the omission of the information.[26] The limited procedures to be applied in reviewing such **supplemental information required by the FASB** consist of the following:

1. Inquire of management as to methods used in preparing the information;
2. Compare the supplemental information for consistency with management's responses, with the audited statements, and with other knowledge obtained during the audit;
3. Consider whether representations concerning supplementary data should be included in the client representation letter;
4. Apply other procedures specifically required by FASB; and
5. Make additional inquiries if these procedures lead the auditor to suspect that the information is not properly presented within the applicable guidelines.[27]

The auditor should *not* refer, in the audit report, to the supplemental information or the procedures applied except when the required information is omitted or in error or the auditor is unable to complete the prescribed procedures. Reference in the audit report, under these circumstances, should be made in an explanatory paragraph following the opinion paragraph. Because the audit opinion does *not* extend to the

25 Ibid, section AU 550.04.
26 Ibid, section AU 558.06.
27 Ibid, section AU 558.07.

EXHIBIT 14.16

Partial Management Discussion and Analysis

OWENS CORNING
MANAGEMENT DISCUSSION AND ANALYSIS

RESULTS OF OPERATIONS

Financial Statements
Years Ended December 31, 1998, 1997, and 1996

Sales and Profitability

Net sales for the year ended December 31, 1998, were $5.009 billion, reflecting a 15 percent increase from the 1997 level of $4.373 billion. Net sales in 1996 were $3.832 billion. The year-to-year increases are primarily due to the acquisitions of Fibreboard and AmeriMark, which were completed in the second and fourth quarters of 1997, respectively. Continued strength in U.S. residential roofing markets resulted in increased volume and price during 1998. Volume declines in North American and European residential insulation markets were partially offset by volume increases in mechanical and other insulation markets. Although average price levels for insulation products were lower in 1998 than 1997 when calculated on an annual basis, residential insulation price levels were higher in the fourth quarter of 1998 compared to the fourth quarter of 1997, indicating the benefits of the price increases implemented throughout 1998 and the establishment of an upward price trend which is expected to continue into 1999. This represents a reversal of the downward trend in insulation pricing experienced during 1997 and 1996. In the vinyl siding market, volume increases were largely offset by declines in pricing during 1998. Volume increases in North American composites markets during 1998, particularly during the fourth quarter, helped to offset price declines in European and Asian markets during the year. On a consolidated basis, there was virtually no impact of currency translation on sales in foreign currencies during 1998. Please see Note 1 to the Consolidated Financial Statements.

Sales outside the U.S. represented 20 percent of total sales for the year ended December 31, 1998, compared to 24 percent during 1997 and 25 percent during 1996. The decline in non-U.S. sales as a percentage of total sales in 1998 compared to 1997 and 1996 is due to the 1997 acquisitions of Fibreboard and AmeriMark, which are primarily U.S. operations, and volume declines in Europe during 1998. Gross margin for the year ended December 31, 1998, was 21 percent of net sales, compared to 20 percent and 26 percent in 1997 and 1996 respectively. The decline in gross margin as a percentage of sales in 1998 and 1997 compared to 1996 and prior years is largely attributable to the lower-margin businesses of the 1997 acquisitions. Cost of sales in 1998 includes a $65 million charge as part of the $243 million charge for restructuring and other actions described below. Gross margin during 1998 reflects the benefits of price improvements, cost reductions resulting from the Company's strategic restructuring program, and continuing productivity improvements across the Company's businesses. Cost of sales in 1997 includes a $38 million charge as part of the $143 million charge for restructuring and other actions described below.

For the year ended December 31,1998, the Company reported a net loss of $705 million or $13.16 per share, compared to net income of $47 million, or $.88 per share, for the year ended December 31, 1997, and a net loss of $284 million, or $5.54 per share, for the year ended December 31, 1996. Included in the 1998 net loss are a $1.415 billion pretax charge ($906 million after tax) for asbestos litigation claims, a $243 million pretax charge ($171 million after tax) for restructuring and other actions, and a $359 million pretax gain ($217 million after tax) from the sale of certain businesses. Net income in 1998 also reflects manufacturing and operating expense reductions of approximately $110 million on a pretax basis, resulting from the Company's strategic restructuring program. Cost of borrowed funds during 1998 was $140 million, $29 million higher than the 1997 level, due to higher levels of average debt, offset partially by a reduction in average interest rates during 1998. The reduction in equity in net income of affiliates for the year ended December 31, 1998, reflects the first quarter 1998 sale of the Company's 50 percent ownership interest in Alpha/Owens-Corning, LLC. As part of the Company's debt realignment strategy, the Company repurchased, via a tender offer, certain debt securities during the third quarter of 1998 and recorded an extraordinary loss of $39 million, or $.72 per share, net of related income taxes of $25 million. Please see Notes 2, 4, 5 and 22 to the Consolidated Financial Statements.

Source: SEC EDGAR database.

supplementary information, the opinion paragraph is not affected, and the fourth paragraph may be categorized as *emphasis of a matter*.[28]

Related-Party Transactions

Chapter 13 defined related-party transactions, gave examples, and considered the auditor's responsibility for locating and examining the transactions. Related-party transactions also have audit report implications. First, the auditor may choose to add an explanatory paragraph describing the related party and the related-party transactions and direct the reader's attention to the footnote that more fully explains the matter (refer to Exhibit 14.12). Second, if the transactions are not properly represented by management or disclosure is inadequate, the auditor must express a qualified or adverse opinion because of a departure from GAAP.[29] A less than arm's-length transaction represented by management as an arm's-length transaction, for example, would be considered misrepresentation and, if material, should lead to a modification of the audit opinion.

Omitted Procedures Discovered After the Date of the Audit Report

After release of the audit report, the auditor may discover that one or more auditing procedures, considered necessary at the date of the audit report, were omitted. CPA firms' internal inspection programs or peer review are the most frequent means for detecting **omitted procedures**.

The auditor should assess the importance of the omitted procedures in terms of support for the audit opinion. If the omitted procedures are necessary to support the opinion, and the auditor believes persons are still relying on the report, he or she should proceed as follows:

1. If the omitted procedures can be applied, they should be so applied. If they reveal facts that would have affected the audit opinion, the auditor should take those steps described in the section entitled "Subsequent Discovery of Facts Existing at the Date of the Audit Report."
2. If unable to apply omitted or alternate procedures, the auditor should consult an attorney to determine the appropriate course of action with regard to persons thought to be relying on the financial statements and audit report.[30]

KEY TERMS

Ability to continue as a going concern, 598
Adverse opinion, 590
Client-imposed scope restrictions, 591
Comprehensive basis of accounting other than GAAP, 603
Continuing auditor, 605

Departure from a designated principle, 597
Disclaimer of opinion, 591
Divided responsibility, 594
Dual-dated audit report, 586
Emphasis of a matter, 601
Explanatory paragraph between the scope and opinion paragraphs, 588

28 Ibid, section AU 558.08.
29 Ibid, section AU 334.12.
30 Ibid, section AU 390.05–07.

REVIEW QUESTIONS

1. Describe the components of the audit report.

2. Define *dual-dated audit reports*.

3. List the conditions necessary for an unqualified audit opinion.

4. Why might an auditor decide to disclaim an opinion?

5. Define *material scope restriction*. Must a material scope restriction always lead to a modification of the audit opinion?

6. Why is a client-imposed scope restriction considered more serious than other forms of scope restrictions?

7. Differentiate between an explanatory paragraph following the opinion paragraph of the audit report and a qualified opinion.

8. Under what circumstances might an explanatory paragraph follow the opinion paragraph of an audit report?

9. Define *principal auditor*.

10. What factors influence the auditor's decision to divide responsibility?

11. What purposes are served by a paragraph added between the scope and opinion paragraphs in the audit report?

12. What is meant by "updating the audit report"?

13. What circumstances require modification of a previously issued audit report?

14. What steps should the auditor take upon learning of information that may have existed at the date of the audit report, and that, if known to the auditor, would have affected the wording of the audit report?

15. Define *present fairly in accordance with GAAP*.

16. Under what circumstances might an auditor agree with a departure from a designated principle?

17. What responsibility does the auditor have for other information appearing in documents containing audited financial statements?

18. Does the audit opinion extend to the "other information"?

19. What action should the auditor take upon discovering, after release of the audit report, that certain auditing procedures were *not* performed?

20. Describe the auditor's responsibility relative to the ability of the client to continue as a going concern.

21. What steps should the auditor follow upon learning of a change in accounting principle?

22. Give an example of financial statements prepared on a comprehensive basis of accounting other than GAAP.

23. What type of report does the CPA render when a client's financial statements are prepared on a comprehensive basis of accounting other than GAAP?

MULTIPLE CHOICE QUESTIONS FROM PAST CPA EXAMS

1. An auditor's report on financial statements prepared in accordance with another comprehensive basis of accounting should include all of the following *except*
    a. An opinion as to whether the basis of accounting used is appropriate under the circumstances.
    b. An opinion as to whether the financial statements are presented fairly in conformity with the other comprehensive basis of accounting.
    c. Reference to the note to the financial statements that describes the basis of presentation.
    d. A statement that the basis of presentation is a comprehensive basis of accounting other than generally accepted accounting principles.

2. When reporting on financial statements prepared on the same basis of accounting used for income tax purposes, the auditor should include in the report a paragraph that
    a. Emphasizes that the financial statements are *not* intended to have been examined in accordance with generally accepted auditing standards.
    b. Refers to the authoritative pronouncements that explain the income tax basis of accounting being used.
    c. States that the income tax basis of accounting is a comprehensive basis of accounting other than generally accepted accounting principles.
    d. Justifies the use of the income tax basis of accounting.

3. The existence of audit risk is recognized by the statement in the auditor's standard report that the auditor
    a. Obtains reasonable assurance about whether the financial statements are free of material misstatement.
    b. Assesses the accounting principles used and also evaluates the overall financial statement presentation.
    c. Realizes some matters, either individually or in the aggregate, are important while other matters are *not* important.
    d. Is responsible for expressing an opinion on the financial statements that are the responsibility of management.

4. An auditor may reasonably issue a qualified opinion for a

	Scope limitation	Unjustified accounting change
a.	Yes	No
b.	No	Yes
c.	Yes	Yes
d.	No	No

5. Helpful Co., a nonprofit entity, prepared its financial statements on an accounting basis prescribed by a regulatory agency solely for filing with that agency. Green audited the financial statements in accordance with generally accepted auditing standards and concluded that the financial statements were fairly presented on the prescribed basis. Green should issue a
   a. Qualified opinion.
   b. Standard three paragraph report with reference to footnote disclosure.
   c. Disclaimer of opinion.
   d. Special report.

6. The following explanatory paragraph was included in an auditor's report to indicate a lack of consistency:

   "As discussed in Note T to the financial statements, the company changed its method of computing depreciation in 1996."

   How should the auditor report on this matter if the auditor concurred with the change?

Type of *opinion*	*Location of* *explanatory paragraph*
a. Unqualified	Before opinion paragraph
b. Unqualified	After opinion paragraph
c. Qualified	Before opinion paragraph
d. Qualified	After opinion paragraph

7. After issuing a report, an auditor has no obligation to make continuing inquiries or perform other procedures concerning the audited financial statements, unless
   a. Information, which existed at the report date and may affect the report, comes to the auditor's attention.
   b. Management of the entity requests the auditor to reissue the auditor's report.
   c. Information about an event that occurred after the end of fieldwork comes to the auditor's attention.
   d. Final determinations or resolutions are made of contingencies that had been disclosed in the financial statements.

8. An auditor was unable to obtain sufficient competent evidential matter concerning certain transactions due to an inadequacy in the entity's accounting records. The auditor would choose between issuing a(n)
   a. Qualified opinion and an unqualified opinion with an explanatory paragraph.
   b. Unqualified opinion with an explanatory paragraph and an adverse opinion.
   c. Adverse opinion and a disclaimer of opinion.
   d. Disclaimer of opinion and a qualified opinion.

9. For an entity's financial statements to be presented fairly in conformity with generally accepted accounting principles, the principles selected should
   a. Be applied on a basis consistent with those followed in the prior year.
   b. Be approved by the Auditing Standards Board or the appropriate industry subcommittee.
   c. Reflect transactions in a manner that presents the financial statements within a range of acceptable limits.
   d. Match the principles used by most other entities within the entity's particular industry.

10. In which of the following situations would a principal auditor *least* likely make reference to another auditor who audited a subsidiary of the entity?
    a. The other auditor was retained by the principal auditor and the work was performed under the principal auditor's guidance and control.

b. The principal auditor finds it impracticable to review the other auditor's work or otherwise be satisfied as to the other auditor's work.

c. The financial statements audited by the other auditor are material to the consolidated financial statements covered by the principal auditor's opinion.

d. The principal auditor is unable to be satisfied as to the independence and professional reputation of the other auditor.

11. An auditor issued an audit report that was dual-dated for a subsequent event occurring after the completion of field work but before issuance of the auditor's report. The auditor's responsibility for events occurring subsequent to the completion of field work was

a. Extended to subsequent events occurring through the date of issuance of the report.

b. Extended to include all events occurring since the completion of field work.

c. Limited to the specific event referenced.

d. Limited to include only events occurring up to the date of the last subsequent event referenced.

12. Which of the following phrases should be included in the opinion paragraph when an auditor expresses a qualified opinion?

	When read in conjunction with Note X	*With the foregoing explanation*
a.	Yes	No
b.	No	Yes
c.	Yes	Yes
d.	No	No

13. When an auditor expresses an adverse opinion, the opinion paragraph should include

a. The principal effects of the departure from generally accepted accounting principles.

b. A direct reference to a separate paragraph disclosing the basis for the opinion.

c. The substantive reasons for the financial statements being misleading.

d. A description of the uncertainty or scope limitation that prevents an unqualified opinion.

14. Hernandez, CPA, concludes that there is substantial doubt about JKL Co.'s ability to continue as a going concern. If JKL's financial statements adequately disclose its financial difficulties, Hernandez' auditor's report should

	Include an explanatory paragraph following the opinion paragraph	*Specifically use the words* **going concern**	*Specifically use the words* **substantial doubt**
a.	Yes	Yes	Yes
b.	Yes	Yes	No
c.	Yes	No	Yes
d.	No	Yes	Yes

15. An auditor concludes that there is substantial doubt about an entity's ability to continue as a going concern for a reasonable period of time. If the entity's disclosures concerning this matter are adequate, the audit report may include a(n)

	Disclaimer of opinion	*Qualified opinion*
a.	Yes	Yes
b.	No	No
c.	No	Yes
d.	Yes	No

16. In which of the following circumstances would an auditor most likely add an explanatory paragraph to the standard report while *not* affecting the auditor's unqualified opinion?
    a. The auditor is asked to report on the balance sheet, but not on the other basic financial statements.
    b. There is substantial doubt about the entity's ability to continue as a going concern.
    c. Management's estimates of the effects of future events are unreasonable.
    d. Certain transactions cannot be tested because of management's records retention policy.

17. Cheng, CPA, was engaged to audit the financial statements of Essex Co. after its fiscal year had ended. The timing of Cheng's appointment as auditor and the start of field work made confirmation of accounts receivable by direct communication with the debtors ineffective. However, Cheng applied other procedures and was satisfied as to the reasonableness of the account balances. Cheng's auditor's report most likely contained a(n)
    a. Unqualified opinion.
    b. Unqualified opinion with an explanatory paragraph.
    c. Qualified opinion due to a scope limitation.
    d. Qualified opinion due to a departure from generally accepted auditing standards.

18. Davis, CPA, believes there is substantial doubt about the ability of Hill Co. to continue as a going concern for a reasonable period of time. In evaluating Hill's plans for dealing with the adverse effects of future conditions and events, Davis most likely would consider, as a mitigating factor, Hill's plans to
    a. Accelerate research and development projects related to future products.
    b. Accumulate treasury stock at prices favorable to Hill's historic price range.
    c. Purchase equipment and production facilities currently being leased.
    d. Negotiate reductions in required dividends being paid on preferred stock.

19. A limitation on the scope of an audit sufficient to preclude an unqualified opinion will usually result when management
    a. Is unable to obtain audited financial statements supporting the entity's investment in a foreign subsidiary.
    b. Refuses to disclose in the notes to the financial statements related-party transactions authorized by the board of directors.
    c. Does not sign an engagement letter specifying the responsibilities of both the entity and the auditor.
    d. Fails to correct a reportable condition communicated to the audit committee after the prior year's audit.

20. Delta Life Insurance Co. prepares its financial statements on an accounting basis insurance companies use pursuant to the rules of a state insurance commission. If Wall, CPA, Delta's auditor, discovers that the statements are not suitably titled, Wall should
    a. Disclose any reservations in an explanatory paragraph and qualify the opinion.
    b. Apply to the state insurance commission for an advisory opinion.
    c. Issue a special statutory basis report that clearly disclaims any opinion.
    d. Explain in the notes to the financial statements the terminology used.

21. When disclaiming an opinion due to a client-imposed scope limitation, an auditor should indicate in a separate paragraph why the audit did not comply with generally accepted auditing standards. The auditor should also omit the

	Scope paragraph	Opinion paragraph
a.	No	Yes
b.	Yes	Yes
c.	No	No
d.	Yes	No

22. An auditor decides to issue a qualified opinion on an entity's financial statements because a major inadequacy in its computerized accounting records prevents the auditor from applying necessary procedures. The opinion paragraph of the auditor's report should state that the qualification pertains to
    a. A client-imposed scope limitation.
    b. A departure from generally accepted auditing standards.
    c. The possible effects on the financial statements.
    d. Inadequate disclosure of necessary information.

23. Several sources of GAAP consulted by an auditor are in conflict as to the application of an accounting principle. Which of the following should the auditor consider the most authoritative?
    a. FASB Technical Bulletins
    b. AICPA Accounting Interpretations
    c. FASB Statements of Financial Accounting Concepts
    d. AICPA Technical Practice Aids

24. Which of the following events occurring after the issuance of an auditor's report most likely would cause the auditor to make further inquiries about the previously issued financial statements?
    a. A technological development that could affect the entity's future ability to continue as a going concern.
    b. The discovery of information regarding a contingency that existed before the financial statements were issued.
    c. The entity's sale of a subsidiary that accounts for 30 percent of the entity's consolidated sales.
    d. The final resolution of a lawsuit explained in a separate paragraph of the auditor's report.

INTERNET ACTIVITIES

Go to http://www.tenkwizard.com. This is a search engine that includes SEC filings for more than 68,000 companies. By entering key words in accordance with the rules of the search engine, you can access financial reports of interest. Your assignment is to locate the following types of audit reports:

.com
http://
www.tenkwizard.com

1. Doubt as to ability to continue as a going concern;
2. Comprehensive basis of accounting other than GAAP;
3. Change in accounting principle;
4. Qualified opinion due to scope limitation;
5. Qualified opinion due to departure from GAAP; and
6. Explanatory paragraph emphasizing related-party transactions.

Be sure to read the instructions concerning how to word your search requests.

ESSAY QUESTIONS AND PROBLEMS

14.1   Items 1 through 7 present various independent factual situations an auditor might encounter in conducting an audit. List A represents the types of opinions the auditor ordinarily would issue and List B represents the report modification (if any) that would be necessary. For each situation, select one response from List A and one from List B. Select, as the *best* answer for each item, the action the auditor would normally take. The types of opinions in List A and the report modifications in List B may be selected once, more than once, or not at all.

Assume these conditions:

- The auditor is independent.
- The auditor previously expressed an unqualified opinion on the prior year's financial statements.
- Only single-year (not comparative) statements are presented for the current year.
- The conditions for an unqualified opinion exist, unless contradicted in the factual situations.
- The conditions stated in the factual situations are material.
- No report modifications are to be made *except* in response to the factual situation.

Example:
The following is an example of the manner in which the items should be answered.

Item: The financial statements present fairly, in all material respects, the financial position, results of operations, and cash flows in conformity with generally accepted accounting principles.

Answer: B, Q

Items to Be Answered:
1. In auditing the long-term investments account, an auditor is unable to obtain audited financial statements for an investee located in a foreign country. The auditor concludes that sufficient competent evidential matter regarding this investment cannot be obtained.
2. Due to recurring operating losses and working capital deficiencies, an auditor has substantial doubt about an entity's ability to continue as a going concern for a reasonable period of time. However, the financial statement disclosures concerning these matters are adequate.
3. A principal auditor decides to take responsibility for the work of another CPA who audited a wholly owned subsidiary of the entity and issued an unqualified opinion. The total assets and revenues of the subsidiary represent 17 and 18 percent, respectively, of the total assets and revenues of the entity being audited.
4. An entity issues financial statements that present financial position and results of operations but omits the related statement of cash flows. Management discloses in the notes to the financial statements that it does *not* believe the statement of cash flows to be a useful financial statement.
5. An entity changes its depreciation method for production equipment from the straight-line to a units-of-production method based on hours of utilization. The auditor concurs with the change, although it has a material effect on the comparability of the entity's financial statements.
6. An entity is a defendant in a lawsuit alleging infringement of certain patent rights. Management cannot reasonably estimate the ultimate outcome of the litigation. The au-

ditor believes there is a reasonable possibility of a significantly material loss, but management refuses to disclose the lawsuit in the notes to the financial statements.

7. An entity discloses in the notes to the financial statements certain lease obligations. The auditor believes that the failure to capitalize these leases is a departure from generally accepted accounting principles.

LIST A	**LIST B**
Types of Opinions	*Report Modifications*
A. A qualified opinion	H. Describe the circumstances in an explanatory paragraph preceding the opinion paragraph, without modifying the three standard paragraphs.
B. An unqualified opinion	
C. An adverse opinion	
D. A disclaimer of opinion	
E. Either a qualified opinion or an adverse opinion	I. Describe the circumstances in an explanatory paragraph following the opinion paragraph, without modifying the three standard paragraphs.
F. Either a disclaimer of opinion or a qualified opinion	
G. Either an adverse opinion or a disclaimer of opinion	J. Describe the circumstances in an explanatory paragraph preceding the opinion paragraph, and modify the opinion paragraph.

K. Describe the circumstances in an explanatory paragraph following the opinion paragraph, and modify the opinion paragraph.

L. Describe the circumstances in an explanatory paragraph preceding the opinion paragraph, and modify the scope and opinion paragraphs.

M. Describe the circumstances in an explanatory paragraph following the opinion paragraph, and modify the scope and opinion paragraphs.

N. Describe the circumstances within the scope paragraph without adding an explanatory paragraph.

O. Describe the circumstances within the opinion paragraph without adding an explanatory paragraph.

P. Describe the circumstances within the scope and opinion paragraphs without adding an explanatory paragraph.

Q. Issue the standard auditor's report without modification.

(AICPA adapted)

14.2   Media, Inc., engaged Thomas Blank to audit its financial statements for the year ended December 31, 2002. The financial statements of Media, Inc., for the year ended December 31, 2001, were audited by Shelley Clark, whose March 31, 2002, auditor's report expressed an unqualified opinion. This report of Clark is *not* presented with the 2002–2001 comparative financial statements.

Blank's workpapers contain the following information that does *not* appear in the footnotes to the 2002 financial statements as prepared by Media, Inc.

1. One director, appointed in 2002, was formerly a partner in Blank's accounting firm. Blank's firm provided financial consulting services to Media during 1996 and 1997, for which Media paid approximately $3,000 and $12,000, respectively.
2. The company refused to capitalize certain lease obligations for equipment acquired in 2002. Capitalization of the leases in conformity with generally accepted accounting principles would have increased assets and liabilities by $420,000 and $480,000, respectively; decreased retained earnings as of December 31, 2002, by $83,000; and decreased net income and earnings per share by $83,000 and $0.83, respectively, for the year then ended. Blank has concluded that the leases should have been capitalized.
3. During the year, Media changed its method of valuing inventory from the first-in first-out method to the last-in first-out method. This change was made because management believes LIFO more clearly reflects net income by providing a closer matching of current costs and current revenues. The change had the effect of reducing inventory at December 31, 2002, by $70,000 and net income and earnings per share by $40,000 and $0.40, respectively, for the year then ended. The effect of the change on prior years was immaterial; accordingly, there was no cumulative effect of the change. Blank firmly supports the company's position. After completion of the field work on February 28, 2003, Blank concludes that the expression of an adverse opinion is *not* warranted.

Required:
Prepare the body of Blank's report, dated February 28, 2003, and addressed to the board of directors, to accompany the 2002–2001 comparative financial statements. (AICPA adapted)

14.3   The following auditor's report was drafted by Bauman, a staff accountant of Rust & Seaman, CPAs, at the completion of the audit of the consolidated financial statements of Farber Co. for the year ended July 31, 2002. The report was submitted to the engagement partner, who reviewed the audit workpapers and properly concluded that an unqualified opinion should be issued. In drafting the report, Bauman considered the following:

1. Farber's consolidated financial statements for the year ended July 31, 2001, are to be presented for comparative purposes. Rust & Seaman previously audited these statements and appropriately rendered an unmodified report.
2. Farber has suffered recurring losses from operations and has adequately disclosed these losses and management's plans concerning the losses in a note to the consolidated financial statements. Although Farber has prepared the financial statements assuming it will continue as a going concern, Bauman has substantial doubt about Farber's ability to continue as a going concern.
3. Cellini & Long, CPAs, audited the financial statements of Barnett Services, Inc., a consolidated subsidiary of Farber, for the year ended July 31, 2002. The subsidiary's financial statements reflected total assets and revenues of 15 and 18 percent, respectively, of the consolidated totals. Cellini & Long expressed an unqualified opinion and furnished Bauman with a copy of the auditor's report. Cellini & Long also granted permission to present the report together with the principal auditor's report. Bauman decided *not* to present Cellini & Long's report with that of Rust & Seaman, but instead to make reference to the report of Cellini & Long.

Independent Auditor's Report

We have audited the consolidated balance sheets of Farber Co. and subsidiaries as of July 31, 2002 and 2001, and the related consolidated statements of income and retained earnings for the years then ended. Our responsibility is to express an opinion on these financial statements based on our audits. We did not audit the financial statements of Barnett Services, Inc., a wholly owned subsidiary. Those statements were audited by Cellini & Long, CPAs, whose report has been furnished to us, and our opinion, insofar as it relates to the amounts included for Barnett Services, Inc., is based solely on the report of Cellini & Long.

We conducted our audits in accordance with generally accepted auditing standards. Those standards require that we plan and perform the audit to obtain reasonable assurance about whether the financial statements are free of material misstatement. An audit includes assessing control risk, the accounting principles used, and significant estimates made by management, as well as evaluating the overall financial statement presentation. We believe that our audits provide a reasonable basis for our opinion.

In our opinion, based on our audits and the report of Cellini & Long, CPAs, the consolidated financial statements referred to above present fairly, in all material respects, except for the matter discussed below, the financial position of Farber Co. as of July 31, 2002 and 2001, and the results of its operations for the years then ended.

The accompanying consolidated financial statements have been prepared with the disclosure in Note 13 that the company has suffered recurring losses from operations. Management's plans in regard to those matters are also discussed in Note 13. The financial statements do not include any adjustments that might result from the outcome of this uncertainty.

Rust & Seaman, CPAs
November 4, 2002

Required:

Identify the deficiencies in the auditor's report as drafted by Bauman. Group the deficiencies by paragraph and in the order in which the deficiencies appear. Do *not* redraft the report. (AICPA adapted)

14.4   Consistent application of GAAP enhances comparability of financial statements. Auditors, therefore, must add an explanatory paragraph following the opinion paragraph of the audit report whenever GAAP are *not* consistently applied.

Required:
a. Identify the accounting changes that require a consistency explanation.
b. An unqualified opinion may be issued only if the auditor concurs with the change. Explain why.

14.5   The following auditor's report was drafted by a staff accountant of Light & Dark, CPAs, at the completion of the audit of the financial statements of Stone Computers, Inc., for the year ended March 31, 2002. It was submitted to the engagement partner, who reviewed matters thoroughly and properly concluded that Stone's disclosures concerning its ability to continue as a going concern for a reasonable period of time were adequate.

To the Board of Directors of Stone Computers, Inc.

We have audited the accompanying balance sheet of Stone Computers, Inc., as of March 31, 2002, and the other related financial statements for the year then ended. Our responsibility is to express an opinion on these financial statements based on our audit.

We conducted our audit in accordance with standards that require that we plan and perform the audit to obtain reasonable assurance about whether the financial statements are in conformity with generally accepted accounting principles. An audit includes examining, on a test basis, evidence supporting the amounts and disclosures in the financial statements. An audit also includes assessing the accounting principles used and significant estimates made by management.

The accompanying financial statements have been prepared assuming that the Company will continue as a going concern. As discussed in Note X to the financial statements, the Company has suffered recurring losses from operations and has a net capital deficiency that raises substantial doubt about its ability to continue as a going concern. We believe that management's plans in regard to these matters, which are also described in Note X, will permit the Company to continue as a going concern beyond a reasonable period of time. The financial statements do not include any adjustments that might result from the outcome of this uncertainty.

In our opinion, subject to the effects on the financial statements of such adjustments, if any, as might have been required had the outcome of the uncertainty referred to in the preceding paragraph been known, the financial statements referred to above present fairly, in all material respects, the financial position of Stone Computers, Inc., and the results of its operations and its cash flows in conformity with generally accepted accounting principles applied on a basis consistent with that of the preceding year.

Light & Dark, CPAs
April 28, 2002

Required:
Identify the deficiencies contained in the auditor's report as drafted by the staff accountant. Group the deficiencies by paragraph. Do *not* redraft the report. (AICPA adapted)

14.6   Audit reports frequently contain an explanatory paragraph following the scope paragraph or the opinion paragraph.

Required:
a. Describe the conditions under which one might expect to find an explanatory paragraph following the opinion paragraph of the audit report.
b. Describe the conditions under which an explanatory paragraph is mandatory.
c. Draft an explanatory paragraph for each of the following situations.
   1. Greg Grant, the chief executive officer of Ganges Brothers, Inc., hardware manufacturers, also owns a large plumbing supplies outlet, Ace Plumbing. Several material transactions have been completed between Ganges Brothers and Ace Plumbing, and a sizeable receivable from Ace Plumbing appears on Ganges' balance sheet. As auditor, you have concluded that the transactions have been properly reflected in the financial statements and adequately described in Note 4 to the financial statements.
   2. Jolly Amusements, Inc., an audit client, was sued by persons injured in the collapse of one of its amusement park rides. A jury found for the plaintiffs, and the damages awarded by the action raise doubt as to Jolly Amusements' ability to continue as a going concern. The financial statements properly reflect the damages as a nonrecurring loss on the income statement.

14.7   Because the audit report reflects the degree of responsibility assumed, the independent auditor must exercise caution in choosing the appropriate wording. The following report alternatives are available:

1. Unqualified opinion
2. Opinion qualified because of departure from GAAP
3. Opinion qualified for lack of evidence (scope restriction)

4. Disclaimer of opinion—scope restriction
5. Disclaimer of opinion—uncertainty
6. Adverse opinion
7. Explanatory paragraph following opinion paragraph:
   a. Doubt as to ability to continue as a going concern
   b. Emphasis of a matter
   c. Agreed-upon departure from accounting principle
   d. Change in accounting principle

Required:

For each of the following situations, indicate by number and letter the appropriate form of audit report. More than one choice may apply to a given situation. For example, an unqualified opinion followed by an explanatory paragraph for emphasis of a matter would be answered as 1, 7b.

A. The auditors were able to gather all of the evidence necessary to support an audit opinion; the financial statements contain no material departures from GAAP, but oil and gas reserve information required by FASB as supplemental information has been omitted.

B. The client refused to capitalize certain leases meeting one or more of the criteria that define capital leases. The auditors are also in doubt as to the recoverability of purchased patents, the cost of which are material in relation to the company's net assets.

C. The client refused the auditors' request to confirm trade accounts receivable. The unaudited balance in this account is significant in relation to total assets, and the auditors were unable to satisfy themselves by other means.

D. Certain subsidiary companies were audited by other independent CPAs. The principal auditors decided to divide responsibility.

E. A land development company decided to write up all of its assets from cost to current market value and recognize the appreciation as part of current income. Management believed that the increase in earnings would facilitate a public offering of the company's stock.

F. Although Company A is virtually insolvent, its financial statements are based on the going concern assumption. Given the gravity of the situation, the auditors do *not* believe that adding an explanatory paragraph is adequate in the circumstances.

G. During the year, Company B changed its method of inventory costing from FIFO to LIFO. Although proper accounting treatment was accorded the change, management refuses to include a footnote describing the change.

H. Although Company C permitted the auditors to confirm accounts receivable, the results of the confirmation process were disappointing. Only 20 percent of customers responded, and more than half of these were unable to confirm their outstanding balances. The auditors were unable to satisfy themselves by other means. In addition, Company C completed several significant transactions with related parties. Although the auditors determined that these transactions were recorded correctly and adequately disclosed in the financial statements, they wish to bring the existence of the transactions to the attention of the stockholders.

I. Company D debited significant amounts of leasehold improvements to repairs expense. The auditors determined that these expenditures should have been debited to asset accounts and amortized over the remaining term of the lease. Management refuses to accept the auditors' proposed adjustments. In addition, the company's liquidity position is so precarious that the auditors are not certain as to whether it will be able to meet its obligations in the short run.

J.   For many years Company G followed the practice of recognizing revenue at the point of sale. Given increasing uncertainty regarding collectibility, the company, with the auditors' approval, decided to change to the installment method of accounting for sales. Rather than recognizing the cumulative effect of the change as a component of current income, however, the company decided to debit the amount to beginning retained earnings and restate prior earnings to reflect the new method. The auditors agreed with this departure on the basis that, given the magnitude of accounts receivable at the date of change, the designated treatment would cause the financial statements to be materially misleading. Also, in conducting the current examination, the auditors were unable to obtain sufficient evidence to evaluate the reasonableness of the company's provision for inventory obsolescence.

K.   Company H changed its method of depreciation from straight line to the appraisal method for all of its property, plant, and equipment. Footnote 8 fully described the change and the effect on current earnings. Property, plant, and equipment comprise 60 percent of the company's total assets.

L.   Company X changed its method of determining inventory cost from specific identity to moving average. Footnote 6 fully described the change and its impact on current earnings.

M.   Company Y changed its method of accounting for postretirement benefits to conform to SFAS No. 106. In addition, the company has sustained significant losses over the past three years, raising doubts concerning short-term debt paying ability.

14.8   The CPA firm of Crest & Shield has audited the consolidated financial statements of Happy Corporation. Crest & Shield performed the audit of the parent company and all subsidiaries except for Toytown, Inc., which was audited by the CPA firm of Hope & Glory. Toytown constituted approximately 12 percent of the consolidated assets and 8 percent of the consolidated revenue.

Hope & Glory issued an unqualified opinion on the financial statements of Toytown. Crest & Shield will be issuing an unqualified opinion on the consolidated financial statements of Happy.

Required:

a.   What procedures should Crest & Shield consider performing with respect to Hope & Glory's examination of Toytown's financial statements that will be appropriate whether or not reference is to be made to the other auditors?

b.   Describe the various circumstances under which Crest & Shield could take responsibility for the work of Hope & Glory and make no reference to Hope & Glory's examination of Toytown in Crest & Shield's auditor's report on the consolidated financial statements of Happy.

(AICPA adapted)

14.9   The following auditor's report was drafted by Thomas, a staff accountant of Sinclair & Lewis, CPAs, at the completion of the audit of the financial statements of Cramer Industrial Cleaning, Inc., for the year ended September 30, 2002. The report was submitted to the engagement partner, who reviewed the audit workpapers and properly concluded that an unqualified opinion should be issued. In drafting the report, Thomas considered the following:

1.   During fiscal year 2002, Cramer changed its depreciation method. The engagement partner concurred with this change in accounting principle and its justification, and Thomas included an explanatory paragraph in the auditor's report.

2. The 2002 financial statements are affected by an uncertainty concerning a lawsuit, the outcome of which cannot presently be estimated. Thomas has included an explanatory paragraph in the auditor's report.

3. The financial statements for the year ended September 30, 2001, are to be presented for comparative purposes. Sinclair & Lewis previously audited these statements and expressed an unqualified opinion.

Independent Auditor's Report

To the Board of Directors of Cramer Industrial Cleaning, Inc.

We have audited the accompanying balance sheets of Cramer Industrial Cleaning Inc., as of September 30, 2002 and 2001, and the related statements of income and cash flows for the years then ended. These financial statements are the responsibility of the Company's management.

We conducted our audits in accordance with generally accepted auditing standards. Those standards require that we plan and perform the audit to obtain reasonable assurance about whether the financial statements are fairly presented. An audit includes examining, on a test basis, evidence supporting the amounts and disclosures in the financial statements. An audit also includes assessing significant estimates made by management, as well as evaluating the overall financial statement presentation. We believe that our audits provide a basis for determining whether any material modifications should be made to the accompanying financial statements.

As discussed in Note X to the financial statements, the company changed its method of computing depreciation in fiscal 2002.

In our opinion, except for the accounting change, with which we concur, the financial statements referred to above present fairly, in all material respects, the financial position of Cramer Industrial Cleaning as of September 30, 2002, and the results of its operations and its cash flows for the year then ended in conformity with generally accepted accounting principles.

As discussed in Note Y to the financial statements, the company is a defendant in a lawsuit alleging infringement of a machine cleaning process patent. The company has filed a counteraction, and preliminary hearings on both actions are in progress. Accordingly, any provision for liability is subject to adjudication of this matter.

Sinclair & Lewis, CPAs
November 5, 2002

Required:
Identify the deficiencies in the auditor's report as drafted by Thomas. Group the deficiencies by paragraph and in the order in which the deficiencies appear. Do *not* redraft the report. (AICPA adapted)

14.10 Jennifer Beal, CPA, is the continuing auditor for Christine's Fashions, Inc. The current year end is January 31, 2002. Last year's audit report contained an explanatory paragraph because of uncertainty regarding the ability of Christine's Fashions to continue as a going concern. The company had defaulted on two major loan agreements and appeared to be losing in the competition to introduce popular fashions. Since the date of last year's audit report, however, company management has changed. Significant new procurement and marketing strategies, which already have proven successful in the markets served by Christine's Fashions, have been developed. Creditors have agreed to major debt restructuring agreements, and the company appears to be "out of the woods."

Required:

Assuming the company presents comparative financial statements for 2001 and 2002, present the audit report. Remember, you are updating—*not* reproducing—last year's audit report.

14.11   On March 12, 2003, Chandy & Lear, CPAs, completed the audit engagement of the financial statements of Vixley Libraries for the year ended December 31, 2002. Vixley Libraries presents comparative financial statements on a modified cash basis. Assets, liabilities, fund balances, support, revenues, and expenses are recognized when cash is received or disbursed, except that Vixley includes a provision for depreciation of buildings and equipment. Chandy & Lear believes that Vixley's three financial statements, prepared in accordance with a comprehensive basis of accounting other than generally accepted accounting principles, are adequate for Vixley's needs and wishes to issue an auditor's special report on the financial statements. Chandy & Lear has gathered sufficient competent evidential matter in order to be satisfied that the financial statements are fairly presented according to the modified cash basis. Chandy & Lear audited Vixley's 2001 financial statements and issued the auditor's special report expressing an unqualified opinion.

Required:

Draft the auditors' report to accompany Vixley's comparative financial statements. (AICPA adapted)

14.12   In accordance with GAAP, Drako, Inc., a large audit client, discloses certain information regarding oil and gas reserves.

Required:

a. What procedures would you apply to the supplemental data required by the FASB pronouncement?
b. What effect would omitted or improperly presented information have on your audit report? On your audit opinion?
c. Draft the audit report assuming that Drako refuses to include the required supplemental information.

14.13   For each of the following situations, indicate the type of audit report to be issued and the reasons for your choice. Assume the amounts involved in each case are material.

• Martin, Inc., your audit client, is being sued in a product liability action. As of the audit report date, the outcome cannot be predicted with certainty. The probability for an unfavorable decision, however, has been estimated as reasonably possible.
• Gaylord, Ltd., an Australian mining company, has participated with Harken, Inc., your audit client, in a joint copper exploration venture. Jeremy Tunnel, the chairman of Harken, is also the principal stockholder of Gaylord. Several transactions, some of them material, have occurred between Gaylord and Harken for the year under examination. You are satisfied that all of the transactions have been properly reflected in the financial statements and adequately disclosed in footnotes.
• Crowe Construction, another audit client, is engaged in buying land, building shopping centers, and leasing space in the centers. In an effort to raise capital, the company has been selling certain of its properties and leasing them back. Because the selling prices have materially exceeded Crowe's cost to build and develop the properties, substantial profits have been recognized and reflected in the financial statements.
• On October 30, 2002, you were engaged to audit the financial statements of Spandley, Inc., a wholesale distributor of automotive parts and accessories. Spandley has *not* been

previously audited, and its fiscal year ends November 30, 2002. Spandley plans to take a complete physical inventory as of November 30, 2002, and agrees to provide you with all of the documentation in support of the November 30, 2001, physical inventory.

14.14 On July 23, 2002, Beaudry and Berschback, CPAs, completed the field work relating to the 2002 audit of Wellness Hospital, a 700-bed facility located in a large metropolitan area. Beaudry and Berschback also audited Wellness's fiscal 2001 financial statements. Wellness closes its books annually on June 30. In deciding on the appropriate form and wording for the audit report, Bruce Beaudry, the partner in charge of the audit, considered the following matters:

1. The hospital changed its method of accounting for Medicare reimbursements in 2002 and now recognizes reimbursements upon approval rather than when submitted. Both methods conform to GAAP and the hospital has agreed to the auditors' recommended accounting for the change, including appropriate footnote disclosure.
2. The hospital capitalized certain small-equipment expenditures in 2002 that, based on past practice and company policy, should have been expensed. Although the expenditures ($273,000) were material in relation to Wellness's financial position and operations, Beaudry did not feel that an adverse opinion was warranted.
3. According to Wellness's outside legal counsel, the hospital is a defendant in a $10 million lawsuit brought by the family of a patient who died while under the hospital's care. Although the ultimate outcome is uncertain, legal counsel is of the opinion that any resulting judgment will *not* materially affect Wellness's financial position or operations.
4. The audit report covering the fiscal 2001 financial statements was a standard three-paragraph unqualified report.

Required:
Draft an audit report covering the fiscal years ended June 30, 2001 and 2002.

DISCUSSION CASE

Cascade International

Cascade International, a women's clothing and cosmetics retailer, masked a $7 million loss as an $11 million profit for the year ended June 30, 1991. The fraud was perpetrated by fabricating revenues for nonexistent cosmetics sales. The company, controlled by Victor Incendy and his wife, Jeanette, went public in 1985 by merging Jean Cosmetics into Cascade Importers, an existing public shell company. This form of "going public" avoided both SEC scrutiny and heavy underwriting costs associated with initial public offerings. The company then proceeded to buy bankrupt women's clothing stores, such as Conston Corp., a chain of 226 stores selling clothes primarily to large women, as outlets for its cosmetics. Cascade also marketed Jean Cosmetics through independent retailers. Among the company's own outlets were J.B.'s Boutiques, Diana Shops, and Allison's Place.

With the retailing downturn of 1989, Cascade found its cosmetics revenues declining rapidly as many of the independent retailers dropped the Jean Cosmetics counters from their stores, and as the company's own outlets began losing money.

To keep investors happy, Victor Incendy allegedly fabricated cosmetics sales by claiming cosmetic counters that didn't exist. In 1991, for example, of the 255 counters and 17 stores represented by the company, only six counters and one store actually existed. At the same time, as a means for raising needed capital, Incendy issued unauthorized shares of Cascade International stock.

By July of 1992, Victor and Jeanette Incendy had disappeared, the stock was worthless, and the remaining counters and stores had been closed and were to be auctioned off. The company ultimately was liquidated and recovered approximately $2 million for its creditors, leaving them with sizeable losses. Investors also lost significant sums. Safeco Growth Fund, Inc., for example, a $155 million mutual fund, lost $2 million from its investment in Cascade stock. In November 1992, Robert Morgenthau, the district attorney for Manhatten, indicted Cascade and its management, charging that the company was a "criminal enterprise" engaged in defrauding investors and creditors.

The auditor for Cascade International, Bernard Levy, had prepared Victor Incendy's personal tax returns for years. Cascade maintained a private office for him at its Boca Raton headquarters and leased a private car for him. As for the audit, Victor Incendy told Levy not to worry about the Jean Cosmetics unit, inasmuch as that subsidiary was audited by other independent CPAs. (In fact, the Jean Cosmetics unit did not exist.) For the year ended June 30, 1991, Levy, as principal auditor, issued an unqualified opinion, covering the company's reported profit of $11.1 million. Cascade, in fact, had sustained a loss of $7.1 million for this period.

Required:

a. Can principal auditors be expected to detect frauds perpetrated at divisions or subsidiaries audited by other CPAs? What is the principal auditor's responsibility in cases such as the one described above?

b. Assuming that Levy actually audited Jean Cosmetics and that sales documents were fabricated, would he have detected the fraud? Based on generally accepted auditing standards, should he have detected the fraud?

c. Are independent auditors permitted, under the Professional Code of Conduct, to maintain offices provided by clients and to accept private cars from their clients?

part 5

Other Attestation and Assurance Services

biltrite

Other Assurance Services

chapter 15

biltrite

learning objectives

After reading this chapter, you should be able to

1 Define assurance services and differentiate among assurance, auditing, and attestation.

2 Differentiate among audits, compilations, and reviews in terms of procedures applied and assurance provided.

3 Identify the eleven attestation standards and contrast them with the ten auditing standards.

4 Give examples of other assurance services covered by the accounting and review standards, the auditing standards, and the attestation standards.

5 Describe the newer types of assurance services that will help define the future of the assurance function.

OVERVIEW

The AICPA Committee on Assurance Services has defined **assurance services** as "independent professional services that improve the quality of information, or its context, for decision makers."[1] This is a broader definition than auditing and attestation and therefore embraces these functions as well as other assurance services. In performing certain of these services, the independent CPA conducts an examination, which is similar in breadth and depth to an audit, and offers positive assurance at the conclusion of the examination. In other engagements, limited procedures are applied and the CPA offers only limited assurance. In yet other engagements, the CPA provides no assurance.

Some of the other assurance services performed by independent CPAs, such as agreed-upon procedures engagements and special reports, are covered by auditing standards. Other assurance service engagements, such as examinations of prospective financial statements and reports on internal control, are covered by attestation standards. Engagements relating to the financial statements of nonpublic entities are covered by accounting and review standards. Certain new types of assurance services not presently covered by existing AICPA standards include providing assurance regarding the integrity and security of electronic transactions and assessing the relevance and reliability of an entity's performance measures.

These other assurance services, both old and new, are the topic of this chapter and are considered in terms of the level of assurance associated with each type of engagement, necessary procedures, and reporting requirements.

The chapter begins by considering the changing nature of the assurance function and future assurance prospects. Assurance services, other than audits, covered by the auditing standards are then considered (e.g., letters for underwriters and review of interim financial information) and inasmuch as these services are typically extensions of audit engagements, they are covered under the auditing standards.

Compilations and reviews of financial statements for nonpublic entities are described next. These services are covered by the Statements on Standards for Accounting and Review Services, which cover most financial statement engagements performed for small clients not requiring audits. The standards clearly define and differentiate among the concepts of positive assurance, limited assurance, and no assurance as related to audits, compilations, and reviews. The standards also describe the procedures associated with each type of engagement; since these distinctions are applicable to many other types of assurance services, compilations and reviews are considered first.

Next, the eleven attestation standards are listed and compared with the auditing standards. Engagements covered by the attestation standards are briefly described; these engagements require some form of attestation, but the assertions being evaluated are outside the financial statements. A table summarizing all of the services covered by existing standards follows this section of the chapter. The chapter concludes by considering the newer types of assurance services not yet covered by any structured set of standards.

CHANGING NATURE OF THE ASSURANCE FUNCTION

Change has impacted the traditional financial statement audit in two ways. First, as companies have merged and pressures to reduce costs have intensified, CPA firms have experienced a significant decline in audit fees as a percentage of total revenue. Second, advances in information technology have rendered financial statements less useful to investment decisions than they were previously. Examples of these technological advances include public and proprietary databases accompanied by computer software permitting financial analysts broader and more timely access to data; technology

---

1 See *The Journal of Accountancy*, September 1996, p. 16.

permitting more frequent and timely financial reports, thereby rendering the annual printed financial statements less useful; and electronic data interchange (EDI) extending to capital providers (banks and investors) as well as to other suppliers. The form of linking capabilities provided by EDI permits the capital provider to assess cash needs and the repayment ability of investees.[2]

Given the constraints on the traditional financial statement audit, combined with the desire by information recipients for improvements in the quality of information, most accounting firms have expanded into other kinds of assurance services. Some of these are similar in approach to traditional auditing; others require more creative approaches to evaluating the relevance and reliability of information.

In light of the diverse nature of these other services, a critical component of the client acceptance decision is the understanding between the CPA and the client regarding the precise nature of the services to be rendered. Recent pronouncements of the Auditing Standards Board require that the understanding be documented in the working papers, preferably through a written communication with the client.[3]

In the future auditors may find themselves attesting to a much broader array of information, transcending the traditional financial statements and likely encompassing nonfinancial information such as company codes of ethics, customer satisfaction, product quality, and risk assessment.[4] The auditor's role may even extend to the interpretation of financial statements and the inclusion of qualitative information. To this end, in 1994, the AICPA appointed a special Committee on Assurance Services to address issues relating to forms of assurance and to develop a future framework for the attestation-assurance function.[5] The work of this committee is considered in the concluding paragraphs of this chapter.

OTHER ASSURANCE SERVICES COVERED BY THE AUDITING STANDARDS

In addition to financial statement audits, CPAs perform other services related to their clients' financial statements. These services are embraced by the auditing standards and are considered in the following paragraphs.

Agreed-Upon Procedures Applied to Specified Elements of the Financial Statements

In lieu of or in addition to an audit, a CPA may be asked to apply **agreed-upon procedures** to specified elements of the financial statements. For example, the CPA may be asked to apply agreed-upon procedures to the cash accounts as of a certain date, a schedule of accounts receivable of an entity, the amounts included in the caption "property and equipment," or the gross income component of the income statement. The application of the agreed-upon procedures *does not provide sufficient evidence to support either an opinion or limited assurance* on the specified elements.

---

2   For an excellent discussion of these issues confronting CPAs, see Elliot, Robert K., "Assurance Services and the Audit Heritage," *Auditing: A Journal of Practice & Theory*, American Accounting Association, Vol. 17, Supplement 1998.
3   See *AICPA Professional Standards*, sections AT 100 and AU 333, for a fuller discussion of this topic.
4   See AICPA Committee on Assurance Services, op. cit., *The Journal of Accountancy*, September 1996, p. 16.
5   Elliot, Robert K., "The Future of Assurance Services: Implications for Academia," op. cit. For reports issued by the Committee, the reader is referred to the following web site: http://www.aicpa.org/assurance/index.htm

The CPA may accept the engagement provided the conditions listed in Table 15.1 are met. The report issued at the culmination of the engagement should be in the form of procedures and findings. It should contain a clear disclaimer of opinion and should *not* include any form of assurance. Moreover, the report, given the unique nature of the engagement, should be restricted to the specified parties.[6] Exhibit 15.1 illustrates the appropriate wording for the CPA's report on the application of agreed-upon procedures to specified elements of the financial statements.

Letters for Underwriters: Comfort Letters

Publicly held companies are required by law to register new securities offerings with the Securities and Exchange Commission (SEC). A registration statement and prospectus must be completed by the company and approved by the SEC. The primary purpose of the registration statement and prospectus is to provide prospective investors with financial and other information concerning the registrant.

Financial statements must be included as part of the documentation. In addition to the most recent audited financial statements, unaudited financial statements as of a date within ninety days of the filing date must be included if the most recent audited statements do not fall within that period.

Although not required by the SEC, a **comfort letter** from the auditors is frequently provided for in the agreement between the underwriters and the registrant.[7] The letter

---

TABLE 15.1

Conditions for Performing Agreed-Upon Procedures to Specified Elements of a Financial Statement

1. The accountant is independent.
2. The accountant and the specified parties agree upon the procedures performed or to be performed by the accountant.
3. The specified parties take responsibility for the sufficiency of the agreed-upon procedures for their purposes.
4. The procedures to be performed are expected to result in reasonably consistent findings.
5. The basis of accounting of the specified elements, accounts, or items of a financial statement is clearly evident to the specified parties and the accountant.
6. The specific subject matter to which the procedures are to be applied is subject to reasonably consistent estimation or measurement.
7. Evidential matter related to the specific subject matter to which the procedures are applied is expected to exist to provide a reasonable basis for expressing the findings in the accountant's report.
8. Where applicable, the accountant and the specified parties agree on any materiality limits for reporting purposes.
9. Use of the report is restricted to the specified parties.

Source: AICPA Professional Standards, New York: AICPA, section AU 622.09.

---

6 SAS No. 87 describes the conditions under which the distribution of a CPA's report must be restricted. Ordinarily, reports on financial statements prepared in conformity with GAAP or a comprehensive basis of accounting other than GAAP are considered *general* use reports. The term *restricted use* applies to CPA reports intended only for specified parties.
7 The underwriter is responsible for issuing the registrant's securities upon approval of the SEC. Securities brokers and investment bankers are the most common underwriters of securities issues.

EXHIBIT 15.1

Agreed-Upon Procedures Report: Applied to Elements of the Financial Statements

**Independent Accountant's Report
on Applying Agreed-Upon Procedures**

To the Trustee of XYZ Company:

We have performed the procedures described below, which were agreed to by the Trustee of XYZ Company, with respect to the claims of creditors to determine the validity of claims of XYZ Company as of May 31, 2001, as set forth in accompanying Schedule A. This engagement to apply agreed-upon procedures was performed in accordance with standards established by the American Institute of Certified Public Accountants. The sufficiency of these procedures is solely the responsibility of the Trustee of XYZ Company. Consequently, we make no representation regarding the sufficiency of the procedures described below either for the purpose for which this report has been requested or for any other purpose.

The procedures and associated findings are as follows:

1. Compare the total of the trial balance of accounts payable at May 31, 2001, prepared by XYZ Company, to the balance in the related general ledger account.

    The total of the accounts payable trial balance agreed with the balance in the related general ledger account.

2. Compare the amounts for claims received from creditors (as shown in claim documents provided by XYZ Company) to the respective amounts shown in the trial balance of accounts payable. Using the data included in the claims documents and in XYZ Company's accounts payable detail records, reconcile any differences found to the accounts payable trial balance.

    All differences noted are presented in column 3 of Schedule A. Except for those amounts shown in column 4 of Schedule A, all such differences were reconciled.

3. Examine the documentation submitted by creditors in support of the amounts claimed and compare it to the following documentation in XYZ Company's files: invoices, receiving reports, and other evidence of receipt of goods or services.

    No exceptions were found as a result of these comparisons.

We were not engaged to, and did not, perform an audit, the objective of which would be the expression of an opinion on the specified elements, accounts, or items. Accordingly, we do not express such an opinion. Had we performed additional procedures, other matters might have come to our attention that would have been reported to you.

This report is intended solely for the use of the Trustee of XYZ Company and should not be used by anyone other than this specified party.

Source: *AICPA Professional Standards*, New York: AICPA, section AU 622.49.

is issued by the auditor at the request of the underwriter to assist the underwriter in conducting a "due diligence" review. The following matters and items are commonly covered (included) in the comfort letter:

1. The independence of the accountants;
2. Whether the audited financial statements and financial statement schedules included in the registration statement comply as to form in all material respects with the applicable accounting requirements of the Act and the related published rules and regulations;
3. Unaudited financial statements, condensed interim financial information, capsule financial information, pro forma financial information, financial forecasts, management's discussion and analysis, and changes in selected financial statement items

during a period subsequent to the date and period of the latest financial statements
in the registration statement;

4. Tables, statistics, and other financial information included in the registration statement; and

5. Negative assurance as to whether certain nonfinancial statement information included in the registration statement complies as to form in all material respects with
Regulation S-K.[8]

If limited procedures have been applied to the unaudited data, these procedures
should be described in the comfort letter, and the CPA may give limited (negative) assurance with respect to the data. As with a review of financial statements, a limited assurance report disclaims an opinion of the financial data because the procedures are
less extensive than those applied in an audit. The disclaimer is followed, however, by
limited assurance, inasmuch as the procedures are considered adequate for that purpose. The procedures applied to the unaudited data consist mainly of inquiry and analytical procedures. Exhibit 15.2 illustrates a partial comfort letter covering unaudited
data that have been reviewed by the CPA.

A CPA should *not* give limited assurance with respect to unaudited financial statements without having obtained knowledge of the client's accounting and financial reporting practices and its internal control policies and procedures relating to the
preparation of financial statements.[9] Given this requirement, a CPA who has *not* previously audited the client's financial statements should *not* give limited assurance in the
comfort letter.

Review of Interim Financial Information

Interim financial information may be defined as financial statements or condensed information covering less than a year. Interim financial information may be presented
alone or as a note to audited financial statements. Public companies are required by the
SEC to file quarterly financial information (Form 10-Q) and to include some of this information in the annual report to shareholders.[10] In addition, independent auditors
often are asked to apply limited procedures to the data. The information usually is presented in the annual report in the form of a footnote and should be clearly marked as
unaudited.[11] If limited procedures have *not* been applied, the audit report must be modified to include a statement that such procedures were not applied to the interim financial information. Report modification would assume the form of an explanatory
paragraph following the opinion paragraph, and would *not* constitute a qualification of
the audit opinion.

The objective of reviewing interim financial information is to determine whether
any material modifications are necessary in order for the information to conform to
GAAP. The review does *not* contemplate a study and evaluation of internal control or
tests of the accounting records through inspection, observation, or confirmation.[12] Like
other reviews, therefore, it is considerably more limited in scope than an audit.

---

8 *AICPA Professional Standards,* op. cit., section AU 634.22.
9 Ibid, section AU 634.
10 Ibid, section AU 722.36.
11 Ibid, section AU 722.38.
12 Ibid, section AU 722.09.

EXHIBIT 15.2

Partial Comfort Letter: Negative Assurance with Respect to Unaudited Data

a. With respect to the three-month periods ended March 31, 20X6 and 20X5, we have—
 (i) Performed the procedures specified by the American Institute of Certified Public Accountants for a review of interim financial information as described in SAS 71, *Interim Financial Information*, on the unaudited condensed consolidated balance sheet as of March 31, 20X6, and unaudited condensed consolidated statements of income, retained earnings (stockholders' equity), and cash flows for the three-month periods ended March 31, 20X6 and 20X5, included in the registration statement.
 (ii) Inquired of certain officials of the company who have responsibility for financial and accounting matters whether the unaudited consolidated condensed financial statements referred to in (a) comply in form in all material respects with the applicable accounting requirements of the Act of the related published rules and regulations.

b. With respect to the period from April 1, 20X6 to May 31, 20X6, we have—
 (i) Read the unaudited consolidated financial statements of the company and subsidiaries for April and May of both 20X5 and 20X6 furnished us by the company, officials of the company having advised us that no such financial statements as of any date, or for any period subsequent to May 31, 20X6, were available.
 (ii) Inquired of certain officials of the company who have responsibility for financial and accounting matters whether the unaudited consolidated financial statements referred to in b(i) are stated on a basis substantially consistent with that of the audited consolidated financial statements included in the registration statement.

The foregoing procedures do not constitute an audit conducted in accordance with generally accepted auditing standards. Also, they would not necessarily reveal matters of significance with respect to the comments in the following paragraph. Accordingly, we make no representations regarding the sufficiency of the foregoing procedures for your purposes.

Nothing came to our attention as a result of the foregoing procedures, however, that caused us to believe that—

a. (i) Any material modifications should be made to the unaudited condensed consolidated financial statements described in 4a(i), included in the registration statement, for them to be in conformity with generally accepted accounting principles.
 (ii) The unaudited condensed consolidated financial statements described in 4a(i) do not comply as to form in all material respects with the applicable accounting requirements of the Act and the related published rules and regulations.

b. (i) At May 31, 20X6, there was any change in the capital stock, increase in long-term debt, or decrease in consolidated net current assets or stockholders' equity of the consolidated companies as compared with the amounts shown in the March 31, 20X6, unaudited condensed consolidated balance sheet included in the registration statement, or
 (ii) For the period from April 1, 20X6 to May 31, 20X6, there were any decreases, as compared to the corresponding period in the preceding year, in consolidated net sales or in the total or per-share amounts of income before extraordinary items or of net income, except in all instances for changes, increases, or decreases that the registration statement discloses have occurred or may occur.

  This letter is solely for the information of the addressee and to assist the underwriters in conducting and documenting their investigation of the affairs of the company in connection with the offering of the securities covered by the registration statement, and it is not to be used, circulated, quoted, or otherwise referred to within or without the underwriting group for any other purpose, including but not limited to the registration, purchase, or sale of securities, nor is it to be filed with or referred to in whole or in part in the registration statement or any other document, except that reference may be made to it in the underwriting agreement or in any list of closing documents pertaining to the offering of the securities covered by the registration statement.

(Signature and Date)

Source: Adapted from Auditing Standards Board, *Codification of Statements on Auditing Standards*, New York: AICPA, section AU 634.63.

The procedures to be applied in the review consist primarily of inquiry and analytical procedures concerning accounting matters relating to the interim information. Recommended procedures are as follows:

1. Inquiry concerning the internal control structure and any significant changes in internal control;
2. Application of analytical procedures to the interim information;
3. Reading of the minutes of stockholders' and directors' meetings;
4. Reading of the interim financial information; and
5. Inquiry of and obtaining written representations from management concerning its responsibility for the financial information and other matters.[13]

As with comfort letters, knowledge of a client's internal control policies and procedures relating to financial reporting and of its financial reporting practices is considered vital to performing a review of interim financial information. This knowledge usually is obtained by having audited the most recent financial statements of the company. If the CPA has *not* audited the most recent annual financial statements and has *not* acquired sufficient knowledge about internal control, he or she should perform procedures to obtain that knowledge.[14]

If interim financial information that has been reviewed is presented alone (rather than in an unaudited footnote to the annual financial statements), a review report must accompany the statements. Exhibit 15.3 illustrates the recommended form of the report. The report contains a statement that the review was made in accordance with standards established by the AICPA. It identifies the interim financial information or statements

---

EXHIBIT 15.3

Report on Review of Interim Financial Information or Statements Presented Alone

INDEPENDENT ACCOUNTANT'S REPORT

(Addressee)

We have reviewed (describe the statements or information reviewed) of ABC Company and consolidated subsidiaries as of September 30, 20XX, and for the three-month and nine-month periods then ended. These financial statements (information) are (is) the responsibility of the company's management.

We conducted our review in accordance with standards established by the American Institute of Certified Public Accountants. A review of interim financial information consists principally of applying analytical procedures to financial data and making inquiries of persons responsible for financial and accounting matters. It is substantially less in scope than an audit in accordance with generally accepted auditing standards, the objective of which is the expression of an opinion regarding the financial statements taken as a whole. Accordingly, we do not express such an opinion.

Based on our review, we are not aware of any material modifications that should be made to the accompanying financial statements (information) for them (it) to be in conformity with generally accepted accounting principles.

(Signature and Date)

Source: *AICPA Professional Standards*, New York: AICPA, section AU 722.28.

---

13 Ibid, section AU 722.13.
14 Ibid, section AU 722.10.

reviewed and describes the review procedures. The report provides limited (negative) assurance by stating that the accountant is *not* aware of any material modifications that should be made to the interim information in order for it to conform to GAAP.

If the interim information is known by the accountant to contain a departure from GAAP, the report must be modified to disclose this. The modification should describe the nature of the departure and, if practicable, should state the effects on the interim information.[15]

Unaudited Financial Statements of Public Entities

A CPA who is associated with **unaudited financial statements** of a public entity (i.e., an entity whose shares are publicly traded) should disclaim an opinion, and each page of the statements should be marked "unaudited."[16] A state of association exists whenever

1. The CPA's name is used in a document containing the statements; or
2. The CPA has prepared or assisted in preparing the statements.[17]

This type of association might arise, for example, where the independent CPA does not review interim financial statements.

The general form of disclaimer accompanying unaudited statements is as follows:

> *The accompanying balance sheet of X Company as of December 31, 20XX, and the related statements of income, retained earnings, and cash flows for the year then ended were not audited by us and, accordingly, we do not express an opinion on them.*
>
> *(Signature and date)*[18]

If the financial statements are known by the CPA to contain a material departure from GAAP, the client should be encouraged to revise the statements accordingly. If the client refuses, the disclaimer must additionally describe the departure and state the effects on the financial statements, if practicable. If the client doesn't agree to this, the CPA should refuse to be associated with the statements.[19]

Lack of Independence

A CPA who lacks independence with respect to the client may *not* conduct an audit or a review, but may perform a compilation.[20] When a CPA is associated with financial statements but is not independent and has not compiled the statements, the accompanying disclaimer should be modified to indicate the lack of independence. The following report form is recommended:

> *We are not independent with respect to XYZ Company, and the accompanying balance sheet as of December 31, 20XX, and the related statements of income, retained earnings, and cash flows for the year then ended were not audited by us and, accordingly, we do not express an opinion on them.*
>
> *(Signature and Date)*[21]

15 Ibid, section AU 722.31.
16 Ibid, section AU 504.05.
17 Ibid, section AU 504.03.
18 Ibid, section AU 504.05.
19 Ibid, section AU 504.11–13.
20 Ibid, section AR 100.22.
21 Ibid, section AU 504.10.

For compiled statements, lack of independence should be disclosed in a final paragraph stating "We are not independent with respect to XYZ Company."[22]

SERVICES COVERED BY THE ACCOUNTING AND REVIEW STANDARDS

Nonpublic entities—generally those whose securities are not traded in a public market—may request the CPA to compile or review their financial statements. These requests often occur when entities are applying for loans or attempting to attract outside investors. The potential lenders or investors, in reaching credit or investment decisions, may want more than the basic unaudited financial statements, but be willing to accept less than an audit. Compilations and reviews are designed to fill this need. Standards governing compilations and reviews for nonpublic entities are contained in the **Statements on Standards for Accounting and Review Services (SSARSs)** issued by the Accounting and Review Services Committee of the AICPA. We should note that these statements prohibit a CPA member from being associated with the unaudited financial statements of a nonpublic entity unless she or he has at least compiled or reviewed the statements, or includes a statement that she or he has not compiled or reviewed the statements and assumes no responsibility for them.[23]

The following paragraphs define compilations and reviews and are based on the SSARSs.

Compilation of Financial Statements for Nonpublic Entities

In compiling financial statements for a client, the CPA presents information that is the representation of management without undertaking to express any assurance on the statements.[24] To perform a **compilation**, the CPA must possess a level of knowledge of the accounting principles and practices of the client's industry that will result in compiled financial statements appropriate to that industry.[25] A general understanding of the nature of the entity's business transactions and accounting records, the qualifications of the accounting personnel, and the accounting basis on which the financial statements are to be presented are the necessary requirements for a compilation. Table 15.2 is a listing of the procedures to be applied in a compilation. One should note that such procedures as inquiry, observation, confirmation, vouching, reconciling, and recalculating ordinarily associated with audits are *not* required in compilations.

Exhibit 15.4 illustrates the recommended wording to be used in a compilation report. Note that no form of assurance is given by the CPA.

The CPA should encourage the client to correct the financial statements for known errors or departures from GAAP. If the client refuses, the compilation report should disclose the information. If the client declines to permit disclosure in the compilation report, the CPA should refuse to be associated with the statements.

Review of Financial Statements for Nonpublic Entities

More extensive than a compilation but less so than an audit, a **review** consists mainly of performing inquiry and analytical procedures. In reviewing loan applications for small businesses, many banks accept reviews in lieu of more expensive audited financial statements.

22 Ibid, section AR 100.22.
23 Ibid, section AR 100.06.
24 Ibid, section AR 100.04.
25 Ibid, section AR 100.10.

TABLE 15.2

Procedures to Be Applied in a Compilation Engagement

1. Study sources of industry accounting principles and practices, such as AICPA industry accounting and auditing guides;

2. Study the client's accounting manuals and chart of accounts to become familiar with the types of business transactions and the nature of the accounting records;

3. Read job descriptions to obtain knowledge about stated qualifications of accounting personnel; and

4. Read the financial statements to determine that they are free from obvious errors and to ascertain that necessary footnote disclosures are included.

Source: *AICPA Professional Standards*, New York: AICPA, section AR 100.10–12.

EXHIBIT 15.4

Compilation Report

To: Board of Directors
       XYZ Company

We have compiled the accompanying balance sheet of XYZ Company as of December 31, 20XX, and the related statements of income, retained earnings, and cash flows for the year then ended, in accordance with standards established by the American Institute of Certified Public Accountants.

A compilation is limited to presenting in the form of financial statements information that is the representation of management. We have not audited or reviewed the accompanying financial statements and, accordingly, do not express an opinion or any other form of assurance on them.

Lowell & Durbin
Certified Public Accountants

Source: *AICPA Professional Standards*, New York: AICPA, section AR 100.17.

Analytical procedures provide the CPA a basis for expressing **limited (negative) assurance** concerning conformance with GAAP. In contrast, an audit provides **positive assurance**. A review does not contemplate a study and evaluation of internal control, confirmation, or other tests of accounting records performed in an audit.

Table 15.3 lists the inquiry and analytical procedures to be applied in a review engagement. Exhibit 15.5 illustrates the recommended wording for a review report. Unlike a compilation report, the review report includes, after the disclaimer, a paragraph expressing limited (negative) assurance on the financial statements.

The review report should be modified to disclose any known and uncorrected deficiencies in the financial statements. If management does not agree to the disclosure, the CPA should refuse to be associated with the statements.

TABLE 15.3

Procedures to Be Applied in a Review Engagement

1. Inquiries concerning the entity's accounting principles and practices and the methods followed in applying them;

2. Inquiries concerning the entity's procedures for recording, classifying, and summarizing transactions and accumulating information for disclosure in the financial statements;

3. Analytical procedures designed to identify relationships and individual items that appear to be unusual;

4. Inquiries concerning actions taken at meetings of stockholders, the board of directors, or committees of the board of directors, or at comparable meetings that may affect the financial statements;

5. Reading of the financial statements to consider whether they appear to conform with generally accepted accounting principles;

6. Obtaining of reports from other accountants, if any, who have been engaged to audit or review the financial statements of significant components of the reporting entity; and

7. Inquiries of persons having responsibility for financial and accounting matters concerning
   a. conformity with GAAP;
   b. changes in activities or accounting principles and practices;
   c. matters as to which questions have arisen in applying the foregoing procedures; and
   d. events subsequent to the date of the financial statements that would have a material effect on the financial statements.

Source: *AICPA Professional Standards*, New York: AICPA, section AR 100.27.

EXHIBIT 15.5

Review Report

To: Board of Directors
      XYZ Company

We have reviewed the accompanying balance sheet of XYZ Company as of December 31, 20XX, and the related statements of income, retained earnings, and cash flows for the year then ended, in accordance with standards established by the American Institute of Certified Public Accountants. All information included in these financial statements is the representation of the management of XYZ Company.

A review consists principally of inquiries of company personnel and analytical procedures applied to financial data. It is substantially less in scope than an audit in accordance with generally accepted auditing standards, the objective of which is the expression of an opinion regarding the financial statements taken as a whole. Accordingly, we do not express such an opinion.

Based on our review, we are not aware of any material modifications that should be made to the accompanying financial statements in order for them to be in conformity with generally accepted accounting principles.

Lowell & Durbin
Certified Public Accountants

Source: *AICPA Professional Standards*, New York: AICPA, section AR 100.35.

To summarize, a *compilation* offers *no assurance*, a *review* offers *limited assurance*, and an *audit* offers *reasonable assurance* regarding fairness of the financial statements. Although it offers less than the reasonable assurance provided by an audit, many lending officers accept the review report as adequate for loan application purposes.

Table 15.4 displays the range of services, the principal procedures, and the level of assurance, if any, related to various forms of association by the CPA with a client's financial statements. Note the absence of any form of assurance in a compilation.

ASSURANCE SERVICES COVERED BY THE ATTESTATION STANDARDS

Many of the nonfinancial services (e.g., reports on internal control) performed by CPAs require some form of attestation by the accountant. **Attestation**, as defined by the AICPA, results in a "written communication that expresses a conclusion about the reliability of a written assertion that is the responsibility of another party."[26] An **assertion** is "any declaration, or set of related declarations taken as a whole, by a party responsible for it."[27] The independent financial audit is a form of attestation but has its own set of standards because financial statement audits embrace a more specific subject matter (historical financial data) than other forms of attestation. The Statements on Standards for Attestation Engagements (SSAEs) cover other assurance functions and set forth eleven standards embracing both positive and limited assurance.

Preconditions for Attestation Services

The attestation standards are the result of a joint project of the Auditing Standards Board and the Accounting and Review Services Committee of the AICPA. These standards require five preconditions for attest services to be performed:

1. The practitioner must have adequate *training and proficiency* in the attest function;

TABLE 15.4

Range of Services of a CPA Associated with Financial Statements

No Assurance	Limited Assurance	Positive Assurance
Compilation:	**Review:**	**Audit:**
Read financial statements	Conduct inquiries	Study and evaluate internal control
Understand industry accounting practices	Perform analytical procedures	Observe, examine, confirm, reconcile, calculate, and vouch
Issue report that disclaims an opinion	Issue report that disclaims an opinion	Issue an audit report

26 Ibid, section AT 100.01.
27 Ibid.

2. The practitioner must have adequate *knowledge* of the subject matter;
3. There must be reasonable *measurement and disclosure criteria* concerning the subject matter;
4. The assertions must be *capable of reasonably consistent estimation or measurement* using such criteria; and
5. The practitioner must be *independent*.

Attestation Standards as Contrasted with Auditing Standards

Because financial statement audits are a form of attestation, the attestation standards do *not* supersede the ten generally accepted auditing standards. Rather, they complement them, in that the attestation standards are broader in scope and are meant to maintain quality in the performance of the services they cover.

Table 15.5 presents both the **attestation standards** and the auditing standards for comparison. Note that the general attestation standards, like the general auditing standards, require *adequate training and proficiency*, *independence*, and *due care*. In addition, given the broader spectrum of services covered, the attestation standards require

---

TABLE 15.5

Attestation Standards Contrasted with Auditing Standards

ATTESTATION STANDARDS	AUDITING STANDARDS
General Standards	**General Standards**
1. The engagement shall be performed by a practitioner or practitioners having adequate technical training and proficiency in the attest function.	1. The audit shall be performed by a person or persons having adequate technical training and proficiency as an auditor.
2. The engagement shall be performed by a practitioner or practitioners having adequate knowledge in the subject matter of the attestation.	2. Not applicable.
3. The practitioner shall perform an engagement only if he or she has reason to believe that the following two conditions exist: A. The assertion is capable of evaluation against reasonable criteria that either have been established by a recognized body or are stated in the presentation of the assertion in a sufficiently clear and comprehensive manner for a knowledgeable reader to be able to understand them. B. The assertion is capable of reasonably consistent estimation or measurement using such criteria.	3. Not applicable.
4. In all matters relating to the engagement, an independence in mental attitude shall be maintained by the practitioner or practitioners.	4. In all matters relating to the engagement, an independence in mental attitude shall be maintained by the auditor or auditors.
5. Due professional care shall be exercised in the performance of the engagement.	5. Due professional care shall be exercised in the performance of the audit and the preparation of the report.

(continued)

TABLE 15.5

(continued)

ATTESTATION STANDARDS	AUDITING STANDARDS
Standards of Field Work	**Standards of Field Work**
1. The work shall be adequately planned and assistants, if any, shall be properly supervised.	1. The work shall be adequately planned and assistants, if any, are to be properly supervised.
2. Not applicable.	2. A sufficient understanding of the internal control system is to be obtained to plan the audit and to determine the nature, timing, and extent of tests to be performed.
3. Sufficient evidence shall be obtained to provide a reasonable basis for the conclusion that is expressed in the report.	3. Sufficient competent evidential matter shall be obtained through inspection, observation, inquiries, and confirmations to afford a reasonable basis for an opinion regarding the financial statements under audit.
Standards of Reporting	**Standards of Reporting**
1. The report shall identify the assertion being reported on and state the character of the engagement.	1. Not applicable.
2. Not applicable.	2. The report shall state whether the financial statements are presented in accordance with generally accepted accounting principles.
3. Not applicable.	3. The report shall identify those circumstances in which such principles have not been consistently observed in the current period in relation to the preceding period.
4. Not applicable.	4. Informative disclosures in the financial statements are to be regarded as reasonably adequate unless otherwise stated in the report.
5. The report shall state the practitioner's conclusion about whether the assertion is presented in conformity with the established or stated criteria against which it was measured.	5. The report shall contain either an expression of an opinion regarding the financial statements taken as a whole, or an assertion to the effect that an opinion cannot be expressed. When an overall opinion cannot be expressed, the reasons therefore should be stated. In all cases where an auditor's name is associated with financial statements, the report should contain a clearcut indication of the character of the auditor's work, if any, and the degree of responsibility the auditor is taking.
6. The report shall state all of the practitioner's significant reservations about the engagement and the presentation of the assertion.	6. Not applicable.
7. The report on an engagement to evaluate an assertion that has been prepared in conformity with agreed-upon criteria or an engagement to apply agreed-upon procedures should contain a statement limiting its use to the parties who have agreed upon such criteria or procedures.	7. Not applicable.

Source: *AICPA Professional Standards*, New York: AICPA, section AT 100.82.

that the CPA have adequate knowledge of the subject matter and ascertain that the *assertions are capable of attestation*.

The field work standards for attestation, like the auditing field work standards, require that the CPA *properly plan the engagement, supervise the work,* and *gather sufficient competent evidence in support of the assertions*. However, the reliability of the assertions covered under the attestation standards, unlike the financial statement assertions covered under GAAS, are *not* dependent on the reliability of internal control. Therefore, unlike the auditing standards, the attestation standards do not require the CPA to obtain an understanding of internal control.

The attestation reporting standards are similar to GAAS reporting standards in requiring the CPA to clearly state any reservations (qualifications) regarding presentation of the assertions. They differ from reporting standards under GAAS in certain other respects. First, the attestation standards say nothing about GAAP, inasmuch as GAAP is not the standard used to measure the reasonableness of assertions covered by the attestation standards. Second, given the diversity of assertions and types of engagements covered by the attestation standards, the standards require that the CPA identify the assertions being reported upon, as well as the nature of the engagement. Finally, as will be discussed later, professional standards prohibit general distribution of some forms of attestation reports. Therefore, the attestation reporting standards require the CPA to state applicable restrictions on distribution.

The following paragraphs describe the more common types of assurance services covered by the attestation standards.

Compliance Attestation

In recent years, a significant growth area in public accounting has been compliance attestation. **Compliance attestation** involves management's written assertions about either an entity's *compliance with requirements* of specified laws, regulations, rules, contracts, or grants or the *effectiveness of an entity's internal control over compliance* with specified requirements.[28]

Having begun as a response to a series of federal requirements relating to entities receiving federal financial assistance, compliance attestation has now extended to other areas. For example, a CPA may be asked to determine a financial institution's compliance with Federal Deposit Insurance Corporation requirements regarding "safety and soundness" laws and regulations, or the CPA may be asked to attest to compliance with the Environmental Protection Agency's specifications concerning the maximum level of contaminants in certain products and processes. Attestation to compliance with Department of Education conditions regarding student financial assistance programs, or with the Mortgage Bankers' Association of America requirements regarding compliance with loan servicing agreements are other examples.

For some time the SEC has required public companies to include a management discussion and analysis (MD&A) report in the annual report to stockholders (see Chapter 14). The rules and regulations governing the preparation of the report, however, have become increasingly complex and demanding. To ensure compliance, companies often ask their independent auditors to either examine, review, or apply agreed-upon procedures to the reports and issue a compliance attestation report. The CPA may accept the

---

28 Ibid, section AT 500.01.

engagement provided he or she has audited the financial statements for at least the latest period covered by the MD&A.

The attestation standards do *not* apply to engagements performed in accordance with government auditing standards. These engagements are covered under the auditing standards and are considered in Chapter 16.

Compliance attestation engagements of the type described above typically involve the application of agreed-upon procedures, which focus more directly on the specific assertions requiring attestation. They allow a given engagement to be tailored more easily to the exact needs of the client. This approach is also more cost effective than a more broadly based examination.

The conditions listed in Table 15.6 must exist if the CPA is to apply agreed-upon procedures for compliance attestation purposes. Because most of the regulatory provisions require attestation as to internal control effectiveness over compliance, the engagements usually require the CPA to apply certain procedures to management's assertions concerning internal control effectiveness and to apply similar and/or different procedures to those assertions related to compliance with the applicable laws and regulations.

Internal control supporting compliance may differ from those controls associated with financial statement reliability. A control related to maintaining contaminant levels, for example, is not part of the internal control system relating to financial reporting. For this reason, the CPA must adopt different procedures for studying and testing internal controls in compliance engagements from those used in financial audits.

The AICPA Professional Standards prohibit CPAs from performing review services related to an entity's compliance or to the effectiveness of internal controls over compliance. As described earlier, review services entail inquiry and the application of analytical procedures, an approach considered ineffective in testing compliance with laws and regulations.

TABLE 15.6

Conditions for Accepting an Engagement to Apply Agreed-Upon Procedures for Compliance Attestation Purposes

1. Management accepts responsibility for the entity's compliance with specified requirements and the effectiveness of the entity's internal control over compliance;

2. Management evaluates the entity's compliance with specified requirements or the effectiveness of the entity's internal control over compliance;

3. Management provides to the practitioner its written assertion about the entity's compliance with specified requirements or about the effectiveness of the entity's internal control over compliance;

4. Management's assertion is capable of evaluation against reasonable criteria that either have been established by a recognized body or are stated in or attached to the practitioner's report in a sufficiently clear and comprehensive manner for a knowledgeable reader to understand them, and the assertion is capable of reasonably consistent estimation or measurement using such criteria; and

5. Sufficient evidential matter exists or could be developed to support management's evaluation.

Source: *AICPA Professional Standards*, New York: AICPA, section AT 500.09–11.

In gathering evidence regarding compliance, the CPA is advised to consider the following sources:

1. Laws, regulations, rules, contracts, and grants that pertain to the specified compliance requirements, including published requirements;
2. Knowledge about the specific compliance requirements obtained through prior engagements and regulatory reports;
3. Knowledge about the specified compliance requirements obtained through discussions with appropriate individuals within the entity (for example, the chief financial officer, internal auditors, legal counsel, compliance officer, or grant or contract administrators); and
4. Knowledge about the specified compliance requirements obtained through discussions with appropriate individuals outside the entity (for example, a regulator or third-party specialist).[29]

Exhibit 15.6 illustrates the proper report wording for an agreed-upon procedures compliance attestation engagement. The report should be drafted in terms of procedures applied and the resulting findings. In addition, the report should contain the elements listed in Table 15.7.

Note the disclaimer of opinion in the second paragraph of the report and the restriction on distribution in the third paragraph.

EXHIBIT 15.6

Compliance Attestation Report: Agreed-Upon Procedures

**Independent Accountant's Report
on Applying Agreed-Upon Procedures**

We have performed the procedures enumerated below, which were agreed to by (list specified users of report), solely to assist the users in evaluating management's assertion about XYZ Company's compliance with (list of specified requirements) during the period ended December 31, 20XX, included in the accompanying (title of management report). This agreed-upon procedures engagement was performed in accordance with standards established by the American Institute of Certified Public Accountants. The sufficiency of these procedures is solely the responsibility of the specified users of the report. Consequently, we make no representation regarding the sufficiency of the procedures described below either for the purpose for which this report has been requested or for any other purpose.

(include paragraph to enumerate procedures and findings)

We were not engaged to, and did not, perform an examination, the objective of which would be the expression of an opinion on management's assertions. Accordingly, we do not express such an opinion. Had we performed additional procedures, other matters might have come to our attention that would have been reported to you.

This report is intended solely for the use of (list or refer to specified users) and should not be used by those who have not agreed to the procedures and taken responsibility for the sufficiency of the procedures for their purposes.

Source: *AICPA Professional Standards*, New York: AICPA, section AT 500.24.

29 Ibid, section AT 500.19.

TABLE 15.7

Reporting Requirements for a Compliance Attestation Report

1. A title that includes the word *independent*;

2. Identification of the specified users;

3. A reference to or statement of management's assertion about the entity's compliance with specified requirements, or about the effectiveness of an entity's internal control over compliance, including the period or point in time addressed in management's assertion, and the character of the engagement;

4. A statement that the procedures, which were agreed to by the specified users identified in the report, were performed to assist the users in evaluating the entity's compliance with specified requirements or the effectiveness of its internal control over compliance, or management's assertion thereon;

5. Reference to attestation standards established by the American Institute of Certified Public Accountants;

6. A statement that the sufficiency of the procedures is solely the responsibility of the specified users and a disclaimer of responsibility for the sufficiency of those procedures;

7. A list of the procedures performed (or reference thereto) and related findings. The practitioner should not provide negative assurance;

8. Where applicable, a description of any agreed-upon materiality limits;

9. A statement that the practitioner was not engaged to, and did not, perform an examination of management's assertion about compliance with specified requirements or about the effectiveness of an entity's internal control over compliance, a disclaimer of opinion thereon, and a statement that if the practitioner had performed additional procedures, other matters might have come to his or her attention that would have been reported;

10. A statement of restrictions on the use of the report because it is intended to be used solely by the specified users. (However, if the report is a matter of public record, the practitioner should include the following sentence: "However, this report is a matter of public record and its distribution is not limited.");

11. Where applicable, reservations or restrictions concerning procedures or findings as discussed in sections 600.35, .37, .41, and .42; and

12. Where applicable, a description of the nature of the assistance provided by the specialist as discussed in sections 600.21 and .23.

Source: *AICPA Professional Standards*, New York: AICPA, section AT 500.23.

Reporting on Internal Control

Certain entities, such as investment companies, brokers, and securities dealers, are required by the Securities Exchange Act of 1934 to submit **reports on internal control**. In addition, the Foreign Corrupt Practices Act of 1977 requires that public companies establish and maintain adequate systems of internal control. Because of these requirements, a CPA may be asked to express an opinion on internal control. AICPA Professional Standards provide the CPA with two alternative approaches to this type of engagement. In the first approach, referred to as **indirect attestation**, the CPA expresses an opinion on the reasonableness of management's assertions regarding the effectiveness of its internal control system. The second alternative, known as **direct attestation**, permits the CPA to express an opinion directly on the effectiveness of the client's internal control system. The scope of the examination and reporting requirements for reports on internal control are discussed in the following paragraphs.

The CPA's objective in reporting on internal control is to either "express an opinion about whether management's assertion regarding the effectiveness of the entity's internal control system is fairly stated, in all material respects, based upon the control criteria" (indirect attestation);[30] or express an opinion on the effectiveness of the entity's internal control system (direct attestation). In either case, the CPA is examining and reporting on controls as of a specified date, and is expressing an opinion on internal control as a whole. This differs from the financial audit, in which control subsets are tested for effectiveness over the period covered by the financial statements. Moreover, engagements for the purpose of expressing an opinion are more extensive than a study of internal control made as part of a financial audit. The CPA, in an engagement to express an opinion, must gather sufficient evidence to provide reasonable assurance to management concerning the control environment, the accounting system, and internal control procedures. The study and evaluation made as part of an audit, on the other hand, is an intermediate step in evaluating the reliability of the financial statements. Exhibit 15.7 illustrates the standard form of report on internal control, given indirect attestation. Exhibit 15.8 illustrates the report form given direct attestation.

EXHIBIT 15.7

Report on Internal Control: Indirect Attestation

INDEPENDENT ACCOUNTANT'S REPORT

(Addressee)

(Introductory paragraph)

We have examined management's assertion included in the accompanying (title of management report), that W Company maintained effective internal control over financial reporting as of December 31, 20XX, based on (identify stated or established criteria). Management is responsible for maintaining effective internal control over financial reporting. Our responsibility is to express an *opinion on management's assertion* based on our examination.

(Scope paragraph)

Our examination was conducted in accordance with attestation standards established by the American Institute of Certified Public Accountants and, accordingly, included obtaining an understanding of internal control over financial reporting, testing, and evaluating the design and operating effectiveness of internal control, and performing such other procedures as we considered necessary in the circumstances. We believe that our examination provides a reasonable basis for our opinion.

(Inherent limitations paragraph)

Because on inherent limitations in any internal control, misstatements due to error or fraud may occur and not be detected. Also, projections of any evaluation of internal control over financial reporting to future periods are subject to the risk that internal control may become inadequate because of changes in conditions, or that the degree of compliance with the policies or procedures may deteriorate.

(Opinion paragraph)

In our opinion, *management's assertion* that W Company maintained effective internal control over financial reporting as of December 31, 20XX, is fairly stated in all material respects based on (identify established criteria).

(Signature)

(Date)

Source: *AICPA Professional Standards*, New York: AICPA, section AT 400.47.

---

30 Ibid, section AT 400.15.

EXHIBIT 15.8

Report on Internal Control: Direct Attestation

INDEPENDENT ACCOUNTANT'S REPORT

(Addressee)

(Introductory paragraph)

We have examined management's assertion included in the accompanying (title of management report), that W Company maintained effective internal control over financial reporting as of December 31, 20XX, based on (identify stated or established criteria). Management is responsible for maintaining effective internal control over financial reporting. Our responsibility is to express an *opinion on the effectiveness of internal control* based on our examination.

(Scope paragraph)

Our examination was conducted in accordance with attestation standards established by the American Institute of Certified Public Accountants and, accordingly, included obtaining an understanding of internal control over financial reporting, testing, and evaluating the design and operating effectiveness of internal control, and performing such other procedures as we considered necessary in the circumstances. We believe that our examination provides a reasonable basis for our opinion.

(Inherent limitations paragraph)

Because of inherent limitations in any internal control, misstatements due to error or fraud may occur and not be detected. Also, projections of any evaluation of internal control over financial reporting to future periods are subject to the risk that internal control may become inadequate because of changes in conditions, or that the degree of compliance with the policies or procedures may deteriorate.

(Opinion paragraph)

In our opinion, W Company maintained, in all material respects, effective internal control over financial reporting as of December 31, 20XX, based on (identify established criteria).

(Signature)

(Date)

Source: *AICPA Professional Standards*, New York: AICPA, section AT 400.46.

When the above conditions are met, no restrictions need be placed on the use of the resulting report. Note that in both forms of attestation the report expresses an opinion as of a particular point in time. Note also that under indirect attestation the opinion is limited to evaluating management's assertion about the effectiveness of the internal control system. In both forms of attestation, the report should be modified if material weaknesses were found or if scope limitations were encountered.

Reports on Prospective Financial Statements

When a company applies for a long-term loan, the lending institution may request, in addition to historical financial statements, future-oriented financial statements incorporating the entity's best estimates relating to the use of the loan proceeds; or when Company A negotiates to acquire Company B, the parties to the proposed combination may request projected pro forma financial statements for the combined entity covering a specified future time period. The AICPA Professional Standards have referred to such pro forma statements as **prospective financial statements**.

A CPA who is associated with prospective financial statements that are expected to be used by a third party should either compile, examine, or apply agreed-upon procedures to the statements.[31] Prospective financial statements may assume one of two forms:

- **Forecast**: Presents the entity's expected financial position, results of operations, and cash flows reflecting *conditions expected to exist*. An example of a financial forecast might be a set of budgeted financial statements for the next quarter.
- **Projection**: Presents financial position, results of operations, and cash flows given one or more *hypothetical assumptions*. Projected revenues and cash flows for a proposed shopping mall, given various assumptions regarding occupancy and rentals, exemplifies a financial projection.

A forecast is appropriate for general distribution to third parties with which the client is not in direct negotiation. A projection, however, is more tentative, and it should be restricted to those parties with whom the client is negotiating directly, and who therefore may ask questions concerning the assumptions. If the client proposes to prepare financial projections for general use, the CPA should refuse to be associated with them.[32]

Compilation of Prospective Financial Statements   Exhibit 15.9 illustrates a standard compilation report that a CPA would issue in conjunction with a financial forecast. Exhibit 15.10 is a compilation report accompanying a financial projection. In neither case is any form of assurance provided by the CPA. Table 15.8 lists the procedures to be applied in compiling prospective financial statements. Note that, with regard to prospective financial statements, the CPA focuses on the reasonableness and consistency of the assumptions used by management in developing the forecast or projection.

EXHIBIT 15.9

Compilation Report for Association with a Financial Forecast

(Addressee)

We have compiled the accompanying forecasted balance sheet, statements of income, retained earnings, and cash flows of XYZ Company as of December 31, 20XX, and for the year then ending, in accordance with standards established by the American Institute of Certified Public Accountants.

A compilation is limited to presenting in the form of a forecast information that is the representation of management and does not include evaluation of the support for the assumptions underlying the forecast. We have not examined the forecast and, accordingly, do not express an opinion or any other form of assurance on the accompanying statements or assumptions. Furthermore, there will usually be differences between the forecasted and actual results, because events and circumstances frequently do not occur as expected, and those differences may be material. We have no responsibility to update this report for events and circumstances occurring after the date of this report.

(Signature and Date)

Source: *AICPA Professional Standards*, New York: AICPA, section AT 200.17.

---

31 Ibid, section AT 200.01.
32 Ibid, section AT 200.09.

EXHIBIT 15.10

Compilation Report for Association with a Financial Projection

(Addressee)

We have compiled the accompanying projected balance sheet, statements of income, retained earnings, and cash flows of XYZ Company as of December 31, 20XX, and for the year then ending, in accordance with standards established by the American Institute of Certified Public Accountants.

The accompanying projection and this report were prepared for (state special purpose, for example, "the DEF National Bank for the purpose of negotiating a loan to expand XYZ Company's plant") and should not be used for any other purpose.

A compilation is limited to presenting in the form of a projection information that is the representation of management and does not include evaluation of the support for the assumptions underlying the projection. We have not examined the projection and, accordingly, do not express an opinion or any other form of assurance on the accompanying statements or assumptions. Furthermore, even if (describe hypothetical assumption, for example, "the loan is granted and the plant is expanded"), there will usually be differences between the projected and actual results, because events and circumstances frequently do not occur as expected, and those differences may be material. We have no responsibility to update this report for events and circumstances occurring after the date of this report.

(Signature and Date)

Source: *AICPA Professional Standards*, New York: AICPA, section AT 200.18.

TABLE 15.8

Procedures to Be Applied in Compiling Prospective Financial Statements

1. Establish an understanding with the client, preferably in writing, regarding the services to be performed;

2. Inquire about the accounting principles used in the preparation of prospective financial statements;

3. Ask how the key factors are identified and how the assumptions are developed;

4. Obtain a list of significant assumptions and consider whether there are any omissions or inconsistencies;

5. Test the mathematical accuracy of the computations that translate the assumptions into prospective financial statements; and

6. Read the statements and determine that they conform to AICPA presentation guidelines in all material respects.

Source: *AICPA Professional Standards*, New York: AICPA, section AT 200.68.

Examination of Prospective Financial Statements   An examination of prospective financial statements, like an audit, requires a form of attestation, and is more extensive than a compilation. The examination involves evaluating the preparation of the prospective statements, examining the support underlying the assumptions, and determining whether the presentation is in conformity with AICPA guidelines.[33]

33 Ibid, section AT 200.27.

In a report on the examination of prospective financial statements, the CPA expresses an opinion as to whether the statements are presented in conformity with AICPA guidelines and whether the assumptions provide a reasonable basis for the forecast or projection. Exhibits 15.11 and 15.12 illustrate the proper forms of reports on the examination of a financial forecast and a financial projection, respectively.

Applying Agreed-Upon Procedures to Prospective Financial Statements   Companies experiencing financial difficulties may be asked by their creditors to submit prospective financial statements to which certain agreed-upon procedures have been applied. Companies involved in acquisition or merger negotiations similarly may request their CPAs to apply certain procedures to prospective financial information. A CPA may accept an engagement to apply agreed-upon procedures provided the conditions listed in Table 15.9 are met. These conditions are similar to those agreed-upon procedures engagements relating to compliance attestation and financial statement elements.

Exhibit 15.13 illustrates a report that might be issued when agreed-upon procedures have been applied. Note the report describes procedures and findings. Note also the absence of any form of assurance regarding the prospective financial statements.

SUMMARY TABLE

Table 15.10 (p. 656) summarizes assurance services other than audits that are covered by existing auditing standards, accounting and review standards, and attestation standards. CPAs who examine, review, or apply agreed-upon procedures must be independent of their clients. Independence is not a requirement for compilations. Examinations provide positive assurance regarding assertions, reviews provide limited assurance, and compilations and application of agreed-upon procedures provide no assurance.

EXHIBIT 15.11

Report on Examination of a Financial Forecast

(Addressee)

We have examined the accompanying forecasted balance sheet, statements of income, retained earnings, and cash flows of XYZ Company as of December 31, 20XX, and for the year then ending. Our examination was made in accordance with standards for and examination of a forecast established by the American Institute of Certified Public Accountants and, accordingly, included such procedures as we considered necessary to evaluate both the assumptions used by management and the preparation and presentation of the forecast.

In our opinion, the accompanying forecast is presented in conformity with guidelines for presentation of a forecast established by the American Institute of Certified Public Accountants, and the underlying assumptions provide a reasonable basis for management's forecast. However, there usually will be differences between the forecasted and actual results, because events and circumstances frequently do not occur as expected, and those differences may be material. We have no responsibility to update this report for events and circumstances occurring after the date of this report.

(Signature and Date)

Source: *AICPA Professional Standards*, New York: AICPA, section AT 200.32.

EXHIBIT 15.12

Report on Examination of a Financial Projection

(Addressee)

We have examined the accompanying projected balance sheet, statements of income, retained earnings, and cash flows of XYZ Company as of December 31, 20XX, and for the year then ending. Our examination was made in accordance with standards for an examination of a projection established by the American Institute of Certified Public Accountants and, accordingly, included such procedures as we considered necessary to evaluate both the assumptions used by management and the preparation and presentation of the projection.

The accompanying projection and this report were prepared for (state special purpose) and should not be used for any other purpose.

In our opinion, the accompanying projection is presented in conformity with guidelines for presentation of a projection established by the American Institute of Certified Public Accountants, and the underlying assumptions provide a reasonable basis for management's projection (describe the hypothetical assumption, for example, "assuming the granting of the requested loan for the purpose of expanding XYZ Company's plant as described in the summary of significant assumptions"). However, even if (describe hypothetical assumption, for example, "the loan is granted and the plant is expanded"), there usually will be differences between the projected and actual results, because events and circumstances frequently do not occur as expected, and those differences may be material. We have no responsibility to update this report for events and circumstances occurring after the date of this report.

(Signature and Date)

Source: *AICPA Professional Standards*, New York: AICPA, section AT 200.33.

TABLE 15.9

Conditions for Accepting an Engagement to Apply Agreed-Upon Procedures to Prospective Financial Statements

1. The accountant is independent;
2. The accountant and the specified parties agree upon the procedures performed or to be performed by the accountant;
3. The specified parties take responsibility for the sufficiency of the agreed-upon procedures for their purposes;
4. The prospective financial statements include a summary of significant assumptions;
5. The prospective financial statements to which the procedures are to be applied are subject to reasonably consistent estimation or measurement;
6. Criteria to be used in the determination of findings are agreed upon between the accountant and the specified parties;
7. The procedures to be applied to the prospective financial statements are expected to result in reasonably consistent findings using the criteria;
8. Evidential matter related to the prospective financial statements to which the procedures are applied is expected to exist to provide a reasonable basis for expressing the findings in the accountant's report;
9. Where applicable, a description of any agreed-upon materiality limits for reporting purposes; and
10. Use of the report is to be restricted to the specified parties.

Source: *AICPA Professional Standards*, New York: AICPA, section AT 200.50.

EXHIBIT 15.13

Report on Prospective Financial Statements Given Application of Agreed-Upon Procedures

**Independent Accountant's Report
on Applying Agreed-Upon Procedures**

Board of Directors—XYZ Company
Board of Directors—ABC Company

At your request, we have performed certain agreed-upon procedures, as enumerated below, with respect to the forecasted balance sheet and the related forecasted statements of income, retained earnings, and cash flows of DEF Company, a subsidiary of ABC Company, as of December 31, 20XX, and for the year then ending. These procedures, which were agreed to by the Boards of Directors of XYZ Company and ABC Company, were performed solely to assist you in evaluating the forecast in connection with the proposed sale of DEF Company to XYZ Company. This agreed-upon procedures engagement was performed in accordance with standards established by the American Institute of Certified Public Accountants. The sufficiency of these procedures is solely the responsibility of the specified users of the report. Consequently, we make no representation regarding the sufficiency of the procedures described below either for the purpose for which this report has been requested or for any other purpose.

(Include paragraphs to enumerate procedures and findings)

We were not engaged to, and did not, perform an examination, the objective of which would be the expression of an opinion on the accompanying prospective financial statements. Accordingly, we do not express an opinion on whether the prospective financial statements are presented in conformity with AICPA presentation guidelines or on whether the underlying assumptions provide a reasonable basis for the presentation. Had we performed additional procedures, other matters might have come to our attention that would have been reported to you. Furthermore, there will usually be differences between the forecasted and actual results, because events and circumstances frequently do not occur as expected, and those differences may be material. We have no responsibility to update this report for events and circumstances occurring after the date of this report.

This report is intended solely for the use of the Boards of Directors of XYZ Company and ABC Company and should not be used by those who have not agreed to the procedures and taken responsibility for the sufficiency of the procedures for their purposes.

Source: *AICPA Professional Standards*, New York: AICPA, section AT 200.57.

NEW TYPES OF ASSURANCE SERVICES AND THE FUTURE OF THE ASSURANCE FUNCTION

In meeting the challenge of broadening the CPA's assurance role, the AICPA, in 1994, appointed a Special Committee on Assurance Services to "analyze and report on the current state, as well as the future, of the audit/assurance function."[34] As observed earlier in this chapter, the Committee agreed that assurance is a more comprehensive concept than either auditing or attestation, and can improve the *reliability*, *relevance*, or *context* of virtually any form of information for decision makers. In addition, the Committee identified several areas offering potential for CPA involvement. Most of these are amenable to a form of agreed-upon procedures engagement. Some of these areas are discussed in the following paragraphs.

.com
http://www.aicpa.org/assurance/index.htm

34 *AICPA Board of Directors Resolution*, New York: AICPA, April 22, 1994.

TABLE 15.10

Summary Table of Nonaudit Services

Nature of Service	Type of Report	Level of Assurance	Distribution of Report	Principle Procedures
Covered by Accounting and Review Standards:				
Compilation of financial statements for nonpublic entities	Compilation	None	General	Understand industry accounting practices Read the financial statements
Review of financial statements for nonpublic entities	Review	Limited	General	Inquiry Analytical procedures
Covered by Auditing Standards:				
Agreed-upon procedures applied to specified elements of the financial statements	Agreed-upon procedures	None	Restricted	As agreed
Letters for underwriters (comfort letters)	Review	Limited	Underwriters	Inquiry Analytical procedures
Review of interim financial information	Review	Limited	General	Inquiry Analytical procedures
Unaudited financial statements of public entities	Disclaimer	None	General	Not specified
Covered by Attestation Standards:				
Compliance attestation	Agreed-upon procedures	None	Restricted	As agreed (usually consist of inquiry and reading of applicable laws, rules, and regulations)
Reports on internal control	Opinion	Positive	General	Obtaining management's written assertion Application of procedures to test assertion
Reports on prospective financial statements: Compilation	Compilation	None	Forecast: General Projection: Restricted	Inquiry as to accounting principles Testing of mathematical accuracy of computations Reading of prospective financial statements Evaluation of assumptions
Examination	Opinion	Positive*	Forecast: General Projection: Restricted	Examination of evidence supporting assumptions Determination whether assumptions provide reasonable basis for the forecast or projection Evaluation of preparation and presentation of prospective data
Application of agreed-upon procedures	Agreed-upon procedures	None	Limited to specified parties	As specified by agreement

*Regarding reasonableness of assumptions, but not achievability of results.

WebTrust

As described in Chapter 8, electronic data interchange (EDI) allows entities to purchase inventory and complete sales transactions with suppliers and customers by computer, and use electronic funds transfers to settle the obligations. In addition, electronic shopping on the Internet and electronic banking have added to the degree of electronic commerce being transacted. Given the risk of electronic information being altered, deleted, or duplicated, the need for control over the security and integrity of the information is a critical factor in safeguarding assets and producing reliable information.

In this context, the AICPA and the Canadian Institute of Chartered Accountants (CICA) jointly developed **WebTrust**. A form of attestation, a WebTrust engagement involves examining and attesting to critical aspects of a client's web site, such as privacy and security of transactions completed between the client and its customers at the web site. An electronic seal is awarded to sites that meet the WebTrust principles and criteria. Every three months, the CPA tests the site to determine that it continues to meet the WebTrust criteria. The WebTrust seal may be revoked for sites that do not maintain the proper level of privacy and security.

In addition to evaluating privacy and security, CPAs are often requested to by their WebTrust clients to perform consulting services such as web site design, systems analysis and design, risk identification and assessment, and information technology audits.

.com
http://www.aicpa.org/
webtrust/index.htm

SysTrust

Recognizing the need for systems reliability reporting, the AICPA and the Canadian Institute of Chartered Accountants, in another joint venture, developed **SysTrust** to provide assurance that a system is reliable.[35] In a SysTrust engagement, the accountant reports on the "availability, security, integrity and maintainability of a system."[36] The scope of the engagement includes a "system description . . ., management's assertions about the system's underlying controls, and an attestation report by the accountant that evaluates the system against specific criteria."[37]

.com
http://www.aicpa.org/
assurance/systrust/
index.htm

Relevance and Reliability of an Entity's Performance Measures

In setting and achieving its goals, an entity establishes performance measurement systems. Depending on the nature of the entity and its objectives, measurement criteria need to be identified for this purpose. Examples of possible measures are customer satisfaction, shareholder value, growth, financial performance, product and service quality, process quality, and employee morale. For selected criteria to properly measure performance, they must possess the characteristics of being *relevant to established goals and reliable measures of performance*.

To assess relevance, the CPA should examine the entity's objectives and evaluate the performance measures against the objectives for consistency. To assess reliability, the CPA can make inquiries, examine results, and compare with entity performance reports. Agreement of the CPA's examination results with entity performance reports provides

35 See Boritz, Efrim, Erin Mackler, and Doug McPhie, "Reporting on Systems Reliability," *The Journal of Accountancy*, November 1999, pp. 75–87.
36 Ibid, p. 75.
37 Ibid.

added assurance as to reliability. If the entity compares its results with competitors' data, the CPA can also examine that data for reliability.

Risk Assessment

.com

http://www.aicpa.org/
assurance/scas/
newsvs/risk/index.htm

The AICPA Special Committee on Assurance Services defined **business risk** as the "threat that an event or action will adversely affect an organization's ability to achieve its business objectives and execute its strategies successfully." A critical aspect of entity success is clear identification of its specific business risk, reasonable measurement of that risk, and an established means for controlling it. The independent CPA can assist in this endeavor by helping the entity identify its specific risks, assess the relevance of risks already identified by the entity, and/or evaluate the entity's systems for identifying and controlling those risks.

CPA involvement might assume the form of agreed-upon procedures applied to assessing the likelihood of significant adverse events and measuring the range of magnitude of events that may occur. Procedures might also be applied to evaluating management's responses to identified risks and to assessing the adequacy of risk-monitoring systems established by the entity.

ElderCare

.com

http://www.aicpa.org/
assurance/scas/
newsvs/elderpl/
index.htm

In performing **ElderCare** services, the CPA evaluates alternate types of services provided to elderly clients and their families and provides assurance as to the suitability of the services given the needs of the recipient. Some of the needs addressed in these engagements are financial, such as managing real estate and other property, ensuring that receipts are properly deposited, insurance claims promptly filed, tax planning, and making disbursements. Some of the needs are medical and residential, such as assisted living or extended care arrangements, finding proper medigap insurance, and arranging for transportation, housekeeping, and other services.

As can be seen from this diverse list of services, ElderCare involves consulting and direct assurance. Its purpose is to assist the elderly to experience a reasonable quality of life and to provide assurance to their children that their parents are being properly cared for. With the growing number of elderly, these services represent a real growth potential for the CPA.

Summary of Other Assurance Services

.com

http://www.aicpa.org/
assurance/sitemap/
index.htm

Demand for the aforementioned services is growing rapidly. CPAs, given their expertise in evidence gathering and evaluation and their general knowledge of information systems, are best qualified to perform the new assurance services. To capture a reasonable share of the market, however, the profession must actively offer and promote continuing education programs in the new assurance services, and CPAs need to participate in the programs and then market these services to existing and potential clients.

KEY TERMS

Agreed-upon procedures, 632

Assertion, 642

Assurance services, 631

Attestation, 642

Attestation standards, 643

Business risk, 658

REVIEW QUESTIONS

1. Define *assurance* and *attestation* as used within the context of the accounting profession.

2. Differentiate between negative assurance and positive assurance.

3. What distinguishes assurance services covered by each of the following body of standards?
   a. Auditing standards
   b. Accounting and review standards
   c. Attestation standards

4. What steps should a CPA, associated with a client's financial statements, take upon learning of a material departure from GAAP?

5. What is the major difference between the eleven attestation standards and the ten auditing standards?

6. Differentiate between compilation, review, and audit.

7. What are the major procedures applied in a review? In a compilation?

8. What type of accounting service may be performed by a CPA who lacks independence?

9. Under what conditions may a CPA accept an engagement to report on the application of agreed-upon procedures to specified elements of the financial statements?

10. Why do underwriters request a comfort letter from the auditors?

11. Name three matters commonly covered in comfort letters.

12. Why should a CPA who has *not* previously audited the client's financial statements ordinarily *not* give negative assurance in the comfort letter?

13. Identify the major difference between a report on internal control as part of the audit engagement and one resulting from a special engagement to report on internal control.

14. What type of assurance may be given when interim financial information is presented alone?

15. If limited procedures have *not* been applied to interim financial information included in the annual report, must the audit report be modified? If so, in what way? Does this constitute a qualified opinion?

16. Differentiate between a forecast and a projection.

17. Why is the distribution of projections to third parties more limited than that of forecasts?

18. Give two examples of assurance services that CPAs might perform that are *not* covered by existing standards. Why do agreed-upon procedures hold the most potential in conducting these newer types of assurance services?

MULTIPLE CHOICE QUESTIONS FROM PAST CPA EXAMS

1. Before issuing a report on the compilation of financial statements of a nonpublic entity, the accountant should
   a. Apply analytical procedures to selected financial data to discover any material misstatements.
   b. Corroborate at least a sample of the assertions management has embodied in the financial statements.
   c. Inquire of the client's personnel whether the financial statements omit substantially all disclosures.
   d. Read the financial statements to consider whether the financial statements are free from obvious material errors.

2. The objective of a review of interim financial information of a public entity is to provide the accountant with a basis for
   a. Determining whether the prospective financial information is based on reasonable assumptions.
   b. Expressing a limited opinion that the financial information is presented in conformity with generally accepted accounting principles.
   c. Deciding whether to perform substantive audit procedures prior to the balance sheet date.
   d. Reporting whether material modifications should be made for such information to conform with generally accepted accounting principles.

3. An accountant's report expressing an opinion on an entity's internal controls should state that
   a. Only those controls on which the accountant intends to rely were reviewed, tested, and evaluated.
   b. The establishment and maintenance of the internal controls is the responsibility of management.
   c. The study and evaluation of the internal controls was conducted in accordance with generally accepted auditing standards.
   d. Distribution of the report is restricted for use only by management and the board of directors.

4. Which of the following professional services would be considered an attest engagement?
   a. A management consulting engagement to provide information systems advice to a client.
   b. An engagement to report on compliance with statutory requirements.
   c. An income tax engagement to prepare federal and state tax returns.
   d. The compilation of financial statements from a client's accounting records.

5. A financial forecast is an estimate of financial position, results of operations, and cash flows that, to the best of management's knowledge, is
   a. At the midpoint of a given precision range.
   b. At the low point of a given precision range.
   c. Conservative.
   d. Most probable.

6. An attestation engagement is one in which a CPA is engaged to
   a. Issue a written communication expressing a conclusion about the reliability of a written assertion that is the responsibility of another party.
   b. Provide tax advice or prepare a tax return based on financial information the CPA has not audited or reviewed.
   c. Testify as an expert witness in accounting, auditing, or tax matters, given certain stipulated facts.
   d. Assemble prospective financial statements based on the assumptions of the entity's management without expressing any assurance.

7. In which of the following reports should a CPA *not* express negative or limited assurance?
   a. A standard compilation report on financial statements of a nonpublic entity.
   b. A standard review report on financial statements of a nonpublic entity.
   c. A standard review report on interim financial statements of a public entity.
   d. A standard comfort letter on financial information included in a registration statement of a public entity.

8. When an independent CPA assists in preparing the financial statements of a publicly held entity, but has *not* audited or reviewed them, the CPA should issue a disclaimer of opinion. In such situations, the CPA has no responsibility to apply any procedures beyond
   a. Ascertaining whether the financial statements are in conformity with generally accepted accounting principles.
   b. Determining whether management has elected to omit substantially all required disclosures.
   c. Documenting that the internal control system is not being relied on.
   d. Reading the financial statements for obvious material misstatements.

9. During an engagement to review the financial statements of a nonpublic entity, an accountant becomes aware of a material departure from GAAP. If the accountant decides to modify the standard review report because management will *not* revise the financial statements, the accountant should
   a. Express negative assurance on the accounting principles that do not conform with GAAP.
   b. Disclose the departure from GAAP in a separate paragraph of the report.
   c. Issue an adverse or a qualified opinion, depending on materiality.
   d. Express positive assurance on the accounting principles that conform with GAAP.

10. An accountant may accept an engagement to apply agreed-upon procedures to prospective financial statements provided that
    a. Distribution of the report is to be restricted to the specified parties involved.
    b. The prospective financial statements are also examined.
    c. The accountant takes responsibility for the adequacy of the procedures performed.
    d. Negative assurance is expressed on the prospective financial statements taken as a whole.

11. Performing inquiry and analytical procedures is the primary basis for an accountant to issue a
    a. Report on compliance with requirements governing major federal assistance programs in accordance with the Single Audit Act.
    b. Review report on prospective financial statements that present an entity's expected financial position, given one or more hypothetical assumption.
    c. Management advisory report prepared at the request of a client's audit committee.
    d. Review report on comparative financial statements for a nonpublic entity in its second year of operations.

12. Accepting an engagement to compile a financial projection for a publicly held company most likely would be inappropriate if the projection were to be distributed to
    a. A bank with which the entity is negotiating for a loan.
    b. A labor union with which the entity is negotiating a contract.
    c. The principal stockholder, to the exclusion of the other stockholders.
    d. All stockholders of record as of the report date.

13. Which of the following is *not* an attestation standard?
    a. Sufficient evidence shall be obtained to provide a reasonable basis for the conclusion that is expressed in the report.
    b. The report shall identify the assertion being reported on and state the character of the engagement.
    c. The work shall be adequately planned and assistants, if any, shall be properly supervised.
    d. A sufficient understanding of the internal controls shall be obtained to plan the engagement.

14. Must a CPA in public practice be independent in fact and appearance when providing the following services?

	Compilation of personal financial statements	Preparation of a tax return	Compilation of a financial forecast
a.	No	No	No
b.	No	No	Yes
c.	Yes	No	No
d.	No	Yes	No

15. If requested to perform a review engagement for a nonpublic entity in which an accountant has an immaterial direct financial interest, the accountant is
    a. Independent because the financial interest is immaterial and, therefore, may issue a review report.
    b. Not independent and, therefore, may *not* be associated with the financial statements.
    c. Not independent and, therefore, may *not* issue a review report.
    d. Not independent and, therefore, may issue a review report, but may *not* issue an auditor's opinion.

16. Which of the following statements is correct concerning both an engagement to compile and an engagement to review a nonpublic entity's financial statements?
    a. The accountant does not contemplate obtaining an understanding of the internal control system.
    b. The accountant must be independent in fact and appearance.
    c. The accountant expresses no assurance on the financial statements.
    d. The accountant should obtain a written management representation letter.

17. In performing an attestation engagement, a CPA typically
    a. Supplies litigation support services.
    b. Assesses control risk at a low level.
    c. Expresses a conclusion about an assertion.
    d. Provides management consulting advice.

18. When an accountant examines a financial forecast that fails to disclose several significant assumptions used to prepare the forecast, the accountant should describe the assumptions in the accountant's report and issue a(n)

a. "Except for" qualified opinion.
b. "Subject to" qualified opinion.
c. Unqualified opinion with a separate explanatory paragraph.
d. Adverse opinion.

19. Compiled financial statements should be accompanied by a report stating all of the following *except*
    a. The accountant does not express an opinion or any other form of assurance on them.
    b. A compilation has been performed.
    c. A compilation is limited to presenting in the form of financial statements information that is the representation of management.
    d. A compilation consists principally of inquiries of company personnel and analytical procedures applied to financial data.

20. Which of the following procedures would most likely be included in a review engagement of a nonpublic entity?
    a. Preparing a bank transfer schedule.
    b. Inquiring about related-party transactions.
    c. Assessing the internal control system.
    d. Performing cutoff tests on sales and purchases transactions.

ESSAY QUESTIONS AND PROBLEMS

15.1   The following is an excerpt from an article appearing in an issue of *The Wall Street Journal*.

> SAN JOSE, Calif.—The semiconductor industry's key sales indicator rose in August, giving analysts hope that the battered chip business is improving.
>
> The Semiconductor Industry Association's closely watched ratio of new orders compared to billings for goods sold rose to 0.90 in August, up from a revised figure of 0.86 for July. That means that for every $100 in shipments, chipmakers received $90 in new orders.
>
> . . . The so-called book-to-bill ratio hit a new low of 0.79 in March when buyers of chips cut back their orders because of slowing sales of personal computers. The recent book-to-bill number is still well below August 1995 levels of 1.16, however.

Required:
a. List three examples (in addition to the above) illustrating how the accounting profession might extend the application of assurance services.
b. What kinds of procedures might an independent CPA apply in attesting to the reliability of the book-to-bill ratio?

15.2   For each of the following engagements, indicate the nature of the service performed (i.e., audit, review, compilation, etc.), the standards covering the engagement (i.e., auditing, attestation, or accounting and review), the type of report to be issued (i.e., opinion, review, compilation), and the principal procedures to be applied.

a. The board of directors of Donner, Inc., has requested the CPA to examine the projected financial statements for the upcoming year. The statements are to be used by Charter Bank as part of a loan application to be submitted by Donner.
b. The board of directors of Crimley Corporation request the CPA to scrutinize certain elements of the financial statements of Zoare, Inc., a candidate for acquisition by Crimley.

c. A nonpublic client asks the CPA to prepare financial statements from the client's records, without auditing or reviewing the statements.

d. George & Henry, Investment Bankers, have requested the CPA to issue a comfort letter relative to the registration of securities of Bendy, Inc., with the Securities and Exchange Commission. The comfort letter is to cover the unaudited financial statements for the three months ending February 28, 2002.

15.3   For the year ending December 31, 2001, Wallender & Creighton, CPAs, audited the financial statements of Dan's Hardware, Inc., and expressed an unqualified opinion dated February 27, 2002. For the year ended December 31, 2002, Wallender & Creighton were engaged to review Dan's financial statements—that is, to "look into the company's financial statements and determine whether there are any obvious modifications that should be made to the financial statements in order for them to be in conformity with generally accepted accounting principles."

Wallender made the necessary inquiries, performed the necessary analytical procedures, and performed certain additional procedures that were deemed necessary to achieve the requisite limited assurance. Wallender's work was completed on March 3, 2003, and the financial statements appeared to be in conformity with generally accepted accounting principles that were consistently applied. The report was prepared on March 5, 2003. It was delivered to Finnegan, the controller of Dan's Hardware, on March 9, 2003.

Required:

Prepare the properly addressed and dated report on the comparative financial statements of Dan's Hardware, Inc., for the years ended December 31, 2002 and 2001. (AICPA adapted)

15.4   In order to obtain information that is necessary to make informed decisions, management often calls on the independent auditor for assistance. This may involve a request that the independent auditor apply certain audit procedures to specific accounts of a company that is a candidate for acquisition and report upon the results. In such an engagement, the agreed-upon procedures may constitute a scope limitation.

At the completion of an engagement performed at the request of Viceroy, Ltd., which was limited in scope as just explained, the following report was prepared by an audit assistant and was submitted to the audit manager for review.

To: Board of Directors of Dromederry, Inc.:

We have applied certain agreed-upon procedures, as discussed below, to the accounting records of Dromederry, Inc., as of December 31, 2002, solely to assist Viceroy, Ltd., in connection with the proposed acquisition of Dromederry, Inc.

We have examined the cash in banks and accounts receivable of Dromederry, Inc., as of December 31, 2002, in accordance with generally accepted auditing standards and, accordingly, included such tests of the accounting records and such other auditing procedures as we considered necessary in the circumstances.

In our opinion, the cash and receivables referred to above are fairly presented as of December 31, 2002, in conformity with generally accepted accounting principles. We therefore recommend that Viceroy, Ltd., acquire Dromederry, Inc., pursuant to the proposed agreement.

Signature

Required:

Comment on the proposed report describing those assertions that are

a. Incorrect or should otherwise be deleted.

b. Missing and should be inserted.

(AICPA adapted)

15.5   a. Contrast the scope and reporting requirements for a report on internal control as part of an audit engagement, and a report on internal control as part of a special engagement to express an opinion.

b. In performing an engagement to express an opinion on General Manufacturing's internal control system, Cosmo Kramer, CPA, discovered material control weaknesses within the company's sales and collections functions. What steps should Kramer take with regard to the weaknesses? (Don't forget to address the reporting implications.)

15.6   Daryl Bean, CPA, issued the following report on the forecasted financial statements for German Donuts, Inc.

Trustee in Receivership
German Donuts, Inc.

At your request, I performed the agreed-upon procedures enumerated below with respect to the forecasted balance sheet, statements of income, retained earnings, and cash flows of German Donuts, Inc., as of December 31, 2002.

a. I assisted the management of German Donuts in assembling the prospective financial statements.

b. I read the prospective financial statements for compliance in regard to format with the presentation guidelines established by the American Institute of Certified Public Accountants for presentation of a forecast.

c. I tested the forecast for mathematical accuracy.

d. I applied other auditing procedures that we considered necessary under the circumstances.

In my opinion, the accompanying forecast is presented in conformity with guidelines for presentation of a forecast established by the American Institute of Certified Public Accountants, and the underlying assumptions provide a reasonable basis for management's forecast.

March 11, 2003
Daryl Bean, CPA

Required:
Comment on the above report. Indicate corrections where appropriate. (AICPA adapted)

15.7   One of your public clients is required by the Securities and Exchange Commission to include unaudited interim financial information in its annual report to shareholders. You have been asked to review the information.

Required:
a. What is the purpose of reviewing interim financial information?

b. Why do you think the SEC requires that interim financial information be included in the annual report to stockholders?

c. How should your audit report be modified if limited procedures have not been applied to the interim information?

15.8   You have been asked by Diamond Men's Wear to review its financial statements for the year ending December 31, 2002. Diamond has requested a substantial loan from a newly formed lenders' consortium. In the past you have compiled Diamond's financial statements, but have never audited or reviewed them.

Required:

a. Differentiate among audits, reviews, and compilations in terms of procedures to be applied and level of assurance provided.

b. Assuming you completed your field work on February 14, 2003, and do *not* find any material cause for modification of the financial statements, draft the review report.

c. Assume that you discover that Diamond has not recognized any liability for employee pensions or other postretirement benefits. What modifications should you make to the standard review report? What should you do if management and the board do *not* agree to these modifications?

15.9   The firm of Sheets & Gilmore, CPAs, has been engaged to examine the internal controls of Costanza, Benis, and Neumann, Securities Brokers, as of January 31, 2003, the end of the firm's fiscal year. Rule 17a-5 of the Securities and Exchange Act of 1934 requires that this type of report, rendered by independent CPAs, accompany the financial statements of brokers and investment companies.

The examination is to cover only those aspects of internal control relating to financial reporting—that is, those policies and procedures pertaining to the company's ability to record, process, summarize, and report financial data consistent with the assertions embodied in the annual financial statements.

The auditors have obtained the firm's written statement of assertions relating to its internal control system and have obtained sufficient competent evidential matter to complete the examination on February 22, 2003. Although the firm's management assertions state that the internal financial controls are effective, the CPAs discovered the following weaknesses:

1. Controls do not provide for a clear distinction between securities held in the name of the brokerage firm and securities held in clients' names;
2. Brokerage commissions are not independently reconciled on a recurring basis; and
3. No provision is made for reconciling the firm's several bank accounts. Although the accounts are usually reconciled at the end of each month, not all of the accounts are reconciled monthly, and some accounts are not reconciled at year end.

Required:

a. What is the difference between an engagement to express an opinion on a client's internal control system and an evaluation of internal control as part of a financial statement audit?

b. Draft the report that Sheets & Gilmore should issue to the management and board of directors of Costanza, Benis, & Neumann, assuming:
    1. Direct attestation
    2. Indirect attestation

15.10   CPAs apply analytical procedures for a variety of purposes. They are applicable to both audit and nonaudit services.

Required:

a. What is the overriding purpose of applying analytical procedures?
b. Give six examples of situations calling for the application of analytical procedures.

15.11   Each of the following narratives describes an engagement performed by a CPA.

- The CPA conducted an audit for the purpose of expressing an opinion on the client's financial statements.
- Same as above but in this instance the client is an electric utility and the financial statements conformed to the requirements of the state public utilities commission.
- The CPA reviewed the financial statements of a small client who is applying for a loan at one of the local banks.
- The corporate controller, who is also a CPA, prepared financial statements for her employer, a small privately held manufacturing company. The financial statements are going to be used by a related party in deciding whether to extend a loan to the corporation.
- The CPA accepted an engagement to perform certain procedures that would establish compliance with a royalty agreement to which the client is a party.
- Conway and Bardi, Securities Brokers, as part of their due diligence responsibility, requested the CPA to review unaudited financial data included in a registration statement accompanying a public offering of securities.
- The CPA was requested to express an opinion on prospective financial data accompanying a loan application. The loan, if granted, will finance the construction of a major apartment and condominium complex. The prospective data reflect varying combinations of assumptions as to level of apartment occupancy and timing of condominium sales.
- The CPA agreed to review the quarterly financial data submitted to the Securities and Exchange Commission.

Required:
a. For each narrative:
  1. Identify the nature of the engagement (e.g., audit, compilation, etc.);
  2. Indicate the type of report to be rendered (e.g., compilation, review, opinion, disclaimer) and the level of assurance provided (e.g., none, limited, positive); and
  3. List the principal procedures to be applied in completing the engagement.
b. Indicate the extent of distribution permitted for each of the reports (i.e., general or restricted). For restricted distribution reports, identify the parties to whom the report may be issued.

15.12 Chapter 15 described the following types of assurance services performed by CPAs:

a. WebTrust engagements;
b. SysTrust engagements;
c. Assessing the relevance and reliability of an entity's performance measures;
d. Assessing business risk; and
e. ElderCare engagements.

For each of the following situations, indicate by letter the appropriate type of engagement:

1. Susan Lopez, CPA, is asked by one of her smaller clients to evaluate its financial and operating leverage to determine if the company is maximizing its return on equity without impairing its long-term debt paying ability.
2. Oblong Planets, a computer game developer, has requested Jason Breese, its independent auditor, to assess the reliability of both financial and nonfinancial reports generated by its CBIS.
3. The family of Doris Rosenberry, age 84 and recently widowed, has engaged Richard Carr, CPA, to manage Ms. Rosenberry's rental properties, oversee her other investments, and generally maintain her financial records.

4. Mledger.com is an Internet company formed to maintain clients' accounting records on the Internet. To assure clients as to data security, the firm has engaged Post Mortem, LLP, a large accounting firm, to attest to the integrity and security of Mledger's web site

5. Heather Gruening has been operting a chain of beauty salons for five years and has only recently encountered unexpected cash flow problems. The salons have all reported increasing profits over the past three years. Concerned about the quality of her existing financial reports, she has asked Janet Johnson, her CPA, to develop a set of reports that will provide a greater degree of advance warning of impending cash flow problems.

c h a p t e r 1 6

biltrite

l e a r n i n g   o b j e c t i v e s

After reading this chapter, you should be able to

1 Define operational auditing as a subset of internal auditing.
2 Differentiate between efficiency and effectiveness auditing.
3 Describe how operational auditing developed to fulfill specific management needs.
4 Recognize that operational auditing exists to assist managers in improving their performance.
5 List and describe the steps in planning and performing an operational audit, including:
  a Identifying audit objectives and establishing evaluation criteria;
  b Developing and applying the audit program;
  c Appraising efficiency and effectiveness;
  d Formulating conclusions and recommendations; and
  e Reporting findings.
6 Describe governmental compliance auditing as applied to the audits of state and local governmental units, colleges and universities, and other not-for-profit entities receiving federal financial assistance.
7 Define auditor responsibility under "yellow book" standards and the Single Audit Act of 1984, as amended in 1996, and interpreted by OMB Circular A-133.

OVERVIEW

This chapter considers operational auditing and governmental compliance auditing. Operational auditing is a subset of internal auditing and assists managers by reviewing and evaluating their activities and recommending improvements, focusing on efficiency and effectiveness of operations. Governmental compliance auditing, a form of compliance attestation, involves testing and reporting on compliance with various federal and state laws and regulations. These two forms of auditing have assumed greater importance in recent years, given decentralization of entity operations and the increasing number of laws and regulations affecting both profit and not-for-profit entities.

The first section of this chapter addresses operational auditing and describes how it developed over several years as a monitoring device for top management. A case study then is presented to describe how a typical operational audit is planned and performed. The importance of developing specific audit objectives and identifying appropriate evaluation criteria is emphasized in the case study. An audit program is prepared as part of the case, and the various steps in performing the audit field work are identified and described. An audit report containing the auditors' findings and recommendations also is presented.

The second part of the chapter focuses on governmental compliance auditing as applied by the independent auditor when engaged in audits of state and local governmental units, colleges and universities, and other not-for-profit entities that are the recipients of federal financial assistance. Within this context, the auditor must observe governmental auditing standards as defined in the General Accounting Office's "yellow book," as well as comply with generally accepted auditing standards. Additionally, if the amount of financial assistance exceeds specified minimum levels, the auditor must comply with the requirements of the federal Single Audit Act of 1984, as amended in 1996, and OMB (Office of Management and Budget) Circular A-133.

INTRODUCTION

Internal auditing was described in Chapter 1 as a service function established within an organization to examine and evaluate its activities. Internal audits may focus on financial reporting (financial audits); compliance with policies, procedures, laws, or regulations (compliance audits); fraud detection (fraud audits);[1] or operational efficiency and effectiveness (operational audits). Most internal audit staffs engage in all of these endeavors (see Figure 16.1).

To guide the practice of internal auditing, the **Institute of Internal Auditors** has established general and specific standards, which are presented in an appendix following this chapter. Although not enforceable in the same sense as the AICPA auditing and attestation standards, they do provide helpful guidance for the internal auditor concerning such matters as maintaining necessary independence, required proficiency, audit scope, performing the audit, and administering the internal audit function.

Although they are an important subset of internal auditing, operational audits also are performed by the **General Accounting Office (GAO)** and by the management consulting units of accounting firms. The first part of this chapter addresses operational auditing within the context of the internal auditing function. The second part describes governmental compliance auditing as applied by independent auditors during audits of state and local governmental entities and other not-for-profit entities. Governmental

.com

http://www.gao.gov/

---

1   Often referred to as *forensic accounting,* fraud audits are becoming an increasingly significant factor in the business of CPA firms. For examples of forensic accounting engagements, see "Green Eyeshades and Private Eyes?" *Business Week,* January 20, 1997, p. 74, and "Accounting Sleuths Ferret Hidden Assets," *The Wall Street Journal,* December 18, 1996, p. B1.

FIGURE 16.1

Internal Auditing—A Management Service Function

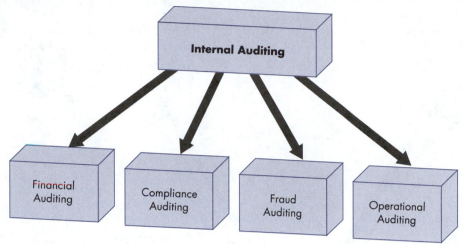

compliance auditing, within this context, involves testing and reporting on an entity's internal controls over federal financial assistance programs, as well as testing and reporting on conformity with laws and regulations relating to those programs, where the state or local entity, or other not-for-profit entity, is a recipient of federal financial assistance.

OPERATIONAL AUDITING

Operational Auditing Defined

Operational auditing, as a subset of internal auditing, reviews an entity's activities for efficiency and effectiveness and may evaluate any type of activity at any level within the organization. Unlike financial auditing, operational auditing focuses on activities rather than financial statement assertions. The audited activities may be related to a function (e.g., why is employee turnover so high?) or they may be part of an organizational unit (e.g., why is the Nashville plant producing a high percentage of defective parts?). The overall objective, common to all operational audits, is maximizing organizational welfare.

Management auditing is a subset of operational auditing that attempts to measure the effectiveness with which an organizational unit is administered, and that concentrates more on effectiveness than on efficiency. Efficiency and effectiveness, as used to describe operational auditing, are distinct terms (see Figure 16.2). **Efficiency** may be viewed as an input measure that relates to cost control and is concerned with the performance of recurring functions at a minimum of cost to the entity. **Effectiveness** is output oriented; it is viewed as a measure of productivity in utilizing the firm's resources and in terms of long-run profitability. As one audits at progressively higher levels within an entity, effectiveness becomes more important relative to efficiency.

Because management audits are about management effectiveness, they can be potentially dangerous to the internal auditor. In performing these audits, the auditor must

FIGURE 16.2

Management Auditing—A Subset of Operational Auditing

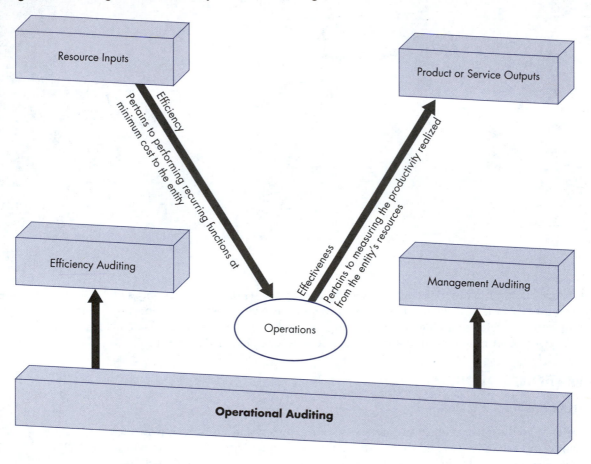

avoid disrupting the harmonious working of the management team and must take care to maintain cooperative relations between auditor and auditee. Obtaining the auditee's input, participation, and support also increases the probability of implementation of the auditor's recommendations. A partnership approach is most important in management audits.

The Evolution of Internal Auditing

As first conceived, **internal auditing** focused on asset safeguards and fraud detection. Later, as laws, regulations, and policies became more numerous, compliance auditing was added to the internal auditor's responsibilities.

With the growth and diversification of companies, management encountered increasing difficulty in monitoring operations and activities that were often far removed from corporate headquarters. At first, decentralization and divisional autonomy relieved corporate management of the need to administer the entire breadth and depth of operations. Product managers, regional vice presidents, and divisional managers emerged as firms' chief line-operating managers. The distancing of top management from much of the operating activity, however, created a need for a monitoring device. Although elaborate systems of budgeting and performance reporting provided some degree of control, corporate management needed to monitor the activities of the divisions and product lines more closely. Operational auditing, as part of the internal audit function, emerged to fill this need.

The **Foreign Corrupt Practices Act of 1977 (FCPA)** also played an important role in increasing the resources devoted to internal auditing by publicly held companies. Congress passed the FCPA in response to a 1976 SEC report on investigations into questionable and illegal corporate payments and practices; the report was submitted to the Senate Committee on Banking, Housing, and Urban Affairs, and recommended legislation to prevent bribes and other illegal payments to foreign officials by public companies as a means for obtaining business. The act contains provisions requiring companies to maintain accounting records that fairly and accurately reflect transactions. The act also requires companies to develop and implement internal controls that permit preparation of financial statements in accordance with GAAP and to maintain accountability over assets.

Given the severity of penalties imposed for violation of FCPA provisions, companies began to enlarge their internal audit staffs as a means for monitoring FCPA compliance. At the same time, the reporting level was raised; today, many internal auditors report to the chief executive officer and the audit committee of the board of directors.

Operational Auditing Today

Operational auditing has emerged as an integral part of internal auditing. As it exists today, operational auditing has become an important part of top management's monitoring effort. With the addition of the operational auditing function to their management service role, internal auditors frequently are referred to as the "eyes and ears of management."

Operational audits typically answer such questions as:

- Are specified employees functioning efficiently?
- Are current approaches still effective in achieving the entity's goals in light of changing conditions?

Until recently, operational auditing followed a practice of performing recurring efficiency and effectiveness audits on different functions or units in a company. The audits were conducted regardless of whether or not the auditors were aware of special problems. Now, the emphasis has shifted from recurring audits to focus more on management's special problems and the means of solving them. For example, instead of auditing the human resources function every three years, the internal audit team, at management's request, may investigate why the company has experienced increasing employee turnover in the appliance division within the past year. One might view this approach as **risk-based operational auditing**. Other problem areas targeted for operational audits might include inability to meet production quotas, unfilled customer backorders, cost overruns, low rate of return on products, a reporting system not providing management with adequate information for decision-making purposes, and possible violation of environmental laws and regulations.

Given its wide breadth of focus, operational auditing requires other forms of expertise in addition to expertise in accounting and auditing. Many operational audit engagements now involve industrial engineers, economists, statisticians, mathematicians, data processing specialists, and lawyers, as well as accountants. While these experts are not necessarily a permanent part of the internal audit staff, they often are borrowed from other units in the organization for the performance of operational audits requiring their particular skills.

Currently, the scope of operational auditing is virtually unlimited; it may cover all functional areas and all levels of the organization. Table 16.1 lists possible operational audits by functional area.

As a by-product of their upgraded role, internal auditors have also acquired an enhanced image in the eyes of the independent auditors. Most public accounting firms consider internal auditors vital to an effective independent audit, and will hesitate to accept a large-client engagement if the client lacks an audit committee and a capable internal audit staff. Indeed, as discussed in Chapters 5 through 7, after obtaining satisfaction concerning competence and objectivity, the independent auditor frequently utilizes the work of the internal auditors in completing the audit.

Operational Audit Approach

Operational auditing focuses on helping management to improve the way entity activities are performed. In this section, a hypothetical internal audit engagement is used to

---

TABLE 16.1

Functional Areas Typically Covered by Operational Audits

Purchasing	Financial Management
Proper determination of the entity's needs for goods and services	Separation between controller and treasurer
Selecting vendors	Flexible budgeting
Receiving goods	Budget coordination
Emergency purchases	Performance reporting by cost and profit center
Controlling vendor influence	Cash control
	Working capital management
Transportation	Investment policy
Reviewing freight costs	**Electronic Data Processing**
Processing claims against carriers	Range of computer usage:
	Underutilization of the computers
Human Resources	Manual rather than computerized report
Adequacy of job analysis, job descriptions, and compensation	Failure to place databases on computer (e.g., customers, creditors, inventories, and payroll)
Recruitment practices	Organizational status for computer head (should be fairly high—otherwise range is too narrow)
Screening procedures	
Training programs	
Adequacy of personnel records	Effectiveness in serving management's needs
Benefits	Adequacy of documentation (systems analysis, programs, modifications, and operator instructions)
Affirmative action	
Computerization	
Exit interviews	Proper controls

illustrate the various steps in planning and performing an operational audit. A simple operational audit report is presented at the conclusion of the exercise.

Vector, Inc., is a diversified manufacturing company consisting of the following three divisions:

- EZ Parts—Automobile replacement mufflers and exhaust pipes
- Excel—Sporting goods
- Staywell—Infant products

The divisions are autonomous and are accountable to corporate headquarters on the basis of divisional budgets, monthly performance reports, and annual headquarters meetings requiring formal presentations by divisional managers. A partial organization chart is presented in Figure 16.3.

The internal audit staff consists of twenty-five members, most of whom are accountants, and is headed by Thomas Layne, Vector's internal audit director. Layne's reporting responsibility extends to the board of directors (refer to Figure 16.3). Audit teams visit the divisions on a recurring basis and examine such functions as budgeting and profit planning, production control, receiving and distribution, and data processing. The cycling process permits each function within each division to be audited every three years. In addition, Layne assigns audit teams to special problem engagements as requested by headquarters management. John Sparks, the corporate controller, currently is concerned that selling prices within the sporting goods division are not producing adequate profits, and so informs Jacquelyn Shoemaker, Vector's marketing vice president. Shoemaker, in turn, requests Layne to conduct a special investigation.

The sporting goods division operates under the trade name of Excel and manufactures and sells baseballs, golf balls, baseball bats, baseball gloves, golf clubs, footballs, tennis rackets, basketballs, soccer balls, and tennis balls. These products are divided into three lines, and each product manager is responsible for pricing her or his line. The three lines and the product managers are as follows:

Line	Product Manager
Baseball bats and gloves	Jeffrey Archer
Baseballs, basketballs, soccer balls, footballs, golf balls, and tennis balls	Jennifer Hill
Golf clubs and tennis rackets	Susan Knox

Kenneth Johns has been designated the in-charge field auditor for the Excel "selling price audit." He is being assisted by Donald Krause, who has been on the staff for two years, and Marjory Mason, a newly hired member of Vector's internal audit staff. Krause is a CPA and was employed previously as a staff auditor by a regional accounting firm. Mason recently earned her baccalaureate degree in accounting; this is her first position. Johns is a CPA and has been with Vector for three years, having spent the preceding four years with a national accounting firm as a senior staff auditor.

Planning the Audit

As in any type of audit, the first step in performing an operational audit is the planning phase. In a properly planned audit, audit objectives and evaluation criteria must be established. In the Vector engagement, Johns has identified the audit objectives as determining whether product prices are set in such a way as to promote Vector's overall

FIGURE 16.3

Vector, Inc., Partial Organization Chart

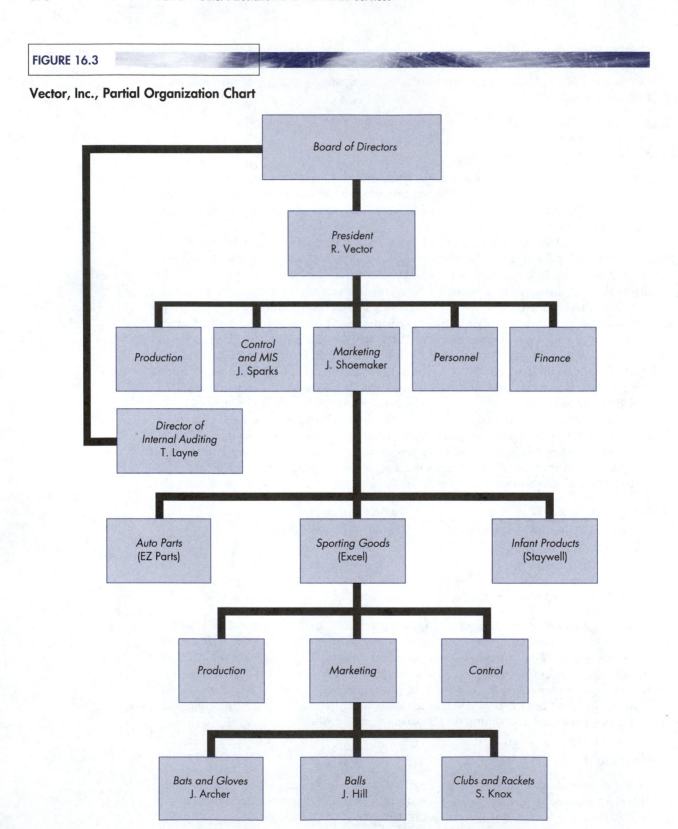

profitability, and whether prices being charged to customers are in accordance with company policy.

Evaluation criteria define the process or activity being audited. Identifying evaluation criteria is necessary if ultimately the auditor is to determine the cause of discovered inefficiencies. For the Vector sales price audit, Johns has established the following criteria:

How do product managers set selling prices?
> Is market analysis undertaken?
> Does market analysis include demand analysis?
> Does market analysis include consideration of competitor pricing strategies?
> Is cost analysis performed?
> Are Vector's cost accountants involved in the process?
> Are indirect costs considered in the decision?
> Is a contribution margin approach applied?

How frequently are selling prices reviewed for adequacy?
> Are selling prices subject to approval by the marketing vice president?
> Once selling prices are set, how does the company ensure that customers are charged correctly?
> Does Excel maintain official price lists by product line?
> Are the price lists stored in the computer?
> What is the process for updating price lists to reflect modifications by product managers?
> Do computer programs contain proper input editing controls that reject quoted prices *not* in conformity with official prices?

The list of evaluation criteria is similar to the internal control questionnaire described in Chapter 7. Instead of serving as a risk assessment device, however, it provides a focal point for developing the audit program.

As a final step in the planning phase, the auditor should discuss the timing and scope of the audit with the official to whom the auditee reports and should review the audit itself with the auditee. In the Excel sales price audit, the three product managers constitute the auditee. Jacquelyn Shoemaker, Vector's marketing vice president, is the officer to whom they report. Johns needs to determine, in conjunction with Shoemaker, whether all product lines and all products within each line, or only a sample, are to be tested. All product lines and products are chosen, in this instance, given the small number of products and the significance of each to total revenue. With regard to timing, Johns and Shoemaker agree that July will be selected for the performance of the audit field work; July is usually a slow sales period and the product managers will have ample time to work with the audit team.

In reviewing the audit with Excel's three product managers, Johns must make every effort to gain their cooperation; cooperation of the auditee is critical to a successful operational audit. A harmonious relationship is necessary if everyone is to work toward promoting the best interests of the entity. Auditees frequently feel threatened and may view the internal audit as a policing exercise, when in fact the internal auditor is trying to help the auditee to better perform his or her assigned role. In gaining the product managers' cooperation, Johns discusses the nature and scope of the audit with each of them. He also requests and encourages their participation in the audit. The product managers' role will consist mainly of answering questions, explaining and illustrating the pricing process, and providing necessary documentation. Involving operating management in the audit develops trust and creates a problem-solving partnership rather than an adversarial relationship.

Performing the Audit Field Work

The field work for an operational audit engagement consists of the following steps, which are addressed in the ensuing sections.

1. Conduct a preliminary survey of the activity or functional unit to be audited;
2. Develop the audit program;
3. Perform the audit;
4. Appraise the efficiency and effectiveness of the activity or unit;
5. Evaluate the findings; and
6. Develop conclusions and recommendations.

Conduct a Preliminary Survey   The purpose of the **preliminary audit survey** is to familiarize the audit team with the unit or activity being audited and the auditee's perception of those operations being reviewed. Sources of information include policies and procedures manuals, discussions with the auditee, organizational charts, written mission statements, minutes of meetings, job descriptions, and reports issued by and to the auditee.

In the Excel sales price audit, the preliminary survey consisted mainly of discussions between Johns and each of the product managers. Krause and Mason, Johns' assistants on the audit, obtained copies of pricing analyses, divisional price lists for the sporting goods division, and organizational charts. The documentation and discussions produced the following preliminary findings:

1. Product prices initially are based on the product manager's evaluation of the market;
2. Although the prices must be set to cover "full" cost, Excel's cost accountants have not been involved in the process and contribution margin is not generally considered;
3. The marketing vice president reviews and approves all selling prices and modifications of existing prices;
4. Selling prices are reviewed on a quarterly basis;
5. Official price lists are included in the computer database and are updated on the basis of change authorizations approved by the marketing vice president; and
6. The computer will *not* accept customer orders containing selling prices at variance with official prices.

Develop the Audit Program   The audit program consists of those procedures necessary to satisfy the audit objectives and produce sufficient and competent evidence to corroborate or refute the auditor's preliminary findings. Exhibit 16.1 contains the audit program developed by Johns for the Vector sales price audit. Procedures 1 through 8 test the preliminary findings and provide further insight into the price-setting process. These audit procedures also determine whether the process complies with company policy. Step 9 tests the process in terms of its effectiveness in maximizing Vector's profits. Step 10 assists the auditor in formulating preliminary findings and recommendations to be discussed with each of the auditees.

EXHIBIT 16.1

Audit Program for Excel Division Sales Price Audit

1. Conduct interviews with each of the product managers regarding the analysis and thought processes leading to the pricing decision.

2. Examine pricing analyses within each product manager's line to obtain further insight into the decision process and to substantiate the information obtained in the interviews:
   a. Obtain cost data for each product from cost accounting; and
   b. Determine that sales price covers cost plus markup.

3. Trace prices from pricing analyses to change authorizations noting agreement of prices and signature of marketing vice president denoting approval.

4. Compare latest price change authorization with computer printout of official price lists and determine agreement.

5. Examine the current year's quarterly price reviews for each line:
   a. Establish that prices are being reviewed quarterly in compliance with company policy; and
   b. Determine the process followed in conducting the review.

6. Prepare customer orders containing incorrect selling prices and enter them into the computer to determine proper functioning of input controls.

7. Inquire of product managers as to procedures followed when the computer rejects the customer order. Are specially priced orders subject to product manager approval?

8. Based on the results of (6) and (7), select a sample of sales invoices and trace billed prices to the computer printout of prices existing at the dates of the respective sales. Determine proper product manager approval of exceptions.

9. Perform independent profitability analysis to determine whether correct prices are producing satisfactory margins:
   a. Select two products from each of the three product lines for testing; and
   b. With assistance from the market economist, determine demand elasticity for each product;
   c. Have market economist describe major competitors' pricing strategies, including probable reaction to price changes within the industry;
   d. Calculate contribution margin per unit at varying selling prices after establishing reasonableness of unit cost data inputs;
   e. Apply cost-volume-profit analysis on basis of (b) to (d) above and determine optimum price; and
   f. Compare "best" price obtained from (e) with official price list. Discuss exceptions with product managers.

10. Summarize exceptions and evaluate findings.

Perform the Audit   The auditor carries out the audit program by:

1. Gathering and evaluating factual evidence; and
2. Comparing the facts against established evaluation criteria.

Like financial statement auditing, the audit evidence must be sufficient to support the auditor's findings and recommendations, and the evidence must be valid and relevant to the stated audit objectives. For the Excel division sales price audit, evidence gathering consists of conducting interviews with the auditees and examining underlying documentation (pricing analyses, cost data, change authorizations, official price lists, and quarterly price reviews). It also involves independent calculations and analyses performed by the auditors (profitability analysis).

The evidence should be evaluated in terms of whether it is sufficient and competent relative to the evaluation criteria set by the auditor. Johns, for example, will need sufficient competent evidence to determine the following:

1. Are the market analysis and the cost analysis performed by the product managers adequate to enable them to set optimum selling prices?
2. Are all selling prices reviewed quarterly in accordance with company policy?
3. Are new product selling prices and selling price changes approved by the marketing vice president?
4. Does the computer price list include the latest change authorizations?
5. Does the computer reject customer orders containing selling prices not in agreement with the official price list?
6. Does the product manager review all customer orders rejected by the computer?

Appraise the Efficiency and Effectiveness of the Activity or Unit   Efficiency and effectiveness appraisals generally involve evaluating reports submitted by auditees, assessing the goal-setting process, determining the extent to which goals are being achieved and the degree of goal congruence (similarity of individual and entity goals), appraising the effectiveness of resource utilization within the unit or activity, and ascertaining whether fraud control is effective. For the Excel pricing engagement specifically, Johns must evaluate the following:

1. Reasonableness of the pricing strategy in terms of profit maximization; and
2. Effectiveness of internal control in preventing fraudulent and erroneous customer billing.

In evaluating the reasonableness of the existing pricing strategy, Johns will compare the established prices against the profitability analyses developed by the audit team. The quality of the existing internal control will be determined by the results of document examination and tests of controls as described above.

Evaluate the Findings   To evaluate **audit findings**, the auditor needs to answer these questions: How well is the activity presently being performed? How might it be improved? The first question can be answered by considering the results of the efficiency and effectiveness appraisals described above. The second question needs to be carefully addressed in consultation with the auditee.

Assume that Johns arrives at the following conclusions regarding Vector's selling price strategy as practiced by the Excel division:

1. Pricing decisions are not systematic and the resulting prices often fail to maximize Vector's profits. Product managers generally set prices in the absence of formal demand analysis, cost analysis, and competitor actions. Neither Vector's economists nor the cost accountants are involved in the process.
2. The existing internal control provides adequate assurance that customers are being billed at official prices.
   a. Selling prices are reviewed on a quarterly basis and the marketing vice president approves all selling prices and modifications of existing prices;
   b. Official price lists contained in the computer reflect the most current prices, and input controls are effective in rejecting prices not in agreement with official prices; and
   c. Sales invoices containing prices other than official prices, and rejected by the computer, are subject to approval by the respective product managers.

Although Johns is convinced that the price-setting process in the sporting goods division could be improved through demand analysis and cost–volume–profit analysis, he wants to obtain the input of the product managers and gain their cooperation and commitment to any suggested change in methodology. To this end, he conducts additional meetings with each of the product managers. At these meetings, Johns emphasizes the internal financial controls that help to ensure that customers are charged correctly and that only authorized prices are included in the computer database. He then addresses the price-setting weaknesses by illustrating several examples in which profitability could have been improved by setting higher or lower prices. He also assists the product managers in developing alternate strategies that consider supply and demand factors, competitors' pricing strategies, and marginal cost analysis. In the process of suggesting and assisting, Johns emphasizes the impact that the increased profitability will have on the product managers' annual bonus and profit sharing. Each product manager agrees and all are appreciative of the audit team's assistance in improving their respective pricing strategies.

Develop Conclusions and Recommendations   Audit conclusions and recommendations are the culmination of the audit field work. They should be developed only after the auditor has collected and evaluated all necessary evidence and discussed the findings with the auditee. Hopefully, the auditee has agreed with the findings and suggested improvements. The absence of agreement, however, should *not* preclude the auditor from recommending appropriate courses of action. The formal conclusions and recommendations should be presented to the auditee before being incorporated into the audit report.

Having discussed the audit team's findings with each of the product managers, and having assisted them in developing appropriate pricing strategies, Johns decides to present the auditors' conclusions and recommendations formally in the form of a conference at Vector's headquarters office. The presentation is given in a daylong meeting conducted by the audit team in one of the company's meeting rooms. The following persons are in attendance: Excel's three product managers, the audit team, Jeremy Jiles (Excel's chief cost accountant), and Judy Smolen (Vector's market economist). The audit team, with the assistance of the cost accountant and market economist, plans to present an actual pricing case applicable to each product line and to demonstrate how a different price would have improved profits. To support the presentation, Johns and his assistants, with the help of Jiles, Smolen, and one of Vector's CBIS specialists, have developed a computer simulation in the form of a game based on different assumptions regarding supply and demand and competitors' pricing strategies. Additionally, marginal cost and revenue data are included in the simulation.

At the end of the presentation, the following conclusions and recommendations, also to be included in the audit report to the marketing vice president, are summarized for the product managers:

1. Controls are effective in ensuring that proper prices are being charged customers. The controls include required approval of prices by the marketing vice president, quarterly review of existing product prices, and computerization of Vector's official price list, together with strict controls preventing unauthorized modification of prices included in the database.
2. Current pricing strategies for Vector's sporting goods division are not producing selling prices that maximize the company's profitability. Neither cost coverage nor market demand is considered adequately in reaching pricing decisions.
3. The following approach to setting and modifying selling prices is recommended:
   a. Direct costs of producing and selling products should be identified;

b. Demand analysis should be conducted to estimate the market for the product at varying prices;

c. Vector's share of market should be estimated on the basis of demand analysis and predicted competitor pricing strategies;

d. The computer simulation should be utilized to view the profit effects of various combinations of cost, price, demand, and market share; and

e. The cost accounting staff and the market economist should be utilized to assist in cost, demand, and market share analysis.

Reporting Audit Findings and Recommendations

The audit report is the culmination of the audit process. Assuming that the audit team has discussed all findings with the auditee and has obtained the auditee's concurrence with the resulting conclusions and recommendations, the audit report should contain no surprises for the auditee. At the same time, however, the auditors should not compromise findings to assuage the auditee's feelings. Instead, the audit process and the resulting report should be viewed by all parties as a means of assisting responsible managers at the field level to take the necessary corrective action.

To avoid any misunderstandings resulting from the formal audit report, auditors follow the practice of reviewing the report draft with the auditee at a postaudit meeting prior to the release of the audit report. Johns has prepared the first draft of a proposed audit report and discussed it with each of the product managers during postaudit meetings. He has gained their concurrence and is now ready to release the final audit report, contained in Exhibit 16.2.

Unlike an independent financial statement audit, an **operational audit report** is not constrained to a single standard reporting format. To be effective, however, the report should exhibit certain characteristics. First, the audit report should be *clear and concise* and should *not* contain any unnecessary technical language. The audit report should be *constructive* by suggesting ways to help the auditee in improving operations where necessary. The reporting style should be *positive and unbiased*. It should neither praise nor criticize, but rather should *focus on results*. Auditors should avoid using personal pronouns (e.g., he, she, him, her) or proper nouns (e.g., John, Kenneth, Susan, Jacquelyn).

If the auditors' findings are to be implemented, results and conclusions must be presented convincingly. Differences between actual and expected conditions should be presented as to *cause* (reason for the difference) and *effect* (risk or exposure produced by the difference). *Auditee efforts* toward improvement should be presented along with the auditors' recommendations. Lastly, the audit report should be *reviewed by the director of internal auditing* before issuance.

Most operational audit reports contain the following components (refer to Exhibit 16.2):

1. Letter of transmittal (including summary of findings and recommendations);
2. Scope of the audit;
3. Findings and conclusions; and
4. Recommendations.

Summary of Operational Auditing

Operational auditing assists operating managers in identifying and solving problems by setting audit goals and collecting evidence relating to the evaluation criteria. The auditor

EXHIBIT 16.2	

Operational Audit Report for the Vector Sales Price Audit

April 19, 2002

To: Jacquelyn Shoemaker,
        Vice President—Marketing

From: Kenneth Johns,
        Senior Internal Auditor

Subject: Audit Report—Vector Sales Price Audit, Excel Division

Attached is your copy of the audit report on our examination of the sales price-setting process as practiced in the Excel division. The purpose of our audit was to determine whether established selling prices for the sporting goods lines are optimal in terms of maximizing Vector's profitability. We previously have discussed a draft of this report with you.

Although the existing internal control provides adequate assurance that customers are being billed at established prices, those prices are less than optimal in maximizing profits. More attention by the product managers to demand and cost analysis will greatly improve pricing decisions. The product managers agree and are committed to appropriate revision in their approach to price setting. Our findings and conclusions, along with recommendations agreed to by the product managers, are described in the body of this report.

Kenneth Johns
Signature

cc: Raymond Vector, President and CEO
    Members of the Audit Committee of the Board:
        Joel Haynes, Chairman
        Lucille Jones
        Harold Allen
        James Todd
    Product Managers—Excel Division:
        Jennifer Hill: Balls
        Jeffrey Archer: Bats and Gloves
        Susan Knox: Golf Clubs and Tennis Rackets

SCOPE OF THE AUDIT

Our audit was limited to two areas within the sporting goods division:

1. Determining whether prices are set such that company profits are maximized; and
2. Determining whether prices charged customers are in compliance with established company prices.

In satisfying the above requirements, we conducted extensive interviews with the product managers who are responsible for the price-setting process; we examined documentation supporting the analysis leading to the setting of specific product prices; we examined the quarterly selling price reviews on a test basis; with the assistance of the product managers, along with Jeremy Jiles, Excel's chief cost accountant, and Judy Smolen, market economist, we developed a set of optimum prices for specific products for comparison with actual prices in terms of profitability; and we compared actual prices appearing on sales invoices with established prices from a random sample of sales invoices.

FINDINGS AND CONCLUSIONS

Selling prices within the sporting goods lines are not maximizing profitability.

We have found that current pricing strategies are not producing selling prices that maximize profitability within the Excel division. Product managers presently set selling prices on the basis of the following inputs:

1. Best estimate of total demand and market share at varying prices; and
2. Total product cost as supplied by cost accounting.

Little attention has been devoted to contribution margin analysis (i.e., selling price minus variable manufacturing and selling costs), demand analysis (including demand elasticity), competitor reactions to price changes, and economic conditions. In our opinion, the resulting prices are not optimal in terms of maximizing Vector's profitability.

(continued)

EXHIBIT 16.2

(continued)

Controls are adequate to provide reasonable assurance that prices charged customers are in compliance with official company prices.

Our tests of the internal control system related to customer billing suggest that customers are being billed in accordance with company policy. All product prices and product price modifications must be approved by the marketing vice president and the product pricing analyses must be signed by the marketing vice president as evidence of such approval. Approved prices are forwarded to EDP for updating of the computerized price list. Updated price lists are forwarded by EDP to marketing at the beginning of each month for review. As part of our audit, we obtained the latest printout of product prices for the sporting goods division and compared them with the pricing analyses provided by marketing. We found no exceptions.

We also established that all product prices are reviewed quarterly. Although these reviews were found to be rather cursory, the product managers have assured us that economic analysis, demand analysis, and cost analysis will be applied in future reviews.

Our audit included selecting a random sample of sales invoices and tracing the billed prices to the computer printout of selling prices existing on the date of sale. The billed prices agreed with the official price list in all cases. We also introduced test data consisting of hypothetical customer orders containing incorrect selling prices. The computer rejected such orders and intervention by the EDP control group was necessary for removal of the orders from the system.

RECOMMENDATIONS

We recommend the following approach to sales price setting within the Excel division. This approach has been developed during our audit with the help and support of the product managers, and with the assistance of the cost accounting staff, the market economist, and the EDP systems and programming personnel. It has the full support of the product managers and presently is being implemented by Susan Knox in pricing the new golf club line.

The first step in the process is information gathering. Cost accounting will provide detailed cost data regarding the product being priced, including:

- Variable manufacturing cost per unit
- Direct fixed manufacturing cost related to the product
- Direct selling expense related to the product
- Share of indirect manufacturing, selling, and administrative overhead

The market economist will assist the product manager in gathering and developing marketing data, including the following:

- Projected total market demand for the product
- Demand elasticity (market sensitivity to price changes)
- Excel's projected share of market given varying levels of advertising and promotion
- Predicted competitor reactions to price changes

The information so developed will serve as input into the "Marketing Strategy" computer program developed as a result of our sales price audit. Having received cost and market inputs, the program predicts contribution margin given varying assumptions regarding:

- Selling price
- Market demand
- Demand elasticity
- Market share
- Level of advertising
- Competitors' pricing strategies

The best selling price, in terms of profitability, under each combination of demand elasticity, advertising level, and competitor reaction then is provided by the program. The product manager is responsible for selecting the best price among the alternatives. The decision will be based generally on the product manager's judgment as to which combination is most realistic.

evaluates the activity in light of the evidence, consults with the auditee, and recommends corrective action. Consulting and recommending are ongoing processes occurring throughout the audit field work as necessary. At the conclusion of the field work, an audit report, addressed to the person to whom the auditee is responsible, is drafted and discussed with the auditee before being released. The report serves the purpose of informing management as to problem areas relating to specific activities, the auditors' recommendations for solving the problems, and the auditee's progress in implementing the recommendations. Perhaps most important is the need for the auditees to perceive that the internal auditor's goal is to assist in—and not to police—the auditee's operations.

GOVERNMENTAL COMPLIANCE AUDITING

Governmental Compliance Auditing Defined

Governmental compliance auditing may be defined as testing and reporting on conformity with laws and regulations relating to recipients of federal financial assistance. As used in this chapter, the term refers to the independent auditor's responsibility for determining compliance with laws and regulations when engaged in audits of state and local governmental units, as well as other not-for-profit entities, such as colleges and universities, that are the recipients of federal financial assistance. In 1989, following a General Accounting Office study that identified a large number of substandard audits of federal financial assistance, the Auditing Standards Board issued Statement on Auditing Standards No. 63, entitled "Compliance Auditing Applicable to Governmental Entities and Other Recipients of Governmental Financial Assistance." SAS No. 74, issued in 1995, and No. 75, issued in 1996, together with the audit and accounting guide, "Audits of State and Local Governmental Units," and Statement of Position 92-9, "Audits of Not-for-Profit Organizations Receiving Federal Awards," superseded SAS No. 63 by adding institutions of higher education and other not-for-profit entities receiving federal financial assistance to the compliance auditing "umbrella." These pronouncements were intended to strengthen this form of compliance auditing.

The independent auditor's compliance auditing responsibility is a function of the type of engagement, but may encompass any or all of the following:

1. Responsibility under generally accepted auditing standards (GAAS);
2. Responsibility under **governmental auditing standards** as set forth in the General Accounting Office's (GAO) "yellow book"; and
3. Responsibility under the federal Single Audit Act of 1984 (and amended in 1996), as defined and interpreted in OMB Circular A-133, issued by the U.S. Office of Management and Budget.

Auditor's Responsibility Under GAAS

In addition to the auditor's responsibility for detecting and reporting on illegal acts and the auditor's responsibility for detecting errors and fraud, as described in earlier chapters, the two SASs (Nos. 74 and 75) mentioned above further define the auditor's responsibilities when state and local governmental units, and other not-for-profit entities that are the recipients of federal financial assistance, are audited. Assistance may assume the forms of contracts, grants, loans, and/or interest rate subsidies. The reason compliance auditing is necessary in this type of environment is that federal assistance is accompanied by federal requirements. SAS Nos. 74 and 75, along with the audit and accounting guide, identify the kinds of laws and regulations to which these entities may be subject and provide guidance as to the proper audit approach in determining compliance with the various requirements. In addition, SAS No. 74 recommends that the auditor obtain written representation from management. A related audit and accounting guide suggests that the written representation include statements that:

1. Management is responsible for the entity's compliance with laws and regulations applicable to it; and
2. Management has identified and disclosed to the auditor all laws and regulations that have a direct and material effect on the determination of financial statement amounts.[2]

Yellow Book Responsibility

When auditing state and local governmental units and other not-for-profit entities that are recipients of federal financial assistance, auditors must comply, in addition to GAAS, with governmental auditing standards, as defined in the GAO's "yellow book." These standards assign greater responsibility to the auditor than is required under GAAS. For example, under the **yellow book** standards, auditors must *report on the entity's compliance with laws and regulations* imposed by the assistance program, and must also *report on the entity's internal control system, regardless of whether material weaknesses are found.* Under GAAS, the auditor need include in the reportable conditions letter only material weaknesses that are discovered in the course of the audit. Also, when reporting on compliance with laws and regulations, the auditor must *give positive assurance on items tested, must give negative assurance on items not tested, and must describe material instances of noncompliance.* Given these requirements, the audit and accounting guide provides guidance to the auditor in meeting them.[3]

Single Audit Act Responsibility as Interpreted by OMB Circular A-133

State and local government entities, colleges and universities, and other not-for-profit entities that receive $300,000 or more in **federal financial assistance** in a single fiscal year must be audited in accordance with the **Single Audit Act of 1984 (as amended in 1996)**, in addition to GAAS and the yellow book standards. The Single Audit Act, amended in 1996, is a federal law that establishes audit requirements for state and local governmental bodies and other not-for-profit entities receiving federal financial assistance. The major provisions of this act are interpreted and explained in **Circular A-133**, issued by the U.S. Office of Management and Budget (OMB).

Audit Requirements   Under the Single Audit Act, the auditor must identify major programs financed by federal funding utilizing a process that considers risk of errors and fraud, as well as dollar volume of expenditures. The process consists of three steps:

1. Identify those programs that meet a stated dollar threshold, referred to as "type A" programs;
2. Identify those type A programs that are classified as low risk; and

---

2   AICPA Audit and Accounting Guide, *Audits of State and Local Governmental Units*, New York: AICPA, section AAG-SLG 5.25.
3   Ibid, section AAG-SLG 5.01–5.43.

3. Identify those programs that fall below the type A dollar threshold, but are classified as high-risk programs, and label as "type B" programs.

In addition to auditing the type A programs classified as high risk and at least 50 percent of the high-risk type B programs, the auditor must also conform to the **percentage-of-coverage rule**, which requires that at least 50 percent of federal expenditures be covered by the audit.[4]

In identifying high-risk programs, the auditor should consider prior audit history, federal oversight, and the inherent risk of the program. The AICPA, in conjunction with the OMB and the GAO, is in the process of developing more specific risk indicators to guide auditors in this regard.

With respect to internal controls over federal expenditures, the auditor is responsible for understanding internal controls over major programs, testing those controls, and reporting the results of their tests.[5]

Reporting Requirements   The auditor is required to describe in the audit report the type of report issued on the financial statements, list any material matters of noncompliance related to the financial statements, describe the type of report issued on compliance for major programs, and state whether reportable conditions were disclosed.[6]

The audit and accounting guide provides guidance in performing compliance audits under these circumstances and covers topics such as how to identify major programs, how to determine materiality, how to assess audit risk relative to type A and type B programs, and how to evaluate the results of auditing procedures.

As with the yellow book requirements, the audit and accounting guide recommends added topics to be covered in the client representation letter, given applicability of the Single Audit Act. These topics relate to such matters as management identification of all sources of federal financial assistance, as well as requirements under the programs; management compliance with reporting requirements; adequate documentation of information contained in financial reports; notification of the independent auditor as to noncompliance; and appropriate action in instances of noncompliance.[7]

Compliance Auditing and Audit Risk

The three components of audit risk, as addressed in Chapter 5, are essentially the same for all types of audits performed by CPAs. For compliance audits related to major federal financial assistance programs, however, the audit and accounting guide expands upon the components of audit risk as follows:

Inherent risk: The risk that material noncompliance with requirements applicable to a major federal financial assistance program could occur assuming there are no related internal control policies and procedures.

Control risk: The risk that material noncompliance that could occur in a major federal financial assistance program will not be prevented or detected on a timely basis by the entity's internal control policies and procedures.

---

4   Jackson, Norwood and Jerry Skelly, "Auditing Federal Awards: A New Approach," *The Journal of Accountancy,* November 1996, pp. 53–60.
5   Ibid.
6   Ibid.
7   AICPA Audit and Accounting Guide, *Audits of State and Local Governmental Units,* op. cit., section SLG 23.82.

Detection risk: The risk that an auditor's procedures will lead him or her to conclude that noncompliance that could be material to a major federal financial assistance program does not exist when in fact such noncompliance does exist.[8]

As discussed in Chapter 5, during the audit planning phase the auditor must carefully evaluate and assess inherent risk and control risk, and then set detection risk at a level that minimizes overall audit risk. In assessing inherent risk for entities receiving federal financial assistance, the auditor must focus on programs by gaining a thorough understanding of them and of the applicable laws and regulations. The auditor also should assess the probability of management override as a possible attempt to circumvent program requirements. In assessing control risk, the auditor must study and evaluate those internal controls that prevent and/or detect noncompliance with the laws and regulations applicable to the major programs. The auditor should direct particular attention toward the control environment, to determine that management supports the concept of compliance.

In a case settled in 1997, New York University Medical Center agreed to pay $15.5 million to the federal government for allegedly submitting false financial information regarding certain costs associated with federally sponsored research grants and contracts.[9] The government appropriates billions of dollars each year for universities to spend on various kinds of approved research. Under most of the contracts and grants, the government allows the universities to add a fixed percentage of the direct costs to cover indirect costs, applicable to all of the contracts and grants. Examples of indirect costs are utilities, building maintenance, libraries, and staff support.

The problem at NYU arose as the result of negotiations with the government permitting increases above the standard indirect cost percentage. NYU was alleged to have inflated overhead charges to the federal government as part of government reimbursement to the center under the grants. Specifically, the government alleged in the lawsuit that from 1982 onward NYU Medical Center negotiated and obtained an inflated indirect cost rate through its submission of false information.[10] The institution misrepresented the amounts of faculty services that were donated at no cost to the research grant project, and allegedly submitted duplicate claims for utility costs, Medicare reimbursement costs, and certain environmental services costs. Other alleged violations included certain expenses that shouldn't have been allowed such as entertainment, capital interest, and overstated housekeeping expenses.[11]

In an earlier case, reported in 1991, Stanford University was similarly alleged to have inflated overhead charges to the federal government under federally sponsored research grants. GAO auditors, in this instance, estimated that Stanford may have overcharged the government nearly $500 million in improper indirect costs. Some of these charges included salaries and other expenses from a university-owned shopping center, a share in a Lake Tahoe retreat for the Stanford board of trustees and guests, and a shower curtain and two window shades for the university president's official residence.[12]

8 Ibid, section AAG-SLG 23.07.
9 "NYU Medical Center Is to Pay $15.5 Million to Settle U.S. Suit," *The Wall Street Journal*, April 8, 1997, p. B3. (A former employee who brought the "whistleblower lawsuit" against NYU received $1.5 million as a reward.)
10 Ibid.
11 Ibid.
12 "Stanford Braces for U.S. Debt of $480 Million," *The Wall Street Journal*, January 2, 1992.

The lesson for auditors in these cases is the need for tailoring risk analysis to the specific needs of the audit engagement. In auditing the NYU and Stanford government contracts and research grants, the auditors should have been concerned with the constant increase in indirect cost reimbursement as a percentage of the operating budget. Given this concern, the auditors should have devoted considerable resources to analyzing the contract charges for compliance with the provisions of the applicable grants and contracts. Inquiring of university officials, reading the contracts and agreements, examining documentation supporting the charges, and confirming a sampling of major reimbursement charges with the reimbursing agencies are some of the procedures that should have been applied under these circumstances.

In today's expanded environment of federal financial assistance programs, compliance auditing is assuming ever-increasing importance. Auditors, therefore, must continue to expand their efforts in the areas of risk analysis and audit program development for compliance auditing purposes.

APPENDIX

INTERNAL AUDITING STANDARDS AS PROMULGATED BY THE INSTITUTE OF INTERNAL AUDITORS

Summary of General and Specific Standards for the Professional Practice of Internal Auditing

100 **INDEPENDENCE**—INTERNAL AUDITORS SHOULD BE INDEPENDENT OF THE ACTIVITIES THEY AUDIT.

110 **Organizational Status**—The organizational status of the internal auditing department should be sufficient to permit the accomplishment of its audit responsibilities.

120 **Objectivity**—Internal auditors should be objective in performing audits.

200 **PROFESSIONAL PROFICIENCY**—INTERNAL AUDITS SHOULD BE PERFORMED WITH PROFICIENCY AND DUE PROFESSIONAL CARE.

The Internal Auditing Department

210 **Staffing**—The internal auditing department should provide assurance that the technical proficiency and educational background of internal auditors are appropriate for the audits to be performed.

220 **Knowledge, Skills, and Disciplines**—The internal auditing department should possess or should obtain the knowledge, skills, and disciplines needed to carry out its audit responsibilities.

230 **Supervision**—The internal auditing department should provide assurance that internal audits are properly supervised.

The Internal Auditor

240 **Compliance with Standards of Conduct**—Internal auditors should comply with professional standards of conduct.

250 **Knowledge, Skills, and Disciplines**—Internal auditors should possess the knowledge, skills, and disciplines essential to the performance of internal audits.

260 **Human Relations and Communications**—Internal auditors should be skilled in dealing with people and in communicating effectively.

270 **Continuing Education**—Internal auditors should maintain their technical competence through continuing education.

280 **Due Professional Care**—Internal auditors should exercise due professional care in performing internal audits.

300 **SCOPE OF WORK**—THE SCOPE OF THE INTERNAL AUDIT SHOULD ENCOMPASS THE EXAMINATION AND EVALUATION OF THE ADEQUACY AND EFFECTIVENESS OF THE ORGANIZATION'S INTERNAL CONTROL AND THE QUALITY OF PERFORMANCE IN CARRYING OUT ASSIGNED RESPONSIBILITIES.

310 **Reliability and Integrity of Information**—Internal auditors should review the reliability and integrity of financial and operating information and the means used to identify, measure, classify, and report such information.

320 **Compliance with Policies, Plans, Procedures, Laws, and Regulations**—Internal auditors should review the systems established to ensure compliance with those policies, plans, procedures, laws, and regulations which could have a significant impact on operations and reports and should determine whether the organization is in compliance.

330 **Safeguarding of Assets**—Internal auditors should review the means of safeguarding assets and, as appropriate, verify the existence of such assets.

340 **Economical and Efficient Use of Resources**—Internal auditors should appraise the economy and efficiency with which resources are employed.

350 **Accomplishment of Established Objectives and Goals for Operations or Programs**—Internal auditors should review operations or programs to ascertain whether results are consistent with established objectives and goals and whether the operations or programs are being carried out as planned.

400 **PERFORMANCE OF AUDIT WORK**—AUDIT WORK SHOULD INCLUDE PLANNING THE AUDIT, EXAMINING AND EVALUATING INFORMATION, COMMUNICATING RESULTS, AND FOLLOWING UP.

410 **Planning the Audit**—Internal auditors should plan each audit.

420 **Examining and Evaluating Information**—Internal auditors should collect, analyze, interpret, and document information to support audit results.

430 **Communicating Results**—Internal auditors should report the results of their audit work.

440 **Following Up**—Internal auditors should follow up to ascertain that appropriate action is taken on reported audit findings.

500 **MANAGEMENT OF THE INTERNAL AUDITING DEPARTMENT**—THE DIRECTOR OF INTERNAL AUDITING SHOULD PROPERLY MANAGE THE INTERNAL AUDITING DEPARTMENT.

510 **Purpose, Authority, and Responsibility**—The director of internal auditing should have a statement of purpose, authority, and responsibility for the internal auditing department.

520 **Planning**—The director of internal auditing should establish plans to carry out the responsibilities of the internal auditing department.

530 **Policies and Procedures**—The director of internal auditing should provide written policies and procedures to guide the audit staff.

540 **Personnel Management and Development**—The director of internal auditing should establish a program for selecting and developing the human resources of the internal auditing department.

550 **External Auditors**—The director of internal auditing should coordinate internal and external audit efforts.

560 **Quality Assurance**—The director of internal auditing should establish and maintain a quality assurance program to evaluate the operations of the internal auditing department.

Source: Institute of Internal Auditors: *Codification of Standards for the Professional Practice of Internal Auditing*, Altamonte Springs, FL, 1993.

KEY TERMS

Audit conclusions and recommendations, 681
Audit findings, 680
Circular A-133, 686
Effectiveness, 671
Efficiency, 671
Evaluation criteria, 677
Federal financial assistance, 686
Foreign Corrupt Practices Act of 1977 (FCPA), 673
General Accounting Office (GAO), 670
Governmental auditing standards, 685

Governmental compliance auditing, 685
Institute of Internal Auditors, 670
Internal auditing, 672
Management auditing, 671
Operational audit report, 682
Operational auditing, 671
Percentage-of-coverage rule, 687
Preliminary audit survey, 678
Risk-based operational auditing, 673
Single Audit Act of 1984 (as amended in 1996), 686
Yellow book, 686

REVIEW QUESTIONS

1. Differentiate between operational auditing and internal auditing.

2. Differentiate between efficiency and effectiveness as they relate to operational auditing.

3. What is management auditing? Why must internal auditors exercise particular care in performing management audits?

4. What is risk-based operational auditing?

5. How has the Foreign Corrupt Practices Act influenced internal auditing?

6. Internal auditors are frequently referred to as the "eyes and ears of management." Explain.

7. Why does operational auditing require a broader base of expertise than accounting and auditing?

8. Describe the steps in planning an operational audit.

9. What are evaluation criteria as related to operational auditing, and how does their identification assist the auditor in conducting the examination?

10. Why is the cooperation of the auditee critical to a successful operational audit?

11. What is the nature of the preliminary survey as it relates to operational auditing? What purpose does it serve?

12. How are sufficiency and competence of evidence determined in operational audits?

13. How does the auditor appraise efficiency and effectiveness in an operational audit?

14. What two questions must the auditor answer to evaluate operational audit findings?

15. The auditor should discuss operational audit findings with the auditee before making formal recommendations. Explain.

16. What course of action should the auditor pursue if the auditee disagrees with the audit findings and preliminary recommendations?

17. The audit report should contain no unknown surprises for the auditee. Explain.

18. Why is it essential that auditees view the operational audit as a device for assisting them?

19. What is the purpose of the postaudit meeting? How does it differ from the preaudit meeting?

20. Describe the attributes of a good operational audit report.

21. Define *governmental compliance auditing*.

22. How does governmental compliance auditing relate to entities receiving federal financial assistance?

23. How is risk analysis within the context of governmental compliance auditing different from that in financial auditing?

MULTIPLE CHOICE QUESTIONS FROM PAST CPA AND CIA EXAMS

1. During an operational audit, the auditor compares the current staffing of a department with established industry standards in order to
   a. Assess the adequacy of the controls over payroll processing for the department.
   b. Assess the current performance of the department and make appropriate recommendations for improvement.
   c. Evaluate the adequacy of the established internal controls for the department.
   d. Determine whether the department has complied with all laws and regulations governing its personnel.

2. Auditors can usually achieve better relations with auditees if they
   a. Emphasize their role as management advisors.
   b. Concentrate on uncovering errors made by lower-level employees.
   c. Concentrate on uncovering frauds and embezzlements.
   d. Emphasize their role as an insurance policy against potential frauds and embezzlements.

3. The best source of information for planning the audit approach and developing the audit program would probably be
   a. Information contained in prior audit reports.
   b. Audit procedures found in the permanent audit files.
   c. The results of a preliminary survey.
   d. The long-range audit plan as it applies to this specific audit.

4. A car rental agency has branch offices throughout the world. Each branch is organized into three separate departments: maintenance, operations, and accounting. What information would be most useful in establishing the objectives for an operational audit?
   a. The objectives of each department.

    b. The most recent financial data for each department.

    c. Activity reports showing rental information for the different branches.

    d. A complete listing of the perpetual inventory for the branch to be audited.

5. When management agrees with a finding and has agreed to take corrective action, the appropriate treatment is to

    a. Report that management has agreed to take corrective action.

    b. Omit the finding and recommendation.

    c. Report that management has already taken corrective action.

    d. Include the finding and recommendation, irrespective of management's agreement.

6. Disclosure of fraud to parties other than a client's senior management and its audit committee or board of directors ordinarily is not part of an auditor's responsibility. However, to which of the following outside parties may a duty to disclose fraud exist?

	To the SEC when the client reports an auditor change	*To a successor auditor when the successor makes appropriate inquiries*	*To a government funding agency from which the client receives financial assistance*
a.	Yes	Yes	No
b.	Yes	No	Yes
c.	No	Yes	Yes
d.	Yes	Yes	Yes

7. Because of the pervasive effects of laws and regulations on the financial statements of governmental units, an auditor should obtain written management representations acknowledging that management has

    a. Implemented internal control policies and procedures designed to detect all illegal acts.

    b. Documented the procedures performed to evaluate the governmental unit's compliance with laws and regulations.

    c. Identified and disclosed all laws and regulations that have a direct and material effect on its financial statements.

    d. Reported all known illegal acts and material weaknesses in internal control to the funding agency or regulatory body.

8. A governmental audit may extend beyond an examination leading to the expression of an opinion on the fairness of financial presentation to include

	Program results	*Compliance*	*Economy & efficiency*
a.	Yes	Yes	No
b.	Yes	Yes	Yes
c.	No	Yes	Yes
d.	Yes	No	Yes

9. The GAO standards of reporting for governmental financial audits incorporate the AICPA standards of reporting and prescribe supplemental standards to satisfy the unique needs of governmental audits. Which of the following is a supplemental reporting standard for government financial audits?

    a. A written report on the auditor's understanding of the entity's internal control system and assessment of control risk should be prepared.

b. Material indications of illegal acts should be reported in a document with distribution restricted to senior officials of the entity audited.

c. Instances of abuse, fraud, mismanagement, and waste should be reported to the organization with legal oversight authority over the entity audited.

d. All privileged and confidential information discovered should be reported to the senior officials of the organization that arranged for the audit.

10. Kent is auditing an entity's compliance with requirements governing a major federal financial assistance program in accordance with the Single Audit Act. Kent detected noncompliance with requirements that have a material effect on that program. Kent's report on compliance should express a(n)

a. Unqualified opinion with a separate explanatory paragraph.

b. Qualified opinion or an adverse opinion.

c. Adverse opinion or a disclaimer of opinion.

d. Limited assurance on the items tested.

Use the following information for questions 11 through 16.

Each audit objective listed in questions 11 through 16 is independent of the other audit objectives. Select the letter designating the *single* best audit technique for meeting the audit objective specified from the audit techniques listed below.

Audit Techniques
a. Inspection of documents
b. Observation
c. Inquiry
d. Analytical procedures

11. Ascertain the reasonableness of the increases in rental revenue resulting from operating costs passed on to the lessee by the landlord. The auditor has already inspected the lease contract to determine that such costs are allowed.

12. Identify the existence of personality conflicts that are detrimental to productivity.

13. Determine whether research and development projects were properly authorized.

14. Ascertain compliance with city ordinance forbidding city purchasing from vendors affiliated with elected city officials.

15. Determine whether planned rate of return on investment in international operations has been achieved.

16. Determine whether mail room staff is fully utilized.

17. When engaged to audit a governmental entity in accordance with government auditing standards, an auditor prepares a written report on the internal control system

a. In all audits, regardless of circumstances.

b. Only when the auditor has noted reportable conditions.

c. Only when requested by the governmental entity being audited.

d. Only when requested by the federal government funding agency.

18. Hill, CPA, is auditing the financial statements of Helping Hand, a not-for-profit organization that receives financial assistance from governmental agencies. To detect misstatements in

Helping Hand's financial statements resulting from violations of laws and regulations, Hill should focus on violations that

a. Could result in criminal prosecution against the organization.
b. Involve reportable conditions to be communicated to the organization's trustees and the funding agencies.
c. Have a direct and material effect on the amounts in the organization's financial statements.
d. Demonstrate the existence of material weaknesses in the organization's internal control.

19. An auditor most likely would be responsible for assuring that management communicates significant deficiencies in the design of the internal control system

a. To a court-appointed creditors' committee when the client is operating under Chapter 11 of the Federal Bankruptcy Code.
b. To shareholders with significant influence (more than 20 percent equity ownership) when the reportable conditions are deemed to be material weaknesses.
c. To the Securities and Exchange Commission when the client is a publicly held entity.
d. To specific legislative and regulatory bodies when reporting under governmental auditing standards.

20. Tell, CPA, is auditing the financial statements of Youth Services Co. (YSC), a not-for-profit organization, in accordance with government auditing standards. Tell's report on YSC's compliance with laws and regulations is required to contain statements of

	Positive assurance	Negative assurance
a.	Yes	Yes
b.	Yes	No
c.	No	Yes
d.	No	No

ESSAY QUESTIONS AND PROBLEMS

16.1 The internal audit staff of a consumer products company recently completed an audit of the company's centralized marketing department. The audit objective was to assess the effectiveness of the marketing department in contributing to company profitability. The company's three divisions manufacture and distribute consumer-oriented electronics, sporting goods/recreational products, and small household appliances. All three divisions are dependent upon aggressive marketing to retain their market share in a highly competitive environment. The audit field work identified, and management agrees with, the following:

Sales Promotion
1. The procurement of outside printing services is subject to competitive bidding if the dollar amount is greater than $4,000 and deadlines permit. Otherwise, the media manager selects the printer based on past experience. The contract is handled via the phone and the media manager informs the accounts payable supervisor that payment to the printer is authorized.
2. Last year's advertising expenditures exceeded the budgeted amount by 8 percent in all three divisions. An overall advertising strategy for the company's products has not been developed; each divisional director plans its own advertising activities.
3. Advertising activities are not studied for overall cost/sales effectiveness. The marketing managers believe that the time between placing ads and seeing any response is too long to permit a useful measure.

Distribution Channels

4. Although each product line is distributed through several channels, distribution costs are accumulated by product line; the product line manager decides what the appropriate channels are for each product within the line.

5. The company uses multiple warehouse facilities and each product line uses an expediter to release products from each warehouse. To date, no storage or transportation studies have been done to ensure product delivery at the lowest possible cost.

6. Product prices are determined by each division subject to committee approval from headquarters. Pricing strategy usually focuses on competitors' pricing; other pricing determinants are seldom examined.

Required:

For each of these situations, prepare the finding and the audit recommendation section of the audit report. (IIA adapted)

16.2 The preliminary meeting between the auditor and auditee management prior to the start of an audit enables the parties to exchange information.

Required:

a. Prepare the auditor's memorandum to the auditee proposing an agenda of topics to be discussed at a preliminary meeting.

b. How might the exchange of information on the topics you described in part (a) affect the audit?

(IIA adapted)

16.3 The results of a preliminary survey of the personnel function are as follows:

Audit Area	*Survey Results*
I. Personnel Projections	Policies and procedures for developing personnel projections appeared to be lacking. There was no evidence of communications from top management on new or expanded business opportunities that might affect personnel projections. There was no indication that operating managers had any input regarding projections. Tests for reasonableness of projections based on economic trends were not evident.
II. Securing New Personnel	Each department recruits for its open positions without regard to other departments. Policies and procedures pertaining to selection of personnel were not evident. User department satisfaction with the personnel function was not known.
III. Position Descriptions	Dates of revisions and signatures of approval did not appear on position descriptions sampled in the survey. There was no evidence of job analysis, nor were criteria established to permit subsequent maintenance of descriptions.
IV. Compensation	No evidence indicating a review of compensation levels for soundness or compliance with established industry standards was found. Compensation levels did not appear to be related to performance. Compensation levels within job classifications were not reviewed or evaluated by the personnel department.

Required:

Develop audit objectives for each audit area in the preliminary survey described. For each objective you develop, give two audit steps that would be appropriate to follow up on the results of the preliminary survey, and give one additional audit step that could apply to each audit area. Use the following format for your answer.

Objective	*Audit Steps*
I.	1.
	2.
	3.
II.	1.
	2.
	3.
III.	1.
	2.
	3.
IV.	1.
	2.
	3.

(IIA adapted)

16.4   As an audit supervisor you are about to assign a less experienced auditor to the task of developing an audit program for the purchasing department. The purchasing department has been audited five times in the last ten years. Prior audits were limited to the financial aspects of the department's operations, but the current audit is to be directed toward operating efficiency and effectiveness. Thus, some preliminary research will be necessary to determine the scope of the audit and the audit methodology. You want the audit to be done efficiently and to be properly focused. You are especially interested in identifying potential risk areas and in evaluating controls over them.

Required:
a. Prepare guidelines for the auditor to follow in gathering the necessary information and writing the audit program.
b. For each guideline listed in part (a) indicate its objective. Use the following format for your answer:

Guidelines   Objectives

(IIA adapted)

16.5   The quality control (QC) group in a large manufacturing company reports directly to the manager of the production department. The QC group's objective is to enforce quality standards established by management. The director of QC has the authority to reject completed production and to interrupt the production process as necessary to correct quality problems. The company views QC in terms of a four-part control cycle as follows:

1. Design engineering establishes acceptable quality levels for components and finished products. In this part of the cycle, the QC group's responsibility is to make sure that specified ranges of quality levels have been established and have been determined on a reasonable basis considering all pertinent factors.
2. The QC group determines how quality assurance will be achieved. The control group's responsibilities in this part of the cycle include establishing programs for preventive

measures and determining needs for facilities, equipment, and personnel to operate the programs.

3. The QC group performs its programs and makes quality decisions based on inspection of parts and products as necessary.

4. The QC group evaluates the results of monitoring activities. In this part of the cycle, the group analyzes the extent of deviations from acceptable quality levels, studies implications, and takes appropriate corrective actions.

Required:

a. State the objectives for an audit of this function.

b. List the audit steps needed to achieve these objectives.

(IIA adapted)

16.6   Your company's management is concerned with the purchasing function. The company has experienced rapid growth created by expansion of its product lines and acquisition of several subsidiaries. Each subsidiary and company operating plant has its own purchasing department. The company deals with many vendors. Supplies are warehoused in multiple locations. Senior management has asked you to do a special study of the function. They have concerns over the apparent inefficient use of resources, based on such factors as (1) increasing inventories, (2) growing vendor lists, (3) increasing number of sole source of procurement items, and (4) an increasing average cost per purchase order.

Required:

a. What are the main components of an operational audit?

b. Explain the difference between a special and a recurring operational audit.

c. Based on the case description, list the steps you would take to complete the special audit. Relate these steps to the case situation by giving possible examples of the steps in the context of the case.

(IIA adapted)

16.7   To speed up tax return processing and reduce data entry costs, a state tax agency has installed a new feature that permits taxpayers to transmit tax returns and inquire about return processing status electronically. Taxpayers still submit payment and receive refund checks by mail. Taxpayers using the new system must request its use. The agency authorizes its use by sending taxpayers user codes, passwords, and directions for formatting their electronic tax returns. Taxpayers are responsible for using the system to inquire about the status of their returns and to submit additional information for incomplete returns.

Required:

Explain the audit objectives of an audit to determine if the new electronic processing feature is (a) effective and (b) efficient. For each audit objective, describe appropriate audit procedures. Identify objectives in the left-hand column and the corresponding audit procedures in the right-hand column as shown below. Indicate by each objective whether it applies to effectiveness or efficiency, or to both.

Audit Objective Category	Effectiveness, Efficiency, or Both	Audit Procedures

(IIA adapted)

16.8   As the director of auditing for a municipality, you have received the following draft audit report from a member of your staff. The report is intended to present the results of an audit of the city's civic center operations. The report is to be presented to the city manager only. The city manager has no familiarity with civic center operations, having moved only recently to his current position from another city.

To: *City Manager*

From: *Director of Auditing*

Subject: *Civic Center Operations*

Findings: *The civic center is poorly managed. One piece of equipment valued at $112 could not be readily located. The civic center entered into legal contracts without review by the city attorney.*

Recommendation: *Civic center management should be improved. We recommend that you fire the present civic center manager.*

Recommendation: *If it has not already been done, someone should locate the missing equipment.*

Recommendation: *Civic center contracts should be reviewed by the city attorney.*

Conclusion: *The above information is based on standard audit procedures and included all appropriate tests. We did not audit maintenance operations.*

The auditor has the following information:

1. The civic center manager entered into contracts valued at $2.8 million for goods and services of the year audited.
2. The civic center manager is responsible for equipment valued at $970,000.
3. An inventory of equipment valued at $656,000 was performed by the auditor.
4. The city attorney is paid a salary of $85,000 per year.
5. City policy requires prior review and approval by the city attorney of all contracts obligating the city.
6. Contracts valued at $480,000 were breached by suppliers. These contracts were found to be invalid and unenforceable by the city attorney subsequent to the breach.
7. Unable to require specific performance on the breached contracts, the city suffered a loss of $225,000.
8. The city policy on contracting was never formally communicated to the civic center management.

Required:

a. Identify and briefly describe the appropriate parts of an audit report.

b. Identify five deficiencies in the draft audit report and explain why they are deficiencies.

(IIA adapted)

16.9   The audit department of a large manufacturing company has just completed an audit of the company's Centralized Computer Support Services (CCSS), which is responsible for all data processing, except for special analysis programs run on personal computers in the R&D, engineering, marketing, and accounting departments. CCSS is responsible for coordinating the acquisition and maintenance of all equipment, including personal computers and associated equipment and software.

The audit of CCSS was limited to a review and evaluation of its responsiveness to the needs of the various personal computer users. This audit was requested by the vice president of operations as a result of frequent complaints by the various departments about CCSS's unresponsiveness. Specifically, the various departments charged that CCSS failed to acquire requested personal computers in a timely fashion, even when funds were readily available. As a result, the departments were frequently unable to do desired analytical work.

Using questionnaires, interviews, and tests of transactions, the auditors discovered that CCSS's role is limited to monitoring corporate usage of personal computers and consolidating departmental requests for personal computers before sending the requests to the purchasing department. The purchasing department actually ordered the computers and worked with the vendor. The audit revealed that CCSS took as long as five months (past the due date of a request) waiting on various requests for similar equipment so that one large request could be sent to purchasing. Once the purchase request was received by purchasing, the order was properly placed and the ordered equipment promptly received.

Required:
Write a short report based on the data given. Your report should be classified as to the main elements of an operational audit report. (IIA adapted)

16.10   Internal auditing can be classified as to financial auditing, compliance auditing, fraud auditing, and operational auditing. Operational auditing may be further categorized as to efficiency auditing and effectiveness auditing.

Required:
Classify each of the following audits as compliance, financial, fraud, or operational. If operational, indicate whether it is an efficiency audit or an effectiveness audit.

a. Determining the cause of excessive employee turnover in a division's manufacturing operations.
b. Recalculating royalties resulting from an existing franchise agreement that calls for payment of sales-related royalties.
c. Searching for the cause of a major branch's decline in profitability and making recommendations for improvement. The auditor's recommendations could lead to the closing of the branch.
d. Auditing travel expenditures at the company's 35 branches located throughout the United States to determine whether personal expenditures are being charged as company travel.
e. Spot-checking inventory at the company's eastern warehouse and comparing with perpetual records for possible major shrinkage.
f. Reviewing the year-end adjustments to the general ledger. These adjustments had been drafted by the general accounting staff preparatory to drafting the unaudited financial statements.
g. Evaluating the adequacy of EDP controls related to transaction processing. More specifically, the auditors are interested in determining that the controls provide for accurate processing of only properly approved transactions.
h. Determining the extent to which the internal reporting system is supporting the management decision process.
i. Examining existing loan agreements for possible violations of restrictive covenants.
j. Ascertaining why sewage costs have nearly doubled in the past year.
k. Evaluating the adequacy of the loan loss reserve of a savings and loan association (a request made by management to the director of internal auditing).
l. Auditing the purchasing function in terms of adequacy of supply sources, reasonableness of vendor prices and whether competitive bids are required where appropriate, and quality and cost of transportation services.

16.11 Discuss the auditor's compliance auditing responsibility under each of the following sets of standards:

1. Generally accepted auditing standards;
2. GAO yellow book; and
3. Single Audit Act of 1984 as interpreted by OMB Circular A-133.

16.12 The College of Agriculture at Watertown State University, a large university located in the Midwest, received a $2 million grant from the U.S. Department of Agriculture in July 2002. The purpose of the grant is further research into developing chickens producing mainly white meat. Direct costs permitted under the grant consist of compensation of faculty while on leave and assigned to the project; fringe benefits related to these faculty; graduate assistants' stipends and other support staff costs; travel directly associated with the research; telephone and fax costs applicable to the grant; and other direct costs such as computer software, chickens used in the research, and postage. In addition to the direct costs, the grant permits the university to add 25 percent of direct costs to billings submitted to the Department of Agriculture to reimburse for such indirect costs as utilities, building space, and administration.

The firm of Orens and Smead, CPAs, has been retained to audit the financial statements of Watertown State for the fiscal year ended June 30, 2003. In addition to requesting the financial audit, the engagement letter requests the firm to audit for compliance, as necessary. Although the university has several contracts and grants from the federal government, you have been assigned to perform the compliance audit for the "chicken grant." You have requested and obtained the following analysis from Dr. Leghorn, the faculty member in charge of the research project.

Watertown State University
College of Agriculture
Poultry Research Grant Analysis
For the Year Ended June 30, 2003

7/11/02	Grant award		$2,000,000
7/11–6/30	Direct costs:		
	Faculty salaries	$300,000 (1)	
	Faculty fringes	60,000 (2)	
	Support staff + fringes	72,000 (3)	
	Graduate assistants	48,000 (4)	
	Travel	6,000	
	Telephone, postage, fax	1,000	
	Computer simulation	2,000	
	Chickens and feed	3,000	
	Total direct costs	$492,000	
	Indirect costs (25%)	123,000	
	Total billings		$ 615,000
6/30/03	Unexpended portion of grant:		
	($2,000,000 – $492,000)		$1,508,000

(1) Five faculty at $60,000 each
(2) 20% of salaries
(3) Two secretaries at $30,000 + 20% fringes
(4) Four secretaries at $12,000

Required:

a. In addition to generally accepted auditing standards, cite the other source(s) of auditor responsibility in performing the compliance audit relative to the "chicken grant." Assuming Watertown State has a resident federal auditor, is the responsibility for performing the compliance audit that of the resident auditor or the independent auditor?

b. Identify internal control policies and procedures that should serve to prevent and/or detect noncompliance with the terms of the grant.

c. Develop an audit program that will provide reasonable assurance of detecting material instances of noncompliance with the terms of the grant.

16.13 An internal auditor with a landscaping company is preparing an audit program for the billing and accounts receivable functions. It was determined that the following objectives should be met by the appropriate operating department:

a. Customer credit reviewed and approved before orders are accepted.
b. Sales billed promptly and in the correct amount.
c. Accounts receivable recorded promptly and accurately.
d. Uncollectible accounts identified in a timely manner and processed properly.
e. Customer discounts approved and accurately recorded.

Required:

Develop three audit procedures for each of the listed objectives to determine whether the billing and accounts receivable functions are accomplishing those objectives. Use the following format:

Objective	*Procedures*
a.	1.
	2.
	3.

(IIA adapted)

b i l t r i t e

A Computerized Audit Practice Case

biltrite

DESCRIPTION OF THE PRACTICE CASE

This case has two learning objectives. First, it provides the student an opportunity to apply auditing concepts to a "real-life" audit client. The client, Biltrite Bicycles, Inc., operates within a unique business climate and internal control environment, and the student must assess inherent risk and control risk accordingly. The student also is asked to evaluate materiality and set individual item and aggregate materiality thresholds. In addition, the case contains modules involving sampling applications, audit program design, audit workpaper completion, audit adjustments, and an audit report upon completion of the 2001 examination.

The second purpose served by the practice case is to enable the student to utilize the PC as an audit assist device. The student may use the computer in the Biltrite case to both automate the audit field work and assist in audit decision making. New to this edition, the student will be asked to perform comparative analyses by accessing the annual report on the web site of Cannondale, an actual company.

The case consists of modules. At the end of each module is a set of requirements. The student will need an IBM-compatible PC, an Excel or Excel-compatible spreadsheet program, and the data CD provided with this textbook.

The modules parallel the phases of a financial statement audit. Many of the modules require both qualitative and quantitative analyses. Based on narrative material and on partially completed audit workpapers, the student will be asked to complete the workpapers, arrive at audit conclusions, and/or answer questions relating to specific auditing standards and interpretations. The following modules make up the Biltrite case:

Module I: Assessment of inherent risk
Module II: Assessment of control risk
Module III: Control testing the sales processing subset of the revenue cycle
Module IV: PPS sampling—factory equipment additions
Module V: Dallas Dollar Bank—bank reconciliation
Module VI: Analysis of interbank transfers
Module VII: Accounts receivable aging analysis and adequacy of allowance for doubtful accounts
Module VIII: Sales and purchases cutoff tests
Module IX: Search for unrecorded liabilities
Module X: Estimated liability for product warranty
Module XI: Plant asset additions and disposals
Module XII: Analysis of marketable securities
Module XIII: Mortgage note payable and note payable to Bank Two
Module XIV: Working trial balance
Module XV: Audit report

For maximum learning benefit, the modules should be completed as follows:

Module I:	Following Chapter 5
Module II:	Following Chapter 8
Module III:	Following Chapter 9
Module IV:	Following Chapter 10
Modules V, VI, and VII:	Following Chapter 11
Modules VIII, IX, X, and XI:	Following Chapter 12
Modules XII, XIII, and XIV:	Following Chapter 13
Module XV:	Following Chapter 14

For purposes of this case, the income tax effects of audit adjustments have been ignored.

Description of the Company

Biltrite was incorporated in 1970 to manufacture ten-speed touring bikes. An exercise bike was added to the product line in 1980, and mountain bikes were added in 1987. Currently, the company makes the following products:

Grand Prix: Ten-speed touring bike
Phoenix: Deluxe eighteen-speed racing bike
Pike's Peak: Twelve-speed mountain bike
Himalaya: Eighteen-speed deluxe mountain bike
Waistliner: Stationary exercise bike

All of these products are manufactured in one plant, which is located in eastern Texas. Derailleurs (front and rear) comprise a major portion of the parts inventory. Other purchased parts consist of tires, handle grips, pedals, wheels, and spokes. Materials and supplies consist primarily of paint and steel. Biltrite manufactures the frames and handlebars, and assembles and paints the bikes.

The factory, which employs 2,000 workers, was built in 1970, was refurbished and updated in 1997, and is now quite automated. Biltrite's administrative offices are located in another building in the same complex. The company has ten regional locations in various parts of the United States; each location consists of a warehouse headed by a warehouse superintendent and a sales office directed by a regional sales manager.

Products are shipped to the warehouses upon completion, and from the warehouses they are shipped to licensed dealers in the respective regions. The dealer network consists of approximately 1,500 outlets located throughout the United States and Canada.

All products carry a full one-year warranty covering parts and labor. The company is known for the quality of its products and for its strong service support.

As of the end of 2001, the company had a total of 60 customer accounts ranging in amounts from $2,200 to approximately $1,350,000. The cumulative accounts receivable at year end December 31, 2001, was $12 million.

Biltrite experienced steady growth in sales and profitability of all product lines from the date of incorporation until the beginning of 1986. From early 1986 until the present time, competition from Asian and European manufacturers has had a significant impact on Biltrite's revenue. This trend has continued through the current year (see Table BR.1).

Your firm, Denise Vaughan & Co., Certified Public Accountants, has audited Biltrite since its incorporation in 1970. Denise Vaughan is presently the partner in charge of

TABLE BR.1

Biltrite Bicycles, Inc., Comparative Income Statements 1992–2001 (in thousands of dollars)

	2001*	2000	1999	1998	1997	1996	1995	1994	1993	1992
Sales	$335,000	$280,000	$272,000	$274,500	$266,800	$269,300	$268,700	$265,570	$263,440	$262,890
Cost of Goods Sold	227,800	215,600	209,440	211,365	205,436	188,510	188,090	185,899	184,408	184,023
Gross Profit	107,200	64,400	62,560	63,135	61,364	80,790	80,610	79,671	79,032	78,867
Operating Expenses	45,770	42,330	41,400	42,000	40,680	39,997	40,100	38,965	38,670	37,700
Operating Income	61,430	22,070	21,160	21,135	20,684	40,793	40,510	40,706	40,362	41,167
Other Expenses (net)	15,668	8,960	8,700	8,240	8,150	7,890	7,940	7,760	7,240	7,123
Net Income before Taxes and Extraordinary Item	45,762	13,110	12,460	12,895	12,534	32,903	32,570	32,946	33,122	34,044
Income Taxes	13,729	4,542	4,150	3,869	3,760	9,871	9,771	9,884	9,937	10,213
Net Income before Extraordinary Item	32,033	8,568	8,310	9,026	8,774	23,032	22,799	23,062	23,185	23,831
Extraordinary Gain (Loss)—Net of Tax	0	1,235	0	(2,650)	0	0	(1,540)	0	3,400	0
Net Income	$ 32,033	$ 9,803	$ 8,310	$ 6,376	$ 8,774	$ 23,032	$ 21,259	$ 23,062	$ 26,585	$ 23,831

*Unaudited

the engagement and Carolyn Volmar is the audit manager. The audit team consists of Richard Derick, senior auditor in charge of the Biltrite audit; Cheryl Lucas, assistant auditor, in her third year with the firm and her third year on the Biltrite audit; Shelly Ross, assistant auditor in her second year with the firm and her second year on the Biltrite audit; and a student (you), assistant auditor, newly hired. Biltrite will be your first audit.

Derick has been in charge of the Biltrite audit field work for the past two years. Prior to that time he had been a part of the Biltrite audit team as an assistant. He is very familiar with the client's operations and internal controls and works well with Biltrite personnel.

Gerald Groth, the corporate controller of Biltrite, has been with the company since receiving his MBA in 1983. Groth is also a CPA and was a staff accountant with Denise Vaughan & Co. from 1978 to 1983. Other Biltrite personnel are Trevor Lawton, president and chief executive officer; Elmer Fennig, vice president, production; Charles Gibson, vice president, marketing; Marlene McAfee, treasurer; Laura Schroeder, director of human resources; John Mesarvey, chief accountant; Glenn Florence, director of internal auditing; and Malissa Rust, director of computer based information systems. Mesarvey, Florence and Rust report to Groth. Emil Ransbottom, the director of purchasing, as well as the plant manager and the factory supervisors, report to Fennig. Biltrite has three product managers—one for touring bikes, one for mountain bikes, and one for stationary bikes. The sales staff report to the product managers and the product managers report to Gibson. Under Mesarvey, the chief accountant, are Harriet Smith, transaction processing; Oliver Perna, cost accounting; and Janice Hollins, financial statements. Transaction processing is divided into the following sections: General ledger, accounts receivable, accounts payable, and payroll. The managers of these sections report to Smith. Three staff auditors report to the director of internal auditing; three personnel officers report to the director of human resources. Harold Cannon, information technology manager, and Nancy Karling, management information systems manager, report to the CBIS director. Cannon's department is divided into four sections: data entry, data processing, control, and systems analysis and programming. Karling's department is divided into three sections: statistical analysis, budget coordination, and report generation. Reporting to the treasurer are Lawrence White, credit manager; Paula Penelee, portfolio manager; and Mark Wilkins, cashier.

Biltrite closes its general ledger on a calendar-year basis. Unaudited financial statements are prepared quarterly and are reviewed by Denise Vaughan & Co. The accounting information system, including the general ledger, inventories, receivables, payables, and plant assets, was computerized in 1977, and was upgraded to a real-time system in 1999. After extensive "debugging," the real-time system seems to be functioning smoothly. The company employs approximately 2,000 production workers and 200 salaried administrative employees, including the corporate management staff, warehouse superintendents, and regional sales managers. In addition, 100 warehouse personnel and 120 salespersons are employed by the regional units. Hourly employees, consisting of the production workers and warehouse personnel, are paid weekly; salaried employees are paid biweekly. Salespersons receive a salary plus 5 percent commission, based on gross sales.

All bank accounts have been reconciled on a monthly basis, including the December 31, 2001, reconciliation. The company has provided the auditors with a year-end adjusted trial balance and a complete set of financial statements, together with supporting schedules (see Exhibits BR.1–BR.5). Richard Derick and his audit team were present at Biltrite's year-end physical inventory.

| EXHIBIT BR.1 |

Biltrite Bicycles, Inc., Adjusted Trial Balance as of December 31, 2001

	Account Number	Debit (in thousands of dollars)	Credit (in thousands of dollars)
Bank Two Demand Deposit	1001	$ 10,200	
Dallas Dollar Bank Demand Deposit	1002	2,100	
Dallas Dollar Bank Payroll Account	1008	57	
Petty Cash	1012	5	
Investments in Marketable Securities	1101	7,000	
All for Decline in Market Value of Securities	1102		$ 2,800
Accounts Receivable—Trade	1201	11,920	
Notes Receivable—Trade	1202	80	
Notes Receivable—Officers	1203	0	
Allowance for Doubtful Accounts	1250		220
Raw Materials Inventory	1310	6,200	
Derailleurs Inventory	1320	5,500	
Purchased Parts Inventory	1330	15,100	
Goods in Process—Grand Prix Touring Bike	1350	800	
Goods in Process—Phoenix Touring Bike	1351	700	
Goods in Process—Pike's Peak Mountain Bike	1352	1,500	
Goods in Process—Himalaya Mountain Bike	1361	1,200	
Goods in Process—Waistliner Stationary Bike	1365	300	
Finished Goods—Grand Prix Touring Bike	1371	1,616	
Finished Goods—Phoenix Touring Bike	1372	2,300	
Finished Goods—Pike's Peak Mountain Bike	1373	5,800	
Finished Goods—Himalaya Mountain Bike	1376	4,600	
Finished Goods—Waistliner Stationary Bike	1379	1,200	
Indirect Materials	1385	800	
Repair Parts Inventory	1390	2,600	
Prepaid Insurance	1410	600	
Deferred Taxes—Warranty	1440	400	
Land	1510	4,000	
Factory Building	1520	50,000	
Accumulated Depreciation—Building	1525		14,140
Warehouses and Sales Offices	1527	200,000	
Accumulated Depreciation—Warehouses and Sales Offices	1529		105,000
Factory Equipment	1530	360,000	
Accumulated Depreciation—Factory Equipment	1535		144,660
Office Building	1540	20,000	
Accumulated Depreciation—Office Building	1545		8,000
Office Fixtures and Equipment	1550	10,000	
Accumulated Depreciation—Office Fixtures and Equipment	1555		6,150
Autos and Trucks	1560	1,000	
Accumulated Depreciation—Autos and Trucks	1565		620
Patents	1610	4,000	
Copyrights	1620	2,000	
Deposits	1710	340	
Cost of Goods Sold—Grand Prix Touring Bike	5100	34,448	

(continued)

EXHIBIT BR.1

(continued)

	Account Number	Debit (in thousands of dollars)	Credit (in thousands of dollars)
Cost of Goods Sold—Phoenix Touring Bike	5200	$ 32,903	
Cost of Goods Sold—Pike's Peak Mountain Bike	5300	89,584	
Cost of Goods Sold—Himalaya Mountain Bike	5400	22,075	
Cost of Goods Sold—Waistliner Stationary Bike	5500	48,790	
Direct Labor	6100	35,600	
Direct Labor Applied	6200		35,600
Indirect Labor	7201	5,500	
Depreciation—Factory Building	7205	2,000	
Depreciation—Factory Equipment	7206	42,060	
Real Estate Taxes	7210	4,400	
Personal Property Taxes	7211	1,600	
Manufacturing Supplies	7220	15,042	
FICA Tax Expense	7230	3,980	
Sate Unemployment Tax Expense	7231	1,120	
Federal Unemployment Tax Expense	7232	880	
Workers' Compensation Premiums	7233	550	
Health Insurance Premiums—Factory	7234	2,860	
Employee Pension Expense	7235	3,810	
Repairs and Maintenance Expense	7236	1,222	
Utilities Expense	7241	16,100	
Miscellaneous Factory Expense	7242	2,200	
Manufacturing Overhead Applied	7250		103,324
Sales Commissions	8310	16,500	
Sales Salaries	8320	1,200	
Bad Debts Expense	8325	500	
Product Warranty	8330	1,139	
Advertising	8340	3,311	
Miscellaneous Selling Expense	8350	420	
Administrative Salaries	9410	7,550	
Research and Development Costs	9420	1,050	
Patent Amortization	9425	700	
FICA Tax Expense	9431	856	
State Unemployment Tax Expense	9432	224	
Federal Unemployment Tax Expense	9433	120	
Workers' Compensation Premiums	9434	100	
Health Insurance Premiums—Administrative	9435	500	
Employee Pension Expense	9436	100	
Employee Profit Sharing Expense	9437	345	
Depreciation—Office Building	9440	800	
Depreciation—Office Fixtures and Equipment	9445	1,875	
Depreciation—Autos and Trucks	9447	320	
Depreciation—Warehouses and Sales Offices	9449	10,000	
Accounting Fees	9450	320	
Legal Fees	9451	430	

EXHIBIT BR.1

(continued)

	Account Number	Debit (in thousands of dollars)	Credit (in thousands of dollars)
Other Professional Services	9452	$ 20	
Supplies Expense	9460	200	
Insurance Expense	9470	450	
Printing and Copying Expense	9480	235	
Postage Expense	9481	285	
Gain/Loss on Disposal of Plant Assets	9485		4,000
Miscellaneous Administrative Expense	9490	220	
Interest Expense	9701	12,890	
Loss on Decline in Market Value of Securities	9702	2,800	
Federal Income Tax Expense	9990	10,329	
State Income Tax Expense	9991	1,923	
City Income Tax Expense	9992	1,477	
Notes Payable—Trade	2010		3,660
Accounts Payable—Trade	2020		10,200
Interest Payable	2030		3,400
Sales Salaries Payable	2041		30
Administrative Salaries Payable	2042		870
Factory Wages Payable	2043		1,290
FICA Payable	2051		310
State Income Taxes Withheld	2052		150
City Income Taxes Withheld	2053		50
Unemployment and Workers' Compensation Premiums Payable	2054		25
Accrued Profit Sharing Payable	2055		345
Federal Income Taxes Payable	2061		4,000
State Income Taxes Payable	2062		1,200
City Income Taxes Payable	2063		800
Estimated Product Warranty Liability	2070		544
Accrued Commissions Payable	2080		1,400
Mortgage Note Payable (10%)	2110		60,000
Deferred Tax Liability—Depreciation	2120		10,600
12% Note Payable to Bank Two	2130		45,000
10% Preferred Stock	3110		120,000
Common Stock	3120		100,000
Additional Paid-in Capital	3130		50,000
Treasury Stock	3140	8,153	
Retained Earnings	3150		29,574
Dividends	3160	15,000	
Sales—Grand Prix Touring Bike	4100		50,659
Sales—Phoenix Touring Bike	4200		47,360
Sales—Pike's Peak Touring Bike	4300		132,892
Sales—Himalaya Mountain Bike	4400		34,299
Sales—Waistliner Stationary Bike	4500		69,790
Interest Earned	4901		115
Dividends Earned	4902		105
Loss on Disposal of Investments	4903	198	
		$1,203,182	$1,203,182

EXHIBIT BR.2

Biltrite Bicycles, Inc., Income Statements for the Years Ended December 31, 2000 and 2001 (in thousands of dollars)

	Year Ended 12/31/01*	Year Ended 12/31/00
Sales Revenue	$335,000	$280,000
Cost of Goods Sold:		
Beginning Inventories	$ 10,142	$ 6,690
Cost of Goods Manufactured (Schedule 1)	233,174	219,052
Cost of Goods Available for Sale	243,316	225,742
Ending Inventories	15,516	10,142
Cost of Goods Sold	227,800	215,600
Gross Profit on Sales	107,200	64,400
Operating Expenses (Schedule 2)	45,770	42,330
Operating Income	61,430	22,070
Financial Income and Expense:		
Interest Expense	12,890	9,682
Interest and Dividends Earned	(220)	(1,022)
Loss (Gain) on Disposal of Investments	198	(100)
Loss on Decline in Market Value of Securities	2,800	400
Net Financial Expense	15,668	8,960
Net Income before Taxes and Extraordinary Items	45,762	13,110
Income Taxes	13,729	4,542
Net Income before Extraordinary Items	32,033	8,568
Extraordinary Gain from Eminent Domain Sale (net of tax)		1,235
Net Income	$ 32,033	$ 9,803

SCHEDULE 1
Cost of Goods Manufactured
(in thousands of dollars)

	Year Ended 12/31/01*	Year Ended 12/31/00
Beginning Work-in-Process Inventories	$ 4,000	$ 4,663
Manufacturing Costs:		
Direct Materials:		
Beginning Inventories of Materials and Purchased Parts	$ 16,150	$ 15,320
Purchases	105,400	86,200
Available for Production	121,550	101,520
Ending Inventories of Materials and Purchased Parts	26,800	16,150
Cost of Materials Used in Production	94,750	85,370
Direct Labor	35,600	31,300
Manufacturing Overhead (Schedule 1A)	103,324	101,719
Total Manufacturing Costs	233,674	218,389
Total Work in Process	237,674	223,052
Ending Work-in-Process Inventories	4,500	4,000
Cost of Goods Manufactured	$233,174	$219,052

EXHIBIT BR.2

(continued)

SCHEDULE 1A
Manufacturing Overhead

	Year Ended 12/31/01*	Year Ended 12/31/00
Indirect Labor	$ 5,500	$ 5,300
Depreciation of Factory Building	2,000	2,000
Depreciation of Factory Equipment	42,060	42,860
Property Taxes	6,000	5,800
Manufacturing Supplies	15,042	14,600
Payroll Taxes and Fringe Benefits	13,200	12,400
Utilities	16,100	15,600
Repairs and Maintenance	1,222	1,159
Miscellaneous	2,200	2,000
	$103,324	$101,719

SCHEDULE 2
Operating Expenses
(in thousands of dollars)

	Year Ended 12/31/01*	Year Ended 12/31/00
Selling Expenses:		
Sales Commissions	$ 16,500	$ 13,800
Sales Salaries	1,200	1,180
Bad Debts Expense	500	900
Product Warranty	1,139	1,078
Advertising	3,311	2,522
Miscellaneous Selling	420	146
	$ 23,070	$ 19,626
General Expenses:		
Administrative Salaries	7,550	6,677
Research and Development	1,050	2,200
Patent Amortization	700	700
Payroll Taxes and Fringe Benefits	2,245	2,200
Depreciation—Office Building	800	800
Depreciation—Office Fixtures and Equipment	1,875	2,260
Depreciation—Autos and Trucks	320	300
Depreciation—Warehouses	10,000	10,000
Accounting and Legal Fees	750	720
Other Professional Services	20	18
Supplies	200	280
Insurance	450	240
Printing and Postage	520	115
Gain/Loss on Disposal of Plant Assets	(4,000)	(3,850)
Miscellaneous Administrative	220	44
	22,700	22,704
	$ 45,770	$ 42,330

*Unaudited

EXHIBIT BR.3

Biltrite Bicycles, Inc., Balance Sheets as of December 31, 2000 and 2001 (in thousands of dollars)

	12/31/01*		12/31/00	
ASSETS				
Current Assets				
Cash on hand and in banks		$ 12,362		$ 15,800
Investments in marketable securities		4,200		5,300
Accounts and notes receivable—trade	$ 12,000		$ 13,200	
Less allowance for doubtful accounts	(220)		(800)	
		11,780		12,400
Inventories:				
Materials and purchased parts	26,800		16,150	
Goods in process	4,500		4,000	
Finished goods	15,516		10,142	
Indirect materials and repair parts	3,400		3,200	
		50,216		33,492
Prepaid expenses		600		560
Deferred tax asset—warranty		400		460
Total currents assets		79,558		68,012
Property, Plant, and Equipment:				
Land		4,000		4,000
Factory building	50,000		50,000	
Less accumulated depreciation	(14,140)		(12,140)	
		35,860		37,860
Warehouses and sales offices	200,000		200,000	
Less accumulated depreciation	(105,000)		(95,000)	
		95,000		105,000
Factory equipment	360,000		320,000	
Less accumulated depreciation	(144,660)		(147,460)	
		215,340		172,540
Office building	20,000		20,000	
Less accumulated depreciation	(8,000)		(7,200)	
		12,000		12,800
Office fixtures and equipment	10,000		9,000	
Less accumulated depreciation	(6,150)		(5,075)	
		3,850		3,925
Autos and trucks	1,000		900	
Less accumulated depreciation	(620)		(300)	
		380		600
Total property, plant, and equipment		366,430		336,725
Investments and other assets:				
Patents and copyrights (net of accumulated amortization)	6,000		6,700	
Deposits	340		340	
Total investments and other assets		6,340		7,040
TOTAL ASSETS		$452,328		$411,777

EXHIBIT BR.3

(continued)

	12/31/01*	12/31/00
LIABILITIES		
Current Liabilities		
Notes payable	$ 3,660	$ 14,890
Accounts payable	10,200	18,600
Interest payable	3,400	2,200
Salaries and wages payable	2,190	2,018
Payroll withholdings	510	490
Taxes and fringe benefits payable	370	345
Income taxes payable	6,000	1,800
Estimated product warranty liability	544	860
Accrued commissions payable	1,400	1,200
Total current liabilities	28,274	42,403
Long-Term Liabilities		
Mortgage note payable (10%)	60,000	60,000
Deferred tax liability—depreciation	10,600	9,800
12% note payable to Bank Two	45,000	
Total long-term liabilities	115,600	69,800
TOTAL LIABILITIES	143,874	112,203
STOCKHOLDERS' EQUITY		
Invested Capital		
Preferred stock—$100 par value, 10%		
cumulative, 10,000,000 shares authorized,		
1,200,000 shares issued and outstanding	120,000	120,000
Common stock, $10 par value, 90,000,000		
shares authorized, 10,000,000 shares issued,		
of which 220,000 shares are in the treasury	100,000	100,000
Paid-in capital in excess of par value		
of capital stock	50,000	50,000
Total invested capital	270,000	270,000
Retained Earnings	46,607	29,574
Total	316,607	299,574
Less cost of 220,000 shares of treasury stock	(8,153)	0
TOTAL STOCKHOLDERS' EQUITY	308,454	299,574
TOTAL LIABILITIES AND		
STOCKHOLDERS' EQUITY	$452,328	$411,777

*Unaudited

EXHIBIT BR.4

**Biltrite Bicycles, Inc., Statements of Retained Earnings
for the Years Ended December 31, 2000 and 2001**

	(in thousands of dollars)	
	Year Ended 12/31/01*	Year Ended 12/31/00
Retained Earnings—beginning of year	$ 29,574	$ 29,771
Net Income	32,033	9,803
Dividends	(15,000)	(10,000)
Retained Earnings—end of year	$ 46,607	$ 29,574

*Unaudited

MODULE I: ASSESSMENT OF INHERENT RISK

In this module, you will be asked to assess inherent risk after you have done the following:

1. Analyzed Biltrite's organizational structure and prepared an organization chart;
2. Applied analytical procedures to Biltrite's financial data; and
3. Studied Biltrite's business operations and the bicycle manufacturing industry generally.

In addition, you will be asked to set individual item and aggregate materiality thresholds. These thresholds will be used in deciding whether potential audit adjustments are to be

1. Proposed;
2. Accumulated in an aggregate materiality workpaper for later consideration; or
3. Ignored.

In completing this assignment, you may assume that Derick has decided on the following initial risk assessments:

Inherent risk: 100%
Control risk: maximum
Audit risk: 5%

Study of the Business and the Industry

As part of his continuing study of Biltrite's operations, Derick has extracted the following data from the computerized permanent file entitled "Business and Industry."

1. Charles Lawton founded Biltrite in 1970 and successfully led the company during the ensuing twenty-five years. He retired in 1994 and his only son, Trevor, assumed control of the company. The Lawton family presently owns 25 percent of the outstanding Biltrite common stock; the remaining 75 percent is publicly held.

EXHIBIT BR.5

Biltrite Bicycles, Inc., Statements of Cash Flows for the Year Ended December 31, 2001

CASH PROVIDED BY OPERATING ACTIVITIES:		
Net Income	$ 32,033	
Add (Deduct):		
Increase in inventories	(16,724)	
Decrease in accounts and notes receivable	620	
Increase in prepaid expenses	(40)	
Increase in deferred tax liability	800	
Decrease in deferred tax asset	60	
Decrease in accounts payable	(8,400)	
Increase in interest payable	1,200	
Increase in salaries and wages payable	172	
Increase in payroll withholdings	20	
Increase in taxes and fringe benefits payable	25	
Increase in income taxes payable	4,200	
Decrease in product warranty liability	(316)	
Increase in accrued commissions payable	200	
Depreciation and amortization	57,755	
Loss on sale of investments	198	
Gain on disposal of plant assets	(4,000)	
Loss on decline in market value of securities	2,800	
Total Cash Provided by Operating Activities		$ 70,603
CASH USED IN INVESTING ACTIVITIES:		
Disposal of Property and Equipment:		
Factory equipment	9,000	
Office equipment	200	
Purchase of Plant Assets:		
Factory equipment	(89,860)	
Office fixtures and equipment	(2,000)	
Autos and trucks	(100)	
Sale of Marketable Securities	1,102	
Purchase of Marketable Securities	(3,000)	
Purchase of Treasury Stock	(8,153)	
Total Cash Used in Investing Activities		(92,811)
CASH PROVIDED BY FINANCING ACTIVITIES:		
Issuance of 12% note payable to Bank Two	45,000	
Payment of dividends	(15,000)	
Payment of mortgage note installment	(10,000)	
Payment of notes payable	(1,230)	
Total Cash Provided by Investing Activities		18,770
INCREASE (DECREASE) IN CASH		$ (3,438)

2. Biltrite has been known for the quality of its products and its strong after-sale service support. (All bicycles are under 100 percent parts and labor warranty for one

year following sale.) These attributes led to many years of steadily increasing sales and profits.

3. Beginning in 1985, imports of bicycles significantly increased industry competition. As a result, from 1985 to 1991, domestic manufacturers, including Biltrite, experienced declining sales and profits; from 1992 until recently, earnings stabilized for both Biltrite and the industry. In response to foreign competition, Biltrite updated its manufacturing facility in 1997, incorporating the latest technology into its products. These efforts produced a modest increase in 2000 sales and profits and, based on unaudited data, a more dramatic increase in 2001.

4. The increased automation resulting from the 1997 manufacturing update enabled Biltrite to decrease its factory labor force from 3,000 in 1996 to 2,000 in 2001, and to reduce its sales force from 150 to 120 in response to declining sales volume.

   Elmer Fennig, production vice president, observed that the factory refurbishing has enabled the company to increase significantly the productivity of its production employees. Charles Gibson, marketing vice president, agrees, and predicts a continued increase in revenues and profits, at least through 2003. However, Gerald Groth, corporate controller, is concerned about the decline in the operating income margin as a percent of sales. He attributes the decline to the increased proportion of fixed overhead to total manufacturing costs, given increased automation.

5. In 2001, in the face of increasing liquidity problems accompanying the automation, payment of trade accounts payable within the specified credit terms became increasingly difficult. After much discussion with Harvey Bombenmyr, the president of Bank Two, and Bank Two's lending officers, Lawton was able to negotiate a ten-year 12% note payable for $45 million. The note is unsecured and is payable in equal annual installments, together with interest, beginning March 1, 2002, and contains restrictive covenants. Those relevant to the Biltrite audit are the following:
   a. A minimum balance of $10 million must be maintained in Biltrite's demand deposit account with Bank Two;
   b. Further borrowing is prohibited until the Bank Two note has been amortized below $10 million; and
   c. Dividends may be declared only from retained earnings in excess of $45 million.

6. In April 2000, Lawton borrowed $3 million from the company in exchange for an unsecured note. The transaction resulted in a debit to Account 1203—Notes Receivable, Officers. According to Groth, Lawton plans to repay this note prior to December 31, 2001.

7. Legal action against the company was initiated by Rollfast, a competitor, in late 2000. The suit alleges that Biltrite infringed on a process already patented by Rollfast. The process, according to Rollfast's attorneys, enables a bicycle manufacturer to produce a frame in one piece, thereby adding strength to the bicycle by eliminating welding. Biltrite has responded to the action by demonstrating the unique characteristics of its patented bicycle frame. By July 2001, the suit had neither been heard by the court nor settled outside the courts by the litigants. Rollfast is suing Biltrite for $50 million.

8. Although Lawton and Groth have intensified efforts in recent years to establish and implement a sound internal control system, the independent auditors have not seen fit to reduce the assessed level of control risk below the maximum level. If the auditors' 2000 recommendations have been implemented, however, Derick anticipates a reduction in the assessed level of control risk in one or more of the transaction cycle subsets.

9. Biltrite's internal audit staff, directed by Glenn Florence, is viewed by our firm as competent, but not outstanding. Because the company does *not* have an audit committee, Florence reports directly to Groth, the controller. In the past, our audit team has utilized Florence and his three staff auditors only when necessary to assist in various phases of the Biltrite audit.

Requirements

1. Prepare an organizational chart for Biltrite and identify the major strengths and weaknesses in Biltrite's organizational structure.
2. Using the data CD and the spreadsheet program, retrieve the file titled "Analy1." Scroll through the file and locate the following workpapers:
   - WP A.1—Comparative income statements;
   - WP A.2—Sales and cost of goods sold—by product line;
   - WP A.3—Comparative schedule of manufacturing overhead and operating expenses; and
   - WP A.4—Inventories.
3. After scrutinizing the workpapers, perform the following:
   a. Using the "Comparative Income Statements" data in WP A.1, calculate each income statement component as a percentage of sales for 2001. (*Hint*: For help with the cell equations, examine the comparable cells for 2000.)
   b. Using the "Sales and Cost of Goods Sold—By Product Line" data in WP A.2, calculate the cost per unit as a percentage of sales price for 2001 by product line. (You may examine the comparable 2000 cell equations as you did in requirement (a).)
   c. Using the "Comparative Schedule of Manufacturing Overhead and Operating Expenses" data in WP A.3, calculate each component as a percentage of sales for 2001. (You may examine the comparable 2000 cell equations as you did in requirements (a) and (b).)
   d. Using the product line data from requirement (b) and the "Inventories" data from WP A.4, calculate finished goods inventory turnover for 2001 by product line. Calculate materials and purchased parts turnover for 2001 by component. (Again, you may refer to comparable cell equations for 2000.)
   e. Print the results of your analytical procedures.
4. Using the data CD and spreadsheet program, load the file titled "Budget." Examine the worksheet carefully and locate the following schedules:
   - WP A.6—Budgeted vs. actual income statements for 2001;
   - Schedule 1—Cost of goods manufactured; and
   - Schedule 2—Operating expenses.

   Compare with the results of requirement (2). Do any of the variances, when considered in relation to the results of requirement (2), raise warning signals? Print the budget.
5. Using the data CD and spreadsheet program, load the file titled "Analy2" and locate the following in WP A.5:
   - Comparative percentage balance sheets for 2001 and 2000; and
   - Comparative ratios:
     2001 vs. 2000
     Industry ratios for 2001

   After reviewing the workpaper, perform the following:

a. Using the "Balance Sheets" data, calculate the percent of each asset component as a percentage of total assets for 2001, and calculate each liability and stockholders' equity component as a percentage of total liabilities and stockholders' equity for 2001. (*Note*: This has been done for 2000; as in requirement (2), you may refer to the comparable cell equations for 2000 to expedite calculating the 2001 percentages.)

b. Using the "Balance Sheets" and "Comparative Income Statements" data, calculate the following ratios for 2001:
   - current ratio;
   - quick ratio;
   - times interest earned; and
   - return on stockholders' equity.
   (*Note*: The 2000 calculations already have been done for you.)

c. Compare pertinent ratios with industry averages (these are located next to the 2000 Biltrite ratios). Are there any significant disparities between Biltrite's ratios and the industry averages?

d. Print the results of your analytical procedures.

e. Cannondale, an actual company, is also a bicycle manufacturer. At this time go to Cannondale's web site at http://www.cannondale.com/company/. Click on "investor info" and retrieve Cannondale's latest annual report. Because web addresses may change, you will also be able to find Cannondale's current annual report in the Student Resources section of the Konrath Auditing web site at http://konrath.swcollege.com. Using the data contained in that report, perform the following:

   1. Compare Cannondale's percentage income statements with Biltrite's percentage income statements for the same years.
   2. Go to Cannondale's comparative balance sheets and income statements and calculate the same ratios that you calculated for Biltrite in (b) above
   3. On the basis of (1) and (2) above, what strengths and weaknesses of Biltrite relative to Cannondale can you identify?

6. What is the purpose of performing analytical procedures during the planning phase of the audit? What is the purpose of including budgets and performance reports in the application of analytical procedures? Based on your analytical procedures performed in requirements (2), (3), (4), and (5), what, if any, concerns do you have? Relate your concerns to management's assertions contained in the financial statements (i.e., existence or occurrence, completeness, rights and obligations, valuation, and presentation and disclosure). Can you suggest some specific audit procedures to allay your concerns?

7. Based on analytical procedures and study of the business and industry, in what specific transaction areas are you willing to reduce inherent risk below 100 percent? In deciding whether or not to reduce inherent risk, consider audit complexity and the probability of management misrepresentation fraud.

.com
http://www.
cannondale.com/
company/

.com
http://konrath.
swcollege.com

MODULE II: ASSESSMENT OF CONTROL RISK

In this module, you will be asked to assess control risk after obtaining a basic understanding of Biltrite's financial controls, including the control environment, the accounting information system, and the control procedures.

The Control Environment, the Accounting Information System and Control Procedures

Biltrite's real-time accounting system has been in operation since the beginning of 1999. By early 2000, the system had been debugged adequately, permitting discontinuation of the old manual system. All CBIS and accounting functions are centralized at the Texas home office. Some of the more significant features of the system are discussed in the following paragraphs.

Computerized Ledger   The general ledger software package, revised as part of the 1999 upgrade project, contains the following integrated modules: accounts receivable, accounts payable, inventories, plant assets, payroll, and general ledger.

Sales Processing   Customer sales orders received by salespersons are input directly into the system via terminals from each of the regional locations. The regional sales manager is responsible for entering the orders after checking for proper credit approval and determining the maximum credit limit. A transaction log is maintained at each remote terminal; the log shows date of order entry, identification number of the salesperson receiving the order, customer number, stock number, and quantity ordered. After determining stock availability, the computer prepares a consecutively numbered, three-part sales invoice. As part of the sales processing, the computer inserts the customer's name and address, product descriptions and prices, and extensions and footings. Terms of payment and discount availability also are determined by the computer and included on the invoice. For each order processed, the computer records the transaction, including costing the sale, and updates the accounts receivable and inventory modules. The original invoice is mailed to the customer, the first copy is faxed to the warehouse as shipping authorization, and the second copy is retained awaiting a signed bill of lading evidencing shipment. Upon its receipt from the regional unit, the bill of lading is attached to the second invoice copy and placed in a numeric file. Figure BR.1 describes the sales processing function in the form of a flowchart.

Cash Receipts   All mail is centrally received in the mailroom, opened, and distributed. Checks from customers are forwarded to CBIS, where the customer number, invoice numbers paid, discount taken, and net amount remitted are entered into the system based on the remittance advice information. The computer then updates the customer accounts, as well as the accounts receivable control and cash in bank accounts. At the end of the day, the computer produces a printout of detail and totals by customer, as well as a grand total.

The checks and remittance advices are then separated and the checks are forwarded to Mark Wilkins, cashier. Wilkins prepares the deposit and deposits each day's remittances intact. Receipted deposit tickets are forwarded by the bank to the controller's office where a comparison is made with the daily printout of cash receipts.

Miscellaneous cash receipts are processed in a fashion similar to that accorded customer remittances, except that a recording form is prepared by the general ledger section and forwarded daily to CBIS for entry into the computer. Prepared from the remittance advice, the recording form contains the date, amount remitted, account number(s), and amount(s) to be credited. Figure BR.2 is a flowchart describing processing of customer cash receipts.

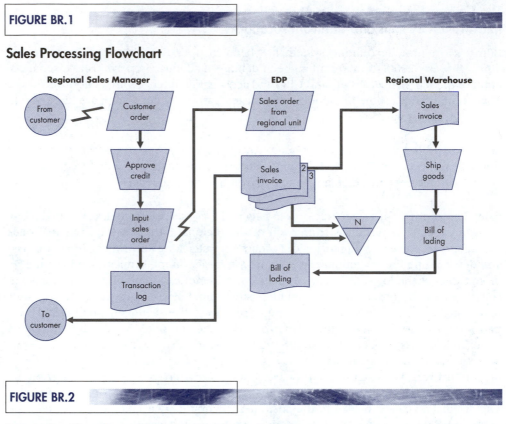

FIGURE BR.1

FIGURE BR.1

Sales Processing Flowchart

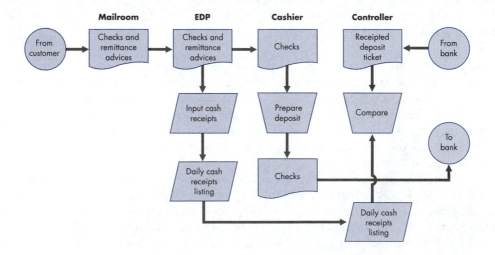

FIGURE BR.2

Processing Flowchart: Cash Receipts from Customers

Purchases and Accounts Payable   Biltrite buys its derailleurs and other bicycle parts from three unrelated vendors; steel and paint are purchased from selected vendors, based on a bidding process. Supplies are purchased from various vendors. All parts, materials, and supplies are ordered as reorder points are reached on the basis of a three-part purchase order generated by the computer.

Emil Ransbottom, director of purchasing, reports to Elmer Fennig, production vice president. Prices, as agreed upon by Ransbottom and the respective vendors, also appear on the purchase order, which is mailed to the vendor after being reviewed and approved by Fennig. A copy of the purchase order is sent to accounts payable and another goes to the purchasing department for later comparison with the incoming goods.

When goods are received, they are counted and inspected by employees in the receiving department and a two-part receiving report is prepared. The original accompanies the goods to stores, where quantities and types of goods are compared with the receiving report, and the copy is filed numerically in the receiving department. The store's manager then signs the receiving report and forwards it to the director of purchasing for comparison with the purchase order for type, quantity, price, and discount terms. After signing for agreement, the director of purchasing forwards the receiving report to accounts payable, where it is filed by vendor, along with the purchase order copy, awaiting receipt of a vendor's invoice.

When the vendor's invoice is received, an accounts payable clerk compares it with the purchase order and receiving report, then prepares a voucher for processing the invoice. The voucher contains the vendor number, vendor invoice number, stock number, quantities, price, and terms. Voucher copies are forwarded to CBIS for daily processing of vendors' invoices. A daily control tape of dollar totals appearing on the invoices is retained by accounts payable for later comparison with computer output. During the input of vouchers, the accounts payable software module of the general ledger package edits for the following characteristics: valid vendor number, valid stock number, price in agreement with vendor price, and agreement with discount and payment terms stored in the computer. During the processing run, the computer updates the accounts payable ledger, the manufacturing overhead detail, the operating expense detail, and the perpetual inventory records for purchased parts, materials, and supplies. The computer also performs a record count and compares output with input at the end of the processing run. Lastly, the due date of the invoice is stored in the computer for purposes of generating daily disbursement checks for invoices to be paid on that date.

Computer output consists of a purchases summary that is forwarded to accounts payable for review and comparison with the control tape. Accounts payable also files alphabetically the voucher, along with the attached purchase order, receiving report, and vendor's invoice in an unpaid vouchers file. All of these documents are prenumbered.

Figure BR.3 is a flowchart depicting the documents and procedures just described.

Payments to Vendors   The daily computer checkwriting process produces a two-part check/remittance advice set. The remittance advice, indicating invoice number(s) being paid, gross amount, discount, and net amount of the check constitutes the lower part of the set. The check/remittance advice set is sent to accounts payable for comparison with the documents contained in the alphabetic vendors' invoice file. If the amounts appearing on the remittance advice agree with the vendor's invoice, an accounts payable clerk initials the voucher, attaches the purchase order, vendor's invoice, and receiving report, and forwards the documents to the treasurer. The treasurer examines the documentation received from accounts payable for agreement among the invoice, purchase order, and receiving report as to type, quantities, and prices. If everything is in

FIGURE BR.3

Purchases and Accounts Payable Processing Flowchart

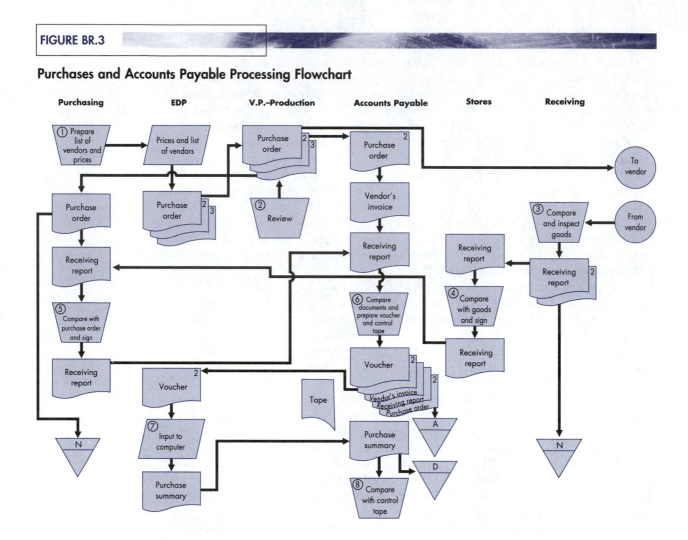

agreement and the documents include initials evidencing proper approvals, the check is approved for signature. The checks then are signed by a check-signing machine and mailed directly to the vendor by the treasurer's office. The documents are effectively canceled to prevent reuse and are returned to accounts payable for filing in a numeric paid vouchers file.

Responsibility for operating the check-signing machine is assigned to one individual. The machine is locked at all times when not being used to sign checks, and the key is in the custody of the check signer. Figure BR.4 is a flowchart describing the payment process.

Payroll   Hourly production employees are paid weekly. Nonproduction employees are salaried and are paid biweekly. Salespersons also are paid biweekly, on a combination salary and commission compensation basis.

The total time worked is accumulated for hourly employees by a time clock located at the factory entrance. The employee's name, social security number, and department number appear on the clock card. Factory supervisors approve the clock cards at the

FIGURE BR.4

Payment Processing Flowchart

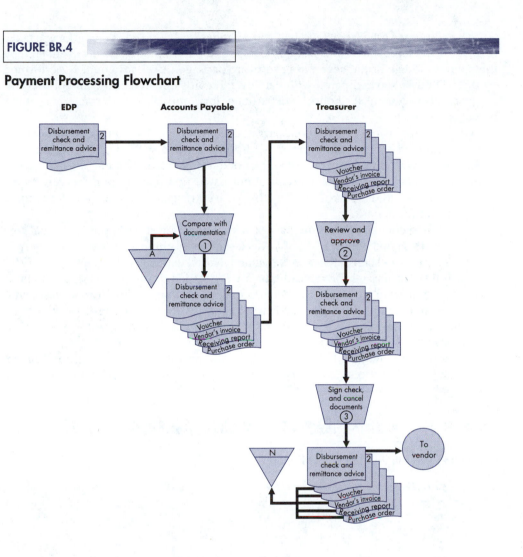

end of each week for employees working in their respective departments, before submitting them to payroll.

Each Monday morning the timekeepers summarize and assemble the clock cards by department number and forward the packets to payroll. The clock cards are examined in payroll for proper approval, a tape is run of total hours by department, and then the cards and tape are forwarded to CBIS for processing.

A data entry clerk enters via a terminal the employee number, the department number, and the hours worked. Input editing consists of checking for valid employee number, valid department, and reasonableness of hours worked. The employee computer files contain current pay rates, as well as employee and department numbers. Adjustments to the employee database for any rate changes, additions of new employees, and deletions of terminated employees are made only on the basis of authorization slips obtained from Laura Schroeder, director of human resources. Withholding information is also included in the database and is updated on the basis of authorization received from the human resources division.

The computer calculates gross pay, withholdings, and net pay. The employer's taxes (e.g., FICA, unemployment, and workers' compensation premium) also are calculated by the payroll module of the accounting software package. A record count is performed by the computer and compared with employee records updated at the end of the run. A register also accumulates hours by department for comparison with total hours at the end of the run.

Output consists of prenumbered payroll checks, a payroll summary, and a cost distribution summary. The control group is responsible for distributing the output. The checks, along with the summaries, are forwarded to the treasurer for signature and distribution. A check for the total amount of net pay is first drawn upon the general account for deposit in the payroll account; the treasurer signs this check and forwards it to the cashier for deposit.

After being compared with the payroll summary, on a test basis, the individual payroll checks are signed with the aid of a check-signing machine and distributed by treasury personnel. Unclaimed checks are retained in safekeeping by the treasurer's office. The payroll summary and the control tape are forwarded to the payroll department as a basis for comparing total hours by department and for completing the various payroll tax returns and reports. The cost summary is sent to Oliver Perna, director of cost accounting, for review and filing. Figure BR.5 is a flowchart describing the production payroll process.

As part of the integrated software package, the payroll data serves as input for updating the goods-in-process inventory accounts. To complete the updating of goods-in-

FIGURE BR.5

Production Payroll Processing Flowchart

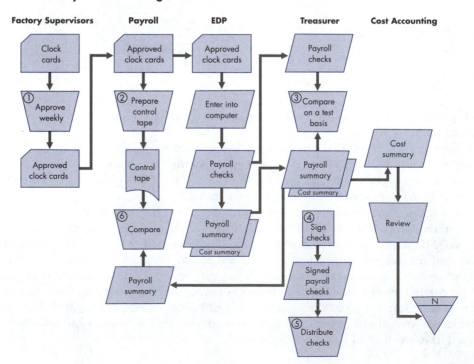

process and finished goods inventory, production reports and materials requisitions are entered into the system on a weekly basis. In addition to the perpetual inventory ledgers, the database includes a manufacturing overhead detail and an operating expense ledger. Current standard costs are also incorporated into the database. This enables the computer to calculate and print daily, weekly, and monthly variance reports for analysis by Perna and Malissa Rust, director of information systems and data processing.

The salaried payroll is prepared in a similar fashion. CBIS updates the employee database as written authorizations are received from human resources. As with production employees, the authorizations relate to changes in employee salaries, new employees, and terminated employees. Any overtime for salaried employees must be approved in writing by the respective department heads and routed to CBIS through payroll; the payroll department reviews the overtime for proper authorization and for reasonableness before transmitting the information to CBIS.

Other Accounting System Features   Monthly financial statements consist of a balance sheet, an income statement, and a statement of cash flows and are generated automatically by the computer. Month-end adjustments for accruals (payroll, taxes, warranty, commissions, pension, profit sharing, interest, and fringe benefits) and apportionments (depreciation, insurance, bad debts, and amortization) are determined by John Mesarvey, Biltrite's chief accountant, and submitted to CBIS on standard recording forms. CBIS enters the data and invokes the command for printing the financial statements. In addition to the financial statements, the adjusting entries are printed and forwarded by the control group to Mesarvey for comparison with his copy of the adjustments as originally submitted to CBIS. Exhibit BR.6 contains the December 31, 2001, adjustments for inventories (perpetual records adjusted to year-end physical inventory) and unrecorded liabilities. Exhibits BR.7–BR.10 (pp. 727–730) contain beginning and ending entries in the December 2001 transaction registers.

Sales invoices, purchase orders, disbursement checks, and payroll checks are prenumbered and generated by computer, as described previously. All manually prepared documents, such as vouchers and receiving reports, are also prenumbered. They are safeguarded and under the responsibility of designated individuals. Used documents are canceled to prevent reuse. Bills of lading are not prenumbered or otherwise accounted for. The internal auditing department regularly accounts for the numeric sequence of used documents. All voided documents are retained until the annual independent audit has been completed.

Within the CBIS department, duties are separated among the following functions:

1. Systems analysis and programming;
2. Data entry;
3. Data processing; and
4. Control.

Systems analysts and programmers provide extensive documentation of all programs and systems, as well as program changes. Complete instructions are provided for the computer operators who enter data as part of the various processing modules. All program changes must be approved in writing by Rust, director of information systems and data processing, as well as by affected user departments. Current backup programs and data files are maintained in a location outside data processing. The internal auditors presumably have current copies of the programs, but rarely test transaction processing on an unannounced basis.

EXHIBIT BR.6

Biltrite Bicycles, Inc., Selected Client Adjusting Entries, December 31, 2001

Unrecorded Invoices

7210	Real Estate Taxes	$ 468,000	
7241	Utilities Expense	1,322,400	
7234	Health Insurance Premiums—Factory	240,980	
9435	Health Insurance Premiums—Administrative	47,560	
1320	Derailleurs Inventory	788,300	
1390	Repair Parts Inventory	177,650	
7220	Manufacturing Supplies	977,500	
9450	Accounting Fees	150,000	
9451	Legal Fees	212,000	
2020	Accounts Payable—Trade		$4,384,390

Client's entry to adjust for unrecorded invoices at 12/31/01

Inventory Adjustment

5100	Cost of Goods Sold—Grand Prix Touring Bike	$ 456,000	
5200	Cost of Goods Sold—Phoenix Touring Bike	244,300	
5300	Cost of Goods Sold—Pike's Peak Mountain Bike	455,690	
5400	Cost of Goods Sold—Himalaya Mountain Bike	88,700	
5500	Cost of Goods Sold—Waistliner Stationary Bike	22,300	
1310	Raw Materials Inventory	33,560	
1330	Purchased Parts Inventory	333,670	
1376	Finished Goods—Himalaya Mountain Bike	66,340	
1385	Indirect Materials	33,500	
1390	Repair Parts Inventory	61,140	
1320	Derailleurs Inventory		$ 222,600
1371	Finished Goods—Grand Prix Touring Bike		625,700
1372	Finished Goods—Phoenix Touring Bike		366,800
1373	Finished Goods—Pike's Peak Mountain Bike		557,800
1379	Finished Goods—Waistliner Stationary Bike		22,300

Client's entry to adjust perpetual inventory records to physical inventory taken as of 12/31/01. (Adjustments to materials and parts inventories were allocated proportionately to the five cost-of-goods-sold accounts.)

All computer output is distributed by the control group to authorized recipients. Any errors occurring during processing runs are logged into the console and are accessible only by the control group. The control group then monitors the reprocessing of the errors after satisfying themselves that the errors were unintentional. Data processing personnel have no access to the error log and must contact the control group, inasmuch as processing cannot continue until an error is corrected.

An accounts receivable aging analysis is produced monthly by the computer. This analysis is used by Lawrence White, credit manager, and John Mesarvey, chief accountant, for determining the monthly adjustment to the allowance for doubtful accounts; White also performs extensive follow-up of customers whose accounts are past due.

(continued on page 731)

EXHIBIT BR.7

Biltrite Bicycles, Inc., Voucher Register, December 2001

Date	Voucher No.	Vendor	Accounts Payable Credit	Raw Materials Debit	Derailleurs Debit	Purchased Parts Debit	Indirect Materials Debit	Repair Parts Debit	Other Account Number	Other Debit
Dec. 1	12222	LaPrix Derailleurs, Ltd.	$ 415,000		$ 415,000					
Dec. 1	12223	Kryolock Steel Supply	212,480	$ 212,480						
Dec. 1	12224	Crown Manufacturing	122,169			$ 78,000	$ 44,169			
Dec. 30	12448	Crystal Manufacturing, Inc.	589,600		589,600					
Dec. 30	12449	Kryolock Steel Supply	266,800	266,800						
Dec. 31	12450	Crown Manufacturing	318,600			215,000	93,000	$ 10,600		
Dec. 31	12451	Palmer & Nile Advertising	112,800						8340	$ 112,800
Dec. 31	12452	MedCare HMO, Inc.	41,600						9435	41,600
Dec. 31	12453	Denise Vaughan & Co., CPAs	122,500						9450	122,500
Dec. 31	12454	Joelson & Wicks, Attorneys at Law	233,000						9451	233,000
Dec. 31	12455	Zebra Cleaning Supplies	7,865						9460	7,865
Dec. 31	12456	Crew Brothers Manufacturing	1,445,900			1,445,900				
Dec. 31	12457	LaPrix Derailleurs, Ltd.	962,200		962,200					
			$25,774,213	$3,822,900	$4,376,000	$12,430,975	$883,411	$776,500		$3,484,427

EXHIBIT BR.8

Biltrite Bicycles, Inc., Sales Summary, December 2001

Date	Invoice No.	Customer	Accounts Receivable Debit	Sales—Credit				
				Grand Prix	Phoenix	Pike's Peak	Himalaya	Waistliner
Dec. 1	31662	Bikes and Parts	$ 67,000	$ 21,750	$ 12,600	$ 27,100	$ 5,550	$ 0
Dec. 1	31663	L Mart Department Stores	325,600	185,200	0	89,600	21,500	29,300
Dec. 30	33002	Texas Bike Emporium	266,800	55,300	42,800	92,300	44,600	31,800
Dec. 30	33003	Rear and Sawbuck	881,870	322,550	23,400	466,740	32,500	36,680
Dec. 30	33004	Southwest Spokes, Inc.	443,760	77,200	55,900	223,060	87,600	0
Dec. 31	33005	Great Lakes Fitness Centers	144,600	0	0	0	0	144,600
Dec. 31	33006	Big Mart Discount Centers	773,200	288,700	0	410,650	22,300	51,550
Dec. 31	33007	Leisure Time	338,700	44,860	62,375	122,400	88,500	20,565
Dec. 31	33008	Truly Bikes	122,900	15,600	31,600	35,500	40,200	0
Dec. 31	33009	L Mart Department Stores	1,322,800	497,310	88,760	714,580	22,150	0
			$21,656,900	$2,356,700	$9,234,500	$1,329,800	$7,988,600	$747,300

EXHIBIT BR.9

Biltrite Bicycles, Inc., Cash Summary, December 2001

Date	Received From	Cash Debit	Sales Discounts Debit	Accounts Receivable Credit	Account Number	Miscellaneous Debit	Miscellaneous Credit	Deposits
Dec. 1	Rear and Sawbuck	$ 662,461	$ 3,329	$ 665,790				
Dec. 1	Texas Bike Emporium	187,398	942	188,340				
Dec. 1	Florida Bike World	759,583	3,817	763,400				$ 1,609,442
Dec. 30	Major Acres Discount Centers	684,162	3,438	687,600				
Dec. 30	New England Bike Shops	88,177	443	88,620				
Dec. 30	Exercise World	43,979	221	44,200				
Dec. 30	Kaiser and Peabody Brokerage	24,223			4902		$ 24,223	
Dec. 30	West Coast Distributors	729,624	3,666	733,290				1,570,165
Dec. 31	L Mart Department Stores	287,207	1,443	288,650				
Dec. 31	Bikes and Parts	75,864	336	76,200				
Dec. 31	T. Lawton	3,000,000			1203		3,000,000	
Dec. 31	Dollar Discount Stores	335,017	1,683	336,700				
Dec. 31	Jimbob's Recreation & Leisure	86,230	0	86,230				
Dec. 31	Big Mart Discount Centers	887,640	4,460	892,100				4,641,958
		$20,006,675	$152,654	$15,988,652		$63,546	$4,234,223	$20,006,675

EXHIBIT BR.10

Biltrite Bicycles, Inc., Check Register, December 2001

Date	Payee	Voucher Number	Bank Two Check Number	Dollar Bank Check Number	Accounts Payable Debit	Purchases Discounts Credit	Bank Two Credit	Dollar Bank Credit
Dec. 1	Kryolock Steel Supply	12188		44263	$ 388,700	$ 2,444		$ 386,256
Dec. 1	Crystal Manufacturing	12193		44264	654,980	3,228		651,752
Dec. 1	MedCare HMO, Inc.	12179	126880		46,400		$ 46,400	
Dec. 30	Crew Brothers Manufacturing	12378		44678	1,890,000	9,450		1,880,550
Dec. 30	Crown Manufacturing	12382		44679	422,300	2,112		420,188
Dec. 30	East Texas Power Company	12390	127329		455,380		455,380	
Dec. 31	Bell Southwest	12391	127330		75,688		75,688	
Dec. 31	LaPrix Derailleurs, Ltd.	12383		44680	1,340,000	6,700		1,333,300
Dec. 31	Zebra Cleaning Supplies	12344		44681	12,460	125		12,335
Dec. 31	Internal Revenue Service	12277		44682	3,600,000			3,600,000
Dec. 31	Jones Equipment	12198	127331		896,000	4,498		891,502
Dec. 31	Jolly Roger Paints	12264		44683	326,000	1,630		324,370
Dec. 31	Rolla Deal Tires, Inc.	12234		44684	667,500	3,338		664,162
					$24,521,003	$87,665	$1,780,000	$22,653,338

Other Controls   In addition to the control environment and the accounting information system, other policies and procedures support Biltrite's financial control system:

1. Laura Schroeder, director of human resources, instituted a program for completely updating job descriptions after the data processing system was converted to real-time in 1999. This program is now finished, and training programs have been developed for data processing, as well as for new and existing employees in other functional areas.
2. Inventories of materials, purchased parts, and finished goods are secured, and inventory managers have been assigned responsibility for their safekeeping. The internal audit staff, however, performs only infrequent test counts and comparisons with the perpetual records. Moreover, when they do plan for these counts, the auditors notify the inventory managers weeks in advance.
3. Directors and department heads are responsible for making hiring recommendations. The human resources division, however, screens and investigates all applicants for proper background and required education, training, and experience for the positions. In addition, final hiring and termination authority rests with the human resources director.

Requirements

1. Given the description of the company, the industry, the control environment, the accounting information system, and control procedures, identify strengths and weaknesses in the financial controls. Relate the strengths and weaknesses to management's assertions contained in the financial statements.
2. Based on your review of the accounting information system and existing control procedures, in what specific transaction areas are you willing to assess control risk below the maximum level? For purposes of this requirement, consider the probability of material financial statement errors caused by control weaknesses.
3. Assuming Richard Derick has established materiality criteria of 2 percent of net income and 0.5 percent of net assets, calculate the individual item materiality thresholds for audit adjustments and reclassifications, respectively. How did Derick arrive at these percentages? Will auditor suspicion of earnings inflation affect the materiality thresholds? In what way? Assuming Derick tentatively wishes to draft potential adjustments of 5 percent of individual item materiality or greater for later consideration, calculate the aggregate materiality threshold. What factors did Derick consider in arriving at the 5 percent figure? How does the internal control system affect aggregate materiality thresholds?

MODULE III: CONTROL TESTING—SALES PROCESSING

In this module you will be asked to apply attribute sampling to Biltrite's prenumbered sales invoices to evaluate whether sales have been processed properly. Recall from Module I that several control weaknesses suggest a high error incidence. However, nothing surfaced during the application of analytical procedures (other than the large 2001 sales increase) that indicated the existence of significant errors. For this reason, the audit team has decided to test sales transactions as a means for reducing the assessed level of control risk, thereby enabling them to decrease the extent of accounts receivable confirmation and other substantive procedures related to the revenue cycle.

Specifically, your first sampling objective is to determine that all recorded sales were shipped and that all shipments were invoiced and recorded. As discussed previously in the case, invoices are mailed to customers prior to shipment; therefore, customers may have received invoices for goods never shipped. Also, in the absence of prenumbered bills of lading, goods may have been shipped but never billed to the customer. The second possible processing problem is that customers may have exceeded existing credit limits without home office knowledge; you need to test the degree to which this has occurred. Finally, due to lack of input editing, prices, customer number, and/or product number may be incorrect; you will test for this as well.

Derick has asked you to complete the sampling plan worksheet that he began earlier. He has defined the sampling unit as the prenumbered sales invoice, and the relevant attributes as

1. Bill of lading attached and signed by the carrier;
2. Product prices in agreement with master price list stored in computer;
3. Extensions and footings correct;
4. Quantities and product type in agreement with customer order; and
5. Customer balance within the authorized credit limit.

The population for attribute sampling purposes is the numeric file of sales invoices. During 2001, 22,400 sales invoices were processed, with document numbers ranging from 10610 to 33009. For each sales invoice number drawn at random and included in the sample, you will request the client to supply the invoice/bill of lading packet and the corresponding customer order. The sales invoice/bill of lading packet can be obtained from the numeric file maintained in CBIS. The customer order, the number of which appears on the face of the invoice, is stored in the computer and can be printed out on demand. You then will examine the documents for the above attributes.

Requirements

1. Based on the control weaknesses identified in the sales processing subset of the revenue cycle, does the above sampling plan test for all significant weaknesses? If not, how might you test for any weaknesses not considered in the initial plan?
2. Using the spreadsheet program and data CD, retrieve the file titled "Attrib." Using the sample size and sample evaluation tables in Chapter 9 and the following data, complete the attribute sampling plan worksheet (in using the "Sample Results Evaluation" table, select the sample size that is closest to your sample size):
   a. A 5% risk of underassessment has been decided on for all attributes;
   b. Errors have been defined, and expected error rates set for each attribute as follows:
      1. Bill of lading not attached to packet—1%
      2. Incorrect prices—1%
      3. Extension and/or footing errors—0.5%
      4. Quantities and/or product type not in agreement with customer order—1%
      5. Customer balance exceeds authorized credit limit—1.5%
   c. Tolerable occurrence limits of 4% have been set for all attributes; and
   d. The following errors were discovered in examining the sample:

Sales Order Number	Error
12511	Bill of lading not signed by carrier
15439	Invoice causing customer to exceed authorized credit limit
18616	Bill of lading missing
23468	Bill of lading missing
27891	Bill of lading missing

3. Print your completed workpaper. (You will need to compress print size or otherwise accommodate a wide workpaper.)
4. What conclusions can you draw based on your completed sampling plan worksheet? What impact might your findings have on the substantive audit programs for Biltrite? Based on the results of your testing, should the aggregate materiality threshold be changed for any part of the revenue cycle? Be as specific as you can in answering this question.

MODULE IV: PPS SAMPLING—FACTORY EQUIPMENT ADDITIONS

Richard Derick has asked you to develop a sampling plan to determine the extent of errors in classifying expenditures as repairs and maintenance expense or factory equipment additions. Given the failure to double-check debits on the face of vouchers, as described in Module I, Derick believes that significant errors may have occurred.

The same vendor's invoice frequently contains charges for parts and supplies as well as equipment, and the Biltrite employees preparing the vouchers sometimes fail to distinguish among the charges and simply indicate "factory equipment" as the debit if the invoice amount is large. Inasmuch as this type of error would cause an overstatement in the factory equipment account, Derick instructs you to use PPS sampling to determine the extent to which such errors have occurred during 2001.

Of the total debits—$89,860,000 to factory equipment during 2001—major additions in the amount of $77,260,000 have been made to replace worn-out equipment. Derick has decided to audit the major additions in their entirety and sample the remainder.

Requirements

1. What is the sampling objective for the purposes of this exercise? What is the sampling unit? What is the population?
2. Using the spreadsheet program and data CD, retrieve the file labeled "PPS." Locate the following workpapers in the file:
    *   WP 11.3A—Probability-proportional-to-size sampling plan;
    *   WP 11.3B—Probability-proportional-to-size sampling plan—projected error; and
    *   WP 11.3C—Probability-proportional-to-size sampling plan—computed precision and upper error limit.

    Scroll to WP 11.3A, "Probability-Proportional-to-Size Sampling Plan." Calculate sample size and sampling interval assuming Derick has set the following parameters:

Risk of incorrect acceptance: 5%
Anticipated error: $100,000
Tolerable error: $640,000

3. What factors did he consider in setting these parameters? Print the workpaper.
4. Scroll to WP 11.3B, "Probability-Proportional-to-Size Sampling Plan—Projected Error." This workpaper summarizes all invoices containing posting errors and calculates the projected error. Note the equations that have been incorporated into the workpaper template.
   a. What factor determines whether a "tainting percentage" appears in column 4?
   b. Print the workpaper. (Compress print size or otherwise accommodate a wide workpaper.)
5. Scroll to WP 11.3C, "Probability-Proportional-to-Size Sampling Plan—Computed Precision and Upper Error Limit." Complete the "Incremental Allowance for Sampling Risk" schedule by ranking the projected errors as appropriate. (*Hint*: If you forgot how to do this, refer to Chapter 10 and the PPS application presented at the end of the chapter. Also refer to Exhibit 10.4, which is a completed schedule calculating the incremental allowance.)
6. Print the workpaper.
7. Explain the meaning of the following amounts:
   a. Basic precision;
   b. Incremental allowance for sampling risk;
   c. Allowance for sampling risk; and
   d. Upper error limit.
8. Evaluate the sampling results. Do they support Derick's sampling objectives? Note the audit adjustment based on errors discovered while examining the sample. Is this adjustment adequate to bring the population into acceptable bounds? If not, what alternate actions might you choose to pursue, based on the sampling results?

MODULE V: DALLAS DOLLAR BANK RECONCILIATION

Biltrite maintains two general demand deposit accounts and a payroll account. One of the general demand deposit accounts and the payroll account are with Dallas Dollar Bank. The second demand deposit account is with Bank Two, the Chicago bank from which Biltrite obtained the $45 million loan referred to previously. As part of the cash audit, Derick has asked you to reconcile all three of the bank accounts for December 2001, and to do an analysis of interbank transfers between Dollar Bank and Bank Two. Recall that Biltrite has reconciled all bank accounts for each of the twelve months. You will begin, therefore, with the company's December 2001 reconciliations.

Requirements

1. Using the spreadsheet program and data CD, retrieve the file labeled "Bank." Briefly examine the following workpapers in this file:
   • WP 1—Cash on hand and in banks;
   • WP 1.B—Bank reconciliation—Dallas Dollar Bank; and
   • WP 1.C—Interbank transfer schedule.
   Scroll to WP 1.B, "Bank Reconciliation—Dallas Dollar Bank." Does the Dollar Bank account reconcile for December? What are the possible causes for nonreconciliation?
2. In tracing cash disbursements from the December check register to the bank statement, you learn that check 44264, in the amount of $642,752, was recorded incorrectly as $651,752. Incorporate this error into the appropriate section of the bank reconciliation. Does the account reconcile after you have made this correction?

Assuming check 44264 was in payment of accounts payable (refer to Exhibit BR.10), draft the necessary audit adjustment at the bottom of your workpaper.

3. Print the bank reconciliation workpaper.
4. Scroll to WP 1 and record the audit adjustment in the "audit adjustments" column of the lead schedule.
5. The deposit in transit, as well as all but the last two checks outstanding at December 31, cleared with the bank cutoff statement. What specific audit objectives are supported by obtaining a cutoff statement directly from the bank? If the cutoff bank statement covered the period 1/1/02 through 1/21/02 and the deposit in transit was credited 1/12/02, would you be concerned? If so, why? What additional procedures would you apply to allay your concerns? Note on workpaper WP 1.B that the deposit in transit was credited by Dollar Bank on 1/3/02.

MODULE VI: ANALYSIS OF INTERBANK TRANSFERS

Requirements

1. Using the spreadsheet program and data CD, retrieve the file labeled "Bank." Scroll to WP 1.C, "Interbank Transfer Schedule." This workpaper was prepared by Cheryl Lucas, a member of the Denise Vaughan & Co. audit team. As part of your audit training, Derick asks that you examine and review the workpaper and determine the need for possible audit adjustments and reclassifications. What is the purpose of analyzing interbank transfers for a short period before and after the balance sheet date? Identify possible audit adjustments and reclassifications by examining WP 1.C. Assume that Bank Two check 127332 was dated December 31, 2001, deposited on that date, and also credited by Dollar Bank on December 31, 2001. As noted previously, Lawton had borrowed $3 million from Biltrite in April 2000, and had planned to repay the loan before December 31, 2001. Did he really repay the loan in December? Do you think the check drawn on Bank Two was reflected as an outstanding check in the 12/31/01 Bank Two reconciliation? Do you think the check was recorded as a December disbursement? If not, why not? (*Hint*: Remember that the loan agreement with Bank Two requires a $10 million compensating balance at all times.)
2. Draft Audit Reclassification A at the bottom of WP 1.C.
3. Print the interbank transfer workpaper.
4. Scroll to WP 1. Record Reclassification A from requirement (2) in the reclassification column of the lead schedule. Does the reclassification place Biltrite in default on the loan agreement? If so, what further audit procedures might you elect to apply at this time?
5. Print the lead schedule.

MODULE VII: ACCOUNTS RECEIVABLE AGING ANALYSIS

Richard Derick has asked you to review the accounts receivable aging analysis and the allowance for doubtful accounts, and to recommend any audit adjustments or reclassifications you consider necessary. Shelly Ross had prepared the aging analysis and the allowance for doubtful accounts workpaper before being temporarily transferred to the Joplin Mills audit. She should be back early next week, but Derick would like to "wrap up" accounts receivable this week.

Based on the aging analysis prepared by Ross, you have decided to confirm all large accounts and a sampling of the smaller accounts, using positive confirmations.

Requirements

1. Using the spreadsheet program and data CD, retrieve the file labeled "AR." Locate the following workpapers in this file:
   - WP 3—Accounts and notes receivable—trade;
   - WP 3.A—Accounts receivable aging analysis; and
   - WP 3.C—Allowance for uncollectible accounts.

   Scroll to WP 3.A, "Accounts Receivable Aging Analysis."
   a. What proportion of the total dollar amount of accounts receivable have you included in your confirmation requests?
   b. What procedures should you apply in the event of no reply to a request for positive confirmation?
   c. What is the purpose of analyzing subsequent collections?
2. Based on your analysis of subsequent collections and the results of the confirmation process, are you satisfied that you have sufficient evidence to evaluate the existence and valuation assertions?
3. Draft the suggested Reclassification Entry B.
4. Scroll to WP 3.C, "Allowance for Uncollectible Accounts."
   a. What type of correspondence would you examine to satisfy yourself as to the accounts receivable write-offs?
   b. Draft the suggested Audit Adjustment 3. Are you satisfied that the balance in the allowance is adequate after your recommended adjustment?
   c. Scroll to WP 3, "Accounts and Notes Receivable—Trade" (lead schedule). Post Reclassification Entry B and Audit Adjustment 3 to the appropriate locations in the lead schedule.
5. Print the workpapers 3, 3.A, and 3.C

MODULE VIII: SALES AND PURCHASES CUTOFF TESTS

Along with Richard Derick and the rest of the audit team, you observed Biltrite's December 31, 2001, physical inventory. Derick is satisfied with the inventory-taking procedures and has considerable confidence in the reliability of the ending inventory quantities. He is concerned, however, with the methods used to value the ending inventories (especially the disposition of unfavorable budget variances) and with possible errors relating to sales and purchases cutoff. With regard to cutoff, Derick is particularly interested in learning why customers could not confirm details of sales transactions recorded by Biltrite on December 31, 2001. In response to the confirmation and cutoff concerns, he has asked you to examine the appropriate books of original entry and underlying documentation for a few days before and after the balance sheet date. Specifically, you are interested in the following:

1. Were purchases and sales recorded in the proper accounting period?
2. Were purchases recorded at year end included in the physical inventory?
3. Were all materials and purchased parts included in inventory recorded as purchases?
4. Were the finished goods inventory accounts properly relieved for all recorded sales?

Using your PC, you were able to "download" Biltrite's December voucher register and sales summary. These are partially reproduced in Exhibits BR.7 and BR.8, referred to in Module I. Using these as a focal point, you requested that the client provide you with the documentation supporting certain of the recorded transactions. You now are prepared to record any necessary audit adjustments and reclassifications.

Requirements

1. Using the spreadsheet program and data CD, retrieve the file labeled "Cutoff." Study WP 6.4, "Inventory Cutoff," and compare it with the voucher register and sales summary portions reproduced in Exhibits BR.7 and BR.8. Comment on any cutoff errors that you detect and determine their effect on net income. Do the errors appear to be intentional or unintentional? Explain.
2. Draft any audit adjustments suggested by the analysis performed in requirement (1). (Remember that Biltrite maintains perpetual inventory records and adjusts its perpetual inventory to the physical inventory through the appropriate "Cost of Goods Sold" accounts.)
3. Print the completed workpaper with the proposed cutoff audit adjustments.

MODULE IX: SEARCH FOR UNRECORDED LIABILITIES

An important part of every audit is examining vendors' invoices processed after year end. Related to cutoff, as discussed in Module VIII, this set of procedures has the purpose of determining that no significant invoices pertaining to the year being audited have been omitted from recorded liabilities. Derick has asked that you examine the workpaper prepared by Cheryl Lucas and entitled "Search for Unrecorded Liabilities," and review it for necessary audit adjustments.

Requirements

1. Using the spreadsheet program and data CD, retrieve the file labeled "Liab." Comment on the adequacy of the procedures performed by Lucas.
2. Assuming that you found the following additional unrecorded charges pertaining to 2001, draft Audit Adjustment 7 at the bottom of WP 15.1:
   a. Sales commissions $366,900
   b. Employer's payroll taxes:
      FICA $94,000
      State unemployment $126,000
   c. Printing and copying $27,800
   d. Postage $22,300
   e. Office supplies $18,600
3. Print the workpaper.

MODULE X: ESTIMATED LIABILITY FOR PRODUCT WARRANTY

All Biltrite products are sold under a one-year warranty covering all parts and labor. Repairs are performed locally, either by the dealer who sold the bicycle or by local entities licensed as official Biltrite bicycle repair shops. Biltrite reimburses the dealers and shops for labor and parts. Reimbursement is based on work orders submitted by the repairing agency. The work orders are signed by the customer, and the serial number of the product repaired also appears on each work order. Defective parts or products replaced must be returned with the accompanying work order. The parts and products are received and logged in on color-coded receiving reports designed for returns.

At the end of each month, the following standard journal entry is posted as an adjustment to estimated product warranty.

8330   Product Warranty Expense
2070   Estimated Product Warranty Liability

For 2001, the company applied 0.5 percent to cost of goods sold in determining the amount of the monthly adjustment. Debits to account 2070 are for reimbursements and for product and parts replacements. Defective parts and products are "zero valued" and placed in the rework department. Derick has asked you to analyze product warranty and determine the appropriate balance in the liability account. He already has provided you with a partially completed workpaper and a client-prepared analysis of returns over the past four years. You have completed the workpaper and are now ready to evaluate the adequacy of the balance.

Requirements

1. Using the spreadsheet program and data CD, retrieve the file labeled "Warranty." Examine the workpaper carefully and comment on its adequacy and completeness. (Note that the 12/31/01 audited balances appear to be unreasonable because you have not yet selected an appropriate provision percentage based on the "data from client-prepared analysis of warranty claims.")
2. Scroll to the bottom of WP 20 and enter audit adjustments already made in previous modules that affect cost of goods sold for 2001. You should identify the following adjustments. (If you weren't assigned the respective modules, ask your instructor for details regarding amounts and accounts.)
   - AJE No. 1 (Module IV correction of repairs expense capitalized as factory equipment); and
   - AJE No. 4 (2001 purchase recorded in 2002, detected in completing Module VIII).
3. What comprises the documentation examined by the auditor (audit legend E) supporting the debits to account 2070?
4. How would you audit the client-prepared analysis of warranty claims? (See "Year of Claim/Year of Sale" analysis in the middle of WP 20.)
5. Enter equations in cells C44, D44, and E44 that will calculate the percentage of warranty claims to cost of goods sold for each of the three years 1998–2000.
6. Note the percentage that now appears in cell B46 and the resulting adjustment to product warranty expense.
7. Draft AJE No. 8 on the workpaper.
8. Print the workpaper.
9. Shelly Ross, the other assistant auditor on the engagement, asks why you didn't adjust the prior years under provision through beginning retained earnings. What is your response?

MODULE XI: PLANT ASSET ADDITIONS AND DISPOSALS

In Module IV, you applied PPS sampling procedures in evaluating the correctness of a subset of debits to the "Factory Equipment" account. You will recall that the debits to account 1530 totaled $89,860,000 for 2001. You also will recall that Derick decided to stratify the population of debits such that $77,260,000 of major additions, representing replacements of worn-out equipment, were to be audited in detail. In Module XI, you will analyze this subset of additions, as well as disposals. You also will be asked to complete the "Plant Assets" lead schedule.

Requirements

1. Using the spreadsheet program and data CD, retrieve the file labeled "Plant." Locate the following workpapers in this file:
    - WP 11—Plant assets and accumulated depreciation—lead schedule (note that AJE 1 from Module IV has already been posted); and
    - WP 11.4—Factory equipment—additions and disposals.

    Scroll to WP 11.4, "Factory Equipment—Additions and Disposals." What is the nature of the "underlying documentation" referred to in the explanation of audit legends E and W?
2. In recording the 2001 disposals, Janel James, Biltrite's plant assets accountant, miscalculated the accumulated depreciation on the assets sold and thereby overstated the gain on disposal by $3,090,000. Draft Audit Adjustment 9 at the bottom of WP 11.4 to correct for this error. In addition, James did not change the standard journal entry for monthly depreciation to reflect additions and disposals during the year. As a result depreciation expense for the year is understated by $800,000. Biltrite depreciates factory equipment on a straight-line basis over a ten-year estimated useful life with zero salvage value. One-half year's depreciation is taken on all additions and disposals. Draft Audit Adjustment 10 at the bottom of WP 11.4 to reflect the depreciation understatement. In recording the underdepreciation, debit account 5300, "Cost of Goods Sold—Pike's Peak Mountain Bike," inasmuch as all overhead accounts have been closed. Any further adjustments, therefore, must be reflected in the cost of sales accounts. Although in Module IV we allocated the adjustment to the five product cost of sales accounts, the present adjustment is less significant in amount, and therefore we will reflect the entire amount in account 5300. (*Note:* Don't forget to enter Audit Adjustments 9 and 10 in the body of the workpaper to arrive at correct adjusted balances.)
3. Scroll to WP 11, "Plant Assets and Accumulated Depreciation—Lead Schedule." Post Audit Adjustments 9 and 10 to the lead schedule.
4. Print workpapers 11 and 11.4.

MODULE XII: ANALYSIS OF MARKETABLE SECURITIES

Although the addition of the Waistliner Stationary Bike to the product line in 1980 helped somewhat in increasing Biltrite's fall and winter revenue, business remains quite seasonal, producing large amounts in idle funds to be invested temporarily after the spring and summer bicycle sales season has ended. Marlene McAfee, the Biltrite treasurer, usually invests in marketable securities in mid-August and holds them until mid-January. They are sold in late January and February to finance spring inventories of bicycles. McAfee's goals in acquiring short-term investments are to maximize return while minimizing risk of loss from wide temporary price fluctuations. For this reason, the portfolio is limited to debt securities rated AA and above, and common stocks of "blue-chip" companies.

As of December 31, 2001, the portfolio consisted of the following holdings:

Security	12/31/01 Carrying Value	12/31/01 Market Value
Transco, Inc. Preferred	$ 804,024	$ 810,000
Jolly Roger Amusement Parks Common	720,000	660,000
Pets 'R' Us Common	736,000	742,000
General Department Stores Common	660,000	550,000
Bell South 8% Debenture Bonds	930,000	942,000
Chrysler 11% Debenture Bonds	1,150,000	1,131,000
Cleveland Electric 9% Debenture Bonds	2,000,000	2,066,000

Requirements

1. Using the spreadsheet program and data CD, retrieve the file labeled "Security." Do you think McAfee's securities portfolio is consistent with her stated goals of "maximizing return while minimizing risk of loss from temporary price fluctuations"? Justify your answer.
2. What determines whether marketable securities are to be classified as current or noncurrent on the balance sheet?
3. What are the objectives in the audit of marketable securities? Examine the audit legends at the bottom of workpaper 2. Have the objectives been satisfied?
4. Enter the carrying value and market data for each security held at December 31, 2001.
5. Add an audit legend (and explain it at the bottom of the worksheet) regarding how market was determined.
6. Draft Audit Adjustment 11 at the bottom of WP 2 to recognize the understatement of interest revenue. The discrepancy results from failure to recognize accrued interest at 12/31/01 (debit account 1205, "Accrued Interest Receivable").
7. Draft Audit Adjustment 12 to adjust the loss on decline of market value to reflect the corrected amount. The wide disparity in this instance arises because Biltrite, in adjusting to market at 12/31/01, compared market at 12/31/01 with the cost of the 12/31/00 portfolio, rather than comparing 12/31/01 market with 12/31/01 carrying values. For this adjustment, use account 9702, "Loss on Decline of Market Value of Securities," and account 1102, "Allowance for Decline of Market Value of Securities."
8. Print your workpaper.

MODULE XIII: MORTGAGE NOTE PAYABLE AND NOTE PAYABLE TO BANK TWO

In addition to a deferred tax liability relating to temporary book and tax depreciation differences, Biltrite's long-term liabilities consist of the following:

- 10% mortgage note payable to Dallas Dollar Bank—$60 million; and
- 12% note payable to Bank Two—$45 million.

In 1997, Biltrite upgraded its manufacturing facilities at a cost of $150 million. The project was financed by issuing 2 million shares of common stock at $25 per share, and by issuing a $100 million 10% mortgage note payable to Dallas Dollar Bank. The mortgage agreement requires repayment in ten annual installments of $10 million each. Interest on the unpaid principal is payable on the first day of each month. The principal installments are due on January 1. The next payment is due on 1/1/02.

The 12% note payable to Bank Two was issued to alleviate the effects of the liquidity problems encountered in 2001. This note is unsecured and requires repayment in ten equal annual installments. Unlike the Dollar Bank mortgage loan, interest on the Bank Two loan is payable annually. The first principal installment, together with interest, is due 3/1/02. This note contains restrictive covenants, as described earlier, relating to a $10 million compensating balance requirement and restrictions regarding further borrowing and dividend payments.

Derick has asked that you analyze the long-term notes payable, being particularly alert to any violations of the restrictive covenants contained in the Bank Two loan agreement.

Requirements

1. Using the spreadsheet program and data CD, retrieve the file labeled "Notes." Locate the following workpapers in this file:
   - WP 14—Notes payable and accrued interest—lead schedule; and
   - WP 14.3—Notes payable—long-term.
   Scroll to WP 14.3, "Notes Payable—Long-Term." What are the audit objectives in the examination of long-term notes payable? Have they been achieved by the evidence provided in the workpaper?
2. Record Reclassification Journal Entry C for the current portion of both notes as of 12/31/01, and enter the amounts in WP 14.3. Now scroll up to WP 14, the lead schedule for notes payable and interest. Post your reclassifications to the lead schedule.
3. Print workpapers 14 and 14.3.
4. What is the probable nature of the adjustment to "notes payable—trade" and to "interest payable" appearing in the adjustments column of the lead schedule?

MODULE XIV: WORKING TRIAL BALANCE

Upon completion of substantive audit testing, the auditor should post all audit adjustments and reclassification entries to the working trial balance and extend the audited balances. The extended balances then form the nucleus for the audited financial statements.

Selected analytical procedures also should be applied at the conclusion of the audit field work. The results may be compared with those developed during the audit planning phase. This approach provides added support for audit conclusions contained in the workpapers.

Derick has asked you to post the adjustments and reclassifications, and to perform the review phase analytical procedures.

Requirements

1. The instructor's CD contains a file labeled "AJE" (adjusting journal entries). It contains all of the audit adjustments and reclassifications that you developed in prior

modules of this practice case. At this time your instructor will supply you with a printout of this file. Review the adjustments. Some of these adjustments meet or exceed the individual item materiality threshold. These adjustments will be presented to the client as proposed audit adjustments. Other adjustments fall below the individual item materiality threshold and must be analyzed separately as to whether they are to be considered as potential audit adjustments in the aggregate, or ignored. As you may recall, Derick set the following materiality thresholds in Module I:

Individual item materiality—income statement	$640,660
Aggregate materiality consideration	$32,033
Ignore as immaterial	<$32,033
Individual item materiality—balance sheet	$1,542,270

In light of the earnings overstatements revealed in previous modules, Derick has decided to reduce the materiality thresholds for the income statement as follows:

Individual item materiality—income statement	$435,000
Aggregate materiality consideration	$22,000
Ignore as immaterial	<$22,000

He has elected to maintain the individual item balance sheet materiality threshold at $1,542,270. Given the revised thresholds and referring to the proposed audit adjustments and reclassifications, perform the following:

a. Identify those adjustments falling between the aggregate and individual item materiality thresholds.

b. Determine whether the potential adjustments that you identified in requirement (a) equal or exceed the individual item threshold in the aggregate. For aggregate purposes, treat income overstatements and income understatements separately. Do *not* net understatements against overstatements. That is, if aggregate overstatements are $600,000 and aggregate understatements are $500,000, the adjustments should be proposed to Biltrite management, inasmuch as both exceed the individual item materiality threshold.

c. Decide which audit adjustments you wish to have reflected in the audited financial statements. Have you omitted any of the thirteen adjustments originally proposed? Why? Have you included any adjustments that failed to meet the individual item materiality threshold? Why?

d. Decide which of the audit reclassifications you wish to have reflected in the audited financial statements. Do all three of the proposed reclassifications meet the individual-item balance sheet materiality threshold?

2. Retrieve the file labeled "WTB." Post the adjustments and reclassifications to the working trial balance. Observe the following rules in making your postings:

a. Post account increases as positive amounts, and post account decreases as negative amounts;

b. Postings are in "thousands of dollars," whereas the adjustments and reclassifications are rounded to the nearest dollar. Therefore, in posting the adjustments and reclassifications, round to the nearest $1,000; and

c. Do *not* foot the adjustments and reclassifications columns (they will automatically be reflected in the audited column as you post them).

3. Save your file under the title "WTB," then print it.

4. Retrieve the file labeled "AUDBS." Using your printout of the working trial balance, enter the amounts from the audited column in the 2001 balance sheet. Calculate the percentages of individual balance sheet items and components relative to totals for 2001.
5. Calculate the new ratios for 2001 based on the audited financial statements. What is the purpose of applying analytical procedures in the evaluation and review phase of the audit?
6. Print the comparative audited balance sheets together with the related ratios. Compare them with the balance sheets and ratios that you developed and printed in requirement (4b) of Module I. What conclusions can you draw regarding the comparison?
7. Retrieve the file labeled "Budget," which you reviewed as part of your assignment in Module I. You will recall that the purpose for this review was to identify significant budget variances that could be the result of under- or overbudgeting, errors in recording data, or intentional misstatement. The auditor, of course, is concerned with the latter two possibilities.
    a. Substitute the audited amounts from your adjusted working trial balance for the unaudited figures in the "Actual 12/31/01" column. Save your file, as revised, under a new file name (for example, "Biltbudg"), so as not to lose the original Module I file. Print the revised budget/actual comparison.
    b. Do significant variances still exist? If so, are you satisfied that the audit has resolved the causes of the significant variances? (*Hint*: Compare the variances resulting from this analysis with those calculated in Module I.)
    c. If you continue to have concerns about certain of the variances, what additional evidence gathering and evaluation procedures do you suggest?

MODULE XV: AUDIT REPORT

The Denise Vaughan audit team completed its audit field work on February 15, 2002. A conference was held on that date involving members of the audit firm and Biltrite management. Participants in the conference were Denise Vaughan, partner in charge of the Biltrite engagement; Carolyn Volmar, audit manager; Richard Derick, in-charge auditor; Trevor Lawton, Biltrite's CEO; Gerald Groth, Biltrite's controller; and Marlene McAfee, Biltrite's treasurer. The Biltrite representatives agreed to all of the audit adjustments and reclassifications proposed by the audit team, and agreed to reflect them in the December 31, 2001, financial statements. They also agreed to modify and/or add footnote disclosures as recommended by the audit team.

At the conclusion of the conference, the audit team obtained a client representation letter from Biltrite management, and presented management with a copy of the "reportable conditions" letter outlining discovered internal control weaknesses. The original of this letter was sent to Biltrite's board of directors. (You will recall that Biltrite does not have an audit committee.)

The legal action initiated against Biltrite by Rollfast, a competitor, for alleged patent infringement, was not yet settled as of February 15. Because the letter obtained by Derick from Biltrite's outside legal counsel was inconclusive as to the probable outcome of this action, Derick requested an informal conference with the attorney handling Biltrite's case. This conference was convened on February 12, and the participants were Joel Haskins, the attorney, Gerald Groth, Denise Vaughan, and Richard Derick.

Haskins exhibited a degree of pessimism that produced considerable uncertainty as to the probable outcome of the litigation. Inasmuch as the amount of loss could be quite substantial, and the probability of an unfavorable outcome was more than remote but less than likely, Groth agreed to disclose the matter in a footnote to the 2001 financial statements.

Notwithstanding the liquidity problems and loan default, Biltrite has been assured by Bank Two management that the bank plans no foreclosure action, provided Biltrite can restore the minimum required bank balance and continues to earn profits. Moreover, management's expressed plans for dealing with the crisis and continued sales growth during January 2002 have convinced Denise Vaughan that an explanatory paragraph expressing substantial doubt as to continued existence is not necessary.

No scope restrictions were encountered during the audit, either imposed or otherwise. Moreover, Biltrite did not change accounting principles in either 2000 or 2001.

Requirements

1. Using the spreadsheet program and data CD, retrieve the file labeled "Report."
2. Modify the report as appropriate to conform to the Biltrite audit results.
3. Print the audit report.
4. Sign the audit report.

answers to multiple choice questions

CHAPTER 1

1. d. Validity and relevance are the two components comprising competence. (a) is incorrect because external evidence may be valid but not relevant. (b) is incorrect because good internal control promotes validity, but not relevance. (c) is incorrect because hearsay evidence is often valid and relevant.

2. d. During the interim audit work, the auditor performs tests of controls as necessary, and applies substantive testing procedures to transactions. By performing substantial amounts of the audit work during the interim phase, the final audit can be completed in a more timely manner. (a) is incorrect because initial audits are frequently accepted after year end. (b) is incorrect because inventories may be immaterial, in which instance, the auditor need not observe inventory taking; or the auditor and client may agree to inventory taking and observation at an interim date. (c) is incorrect because the independent auditors frequently discuss the scope of the audit with the audit committee.

3. a. Although (b), (c), and (d) are subclass in the audit, the primary reason for applying auditing procedures is to gather "sufficient, competent evidence" to support the auditor's opinion on the financial statements.

4. c. Operational auditing serves management and the auditee by helping the audited units to increase their efficiency and thereby improve their performance.

5. d. An adverse opinion conveys the auditor's view that the financial statements do not fairly present financial position, results of operations, and cash flows. (a) is incorrect because a qualified opinion would be too mild in this situation. (b) is incorrect because special reports are not related to material departures from GAAP. (c) is incorrect because disclaimers are warranted when material scope restrictions are encountered by the auditor.

6. c. An adverse opinion is rendered when the financial statements contain a material departure from GAAP. Only (c) involves a departure from GAAP.

7. c. The study of internal control helps the auditor to determine the reliability of the accounting system that produces the data contained in the financial statements. Reliability of the system, in turn, helps the auditor determine the nature, timing, and extent of substantive audit testing to be performed.

8. c. The engagement letter summarizes the agreement between the auditor and the client and clarifies the type of engagement to be undertaken by the auditor. (a) is incorrect because the management letter is issued by the auditor to the client at the end of the engagement and contains suggestions for improving the information system. (b) is incorrect because the scope paragraph is a brief description of what the auditor did in completing the audit engagement. (d) is incorrect because the introductory paragraph of the audit report is a brief summary of the respective responsibilities of management and auditor relative to the financial statements.

CHAPTER 2

1. b. The auditor cannot audit something he/she doesn't understand. Therefore, before beginning the audit, the necessary knowledge must be obtained.

2. c.   The Accounting and Review Services Committee is the AICPA body responsible for issuing Statements on Standards for Accounting and Review Services. These are nonaudit engagements typically performed for clients not required to register their securities with the SEC and who, therefore, are not required to have their financial statements audited by independent CPAs.

3. b.   The Statements on Responsibilities in Tax Practice (TXs), covered under Rule 202 of the Code of Conduct, specifically require a CPA to advise the client of any errors detected in a previously filed tax return. (a) is incorrect because death and disability are beyond the control of the CPA and he/she, therefore, has no obligation to provide for such unforeseen events. (c) is incorrect because, although the CPA does have responsibility for detecting and disclosing major fraud, this responsibility does not necessarily extend to notifying specific third parties. (d) is incorrect because audits are to be conducted in accordance with GAAS, not GAAP.

4. d.   The SASs, defined as interpretations of the auditing standards, are binding upon the CPA, who must justify any departures from them.

5. c.   In all professional engagements, the CPA should properly plan the engagement and should exercise due professional care. In consulting engagements, however, the CPA need not be independent.

6. a.   The Auditing Standards Board is responsible for promulgating both auditing and attestation standards. Auditing, after all, is a form of attestation. (b) and (c) are incorrect because FASB and GASB are responsible for promulgating accounting standards, but not auditing or other forms of attestation standards. (d) is incorrect because GAO is an audit agency performing management, financial, operational, and compliance audits and reporting the results to Congress.

7. c.   The third general standard requires the auditor to exercise due care in the performance of the examination. A critical aspect of due care is supervision of the work of assistants. (a) is incorrect because experience and education relate more to training and proficiency rather than to due care. (b) is incorrect because the auditor is not an attorney and cannot, therefore, be expected to detect all instances of illegal acts. (d) is incorrect because the auditor need not examine all evidence to meet the due care standard, but rather an amount sufficient to support the audit opinion.

8. b.   The CPA firm is responsible for the work of the systems specialist and is also accountable for any violations of the Code of Conduct committed by the non-CPA employee. Nothing in the Code, however, prohibits a CPA firm from hiring nonaccounting personnel for specialized purposes.

9. b.   AICPA bylaws specifically provide for the Management Advisory Services Executive Committee to issue Statements on Standards for Consulting Services to govern the rendering of consulting services by members. Assistance in the implementation of the new computer system is an example of such a service.

CHAPTER 3

1. b.   Under breach of contract actions, the plaintiff (client) must prove negligence. In the present case, the fact that the fraud was highly sophisticated and novel

relieves the auditor of detection responsibility, and, therefore, the accountants were not negligent.

2. d. If the false statements are immaterial, they cannot cause significant harm to financial statement users, and, therefore, they have no basis in action against the CPA. (a) is incorrect because privity need not be present in third party actions alleging gross negligence or fraud. (b) is incorrect because the law does not permit a CPA to disclaim liability for failure to exercise due care by making a statement to that effect in the engagement letter. (c) is incorrect because third parties can sue the company and the auditors jointly or severally, and, therefore, contributory negligence is not a valid defense for the auditor.

3. c. Under *Ernst & Ernst v. Hochfelder*, the Supreme Court held that CPAs may be held liable under 10B-5 of the 1934 Act only if scienter (intent to deceive) is present.

4. b. AICPA professional standards require that firms maintain adequate systems of quality control. (a) is incorrect because it applies only to auditing engagements. (c) is incorrect because enforcement is a remedial rather than a preventive measure. (d) is incorrect because independence is but one standard and does not apply equally to all engagements.

5. c. Constructive fraud is present where there is no actual intent to deceive, but where the auditor's conduct was so grossly negligent that it bordered on fraud. (c) "reckless conduct" falls into this category.

6. b. In this case, privity extends to the known third party beneficiary of the audited financial statements, Rhodes Corp. Therefore, Johnson is liable for ordinary negligence, as well as for gross negligence and fraud. For this reason, Rhodes need only prove negligence (not gross negligence or fraud).

7. d. Injured third parties must prove that the financial statements were materially misstated, that the CPAs were negligent in the conduct of their audit, that the third parties relied on the statements, and that they were injured by such reliance.

8. a. Section AU 315.04 requires that the successor auditor attempt to communicate with the predecessor auditor after obtaining the prospective client's permission. (b) and (c) may be desirable, but are not required by the professional standards. (d) is incorrect because the client representation letter is obtained at the conclusion of audit field work and is not relevant to the acceptance decision.

9. d. Scienter means "intent to deceive." Only in (d) is scienter absent. (a) is incorrect because in the case of *MacClean v. Alexander*, the court held that "reckless misconduct" can be construed as fraud (scienter).

10. b. Section AU 317.20 states that if the client refuses to accept the auditor's recommended actions regarding an illegal act, the auditor should withdraw from the engagement and indicate the reasons in writing to the audit committee or board of directors. (a) is incorrect because a violation of GAAP does not constitute an illegal act. (c) is incorrect because an illegal act committed during a prior year may or may not have an impact on the current year's financial statements. (d) is incorrect because assessment of control risk and the presence of illegal acts are unrelated.

11. a.   Under the law of contract, the CPA is liable to his/her client for ordinary negligence, gross negligence, and fraud. Therefore, the best defense in breach of contract actions is to demonstrate due care, i.e., the audit was conducted in accordance with GAAS.

12. d.   Quality control guidelines suggest advancement and promotion of firm personnel to provide reasonable assurance that positions within the firm will be occupied by competent persons. Although these are guidelines only, the professional standards do require that firms design and implement systems of quality control.

13. b.   Under the 1933 Act, the burden of proof shifts from plaintiff to defendant to demonstrate lack of scienter and the exercise of due care. The plaintiff, of course, must demonstrate that the financial statements were materially misstated and that he/she suffered injury by relying on them.

14. a.   Hall, Inc. is a specifically identified third party and is known by Locke to be the primary beneficiary of the audited financial statements. For this reason, Locke is liable for possible breach of contract as well as for negligence.

CHAPTER 4

1. d.   Lead schedules are summaries of two or more supporting schedules and the lead schedule total is transferred to the working trial balance as a major financial statement component.

2. a.   Although materiality, relative risk, and reasonable assurance are factors to be considered, auditor judgment ultimately determines the nature, timing, and extent of audit procedures to be applied in specific circumstances.

3. c.   (c) is correct because if the assumption of continuity were not valid, the evidence produced by the application of analytical procedures would not be relevant. This assumption permits the auditor to identify abnormalities as indicative of possible errors or fraud. (a) is incorrect because the study of ratios leads to the investigation of unusual fluctuations. Although (b) is true, it is not a basic premise underlying the application of analytical procedures. (d) is incorrect because under rare circumstances, discussed in a later chapter, the results of analytical procedures can replace tests of transactions and balances.

4. c.   Although (a) appears correct, one must remember that a line on the financial statements consists of an aggregation of items. (c), however, begins with the accounting records (a debit posting to the machinery and equipment subsidiary ledger, for example) and traces backward to the supporting evidence (the machine on the factory floor, for example). (b) is incorrect as a test for completeness for the same reason that (a) is incorrect as a test for existence. (d) is incorrect because this form of tracing results in a test for completeness, not existence.

5. a.   The working trial balance is the auditor's "table of contents." As such, it contains columns for the beginning balances, audit adjustments, audit reclassifications, and ending balances. Cross references to lead schedules and supporting schedules are also included to complete the indexing schema.

6. c.   In performing a risk-based audit, the auditor must be alert to possible earnings inflation, a form of fraudulent financial reporting. Earnings inflation may be accomplished by either overstating assets and revenues or understating liabilities and expenses. Therefore, (c) is correct.

7. a.   The bank reconciliation has current year significance only, whereas the items identified in (b), (c), and (d) have ongoing significance and would therefore be contained in the permanent file.

8. d.   The purpose for applying analytical procedures is to identify abnormal conditions that may suggest errors or fraud. (a) and (b) are incorrect because evaluating management performance and evaluating operating plans are not proper objectives in performing an independent audit. (c) is incorrect because an abnormal trend may or may not be indicative of a need for footnote disclosure.

9. d.   The purpose of analytical procedures in the audit planning stage is to detect significant abnormalities in relationships among financial data. A standard cost system that produces variance reports facilitates the auditor's identification of these abnormalities.

10. a.   Effective internal control enhances the validity (reliability) of audit evidence, thereby providing greater assurance concerning the resulting accounting data and financial statements. (b) is incorrect because competence relates to the quality of audit evidence, not the amount obtained. (c) is incorrect because indirect evidence is less persuasive than auditor observation, which is a form of direct audit evidence. (d) is incorrect because competence of audit evidence is considered by the auditor regardless of source.

11. d.   A client's accounting data represents internal evidence and, as such, needs to be further corroborated to a greater or lesser extent, depending on the quality of existing internal control. (a) is incorrect because evidence does not have to be convincing to be competent. The audit report provides reasonable—not absolute—assurance regarding the fairness of the financial statements. (b) is incorrect because effective internal control contributes greatly to the reliability of internal evidence. (c) is incorrect because, given two or more equally effective alternatives for attaining one or more audit objectives, the auditor should select the least costly alternative.

12. d.   By definition, evidence must be valid and relevant to be competent. (a) is incorrect because evidence gathered outside the enterprise may or may not be reliable, depending on the source of the evidence. (b) is incorrect because evidence gathered under satisfactory conditions of internal control may be more reliable, but not necessarily more relevant than evidence gathered under conditions of weak internal control. (c) is incorrect because oral representations of management possess greater or lesser validity as a function of management's competence, knowledge, and integrity.

13. c.   Although (a) is important, it is not the primary purpose of the audit procedures. Gathering corroborative evidence is the primary purpose. (b) is incorrect because the financial statements, not the auditor, must be in conformity with GAAP. (d) is incorrect because audits are test-based and, therefore, can verify the reasonableness, but not the accuracy, of account balances.

14. a.   In performing audit risk analysis, the auditor is alert to indicators of possible errors and/or fraud. Of the choices listed in this question, only (a) is so indicative. (b) is incorrect because low turnover of senior accounting personnel supports low error incidence. (c) is incorrect because heavy (not little) emphasis on meeting earnings projections is the condition alerting the auditor to possible fraudulent financial reporting. (d) is incorrect because division of functions among several individuals prevents undue dominance by a single individual who could more readily effect fraudulent financial reporting.

CHAPTER 5

1. c.   Although the independent auditor may utilize the internal audit staff in conducting the examination, all audit judgment decisions must be made by the independent auditor. Assessing materiality and evaluating the reasonableness of accounting estimates both fall within the realm of audit judgment.

2. b.   Given the equation $DR = AR/IR \times CR$, where:
DR = detection risk;
AR = overall audit risk;
IR = inherent risk; and
CR = control risk,
the level of control risk assessed by the auditor directly influences detection risk. As control risk increases, detection risk decreases, and as control risk decreases, the acceptable level of detection risk increases.

3. a.   A reduction in the acceptable level of detection risk requires an increase in the quality and/or amount of audit evidence. Therefore, as stronger and increasing quantities of evidence are gathered, given a decrease in detection risk, the level of assurance increases accordingly.

4. d.   The auditor studies the business and industry, performs analytical procedures, and studies and evaluates the system of internal control in assessing inherent risk and control risk. The auditor then sets detection risk accordingly. Detection risk, therefore, is the dependent variable and may be increased or decreased by the auditor. (a) is incorrect because all three components are elements of audit risk. (b) is incorrect because inherent risk and control risk are independent variables and cannot be changed by the auditor. (c) is incorrect because all components of audit risk may be considered at different levels of aggregation.

5. d.   Analytical procedures applied as part of audit planning are intended to identify significant abnormalities that may be indicative of possible errors or fraud. These abnormalities are termed "high risk" areas. Therefore, (d) is the correct answer.

6. a.   The purpose for communicating with the predecessor auditor is to obtain information helpful in deciding whether to accept the engagement. Only (a) directly influences that decision. Although the information described in (b), (c), and (d) may be relevant in conducting the audit, it does not impact the acceptance decision.

7. b.   A decrease in detection risk requires an increase in the amount and/or quality of audit evidence. (b) is correct because a change from less effective to more effective types of evidence increases its quality. (a) is incorrect because a reduction in the acceptable level of detection risk precludes performing significant substantive tests at interim dates. (c) and (d) are incorrect because the setting of detection risk presumes that the assessed levels of inherent risk and control risk have already been established.

8. c.   The primary purpose of workpaper review is to determine that sufficient, competent evidence was obtained to support the audit opinion. (a) and (b) are incorrect because these conditions must be present before any audit engagement is accepted. (d) is incorrect because the professional standards do not generally dictate specific audit procedures.

9. a.   One of the preliminary matters to be discussed with the client is the timing and nature of inventory taking and the formulation of proper instructions for those performing the inventory taking and documentation procedures. (b) and (c) are incorrect because, as an independent intermediary between management and financial statement users, the auditor should not discuss audit procedures with the client. (d) is incorrect because the lawyer's letter is usually drafted towards the end of the audit field work when the status of pending litigation is most current.

10. d.   Given the equation AR = IR × CR × DR, if control risk (CR) increases, and inherent risk (IR) remains constant, the only means for holding overall audit risk (AR) at the planned level is to decrease detection risk (DR).

11. a.   The lower the detection risk, the greater the amount of substantive testing necessary to maintain overall audit risk at an acceptable level. Low detection risk is associated with high control and/or inherent risk. (c) and (d) are incorrect because control testing provides an input into determining an acceptable level of detection risk.

12. a.   All of the audit risk components, either individually or collectively, may be assessed in quantitative or nonquantitative terms.

13. b.   The purpose for applying analytical procedures is to enable the auditor to detect abnormal conditions indicative of possible errors or fraud.

14. a.   A level higher than $10,000 risks overlooking material income statement misstatements.

15. c.   This choice describes a control testing procedure that would be applied after planning the audit. (a), (b), and (d), however, are all relevant to the audit planning process.

16. d.   (d) is virtually a direct quote from SAS 82, which requires the auditor to plan the audit to provide reasonable assurance of detecting material errors and fraud.

17. c.   A comparison of actual with budgeted revenue provides a measure of how closely the entity met the revenue portion of its operating plan for the year. (a) is incorrect because changes in accounts payable assist in measuring liquidity

but have no direct bearing on operations. (b) is incorrect because neither prior year's expense nor current budget amount has a bearing on current year's actual operations. (d) is incorrect because warranty expense is but one component of operations and one of perhaps several contingencies.

CHAPTER 6

1. d.   Signed disbursement checks are financial assets and, to maintain proper separation between accounting and treasury, should not be returned to accounting, but should be mailed directly by the treasurer's office upon signing.

2. a.   (a) provides the best control in that the functions of asset custody and asset accountability are effectively separated. (b) is undesirable because an annual verification of securities is not sufficiently adequate or timely to prevent loss from misappropriation of securities. (c) is not a control procedure but is rather a part of the independent audit. (d) represents an inappropriate assignment of functions to the board of directors.

3. d.   Although (a), (b), and (c) are helpful in detecting misappropriation of incoming customer checks, (d), the lock box system, is the best preventive control in that it avoids employee handling of checks in the first instance.

4. b.   The debit memo from purchasing notifies accounting that the goods have been returned to the vendor. Accounting should then record the return and file the debit memo awaiting receipt of a credit memo from the vendor. (a) and (c) are incorrect because the unpaid voucher and the vendor's invoice are not in possession of the purchasing department. (d) is incorrect because the vendor will issue the credit memo, not purchasing.

5. a.   Effective internal control over payroll requires that all hiring, termination, and pay rate and deduction decisions be approved by personnel. Payroll should prepare payroll, the controller is responsible for accounting for the payroll, and the treasurer should sign payroll checks and distribute the payroll.

6. d.   Proper internal control over purchasing and receiving should require an approved purchase order acknowledging the requisition. The purchase order may then be used by receiving to assure that only ordered goods be accepted upon receipt. (a) is incorrect because the vendor's invoice usually follows shipment and may include goods not received or ordered. (b) is incorrect because a requisition must be approved and accompanied by a purchase order for proper authorization. (c) is incorrect because the bill of lading only supports the goods received and does not provide information regarding goods ordered.

7. d.   An audit committee, the internal audit function, and a sound organization structure are all components of an effective control environment.

8. b.   The purpose of listing incoming cash receipts is to assure that all incoming cash receipts are recorded and deposited intact. When this control is combined with a comparison of the listing, recorded cash and the receipted bank deposit slip, the control loop is completed.

9. c.   Adequate separation between accounting and treasury requires controller approval of vouchers for payment. (a), (b), and (d) are proper treasury functions.

10. b.   Establishing agreement among the invoice, receiving report, and purchase order prevents errors in pricing goods and adds further verification that the entity received what it ordered and is being billed for what it received. Although (a), (c), and (d) are important controls, they are performed by the purchasing department, the treasurer's office, and manufacturing, respectively, and not by accounts payable.

CHAPTER 7

1. b.   GAAS defines reportable conditions as "matters coming to the auditor's attention, relating to internal control deficiencies, which could adversely affect the entity's ability to record, process, summarize, and report financial data consistent with management's assertions contained in the financial statements.

2. b.   The auditor tests controls to ascertain their operating effectiveness for the period under audit. Knowledge of operating effectiveness is necessary if the auditor wishes to reduce the assessed level of control risk below maximum. (a) is incorrect because substantive, not control, tests detect material misstatements in the financial statements. (c) is incorrect because the auditor must ultimately assess control risk before determining the nature, timing, and extent of substantive audit procedures. (d) is incorrect because control tests may afford a basis for reducing control risk, but will not impact inherent risk.

3. a.   Ineffective control procedures require an increase in the amount of substantive testing (tests of details) in order to maintain overall audit risk at the desired level. (b) is incorrect because control weaknesses may be the result of inherent risk, but not the cause of it. (c) is incorrect because an auditor does not test controls that are already found to be ineffective. (d) is incorrect because weak internal control should prompt the auditor to reduce, not increase, the level of detection risk.

4. b.   If the auditor assesses control risk at maximum, he/she need only document his/her understanding of internal financial control. If he/she wishes to assess control risk below maximum, however, he/she must additionally document the basis for such reduction.

5. c.   Knowledge about operating effectiveness can be obtained only through control testing, which is not considered to be part of the initial understanding of internal control.

6. a.   The only controls relevant to an audit are those that affect management's financial statement assertions. (b) is incorrect because management override is an inherent limitation of internal control, and therefore cannot be prevented by internal control policies and procedures. (c) and (d) are incorrect because, although the auditor is interested in the control environment, of which management's philosophy and operating style are an integral part, that is not the primary consideration in assessing control risk.

7. c.   The internal control questionnaire, along with the internal control memorandum and the internal control flowchart, are the means used by the auditor in documenting his/her understanding of the client's internal control.

8. a. (a) is correct and (b), (c), and (d) are incorrect because, under GAAS, the auditor must obtain an understanding of the design and implementation of internal control, but need not obtain knowledge about operating effectiveness.

9. b. The visual portrayal of transaction cycle subsets helps the auditor gain a broader understanding of the system. When used in conjunction with the questionnaire and memorandum approaches, the combination is most useful in obtaining a thorough understanding of a client's internal control system. (a) is an advantage of the questionnaire approach, given that "no" answers indicate control weaknesses. (c) is incorrect because, generally, control testing is the only means for determining operating effectiveness. (d) is incorrect because, regardless of approach, some observation is necessary to gaining an understanding of internal control.

10. b. When control risk is assessed at maximum, the auditor must document his/her understanding and a conclusion stating that control risk is assessed at maximum. (a) is incorrect because the conclusion is not contemplated in this answer. (c) is incorrect because it does not contemplate documentation of the understanding. (d) is incorrect because it requires the auditor to document his/her reasons for assessing at maximum.

11. d. Assessing control risk at a low level requires a determination of operating effectiveness, generally by testing the relevant controls. Assuming the control tests support the auditor's plan to reduce control risk assessment, only limited substantive testing need be performed. (a) and (c) are incorrect because analytical procedures are more pertinent to assessing inherent risk than control risk. (b) is incorrect because tests of controls combined with extensive tests of the asset accounts would not be cost effective.

12. b. The second standard of audit field work requires the auditor to obtain an understanding of the client's internal control policies and procedures sufficient to plan the audit.

13. a. If internal controls are unlikely to be effective, a risk-based approach suggests that the auditor plan a primarily substantive audit and not test the controls. (b) is incorrect because lack of documentation does not necessarily preclude control testing to reduce the assessed level below maximum. (c) is incorrect because control tests are not cost effective where control risk is assessed at maximum. (d) is incorrect because an auditor is not likely to assess control risk at maximum if the internal controls are effective in preventing material misstatements. Instead, the auditor is more likely to test those controls in an effort to reduce the assessed level of control risk below maximum.

14. d. Operating effectiveness of internal controls can be evaluated through the techniques of observation, reprocessing, or document examination, depending on the procedure being examined and the nature of the client's accounting system. (a) and (c) are substantive auditing procedures and are not relevant to determining operating effectiveness. (d) is a technique for gaining an understanding of internal control, but it is not useful for determining operating effectiveness.

15. d. The purpose for assessing control risk is to afford the auditor a basis for determining the nature, timing, and extent of substantive audit procedures. (a) is in-

correct because determining the existence of asset safeguards is part of the auditor's understanding, and not a use of the knowledge gained from such understanding. (b) is incorrect because detecting fraud opportunities caused by control weaknesses is not a primary purpose of obtaining an understanding. (c) is incorrect because inherent risk is not affected by internal control strengths or weaknesses.

16. a. In assessing control risk as part of audit planning, the auditor recognizes that inherent risk factors, such as collusive fraud, exist and therefore provide reasonable but not absolute assurance of error prevention and detection. This, in turn, when combined with test-based auditing, provides only reasonable assurance that the independent auditor will detect material misstatements, notwithstanding a properly designed and executed audit. (b) is incorrect because a properly designed audit should enable the auditor to detect material irregularities as well as material errors. (c) is incorrect because an increased risk of intentional misstatements should cause the auditor to concentrate efforts in those areas. (d) is incorrect because the auditor should consider factors having a pervasive effect on the financial statements.

17. b. After obtaining the initial understanding, the auditor must decide whether to perform control tests in an effort to reduce the assessed level of control risk. This decision requires the auditor to identify available means and the cost effectiveness of those means. (a) is incorrect because substantive, not control, tests verify management's assertions. (c) is incorrect because analytical procedures assist in assessing inherent risk, but not control risk. (d) is incorrect because evaluating the detection capabilities of internal controls is but one aspect of obtaining the initial understanding of internal control, but it is not the next step after the understanding.

18. d. In developing an audit strategy, the auditor should consider audit risk in terms of its three components, i.e., inherent risk, control risk, and detection risk. (a), (b), and (c) are important considerations; but they pertain to audit work performed after an audit strategy has been developed.

19. d. In evaluating internal control, the auditor is interested only in those controls relevant to an audit, i.e., those controls affecting management's assertions relating to the reliability of the financial statements. (a) and (b) are incorrect because the auditor must always be aware of inherent limitations in internal control, such as collusion and management override of internal control. (c) is incorrect because the auditor tests only those controls that are relevant to assertions.

CHAPTER 8

1. d. For the test data approach to provide reliable evidence about operating effectiveness, the auditor must control the process and must use the client's application programs. (d), therefore, is the correct response. (a) is incorrect because the auditor wishes to test only those controls relevant to financial statement assertions, and these do not necessarily encompass all valid and invalid conditions. (b) is incorrect because if the program is different from the program used by the client, no assurance as to control effectiveness is gained from the

test. (c) is incorrect because only one transaction of each type need be tested so long as it tests the relevant controls.

2. b.   Accessing programs and files from terminals is a characteristic of real-time systems. Given the heightened danger of data manipulation and/or destruction resulting from unlimited access, data security in the form of properly controlled user identification codes becomes critical. (b), therefore, is the correct response. (a), (c), and (d) are hardware controls and are not dependent on any form of user entry.

3. b.   In applying ITF, the client's employees should not be made aware that the auditor's simulated transactions are being simultaneously processed alongside actual transactions. Such awareness could enable client personnel to temporarily alter program controls to provide the appearance of effectiveness.

4. b.   Systems analysts and programmers should not be involved in the processing of actual transactions. Maintaining output controls violates this control principle. (a), (c), and (d) describe conditions properly performed by the respective individuals.

5. c.   The most cost-effective means for determining adequate online data access control is for the auditor to introduce invalid passwords. If the computer rejects them, the auditor has increased satisfaction concerning data input controls.

6. a.   A systems flowchart, with only slight modification, can be transformed into an internal control flowchart. Both flowcharts display documents, people, and functions performed in processing transactions through the system. The flowchart is one of the means used by the auditor to obtain and document his/her understanding of the essential internal financial controls. (b), (c), and (d) are part of the overall systems documentation, but represent minute detail that are not of particular concern to the auditor in obtaining an overall understanding of internal control.

7. a.   The simplest and most cost-effective way to test proper functioning of user identification and password controls is for the auditor to attempt to "sign on" the computer by inputting an unauthorized number. (a), therefore, is the correct choice. (b) and (c) may provide some evidence as to password security, but are not as cost effective as (a) and do not provide evidence as conclusive. (d) may provide some assurance that nonauthorized persons are not currently using authorized passwords or identification codes; but this technique provides no evidence concerning ability of a person to sign onto the system with an unauthorized code or password.

8. d.   Controls providing for adequate documentation of systems and programs are vital to effective internal control policies and procedures in CBIS. (a), (b), and (c) describe substantive auditing procedures and are not designed primarily to test controls for operating effectiveness.

9. d.   Tagging and tracing consists of programmed controls designed to identify unusual transactions or any other characteristic, such as processing steps, considered relevant by the auditor. The transactions or steps so tagged are available only to the auditor. (d), therefore, is the correct choice.

10. d.   Unless strict password control is in place, data files housed in microcomputers may be easily accessed by anyone knowing how to operate the computer. Access to manual files, in contrast, is more easily controlled through physical means, such as locked files and assignment of responsibility. (a) is incorrect because computer processing reduces, rather than increases, the incidence of random error. (b) and (c) are incorrect because these conditions do not apply differently to computerized vs. manual files.

11. c.   To obtain evidence about control risk, the auditor may decide to perform tests of internal financial controls. These tests may assume the form of observation, reprocessing, and/or document examination and testing. Of these three alternatives, only (c), reprocessing, represents a control test. (a), (b), and (d) are substantive testing techniques and are therefore incorrect responses.

12. b.   The ITF approach involves the introduction of "dummy" transactions by the auditor during live processing by the client. (a) and (c) use actual rather than simulated transactions. (d) does not involve the processing of either live or simulated data.

13. c.   CBIS controls can check for invalid numbers, incorrect prices, customers exceeding credit limits, unreasonable amounts, or other comparisons of number sets. These controls, however, cannot check for proper authorizations, approvals, and/or signatures. Controls outside CBIS must be designed and implemented to achieve these objectives. (c), therefore, is the correct choice. (a), (b), and (d) are incorrect because they do not compare number sets and therefore cannot be programmed as input editing controls.

14. a.   User identification codes and passwords help to prevent unauthorized access to databases. Such unauthorized access could result in manipulation, loss, or destruction of information contained in these files. (a), therefore, is the correct choice.

15. c.   If a visible trail of documentary evidence is available, the auditor may choose to examine and test documents as a technique for testing a client's internal financial controls. In the absence of a documentary audit trail, the auditor may elect the techniques of reprocessing and/or observation. (c), therefore, is the best choice. (a), (b), and (d) are substantive testing techniques and, are, therefore, incorrect responses.

16. b.   Backup files stored away from the originals—preferably off the premises—enable the entity to reconstruct files and records following loss of the originals from whatever cause. (a), (c), and (d) are proper controls, but are not relevant to data reconstruction.

17. c.   Application controls are categorized as to input, processing, and output controls. (a) is a processing control. (b) is a general control relating to organization and access security. (d) is the objective of output controls. (c) defines the goal of input controls and is therefore the correct response.

18. c.   The CBIS control group should be independent of programmers, operators, and systems analysts. Their responsibilities include distributing output to authorized users and monitoring the reprocessing of errors. (c), therefore, is the correct choice. (a) is incorrect because a proper system of double check would

be violated were the computer operator to be responsible for both entering data and reviewing error conditions. (b) and (d) are incorrect because proper separation within CBIS precludes systems analysts and computer programmers from being involved in the data processing operation.

19. c.   A large number of geographically dispersed and networked microcomputers linked to a headquarters mainframe computer characterize distributed data processing systems. Given the large number and geographic dispersion of the microcomputers, access controls are most critical to database protection. (a), (b), and (d) are incorrect because, although important controls, they are not more or less critical to distributed systems.

20. c.   Adequate systems documentation will enable a new systems analyst to more readily determine the work to date on the project and proceed forward from that point. (a), although a valuable general control, would be of little help in carrying forward a partially completed systems project. (b) and (d) are incorrect because they are application controls rather than general controls.

21. c.   The responsibilities of the CBIS function encompass software acquisition, documentation of systems and system changes, as well as programs, program changes, operator instructions, and file security. Originating changes in master files, however, is an operating function that must be kept separate from CBIS. (c), therefore, is the correct response.

22. b.   Computers can be programmed to check for reasonableness and correctness of numbers, such as employee number (a), job number (c), and hours (d). The computer cannot, however, check for proper approvals (b) because this control does not contain a number set for comparison purposes.

23. a.   (a) is the correct response because adequate separation within CBIS suggests that systems analysts be responsible for designing operating systems, but that they not process transactions through the system (computer operators), or review and distribute output (control clerk). (b) is incorrect because preparing data for computer input and entering the data into the computer are appropriate responsibilities of the accounts payable clerk. (c) is incorrect because programmers' functions include designing and testing programs. (d) is incorrect because reconciling control totals and distributing output are proper functions of the control clerk.

24. c.   An audit trail is necessary in any accounting system, whether computerized or manual, for the purpose of reconstructing recorded transactions. Such reconstruction supports the functions described in (a), (b), and (d). An audit trail, however, is not necessary for purposes of performing analytical procedures, inasmuch as these are based on the end product—financial statement components.

25. d.   General controls are more pervasive than application controls, and, therefore, general control weaknesses are considered more serious than application control weaknesses. For this reason, an auditor who wishes to assess control risk below maximum should concentrate on general controls first. (a) and (c) are incorrect because (a), programmed controls, represents a subset of general controls, and (c), output controls, are a subset of application controls.

CHAPTER 9

1. a.   Sample size for attribute sampling purposes is a function of the expected occurrence rate, the tolerable occurrence rate, and the risk of underassessment of control risk. (b) is incorrect because the upper precision limit is given once the expected occurrence rate and the tolerable occurrence rate are set. (c) is incorrect because risk of incorrect acceptance is another term for risk of underassessment. (d) is incorrect because setting the tolerable occurrence rate sufficiently high addresses risk of incorrect rejection.

2. c.   Risk of underassessment and the tolerable occurrence rate are inversely related to sample size. Therefore, increasing these factors reduces sample size. The expected occurrence rate is positively related to sample size. Therefore, decreasing this factor reduces sample size. Given these rules, (a), (b), and (d) are incorrect because they either result in increased sample sizes or else the combination of factor changes makes the direction of change indeterminate.

3. a.   If the joint probability of inherent risk (IR) times control risk (CR) is less than overall audit risk (AR) set by the auditor, further substantive testing is not necessary. That is, the product of the two risk factors has reduced audit risk below the specified maximum. Only in (a) is this condition true.

4. a.   A calculated upper occurrence limit, based on sample evaluation, that exceeds the tolerable rate means that the controls are less effective than the auditor first expected. This suggests increasing the assessed level of control risk beyond the initial level, or at least not reducing it below maximum. (b) is incorrect because the expected occurrence rate was 2 1/2%, not 7%; and the sample error rate, at 3 1/2%, exceeded the expected rate. (c) and (d) are incorrect because (c) considers actual results only and (d) considers anticipated results only; whereas an evaluation of results requires a comparison between actual and anticipated results.

5. b.   The allowance for sampling risk, achieved precision, equals the upper occurrence limit (8%) minus the sample error rate (3 1/2%), which equals 4 1/2%.

6. c.   The sample rate of error plus the allowance for sampling risk equals the upper occurrence limit; and if the upper occurrence limit exceeds the tolerable rate, the auditor should reject the population and increase the assessed level of control risk. (a) is incorrect because if the sample error rate is less than the expected rate, a lowering of assessed control risk is suggested. (b) is incorrect for the same reason because the tolerable rate less the allowance for sampling risk equals the expected error rate. (d) is incorrect because the sample error rate plus the allowance for sampling risk equals the upper occurrence limit. If the upper and tolerable limits are equal, a change in the assessed level of control risk is not indicated.

7. b.   The auditor should reject the population and not reduce the assessed level of control risk for two reasons. First, the sample error rate (4%) exceeds the expected rate (3%). Second, the upper occurrence limit, sample error rate plus allowance for sampling risk, equals 6% and this exceeds the tolerable rate of 5%.

8. b.   This question illustrates the importance of correctly defining "error" with regard to each attribute tested by the auditor. Inasmuch as the auditor cannot

establish existence of a proper countersignature, a missing check must be considered an error. (a) and (d) are incorrect because they ignore the presence of a possible error. (c) is incorrect because the dominant condition relative to the other 19 checks is not relevant to the missing check.

9. d.   (d) is the best answer because the combination of the purchase order, receiving report, and vendor's invoice documents all aspects of the purchase. An independent review of these documents for correctness and agreement, prior to preparing and recording the voucher, is the best means for minimizing recording errors. (a), (b), and (c) are incorrect because they only perform a portion of the comparison function.

10. c.   This is a test for completeness. Specifically, the objective is to determine that all merchandise received has been recorded by a debit to inventory and a credit to accounts payable. Inasmuch as the receiving report documents merchandise received, these documents are the population for purposes of this test.

11. d.   The objective here is to test for existence. Specifically, the auditor wishes to determine that all entries in the payroll register represent actual employees and actual hours worked. The direction of testing, therefore, should proceed from the payroll register entry to the employee earnings record and the time card.

12. a.   The objective of control testing is to evaluate operating effectiveness of those internal control policies and procedures for which the auditor wishes to reduce the assessed level of control risk. The auditor obtains an understanding, prior to testing the controls, to ascertain proper design and implementation of the controls.

13. b.   This situation illustrates alpha risk, the risk of incorrect rejection. In this case, the auditor overassessed control risk and did more substantive testing than necessary. Although overauditing is not cost efficient, it is preferred to underauditing (underassessing control risk), which can lead to expressing an unqualified opinion on financial statements that are materially misstated.

14. d.   When the auditor reduces the tolerable occurrence rate, the sample size increases to accommodate the narrower precision range. (a) is incorrect because, although deviations from control procedures will increase the estimated population deviation rate, the resulting population rate should not vary from the sample error rate. (b) is incorrect because population size has a negligible impact on sample size. (c) is incorrect because the auditor does consider qualitative factors in evaluating the significance of sample deviations.

15. d.   In deciding whether to modify the assessed level of control risk as a result of attribute sampling, the auditor compares the achieved upper occurrence limit with the tolerable occurrence rate. If the achieved upper limit exceeds the tolerable rate, the auditor may need to increase the assessed level of control risk and extend substantive audit testing. In the present case, the upper limit, which equals the sample deviation rate, 6%, plus the allowance for sampling risk, 2%, does exceed the tolerable rate, 7%. Therefore, (d) is the correct choice.

16. b.   The audit objective is to ascertain whether checks are being issued without proper approval and/or documentation. The auditor should start, therefore,

with a sample of canceled checks and work back to the underlying documentation evidencing authenticity and approvals.

17. d.   Assuming all other factors remain the same, an increase in the expected occurrence rate should produce an increase in the sample size. Increasing the tolerable rate (a), the allowance for sampling risk (b), or the risk of underassessing control risk (c) would only serve to increase overall audit risk beyond the level considered satisfactory in the prior year's audit.

18. b.   This is an example of sampling error. As a result of examining a sample rather than the population, the auditor must assume the risk that the sample will not be representative of the population. In this instance, the auditor underassessed control risk and incorrectly reduced substantive testing. Although (d) is also an example of sampling error, it illustrates the risk of overassessing control risk and, as a result, the auditor would increase, rather than decrease, substantive testing.

19. d.   In virtually all instances of statistical sampling for control testing purposes, some form of attribute sampling that estimates frequency of occurrence of errors is the preferred method.

20. c.   This situation describes the risk of underassessing control risk, and occurs when the sample occurrence rate is less than the population error rate. The low sample occurrence rate leads the auditor to understate the upper error limit, thereby assessing control risk too low. (a) is incorrect because a high sample occurrence rate should lead to an increase in the assessed level of control risk. (b) is incorrect because a low population deviation rate justifies a lowering of the assessed level of control risk. (d) should lead to overassessing control risk.

CHAPTER 10

1. a.   Alpha risk is the risk of rejecting a population that is not materially misstated. If the auditor's sample results lead him/her to believe that the population is materially misstated, he/she will reject the book value of that population. If, in fact, the book value is reasonably stated, the auditor has incorrectly rejected the population book value.

2. b.   Given that the book value of the sample, $10,000, exceeds the sampling interval, $5,000, the projected error is the same as the detected error ($10,000 minus $8,000 equals $2,000).

3. c.   By dividing the population into subsets (large items in one subset, remainder in a second subset), the standard deviation (degree of variability about the mean) will be less for each subset than if they were commingled. Also, stratification enables the auditor to apply different sampling strategies to the subsets (e.g., auditing the larger items 100% and randomly sampling the smaller subset).

4. d.   By stratifying the population, the auditor is testing larger dollar amounts in the most cost effective manner. Although (a) and (b) will also result in examining large disbursements, these approaches are not as cost effective as (d). (c) simply

increases the sample size without assuring the inclusion of the larger disbursements.

5. a. Precision is defined as the range within which the true answer lies. The precision range may be expressed as the calculated mean plus or minus computed precision. This is another way of expressing possible error. (b) is incorrect because reliability is the probability that the true population value lies within the precision range. (c) is incorrect because projected error is the auditor's most likely estimate of error, but it does not express a range of error. (d) is incorrect because standard deviation is a measure of variability but not a measure of error.

6. c. PPS sampling is best suited to populations for which the auditor suspects a few significant overstatement errors. If the population contains both over- and understatement errors, classical variables sampling is generally preferred. (a) and (d) are advantages—not disadvantages—of PPS sampling. (b) is incorrect because the auditor may or may not use computer programs in designing, selecting, and evaluating samples.

7. d. Statistical sampling is defined as a mathematical approach to inference. As such, it adds consistency to determining the sufficiency of audit evidence. (a) is incorrect because the auditor, not statistical sampling, defines materiality. (b) is incorrect because statistical sampling, per se, neither increases nor decreases the amount of substantive testing. (c) is incorrect because, although statistical sampling provides a consistent approach to audit judgment, the auditor applies judgment in setting the sampling parameters.

8. a. The reason for comparing achieved precision with the desired (specified) range is to ascertain that achieved beta risk is not greater than specified beta risk. If achieved precision is wider than specified precision, the preliminary estimate of standard deviation was too low (actual standard deviation is greater) and further sampling is indicated. (b) is incorrect because under this condition, achieved precision would be narrower than the desired range. (c) and (d) are incorrect because population size, by itself, is not the sole determinant of either desired or achieved precision.

9. d. Sampling for variables enables one to estimate the value of a population, e.g., volume, number, or dollar value. (a), discovery sampling, is used when one wishes to find a single event occurring in a population, e.g., a fraud. (c), attribute sampling, is used to estimate the rate of frequency of one or more characteristics of a population. (b), numerical sampling, is not a term commonly used in sampling methodology.

10. a. To calculate sample size for mean-per-unit and difference estimation purposes, the auditor must estimate population variability. This can be done by drawing a pilot sample of 40 or 50 items at random and calculating a standard deviation for the sample. The calculated standard deviation is then used in the equation for sample size and compared later with the standard deviation of the sample.

11. d. In skewed populations, the auditor's sample may not be normally distributed. (a) is incorrect because approximately 2/3 of the sample means will be within one standard deviation of the mean. (b) is incorrect because a sample distrib-

ution is defined by its mean and standard error. (c) is incorrect because 95% of the area under a normal curve is within two standard deviations of the mean.

12. a. Discovery sampling is a means of locating an instance of error when error is suspected. In auditing for fraud, discovery sampling is frequently the most efficient way to locate a single occurrence.

13. c. Tolerable occurrence limit is the maximum misstatement allowable by the auditor while accepting the book value as reasonably stated. The auditor's judgment concerning materiality will be the major factor in setting this limit. (a) is incorrect because inherent risk, as well as control risk, will influence the desired precision level but does not enter into the determination of tolerable misstatement. (b) is incorrect because materiality considerations encompass both quantitative and qualitative factors. (d) is incorrect because all parameters used in statistical sampling are subject to change as additional information comes to the auditor's attention.

14. c. To calculate projected error for logical units having a book value less than the sampling interval, a tainting percentage must be calculated and applied to the sampling interval. In the present case the tainting percentage is 60 percent [($5,000 − $2,000)/$5,000]. The sampling interval, $10,000 times the tainting percentage, 60 percent, equals the projected error, $6,000.

15. d. Probability-proportional-to-size sampling is most appropriate where the auditor suspects overstatement errors.

16. a. Variables sampling, whether mean-per-unit or difference estimation, is used by the auditor to estimate the dollar value of populations by examining a sample and extending the sample results to the population. (b) is incorrect because attribute sampling is used to estimate error rates but not population values. (c) is incorrect because discovery sampling is used to locate an instance of error or fraud when the auditor's suspicions are aroused. (d) is incorrect because the term "numerical sampling" is not a sampling term.

17. c. PPS sampling is most useful where the auditor suspects a few significant overstatement errors. If the auditor believes understatement as well as overstatement errors are present, some other sampling method, e.g., mean-per-unit or difference estimation, should be applied. (a), (b), and (d) are incorrect because none of these conditions affect the efficiency of PPS sampling.

CHAPTER 11

1. b. If credit sales made before year end were not recorded until the next year, revenues are incomplete for the year, and cutoff tests should enable the auditor to detect the understatements.

2. c. Sales cutoff procedures include examining journal entries and documents supporting sales transactions recorded a few days before and after year end. Such procedures should assist in detecting unrecorded year-end sales, inasmuch as the shipping documents and freight terms establish the date on which title to the goods passed from seller to buyer. (a) is incorrect because, lacking

documentation, the auditor is unlikely to detect unrecorded shipments. (b) and (d) are incorrect because cutoff tests, by their nature, do not assist in identifying excessive write-offs or lapping of accounts receivable.

3. b.   If the check was written and mailed the last week of the year, it will likely have cleared by the date of the cutoff bank statement. Therefore, it will be included with the checks returned with the cutoff bank statement and examined by the auditor. (a) is incorrect because if the check is unrecorded, it will not appear in the check register. (c) is incorrect because bank confirmations do not confirm details concerning checks or deposits. (d) is incorrect because an unrecorded liability is not involved, given that the disbursement has been made.

4. d.   The purpose of confirming accounts receivable is to establish existence and valuation of the accounts. If replies are not received, the auditor must obtain satisfaction by other means. Among these other means is inspection of documents evidencing shipments to the customer. (a) is incorrect because the auditor will examine cash receipts subsequent to the balance sheet date to establish existence and valuation at the balance sheet date; but examining cash records prior to the balance sheet date is not relevant to this set of audit objectives. (b) is incorrect because further study of internal control will not contribute to the existence and valuation assertions relative to accounts receivable. (c) is incorrect because it only serves to increase detection risk to an unacceptably high level and does nothing to satisfy the stated objectives.

5. c.   Kiting is a means for overstating bank accounts. It occurs when a check is drawn on one bank at year end for deposit in another bank. The transfer is either not recorded until the following period or only the receipt is recorded in the current period.

6. b.   The standard bank confirmation form, as recommended by the Auditing Standards Board, is used to confirm deposit and loan balances only. (a) is incorrect because the auditor utilizes cutoff bank statements and analysis of interbank transfers to detect kiting. (c) is incorrect because bank statements and cash receipts and disbursements records are needed to prepare a proof of cash. (d) is incorrect because separate confirmation letters are used for obtaining information about contingent liabilities and secured transactions.

7. c.   Understating liabilities is a means of intentionally inflating earnings. For this reason, auditors test extensively for unrecorded liabilities. As described in the balanced audit approach, auditors also emphasize testing revenues for understatement, but these tests are not so extensive as those applied to possible liability understatement. (b) is incorrect because, under the balanced audit approach, auditors test assets for overstatement. (d) is incorrect because capital stock and retained earnings are tested more for proper classification and disclosure than for either understatement or overstatement.

8. a.   Tracing from shipping documents to sales invoices will help establish that all shipments to customers were billed and recorded as sales—the completeness assertion. (b), (c), and (d) are concerned with existence or occurrence, and with valuation, but not completeness.

9. c.   (c) is the definition of substantive audit tests as stated in the AICPA Professional Standards. (a) is incorrect because the concept of a minimum audit requires

some substantive testing. (b) is incorrect because the search for subsequent events is but one of many sets of substantive tests applied by the auditor. (d) is incorrect because substantive tests will increase with an increase in control risk, but not proportionately.

10. c.   Recording of liabilities in the proper accounting period is a cutoff issue that can be tested only as of the balance sheet date. (b) is incorrect because the auditor reviews internal control before applying substantive tests of transactions and balances. (a) and (d) are incorrect because under conditions of good internal control, inventory observation and accounts receivable confirmation may be performed prior to the balance sheet date.

11. a.   If internal control were strong and customers were likely to respond to confirmation requests, Cooper might elect to mail negative requests. But in this case control is weak and, under conditions of weak internal control over receivables, the positive form of confirmation requests should be used. (a), therefore, is correct and (b) is incorrect. (c) is incorrect because although analysis of subsequent receipts does provide evidence of existence it is not a substitute for confirmation. (d) is incorrect because under conditions of weak internal control internal documentation possesses less validity than under strong internal control.

12. d.   A sales overstatement results from recording sales that did not occur. Tracing from sales journals and/or subsidiary ledger accounts (accounting records) to the sales invoices and shipping orders (source documents) is the most effective way of detecting the overstatements.

13. d.   Inasmuch as the allowance for uncollectible accounts is a valuation allowance, determining its adequacy is directly related to the valuation assertion. (a) is incorrect because it relates to existence or occurrence assertions. (b) relates to both existence and valuation, but is not as directly related to valuation as (d). (c) concerns presentation and disclosure, but does not impact valuation.

14. b.   Because these checks were recorded in December and cleared the bank in January, they should have appeared on the December 31 bank reconciliation as outstanding checks. (a) and (c) are incorrect because tracing to the December or January cash disbursements records will not provide information regarding bank clearing dates. (d) is incorrect because year-end bank confirmations do not provide details as to receipts or disbursements.

15. a.   Because the cash receipts were recorded in December and cleared the bank in January, they should have appeared on the December 31 bank reconciliation as deposits in transit. (b), (c), and (d) are incorrect for the same reasons cited in question 14.

CHAPTER 12

1. d.   A decrease in inventory turnover may be indicative of obsolete or slow-moving inventory carried at amounts in excess of net realizable value—a valuation question.

2. c.   Payroll transactions are typically numerous and individually small. Therefore, unless analytical procedures produce significant abnormalities (e.g., in choice

(c)), auditors generally confine payroll auditing to evaluating internal control over payroll, perhaps testing the controls for operating effectiveness and recalculating year-end payroll accruals. If the assessed level of control risk is low as in (b) the auditor is less likely to perform substantive tests of payroll transactions.

3. d.   To help assure that all purchases are recorded (the completeness assertion), transactions should be fully documented and documents should be prenumbered. Prenumbered documents provide an "audit trail," thereby facilitating the tracing of transactions from document to accounting records (tests for completeness) and the vouching of transactions from accounting records to documents (tests for existence or occurrence). Although the other choices illustrate significant control techniques, they do not address the question of completeness.

4. d.   High control risk is associated with weak internal control. Under conditions of weak internal control over perpetual inventory records, the auditor would encounter difficulty in working an interim physical inventory forward to the balance sheet date. For this reason, generally accepted auditing standards recommend conducting a physical inventory prior to the balance sheet date only under conditions of strong internal control. (a) is incorrect because frequent physical counts during the year are no substitute for an accurate year-end physical count. (b) is incorrect because gross profit tests are applied to the final inventory values regardless of whether internal control is strong or weak. (c) is incorrect because audit efficiency suggests that the auditor not conduct further tests of controls that are perceived as weak.

5. c.   To satisfy the existence and valuation objectives, the auditor should start with the recorded entry or posting and work back to the underlying documentation (purchase order, receiving report, and vendor's invoice.) (a), (b), and (d) are incorrect because the described procedures relate more to the completeness assertion than to the existence assertion. Also, (b), opening the client's mail, is not a recommended audit procedure under normal conditions.

6. b.   To test for completeness of purchases transactions, the auditor should begin with the documentation of merchandise receipts, as evidenced by receiving reports, and trace forward to entries in the voucher register and postings to creditors' accounts in the accounts payable subsidiary ledger.

7. c.   Recording of liabilities in the proper accounting period is a cutoff issue that can be tested only as of the balance sheet date. (a) is incorrect because the auditor reviews internal control before applying substantive tests of transactions and balances. (b) and (d) are incorrect because under conditions of good internal control, inventory observation and accounts receivable confirmation may be performed prior to the balance sheet date.

8. d.   By examining cash disbursements after year end, along with the supporting documentation, the auditor can ascertain whether the related debit was recorded in the proper accounting period. (a) is a test for existence—not omission—and is therefore incorrect. (b) may lead to ultimate detection of unrecorded purchases, but, by itself, is not a valid procedure for detecting unrecorded liabilities. (c) is incorrect because the period covered—a few

days—is not adequate to provide assurance as to omission of significant year-end liabilities.

9. a. The purpose for reviewing sales cutoff is to determine that sales transactions were recorded in the proper accounting period. Therefore, application of this test should detect significant amounts of year-end sales recorded in the following accounting period. (b), (c), and (d) are incorrect inasmuch as sales cutoff tests focus on the sales accounts and therefore provide little, if any, evidence regarding lapping, sales discounts, or sales returns.

10. a. Evidence relevant to fixed asset additions should relate primarily to existence and valuation. Examining documents underlying purchases and inspecting the assets on a test basis are the most effective means for meeting these objectives. Although (b), (c), and (d) are relevant to fixed asset auditing, they are not as strong as (a) in establishing existence and valuation.

11. c. This is a test for existence and validity of recorded liabilities. By proceeding from an entry in the voucher register to the underlying documentation, including the vendor's invoice, the auditor obtains satisfaction that the credit to vouchers payable represents a valid expenditure. (a) and (d) are incorrect because tracing from the voucher register to voucher and invoice provides no evidence as to payment. (b) is incorrect because the auditor must also examine vouchers and cash disbursements in the subsequent period to obtain evidence as to recording in the proper accounting period.

12. a. The most effective means for determining whether recorded inventories exist (existence or occurrence of manufacturing transactions) is to compare the perpetual inventory records with actual goods on hand. (b) and (c) are relevant to the goal of physically safeguarding inventories, but do not establish existence or occurrence of inventory transactions. (d) supports proper valuation of completed transactions and contributes to error detection, but like (b) and (c) does not contribute to the existence assertion.

13. d. Obsolete or slow-moving inventory reported at full cost by the client represent assets valued above net realizable value.

CHAPTER 13

1. b. Investments accounted for under the equity method are initially recorded at cost and then adjusted for the investor's share of investee income and dividends. The most effective means for auditing for proper valuation, therefore, is to examine the audited financial statements of the investee. (a) establishes existence and ownership, but does not help in determining proper valuation. (c) and (d) contribute to the valuation objective for investments for which the investor does not have effective control.

2. b. A note payable, otherwise classified as a current liability, should be reclassified as long-term if it is renewed on a long-term basis shortly after the balance sheet date. Renewal of the note, however, does not affect existence or occurrence, completeness, or valuation as of the balance sheet date. (a), (c), and (d), therefore are incorrect.

3. c. Regardless of amount, frauds involving management raise questions of management integrity and suggest reconsideration of the client acceptance decision. Moreover, detection of small management fraud could be indicative of clever concealment schemes that "spread" material misstatements over several financial statement components.

4. a. Only (a) lends itself to analytical procedures. An abnormal decrease in investment income for the current year in relation to the prior year, for example, may be indicative of unrecorded income—the completeness assertion. (b) is incorrect because marketability and management intent govern classification. (c) is incorrect because the auditor determines valuation by reference to underlying purchases and sales documentation and to market quotations. (d) is incorrect because the auditor obtains satisfaction regarding unrealized gains or losses in the portfolio by comparing beginning of the year valuation with end of year market values.

5. a. Analytical procedures in the planning stage are necessary to provide guidance as to the direction of auditing and are important to risk-based auditing. Analytical procedures in the review stage are vital to the auditor's evaluation as to the adequacy of evidence obtained. Therefore, AICPA Professional Standards require the auditor to apply the procedures in the planning and review stages of the audit.

6. a. AICPA Professional Standards require the auditor to communicate significant audit adjustments and changes in significant accounting policies to the audit committee of the board of directors (See AU Section 380).

7. c. The most efficient and effective way to verify the amount of interest earned is to recalculate it. (a) is incorrect because interest received and deposited may not equal interest earned. (b) is incorrect because the bond interest rate is but one component of the interest calculation. (d) is incorrect because, like (a), cash received is not synonymous with interest earned during the period.

8. a. In both the planning and review stages of the audit, analytical procedures are for the purpose of identifying abnormalities. In audit review, the objective is to determine that all planning stage suspicions have been satisfactorily resolved and that no new abnormalities have surfaced for which the auditor has not gained satisfaction. (b) is simply a definition of substantive audit testing. (c) describes procedures that should be performed prior to audit review. (d) describes procedures that are not cost effective, inasmuch as weak controls should not be tested.

9. c. Section AU 560.12 is quite explicit as to procedures the auditor should perform in searching for subsequent events. Of the choices, only (c) is included in the listing. Moreover, (a) and (d) are procedures applicable to the following year's audit and are not relevant to the current year.

10. c. Assessing the validity of conclusions reached is analogous to evaluating the adequacy of evidence obtained. If sufficient, competent evidence has been obtained, application of analytical procedures, as part of audit review, should produce no significant abnormalities that have not been resolved to the auditor's satisfaction. (a) is incorrect because analytical procedures do not produce evidence from details. (b) is incorrect because this statement defines the pur-

pose for applying analytical procedures in the planning stage of the audit, while the question relates to the review stage. (d) is incorrect because other procedures are more relevant than analytical procedures in evaluating the ability of a client to continue as a going concern.

11. c.   Inventory pledging as loan collateral requires disclosure either in the body of the financial statements or in a footnote.

12. d.   Although (a), (b), and (c) are suggested, only (d) is required by AICPA Professional Standards. (See AU Section 333.)

13. c.   The purpose of the client representation letter is to emphasize that the financial statements are the primary responsibility of management. (a), (b), and (d) are incorrect because they incorrectly imply that the letter somehow reduces the auditor's responsibility and/or risk.

14. b.   Recalculating interest on long-term debt provides independent verification as to the proper valuation of interest expense for the period and accrued interest payable at the balance sheet date. This procedure, therefore, is most likely to be applied, at least on a test basis. (a) is incorrect because long-term debt should approximate net present value, but not market value, as of the balance sheet date. (c) is incorrect because auditors do not need to verify the existence of individual holders of long-term debt. (d) is incorrect because long-term debt erroneously included in the accounts payable subsidiary ledger is misclassified; but it is not unrecorded.

15. d.   An arm's-length borrowing transaction between independent parties is not likely to include an interest rate significantly below the market rate. The transaction described in (d), therefore, is evidence of a possible related-party transaction. Although (a), (b), and (c) are of interest to the auditor, they do not suggest the existence of related-party transactions.

16. d.   (d) is correct because management has primary responsibility for the fairness of financial presentation. Management, therefore, should be responsible for evaluating litigation, claims, or assessments. The lawyer's letter is for the purpose of reviewing management's evaluations and reporting directly to the auditors and either corroborating or disagreeing with those evaluations.

17. c.   The purpose of the client representation letter is to emphasize to management that fairness of financial presentation, i.e., adherence to both measurement and disclosure aspects of GAAP, is primarily their responsibility. Of the choices, only (c), disclosure of compensating balances and other restrictions, is required by GAAP. (a) is incorrect because material internal control weaknesses may be present and do not necessarily preclude an audit in accordance with GAAS. (b) is incorrect because sufficiency of evidence does not guarantee an unqualified opinion. (d) is incorrect because management acknowledgment of responsibility for employees' illegal actions has no impact on financial statement assertions.

18. d.   Generally accepted accounting principles require that retained earnings restrictions be disclosed either parenthetically or in footnotes to the financial statements. This procedure, therefore, supports the presentation and disclosure assertion.

19. d.   The auditor must identify related parties and audit related-party transactions to determine that the financial statements properly reflect the substance of the transactions. Understanding the subsidiary's relationship to the total entity is a necessary prerequisite if the auditor is to distinguish between form and substance of the transactions between the related parties. (a) is incorrect because understanding the relationship does not facilitate audit of balances as of concurrent dates. (b) and (c) are incorrect because arm's-length transactions and transactions that would have taken place if the parties were not related do not pose problems for the auditor.

CHAPTER 14

1. a.   AICPA Professional Standards do not require the CPA to justify the appropriateness of the other basis—only whether the statements conform to the other basis. (b), (c), and (d) are incorrect because these matters must be covered in the auditor's report.

2. c.   AICPA Professional Standards require the CPA to state that any basis other than generally accepted accounting principles, used for evaluating fairness, is a comprehensive basis other than GAAP. (a) is incorrect because the financial statements are intended to be examined in accordance with GAAS. (b) and (d) are incorrect because the standards do not require the CPA to make reference to authoritative pronouncements describing the other basis or to justify the other basis.

3. a.   Audit risk is defined as the risk of expressing an unqualified opinion on financial statements that are materially misstated. (a) contains the only statement in the audit report referring directly to the risk of undetected error.

4. c.   A material scope limitation, resulting in insufficient audit evidence, should cause the auditor to either disclaim an opinion or to issue a qualified opinion. An unjustified accounting change is a departure from generally accepted accounting principles and should cause the auditor to issue either a qualified or adverse opinion. In both instances, if qualified, the opinion should contain the words "except for."

5. d.   Whenever a client prepares financial statements on a basis other than GAAP, and requests an audit, the CPA accepting the engagement should evaluate the financial statements according to whether they conform, in all material respects, to the other basis and issue a report referring to conformity with the basis. These reports are referred to in the professional standards as "special reports."

6. b.   A change in accounting principle, if agreed to by the auditor, does not constitute a departure from GAAP. Therefore, the opinion should be unqualified. An explanatory paragraph should be added after the opinion paragraph, however, referring to the footnote that describes the change. (a) is incorrect because an explanatory paragraph placed before the opinion paragraph designates a qualification of the audit opinion. (c) and (d) are incorrect because the change should not cause the auditor to qualify the opinion.

7. a.   If the information existed at the report date and could affect the audit report, the auditor has a responsibility to those persons relying on the financial statements to evaluate the information and reissue the audit report if deemed necessary. (b) is incorrect because it does not entail added inquiries or procedures. (c) and (d) are incorrect because the auditor does not have further responsibility for events occurring after the completion of audit field work.

8. d.   Inability to obtain sufficient competent evidence represents a scope limitation and, if material, should lead to a qualified or disclaimer of opinion.

9. c.   (c) describes the overriding goal of applying generally accepted accounting principles. (a) is incorrect because a change in accounting principle, if properly reflected, does not detract from GAAP. (b) is incorrect because the ASB does not approve accounting principles. (d) is incorrect because GAAP does not require entities in the same industry to use the same accounting principles.

10. a.   If the principal auditor controls the work of the other auditor, he/she may elect to assume full responsibility. (b) and (c) are incorrect because they describe conditions under which the principal auditor should choose to divide responsibility. (d) is incorrect because the principal auditor, if unable to obtain satisfaction as to the independence and professional reputation of the other auditors, should qualify or disclaim an opinion or refuse to be associated with the financial statements.

11. c.   When an auditor dual dates an audit report, an event occurring after the completion of field work has come to his/her attention that needs to be reflected in the financial statements. The later date refers only to the single event and extends no further responsibility to the auditor.

12. d.   The only phrase universally used in the opinion paragraph of a qualified opinion is "except for."

13. b.   (a) and (c) are incorrect because they describe information contained in the separate paragraph referred to in (b). (d) is incorrect because an uncertainty or scope limitation may lead to a disclaimer of opinion, but not to an adverse opinion.

14. a.   Inasmuch as the opinion is unqualified, given adequate disclosure, the explanatory paragraph follows the opinion paragraph. Moreover, professional standards require the use of the phrases "substantial doubt" and "going concern" in the explanatory paragraph.

15. d.   An "except for" qualified opinion is issued when the auditor discovers a departure from GAAP, or has gathered insufficient evidence to support an unqualified opinion. Neither of these circumstances exists in the present case. The uncertainty surrounding the client's ability to continue, however, could be sufficiently high to suggest a disclaimer of opinion.

16. b.   (a), (c), and (d) all describe conditions requiring a qualified, adverse, or disclaimer of opinion. (b), in contrast, assuming the financial statements clearly reflect and disclose the uncertainty, requires only an explanatory paragraph following the opinion paragraph.

17. a.   Inasmuch as Green obtained satisfaction by other means, no mention need be made in the auditor's report.

18. d.   (d) is the only action that relieves cash flows in the short run, and is therefore a mitigating factor. (a), (b), and (c) require added cash flows and therefore exacerbate, rather than mitigate, the situation.

19. a.   Assuming the foreign subsidiary's assets and income are material to the entity's combined financial position and results of operations, inability to obtain the audited statements constitutes lack of evidence sufficient to result in either a qualification or disclaimer of the auditor's opinion. (b) describes a departure from generally accepted accounting principles rather than a scope limitation. (c) and (d), as such, will not affect the auditor's opinion.

20. a.   Use of an inappropriate title is a departure from generally accepted accounting principles and the auditor should qualify the opinion accordingly.

21. d.   Inasmuch as an audit was not performed, the scope paragraph would only serve to mislead readers.

22. c.   All audit opinion qualifications, whether due to scope limitations or departures from GAAP, should be based on possible financial statement effects. (a) is incorrect because the limitation is not client-imposed. (b) and (d) are incorrect because there have been no departures from auditing standards and there is no indication of inadequate disclosure.

23. a.   FASB Technical Bulletins are listed in Category IB in the AICPA ranking of GAAP. AICPA Accounting Interpretations are also included in Category I but below FASB Technical Bulletins. FASB Statements of Financial Accounting Concepts and AICPA Technical Practice Aids are listed in Category II.

24. b.   Only information available at the date of the audit report, and that may have affected the audit report, would cause the auditor to inquire further to determine whether an audit report modification might be necessary. (a), (c), and (d) describe information that did not exist at the date of the audit report.

CHAPTER 15

1. d.   A financial forecast presents expected results, whereas a projection contains one or more hypothetical assumptions. A projection is more tentative than a forecast. Moreover, forecasted data represents management's best estimate of expected results. (a), (b), and (c) are incorrect because, although a projection may be based on these kinds of ranges, a forecast must be based on expected results.

2. a.   A compilation report provides no assurance. Therefore, expressing negative or limited assurance on compiled financial statements is prohibited by AICPA Professional Standards. (b), (c), and (d) are incorrect because reviews and comfort letters to underwriters are intended to provide limited assurance regarding the financial data reviewed.

3. d.   A financial projection, which a CPA has compiled, given its tentative nature, should be restricted to management and those parties with whom manage-

ment is negotiating directly. Distributing the projection to all stockholders violates the rule of restricted distribution. (a), (b), and (c) are incorrect because presumably these parties are in direct negotiation with management.

4. a. A CPA may accept an engagement to apply agreed-upon procedures provided (among other things) distribution of the report is restricted to the specified users. (See AICPA Professional Standards, Section AT 200.50.) (b) is incorrect because an examination presumes application of more than the agreed-upon procedures, and this is not required by AICPA guidelines. (c) is incorrect because determining the adequacy of the procedures is the responsibility of management, and not the CPA. (d) is incorrect because AICPA guidelines do not provide for giving negative assurance based on application of agreed-upon procedures.

5. d. If the significant assumptions are not disclosed, the forecast is not presented in accordance with AICPA guidelines, which expressly require inclusion of all major assumptions on which the forecast is based. Therefore, an adverse opinion is appropriate. (a) is incorrect because omission of the major assumptions is too material to warrant a qualification. (b) is incorrect because subject to opinions are not permitted by GAAS. (c) is incorrect because an unqualified opinion, in light of a major departure from the guidelines, is inappropriate.

6. b. Attestation occurs when the CPA expresses an opinion on the reliability of a written assertion by a third party. Only (b) results in an opinion related to an assertion. (a) is incorrect because EDP advice does not constitute an opinion as to the reliability of third-party assertions. (c) is incorrect because the CPA is attempting to comply with the tax laws in preparing the returns, but is not expressing an opinion on another's compliance. (d) is incorrect because a compilation, by definition, offers no assurance, and is therefore not a form of attestation.

7. b. A review consists mainly of inquiry and analytical procedures. (a) is incorrect because a bank transfer schedule is associated with an audit, but is beyond the scope of a review. (c) is incorrect because a review does not contemplate a study and evaluation of the client's existing internal control. (d) is incorrect because sales and purchases cutoff tests, like the bank transfer schedule, are procedures associated with an audit, but not with a review.

8. d. The CPA's review of a nonpublic entity consists mainly of making inquiries of management and employees and performing analytical procedures. (a) is incorrect because a compliance report is a form of attestation and therefore encompasses a broader spectrum of procedures than inquiry and analytical procedures. (b) is incorrect because a review of prospective financial statements is not permitted by AICPA guidelines. (c) is incorrect because a management advisory report is associated with a consulting engagement and is covered by AICPA guidelines for consulting engagements, rather than guidelines for accounting and review services.

9. d. Since a compilation provides no assurance, the CPA's responsibility is limited to reading the financial statements and ascertaining that obvious errors do not exist. (a) and (c) are incorrect because these procedures are associated with reviews but not compilations. (b) is associated with audits of financial statements.

10. c. A CPA with a direct financial interest in a client is considered to lack independence even where the interest is immaterial to the client's total capitalization. A CPA who lacks independence may compile financial statements, but may not review or audit those statements. (a) is incorrect because the CPA is not independent. (b) is incorrect because the CPA may be associated to the extent of compiling the financial statements. (d) is incorrect because a CPA who is not independent may not issue a review report.

11. d. Analytical procedures are associated with reviews, but not with compilations. (a), (b), and (c) are incorrect because all of these statements contain language recommended for inclusion in compilation reports.

12. d. A review of interim financial information entails applying limited procedures to the data to determine whether it needs to be modified to conform to GAAP. (a) is incorrect because interim data is not prospective. (b) is incorrect because CPAs do not express limited opinions. (c) is incorrect because the auditor's decision to perform substantive procedures prior to the balance sheet date is not contingent on a limited review of interim information.

13. a. In neither a compilation nor a review does the auditor evaluate internal control. (b) is incorrect because the accountant need not be independent to compile financial statements. (c) is incorrect because the accountant does express limited assurance upon completion of a review engagement. (d) is incorrect because the representation letter is not required in nonattest engagements.

14. d. Under Section AU 504.05, when an accountant is associated with unaudited financial statements, he/she must issue a disclaimer of opinion and has no responsibility to apply any procedures beyond reading the financial statements for obvious material misstatements.

15. b. An engagement to express an opinion on a client's internal controls is a form of attest engagement and must, therefore, conform to the standards relating to attest engagements. According to these standards and interpretations, a report on internal control must state that management is responsible for establishing and maintaining the controls. (a) is incorrect because, in an engagement to express an opinion on internal control, unlike an audit, the accountant is not attempting to rely on the controls. (c) is incorrect because auditing standards apply to audits only. (d) is incorrect because reports on internal control may be distributed generally.

16. a. According to the attestation standards, a CPA need not be independent in order to compile financial statements or financial forecasts. Moreover, the Statements on Responsibilities in Tax Practice do not require independence in preparing tax returns and in representing clients in tax court.

17. a. (a) defines attestation. Auditing is also a form of attestation but is covered by a separate set of standards. (b), (c), and (d) are incorrect because none requires a conclusion regarding the reliability of another party's assertion.

18. d. This choice describes the second standard of audit field work. For attestation engagements, other than audits, the CPA need not obtain an understanding of internal control. (In an engagement to express an opinion on internal control,

the CPA would need to gain a greater understanding of internal control than that contemplated by the second audit field work standard.)

19. c.   The AICPA defines attestation as "... a conclusion about the reliability of an ... assertion that is the responsibility of another party." (a) is incorrect because CPAs do not typically provide litigation support services. (b), assessing control risk, is an integral part of an audit engagement, but is not relevant to attestation engagements. (d), management consulting, is not a form of attestation.

20. b.   Even though the CPA is not conducting an audit, known departures from GAAP must be disclosed in a separate paragraph of the review report. (a) is incorrect because negative assurance is provided in cases where no material departures from GAAP have been detected. (c) and (d) are incorrect because these choices pertain only to audits.

CHAPTER 16

1. b.   A measure of performance is whether the department is over- or understaffed. Comparing the department's staffing with available industry standards is a means for making this determination. (a), (c), and (d) are incorrect because established industry staffing standards will shed no light on adequacy of internal control or the degree of compliance with laws and regulations.

2. a.   As a management advisor, the auditor is attempting to help the auditee to do a better job, thereby enhancing the status of the auditee. This approach facilitates auditee cooperation and promotes harmonious relations between auditor and auditee. (b), (c), and (d) are incorrect because they cast the auditor in the role of "policeman" and this role tends to promote disharmony and lack of cooperation.

3. c.   The purpose of a preliminary survey is to familiarize the audit team with the unit and activities being audited. This familiarity, of necessity, precedes and facilitates audit planning and program development. (a) and (b) are incorrect because operational audits vary so widely that prior audit reports and permanent files are not likely to contain useful information for planning purposes. (d) is incorrect because the long-range audit plan is unlikely to contain the level of detail needed to plan the current audit and develop audit programs.

4. a.   Since operational auditing focuses on whether established objectives are being attained, a knowledge of departmental objectives is a necessary prerequisite to planning the audit and developing audit programs. (b) is incorrect because financial data may be examined as part of the audit, but is not particularly useful in setting audit objectives. (c) and (d) are incorrect because, like financial data, activity reports showing rental information and perpetual inventory listings are not very useful in setting audit objectives.

5. a.   If the auditor properly enlists the cooperation of the auditee, obtaining agreement as to audit conclusions will likely lead to a commitment by the auditee to take corrective action, and the audit report should state this. (b) and (c) are incorrect because they are untrue and represent improper compromises by the auditor. (d) is incorrect because if management has agreed with the

auditor's conclusions and recommendations, this should be stated in the audit report.

6. d.   Confidentiality generally precludes auditor reporting of fraud outside the company. However, various laws and regulations as well as the Code of Professional Conduct make exceptions for the conditions listed in this question.

7. c.   SAS Nos. 74 and 75 discuss expansion of the client representation letter as it applies to compliance audits of state and local governmental units. Of the four choices given in this question, only (c) is required by these SASs.

8. b.   Governmental audits, as performed by such agencies as the General Accounting Office, are very broad based. As such they frequently test for compliance, efficiency, and effectiveness as evidenced by program results.

9. a.   The GAO "yellow book" standards specifically require that the auditor report on the entity's compliance with laws and regulations imposed by applicable assistance programs, and on the entity's internal control system. (b), (c), and (d) are not contained in the yellow book standards.

10. b. Since a principal objective of the audit is to determine compliance with laws governing the assistance programs, detection of material noncompliance requires a qualified or adverse opinion. (a) is incorrect because of the materiality of the particular noncompliance. (c) is incorrect because a disclaimer is appropriate only where the auditor has not obtained sufficient evidence to determine compliance. (d) is incorrect because limited assurance is not permitted in compliance audits under the Single Audit Act.

11. d. Analytical procedures consist of auditing by comparison. In this instance comparing the current period's rental revenue with those of the previous period, and comparing the difference with operating costs passed on to lessees, is the most effective way to determine reasonableness.

12. c. The only effective means to identify personality conflicts is to engage in discourse with the relevant parties.

13. a. A sound internal control system requires written authorizations. Examining the pertinent documents, such as project authorizations, and minutes of meetings of the board of directors and the executive committee should provide the needed evidence.

14. a. The relevant documents are the city ordinance prohibiting such transactions, conflict of interest statements from elected city officials as to outside affiliations, and a list of vendors with whom the city conducted business.

15. d. Recalculating the actual rate of return and comparing with the planned rate is a form of analytical procedures.

16. b. A site inspection of the mailroom at various hours in a typical working day should enable the auditor to determine adequacy of utilization.

17. a. Under Section 325 of Generally Accepted Auditing Standards, the auditor is required to communicate reportable conditions; however Government Auditing Standards require a written report on the internal control system in all audits.

18. c.   Although Hill is responsible for reporting on internal control and detecting material weaknesses, his responsibility regarding the financial statements is to detect violations that would have a material effect on the assertions contained therein.

19. d.   Under Government Auditing Standards, the auditor must include significant design deficiencies in the reportable conditions letter to management and appropriate legislative and regulatory bodies.

20. a.   Under Government Auditing Standards, the CPA must give positive assurance on those items that were tested and must provide negative assurance on items not tested.

glossary

(Numbers in parentheses denote chapter(s) in which the term is used.)

A

Ability to continue as a going concern (14) The ability of an entity to continue to meet its obligations as it matures.

Access controls (6) Controls that limit access to assets, documents, computer files, programs, documentation, and hardware.

Account (4) A reference to financial statement components as representations of the underlying substance to which they relate.

Account distribution (8) The accounts debited and credited in the recording of a given transaction.

Account distribution errors (8) Debits or credits to incorrect accounts during the recording of a given transaction.

Account versus substance (4) This term differentiates between the representation of something and the thing itself. For example the account, "raw materials inventory" represents the investment in the physical items of inventory.

Accountability controls (6) Control procedures that fix responsibility for the custody of assets, documents, accounting records, and elements of electronic databases.

Accounting and Review Services Committee (2) A committee of the AICPA charged with promulgating standards and interpretations governing nonattest engagements, such as compilations and reviews.

Accounting estimates developed by management (4) Of particular concern to the auditor, these estimates relate to such financial statement components as product warranty, bad debts, pensions, and compensated absences. Auditing standards outline auditor requirements in evaluating the reasonableness of the estimates.

Accounting manual (6) A set of instructions and definitions that describe the kinds of transactions affecting the debit and credit sides of each of an entity's accounts, and gives instructions for the proper recording of unique transactions. The accounting manual, together with the chart of accounts, facilitates proper recording of an entity's transactions and events.

Accounting symmetry (13) A state whereby both sides of a transaction have been consistently recorded in accordance with GAAP. Auditors are concerned with symmetry when examining intercompany and intracompany transactions.

Accounting system (6) The methods and records established to identify, assemble, analyze, classify, and disclose components of financial statements.

Accounts payable confirmation (12) *See* confirmation of accounts payable

Accounts receivable aging analysis (11) A schedule displaying customers' account balances by length of time outstanding. As an audit tool, the aging analysis facilitates evaluation of the adequacy of the client's allowance for uncollectible accounts.

Accuracy controls (6) Controls that support the reliability of recorded transactions. Examples of accuracy controls are assignment of competent persons to tasks involving account distribution and cost allocation, and a system of double check.

Achieved precision (10) The calculated range within which the true value of the population most likely falls.

Adverse opinion (14) An audit opinion issued whenever financial statements contain departures from GAAP which are too material to warrant only a qualification.

Aggregate materiality (5) The total effect of two or more errors each of which, by itself, is not material.

Agreed-upon procedures (15) A situation in which the CPA and the client have agreed that procedures be applied either to specified elements of the financial statements or to nonfinancial statement subject matter. Application of the agreed-upon procedures does not provide sufficient evidence to support either an opinion or limited assurance on the specified elements. Examples are bank directors' examinations, examinations for proposed acquisitions, and examinations for creditors' committees or trustees in bankruptcy proceedings.

AICPA/FTC Consent Agreement of 1991 (2) An agreement entered into by the AICPA and the Federal Trade Commission whereby the Institute agrees to permit greater latitude to members regarding the form of organization, advertising, firm name, referral commissions, and contingent fees.

AICPA Quality Control Standards Committee (3) The body responsible for issuing Statements on Quality Control Standards.

Allocation (4) Allocation, in an accounting sense, is the process of distributing an outflow between asset and expense; and distributing an inflow between liability and revenue.

Allowance for sampling risk (10) A statistical sampling term meaning the sum of basic precision plus the incremental allowance for sampling risk. Also referred to as "achieved precision" or "computed precision."

Alpha risk (9 and 10) The risk of incorrect rejection of a population based on the results of sampling.

Alteration of accounts (6) A means of concealing misappropriation whereby the perpetrator changes the balance in one or more accounts. For example, to conceal misappropriation of unrecorded cash receipts from customers, the dishonest employee might debit "allowance for doubtful accounts" and credit "accounts receivable" for the missing amounts.

Alteration of substance (6) A means of concealing misappropriation whereby the perpetrator changes the physical substance underlying the misstated account balance(s). For example, to conceal an inventory overstatement, the perpetrator might temporarily substitute similar goods for stolen inventory.

Analysis of interbank transfers (11) An examination of cash transfers between two or more bank accounts for a few days before and after the balance sheet date. The purpose of the analysis is to assist in detecting year-end kiting and other forms of errors or fraud.

Analytical evidence (4) Audit evidence obtained by studying and comparing relationships among data. GAAS requires the auditor to apply analytical procedures in both the planning and review stages of the audit.

Anticipated error (10) A term used in PPS sampling—the amount of error expected by the auditor.

Application controls (8) Control procedures designed to achieve specific control objectives. Application controls relate to individual computerized accounting applications.

Assertions (1 and 15) Representations of management as to the fairness of the financial statements.

Assessed level of control risk (7) That level of control risk used by the auditor, in conjunction with the assessed level of inherent risk, in determining the detection risk to accept for a financial statement assertion and, accordingly, in determining the nature, timing, and extent of substantive tests.

Asset management ratios (4) Calculations designed to show how effectively management has controlled operating assets.

Asset safeguards (6) Procedures, which are part of the overall control structure, designed to protect the entity's assets. Safeguards may be further classified as to "limited access" controls and "accountability" controls.

Assurance services (1 and 15) Independent professional services that improve the quality of information or its context for decision makers.

Attestation (1 and 15) Any service performed by a CPA resulting in a written communication that expresses a conclusion about the reliability of a written assertion that is the responsibility of another party.

Attestation standards (2 and 15) Standards defining the quality of attest services other than audits; for example, reports on internal control or compliance with contractual requirements.

Attribute (9) A characteristic of interest in sampling. In auditing applications, attributes usually assume the form of types of errors having a material impact on control risk assessment.

Attribute sampling (9) A sampling approach that estimates the frequency of events. As used for control testing purposes, this method estimates the upper error limit, expressed as a percentage, for specified attributes related to a population of documents.

Audit adjustments (4) Journal entries proposed by the auditor to the client. The purpose of the entries is to correct the financial statements for material errors discovered during the examination.

Audit committee (1 and 3) A committee of the board of directors comprised mainly of outside directors having no management ties to the organization.

Audit conclusions and recommendations (16) Culmination of the audit field work where the auditor has collected and evaluated all necessary evidence and discussed the findings with the auditee.

Audit effectiveness (10) Related to beta risk and the sufficiency and competence of audit evidence, audit effectiveness is reduced if the auditor gathers too little evidence.

Audit efficiency (10) Related to alpha risk and the sufficiency and competence of audit evidence, audit efficiency is reduced if the auditor gathers too much evidence.

Audit evidence (1 and 4) The underlying accounting data and all corroborating information available to the auditor.

Audit field work (1) That part of the audit performed mainly on the client's premises.

Audit findings (16) The results the auditor found during the audit process.

Audit objectives (4) Relating to management's financial statement assertions of existence or occurrence, completeness, rights and obligations, valuation or allocation, and presentation and disclosure, audit objectives are goals to be attained in completing an audit. Audit objectives may be classified as information system objectives and transaction and balance objectives.

Audit of client's environment (4) That part of the audit that concentrates on assessing inherent risk and control risk through study of the business and industry, application of analytical procedures, and study and evaluation of internal control policies and procedures pertaining to an audit.

Audit of transactions and balances (4) That part of the audit that concentrates on gathering and evaluating evidence in support of recorded transactions and events. (Also referred to as substantive audit testing.)

Audit planning (1, 4, and 5) The process of assessing audit risk, identifying audit resources, and developing audit programs.

Audit program (1 and 4) An audit plan containing the procedures designed to achieve the audit objectives developed during the planning phase of the audit. Audit programs are usually classified according to transaction cycles.

Audit reclassifications (4) Entries (usually affecting a single account) to ensure proper presentation of items in the financial statements. The reclassifications are not posted by the client to the accounts, but rather are displayed only in the auditor's working trial balance—usually in a column separate from audit adjustments. Examples of reclassifications are credit balances in customers' accounts and current installments of long-term indebtedness.

Audit report (1) The mechanism for communicating the results of the audit to interested users. The standard audit report contains three paragraphs—an introductory paragraph, a scope paragraph, and an opinion paragraph.

Audit risk (1, 4, and 5) The probability of rendering an unqualified opinion on financial statements that are materially misstated.

Audit risk analysis (1) A methodical approach to identifying and assessing the components of audit risk, and allocating audit resources to those subsets of transaction cycles presenting the highest risk levels.

Audit trail (4) A "stream" of evidence that permits one to trace a transaction or event forward from its inception to the appropriate ledger account(s) or, conversely, to vouch from the ledger account to the inception of the transaction.

Audit workpapers (4) The record of evidence that the auditor has gathered and evaluated in support of the audit opinion.

Auditing (1) A systematic process of objectively obtaining and evaluating evidence regarding assertions and communicating the results to interested users.

Auditing around the computer (8) Assessing control risk by comparing input and output and ignoring the specifics of how the computer processes data.

Auditing standards (2) Define the quality of the audit and consist of three general standards, three field work standards, and four reporting standards.

Auditing through the computer (8) Identifying and testing programmed controls used in processing specific applications.

Auditing with the computer (8) Using the computer to assist in gathering and evaluating audit evidence.

Auditor/client conference (13) A meeting with the top officers of the client entity, convened by the auditor. The purpose of the meeting is to present the client with a set of proposed audit adjustments and reclassifications, along with suggested footnote disclosures. Reportable conditions (internal control weaknesses) are also covered during this meeting.

Auditor independence (2) A state of separation between the auditor and client management. Independence consists of two aspects—independence in fact, which is a state of mind; and independence in appearance, which precludes the auditor from serving in any capacity that would convey to the public an apparent compromise of independence (such as serving on the client's board of directors).

B

Balanced audit approach (11) An approach to substantive audit testing designed to avoid overemphasizing either overstatement or understatement at the expense of the other. This approach tests assets and expenses for overstatement, and liabilities and revenues for understatement.

Bartered web-site advertising (11) A practice prevalent among dot-com companies that involves the trading of advertising with other dot-com companies.

Base case system evaluation (BCSE) (8) BCSE is a special application of the test data approach to control testing whereby a comprehensive set of test data is developed to test all possible data processing conditions within a given application.

Basic precision (10) BV × RF (book value times the reliability factor). Used in probability-proportional-to-size sampling to represent the precision range assuming zero errors.

Batch processing (8) A data processing system in which transactions are accumulated and processed in groups, as contrasted with a real-time system in which transactions are processed as they occur.

Beta risk (9 and 10) The risk of incorrectly accepting a population value based on the results of sampling.

Bill of lading (7) A document describing goods shipped to customers. The document should be signed and dated by the carrier, thereby providing evidence of shipment.

Budget and time summary (1 and 5) An audit planning and control device that classifies projected and actual time according to audit staff level.

Business risk (6) The risk that an entity's business objectives will not be attained as a result of the external and internal factors, pressures, and forces brought to bear on the entity.

C

Cash receipts cutoff (11) A set of procedures to ensure that cash receipts have been recorded in the proper accounting period. The procedures include counting and listing cash at year end; tracing ending cash to the cash receipts record and the cutoff bank statement; examining cash receipts listings, journal entries, and bank deposit tickets for a few days before and after the balance sheet date; and confirming bank balances directly with banks.

CBIS manager (8) The person in charge of the data processing function.

Centralized data processing (8) Processing controlled by a data processing group that records the transactions at a central location utilizing one or more large computers.

Chart of accounts (6) A listing of account numbers and titles for all accounts appearing in the general ledger, as well as in the detail ledgers. The chart of accounts, together with the accounting manual, facilitate proper recording of transactions and events.

Check digit (8) A value computed by a formula when data are entered into a data processing system, then recomputed and compared to the original value whenever the field is used. Check digits detect data entry errors.

Chief Accountant of the SEC (3) An appointed official of the Securities and Exchange Commission, the chief accountant is responsible for investigating alleged "audit failures," overseeing financial reporting practices of public companies, and monitoring the activities of the Financial Accounting Standards Board, as well as the peer review programs of the SEC Practice Section of the Division for CPA Firms.

Circular OMB A-133 (16) This circular was issued by the U.S. Office of Management and Budget in 1991 and amended in 1996. It interprets the Single Audit Act of 1984 (as amended in 1996) and sets forth requirements relative to compliance audits of state and local government entities, colleges and universities, and other not-for-profit entities receiving over $300,000 of federal financial assistance in a single fiscal year.

Civil liability (3) Liability to third persons who are not parties to a contractual agreement. Under common law, auditors are liable to third-party financial statement users for gross negligence and fraud in the conduct of an examination.

Client acceptance (1 and 5) A decision process relating to a CPA's determination of whether to continue servicing an existing client or accept a new client. Inputs to the process include evaluating management integrity, as well as the CPA's competence to complete the engagement.

Client-imposed scope restriction (14) A scope restriction imposed by management or circumstantially imposed.

Client representation letter (13) A letter obtained by the auditor from the client confirming the fairness of the representations and the adequacy of informative disclosures contained in the financial statements.

Code of corporate conduct (6) A written statement defining conflicts of interest, illegal acts, improper payments, and other behavior considered unacceptable to the entity.

Code of Professional Conduct (2) Principles and rules of conduct formulated by the AICPA to provide guidance to the CPA in the performance of all types of professional accounting and auditing services.

Codification of Professional Standards (2) A project whereby the AICPA has codified all professional standards relating to the practice of public accounting. The codification consists of sections containing abbreviations and section numbers according to the various types of public accounting service rendered by CPAs.

Collateral (13) Security for loans or other forms of indebtedness. In conducting an audit, the CPA must determine that the value of collateral is adequate to prevent material loss from loan defaults.

Collusion (6) One of the limitations inherent in a given system of internal control, collusion involves two or more individuals working together to effect misappropriation and concealment.

Comfort letter (3 and 15) A letter issued by the CPA at the request of the underwriter to assist the underwriter in conducting a due-diligence review. The letter commonly covers such matters as the independence of the CPA, compliance of the audited statements with SEC requirements, and unaudited financial data. If analytical procedures have been applied to the unaudited data, the CPA may give negative (limited) assurance in the comfort letter with respect to the data.

Commissions and referral fees (2) Fees charged by the auditor for referrals. The AICPA has seen fit to discourage this charging relating to audits and other attest engagements, as well as to tax services and compilations where third-party use of the financial statements is expected.

Common size financial statements (4) Financial statements that express all components as a percentage of a common base, such as a percent of total assets on a common size balance sheet, or a percent of net sales on a common size income statement.

Communication (6) Clear job descriptions, accounting manuals, policy and procedures manuals, and employee training programs are examples.

Communication with audit committee (13) A GAAS requirement that compels the auditor to convey to the audit committee, preferably in writing, certain specified matters discovered in the course of the audit.

Communication with predecessor auditor (3 and 5) Occurs when an entity changes auditors and the new (successor) auditor initiates contact with the prior (predecessor) auditor. The successor auditor must attempt to contact the predecessor after obtaining the client's permission. Matters to be discussed might include reasons for the change in auditors, management integrity, prior disagreements between management and auditors, and difficulties encountered in conducting audits in the past.

Compensating balance requirements (13) Provisions in loan agreements requiring the borrower to maintain minimum cash balances with the lending institution.

Compensating controls (6 and 7) A control that remedies a control weakness suggested by the absence of an accuracy or safeguard control at a specified control point.

Competent evidence (4) Competence determines the adequacy of audit evidence and is a function of validity (quality) and relevance.

Compilation (15) A professional service in which the CPA presents information that is the representation of management without undertaking to express any assurance on the statements.

Completeness (1 and 4) A state in which the financial statements contain the results of all transactions that have occurred since the inception of the entity.

Completeness tests (8) Routines that determine that all necessary fields contain data.

Compliance attestation (15) Attestation that concerns testing and reporting on conformity with laws and regulations.

Compliance auditing (1) Testing and reporting on conformity with laws and regulations relating to a specific entity or activity.

Compliance controls (6) Relates to the entity's compliance with applicable laws and regulations.

Comprehensive basis of accounting other than GAAP (14) An accounting basis not in conformity with generally accepted accounting principles; for example, financial statements prepared to conform to the financial reporting requirements of a regulatory body, financial statements prepared on a tax basis, and financial statements prepared on a cash basis.

Computed precision (10) As contrasted with desired precision, the precision range based on the results of statistical sampling.

Computer audit specialist (8) An employee of the CPA firm who, typically, will have served on the audit staff for a period of time, followed by specialized training in computer system design and control and CBIS auditing.

Computer editing (8) The process of including programmed routines for computer checking as to validity and accuracy of input.

Computer operators (8) Persons within the CBIS function who process transactions through the system in accordance with the operator instructions for the application being updated.

Conditioned telecommunication lines (8) Used in transmitting data over long distances, conditioned telecommunication lines are clearer and less likely to produce loss through partial outages.

Confidence level (10) The likelihood that the sample range contains the true value; synonymous with reliability. It is based on the degree of confidence the auditor wishes to place in the sampling results.

Confidential client information (2) As defined by the Code of Conduct, confidential client information encompasses all information obtained by the CPA in the course of an audit. That is, the CPA may not disclose information to third parties unless it is necessary to a fair presentation of the audited financial statements.

Confirmation evidence (4) Audit evidence obtained directly from third parties, external to the client.

Confirmation of accounts payable (12) The act of obtaining evidence of completeness and valuation directly from creditors.

Confirmation of accounts receivable (11) The act of obtaining evidence of existence, ownership, and valuation directly from customers.

Confirmation of securities (13) Determining, by obtaining direct verification from the holder, that securities purported to be owned by the client at the balance sheet date exist and are indeed owned by the client. The holder may be a bank, a brokerage firm, or a lender holding the securities as collateral for an existing loan.

Consistency (14) A state of using the same accounting principles during the current period as were used in the immediately preceding period.

Constructive fraud (3) Negligence so gross as to border on intentional deceit. Invoked by the law when the auditor appears to ignore that which was obvious, or if the auditor has no reason to believe that the financial statements fairly present financial position, results of operations, and cash flows. (*See also Ultramares vs. Touche* in the appendix to Chapter 3.)

Consulting services (2) Services, other than auditing and other forms of attestation, performed by CPAs for their clients. Consulting services include such engagements as analyzing an accounting system, reviewing a profit plan, installing a computer system, analyzing a merger proposal, and providing staff for computer programming services.

Contingent fees (2) Fees based on findings or outcomes. Contingent fees are prohibited in auditing and other attestation engagements.

Continuing auditor (14) One who has audited the financial statements of the current period and one or more consecutive periods immediately prior to the current period.

Continuing professional education (3) A means for CPAs to keep abreast of changes occurring within the profession.

Continuous auditing (1 and 8) An auditing approach whereby the auditor tests controls and transactions at frequent intervals throughout the year. Especially applicable to clients with complex CBIS accounting applications.

Contractual liability (3) Liability to the client resulting from the contractual agreement between the CPA and the client. Contractual liability encompasses ordinary negligence, as well as gross negligence and fraud.

Contributory negligence (3) A defense frequently invoked in breach of contract cases involving employee fraud, whereby the auditor counters the client's charges of negligence by claiming that the client's own negligence gave rise to the misappropriation and concealment.

Control activities (6) Policies and procedures that help ensure management directives are carried out. They also help ensure that necessary actions are taken to address risks to the achievement of entity objectives.

Control environment (6) The collective effect of various factors on establishing, enhancing, or mitigating the effectiveness of specific policies and procedures.

Control point (7) The moment at which an error or fraud could occur in capturing and processing data or at which assets need to be safeguarded against loss from theft or other causes.

Control risk (5) The risk that material errors or fraud are not prevented or detected by the internal financial control system.

Control testing (7 and 8) An approach to further reducing the assessed level of control risk by testing a sample of transactions and estimating pertinent error rates. Control testing may assume the form of observation, reprocessing, or document testing.

Control total (8) A calculated total to be compared with output.

Corroborating information (4) Audit evidence consisting of such documentation as canceled checks, bank statements, sales invoices, vendors' invoices, vouchers, time cards, requisitions, purchase orders, bills of lading, and shipping orders. Auditor-developed evidence, such as confirmations, reconciliations, calculations, and observation, also is considered corroborating information.

Cost–benefit (4) The process of determining that the benefit of an act or series of acts exceeds the cost of performing the act(s). In auditing, cost–benefit analysis is applied in selecting among alternate procedures for achieving stated audit objectives. It also is applied in determining whether to test control procedures for the purpose of lowering the assessed level of control risk.

Current file (4) Those audit workpapers that support the period currently being examined.

Cutoff (12) The act of recording transactions in the proper accounting period.

Cutoff bank statement (11) A bank statement covering a two- or three-week period immediately following year end. If mailed directly to the auditor by the bank, the statement permits the auditor to examine evidence in support of the reconciling items appearing on the year-end bank reconciliation.

Cutoff tests (12) Substantive tests performed by the auditor to determine that transactions were recorded in the proper accounting period. These tests are applied to cash receipts and disbursements, sales, and purchases transactions. In performing the tests, the auditor examines substance, documents, and journal entries for agreement.

D

Data and procedural controls (8) Controls designed to manage daily computer operations. Two examples are a system of backup files and environmental controls.

Database management system (8) The software used by integrated database systems to control input, processing, and output.

Data control group (8) Persons within the CBIS function who distribute output, monitor reprocessing of errors, and compare input with output on a test basis.

Data encryption (8) An electronic data interchange control whereby an encoding key is used by the sender to "scramble" a message. The receiver then must have the corresponding key to unscramble and read the message. Encryption is designed to prevent unauthorized access to EDI systems.

Defense Contract Audit Agency (DCAA) (1) A federal agency that examines the records of entities fulfilling defense contracts for the federal government to determine that only those costs pertaining to the fulfillment have been charged to the contracts and that the entities have conformed to the contract terms.

Departure from designated principal (14) A departure from an accounting standard or principal promulgated by the body (currently FASB) designated by the Council of the AICPA.

Derivatives (13) Complex financial instruments whose values depend on the values of one or more underlying assets or financial indexes. The auditor must determine that the client has recognized all material losses from holding derivatives during periods when the prices of the related instruments have declined. The auditor also should ascertain adequacy of footnote disclosure regarding company policy relating to investments in derivatives.

Design phase auditing (8) Involvement of the auditor in designing the client's data processing system. The goal is to ensure inclusion of controls that will detect exception or unusual conditions and record and log information about the initiating transactions.

Desired precision (10) The range of precision specified by the auditor in developing a particular sampling plan. The desired range is a function of materiality and acceptable risk levels.

Detection controls (6) Internal controls that provide for a double check to locate significant errors and/or fraud after the fact.

Detection risk (5) The risk that errors or fraud that are not prevented or detected by the internal control system are not detected by the independent audit.

Difference estimation (10) A variables sampling method that calculates the average difference between the audited value and the client's book value and multiplies by the number of items in the population. The result is the estimated total difference between the audited and book values.

Direct attestation (15) Permits the CPA to express an opinion directly on the effectiveness of the client's internal control system.

Direct evidence (4) Evidence that permits the auditor to draw conclusions. Observing inventory, for example, provides the auditor with direct evidence as to the existence assertion.

Disclaimer of opinion (14) Inability to render an audit opinion because of lack of sufficient evidence or lack of independence.

Disclosure (4) Associated with the footnotes to the financial statements.

Discovery sampling (9) An orderly approach to locating a particular event. Discovery sampling is used in auditing to find an example of an error or fraud when the auditor's suspicions are aroused.

Discreditable act (2) An act that could lead to suspension or termination of the auditor. These include unauthorized retention of clients' records, discrimination in employment practices, failure to follow required standards in conducting government compliance audits, and unauthorized disclosure of CPA exam questions and answers.

Disposal of a segment (13) When a client reports a segment disposal for the period under examination, the auditor determines whether the transaction meets the requirements, as set forth in APBO No. 30.

Distributed data processing (8) Processing transactions at remote locations by microcomputers or terminals and transmitting to a home office mainframe via communication links. Additionally, the microcomputers may be linked to one another through a system of networking, thereby facilitating communication and permitting the sharing of workload among locations.

Divided responsibility (14) An audit reporting situation in which the principal auditors accept responsibility for the components audited by them, and other auditors are responsible for the subsidiaries audited by them.

Division for CPA Firms (3) A body created by the Securities and Exchange Commission and monitored by the Public Oversight Board, for the purpose of promoting quality and consistency in the rendering of professional services by CPAs.

Document examination and testing (7) The process of testing control procedures by selecting and examining documents and transactions for errors, and projecting error rates based on such examination and testing.

Document management system (8) Used in paperless office systems to scan, retrieve, and manage documents stored in computer file cabinets.

Documentary evidence (4) Evidence consisting of the accounting records and all of the underlying documentation supporting the transactions and events recorded in these records.

Document management systems (8) Software used to scan and retrieve documents that have been stored electronically.

Dual-dated audit report (14) An audit report containing a second date following the date of completion of audit field work. The second date pertains to a specific event that occurred subsequent to the completion of field work, and of which the auditor has become aware prior to the release of the audit report. For the report to be dual-dated, the event must be adequately disclosed in a footnote to the financial statements.

Due professional care (2) The act of exercising reasonable diligence in the conduct of auditing and other professional services.

E

Early revenue recognition (11) The act of recognizing revenues before they are earned or realized.

Echo check (8) A computer processing control whereby the computer sends the message back to the sender for verification. As used in electronic data interchange environments, the receiving computer returns the message to the sending computer for confirmation that information received is the same as information sent.

Economic substance (13) The "real" nature of a transaction, as opposed to its legal form. For example, in a sale and leaseback transaction between parties, the gain on sale by the lessee to the lessor may not have been realized in an "arms-length" transaction, notwithstanding conformity with the legal definition of a sale. Whenever legal form and economic substance are in conflict, economic substance should prevail.

EDGAR (14) An SEC electronic database that can be accessed at web site http://www.sec.gov/edaux/searches.htm and that contains all company filings with the SEC.

Effectiveness (16) A measure of productivity in utilizing an entity's resources. Related to management auditing, effectiveness is output oriented.

Efficiency (16) A measure of cost control in performing recurring functions within an entity. Related to operational auditing, efficiency is input oriented.

ElderCare (15) An assurance service wherein the CPA evaluates alternate types of services provided to elderly clients and their families.

Electronic commerce (8) Involves the trading of goods and services through the use of computers.

Electronic data interchange (EDI) (8) A technique whereby a company's computer system is linked to those of its suppliers and customers, and transactions, such as purchases, sales, cash receipts, and cash payments, may be initiated automatically by the system.

Electronic workpaper files (4) Audit workpapers prepared with the assistance of a computer.

Emerging Issues Task Force (3) A committee of the FASB, EITF consists of seventeen members from within and outside the accounting profession. Its purpose is to reach consensus on how to account for new and unusual financial transactions. Given SEC representation on the committee, its recommendations carry considerable weight with the FASB.

Emphasis of a matter (14) A fourth paragraph added after the opinion paragraph of the audit report. Used whenever the auditor wishes to bring a matter of importance that has already been adequately disclosed in the financial statements or footnotes to the financial statement reader's attention.

Engagement letter (1) A letter from the CPA to the client—signed by the client—clearly stating the mutual understanding of the nature of the engagement.

Errors (5) Unintentional mistakes. Errors may be further classified as to errors of omission and errors of commission.

Ethics (2) Moral principles that concern such characteristics as honesty and integrity, reliability and accountability, as well as all other aspects of right versus wrong behavior.

Ethics rulings and interpretations (2) Rulings and interpretations issued by the Executive Committee of the Professional Ethics Division of the AICPA, which represent further clarification of the principles and rules contained in the Code of Professional Conduct.

Evaluation criteria (16) Criteria that define the process or activity being audited. The term is associated with operational auditing. Identifying evaluation criteria is necessary if the auditor is ultimately to determine the cause of discovered inefficiencies.

Evidence (1) The underlying accounting data and all corroborating information available to the auditor.

Examination of debt agreements (13) Examination by the auditor of long-term liabilities (bonds, notes, leases, and mortgages payable), which are supported by contracts or agreements entered into by the client.

Examination of securities (13) Comparison by the auditor of serial numbers as recorded in the investment records with those appearing on the securities.

Existence or occurrence (1 and 4) A state in which all of the transactions reflected in the financial statements actually have occurred at or prior to the current year end.

Expansion factor (10) This is a term used in probability-proportional-to-size sampling. It is related to the reliability factor and provides for additional sampling error where some errors are expected.

Expectations gap (3) The disparity between users' and CPAs' perceptions of professional services, especially audit services rendered by CPAs.

Expected occurrence rate (9) The anticipated error rate. Used in attribute sampling.

Expenditure cycle (4) That transaction cycle comprising purchases, payroll, cash payments, operating expenses, inventories, plant assets, intangible assets, and accounts payable.

Expert systems (8) Software packages that extend to the computer the ability to make expert quality decisions within specialized domains.

Expert systems shell (8) A software package containing a knowledge representation framework of decision parameters. The shell is basically an expert system awaiting a knowledge base.

Explanatory paragraph between the scope and opinion paragraphs (14) A paragraph explaining the reasons for, and financial statement effects of (if determinable), a qualified or adverse audit opinion.

Explanatory paragraph following the opinion paragraph (14) A paragraph added after the opinion paragraph of the audit report for the purpose of elaborating on one or more of the following conditions: departure from a principle promulgated by the body designated by the AICPA council, material uncertainties, ability of the entity to continue as a going concern, a change in accounting principle, or emphasis of a matter.

External auditing (1) *See* independent auditing.

External regulation (3) Regulation of the accounting profession in the form of oversight and corrective action by the SEC and the courts.

F

Factual evidence (4) *See* direct evidence.

Federal financial assistance (16) Assistance given to state and local government entities, colleges and universities, and other not-for-profit entities. If they receive $300,000 or more in in a single fiscal year, they must be audited in accordance with the Single Audit Act of 1984 (as amended in 1996), in addition to GAAS and the yellow book standards.

Fiber optic cable (8) An information processing mechanism whereby data is transmitted in the form of high speed pulses of light.

Field work (1) *See* audit field work.

Field work standards (2) Those auditing standards that relate to the audit process.

Final audit (1) Those audit procedures performed after the balance sheet date, consisting primarily of tests of transactions and balances.

Financial reporting controls (6) Relates to the preparation of reliable published financial statements.

Financial statement assertions (6) Existence or occurrence, completeness, rights and obligations, valuation or allocation, and presentation and disclosure.

Financial statement auditing (1) A historically oriented evaluation for the purpose of attesting to the fairness of financial statement presentation.

Financial fraud (5) Misstatements of financial statements caused by intentional acts. Fraud may be further classified into misappropriation and misrepresentation.

Financing and investing cycle (4) That transaction cycle comprising borrowing from others, lending to others, interest expense, interest revenue, dividend revenue, notes payable, bonds payable, notes receivable, capital stock, and retained earnings.

Finite correction factor (10) A downward adjustment of sample size applied whenever the initial sample size exceeds a specified percentage of the population size.

Flat file system (8) An environment in which users own their own data and have exclusive access to and use of the data.

Float (11) The time lag for cash transfers between the disbursing bank and the payee bank. A term associated with kiting.

Forecast (15) A form of prospective financial statements that presents the entity's expected financial position, results of operations, and cash flows reflecting conditions expected to exist.

Foreign Corrupt Practices Act of 1977 (16) An act passed by Congress to prevent bribes and other illegal payments to foreign officials by public companies as a means for obtaining business. As such, the Act contains provisions requiring companies to maintain accurate accounting records and adequate internal control systems.

Form vs. substance (13) Form refers to the legal nature of a transaction or event; substance refers to the economic aspects of the transaction or event. When form and substance are in conflict relative to material transactions or events, substance should take precedence over form. Auditors are particularly alert to possible conflicts between form and substance when auditing related-party transactions.

Fraud (3 and 5) Intent to deceive.

Fraud on the market theory (3) The theory that if a fraudulent statement or act causes the market to price a security improperly, the parties responsible for the fraud can be held liable to any investor relying on the efficient market. Invoked by plaintiffs in negligence actions against CPAs and related to the "efficient market hypothesis."

Fraudulent financial reporting (1, 5, and 6) Deliberate attempts by management to misstate the financial statements by omitting significant information from the records, recording transactions without substance, or intentionally misapplying accounting principles.

Full responsibility (14) An audit reporting situation when one or more subsidiaries are audited by other CPAs, in which the principal auditor, after obtaining satisfaction as to the other CPAs' independence, professional status, and quality of work, may elect to assume responsibility for all work performed on the audit, including that of the other CPAs. Contrasted with *divided responsibility*.

G

General Accounting Office (GAO) (1 and 16) A federal agency reporting directly to Congress on the efficiency, effectiveness, and compliance of entities either receiving federal funds or under some degree of federal regulation.

General controls (8) Procedures designed to contribute to the achievement of specific control objectives through their interdependence with specific control procedures. General controls are broader in scope than application controls and relate to all or many computerized accounting activities.

General standards (2) Those auditing standards that relate to the character and competence of the auditor.

Generally accepted auditing standards (2) The set of standards developed by the Auditing Standards Board of the AICPA that defines the quality of independent audits.

Government compliance auditing (16) Testing and reporting on conformity with laws and regulations relating to recipients of federal financial assistance.

Governmental auditing standards (16) Standards set forth in the General Accounting Office's (GAO) "yellow book."

Gross negligence (3) Failure to exercise minimum care.

H

Hash total (8) A user control consisting of a meaningless sum (e.g., the sum of customer account numbers) to be compared with a computer generated total to determine that all records have been updated in a given computer processing run.

Header and trailer label information (8) A computer processing control whereby the file name, record counts, and other data are included for comparison purposes.

Hearsay evidence (4) Evidence consisting of answers to questions posed by the auditor to client personnel. This is the weakest form of audit evidence and usually must be further corroborated.

I

Inconsistency (1 and 14) A change in accounting principle from one period to the next requiring an explanatory paragraph following the opinion paragraph of the auditor's report.

Incorporation by reference (3) Directs the reader's attention to information included in the annual report to shareholders rather than reporting such information in Form 10-K.

Incremental precision allowance (10) The incremental allowance is calculated in probability-proportional-to-size sampling to express the increase in the precision range, given logical units containing error and having book values less than the sampling interval. The increment recognizes the increased standard error when projecting sample results to a larger interval.

Independence in fact vs. appearance (2) Independence in fact is a state of mind. Independence in appearance requires the auditor to avoid situations that appear to compromise auditor independence (such as serving on the client's board of directors).

Independence Issues Committee (3) A nine-member body composed of CPAs from accounting firms that audit SEC registrants; the committee was established for the purpose of monitoring the Independence Standards Board.

Independence Standards Board (2 and 3) A body established by the AICPA in 1997 for the purpose of setting independence standards for auditors of public companies. The board is responsible for issuing standards and rules that prevent public accounting firms from accepting engagements that could affect the quality and independence of their audits of public companies' financial statements.

Independent audit (1) An examination conducted by auditors who are independent of the persons whose assertions are being evaluated.

Indexing (4) A system of classifying and integrating audit workpapers according to a predetermined schemata.

Indirect attestation (15) A form of attestation wherein the CPA expresses an opinion on the reasonableness of management's assertions concerning the effectiveness of its internal control system.

Indirect evidence (4) Evidence that permits the auditor to infer certain states by examining the evidence, but that does not permit the auditor to draw conclusions from the evidence. For example, the existence of inventory on the client's premises provides conclusive evidence of existence, but only inferential evidence of ownership. Further evidence, in the form of documentation, must be obtained by the auditor to further support the ownership objective.

Individual item materiality (5) The impact of a single error or fraud on the financial statements.

Inferential evidence (4) *See* indirect evidence.

Information and communication (6) A system identifying the information requirements and creating an information system that provides the needed data and reports.

Information system (6) The system that produces the data appearing on the financial statements.

Information system elements (6) Those segments of an entity's internal control system designed to identify, capture, process, and report information in a reliable and timely manner.

Inherent limitations (6) Limitations causing an otherwise effective system of internal control to provide reasonable, rather than absolute, assurance of preventing and detecting errors and fraud. (*See also* collusion, management override, and temporary breakdown.)

Inherent risk (5) The susceptibility of an account balance or class of transactions to misstatement that could be material, assuming that there were no related internal controls.

Initial audit (4) A first-time audit. The client's financial statements may or may not have been audited in prior years by other CPAs.

Input controls (8) Controls concerned with the accuracy and completeness of data fed into the data processing system.

Input preparation group (8) Persons within the CBIS function who convert input data to a machine-readable form.

Institute of Internal Auditors (16) An organization of internal auditors formed to provide guidance in the practice of internal auditing.

Integrated database system (8) A system that updates many files—for example, sales, accounts receivable, and inventory—as transactions are entered into the system.

Integrated disclosure (3) An SEC provision that permits companies registered with the SEC to incorporate data by reference from the annual report to stockholders to Form 10-K filed with the SEC.

Integrated test facility approach (8) A means for auditing through the computer whereby the auditor creates a fictitious entity within the client's actual data files. Hypothetical data then are processed as part of the client's regular data processing activity. The auditor then compares the results with the anticipated results as a basis for evaluating control effectiveness.

Interim audit (1) Procedures applied prior to the client's year end, primarily for the purpose of lowering the assessed risk level.

Interim financial information (15) Financial statements or condensed information covering less than a year.

Internal auditing (1 and 16) An independent appraisal function established within an organization to examine and evaluate its activities as a service to the organization.

Internal control (1 and 6) The process effected by an entity's board of directors, management, and other personnel designed to provide reasonable assurance regarding the achievement of objectives. It consists of three parts—operations controls, financial reporting controls, and compliance controls, and five components—the control environment, risk assessment, control activities, information and communication, and monitoring.

Internal control checklist (7) A listing of controls necessary to provide reasonable assurance of effective internal control within a given transaction cycle subset.

Internal control flowchart (7) A means for documenting the auditor's understanding of internal control, the flowchart represents a pictorial presentation of the processing steps within a transaction cycle subset. Actions, documents, and people performing the control procedures are depicted in the flowchart.

Internal control memorandum (7) A narrative description of a transaction cycle, together with a statement describing control strengths and weaknesses.

Internal control questionnaire (7) A list of questions designed to cover all pertinent control points in a transaction cycle subset. "Yes" answers denote strengths; "no" answers denote weaknesses.

Internal evidence (4) Audit evidence, mainly documentary, obtained from within the client entity. Its validity is a function of existing internal control.

Introductory paragraph (14) The first paragraph of the standard audit report that identifies the financial statements covered by the audit report and clearly differentiates management's responsibility for preparing the financial statements from the auditor's responsibility for expressing an opinion on them.

Inventory confirmation (12) Evidence of inventory existence obtained directly by the auditor from third parties having custody of the client's inventory. This audit procedure typically is applied to inventory on consignment and to inventories in public warehouses.

Inventory cutoff (12) The state of consistency among the physical inventory, recorded sales, and recorded purchases whereby recorded purchases have been received and included in the physical inventory, and recorded sales have been shipped and excluded from the physical inventory.

Inventory cutoff tests (12) Substantive tests performed by the auditor to determine that purchases and sales transactions were recorded in the proper accounting period.

Inventory instructions (12) A set of directions for the purpose of ensuring a reliable physical inventory. The instructions are written by the client and reviewed by the auditor. They cover such matters as location and timing of inventory taking; procedures for counting, double-checking counts, and documenting the counts; and the auditors' participation as observers of the inventory.

Inventory in transit (12) Inventory en route to customers or from suppliers. Inventory in transit is of particular concern to the auditor at the client's year end. The auditor, by reference to freight terms, must determine whether the client owns the inventory, and if so, whether it has been properly included in the physical count.

Inventory observation (1 and 12) The performing of test counts, controlling the auditor's copies of the physical inventory documentation, and otherwise evaluating the year-end inventory taking by the client. Inventory observation requires that the audit team be present during the client's annual physical inventory.

Inventory pricing tests (12) A set of audit procedures designed to ascertain whether the client has properly costed the ending inventories.

Inventory tags or sheets (12) Instruments for documenting the physical inventory. The tags or sheets should be prenumbered and provide for a description of the inventory item, stock number, location, and condition.

Inventory test counts (12) Counts of the client's inventory performed by the auditor following the client's original counts and double checks.

Investment ledger (13) A subsidiary ledger containing the detail supporting the investment account in the general ledger.

K

Kiting (11) A type of misrepresentation fraud used to conceal bank overdrafts or cash misappropriations. Kiting occurs when a company draws a check on one bank for deposit in another bank but does not record the transaction, or records only a part of the transaction, before year end.

Knowledge base (8) The body of expert knowledge (tax, audit, CBIS) incorporated into an expert systems shell, thereby forming a workable expert system.

L

Lapping (11) A form of concealment that involves crediting current customer remittances to the accounts of customers who have remitted previously. The purpose is to keep all accounts current in order to avoid auditor suspicion.

Lawyer's letter (4 and 12) *See* letter of audit inquiry to client's legal counsel.

Lead schedule (4) A schedule that lists all of the general ledger accounts comprising a single line item on the financial statements.

Legal form (13) The nature of a transaction as defined in the law. Legal form may be at variance with the "real" nature (economic substance) of the transaction. When this occurs, substance should take precedence over form in the financial statements. (*See also* Continental Vending Machine Corporation [*U.S. vs. Simon*] case in the appendix following Chapter 3.)

Letter of audit inquiry to client's legal counsel (12) A letter obtained directly by the auditor from the client's outside legal counsel. The purpose of the letter is to provide evidence regarding pending litigation and the possible need for journal entries or footnotes relating to asserted and unasserted claims.

Leverage ratios (4) A set of calculations designed to portray the firm's financial flexibility. Examples of leverage ratios include debt/equity ratio and times interest earned.

Librarian (8) The staff member who maintains custody over master files and computer programs and permits access only on the basis of proper authority. Related to off-line storage of data and files.

Limited access controls (6) Control procedures that prevent other than authorized personnel from gaining access to specified assets, documents, and/or database elements.

Limited (negative) assurance (15) A report that expresses conclusions on the basis of a review, or other form of limited procedures.

Liquidity ratios (4) A set of calculations designed to indicate a firm's short-term debt paying ability. Examples are the current ratio and the quick ratio.

Loan defaults (13) Violations of loan agreements that could result in loan principal and interest becoming immediately due. Such defaults may assume the form of either violations of restrictive covenants or failure to meet principal or interest payments when due.

Logical sampling unit (10) A term used in PPS sampling to describe the item to which the randomly selected dollar attaches; for example, a customer account, a line item on an inventory listing, or a posting to a plant asset account.

M

Management auditing (16) An examination and evaluation of the activities of management. Also referred to as effectiveness or performance auditing.

Management letter (13) A letter from the auditor to the client covering all material auditor-discovered weaknesses in the client's internal controls. The purpose of the letter is to provide constructive suggestions to management concerning improvements in internal control.

Management override (6) One of the limitations inherent in a given system of internal control. Management override involves management circumvention of internal control for the purpose of perpetrating one or more fraudulent acts.

Management's assertions (6) Management's representations concerning data contained in the financial statements. The assertions include existence or occurrence, completeness, rights and obligations, valuation or allocation, and presentation and disclosure.

Management's discussion and analysis (14) A supplemental letter from management in the annual report to stockholders. The letter elaborates on the audited financial statements by explaining the more significant changes in financial statement components occurring during the year.

Materiality (4 and 5) As used in financial auditing, materiality relates to the impact of errors or fraud on the decisions of financial statement users.

Materiality threshold (5) The smallest aggregate level of errors or fraud that could be considered material to any one of the financial statements.

Mathematical evidence (4) Audit evidence consisting of calculations, recalculations, and reconciliations performed by the auditor. Mathematical evidence is a direct form of audit evidence.

Maximum control risk (7) A high assessed level of control risk suggesting a primarily substantive audit approach.

Mean per unit (10) A method of sampling for variables whereby a sample mean is calculated and extended to the population.

Minimum audit (6) The concept that requires the application of some minimum degree of substantive audit testing regardless of the effectiveness of the client's system of internal control. The concept of a minimum audit recognizes that effective internal control provides reasonable, but not absolute, assurance concerning the reliability of the financial statements.

Minimum care (3) The least amount of diligence expected of the CPA in performing accounting and auditing services, below which reckless misconduct may be construed.

Misappropriation (5) The fraudulent transfer of assets from the firm to one or more dishonest employees. The transfer is either preceded or followed by some form of concealment involving alteration of accounts or substance.

Misstatements due to commission (4) Inclusion of nonexistent items in the financial statements. Misstatements due to commission result in overstatement of financial statement components.

Misstatements due to omission (4) Misstatements resulting in understatements of financial statement components.

Monitoring (6) The checking of internal controls to ensure their effectiveness.

Multi-user system (8) A CBIS wherein functional and geographical units share a single operating system housed in a central location.

N

Negative confirmation (11) A form of accounts receivable confirmation that requests the customer to respond only in the event of disagreement with the reported balance.

Network monitoring software (8) Software designed to monitor data flow and detect weak points in hardware and software configurations that are likely to cause transmission errors.

Networking (8) The act of connecting two or more computers together for the purpose of communicating and sharing workloads.

Neural network (8) Computer systems designed to replicate the functioning of the human brain. Used by accounting firms to evaluate clients' internal control and to detect various types of fraud.

Nonstatistical sampling (9) A subjective approach to inference, in that mathematical techniques are not used consistently in determining sample size, selecting the sample, or evaluating sample results. Smaller populations, or populations containing items not so readily accessible by the auditor, are often more conducive to testing through nonstatistical sampling techniques.

Numeric field tests (8) Tests that determine only numeric data were entered in numeric fields, and that only alphabetic data were entered in alphabetic fields.

O

Observation (7) Control testing whereby the auditor is present during transaction processing and observes for proper functioning of pertinent controls at the input stage of transaction processing.

Omitted procedures (14) Necessary procedures not applied by the auditor. The term is used in the context of auditor discovery of the omission after the date of the audit report.

Ongoing monitoring (6) That part of the internal control monitoring mechanism that operates in a virtually automatic fashion. It is often referred to as "real-time" monitoring.

Online real-time processing system (8) A CBIS that processes transactions as they occur (some automatically), and several files (e.g., sales, accounts receivable, inventory) are updated simultaneously by a single transaction input.

Open items (13) Questions that have arisen during the audit for which answers were not immediately available. All open items should be cleared prior to completion of audit field work.

Operating effectiveness of financial reporting controls (7) Part of the auditor's assessment of control risk where control tests are performed. Operating effectiveness reflects how well controls functioned during the period under audit.

Operational audit report (16) This is the document summarizing the internal auditor's conclusions and recommendations resulting from an operational audit.

Operational auditing (1 and 16) A future-oriented, independent, and systematic evaluation performed by the internal auditor for management of the operational activities controlled by top-, middle-, and lower-level management for the purposes of im-

proving organizational profitability and increasing the attainment of the other organizational objectives. A subset of internal auditing, operational auditing reviews an entity's activities for efficiency and effectiveness.

Operations control (6) Relates to the effective and efficient use of the entity's resources.

Opinion paragraph (14) The paragraph in the audit report that reflects the auditor's findings.

Optical scanning devices (11) A computer hardware device that can read hard copy data and enter it into the computer without the need for "keyboarding."

Ordinary negligence (3) Failure to exercise reasonable care.

Output controls (8) Controls that are concerned with the verification and distribution of computer output.

P

Panel on Audit Effectiveness (3) A panel formed at the urging of SEC Chairman Arthur Levitt to determine whether the audit practices of CPA firms adequately serve the interests of investors and creditors.

Paperless office (8) An accounting system wherein optical scanners are used to transfer transaction documents to computer file cabinets.

Parallel simulation (8) A control testing technique that requires the auditor to create a set of application programs that simulate the processing system, and compare output from the real and simulated systems.

Passwords (8) A form of control over access to databases. Passwords are codes used for accessing various parts of the database. Some passwords permit read-only capability, while others permit updating of files (read and write capability).

Peer review (3) The examination of one professional's work by others in the same profession. The purpose is to promote quality in the performance of professional services through self-regulation.

Percentage-of-coverage rule (16) This rule applies to audits conducted under the Single Audit Act, and requires that at least 50% of federal expenditures be covered by the audit.

Periodic counts and comparisons (6) The act of comparing accounts and related substance on a recurring basis.

Permanent file (4) The file containing those audit workpapers that have ongoing significance.

Personal computer systems (8) Data processing systems utilizing personal computers (PCs). A PC is a small computer, ordinarily used by a single individual. PCs may be used as "stand-alone" computers or they may be connected to mainframe computers through a form of networking.

Personal computer audit packages (11) Software packages, either generalized or custom-designed, used to analyze client data and generally automate the audit. These packages assist the auditor in performing substantive testing.

Phases of processing (8) The steps required to process a given subset of a transaction cycle; for example, cash receipts from customers.

Physical evidence (4) Audit evidence consisting of everything that can be counted, examined, observed, or inspected. It provides as direct evidence, primary support for the existence assertion.

Pilot sample (10) Random selection of 30 to 40 items from the population. In mean per unit sampling, the pilot sample is drawn for the purpose of estimating the standard deviation, which, in turn, is used in the sample size equation.

Planning and supervision (2) The act of predetermining the audit approach and directing and reviewing the activities of assistants assigned to the audit. The major tasks involved in planning and supervision are usually assigned to the in-charge senior auditor.

Plant assets lead schedule (12) An audit lead schedule workpaper listing the components of the "plant assets" line item from the working trial balance.

Population size (9) The size of the entire process being sampled.

Positive assurance (15) A report that expresses conclusions on the basis of an audit.

Positive confirmation (11) A form of accounts receivable confirmation that requests the customer to respond as to agreement or disagreement with the reported balance.

Preaudit conference (1, 4, and 5) A meeting of the audit team prior to commencing field work for the purpose of increasing the effectiveness of the audit by discussing the results of risk analysis with the staff assigned to the audit.

Precision (9 and 10) A statistical sampling term defined as the range within which the true answer most likely falls.

Predecessor auditor (14) One who has audited the financial statements of one or more consecutive periods immediately prior to the current period, but who has not audited the financial statements of the current period.

Preliminaries (1) Inquiries occurring at the beginning of the audit process. Preliminaries consist of auditor inquiry of the client's management and employees concerning general information about the entity. Questions should address the nature of the entity's operations, its organizational structure, its financial control system, and the existence of electronic data processing applications.

Preliminary audit programs (5) Initial audit programs prepared after the auditor's study of the business and industry, application of analytical procedures, and preliminary assessment of control risk. These programs may be further modified on the basis of internal control testing.

Preliminary audit survey (16) As used in internal auditing, a survey done to familiarize the audit team with the unit or activity being audited and the auditee's perception of those operations being reviewed. Sources of information include policies and procedures manuals, discussions with the auditee, organization charts, mission statements, job descriptions, and reports issued by and to the auditee.

Presentation and disclosure (1 and 4) A state in which all of the financial statement components have been properly classified and in which disclosure, in the form of footnotes or in the body of the statements, is adequate so as not to make the financial statements misleading.

Prevention controls (6) Internal controls that avoid the occurrence of errors and/or fraud.

Primarily substantive audit (5 and 7) An audit approach that emphasizes substantive testing rather than some combination of control testing and substantive testing. This approach usually is followed for transaction cycle subsets where control risk is assessed at maximum.

Principal auditor (14) The firm that has audited the major portion of the combined entity, where two or more auditing firms have participated in the audit. The decision of which firm is principal auditor is necessary for a proper division of responsibility.

Principles of conduct (2) Part of the Code of Professional Conduct of the AICPA. The principles provide the framework within which the rules of conduct and interpretations are formulated.

Private Companies Practice Section (3) That section of the Division for CPA Firms comprising CPAs with non-SEC clients.

Private Securities Litigation Reform Act of 1995 (3) An act that changes auditor liability, under statutory law, from joint and several to proportionate.

Privity of contract (3) Limitation of liability to the parties to a given contract. Under privity, the CPA is not liable to third parties for ordinary negligence. (*See also Ultramares vs. Touche* and *Rhode Island Hospital Trust National Bank vs. Swartz* in the appendix to Chapter 3.)

Probability-proportional-to-size sampling (10) A variation of attribute sampling. PPS is used to estimate the dollar amount of errors in a population.

Applicable only to populations for which the auditor suspects a few errors of overstatement.

Procedures-driven audit (5) An audit approach that utilizes standard audit programs regardless of varying levels of audit risk. This approach is no longer considered acceptable in today's audit environment.

Processing controls (8) Those controls concerned with the manipulation of data once it is entered into the computer.

Professional skepticism (5) An attitude that includes a questioning mind and critical assessment of audit evidence.

Profitability ratios (4) A set of calculations designed to measure operating efficiency and effectiveness. Examples are operating margin and return on assets.

Programmers (8) Persons within the CBIS function who write and test programs based on the system design and/or modification.

Projected error (10) The estimated population overstatement error as calculated from the sample. Related to probability-proportional-to-size sampling.

Projection (15) A form of prospective financial statements that presents financial position, results of operations, and cash flows given one or more hypothetical assumptions.

Proof of cash (11) A form of bank reconciliation that agrees recorded receipts and disbursements for a given time period with bank statement credits and debits. As an audit procedure, the proof of cash helps to detect errors in recording cash receipts or disbursements.

Prospective financial statements (15) Financial statements containing nonhistorical data. Prospective financial statements usually assume the form of forecasts or projections.

Protocol controls (8) Protocol controls direct the receiving and sending computers to acknowledge the transmission link and verify the accuracy of the data transmitted. Used as a means for controlling data transmission.

Public Oversight Board (3) A body of the AICPA consisting mainly of nonaccountants that supervises the activities of the SEC Practice Section of the Division for CPA Firms. The POB is monitored by and reports to the SEC.

Purchases cutoff (12) The process of determining whether purchases were recorded in the proper accounting period.

Q

Qualified audit opinion (14) An audit opinion rendered under circumstances of one or more material scope restrictions or departures from GAAP.

Qualitative approach (7) An approach to determining the nature and timing of substantive audit procedures to apply in the circumstances.

Quality review (3) *See* peer review.

Quality control (3) The policies adopted and procedures established to provide an accounting firm with reasonable assurance of conforming with professional standards. A system of quality control is required for CPA firms by the bylaws of the AICPA.

Quantitative approach (7) An approach to determining the extent of substantive audit procedures to apply in the circumstances.

R

Random selection (9) A term used to describe the process of selecting items to be included in a sample on a probability basis. Given random selection, every item in the population has a known or equal chance of being included in the sample.

Range of acceptability (10) The range of possible book values considered acceptable to the auditor. The upper end of precision minus materiality equals the lower end of the range; the lower end of precision plus materiality equals the upper end of the range. Used in variables sampling.

Ratio analysis (4) A comparison of relationships among account balances. Ratios are most useful when compared with other entities and industry averages and when compared within a single entity over time.

Real-time processing (8) The entering of transactions into the computer as they occur and their processing as they are entered.

Reasonable assurance (6) The level of confidence one may place in the ability of an effective system of internal control to prevent and detect errors and fraud.

Reasonable care (3) The act of exercising reasonable diligence in the conduct of auditing and other professional services. That degree of care exercised by the "prudent" CPA in conducting an examination of financial statements or other professional services.

Reconciliation (4) A comparison of two independently calculated amounts. Examples of reconciliations, as used in accounting and auditing, are bank reconciliations and agreeing subsidiary ledgers to control accounts.

Recording forms (8) Input forms used to ensure consistency and completeness of recurring inputs such as purchases and sales.

Recurring audit (4) A repeat audit of the financial statements of a client whose prior financial statements also were audited by the same accounting firm.

Related party (4) A person or entity having the potential to influence the auditee and to prevent the auditee from fully pursuing its own interests.

Related-party transactions (13) Transactions between the client and persons or entities related to the client through family ties, common stock ownership, or other means. Related-party transactions often produce variances between legal form and economic substance. When the two are in conflict, GAAP requires that substance take precedence over form.

Relational database software package (11) Software packages that permit multi-classifications of large volumes of data. Having greater storage capacity than spreadsheets, these packages are being used to an increasing extent by auditors in audit workpaper preparation and linking.

Relevance (4) The usefulness of audit evidence in satisfying stated audit objectives.

Reliability (10) Confidence level. Reliability is a statistical sampling term meaning the likelihood that the sample range contains the true value.

Reliability factor (10) Corresponds to the level of incorrect acceptance (beta risk) as set by the auditor, and assumes zero errors.

Remittance advice (7) The lower half of a customer remittance document. This part of the document describes the invoices covered by the customer check (the upper half of the document).

Reportable conditions (7 and 13) Matters coming to the auditor's attention that in his or her judgment should be communicated to the audit committee, because they represent significant deficiencies in the design or operation of the internal financial control system.

Reportable conditions letter (13) A letter from the auditor to senior management and the audit committee of the board of directors. The letter describes internal control weaknesses discovered during the course of the audit, together with recommendations for improvement.

Reporting standards (2) Those auditing standards that relate to the attest function.

Reports on internal control (15) Reports submitted by certain entities, such as investment companies, brokers, and securities dealers, as required by the Securities Exchange Act of 1934.

Reprocessing (7) Control testing whereby the auditor introduces hypothetical transactions into the client's accounting system to test the system's ability to identify and correct errors in the capturing and processing of data. Reprocessing may be done separately or during live processing of client data.

Request for vendor's statement (12) A draft by the client mailed to the vendor with a request that the statement be returned directly to the auditor.

Results of processing (8) The output, in the form of recorded transactions and balances, of a given transaction cycle; for example, sales revenue and accounts receivable balances.

Revenue cycle (4 and 11) The transaction cycle comprising sales revenue, cash receipts, cash balances, and accounts receivable.

Review (15) The application of procedures, mainly in the form of inquiry and analytical procedures, adequate to provide the CPA a basis for expressing limited assurance concerning the conformance of a set of financial statements with GAAP. More than a compilation, but less than an audit.

Rights and obligations (1 and 4) A state in which all assets reflected in the balance sheet are owned by the client at the balance sheet date and in which all liabilities reflected in the balance sheet are obligations of the client at the balance sheet date.

Risk analysis matrix (5) A diagrammatic means for matching "warning signs" with the sources of information available to the auditor for identifying the warning signs. See Table 5.1 for a comprehensive example of a risk analysis matrix.

Risk assessment (6 and 15) Identification, analysis, and management of risks relevant to the preparation of financial statements.

Risk-based audit (1) An audit in which the auditor carefully analyzes the entity and its existing internal control, identifies areas that pose the highest risk of financial statement errors, and allocates a greater proportion of audit resources to those areas.

Risk-based operational auditing (16) An operational audit focus that responds to efficiency and effectiveness problem areas within the entity as they arise.

Risk-driven audit (5) An audit approach that carefully analyzes audit risk, sets materiality thresholds based on audit risk analysis, and develops audit programs that allocate a larger proportion of audit resources to high-risk areas. The risk-driven audit is the preferred approach in today's financial environment and, therefore, is the main focus of this textbook.

Risk of underassessment (9) The risk that the sample results support the auditor's lowering of assessed control risk when the true error rate does not justify such reduction. In nonstatistical terms, it is the probability that the auditor will assess control risk at a lower level than justified for a given subset of the client's system of internal control.

Rules of conduct (2)   That part of the Code of Professional Conduct that governs the performance of auditing and other services rendered by CPAs. The Code contains principles and rules. The principles provide a framework, while the rules are concerned with proper adherence to the principles.

S

S-1 review (3) An auditor's review of subsequent events up to the effective date of a registration statement pursuant to the Securities Act of 1933 involving new securities offerings. (*See also Escott vs. Bar Chris Construction Corporation* in the appendix following Chapter 3.)

Safeguard controls (6)   Controls designed to protect assets against misappropriation or other forms of loss. Examples include password controls securing the integrity of computer databases, restricted access to assets and documents, cash registers, and separation of duties. (*See also* access controls and accountability controls.)

Sales cutoff (11 and 12)   The process for ensuring that sales are recorded in the proper accounting period.

Sampling for attributes (9)   An estimate of frequency of occurrence of events (errors or fraud). In auditing, attribute sampling is frequently used to further test control procedures.

Sampling interval (10)   A term used in PPS sampling to describe the distance between two consecutive sample items.

Sampling risk (9 and 10)   The combined influence of alpha and beta risk. The probability that the auditor's conclusions about a population will be incorrect.

Sampling unit (9)   A defined population item (e.g., a line item in an inventory listing or a bill of lading evidencing shipment of goods) representing the focal point for sampling applications.

Scienter (3)   Intent.

Scope paragraph (14)   That paragraph of the audit report that tells what the auditor did. Specifically, it states whether or not the audit was conducted in accordance with GAAS.

Scope restriction (14)   A failure by the auditor to apply auditing procedures considered necessary in the circumstances. Scope restrictions may be imposed by the client, or they may be unimposed (e.g., when the auditor is engaged after fiscal year end and cannot observe the year-end physical inventory).

Search for unrecorded liabilities (12)   A set of auditing procedures designed to locate misstatements due to omission involving unrecorded year-end liabilities.

Securities Act of 1933 (3)   A federal statute governing the registration of new securities issues traded in interstate commerce.

Securities Exchange Act of 1934 (3)   A federal statute establishing recurring reporting requirements for public companies once their securities have been registered with the SEC.

SEC Practice Section (3)   That section of the Division for CPA Firms consisting of CPAs with SEC clients.

Self-regulation (3)   The state whereby the accounting profession regulates its own activities and performance without intervention by public bodies, such as Congress or the SEC.

Separate evaluations (6)   A means of monitoring those internal controls not conducive to real-time (recurring and automatic) monitoring.

Single Audit Act of 1984 (as amended in 1996) (16)   An act of Congress applicable to the audits of state and local government entities, colleges and universities, and other not-for-profit entities receiving $300,000 or more of federal financial assistance in a fiscal year. The act requires the auditor to evaluate internal controls over federal financial assistance, audit compliance with specific requirements, and report on compliance with laws and regulations that may have a material effect on each major federal financial assistance program.

Smoothing (12)   When an entity attempts to minimize peaks and valleys in earnings over time.

Special report (14)   An audit report covering financial statements prepared on a comprehensive basis of accounting other than GAAP.

Standard audit report (14)   The form of audit report recommended by the Auditing Standards Board of the AICPA. This report is rendered at the conclusion of an audit in which the auditor encountered no material scope limitations, and the financial statements conform to GAAP in all material respects.

Standard bank confirmation (11)   A confirmation form recommended by the AICPA by which the bank provides information directly to the auditor concerning bank balances and outstanding loans relative to a specified client.

Standard deviation (10)   A measure of population variability. Standard deviation may be defined as the degree of variation of individual item values about the population mean.

Standard journal entries (6)   A set of predetermined journal entries for recording recurring month-end transactions and events. Standard journal entries provide control by preventing oversights in the form of omitted accruals and/or apportionments.

Statements on Auditing Standards (2) Pronouncements of the Auditing Standards Board of the AICPA that constitute interpretations of the ten generally accepted auditing standards.

Statements on Quality Control Standards (3) Guidelines issued by the AICPA Quality Control Standards Committee that accounting firms must follow.

Statements on Responsibilities in Tax Practice (2) Pronouncements issued by the Committee on Federal Taxation of the AICPA. They provide guidance for CPAs in performing tax services and in representing clients before the Internal Revenue Service.

Statements on Standards for Accounting and Review Services (2 and 15) Pronouncements of the Accounting and Review Services Committee of the AICPA that establish the framework for performing other accounting services for clients, such as compilations and reviews.

Statements on Standards for Consulting Services (2) Pronouncements of the AICPA Management Advisory Services Executive Committee that provide guidance for maintaining standards of quality in the performance of consulting services for clients.

Statistical sampling (9) A mathematical approach to inference. In determining sample size, in selecting the sample, and in evaluating the sample results, a consistent and orderly approach is followed.

Statutory law (3) Auditors may be held liable for violating the provisions of the Securities Act of 1933 and the Securities Exchange Act of 1934.

Statutory liability (3) Legal liability imposed by statutes. CPAs are liable to third parties under the Securities Act of 1933 and under Section 10B-5 of the Securities and Exchange Act of 1934 for negligence and fraud.

Stratified sampling (10) A statistical sampling approach whereby a population is divided into two or more subsets, the parameters for each to be set differently. Used primarily in variables sampling, stratification permits the auditor to examine larger items in the population more intensively than less significant items.

Study and evaluation of internal control (2) This phrase describes that element of the independent financial audit that permits the CPA to evaluate the reliability of the client's financial information system. This evaluation, in turn, assists the CPA in determining the nature, timing, and extent of substantive audit procedures to apply in the circumstances.

Subsequent discovery of facts (14) Discovery by the auditor, after issuing the audit report, of facts existing at the date of the audit report. The facts may or may not have changed the audit report had they been known at the date of the report.

Subsequent events (13) Events or transactions occurring after the balance sheet date, but before the completion of audit field work. Subsequent events may have a material impact on the audited financial statements and may require adjustment or disclosure.

Subsequent events review (3) A review of events following the balance sheet date. Under the Securities Act of 1933, the review must extend to the effective date of the securities registration.

Substantive tests (1) Tests where the auditor examines evidence representing the substance underlying the transactions and balances.

Substance (4) That which is represented by an account. The inventory in the warehouse, for example, is the substance represented by the account, "finished goods inventory."

Substantive audit testing (1, 4, and 11) The process of obtaining evidence in support of transactions and balances.

Successor auditor (14) An auditor engaged to conduct an audit for a client whose financial statements have been previously examined by other auditors.

Sufficiency of audit evidence (1 and 4) Enough evidence to support the auditor's opinion on the financial statements.

Sufficient competent evidential matter (2) Identifies the various types of evidence available to the auditor, and offers guidelines for the auditor to follow in judging *sufficiency* and *competence* of evidential matter.

Sufficient evidence (4) Evidence that is adequate to support the auditor's opinion on the financial statements.

Supplemental information required by FASB (14) Additional information that must accompany the financial statements but that is not part of the financial statements. Disclosure of mineral reserves is an example.

Supporting schedule (4) A schedule containing evidence of substantive tests performed by the auditor together with the results of those tests and the auditor's conclusions.

Surprise audit (8) A control testing procedure for CBIS whereby the auditor, on an unannounced basis, requests duplicate copies of client programs at the completion of data processing runs for comparison with the auditor's copies of "authorized" versions.

Systematic sampling (9) A random selection means whereby the sample is drawn by selecting every nth item in the population until the required sample size is reached. In applying systematic selection, the starting point must be at random and the entire field must be covered.

Systems analyst (8) A person within the CBIS function who designs new systems and modifies existing systems in accordance with the information needs of the users.

Systems control audit review file (SCARF) (8) An audit log used to collect information for subsequent analysis and review. SCARF is a technique used by auditors for testing CBIS controls.

Systems development and documentation controls (8) Controls over the definition, design, development, testing, and documentation of the systems and programs constituting each application. Associated with CBIS.

SysTrust (15) An assurance service wherein the CPA evaluates the client's information system for reliability.

T

Tagging and tracing (8) A control testing technique whereby an identifier or "tag" is affixed to a transaction record. The tag triggers "snapshots" during the processing of transactions. The snapshots are stored, are accessible only by the auditor, and enable the auditor to examine transactions at the intermediate steps in processing.

Tainting (10) A logical unit containing one or more errors is said to be "tainted." If the book value of the logical unit is less than the sampling interval, a "tainting" percentage must be applied in order to project the error for the entire sampling interval containing the logical unit.

Tainting percentage (10) (BV – AV)/BV, calculated for any logical unit ≤ sampling interval and containing error.

Temporary breakdown (6) One of the limitations inherent in a given system of internal control. Relates to the occasional failure of internal control to prevent or detect an error or fraud. Such failures are due to oversight by individuals responsible for performing control procedures, as well as by changes in the control environment.

Test-based audit (2) An audit of a sampling of transactions as contrasted with a detailed audit requiring the examination of all transactions. A test-based audit is designed to provide reasonable, but not absolute, assurance as to fairness of financial statement presentation.

Test data approach (8) A means for auditing through the computer whereby the auditor prepares simulated input data (transactions) that are processed, under the auditor's control, by the client's processing system. The test data should contain a combination of all inputs required to execute all of the logic contained in the process.

Tests for inventory obsolescence (12) Audit procedures applied for the purpose of determining whether inventories should be written down to reflect a decline in value below cost. Causes of obsolescence might be overstocking, changes in technology, physical deterioration due to improper storage, and style changes. Obsolescence tests may assume the form of inquiry, observation, and turnover tests.

Tests for reasonableness (8) Routines that cause the computer to reject input that is abnormal in amount.

Tests for valid codes (8) Routines that test the accuracy of code numbers entered as input into the system.

Tests of controls (7) The identification of the pertinent financial reporting controls in a given transaction cycle subset and the examination of them on a test basis for the period covered by the audit.

Time budget (1 and 5) An audit planning and control device that classifies projected and actual time according to audit staff level.

Tolerable error (10) The maximum dollar amount of error acceptable to the auditor. Used in PPS sampling.

Tolerable occurrence rate (9) The maximum rate of error acceptable to the auditor, while still warranting a lowering of assessed control risk below the maximum level. Used in attribute sampling.

Tracing (4) The act of following transactions or events forward from documents to journal entries and postings.

Training and proficiency as an auditor (2) Assures clients that CPAs are able to adequately perform the services for which they represent themselves.

Transaction cycle (4) A group of related transactions affecting essentially the same set of general ledger accounts.

Transaction documentation (6) The requirement that some form of underlying document support any given transaction or event. Documentation may assume the form of vendors' invoices, sales invoices, time cards, production reports, journal vouchers, transaction logs, and workpaper analyses supporting adjusting journal entries. An important ingredient of the audit trail.

Transaction log (8) An input record used to trace computerized transactions to their source.

Transaction review (6) An examination of transaction documentation and approvals after completion to ensure that the transaction was properly approved, executed, and recorded. Transaction review should be performed by someone who was not involved in the approval, execution, or recording of the transaction.

Transaction testing (1) That part of the auditor's study of internal control policies and procedures that encompasses examination of transactions on a test basis. The purpose of such testing is to enable the auditor to project an upper error rate as input into the assessment of control risk and design of audit programs. Transaction testing may assume the form of observation, reprocessing, or document testing.

Treadway Report (2) A study released in 1987 under the joint sponsorship of the AICPA, the AAA, the FEI, the IIA, and the IMA. The document contains far-reaching recommendations regarding the direction and performance of the public accounting profession and has significantly influenced accounting, auditing, and other professional pronouncements since its publication.

Trend analysis (4) A form of financial analysis that requires examining changes in data over time. The underlying premise is that past trends may be expected to continue into the future unless conditions change materially.

Troubled debt restructuring (13) Revision of loan terms for the purpose of enabling the borrower to continue amortizing the obligation in a manner mutually acceptable to the lender and borrower. The restructuring may include extending the payment date for the loan, reducing the interest rate, reducing principal, forgiving accrued interest, or settling all or part of the obligation by the transfer of non-cash assets.

Type I subsequent events (13) Events occurring between the balance sheet date and close of audit field work that provide additional evidence with respect to conditions that existed at the date of the balance sheet and affect the estimates inherent in the process of preparing the financial statements. These require adjustment if material.

Type II subsequent events (13) Events that provide evidence with respect to conditions that did not exist at the date of the balance sheet, but arose subsequent to that date. These may require disclosure.

U

Unaudited financial statements (15) Financial statements that have not been audited. Whenever associated with unaudited financial statements of a public entity, a CPA should disclaim an opinion and mark each page of the statements as unaudited. When associated with the financial statements of a nonpublic entity, the CPA at least should compile or review the statements, or state on each page of the financial statements that they were not compiled or reviewed and that the CPA assumes no responsibility for their fairness.

Uncertainty (14) A situation in which the outcome of future events that may affect the financial statements cannot reasonably be estimated by management.

Underlying accounting data (4) Internal evidence consisting of books of original entry, ledgers, and supporting work sheets.

Understanding of internal control (7) Knowledge obtained by the auditor relative to the client's internal financial controls. The understanding so obtained must be sufficient for the auditor to assess control risk as a basis for designing substantive audit programs.

Understanding the client's environment (4) Involves the understanding by the auditor of the client's business and the industry of which it is a part and the existing internal control system.

Unqualified opinion (14) An audit opinion not qualified for any material scope restrictions or departures from GAAP.

Updating the audit report (14) The act of a continuing auditor reporting on financial statements of prior years that are presented together with those of the current year.

Upper error limit (10) The sum of the projected error and the allowance for sampling risk. The upper error limit represents the maximum overstatement error at the reliability level specified by the auditor.

Upper occurrence limit (9) The calculated maximum error rate based on the results of sampling.

User controls (8) Manual control procedures applied by organizational units (user groups) whose data is processed by CBIS. These controls consist mainly of control totals developed prior to submission of data for processing.

V

Validity (4) A measure of the quality of audit evidence. Validity is enhanced by an effective system of internal control.

Valuation or allocation (1) A state in which all components of the financial statements have been properly valued in accordance with GAAP.

Variables sampling (9 and 10) An estimate of amount (account balance or dollar amount of errors). In auditing, variables sampling is used for substantive testing. More specifically, it is used to estimate the dollar amount of transactions or account balances by examining a sample and extending the results to the population.

Vouching (4) The act of following transactions or events backward from journal entries and postings to underlying documentation.

W

Warning signs (5) Signals or "flags" produced by the application of analytical procedures, study of the business and industry, or by other means that are indicative of significant audit risk.

WebTrust (15) An assurance service wherein the CPA examines and attests to critical aspects of a client's web site.

Working trial balance (4) The focal point of the current file. The working trial balance may be thought of as a table of contents showing unaudited balances, adjustments and reclassifications, audited balances, and the workpapers in which the accounts are analyzed.

Workpaper review (13) The process whereby audit workpapers for a given engagement are reviewed by those not preparing the workpapers. Workpapers completed by assistants are usually reviewed by the in-charge senior auditor, the senior auditor's workpapers are reviewed by the audit manager, and the workpapers as a whole are reviewed by the audit partner on an aggregate basis.

Y

Yellow book (16) Publication issued by the General Accounting Office, that sets forth auditing standards to be followed in auditing recipients of federal financial assistance.

index